Student *t* for Selected Upper-Tail Probabilities

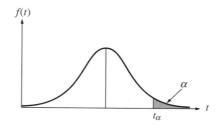

DOF	α					
	0.25	0.10	0.05	0.025	0.01	0.005
1	1.000	3.078	6.314	12.706	31.821	63.657
2	0.816	1.886	2.920	4.303	6.965	9.925
3	0.765	1.638	2.353	3.182	4.541	5.841
4	0.741	1.533	2.132	2.776	3.747	4.604
5	0.727	1.476	2.015	2.571	3.365	4.032
6	0.718	1.440	1.943	2.447	3.143	3.707
7	0.711	1.415	1.895	2.365	2.998	3.499
8	0.706	1.397	1.860	2.306	2.896	3.355
9	0.703	1.383	1.833	2.262	2.821	3.250
10	0.700	1.372	1.812	2.228	2.764	3.169
11	0.697	1.363	1.796	2.201	2.718	3.106
12	0.695	1.356	1.782	2.179	2.681	3.055
13	0.694	1.350	1.771	2.160	2.650	3.012
14	0.692	1.345	1.761	2.145	2.624	2.977
15	0.691	1.341	1.753	2.131	2.602	2.947
16	0.690	1.337	1.746	2.120	2.583	2.921
17	0.689	1.333	1.740	2.110	2.567	2.898
18	0.688	1.330	1.734	2.101	2.552	2.878
19	0.688	1.328	1.729	2.093	2.539	2.861
20	0.687	1.325	1.725	2.086	2.528	2.845
21	0.686	1.323	1.721	2.080	2.518	2.831
22	0.686	1.321	1.717	2.074	2.508	2.819
23	0.685	1.319	1.714	2.069	2.500	2.807
24	0.685	1.318	1.711	2.064	2.492	2.797
25	0.684	1.316	1.708	2.060	2.485	2.787
26	0.684	1.315	1.706	2.056	2.479	2.779
27	0.684	1.314	1.703	2.052	2.473	2.771
28	0.683	1.313	1.701	2.048	2.467	2.763
29	0.683	1.311	1.699	2.045	2.462	2.756
30	0.683	1.310	1.697	2.042	2.457	2.750

APPLIED STATISTICAL METHODS

APPLIED
METHODS

for Business, Eco...

William L. Carlson
...College

Betsy Thorne
...University

APPLIED STATISTICAL METHODS

for Business, Economics, and the Social Sciences

William L. Carlson
St. Olaf College

Betty Thorne
Stetson University

Prentice Hall, Upper Saddle River, New Jersey 07458
http://www.prenhall.com

Library of Congress Cataloging-in-Publication Data

Carlson, William L. (William Lee),
    Applied statistical methods / William L. Carlson, Betty Thorne.
      p. cm.
    Includes index.
    ISBN 0-13-570847-8 (alk. paper)
    1. Mathematical statistics.   I. Thorne, Betty.   II. Title.
QA276.C2852   1997
519.5—dc20   96-20962
                                           CIP

Acquisition Editor: Ann Heath
Editorial Director: Tim Bozik
Editor-in-Chief: Jerome Grant
AVP, Production and Manufacturing: David W. Riccardi
Development Editor: Millicent Treloar
Production Editor: Elaine W. Wetterau
Managing Editor: Linda Mihatov Behrens
Marketing Manager: Evan Girard
Creative Director: Paula Maylahn
Art Director: Jayne Conte
Cover Designer: Bruce Kenselaar
Manufacturing Buyer: Alan Fischer
Manufacturing Manager: Trudy Pisciotti
Cover Photograph: Mark Newman / Superstock 4
Composition: Windfall Software, using ZzTeX

Printed in the United States of America
10 9 8 7 6 5 4 3 2

0-13-570847-8

PRENTICE-HALL INTERNATIONAL (UK) LIMITED, *London*
PRENTICE-HALL OF AUSTRALIA PTY. LIMITED, *Sydney*
PRENTICE-HALL CANADA INC., *Toronto*
PRENTICE-HALL HISPANOAMERICANA, S.A., *Mexico*
PRENTICE-HALL OF INDIA PRIVATE LIMITED, *New Delhi*
PRENTICE-HALL OF JAPAN, INC., *Tokyo*
SIMON & SCHUSTER ASIA PTE. LTD., *Singapore*
EDITORA PRENTICE-HALL DO BRASIL, LTDA., *Rio de Janeiro*

Dedicated with Love and Thanks by

Bill Carlson
in memory of his parents Ruth and Leslie
and
to his wife Charlotte
and his children Andrea, Douglas, and Larry

and

Betty Thorne
in memory of her father Westley
and
to her mother Jennie,
her husband Jim,
and her children Jennie, Ann, Renee, and Jon

Contents

18 QUALITY 866

Preface

APPROACH

This book provides a strong introduction to statistical procedures for solving applied problems. A wide range of applications, including a number from business and economics, is presented. Emphasis is placed on analyzing the process providing the data along with the important questions under study. Problem solving requires clear understanding of present and proposed systems. An understanding of statistical methodologies, including the computational procedures used by statistical programs, is necessary to study systems and processes.

Statistical methods are presented in sufficient depth to provide the understanding required for good analysis and interpretation of results. Conceptual understanding in the applications context is emphasized. Solved examples and graphical and mathematical tools are all used for clear presentation of the statistical procedures. Of equal importance are the included discussions of the reasoning and philosophy that make statistics an exciting and effective problem-solving skill. The use of computers for computations is assumed in most examples and homework problems.

This book has been written to implement the ideas being developed in the annual conference, "Making Statistics More Effective in Schools of Business," by authors who are long-term participants and members of the organizing board. Emphasis is placed on problem solving and the importance of interdisciplinary partnerships. This theme is emphasized by our cover showing a dedicated, hard-working team of sled dogs in the Iditorad 1000-mile Alaskan race.

Based on our many years of teaching, we believe the best way to learn to solve problems is by the practice of solving problems. The text begins each topic with problems posed in applications, followed by a discussion of broad concepts, then by layers of deeper detail. Each topical discussion includes Key Idea boxes summarizing a concept or procedure. Discussions comprehensively cover concepts, assumptions, objectives, and computational details. Solved examples show and interpret specific applications. As you develop your statistical understanding in progressing through this course, you may need to refer back to ideas from previous chapters. Quick referencing is aided by chapter indexes to the Key Idea boxes.

The material has been class tested with a wide range of students from those with strong mathematical skills to those with math anxiety. Students from all backgrounds have developed a clear understanding of statistics. Students learn because they see a wide range of realistic examples for every new topic. "I did not realize statistics could be so interesting," is a common quote.

This book is intended to serve you as a useful reference in your professional career. You will recognize problems that arise on the job as similar to those you worked in college. By going back to this textbook, you will be able to quickly refresh your memory and insightfully solve the problems.

WHO SHOULD USE THIS BOOK?

This book was designed to provide a strong resource for a wide range of statistics classes and to be a reference for students during their professional career. Thus it contains more topics than can be covered in a typical one-semester course. By selecting appropriate chapters and sections, this book is suitable for courses that emphasize data analysis with a limited study of probability and courses that use a probability base for data analysis. For those who have a calculus background, "*" sections provide a discussion of the concepts using calculus. For the entire range of users the emphasis is on learning to apply statistical procedures in problem-solving situations.

Depending on your course structure, we suggest the following organizational selections.

Chapters 1 Through 3 and 8

These chapters introduce analysis concepts, sampling and data acquisition, and basic descriptive statistics and procedures. Our sense, and that of most teachers we have talked to, is that all statistics courses should include this material.

Chapters 4 Through 7

This material covers probability and random variables. Courses that emphasize data analysis and wish to reduce the study of probability could select only the discussion of the binomial distribution (Section 5.6) and the normal distribution (Sections 6.5 and 6.6). Other courses could select a wide range of material dealing with probability and random variables. For example, Chapter 7 provides extensive coverage of correlated random variables and linear combinations of random variables. This material is extremely important for financial analysis and is not covered in most books at this level.

Chapters 9 Through 11

This material covers statistical inference with emphasis on acceptance intervals (Chapter 9), confidence intervals (Chapter 10), and hypothesis testing (Chapter 11). Material could be selected to provide for a wide range of course requirements including the analysis of single-population statistics (means and proportions), differences between two populations (means and proportions), analysis of sample variances, portfolio analysis, and even maximum likelihood estimators.

Chapters 14 Through 16

This material covers simple and multiple regression, including many analysis examples. Chapters 14 and 15 both include a detailed example that indicates how regression is applied using computer output and clear analysis. A wide range of options could be selected from basic applications through a number of important extensions, including transformations, categorical variables, experimental design, serial correlation, and heteroscedasticity. In particular, Chapter 16 contains material typically found only in specialized regression and econometrics books. Chapter appendices include the mathematical development of the regression model for students with a calculus background.

Chapters 12, 13, and 17

These chapters provide an introduction to topics that are important for certain courses: Chapter 12, Chi-Square nonparametric tests; Chapter 13, Analysis and Variance procedures; and Chapter 17, Introduction to Time-Series analysis. These topics can be included or excluded without affecting the continuity of any course.

Chapter 18

This chapter provides an extensive discussion of the philosophy and methods used in modern Quality Assurance work. The importance of this topic in business, government, and nonprofit sectors suggests that it be included in a wide range of courses. We suggest that all students in statistics courses should study this material.

UNIQUE FEATURES

- Emphasis on problem solving using interesting and realistic applications.
- Early coverage of problem analysis, data collection, experiments, surveys, bivariate data, and scatterplots.
- Rigorous presentation of statistical methods and procedures, providing the basics for good problem solving.
- Presentation of each topic on several levels, from broad concepts, to definitions, to assumptions, and to solved examples.
- Solved examples structured to present computer analyses of supplied data sets and to reveal the important features of statistical analysis using computers.
- Key Ideas summarize important methods and procedures.
- Does It Make Sense? sections provide practical insights from experienced analysts and point out judgmental elements of problem solving.
- Over 1000 student problems, including Practice Problems dispersed through the discussions, allow immediate feedback to a student's understanding of concepts up to that point. Solutions to the Practice Problems appear at the end of each chapter. The ends of sections provide short problems focusing on single ideas

and eliciting short answers. The answers to these appear at the end of the book. Last, problems at the ends of the chapters require students to integrate concepts in problem solving. A separate volume, the Student Solutions Manual, contains detailed solutions to the odd-numbered end-of-chapter problems in the text.

· Quality Assurance topics are contained in an extended separate chapter as well as appear in many applications throughout the book.

· Extensive coverage of linear combinations of random variables and correlated random variables are covered in the probability chapters.

ACCOMPANIMENTS

Ancillary publications to this textbook are a Student Solutions Manual containing step-by-step solutions to odd-numbered end-of-chapter problems, which can be purchased through your bookstore. Your instructor has a data disk available either for duplication or for downloading from the local server.

There also is an Instructor's Solutions Manual containing step-by-step solutions to the even-numbered end-of-chapter problems.

ACKNOWLEDGMENTS

There are many people who have made important contributions to this book. First, we must recognize the efforts of our editor Millicent Treloar, whose professional guidance and long-term support brought this project to fruition. In addition, Scott Isenberg and Ann Heath provided the vision and support that made the project possible. Douglas Scholz-Carlson provided the original TEX macros that provided an excellent environment for preparing the manuscript. Numerous business firms provided data and example problems. Kevin Ackley and Eric Lind, former St. Olaf student assistants, provided important editorial perspectives and were co-authors of the extended solutions manual. Jay Stryker, a former Stetson student, provided important technical assistance. Numerous former students were the context for this book, and they contributed many suggestions to the text as they used preliminary copies in their study of statistics. The book is ultimately a statement of their dedication to learning.

Numerous reviewers made major contributions to this book as it developed. These include Ajay K. Aggarwal, Millsaps College; Peter Von Allmen, Moravian College; Bradley C. Baird, University of Utah; David Booth, Kent State University; Michael Broida, Miami University; Myron Cox, Wright State University; Mary E. Deily, Lehigh University; Frederick Derrick, Loyola College in Maryland; Jamie Eng, San Francisco State University; Charles Feinstein, Santa Clara University; Joel Goldstein, Western Connecticut State University; Jane Harvill, Bowling Green State University; Don Johnson, University of Northern Iowa; Roger Johnson, Carleton College; Thomas Johnson, North Carolina State University; Jeffrey Jung, University of Phoenix; Mark Kanazawa, Carleton College; David Krueger, St. Cloud State University; Ernest Kurnow, New York University; John Loucks, St. Edward's University;

Dale McFarlane, Oregon State University; Steven Nahmias, Santa Clara University; Patrick Philipoom, University of South Carolina; Fatollah Saliman, Salisbury State University; Hedayeh Samavati, Indiana University–Purdue University at Fort Wayne, Indiana; Thomas A. Severinc, Northwestern University; Jack Siler, Wharton School of Business, University of Pennsylvania; Clifford Sowell, Berra College; William Straley, Oglethorpe University; and Mary Sue Younger, University of Tennessee.

Bill Carlson recognizes the love and support of Charlotte and their children Andrea, Douglas, and Larry. Betty Thorne acknowledges the love and support of Jim and their children Jennie, Ann, Renee, and Jonathan. Their sacrifices of our time made this project possible.

W. C.
B. T.

APPLIED STATISTICAL METHODS

1

Introduction

Statistics is a participation sport.

1.1 WHY STUDY STATISTICS?

When we tell people that we teach statistics, they immediately tell us a horror story of their college experience with a statistics course. Or they say that it must be terribly difficult. Their experience is unfortunate, because statistics is an exciting tool for learning about many different subjects. More important, an understanding of statistics is an increasingly important asset to you in understanding and managing your business. A quality control manager at a cereal factory recently explained to local college students how they must become more scientific—making extensive use of statistical procedures—if they expect to survive in the new competitive world. Such comments are repeated often during conversations with managers in a wide variety of businesses. At times you will find that learning new concepts is difficult. However, the rewards of discovery are great. Furthermore, statistical methods are often a key for success and even in some cases for survival in the emerging competitive world of business.

Statistics is a set of tools or techniques that provide the user with input to make wise decisions in the face of uncertainty. In the following sections the basic building blocks for statistical analysis are developed. We will see that statistics is a "team sport" that requires both practice and participation. In addition, we will learn about descriptive and inferential statistics, enumerative and analytic studies, and systems and process models.

1.2 STATISTICS IS A PARTICIPATION SPORT

Statistical methods provide the tools for discovery and evaluation in business and economics in much the same way as physicists and chemists use laboratory experiments for discovery and evaluation. The "laboratory" for the economist and the manager is the dynamic competitive world. "Experiments" take place in the factory, the bank, the supermarket, the stock market, corporate meetings, legislative bodies—whenever actions are taken and outcomes occur. Business experiments produce outputs that can

1

be measured, thus providing statistics—our raw material. These statistics are analyzed using statistical methods, which are our "laboratory tools" for discovery and evaluation. The excitement of discovery makes statistics both an important and an interesting area.

Today, statistics has become a participation sport extending to the factory floor. Recent years have seen a renewed interest in quality control as business moves to compete in a dynamic world economy. This has led to increased data collection and statistical analysis. In this new business environment production workers are members of teams who monitor and discuss statistical measures of their machines' processes and the relationship between these measures and quality and productivity. These teams learn basic statistical concepts and use them regularly to operate and control their production operations.

Statistical methods provide the link between the growing body of management theory and applications to business and public-sector problems. Electronic data collection and storage, computational power, and flat organizational reporting structures allow many theories to be investigated that otherwise would be only hunches. For instance, what is the relationship between advertising and sales? Are a company's books in compliance with accounting procedures? How many bank tellers should be on duty at different times of the day? Does an increased income gap in cities lead to a higher tax base? These and similar questions are under frequent reexamination in today's business climate. As a future participant on a team in the business world, you can expect to be a participant in the discovery and evaluation of these questions.

Team effort combined with individual qualities such as dedication, motivation, discipline, practice, and training are obvious requirements for a successful musical performance, athletic competition, or theatrical production. Today, modern managers facilitate and encourage workers in a manner similar to the "conductor," "coach," or "director." Workers are viewed as "players," and customers are either the "fans" supporting the team, the "audience" applauding the performance, or the "referees" calling the "fouls" when customer satisfaction is not attained. Annually, mushers with their team of dogs compete in the famous Iditarod Trail Sled Dog Race from Anchorage to Nome, Alaska. This race, which is over 1000 miles in length, will take the team through blizzards, blinding winds, and freezing temperatures. The virtues of courage, determination, and team cooperation that are required in the Iditarod Race must also be present in today's business world.

1.3 THE INFORMATION AGE

Information and analysis are key driving forces in our modern economy. Developed countries have very few people growing their food and a rapidly decreasing number producing manufactured goods. Most jobs involve processing information in some way. Many authors have identified the present period of history as the *information age*.

We are at a point where economic growth often results from the analysis of systems. Thus there is a great need for problem solving that uses data gathered from existing systems.

People who study information systems have developed a hierarchy to help understand the development of information systems (Key Idea 1.1). This hierarchy begins with "data," which is processed and summarized to provide "information," and in turn information is organized selectively and combined with experience and theory to provide "knowledge."

Key Idea 1.1: Hierarchy of Information

1. **Data:** specific observations of measured numbers.
2. **Information:** processed and summarized data yielding facts and ideas.
3. **Knowledge:** selected and organized information that provides understanding, recommendations, and the basis for decisions.

Figure 1.1 describes the role of statistical analysis in this hierarchy. We begin with data produced by a process and collected according to a design. These data are analyzed by using one or more statistical procedures. From this analysis we produce information that is converted to knowledge using structured understanding based on specific experience and theory. In our case this structure is based on the techniques and functional analyses drawn from business and economics.

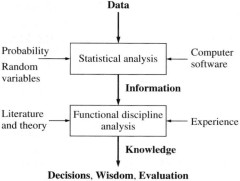

Figure 1.1   The Information Process and Statistical Analysis

1.4 DESCRIPTIVE AND INFERENTIAL STATISTICS

Two branches of statistics that are used in business and economics are descriptive statistics and inferential statistics (Key Idea 1.2).

Key Idea 1.2: Descriptive and Inferential Statistics

Descriptive statistics are numerical and graphical methods used to summarize and process data, and to transform data into information.

    Inferential statistics are procedures used to provide business managers and economists with a basis for predictions, forecasts, estimates, and other forms of decision making, and to transform data and information into knowledge.

The Bureau of the Census provides a wealth of descriptive statistics. From the 1990 Census, we learned that 9 of the top 10 fastest-growing metropolitan areas in the United States are located in Florida; that the population of Daytona Beach, Florida, in 1990 was 399,413; and that New York City ranked first in population in 1990.[1] From the daily newspapers, you can find numerous descriptive statistics such as that during the first six months of 1994, there were 36,790 business failures in the United States.[2]

Economists often use statistics released by the Labor Department, the Commerce Department, the National Association of Purchasing Management (NAPM), and other organizations to make inferences and to draw conclusions about the U.S. economy. For example, on March 5, 1993, the Labor Department reported that the "unemployment rate in February had edged downward from 7.1% to 7.0% and that 365,000 new jobs had been created."[3] Based on this information, the following inference was made: "Data suggests inflationary pressures—statistics released in March suggested that inflation might become a problem for the U.S. economy."[4] In July 1994 the Commerce Department reported that "consumers boosted their spending for a second straight month in June, up 0.4% to a seasonally adjusted annual rate of $4.6 trillion." Economists concluded that this was a new sign of "moderate but steady economic growth."[5] Similarly, in July 1994, NAPM concluded that "manufacturing

---

[1] R. Famighetti, ed., *The World Almanac and Book of Facts: 1994*, Funk & Wagnalls, Mahwah, NJ, 1993, p. 366.

[2] *The Orlando Sentinel*, Tuesday, August 2, 1994, p. B1.

[3] *The World Almanac and Book of Facts: 1994*, p. 48.

[4] Ibid.

[5] "Economy plods at steady pace," *The Orlando Sentinel*, Tuesday, August 2, 1994, p. B1.

activity rose to the highest level in six years . . . possibly shedding light on what to expect in the third quarter."[6]

In addition to economists, market researchers, pollsters, and other groups often use inferential statistics to draw conclusions based on surveys. For instance, does American management monitor workers electronically on the job? This question was asked of 301 American businesses by the International Labor Organization, an agency of the United Nations. The results showed that more than 40% of the companies polled searched worker's E-mail, 28% searched network mail, and 15% tapped into voice mail.[7] Some conclusions drawn from this report were distrust between workers and supervisors, employee stress, demotivation of workers, and a need to develop guidelines for the information superhighway.

Throughout this book you will study various procedures to summarize and process data as well as to make forecasts and predictions. As a result of your study of descriptive and inferential statistics, you will be better prepared to make important business decisions.

1.5 ENUMERATIVE VERSUS ANALYTIC STUDIES

Statistical studies can be classified in two major groupings, enumerative and analytic, each of which has important differences in assumptions and the strength of the resulting conclusions[8] (Key Idea 1.3).

Key Idea 1.3: Enumerative and Analytic Studies

Enumerative studies reach conclusions about a specific set of items. For example, an election poll measures the present attitudes of voters in defined population with respect to a specific candidate.

An **analytic study** measures a group of items and uses those results to infer characteristics outside the group studied. For example, we might measure the reaction of a group to a proposed new product. Then from that measurement we infer the number of people in an extended group who are potential future buyers of the product.

---

[6] Ibid.

[7] "Privacy eroding in workplaces, U.N. report says," *The Orlando Sentinel*, Tuesday, August 2, 1994, p. B1.

[8] Gerald J. Hahn and William Q. Meeker, "Assumptions for statistical inference," *The American Statistician*, Vol. 47, No. 1, February 1993.

Enumerative studies are the ideal base from which statistical sampling strategies and statistical inference are developed. However, analytic studies are more widely used in business and form the basis for many management decisions.

Enumerative studies work with a defined set of items and they alone are the focus. For instance, a shipment of frozen-meat packages might be studied for fat content or the presence of dangerous bacteria. A shipment of iron ore could be studied to determine the iron content. In these instances the conclusions refer only to the particular shipments that are the defined groups for the enumerative study. As a result, statements can be made with greater certainty.

Analytic studies also begin with a complete measurement of a specific group. However, the difference is that the conclusions apply to a related group. For example, test marketing studies measure the reaction to a new product of a group brought together in a shopping mall or an advertiser's office. However, the objective of the study is to determine if a related group will purchase the new product. A production manager conducts experiments to determine conditions in the factory that result in the highest production and lowest number of defective pieces. These experiments provide conclusions concerning changes in factory conditions; then we infer that the changes will result in high production and quality in future factory operations.

Analytic studies do not have the same precision as enumerative studies. However, analytic studies make assumptions concerning the link between the group actually measured and the extension of interest. These linking assumptions require the judgment of someone who understands the underlying behavior of the groups being studied. For example, a marketing analyst can make judgments concerning the behavior of future buyer groups based on the results from an analysis of a present buyer group. In these analytic studies it is important that the subject expert be available to help decide which groups should be measured to obtain the best understanding of the desired group. Similarly, a production engineer needs to be consulted when designing experiments whose ultimate objective is increased production and quality.

The discussion above emphasizes the importance of a close link between a statistical analyst and a person with subject area understanding. This link is fundamentally important for analytic studies. Statistical studies regularly provide businesses with guidance for decisions that lead to cost reductions and increased sales. These studies are analytic and thus require major inputs from subject area experts. The ideal statistical study in business is composed of a team of area experts working with a statistician. All members of the group become familiar with the insights provided by the others. Statisticians learn about the different subject areas and engineers, market analysts, and accountants learn about statistics.

Problem Exercises

1.1   Why do many people call this the information age, and what are the implications of the information age for statistical methods?

1.2   What are the potential effects of statistical analysis on the hierarchy of information?

1.3   A medical researcher was working on a cure for cancer and she developed a drug that proved successful in several animal tests. She then proceeded to administer the drug to 500 persons who had cancer. Was she conducting an enumerative study or an analytic study?

1.4   A petroleum engineer was searching for oil in northern Russia. As part of the exploration he supervised the drilling of 50 test holes. Was he conducting an enumerative or an analytic study?

1.6 SYSTEMS MODELS AND ANALYSIS

Business activity can be represented by a system model. Interpretation of statistical results is clearer if we focus on the particular system or subsystem that is generating the data. Although the terms *system* and *process* are often used interchangeably, we make the definitional distinctives given in Key Idea 1.4.

Key Idea 1.4: System and Process

A **system** is a number of components that are logically and sometimes physically linked together for some purpose.
    A **process** is a set of activities operating on a system that transforms inputs to outputs.

Your computer system consists of a processor chip that performs simple tasks, other chips that store information, a keyboard, a screen, a disk storage drive, possibly a printer, and/or connections to the world. A statistical computer program, such as Minitab, is a system that contains a number of calculation modules that can be linked together. An automobile assembly line is a system that has many machine and human components that link together.

When you enter numbers into your statistical computer program, a number of steps transform the entries into an output such as a graphical plot. Similarly, steel, plastic, paint, energy, and human efforts are part of the inputs to an automobile assembly line and a process converts them to automobiles.

Figure 1.2 is a schematic diagram of a process model. This process converts the inputs to a set of one or more outputs. The outputs can be measured and the measurements can be analyzed using statistical methods. But the analysis must relate to the process problem that is our primary interest. Since systems and processes are studied so that we can predict and/or modify their behavior, it is very important that people who understand the process be included on a team to help to define the measurements and interpret the results.

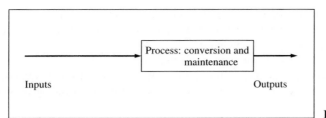

Figure 1.2   General Process Model

As an illustration, Sally Wahl is the production manager of Wheat Cereals. To better understand the cereal manufacturing process and to solve process problems, Sally formed a team of employees to determine if quality standards were being maintained and to find out if there were significant differences in the number of cereal packages produced each day. In addition to herself, Sally added to the team a representative from personnel, a supervisor, a machine operator, a supplier of grain stocks, and a statistical consultant. The team's study would require understanding of the production process and the cooperation of all persons working with the production operation.

Following the consultant's advice, the team first developed a process model (see Figure 1.3) for the cereal manufacturing operation. The team identified the process inputs as various grain stocks, energy, labor, transportation, management, capital equipment, training, and technology in the form of the recipe for combining inputs into cereal. Note that some of the outputs are used for system maintenance. The primary output is a set of cereal packages.

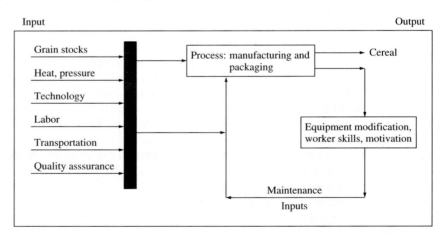

Figure 1.3   Cereal Production System

To determine if quality standards are being maintained, the team obtained "data," that is, specific observations of input and output measurements. For instance, packages were weighed and the density of the cereal product was measured. In later chapters we study statistical analysis procedures used by the team to summarize and to process these data into "information." In turn, we learn how the team then transformed this information into recommendations, "knowledge."

The second phase of the team's inquiry concerned difference in daily production. Was there evidence of large day-to-day differences in the number of cereal packages produced? What conditions resulted in higher production? What conditions were associated with lower production?

The team obtained the number of 16-ounce packages produced each day for the past two workweeks and prepared the graph shown in Figure 1.4. The vertical axis indicates the number of packages produced on a particular day, and the horizontal axis indicates the sequential days. Each point on the graph represents two important measurements: the production level and the day.

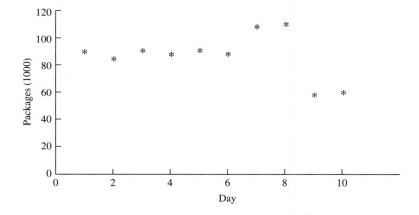

Figure 1.4   Daily Cereal Production

The team examined the graph to learn more about daily production. There did not seem to be much difference in the number of packages produced on each of the first six days. There were variations from day to day, but all six points had numerical values that were very close. However, on days 7 and 8 the production level appeared to be higher. In contrast, on days 9 and 10 production appeared to be lower. Based on these observations, the team attempted to identify the conditions that resulted in higher and lower productivity.

The operating personnel member of the team indicated that key workers were absent on days 9 to 10. Another member of the team, the supervisor, reported that during the same days the production method had been modified. The supplier contributed the information that the raw materials were different during the period of lower production. From the cooperation of the team, conditions that contributed to lower productivity were identified. Through similar efforts, the team next studied the days of higher productivity. Analysis of the data indicated where to look, but the looking required specific production expertise.

This illustration demonstrates a basic approach for statistical studies. The study begins with a process model. Data related to that process are collected and analyzed. In the example the analysis consisted of visual inspection of a graphical plot. This analysis led to certain conclusions that became the basis for action and further work.

Problem Exercise

1.5   Sketch a graphical system model for your college's cafeteria. Define some of the major processes and indicate measurements that might be made to obtain system performance.

SUMMARY OF KEY IDEAS

CHAPTER PROBLEMS

1.1   How does the use of systems analysis help in the design of statistical studies?

1.2   Alfred Smith wants to know if the gasoline consumption for his new car agrees with the manufacturer's claim of 35 miles per gallon. After he has driven the car 2000 miles, he begins to collect gasoline consumption data. After every 200 miles he refills the tank and records the amount of gasoline required. Using these data, he computes the consumption in miles per gallon recorded in Table 1.1. The first seven observations are in column 1, the next seven in column 2, and so on. Gasoline consumption appears to vary considerably from one tank to the next. Alfred asks you to help him analyze the data.

TABLE 1.1   Gasoline Consumption for Alfred Smith's Car

| | Week | | | |
Day	1	2	3	4
Sunday	25.3	28.9	32.5	37.1
Monday	32.0	24.4	33.8	36.5
Tuesday	30.2	23.6	42.8	34.0
Wednesday	36.9	28.7	48.3	34.0
Thursday	37.2	36.6	46.8	32.8
Friday	42.9	30.2	48.2	30.1
Saturday	32.5	35.8	36.6	33.9

(a) List five different factors that might influence the gasoline consumption. Which of these factors could have been easily identified and associated with each tank of gasoline consumed?

(b) Prepare a graphical plot of these data over the time period during which the data were collected (e.g., a plot similar to Figure 1.4).

(c) Based on an examination of your graph, what is the gasoline consumption during most of the typical driving periods?

(d) Based on an examination of your graph, what is the range of consumption during most typical driving periods?

(e) Examine the graph and indicate which driving periods appear to be different from the typical periods. Write some possible explanations for these different periods.

(f) Does Alfred Smith have evidence to dispute the manufacturer's claim concerning mileage?

2

Describing the Data

The world is afloat in data.

2.1 TYPES OF DESCRIPTIVE METHODS

An early point in any statistical study is to prepare a summary and description of data. In this chapter we concentrate on graphical and numerical procedures to accomplish this initial phase of analysis. We study frequency distributions, graphs, measures of central tendency, and measures of dispersion. In addition, we introduce some special data analysis procedures, such as the box-and-whisker plot.

In Chapter 3 we learn how to describe relationships in the data. After describing the data, more sophisticated methods are often used in analysis. These procedures are developed in subsequent chapters.

As you conduct analyses, remember that numbers used in the study of business and economic problems are a summary of complex human processes. There is a conflict between the apparent precision of statistics and the difficulty of measuring behavior. Statistics provide the capability to turn a spotlight on an important idea or relationship, but the associated darkness may hide other important relationships.

2.2 MAKING SENSE OUT OF A SEA OF DATA

The world is afloat in data! Public- and private-sector managers seek data before making decisions. A major percentage of U.S. workers use data as part of their normal duties. Quality assurance activities rely heavily on statistical measures. It is not unusual to find factory workers talking about the central tendency and dispersion of their process. As a future manager you must also understand and be able to communicate using statistical measures and procedures. Government and business spend billions collecting data. The computer age has given us both the power to analyze data rapidly and the encouragement to produce and store more data.

Statistical procedures help us to convert data into information. The analysis begins with a clear objective and an understanding of how the data were created and collected. Recall that in Chapter 1 systems models and process analysis were introduced as concepts used to study the source and generation of data. Thus, we saw how data are generated as part of a process that we wish to study and understand. Using systems models the measurements and resulting data can be related to specific questions. Then the data from the process are examined and summarized as the first step in the analysis.

Data sets contain observations. A data set is either a population (Key Idea 2.1) or a sample (Key Idea 2.2) depending on its contents. Examples of populations include all the people in the United States who are over age 18, all the boxes of cereal produced in a cereal factory over a specific time interval, or all the workers in a factory. Population sizes are often so large that they are unwieldy to analyze. Other factors, such as the excessive costs of collecting population data or the time required to obtain population data, make the use of a sample one of the most important procedures of statistics.

Key Idea 2.1: Population

A **population** is the set that contains all the outcomes from a system or process that is being studied.

Key Idea 2.2: Sample

A **sample** is a subset of a population.

A statistical study typically begins with a data set selected as a sample from a population. Each observation is obtained by a measurement process that has a careful, complete definition. For example, in a cereal factory the number of cereal boxes reported from each shift is based on an agreement concerning when to start and stop counting and which items should be counted. The measurement of economic variables such as investment, consumption, and income produce data sets using a complex process of collecting and recording that is operated by the U.S. Department of Commerce. Applications of sample data sets follow.

1. *Insurance claims data.*   Blue Cross/Blue Shield of Minnesota routinely record claims data for each policyholder. The data represent outcomes from the health care system for the entire Blue Cross/Blue Shield population in Minnesota.

2. *Market studies.*   NPL Research of Dallas does market feasibility studies for shopping center developers in the Dallas/Fort Worth metropolitan area. From their experience they know that the success of a new center is linked to disposable income, so their studies must determine family disposable income. All families in the city are in the study population. The disposable income for every family in the population can be measured and placed in a data file. Alternatively, samples of families are obtained from the population and their disposable incomes placed in data files.

3. *Traffic fatalities.*   The U.S. Department of Transportation collects data on automobile deaths. They define their population as the 50 states and compute the death rate per 100,000 persons for each state. Each state is a system of counties and municipalities that are sampled to obtain data to represent the entire state.

Because of their typically large size, analysis of populations or samples usually requires computer software. Powerful statistical software is available for most personal computers, which combine many individual computational procedures with data management and data manipulation routines. In this chapter and the remainder of the book we present many examples using output from the Minitab statistical system.[1] There are many other excellent statistical packages that can be used for analyzing statistical data.

2.3 CLASSIFICATION OF VARIABLES

Recall from Chapter 1 that systems and processes are studied so that we can predict and/or modify their behavior. Process inputs and outputs are defined using variables. Variables can be classified in several ways. One method of classification refers to the type and amount of information contained in the data. Another method refers to the error component.

2.3.1 Qualitative and Quantitative Variables

Variables are either qualitative or quantitative, depending on the scale of measurement of the data. There are four scales of measurement: nominal, ordinal, interval, and ratio. As you see from Key Idea 2.3, qualitative variables include nominal and ordinal data, whereas quantitative variables include data measured on an interval or ratio scale. This classification system provides a good point of reference in your initial analysis.

Examples of qualitative variables include the model of automobile that one owns, a voter's political affiliation, or a student's favorite basketball team. However, if we are interested in the price of the automobile, the age of the voter, or the cost of a ticket to a basketball game, we have quantitative data.

---

[1] Minitab is a popular statistical program sold by Minitab, Inc. of State College, PA.

Key Idea 2.3: Qualitative and Quantitative Variables

Variables can be classified by the type of information provided.

1. **Qualitative variables** include data measured on nominal or ordinal scales.
    (a) **Nominal scale:** indicates assignments to groups or classes such as gender, geographic region, business type, or numbers on an athletic uniform. Numerical identification is chosen strictly for convenience.
    (b) **Ordinal scale:** indicates rank ordering of items. Examples include job class, product quality ratings (1, best; 2, average; 3, poor), degrees of agreement (1, strongly agree; 2, agree; 3, neutral; 4, disagree; 5, strongly disagree). An ordinal variable indicates only the order and does not indicate the amount of difference between ranks.
2. **Quantitative variables** include data measured on interval or ratio scales.
    (a) **Interval scale:** indicates rank and distance from an arbitrary zero measured in unit intervals. Examples include temperature in Fahrenheit and Celsius scales or placement test scores.
    (b) **Ratio scale:** indicates both rank and the distance from a natural zero, with ratios of two measures having meaning. Examples include height (0 is the lower limit, and 6 feet is twice as tall as 3 feet), total U.S. investment, total consumption, speed, and annual sales.

2.3.2 Error Component

As mentioned earlier, in most cases we use a sample to provide the data for analysis. The sample must represent the population if we want the sample results to apply to the population. Through the use of representative samples, statisticians can make educated, informed comments about the population in the face of uncertainty. The best way to ensure that the sample represents the population is to obtain a simple random sample[2] (Key Idea 2.4).

---

[2] There are many other sampling techniques that obtain samples which also represent the population. They are used to overcome various applied sampling problems and/or to increase the information that can be obtained from a single sample. Some of these procedures are discussed in Chapter 8.

Key Idea 2.4: Simple Random Sample

A **simple random sample** is selected such that each element of the population has an equal chance of being selected and the selection of one element does not affect the selection of any other element.

Simple random samples are the ideal sample and are the assumed data sources for many statistical procedures.

Conclusions based on an analysis of data from a simple random sample apply to the populations. For example, the random sample average will be a close approximation of the population average. The same cannot always be said for analyses based on other samples. Samples that exclude or reduce the chance of selection for certain elements are likely to produce incorrect conclusions. Persons without a clear understanding of sampling methods will often collect observations improperly. When this occurs, the results of subsequent analysis are misleading. In Chapter 8 we discuss sampling techniques in detail.

Statistical analysis assumes a mathematical model for each observation and for each measure computed from the data. In this model each observation or measure contains both an information and an error component. Information refers to the typical operation of the process, which we call the *central tendency* component. *Error* refers to the difference between each observation and the typical observation of the process, such as the mean. Error is the variation in the process. The error component cannot be predicted from one observation to another.

The objective of statistical studies is to isolate the information in order to understand the system being studied. To do this we need to separate information from error. If the information contained in a number is larger than the error, the information can contribute to our understanding. But a large error component will make it very difficult to isolate the information. In general, we would like the information component to be large and the error component to be small.

The error component can generally be divided into two categories: bias and random error (Key Idea 2.5). If the person counting boxes of cereal in a factory takes two boxes home every day, the reported production would be negatively biased compared to the actual number of boxes produced. Bias can also occur in survey samples if certain groups are always excluded. A survey of college students conducted only in sophomore-level classes would yield biased results.

The first step in a quality control program is to reduce and control random error. This is done by carefully examining and correcting potential sources of variation, including raw materials, work procedures, worker training, and machine setting. After random error is reduced as much as possible, the process is defined as being *stable* or *in control*. A process that remains in control will produce products with

---

Key Idea 2.5: Bias and Random Error

Bias is a predictable deviation that results from incorrect sampling or measurement procedures.

Random error is an unpredictable deviation.

---

a predictable quality standard. We study stable processes in more depth in Chapter 18.

In statistical studies random error can be estimated and controlled with greater precision if larger samples are obtained. Random error will have both positive and negative values, and the typical value of the errors will approach zero as the number of observations is increased. It is usually true that the more times we observe a process, the greater is our confidence that we understand the process. Increasing the sample size does not remove bias, because bias is a fixed quantity contained in each observation.

The second method of classification of variables refers to the error component. Variables are either deterministic or random (Key Idea 2.6).

Key Idea 2.6: Deterministic and Random Variables

A **deterministic variable** is assumed to be known without error and thus contains pure information.

A **random variable** contains both information and error. Statisticians use random variables and statistical methods to attempt to estimate information and error for processes that are stable and to identify reasons for an unstable process.

In the remainder of this chapter we study numerical and graphical techniques for qualitative and quantitative variables. We also develop measures of central tendency and measures of dispersion that are more formal and precise procedures for separating the information and error components of random variables.

2.4 COMMUNICATION USING DATA PICTURES: QUALITATIVE VARIABLES

The results of good statistical and data analysis in business and economics needs to be **communicated** to decision makers and the general public. This communication is improved by using a variety of tabular and graphical techniques to drive home the key ideas generated by careful analysis. A few important examples will be presented here to emphasize the value of such techniques. Our hope is that these examples will encourage you to use your creative abilities to develop effective ways of communicating the results of your analysis.

One of the simplest tabular techniques used to summarize large sets of qualitative data is the **frequency distribution table**. In this table, a set of data is classified into subgroups, called *classes*, and the frequency or number of observations in each class is recorded. Suppose that a random sample of 50 spectators at this year's Super Bowl are asked to identify in which region of the United States they live. Categories in all frequency distribution tables must be both **inclusive** and **mutually exclusive**. For this example, this means that each possible region must be represented, and a spectator can live in one and only one region. The responses include *north*, *south*, *east*, *west*, and *international* (for the nonresident fans). A list of the categories together with the number of spectators in each region is given in Table 2.1. When the number of spectators for each category is converted to a percentage of the sample size, the resulting table is called a **relative frequency distribution table**, as shown in Table 2.2.

TABLE 2.1   Frequency Table of Residence

Region	Number of Spectators Who Live in This Region
North	10
South	21
East	12
West	4
International	3

TABLE 2.2   Relative Frequency Table of Residence

Region	Percentage of Spectators Who Live in This Region
North	20
South	42
East	24
West	8
International	6

Other graphical techniques, such as pie charts, bar charts, pictorial graphs, and Pareto diagrams, can easily be prepared using statistical programs, spreadsheet programs, and special graphics packages. All of these packages provide useful and impressive graphical displays that can easily be prepared within their systems. The following pie and bar charts were constructed using Lotus 1-2-3 for Windows and Microsoft Excel.[3]

2.4.1 Pie Charts and Bar Charts

Pie and bar charts are two of the most common data pictures for qualitative data. In the following example we see how a team used these graphs to study solid waste reduction.

Example 2.1   Solid Waste Reduction

A task force was appointed by a regional solid waste authority to study the county solid waste system and to determine the costs of alternatives to landfill disposal. This is an increasingly severe problem for local governments as more valuable land is allocated to garbage disposal and the cost of minimizing landfill damage to groundwater supply increases. The project required considerable data analysis and the communication of important results to the decision-making board.

   Solution   The first step taken by the task force was to determine the major categories of waste. From records and experience they concluded that the categories of solid waste composition included recyclable waste, yard waste, compostable waste, residual landfill waste, and demolition waste. Figure 2.1 is a pie chart that indicates the percentage of various categories of solid waste composition.

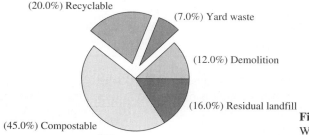

Categories by Percentage

(20.0%) Recyclable

(7.0%) Yard waste

(12.0%) Demolition

(16.0%) Residual landfill

(45.0%) Compostable

Figure 2.1   Pie Chart Showing Solid Waste Composition

   Next, the task force would need to develop strategies for handling these categories. Recall that categories of waste such as recyclable and yard waste are qualitative variables. Notice how the various categories are immediately apparent because of the relative size of the segments. Well-known strategies for reducing landfill waste include recycling and open composting of yard waste (leaves, grass, branches, etc.). Thus in Figure 2.1 these two sections were shown as cut out of the pie to emphasize immediate solid waste reductions. One can easily see that over one-fourth of

---

[3] Lotus 1-2-3 for Windows is a registered trademark of the Lotus Development Corporation. Microsoft Excel is a registered trademark of the Microsoft Corporation.

the waste can be removed from the landfill by these two procedures. Another strategy being considered was the composting of household garbage using a more complex procedure. Analysis of the waste stream indicated that 45% of the material was in the "compostable" category. Again note how dramatically this fraction is identified and emphasized in the pie chart. A quick glance at this chart indicates that almost three-fourths of the present landfill material could be removed by the strategies proposed.

Another part of the analysis consisted of comparing the total solid waste disposal costs using the present landfill operation versus developing a facility for composting household waste. Figure 2.2 is a bar chart that shows the cost comparison between alternatives over time. The bar chart makes the comparison clear and easy to follow. The cost differences expand more rapidly into the future, because there are larger initial fixed costs for the composting facility.   □

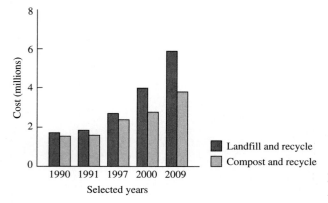

Figure 2.2   Bar Chart: Comparison of Annual Costs

2.4.2 Pictorial Graphs

Another type of graphical display, which is often used in magazines and newspapers, is the pictorial graph, shown in Figures 2.3 and 2.4. These graphs are designed to emphasize context and conclusions in an easy-to-interpret artistic form.

The preparation of such charts previously required a skilled graphic artist. However, now there are a number of computer packages that provide standard picture components that can be used to prepare pictorial graphs. Figure 2.3 provides a comparison of productivity growth for the past 50 years. This graph appeared in the *New York Times* as part of an article dealing with problems in the U.S. economy.[4]

The author wanted to indicate that the rate of productivity increase was growing again after declining in the 1970s and 1980s. However, productivity growth had not reached the level of 2% per year that occurred in the 1950s and 1960s. The message about the major downturn in productivity growth that weakened the economy and the

---

[4] "The Economy: Problems . . . ," *The New York Times*, National, Sunday, February 14, 1993.

Average Yearly Growth in Productivity

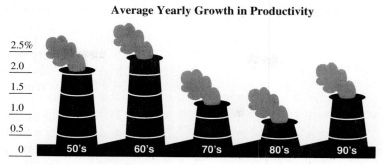

Source: Bureau of Labor Statistics.

Figure 2.3   Productivity Still Lags: Comparison of Productivity Growth

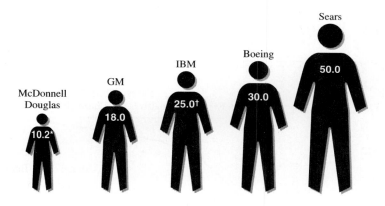

*All figures in thousands.
†IBM is said to be contemplating cutting another 15,000 jobs.

Figure 2.4   Big Companies, Big Cuts: Planned Layoffs Recently Announced
by Large Companies

recent evidence of renewed growth is clear. There is one subtle problem in this display. The smokestack symbol emphasizes industrial productivity. However, the 1990s economy contains information-processing and service sectors that are substantially larger than the industrial sector. Thus productivity growth must come in nonindustrial sectors.

In a related part of the same article the author wanted to indicate that large firms were reducing their workforce in response to reduced sales. Figure 2.4 uses a generic worker of various sizes to indicate the relative size of work force reduction by large firms. The emphasis here is on the magnitude of layoffs, not on the percentage reduction within the firms.

2.4.3 Pareto Charts

One responsibility of quality control managers is to identify the major causes of problems and attempt to correct them quickly at minimum cost. A statistical quality control tool that is frequently used to accomplish this task is called the Pareto chart (Key Idea 2.7), named for an Italian economist, Vilfredo Pareto (1848–1923), who identified the result that in most cases a small number of factors are responsible for most problems. In a Pareto chart, which is introduced in Figure 2.5, bars are arranged to emphasize the most frequent causes of defects.

Key Idea 2.7: Pareto Chart

The **Pareto chart** is a bar chart that displays the frequency of defect causes. The bar at the left indicates the most frequent cause and bars to the right indicate causes in decreasing frequency.

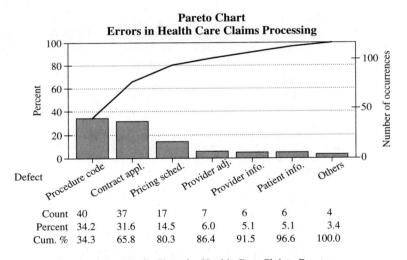

Defect	Procedure code	Contract appl.	Pricing sched.	Provider adj.	Provider info.	Patient info.	Others
Count	40	37	17	7	6	6	4
Percent	34.2	31.6	14.5	6.0	5.1	5.1	3.4
Cum. %	34.3	65.8	80.3	86.4	91.5	96.6	100.0

Figure 2.5   Pareto Chart for Health Care Claims Process

Pareto analysis is used to search for significant causes of problems—to separate the vital few from the trivial many. Pareto's result applies to a wide variety of behavior over many systems and is sometimes referred to as the *80–20 rule*. A common observation is that 80% of a systems improvement can be made for 20% of the cost of making all possible improvements, because 80% of the problems result from 20% of the causes. The use of a Pareto chart can also improve communication with employees, management, and within production teams. The use of Pareto charts in data analysis and communication is illustrated below in the context of insurance claims processing.

Analysis and payment of health care insurance claims is a complex process that can result in a number of incorrectly processed claims. These errors lead to an increase in staff time to obtain the correct information and/or errors in actual payment. Errors resulting in underpayment are usually detected by the payee. Overpayments may often be overlooked by the recipient. These errors can increase costs substantially, in addition to having negative effects on customer relationships. Considerable effort is devoted to analyzing the reporting and claims processing activity so that procedures for minimizing errors can be developed. A major health insurance company set a goal to reduce errors by 50%.

The health insurance company conducted an intensive investigation of the entire claims submission and payment process. The investigation was designed and directed by a committee of key staff people from the claims processing, provider relations, marketing, internal audit, data processing, and medical review departments. The committee first prepared a list of the most common problems based on their experience and review of the process. The committee finally agreed on a list of seven types of error. Three of these—procedure and diagnosis codes, provider information, and patient information—are related to the submission process and must be checked by reviewing patient medical records in clinics and hospitals. The other four—pricing schedules, contract applications, provider adjustments, and program and system errors—are related to the processing of claims for payment within the insurance company offices. A detailed description of each of these error types is in Appendix A of this chapter.

A random sample of 1000 claims was selected for complete audit. This audit began with checking the claim against medical records in clinics and hospitals and proceeded through the final payment stage. Claims with errors were separated and the total number of errors of each type was recorded. If a claim had a number of errors, each error was recorded. In this process many decisions were made concerning error definition. For example, if a child was coded for a procedure typically used for adults and the computer processing system did not detect this, this error was recorded as error 7 (program and system errors) and also as error 3 (patient information error). If treatment for a sprain was coded as a fracture, this was recorded as error 1 (procedure code error). The number of errors by type is shown in Table 2.3.

TABLE 2.3   Errors in Health Care Claims Processing

Code	Category	Error Type	Frequency
A	1	Procedure and diagnosis code	40
B	2	Provider information	6
C	3	Patient information	6
D	4	Pricing schedules	17
E	5	Contract application	37
F	6	Provider adjustments	7
G	7	Program and system errors	4

Next, the team constructed a Pareto chart (Figure 2.5) to depict the frequency of errors visually and to indicate areas needing the most improvement. In most cases the vertical axis on the Pareto chart indicates the frequency or the percentage of problems that resulted from this cause. Notice the line, called a *cumulative frequency line graph*, which is sketched above the various bars. Reading from left to right, this line tells the reader that 34.2% of the errors in the health care claim processing result from procedure and diagnosis code errors, and that when procedure and diagnosis code errors are *combined* with the contract application errors, we can account for a total of 65.8% of all the defects. As we add (cumulate) the defect percentages for each type of error (from left to right), we notice that the increase in this cumulative frequency line indicates the relative improvement that would result from correcting each of the most frequent problems. From the Pareto chart the analysts saw that error 1 (procedure and diagnosis code error) and error 5 (contract application error) were the major causes of error. The combination of errors 1, 5, and 4 (pricing schedules error) resulted in over 80% of the errors. By examining the Pareto chart, the analyst can quickly determine which causes should receive most of the problem correction effort.

Armed with this information, the task force made a number of recommendations to reduce errors and bring the process into control. Following are some of these recommendations:

1. Hold special training sessions for hospital and clinic claims processors.
2. Conduct surprise random audits to check for coding errors.
3. Impose monetary penalties for organizations with excessive errors.
4. Have two people prepare the complete set of contract application tables separately. Next, compare all the table entries using a computer program and resolve any differences.
5. Prepare a master set of model claims to be used to test for correct contract application.
6. Apply recommendations 4 and 5 to the preparation of pricing schedules.

Use of the Pareto chart and the subsequent recommendations resulted in substantially fewer errors. Overpayments on claims, as well as the staff work required to correct the errors, were reduced.

2.5 FREQUENCY DISTRIBUTIONS FOR QUANTITATIVE DATA

Statistical studies often begin with small samples to explore intuitive links between observed data and frequency distributions. After analyzing intuitive links in a small sample, the study is extended by collecting and analyzing larger samples. Among the first analytical tools used in a statistical study is the frequency distribution (Key Idea 2.8).

Key Idea 2.8: Frequency Distributions

A **frequency distribution** records the number of observations contained in subgroups (called *classes*), which are defined by numerical intervals on a variable being studied. Intervals normally are of equal size and must cover the range of sample observations.

The purpose of a frequency distribution is to summarize large data sets and to organize and present the data in tabular form. A set of data is classified into subgroups, called *classes*, and the frequency or number of observations in each class is recorded. It might not be feasible or desirable to use equal-width intervals for distributions with extreme outliers. Consider the following illustration from a tourism survey conducted in the Orlando, Florida, area during the 1994 World Cup Games.

The tourism industry in Florida surveys visitors to the state to obtain information on tourists' vacation plans and spending habits. Such information is helpful to the chambers of commerce in local communities; to beach patrols; to the managers of restaurants, hotels, and main attractions; and even to the department of transportation in planning repairs to major interstates. Variables of interest include the age of tourists, their expected length of stay, their average daily food budgets, and the percentage of tourists who plan to visit Disney World, Sea World, or the NASA Space Center.

Suppose that the ages of tourists in the Orlando area during the 1994 World Cup Games is of interest to the retailers at Church Street (Orlando's restored historic district, which offers entertainment, restaurants, and shops). Advertising and sales are often targeted to specific age markets. The data in Table 2.4 record the ages of a random sample of 100 tourists visiting in the metro-Orlando area during the World Cup Games.

Unfortunately, the data in their present form are of little value to the Church Street retailers. We will first develop a frequency distribution to present these data in a table. Throughout this chapter we present other tabular forms (such as cumulative frequency distributions), graphical forms (including histograms and ogives), and descriptive measures to summarize this data set and to provide useful information to the Church Street merchants.

2.5.1 Basic Rules for Frequency Distributions

Certain questions arise immediately in the construction of a frequency distribution. How many class intervals should be used? How wide is each interval? Should all intervals be of the same width? Where does the first interval begin? There are some

TABLE 2.4   Ages of 100 Tourists

20	20	30	41	35	46	47
61	12	34	36	19	27	46
32	6	65	37	63	25	28
11	64	48	29	15	39	44
70	31	39	18	21	35	22
42	48	23	14	35	36	44
70	49	39	6	34	16	28
3	61	12	23	27	45	48
40	33	50	58	53	15	18
30	31	39	29	45	14	38
50	20	29	20	17	55	37
73	5	79	19	8	59	18
43	78	53	21	59	43	16
22	26	26	27	36	38	67
38	38					

general rules for preparing frequency distributions that make it easier to analyze data and to communicate results.

Inclusive and nonoverlapping intervals.   Interval classes *must* be established to be inclusive and nonoverlapping. Every observation must belong to one and to only one class interval. The problem of overlapping may occur if the interval endpoints are actual observations from the data set. For example, in the tourism survey, suppose that two class intervals are "age 10–age 20" and "age 20–age 30." To which of these two classes would a person age 20 belong?

To avoid overlapping, two approaches can be taken. One method is to construct the intervals with a "less than" sign. For example, instead of the interval "age 10–age 20," one would use the interval "age 10 but less than age 20." Another approach is to add a decimal place to the data and to use intervals such as "age 9.5–age 19.5."

Number of intervals.   There are no absolute rules to determine the exact number of classes to use in a frequency distribution. Practitioners often use guidelines similar to the ones listed in Key Idea 2.9. Practice and experience are the best guidelines with larger data sets requiring more class intervals. Since the sample size for the tourism survey is 100, we will select eight intervals for the tourism study of ages.

As you gain experience in developing frequency distributions, you will see that if you select too few classes, the pattern and various characteristics of the data may be hidden. If you select too many classes, you will discover that some of your intervals may contain no observations or a very small number of frequencies. We address these problems again in Section 2.6 in the study of histograms.

Key Idea 2.9: Guidelines for Number of Intervals

Sample Size	Number of Intervals
Fewer than 50	5–6
50 to 100	6–8
Over 100	8–10

You may find it helpful as you become more proficient with the construction of frequency distributions to use Sturges's rule (Key Idea 2.10) as a guide to the number of intervals. Using Sturges's rule to determine the number of classes for the tourism survey, we find that

$$1 + 3.322(\log 100) = 1 + 3.322(2) = 7.644$$

or approximately eight classes, which is the same number as that of our guideline in Key Idea 2.9.

Key Idea 2.10: Sturges's Rule

Let k = approximate number of classes to use in a frequency distribution

n = number of observations

$$k = 1 + 3.322(\log n)$$

Interval width.   After choosing the number of intervals, the next step is to choose the interval width using the basic rule given in Key Idea 2.11. In most situations the interval width will be rounded or truncated to a convenient whole number to provide for easy interpretation. In the tourism illustration, the oldest tourist in the sample was age 79 and the youngest tourist in the sample was only 3 years old. Using eight classes, the width rounds to 10.

An example of a frequency distribution following the basic rules in Key Ideas 2.9 to 2.11 is given in Table 2.5. Notice that we also converted the number of observations to percentages (here we used decimal equivalents). You will recall that the resulting table, as discussed in Section 2.4 for qualitative data, is called the relative frequency distribution.

Key Idea 2.11: Interval Width

$$\text{Interval width} = \frac{\text{largest number} - \text{smallest number}}{\text{number of intervals}}$$

Intervals normally are of equal size.

TABLE 2.5   Frequency Distribution of Ages
of 100 Tourists

Ages	Number of Tourists	Relative Frequency (%)
0–under 10	5	0.05
10–under 20	15	0.15
20–under 30	21	0.21
30–under 40	24	0.24
40–under 50	16	0.16
50–under 60	8	0.08
60–under 70	6	0.06
70–under 80	5	0.05
	100	**1.00**

2.5.2 Cumulative Frequency Distributions

The Church Street merchants may want to know how many tourists are younger than
a certain age (e.g., younger than 30 years old). In situations like this, we want to
know the number of observations that are less than a particular value. The appropriate
distribution to use is called a cumulative frequency distribution (Key Idea 2.12).

Key Idea 2.12: Cumulative Frequency Distributions

A **cumulative frequency distribution** contains the total number of observations whose values are less than the upper limit for each interval. It is
constructed by adding the frequencies of all frequency distribution intervals up to and including the present interval.

From Table 2.6, the merchants can readily determine information such as that 20% of the sample were younger than 20 years of age or that 41% of those sampled were younger than 30. This type of information provides a basis for advertising and marketing and was not readily available when the data were presented in raw form (Table 2.4).

TABLE 2.6   Cumulative Frequency
Distribution for Tourists' Ages

Age	Cumulative Frequency	Relative Cumulative Frequency
Less than 10	5	0.05
Less than 20	20	0.20
Less than 30	41	0.41
Less than 40	65	0.65
Less than 50	81	0.81
Less than 60	89	0.89
Less than 70	95	0.95
Less than 80	100	1.00

It is important to note that the final interval in a cumulative frequency distribution must contain the total number of observations in the sample and a cumulative percentage of 100%. In Section 2.6.3 we discuss a graph of the cumulative frequency distribution called an ogive.

Practice Problem 2.1

Construct a frequency distribution of the data in Table 2.4 using 10 classes. Compare and contrast your answer with the frequency distribution in Table 2.5. Which frequency distribution do you think presents a clearer picture of the data? Why?
□

The solutions for all Practice Problems are given at the end of the chapter.

2.6 COMMUNICATION USING DATA PICTURES: QUANTITATIVE VARIABLES

In Section 2.4 we discussed various tabular and graphical pictures used to summarize qualitative data. In this section we study data pictures of quantitative data: the histogram, the stem-and-leaf display, and the ogive.

2.6.1 Histograms

In continuing their efforts to make sample data sets meaningful, analysts construct graphs of the frequency and cumulative frequency distributions. Sample data sets are often displayed in graphical forms to improve understanding and communication. The data from a frequency distribution can be used to construct a graph called a histogram (Key Idea 2.13). Essentially, a histogram provides the same information as a frequency distribution but in pictorial form.

Key Idea 2.13: Histograms

A **histogram** consists of vertical bars constructed on a horizontal line marked off with intervals for the variable being displayed. The intervals correspond to those in a frequency distribution table. The heights of the bars are proportional to the number of observations in that interval. In some cases the number of observations are displayed above the bars.

Since histograms are pictures of frequency distributions, the same basic rules of frequency distributions discussed in Section 2.5.1 apply to the construction of histograms. The number of bars increases with the sample size. Too few or too many bars may hide the characteristics of the data sets. We continue the Tourist Example, and in Figure 2.6 we used Minitab for Windows [**Graph** > **Histogram**][5] to construct histograms of the tourists' ages. Graph (a) illustrates that too few bars hide the overall picture of the data; graph (b) exhibits the confusion of too many bars; and graph (c) follows the basic rules of Key Ideas 2.9 to 2.11.

2.6.2 Stem-and-Leaf Display

Exploratory data analysis (EDA) is concerned with describing data in simple arithmetic terms with easy-to-draw pictures. One useful technique for exploratory data analysis is the stem-and-leaf display (Key Idea 2.14). It was developed by John Tukey, a famous mathematical statistician, as a technique for summarizing a data set without losing the individual observations.[6] This technique was originally proposed as an easy pencil-and-paper procedure for quickly identifying the pattern of a newly acquired set of data. Subsequently, stem-and-leaf displays have become a standard component of most computer statistical software.

---

[5] Throughout the book we present the Minitab for Windows menu steps in brackets and in boldface. Follow these steps, selecting each menu from left to right. Readers who are unfamiliar with Minitab for Windows may refer to Appendix C at the end of the chapter for additional information.

[6] John Tukey, *Exploratory Data Analysis*, Addison-Wesley, Reading, MA, 1977.

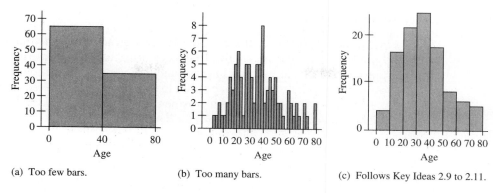

(a) Too few bars.   (b) Too many bars.   (c) Follows Key Ideas 2.9 to 2.11.

Figure 2.6   Histograms of Tourists' Ages [**Graph** > **Histogram**]

Key Idea 2.14: Stem-and-Leaf Display

The **stem-and-leaf display** provides a graphical picture of a set of data. It is constructed by establishing subsets based on the leading digits (called the *stem*) of the numbers. The trailing digits (called the *leaf*) are displayed individually in ascending order after each of the stem-defined subsets. The number of digits in each subset indicates the subset frequency. The individual digits indicate the pattern of values within each subset. Except for data with extreme outliers, all stems are included even if there are no observations in the corresponding subset.

The number of digits in the stem varies according to the data set. In the following examples, we first work with a one-digit stem (Example 2.2). Example 2.3 involves a two-digit stem.

Example 2.2   Time to Complete an Assignment

In a random sample of 25 students, the students were asked to record the time (in minutes) to complete a particular homework assignment. They were then to examine patterns in the data. The times (in minutes) to complete the assignment were

32	26	45	28	49
19	38	41	63	46
24	42	37	40	64
47	34	30	45	18
33	45	61	42	30

Solution   In this problem we select a one-digit stem (the number in the ten's position) and construct the stem-and-leaf display shown in Table 2.7. Note that the leaves after each stem have been arranged in ascending order and that we included the stem of "5" even though there were no values in this subset. To see the pattern of the data quickly, we only need to rotate the stem-and-leaf display 90°.   □

TABLE 2.7   Stem-and-Leaf Display for Homework Time (minutes)

Stem	Leaf
1	8 9
2	4 6 8
3	0 0 2 3 4 7 8
4	0 1 2 2 5 5 5 6 7 9
5	
6	1 3 4

Example 2.3   GPAs of Graduating Economics Majors

In this example we examine patterns in the grade-point averages (GPAs) of 112 graduating economics majors.

Solution   Rather than list the individual GPAs as a beginning point, we have constructed the stem-and-leaf display (Table 2.8) using Minitab for Windows [**Stat > EDA > Stem-and-Leaf**]. The lowest GPA in our data set was 2.12 and the highest GPA was 3.87. We now use a *two-digit* stem (i.e., 21 represents a GPA of 2.10, or 38 is a 3.80 GPA). The first two digits in the stem represent the GPA to the nearest 0.1. The first row represents those students with GPAs between 2.10 and 2.19. Within that subgroup there was one student with a GPA of 2.12, as indicated by the digit 2 in the leaf section. The second-row subgroup contains two students, with GPAs of 2.22 and 2.29.

As you can readily see, the pattern and shape of the distribution are apparent. In addition to the stem and leaf columns, you notice that the left column in Minitab provides a cumulative frequency of observations from the extremes to the center. For example, 40 students had GPAs at or below 2.89. From the upper extreme of the distribution, 42 students had GPAs at or above 3.20, while 13 had GPAs at or above 3.60.

The middle of the data is centered in the interval from 3.00 to 3.09. Examination of this graph indicates that these GPAs are approximately symmetric about the center. In Section 2.9 we study another technique of exploratory data analysis called box-and-whisker plots.

Since the purpose of this technique is to communicate information, simply constructing a stem-and-leaf display is not sufficient. Certainly, statistical packages can prepare the graphs. You must also be able to write a summary of the significant results

TABLE 2.8   Stem-and-Leaf Display for
GPAs of Economics Majors

Cumulative Frequency	Stem	Leaf
1	21	2
3	22	2 9
7	23	3 4 5 9
13	24	0 1 3 4 7 9
19	25	1 2 3 5 5 7
24	26	1 1 1 2 6
30	27	1 2 3 5 6 8
40	28	0 2 3 4 4 4 5 6 9 9
51	29	0 1 2 2 4 4 4 5 7 7 7
(10)	30	1 1 1 2 6 7 8 8 8 9
51	31	0 1 1 1 2 4 5 6 8
42	32	1 1 4 5 6 8 9
35	33	1 2 3 5 7 8 8 9
27	34	0 0 1 1 1 3 3 3 4 6
17	35	1 6 7 7
13	36	0 1 2 5 5 6 6 8 8
4	37	2 3
2	38	0 7

apparent from the graph. We suggest that you develop your written communication skills at the same time that you are also developing your statistical skills.   □

Practice Problem 2.2

Use a statistical package, such as Minitab for Windows, to analyze the data in the tourism illustration by constructing a stem-and-leaf display.   □

Problem Exercises

2.1   Analyze the following random sample of 12 retail clothing stores' daily sales using a stem-and-leaf display.

2000	2500	2100	1900	1800	2200
1700	2000	2300	2400	2600	1400

2.2   The number of hours to negotiate a sales contract for medium-sized computer systems are

10	24	29	32	36	15	29	12	14	16
11	17	24	18	26	15	18	34	31	35

Analyze the sales contract negotiation data using a stem-and-leaf display.

2.3   Analyze the weight of shipments in pounds for the following random sample of food
       distribution warehouses to small-town supermarkets:

2800	3500	2100	1300	2800	2200
700	3300	4300	1400	1100	1600

2.4   A random sample of delivery time in days was obtained for packages mailed from a
       large urban post office. The times are

10	4	8	12	6	5	9	12	14	15
10	14	13	8	6	15	18	14	11	16

Prepare a frequency distribution and histogram using:
(a) Intervals of 5 beginning with 1.
(b) Intervals of 2 beginning with 1.
(c) In your opinion, does part (a) or part (b) result in a better presentation of the data?

2.5   The management of a medium-sized chair factory is concerned about the daily output. A
       random sample of days from the past year is selected and the number of chairs produced
       on each day is

108	48	98	122	66	95	94	123	144	125
109	148	132	88	96	135	128	134	141	126

Prepare a frequency distribution and histogram using:
(a) Intervals of 50 beginning with 1.
(b) Intervals of 20 beginning with 1.
(c) In your opinion, does part (a) or part (b) result in a better presentation of the data?

2.6   The aptitude test scores for 30 applicants are

110	94	88	126	96	95	119	128	143	152
109	114	113	98	86	152	148	134	119	136
109	94	78	132	96	115	129	127	144	153

Prepare a frequency distribution and histogram using:
(a) Intervals of 10.
(b) Intervals of 30.
(c) In your opinion, does part (a) or part (b) result in a better presentation of the data?

2.7   A major resort is studying its occupancy rates for various seasons. A random sample of
       the number of days stayed by family groups is

10	4	9	12	16	15	9	12	14	16
10	17	14	8	16	15	18	14	11	15

Prepare a frequency distribution and histogram using:
(a) Intervals of 5 beginning with 1.
(b) Intervals of 2 beginning with 1.
(c) In your opinion, does part (a) or part (b) result in a better presentation of the data?

2.6.3 Ogives

In Section 2.5.2 we discussed cumulative frequency distributions, and in this section
we learn to construct an ogive, which is a graph of a cumulative frequency distribution
(Key Idea 2.15). Figure 2.7 shows the ogive for the cumulative frequency distribution
of tourists' ages (see Table 2.6). Again, we used Minitab for Windows [**Graph** >

Histogram > Options ... > Cumulative Frequency or Cumulative Percent].
The ogive indicates the percentage of observations that are below certain values. For
instance, in this example the Church Street retailers know that 65% of the tourists in
this survey were younger than 40.

Key Idea 2.15: Ogive

An **ogive** is a line graph connecting points that are the cumulative percentage of observations below the upper limit of each class in a cumulative
frequency distribution.

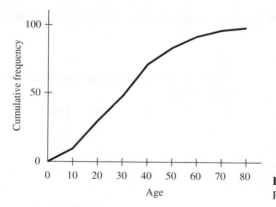

Figure 2.7 Ogive of Cumulative
Frequency Distribution of Age

What if the Church Street merchants want to know what percent of the sample
were at least 40 years old? It is possible to construct a "greater than or equal to" cumulative frequency distribution and an ogive of that table. It is easier to subtract from
100% and quickly conclude that 35% of the sample are at least 40 years old. This kind
of data provides relevant information to the merchants in preparing advertisements and
in planning promotional sales.

Problem Exercises

2.8   The percentage of defective parts produced on a random sample of 8-hour production
shifts are

1.0	4.2	5.9	1.2	1.6	5.4	2.9	1.2	1.4	4.6
1.9	1.7	3.4	4.8	1.6	3.5	1.8	5.4	1.1	3.5

Prepare a frequency distribution and histogram using:
(a) Intervals of 1.0.
(b) Intervals of 2.
(c) Prepare a cumulative frequency distribution.
(d) Draw an ogive corresponding to the cumulative frequency distribution.

2.9 Refer to Problem 2.7.
(a) Construct a cumulative frequency distribution using intervals of 2.
(b) Draw an ogive corresponding to the cumulative frequency distribution.
(c) What percentage of the sample stayed 8 days or less?
(d) What percentage of the sample stayed for more than 14 days?

2.7 COMPUTER USE FOR DATA ANALYSIS

In the first part of this chapter we developed various graphical procedures to summarize and describe data. In the remainder of the chapter we study numerical procedures to summarize data. Although manual computation of these numerical descriptors is possible for smaller data sets, most often summarization of data is easiest to accomplish with computer software such as Minitab, SAS (Statistical Analysis System), SPSS (Statistical Package for the Social Sciences), BMDP (UCLA Biomedical Statistical Package), or Systat. These programs include a user-friendly interface that provides access to a number of analytical procedures and data files. With technological advances, nearly everyone has immediate access to the computation of these statistics. But not everyone understands what the data are saying! *To have a competitive advantage in today's business environment, you must become proficient in data interpretation and analysis.*

Most of your analysis will be performed using an interactive statistical program. Interactive programs take one instruction at a time and present the output before the next instruction is entered. The user views the results and then may enter the next instruction based on the results of the previous analysis. In that way the user "interacts" and can work more closely with the data from the terminal. Interactive programs enable users to try different options and to correct mistakes immediately. The entering of commands can range from typing an instruction line to clicking a mouse on an icon or possibly even a voice command.

Most computer packages provide a capability for using a set of commands that are written in a computer file and then executed in sequence. These command files, often called *macros*, are extremely useful if an analysis procedure is to be executed a number of times on different data sets. Macros increase the speed of analysis because the user does not have to retype each step. They also ensure that the same analysis is performed on each data set. Thus differences in results are due to differences in the data, not to mistakes in entering analysis commands.

Computer analysis requires data files that are often structured as a rectangular table or data matrix containing the observations for several variables. Each row contains one observation and each column contains a different variable. Variables are often defined in a data dictionary (Key Idea 2.16).

> **Key Idea 2.16: Data Files and Data Dictionaries**
>
> A **data file** contains the observations for the variables that are being described and analyzed. A **data dictionary** contains descriptions for the variables in a data file.

The U.S. Department of Commerce, the Economics and Statistics Administration, and the Bureau of the Census annually publish the *Statistical Abstract of the United States*.[7] The *Abstract* provides data and information to researchers, economic forecasters, government agencies, politicians, educational institutions, hospital managers, insurance companies, marketing agencies, manufacturers, service industries, and many others. A sample of the data included annually for each state and the District of Columbia follows:

1. Total resident population (both number and rank)
2. Unemployment percentage of civilian labor force
3. Median household income
4. Business failure rate per 10,000 concerns
5. Violent crime rate per 100,000 population
6. Average cost per patient per day in community hospitals
7. State gasoline tax rate in cents per gallon
8. Percent of population receiving Social Security benefits
9. Educational attainment of residence
10. Public elementary and secondary teachers' average salary
11. Infant mortality rate

An interesting activity for the reader is to use the most recent publication of the *Abstract* to find the values of the variables listed above for the state of your residence. As an illustration, consider the following situation.

The store location division of a national retail firm wanted to identify variables that would provide some of the information for selecting new store locations. The data dictionary and the data file used were taken from the *Statistical Abstract of the United States, 1993*:

1. STATE: a code number that identifies each state as defined in the *Abstract*. The code definition has been added to the file.

---

[7] *Statistical Abstract of the United States, 1993*, 113th ed., Washington, DC: U.S. Bureau of the Census, 1993.

2. TOTPOP92: total state residential population (1992) in thousands.
3. UNEMP92: unemployment percentage of the civilian labor force.
4. BUSFAIL: business failure rate per 10,000 concerns (1992).

The variables in the data file are listed in Appendix B of this chapter. The computer output in Exhibit 2.1 is a sneak preview of the exciting material you will learn to interpret and analyze. We obtained this printout using Minitab for Windows [**Stat** > **Basic Statistics** > **Descriptive Statistics**]. The column labels identify major descriptive statistics (descriptors) that we study in the remainder of the chapter. Some column labels are probably obvious to you (such as MEAN for the average, MIN and MAX for the smallest and largest values in a data set). We will not use the columns TRMEAN and SEMEAN at this time. As you learn each descriptor, think about this printout. For now, simply observe the data. Just as medical students are trained to read x-rays, so you are being trained to read an x-ray of the data. As you progress in this chapter, the numbers in the exhibit will take on new meaning. We will revisit this file periodically.

EXHIBIT 2.1   State Survey: Descriptive Statistics

	N	MEAN	MEDIAN	TRMEAN	STDEV	SEMEAN
TOTPOP92	51	5002	3470	4151	5599	784
UNEMP92	51	6.798	6.900	6.820	1.592	0.223
BUSFAIL	51	95.25	90.00	93.49	29.72	4.16

	MIN	MAX	Q1	Q3
TOTPOP92	466	30867	1235	5996
UNEMP92	3.000	11.300	5.700	7.500
BUSFAIL	47.00	169.00	74.00	111.00

2.8 MEASURES OF CENTRAL TENDENCY

In addition to graphical methods, businesspeople and economists use measures of central tendency, measures of variability, and measures of relative standing to summarize data. Each of these descriptors serves a different purpose in the analysis of data. Measures of central tendency provide the analyst with information about a "typical" observation in the data. Measures of variability indicate the amount of spread, dispersion, or deviation among the observations. This information tells the analyst the risk of extremely large or small numbers. The position of a single observation in relation to the remainder of the values is expressed by measures of relative standing. Both graphical and numerical methods provide a picture of the data and are valuable tools in the analysis of processes and systems.

The three most common measures of central tendency are the arithmetic mean (simply called the mean), the median, and the mode. There are some useful guidelines as to which measure of central tendency should be used. Analysts often base their choice on the type of variables in the data. For quantitative data, all three measures of central tendency can be computed, but the mean is most frequently used. However, the median is computed for nonsymmetric quantitative data or for ordinal variables. If the data are nominal, the mode is often used as a measure of central tendency.

2.8.1 Arithmetic Mean

The mean, or average, is the most frequently used measure of central tendency, and can be computed for both samples and populations (Key Idea 2.17). Note that although both μ and $\overline{X}$ are averages, most of the time it will not be practical or possible to calculate the population mean, μ. Thus we find the sample mean, $\overline{X}$. Because the sample mean is calculated on only a subset of the population data, we expect some deviation between these two measures. Statistics, as stated in Chapter 1, will give us tools to make wise decisions about the population by using sample estimates.

Key Idea 2.17: Arithmetic Mean

The **arithmetic mean**, or **average**, is the sum of the data values divided by the number of observations. If the data set is a sample, the sample mean, $\overline{X}$, is

$$\overline{X} = \frac{\sum_{i=1}^{n} x_i}{n} = \frac{x_1 + x_2 + \cdots + x_n}{n}$$

where n is the sample size and $\sum$ means "to add." If the data set is a population, the **population mean**, μ, is

$$\mu = \frac{\sum_{i=1}^{N} x_i}{N} = \frac{x_1 + x_2 + \cdots + x_N}{N}$$

where N is the population size.

Since a descriptor refers to either a sample or a population, it is important to understand the difference between a statistic and a parameter (Key Idea 2.18). The sample mean, $\overline{X}$, is a statistic, and the population mean, μ, is a parameter. Since the mean uses all the observations and the actual size of each observation, a few extremely large or small observations will influence the value of the mean.

Key Idea 2.18: Statistic and Parameter

A **statistic** is a numerical measure computed from a sample. A **parameter** is a numerical measure computed from a population.

Example 2.4   Analysis of Convenience Food Stores

During the past three years Consolidated Oil Company has converted a number of its gasoline stations into convenience food stores (CFSs) to increase total sales revenue. Gasoline sales have not been increasing, so it was decided to expand into related business areas.

Roy Brady, the general manager of the CFS Division, has asked a senior statistician, Susan Smith, to assist with his analysis of daily sales at the convenience stores.

Solution   Susan obtained a random sample of 10 weekdays from each of four stores. The daily sales, in hundreds of dollars, for the stores is shown in Table 2.9. Susan calculated the mean daily sales for each of the four stores. She found that the mean daily sales for store 1, $\bar{X}_1$, was

$$\bar{X}_1 = \frac{6 + 8 + \cdots + 11}{10} = 10.1$$

or $1010. The average daily sales for store 2 was 10.1, for store 3 was 30.1, and for store 4 was 12.1.

TABLE 2.9   CFS Sales ($100 Units)

Day	Store 1	Store 2	Store 3	Store 4
1	6	1	26	6
2	8	19	28	8
3	10	2	30	10
4	12	18	32	12
5	14	10	34	24
6	9	10	29	9
7	11	3	31	11
8	7	17	27	7
9	13	4	33	23
10	11	17	31	11

Roy noticed that the observations in store 3 were merely the store 1 observations plus 20. He then realized that the mean sales for store 3 ($3010) was the mean sales for store 1 increased by the same constant 20, or $2000. Susan informed Roy that whenever a constant is added to all the observations in a sample, the resulting mean is increased by that same constant. (We discuss transformations of data in Section 2.10.) □

Sample observations that are either much larger or much smaller than all the other observations are called *outliers*. Compare store 4 sales to store 1 sales. What do you notice? Susan pointed out to Roy that although the two stores have identical sales for 8 of the 10 sample days, the presence of outliers on days 5 and 9 increased the mean sales for store 4 significantly. Susan first recommended that Roy check the accuracy of the data for those days. If there were no errors, Roy certainly needs to find the factors that contributed to the increased sales on those days. *Whenever there are outliers in the data, you need to look for possible causes.* Susan also suggested that since the mean is influenced by these outliers, another measure of central tendency, the median, might be more appropriate.

2.8.2 Median

The median uses only the relative size of the observations and not their actual numerical values (Key Idea 2.19). As a result, outliers have less effect on the median than on the mean. As an illustration, note that for stores 1 and 4 in Example 2.4, the medians are identical. In both stores, the median daily sales were $1050.

Key Idea 2.19: Median

If the sample size, n, is an odd number, the **median**, X_m, is the value of the middle observation when the data are arranged in ascending (or descending) order.

    If the sample size, n, is an even number, the **median**, X_m, is the average of the two middle observations when the data are arranged in ascending (or descending) order.

Store 1:   6,   7,   8,   9,   10,   11,   11,   12,   13,   14

$$\text{Median daily sales for store 1} = \frac{10 + 11}{2} = 10.5, \text{ or } \$1050$$

Store 4:   6,   7,   8,   9,   10,   11,   11,   12,   23,   24

$$\text{Median daily sales for store 4} = \frac{10 + 11}{2} = 10.5, \text{ or } \$1050$$

    Recall the difference in the means due to the outliers on days 5 and 9 (store 1 had mean daily sales of $1010 and store 4 had mean daily sales of $1250). The choice between the mean and the median depends on the distribution of the observations. The mean or per capita income for a developing country provides a measure of purchasing power. However, it does not show the income of a typical person because the mean is increased greatly by the 10 or 15% of the population who have very large incomes. The same result occurs for housing prices in large cities. For data with outliers, the median should be used. Other measures, such as package weights, component part dimensions, and test scores, tend to have symmetric distributions. In those cases the mean and the median are very close, and we use the mean because it uses all the sample observations.

For large data sets, the median is easier to locate if the stem-and-leaf display is constructed first. For moderate sample sizes, manual ranking of data by use of a stem-and-leaf display is quite simple. Computer software, such as Minitab for Windows, can also be used. Once the data are in ascending order, the median will be located in the $0.5(n + 1)$st position. Recall Example 2.3, the grade-point averages of the 112 graduating economics majors and the stem-and-leaf display in Figure 2.6. The median is found in the 56.5th position:

$$0.5(112 + 1) = 56.5\text{th position} \qquad \text{or}$$

$$\text{median} = \frac{3.06 + 3.07}{2} = 3.065$$

We know from the median that 50% of the graduating economics majors have a GPA below 3.065.

2.8.3 Mode

A third measure of central tendency is the mode (Key Idea 2.20). For the daily sales in Example 2.4, we see that for stores 1 and 4 the value 11 occurs twice (days 7 and 10) and that all the other observations have unique values. Therefore, the modal sales for these two stores is found to be $1100. Store 2 is bimodal, with two modes 10 and 17, and store 3 had a mode of 31. Stores 1, 2, and 3 are unimodal (only one mode).

Key Idea 2.20: Mode

The **mode**, if one exists, is the most frequently occurring observation in the sample or population.

Suppose that the sales on day 10 for store 1 had been 15 instead of 11. Then there would be no mode since each of the observations would have occurred only once.

Recall the frequency distributions in Tables 2.1 and 2.2. The region in which most of this year's Super Bowl spectators lived is the south. We can conclude that the south is the modal region. This is an example of how the mode is the appropriate measure of central tendency for nominal data.

2.8.4 Skewness

We have seen how samples and populations can be described using statistics that measure central tendency. Symmetry (Key Idea 2.21) is one such characteristic. Skewness (Key Idea 2.22) is another property that should be examined. Skewness indicates that a distribution of observations is not symmetric.

Skewness indicates that there are either a few very large or a few very small observations in the data. Positive skewness indicates that there are some very large observations, which, you recall, will increase the mean. Negative skewness, which

---

Key Idea 2.21: Symmetry

The shape of a distribution is said to be **symmetric** if the observations are balanced about the mean. In a symmetric distribution the mean and the median are equal.

Key Idea 2.22: Skewness

A distribution is said to be **skewed** if the observations are not symmetrically distributed above and below the mean.

Positive skewness is identified by $\bar{X} > X_m$. Negative skewness is identified by $\bar{X} < X_m$.

---

indicates the presence of some very small observations, reduces the value of the mean. Skewness can be identified by comparing the mean and the median. From the sales data of Example 2.4, we observe that the distribution of sales for store 4 is positively skewed since:

$$\text{Store 4:}\quad \text{mean} = 12.1 > 10.5 = \text{median}$$

Symmetric and positively and negatively skewed distributions are illustrated in Figure 2.8.

You might ask what business examples are expected to be positively skewed, negatively skewed, or symmetric. Recall the state data survey example from Section 2.7 and the Minitab printout in Exhibit 2.1. We repeat the printout as Exhibit 2.2 to show you clearly how skewness in total state residential population is apparent from the data. *Remember that you are learning to analyze data.*

Notice that the total state residential population mean (5002 in thousands) is much larger than the median (only 3470 in thousands). *This indicates a positively skewed distribution.* You would expect to find a few large observations in the data set. Look at the data in Appendix B of this chapter. Notice the large total state residential population of California. In the following sections we study quartiles and a graph called a box-and-whisker plot. You will then see another way to look at the printout and notice the apparent skewness of the distributions. From the printout you also know that half the states have a total state residential population below 3,470,000 and that half of the total state residential populations exceed this value.

With respect to the unemployment rate, *the mean is only slightly less than the median of 6.9%, indicating a slight negative skewness in the unemployment data.*

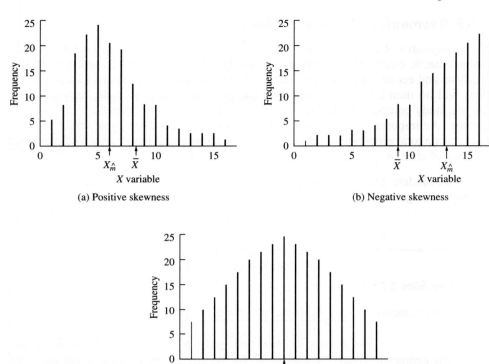

Figure 2.8   Symmetry Versus Skewness

EXHIBIT 2.2   MTB 2.1 State Survey: Descriptive Statistics

	N	MEAN	MEDIAN	TRMEAN	STDEV	SEMEAN
TOTPOP92	51	5002	3470	4151	5599	784
UNEMP92	51	6.798	6.900	6.820	1.592	0.223
BUSFAIL	51	95.25	90.00	93.49	29.72	4.16

	MIN	MAX	Q1	Q3
TOTPOP92	466	30867	1235	5996
UNEMP92	3.000	11.300	5.700	7.500
BUSFAIL	47.00	169.00	74.00	111.00

Examining the descriptive results for the business failure rate per 10,000 concerns, we find that *the average failure rate of 95.25 is larger than the median failure rate of 90.00—again, a positively skewed distribution.*

2.8.5 Geometric and Harmonic Mean

Other measures of central tendency that are important in business and economics are the geometric mean and the harmonic mean. The geometric mean is used by business analysts and economists who are interested in growth over a number of time periods. You will no doubt find applications for the geometric mean in your finance classes as you study compound interest over several years, total sales growth, or population growth. An important question concerns the average growth each year that will result in a certain total growth over several years. The harmonic mean is used with measures of rates of change.

Geometric mean.   The geometric mean is defined in Key Idea 2.23. As an example, the geometric mean of 1.05, 1.02, 1.10, and 1.06 is

$$X_g = [(1.05)(1.02)(1.10)(1.06)]^{1/4} = 1.0571$$

Key Idea 2.23: Geometric Mean

The **geometric mean**, X_g, is the nth root of the *product* of n numbers:

$$X_g = (x_1 \times x_2 \times \cdots \times x_n)^{1/n}$$

The geometric mean is used for computing mean growth over several periods given compounded growth from each period.

Example 2.5   Annual Growth Rate

If sales have grown 25% over five years, determine the average annual growth rate.

Solution   The intuitive but naive temptation is simply to divide total growth, 25%, by the number of time periods, five, and conclude that the average annual growth rate is 5%. This result is incorrect because it ignores the compound effect of growth.

Suppose that the annual growth rate were actually 5%; then the total growth over five years would be

$$(1.05)(1.05)(1.05)(1.05)(1.05) = 1.2763 \quad \text{or} \quad 27.63\%$$

However, the annual growth rate, r, that would yield 25% over five years must satisfy the equation $(1 + r)^5 = 1.25$. First, solve for the geometric mean, $X_g = 1 + r$:

$$1 + r = (1.25)^{1/5}$$
$$= 1.046$$

The growth rate is $r = 0.046$, or 4.6%.   □

Harmonic mean.   The harmonic mean is defined in Key Idea 2.24.

Key Idea 2.24: Harmonic Mean

The **harmonic mean** of a sample of n observations is defined as the quotient of the sample size n divided by the sum of the reciprocals of the sample observations:

$$\text{harmonic mean} = \frac{n}{\sum_{i=1}^{n} 1/x_i}$$

Suppose that a turkey gains weight at the rate of 10 pounds per month over the first 5 pounds of growth, 5 pounds per month in the next 5 pounds of growth, and a rate of 4 and 2 in the next two 5-pound intervals. What is the average growth rate? The average growth is 10, 5, 4, 2; the harmonic mean is

$$\frac{4}{0.25 + 0.20 + 0.50 + 0.10} = 3.81$$

The mean growth rate is 3.81 pounds per month. As we stated earlier, this measure of central tendency is also used in more advanced statistical procedures (such as in ANOVA multiple pairwise testing).

Problem Exercises

2.10 Sally Strom, an investment counselor, has reported the following annual growth rates in the price of Amalgamated Roofing stock: 4.3%, 6.0%, 3.5%, 8.2%, and 7.0%.
(a) What is the mean growth rate over the five-year period?
(b) If this growth rate continued, how many years would be required for the price to double?

2.11 The U.S. Agency for International Development (AID) has been studying the population growth rates for a small African country. For the past four years the annual reported population growth rates were 2.5%, 2.1%, 2.8%, and 2.6%.
(a) What is the average annual population growth rate?
(b) Suppose that the projected rate of increase in food production annually is 2%. Should AID consider a project to increase food production in this country? Explain.

2.12 Inflation rates in a small country for the past five years have been 10%, 7%, 13%, 9%, and 12%.
(a) What is the average annual rate of inflation?
(b) If this rate of inflation continues, how long will it take for prices to double?

2.13 Millicent Treloar has been studying the economics of her local delivery business for the past five years. During that time she granted annual wage increases of 4%, 6%, 3%, 5%, and 4%. In addition, she has increased unit delivery prices annually by 1%, 0%, 5%, 6%, and 3%. Determine the average annual rate of:
(a) Wage increase.

(b) Price increase.

(c) Does she have a problem? Explain.

2.9 MEASURES OF DISPERSION

The measures of central tendency do not tell the analyst how closely the observations in the data are to the "typical" observation, or center of the distribution. Thus statisticians searched for a single number that would indicate the amount of deviation in the data. For instance, if an instructor announces to a class that the average grade on the last exam was 80, does this mean that most students scored close to 80, or were there a few outliers, the one or two perfect papers, that raised the value of the mean significantly?

Analysts know the importance of dispersion for describing data instead of reporting only the central tendency: For instance, an economic planner in a poor country would be pleased to know that the mean food consumption is 2500 calories per day, which is well above the subsistence level. However, if one-fifth of the population is starving while another one-fifth are overeating, he would question the fairness of the economic policies. Or suppose that the owner of a small factory knows that the average monthly cash flow is positive. She would be very unhappy to know that in some months there is a negative cash flow, which risks foreclosure by the banks.

From the data in Example 2.4, Roy Brady noticed how sales varied from day to day within each store. Good managers know that the variation from day to day is an important indicator of performance. Stores with a wide sales variation have some days when the staff has little work and other days when customers leave because the delays are too long. Sales variation could be indicated by using measures of dispersion, which include the range, the variance, and the standard deviation.

2.9.1 Range

The range (Key Idea 2.25) of a set of data uses only two of the actual observations and is therefore the easiest of the measures of dispersion to compute. Looking at the illustrations and examples in this chapter, we see that the range of ages for the tourism survey is 76, while the range of GPAs in Example 2.3 is 1.75. Roy Brady discovered that stores 1 and 3 both had ranges of 8. Stores 2 and 4, with ranges of 18, are more erratic in their sales pattern. From this information, Roy understood why stores 2 and 4 had more difficulties with staffing and inventory.

Key Idea 2.25: Range

The **range** is defined as the difference between the largest and the smallest observations in a sample or population.

As you see, the range is easy to obtain by inspecting the sample, and it has some intuitive appeal because it indicates the limits of a sample or population. However, because only two observations are used, it can vary greatly between samples.

In Chapter 18 you will learn that quality control monitoring of processes makes extensive use of range or R charts to ensure that variability is kept at minimum levels. To produce high-quality goods or offer high-quality services, the variability or dispersion of critical measurements must be kept as small as possible. Processes are first adjusted to obtain the minimum variability. Random samples of three to eight observations are obtained at regular intervals and the range is computed and plotted on the graph. If there appears to be a problem, the process is stopped and the problem is identified and corrected. The range was chosen as the measure of dispersion before computers were widely available. With improved software, the standard deviation is now often chosen as the measure of variability in the monitoring of processes.

2.9.2 Variance and Standard Deviation

Although the range gives a measure of the spread of data, statisticians searched for another measure that would consider each data value rather than only the two extremes. This measure would average the total ($\sum$) distance between each observation and the mean, and since distance is not negative, each difference must be squared, $(x_i - \bar{X})^2$. Thus each observation—above and below the mean—contributes to the sum of the squared terms. Next, the average of this sum of squares is obtained by dividing by N for population data and by $(n - 1)$ for sample data. Mathematical statisticians have shown that the sample variance is a better estimator of the population variance if the denominator is $(n - 1)$ rather than n. The result is the variance (Key Idea 2.26).

Key Idea 2.26: Variance

The **sample variance**, s^2, is defined as

$$s^2 = \frac{\sum_{i=1}^{n} (x_i - \bar{X})^2}{n - 1}$$

The **population variance**, σ^2, is defined as

$$\sigma^2 = \frac{\sum_{i=1}^{N} (x_i - \mu)^2}{N}$$

You will also note that the variance is influenced by the size of each observation and therefore uses all the information in the data set. Observations that are a greater distance from the mean increase the sample variance significantly.

To compute the variance requires squaring the distances, which then changes the unit of measurement to square units. The standard deviation (Key Idea 2.27), which is the square root of variance, restores the data to their original measurement unit. For instance, if the original data were in feet, the variance would be in feet squared, but the standard deviation would be in feet.

Key Idea 2.27: Standard Deviation

The **sample standard deviation**, s, and the **population standard deviation**, σ, are defined as

$$s = \sqrt{s^2} = \sqrt{\frac{\sum_{i=1}^{n} (x_i - \bar{X})^2}{n - 1}}$$

and

$$\sigma = \sqrt{\sigma^2} = \sqrt{\frac{\sum_{i=1}^{N} (x_i - \mu)^2}{N}}$$

To illustrate computation of these measures, recall the sales data for Example 2.4. In Table 2.10 we show the steps to find the variance and the standard deviation. Thus

$$s^2 = \frac{\sum_{i=1}^{n} (x_i - \bar{X})^2}{n - 1} = \frac{60.9}{9} = 6.7\bar{6}$$

and the standard deviation $s = 2.60$.

TABLE 2.10   Variance and
Standard Deviation of Store 1

x_i	$(x_i - \bar{X})$	$(x_i - \bar{X})^2$
6	−4.1	16.81
8	−2.1	4.41
10	−0.1	0.01
12	1.9	3.61
14	3.9	15.21
9	−1.1	1.21
11	0.9	0.81
7	−3.1	9.61
13	2.9	8.41
11	0.9	0.81
101	0	60.9

Similar computation for the other stores indicates that the standard deviation is 7.25 for store 2, 2.60 for store 3, and 6.30 for store 4. Notice that although stores 1 and 2 have the same mean daily sales ($1010), the larger standard deviation for store 2 indicates that there were more high and low sales days for store 2 than for store 1. As we will see in Section 2.10, adding a constant of 20 to each observation in store 1 had no effect on the variance of store 3. In both stores, the variance was 2.60.

It is often easier to compute sample variance by the shortcut formulas presented in Key Idea 2.28. In Table 2.11 we calculate the variance for store 1 using these shortcut procedures.

Key Idea 2.28: Shortcut Formulas for s^2

Two shortcut formulas for the sample variance are

$$s^2 = \frac{\sum X_i^2 - \left[\frac{(\sum X_i)^2}{n}\right]}{n-1} \quad \text{or} \quad s^2 = \frac{\sum X_i^2 - n\bar{X}^2}{n-1}$$

TABLE 2.11   Shortcut Procedures to Calculate Sample Variance for Store 1

X_i	X_i^2
6	36
8	64
10	100
12	144
14	196
9	81
11	121
7	49
13	169
11	121
Total = 101	Total = 1081
Mean = 10.1	Mean = 10.81

Using these shortcut procedures, we see that

$$s^2 = \frac{\sum X_i^2 - \left[\dfrac{\left(\sum X_i\right)^2}{n}\right]}{n-1} = \frac{1081 - \left[\dfrac{(101)^2}{10}\right]}{9} = \frac{60.9}{9} = 6.7\bar{6}$$

or

$$s^2 = \frac{\sum X_i^2 - n\bar{X}^2}{n-1} = \frac{1081 - 10(10.1)^2}{9} = \frac{60.9}{9} = 6.7\bar{6}$$

In both cases we obtain the same value for the sample variance for store 1 as we found in Table 2.10.

The variances and standard deviations can easily be found with Minitab and other software. The descriptive data shown in Exhibits 2.3 and 2.4 were obtained with Minitab for Windows for both the tourism illustration and for the convenience food store data (Example 2.4). Notice that these printouts are similar to the state survey printout (Exhibit 2.1) introduced in Section 2.7. Although you do not know all of the descriptors yet, you should be improving in your interpretation of the data.

EXHIBIT 2.3   Minitab Printout for Tourism Illustration

	N	MEAN	MEDIAN	TRMEAN	STDEV	SEMEAN
Age	100	35.32	35.00	34.82	17.49	1.75

	MIN	MAX	Q1	Q3
Age	3.00	79.00	21.00	46.00

EXHIBIT 2.4   Minitab Printout for Convenience Food Stores, Example 2.4

	N	MEAN	MEDIAN	TRMEAN	STDEV	SEMEAN
Store 1	10	10.10	10.50	10.125	2.601	0.823
Store 2	10	10.10	10.00	10.120	7.250	2.290
Store 3	10	30.10	30.50	30.125	2.601	0.823
Store 4	10	12.10	10.50	11.370	6.300	1.990

	MIN	MAX	Q1	Q3
Store 1	6.00	14.00	7.75	12.25
Store 2	1.00	19.00	2.75	17.25
Store 3	26.00	34.00	27.75	32.25
Store 4	6.00	24.00	8.75	14.75

The following example demonstrates one application of variances and standard deviations in the area of finance.

Example 2.6   Risk of a Single Asset

Wes and Jennie Moore, owners of Moore's Foto Shop in western Pennsylvania, are considering one of two investment alternatives, investment A or investment B. They are not sure which of these two single assets is better, and ask Sheila Morris, a financial planner, for some assistance in analyzing the performances of both assets.

Solution   Sheila knows that the standard deviation, s, is the most common single indicator of the risk or variability of a single asset. In financial situations, the difference between a stock's actual rate of return and its expected rate of return is called the *risk* of the stock. The standard deviation measures the variation of returns around an asset's average. Sheila obtained the rates of return on each asset for the last five years, and calculated the means and standard deviations of each asset. The results are shown in Table 2.12. Note that each asset had the same average rate of return of 12.2%. However, once Sheila obtained the standard deviations, it became apparent that asset B was a more risky investment.   □

TABLE 2.12   Rates of Return for A and B

| Year | Rate of Return (%) | |
	Asset A	Asset B
1989	11.3	9.4
1990	12.5	17.1
1991	13.0	13.3
1992	12.0	10.0
1993	12.2	11.2
	61.0	61.0
Average rate of return:	12.2	12.2
Standard deviation:	0.63	3.12

2.9.3 Coefficient of Variation

In some applications it is useful to use a measure of relative dispersion, and the coefficient of variation is often chosen (Key Idea 2.29). The CV is the standard deviation divided by the mean. This measure is particularly useful when the dispersion varies with the total magnitude. If we compared the standard deviation in sales in large and small stores selling similar goods, the standard deviation for large stores would almost always be bigger. A simple explanation is that a large store could be modeled as a number of small stores. Comparing variation using the standard deviation would be

---

Key Idea 2.29: Coefficient of Variation

A measure of relative dispersion is the **coefficient of variation** (CV), defined as

$$CV = \frac{s}{\bar{X}} \qquad \text{when} \quad \bar{X} > 0$$

misleading. The coefficient of variation overcomes this problem by adjusting for the scale of units in the population.

Problem Exercises

2.14 A random sample of 11 cereal packages had the following weights in grams:

440	448	455	442	446	450
454	456	452	457	449	

Compute:
(a) The sample mean.
(b) The sample variance and standard deviation.
(c) The median.
(d) The coefficient of variation.
(e) The range.

2.15 Recall the sample of daily sales in Problem 2.1. Compute:
(a) The sample mean.
(b) The sample standard deviation.
(c) The coefficient of variation.
(d) What is the store median?

2.16 Recall the delivery times in days for the data in Problem 2.4. Compute:
(a) The mean and the median delivery times.
(b) The variance and the standard deviation for delivery times.

2.9.4 Interquartile Range

In Section 2.5 we studied measures of central tendency. It is often important to determine values that are not necessarily located in the center of the data. Instead, individual observations are sometimes compared by using their relative ranking. For this purpose percentiles and quartiles are often used (Key Idea 2.30).

Key Idea 2.30: Percentiles and Quartiles

The Pth **percentile** is a number such that $P\%$ of the observations are at or below that number.

   Some special percentiles are

The 25th percentile is called Q_1, the first quartile.
The 50th percentile is Q_2, the median.
The 75th percentile is called Q_3, the third quartile.

Percentiles are widely used for ranked data. For example, a college entrance examination 80th percentile test score is the score such that 80% of all tests had scores less than or equal to that score. And, of course, 20% had higher scores. Percentiles indicate the relative position of individuals on a scale instead of the actual score received. It is difficult to explain a specific test score without providing considerable data about the design and construction of the test. However, a 90th percentile test score indicates that the person scored in the upper 10% of all persons taking the test.

Another measure of dispersion, the interquartile range, is based on the first and third quartiles (Key Idea 2.31). Because the interquartile range excludes the largest and the smallest observations, it has greater stability between samples.

Key Idea 2.31: Interquartile Range

The **interquartile range** (IQR) is the difference between the observations at the 25th and the 75th percentiles:

$$IQR = Q_3 - Q_1$$

The IQR indicates the boundaries for the center 50% of the observations.

Once the data are in ascending order, Q_1 and Q_3 are found in the following locations:

Q_1 is in the $0.25(n + 1)$st position.

Q_3 is in the $0.75(n + 1)$st position.

There are several names for the quartiles. For instance, the first quartile, Q_1 (the 25th percentile), is also called the lower quartile or the lower hinge. The third quartile, Q_3 (the 75th percentile), is also called the upper quartile or the upper hinge. These quartiles can easily be found with Minitab for Windows using [**Stat > Basic Statistics > Descriptive Statistics**], or we can compute these values as:

Q_3 is in the $0.75(101)$st position $= 75.75$th position $= 46$.

Q_1 is in the $0.25(101)$st position $= 25.25$th position $= 21$.

The Church Street merchants can conclude that the middle 50% of the tourists in the survey were between the age of 21 and 46 (IQR $= 25$).

Problem Exercises

2.17 Recall the occupancy rates for various seasons at a major resort given in Problem 2.7. Determine:

(a) The median and the interquartile range.

(b) The 80th percentile occupancy rate.

   (c) The percentage of the sample who stayed 8 days or less.
   (d) The percentage of the sample who stayed for more than 14 days.

2.18   Recall the aptitude test scores for the 30 applicants given in Problem 2.6. Determine:
   (a) The 50th percentile test score.
   (b) The 20th percentile.
   (c) The 80th percentile.
   (d) A student received a score of 120. What is the percentile for this score?

2.9.5 Box-and-Whisker Plots

We have already introduced one exploratory data analysis technique, the stem-and-leaf display. The box-and-whisker plot is another EDA technique introduced by John Tukey as an easy-to-draw picture of data (Key Idea 2.32).

Key Idea 2.32: Box-and-Whisker Plots

The box-and-whisker plot is a graphical procedure that uses five statistical measures: the minimum, the 25th percentile, the median, the 75th percentile, and the maximum value. The inner box shows the numbers that span the range from the 25th to the 75th percentiles. A line is drawn through the box at the median. Tukey has defined the 25th and 75th percentiles as the lower and upper hinges. The "whiskers" are the lines from the 25th and 75th percentiles to the minimum and maximum values.

All five of the statistical measures described in Key Idea 2.32 can be obtained directly from the typical descriptive statistics output produced by programs such as Minitab for Windows. In addition, many statistical programs have routines that produce box-and-whisker plots directly. The subinterval covered by each 25% of the sample provides a good picture of the "shape" of the data distribution. Table 2.13 shows these five measures for the four stores from Example 2.4. Throughout this chapter we have attempted to show you various ways to look at computer printouts and to understand the distribution. Before you look at the box-and-whisker plot in Figure 2.9, study the five descriptors below, comparing the distance between Q_1 and the minimum (this is the bottom 25% of the data) with the distance between the maximum and Q_3 (this is the top 25% of the distribution) for each of the stores. Are these distances (whiskers) about equal or do you notice that one whisker is significantly greater than the other whisker? What do you think these whiskers suggest about the shape of the distribution? For instance:

1. Consider store 1. (Q_1–minimum) = 1.75; (maximum–Q_3) = 1.75. Here the whiskers are equal. Do you think the data are symmetric? Positively skewed? Negatively skewed?

TABLE 2.13   Descriptive Statistics for Box-and-Whisker Plots

Store	Minimum	Q_1	Median	Q_3	Maximum
1	6.00	7.75	10.5	12.25	14.0
2	1.00	2.75	10.0	17.25	19.0
3	26.00	27.75	30.5	32.25	34.0
4	6.00	8.75	11.0	14.75	24.0

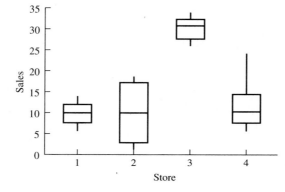

Figure 2.9   Box-and-Whisker Plots: Stores 1, 2, 3, and 4 [**Stat** > **EDA** > **Boxplot**]

2. Consider store 4. (Q_1–minimum) $= 2.75$; (maximum–Q_3) $= 9.25$. The whiskers differ greatly. Is the graph symmetric? Positively skewed? Negatively skewed?

Now let's examine the box-and-whisker plot to see the shape of the distributions. By examining the graphs in Figure 2.9, the center and extreme portions of the distribution can be compared. Central tendency, dispersion, and skewness are immediately obvious.

Notice how the four stores compare. Stores 1, 2, and 4 have the same median. Store 1 has a small dispersion over both the overall range and the distance between hinges (interquartile range). Store 3 shows a similar pattern. Notice the tails (whiskers) of store 4. What can you conclude about the shape of store 4's distribution? Correct! The distribution is positively skewed. Notice the extreme skewness toward higher values. Store 2 shows wide dispersion for both its overall and interquartile range, and store 3 shows a shape similar to that of store 1.

Practice Problem 2.3

Using the descriptive statistics in Exhibit 2.1 for the state survey data example, determine the shape of the distributions for each of the three variables given by looking at the whiskers. Do your results agree with the shapes we determined by comparing the mean and the medians? Use a software package and the data from Appendix B of this chapter to construct the box-and-whisker plots for:

(a) Total state residential population (1992).

(b) Unemployment percentage of the civilian labor force (1992).

(c) Business failure rate per 10,000 concerns (1992).

The Minitab for Windows menu steps are [**Stat** > **EDA** > **Boxplot**].   □

Problem Exercises

2.19   Recall the retail clothing data in Problem 2.1. The following sample of daily sales was reported from 12 randomly selected retail clothing stores:

2000	2500	2100	1900	1800	2200
1700	2000	2300	2400	2600	1400

Prepare a box-and-whisker plot.

2.20   Recall the weights of shipments in pounds from a food distribution warehouse to small-town supermarkets in Problem 2.3. These weights were:

2800	3500	2100	1300	2800	2200
700	3300	4300	1400	1100	1600

Prepare a box-and-whisker plot.

2.10 APPLICATIONS OF THE MEAN AND STANDARD DEVIATION

Throughout the book we study numerous applications of the mean and the standard deviation. In this section we discuss the detection of outliers using these two numerical measures.

In the early nineteenth century a Russian mathematician by the name of Chebyshev (sometimes spelled Tchebysheff) established data intervals for any data set *regardless* of the shape of the distribution. The rule developed by Chebyshev (see Key Idea 2.33) provided the first boundaries on data, and hence introduced the original method for detecting outliers. Chebyshev's rule is limited in that he could determine boundaries within $\pm k$ standard deviations of the mean only when $k > 1$. The empirical rule for mounded distributions (Key Idea 2.34) was unknown in Chebyshev's time.

Key Idea 2.33: Chebyshev's Rule

At least $1 - (1/k^2)$ of the observations in a data set must be within k standard deviations of the mean, where $k > 1$.

Key Idea 2.34: Empirical Rule (Mounded Distributions)

If the data set is mounded (bell shaped), we can conclude that:

$\mu \pm 1\sigma$ includes approximately 68% of the observations.
$\mu \pm 2\sigma$ includes approximately 95% of the observations.
$\mu \pm 3\sigma$ includes almost all of the observations.

As an example of applying Chebyshev's rule, for $k = 2$ and $k = 3$, the intervals are:

$\mu \pm 2\sigma$ includes at least 75% of the observations.
$\mu \pm 3\sigma$ includes at least 88.9% of the observations.

Suppose we know that the mean grade on an exam is 72 with a standard deviation of 4. Then according to Chebyshev's rule, we can conclude that at least 75% of the grades are in the interval between 64 and 80, or at least 88.9% of the grades are between 60 and 84.

The intervals of the empirical rule (Key Idea 2.34) can be used to detect outliers, observations that deviate a great deal from the central tendency. Any observation that deviates by more than $\pm 3\sigma$ from the mean can usually be considered an outlier. Points outside the $\pm 3\sigma$ interval should be examined. They could be the result of an error in data recording or measurement, or they might indicate unusual conditions in the process that generated the data. In Chapter 18 we learn how quality assurance procedures use these limits to detect problems in a production process. In the example of exam grades above, if we knew that the distribution of scores were symmetric, we could conclude that approximately 95% of the grades were in the interval between 64 and 80, or that almost all of the grades are in the interval between 60 and 84.

Practice Problem 2.4

A group of 13 students are studying in Istanbul, Turkey for five weeks. As part of their study of the local economy, they each purchased an oriental rug and arranged for its shipment to the United States. The shipping time, in days, for each rug was

| 81 | 31 | 42 | 39 | 72 | 43 | 74 |
| 30 | 28 | 36 | 37 | 35 | 45 | |

You have been asked to analyze the shipping experience of these students to provide advice to future students. In your analysis, answer the following questions.

(a) What are the mean and median for this data set?
(b) What are the range, the sample variance, and the sample standard deviation?
(c) Is the distribution symmetric or skewed?

(d) Use both the empirical rule and Chebyshev's rule to estimate the percentage of days that are within two standard deviations of the mean. How do these estimates compare to the actual percentage of data within the 2 standard deviation interval?

(e) What advice would you give to future study groups concerning the time to ship rugs?   □

Problem Exercises

2.21   Refer to the aptitude test scores for the 30 applicants in Problem 2.6. Determine:
        (a) The sample mean and median test scores.
        (b) The sample standard deviation and the range for the test scores.
        (c) The percentage of observations that are within ±2 standard deviations of the mean.

2.22   Refer to the occupancy rates for various seasons at a major resort in Problem 2.7. Determine:
        (a) The sample mean, median, and mode.
        (b) The sample variance and the standard deviation.
        (c) The percentage of observations that are within ±3 standard deviations of the mean.
        (d) An approximate symmetric interval that includes 95% of the observations.
        (e) The Chebyshev interval that contains 85% of the observations.

2.23   Refer to the percentage of defective parts produced on a random sample of 8-hour production shifts in Problem 2.8. Determine:
        (a) The mean and median for the sample.
        (b) The variance and the standard deviation for the sample.
        (c) The coefficient of variation for the sample.
        (d) The approximate symmetric interval, assuming an approximate bell-shaped distribution, which includes 95% of the observations.
        (e) The approximate Chebyshev interval that includes 90% of the observations.
        (f) Why is the first interval of part (e) so much narrower?

2.24   Refer to the daily output at the medium-sized chair factory in Problem 2.5. Determine:
        (a) The sample mean number of chairs produced each day.
        (b) The sample variance and standard deviation.
        (c) An approximate symmetric interval within which 95% of the observations would occur.

2.11 TRANSFORMATIONS OF DATA

Business and economic problems often use functions of sample data. For instance, the total cost per day to operate a factory unit is the sum of variable labor costs and fixed costs. The mean and variance of labor costs are computed from a random sample. However, we also need the mean and variance of total costs. In another situation, although the mean and standard deviation of a single stock may be known, we may want the mean and standard deviation for the total value of 100 shares of that stock. An automobile manufacturer may either increase the price of all cars by $100 or increase the price by 10% for all cars. In each of these illustrations, questions arise concerning the mean and the standard deviation of a data set in which each observation has either been (1) increased (decreased) by a given constant or (2) multiplied by a given constant.

2.11.1 Addition of a Constant

Recall Example 2.4, the analysis of convenience food stores. When stores 1 and 3 were compared, we saw that the observations in store 3 were merely the store 1 observations plus 20. We also saw that the mean for store 3 was the store 1 mean plus 20 and that the standard deviation of the two samples were exactly the same. Did these results just happen, or do they indicate important results?

The principle of addition of a constant is described in Key Idea 2.35. Algebraic verification of the principle is left to the reader. Adding a constant shifts every observation while maintaining their relative location and the variability. This insight reduces the number of computations for a particular analysis. For the automobile manufacturer who increased price by $100 for all cars, the average price also increased by $100, but the variance remained the same.

Key Idea 2.35: Addition of a Constant

When a constant is added to (or subtracted from) each observation in a sample:

1. The resulting mean is increased (decreased) by that constant.
2. The resulting variance and standard deviation are unchanged.

Expressed in symbols, if a constant Δ is added to a random variable X,

$$y_i = x_i + \Delta$$

the mean, variance, and standard deviation become

$$\bar{Y} = \bar{X} + \Delta$$
$$s_Y^2 = s_X^2$$
$$s_Y = s_X$$

Example 2.7   Stryker Computer Services, Inc.

Stryker Computer Services, Inc. is an international company offering not only computer hardware and software, but also extensive training to its customers. Jay Stryker, president and CEO, knows that to compete globally he must not only meet but exceed customer expectations and provide high-quality products and services. Jay requested information about daily sales and services in one of his new stores.

Solution   James Thorne, a computer analyst with Stryker, gathered the following random sample of daily sales: \$8950, \$8960, \$8954, \$8965, and \$8955. By subtracting the constant 8950, Jim quickly computed the mean and variance as

$$\frac{0 + 10 + 4 + 15 + 5}{5} = 6.8$$

and then added the constant 8950 back to arrive at the mean daily sales of \$8956.80:

$$\frac{(0 + 100 + 16 + 225 + 25) - [(34)^2/5]}{4} = 33.7 \qquad \square$$

2.11.2 Multiplication by a Constant

In numerous business and economic problems, a data set is multiplied by a constant (Key Idea 2.36). Again, we want to find the effect on the mean, the variance, and the standard deviation. By simple algebra, Key Idea 2.36 can be verified. As an example of multiplication by a constant, if the automobile manufacturer increases the price of all cars by 10%, which is equivalent to multiplying the original prices by the multiplier $b = 1.1$, the mean price will increase (1.1) times the original mean price. Similarly, the variance will increase by $(1.1)^2 = 1.21$ or 21%.

Key Idea 2.36: Multiplication by a Constant

If each sample observation is multiplied by a constant, b, then:

1. The resulting mean is the original mean multiplied by the constant.
2. The resulting variance is the original variance multiplied the square of the constant.
3. The resulting standard deviation is the original standard deviation multiplied by the absolute value of the constant.

Let $y_i = bx_i$. Then the mean, variance, and standard deviation are

$$\bar{Y} = b\bar{X}$$
$$s_Y^2 = b^2 s_X^2$$
$$s_Y = |b|\, s_X$$

Example 2.8   Income and Consumption

An economist calculates the mean disposable family income to be $X = \$30,000$ and the standard deviation to be $s = \$5000$. What are the mean and standard deviation of clothing expenditures for these families if clothing expenditures are 10% of disposable income?

Solution   In this problem the multiplier $b = 0.10$. Therefore, the mean clothing expenditure is $3000[(0.1) \times (30,000)]$, and the standard deviation is $500[(0.1) \times (5000)]$.   □

2.11.3 Transformation of a Linear Equation

If each observation were multiplied by the constant, b, and then were added to the observation, we would obtain the linear equation

$$y_i = bx_i + \Delta$$

See Key Idea 2.37. The results of Key Idea 2.37 could be obtained from Key Ideas 2.34 and 2.35. However, we will verify these results algebraically. The mean of this linear equation is found by

$$\bar{Y} = \frac{\sum y_i}{n} = \frac{\sum bx_i + \Delta}{n} = \frac{\sum bx_i + \sum \Delta}{n} = \frac{b\sum x_i + n\Delta}{n} = b\bar{X} + \Delta$$

Key Idea 2.37: Transformation of a Linear Equation

The mean of the linear equation, $Y = bX + \Delta$, is

$$\bar{Y} = b\bar{X} + \Delta$$

The variance and standard deviation of the linear equation, $Y = bX + \Delta$, are

$$S_Y^2 = b^2 s_X^2 \quad \text{and} \quad S_Y = |b| s_X$$

Similarly, the variance is derived algebraically:

$$S_Y^2 = \frac{\sum (y_i - \bar{Y})^2}{n-1}$$
$$= \frac{\sum bx_i + \Delta - b\bar{X} - \Delta)^2}{n-1}$$
$$= \frac{\sum (bx_i - b\bar{X})^2}{n-1}$$
$$= \frac{\sum b^2(x_i - \bar{X})^2}{n-1}$$
$$= b^2 S_x^2$$

Practice Problem 2.5

Arnold Johnson, an economist, concluded that the demand function for $3\frac{1}{2}$-inch floppy disks was

$$Q = 500 - 40P$$

where Q is the quantity demanded and P is the price. From a random sample of stores he calculated the mean price, $P = 1$, and the standard deviation, $s_p = 0.5$. What are the mean and standard deviation for the quantity demanded, Q?

Problem Exercises

2.25   Consider the daily sales for the retail clothing stores in Problem 2.1:

2000	2500	2100	1900	1800	2200
1700	2000	2300	2400	2600	1400

After computing statistics for the daily samples you are asked to compute descriptive statistics assuming that all prices are reduced by 20%. Compute:
(a) The sample mean.
(b) The sample standard deviation.
(c) The coefficient of variation.

2.26   For the retail clothing sales data of Problem 2.25 you are asked to compute descriptive statistics for operating costs. From historical accounting studies you know that the operating costs are equal to 500 plus the cost of goods sold. The cost of goods sold are 60% of total sales revenue. Using the sample daily sales, derive the following descriptive statistics for the daily operating costs:
(a) The sample mean for daily operating costs.
(b) The sample standard deviation for daily operating costs.
(c) The coefficient of variation for daily operating costs.

2.27   The mean and standard deviation of a stock price for Mountain Top Personal Computers are $\bar{X} = 25$ and $s = 8.5$. Compute the mean and standard deviation for the total value of 100 shares of that stock.

2.28   The total cost per day to operate a factory unit is the sum of variable labor costs plus fixed costs. The mean and variance of labor costs are computed from a random sample as $\bar{X} = 1200$ and $s = 125$. The fixed costs are $1000. What are the mean and variance of total costs?

2.29   Each week Manitou Manufacturing, Inc. purchases 134 gallons of a special lubricant for its manufacturing process. The total weekly cost consists of the fixed cost of $200 for the delivery truck plus the price per gallon times 134. The price per gallon each week has a mean of $\bar{X} = \$5.50$ and a standard deviation of $s = \$0.75$. What are the mean and standard deviation of the total weekly cost to obtain the lubricant?

2.30   Recall the number of chairs produced each day in the medium-sized chair factory of Problem 2.5. The cost of operating the chair factory each day consists of a fixed cost of $1000 and a variable cost per chair of $90. Determine:
(a) The sample mean number of chairs produced each day.
(b) The sample variance and standard deviation.

(c) The sample mean for total cost per day to operate the factory.

(d) The standard deviation for total cost per day to operate the factory.

2.31   Use the data for the aptitude test scores for the 30 applicants in Problem 2.6. The placement score for accounting analysts is computed by multiplying the aptitude test score by 1.5 and adding 100. Determine:

(a) The sample mean and sample median test scores.

(b) The sample standard deviation and the range for the test scores.

(c) The sample mean and standard deviation for the placement score for accounting analysts.

(d) The approximate symmetric interval that includes 95% of the placement scores.

2.32   Use the data from Problem 2.7, where we looked at the occupancy rates for various seasons at a major resort. The price per day for family groups is $100. The housekeeping costs for a family room are a fixed cost of $50 plus $20 per day. Determine:

(a) The sample mean for the number of days stayed.

(b) The sample standard deviation for the number of days stayed.

(c) The sample mean and standard deviation for the revenue per family stay at the resort.

(d) The sample mean and standard deviation for the housekeeping cost per family.

SUMMARY OF KEY IDEAS

PRACTICE PROBLEM SOLUTIONS

2.1 The frequency distribution of the tourism illustration using 10 classes is given in Table 2.14. It is a matter of opinion whether a clearer picture of the data is provided by the frequency distribution in Table 2.5 using eight classes or by this frequency distribution using 10 classes. Since we most often think of ages in groups of 10 years (e.g., people in their 20s or 30s), practitioners might find the distribution with eight classes easier to read.

2.2 The stem-and-leaf display is given in Table 2.15. The Church Street merchants can readily draw conclusions such as: 1 out of every 5 people surveyed were younger than 20; or 35% of the sample were at least 40.

2.3 First, let's look at Exhibit 2.5.

(a) *Total population*. The positive skewness of the total state residential population (1992) is evident by observing that 25% of the state populations are between the minimum, 466, and the lower quartile, 1235. Another 25% are between the upper quartile, 5996, and the maximum, 30,867. Again, the large difference in the size of the whiskers indicates skewness, and the direction is positive since the upper whisker is longer. From the data in Appendix B of this chapter we also note that there are some outliers—such as California, with a total state residential population of 30,867 (in

TABLE 2.14   Frequency
Distribution of Tourists'
Ages: 10 Classes

Ages	Frequency
0–under 8	4
8–under 16	8
16–under 24	18
24–under 32	16
32–under 40	19
40–under 48	12
48–under 56	9
56–under 64	6
64–under 72	5
72–under 80	3

TABLE 2.15   Stem-and-Leaf Display of Tourists' Ages

Cumulative Frequency	Stem	Leaf
5	0	3 5 6 6 8
20	1	1 2 2 4 4 5 5 6 6 7 8 8 8 9 9
41	2	0 0 0 0 1 1 2 2 3 3 5 6 6 7 7 7 8 8 9 9 9
(24)	3	0 0 1 1 2 3 4 4 5 5 5 6 6 6 7 7 8 8 8 8 9 9 9 9
35	4	0 1 2 3 3 4 4 5 5 6 6 7 8 8 8 9
19	5	0 0 3 3 5 8 9 9
11	6	1 1 3 4 5 7
5	7	0 0 3 8 9

EXHIBIT 2.5   State Survey: Descriptive Statistics

	N	MEAN	MEDIAN	TRMEAN	STDEV	SEMEAN
TOTPOP92	51	5002	3470	4151	5599	784
UNEMP92	51	6.798	6.900	6.820	1.592	0.223
BUSFAIL	51	95.25	90.00	93.49	29.72	4.16

	MIN	MAX	Q1	Q3
TOTPOP92	466	30867	1235	5996
UNEMP92	3.000	11.300	5.700	7.500
BUSFAIL	47.00	169.00	74.00	111.00

thousands); also New York and Texas are much larger in populations. In the box-and-whisker plot (Figure 2.10), you can observe the size of the whiskers, note the asterisks for the outliers, and observe the positive skewness.

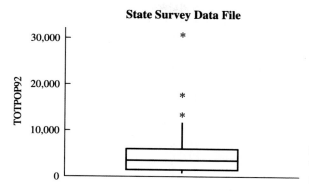

Figure 2.10 Box-and-Whisker Plot: Total State Residential Population (1992)

(b) *Unemployment percentage of the civilian labor force.* This is an interesting variable. From the descriptive statistics in Exhibit 2.5, note that the mean rate and the median rate of unemployment are quite close, with the mean of approximately 6.8% only slightly less than the median of 6.9%. Thus we would expect some negative skewness. In the box-and-whisker plot in Figure 2.10, we can see this skewness better. Note the one outlier (from Appendix B, this large unemployment rate of 11.3% is in the state of West Virginia). Remember that outliers tend to affect the value of the mean. This explains why the two measures of central tendency are so close in value. The negative skewness is better seen in a box-and-whisker plot (Figure 2.11).

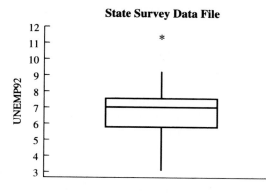

Figure 2.11 Unemployment Percentage of the Civilian Labor Force (1992)

(c) *Business failure rate per 10,000 concerns.* With respect to business failure rates, positive skewness is also evident by observing that 25% of the rates are between the minimum of 47 and the first quartile of 74, with another 25% of the failure rates between the third quartile, 111, and the maximum of 169 failures per 10,000 concerns. The box-and-whisker plot of this variable is shown in Figure 2.12.

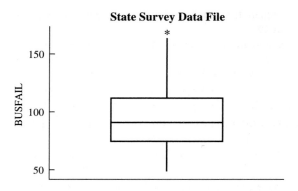

Figure 2.12   Box-and-Whisker Plot: Business Failure Rate per 10,000
Concerns (1992)

2.4   (a) Mean, $\bar{X} = 45.6$ days; median, $X_m = 39$.
(b) Range $= 53$; $s_X^2 = 322.2$ and $s_X = 18$.
(c) The distribution is positively skewed.
(d) By the empirical rule, we would expect approximately 95% of the observations to be in the interval

$$\bar{X} \pm 2S = 45.6 + 36$$

By Chebyshev's rule, at least 75% of the observations would be in this interval. The actual number from the data set is 100%.
(e) Tell the students to expect around 39 days (the median) for the shipment. However, be aware that in some cases shipments could take as long as 70 or 80 days.
2.5   Using Key Idea 2.36, $\bar{Q} = 500 - 40(1) = 460$ and $S_Q = 40(0.5) = 20$.

CHAPTER PROBLEMS

2.1   John Smith, president of a large automobile parts firm, wants to know the quality performance in the two factories operated by his firm. In factory A his staff obtained a random sample of days and determined the number of defective parts produced on those days. The number of defective parts for each day were

   10,   12,   8,   9,   11,   14,   7,   6,   15,   10,   8,   11,   9,   10,   12

A random sample was also obtained in factory B. The number of defective parts on each day were

   2,   3,   4,   21,   20,   9,   10,   18,   15,   7,   12,   9,   11,   8,   10

(a) Prepare frequency distributions and histograms for the number of defective parts from each factory that start with 1 and have an interval of 2.

    (b) Prepare frequency distributions and histograms that start with 1 and have an interval of 10.

    (c) Compare the frequency distributions in parts (a) and (b). Indicate which set of frequency distributions provides the best comparison between the two factories. Explain your conclusion.

    (d) Write a short paragraph that explains the differences between factories A and B.

2.2   What is the difference between a population and a sample?

2.3   Define a simple random sample and explain its importance in statistical analysis.

2.4   Name the two most important characteristics or properties that are used to summarize the distribution of a sample of observed numbers. Name the statistics that are used to describe or measure these observed characteristics or properties.

2.5   You have been assigned the task of evaluating a work incentive program whose objective is to help families to move out of the poverty cycle. The program involves a complex set of counseling, job training, and job placement activities. The agency funding the project is particularly interested in knowing if the families have been able to increase their total income above the poverty level, which is $10,000 per year. A random sample of 25 families who are program participants was selected and their family incomes were carefully measured. The family incomes are contained in Table 2.16.

TABLE 2.16   Random Sample of Family Income: Program Evaluation

7,500	8,900	9,600	13,000	9,100
12,900	10,800	8,700	9,500	9,900
11,900	12,800	13,800	10,900	10,500
11,400	8,500	11,700	11,300	10,300
10,700	11,600	13,900	11,100	11,800

    (a) Prepare a frequency distribution and histogram using the intervals 6001–8000; 8001–10,000; 10,001–12,000; 12,001–14,000.

    (b) Prepare a frequency distribution and histogram using the intervals 6001–7000; 7000–8000; . . . ; 13,001–14,000.

    (c) Prepare a frequency distribution and histogram using all of the following intervals: 6001–6500; 6501–7000; 7001–7500; . . . ; 13,500–14,000.

    (d) Compare the results obtained using the three different intervals, indicating what you can tell about the income distribution from each frequency distribution and histogram. Which result do you find most useful? Explain your conclusion.

    (e) Using the results above, discuss why the program is either successful or not successful.

2.6   You have been assigned the task of evaluating a work incentive program whose objective is to help families to move out of the poverty cycle. The program involves a complex set of counseling, job training, and job placement activities. The agency funding the program is interested in determining if the program participants have raised their family income more than would have occurred from normal growth in the overall economy.

Table 2.16 is a random sample of families that participated in the program. Table 2.17 contains a random sample of families from the same neighborhood who did not participate in the program.

TABLE 2.17   Family Incomes of Nonparticipants in Program

9,800	9,100	11,900	9,600	8,700
5,500	6,900	7,600	11,000	7,100
8,300	9,300	9,700	6,500	9,400
10,900	8,800	6,700	7,500	7,900
8,500	8,900	11,600	10,800	9,900

(a) Prepare a frequency distribution and histogram using the sample of program participants contained in Table 2.16. In the histogram use all of the following intervals: 5001–6000; 6001–7000; . . . ; 13,001–14,000.

(b) Prepare a frequency distribution and histogram using the sample of families who are not program participants contained in Table 2.17. Use the intervals 7001–8000; 8001–9000; . . . ; 13,001–14,000.

(c) Compare the results from parts (a) and (b). Discuss your conclusions concerning the effect of the program using the frequency distributions and histograms.

2.7   Using the data from Table 2.18, prepare a frequency distribution and histogram with intervals that are 4 units wide.

TABLE 2.18   Gasoline Consumption for Alfred Smith's Car

	Week			
Day	1	2	3	4
Sunday	25.3	28.9	32.5	37.1
Monday	32.0	24.4	33.8	36.5
Tuesday	30.2	23.6	42.8	34.0
Wednesday	36.9	28.7	48.3	34.0
Thursday	37.2	36.6	46.8	32.8
Friday	42.9	30.2	48.2	30.1
Saturday	32.5	35.8	36.6	33.9

(a) Based on an examination of your graph, what is the gasoline consumption during most of the typical driving periods?

(b) Based on an examination of your graph, what is the range of consumption during most of the typical driving periods?

(c) Discuss the advantages and disadvantages of the time-series graphical plot prepared for Problem 1.4 compared to the frequency distribution prepared for this problem.

(d) What can you say about the manufacturer's mileage claims?

For Problems 2.8 and 2.9 you will first enter the data from Table 2.19 into a statistical package such as Minitab and use the computer to prepare the graphs.

TABLE 2.19   Gasoline Consumption for Betty Jackson's Car

	Week			
Day	1	2	3	4
Sunday	34.9	31.5	32.8	21.9
Monday	32.0	35.0	25.4	25.0
Tuesday	27.3	28.8	27.7	19.6
Wednesday	33.0	28.7	31.9	32.7
Thursday	30.0	24.4	33.3	21.3
Friday	29.8	30.3	33.5	32.4
Saturday	29.5	29.6	24.5	33.2

2.8   Betty Jackson wants to know if the gasoline consumption for her new car agrees with the manufacturer's claim of 30 miles per gallon. After she has driven the car 2000 miles she begins to collect gasoline consumption data. After every 200 miles she refills the tank and records the amount of gasoline required. Using these data, she computes the consumption in miles per gallon recorded in Table 2.19. The first seven observations are in column 1, the next seven in column 2, and so on. Gasoline consumption appears to vary considerably from one tank to the next. She asks you to help her analyze the data.
   (a) Prepare a graphical plot of these data over the time sequence during which the data were collected.
   (b) Based on an examination of your graph, what is the gasoline consumption during most of the typical driving periods?
   (c) Based on an examination of your graph, what is the range of consumption during most of the typical driving periods?
   (d) Examine the graph and indicate which driving periods appear to be different from the typical periods. Write some possible explanations for these different periods.
   (e) Does Betty Jackson have evidence to reject the manufacturer's claim concerning gasoline mileage?
2.9   Using the data from Table 2.19, prepare a frequency distribution and histogram with intervals that are 2 units wide.
   (a) Based on an examination of your graph, what is the gasoline consumption during most of the typical driving periods?
   (b) Based on an examination of your graph, what is the range of consumption during most of the typical driving periods?
   (c) Discuss the advantages and disadvantages of a time-series graphical plot compared to the frequency distribution prepared for this problem.

In Problems 2.10 to 2.12 we study a very simple production and quality control problem. Although the problem appears to be very simple, it contains some very important lessons about probability and production. Because of the amount of work, you may wish to invite one or two classmates to join you and turn in a common solution. It could also be a fun activity.

2.10   In this factory we produce flippers, a fun new game that promises high sales. The production process consists of flipping a "fair coin." (A penny will do. However, using a deutsche mark would make this a multinational factory.) You must be careful in your production process to provide the proper spin to the coin so that it turns over the proper number of times. If the coin lands with a head up, you have produced a good piece that can be shipped. But a tail is a defect that must be scrapped. Each worker completes 20 pieces each day. The output is the number of heads from the 20 pieces completed each day. A tail results in a defective piece that must be scrapped. The factory manager wants to increase output by reducing the number of defective parts.

(a) Prepare 25 days of production and plot the output for each day in a time-series plot.

(b) Prepare a frequency distribution and a histogram for the 25 days of output.

(c) Examine the output patterns and fluctuations using the analysis developed above. Discuss the central tendency and variation that result from the process.

2.11   The factory manager decides to establish an incentive plan for workers producing flippers (Problem 2.10). They know from the analyses that you prepared and other experience that the average worker will produce 10 good pieces each day out of 20 completed. Therefore, they decide to pay $10 to an employee on each day that he or she produces more than 10 good pieces. They also decide to provide even more encouragement for increased output by reducing an employee's wages by $10 for each day that the number of good pieces drops below 10. Discuss the probable effect of this incentive plan on total output and on employee morale.

2.12   After the experience of the previous incentive plan, the manager decides to try another scheme, which he believes will certainly increase output. The scheme has the following rules:

1. If an employee produces more than 10 good pieces, she can reduce the number of pieces processed on the next day. The reduction will be equal to twice the number of good pieces above 10. For example, if a worker produces 12 good pieces, she will only need to work on 16 pieces the next day. This break should give employees the opportunity to go home early and possibly do some fishing.

2. If an employee produces less than 10 good pieces, he must increase the number of pieces processed on the next day. The increase will be equal to twice the number of good pieces less than 10. For example, if a worker produces 8 good pieces, he will have to work on 4 additional units on the next day. If he worked on 18 pieces and obtained only 8 good pieces, he would have to work on 22 pieces on the next day. The manager reasons that the punishment of working harder and longer should encourage most people to produce more good pieces.

(a) Work through 20 days of production using this new incentive plan. Prepare a time-series plot for the 20 days of production.

(b) Prepare a frequency distribution for the 20 days of production. Compare the output with that obtained for Problem 2.10.

(c) Based on the analysis above, how has the new incentive plan affected average output? How has the new incentive plan affected the average level of output and the variation in output from one day to the next?

2.13   Show that

$$\sum_{i=1}^{n}(x_i - \bar{X})^2 = \sum_{i=1}^{n}x_i^2 - n \times (\bar{X})^2$$

2.14   Natalie Numbers, manager of market research, wishes to compare cereal sales between two stores located on the east and west sides of a major city. In the east store the number of cases sold during the last six days were 4, 5, 6, 7, 8, and 9. Sales in the west store for the same time period were 9, 10, 8, 11, 9, and 11.
   (a) Please help Natalie by computing the mean, median, and variance for the two stores.
   (b) Explain the differences between sales in the east and west stores using the mean and variance.

2.15   An extensive quality control program has been installed at a large factory to monitor each of various production lines. The production line that produces gears for large machine tools generated the following number of defective gears during the day shifts over the past seven days: 5, 4, 3, 6, 4, 5, and 15. The process has been stable for the past several months.
   (a) Compute the mean, median, and standard deviation.
   (b) Explain the pattern of defects using only the three descriptive statistics computed in part (a).

2.16   Rita Reamano, an economist, is studying the costs of housing in small towns and large cities. In the process of her study she has obtained random samples of rent costs for two-bedroom apartments in a small town in Minnesota and in Chicago. The data for the small town in Minnesota are 250, 200, 300, 275, 300, and 325, and for the Chicago apartments, 700, 600, 800, 650, 750, and 625. Analyze these data using your understanding of descriptive statistics. Write a short explanation of the differences between rent costs in small versus large cities based on your summary statistics.

2.17   Green Christmas, Inc. is a large producer of Christmas trees located in northern Wisconsin. Robert Thrash, production manager, has asked you to prepare a statistical study to assist in the estimation of potential production for the coming Christmas season. Contracts with retailers require that the trees be at least 72 inches tall. A random sample of tree heights provided the following result:

71	72	63	66	65	53	54	81	83
80	79	51	62	55	54	58	62	

   Robert has asked for the following information based on this sample.
   (a) What is the percentile for a 72-inch-tall tree?
   (b) Based on the sample data, what percentage of the trees can be sold?

2.18   Given the random sample 8001, 8003, 7999, 7997, and 8000, compute the sample mean and variance.

2.19   Refer to the family income program evaluation in Problem 2.6.
   (a) Compute the mean, median, sample standard deviation, and range for the program participants in Table 2.16 and nonparticipants in Table 2.17.
   (b) Compare the two samples in terms of central tendency, dispersion, and skewness using the statistics from part (a).
   (c) Using the results above, discuss the program effectiveness using the descriptive statistics computed above.

2.20   Random samples of 1000 persons have been obtained for three countries and their individual incomes have been measured. Table 2.20 presents summary statistics for the per capita income distribution over the three countries.

TABLE 2.20   Summary Statistics for Problem 2.20

| | Country | | |
Statistic	A	B	C
Mean	10,000	10,000	10,000
Median	14,000	8,000	10,000
Standard deviation	2,000	1,500	1,000
Lower hinge	9,000	7,000	8,500
Upper hinge	15,000	12,000	12,000

(a) Discuss differences and similarities of the income patterns in the three countries.

(b) Indicate which country you would prefer for your residence given that you would be randomly assigned a job and a wage. Explain your reasoning using the summary statistics.

2.21   A small college was interested in analyzing the academic performance of its graduates. In the process it prepared the Minitab computer output shown in Exhibit 2.6. This analysis contains the descriptive statistics for variables contained in the data file "Student."

(a) Compare the grade-point average overall with the economics grade-point average, using the mean, standard deviation, and a standard deviation interval of ± 2.

(b) Are the two grade-point-average distributions symmetric? Indicate any differences, and present your evidence for differences in their distribution.

(c) Compare the SAT verbal and mathematics scores using the mean, median, standard deviation, and quartile points. Comment on differences between the distribution of the two test scores.

2.22   The following random sample of housing prices was obtained from a suburban community:

801,000   900,000   750,000   960,000   800,000
780,000   990,000   1,200,000   840,000   1,250,000

(a) Compute $\bar{X}$, S_X^2, and the median.

(b) Is this sample symmetric, skewed high, or skewed low?

2.23   You have been asked by Consolidated Foods, Inc. to investigate the feasibility of opening a new specialty supermarket in Gotham Village. As a first step you have obtained information from a sample of 10 families. Included in the information are 10 observations of disposable family income as follows:

20,900   31,000   47,800   65,000   80,000
32,000   25,000   38,000   35,000   45,000

The decision regarding store development is related directly to the family disposable income.

EXHIBIT 2.6   Minitab Output for Student Academic Performance Study

```
MTB > info
```

COLUMN	NAME	COUNT	MISSING
C1	sex	112	
C2	GPA	112	
C3	SATverb	112	45
C4	SATmath	112	45
C5	Acteng	112	39
C6	ACTmath	112	39
C7	ACTss	112	39
C8	ACTcomp	112	39
C9	HSPct	112	6
C10	EconGPA	112	

```
CONSTANTS USED: NONE

MTB > describe c1 - c10
```

	N	N*	MEAN	MEDIAN	TRMEAN	STDEV	SEMEAN
sex	112	0	0.3125	0.0000	0.2900	0.4656	0.0440
GPA	112	0	3.0436	3.0650	3.0475	0.4114	0.0389
SATverb	67	45	52.642	52.000	52.689	8.080	0.987
SATmath	67	45	61.28	62.00	61.61	8.42	1.03
Acteng	73	39	22.425	22.000	22.462	3.171	0.371
ACTmath	73	39	26.630	26.000	26.708	3.991	0.467
ACTss	73	39	25.562	25.000	25.723	4.570	0.535
ACTcomp	73	39	25.767	26.000	25.769	2.932	0.343
HSPct	106	6	84.54	88.50	85.93	13.72	1.33
EconGPA	112	0	2.9839	2.9325	2.9877	0.5451	0.0515

	MIN	MAX	Q1	Q3
sex	0.0000	1.0000	0.0000	1.0000
GPA	2.1200	3.8700	2.7525	3.3875
SATverb	31.000	69.000	48.000	58.000
SATmath	35.00	80.00	57.00	66.00
Acteng	14.000	29.000	20.000	25.000
ACTmath	15.000	36.000	24.000	29.000
ACTss	14.000	34.000	23.000	30.000
ACTcomp	19.000	32.000	23.000	28.000
HSPct	31.00	99.00	77.75	94.00
EconGPA	1.8000	4.0000	2.5406	3.4854

(a) Prepare a description of this sample by computing the mean, median, sample variance, and coefficient of variation.

(b) Briefly discuss the characteristics of family income in Gotham Village.

2.24 You are walking home along a dark street late at night. Suddenly, three masked women leap from behind the bushes and present you with the following sample of 10 numbers:

8000	8001	7999	7997	7996
8004	8003	8005	7995	8000

They indicate that they want you to determine the mean, median, and sample variance within the next 12.5 minutes or they will injure you. Naturally, you do not have your calculator or a computer, but they do give you some paper. Please proceed quickly since we are worried about your safety.

2.25 You have been studying the sales for Yellow and Black cereals. Based on a sample of 121 stores, the sample mean is 100 boxes and the variance is 100. As you are presenting your results to the marketing vice president, Ms. U. Otta Sellitall, she asks for the mean and variance of the sales revenue.

(a) What are the mean and variance of the sales revenue if the price per box is $2.00?

(b) What would 'be the mean and variance of sales revenue if the price were $1.50 per box and the demand curve for mean sales was $Q = 200 - 50 \times P$, where Q is the mean quantity sold and P is the price per box. Assume that the variance of boxes sold is not influenced by the mean sales level.

(c) Repeat part (b) using $P = \$2.00$ and $P = \$3.00$. The coefficient of variation for Q is 0.2.

2.26 Refer to the family income program evaluation in Problem 2.6. A second incentive is to be applied to both the program participants and nonparticipants. The incentive is expected to increase the income of program participants by 10% and nonparticipants by 25%. Using the results from Problem 2.6, determine the mean, median, sample standard deviation, and range for each group, assuming that the second incentive program was successful. Discuss the comparison of the two groups after this second incentive has been applied.

2.27 Eric Lind, financial vice-president, is preparing an analysis of monthly cash flows for the next fiscal year. Based on a manufacturing cost analysis for the production of high-performance computer processor chips, it is known that the setup fixed costs are $5000 and the cost per unit is $5.00. A random sample of past monthly demand resulted in a sample mean, $\bar{X} = 1000$, and a sample variance, $S_X^2 = 10,000$. Eric believes that the past demand is a good model for future demand because the demand is stable. Using the information above, what are the mean and variance of total monthly production costs for the processor chips?

2.28 Kevin Ackley, portfolio manager for Consolidated Investments, has asked you to determine the daily mean and variance for a portfolio of 75 shares of stock. He assures you that the prices are not increasing or decreasing but vary about a central tendency. A random sample of daily stock prices results in a sample mean, $\bar{X} = 50$, and a sample variance, $S_X^2 = 100$. What are the mean and variance for the entire 75-share portfolio?

2.29 Robert Thrash, financial manager, has set up purchasing funds for lower-priced capital equipment. These units are purchased through direct negotiation between the manufacturing engineer and various retail suppliers. During the next six months, 10 units will be purchased. A random sample of past purchase prices results in a mean, $\overline{X} = 600$, with a sample variance, $S_X^2 = 400$. The beginning balance of the fund is $10,000. What are the mean and variance of the fund balance after 10 units have been purchased?

2.30 The following random sample of housing prices was obtained from a suburban community:

801,000	900,000	750,000	960,000	800,000
780,000	990,000	1,200,000	840,000	1,250,000

(a) Draw and label a box-and-whisker plot.
(b) Is this sample symmetric, skewed high, or skewed low?

2.31 Refer to the family income program evaluation in Problem 2.6.
(a) Prepare a box-and-whisker plot for both the participant and nonparticipant groups. Label the plot clearly.
(b) Compare the two groups using the box-and-whisker plots. Discuss the program effectiveness using the two box-and-whisker plots.
(c) Use the box-and-whisker plot for the participant group to judge whether the program is successful in raising family incomes above the poverty level of $10,000.

2.32 We return again to northern Wisconsin. Green Christmas, Inc. is a large producer of Christmas trees located in northern Wisconsin. Robert Thrash, production manager, has asked you to prepare an additional statistical study to assist in the estimation of potential production for the coming Christmas season. Contracts with retailers require that the trees be at least 72 inches tall. A random sample of tree heights provided the following result:

71	72	63	66	65	53	54	81	83
80	79	51	62	55	54	58	62	

Robert has asked for the following information based on this sample.
(a) Construct a stem-and-leaf diagram for the tree height data.
(b) Describe the pattern of observations. If trees have an average growth of 12 inches per year, what percentage of the trees can be harvested during each of the next two years?

2.33 You are preparing a study of a developing country for the World Bank as part of the evaluation of a loan request. A random sample of annual family incomes from persons in the northern region provided the following data:

900	1100	800	1200	800	1300	1900	1600
1700	9000	15,000	1500	1250	1400	1800	

(a) Prepare a box-and-whisker plot.
(b) Describe the pattern of income in this country.

2.34   Speedy package delivery service is attempting to determine the distribution of package weights from its Minneapolis collection area. This information is required to develop truck and airplane loading requirements as their business grows. In addition, employee workloads and physical requirements are determined by these distributions. The following random sample of package weights, in pounds, was collected:

8	7	5	15	16	17	19	18	19
27	28	29	27	29	35	36	38	

    (a) Prepare a stem-and-leaf diagram.

    (b) The company pricing policy sets a single rate for all packages weighing 1 to 9 pounds, another single rate for packages weighing 10 to 19 pounds, and so on. Does knowledge of this pricing rule suggest an explanation for the pattern observed in the stem-and-leaf diagram developed in part (a)?

2.35   You have been asked by Consolidated Foods, Inc. to investigate the feasibility of opening a new specialty supermarket in Gotham Village. As a first step you have obtained information from a sample of 10 families. Included in the information are 10 observations of disposable family income as follows:

20,900	31,000	47,800	65,000	80,000
32,000	25,000	38,000	35,000	45,000

The decision regarding store development is related directly to the family disposable income.

    (a) Prepare a box-and-whisker plot for this sample.

    (b) Briefly discuss the characteristics of family income in Gotham Village.

2.36   Consolidated Foods, Inc. has also asked you to investigate the feasibility of opening a supermarket in Gotham Village. Select a random sample of 100 observations of disposable family income from the data file "Consb," which is available on your data disk and described in Appendix B.

    (a) Use the computer to prepare a box-and-whisker plot for this sample.

    (b) Briefly discuss the characteristics of family income in Gotham Village.

2.37   In this problem you will use the state survey data file in the data file "State87," which is provided on your data disk. Define four geographic regions: northeast (rows 1–9), north central (rows 10–21), southeast (rows 22–36), and west (rows 37–49). The regions will be compared using the mean, median, standard deviation, and range.

    (a) Compare the state populations in the four regions in terms of central tendency, dispersion, and skewness.

    (b) Compare the percent unemployment by state in the four regions in terms of central tendency, dispersion, and skewness.

    (c) Compare the state per capita income in the four regions in terms of central tendency, dispersion, and skewness.

    (d) Compare the state per capita retail sales in the four regions in terms of central tendency, dispersion, and skewness.

2.38   In this problem you will use the state survey data file in the "State87" data file on your data disk. Define four geographic regions: northeast (rows 1–9), north central (rows 10–21), southeast (rows 22–36), and west (rows 37–49). The regions will be compared using box-and-whisker plots.

    (a) Compare the state populations in the four regions in terms of central tendency, dispersion, and skewness.

    (b) Compare the percent unemployment by state in the four regions in terms of central tendency, dispersion, and skewness.

    (c) Compare the state per capita income in the four regions in terms of central tendency, dispersion, and skewness.

    (d) Compare the state per capita retail sales in the four regions in terms of central tendency, dispersion, and skewness.

2.39   This problem will require you to use the statistical program on your local computer. Peter Lapin is considering the purchase of a small sporting goods store in a midwestern city. The owners have supplied him with daily sales data from the past two years. The data are contained in a data file named "Stordata," which is located on your disk. The description of the variables is given in the file and can be read using any text editor. Peter has asked you to analyze the data so that he will be better able to decide if this is a profitable business. To answer Peter's question, you proceed with your analysis.

    (a) Prepare a frequency distribution and histogram and discuss the pattern of daily sales.

    (b) Compute the descriptive statistics: mean, median, standard deviation, and range. Discuss the central tendency, dispersion, and skewness based on the descriptive statistics.

    (c) Prepare a box-and-whisker plot. Compare the conclusions from the box-and-whisker plot with those obtained in parts (a) and (b).

    (d) Prepare a discussion for Peter that will help him to better understand the daily sales performance for this store.

2.40   This problem will require you to use the statistical program on your local computer. Peter Lapin is considering the purchase of a small sporting goods store in a midwestern city. The owners have supplied him with daily sales data from the past two years. The data are contained in a data file named "Stordata," which is located on your disk. The description of the variables is contained in the file and can be read using any text editor. Peter has asked you to analyze the data so that he will be better able to decide if this is a profitable business. He wants to know how the daily sales patterns differ over different periods of the week. In particular, he wants you to divide the data into two subsets: (1) Friday, Saturday, and Monday, and (2) Tuesday, Wednesday, and Thursday. He suspects that sporting goods sales may be higher close to the weekend, when people have more opportunity to think about recreation. Use your local statistical computer program to divide the data file into the two subsets.

    (a) For each subset prepare a frequency distribution and histogram. Compare the pattern of daily sales between the two subsets.

    (b) For each subset compute the descriptive statistics: mean, median, standard deviation, and range. Compare the pattern of daily sales between the two subsets using the central tendency, dispersion, and skewness.

    (c) For each subset prepare a box-and-whisker plot. Compare the conclusions from the box-and-whisker plots with those obtained in parts (a) and (b).

    (d) Prepare a discussion for Peter that will help him to better understand the daily sales performance for this store.

2.41 The Federal Bureau of Investigation has asked you to study 1984 crime rates as part of a larger study of patterns and trends in crime rates by state. Specifically, you are to analyze the following crime rates for 1984: total crime, murder, robbery, assault, and rape. For the study you have been provided with the cross-section crime rate data file called "Crime," which is located on your data disk or in the file designated by your instructor. The description of the variables is given in Appendix B and at the beginning of the data file. The computational work will be performed using your local computerized statistical package.

(a) Prepare frequency distributions, histograms, and box-and-whisker plots for crime rates.

(b) Locate the mean and median on each histogram. By examining the histograms, which now include the mean and median, determine if the distributions are skewed or symmetric.

2.42 A midwestern manufacturer has asked you to analyze their production data for flaked cereal. They present you with data collected for 22 production runs conducted during a recent year. These data are in the file "Cereal," which is on your data disk. The four column variables are: C1, percent yield; C2, percent grits; C3, pounds of grits; and C4, pounds of cereal. The production facilities are used to produce several different cereal products. Thus whenever the warehouse inventory and/or anticipated demand indicate a need for additional flaked cereal, a production run is scheduled.

(a) Prepare a frequency distribution and a histogram for the percent yield. Select the intervals so that there are 8 to 10 equal-width cells.

(b) Prepare a frequency distribution and a histogram for the pounds of cereal produced during each production run. Select the intervals so that there are 8 to 10 equal-width cells.

(c) Briefly discuss the percent yield and the total output for these production runs.

2.43 A midwestern manufacturer has asked you to analyze their production data for flaked cereal. They present you with data collected for 22 production runs conducted during a recent year ("Cereal"). The production facilities are used to produce several different cereal products. Thus whenever the warehouse inventory and/or anticipated demand indicates a need for additional flaked cereal, a production run is scheduled.

(a) Compute the mean, median, standard deviation, and range for the percent yield.

(b) Compute the mean, median, standard deviation, and range for the total output.

(c) Briefly discuss the percent yield and the total output based on the descriptive statistics above.

2.44 Jonathan Livingston, a labor economist, is studying labor force participation rates for married women. Use the data file "Labor2," which is described in your data dictionary, and your computer statistics package to compute descriptive statistics for percent labor participation for married women in age groups 15–24, 25–34, 35–44, 45–54, and 55–64.

(a) Compare the age subgroups by mean and indicate groups that are highest and lowest.

(b) Compare the groups using box-and-whisker plots. Discuss differences between the subgroups.

(c) Compute the mean ± 2 standard deviation interval for each subgroup. Compare these intervals with the quartile intervals from part (b). Do these two groups of intervals have the same relative size?

2.45 This problem uses the data file "Labor2" described in your data dictionary to help you study labor force participation of married women. You are interested in the influence of children on labor participation of married women. Compute appropriate statistics for the three subgroups: no children, children under age 6, and children age 6 to 17. Discuss the differences using appropriate descriptive statistics.

2.46 This problem continues the academic performance study in the small college. Use the data file "Student" to obtain the data for analysis using your computer statistical package.
(a) Prepare histograms for the overall grade-point average and the economics grade-point average. Discuss differences in the distributions.
(b) Compare the overall grade-point averages for men and women using histograms and box-and-whisker plots. What differences do you observe?
(c) Compare the economics grade-point averages for men and women using histograms and box-and-whisker plots. What differences do you observe?
(d) Compare the economics grade-point averages for men and women using the mean, standard deviation, and the mean ± 2 standard deviation interval. Are your conclusions the same as those obtained in part (c)?

2.47 The federal government is interested in studying the automobile death rate patterns over the various states. The data file "Crash" is to be used to prepare analyses for this problem. They are interested in comparing the mileage death rate (deaths divided by miles driven) in all automobile-related accidents and the population death rate in automobiles and pickups.
(a) Compute the mean, standard deviation, 2 standard deviation interval, and box-and-whisker plot for both death rates. Discuss differences in the distribution patterns.
(b) Compare the 2 standard deviation interval for states with the oldest cars and newest cars. (*Hint:* Group the observations into subgroups below and above the median on the "average age of automobiles" variable. Then run the statistics for each subgroup.)
(c) Compare the 2 standard deviation interval for states with the smallest and the largest population density per square mile. Note differences and suggest reasons for these differences.

2.48 The state planning agency is studying taxation and spending patterns for small cities outside the major metropolitan area, and they have hired you as a consultant. For this analysis you are to use the data file "Citydat." They want you to compare per capita government expenditures, the property tax rate, and the assessment base divided by population.
(a) Prepare appropriate measures to describe the pattern of the distributions for the variables of interest, and discuss your results.
(b) Repeat the analysis in part (a) using subsets defined by the largest and smallest populations.

2.49   Examine the summary statistics for samples I, II, and III shown in Table 2.21 and answer
the following questions.

TABLE 2.21   Description of Samples I,
II, and III

| | Sample | | |
Statistic	I	II	III
Maximum	1000	1000	597
75th percentile	800	900	516
Median	700	400	463
25th percentile	400	300	408
Minimum	200	200	329

(a) Sketch the form of the approximate histogram for each sample. The bars should
indicate relative frequency.
(b) For each sample indicate whether the mean is larger or smaller than the median.

APPENDIX A: ERRORS IN HEALTH CARE CLAIMS PROCESSING

1. Procedure and Diagnosis Code Errors

There are several hundred different medical procedures that might be performed, and
each has an agreed payment. In some cases, providers might submit a procedure code
that calls for a higher payment than is actually deserved for the service performed
(e.g., complete rather than partial physical examination). In other cases, provider staff
may simply copy the code incorrectly. Correct payment requires accurate reporting of
procedure and diagnosis codes.

2. Provider Information Errors

Insurance plans often limit the patient to a set of authorized providers at a specific
location who have agreed to a payment schedule. Claims submitted for unauthorized
providers cannot be paid or possibly are paid at a reduced rate. Errors usually result
from provider staff who do not know the contract rules or from a coding mistake.
However, the error could also be an attempted case of fraud.

3. Patient Information Errors

Each insurance contract has a patient code for the contract holder and a separate code
for each of his or her dependents. Only persons with a patient code can receive benefits, and there are logical restrictions on benefits (e.g., a male cannot receive payment
for maternity procedures). Most of these errors are the result of submitting the wrong
code or a clerical error in recording the number. However, there are situations in which
a claim for an unauthorized patient is submitted.

4. Pricing Scheduling Errors

Most health insurance contracts include a list of authorized providers who have agreed to a specific schedule of payments for procedures that are authorized by the contract. Thus a pricing schedule must be prepared and maintained for each contract group (e.g., all employees of a particular company). Each schedule is extensive, complex, and unique. There are many possible chances for error by the person or persons who prepare and maintain the schedule.

5. Contract Application Errors

Group contracts are sold by a marketing representative and maintained by a contract manager. In most cases a unique set of procedures and providers are specified in the details of the contract. Providers often are paid on different schedules for different contracts. Again, the details must be coded into a number of long and complex tables. Any entry could be in error because of a failure to understand the contract or simply because of a coding error. In addition, changes might occur during the contract period because of legal rulings or mutual agreements between the insurance company and the provider or the group contract holder. The complexity of the contract administration process has many opportunities for error.

6. Provider Adjustment Errors

There are a number of special payment adjustments that might be applied permanently or temporarily for certain providers. These might include partial withholding for provider incentives, penalties for overpayment, and/or special conditions. These adjustments are recorded in tables and must be maintained. Again, the complexity provides many possibilities for error.

7. Program and System Errors

The complex payment system is coded into very large computer programs that are designed to process as many claims as possible without human intervention. The programs include procedures to send claims with unusual conditions to a trained claims examiner. The computer programs are modified as insurance regulations and company contract administration policies change. Again, there are many possibilities for error.

APPENDIX B: STATE SURVEY DATA FILE

STATE	TOTPOP92	UNEMP92	BUSFAIL
ME 1	1235	7.1	90
NH 2	1111	7.5	146
VT 3	570	6.6	94
MA 4	5998	8.5	135
RI 5	1005	8.9	133

STATE	TOTPOP92	UNEMP92	BUSFAIL
CT 6	3281	7.5	86
NY 7	18119	8.5	117
NJ 8	7789	8.4	103
PA 9	12009	7.5	109
OH 10	11016	7.2	82
IN 11	5662	6.5	93
IL 12	11631	7.5	74
MI 13	9437	8.8	77
WI 14	5007	5.1	73
MN 15	4480	5.1	87
IA 16	2812	4.6	47
MO 17	5193	5.7	109
ND 18	636	4.9	55
SD 19	711	3.1	63
NE 20	1606	3.0	94
KS 21	2523	4.2	99
DE 22	689	5.3	87
MD 23	4908	6.6	111
DC 24	589	8.4	64
VA 25	6377	6.4	116
WV 26	1812	11.3	85
NC 27	6843	5.9	77
SC 28	3603	6.2	52
GA 29	6751	6.9	169
FL 30	13488	8.2	130
KY 31	3755	6.9	104
TN 32	5024	6.4	120
AL 33	4136	7.3	86
MS 34	2614	8.1	70
AR 35	2399	7.2	65
LA 36	4287	8.1	74
OK 37	3212	5.7	124
TX 38	17656	7.5	108
MT 39	824	6.7	51
ID 40	1067	6.5	77
WY 41	466	5.6	60

STATE	TOTPOP92	UNEMP92	BUSFAIL
CO 42	3470	5.9	114
NM 43	1581	6.8	85
AZ 44	3832	7.4	164
UT 45	1813	4.9	82
NV 46	1327	6.6	106
WA 47	5136	7.5	104
OR 48	587	9.1	51
HI 51	1160	4.5	87

APPENDIX C: MINITAB FOR WINDOWS INSTRUCTIONS

For those readers unfamiliar with Minitab for Windows, we give the following short explanation of how the histograms in this chapter were constructed. Hopefully, this will be sufficient to start you in the exciting area of statistical graphics.

- You must first enter your data into a Minitab worksheet. You can name your variable or leave it as C1. We labeled C1 as "Ages."
- Select Graph from the main Menu bar.
- From the Graph menu, choose Histogram . . . . The ellipsis indicates that a dialog box will appear. You will be prompted to provide additional information. Double-click to select the variable in the C1 column.
- In the Histogram dialog box, select OPTIONS . . . .
- The Options dialog box appears. Choose the type of interval you prefer (either MIDPOINT, which gives the midpoint of the classes on the x-axis; or CUTPOINT, which gives the endpoints of the classes on the x-axis). We used the cutpoint for the histograms in Figure 2.6.
- In the Options dialog box, define the interval you desire using the format a:b/c, where "a" is the starting value of the histogram, "b" is the ending value, and "c" is the width of the intervals for your histogram. For example, in Figure 2.6c we defined our intervals as 0:80/10. Click on "OK" when you are finished in the Options dialog box. This will return you to the Histogram dialog box.
- If you wish to add a title or footnote, select the Annotations pulldown box. When you have finished designing your histogram, select "OK" and Minitab will begin to initialize the graphics.

3

Descriptive Relationships

Everything depends on everything!

3.1 RELATIONS BETWEEN VARIABLES

In this chapter we present descriptive techniques for using data to study relation-ships between variables. In Chapter 2 we learned how to summarize and describe populations and samples using descriptive statistics, frequency distributions, and various graphical devices. Those descriptions provided information about single variables. Here we build upon and extend those results. Analysis of business and economic problems places us in the world where everything depends on everything. Our problem as future analysts and managers is to determine which of these re-lationships are truly important. We begin our study of tools that will help in that task.

Brooke Mohn is product manager for Plaito brand yogurt. In this competitive market she uses a number of different strategies to encourage consumers to purchase Plaito yogurt. One of these strategies is periodic price reductions from the "official" price. Brooke would like to know how price reductions have affected weekly sales. She obtained a data set from A.C. Nielsen, Inc., which was a sample of weekly price and sales data from randomly selected supermarkets. She now has 52 pairs of unit price and number of units sold and wants to use this to understand the past behavior of the market. How should she analyze the data? Did lower prices usually result in higher sales? How much increase in sales occurred for each 1-cent reduction in price? In this chapter we develop procedures to answer these questions.

Beginning in Chapter 14 you will learn to use these procedures in more sophisti-cated statistical analyses. These descriptive procedures are not merely an intermediate learning step on the road to the more powerful procedures. Professional statisticians, analysts, managers, and executives spend considerable time examining data, using the descriptive procedures developed in Chapters 2 and 3, before applying more sophisti-cated procedures.

Economists and business people devote considerable effort to studying relationships between variables. Typical questions include:

1. If a florist's prices are lowered by 10%, what will happen to sales?
2. Will U.S. exports increase if the value of the dollar is decreased relative to the deutsche mark?
3. How much can the production of golf clubs for a sporting goods manufacturer be increased by adding workers?

To answer questions such as these, business and economic analysis makes extensive use of linear equations of the form

$$Y = \beta_0 + \beta_1 X$$

Examples include:

1. Sales, Y, as a function of price, X.
2. Exports, Y, as a function of the value of the dollar, X.
3. Production, Y, as a function of the number of workers, X.

The linear equation includes two constant parameters: β_0 and β_1, where β_1 is the slope coefficient that indicates rate of change. For every 1-unit change in X the value of Y will change by β_1 units. In most applications the variable Y is called the *dependent variable* and X the *independent variable*. Economists also use the special terms *endogenous* (determined by the model) for Y and *exogenous* (determined outside the model) for X.

3.2 SCATTER PLOTS

In beginning algebra courses you plotted points to obtain pictures representing mathematical functions, including linear, quadratic, exponential, and various polynomials. Statistical analysts plot individual points and examine the entire pattern to determine the type of relationship between two variables. These scatter plots (Key Idea 3.1) can be prepared using a pencil and graph paper. However, almost all statistical analysis uses computer-generated scatter plots that are routinely examined as part of any statistical study involving relationships between variables (Key Idea 3.2).

Key Idea 3.1: Scatter Plot

A **scatter plot** is prepared by placing one point for each observation using the values of the two variables included in the observation.

Key Idea 3.2: Information from Graphs

1. Range of each variable
2. Spread of values over the range
3. Whether there is a relationship between the two variables
4. Mathematical form of the relationship
5. Indication of outliers (extreme points) from linear equation

The scatter plot of points for all observations, shown in Figure 3.1, provides a "picture" of the relationship between variables. Scatter plots provide a great deal of information. Each point on the plot represents a combination of quantity and price that occurred in a particular quarter. The point is plotted at the intersection of perpendicular lines drawn from the axis at specific quantity and price values.

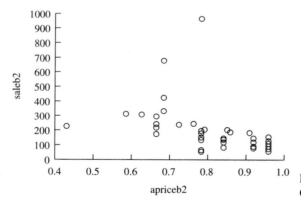

Figure 3.1 Plot of Quantity Sold Versus Price

Example 3.1 Quantity and Price

Using economic theory we know that the quantity of a good purchased will decrease with higher prices. This is the basic demand function. Figure 3.1 presents a scatter plot of weekly quantities sold in a supermarket versus actual price for a consumer food product. These data were collected by A.C. Nielsen, Inc. as part of its regular supermarket scanning survey conducted for food producers. This plot was prepared using Minitab, but all good statistical computer programs have similar capability. We used the ranges of the variables to set its boundaries. However, it is easy to instruct the computer to use different boundaries if, for example, you wish to compare several plots all drawn to the same scale. Examine the relationship between price and quantity sold in Figure 3.1. Does it follow the pattern you would expect from economic theory?

Solution   Using this scatter plot we can study the relationship between the number of units sold ("saleb2") and the price charged during that week ("apriceb2"). The quantity sold varied from about 40 to just over 900 units per week. The price was in dollars and generally varied from 60 to 98 cents, with one week having a price of 45 cents. Examination of the plot indicates a downward linear pattern with the exception of three points. The weekly quantities sold for two weeks were much higher than suggested by the linear pattern. In addition, the quantities sold when the price was 45 cents were lower than would be predicted by a price that low. An analyst would examine the week for each of these unusual points and attempt to determine if anything could be learned from the unusual combinations of quantity and price. Alternatively, these points could have resulted from recording errors and thus should be corrected.   □

Example 3.2   Comparison of Imports and Exports

The International Trade Division of the U.S. Department of Commerce has been considering strategies to improve the U.S. balance of trade (exports minus imports). Some politicians have argued that as we import more items there will be a natural tendency to export more items. To test this argument, George Gatt, the chief economist, plotted imports versus exports using quarterly data from 1977 to 1986. Figure 3.2 shows the scatter plot. Discuss the evidence for or against the argument made by the politicians.

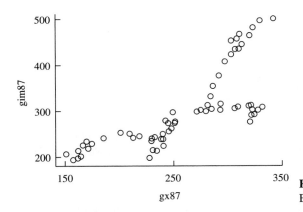

Figure 3.2   Plot of Imports Versus Exports (1977–1986)

Solution   The results from this example provide an interesting contrast to Example 3.1. There is no obvious relationship between exports and imports. Instead, there is one group of points spread horizontally, with another group extending upward. The points that extend upward occur for time periods in which exports range from about 280 to 350 while imports range from about 300 to 500. Therefore, all these points would result in negative trade balances (trade balance = exports − imports). This analysis clearly indicates that increased exports do not necessarily lead to increased imports. Nor do changes in imports imply changes in exports.   □

Example 3.3   Income Versus Age of Head of Household

Exhibit 3.1 shows the plot of family income versus age of head of household for the random sample of households.

EXHIBIT 3.1   Plot of Income Versus Age of Head of Household

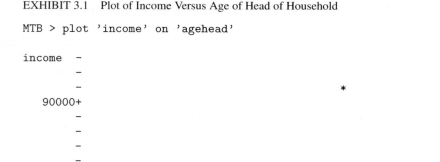

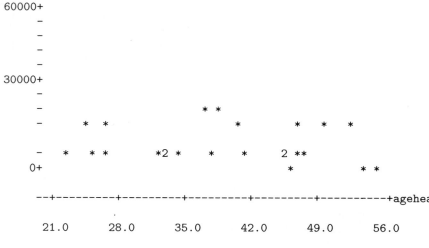

```
MTB > plot 'income' on 'agehead'


income  -
        -
        -                                                        *
  90000+
        -
        -
        -
        -
  60000+
        -
        -
        -
        -
  30000+
        -
        -                                  *  *
        -          *   *                *            *    *    *
        -      *     *  *         *2  *      *      *     2 **
      0+                                                *         *  *

      --+---------+---------+---------+---------+----------+agehead
        21.0      28.0      35.0      42.0      49.0       56.0
```

Solution   The general pattern is that income remains essentially the same over the range of ages. Special interest is directed to the single very high family income for a family whose head is about 45. This large outlier was discovered by using a scatter plot. A single outlier can distort the pattern of the other points because the range must be very wide to accommodate an outlier. The analyst should double-check the data for accuracy and then try to determine if there are any special conditions associated with that observation. In some cases a few observations that produce outliers provide important information that cannot be obtained using conventional statistical procedures. Experience indicates that family income samples typically include some positive outliers.   □

3.3 COVARIANCE AND CORRELATION

Now that we have seen how to look for relationships between variables using scatter plots, we learn how to use statistics to describe relationships between variables. *Covariance* is a measure of the linear relationship between two variables, and *correlation* is a standardized measure of the linear relationship. We introduce these statistics with an example to demonstrate how and where they are applied.

Example 3.4   Demand for Plywood

Ms. Agnes Larson is the regional manager for a chain of building supply stores. She is interested in determining the relationship between the price charged for plywood and the quantity sold. She recalls from her study of economics that this relationship is called a *demand function* and that demand functions can often be approximated by linear equations. From past store records she discovers the number of pieces of plywood sold per day and the prices charged on those days. These data are shown in Table 3.1. How should she proceed with analyzing these data?

TABLE 3.1   Plywood
Sales Versus Price

Price per Piece, X	Thousands of Pieces, Y
$6	80
7	60
8	70
9	40
10	0

Solution   To understand the data better she prepares Figure 3.3, which is a plot of Y versus X. The scatter plot, with a line drawn for emphasis, shows an approximate linear relationship with a negative slope. Agnes shows these results to the manager of market research, Sally Goldberg, who suggests that she compute the covariance and then the correlation for her data. Agnes asks for an explanation and some assistance. (This example continues below.)

3.3.1 Covariance Calculation

The covariance uses sample observations that contain pairs of x_i and y_i values. The sample means, $\bar{X}$ and $\bar{Y}$, are subtracted from each of the x and y values in the observation to obtain deviations from the mean; the products of these deviations are added together and divided by the sample size, n, minus 1 (Key Idea 3.3). The covariance has some similarities to the variance. If x and y were both the same variable, the covariance would be equal to the variance.

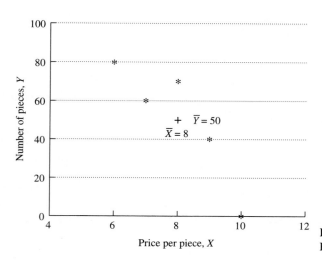

Figure 3.3 Plywood Sales Versus Price

Key Idea 3.3: Covariance

The **covariance**, S_{XY}, is a measure of the linear relationship between two variables. A positive value indicates that both variables increase together, and a negative value indicates that variables move in opposite directions.

For sample data the formula is

$$S_{XY} = \frac{\sum_{i=1}^{n} (x_i - \bar{X})(y_i - \bar{Y})}{n - 1}$$

where x_i and y_i are observed values, $\bar{X}$ and $\bar{Y}$ are the sample means, and n is the sample size.

For population data the formula is

$$\sigma_{XY} = \frac{\sum_{i=1}^{n} (x_i - \mu_x)(y_i - \mu_y)}{N}$$

where μ_x and μ_y are the population means. Here we use the sample definition that is used by most computer software.

Solution (continued, Example 3.4)   Sally helps Agnes compute the covariance for the price and quantity data in Table 3.1. Price is labeled by X and quantity of plywood by Y. First they computed the sample means:

$$\bar{X} = \frac{\sum_{i=1}^{n} x_i}{n}$$

$$= \frac{6 + 7 + 8 + 9 + 10}{5}$$

$$= 8.0$$

$$\bar{Y} = \frac{\sum_{i=1}^{n} y_i}{n}$$

$$= \frac{80 + 60 + 70 + 40 + 0}{5}$$

$$= 50$$

Next they computed the covariance:

$$S_{XY} = \frac{\sum_{i=1}^{n} (x_i - \bar{X})(y_i - \bar{Y})}{n - 1}$$

$$= \frac{(6 - 8)(80 - 50) + (7 - 8)(60 - 50) + \cdots + (10 - 8)(0 - 50)}{5 - 1}$$

$$= -45$$

In this example, the downward-sloping relationship between price and quantity, shown in Figure 3.1, results in a negative covariance. The x and y deviations from the mean have opposite signs. This occurs because the points are located in the upper left and lower right sections of the graph. As a result, the covariance is negative. The scatter plot indicates a downward (negative) slope from left to right. Similarly, if the points were in the lower left and the upper right sections, the x and y deviations would have the same sign and the result would be a positive covariance. A plot of those points would have an upward (positive) slope from left to right. The details of the calculation and Figure 3.1 reveal how the negative covariance is obtained.   □

3.3.2 Correlation Calculation

In contrast to the covariance the correlation coefficient is a standardized measure of correlation whose value ranges from -1.0 to $+1.0$. Thus the correlation is a more useful measure of the linearity and direction of the relationship between two variables.

The correlation is computed by dividing the covariance by the product of the standard deviations of the two variables X and Y (Key Idea 3.4). Dividing the covariance by the two standard deviations standardizes the correlation to the range -1 to $+1$ regardless of the variances for the two variables. The standard deviations are always positive, and the correlation r_{xy} has the same sign as the covariance.

Key Idea 3.4: Correlation

The **correlation** is a standardized measure that indicates the strength of the linear relationship between two variables.

1. The correlation coefficient varies from -1 to $+1$ with:
   (a) $+1$ indicates a perfect direct (X increases, Y increases) linear relationship.
   (b) 0.0 indicates no linear relationship (X and Y have no pattern).
   (c) -1 indicates a perfect inverse relationship (X increases, Y decreases).
2. Positive correlations indicate direct linear relationships with values closer to 1 indicating data points closer to a straight line and smaller values indicating a more scattered pattern of points.
3. Negative correlations imply inverse linear relationships with values closer to -1 indicating data points closer to a straight line and values between -1 and 0 indicating a more scattered pattern of points.

The correlation, r_{xy}, is computed by

$$r_{xy} = \frac{S_{XY}}{S_X S_Y}$$

Solution (continued, Example 3.4)   Returning to the plywood problem, Sally and Agnes computed the standard deviations as

$$S_X = \sqrt{\frac{\sum_{i=1}^{n}(x_i - \bar{X})^2}{n-1}}$$

$$= \sqrt{\frac{(6-8)^2 + (7-8)^2 + (8-8)^2 + (9-8)^2 + (10-8)^2}{5-1}}$$

$$= 1.58$$

$$S_Y = \sqrt{\frac{\sum_{i=1}^{n}(y_i - \bar{Y})^2}{n-1}}$$

$$= \sqrt{\frac{(80-50)^2 + (60-50)^2 + (70-50)^2 + (40-50)^2 + (0-50)^2}{5-1}}$$

$$= 31.62$$

Using these results with the covariance computed previously, they found that

$$r_{xy} = \frac{S_{XY}}{S_X S_Y}$$

$$= \frac{-45}{(1.58)(31.62)}$$

$$= -0.90$$

The correlation of -0.90 indicates that the relationship is downward sloping and that it is close to a straight line. Figure 3.3 provides a mental image of a "strong" negative correlation. □

Table 3.2 contains some very simple samples that are also plotted in Figure 3.4. From these samples we see some idealized examples of $+1$, 0.0, and -1.0 correlations. Sample 1 has a correlation of $+1.0$, which indicates a perfect direct relationship, as shown in the plot. Sample 2 has a correlation of -1, corresponding to the plotted perfect inverse relationship. Finally, sample 3 has a correlation of 0 and has a plot that indicates no relationship.

TABLE 3.2   Small Samples for Correlation Calculation

Observation	Sample 1		Sample 2		Sample 3	
	X	Y	X	Y	X	Y
1	-1	-1	-1	$+1$	-1	0
2	0	0	0	0	0	0
3	$+1$	$+1$	$+1$	-1	$+1$	0

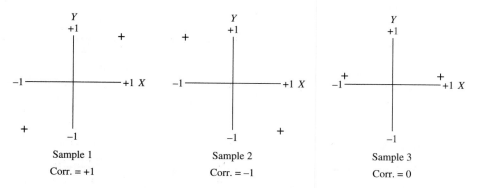

Figure 3.4   Graphs for Simple Samples

Figure 3.5 presents plots of data for six different correlations, which provide rough scaling pictures to give you an intuitive feeling for the correlation coefficient when there are more observations. The correlations indicated were computed using computer software.

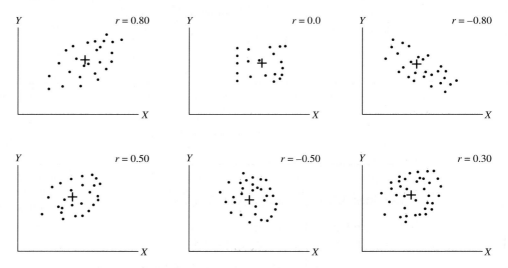

Figure 3.5   Examples of Various Correlations

As the points on a graph approach a straight line, the absolute value of the correlation approaches 1.0. When correlations are closer to +1 or −1, the prediction of the dependent variable Y, by using a value for the independent variable X, yields a more precise value for Y. With a correlation of 0 the Y's have the same pattern for every value of X. By contrast with $r = +0.8$ or $r = -0.8$, the central tendency of Y changes substantially with changes in X.

Correlation only provides information about linear relationships: those that are continuously increasing or decreasing at the same rate. Figure 3.6 is a typical plot of average costs per unit versus number of units produced. Point A is the most efficient production level. These data, which have a quadratic relationship, would have a correlation $r = 0$. The correlation without the plot is misleading (Key Idea 3.5).

Figure 3.7 shows the sales of lawn mowers as a function of time in a city with a stable population. Demand is seasonal. These data have a correlation $r = 0.0$. Seasonal demand increases and decreases would be missed if a scatter plot were not included with the correlation.

Does It Make Sense?

We have seen that correlations provide useful information only about linear relationships. If a correlation is at or close to zero, we cannot say that there is no relationship between the variables. We can only say that there is not a linear relationship between

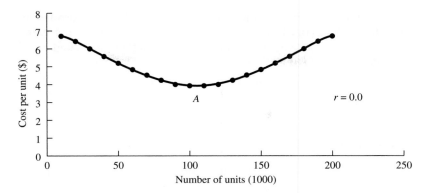

Figure 3.6   Average Production Cost

Key Idea 3.5: Correlations and Graphs

The correlation coefficient and a scatter plot applied together provide a simple but powerful data analysis tool.

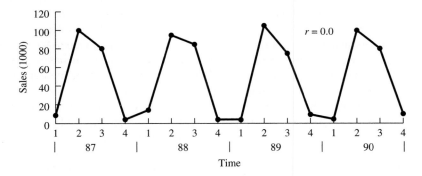

Figure 3.7   Lawn Mower Sales by Quarter

the variables. Although linear relationships are very important for business and economic analysis, they are not the only type of relationship. A correlation close to zero does indicate the absence of a linear relationship.

Correlation coefficients have also been computed for the data presented in Figures 3.1 and 3.2. Figure 3.1 is a plot of quantity purchased versus price, which indicates a downward-sloping linear relationship. The correlation coefficient, computed using a computer, was -0.509. In contrast, the scatter plot for exports and imports shown in Figure 3.2 does not appear to be linear. The correlation coefficient computed was 0.329. The correlation coefficient for Exhibit 3.1 was approximately 0.

Practice Problem 3.1: Covariance and Correlation

For the (x, y) pairs of data points $(1, 5)$, $(3, 7)$, $(4, 6)$, $(5, 8)$, and $(7, 9)$:

(a) Compute the covariance.

(b) Compute the correlation coefficient.

(c) Discuss briefly the relationship between X and Y.   □

The solutions for all Practice Problems are given at the end of the chapter.

Problem Exercises

3.1   Rising Hills Manufacturing wishes to study the relationship between the number of workers, X, and the number of tables, Y, produced in its Redwood Falls plant. They have obtained a random sample of 10 days of production. The following (X, Y) combinations of points were obtained:

(12, 200)	(30, 600)	(15, 270)	(24, 500)	(14, 210)
(18, 300)	(28, 610)	(26, 540)	(19, 320)	(27, 570)

(a) Prepare a scatter plot of the points.
(b) Compute the covariance.
(c) Compute the correlation.
(d) Discuss briefly the relationship between the number of workers and the number of tables produced per day.

3.2   River Hills Hospital is interested in determining the effectiveness of a new drug for reducing the time required for complete recovery from knee surgery. Complete recovery is measured by a series of strength tests that compare the treated knee with the untreated knee. The drug was given in varying amounts to 18 patients over a six-month period. For each patient the number of drug units, X, and the days for complete recovery, Y, are given by the following (X, Y) data:

(5, 53)	(21, 65)	(14, 48)	(11, 66)	(9, 46)	(4, 56)
(7, 53)	(21, 57)	(17, 49)	(14, 66)	(9, 54)	(7, 56)
(9, 53)	(21, 52)	(13, 49)	(14, 56)	(9, 59)	(4, 56)

(a) Prepare a scatter plot of the points.
(b) Compute the covariance.
(c) Compute the correlation.
(d) Briefly discuss the relationship between the number of drug units and the recovery time. What dosage would you recommend based on this initial analysis?

3.3   Acme Delivery offers three different shipping rates for packages under 5 pounds delivered from Maine to the west coast: regular, $3; fast, $5; and lightning, $10. To test the quality of these services, a major mail-order retailer shipped 15 packages at randomly selected times from Maine to Tacoma, Washington. The packages were shipped in groups of three by the three services at the same time to reduce variation resulting from the shipping day. The following data show the shipping cost, x, and the number of days, y, in (x, y) pairs:

(3, 7)   (5, 5)   (10, 2)   (3, 9)   (5, 6)   (10, 5)   (3, 6)   (5, 6)

(10, 1)   (3, 10)   (5, 7)   (10, 4)   (3, 5)   (5, 6)   (10, 4)

(a) Prepare a scatter plot of the points.
(b) Compute the covariance.
(c) Compute the correlation.
(d) Discuss the value of the higher-priced services in terms of quicker delivery.

3.4   The human resources department of a large firm conducted a study of its salary structure. As part of this study the years of experience and monthly wages were collected for a sample of 12 employees. These employees were in various administrative and management positions. The first number in the following pairs is the years of experience.

(5, 2500)   (9, 6200)   (14, 8000)   (12, 6400)   (2, 2200)   (8, 4000)

(6, 4500)   (10, 6600)   (15, 10,000)   (11, 6900)   (1, 2000)   (8, 4800)

(a) Prepare a scatter plot of the points.
(b) Compute the covariance.
(c) Compute the correlation.
(d) Is it correct for the company to conclude that wages tend to increase directly with years of experience?

3.5   Consumer Foods, Inc. wishes to evaluate the effectiveness of its advertising expenditures. Advertising effectiveness is measured by the percentage of randomly selected households that have seen an advertisement and have purchased the product. Expenditures are measured by the cost per 10,000 viewers in a region. The following data were collected in 10 major urban markets, with the first number being the expenditures and the second being the effectiveness:

(50, 10.2)   (40, 8.1)   (64, 11.4)   (76, 14.7)   (66, 13.8)

(36, 6.1)   (55, 15.0)   (62, 12.1)   (48, 10.8)   (59, 14.8)

(a) Prepare a scatter plot of the points.
(b) Compute the covariance.
(c) Compute the correlation.
(d) Discuss the relationship between advertising cost and effectiveness for Consumer Foods, Inc.

3.4 LEAST-SQUARES REGRESSION LINES

By working with Sally Goldberg and her marketing research staff, Agnes Larson has learned to use scatter plots and correlation for analyzing the relationship between quantity and price variables. She now knows that the relationship between price and quantity sold is nearly linear. Could she estimate a linear equation that represents the demand function? With such an equation she could compute the quantity demanded for various prices.

Agnes asked Sally to meet with her to provide some guidance. Sally says that *regression analysis* is the procedure to use for describing linear relationships more precisely than the scatter plot and correlation procedure. We concentrate on using regression analysis as a procedure for describing relationships between X, Y data points.

The following introductory development of regression will provide a basic understanding of the objectives and outcomes of regression analysis. You will understand how to obtain and interpret a regression equation using the computer. You will not know how to use it for advanced statistical analysis. Those skills will come in Chapters 14 to 16. As you read the following sections, focus on regression as another tool for describing and summarizing data.

3.4.1 Simplified Regression for Data Description

Early courses in algebra have shown you that a linear relationship between variables Y and X can be represented by an equation of the form

$$\hat{Y} = \hat{\beta}_0 + \hat{\beta}_1 X$$

In the discussion of regression analysis we use the terms $\hat{\beta}_0$ and $\hat{\beta}_1$ whenever specific values for these coefficients are computed from a sample of data. Thus the general form of the linear equation is (Key Idea 3.6)

$$Y = \beta_0 + \beta_1 X_1$$

while the equation form

$$Y = \hat{\beta}_0 + \hat{\beta}_1 X_1$$

contains specific values of the coefficients computed from the sample data. In general, any time the ˆ symbol appears over a variable, the variable represents a value computed from sample data instead of simply the general variable.

Key Idea 3.6: Least-Squares Regression

Least-squares regression is a technique for obtaining estimates of coefficients β_0 and β_1 in the linear equation

$$Y = \beta_0 + \beta_1 X$$

from sample or population data that contain (x_i, y_i) pairs for each observation.

Using this equation, values of Y can be predicted for given values of X. The coefficient $\hat{\beta}_1$ indicates the rate of change of Y with respect to X. Thus if X changes by 1 unit, Y will change by $\hat{\beta}_1$ units. The change in Y will be positive or negative depending on the sign for the coefficient $\hat{\beta}_1$. $\hat{\beta}_0$, which is also the Y intercept, shifts the equation up or down in the Y direction. If $\hat{\beta}_0$ and $\hat{\beta}_1$ are known, the equation representing the relationship between X and Y is known.

Analysts should use caution when interpreting $\hat{\beta}_0$. From high school algebra we know that $\hat{\beta}_0$ is the intercept of the Y axis when $X = 0$. However, regression models should only be used over the range of the X variable that was used to develop the equation coefficients, $\hat{\beta}_0$ and $\hat{\beta}_1$. Literal interpretations of $\hat{\beta}_0$ as the value of Y when $X = 0$ can be misleading if the original data do not include values of X at 0 or very close to 0.

One of the important objectives of regression is to estimate the values of $\hat{\beta}_0$ and $\hat{\beta}_1$ from a set of data. Other objectives include determining if X and Y are related and computing measures of error associated with the estimation of $\hat{\beta}_0$ and $\hat{\beta}_1$.

Obtaining estimates $\hat{\beta}_0$ and $\hat{\beta}_1$ in a linear equation is complicated because all (X, Y) points do not lie on a straight line. They do not have a correlation equal to 1.0. The data from Agnes Larson's plywood demand function are plotted again in Figure 3.8. None of these points are exactly on the straight line, but they are all close and the pattern is approximately linear.

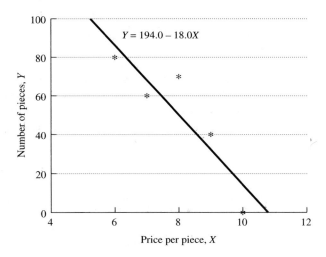

Figure 3.8 Plywood Demand Function

In Chapter 2 we developed data models that included *information* and *error*. For linear regression models the information is $\hat{Y}$, defined by the linear function of the coefficients $\hat{\beta}_0$, $\hat{\beta}_1$, and X. The error is the difference between the observed value of Y_i and the value predicted by the equation, $\hat{Y}_i$. This difference is defined as the *residual*, $\hat{e}_i$ (Key Idea 3.7).

Key Idea 3.7: Least-Squares Residual

The **residual** $\hat{e}_i$ is the deviation of a point from the linear equation measured in the Y or vertical direction.

In algebraic terms,

$$\hat{e}_i = y_i - \hat{Y}_i$$

where y_i is the observed value of Y from the data set and $\hat{Y}_i$ is the computed value of Y from the regression equation. In regression analysis the error term is called the residual.

Early mathematical statisticians struggled with the problem of obtaining the most accurate number for the dependent variable, Y, given that a set of points did not all line on a straight line. After many years there was general agreement that the most accurate estimate could be obtained from a linear equation developed using the least-squares regression procedure presented in Key Idea 3.8.

Minimizing the sum of squared residuals results in an equal influence for both positive and negative residuals. Therefore, the resulting coefficients provide a regression equation that goes through the middle of the data plotted on a graph.

However, outlier points with large residuals will have a greater influence than points with small residuals. Because we square the residuals, a point that has a residual twice as large will contribute four times as much influence on an estimation of the coefficients $\hat{\beta}_0$ and $\hat{\beta}_1$. Thus in a small sample one very deviant observation would substantially change the regression slope, $\hat{\beta}_1$. Always prepare a scatter plot with the regression. Among other benefits the scatter plot would indicate when the slope is influenced by a few extreme outliers.

Does It Make Sense?

The regression line could be closely approximated by drawing a line on a scatter plot. Using such a line and techniques from introductory algebra, estimates of the coefficients $\hat{\beta}_0$ and $\hat{\beta}_1$ could be computed. However, regression analysis provides a more precise method for computing the coefficients because it uses all the data points, not just the trend indicated by the pattern of the points.

The regression is computed using descriptive statistics. Key Idea 3.8 shows that the slope coefficient, $\hat{\beta}_1$, is obtained by multiplying the correlation, r_{xy}, by the ratio of the standard deviation of Y, S_Y, to the standard deviation of X, S_X. The correlation coefficient r_{xy} and the slope coefficient $\hat{\beta}_1$ both describe the relationship between X and Y. The slope coefficient is the rate of change in Y as a function of X. Economic and business applications make considerable use of *rates of change*, including the rate of change of the quantity of plywood as a function of price in our example.

Key Idea 3.8: Least-Squares Procedure

The **least-squares regression procedure** uses the data points (x_i, y_i) to compute coefficients $\hat{\beta}_0$ and $\hat{\beta}_1$ by minimizing the sum of squared deviations $\hat{e}_i$ (the residual) from the line. The least-squares rule is:

Choose $\hat{\beta}_0$ and $\hat{\beta}_1$ to minimize

$$Q = \sum_{i=1}^{n} \hat{e}_i^2$$

$$= \sum_{i=1}^{n} (y_i - \hat{Y}_i)^2$$

$$= \sum_{i=1}^{n} [y_i - (\hat{\beta}_0 + \hat{\beta}_1 x_i)]^2$$

where Q is the sum of the squared residuals about the line, $\hat{e}_i$ is the deviation of points from the equation

$$\hat{Y}_i = \hat{\beta}_0 + \hat{\beta}_1 x_i$$

$\hat{\beta}_0$ is the linear equation constant, and $\hat{\beta}_i$ is the linear equation slope coefficient.

Equations for computing estimates of $\hat{\beta}_0$ and $\hat{\beta}_1$ can be obtained by using calculus as shown in Chapter 14. The results are

$$\hat{\beta}_1 = r_{xy} \frac{S_Y}{S_X}$$

$$\hat{\beta}_0 = \bar{Y} - \hat{\beta}_1 \bar{X}$$

The regression equation always goes through the mean of X and the mean of Y.

Figure 3.8 shows that the residuals from the line for the plywood problem are small compared to the differences in sales at different prices. If the change in Y as X goes from its smallest to largest value is greater than the residuals from the line, we conclude that there is a relationship between X and Y.   □

Example 3.5   Regression of Quantity on Price

With an understanding of regression analysis, Sally and Agnes now need to compute the constant and slope coefficient for the plywood demand function. Discuss the resulting price/quantity results.

Solution   They know that

$$\hat{\beta}_1 = r_{xy} \times \frac{S_Y}{S_X}$$

$$= (-0.90) \times \frac{31.61}{1.58}$$

$$= -18.0$$

$$\hat{\beta}_0 = \bar{Y} - \hat{\beta}_1 \bar{X}$$

$$= 50.0 - (-18.0) \times 8.0$$

$$= 194.0$$

The means, standard deviations, and correlation coefficient were computed in Section 3.3. With these results the demand equation is

$$\hat{Y} = 194.0 - 18.0X$$

where $\hat{Y}$ is the predicted plywood quantity in thousands of sheets and X is the price per sheet in dollars. Regression equation variables should be defined immediately following the equation. It is also helpful to show the regression equation and the data points on a graph such as Figure 3.8.

The regression-derived demand function can be used to compute the central tendency of demand for various prices. For example, at a price of $8.00, the central tendency of demand is 50,000 [(194 − 18 × 8) × 1000] sheets of plywood. The slope $\hat{\beta}_1 = -18.0$ indicates that each $1 increase in price will lower the quantity of plywood demanded by 18,000 sheets. If the price is decreased by $1, the quantity demanded will increase by 18,000 sheets. Experienced statisticians use regression equations only over the range defined by the original values of the X variables. Thus Sally should caution Agnes that her demand equation applies only when the price per sheet is between $6 and $10. There are no data outside this range that might indicate a continuing linear relationship.   □

Exhibit 3.2 presents a typical computer output for a simple regression analysis, which computes a demand function. Demand ("saleb2") is the dependent, or Y, variable, and price ("apriceb2") is the independent, or X, variable. This computer output was prepared using the Minitab program. However, other statistical computer programs provide similar output. The data for this example were plotted in Figure 3.1. The computer output shows the constant ($\hat{\beta}_0 = 685.7$) and the slope coefficient ($\hat{\beta}_1 = -603.5$) displayed in equation form. These estimated regression statistics are also displayed in the coefficient ("Coef") column. The remaining parts of the output provide a number of statistics that are used to determine the quality of the relationship between the variables when sample data are used. These other parts of the computer output will be ignored for the present discussion because we are only concerned with describing the relationship. The entire computer output will be explained in Chapter 14.

EXHIBIT 3.2   Regression Analysis: Quantity Sold ("saleb2") on Price ("apriceb2")

```
MTB > regr 'saleb2' on 1 independent variable 'apriceb2'

The regression equation is
saleb2 = 686 - 604 apriceb2
```

Predictor	Coef	Stdev	t-ratio	p
Constant	685.7	124.3	5.52	0.000
apriceb2	-603.5	144.2	-4.19	0.000

```
s = 134.6       R-sq = 26.0%     R-sq(adj) = 24.5%
```

Analysis of Variance

SOURCE	DF	SS	MS	F	p
Regression	1	317750	317750	17.53	0.000
Error	50	906442	18129		
Total	51	1224192			

Unusual Observations

Obs.	apriceb2	saleb2	Fit	Stdev.Fit	Residual	St.Resid
24	0.430	223.0	426.2	63.7	-203.2	-1.71 X
38	0.690	673.0	269.3	30.0	403.7	3.08R
49	0.790	961.0	208.9	20.7	752.1	5.65R

R denotes an obs. with a large st. resid.
X denotes an obs. whose X value gives it large influence.

3.4.2 Interpretation of Regression Relationship

The equations for computing the regression slope $\hat{\beta}_1$ and constant $\hat{\beta}_0$ can be applied to any set of X and Y points. Therefore, it is possible to compute coefficients even if there is no linear relationship between X and Y. Additional statistical results are helpful in understanding the linearity of the relationship.

In practice most statistical analysts use a t ratio greater in absolute value than 2.0 as an indicator of a relationship (Key Idea 3.9). The t ratio for the demand example in Exhibit 3.2 is -4.19, which indicates a strong negative relationship. Look at the plot in Figure 3.1 to obtain a visual image of the relationship. In contrast, a regression analysis for the data plotted in Exhibit 3.1 (income regressed on age of head of household) has a t ratio of 0.16, which indicates that there is not a relationship.

Another useful regression output is labeled *unusual observations*. These are the observations with large residuals. A careful analyst will examine the original source of these observations to check for errors in the data or for unusual conditions in the system that generated the data. In the demand function example, observations 24, 38, and 49 were listed as unusual observations. Recall that these points appeared as

Key Idea 3.9: Least-Squares Approximate Rule

One statistic, the *t* **ratio** for the slope coefficient ($\hat{\beta}_1$), indicates the strength of the relationship between the two variables. A good rule of thumb is: If the absolute value of the *t* ratio is greater than 2, and the number of observations is 25 or more, there is strong evidence to support the conclusion that a relationship exists between the two variables. This result is developed in Chapter 14.

outliers in the scatter plot (Figure 3.1). Observation 24 had a very low price of 43 cents, but the actual sales value of 223 was substantially lower than the predicted value of 426.2 from the linear regression equation. Observations 38 and 49 represent weeks where sales were substantially higher than would be predicted from a simple linear equation. The sales activity for these weeks should be investigated more carefully either to determine that these sales figures were not correct or to discover the unusual circumstances that might help future marketing activity.

Practice Problem 3.2: Regression Computations

Use the (x, y) pairs of data points from Practice Problem 3.1, $(1, 5)$, $(3, 7)$, $(4, 6)$, $(5, 8)$, and $(7, 9)$, to determine:

(a) $\hat{\beta}_0$ and $\hat{\beta}_1$ for the regression equation.
(b) The predicted value of $\hat{Y}$ when $X = 4$; $X = 1$; $X = 6$. □

Problem Exercises

3.6   Refer to the demand equation in Example 3.5 and Exhibit 3.2. You are interested in determining the effect of different pricing strategies. Answer the following questions that are required to evaluate price change effects.
    (a) What is the change in sales for each 1-cent reduction in price? (Remember that the price units are dollars.)
    (b) What is the predicted quantity sold if the price is 80 cents?
    (c) What is the predicted total revenue at a price of 80 cents? (Remember that total revenue is price times quantity.)
    (d) What is the predicted total revenue at a price of 60 cents?
    (e) What is the price that will result in the maximum predicted total revenue? (*This can be determined using calculus or by preparing a graph of total revenue versus price.[1])

[1] Many of the concepts developed in this and later chapters will include sections that use calculus in the development. These sections are indicated by a star. You can learn the statistical procedures without these sections. However, your understanding will be increased if you can use these calculus-based sections.

3.7   Refer to the demand equation in Example 3.5. You are asked to study the effect of price on quantity sold. Determine:
(a) The predicted quantity sold when the price is $6.
(b) The predicted quantity sold when the price is $9.50.
(c) The total revenue when the price is $7.50.
(d) The total revenue when the price is $9.50.

3.8   Rising Hills Manufacturing wishes to study the relationship between the number of workers, X, and the number of tables, Y, produced in its Redwood Falls plant. They have obtained a random sample of 10 days of production. The following (X, Y) combinations of points were obtained:

(12, 200)	(30, 600)	(15, 270)	(24, 500)	(14, 210)
(18, 300)	(28, 610)	(26, 540)	(19, 320)	(27, 570)

(a) Prepare a scatter plot of the points.
(b) Compute the regression constant, $\hat{\beta}_0$, and slope coefficient, $\hat{\beta}_1$.
(c) What is the predicted number of tables when there are 20 workers?
(d) Discuss briefly the relationship between the number of workers and the number of tables produced per day.

3.9   River Hills Hospital is interested in determining the effectiveness of a new drug for reducing the time required for complete recovery from knee surgery. Complete recovery is measured by a series of strength tests that compare the treated knee with the untreated knee. The drug was given in varying amounts to 18 patients over a six-month period. For each patient the number of drug units, X, and the days for complete recovery, Y, are given in the following (x, y) data:

(5, 53)	(21, 65)	(14, 48)	(11, 66)	(9, 46)	(4, 56)
(7, 53)	(21, 57)	(17, 49)	(14, 66)	(9, 54)	(7, 56)
(9, 53)	(21, 52)	(13, 49)	(14, 56)	(9, 59)	(4, 56)

(a) Prepare a scatter plot of the points.
(b) Compute the regression constant, $\hat{\beta}_0$, and slope coefficient, $\hat{\beta}_1$.
(c) What is the predicted recovery time when drug use is 6 units and when drug use is 15 units?
(d) Discuss briefly the relationship between the number of drug units and the recovery time. What dosage would you recommend based on this initial analysis?

3.10   Acme Delivery offers three different shipping rates for packages under 5 pounds delivered from Maine to the west coast: regular, $3; fast, $5; and lightning, $10. To test the quality of these services, a major mail-order retailer shipped 15 packages at randomly selected times from Maine to Tacoma, Washington. The packages were shipped in groups of three by the three services at the same time to reduce variation resulting from the shipping day. The following data show the shipping cost, x, and the number of days, y, in (x, y) pairs:

(3, 7)	(5, 5)	(10, 2)	(3, 9)	(5, 6)	(10, 5)	(3, 6)	(5, 6)
(10, 1)	(3, 10)	(5, 7)	(10, 4)	(3, 5)	(5, 6)	(10, 4)	

(a) Prepare a scatter plot of the points.
(b) Compute the regression constant, $\hat{\beta}_0$, and slope coefficient, $\hat{\beta}_1$.

(c) Compute the predicted delivery time for each of the three delivery categories.

(d) Discuss the value of the higher-priced services in terms of quicker delivery.

3.11 The human resources department of a large firm conducted a study of its salary structure. As part of this study the years of experience and monthly wages were collected for a sample of 12 employees. These employees were in various administrative and management positions. The first number in the following pairs is the years of experience.

(5, 2500)   (9, 6200)   (14, 8000)   (12, 6400)   (2, 2200)   (8, 4000)

(6, 4500)   (10, 6600)   (15, 10,000)   (11, 6900)   (1, 2000)   (8, 4800)

(a) Prepare a scatter plot of the points.

(b) Compute the regression constant, $\hat{\beta}_0$, and slope coefficient, $\hat{\beta}_1$.

(c) What is the expected increase in monthly salary for each year of experience?

(d) What is the expected annual salary increase for each year of experience?

(e) What is the predicted monthly salary with 10 years of experience?

(f) Is it correct for the company to conclude that wages tend to increase directly with years of experience?

3.12 Consumer Foods, Inc. wishes to evaluate the effectiveness of its advertising expenditures. Advertising effectiveness is measured by the percentage of randomly selected households that have seen an advertisement and have purchased the product. Expenditures are measured by the cost per 10,000 viewers in a region. The following data were collected in 10 major urban markets, with the first number being the expenditures and the second being the effectiveness.

(50, 10.2)   (40, 8.1)   (64, 11.4)   (76, 14.7)   (66, 13.8)

(36, 6.1)   (55, 15.0)   (62, 12.1)   (48, 10.8)   (59, 14.8)

(a) Prepare a scatter plot of the points.

(b) Compute the regression constant, $\hat{\beta}_0$, and slope coefficient, $\hat{\beta}_1$.

(c) What is the predicted effectiveness when the expenditure is 50?

(d) What is the increase in advertising effectiveness for each unit of expenditure?

(e) Discuss the relationship between advertising cost and effectiveness for Consumer Foods, Inc.

3.5 TIME-SERIES GRAPHS

Much of the data used for economic and business analysis is generated over time. Variables such as sales, stock prices, material costs, labor costs, and interest rates are measured on a monthly or sometimes even a weekly interval. Other measures, such as gross domestic product, consumption, imports, exports, and investment, are usually measured quarterly. This time series contains additional information because of the sequence of the observations and therefore requires that we consider patterns of the observations over time.

Sequential arrangement of data was introduced in Chapter 1 and represents additional information that should be considered in an analysis. In Chapter 2 we ignored the sequential arrangement of the data over time as we developed descriptive statistics and frequency distributions. Those analyses were concerned only with the variable by itself. For every variable that is collected over time there is also a time variable associated with each observation. We learn next how time-series graphs provide additional information from a set of data (Key Idea 3.10).

Key Idea 3.10: Time-Series Graphs

Business and economic data are often generated over time, producing a **time series**. Examination of their patterns over time often provides improved understanding of the system or process that is being studied.

1. A time series is a data set whose observations are generated sequentially over time.
2. A time-series plot is a scatter plot of a time-series variable versus time.
3. Time-series plots are extremely useful for revealing important patterns in the data.

A time series is generated by a dynamic, or ever-changing, system. For this reason measures of central tendency and dispersion can be expected to be different for different time intervals. For example, the mean gross national product was much lower in the 1970s than in the 1990s. Studying the patterns of change over time increases our understanding of economic behavior.

Time-series plots are extremely important economic analysis tools. All time-series analyses begin with time-series plots. These plots provide insights concerning the behavior of the system that generated the data. For example, increasing or decreasing trends, cyclical variations, or seasonal patterns can be seen in the plot. More sophisticated techniques (developed in Chapter 17) often confirm results obtained from examining time-series plots but also provide procedures to forecast future behavior.

Example 3.6   Time-Series Comparison of Imports and Exports

Shirley Preston, a U.S. Department of Commerce economist, is preparing a study of U.S. trade policy. As part of this study she wants to examine the patterns of exports and imports over time. Exhibit 3.3 presents an example of a time-series plot, with both exports and imports plotted over time. Examine the time-series plot and discuss some important insights revealed in it.[2]

---

[2] Note that the time variable was generated using the "let" statement. The time variable has a value of 1 for the first quarter of 1977, 8 for the fourth quarter of 1978, and 40 for the fourth quarter of 1986. This simple transformation provides an easy way to include time as a variable.

EXHIBIT 3.3   Exports and Imports Versus Time

```
MTB > let c10 =('year' -77)*4 +'quarter'
MTB > name c10 'time'
MTB > mplot 'GEX82' vs 'time' and 'GIM82' vs 'time'
```

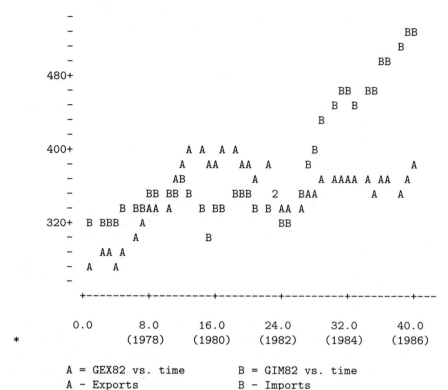

```
   *
        A = GEX82 vs. time        B = GIM82 vs. time
        A - Exports               B - Imports
   * The dates on this line are not part of the Minitab output and
   were inserted to simplify the grapical analysis.
```

Solution   Imports (plotted as B) and exports (plotted as A) were nearly equal until 1983. At that point imports began to increase rapidly while exports remained stable. In addition, we can see that exports (A's) follow a cyclical pattern, but the upward cycle appears to be flattened during the period 1983–1986. Examination of other economic information for this period provides possible explanations for the patterns in the data. For instance, the economy was coming out of a recession and consumer demand was stimulated by large federal government deficits. Concurrently, manufacturers increased imports of component parts as part of the move toward global manufacturing. At this time the U.S. dollar was strong relative to other major currencies. Imports, B, were relatively cheap, and U.S. exports, A, were relatively expensive. A large U.S. appetite for imported consumer goods was not matched by a comparable foreign demand for U.S. goods. The increase in imports is clearly shown in this plot. Would a comparison of imports and exports using sample means and other descriptive statistics or frequency distributions have revealed these relationships between exports and imports over time as clearly as revealed in this plot?   □

Problem Exercises

3.13   You have been asked to study the weekly sales pattern over the year for a consumer product. Use the data file "Chain" and prepare a time-series plot of the variable "Saleb3." In addition, prepare a time-series plot of the weekly prices, "Apriceb3." The data file "Chain" is described in Appendix B at the end of the book.
(a) Discuss the pattern of weekly sales data.
(b) Compare the pattern of weekly sales data with the weekly price data.

3.14   Use the data file "Cotton" to prepare a plot of quarterly cotton production data "Cotprod."
(a) Discuss the pattern of cotton production over time.
(b) What value would you forecast for the next observation in the series?

3.15   You have been asked to study the pattern of the prime interest rate. Use the data file "Macrel95" described in Appendix B at the end of the book. Prime interest rate is the variable "Fyprq." Prepare a time-series plot for the prime interest rate. Discuss the pattern of the series and make a forecast for the next observation in the series.

3.6   TWO-WAY TABLES

In this chapter we have presented a number of techniques for describing relationships between variables. All of those techniques assume that we have interval variables. However, there are also a number of situations in which there is a need to describe relationships between categorical and/or ordinal variables. Market research organizations describe attitudes toward products, measured on an ordinal scale, as a function of educational levels, social status measures, geographic areas, and other ordinal or categorical variables. Personnel departments study employee evaluation levels versus job classifications, educational levels, or other employee variables. Production analysts study relationships between departments or production lines and performance measures, such as reason for product change, reason for interruption of production, and quality of output. These situations are usually described and analyzed using two-way tables (Key Idea 3.11).

Key Idea 3.11: Two-Way Tables

A **two-way table** presents the number of observations that are defined by the joint occurrence of specific intervals for two variables. The combination of all possible intervals for the two variables defines the cells in a table.

Example 3.7   Product Demand by Residential Area

Agnes Larson has been working on a plan for new store locations as part of her regional expansion. In one city proposed for expansion there are three possible locations: north, east, or west. From past experience she knows that the three major profit centers in her stores are tools, lumber, and paint. In selecting a location the demand patterns in the different parts of the city were important. Thus she again requested help from Sally Goldberg and her market research department to obtain and analyze relevant data.

Solution   Table 3.3 is a two-way table for the variables "residential location" versus "product purchased." This table was prepared by the market research personnel using data obtained from a random sample of households in the three major residential areas of the city. Each residential area had a separate phone number prefix, and the last four digits were chosen using a computer random number generator. If the number was not a residence, another phone number was generated randomly. If the phone number was not answered, the number was called again up to a maximum of five times to ensure a high participation rate.

TABLE 3.3   Two-Way Table of Household Demand for Products by Residential Area

Area	Tools	Lumber	Paint	None	Total
East	100	50	50	50	250
North	50	95	45	60	250
West	65	70	75	40	250
	215	215	170	150	750

In each residential area 250 households were contacted by telephone and asked to indicate which of three categories of products they had purchased during their last trip to a building supply store. The survey was conducted to determine the demand for tools, lumber, and paint by people from the various neighborhoods. The three residential areas contain the same number of households, and thus the random sample of 750 represents the population of households in the entire city.

Every cell in the table shows the number of sampled households in each of the residential areas that had purchased tools, lumber, or paint in the past month. If they had purchased from more than one category, they indicated the category with the largest sales value. For example, 100 sampled households in the east area had purchased tools, and 75 sampled households in the west area had purchased paint. At the right side of each row we see the total number of sampled households (250) in that row. Similarly, the number of sample households that have purchased from each product category are displayed at the bottom of each column. The displays at the right-hand side of the rows and the bottom of the columns are referred to as *marginal distributions*. These numbers are the frequency distributions for each of the two variables presented in the two-way table.

The table provides a summary of the purchase patterns for households in the three neighborhoods. Ms. Agnes Larson now knows that people in the east area are more frequent purchasers of tools, whereas households in the north purchase more lumber. Demand for paint is highest in the west and they also tend to purchase more from each product category. They are also more likely to purchase something.

In addition to store location information, these data indicate which products should be emphasized in advertisements directed toward each geographic area. Ms. Larson decides to emphasize tools when distributing advertising material to the east and to emphasize lumber in the north. Advertising directed to the west will emphasize that all three product categories are in the same store. From the column marginal totals she also observes that tools and lumber will be purchased by about the same number of households in the city, while the demand for paint will be lower.   □

3.7 SOURCES OF DRINKING DRIVERS

As a final illustration of data analysis, we will look at data from a study of alcohol and driving, shown in Table 3.4. This table displays the relationship between blood alcohol concentration and the location of the first drinking episode for night drivers who had been drinking. The data for this table were obtained from a random sample of drivers in Washtenaw County, Michigan, collected during the hours 7 P.M. to 3 A.M. The columns indicate the blood alcohol concentration (BAC) of the driver, obtained from a breath test. Common interpretations of these concentrations are: $\leq 0.02\%$, essentially no blood alcohol and no driving impairment; 0.03–0.04%, social drinking with no impairment for most drivers; 0.05–0.09%, almost all drivers will have noticeable impairment and could be convicted by a court; $\geq 0.10\%$, all drivers are seriously impaired and represent a threat to other vehicles and pedestrians. The table also includes the percentage of drivers, in each intoxication category, for each row. This makes it possible to compare the various sources of drinking drivers easily, even though the number of drivers from each drinking source is different.

From Table 3.4 it was possible to obtain some important indications concerning drinking and driving behavior. The sample contained only drivers who had consumed at least one alcoholic beverage during the day. From the bottom row, which summarizes the entire set, over 70% did not have blood alcohol concentrations (BACs) that would seriously reduce their driving ability (e.g., $\leq 0.02\%$ and 0.03–0.04%). The most likely source of seriously impaired drivers was bars. For the 78 people who drank first in a bar, 17.9% had BACs at or above 0.10%. For the 82 drivers who began drinking at home, 12.2% were at the highest BAC level. However, in this group of home drinkers almost 75% were in the lowest two BAC categories and thus not seriously impaired. Those people who had their first drink in another home were least

TABLE 3.4   Two-Way Table of Driver BAC by Location of First Drinking
Episode

| Location | Driver BAC % | | | | Total |
	≤ 0.02	0.03–0.04	0.05–0.09	≥ 0.10	
Bar					
Number	22	25	17	14	78
Percent	28.2	32.1	21.8	17.9	100.0
Restaurant					
Number	11	3	9	1	24
Percent	45.9	12.5	37.5	4.1	100.0
Own home					
Number	45	16	11	10	82
Percent	54.9	19.5	13.4	12.2	100.0
Another home					
Number	42	10	6	0	58
Percent	72.5	17.2	10.3	0	100.0
Total					
Number	120	54	43	25	242
Percent	49.6	22.3	17.8	10.3	100.0

Source: W. L. Carlson, "Alcohol usage of the nighttime driver," *Journal of Safety Research*, Vol. 4, No. 1, March 1972.

likely to have high BAC levels. One important outcome of this analysis is that efforts to reduce the number of seriously impaired drivers should consider bars as a major source.

Does It Make Sense?

Many statistical studies begin with an examination of two-way tables, and these tables provide important understandings of the relationships between variables. We have presented some examples that show how two-way tables can be used to study relationships between qualitative variables. Two-way tables are also used with quantitative variables when the relationships between variables are expected to be nonlinear and complex. In those cases quantitative variables are assigned to subgroups using defined subranges.

Most of these tables are prepared by statistical computer programs. Chapter exercises will provide you with the opportunity to prepare two-way tables. Notice that two-way tables cannot be summarized by statistics such as the correlation coefficient or the regression line (Key Idea 3.12). In addition, they do not have the strong visual impact of a scatter plot. Many statistical computer packages provide graphical devices, such as three-dimensional histograms, which provide clear intuitive visual displays. Contact your local computer system for locally available procedures. In Chapter 12 more powerful statistical procedures for analyzing two-way tables will be presented. □

Key Idea 3.12: Two-Way Table Applications

Two-way tables can be used to describe relationships between qualitative variables that cannot be described using correlation and regression analysis.

Problem Exercises

3.16 Refer to Example 3.7. Suppose that the market survey data had resulted in Table 3.5 instead of Table 3.3. Explain the conclusions from this survey in terms of the product strategy.

TABLE 3.5 Revised Two-Way Table of Household Demand for Products by Residential Area

Area	Tools	Lumber	Paint	None	Total
East	100	40	60	50	250
North	70	45	95	40	250
West	75	70	65	40	250
	245	155	220	130	750

3.17 You have been asked to study the patterns of daily sales in dollars by day of week for a sporting goods store. Sales by day of the week are contained in the "Stordata.mtw" data file, which is described in the data file dictionary in Appendix B at the end of the book. Using either your statistical computation program or an electronic spreadsheet, group the data by day of week and four different groups of sales data. The daily sales data should be divided into groups by quartile. Prepare a two-way table that contains the days of the week as rows and the four sales quartile intervals as columns.
(a) Compute the row percentages.
(b) What are the major differences in sales level by day of week as indicated by the row percentages?
(c) Describe the expected sales volume patterns over the week based on this table.

SUMMARY OF KEY IDEAS

PRACTICE PROBLEM SOLUTIONS

3.1

(a) *Covariance.* Computation of means:

$$\bar{X} = \frac{1+3+4+5+7}{5}$$
$$= 4.0$$
$$\bar{Y} = \frac{5+7+6+8+9}{5}$$
$$= 7.0$$

Computation of covariance:

$$S_{XY} = \frac{(1-4)(5-7)+(3-4)(7-7)+(4-4)(6-7)+(5-4)(8-7)+(7-4)(9-7)}{4}$$
$$= \frac{6+0+0+1+6}{4}$$
$$= 3.25$$

(b) *Correlation.* Computation of sample variances:

$$S_X^2 = \frac{(1-4)^2+(3-4)^2+(4-4)^2+(5-4)^2+(7-4)^2}{4}$$
$$= \frac{9+1+0+1+9}{4}$$
$$= 5$$
$$S_Y^2 = \frac{(5-7)^2+(7-7)^2+(6-7)^2+(8-7)^2+(9-7)^2}{4}$$
$$= \frac{4+0+1+1+4}{4}$$
$$= 2.5$$

Computation of correlation:

$$r_{XY} = \frac{S_{XY}}{S_X S_Y}$$
$$= \frac{3.25}{\sqrt{5}\sqrt{2.5}}$$
$$= 0.92$$

(c) There is a strong direct relationship.

3.2

(a) Using the results from Practice Problem 3.1, the coefficient estimates are

$$\hat{\beta}_1 = r_{XY}\frac{S_Y}{S_X}$$
$$= 0.92\frac{\sqrt{2.5}}{\sqrt{5}}$$
$$= 0.65$$
$$\hat{\beta}_0 = \bar{Y} - \hat{\beta}_1\bar{X}$$
$$= 7 - (0.65)(4)$$
$$= 4.4$$

The equation is

$$\hat{Y} = \hat{\beta}_0 + \hat{\beta}_1 X$$

(b) Computation of predicted values: When $X = 4$,

$$\hat{Y} = 4.4 + (0.65)(4)$$
$$= 7$$

When $X = 1$,

$$\hat{Y} = 4.4 + (0.65)(1)$$
$$= 5.05$$

When $X = 6$,

$$\hat{Y} = 4.4 + (0.65)(6)$$
$$= 8.3$$

CHAPTER PROBLEMS

3.1 Ms. Agnes Larson wants you to study the demand for paint as a function of price. She has obtained (price, quantity) data for seven days of operation. These data are

(10, 100)   (8, 120)   (5, 200)   (4, 200)   (10, 90)   (7, 110)
(6, 150)

(a) Prepare a plot of quantity of paint versus price. Describe the relationship between quantity and price, with emphasis on any unusual observations.

(b) Compute the correlation coefficient for quantity versus price. Describe the relationship between quantity and price by interpreting the correlation coefficient.

3.2   George B. Smith, president of Forcasters, Inc., reported that the correlation between annual investment in the textile industry and the average temperature in Minnesota during January is -0.60. He then explains that investment in textiles is strongly influenced by the demand for clothing. He also visited Minnesota in January and discovered that people wear more clothing when the temperature is low. Explain the value of this forecast and either support or reject the reasoning.

3.3   A large consumer goods company has been studying the effect of advertising on total profits. As part of this study, data on advertising expenditures and total sales were collected for a six-month period and are as follows:

$$(10, 100) \qquad (15, 200) \qquad (7, 80) \qquad (12, 120) \qquad (14, 150)$$

The first number is advertising expenditures and the second is total sales.

(a) Plot the data and compute the correlation coefficient.

(b) Do these results provide evidence that advertising has a positive effect on sales?

(c) Present an alternative to the argument that advertising increases sales given the results from part (a).

3.4   In Problem 3.1, recall that Ms. Agnes Larson wants you to study the demand for paint as a function of price. She had obtained (price, quantity) data for seven days of operation. These data are

$$(10, 100) \qquad (8, 120) \qquad (5, 200) \qquad (4, 200) \qquad (10, 90) \qquad (7, 110)$$
$$(6, 150)$$

(a) Compute the constant and slope coefficient for the least-squares regression line of quantity on price.

(b) Compute the predicted values of quantity sold using the regression equation and the prices 5, 7, and 10. Compute the residual $\hat{e}$ for each of the three prices.

(c) Discuss the additional information about the demand for paint that you can obtain with results from parts (a) and (b), compared to the results obtained in Problem 3.1.

3.5   You are the economic adviser to a U.S. Senator. She has asked you to study the relationship between consumption and gross domestic product. As part of your study you have obtained the regression analysis in Exhibit 3.4 for the United States from 1977 through 1986.

(a) Compute predicted consumption from the regression equation for the time periods: 1977 quarter 1 (GDP = 2896.0, GC = 1864), 1984 quarter 1 (GDP = 3233, GC = 2015), and 1986 quarter 1 (GDP = 3721, GC = 2411). Compute the residuals for each of these time periods.

(b) What is the correlation between consumption and gross domestic product for this time period? (Exhibit 3.4 includes means and standard deviations.)

(c) Sketch the regression line on a graph.

(d) Explain the regression equation to the Senator and explain how she might use it to answer additional economic questions.

EXHIBIT 3.4   Regression Analysis Consumption ("GC82") on GDP ("GDP82")

```
MTB > regress 'GC82' on 1 independent variable 'GDP82'
```

The regression equation is
Gc82 = - 355 + 0.748 Gdp82

Predictor	Coef	Stdev	t-ratio	p
Constant	-355.13	80.64	-4.40	0.000
Gdp82	0.74798	0.02439	30.67	0.000

s = 35.38   R-sq = 96.1%   R-sq(adj) = 96.0%

Analysis of Variance

SOURCE	DF	SS	MS	F	p
Regression	1	1177583	1177583	940.66	0.000
Error	38	47571	1252		
Total	39	1225153			

Unusual Observations

Obs.	Gdp82	Gc82	Fit	Stdev.Fit	Residual	St.Resid
24	3159	2078.70	2007.95	6.54	70.75	2.03R

R denotes an obs. with a large st. resid.
```
MTB > describe c2 c3
```

	N	MEAN	MEDIAN	TRMEAN	STDEV	SEMEAN
Gdp82	40	3298.5	3213.2	3295.8	232.3	36.7
Gc82	40	2112.1	2031.3	2105.8	177.2	28.0

	MIN	MAX	Q1	Q3
Gdp82	2896.0	3733.6	3159.2	3515.0
Gc82	1863.7	2477.8	1994.7	2254.6

3.6   Sam Kowalski, president of Floor Coverings Unlimited, has asked you to study the
relationship between market price and the tons of rugs supplied by his competitor, Best
Floor, Inc. He supplies you with the following observations of price per ton and number
of tons, obtained from his secret files:

   (2, 5)   (4, 10)   (3, 8)   (6, 18)   (3, 6)   (5, 15)   (6, 20)   (2, 4)

(The first number for each observation is price and the second is quantity.)
(a) Prepare a graphical plot of quantity versus price, with price on the horizontal axis.
(b) Compute the covariance and correlation.
(c) Compute the constant and slope coefficients for the regression equation and draw
    the equation on the graph prepared in part (a).

(d) Write a short explanation of the regression equation that tells Sam how the equation can be used to describe his competition. Include an indication of the range over which the equation can be applied.

3.7   Examine the four graphical plots in Figure 3.9.

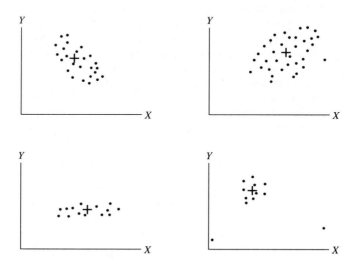

Figure 3.9   Graphical Plots for Problem 3.7

(a) Indicate an approximate value for the correlation coefficient.
(b) What sign would you expect for the regression slope coefficient if you were to compute it?
(c) Suppose that the data from the four graphical plots represented product demand in four different market regions. An analyst offers to compute regression equations that could be used as demand functions for the four different regions. Which regression equation would provide the best demand function? (*Note:* You first need to define best in terms of the problem and the data available.)

3.8   The following 32 data points were obtained from a random sample of households. The first number indicates the response to the question: Would you purchase a used car from Charlie Levine (no, 0; yes, 1)? The second number indicates the neighborhood (1, west; 2, south; and 3, north).

(0, 3)	(1, 4)	(0, 1)	(0, 2)	(1, 1)	(0, 2)	(1, 3)	(0, 4)
(1, 3)	(1, 4)	(1, 1)	(1, 2)	(0, 1)	(0, 3)	(1, 4)	(0, 4)
(0, 3)	(1, 4)	(0, 4)	(0, 3)	(1, 1)	(0, 1)	(1, 2)	(0, 4)
(0, 2)	(1, 2)	(0, 1)	(0, 3)	(1, 2)	(0, 1)	(1, 2)	(0, 2)

(a) Prepare a two-way table that shows the frequency of buyers and nonbuyers by neighborhood.

(b) Compute the percentage of buyers for each of the neighborhoods.
(c) Which neighborhood should Charlie select for opening his used car lot? State why you have made this recommendation.

3.9   Robert Johnson, Rice County solid waste director, wanted to establish a household garbage collection fee based on the weight of garbage collected at each household. Economic theory indicates that such a pricing strategy would encourage households to recycle and to reduce the total amount of waste generated. However, he wanted the rate to provide the same revenue for the garbage collectors as they experienced with the old flat rate per household. He was also interested in developing a payment plan for haulers that would be consistent with neighboring counties. He obtained the annual garbage collection data from neighboring communities, which is shown in Table 3.6. To help with his planning, he wanted to know the relationship between total revenue and total number of households. In addition, he wanted to know the relationship between total revenue and total tons collected.

TABLE 3.6   Annual Solid Waste Collection Data

City	Number of Households	Total Tons	Revenue
A	2,200	3,080	$118,800
B	2,500	3,500	200,000
C	2,700	3,780	250,560
D	4,000	5,600	201,600
E	4,000	5,600	308,800
F	4,000	5,600	268,000
G	5,500	7,700	452,100
H	6,000	8,400	277,200
I	9,000	12,600	358,200

(a) Enter the observations for revenue, households, and tons into a computer data file and plot the relationship between revenue and households and between revenue and tons collected. Visually estimate the best-fit line and draw it on the graph.
(b) Use the computer to compute the correlations between revenue and number of households and between revenue and total tons collected. In addition, compute the regression equations for each relationship.
(c) Mr. Johnson is interested in estimating the annual revenue for a city that had 2900 households and 12,600 tons of solid waste. Estimate the revenue using both of the regression equations from part (b).
(d) What is the marginal revenue for haulers per ton of solid waste?

3.10   A random sample of 12 college baseball players participated in a special weight-training program in an attempt to improve their batting average. The program lasted for 20 weeks immediately prior to the start of the baseball season. The average number of hours

per week and the change in their batting averages from the preceding season are as
follows:

(8.0, 10)   (20.0, 100)   (5.4, −10)   (12.4, 79)   (9.2, 50)   (15.0, 89)

(6.0, 34)   (8.0, 30)   (18.0, 68)   (25.0, 110)   (10.0, 34)   (5.0, 10)

(a) Plot the data. Does it appear that the weight-training program was successful?

(b) Estimate the regression equation. What is the marginal value of each hour of weight training?

3.11 You have been asked to estimate a demand function for the production of cotton fiber. The data file "Cotton," which is on your data disk and described in the data dictionary in Appendix B at the end of the book, contains data that can be used by your computer.

(a) Plot cotton production versus wholesale price. Sketch an approximate linear relationship.

(b) Use the computer program to compute the constant and slope for your regression equation. What is the marginal effect on quantity produced for each unit change in price?

3.12 You have also been asked to estimate the relationship between exported cotton fabric and the production of cotton fiber. The data file "Cotton," which is on your data disk and described in the data dictionary in Appendix B at the end of the book, contains data that can be used by your computer.

(a) Plot cotton production versus amount of exported cotton fabric. Sketch an approximate linear relationship.

(b) Use the computer program to compute the constant and slope for your regression equation. What is the marginal effect on quantity produced for each unit change in exported fabric?

3.13 The production manager of Amalgamated Cereals Ltd. wishes to study the relationship between the amount of grits or broken cereal and the total cereal produced during a production run. These data are in the file "Cereal," which is on your data disk. The four column variables are C1, percent yield; C2, percent grits; C3, pounds of grits; and C4, pounds of cereal. Use this data file with your local computer system to prepare a graph of total production (pounds) on the horizontal axis (abscissa) versus the amount of grits (pounds) on the vertical axis (ordinate). Label the graph so that it can easily be interpreted. Write a short description of the relationship between the total production and the amount of grits. Discuss the linear trend and the amount of variation about that trend.

3.14 Refer to the cereal production situation discussed in Problem 3.13.

(a) Use the computer program to compute the correlation between the amount of grits and total production.

(b) Compute the coefficients of the linear regression between total production and the amount of grits produced.

(c) What quantity of grits would be expected for each additional pound of cereal produced?

3.15 Refer to the cereal production discussed in Problem 3.13. The production manager also wished to determine the relationship between the percentage of grits produced and the percent yield of finished cereal product. The yield variable, which is included in the data file "Cereal.mtw," is computed by dividing the pounds of finished cereal divided by the total weight of wet ingredients used in the production run.

(a) Plot the relationship between yield on the vertical axis and percent grits on the horizontal axis.

(b) Compute the regression coefficients for the regression of yield on percent grits—the relationship plotted above.

(c) Draw the linear regression equation on the graphical plot.

(d) What change in yield do you expect for each percentage point increase in grits?

In Problems 3.16 and 3.17 we will use the data file "State87," which is described in Appendix B at the end of the book and stored on your data disk. The observations are individual states and the District of Columbia. The data variables were obtained from *Statistical Abstracts*.

3.16 Study the relationship between per capita personal income and the following variables: per capita health care expenditures, per capita retail sales, and per capita energy consumption.

(a) Plot the relationships with per capita personal income on the horizontal axis and each of the other variables on the vertical axis.

(b) Compute the regression coefficients for each of the expenditure variables regressed on per capita personal income. Sketch the linear regression lines on the graphical plots.

(c) Briefly discuss the relationships based on the analysis above.

3.17 Study the relationship between per capita personal income and the following variables: per capita expenditures on education, per capita expenditures on highways, and per capita expenditures on public welfare. When you examine the variables in the computer file you will discover that the government expenditures are expressed in totals for each state instead of per capita measures. Thus you will have to use your statistical computer package to compute the ratio of total expenditures divided by total state population for each expenditure category. Instructions for performing these calculations will be presented in the computer manual for your statistical program.

(a) Plot the relationships with per capita personal income on the horizontal axis and each of the other variables on the vertical axis.

(b) Compute the regression coefficients for each of the government expenditure variables regressed on per capita personal income. Sketch the linear regression lines on the graphical plots.

(c) Discuss briefly the relationships based on the analysis above.

3.18 Economists do not have uniform agreement concerning the effect of military spending on economic growth. This disagreement has been particularly important for analyses of economic growth in the Middle East. This region contains countries that have benefited from oil revenues and others that struggle greatly to improve conditions for their population but have limited resources. Alan Richards and John Waterbury discuss the issue of economic development in their book, *A Political Economy of the Middle East: State Class and Economic Development* (Boulder, CO: Westview Press, 1990). Included in their analysis are the data shown in Table 3.7. The second column contains the annual percentage growth in gross domestic product (GDP), and the third column contains the annual military expenditures as a percentage of GDP. The data represent the period 1973–1984 except for Iran (1980–1985) and Iraq (1960–1980).

TABLE 3.7   Middle Eastern Military Expenditures and Economic Growth

Country	GDP Growth Rate (%)	Defense Expenditure/ GDP (%)
Algeria	6.4	2.0
Egypt	8.5	11.0
Iran	0.5	8.0
Iraq	5.3	51.0
Israel	3.1	17.0
Jordan	9.6	11.4
Libya	3.0	3.0
Morocco	4.5	4.3
Saudi Arabia	6.0	19.0
Sudan	5.5	3.0
Syria	7.0	18.0
Tunisia	5.5	5.0
Turkey	4.1	4.4
YAR	8.1	18.0

(a) Enter the data into your computer package and plot GDP growth rate versus military expenditures.

(b) Compute the correlation between growth rate and military expenditures.

(c) Compute the coefficients for the simple regression of GDP growth as a function of percent military expenditures.

(d) Based on your statistical analysis, what conclusion can you reach concerning the effect of military expenditures on economic growth in the Middle East?

(e) For the same time period the United States had a GDP growth rate of 2.3% and military expenditures of 6.5%, while Japan had a GDP growth rate of 4.3% and military expenditures of 1.0%. If you considered only these two countries, what would you conclude about military expenditures and growth?

(f) If you added these two countries to the graph of part (a) and the remaining statistical analysis, would your conclusion in part (d) change?

3.19   The following article appeared in *Status Report*, a publication of the Insurance Institute for Highway Safety.

Death Rates Higher in U.S. Than Germany Only Since 1987

Despite longstanding claims about the safety of Germany's autobahns, the death rate on U.S. interstate highways was lower until 1987.

Then speed limits were raised to 65 mph on most rural interstates and beginning in 1987, the death rate on U.S. interstates started exceeding the rate on autobahns. This pattern continued through 1989. . . .

The article implies that U.S. highway death rates have risen above autobahn death rates as a result of increasing the speed limit in 1987. Using the data in Table 3.8, which were also in the article, plot U.S. interstate and German autobahn death rates versus time. Using your plot critically, evaluate the implication of the article.

TABLE 3.8   Deaths per 100 Million Miles: U.S. Interstate Versus German Autobahn

Year	U.S. Interstate	Autobahn
1975	1.24	2.75
1976	1.38	2.24
1977	1.55	2.13
1978	1.54	2.09
1979	1.51	1.75
1980	1.51	1.60
1981	1.48	1.57
1982	1.28	1.52
1983	1.20	1.59
1984	1.22	1.23
1985	1.12	1.14
1986	1.10	1.19
1987	1.11	1.01
1988	1.17	0.95
1989	1.08	0.97

3.20   The sales manager of a large merchandising firm is studying the sales performance of two of her salespersons. The daily sales for one week for salesperson 1 were 41, 42, 39, 38, and 40. The daily sales for the same week for salesperson 2 were 81, 82, 79, 78, and 80.

(a) Compute the mean and the variance for the sales by salesperson 1.
(b) Compute the mean and the variance for the sales by salesperson 2.
(c) What is the sample correlation between the sales for the two salespersons? (*Note:* It is not necessary to compute the covariance.)

3.21   A patient is under intense medical treatment for a major bacterial infection. Treatment includes intravenous drugs, rest, and close monitoring. Two important measures of the patient's condition are body temperature and diastolic blood pressure. These two measures are included in Table 3.9 at specified hourly intervals beginning with the time of admission.

TABLE 3.9   Medical Data for Problems 3.21 and
3.22

Hour	Temperature (°F)	Diastolic Blood Pressure	Pulse
4	104.7	60	92
8	98.6	64	82
12	99.2	64	82
16	101.2	64	80
20	101.7	70	80
24	98.4	68	72
32	101.4	70	88
36	98.3	70	88
40	101.9	60	80
48	98.7	70	72
56	97.7	70	70
64	98.6	70	70
72	99.7	80	72
76	101.3	80	72
80	97.8	72	80

(a) Prepare time-series plots of body temperature and diastolic blood pressure. It will be easier to complete this task if the data are entered into your local computer statistical package.

(b) Describe the pattern of the two series and discuss possible implications regarding the patient's health.

(c) What basis would you have as a physician for releasing the patient from intensive care in the hospital?

3.22 A patient is under intense medical treatment for a major bacterial infection. Treatment includes intravenous drugs, rest, and close monitoring. Two important measures of the patient's condition are body temperature and diastolic blood pressure. These two measures are included in Table 3.9 at specified hourly intervals beginning with the time of admission.

(a) Prepare a plot of body temperature versus diastolic blood pressure.

(b) Regress body temperature on diastolic blood pressure. Is diastolic blood pressure a good predictor of body temperature?

(c) Plot body temperature and pulse rate, then regress body temperature on pulse rate.

(d) Is pulse rate a good predictor of body temperature?

4

Introduction to Probability

The closer the probability is to the number 1,
the more likely the event will occur. . . .

4.1 USES FOR PROBABILITY

In the first three chapters we have studied methods for describing systems and processes by using data. In this chapter we begin our study of probability models, which are used to represent outcomes of a process that we wish to analyze. If we have a useful probability model for a process, the relative frequency of various outcomes can be computed. In that way process behavior can be predicted and decisions can be made to ensure desired process outcomes. The study of probability will assist in the making of wise decisions in the face of uncertainty.

Concepts of probability have a long history, but most applications to business and economic problems have been relatively recent. Probability was developed initially by mathematicians in the seventeenth and eighteenth centuries as they explored games of chance. Only in the last 50 to 60 years have applications of probability increased in the area of business and economic decision making. Today, businesses recognize that an understanding of probability theory and its applications can help in the development of models for studying decisions involving risk and for analyzing data. In this chapter we introduce the basic axioms and methods of determining probability. We develop probability models that focus on the key issues in decision situations. For instance, in this chapter we learn how economic planners use probability to develop a five-year plan to increase average life expectancy in a country; and how a company may use probability in determining if one of its products needs to be modified. A market researcher will use concepts introduced in this chapter to determine if a customer's age influences the purchase of a new product. After this introduction to probability, Chapters 5 to 7 will expand your understanding and introduce additional probability applications.

4.2 BASIC PROBABILITY CONCEPTS

We begin our study of probability with the basic definitions and fundamental probability axioms listed in Key Idea 4.1. An experiment might be selecting two parts from a production process and testing to determine if each part meets quality standards. The outcomes are either good, G, or defective, D. The sample space, S, is

$$S = \{GG, GD, DG, DD\}$$

where the first letter represents the outcome of the first part selected, and the second letter represents the outcome of the second part selected. Consider the following events:

Event A: Both parts selected are good.
Event B: At least one part selected is good.

Event A consists of only one outcome, GG, and is, therefore, a simple event. However, event B is a compound event consisting of the three simple events GG, GD, or DG.

Key Idea 4.1: Experiment, Event, and Sample Space

1. An **experiment** is a process that results in more than one outcome.
2. An **event** is one or more outcomes of an experiment. A simple event corresponds to a single outcome. A compound event is composed of two or more simple events. We use capital letters such as A, B, C to denote events.
3. A **sample space** is the collection of all possible simple events from an experiment. The letter S represents a sample space.

4.2.1 Probability Axioms

The chance, or likelihood, that an event will occur is known as the probability of that event. All probabilities must satisfy the two basic axioms listed in Key Idea 4.2. We are all familiar with weather reports such as "the probability of rain is 70%," or "the probability of rain is 20%." The closer the probability is to the number 1, the more likely the event will occur; similarly, the closer the value is to 0, the less likely that the event will take place.

4.2.2 Definitions of Probability

In Section 4.2.1 we discussed probability from a general understanding and stated two fundamental probability axioms. In this section we present three different formal

---

Key Idea 4.2: Probability Axioms

1. **Probability** is a mathematical function that assigns a number between 0 and 1 inclusively to each event in a sample space. For any event A,

$$0 \leq P(A) \leq 1$$

2. The **sum of probabilities** for all simple events, A_i, in a sample space is equal to 1:

$$\sum_{i=1}^{n} P(A_i) = 1$$

---

definitions of probability: classical probability, relative frequency probability, and subjective probability. The process of counting events and using the classical definition (Key Idea 4.3) is illustrated in the following example.

Key Idea 4.3: Classical Probability

Probability is defined as the theoretical proportion of times an event will occur, assuming that all events in the sample space are equally likely to take place. Probabilities are established by counting the number of events with the desired condition and dividing by the total number of events. The probability of an event A is

$$P(A) = \frac{N_A}{S_n}$$

where N_A is the number of outcomes that satisfy the condition of event A and S_n is the total number of outcomes in the sample space.

Example 4.1   Selection of Cars

You own a used car lot that contains three Saabs and two Toyotas. Two customers come to your lot and each selects a car. You want to know the probability of event A: The customers will select one Saab and one Toyota. The customers do not know each other, and therefore there is no communication between them. You assume that each car is equally likely to be selected (perhaps an unreasonable assumption).

Solution   The classical probability concept can be used to compute the probability. Define the sample space and count the number of outcomes that include exactly one Saab and one Toyota. The sample space contains the following pairs of cars:

$$S = \{S_1T_1, \ S_1T_2, \ S_2T_1, \ S_2T_2, \ S_3T_1, \ S_3T_2, \ S_1S_2, \ S_1S_3, \ S_2S_3, \ T_1T_2\}$$

Examination of the set S indicates that $S_n = 10$ outcomes in the sample space and that the event A contains $N_A = 6$ outcomes or simple events which include exactly one Saab and one Toyota. Thus the probability is $\frac{6}{10} = 0.6$. $\qquad\qquad$ □

There are several drawbacks to the classical definition of probability. First, the assumption of equally likely outcomes in the sample space may be reasonable for gambling problems, but it is not necessarily true in business situations. A second drawback is that we must count the number of outcomes in the sample space as well as the event itself. In the example above, the sample space only contained 10 outcomes—counting was easy. However, counting can be very tedious and time consuming. Recall the definition of the number of combinations developed in previous mathematics courses (Key Idea 4.4). Suppose that we had 10,000 parts on an assembly line and that each part is equally likely to be selected. Recall that $n! = n(n-1)!$ Let's determine the number in the sample space if two parts are randomly selected:

$$C_2^{10,000} = \frac{10,000 \times 9999}{2} = 49,995,000$$

Similarly, if we selected four parts randomly, the number in the sample space would be

$$C_4^{10,000} = \frac{10,000 \times 9999 \times 9998 \times 9997}{4 \times 3 \times 2} = 416.54 \text{ trillion}$$

You can see that the classical definition is not very practical.

Key Idea 4.4: Number of Combinations

The counting process can be generalized by using the following formula for the **number of combinations** of n items taken k at a time:

$$C_k^n = \frac{n!}{k! \ (n-k)!} \qquad \text{where} \quad 0! = 1$$

See Key Idea 4.5 for the relative frequency definition of probability. Using the relative frequency argument, assigned probabilities indicate how often an event will occur compared to other events. For example, if an event A has a probability of 0.40, we know that it will occur 40% of the time. This is more often than an event B that has only a 0.30 probability of occurrence. But we do not know which event, A or B, will occur next. Probabilities provide useful information for decision making. But if we have to make one decision and that decision depends on which event, A or B, will occur, knowing the probability does not guarantee a correct decision. The following example illustrates the relative frequency approach to defining probability.

Key Idea 4.5: Relative Frequency Probability

Probability is defined as the proportion of times that an event occurs in a large number of trials. Given event A,

$$P(A) = \frac{N_A}{N_P}$$

where N_A is the number in the population with condition A and N_P is the total number of trials in the population.

Example 4.2   Income Probability

Earl Jones is considering an opportunity to establish a foreign car dealership in Black River County, which has a population of 150,000 people. Experience from many other dealerships indicates that in similar areas a dealership will be successful if at least 40% of the households have annual incomes over $30,000. He has asked Paula Smith, a marketing consultant, to estimate the proportion or probability that family incomes are above $30,000.

Solution   After considering the problem, Paula decides that the probability should be based on the relative frequency concept. She first examines the most recent census data and finds that there were 50,486 households in Black River County, of which 29,248 had incomes above $30,000. She computed the probability for event A, family income greater than $30,000, as

$$P(A) = \frac{N_A}{N_P} = \frac{29,248}{50,486} = 0.58$$

Since Paula knows that there are various errors in census data, she consulted similar data published by *Sales Management* magazine. From this source she found 48,250 households with 28,543 having incomes above $30,000. Paula computed the probability of event A from this source as

$$P(A) = \frac{28,543}{48,250} = 0.59$$

Since these numbers were close, she could report either. Paula chose to report the probability as 0.58.   ☐

This example points out that probabilities based on the relative frequency approach often can be obtained using existing data sources. It also indicates that different results can and do occur, and that experienced analysts and managers will seek to verify their results by using more than one source. Experience and good judgment are needed to decide if confirming data are close enough.

4.2.3 Future States of Nature

Business and economic decisions require a comparison of alternative strategies and the selection of the "best" strategy. The choice of the best strategy usually depends on the state of nature or environment that will occur in the future. The amount of knowledge that we have about the future state (event) is classified into situations of certainty, risk, and uncertainty (Key Idea 4.6). The following example illustrates a situation of risk and the selection of the best strategy.

Key Idea 4.6: Certainty, Risk, and Uncertainty

1. **Certainty** is defined as a situation in which we know exactly which future state of nature will occur. Actually, situations of certainty do not exist. The assumption of certainty is sometimes a good approximation.

2. **Risk** is defined as a situation in which the probability or relative frequency of various states of nature or events can be estimated from data, experience, judgment, or analysis. These situations are the primary focus of this book and of classical statistical methods. Probabilities are obtained using an assumed model of the process under study.

3. **Uncertainty** is defined as a situation in which we do not know the relative likelihood of the possible future states of nature or events.

Example 4.3   Increasing Average Life Expectancy

Economic planners in a country are required to develop a five-year plan to increase average life expectancy. Politicians have suggested several strategies for accomplishing this. How should the proposed planners proceed in evaluating the strategies?

Solution   The planners have several alternative plans to consider, including the construction of a new hospital, developing a nutrition program, or building a sewage treatment plant. They know that the best strategy to achieve the goal of increasing life expectancy will depend on the major causes of death in the country. They have as a data resource complete records of people who have died. Deaths that doctors have determined could be prevented are assumed to result from one of the following causes, or in the language of probability,

> *Event A:* Deaths result from a failure to provide skilled medical care for normal diseases.
>
> *Event B:* Infant deaths occur because the mother cannot provide enough nutrients prior to birth.
>
> *Event C:* Deaths result from lack of proper diet.
>
> *Event D:* Deaths result from fatal diseases that are transferred through organisms that grow rapidly in human waste.

For each of these events, the planners decided that the best strategies would be

Event	Best Strategy
A	Build a hospital
B	Develop a prenatal nutrition program
C	Develop a nutrition program for infants and adults
D	Build a sewage treatment plant

The planners next gathered data and developed a Pareto diagram of the causes of death. Suppose that the hospital and sewage treatment plant have the same total cost. The planners used historical data to estimate the chance or relative frequency of the future states of nature. They found that 40% of the deaths resulted from human waste (event *D*) and that 25% of the deaths resulted from a lack of skilled medical care (event *A*). The best strategy would then be to build a sewage treatment plant. ☐

Sometimes the chance or relative frequency of various states of nature are unknown (uncertainty). To illustrate, consider the following example.

Example 4.4   Product Modification

A company must decide whether it should modify its product. The choice depends on the potential reaction of customers. How should the company proceed to quantify the potential reaction of customers?

Solution   The population consists of all customers. Each possible customer reaction is a *state of nature* or *event*. For example, the following states of nature could be considered:

> *Event A:* Customers like the present product very much and will continue their purchases.
>
> *Event B:* Customers find competitor's products better and are gradually switching their loyalties to another product. Potential new customers always purchase the competitor's product.

Event C: Customers like the present product, but additional customers can only be attracted by a modified product design.

For each of these states of nature, the best strategies would be

Event	Best Strategy
A	No product change
B	A new product should replace the old
C	Market both new and old products

At the moment, the company does not know the relative likelihood of the possible future state of nature. A market researcher might suggest a survey of all customers, and from the data gathered develop probabilities of the given events.   □

The third approach to defining probability is the subjective definition (Key Idea 4.7). Subjective probabilities are based on the judgment of the decision maker or analyst. A manager believes that there is a 40% chance that next month's sales will exceed $100,000. Thus the manager's subjective probability of sales over $100,000 is 0.40. A state director of public health believes that the probability of an influenza epidemic is 0.70. She cannot be certain, but her belief is strong, and she encourages vaccine production. An enthusiastic Hoosier believes that her alma mater, Indiana University, has a 90% chance of winning the Final Four. All of these are personal, subjective opinions. Some of the methods used to obtain and to apply subjective probabilities are controversial.

Key Idea 4.7: Subjective Probability

Subjective or **personal probabilities** are based on the judgment and experience of a decision maker. They represent the strength of belief in a future outcome and the willingness to bet or commit resources consistent with that outcome. Rational people can have different subjective probabilities for a specific outcome.

Practice Problem 4.1: CD Players

A shipment of 30 compact disc (CD) players is received at a store. Ten of the players have a special sound modulating system that provides improved sound for choral music. The others do not, and there are no exterior markings that provide identification of the two types. Five units are randomly selected for display in the store. Determine the probability that:

(a) Two units have the new system.

(b) Four units have the new system.   □

The solutions for all Practice Problems are given at the end of the chapter.

Problem Exercises

4.1   A store receives 5 red shirts and 10 green shirts. A random sample of 5 shirts is selected. Determine the probability that:

   (a) It contains 3 red shirts.

   (b) It contains 1 red shirt.

   (c) What percentage of the samples contain 3 green shirts?

4.2   Riverwood, Inc. is the manufacturer of high-quality hardwood furniture. During a particular day they shipped 40 chairs: 15 oak, 15 cherry, and 10 maple. Your store received a shipment of 6 randomly selected chairs from that day. Determine the probability of receiving:

   (a) 2 oak chairs.

   (b) 1 oak chair.

   (c) 2 or more chairs that are not oak.

4.3   Continuing the Riverwood, Inc. example from Problem 4.2, and using a random sample of size 5, determine the probability of receiving:

   (a) 2 oak and 3 cherry chairs.

   (b) 1 oak, 2 cherry, and 2 maple chairs.

   (c) 2 maple, 1 cherry, and 2 oak chairs.

   (d) 5 cherry chairs.

4.4   A jury of size 6 is obtained from a pool of 25 citizens. The ethnic background of the pool is 7 Asians, 7 Latinos, 7 blacks, and 4 whites. Determine the probability that:

   (a) The jury contains 3 whites.

   (b) The jury contains 2 Asians, 2 Latinos, and 2 blacks.

   (c) The jury contains 2 whites, 2 blacks, and 2 Asians.

4.5   (a) A midwestern state contains 2,150,123 women and 1,999,550 men, based on the most recent census. Compute the probability that a randomly selected person from the state is a woman.

   (b) A major random sample from the state is obtained and it contains 330,456 women and 325,300 men. What is the probability that a randomly selected person from this sample is a woman?

4.6   A small manufacturer has recently purchased 20 new drill presses: 12 from Amalgamated Tools and 8 from Cellar Works, a new firm based in a low-income neighborhood in a large city. Conventional wisdom across the industry is that Amalgamated produces the highest-quality machines. After the new machines have been in production for a month, they each process 10 units per shift. On a particular shift, 10 defective units are produced. Assume that defects are equally likely from each machine. Determine the probability that:

   (a) Seven of the defective units came from the Cellar Works machines.

(b) Seven of the defective units came from the Amalgamated machines.

(c) Five of the defective units came from Amalgamated and five from Cellar Works machines.

4.3 COMPUTING PROBABILITIES

In this section we study relationships between events and basic probability laws associated with these relationships. Business and economic problems frequently involve such relationships as mutually exclusive events, complementary events, the union of two events, the intersection of two events, or independent events. We use techniques such as contingency tables to organize probability information.

4.3.1 Relationships Between Events

Computation of probabilities in applied situations requires precise and often complex definitions of the sample space. It is helpful to use definitions from set theory to define and compute probabilities. See Key Idea 4.8 for the basic set-theory definitions. Then study the examples of their applications that follow.

Key Idea 4.8: Relationships Between Events

1. The **complement** of an event A is the set of events that are in the sample space S but are not included in event A. We designate the complement of event A by $\bar{A}$.

2. If A and B are two sets in a sample space S, the **union** of A and B, denoted by $A \cup B$, is the event containing either A or B or both.

3. The **intersection** of events A and B, denoted by $A \cap B$, is the compound event that contains both A and B. The probability of the intersection of events A and B, written as $P(A \cap B)$ or simply $P(AB)$, is referred to as the **joint probability** of events A and B.

4. Two events, A and B, are said to be **mutually exclusive** if both events cannot occur at the same time. Mutually exclusive implies that if event A occurs, event B cannot take place, or that there is no compound event that contains both A and B. Events A and B are mutually exclusive if and only if their joint probability is zero: $P(AB) = 0$.

Example 4.5   Rolling a Single Die

Suppose that a single fair die, six-sided, is rolled once. The sample space, S, is

$$S = E_1, E_2, E_3, E_4, E_5, E_6$$

where, for example, E_3 means that a "3" was rolled. Consider each of the following events:

A: A number < 5 occurred.
B: An odd number occurred.
C: A number > 5 occurred.

Define and use the relative frequency definition of probability to calculate the probabilities of each of the following events: $\bar{A}$, $A \cup B$, and $A \cap B$. Also find two mutually exclusive events.

   Solution   We first define each event in terms of the possible outcomes:

$$A = \{E_1, E_2, E_3, E_4\} \qquad B = \{E_1, E_3, E_5\} \qquad C = \{E_6\}$$

1. The *complement* of A is $\bar{A} = \{E_5, E_6\}$. These are all the outcomes in S that are not included in event A. $P(\bar{A}) = \frac{2}{6}$.
2. The *union* of A and B is $A \cup B = \{E_1, E_2, E_3, E_4, E_5\}$. The outcomes in the union occurred either in A or in B or in both events. $P(A \cup B) = \frac{5}{6}$.
3. The *intersection* of A and B is $A \cap B = \{E_1, E_3\}$. The intersection contains events that are in both A and B. $P(A \cap B) = \frac{2}{6}$.
4. Events A and C are mutually exclusive. If event A takes place, then we know that the number on the die was 1, 2, 3, or 4. Therefore, C, which states that the number was a "6," could not have occurred. Since there are no events common to both A and C, these events are mutually exclusive. $P(AC) = 0$.   □

4.3.2 Basic Probability Laws

The laws that are used to develop probabilities in applied business situations are listed as Key Idea 4.9. Let's return to Example 4.5, rolling a single fair die. We will use the complement law and the additive law to calculate $P(\bar{A})$ and $P(A \cup B)$. You will see that our results are the same as the probabilities we found in Example 4.5 by using the relative frequency definition. More complex business problems are often solved more quickly by use of these laws.

1. By the complement law,

$$P(\bar{A}) = 1 - P(A) = 1 - \frac{4}{6} = \frac{1}{3}$$

2. By the additive law,

$$P(A \cup B) = P(A) + P(B) - P(AB) = \frac{2}{3} + \frac{1}{2} - \frac{1}{3} = \frac{5}{6}$$

3. By the additive law for mutually exclusive events,

$$P(A \cup C) = P(A) + P(C) = \frac{2}{3} + \frac{1}{6} = \frac{5}{6}$$

Key Idea 4.9: Basic Probability Laws

1. **Complement law.** The probability of the complement of an event A is

$$P(\bar{A}) = 1 - P(A)$$

2. **Additive law.** The probability of the union of two events A and B is

$$P(A \cup B) = P(A) + P(B) - P(AB)$$

For mutually exclusive events A and B, the additive law becomes

$$P(A \cup B) = P(A) + P(B) - P(AB) = P(A) + P(B)$$

4.3.3 Conditional Probabilities

Conditional probability tells us the chance of an event under different conditions and based on a restricted sample space (Key Idea 4.10). Note that from this definition of a conditional probability, the joint probability of events A and B is

$$P(A \cap B) = P(A \mid B)P(B)$$

Key Idea 4.10: Conditional Probability

Conditional probability is defined as the probability of an event A if we assume that another event B has occurred. We write a conditional probability of A, given B, as $P(A \mid B)$ and compute the conditional probability by the formula

$$P(A \mid B) = \frac{P(A \cap B)}{P(B)} \qquad \text{if } P(B) \neq 0$$

Example 4.6   Pizza Dinners

Suppose that you are trying to decide if you should go to the local pizza restaurant for dinner or cook your own dinner. From past experience you know that if Hans Anderson is cooking, the pizza will be great. If he is not cooking, you would prefer your own cooking. Hans works 40% of the evenings. However, you also know that on Friday and Saturday evenings Hans works 60% of the time. Thus, by checking the day, you can obtain better information for your dining decision. In probability terms we have just stated:

A: Hans Anderson is cooking.
B: It is a Friday or Saturday evening.

$$P(A) = 0.40$$
$$P(A \mid B) = 0.60$$

You can see that the probability of Hans working indeed changes *under different conditions.*   □

In the following example, we illustrate the usefulness of a contingency table (sometimes called a *two-way table*) to analyze probability problems involving two variables. You will note that each cell contains the probability of intersections, while the margins indicate the probabilities of each variable by itself. You will see how contingency tables can be used by a marketing department to help define segments that should be emphasized when developing marketing strategies.

Example 4.7   Market Research

Jennie Thorne, manager of a market research firm in central Florida, has been asked to determine if a person's age influences the purchase of souvenirs during the World Cup games in Orlando. She has asked you to design an analysis to determine the probability of purchase for persons in different age groups. The age groups that are believed to have different purchasing habits are: 16–25; 26–45; and 46 or older. (Note that people younger than 16 were not asked questions about purchasing.) Describe the plan for analysis that you devised for Jennie.

Solution   Your analysis should be similar to the plan that follows.

1. First prepare specific definitions for the events in the sample space:
    A_1:   persons aged 16–25
    A_2:   persons aged 26–45
    A_3:   persons aged 46 or older
    B_1:   persons who will purchase the product
    B_2:   persons who will not purchase the product

2. Next, assume that you conducted a survey of 1000 soccer fans and found that:
    100 persons aged 16–25 indicated that they will purchase soccer souvenirs.
    250 persons aged 26–45 indicated that they will not purchase soccer souvenirs.
    100 persons aged 46 and older indicated that they will purchase the souvenirs.
    450 people were aged 26–45.
    200 people were aged 46–65.

3. From this information you should construct a contingency table (sometimes called a two-way table) of the data. Using the survey information above, basic laws of probability, and arithmetic, you arrive at Table 4.1.

TABLE 4.1   Market Research Contingency Table

	A_1 (16–25)	A_2 (26–45)	A_3 (46 or older)	Total
B_1 (buy)	0.10	0.20	0.10	0.4
B_2 (don't buy)	0.25	0.25	0.10	0.6
	0.35	0.45	0.20	1.0

4. You complete your analysis for the manager with some conclusions.
   (a) **50% of the buyers are in the age group 26–45.** Here we know that the person is a buyer. The sample space is restricted to only the 400 buyers, of which 200 were in the age group 26–45. Thus

   $$P(A_2 \mid B_1) = \frac{P(A_2 \cap B_1)}{P(B_1)} = \frac{0.20}{0.40} = 0.50$$

   (b) **25% of the buyers are age 46 or older** $(0.10/0.40 = 0.25)$. Again, this is a conditional probability with the sample space restricted to the 400 buyers.
   (c) **28.6% of the age group 16–25 would buy the product** $(0.10/0.35)$. This time we restricted the sample space to the 16–25 age group and found

   $$P(B_1 \mid A_1) = \frac{P(B_1 \cap A_1)}{P(A_1)} = \frac{0.10}{0.35} = 0.286$$

   (d) **The age group 46 or older contains the largest percentage of buyers. Each sales contact in this age group has a greater chance of resulting in a purchase.** We already found that 28.6% of the age group 16–25 would buy; by similar conditional probabilities, you can show that 44.4% of the age group 26–45 would buy and that 50% of the age group 46 or older would buy. ☐

4.3.4 Independence

Another relationship that could exist between two events is independence (Key Idea 4.11). Independence in a probability context indicates that the occurrence of one event does not change the probability of the occurrence of another event. If you are tossing coins, a head on the first toss does not change the probability of a head on the second toss.

Independence is a very important concept for business decisions. Suppose that the probability of a sale is independent of radio advertising. Then spending for radio advertising will not increase sales. If the amount charged by different suppliers is independent of the quality of material, one should purchase from the lowest-cost supplier.

Key Idea 4.11: Independent Events

Events A and B are said to be **independent** if and only if the conditional probability of event A given event B is equal to the marginal probability of A. That is,

$$P(A \mid B) = P(A)$$

or if the joint probability of events A and B is equal to the product of the two marginal probabilities:

$$P(A \cap B) = P(A)P(B)$$

Example 4.8   Independent Purchase Probabilities

Consider Example 4.7, but use the data in Table 4.2 instead of the data in Table 4.1.

TABLE 4.2   Revised Market Probabilities: Market Research

	A_1 (16–25)	A_2 (26–45)	A_3 (46 or older)	Total
B_1 (buy)	0.14	0.18	0.08	0.40
B_2 (don't buy)	0.21	0.27	0.12	0.60
	0.35	0.45	0.20	1.00

Solution   The conditional probabilities are

$$P(B_1 \mid A_1) = \frac{0.14}{0.35} = 0.40 = P(B_1)$$

$$P(B_1 \mid A_2) = \frac{0.18}{0.45} = 0.40 = P(B_1)$$

$$P(B_1 \mid A_3) = \frac{0.08}{0.20} = 0.40 = P(B_1)$$

Note that all of the conditional probabilities are equal to 0.40, which is the unconditional probability of B_1. The reader should also verify that the probabilities for all cells in the table are equal to the product of their respective row and column marginal probabilities.

These results imply that the probability of purchase is the same for all age groups. Hence age and purchase decision are independent. That is, information about age groups does not change the probability of purchase. Knowing that age and purchase decision are independent is an important result for selecting market plans. ☐

This property of independence has important implications for sampling and for a number of statistical inference procedures. For the present, recognize that independence implies that information about one event does not change the conditional probability of the other event. The specific definition of independence must be used to determine independence in a probability sense. The commonly used term *independence* has a very specific meaning in probability and statistics. We have discussed some useful intuitive interpretations. However, the final test for independence requires using the definition in Key Idea 4.11.

There is often confusion between the concepts of mutually exclusive and independence. If two events A and B with nonzero probabilities [i.e., $P(A) \neq 0$ and $P(B) \neq 0$] are mutually exclusive, then if A occurs, B cannot occur. Therefore, mutually exclusive implies that the conditional probability

$$P(A \mid B) = \frac{P(A \cap B)}{P(B)} = 0$$

Thus $P(A \mid B) = 0$, but $P(A) \neq 0$, hence A and B are not independent. Mutually exclusive rules out independence, and independence rules out mutually exclusive. In fact, as we see by the discussion above, mutually exclusive actually implies dependence.

4.3.5 Odds

Probability information is also communicated by using odds (Key Idea 4.12). If the odds of reducing the birthrate in a developing country are 7 to 3, or 7:3, the probability, $P(A)$, of reducing the birthrate is

$$\frac{7}{3} = \frac{P(A)}{P(\bar{A})} \quad \text{and} \quad P(A) = 0.70$$

Key Idea 4.12: Odds

The **odds** in favor of a particular event is given by the ratio of the probability of the event divided by the probability of its complement. The odds in favor of A are

$$\text{odds} = \frac{P(A)}{1 - P(A)} = \frac{P(A)}{P(\bar{A})}$$

Suppose that you know that the odds in favor of your favorite team winning a particular game is 3 to 1, or 3:1. This means that your team's chance of winning the game is three times the chance that your team would lose the game. Your team has a 75% chance of winning. Of course, the odds against the occurrence of an event is the reverse of the odds in favor. Your team's odds against winning is 1:3, or 25%.

Practice Problem 4.2: Joint Probability

A large nursery plants shoots equally in three different fields. The shoots are mixed before placing them in the fields. In the entire shipment of shoots, two-thirds are red and one-third are yellow. The probability of field 1 and yellow flowers is 0.067. The probability of field 3 and red flowers is 0.20. Determine the probability of:

(a) Red flowers and field 1.
(b) Red flowers and field 2.
(c) Yellow flowers and field 2.
(d) Yellow flowers and field 3?   □

Practice Problem 4.3: Complex Probability

Students at a midwestern college can participate in three performing arts: orchestra, choir, and theater. A recent survey found that 30% are in choir, 20% are in orchestra, and 10% are in theater. In addition, 15% are in two performing arts, and 5% participate in all three. What is the percentage of students who participate in at least one performing art?   □

Problem Exercises

4.7   Machine Tools, Inc. produces wheel rims for lawn mowers. Wheels are rejected as defects because of either cracking (A_1) or alignment (A_2). The probability of a part with neither defect is 0.80. The probability of a cracking defect is 0.12 and of an alignment defect is 0.15. What is the probability of a part with both defects?

4.8   Given $P(A_1 B_1) = 0.20$, $P(A_2 B_2) = 0.15$, $P(A_1 B_3) = 0.20$, $P(A_2) = 0.40$, and $P(B_1) = 0.30$. Assume that the events A_1 and A_2 are the simple events of experiment A, and that B_1, B_2, and B_3 are the simple events of experiment B. Determine the following probabilities.
(a) $P(A_1 B_2)$.
(b) $P(A_1)$.
(c) $P(A_2 B_3)$.
(d) $P(B_2)$.
(e) $P(A_2 B_1)$.

4.9   Given $P(A_1 B_1) = 0.10$, $P(A_2 B_2) = 0.25$, $P(A_1 B_3) = 0.30$, $P(A_2) = 0.40$, and $P(B_1) = 0.20$. Assume that events A_1 and A_2 are the simple events of experiment A, and that B_1, B_2, and B_3 are the simple events of experiment B. Determine the following probabilities.
(a) $P(A_1 B_2)$.
(b) $P(A_1)$.
(c) $P(A_2 B_3)$.
(d) $P(B_2)$.
(e) $P(A_2 B_1)$.

4.10   Given $P(A_1 B_2) = 0.10$, $P(A_2 B_1) = 0.25$, $P(A_1 B_3) = 0.30$, $P(A_2) = 0.40$, and $P(B_2) = 0.20$. Assume that events A_1 and A_2 are the simple events of experiment A, and that B_1, B_2, and B_3 are the simple events of experiment B. Determine the following probabilities.

(a) $P(A_2 B_2)$.

(b) $P(A_1)$.

(c) $P(A_2 B_2)$.

(d) $P(B_3)$.

4.11 A marketing study determined that 40% of customers want automatic door locks and 50% want power windows. In addition, 30% want both. What is the probability that a customer wants either automatic door locks or power windows, or both?

4.12 The audit of accounts receivable for a medium-sized supplier of computer software support reveals errors in either the number of hours billed or the rate per hour. The probability of either an error in the hours billed or the rate or both is 0.30. Both errors occur for 20% of the claims. Determine the probability of a billed rate error if the hours billed errors occur in:

(a) 20% of the claims.

(b) 40% of the claims.

(c) 15% of the claims.

4.13 A marketing study determined that 40% of customers wanted automatic door locks, 50% wanted power windows, and 60% wanted a sunroof. At least one of the options was desired by 80% of the customers, and 30% wanted all three. The sunroof and one of the other options was desired by 65% of the customers. What is the probability that a customer wants both automatic door locks and power windows?

4.14 Health Claims, a health insurance claims processor, conducts a continuing audit of the claims submitted. Procedure code errors occur in 15% of the claims, provider code errors in 5% of the claims, and patient code errors in 15% of the claims. In addition, 25% of the claims have exactly two of the three errors and 5% have all three errors. What is the probability that a randomly selected claim has at least one error?

4.3.6 Probability Trees

Probability trees (Key Idea 4.13) are a well-known and useful graphical technique for analyzing and solving problems that include conditional probabilities relating several factors. The procedure utilizes a graphical representation that begins with a "trunk" from which "branches" representing the different levels of a factor are drawn. At each branching the sum of probabilities must equal 1.0. It is easier to understand the procedure from examples than from a general explanation. We illustrate both a two-branch and a three-branch probability tree in the following test marketing problem.

Example 4.9   Test Marketing Analysis: Two-Branch Tree

National Brands, Inc. produces and markets a variety of prepared consumer food products. The business is very competitive and National Brands is continuously developing new product ideas and deciding which products should actually be marketed. James Robert, the director of market research for National Brands, conducts extensive focus groups and test markets prior to deciding on full-scale production. From their history of new product development, the company knows that 30% of new product ideas fail

Key Idea 4.13: Probability Trees

1. Probability trees are a useful procedure for solving problems that include several levels of conditional probabilities.
2. The probability tree begins with a series of branches that cover all possible outcomes for an event, and thus the probabilities of the branches must equal 1.0.
3. At the end of each initial branch, additional probability branches may be drawn and the sum of their probabilities must also equal 1.0.
4. The probability tree branches continue until all conditional probabilities have been exhausted on each branching path.
5. The probabilities on each branching path are then multiplied to obtain the probability of the combination of events defined by each path and that probability is written at the end of the final branch.
6. The sum of all probabilities at the end of the final branches must equal 1.0.

at the focus group phase, and that 70% are successful. Some of the products that fail the focus group are still run through a test market. Products that had a successful focus group have a successful test market 60% of the time. Those that fail the focus group have a successful test market 40% of the time. Mr. Robert needed answers to the following three questions:

(a) What is the chance that a new product idea is successful at both the focus group and the test market phases?

(b) What is the probability that a new product idea is successful at the test market phase?

(c) Suppose we know that a new product idea failed the test market phase? What is the probability that the product also failed the focus group?

Solution   Jonathan David, a member of the new product ideas development team at National Brands, recognized that the two branches are the focus group phase and the test market phase, and proceeded to define the events for each phase as follows:

S_1:   success in focus group

F_1:   failure in focus group

S_2:   success in test market

F_2:   failure in test market

After defining the events, Jonathan prepared the two-branch probability tree in Figure 4.1. Using the probability tree, Jonathan provided the following answers to the questions posed by Mr. Robert:

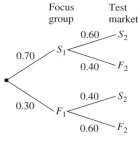

Figure 4.1 Market Analysis: Two-Branch Tree

(a) The probability that a new product idea is successful with both the focus group and the test market is found by following the branches from the starting point to S_1 and then to S_2 and noting that

$$P(S_1 \cap S_2) = (0.70)(0.60) = 0.42$$

(b) To determine the probability that a new product idea is successful at the test market stage means that one of two mutually exclusive events occurred: Either the product was successful with the focus group or it failed the focus group. Thus, using the additive law in Key Idea 2.9, there is a 54% chance that the product idea was successful at the test market phase:

$$P(S_2) = P(S_1 S_2) + P(F_1 S_2)$$
$$= 0.42 + (0.3)(0.4)$$
$$= 0.54$$

(c) Since we know that a particular new product idea has failed with the test market, we have a conditional probability problem. We are asked to find $P(F_1 \mid F_2)$. Jonathan used Key Idea 4.10 to find that

$$P(F_1 \mid F_2) = \frac{P(F_1 F_2)}{P(F_2)} = \frac{0.18}{0.46} = 0.39$$

where $P(F_2) = (0.7)(0.4) + (0.3)(0.6) = 0.46$.   ☐

Example 4.10   Test Marketing Analysis: Three-Branch Tree

Another member of the new product ideas development team at National Brands, Ann Renee Moore, obtained additional information. If a product has success in both the focus group and the test market, there is a 90% probability of success at the national market (this will become branch 3 in our tree). A product with a successful focus group and a failed test market has only a 30% chance of success at the national market. Products that failed the focus group but are successful with the test market have a probability of national market success equal to 0.60. Finally, products that fail with both the focus group and the test market are successful only 10% of the time in the national market. Determine the probability that a new product idea is successful at the national level.

Solution   To answer this question, Ann Renee constructed the three-branch probability tree in Figure 4.2, using success in the national market and failure in the national market. The asterisk indicates the events in which success at the national market could have occurred. Thus

$$P(S_3) = (0.7)(0.6)(0.9) + (0.7)(0.4)(0.3) + (0.3)(0.4)(0.6) + (0.3)(0.6)(0.1)$$
$$= 0.552$$

There is only a 55.2% chance of a product successful in the national market. This company needs to improve its product ideas development.   □

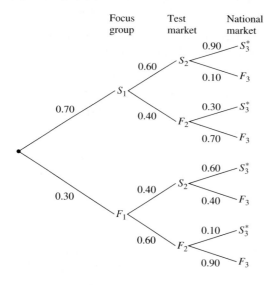

Figure 4.2   Market Analysis: Three-Branch Tree

Example 4.11   Television Game Show

The following problem is based on a television game program and shows that it is not necessary to have symmetric branch structures. In addition, it provides an example that illustrates that careful analysis sometimes results in solutions that are counter to initial intuition. As a game contestant you are asked to choose between one of three doors. Two of the doors hide a very small prize and one hides a very valuable prize. You choose one of the doors and then the host of the program opens one of the other doors and it does not hide the valuable prize. Now you are given the option of either holding with your initial choice or switching to another door. What should you do, and does your choice make a difference?

Solution   The problem involves two steps. First you make an initial choice based on probability information. After the first choice you are provided with additional information and asked to make another choice. The probabilities for the second choice are conditional on the first choice and the information provided by the program host.

The problem analysis can be guided by using the probability tree in Figure 4.3. Label the three doors A, B, and C. Initially, the probabilities of the major prize behind each of the doors is equal to 0.33 given the initial information. Suppose that you initially chose door B. The show host will now open one of the other two doors that does not contain the major prize. If the prize is behind door A and you chose door B, the host will open door C with probability 1, because the host knows the prize location and will open only a door that does not contain the prize. If the prize is behind door B, the host can open either door A or door C and will do so with probability 0.50 for each. Finally, if the prize is behind door C, the host will choose door A with probability 1. The probabilities for each of the branches is shown in Figure 4.3. The probabilities for the various choices are

$$P(\text{prize } A, \text{host } C) = 0.333$$
$$P(\text{prize } B, \text{host } A) = 0.167$$
$$P(\text{prize } B, \text{host } C) = 0.167$$
$$P(\text{prize } C, \text{host } A) = 0.333$$

If the host opens door C, you can either keep door B or switch to A.

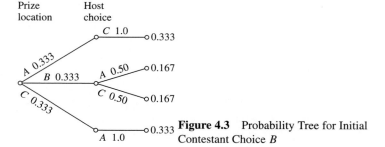

Figure 4.3   Probability Tree for Initial Contestant Choice B

The conditional probabilities of the prize locations given the host chooses C are

$$P(A \mid C_H) = \frac{P(A \cap C_H)}{P(C_H)}$$
$$= \frac{0.333}{0.333 + 0.167}$$
$$= 0.67$$
$$P(B \mid C_H) = \frac{0.167}{0.333 + 0.167}$$
$$= 0.33$$

Since door A has a higher probability, you should switch from door B to door A. If the host opens door A, you can either keep door B or switch to C.

The conditional probabilities of the prize locations given the host chooses A are

$$P(C \mid A_H) = \frac{P(C \cap A_H)}{P(A_H)}$$

$$= \frac{0.333}{0.333 + 0.167}$$

$$= 0.67$$

$$P(B \mid A_H) = \frac{0.167}{0.333 + 0.167}$$

$$= 0.33$$

Since door C has a higher probability, you should switch from door B to door C. Thus we see that in either case the chances of winning increase if you switch from your original choice of B to the unopened door.

You should revise the probability tree in Figure 4.3 and the probability to show that the same result—switch your initial choice of doors—has the highest probability of winning, no matter what your initial choice. □

Practice Problem 4.4: Test Marketing Analysis

National Brands, Inc. produces and markets a variety of prepared consumer food products. The business is very competitive and thus National Brands is constantly developing new product ideas and deciding which products should actually be marketed. Prior to deciding on full-scale production, the company conducts extensive focus groups and test marketing to determine the possibility of success in the national market. From their history of new product development the company knows that 60% of new products fail at the focus group phase and 40% are successful. Some of the products that fail the focus group are still run through a test market. Products that had a successful focus group have a successful test market 60% of the time. Those that fail the focus group have a successful test market 40% of the time. If a product has success in both the focus group and the test market, the probability of success in the national market is 0.90. A product with a successful focus group and a failed test market has a probability of success in the national market equal to 0.30. Products that fail the focus group but are successful in the test market have a probability of national market success equal to 0.60. Finally, products that fail both the focus group and the test market are successful only 10% of the time in the national market.

(a) Prepare a probability tree that defines the possible product outcomes. Label the outcomes S_i success and F_i failure at each stage, where $i = 1$ is the focus group, $i = 2$ is the test market, and $i = 3$ is the national market.

(b) What is the probability of national market success if the focus group test is successful?

(c) If a product is successful, what is the probability that its focus group was successful? □

Problem Exercises

4.15 Given $P(A_1B_1) = 0.20$, $P(A_1B_2) = 0.25$, and $P(A_2B_1) = 0.25$.
(a) What is the conditional probability $P(A_1 \mid B_1)$?
(b) What is the conditional probability $P(A_2 \mid B_1)$?
(c) What is $P(B_2 \mid A_2)$?
(d) Are the A_i and B_i elements independent?

4.16 Given $P(A_1B_1) = 0.20$, $P(A_1B_2) = 0.10$, $P(A_1B_3) = 0.15$, $P(A_2B_1) = 0.25$, and $P(B_3) = 0.35$.
(a) What is the conditional probability $P(A_1 \mid B_1)$?
(b) What is the conditional probability $P(A_2 \mid B_3)$?
(c) What is $P(B_3 \mid A_2)$?
(d) Are the A_i and B_i elements independent?

4.17 Given $P(A_1B_1) = 0.40$, $P(A_1B_2) = 0.25$, and $P(A_2B_2) = 0.25$.
(a) What is the conditional probability $P(A_2 \mid B_2)$?
(b) What is the conditional probability $P(B_2 \mid A_1)$?
(c) What is $P(B_2 \mid A_2)$?
(d) Are the A_i and B_i elements independent?

4.18 Given $P(A_1B_1) = 0.10$, $P(A_1B_2) = 0.35$, $P(A_1B_3) = 0.20$, $P(A_2B_1) = 0.20$, and $P(B_3) = 0.05$.
(a) What is the conditional probability $P(A_1 \mid B_1)$?
(b) What is the conditional probability $P(A_2 \mid B_3)$?
(c) What is $P(B_3 \mid A_2)$?
(d) Are the A_i and B_i elements independent?

4.19 Adams Construction is negotiating a prime contractor proposal with the government of Egypt to build a resort hotel on the Sinai along the Gulf of Aqabah. The international manager, Karen Jenkins, indicates that the odds in favor of the contract are 3.5 to 1. What is the probability of a successful negotiation?

4.20 Gunnar Thorson lives in Warroad, Minnesota, and drives to the local factory for work at 6:30 A.M. During December, January, and February he is concerned about his truck starting in the morning. When the temperature is below $-10°$F, the probability of starting is 0.60. However, when the temperature is $-10°$F or above, the probability of starting is 0.90. The probability of an early morning temperature below $-10°$F is 0.40 during these months.
(a) Prepare a probability tree and use it to compute the probability of the various combinations of temperature range and starting and not starting.
(b) What is the probability that Gunnar's car will start on any given day during this period?
(c) What are the odds in favor of his car starting?

4.4 OVERINVOLVEMENT RATIOS

An *overinvolvement ratio* is the ratio of the probability of an event occurring, given a specific event compared to the probability without that event. If the ratio of probabilities is not equal to 1.0, the event has an influence on the outcome condition.

These ratios have applications in a number of business situations, including marketing, production, and accounting. In this section we develop the theory and application of overinvolvement ratios (Key Idea 4.14).

Key Idea 4.14: Overinvolvement Ratio

The overinvolvement of element A_1 in activity B_1 compared to its involvement in activity B_2 is defined as the **overinvolvement ratio**:

$$\frac{P(A_1 \mid B_1)}{P(A_1 \mid B_2)}$$

An overinvolvement ratio greater than 1,

$$\frac{P(A_1 \mid B_1)}{P(A_1 \mid B_2)} \geq 1.0$$

implies that element A_1 increases the odds in favor of B_1:

$$\frac{P(B_1 \mid A_1)}{P(B_2 \mid A_1)} > \frac{P(B_1)}{P(B_2)}$$

We start by considering a simple example. Suppose we know that 60% of the purchasers of our product and 30% of the nonpurchasers have seen an advertisement. The ratio of 60% to 30% is the overinvolvement of the event "seen an advertisement" in the purchasers group compared to the nonpurchasers group. In the analysis to follow we show how an overinvolvement ratio greater than 1 provides evidence that, for example, advertising influences purchase behavior. The use of overinvolvement ratios is valuable because certain experiments can be very difficult or unethical.

Consider a company that wishes to determine the effectiveness of a new ad. An experiment is conducted in which an ad is shown to one customer group and not to another, followed by observation of the purchase behavior of both groups. Studies of this type can be tricky; they can be biased because people who are watched closely often behave differently than they do when they are not being observed. However, it is possible to measure the percentage of buyers who have seen an ad and to measure the percentage of nonbuyers who have seen the ad. How should the study data be analyzed in order to determine the effectiveness of the new ad?

First let us consider the framework for evaluation of advertising effectiveness. The population can be divided into

B_1:   buyers
B_2:   nonbuyers

In addition, the viewing of advertising can be divided into

A_1:   those who have seen the advertisement
A_2:   those who have not seen the advertisement

Previously, we defined the odds in favor of an event as the probability of the event divided by the probability of its complement. The odds in favor of a buyer are

$$\frac{P(B_1)}{P(B_2)}$$

Now consider the concept of conditional odds, in which we use the ratio of probabilities that are both conditional on the same event. For example, the odds of a buyer conditional on "have seen advertisement" are

$$\frac{P(B_1 \mid A_1)}{P(B_2 \mid A_1)}$$

If the conditional odds are greater than the unconditional odds, the conditioning event is said to have an influence on the event of interest. Thus advertising would be considered effective if

$$\frac{P(B_1 \mid A_1)}{P(B_2 \mid A_1)} \geq \frac{P(B_1)}{P(B_2)}$$

The left-side terms are equal to

$$P(B_1 \mid A_1) = \frac{P(A_1 \mid B_1)P(B_1)}{P(A_1)}$$

$$P(B_2 \mid A_1) = \frac{P(A_1 \mid B_2)P(B_2)}{P(A_1)}$$

By substituting these latter terms, the first equation becomes

$$\frac{P(A_1 \mid B_1)P(B_1)}{P(A_1 \mid B_2)P(B_2)} \geq \frac{P(B_1)}{P(B_2)}$$

Dividing both sides by the right-side ratio, we obtain

$$\frac{P(A_1 \mid B_1)}{P(A_1 \mid B_2)} \geq 1.0$$

This result shows that if a larger percentage of buyers have seen the advertisement compared to nonbuyers, the odds of purchasing conditional on having seen the advertisement is greater than the unconditional odds. Therefore, we have evidence that the advertising is associated with an increased probability of purchase.

From the original problem 60% of the purchasers and 30% of the nonpurchasers had seen the advertisement. The overinvolvement ratio is 2.0 (60/30), and thus we conclude that the advertisement increases the probability of purchase. Market researchers use this result to evaluate the effectiveness of advertising and other sales promotion activities. Purchasers of products are asked whether they have seen certain advertisements. This is combined with random sample surveys of households from which the percentage of nonpurchasers who have seen an advertisement is determined.

Now consider another situation in which it is difficult, illegal, or unethical to obtain probability results.

Example 4.12   Alcohol and Highway Crashes

Researchers at the National Highway Traffic Safety Administration in the U.S. Department of Transportation wished to determine the effect of alcohol on highway crashes. Clearly, it would be unethical to provide one group of drivers with alcohol and then compare their crash involvement with that of a group who did not have alcohol. However, researchers did find that 10.3% of the drivers at night in a specific county had been drinking and that 32.4% of the single-vehicle-accident drivers, during the same time and in the same county, had been drinking. Single-vehicle accidents were chosen to ensure that any driver error could be assigned to only one driver, whose alcohol usage had been measured. Based on these results, they wanted to know if there was evidence to conclude that accidents increased at night when drivers had been drinking. Use these data to analyze whether alcohol usage leads to increased probability of crashes.

Solution   This problem can be solved by using the overinvolvement ratios. First, the conditions need to be defined.

A_1:   Driver had been drinking.
A_2:   Driver had not been drinking.
C_1:   Driver was involved in a crash.
C_2:   Driver was not involved in a crash.

We know that alcohol, A_1, increases the probability of a crash if

$$\frac{P(A_1 \mid C_1)}{P(A_1 \mid C_2)} \geq 1.0$$

From the research the conditional probabilities are

$$P(A_1 \mid C_1) = 0.324$$
$$P(A_1 \mid C_2) = 0.103$$

Using these results, we find that the overinvolvement ratio is

$$\frac{P(A_1 \mid C_1)}{P(A_1 \mid C_2)} = \frac{0.324}{0.103} = 3.15$$

Based on this analysis, there is evidence to conclude that alcohol increases the probability of automobile crashes.[1]   □

Does It Make Sense?

The overinvolvement ratio is a good example of how mathematical manipulations of probabilities can be used to obtain useful results for business decisions. The wide use of automated data collection using bar code scanners, audience segmentation, and census data on tapes and disks provides the possibility to compute many different probabilities, conditional probabilities, and overinvolvement ratios. As a result, analyses similar to those presented in this chapter become part of the daily routine for marketing analysts and product managers.   □

4.5 BAYES' THEOREM

In this section we introduce a very important result that has a number of important implications for decision making and evaluating information. Bayes' theorem (Key Idea 4.15) is used to obtain conditional probabilities. Data are not always properly structured for decision making and Bayes' theorem can be used to revise probabilities. There is also an area of management decision theory that uses Bayes' theorem to determine how new information influences a manager's probability of an outcome. We begin with some interesting background and a public-sector example.

Bayes' theorem was developed by Reverend Thomas Bayes (1702–1761), whose famous paper was published after his death in 1763 and in 1958.[2] Because games of chance and hence probability were considered to be works of the devil, Bayes did not widely publicize his results. Since World War II, a major area of statistics and a major area of management decision theory have developed based on the original works of Thomas Bayes. Before providing a formal definition of Bayes' theorem, we first present an illustration that introduces the basic ideas.

Government agencies assigned to implement public policy often utilize screening tests to select citizens who are eligible for special benefits or are subject to special sanctions, such as in the case of alcohol consumption and driving privileges. An interesting application of Bayes' theorem occurred when researchers were attempting to develop a test to identify potentially dangerous drivers. Highway accident fatalities are a major cause of death, especially for persons under age 30. Research has established that alcohol is related to 50% of the deaths. In addition, there is considerable evidence that alcoholics are responsible for a large fraction of the alcohol-related accidental deaths. Thus a public program that reduces the number of alcoholics licensed to drive would reduce highway fatalities. However, removing driver license privileges reduces a person's freedom and capability to carry on a normal life. In addition, it is

---

[1] William L. Carlson, "Alcohol usage of the nighttime driver," *Journal of Safety Research*, Vol. 4, No. 1, March 1972.

[2] T. Bayes, "Essay towards solving a problem in the doctrine of chances," *Biometrika*, Vol. 45, 1958, pp. 293–315 (reproduction of 1763 paper).

Key Idea 4.15: Bayes' Theorem

Bayes' theorem is

$$P(A_1 \mid T_1) = \frac{P(T_1 \mid A_1)P(A_1)}{P(T_1 \mid A_1)P(A_1) + P(T_1 \mid A_2)P(A_2)}$$

or, in general,

$$P(A_i \mid T_1) = \frac{P(T_1 \mid A_i)P(A_i)}{\sum_{i=1}^{K} P(T_1 \mid A_i)P(A_i)}$$

where A_i defines K mutually exclusive categories. Bayes' theorem is used to determine the probability of an event A_1 given test data T_1. The value of the data depends on its effect on decisions. Thus Bayes' theorem converts the test result data to information. The information is the probability of the event after the data were processed using Bayes' theorem.

---

likely that some alcoholics are not high-risk drivers and that not all persons identified by screening tests as alcoholics are indeed alcoholics. The public policy issues are complex.

Early in the 1970s a psychiatrist developed a simple pencil-and-paper test to identify persons with alcoholic characteristics. The test was evaluated by applying it to several groups of people, with the following results:

1. The test was given to several hundred persons hospitalized for alcoholism treatment and 90% scored positive, indicating correct identification.
2. The test was also given to several hundred persons who were known to be nonalcoholics. In this group 90% scored negative, which is also a correct identification.
3. Experts estimated that 10% of potential drivers were alcoholics. The psychiatrist proposed that the test be given to all persons applying for new and renewal driver licenses in a midwestern state. A positive test would result in a refusal to assign a driver's license.

The secretary of state had to decide if the test would be used. The test appeared to classify most people correctly, and alcohol-related accidents were a major public health problem. Required to advise on the use of this test, the secretary undertook a probability analysis.

The first step was to identify the elements of the sample space. Since the analysis is attempting to identify alcoholics, define

A_1:   The person is an alcoholic.
A_2:   The person is not an alcoholic.

The proposed test also indicates either positive or negative results; define

T_1:   Test says that the person is an alcoholic.

T_2:   Tests says that the person is not an alcoholic.

From the information provided above, the following probabilities can be defined:

$$P(A_1) = 0.10 \qquad P(A_2) = 0.90$$
$$P(T_1 \mid A_1) = 0.90 \qquad P(T_2 \mid A_1) = 0.10$$
$$P(T_1 \mid A_2) = 0.10 \qquad P(T_2 \mid A_2) = 0.90$$

Consider the application of this information to a population of 100,000 drivers. Table 4.3 shows the various combinations of the A's and T's. Since 10% of the population are alcoholics, the first row contains 10,000 persons and the second row contains 90,000 persons. For the 10,000 alcoholics, 9000 would be classified correctly and appear in the T_1 column. This would leave 1000 for the T_2 column. The 90,000 non-alcoholics in the second row would be grouped into 81,000 ($0.90 \times 90,000$) correctly assigned to the T_2 column, and 9000 ($0.10 \times 90,000$) would be incorrectly assigned to the T_1 column. Adding the two columns, we find that there are 18,000 identified by the test as alcoholics (T_1) and 82,000 identified by the test as nonalcoholics (T_2). Now we can examine Table 4.3 and state some conclusions. For those 82,000 identified as non-alcoholics, (T_2), 81,000 or 0.988 (81,000/82,000) are actually nonalcoholics. Thus the test identifies the nonalcoholics with a high probability of being correct. However, the identification of alcoholics poses a problem since 50% (9000/18,000) of those identified as being alcoholics are not alcoholics. Those 18,000 would be refused driver's licenses. One can imagine severe political problems if one-half the people subjected to sanctions did not deserve the sanctions.

TABLE 4.3   Alcoholics and Test Scores

	T_1 (Test Says Alcoholic)	T_2 (Test Says Not Alcoholic)	Total
A_1 (alcoholic)	9,000	1,000	10,000
A_2 (not alcoholic)	9,000	81,000	90,000
	18,000	82,000	100,000

Does It Make Sense?

In general, conditional probabilities such as $P(T_1 \mid A_1)$ and $P(T_2 \mid A_1)$ are complements only if the conditioning variable is the same. Thus

$$P(T_1 \mid A_1) + P(T_2 \mid A_1) = 1$$

However, in general,

$$P(T_1 \mid A_1) + P(T_2 \mid A_2) \neq 1$$

because the conditioning variables A_1 and A_2 are not the same. The specific results in this example are purely coincidental. Note that in Table 4.3,

$$P(A_1 \mid T_1) = \frac{9,000}{18,000} = 0.50$$

$$P(A_2 \mid T_2) = \frac{81,000}{82,000} = 0.988$$

and thus

$$P(A_1 \mid T_1) + P(A_2 \mid T_2) \neq 1.0 \qquad \qquad \Box$$

This example indicates how an initial conclusion concerning the outcome, given certain data, does not hold up after more rigorous analysis. This happens in many Bayes' problems. The general rule that common sense should guide decisions is a good one. However, Bayes' theorem should be part of that common sense.

Development of Bayes' theorem.   The analysis of the test scores of alcoholics and nonalcoholics is an application of Bayes' theorem conducted without using the formal probability statements. The formal structure of this analysis will be developed by considering the same objective: to determine the probability that a person is an alcoholic given that the test indicates alcoholism.

The development of Bayes' theorem is as follows:

$$P(A_1 \mid T_1) = \frac{P(A_1 \cap T_1)}{P(T_1)}$$

which can be expressed as

$$P(A_1 \mid T_1) = \frac{P(T_1 \mid A_1)P(A_1)}{P(T_1)}$$

The denominator $P(T_1)$ is the sum of the probabilities of T_1 occurring with A_1 and then with A_2, which in turn can be written using conditional probabilities:

$$P(T_1) = P(A_1 \cap T_1) + P(A_2 \cap T_1)$$
$$= P(T_1 \mid A_1)P(A_1) + P(T_1 \mid A_2)P(A_2)$$

These results are combined to obtain Bayes' theorem:

$$P(A_1 \mid T_1) = \frac{P(T_1 \mid A_1)P(A_1)}{P(T_1 \mid A_1)P(A_1) + P(T_1 \mid A_2)P(A_2)}$$

or, in general,

$$P(A_i \mid T_1) = \frac{P(T_1 \mid A_i)P(A_i)}{\sum_{i=1}^{K} P(T_1 \mid A_i)P(A_i)}$$

where A_i defines K mutually exclusive categories.

In the alcoholic test illustration there was a prior probability of alcoholism, $P(A_i)$. Using the data from the test, a posterior probability was obtained. Bayes' theorem provides a way to adjust the probability using the test result. The quality of test data is given by conditional probabilities, such as $P(T_1 \mid A_1)$ and $P(T_2 \mid A_2)$.

Application of Bayes' theorem (Key Idea 4.16) requires a careful analysis of the problem. In summary, the first task is to identify the events in the sample space. The sample space in the illustration above consists of drivers separated into A_1, alcoholics, and A_2, nonalcoholics. This required an independent judgment of which people were actually alcoholics and which were not. These events cover the sample space. Elements could also be identified by their test classification. Events are T_1, the test indicates alcoholic, and T_2, the test indicates nonalcoholic. These events also cover the sample space. Note that a test result T_1, which indicates alcoholism, does not guarantee that the person is an alcoholic, A_1.

Key Idea 4.16: Solution Steps: Bayes' Theorem

1. Define the subset events from the problem.
2. Define the probabilities for the events defined in step 1.
3. Compute the complements of the probabilities.
4. Apply Bayes' theorem to compute the probability for the problem solution.

After the events have been defined, we need to determine the capability of the procedure to predict using the data. Thus in the illustration above the test was given to a group of known alcoholics and to a group of nonalcoholics. These test results provided data. These data were converted to information concerning the quality of the psychiatrist's test to predict by using Bayes' theorem.

The final task is to express one or more questions in the form of Bayes' theorem. In the illustration above we were interested in the probability that a driver was alcoholic given that the driver obtained a positive result on the test. We also realized that it was important to know the probability that a person was not an alcoholic given a positive test result.

Example 4.13   Automobile Sales Incentive

A car dealership knows from past experience that 10% of the people who come into the showroom and talk to a salesperson will eventually purchase a car. To increase the chances of success, you propose to offer a free dinner with a salesperson for all people who agree to listen to a complete sales presentation. You know that some people will do anything for a free dinner even if they do not intend to purchase a car. In addition, some people would rather not spend time having dinner with a car salesperson. Thus you wish to test the effectiveness of this sales promotion incentive. The project is conducted for six months and 40% of the people who purchased cars had a free dinner. In addition, 10% of the people who did not purchase cars had a free dinner.

(a) Do people who accept the dinner have a higher probability of purchasing a new car?

(b) What is the probability that a person who does not accept a free dinner will purchase a car?

Solution   Step 1. Define the subset events from the problem.

D_1:   Customer has dinner with the salesperson.
D_2:   Customer does not have dinner with the salesperson.
P_1:   Customer purchases a car.
P_2:   Customer does not purchase a car.

Step 2. Define the probabilities for the events defined in step 1.

$$P(P_1) = 0.10 \qquad P(D_1 \mid P_1) = 0.40 \qquad P(D_1 \mid P_2) = 0.10$$

Step 3. Compute the complements of the probabilities.

$$P(P_2) = 0.90 \qquad P(D_2 \mid P_1) = 0.60 \qquad P(D_2 \mid P_2) = 0.90$$

Step 4. Apply Bayes' theorem to compute the probability for the problem solution.

We now answer the questions posed.

(a) We know that the sales promotion plan increased the probability of a car purchase if more than 10% of those who had dinner purchased a car. Specifically, we ask if

$$P(P_1 \mid D_1) > P(P_1)$$
$$P(P_1 \mid D_1) > 0.10$$

Using Bayes' theorem, we can find that

$$P(P_1 \mid D_1) = \frac{P(D_1 \mid P_1)P(P_1)}{P(D_1 \mid P_1)P(P_1) + P(D_1 \mid P_2)P(P_2)}$$

$$= \frac{0.40 \times 0.10}{0.40 \times 0.10 + 0.10 \times 0.90}$$

$$= 0.308$$

Therefore, the probability of purchase is higher given the dinner with the salesperson.

(b) This question asks that we compute the probability of purchase, P_1, given that the customer does not have dinner with the salesperson, D_2. We again apply Bayes' theorem to compute

$$P(P_1 \mid D_2) = \frac{P(D_2 \mid P_1)P(P_1)}{P(D_2 \mid P_1)P(P_1) + P(D_2 \mid P_2)P(P_2)}$$

$$= \frac{0.60 \times 0.10}{0.60 \times 0.10 + 0.90 \times 0.90}$$

$$= \frac{0.06}{0.06 + 0.81}$$

$$= 0.069$$

We see that those who refuse the dinner have a lower probability of purchase.

To provide additional evaluation of the sales program, we might also wish to compare the six months' sales experience with that of other dealers and with previous sales experience given similar economic conditions.   □

Does It Make Sense?

We have presented a logical step-by-step or linear procedure for solving Bayes' problems. This procedure works very well for persons experienced in solving this type of problem. This procedure can also help you to organize Bayes' problems. However, most real problem solving in new situations does not follow a step-by-step or linear procedure. Thus you are likely to move back to previous steps and revise results. In some cases you may find it useful to write out Bayes' theorem before you define the probabilities. The mathematical form defines the probabilities that must be obtained from the problem description. As you are learning to solve these problems, use the structure but learn to be creative and willing to go back to earlier steps.   □

Practice Problem 4.5: Quality Control

Acme Manufacturers are trying to identify ways to reduce the number of defective parts. The present production procedures produce 10% defectives. After checking the defective parts it was found that 50% were produced on machine 1. They also found that 10% of the nondefective parts were produced on machine 1.

  (a) What is the probability of producing defective parts on machine 1?
  (b) What strategy would you recommend to reduce defective parts?   □

Problem Exercises

4.21 Given $P(A_1) = 0.60$, $P(T_1 \mid A_1) = 0.60$, and $P(T_2 \mid A_2) = 0.50$. Determine:
      (a) $P(A_1 \mid T_1)$.
      (b) $P(A_2 \mid T_2)$.

4.22 Given $P(A_2) = 0.70$, $P(T_1 \mid A_2) = 0.45$, and $P(T_2 \mid A_1) = 0.60$. Determine:
      (a) $P(A_2 \mid T_2)$.
      (b) $P(A_1 \mid T_1)$.

4.23   Northern Manufacturing uses a simple test to screen parts that are suspected of being defective. In their process 10% of the parts are defective. Defective parts score positively with probability 0.90. Alternatively, good parts score positively with probability 0.15. A part is tested and scores positively. What is the probability that the part is defective?

4.24   A television advertisement for a new breakfast cereal is seen by 30% of the households in a major city. The purchasers of the cereal are asked if they had seen the ad, and 50% indicated that they had. (Assume that the percentage of nonbuyers who have seen the ad is the same as that of the entire population.) Is the advertising effective? Indicate why.

4.25   Disease A occurs in 20% of the population who visit their physician complaining of weakness in their legs. A screening test is used as the first step in the diagnostic process. People with disease A score positively 80% of the time on this test. People who do not have disease A score positively 15% of the time.

   (a) A person is given the test and scores positively. What is the probability that she has disease A?

   (b) A second person is given the test and scores negatively. What is the probability that she does not have disease A?

4.6 FORECASTING AND THE VALUE OF INFORMATION

Public- and private-sector managers make many decisions that anticipate a future set of conditions. New factories are built in anticipation of new or increased demand for a product. Airlines order new planes because they anticipate increased passenger loads in the future. In many cases major expenditures must be incurred and funds committed a long time before sales begin. For example, electrical generating plants require five to eight years for development and construction. To improve the chances of correct decisions, managers use the services of forecasters. If the forecast is correct, then of course the decision maker can make a correct decision. Decision makers can also make correct decisions based on incorrect forecasts, but the probability of correct decisions is greatly decreased.

An important part of any decision analysis should include a careful analysis of the quality of forecast. The most direct way to evaluate forecasts is to determine the proportion of times that the forecast has been correct. For example, one could examine all the situations of economic growth and determine the proportion in which the forecaster predicted economic growth. A similar determination could be made for situations in which economic growth did not occur.

There are also many cases in which there is little if any information available concerning the quality of the forecast information. In those cases the manager must make judgments based on her best understanding of the future. This results in a subjective probability that is based on the experience and judgment of the manager and her advisers. For this discussion, label that subjective probability $P(\theta_i)$, the probability of outcome θ_i based on the best prior judgment and experience. The ability to obtain useful subjective probabilities is of course dependent on the specific situation and the experience of the forecaster. That ability can be developed by years of experience with a specific set of economic problems.

Bayes' theorem can be used to adjust a prior subjective probability, $P(\theta_i)$, when new data are made available. The prior probability, $P(\theta_i)$, is adjusted to the posterior probability, $P(\theta_i \mid \text{data})$, by the ratio of the probability of the data given θ_i divided by the unconditional probability of the data (Key Idea 4.17).

Key Idea 4.17: Bayes' Probability Adjustment Using Data

The adjustment of the probability for a specific future outcome, θ_i, as a result of obtaining data is given by the following general result, which is based on Bayes' theorem:

$$P(\theta_i \mid \text{data}) = \frac{P(\text{data} \mid \theta_i) P(\theta_i)}{P(\text{data})}$$

The probability of the outcome, $P(\theta_i)$, is called the **prior probability** because it is stated before the data are obtained. Similarly, $P(\theta_i \mid \text{data})$ is the **posterior probability** because it is obtained after the data are considered. Notice that the prior probability is modified by the ratio of $P(\text{data} \mid \theta_i)$ divided by $P(\text{data})$.

The numerator is the probability of obtaining the data and the parameter θ_i. The denominator is the probability of obtaining the data without knowing about θ_i. The posterior probability $P(\theta_i \mid \text{data})$ increases or decreases from the prior $P(\theta_i)$ depending on the probability of the data given θ_i divided by the unconditional probability of the data.

As an illustration, let us consider how the judgment of a decision maker might be modified as a result of a forecast or new information. Suppose that Joyce Gruber, manager of development, is considering the possibility of building a new shopping center in Brown County. The success of this shopping center will depend on the economic growth in the county over the next 10 years. There are three possible levels: G_1, high growth, G_2, moderate growth, and G_3, no growth. The manager's judgment of the probabilities of these outcomes is

$$P(G_1) = 0.40 \qquad P(G_2) = 0.30 \qquad P(G_3) = 0.30$$

To improve the decision, Joyce conducts a survey of 100 small manufacturers and discovers that 60% plan to locate in Brown County. From her experience with studies from similar counties she knows that the probability of this result given future high growth is 0.70, while under moderate growth the probability is 0.50, and under no growth the probability is 0.30. Given these results, how do the data from the survey of small manufacturers change the probabilities of economic growth?

First we define D_1 as the survey data which indicate that 60% or more plan to locate in the county, and D_2 as the survey data which indicate that less than 60% plan to locate in the county. This results in the following conditional probabilities:

$$P(D_1 \mid G_1) = 0.70$$
$$P(D_1 \mid G_2) = 0.50$$
$$P(D_1 \mid G_3) = 0.30$$

By applying Key Idea 4.16, we can see that the probability of growth, G_i, after the survey data have been considered, is

$$P(G_i \mid D_1) = \frac{P(D_1 \mid G_i)P(G_i)}{P(D_1)}$$

For this example the probability of the data is given by

$$P(D_1) = P(D_1 \mid G_1)P(G_1) + P(D_1 \mid G_2)P(G_2) + P(D_1 \mid G_3)P(G_3)$$
$$= (0.70 \times 0.40) + (0.50 \times 0.30) + (0.30 \times 0.30)$$
$$= 0.52$$

Using these results, we find that the probabilities of the three possible outcomes are

$$P(G_1 \mid D_1) = \frac{P(D_1 \mid G_1)}{P(D_1)} \times P(G_1)$$
$$= \frac{0.70}{0.52} \times 0.40$$
$$= 0.54$$
$$P(G_2 \mid D_1) = \frac{P(D_1 \mid G_2)}{P(D_1)} \times P(G_2)$$
$$= \frac{0.50}{0.52} \times 0.30$$
$$= 0.29$$
$$P(G_3 \mid D_1) = \frac{P(D_1 \mid G_3)}{P(D_1)} \times P(G_3)$$
$$= \frac{0.30}{0.52} \times 0.30$$
$$= 0.17$$

In this illustration we have seen how judgments, in the form of probabilities, can be modified in response to data. This analysis process is powerful and can result in improved decisions. However, to make effective use of the analysis, it is necessary to study the system that forms the context of the decision. Bayesian analysis clearly indicates the issues that need to be considered. The probabilities of obtaining the data under the three possible conditions of economic growth were known from past experience. These results could have been obtained in different ways. In the example, similar counties that had the same growth potential in the past were studied. An analyst could also consult a panel of regional economic development experts. Good decisions are based on a combination of good analysis techniques and careful study of the system.

SUMMARY OF KEY IDEAS

PRACTICE PROBLEM SOLUTIONS

4.1 In this problem, 20 CD players have the standard system and 10 have the new system. Define

N_1:   number of players out of five with new system
N_2:   number of players out of five with the standard system

(a) Probability that two out of five have the new system:

$$P(N_1) = \frac{C_{N_1}^{10} \times C_{N_2}^{20}}{C_5^{30}}$$

$$P(N_1 = 2) = \frac{C_2^{10} \times C_3^{20}}{C_5^{30}}$$

$$= \frac{45 \times 1140}{142,506}$$

$$= 0.36$$

(b) Probability that four out of five have the new system:

$$P(N_1 = 4) = \frac{C_4^{10} \times C_1^{20}}{C_5^{30}}$$

$$= \frac{210 \times 20}{142,506}$$

$$= 0.029$$

4.2   The problem can be solved by preparing a two-way table (Table 4.4). The probabilities given in the problem are identified by an asterisk and the remainder are computed using the procedures for analyzing two-way tables. After computing the cell probabilities, the answers can be read directly from Table 4.4.

TABLE 4.4   Joint Probability for Practice Problem 4.2

Color	Field 1	2	3	Total
Red	0.266	0.200	0.200*	0.67*
Yellow	0.067*	0.133	0.133	0.33
	0.333*	0.333*	0.333*	1.0*

(a) 0.266.
(b) 0.200.
(c) 0.133.
(d) 0.133.

4.3   The first step is to define the events:

A: Student participates in orchestra.
B: Student participates in choir.
C: Student participates in theater.

The probability of participating in at least one art is the union of events A, B, and C and is computed as follows:

$$P(A \cup B \cup C) = P(A) + P(B) + P(C) - P(A \cap B)$$
$$- P(A \cap C) - P(B \cap C) + P(A \cap B \cap C)$$
$$= 0.20 + 0.30 + 0.10 - 0.15 + 0.05$$
$$= 0.50$$

4.4 The first step is to define the events for each stage:

S_1:   success with focus group
F_1:   failure with focus group
S_2:   success with market test
F_2:   failure with market test
S_3:   success in national market
F_3:   failure in national market

(a) The probability tree is contained in Figure 4.4.

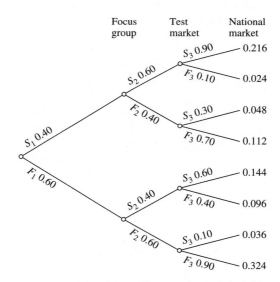

Figure 4.4   Probability Tree for Practice Problem 4.4

(b) The probability of success in the national market given a successful focus group is $P(S_3 \mid S_1)$, which is computed as follows:

$$P(S_3 \mid S_1) = \frac{P(S_3 \cap S_1)}{P(S_1)}$$

$$= \frac{0.216 + 0.048}{0.40}$$

$$= 0.66$$

(c) The probability that a successful product in the national market had a successful test focus group is $P(S_1 \mid S_3)$, which is computed as follows:

$$P(S_1 \mid S_3) = \frac{P(S_1 \cap S_3)}{P(S_3)}$$

$$= \frac{0.216 + 0.048}{0.216 + 0.048 + 0.144 + 0.036}$$

$$= 0.59$$

4.5

(a) Define the subset events from the problem.

D_1:   defective parts
D_2:   nondefective parts
M_1:   produced on machine 1
M_2:   not produced on machine 2

Define the probabilities for the events.

$$P(D_1) = 0.10 \qquad P(M_1 \mid D_1) = 0.50 \qquad P(M_1 \mid D_2) = 0.10$$

Compute the complements of the probabilities.

$$P(D_2) = 0.90 \qquad P(M_2 \mid D_1) = 0.50 \qquad P(M_2 \mid D_2) = 0.90$$

Apply Bayes' theorem to compute the probability for the problem solution.

$$(D_1 \mid M_1) = \frac{P(M_1 \mid D_1)P(D_1)}{P(M_1 \mid D_1)P(D_1) + P(M_1 \mid D_2)P(D_2)}$$

$$= \frac{(0.50)(0.10)}{(0.50)(0.10) + (0.10)(0.90)}$$

$$= \frac{0.05}{0.05 + 0.09}$$

$$= 0.357$$

The probability of a defective part on machine 1 (0.357) is over three times the overall probability of defective parts (0.10).

(b) To reduce the number of defectives you should examine machine 1 carefully because the probability of a defective part is much higher than the probability of defectives on all machines.

CHAPTER PROBLEMS

4.1 Define the sample space for the following examples.
   (a) You wish to purchase a new car, and after visiting dealers you have prepared a list of 20 cars from which you will purchase one.
   (b) You wish to purchase a bed and dresser for your room. The local stores have 10 different beds and 15 different dressers. Define the sample space of bedroom combinations available for your selection and indicate the number of elements.
   (c) You and a friend go to a new restaurant that has five different meals on the menu. Each of you selects a different meal. Define the meal selections as A through E and write out the entire sample space for the combined meal selections brought to your table.
   (d) A new master's of economic management degree program consists of 20 courses, including 10 that are required. The remaining 10 may be selected from 30 elective courses. Define the sample space of degree transcripts and determine the number of elements in the sample space.
   (e) A large parts supplier lists 10,000 auto parts in its catalog. Two customers arrive at the sales desk. The first purchases two different parts, and the second purchases five different parts. Define the sample space for the total of seven parts purchased by the two customers and indicate the number of elements in the sample space.

4.2 A sample space contains outcomes A_1 and A_2 and B_1 and B_2, with both pairs covering all elements. Given are the following probabilities:

$$P(A_1 \cup B_1) = 0.60$$
$$P(A_1) = 0.20$$
$$P(B_1) = 0.40$$

   (a) Are A_i and B_i independent?
   (b) What is $P(A_2 \cap B_2)$?

4.3 Suppose that Sodom had 100 citizens, of whom 80 were "sinners." What is the probability of finding no sinners in a random sample of 2 citizens?

4.4 You are the manager of a large food service operation. On a particular day the main entrees are steak and fish, and the vegetables are carrots and peas. From past data you discover that out of 2000 dinner customers 400 will choose fish and the rest steak. In addition, 1200 will select either fish or carrots. Someone also indicates that the difference between the number of customers who choose carrots and the number who choose fish is 400.
   (a) Define the elements in the sample space and convert the information provided above to probability statements using the relative frequency concept of probability.
   (b) Determine the probability that a customer will take both fish and carrots.
   (c) Determine the probability that a customer will take neither fish nor carrots.

4.5 What is the probability of selecting computer A and computer B from a store that has 10 computer A's, 5 computer B's, and 8 computer C's? Assume that each computer has an equal chance of being selected.

4.6 Uren Clockworks Limited produces 90 clocks per day. As a check on quality they select a random sample of 5 clocks each day and test each clock.

(a) If there are 5 defective clocks in the 90 produced on a given day, compute the probability of 0, 1, 2, 3, 4, and 5 defective clocks in the sample.

(b) Repeat part (a) if there are 30 defective clocks produced on a given day.

4.7   A major auto company has an inventory of 90 cars. Of these, 20 are station wagons. The company ships 20 cars per month to a dealer and last month the dealer's order was lost. Therefore, the 20 cars were selected randomly and shipped. The dealer has sold 6 station wagons and customers are awaiting their delivery. What is the probability that the shipment contains exactly 6 station wagons?

4.8   A major auto company has conducted a study of the desire for automatic transmissions, air conditioning, or tape decks. From the study they found that 20% wanted no options, 60% wanted automatic transmissions, 50% wanted air conditioning, and 30% wanted tape decks. In addition, 25% wanted automatic transmissions and air conditioning, 30% wanted automatic transmissions and tape decks, and 25% wanted air conditioning and tape decks. What is the probability that a customer will order all three?

4.9   McKenzie Ltd. manufactures microprocessor computer chips for various equipment manufacturers. Chipsey Forest, Inc. has purchased 1000 chips for use in its forest product processing equipment. Suppose that a new contract, which guaranteed 10% or less defectives, was negotiated. A shipment of 1000 computers is received and a random sample of 5 computers was obtained for testing.

(a) What are the probabilities of 0, 1, 2, 3, 4, and 5 defective computers in your sample? Assume 10% defectives.

(b) What would you conclude concerning the contract if there were 3 or more defectives in the sample?

4.10   A sample space can be divided into cells identified by A_1, A_2, A_3 and by B_1, B_2, B_3. The following probabilities are known:

$$P(A_1, B_1) = 0.10 \qquad P(A_2, B_2) = 0.30 \qquad P(B_1) = 0.30$$
$$P(A_1, B_3) = 0.20 \qquad P(A_3, B_3) = 0.10 \qquad P(B_2) = 0.40$$
$$P(A_1) = 0.30 \qquad P(A_2) = 0.50$$

Compute the following probabilities.

(a) $P(A_2, B_1)$, $P(A_3, B_1)$.

(b) $P(A_1, B_2)$, $P(A_3, B_2)$, $P(A_2, B_3)$.

4.11   Fireup, Inc. is a major producer of heaters. Each day, 75 heaters are produced. If the production process is operating properly, a maximum of 5 defective heaters would be produced. You are responsible for establishing a sampling procedure to monitor the manufacturing process. Each day a random sample of 6 heaters will be tested. If the number of defective heaters equals or exceeds the upper control limit, K, you will conclude that the process is out of control and producing too many defectives. If manufacturing the process is out of control, it must be stopped and the cause of the problem eliminated. Determine the upper control limit, K, so that the probability of closing down the process when the process is operating correctly is less than 0.07.

4.12   The personnel roster for a large marketing company indicates that 20% of the employees have MBAs and 30% have undergraduate liberal arts degrees. In addition, 40% have either an MBA or an undergraduate liberal arts degree. What is the probability that a randomly selected employee has both an MBA and an undergraduate liberal arts degree? What is the probability that a randomly selected person with an MBA has an undergraduate liberal arts degree?

4.13   The market research department of a major corporation has obtained a random sample of 1000 persons who could purchase a new product. The survey contains 40% men and the remainder are women. The participants were asked if they would purchase 0, 1, 2, or 3 units per year. Of the men, 25% said they would purchase 0 units and 37.5% said they would purchase 2 units. For the women, one-third would purchase 1 unit and one-third would purchase 3 units. In the entire sample, 30% said 1 unit and 30% said 2 units. Determine the probability that:
(a) A person is a man and purchases 1 unit.
(b) A person is a woman and would purchase 0 units.
(c) A person purchases 3 units.
(d) A person is a woman and purchases 2 units.

4.14   A factory has three production processes to produce cereal. Process 1 produces 30% of the total output, process 2 produces 25%, and process 3 produces 45%. Every day 5% of the boxes produced in the entire factory are defective and must be destroyed. Careful examination of the production processes shows that process 3 produces 2% defective boxes, and process 1 produces 5% defective boxes.
(a) What is the probability of a defective cereal box from process 2?
(b) If process 2 was reduced to 15% of the total output and process 3 was increased to 55%, what is the probability of a defective box of cereal being produced in the factory?
(c) Using the probabilities from part (b), suppose that you obtain a defective box of cereal. What is the probability that it came from process 1?

4.15   Shirley Evans, market research manager, has received results from a study on cereal purchase behavior. There were three cereals considered in the survey: Flakes, Puffed, and O's. The survey obtained results from a random sample of 1000 households. The following results were obtained:

   100 households purchase all three cereal types.
   300 households purchase two different cereal types.
   800 households purchase at least one cereal type.
   400 households included children.

Previous research indicates clearly that 40% of households with children purchase Flakes and 30% purchase Puffed. The same data indicate that 20% of the households without children purchase Flakes and 10% purchase Puffed. What is the probability that a household purchases O's?

4.16   You are associated with a research team that is developing an estimate of the probability of major causes of automobile accidents. The three major causes being studied are driver error, slippery road, and worn tires. A random sample of 1000 accidents is obtained and the causes of the accident are identified: 100 accidents had all three causes, 300 accidents had two causes, 800 accidents had a least one of the three causes. It was also noted that 400 of the accidents involve drivers under age 25. National data indicate that 40% of the drivers under age 25 involved in accidents experienced driver error and 30%

had accidents caused by slippery roads. The same data indicate 20% of the drivers age 25 or older had accidents caused by slippery roads and 10% of those same older drivers had accidents caused by driver error. What is the probability that an accident resulted from worn tires?

4.17   Suppose that when the weather is rainy the probability that a customer will purchase an umbrella is 0.80 but when it is not raining the probability is 0.30. The probability of rain is 0.40. Determine the probability that:
(a) The customer will purchase an umbrella today.
(b) It is raining given that a customer has purchased an umbrella.
(c) Tomorrow will be sunny and that the customer will purchase an umbrella.

4.18   The quality assurance department of a large microcomputer company has recently studied two major product defects, exterior scratches and electronic component failure. Their report indicated that 36% of all units have either of these two defects. In addition, 20% have exterior scratches and 20% have electronic defects. Are these two defects independent? The president of the company insists that all computers with exterior scratches should be tested for electronic defects. He argues that if a computer is scratched, it has been subjected to rough treatment and is more likely to have electronic defects. Given the results of this study, how would you react to his rule?

4.19   In a recent speech a congressman stated that mutually exclusive events are also independent events. Using the rules of probability, demonstrate that he is either right or wrong.

4.20   A company produces four different automobile models: model A (20% of output), model B (25%), model C (25%), and model D (30%). The long-term percentages of defectives for each model are model A (5%), model B (10%), model C (2%), and model D (6%).
(a) What is the probability of a defective automobile if automobiles are selected randomly from the entire company output?
(b) A new inspector is hired and she always passes model D automobiles. What is the probability that a defective automobile has been selected?
(c) Can we conclude that automobile models and defectives are independent?

4.21   The manager of a large supermarket has placed a set of new signs that advertise the business. He would like to evaluate the effect of these signs. Presently, the store sells to 30% of the people in the community. A sample of customers indicates that 40% have seen at least one of the signs. The sign company states that 50% of the people in the community have seen the sign. What is the probability that people go to this supermarket given that they have seen one or more of the signs?

4.22   You are attempting to determine the probability of a defective microcomputer in the latest shipment. From your past experience you know that microcomputers are shipped from factories A, B, and C. In addition, you know that factory A produces 20% defective computers, factory B produces 10% defective computers, and factory C produces 5% defective computers. From the shipping labels you discover that 40% are from factory C and 40% are from factory B.
(a) What is the probability of a defective computer in this shipment?
(b) If you find a defective computer, what is the probability that it came from factory A?

4.23   A study of driving accidents in a developing country indicated that 75% of the crashes involved "old" drivers (over age 25) and the remainder involved "young" drivers (16 to 25). In addition, 5% of all drivers have crashes and 20% of all drivers are young.
       (a) Can you conclude that driver age and crash involvement are independent?
       (b) What is the probability that an old driver will have a crash?
       (c) What is the probability that a young driver will have a crash?

4.24   The market research department of a large bicycle manufacturer has been evaluating the effectiveness of a new advertising project. They discovered that 30% of the households in a major city could recall seeing their television ad. Interviews with recent purchasers of their bicycles indicated that 25% of this group could recall seeing their television ad. What recommendation should be made regarding the advertising campaign?

4.25   The Ackley clinic performs tests for potential AIDS victims. When a test is performed on a person who is HIV positive, there are two outcomes. The test says that the person is HIV positive or that the person is not. Show that the sum of the probabilities of these two results must always sum to 1. Let A_1 define the condition that a person is HIV positive, T_1 indicate that the test says the person is HIV positive, and T_2 indicate that the test says the person is not. Prepare a formal argument using probability notation.

4.26   A car dealership knows from past experience that 10% of the people who come into the showroom and talk to a salesperson will eventually purchase a car. To increase the chances of success, you propose to offer a free dinner with a salesperson for all people who talk to a salesperson in the showroom. You know that some people will do anything for a free dinner even if they do not intend to purchase a car. In addition, some people would rather not spend a dinner with a car salesperson. Thus you wish to test the effectiveness of this sales promotion incentive. You run the project for six months and discover that 40% of the people who purchased cars had a free dinner. In addition 10% of the people who did not purchase cars had a free dinner.
       (a) Does the sales promotion plan increase the probability of purchasing a new car?
       (b) What is the probability that a person who does not accept a free dinner will purchase a car?

4.27   An economist is evaluating the effectiveness of a new fertilizer in an agricultural development project. She first discovered that 30% of the farms had high production levels and 70% had low production levels. Further investigation revealed that 50% of the farms with high production had used the new fertilizer. In addition, 60% of the farms with low production had not used the new fertilizer. Determine the probability of high production given first, the new fertilizer, and second, that the new fertilizer was not used. What should she recommend regarding the effect of the new fertilizer on production level?

4.28   A major economic planning group has proposed a program to encourage more people to study economics at the undergraduate level. They point out that their program will lead to significant economic growth if there is a world energy shortage in the next 10 years. As a U.S. Senator, you believe that the probability of such a shortage is 0.40. Shirley Johnson of Economic Forecasters Ltd. has projected that a world energy shortage will occur in the next 10 years. She has correctly predicted 60% of the previous major changes in the world economy. However, she has also predicted change 40% of the time when in fact a change did not occur. How does Ms. Johnson's projection that the world economy will change to an energy shortage economy modify your probability of a world energy shortage and therefore your vote on the proposed educational program?

4.29   The president of an intermediate-sized company is concerned about hiring persons who are alcoholics. She reasons that alcoholics will have poor attendance and work performance. After some study she discovers that 20% of the potential workers in her community are alcoholic. After receiving this disturbing news, she decides to hire Jack Brown to interview all applicants and indicate whether they are alcoholics. When Dr. Brown used his interview technique on a group of alcoholics he was correct 80% of the time. When he used the technique on a group of nonalcoholics he was correct 90% of the time. Recently, a person who was rejected for employment because he was classified as an alcoholic by Dr. Brown has threatened to file a lawsuit if he is not hired. Should the company fight the threatened lawsuit? (The answer will depend, of course, on the probability that the test identifies alcoholics correctly.)

4.30   Jane Smith is considering a major business expansion. However, she knows that the expansion will recover its cost only if the Latin American coffee harvest is small next year. Her initial judgment is that the probability of a small harvest is 0.50. To help guide her decision she hires a forecaster who forecasts that the harvest will be small. After some investigation she discovers that this forecaster has predicted both small and large harvests correctly 75% of the time. What is the probability of a small coffee harvest given the forecast?

4.31   Computer failures in a large university can be modeled by two *Bernoulli processes*, one for the disk drive and the other for the central computer processor. A Bernoulli process has only two states. In this case the computer is either operating or not operating. If the disk drive experiences an electrical overload, the probability of a disk drive failure is 0.20. If the central processor experiences an electrical overload, its probability of failure is 0.30. When an electrical overload occurs to the computer system, either the disk drive or the CPU is overloaded but not both. Given that an electrical overload occurs, the probability of the disk drive being overloaded is 0.60 and the probability of the central processor being overloaded is 0.40. Assume that an electrical overload has occurred and that the computer system has failed. What is the probability that the disk drive has failed? Note that an electrical overload results in a failure of either the disk drive or the central processor.

4.32   You have been asked to advise the National Transportation Safety Board (NTSB) about the causes of airline accidents. In particular, they are interested in the contribution of faulty maintenance to accidents. After every crash an NTSB investigator makes a preliminary judgment concerning the culpability of faulty maintenance as a cause of the accident. After extensive investigation of past accident reports, you discover that the probability that an airplane accident caused by faulty maintenance is diagnosed correctly is 0.90. Similarly, accidents that are not caused by faulty maintenance are diagnosed incorrectly as being caused by faulty maintenance with a probability of 0.40. You also found that 30% of all airplane accidents are caused by faulty maintenance. An airplane accident occurs and the preliminary diagnosis is that it was caused by faulty maintenance. What is the probability that the accident is actually due to faulty maintenance?

4.33   Midwest Food, Inc. is considering a change in the package design for its traditional pancake mix. The marketing manager believes that the probability of increased sales from this product is 0.80. The new package design is tried in a test market and sales are reduced. From past experience they know that this result would occur with probability 0.40 even if sales would increase in the total market. In addition, the test market has correctly predicted sales decreases in the total market with probability 0.80. What should be the manager's revised probability of a sales increase given the test market result?

4.34   Sandy Chadwick, the president of Midwest Bank, believes that the prime interest rate will increase during the next six months with probability 0.70. She asks an economic consultant for his prediction and he predicts that the prime interest will not increase during the next six months. Over the past 10 years the consultant has been correct 80% of the time (e.g., in 80% of the cases in which interest rates eventually increased, he predicted an increase; similarly, in 80% of the cases in which interest rates decreased he predicted a decrease). What is Sandy's modified probability that the prime interest will increase given that the consultant predicts the prime will not increase?

4.35   A manufacturing process produces 10% defective items. An inspector is hired to inspect each item before shipment. He identifies good items correctly with probability 0.80 and bad items as bad items correctly with probability 0.80. If an item is shipped, what is the probability that the item is not defective?

4.36   The Boston Copper Co. is involved in the search for copper ore in South America. Based on preliminary evaluation of the local geology the chief mining engineer believes that there is a 50–50 chance that copper will be discovered in their new exploration. A first test drilling provides positive results. The probability that the test drilling would give incorrect results is 0.25. Based on the first test drilling, what is the revised probability that copper will be discovered?

4.37   Associated Grocers has just received a shipment of 1000 boxes of cereal from Wheat Cereals, Inc. From past experience Associated knows that the shipment has come from either the west factory or the east factory. Each factory ships an equal amount of cereal. They also know that 40% of the boxes from the east factory contain stale cereal and only 10% of the boxes from the west factory contain stale cereal. Associated does not want to accept the shipment if it has come from the east factory. One randomly selected box of cereal is selected, opened, and tasted. It is stale. What is the probability that the shipment came from the east factory?

4.38   A manager who travels a great deal has become concerned about hijacking of airlines. He read a news story which stated that the probability of two passengers with bombs is essentially zero. Therefore, he started to carry a bomb in his suitcase. Comment on his reasoning based on your understanding of conditional probability and independence.

4.39   Consolidated Boat Builders has manufactured 100 special-class sailboats for a northern Minnesota resort. The contract states that at least 90 of the 100 boats will have no hull defects. A random sample of 10 boats was selected. In the sample, two of the boats had a hull defect. What is the probability of two or more boats with hull defects if the contract has been met?

4.40   The marketing vice-president believes that the probability of successful sales for a new CD player is 0.60. This player features 80% oversampling, distortion in the extreme range of less than 10% and 6.2% drive reliability, and a double-digit dipping focal insert and transport mechanism with a 0.50 plastic construction. After examining a preliminary model of the CD player, the senior sales analyst says that this player will not have a successful sales experience. You decide to examine the past forecasts for the senior analyst to help interpret his prediction. For 100 successful product innovations that were introduced, he predicted correctly 30% of the time. For 100 unsuccessful product innovations the senior analyst predicted a successful sales experience for 80 of the products. Given the prediction of the senior sales analyst, what is the marketing vice-president's new probability of success given a Bayesian analysis?

4.41 Consolidated Insurance has devoted considerable time to reducing industrial accidents, so that they can reduce their claims experience. A recent study indicated that 20% of the accidents in the food-processing industry involved workers with blood alcohol levels above the legal limit for driving. In addition, 30% involved workers without a high school education and 50% of these workers had high blood alcohol levels. What percentage of accidents would be reduced if workers with high blood alcohol were sent home and hiring policies were modified to hire only workers with a high school education?

4.42 A pool of citizens selected for a jury trial contains 10 people, four who are black and six who are white. From this pool of citizens, juries of six people are selected randomly.
   (a) A jury was selected and contained five white people and one black person. What is the probability of selecting this jury if the selection is random?
   (b) In a second county the jury pool contained two black and eight white people. A jury containing five white people and one black person was selected. What is the probability of selecting this jury if the selection is random? What is the probability of selecting a jury with 0 black people from this jury pool?
   (c) Comment on the jury selection process in parts (a) and (b).

4.43 Consolidated Machine Tools has conducted an extensive study of its marketing and sales operation. Based on the following specific facts from the study, you are to prepare an analysis of the marketing and sales operation.
   1. A buyer of heavy machine tools may purchase 0, 1, 2, or 3 tools. The probability of purchasing 0 is 0.20. The probability of purchasing 1 is 0.30. The probability of purchasing 2 is 0.30.
   2. The following three sales strategies are used for different potential purchasers.
      (i)   Reduce price by 10%—used 40% of the time.
      (ii) Demonstrate tools using an expert machinist—used 30% of the time.
      (iii) A sales talk by Molly Super, the leading sales agent.
   3. The conditional probability that the price reduction strategy was used given that 3 tools were purchased is 0.40. However, the conditional probability that the sales talk strategy was used given that 3 tools were purchased is only 0.20.
   4. The intersection of the price reduction strategy and 0 tools sold has a probability of 0.05.
   5. The conditional probability of using the sales talk strategy given that 2 sales occurred is 0.10.
   6. The conditional probability of using the demonstration sales strategy given that 1 sale occurred is 0.30.
   7. The conditional probability of using the sales talk strategy given that 0 tools were sold is 0.50. Using all of the facts above, complete the following analysis:

(a) Construct the joint probability distribution of number of sales versus sales strategies.
(b) Are the number of sales independent of sales strategy?
(c) Which sales strategy provides the highest probability of 0 sales?
(d) Which sales strategy provides the highest probability of 2 or 3 sales?

4.44 A congressional committee has recommended mandatory HIV testing for all health care workers. Research shows that 5% of all health care workers are HIV positive. A new test was given to people who are known to be HIV positive and they had positive results (the test says the person is HIV positive) 90% of the time. When the test was given to people who are not HIV positive, it gave correct results 95% of the time.
(a) With this new testing scheme, how often will health care workers with AIDS be identified properly?
(b) How often will the test tell you that health care workers are HIV positive when, in fact, they are not?
(c) Using the results above, comment on the effectiveness of this new test.

4.45 A large marketing study was conducted in three cities, identified as city 1, city 2, and city 3. Each person interviewed was asked if he or she would buy the proposed new oat bran cereal that was the subject of this study. In the entire study 50% of the people indicated that they would buy. However, in city 1, 40% said they would buy, and in city 3, 60% said they would buy. For the entire study, 20% of the people came from city 1 and 40% from city 2. What is the probability that:
(a) A subject is from city 1 and a buyer?
(b) A subject is from city 3 and a nonbuyer?
(c) A subject is from city 2 and a buyer?
(d) A city 2 resident is a buyer?
(e) A subject comes from city 3?

4.46 The manager of Northeast Cereals is examining the accuracy of the forecasts made by its forecaster, Acme Associates. First he collected data on the forecasts that were made in those cases in which the cereal market actually grew. In those cases of subsequent growth the forecasts were (1) the market will expand, 50% of the time; (2) no change in the market, 20% of the time; and (3) the market will decline, 30% of the time. In those cases of subsequent decline, the forecasts were (1) the market will expand, 20% of cases; (2) no change in the market, 30%; and (3) the market will decline, 50%. Assume that the prior probability of growth is 0.60. Determine the revised probability of market growth given a forecast that:
(a) The market will expand.
(b) The market will decline.

5

Discrete Random Variables and Probability Distribution Functions

Developing skills in distribution choice will require problem-solving experience.

5.1 PROBABILITY MODELS

In Chapter 4 we learned about probability and saw some important applications. The concept of outcomes from an experiment or problem situation was developed. The probability of each outcome was computed and the resulting set of probabilities for all outcomes helped to define the system and its outputs.

In this chapter the set of outcomes is defined by a discrete random variable and the probabilities of outcomes by a probability distribution function. By using these variables and functions some useful mathematical tools can be used to develop greater statistical understanding and to simplify problem solving. After developing the basic concepts of random variables, we present the most important discrete probability distributions used in business and economics. These distributions, the binomial and the Poisson, are used with families of problems (i.e., problems with common solution characteristics). As a result, solution development and the computation of probabilities is simplified.

Our goal in this chapter is to understand how to define these discrete probability models and to use these models in business situations. For instance, suppose that an airline has 16 seats remaining seven days before a given flight departs. They sell 20 tickets for those seats. If more than 16 people arrive for the flight, one or more persons will be bumped from the flight, and the airline will have to pay a penalty. We learn how to use the binomial distribution to determine the probability that at least one person will be bumped from the flight, and the airline will have to pay a penalty. We learn how to use the binomial distribution to determine the probability that at least one person will be bumped. In another example we study how a computer center manager uses the Poisson distribution to determine the probability of one or more component failures of a computer system on a given day.

5.2 DISCRETE RANDOM VARIABLES

A precise definition of the random variable, X (Key Idea 5.1), provides the foundation for a number of analysis and decision-making models and is a fundamental step in problem solving. Random variables are either discrete (which we study in this chapter) or continuous (which we study in Chapter 6).

Key Idea 5.1: Discrete Random Variable

A **discrete random variable** assigns distinct values to all outcomes in a sample space. If the number of values for the random variable can be counted, the random variable is discrete.

We have seen in Chapter 4 that if two parts are selected from a production process and tested to determine if they are either good, G, or defective, D, the sample space is

$$S = \{GD, GG, DG, DD\}$$

Let X represent the number of good parts for each outcome in the sample space. The variable discrete random variable X has three possible values: 0, 1, or 2. Note that X assigns a distinct value to each outcome in the sample space and does not distinguish between the outcomes, GD and DG, and thus it loses some information. This loss of information is not important if we are concerned only with the number of good parts in the sample. If order is important, a different random variable would be required. The random sample of parts presented above provides a reference example.

In this book we use the standard convention of defining a random variable with an uppercase letter (e.g., X) and a specific value of the random variable with a lowercase letter (e.g., x). The probability distribution function is defined in Key Idea 5.2. Consider the following examples.

Example 5.1   Production Investment Probability Distribution Function

Mark Goede, Vice-President of Finance for North Star Stoves, is considering a project to increase production. The possible returns from the project are: $1000, $3000, $5000, and $7000, with probabilities 0.30, 0.20, 0.40, and 0.10. Describe the investment model.

Solution   The probability distribution function is defined in Table 5.1. The random variable, X, has four values, corresponding to the four possible outcomes in

---

Key Idea 5.2: Probability Distribution Function

A **probability distribution function** $f(x)$ assigns a probability to each value of the random variable such that the sum of the probabilities totals to 1.

The combination of a random variable and a probability distribution function defines a probability model. The general notation

$$P(X = x) = f(x)$$

is read:

The probability that the random variable, X, equals a specific value, x, is assigned by the function $f(x)$.

---

the sample space. The random variable and probability distribution function define a model of an investment process. $\square$

TABLE 5.1   Probability
Distribution Function for
Investment Project Returns

Return, X	$f(x) = P(X = x)$
1000	0.30
3000	0.20
5000	0.40
7000	0.10
	1.00

Example 5.2   Defective Parts Probability Distribution

Richard Pernecky, Manager of Quality Control, is developing a procedure to test the quality of incoming parts shipments. In one model he assumed that 20% of all parts are defective and that a random sample of four parts is appropriate to make a decision. Describe the probability distribution he is using in this model.

Solution   If we define the random variable, X, to be the number of defective parts in the random sample, X can take on five values: 0, 1, 2, 3, or 4. The probability distribution function is given in Table 5.2. (*Note:* These probabilities were derived using the binomial distribution, which we study in Section 5.6.) $\square$

TABLE 5.2   Probability
Distribution Function for
Defective Parts

Number, X	$f(x) = P(X = x)$
0	0.4096
1	0.4096
2	0.1536
3	0.0256
4	0.0016
	1.0000

5.2.1 Cumulative Distribution Function

In many situations we wish to know the probability that the random variable is less than or equal to a particular value x_*. For instance, we may want to know the probability that sales are below the break-even level. Or perhaps we are interested in the probability that the number of defects is below or above the desired target number. For these situations we use the cumulative distribution function (CDF; Key Idea 5.3). The CDF for a discrete random variable is computed by adding the probabilities for all random variables up to and including the random variable desired.

Key Idea 5.3: Cumulative Distribution Function

The **cumulative distribution function** (CDF) for a discrete random variable, $F(x_*)$, is defined as the probability that the random variable X is less than or equal to a particular value, x_*. In mathematical notation,

$$F(x_*) = P(X \leq x_*)$$

$$= \sum f(x_i) \qquad \text{all } x_i \leq x_*$$

The CDF for a particular random variable, x_*, is computed by adding the individual probabilities for random variable values less than and including x_*.

The complement of the CDF is the probability of outcomes above a specific value. Using this notation, the probability that X is greater than x_* is given by the complement of $F(x_*)$, $1 - F(x_*)$. For example, the probability that the number of defects exceeds 3 is 1 minus the CDF for 3:

$$P(X > 3) = 1 - F(3)$$

Example 5.3   Cumulative Distribution Function

Continuing the example of defective parts, suppose that Richard Pernecky wants to know the probability that at most two parts in the sample of four are defective.

Solution   The CDF provides the solution: Using the probability distribution in Table 5.2 gives

$$F(2) = P(X \leq 2)$$
$$= f(0) + f(1) + f(2)$$
$$= 0.4096 + 0.4096 + 0.1536$$
$$= 0.9728$$

Also, we see that there is only a 2.78% probability that there are more than two defects in the sample. Again using Table 5.2, the probability that the number of defects is greater than 0 is given by

$$P(X > 0) = 1 - F(0)$$
$$= 1 - 0.4096$$
$$= 0.5904$$

Practice Problem 5.1: Cumulative Distribution Function

Prepare the cumulative distribution function for the discrete random variable in Table 5.2. To reinforce your understanding, show how the CDF $F(x)$ can be used to compute the probability that the number of defective parts in Table 5.2 is either 1, 2, or 3.

The solutions for all Practice Problems are given at the end of the chapter.

5.3 PROPERTIES OF DISCRETE RANDOM VARIABLES

In this section two important properties of discrete random variables are developed. These are the expected value or mean, which is a measure of central tendency, and the variance, which is a measure of variability. Expected value and variance have specific mathematical definitions and are used to compare probability models and systems modeled by probability distribution functions.

5.3.1 Expected Value or Mean

Expected values or means are used to summarize the central tendency of probability distributions (Key Idea 5.4). The mean is the long-term average outcome of the process being studied. Thus if we wanted one number to define the process outcome, the mean would usually be used. The mean is computed by weighting all possible outcomes by their probability of occurrence. In this sense it is the best single value to describe the set of outcomes.

Key Idea 5.4: Expected Value

The **expected value**, $E[X]$, or **mean**, μ, is the central tendency of a discrete random variable, defined as

$$\mu = E[X] = \sum x_i f(x_i) \qquad \text{all } x_i$$

Example 5.4   Expected Value: Discrete Random Variable

North Star Stove's banker has asked for a single value for the return on investment. Select the appropriate summary measure and compute its value.

Solution   Given the possible returns and their probabilities as described in Table 5.1, the mean is the best value to submit to the banker. The mean for the discrete random variable is

$$\mu = E[X] = \sum_{x=1000}^{x=7000} xf(x)$$
$$= 1000(1 \times 0.30 + 3 \times 0.20 + 5 \times 0.40 + 7 \times 0.10)$$
$$= 3600$$

The mean or expected return on investment for North Star Stove's production project is $3600.   □

Practice Problem 5.2: Expected Values

Compute the expected values for the discrete random variable defined in Table 5.2.   □

5.3.2 Variance and Standard Deviation

Definition of the system represented by a probability model requires a measure of variability in addition to a measure of central tendency—the mean μ. A smaller variance (and smaller standard deviation) implies a narrower range for most outcomes. Investors and business managers often associate variance with risk. A large variance implies a greater chance of high returns but also a greater chance of low returns. A small variance implies that neither a very high nor a very low return is likely. Venture capital funds have large variance on their returns, whereas conservative retirement funds have a low variance.

The squared deviation from the mean is used (see Key Idea 5.5) so that variations below and above the mean contribute equally to the measure of variability. The variation of each random variable value is weighted by the probability of occurrence. In this sense the variance provides the best average measure of the squared deviation. Note, however, that a random variable that is far away from the mean will make a large contribution to the variance. The standard deviation converts the measure of variability to the same units as the random variable. Later, we see how the standard deviation can be used to compute probabilities.

Key Idea 5.5: Variance and Standard Deviation

The **variability** of a random variable is defined by the variance, σ^2, and the standard deviation, σ:

$$\sigma^2 = E[(X - \mu)^2]$$
$$= \sum (x_i - \mu)^2 f(x_i)$$
$$\sigma = \sqrt{\sigma^2}$$

Example 5.5   Variance for a Discrete Random Variable

Mark Goede is interested in the variability of returns for the proposed North Star Stoves investment. Select the appropriate measure of variability and compute its value.

Solution   Using the investment model defined in Table 5.1, the variance computation for the discrete random variable is

$$\sigma^2 = E[(X - \mu)^2]$$
$$= \sum (x_i - \mu)^2 f(x_i)$$
$$= (1000^2)[(1 - 3.60)^2 0.30 + (3 - 3.60)^2 0.20$$
$$+ (5 - 3.60)^2 0.40 + (7 - 3.60)^2 0.10]$$
$$= (1000^2)(2.028 + 0.072 + 0.784 + 1.156)$$
$$= 4,040,000$$

and

$$\sigma = 2010$$

The variance, 4,040,000, or the standard deviation, 2010, could be compared with the variances or standard deviations from other projects and used to rank projects in terms of risk (e.g., larger variance implies larger risk).   □

5.3.3 Simplified Variance Computation

The work to compute variances can be reduced by applying some simple algebra to the expected value expression for variance (Key Idea 5.6).

$$\sigma^2 = E[(X - \mu)^2]$$
$$= E[X^2 - 2X\mu + \mu^2]$$
$$= E[X^2] - 2\mu\mu + \mu^2$$
$$= E[X^2] - \mu^2$$

In this development we see some of the typical mathematical operations that can be performed using the expected value operator, E. Expressions such as $(X - \mu)^2$ can be expanded within the E operator. The E operator for a linear combination such as

$$E[X^2 - 2X\mu + \mu^2]$$

can be assigned to each individual term and constants can be moved from within the operator,

$$E[X^2] - 2\mu E[X] + \mu^2 = E[X^2] - 2\mu^2 + \mu^2 = E[X^2] - \mu^2$$

These operations on expressions involving the expected value operator reduce the amount of tedious arithmetic.

Key Idea 5.6: Algebraic Simplification

A shortcut formula to compute the variance of a discrete random variable is

$$\sigma^2 = E[(X - \mu)^2]$$
$$= E[X^2] - \mu^2$$

Example 5.6   Simplified Variance Calculation

Using Key Idea 5.6, the variance can be obtained by computing $E[X^2]$ and then combining it with μ, which was computed previously. Confirm this calculation for the example in Table 5.1.

Solution

$$E[X^2] = \sum x_i^2 f(x_i)$$
$$= (1000^2)(1^2 \times 0.30 + 3^2 \times 0.20 + 5^2 \times 0.40 + 7^2 \times 0.10)$$
$$= 17.0 \times 1000^2$$

Combining with $\mu = 3.60 \times 1000$, the variance is

$$\sigma^2 = E[X^2] - \mu^2$$
$$= (1000^2)(17.0 - 3.60^2)$$
$$= 4{,}040{,}000$$

and

$$\sigma = 2010 \qquad \qquad \square$$

Practice Problem 5.3: Variance Computation

Compute the variance for the discrete random variable defined in Table 5.2. $\square$

Problem Exercises

5.1   The number of refrigerators sold by Olson's Appliances each day is:

Number of refrigerators	0	1	2	3	4
Probability	0.15	0.21	0.35	0.17	0.12

   (a) Draw the probability function.
   (b) Draw the cumulative probability function.
   (c) What is the probability of 2 or more sales?

5.2   Refer to the probability distribution of refrigerators sold by Olson's Appliances in Problem 5.1. Determine:
   (a) The mean daily sales of refrigerators.
   (b) The variance and standard deviation of daily refrigerator sales.

5.3   The number of bicycles brought in for repair at Sam's Cycles each day is:

Number of bicycles	0	1	2	3	4	5
Probability	0.07	0.25	0.28	0.19	0.12	0.09

   (a) Draw the probability function.
   (b) Draw the cumulative probability function.
   (c) What is the probability of 3 or more bicycles?

5.4   Refer to the probability distribution of bicycle repairs at Sam's Cycles in Problem 5.3. Determine:
   (a) The mean daily number of bicycle repairs.
   (b) The variance and standard deviation of daily bicycle repairs.

5.5   Flip a coin three times and count the number of heads.
   (a) What is the probability distribution of the number of heads if the probability of a head on each toss is 0.50 and the flips are independent? (*Hint:* Write all the possible combinations of heads and tails in the sets of three coin flips.)
   (b) What is the probability of the number of heads you actually obtained?

(c) Repeat the three-coin-flip 20 times and record the number of heads from each three-coin-flip. Compare the distribution of number of heads you obtained in 20 trials with the probability distribution from part (a). Why are they not exactly the same?

5.6   Consider the three-coin-flip from Problem 5.5. Determine:
(a) The mean number of heads for the probability distribution.
(b) The variance of the number of heads.

5.7   A shipment of CDs are received at Sound's Music Store. The supplier has indicated that 50% of the CDs contain classical music. You randomly select 3 CDs from the shipment and check each label to determine if it is a classical music recording.
(a) What is the probability distribution function for the number of classical CDs in your random sample of 3? (*Hint:* Write all the possible combinations of classical and nonclassical CDs in sets of 3 observations.)
(b) Construct the cumulative probability distribution.
(c) What is the probability of 2 or more classical CDs?

5.8   Refer to Problem 5.7, in which the shipment of CDs to Sound Music Store was analyzed. Determine:
(a) The expected value of the number of classical CDs in the sample.
(b) The variance of the number of classical CDs.

5.4 PARAMETRIC PROBABILITY DISTRIBUTIONS

Next, parametric probability distributions will be developed (Key Idea 5.7). Most applications of probability and statistics use a parametric probability distribution, which provides a standard approach and an easier computation of probabilities.

Key Idea 5.7: Parametric Probability Distributions

Parametric probability distribution functions (pdf's) include one or more parameters that can be selected to define a large number of different pdf's, all of which have a similar form.

In the following sections we study some important discrete parametric probability distributions for business applications. First, discrete parametric distributions, including the Bernoulli, binomial, and Poisson, are presented. In Chapter 6, after continuous random variables have been developed, the exponential and normal distributions are presented. In later chapters additional parametric distributions are introduced as they are needed for problem solving. Parametric probability distributions provide standard model forms that simplify problem analysis and make possible the development of standard solutions. Carefully study the distribution assumptions and the applications presented in this chapter. As you will discover, obtaining probability values for parametric distributions is not difficult. In fact, most probabilities can be obtained from a table or by using a simple computer command. However, developing skills in distribution choice and application will require problem-solving experience and a good understanding of the distributions. We begin with the simple Bernoulli distribution and move to more difficult distributions as our understanding increases.

5.5 BERNOULLI RANDOM VARIABLE

The Bernoulli random variable (Key Idea 5.8) is the simplest distribution and is used to derive more complex distributions. The process being modeled is called a *Bernoulli process* with interpretations such as yes or no, success or failure, on or off. The Bernoulli random variable would be coded yes ($X = 1$), no ($X = 0$); success ($X = 1$), failure ($X = 0$); on ($X = 1$), off ($X = 0$). Early work on this distribution was done by James Bernoulli (1654–1705), one of a Swiss family of mathematicians and scientists, for whom the process and the random variable are named.

Key Idea 5.8: Bernoulli Random Variable

The **Bernoulli random variable** has two values: $x = 0$ and $x = 1$. The probability that the random variable X is equal to 1 is given by a parameter, π, where $0 < \pi < 1$, and the probability that the random variable is equal to 0 is given by $1 - \pi$.

$$P(X = x \mid \pi) = f(x \mid \pi) = \pi^x (1 - \pi)^{1-x}$$
$$\mu_X = \pi$$
$$\sigma_X^2 = \pi(1 - \pi)$$

The Bernoulli distribution provides the first example of a discrete parametric probability distribution. It represents an entire family of probability distributions, which differ only in the value of the parameter π. Following are examples of its application.

1. During election periods, voters will be asked if they support a particular candidate in an election poll. Responses for each voter are modeled yes ($X = 1$) or no ($X = 0$). The parameter π is the probability that a voter will vote for the candidate. The probability distribution function is

$$f(0) = P(X = 0) = 1 - \pi$$
$$f(1) = P(X = 1) = \pi$$

or in parametric form,

$$f(x) = \pi^x (1 - \pi)^{1-x}$$

The value of π is often obtained by using the relative frequency concept from Chapter 4 (Key Idea 4.5).

2. A part produced in a manufacturing process is either acceptable ($X = 1$) or not acceptable ($X = 0$). The Bernoulli probability distribution function is

$$f(x) = \pi^x (1 - \pi)^{1-x}$$

The parameter π is defined as the proportion of acceptable parts produced by the process.

Results such as expected values and variances can be derived as a function of the parameter. The power of parametric probability distributions will become clear as we work with more complex examples. The expected value and variance for the Bernoulli random variable are derived as follows:

$$\mu_X = \sum_{x=0}^{x=1} x f(x)$$
$$= 0(1 - \pi) + 1\pi$$
$$= \pi$$
$$\sigma_X^2 = E[(x - \mu_X)^2]$$
$$= \sum_{x=0}^{x=1} (x - \mu_X)^2 f(x)$$
$$= (0 - \pi)^2 (1 - \pi) + (1 - \pi)^2 \pi$$
$$= \pi(1 - \pi)$$

5.6 BINOMIAL PROBABILITY DISTRIBUTION FUNCTION

The binomial probability distribution (Key Idea 5.9) is the most used discrete parametric probability distribution for business and economic applications. Computation of probabilities using the binomial distribution requires two important assumptions:

1. Each of the trials must have the same probability of success. The process being modeled should be examined to ensure that the assumption of a constant probability is reasonable, given the amount of information available. Thus assuming that the probability of a pedestrian death after being struck by a bicycle or a car is the same would be wrong. However, assuming that the probability of a pedestrian death after being struck by any vehicle is the same would be a reasonable assumption if we did not know what kind of vehicle would strike the pedestrian.

2. Each of the trials is independent. The process must be examined to ensure that a success or a failure in one trial does not change the probability of the next trial. One must also assume that there is not a cyclical phenomenon that changes the probability of success for a subset of trials. Thus the probability of a customer arriving at a restaurant for lunch is not independent of time.

Key Idea 5.9: Binomial Probability Distribution

The **binomial probability distribution** defines the probability of X successes given n independent Bernoulli trials, all with the same probability of success, equal to π. In mathematical terms,

$$P(X = x \mid \pi, n) = C_x^n \pi^x (1 - \pi)^{n-x}$$

where n is the number of independent Bernoulli trials and π is the probability of a success for each Bernoulli trial. C_x^n is the number of combinations of n items taken x at a time:

$$C_x^n = \frac{n!}{(n - x)! \, x!}$$

The mean number of successes is

$$\mu_X = n\pi$$

and the variance is

$$\sigma_X^2 = n\pi(1 - \pi)$$

This distribution has numerous applications, including:

1. *Worker's reporting.* Computing the probability that 8 employees out of a work team of 10 will arrive at work on a particular day given that the probability of each worker arriving is 0.90. In this example there are $n = 10$ trials with probability of success, $\pi = 0.90$. We assume that all workers have the same desire and opportunity to come to work and that workers do not influence each other's decision to arrive at work.

2. *Airline seating.* What is the probability that you will be "bumped" from an airline seat? An airline has 16 seats available on a given flight and sells 20 tickets for those seats. Airlines know from their experience with hundreds of thousands of flights the probability π that passengers will not arrive for a flight, and thus, if possible, they sell more tickets than there are seats on the plane. The number to sell depends on the probability of various numbers of passengers arriving at the gate. If more passengers than the number of available seats arrive, the airline must pay a financial penalty or provide free tickets. If fewer passengers arrive, the airline loses revenue. Define X as the number of ticket holders who actually arrive for a flight. In this case we assume that $n = 20$ independent Bernoulli trials are conducted. There are, of course, events that could invalidate the assumption of independent arrivals, such as a major traffic jam on the road to the airport. If more than 16 persons arrive for the flight, one or more people

will be bumped from the flight and the airline will have to pay a penalty. What is the probability that at least one person will be bumped? (If you are bumped, you may be angry because you will not get home when you want, or you may be happy because you are getting a free ticket.)

3. *Sales samples.* A store owner knows that 40% of the people who ask to see a television set will actually purchase a set. The store owner anticipates that 50 people will ask to see a television set on a particular Saturday. What is the probability that potential sales will be lost if he has exactly 25 sets in the store? For this problem there are $n = 50$ trials, each with probability $\pi = 0.40$ of success. If more than $X = 25$ wish to purchase, sales will be lost. The store owner assumes that π is the same for all customers.

4. *Acceptance sampling.* A company receives 1,000,000 computer chips and the supplier guarantees that there are less than 100,000 defective chips. To check quality the company tests a random sample of 10 computer chips. If two or more chips are defective, the company rejects the shipment. The company president wishes to know the probability of accepting bad shipments using this rule.

5.6.1 Development of the Binomial

The binomial probability distribution will be developed using a simple example.

Example 5.7   College Admissions Acceptance Probability

Three days before the opening of school a college is notified that three first-year students have withdrawn. As a result, the college has three first-year class openings and it offers admission to four students. Experience indicates that 60% of the students offered admission will actually attend. What is the probability that exactly three of the four students will attend?

Solution   The problem can be solved by examining the sample space. Consider a typical event using 1 to represent attendance and 0 to represent nonattendance:

$$[1 \quad 0 \quad 1 \quad 1]$$

All but the second student attends. Because student decisions are independent, the probability of this event—three out of four deciding to attend—is computed by multiplying the probabilities of attendance for each student:

$$P(\text{event}[1 \quad 0 \quad 1 \quad 1] = 0.60 \times (1 - 0.60) \times 0.60 \times 0.60 = 0.0864)$$

The event

$$[0 \quad 1 \quad 1 \quad 1]$$

also has a probability of 0.0864, because the same numbers ($0.40 \times 0.60 \times 0.60 \times 0.60$) are multiplied to obtain the probability. Continuing with this reasoning, the probability of each of the events, which have three students out of four attending, is

$$0.60^3 0.4^{(4-3)} = 0.0864$$

Next we determine the number of different combinations of one 0 and three 1's. That number can be obtained using the counting formula for the number of combinations of four items taken three at a time:

$$C_3^4 = \binom{4}{3}$$

$$= \frac{4!}{(4-3)!\,3!}$$

$$= \frac{4 \times 3 \times 2 \times 1}{1 \times 3 \times 2 \times 1}$$

$$= 4$$

Combining the probability calculation with the counting formula, we find that

$$P(3 \text{ successes}) = C_3^4 (0.60)^3 (1 - 0.60)^1$$

$$= 4 \times 0.0864$$

$$= 0.3456 \qquad \square$$

The definition of the binomial implies that we are not concerned about the order of successes in the n independent trials. This result can be generalized to obtain the binomial probability distribution function:

$$P(X = x \mid \pi, n) = f(x \mid \pi, n)$$

$$= C_x^n \pi^x (1 - \pi)^{n-x}$$

$$= \frac{n!}{(n-x)!\,x!} \pi^x (1 - \pi)^{n-x}$$

where n is the number of independent Bernoulli trials, x is the random variable for number of successes, and π is the probability of success for each trial.

The complete binomial probability distribution function for $n = 4$ and $\pi = 0.60$ is presented in Table 5.3. Notice that the probability for each value of x is computed as the product of the probability of an event that contains x successes and $(n - x)$ failures multiplied by the number of different events that result in x successes.

The computed probability distribution functions for many different values of n and π are readily available in most statistics books. In this book, Table A.5 presents the binomial probability distribution function and Table A.6 presents the cumulative binomial probability distribution function.

Computer statistical packages can also be used to compute binomial probabilities quickly and easily. For example, in Minitab for Windows the probability of 4 successes in 5 trials with $\pi = 0.4$ can be computed either by [**Calc** > **Prob. Distributions** > **Binomial**] or by session commands:

MTB > pdf 4
SUBC > Binomial 5 0.4

TABLE 5.3   Binomial Probability Distribution for $n = 4$ and $\pi = 0.60$

x	$f(x \mid n = 4, \pi = 0.60)$	$C_x^n \pi^x (1-\pi)^{n-x}$	$f(x)$	$F(x)$
0	$\dfrac{4!}{(4-0)!\,0!}\pi^0(1-\pi)^{4-0}$	1×0.0256	0.0256	0.0256
1	$\dfrac{4!}{(4-1)!\,1!}\pi^1(1-\pi)^{4-1}$	4×0.0384	0.1536	0.1792
2	$\dfrac{4!}{(4-2)!\,2!}\pi^2(1-\pi)^{4-2}$	6×0.0576	0.3456	0.5248
3	$\dfrac{4!}{(4-3)!\,3!}\pi^3(1-\pi)^{4-3}$	4×0.0864	0.3456	0.8704
4	$\dfrac{4!}{(4-4)!\,4!}\pi^4(1-\pi)^{4-4}$	1×0.1296	0.1296	1.0000

The resulting probability is

$$P(X = 4 \mid \pi = 0.40, n = 5) = 0.0768$$

5.6.2 Cumulative Binomial Probability Distribution Function

In many problems we want to know the probability that X is less than or equal to a given value x. In this case the cumulative binomial $F(x)$ should be used (Key Idea 5.10). An example is shown in Table 5.3.

Key Idea 5.10: Cumulative Binomial Distribution

$$F(x) = P(X \leq x \mid \pi, n)$$

$$= \sum_{x_i=0}^{x} f(x_i \mid \pi, n)$$

$$= \sum_{x_i=0}^{x} C_{x_i}^n \pi^{x_i}(1-\pi)^{n-x_i}$$

5.6.3 Mean and Variance

The mean, μ, and variance, σ^2, are computed by using the procedure presented in Section 5.3:

$$\mu = E[X]$$

$$= \sum_{i=1}^{n} x_i P(X = x_i \mid \pi, n)$$

$$= \sum_{i=1}^{n} x_i \frac{n!}{x_i!(n - x_i)!} \pi^{x_i}(1 - \pi)^{n - x_i}$$

$$= n\pi$$

$$\sigma^2 = E[(X - \mu_X)^2]$$

$$= \sum_{i=1}^{n} (x_i - n\pi)^2 P(X = x_i \mid \pi, n)$$

$$= \sum_{i=1}^{n} (x_i - n\pi)^2 \frac{n!}{x_i!(n - x_i)!} \pi^{x_i}(1 - \pi)^{n - x_i}$$

$$= n\pi(1 - \pi)$$

The algebra required to carry out these computations is complex and tedious. An easier way to accomplish the task is presented next.

5.6.4 Simplified Computation of Binomial Mean and Variance

Instead of computing the mean and variance directly using the equations above, we can take advantage of the fact that the binomial random variable is the sum of n independent Bernoulli random variables. Let x_i $(i = 1, \ldots, n)$ be a sample of n independent Bernoulli random variables and define X as a binomial random variable:

$$X = X_1 + X_2 + \cdots + X_n$$

The mean for the sum, X, of n independent random variables, $X_i, i = 1, \ldots, n$, is the sum of the means for each X_i. Similarly, the variance for the sum, X, is the sum of the variances for each X_i. The mean for a Bernoulli random variable is π and the variance is $\pi(1 - \pi)$ (Key Idea 5.8). Therefore, the mean and variance for the binomial random variable are

$$\mu_X = E[X_1 + X_2 + \cdots + X_n]$$
$$= \pi + \pi + \cdots + \pi$$
$$= n\pi$$
$$\sigma_X^2 = \sigma^2(X_1 + X_2 + \cdots + X_n)$$
$$= \pi(1 - \pi) + \pi(1 - \pi) + \cdots + \pi(1 - \pi)$$
$$= n\pi(1 - \pi)$$

By using the sum of independent random variables, we were able to present a clear and direct development instead of the more complex development indicated above. This is another example in which more powerful tools provide us with clear and simple results.

Does It Make Sense?

The assumption of independent events is critical when the binomial distribution is used. Recall that in developing the binomial probability we multiplied together the probability of each Bernoulli event to obtain the probability for the total of x successes. If the Bernoulli events are not independent, the binomial distribution will not provide the correct probabilities. In applications, the independence assumption needs to be considered carefully. If the probabilities of the Bernoulli events change with the total number of events or for different events, the binomial is not appropriate.   □

Example 5.8   Workers Reporting

What is the probability that 8 of 10 workers will arrive at work on Monday morning given that the probability of each worker arriving is 0.90? We assume that all workers have the same desire and opportunity and that workers do not influence each other's decision to report.

Solution   Compute the probability of $x = 8$ successes out of 10 independent Bernoulli trials. We assume independent decisions and that the probability of reporting to work is 0.90 for each worker. It is possible that the probability for each worker is different. However, determining individual probabilities would require extensive testing. A constant $\pi = 0.90$ is the best number given the available information. Similar assumptions in comparable problems have resulted in correct answers. The assumption of independent decisions is more likely to be suspect and should be considered carefully in applied problems. After analysis of the assumptions, computation of the probability can be made using Key Idea 5.9:

$$P(X = 8 \mid \pi = 0.90, n = 10) = \frac{10!}{(10 - 8)! \, 8!} 0.90^8 (1 - 0.90)^2$$

$$= \frac{10 \times 9}{2 \times 1} 0.90^8 0.10^2$$

$$= 0.1937$$

Most analysts use tables such as Table A.5 instead of computing the probabilities from the equation. Alternatively, analysts may use a computer or calculator programmed to make the Key Idea 5.9 computations.   □

Example 5.9   Airline Seating

An airline has 16 seats remaining seven days before a given flight departs. They sell 20 tickets for those seats. If more than 16 people arrive for the flight, one or more persons will be bumped from the flight and the airline will have to pay a penalty. Assume that past data indicate that 80% of the people with tickets will actually arrive for the flight. What is the probability that at least one person will be bumped?

Solution   In this problem we assume that there are $n = 20$ independent Bernoulli trials. An unusual situation such as a major traffic jam on the road to the airport could invalidate the independence assumption. We need to compute the sum of the probabilities of 17, 18, 19, and 20 people arriving for the flight. The probability, $\pi = 0.80$, that people will arrive for the flight was estimated using the relative frequency concept developed in Chapter 4. The solution is

$$P(X \geq 17 \mid \pi = 0.80, n = 20) = \sum_{x=17}^{x=20} P(x \mid \pi = 0.80, n = 20)$$

$$= 1 - \sum_{x=0}^{x=16} f(x \mid 0.80, 20)$$

$$= 0.4114$$

This value was obtained from Table A.6 for the cumulative binomial distribution.

☐

Example 5.10   Acceptance Sampling

A company receives 1,000,000 computer chips and the supplier guarantees that there are fewer than 100,000 defective chips. To check quality the company tests a random sample of 10 computer chips. If two or more chips are defective, the company rejects the shipment. The company president wishes to know the probability of accepting bad shipments using this rule.

Solution   In this problem a shipment will be accepted if there is at most one defective chip in the random sample of 10 chips. A bad shipment has 100,000 or more defective chips. In problems such as this, statisticians compute the probability for the extreme case (i.e., the probability of accepting a shipment that has 100,000 defective chips). For shipments with more than 100,000 defectives, the probability of obtaining more than 1 defective increases, and thus the probability of accepting a "bad" shipment decreases. We demonstrate this below.

First compute a value for the parameter π using the relative frequency concept. If there are 100,000 defective chips in the shipment of 1,000,000,

$$\pi = \frac{100,000}{1,000,000} = 0.10$$

The probability of accepting a bad shipment is

$$P(X \leq 1) = \sum_{x=0}^{x=1} P(x \mid \pi = 0.10, n = 10)$$

$$= f(0 \mid \pi = 0.10, n = 10) + f(1 \mid \pi = 0.10, n = 10)$$

$$= 0.3487 + 0.3874$$

$$= 0.7361$$

If there were 110,000 defectives, the probability of accepting a bad shipment would be

$$P(X \leq 1) = \sum_{x=0}^{x=1} P(x \mid \pi = 0.11, n = 10)$$

$$= f(0 \mid \pi = 0.11, n = 10) + f(1 \mid \pi = 0.11, n = 10)$$

$$= 0.3118 + 0.3854$$

$$= 0.6972$$

This is smaller than the probability when the number of defective chips is 100,000.

If the shipment contained 90,000 defectives, the probability of accepting the good shipment would be

$$P(X \leq 1 \mid \pi = 0.09, n = 10) = f(0) + f(1)$$

$$= 0.3894 + 0.3851$$

$$= 0.7745$$

and the probability of rejecting a good shipment would be

$$P(\text{reject}) = 1 - 0.7745 = 0.2255$$

After examining these results, a thoughtful manager would raise serious questions about a sampling strategy that resulted in accepting bad shipments about 74% of the time. As a first step she might change the rule to "accept shipment only if zero defective chips are found in the sample of 10 chips." This would reduce the probability of accepting bad shipments to

$$P(x = 0 \mid \pi = 0.10, n = 10) = 0.3487$$

However, if this rule were applied and there were only 90,000 defective chips, the probability of rejecting a good shipment would be:

$$P(x > 0 \mid \pi = 0.09, n = 10) = 1 - P(x = 0 \mid \pi = 0.09, n = 10)$$

$$= 1 - 0.3894$$

$$= 0.6106$$

Thus we see that 61% of the time we would reject a good shipment that contained only 9% defective chips, compared to rejecting good shipments 23% of the time under the old rule. We would accept only 39% of good shipments. Here we see the classic problem of choosing a correct rule. The rule chosen would be influenced by whether you are the seller or the purchaser of computer chips. The probability of both rejecting bad shipments and accepting good shipments could be increased by using a larger sample size.   □

Does It Make Sense?

Acceptance sampling with small samples has become less popular because of the large probability of incorrect decisions. Modern quality control applications emphasize process monitoring to improve quality instead of accepting or rejecting completed

batches. We discuss this example further and present modern quality control procedures in Chapter 18.   ☐

Practice Problem 5.4: Cake Production

The Fancy Cake shop must decide how many cakes to produce each day. The probability that a customer will purchase a cake is $\pi = 0.4$. Suppose that 10 customers
come into the store on a particular morning and their decisions to purchase a cake or
not purchase are independent. Compute the probabilities that:

(a) More than 6 cakes are purchased.
(b) Less than 3 cakes are purchased.
(c) More than 2 and less than 7 are purchased.   ☐

5.6.5 Distribution of Proportions

In many applied problems, based on binomial assumptions, we wish to compute the
probability of the proportion of successes instead of the number of successes (Key
Idea 5.11).

Key Idea 5.11: Proportion Random Variables

The probability of binomial proportions is exactly equal to the corresponding sum, X, of successes. Expressed mathematically, we have

$$\hat{P} = \frac{x}{n}$$

$$P(\hat{P} \mid \pi, n) = P(x \mid \pi, n)$$

where

$$x = \sum_{i=1}^{n} x_i \qquad x_i = 0, 1$$

$$\mu_{\hat{p}} = \pi$$

$$\sigma_{\hat{p}}^2 = \frac{\pi(1 - \pi)}{n}$$

---

1. *Workers reporting.* Suppose that an employer wishes to know the probability that
   80% of 10 workers, instead of 8 of the 10 workers, will report for work. This is
   the same problem because 8 of 10 is exactly the same as 80% of 10.
2. *Airline seating.* The airline might wish to determine the probability that 85%,
   90%, 95%, or 100% of the 20 persons who are sold seats will actually arrive

for the flight. These probabilities are exactly the same as the probabilities that 17, 18, 19, or 20 of the 20 persons will arrive for the flight. This result occurs because 17 of 20 is exactly 85%, 18 of 20 is exactly 90%, and so on.

3. *College enrollments.* Finally, suppose that the admissions department wishes to know the probability that 75% of the four applicants offered admission will actually accept. Again, this is the same as three of four applicants accepting admission.

We are pleased to find that this section does not require us to learn any new results, even though it provides applications for a large set of new problems. The mean and variance of sample proportions are developed as follows:

$$\hat{P} = \frac{X_1 + X_2 + \cdots + X_n}{n} = \frac{X}{n}$$

where the X_i's are Bernoulli random variables with mean π and variance $\pi(1 - \pi)$. Therefore, using the mean and variance for sample means, we see that

$$\mu_{\hat{P}} = E\left[\frac{X}{n}\right]$$

$$= \frac{n\pi}{n}$$

$$= \pi$$

$$\sigma_{\hat{P}}^2 = \sigma^2\left(\frac{X}{n}\right)$$

$$= \left(\frac{1}{n}\right)^2 \sigma_X^2$$

$$= \left(\frac{1}{n}\right)^2 n\pi(1 - \pi)$$

$$= \frac{\pi(1 - \pi)}{n}$$

Again, linear combinations of random variables provide important results for both specific applications and for the theory of random samples.

Problem Exercises

5.9   Shirley Smith has just flipped 10 silver dollars. Determine the probability of:
(a) Exactly 4 heads.
(b) Exactly 6 tails.
(c) More than 5 heads.
(d) Three or fewer heads.

5.10   During a particular month of the baseball season, Ken Griffey, Jr. had a batting average of 300 (30 hits out of 100 at bat). In a particular game he was at bat 5 times. Assume that hits are independent events. Determine the probability that he gets:
(a) Three hits.
(b) Fewer than 2 hits.
(c) Sketch the probability distribution function.

5.11   Your health insurance claims processor has written your medical clinic a letter complaining that 30% of the claims from your clinic have errors. They ask that this problem be corrected or they will delay payment. To check on the error rate of your claims, you obtain a random sample of 12 claims. Determine the probability of:
(a) Exactly 5 claims with errors.
(b) More than 5 claims.
(c) Three claims or less with errors.

5.12   Refer to Problem 5.11 concerning errors on insurance claims. Suppose that in the random sample of 12 there are only 2 claims with errors. What is the probability of 2 or fewer claims with errors if the insurance company is correct?

5.13   The Great Planes Airline has 80% of its flights arriving on time. Over the next three days, George Brown, a product representative, has a series of 7 flights scheduled on Great Planes Air. Determine the probability that:
(a) Three flights will arrive late.
(b) Two or fewer flights will arrive late.
(c) Five or more flights will arrive late.
(d) Suppose that on the 7 flights George arrives late five times. What should George think about the claim of 80% on-time flights?

5.14   A professional football team has found that 30% of the new players that it signs out of college actually play for more than one year. During a recent year 20 new players were signed to contracts. Determine the probability that:
(a) Eight or more will play for more than one year.
(b) Six or fewer will play for more than one year.
(c) For the 20 players signed last year, exactly 5 are still playing this second year. What is the probability of this event?

5.15   Andrea Johnson is the manager of Speedy Mufflers and Lube, which provides automobile service on a drive-in basis. Andrea believes that on 60% of the days, more than 12 cars will arrive for muffler replacement. What is the probability that a majority of the next five days will have more than 12 cars for muffler replacement?

5.16   A professional football team has found that 30% of the new players that it signs out of college actually play for more than one year. During a recent year 20 new players were signed to contracts. Determine:
(a) The mean number of players who actually play for more than one year.
(b) The variance of the number of players who play for more than one year.

5.17   Shirley Harder believes that 25% of the automobile insurance claims submitted to her regional office will have an error that requires a call to the claims examiner. A random sample of 50 claims is selected. If Shirley is correct, what are the mean and variance of the number of claims with errors?

5.18   A company receives a shipment of 100,000 computer processor chips. The company tests a random sample of 20 chips and will accept the shipment only if 17 or more are not defective. Determine the probability that:
(a) The company will accept a shipment with 10% defectives.
(b) The company will accept a shipment with 20% defective chips.
(c) A shipment with 30% defective chips will be accepted.

5.7 POISSON PROBABILITY DISTRIBUTION

The Poisson probability distribution was first proposed by Simeon Poisson (1781–1840) in a book published in 1837. An increased number of applications began to appear early in the twentieth century. The Poisson probability distribution function (Key Idea 5.12) is an important discrete probability distribution for a number of applications, including the following:

1. The probability of x failures in a large computer system. Such a system has a very large number of components that could fail.

2. The probability of x holes or blemishes in a large continuous roll of woven cloth. If the cloth is sold to a manufacturer of shirts, each defect is likely to result in an imperfect shirt that cannot be sold for full price.

3. The probability of x ships arriving at a loading facility during a 6-hour loading period. This is a very important problem because it influences the number of

---

Key Idea 5.12: Poisson Probability Distribution

The **Poisson probability distribution** computes the probability of X occurrences over an interval of time or space given that the average number of occurrences is a constant λ.

Expressed mathematically,

$$P(X = x \mid \lambda) = f(x \mid \lambda) = \frac{\lambda^x e^{-\lambda}}{x!}$$

where x is the Poisson random variable, λ the parameter, average number of occurrences, and e the base for natural logarithms, $e \approx 2.71828$. The mean and variance are both equal to the parameter λ:

$$\mu_X = \lambda$$

$$\sigma_X^2 = \lambda$$

The parameter λ is specified for a particular time and/or space and is in the same units as x.

loading facilities that should be built and the number of loading crews that should be hired. If more ships arrive than can be loaded by the facilities and crews, costly delays for the ships will occur. Alternatively, if fewer ships arrive, facilities and crews will be idle, thus wasting expensive economic resources.

4. The probability that x customers would like to purchase a loaf of "Friday bread" at the Quality Bakery on a particular Friday. The baker is very interested in this question because if he produces too many, the excess cannot be sold, and if he does not produce enough, he has lost sales and gained unhappy customers.

The Poisson probability distribution can be derived by first dividing the interval into a very large number of subintervals. We assume that the probability of an occurrence in any subinterval is very small and constant for all subintervals. In addition, there can be no more than one occurrence in each subinterval, and occurrences are independent. Using this model, we can define the number of occurrences X as equal to the sum over a very large number of independent Bernoulli random variables—one for each subinterval. Following this approach, the Poisson can be derived from the binomial pdf by assuming that n approaches infinity and π approaches 0, with $n\pi = \lambda$.

Does It Make Sense?

Both the binomial and Poisson probability distributions compute the probability of the number of occurrences of specific events. The Poisson parameter is the average number of occurrences, λ; given a large number of trials, in contrast, the binomial parameter is the probability, π, of an occurrence in each of n trials. If you know the rate or mean of the occurrences, λ, use the Poisson. If you know the probability, π, of a single occurrence and the number of trials, use the binomial.   □

5.7.1 Computing Probabilities

Tables.   Because the Poisson is a parametric probability distribution, the probabilities have been computed and placed in tables, just as they were for binomial probabilities. The probabilities for each of the discrete occurrences can be obtained from Table A.7, and cumulative Poisson probabilities are given in Table A.8.

Computer statistical package computation.   Poisson probabilities can also be computed using statistical computer packages. If you are using Minitab for Windows, Poisson probabilities are found by selecting [**Calc** > **Prob. Distributions** > **Poisson**] or by a command sequence in Minitab similar to the binomial except that Poisson and the parameters are substituted where appropriate. For example, to compute the probability of $X = 4$ occurrences when the parameter $\lambda = 2.0$, the following Minitab commands are used:

> **MTB > pdf 4**
> **SUBC > Poisson 2.0**

The resulting probability is 0.0902.

5.7.2 Poisson Examples

The following examples will help increase your understanding of the Poisson distribution. You will learn faster if you work on each example at least 5 minutes before reading the solution.

Example 5.11   System Component Failure

Joe Smith, the computer center manager, reports that his computer system has experienced 10 component failures during the past 100 days. What is the probability of one or more component failures on a given day?

Solution   A modern computer system has a very large number of discrete components, each of which could fail and thus result in a computer system failure. To compute the probability of failures using the Poisson distribution, assume that each of the millions of components has the same very small probability of failure. Failure of any component results in a system failure. We also assume that the first failure does not affect the probability of a second failure.[1]

Using past experience, compute the average number of failures, or failure rate, over a fixed time period such as a day or a week. This failure rate would be set equal to the parameter λ. The probabilities of 0, 1, or more failures for the fixed time period can then be computed using the Poisson pdf with λ, its only parameter.

The mean component failure rate per day is estimated from the data to be $0.10(10/100)$. Assume that our experience supports the assumption of independent Bernoulli trials with a fixed and very small π. The question requires the probability of 1, 2, 3, or more failures. This probability can be computed by first determining the probability of 0, the complement of the desired probability, and subtracting it from 1. Using the Poisson pdf with $\lambda = 0.1$, we find that

$$P(X \geq 1 \mid \lambda = 0.1) = 1 - P(X = 0 \mid \lambda = 0.1)$$

$$= 1 - \frac{\lambda^x e^{-\lambda}}{x!}$$

$$= 1 - \frac{\lambda^0 e^{-0.1}}{0!}$$

$$= 1 - 0.9048$$

$$= 0.0952$$

where the probability of 0 component failures is obtained from Table A.7.   □

Example 5.12   Product Defects

Shirley Parsons, the quality control manager of Textiles Ltd., wants to know the probability of x holes or blemishes in large continuous rolls of woven cloth. If the cloth were sold to a manufacturer of shirts, each defect would result in an imperfect shirt that could not be sold for full price.

---

[1] In some cases these assumptions do not hold and other much more complex probability distributions must be used.

Textiles Ltd. sells rolls that contain 10,000 lineal yards of cloth. Based on past experience they know that the mean number of holes or blemishes is 2.0. The purchaser, Luxury Shirts, Inc., knows that these defects result in imperfect shirts. In addition, their sales manager points out that imperfect shirts result in bad relationships with major retail companies and can even result in loss of sales. At her urging, Luxury Shirts negotiates a contract that imposes a penalty of $2000 for every roll of cloth that contains more than four defects. Textiles Ltd. has asked you to determine the probability that this penalty will be paid for any given roll of cloth.

Solution   The Poisson pdf is the correct distribution if the cloth production line produces cloth of uniform quality and if defects are not the result of a change in the weaving machines that would cause a group of defects. Given this assumption, the probability with $\lambda = 2$ is

$$P(X > 4 \mid \lambda = 2.0) = 1 - P(X \le 4 \mid \lambda = 2.0)$$
$$= 1 - F(4)$$
$$= 1 - 0.9473$$
$$= 0.0527$$

where the cumulative Poisson probability, $F(4) = P(X \le 4 \mid \lambda = 2.0)$, is obtained from Table A.8. You inform Shirley Parsons that the penalty will be paid on about 5% of the rolls.   □

Example 5.13   Ship Arrivals at a Dock

The Canadian government has built a large grain shipping port at Churchill, Manitoba, on the Hudson Bay. This port loads boats that carry grain from western Canada to world ports. Unfortunately, the harbor is closed by ice for most of the year. This leads to some critical decisions for the port managers. Management can schedule up to seven crews, and thus seven boats could be loaded simultaneously. However, because of the remote location the cost for each crew is very high and management would like to avoid hiring crews that will be idle most of the time. If a boat arrives and all crews are busy, the boat must wait. If a boat is delayed, the boat owner may decide not to come back to this port, which could limit grain shipments and antagonize a number of farmers.

Initial analysis provides some important facts. Each boat requires 6 hours for loading by a single crew and its loading equipment. The port can remain open only 50 days per year, and during this time 500 boats are needed to transport the grain. Each additional crew costs $100,000 and each boat delay costs $5000. How many crews should be scheduled?

Solution   The final decision requires information about crew costs and delay costs. In addition, there are some political issues related to the importance of this port for western grain farmers and for Canada's trade balance. We first determine the probability of different numbers of boats arriving during the 6-hour period required for loading. These probabilities are then used to compute the expected or average cost of delays. This will provide the basis for evaluating the trade-off between boat delays and idle crews.

The problem can be modeled by assuming that there are thousands of boats in the world, any one of which has a small probability of arriving during the 6-hour loading period. Alternatively, we could assume that the probability of a boat arriving during a small time interval such as 0.1 second is constant but very small. In addition, an arrival during one small interval does not influence an arrival in another small interval. In 6 hours there are 216,000 0.1-second time intervals, and thus we have a large number of time intervals during which a boat could arrive. We would also need to assume that boats do not travel together in convoys. Since 500 boats arrive in 50 days, an average of 10 boats arrive each day, or $\lambda = 2.5$ boats per 6-hour loading period. Thus the probability of x boats arriving during a 6-hour period is defined formally by

$$P(X = x \mid \lambda = 2.5) = \frac{2.5^x e^{-2.5}}{x!}$$

Now consider the effect of scheduling exactly four crews. The probability of delaying boats is, from Table A.7,

$$P(\text{delaying 1 boat}) = P(5 \text{ boats arrive}) = 0.0668$$
$$P(\text{delaying 2 boats}) = P(6 \text{ boats arrive}) = 0.0278$$
$$P(\text{delaying 3 boats}) = P(7 \text{ boats arrive}) = 0.0099$$

The probability of idle crews is given by

$$P(1 \text{ crew idle}) = P(3 \text{ boats arrive}) = 0.2138$$
$$P(2 \text{ crews idle}) = P(2 \text{ boats arrive}) = 0.2565$$
$$P(3 \text{ crews idle}) = P(1 \text{ boats arrive}) = 0.2052$$
$$P(4 \text{ crews idle}) = P(0 \text{ boats arrive}) = 0.0821$$

In this problem the probabilities apply to the 6-hour time units required to load a boat. Thus the probability of 0 boats in a 6-hour period is 0.0821. Each shipping season contains 50 days and hence 200 6-hour time periods. The expected total number of boats delayed over the shipping season is

$$200(1 \times 0.0668 + 2 \times 0.0278 + 3 \times 0.0099) = (200)(0.1521) = 30.42$$

The probability of delaying 1 boat in a 6-hour time period is 0.0668; the probability of delaying 2 boats is 0.0278. Thus the calculation above indicates the expected number of boats that are delayed over the 200 6-hour time periods. Since each boat delay costs $5000, the total expected cost of boat delays is

$$(30.42)(\$5000) = \$152{,}100$$

Next consider the cost of boat delays if five crews are scheduled. The probability of delaying boats is

$$P(\text{delaying 1 boat}) = P(6 \text{ boats arrive}) = 0.0278$$
$$P(\text{delaying 2 boats}) = P(7 \text{ boats arrive}) = 0.0099$$

With five crews scheduled the expected cost of delays would be

$$\$5000 \times 200(1 \times 0.02778 + 2 \times 0.0099) = \$47,600$$

Thus the addition of one more crew would result in an expected savings of $104,500 ($152,100 − $47,600) in boat delay costs. Since an additional crew costs $100,000, this analysis indicates that one more crew should be added. □

Does It Make Sense?

The expenditure of $100,000 for an additional crew would be made to increase service level or the quality of the shipping facility. For this shipping facility, service or quality level is measured by the number of boats delayed. The fewer boats delayed, the higher the quality of the operation. Delaying a boat is costly, and the benefit of an additional crew is an improvement in service level and hence quality. Note that the increased idle time for the crews is not the important issue. Instead, we ask if the improved service level or quality is worth the cost. □

Example 5.14   Inventory Level

Don Klinkhammer, owner of the Quality Bakery, produces a special bread every Friday that is called "Friday bread." He wants to know how many loaves to produce each Friday. If he produces too many, the excess cannot be sold, and if he does not produce enough, there are lost sales and unhappy customers. To help with his decision, Don has asked you to compute the probability of various demand levels.

Solution   This is a classic single-period inventory problem. Perishable items are produced to meet anticipated demand for a stated time period. If demand exceeds the number produced, sales are lost. Alternatively, if the items produced exceed the number demanded, these goods cannot be carried over to a second time period.

The analysis begins by recognizing that there are thousands of people who might decide to purchase Friday bread. You do not know individual customer desires on a given Friday. You assume that the probability of each potential customer making a purchase is small and that the probabilities are equal and independent. Thus there is a constant mean purchase rate, $\lambda = nP$. From past sales data an average of $\lambda = 5.5$ loaves of Friday bread are sold each Friday.[2]

The solution requires the probabilities of excess inventory and lost sales for each production level. For example, if exactly 7 loaves are produced, there would be unsold inventory if 6 or fewer were demanded and a shortage if 8 or more loaves were demanded. These probabilities can be obtained from Table A.8.

---

[2] In some cases, average purchase rates are computed separately for different times of the year. For example, the average purchase rate might be higher in the fall than in the summer. This would merely convert the problem into two separate problems.

$$P(\text{unsold bread}) = P(x \le 6 \mid \lambda = 5.5)$$

$$= \sum_{x=0}^{6} P(X = x \mid \lambda = 5.5)$$

$$= 0.6860$$

$$P(\text{bread shortage}) = P(x \ge 8 \mid \lambda = 5.5)$$

$$= 1 - P(x \le 7 \mid \lambda = 5.5)$$

$$= 1 - 0.8094$$

$$= 0.1906$$

From Table A.7, Don also notes that the probability of exactly meeting demand is $P(X = 7 \mid \lambda) = 0.1234$. The solution can be checked by using the basic probability identity:

$$P(\text{unsold bread}) + P(\text{exact demand}) + P(\text{bread shortage}) = 1.0$$

$$0.6860 + 0.1234 + 0.1906 = 1.0$$

This check supports our calculation of individual probabilities.   □

Practice Problem 5.5: Airline Check-in

Flybynight Airlines is attempting to determine how many agents should be assigned to its check-in counters. From past experience we know that on average $\lambda = 10$ customers arrive for flights during each 15-minute period from 3:00 P.M. to 6:00 P.M. on weekdays. Determine the probability that:

(a) More than 12 customers arrive during a particular 15-minute period.
(b) Fewer than 8 customers arrive.
(c) Nine through 13 customers arrive.   □

5.8 COMPARISON OF BINOMIAL AND POISSON PROBABILITY

The Poisson probability can be obtained from the binomial by allowing π to become very small while n becomes very large. In addition, both the binomial and the Poisson provide the probability of the sum of x independent Bernoulli trials. In this section an example is presented that compares the probabilities computed by the Poisson and binomial probability distributions. The following example indicates conditions under which the binomial and the Poisson generate similar probabilities. Whenever the mean of the Poisson and binomial are the same and the number of trials $n \ge 20$ and $\pi \le 0.05$, the binomial and Poisson will generate similar probabilities. This result is important in applied work because there are cases in which it is difficult to choose between the binomial and Poisson assumptions. The service example given below is one example. Other important examples include random arrivals at service facilities, such as bank waiting lines, gasoline stations, and truck-loading warehouses. As shown in the following examples, the choice of bino-mial or Poisson assumptions is not critical. The reader is also encouraged to per-form similar computations if a choice between distributions is not obvious. It may be that the choice of assumptions that you are struggling with may not affect the probabilities.

Example 5.15   Computer Service Problem

Kathy Mandela is the service manager for Integrated Bit Manipulators, Inc., a com-puter manufacturing and marketing company. She wants to determine the number of service persons that are needed for maintaining the company's computers. The com-pany has asked for bids on two service contracts: one for its thousands of personal computers and a second for its 10 superminicomputers. These contracts must provide a service level such that a service person will be available at least 95% of the time that a computer needs repair. Kathy also knows that a computer can usually be repaired in less than one hour. If the repair requires more than one hour, it will be sent to an outside repair vendor.

Solution   (a) For personal computer maintenance, crew size will be determined by the probability distribution of repairs for personal computers. The probability of a single personal computer breakdown is very small and there are a large number of per-sonal computers. After some discussion with the computer engineers, she concludes that there will be an average of one personal computer breakdown each hour. Given the large number of personal computers, the small probability of failure for each, and the fact that all personal computers are the same model, she decides that a Poisson pdf is the appropriate distribution.

(b) For minicomputer maintenance, the superminicomputer maintenance prob-lem is concerned with only 10 computers. Each computer either has a failure or does not during each hour. There is a Bernoulli process for each computer, and failures are independent between computers. Thus the number of superminicomputer breakdowns is a binomial random variable. Analysis of the superminicomputer failure data for computers in a number of applications in other companies showed that the probability of each superminicomputer breakdown during any hour was $\pi = 0.1$, and breakdowns were independent.

(c) *Combined analysis.* Next, Kathy obtains the probability distribution of com-puter breakdowns from the appropriate tables. Table 5.4 shows the probability dis-tribution functions for the Poisson with $\lambda = 1.0$ and the binomial with $n = 10$ and $\pi = 0.1$. Note that both of these distributions have a mean failure rate of 1.0.

From Table 5.4 Kathy sees that she should schedule three service persons for each contract to provide immediate attention for at least 95% of the breakdowns. She also notes that the probability that all three persons from the minicomputer service crew (binomial pdf) will be idle is 0.3487, or approximately 35%. The personal com-puter service crew (Poisson pdf) will have no computers to service approximately 37% (probability = 0.3679) of the time.   □

TABLE 5.4   Binomial pdf ($n = 10$, $\pi = 0.1$) and Poisson pdf ($\lambda = 1.0$)

Number	Binomial	Cumulative Binomial	Poisson	Cumulative Poisson
0	0.3487	0.3487	0.3679	0.3679
1	0.3874	0.7361	0.3679	0.7358
2	0.1937	0.9298	0.1839	0.9197
3	0.0574	0.9872	0.0613	0.9810
4	0.0112	0.9984	0.0153	0.9963
5	0.0015	0.9999	0.0031	0.9994
6	0.0001	1.0000	0.0005	0.9999
7	0.0000	1.0000	0.0001	1.0000
	1.0000		1.0000	

5.8.1 Binomial Approximation Using the Poisson

Examination of Table 5.4 provides a useful result. The Poisson and binomial probabilities are very close when the mean rate is the same, even though the binomial had only 10 trials. Statisticians have performed these comparisons for a number of specific distributions and have compared the mathematical functions for computing probabilities. From those studies we know that the Poisson pdf can be used to approximate the binomial pdf when π is small and n is large. In addition, recall that the Poisson pdf can be derived from the binomial by increasing the number of trials and reducing the probability of each trial. Thus it is not surprising that the Poisson can be used to approximate the binomial when the number of trials, n, is large and the probability of success, π, is small.

A useful rule is given in Key Idea 5.13. This is a useful result because it is difficult to find binomial probability tables for small π and large n. After studying the normal probability function in Chapter 6, we will also show how to use the normal to approximate the binomial when π is larger. These approximations reduce the number of probability tables required. In addition, they demonstrate how the major probability distributions link together over the range of possible applications.

Key Idea 5.13: Binomial Approximation Using Poisson

The binomial pdf can be approximated by the Poisson pdf when $\pi \leq 0.05$ and $n \geq 20$.

Does It Make Sense?

These results also provide important guidance for the choice of models in applications. There are many situations in which the choice between Poisson and binomial is not clear because the actual situation is a mixture of both Poisson and binomial assumptions. As seen here, either model will provide approximately the same results. The approximation rule above could even be relaxed to $\pi \leq 0.10$ and $n \geq 10$, as indicated in the example, without serious errors in estimating probabilities or making decisions.   □

Problem Exercises

5.19   The number of defective parts produced per day follows a Poisson probability distribution with a mean of 3.6. Determine the probability that on a given day:
(a) Four defects occur.
(b) Two defects occur.
(c) Five or more defects occur.
(d) Three or fewer defects occur.

5.20   The number of cars arriving per hour at a car wash in a large city has a mean of 5 and can be modeled by a Poisson distribution. Determine the probability that:
(a) Exactly 5 cars arrive.
(b) More than 5 cars arrive.
(c) More than 7 cars arrive.

5.21   A large office has 100 personal computers. The probability that there will be a software problem for each computer during a particular day is 0.04.
(a) What is the probability that more than 6 computers will have a software problem?
(b) On a recent day 12 computers had software problems. Does this seem unusual?
(c) Compute the mean and variance assuming a binomial probability distribution.
(d) Compute the mean and variance assuming a Poisson probability distribution. Compare the results with those of part (c).

5.22   The number of automobile crashes per week on Highway 19 from Lonsdale to New Prague can be approximated by a Poisson distribution. Over the past year a total of 208 crashes have occurred. Determine the probability of:
(a) Exactly 6 crashes during a particular week.
(b) More than 7 crashes next week.
(c) More than 2 but fewer than 7 crashes next week.

5.23   The number of automobile crashes per week on Highway 96 from Blooming Prairie to New Ulm can be approximated by a Poisson distribution. Over the past year a total of 312 crashes have occurred. Determine:
(a) The mean, μ, number of crashes per week.
(b) The variance, σ^2, of the number of crashes per week.
(c) The probability that the number of crashes is in the interval $\mu \pm 2\sigma$.
(d) The probability that the number of crashes is in the interval $\mu \pm 3\sigma$.

5.24　Assume that the number of fielding errors committed by a major league baseball team can be modeled by a Poisson distribution. Over the past 100 games the Texas Rangers committed a total of 120 errors. Answer the following questions assuming that the error rate remains the same. Determine the probability of:
(a) No errors in a game.
(b) More than 3 errors in a game.
(c) More than 2 errors in a game.

5.25　Assume that the number of fielding errors committed by a major league baseball team can be modeled by a Poisson distribution. Over the past 100 games the New York Yankees committed a total of 100 errors. Answer the following questions assuming that the error rate remains the same. Determine:
(a) The mean, μ, number of errors per game.
(b) The variance, σ^2, of the number of errors per game.
(c) The probability that the number of errors is in the interval $\mu \pm 2\sigma$.
(d) The probability that the number of errors is in the interval $\mu \pm 3\sigma$.

5.26　The medical doctors at a large clinic complete a summary report of their findings and diagnosis for each patient who is seen. Assume that the number of reports per day with errors can be approximated by a Poisson distribution. Over the past 200 days a total of 640 reports had one or more errors. Assume that the same pattern continues. Determine the probability that:
(a) The number of reports with errors per day exceed 6.
(b) The number of errors per day is less than 2.
(c) The number of errors is greater than 2 but less than 7.

5.27　The medical doctors at a large clinic complete a summary report of their findings and diagnosis for each patient who is seen. Assume that the number of reports per day with errors can be approximated by a Poisson distribution. Over the past 200 days a total of 640 reports had one or more errors. Assume that the same pattern continues. Determine:
(a) The mean, μ, number of errors per day.
(b) The variance, σ^2, of the number of errors per day.
(c) The probability that the number of errors per day is in the interval $\mu \pm 2\sigma$.
(d) The probability that the number of errors per day is in the interval $\mu \pm 3\sigma$.

SUMMARY OF KEY IDEAS

PRACTICE PROBLEM SOLUTIONS

5.1 The cumulative probability distribution is shown in Table 5.5.

$$
\begin{aligned}
P(1 \le X \le 3) &= f(1) + f(2) + f(3) \\
&= 0.4096 + 0.1536 + 0.0256 \\
&= 0.5888 \\
&= P(0 < X \le 3) \\
&= F(3) - F(0) \\
&= 0.9984 - 0.4096 \\
&= 0.5888
\end{aligned}
$$

TABLE 5.5   Probability Distribution Function for Defective Parts

Number, X	$f(x) = P(X = x)$	$F(x) = P(X \le x)$
0	0.4096	0.4096
1	0.4096	0.8192
2	0.1536	0.9728
3	0.0256	0.9984
4	0.0016	1.0000

5.2 The expected value obtained from the random variable defined in Tables 5.2 and 5.5 is

$$
\begin{aligned}
E[X] &= \sum_{x=0}^{x=4} x f(x) \\
&= 0 \times 0.4096 + 1 \times 0.4096 + 2 \times 0.1536 + 3 \times 0.0256 + 4 \times 0.0016 \\
&= 0.80
\end{aligned}
$$

5.3   The variance computation for the probability distribution defined by Tables 5.2 and 5.5 is as follows:

$$\sigma^2 = E[(X - \mu)^2]$$

$$= \sum_{x_i=0}^{x_i=4} (x_i - \mu)^2 f(x_i)$$

$$= (0 - 0.80)^2 0.4096 + (1 - 0.80)^2 0.4096 + (2 - 0.80)^2 0.1536$$
$$+ (3 - 0.80)^2 0.0256 + (4 - 0.80)^2 0.0016$$
$$= 0.2621 + 0.0164 + 0.2212 + 0.1239 + 0.0164$$
$$= 0.64$$

The variance may also be computed by first obtaining $E[X^2]$:

$$E[X^2] = \sum_{x_i=0}^{x_i=4} x_i^2 f(x_i)$$

$$= 0^2 0.4096 + 1^2 0.4096 + 2^2 0.1536 + 3^2 0.0256 + 4^2 0.0016$$
$$= 0.00 + 0.4096 + 0.6144 + 0.2304 + 0.0256$$
$$= 1.28$$

and by using Key Idea 5.6 and the mean $\mu = 0.8$:

$$\sigma^2 = E[X^2] - \mu^2$$
$$= 1.28 - 0.80^2$$
$$= 0.64$$

5.4   This problem uses the binomial distribution with $n = 10$ and $\pi = 0.4$. The cumulative binomial probability table (Table A.6) can be used to find the required probabilities, $F(X \mid \pi = 0.4, n = 10)$.

(a)
$$P(X > 6) = 1 - F(6 \mid 0.4, 10)$$
$$= 1 - 0.9452$$
$$= 0.0548$$

(b)
$$P(X < 3) = F(2 \mid 0.4, 10)$$
$$= 0.1673$$

(c)
$$P(3 \le X \le 6) = F(6 \mid 0.4, 10) - F(2 \mid 0.4, 10)$$
$$= 0.9452 - 0.1673$$
$$= 0.7779$$

5.5 This problem uses the Poisson distribution with $\lambda = 10$. The cumulative Poisson probability table (Table A.8) can be used to find the required probabilities, $F(X \mid \lambda = 10)$.

(a)
$$P(X > 12) = 1 - F(12 \mid 10)$$
$$= 1 - 0.7916$$
$$= 0.2084$$

(b)
$$P(X < 8) = F(7 \mid 10)$$
$$= 0.2202$$

(c)
$$P(9 \leq X \leq 13) = F(13 \mid 10) - F(8 \mid 10)$$
$$= 0.8645 - 0.3328$$
$$= 0.5317$$

CHAPTER PROBLEMS

5.1 The random variable Y is defined by $f(0) = 0.10$, $f(1) = 0.20$, $f(2) = 0.30$, $f(3) = 0.20$, and $f(4) = 0.20$. Determine:
(a) $P(1 \leq Y \leq 3)$.
(b) $P(Y < 3)$.
(c) $P(Y \geq 2)$.
(d) $F(y)$.
(e) $E[Y]$ and σ_Y^2.

5.2 Sam Ytterboe has studied the annual demand for luxury ocean liners to make recommendations concerning inventory levels for his company, Splash Ventures, Inc. He has concluded that demand can be represented by the probability model $f(y) = P(Y = y)$, with $f(1) = 0.30$, $f(2) = 0.20$, $f(3) = 0.30$, and $f(4) = 0.20$. The random variable Y is the number of luxury ocean liners demanded.
(a) What is the probability of fewer than 3 ocean liners?
(b) Compute the expected value and variance of Y.
(c) Assume that you are the company president and Sam has recommended that you maintain an inventory level equal to the annual expected value of demand. What is your response?

5.3 The random variable Y is defined by the probability distribution function in Table 5.6. Determine:
(a) $F(y)$.
(b) $P(2 < Y \leq 4)$.
(c) $P(3 \leq Y < 5)$.
(d) $E[Y]$ and σ_Y^2.

TABLE 5.6   Probability
Distribution Function for
Problem 5.3

y	$f(y)$	$F(y)$
0	0.10	?
1	0.20	?
2	0.10	?
3	0.20	?
4	0.20	?
5	0.20	?

5.4   Gertrude Goodeal is the sales manager for Akimoto and Roberg, dealers in fine used cars. On a bright morning she notes that there are three Saabs and two Toyotas on the lot. A customer comes to the lot and randomly selects two cars for purchase. Help Gertrude with her planning by providing the following results.
(a) Construct the probability distribution function for the number of Saabs in the set of two cars purchased by the customer.
(b) Determine the expected value and variance for the number of Saabs purchased.
(c) Construct the probability distribution function for the number of Toyotas in the set of two cars and repeat part (b).

5.5   In Problem 5.4, suppose that there were six Saabs, eight Toyotas, and four Fords on the lot. A customer comes to the lot and randomly selects three cars for purchase. Help Gertrude with her planning by providing the following results.
(a) Construct the probability distribution function for the number of Saabs in the set of three cars purchased by the customer.
(b) Determine the expected value and variance for the number of Saabs purchased.
(c) (*Optional*) Construct the probability distribution function for the number of Toyotas in the set of three cars and repeat part (b).

5.6   Consider the random variable Z defined by $Z = 5 + 2Y$ where the random variable Y is defined in Table 5.6. Determine:
(a) $P(9 < Z \le 13)$.
(b) $P(5 \le Z \le 11)$.
(c) $P(9 \le Z \le 15)$.
(d) $E[Y]$ and σ_Y^2.

5.7   The demand function for plywood in a large midwestern city is $Q = 100 - 5P$, where Q is the quantity demanded in number of sheets and P is the price in dollars. The price, P, is a random variable whose probability distribution function is given in Table 5.7. Determine:
(a) The probability that the quantity demanded ranges from 20 to 40.
(b) The probability that quantity demanded is greater than or equal to 40.
(c) The expected value and variance of quantity demanded.

5.8   Southeast Cooperative Agricultural Distributors has asked you to study the daily demand for fertilizer during the months of March and April. As a result of analyzing their his-

TABLE 5.7   Probability
Distribution Function for
Problem 5.7

p	$f(p)$	$F(p)$
10	0.20	?
12	0.30	?
14	0.30	?
16	0.10	?
18	0.10	?

torical records and talking to the county agricultural agents, you have concluded that daily demand for fertilizer can be modeled by the probability distribution function in Table 5.8, where y is the number of truckloads ordered on a particular day.

TABLE 5.8   Probability
Distribution Function for
Daily Fertilizer Demand

y	$f(y)$	$F(y)$
0	0.05	?
1	0.10	?
2	0.15	?
3	0.40	?
4	0.15	?
5	0.10	?
6	0.05	?

(a) Determine the cumulative probability distribution function $F(y)$.
(b) Compute the mean and variance of fertilizer demand.
(c) If Southeast schedules four truckloads each day during March and April, what is the probability that they will not be able to deliver all orders on the day the order is received?
(d) If Southeast schedules five truckloads each day during March and April, what is the probability that at least one truckload will not be required?
(e) What is the probability that between three and five trucks will be used on a particular day?

5.9   Table 5.9 contains the probability distribution for income in a small midwestern city. The discrete random variable Y is the family income measured in thousands of 1990 dollars. This probability distribution is an approximation because incomes are a continuous random variable. In this probability model all incomes within ±5000 of each integer are assumed to be at that integer value. Thus the first cell contains all incomes between 15,000 and 25,000 and they are all assumed to be 20,000. This approximation is often used to simplify the probability distribution and related computations.

TABLE 5.9   Probability
Distribution Function for
Income Distribution

y	f(y)	F(y)
20	0.10	?
30	0.30	?
40	0.20	?
50	0.10	?
60	0.05	?
70	0.05	?
80	0.05	?
90	0.05	?
100	0.10	?

(a) Construct the cumulative probability distribution function.
(b) Compute the mean and variance of the family income.
(c) Suppose that the city contains 40,000 families and that each family spends 50% of its income at retail stores within the city. What are the mean and variance of each family's retail expenditures?
(d) What is the expected total retail expenditure in the city?
(e) What percentage of the families will spend over $30,000 in the retail stores within the city?

5.10 Eric Lind, manager of Computers Unlimited, has asked for your assistance in analyzing daily computer sales at its retail stores. The sales pattern at each store is similar. Table 5.10 shows the probability distribution of computer sales.

TABLE 5.10   Probability
Distribution Function for
Daily Computer Sales

X	f(x)	F(x)
0	0.10	?
1	0.10	?
2	0.10	?
3	0.20	?
4	0.20	?
5	0.10	?
6	0.10	?
7	0.05	?
8	0.05	?

(a) Compute the cumulative probability distribution.
(b) What is the probability of selling at least two computers but fewer than seven?

(c) The stock of computers at the beginning of a particular day is five computers. What is the probability that sales exceed the available stock?

(d) The inventory at the beginning of a day is 15 computers. What is the probability that the inventory at the end of the day is 10 or more?

5.11 Eric Lind, manager of Computers Unlimited, has asked for your assistance in analyzing daily computer sales at its retail stores. The sales pattern at each store is similar. Table 5.10 shows the probability distribution of computer sales. Determine:

(a) The mean number of computers sold each day.

(b) The variance of computers sold each day.

5.12 Peg Broderson, president of Computers Unlimited, has asked you to help study the sales revenue patterns for its stores. Each computer sells for $1200 and the probability distribution function for sales is given in Table 5.10. Determine:

(a) The mean daily sales revenue.

(b) The variance of the daily sales revenue.

5.13 This problem continues Problem 5.12. Peg Broderson now asks your help in studying the daily pattern of the contribution to profit and overhead. Contribution is the total revenue minus cost of goods sold minus the daily fixed costs of $500. Each computer costs Computers Unlimited $1000. Determine:

(a) The mean contribution to profit and overhead.

(b) The variance of the contribution.

(c) The probability that the contribution is greater than 0.

5.14 A recent survey indicates that 20% of the Norwegian population in New York City eat bagels regularly. In a random sample of 12 New York Norwegians, determine the probability that:

(a) Four eat bagels regularly.

(b) One or fewer eat bagels regularly.

5.15 Given a binomial probability distribution with a mean $\mu = 2$ and $n = 10$. Determine the probability of:

(a) Exactly two successes.

(b) More than four successes.

5.16 A college has offered admission to 10 students. Based on historical patterns, 60% of students offered admission will actually attend.

(a) If exactly 6 of the 10 actually attend, how many different combinations of six students are possible?

(b) What is the probability that seven or more students attend?

(c) Determine $P(5 \leq Y \leq 7)$.

(d) Determine $P(Y > 6)$.

(e) Compute $E[Y]$ and σ_Y^2.

5.17 The Minnesota Twins have five "300" hitters in the lineup. Assume that the probability of a hit by one of these players is independent of a hit by another player. (*Note:* A "300" hitter has a probability $\pi = 0.30$ of getting a hit in any time at bat.)

(a) The manager expects that these players will each get three times at bat in today's game. What is the probability that these players will collect more than seven hits?

(b) The manager decides to have these players bat consecutively in the batting positions 1 through 5. What is the probability of exactly two hits in the first inning? (Assume that a batter either gets a hit or is out. There are no walks or errors. After three outs the inning is over.)

5.18   A building owner in Pipestone, Minnesota purchases three new refrigerators, which are guaranteed by the manufacturer. The probability that each refrigerator is defective is 0.20. Define the total number of defective refrigerators as the random variable X.
   (a) Construct the probability distribution function for X.
   (b) What are the mean and variance of X?
   (c) The cost of repair, to honor the guarantee, consists of a fixed fee of $40 plus a cost of $60 to repair each defective refrigerator. What is the average cost to repair these three refrigerators? Note that the fixed fee of $40 is incurred only if there are one or more defective refrigerators.

5.19   Fifteen students from a prestigious liberal arts college take a graduate school placement exam. Each has a probability of 0.50 of obtaining a superior score. Determine the probability that:
   (a) Exactly 10 students receive a superior score.
   (b) More than 8 receive a superior score.
   (c) More than 6 and less than 12 receive a superior score.

5.20   A shipment of 100,000 computers contains exactly 20,000 defective computers. You obtain a random sample of three computers and test each. Let Y be a random variable that is the number of defective computers in your sample ($Y = 0, 1, 2, 3$). Construct the probability distribution function for Y; $f(y) = P(Y = y)$. Assume that the probability of selecting a defective computer is the same for each of the three observations obtained in your random sample. That is, assume that you are sampling with replacement of each computer after it has been tested. Determine:
   (a) $f(1)$.
   (b) $f(3)$.
   (c) $F(2)$.
   (d) $E[X]$ and σ_Y^2.

5.21   A large commercial kitchen prepares ready-to-eat meals for use on airlines. On a particular day 30% of the meals are fish and 70% are beef. Steve Steward from Over The Hill airlines rushes in and randomly selects 15 meals for the flight he is about to take. What is the probability that at least five people will be able to eat fish on Steve's flight?

5.22   You have received a shipment of 1000 new computers. You know that the computers have been produced at either factory A or factory B. The probability is 0.50 that they were produced at factory A. You know that factory A produces 10% defective computers while factory B produces 40% defective computers. You obtain a random sample of three computers from your shipment and find that exactly one is defective. What is the probability that the shipment was produced at factory A?

5.23   Charlie Sellsmore is the sales representative for Macro Products, Inc. He is beginning to call on new customers in southern North Dakota. He expects to make 20 sales calls on potential customers during the coming week. The experience from other sales regions indicates that 40% of those contacted will purchase a Macro. Charlie also knows that all sales calls are independent.

    (a) If Charlie makes 10 or more sales, he will be promoted to district manager. If he does not, he will be required to return in the second week and make a second set of 20 independent calls. What is the probability of a promotion in week 1?

    (b) What is the probability that he will be promoted after week 2?

5.24 Shirley Wood, purchasing manager of Amalgamated Products, has negotiated an agreement to purchase 100,000 computer chips from Chipsey Forest, Inc. Included in the agreement is a guarantee that 5000 or fewer chips will be defective. Shirley has asked for your assistance in designing a sampling plan to determine if the shipment satisfies the contract guarantee of 5000 or fewer defectives.

    (a) Suppose that you obtain a random sample of 10 chips. What is the probability of one or more defectives if the guarantee is satisfied?

    (b) Suppose that you obtain a random sample of 20 chips. What is the probability of one or more defective chips and of two or more defective chips if the guarantee is satisfied? What recommendation would you make to Shirley if four defective chips were found in the sample of 20?

    (c) Next consider the case with a random sample of size 50 chips. What is the probability of three or more, of four or more, and of five or more defective chips?

5.25 A political candidate campaigned in two different cities and shook hands with 10 voters in each city. In city A the probability of a voter supporting her is 0.60, while in city B the probability of support from a voter is 0.40. Assume that the 10 voters in each city shaking hands are a random sample of all voters in each city.

    (a) What is the expected value and variance of the number of supporters from the random sample of 10 voters from city A and from the random sample of 10 voters from city B?

    (b) If the random sample of voters contacted in the two different cities are independent, what are the expected value and variance of the number of supporters from the sum of supporters obtained in the two random samples?

    (c) What is the probability of obtaining five supporters from the city A random sample and five supporters from the city B random sample if the two samples are independent?

    (d) What is the probability of obtaining six supporters from the city A random sample and four supporters from the city B random sample if the two samples are independent?

5.26 Gertrude James is the director of academic computing at a liberal arts college. She has just completed a very favorable microcomputer purchase contract with her older brother, Jesse. After the contract has been signed, Jesse mentions that she can expect that 20% of the computers will be defective. Gertrude receives her first shipment of five computers. She knows that each computer has a probability of 0.20 of being defective and that defects are independent among the computers. Now she must obtain a budget increase to test and repair the computers. Testing for the five computers will cost a total of $50 and the repair of each defective computer will cost $100.

    (a) Construct the probability distribution function for the number of defective computers.

    (b) What are the mean and variance of the number of defective computers?

    (c) What is the expected cost for testing and repairing the five computers purchased?

(d) The next time Jesse calls with computers he offers her a guarantee that for an additional $200, the next five computers will not be defective. If any computers are defective, they will be replaced without charge. Given her past experience, Gertrude plans to test each computer at a total cost of $50. Should she pay the additional $200 for the guarantee? Explain your answer.

5.27 Assume that X and Y are independent binomial random variables with the following parameters:

$$X: \quad n = 10, \quad P = 0.40$$
$$Y: \quad n = 5, \quad P = 0.20$$

Determine:
(a) $P(X = 4 \cap Y = 2)$.
(b) $P(X = 2 \mid Y = 1)$.
(c) $P(Y = 4 \mid X = 2)$.
(d) $P(X = 3 \cap Y = 3)$.

5.28 The basketball coach at Ole College discovers that her team is 5 points behind with 2 minutes left. After analyzing the situation carefully, she finds that her team will be able to take five shots during the remainder of the game and the other team will not be able to take any. (Arms O'Leary, the top rebounder, guarantees that she will get every rebound during the next 2 minutes.) The coach must decide to set the offense for five 3-point shots or for five 2-point shots. She knows that her team scores on 50% of the 2-point shots and only on 40% of the 3-point shots. Which strategy has the highest probability of winning—that is, of scoring at least 6 points?

5.29 The Acme Ltd. factory receives regular shipment of computer chips from two different suppliers. Shipments of 10,000 chips from supplier A contain a maximum of 500 defectives. Shipments of 10,000 chips from supplier B contain a maximum of 1000 defective chips. Acme's factory regularly receives 70% of its shipments from supplier A and 30% from supplier B.
(a) What is the probability of 0 defectives in a random sample of size 10 from a shipment sent by supplier A?
(b) What is the probability of 0 defectives in a random sample of size 10 from a shipment sent by supplier B?
(c) Suppose that a random sample of size 10 is obtained from a shipment and the sample contains 0 defectives. What is the probability that the shipment came from supplier A?

5.30 Give an example of a problem that can be modeled using a Poisson probability distribution function. Provide a short discussion indicating why the Poisson is appropriate.

5.31 Your automobile company produced 1,000,000 units during the past year. Fifteen of the cars had defective windshield wiper blades. This year you plan to produce 100,000 units of a new model automobile. You have been asked to determine the probability that four or more of the new cars will have defective wiper blades. State the assumptions that you made to complete your analysis.

5.32 Sparky Charge, the general maintenance foreman for the local electric utility, believes that distribution system failures can be modeled using a Poisson probability distribution. Assume that each repair requires one 8-hour shift to complete. From the repair records for the past several years Sparky discovers that there is on average one distribution system failure per 8-hour shift. If two crews are scheduled, determine the probability that:

(a) At least one crew will be idle.

(b) There will be a shortage of crews.

(c) Suppose that four failures occurred on each of three consecutive days. Determine the probability of this result. What does this result tell you about the assumption that failures have a Poisson probability distribution?

5.33 You are the manager of the Hilltop Pizza delivery service in a western university city. Over the past several years you have observed that on average 500 students call to order pizza from 5:00 to 10:00 P.M. You assume that calls are independent. The probability of any student calling at any time during the five hours is the same. During any 12-minute period Hilltop can receive and deliver 20 pizza orders. If more than 20 orders are placed during the 12-minute period, they cannot be filled and the students obtain their pizza from a competitor. Determine the probability that:

(a) Customers cannot be served during any 12-minute period.

(b) Fewer than 17 orders are received during a particular 12-minute interval.

(c) At least 18 and no more than 23 pizza orders are received during a particular 12-minute interval.

(d) On a particular Friday exactly 500 students called to place orders for pizza. Assume that each pizza order contributes $2.00 to the gross operating margin. What is the loss in gross operating margin that results from the limit of 20 pizza orders during any 12-minute period?

5.34 A small village in India has a population of 2000 people. In 1980 a new water system was installed. This system provides clean water from a deep well and the water is piped to various locations in the village. Everyone can now obtain clean water for household use. Prior to the installation of the water system, people obtained water from open irrigation wells. During the 10 years prior to the water system installation, an average of seven people per year died in the village of amebic dysentery. During the year after the water system was installed, only one person died of amebic dysentery. Is there evidence that the level of public health has improved in this village? Present a probability model and an analysis, which includes a clear explanation, to support your conclusion.

5.35 You are the production manager for a factory with 20 robots. Using past records you have observed that on average four robots fail on any given day. Today you discover that eight robots have failed.

(a) Is this an unusual event if it has occurred only once over the past 100 days?

(b) You are very upset about the eight robot failures and decide to take action that will reduce robot failures in the future. You gather the robots together and discuss their poor performance, lack of loyalty to the company, and lack of appreciation for all you have done for them. You also indicate that if this happens in the future, you will feed them lower-quality electrical power. To evaluate your action, you decide to count the number of robot failures on the day after your discussion with the robots. Is it likely that the number of failures is fewer than eight? Please explain your answer.

(c) Given the results above, what do you conclude about your action to prevent failures? Provide a concise explanation that is based on your understanding of probability.

5.36   You are the loan manager of a medium-sized bank and are trying to determine the type of loan that will be requested by your next customer. One-half of the cars that enter your parking lot come from the commercial district and one-half come from the industrial district. Because of the local traffic control system, all cars arriving during a 10-minute period will come from either the commercial or the industrial district. If the cars come from the commercial district, their average arrival rate will be four cars per 10-minute period. If they come from the industrial district, their average arrival rate will be two cars per 10-minute period. Car arrivals from within each district are independent. During a particular 10-minute period, exactly five cars arrive at the parking lot. What is the probability that these five cars came from the industrial district?

6

Continuous Random Variables and Probability Density Functions

The uniform, exponential, and normal models are used in most of the applications you will encounter.

6.1 CONTINUOUS PROBABILITY MODELS

In Chapter 5 discrete random variable models were developed and applied to a variety of problems. Our goal in this chapter is to understand and use continuous probability models: specifically, the uniform, exponential, and normal. In contrast to discrete random variables, continuous random variables can have any value over a range. They are used to compute probabilities for variables such as price, expenditures, sales, investment, productivity, speed, income, and gross domestic product. The uniform, exponential, and normal models are developed in detail because they are used in many of the applications you will encounter. Specific applications to business and economics problems are developed in examples and assigned problems. After finishing this chapter you will understand the probability foundations that support an extensive structure of statistical analysis.

6.2 CONTINUOUS RANDOM VARIABLES

Sheila Thorne is the treasurer of a high-technology development company and is preparing the research budget for the coming year. The research center has been working on a new product and requests funds for continuing the efforts. The research manager, George Maki, indicates that a major success could occur any day and that project success is equally likely early or late in the project year. After some negotiation George agrees that an upper limit on project funding should be $50,000, to be allocated uniformly by day over the next year. He also agrees that project expenditures will stop as soon as the project succeeds.

Based on such scant information, what amount should Sheila budget for this project? If she budgets $10,000, expecting an early breakthrough, and the project runs the entire year, requiring the entire $50,000, Sheila may lose her job. Similarly, if she budgets the entire $50,000 and ends up requiring only $5000, she may also lose her job. How should she approach arriving at an amount that can be defended as responsible?

The amount of actual expenditure in the coming year is a random variable that can take any value between $0 and $50,000. Specifically, the amount is a continuous random variable (Key Idea 6.1).

Key Idea 6.1: Continuous Random Variable

A **continuous random variable** assigns values to any continuous outcome in a sample space. Ranges of outcomes correspond to a range of the continuous random variable.

Because the actual expenditure for the research project is a continuous random variable, probabilities can be assigned only to ranges of specific values that the expenditures might take. Sheila needs several more key ideas to develop a probability model for this budget. Among these are the probability density function (pdf), cumulative distribution function (cdf), mean, and variance.

6.2.1 Probability Density Function

Sheila's budget problem can be modeled by a continuous probability model that consists of a continuous random variable and a probability density function. Figure 6.1 shows this model. The random variable X is the budget measured in units of $10,000, with a range from 0 to 5 ($0 to $50,000). It is not possible to define the probability of a single value. Instead, the probability that the random variable is within a range of specific values or is greater or less than a specific value is determined. The probability is computed using areas under mathematical functions. These functions are called probability density functions (pdf's; Key Idea 6.2).

The probability density function in Figure 6.1 is defined mathematically as

$$f(x) = 0.2 \qquad 0 \le x \le 5.0$$

The random variable, X, is defined over the range from 0 to 5, with the area under the pdf, $f(x)$, equal to 1.0 (0.2×5).

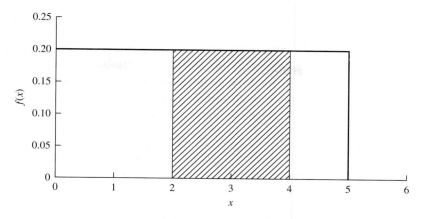

Figure 6.1   Probability Density Function

Key Idea 6.2: Probability Density Function

A **probability density function** (pdf), $f(x)$, is a mathematical function $(f(x) \geq 0)$ defined over the range of a continuous random variable such that the area under the function between two values (a and b) is the probability that the random variable is between a and b. The area under the pdf over the entire range of the random variable is equal to 1.0.

⋆ The probability can also be defined using calculus as

$$P(a \leq X \leq b) = \int_a^b f(x)\, dx$$

If Sheila wanted to know the probability that expenditures are between \$20,000 and \$40,000, she could find the area under probability density function from 2 to 4. The area under the curve from 2 to 4 is 0.40 $[0.2 \times (4 - 2)]$.

⋆The probability can also be computed by using integral calculus to compute this area:[1]

$$P(2 \leq X \leq 4) = \int_2^4 f(x)\, dx = 0.4$$

---

[1] Many of the concepts developed in this and later chapters will include sections that use calculus in the development. These sections are indicated by a star. You can learn the statistical procedures without these sections. However, your understanding will be increased if you can use these calculus-based sections.

Sheila could find the probability that the expenditure is in other ranges by following this procedure.

For business problems that use more complex probability density functions such as the exponential or normal, the area under the curve will be presented in tables or can easily be computed using a computer statistical package. However, to use the tables or the computed probabilities, it is important to understand how continuous probabilities are computed and how to interpret and use them. This understanding will be developed using some simple probability density functions. For these examples the probabilities will be computed using both simple geometry and integral calculus. Intuitive discussion based on simple examples will develop the concepts. However, if you can also follow the calculus, your understanding will be increased.

6.2.2 Cumulative Distribution Function

Now suppose that Sheila wanted to know the probability that expenditures are less than some upper limit (e.g., $30,000). The cumulative distribution function (cdf; Key Idea 6.3) defines this probability. In contrast, the pdf defines the probability over an interval.

Key Idea 6.3: Cumulative Distribution Function

The **cumulative distribution function** (cdf), $F(x^*)$, for continuous random variables is a mathematical function, defined over the range of the continuous random variable, which defines the probability that the random variable is below an upper limit, x^*. The cdf is defined as the area under the probability density function from x_1, the minimum value, up to x^*.
    * The cdf can also be defined using calculus as

$$F(x^*) = P(X \leq x^*)$$

$$= \int_{x_{min}}^{x^*} f(x)\, dx$$

where x_{min} is the minimum value of x.

The probability that a random variable is greater than a value x^*—but less than the upper limit—is computed as the complement $1 - F(x^*)$. Using this result, Sheila could also determine the probability that expenditures will exceed, for example, $40,000.

In Figure 6.1, the cdf $F(4)$ is the area from 0 to 4 and is equal to 0.8 [$0.2 \times (4 - 0)$]:

$$F(4) = P(X \leq 4)$$
$$= (4 - 0) \times 0.2$$
$$= 0.8$$

The probability of expenditures of less than \$40,000 is 0.8, and the probability that expenditures are above \$40,000 is 0.20 $(1 - 0.80)$.

Practice Problem 6.1: Budget Probability

For a second project Sheila and George agree that larger expenditures are more likely to occur early in the budget period. They compared this project with other similar research projects and concluded that the probability density function is

$$f(x) = 0.4 - 0.08x \qquad 0 \leq x \leq 5$$

Figure 6.2 shows its graphical form, which is a triangle beginning at $f(x) = 0.4$ when $x = 0$ and decreasing to $f(x) = 0$ when $x = 5$. Using this probability density function, determine the probability that the project will be completed with a budget expenditure under \$40,000. In addition, determine the probability that the budget expenditure at project completion will be between \$20,000 and \$40,000.   ☐

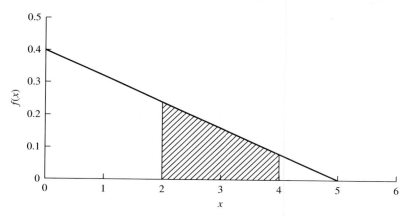

Figure 6.2   Probability Density Function for Practice Problem 6.1

The solutions for all Practice Problems are given at the end of the chapter.

6.2.3 Mean and Variance

Similar to discrete random variables, continuous random variables have a mean and variance (Key Idea 6.4). For Sheila's budget problem the mean indicates the most likely expenditure and the variance provides a measure of risk for comparison with other projects.

The expected value has many interpretations. It is the average of all outcomes weighted by their probabilities. Others view it as the long-run average or central tendency. Some practitioners use the mean when one number is needed to define the outcome.

Key Idea 6.4: Mean and Variance

The mean, μ, is the central tendency of a continuous random variable. It is equal to the expected value, $E[X]$.

$$\mu = E[X]$$

*Using calculus, the mean is defined as

$$\mu = E[X] = \int xf(x)\,dx \qquad \text{all } x$$

The variability of a continuous random variable is defined by the variance, σ^2, and the standard deviation, σ:

$$\sigma^2 = E[(X - \mu)^2]$$
$$= E[X^2] - \mu^2$$
$$\sigma = \sqrt{\sigma^2}$$

*Using calculus, the definition is

$$\sigma^2 = \int (x - \mu)^2 f(x)\,dx$$

The variance provides a measure of risk. Larger variances imply more large and small values in the probability model. Thus there is a greater likelihood that either a very large or a very small value will result. In Sheila's budget problem a larger variance would imply greater uncertainty. Later we see how the mean and variance are used to make inferences about probability models using sample data.

   *The expected value for Sheila's budget problem, whose pdf, $f(x) = 0.20$, is shown in Figure 6.1, is

$$\mu = E[X] = \int_0^5 xf(x)\,dx$$

$$= \int_0^5 x(0.2)\,dx$$

$$= \left[\frac{0.2x^2}{2}\right]_0^5$$

$$= 0.1 \times 5^2 = 2.5$$

The mean budget cost for the research project is $25,000 (2.5 × 10,000).

*In addition, the variance computation for Sheila's continuous random variable can be computed using integral calculus. For the probability density function defined by Figure 6.1,

$$\sigma^2 = E[(X - \mu)^2]$$
$$= \int (x - \mu)^2 f(x)\, dx$$
$$= \int_0^5 (x - 2.5)^2 0.2\, dx$$

The computations can be simplified by using the simplification developed for discrete random variables:

$$\sigma^2 = E[(X - \mu)^2]$$
$$= E[X^2] - \mu^2$$

We first compute $E[X^2]$ and then combine it with $\mu = 2.5$, which was computed above.

$$E[X^2] = \int x^2 f(x)\, dx$$
$$= \int_0^5 x^2 0.2\, dx$$
$$= \left[\frac{x^3 0.2}{3} \right]_0^5$$
$$= \frac{5^3 0.2}{3} - \frac{0^3 0.2}{3}$$
$$= 8.33$$

Using this result, the variance is

$$\sigma^2 = E[(X - \mu)^2]$$
$$= E[X^2] - \mu^2$$
$$= 8.33 - 2.5^2$$
$$= 2.08$$

This variance, 2.08, provides a measure of expenditure variation for the research project. Projects could be ranked by variance to indicate their relative risk.

*Practice Problem 6.2: Expected Value for Research Budget

Compute the expected value for the continuous random variable defined in Figure 6.2. The expected value for continuous random variables requires calculus.   □

Practice Problem 6.3: Variance for Research Budget

Compute the variance for the probability density function:

$$f(x) = 0.4 - 0.08x \qquad (0 \le x \le 5)$$

which is shown graphically in Figure 6.2.   □

The discussion above has developed continuous random variables using an extended example. Sheila would probably likely carry out her analysis using one of the parametric continuous probability models. In the example she actually used a uniform probability model, which is developed in the next section.

6.3 UNIFORM DISTRIBUTION

In Sheila's budgeting problem it was very difficult to determine the probability of various expenditure levels. The research project would continue until a breakthrough occurred. A breakthrough could occur very early in the project or very late. It was agreed that $50,000 would be an upper limit for the project expenditure. If a breakthrough did not occur by that point, the project would be abandoned. Thus the expenditure is a continuous random variable with a range from 0 to 5 ($0 to $50,000). The probability of a completed project between 1.2 and 1.3 is the same as the probability between 4.5 and 4.6. Because the probability is the same over every subinterval, we use a uniform probability distribution (Key Idea 6.5) as a model for the problem.

The parameters can be computed using a uniform distribution such as Figure 6.2. Note that the minimum value is a and the maximum is b. The area under the curve must be equal to 1, and therefore the height or the probability density function must be $1/(b - a)$, so that the area of the rectangle representing the distribution is 1.

$$\frac{1}{b - a} \times (b - a) = 1$$

The cumulative distribution function is the area under the uniform distribution up to the value of the random variable y, and therefore

$$F(x) = (x - a) \times \frac{1}{b - a}$$

*6.3.1 Calculus Derivation of Mean and Variance

The probability density function for the uniform is

$$f(x) = \frac{1}{b - a}$$

Key Idea 6.5: Uniform Probability Distribution

The **uniform probability distribution** indicates the same probability for all intervals on a continuous random variable defined over the range from a minimum to a maximum value. The uniform distribution is called a *no information model* because probabilities are the same over all intervals. The distribution has the following properties:

1. Probability density function (pdf)

$$f(x) = \frac{1}{b-a}$$

where a is the minimum value and b is the maximum value.

2. Cumulative probability function (cdf)

$$F(x) = \frac{x-a}{b-a}$$

3. Mean

$$\mu = E[X] = \frac{b+a}{2}$$

4. Variance and standard deviation

$$\sigma_X^2 = \frac{(b-a)^2}{12}$$

$$\sigma_X = \sqrt{\frac{(b-a)^2}{12}}$$

Using the definition of the mean, we see that

$$\mu_x = E[X]$$

$$= \int_a^b x \frac{1}{b-a}\, dx$$

$$= \frac{1}{2(b-a)}(b^2 - a^2)$$

$$= \frac{b+a}{2}$$

Then using the definition of the variance, we see that

$$\sigma_x^2 = E[(x - \mu_x)^2]$$

$$= \int_a^b (x - \mu_x)^2 \frac{1}{b-a}\, dx$$

$$= \frac{(b-a)^2}{12}$$

or one could first compute

$$E[X^2] = \int_a^b x^2\, dx$$

and then compute the variance using

$$\sigma_x^2 = E[X^2] - \mu_x^2$$

6.3.2 Budget Problem Illustration

In Section 6.2 the analysis of Sheila's budget problem was based on the uniform probability model. Possible expenditures were in the range 0 to 5 (units of $10,000), with any value being equally likely. Since there was no good information on the probability over the range from 0 to 5, a uniform model was a reasonable choice and the probability density function is

$$f(x) = \frac{1}{5-0}$$

$$= 0.2$$

Using this pdf, the probability that x will not exceed 4 ($40,000) is

$$F(4) = \int_0^4 \frac{1}{5-0}$$

$$= (4 - 0) \times 0.2$$

$$= 0.8$$

Sheila can also compute the mean and variance as

$$\mu_x = \frac{b+a}{2}$$

$$= \frac{5+0}{2}$$

$$= 2.5$$

$$\sigma_x^2 = \frac{(b-a)^2}{12}$$

$$= \frac{5^2}{12}$$

$$= 2.08$$

$$\sigma = 1.44$$

The best single value she could use for her budget is the mean 2.5 ($25,000). However, she would need to caution upper management that the standard deviation for the budget value is 1.44 ($14,400), and thus her budget number has a relatively high risk. This risk could be emphasized further by noting that the range of possible values is $0 to $50,000.

Does It Make Sense?

The uniform probability distribution is important because:

1. It provides a simple introduction to continuous probability distributions.
2. It is the probability model that would be used when there is limited information about the pattern of outcomes for a continuous function.

Developing probability distributions for real applications requires considerable historical data measured on a stable process. For new processes such data might not be available, or the cost of obtaining data for new or old processes might be expensive. Thus the analyst should use the data that are available. The most basic data are likely to be upper and lower limits on the possible outcomes. That information can be used to construct a uniform pdf. However, the conclusions based on the uniform pdf provide limited insight because the uniform does not indicate that certain subintervals may have higher or lower probabilities (i.e., an "informationless" probability model).

After obtaining results based on the uniform, one might try to collect additional information that provides a more useful probability model. Certain values over the range might be more likely and a model based on that result could provide better probability estimates and more accurate means and variances. Modern computer-based information systems provide the ability to obtain considerable data from an operating process. These data could be collected and organized to provide better probability distributions. For a new process one might prepare preliminary analyses based on the uniform probability model. Then after the process has been running for a while and appears to be stable, data could be obtained from the computer-based information system and an improved probability model could be developed.   □

6.4 EXPONENTIAL DISTRIBUTION

The exponential probability distribution is used to model a number of waiting line problems, including the time between cars arriving at expressway toll booths, cars arriving at a car wash, customers arriving at a bank teller, machine breakdowns, and telephone calls to a business. The Poisson distribution (Chapter 5) is used to compute the probability of x events in a unit of time. In contrast, the exponential is used to compute the probability that the time between these events is within a particular range. Similar to the Poisson, the exponential is appropriate if:

1. The arrivals are independent. The arrival of one event does not change the probability of the arrival for the next event.
2. The arrival rate λ, the number of arrivals per unit time, is constant.

Many arrival processes can be approximated quite well by using the exponential distribution. In Example 5.13 the Poisson distribution with arrival rate $\lambda = 2.5$ was used to compute the probability that x boats would arrive during a 6-hour period. The exponential distribution can be used, for example, to compute the probability that the next boat will arrive within 3 hours of the previous boat. The elements of the exponential distribution are given in Key Idea 6.6.

Key Idea 6.6: Exponential Probability Distribution

The **exponential probability density function** is

$$f(t) = \lambda e^{-\lambda t}$$

where t is the time between arrivals ($0 \leq t \leq \infty$), λ is the mean arrival rate per unit time, and $1/\lambda$ is the mean time between arrivals. It is used to compute the probability of the time between independent arrivals, which follow the assumptions of the Poisson probability distribution.

1. The probability that the time between arrivals is t_a or less is

$$P(t \leq t_a) = (1 - e^{-\lambda t_a})$$

(Figure 6.3a). The values $e^{-\lambda t}$ can be computed on many mathematical or statistical calculators, and the values of $1 - e^{-\lambda t}$ are in Table A.9 indexed by values of $\lambda \times t$.

2. The probability that the time between arrivals is between t_b and t_a is

$$P(t_b \leq t \leq t_a) = e^{-\lambda t_b} - e^{-\lambda t_a}$$
$$= (1 - e^{-\lambda t_a}) - (1 - e^{-\lambda t_b})$$

(Figure 6.3b).

3. The mean time between arrivals is

$$\mu_t = E[T] = \frac{1}{\lambda}$$

4. The variance of the time between arrivals is

$$\sigma_t^2 = E[(t - \mu_t)^2] = \frac{1}{\lambda^2}$$

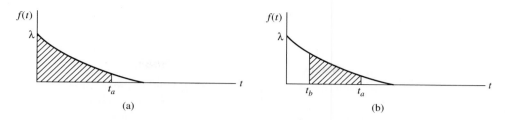

Figure 6.3   Exponential Probability Density Function

Figure 6.3 is a graphical display of the exponential distribution. The distribution intersects with the vertical axis at a value of λ and then approaches 0 asymptotically. The area under the curve is 1. The probability that the time between arrivals, t, is within a certain interval is the area under the curve for that interval.

6.4.1 Computation of Probabilities

There are several ways that the probability can be computed. First, many mathematical and statistical calculators can compute $e^{-\lambda t}$ directly. If your calculator has that capability, you can quickly complete the computation for the probability given by $1 - e^{-\lambda t}$. Alternatively, you can use Table A.9, which provides values for the probability $(1 - e^{-\lambda t})$ for various values of λt. The rows of Table A.9 are indexed by unit values and the columns by the corresponding 0.10 intervals of λt. Each entry is the value for $1 - e^{-\lambda t}$, which is the probability of an arrival within the interval 0 to t. The probability can also be computed using Minitab or most other good statistical packages. Consult the manual for your statistical computer package.

Example 5.13 showed how to compute the probability of x boats arriving in a unit time interval using the Poisson probability distribution. Here, using the exponential, the probability for the time between those same arrivals will be computed for $\lambda = 2.5$ boat arrivals per 6-hour period. To compute the probability that a boat will arrive within 3 hours of the previous boat, we first convert 3 hours into a time unit t based on the time interval for λ, which in this case is 6 hours ($t = 3/6 = 0.5$), and the probability can be computed using

$$P(t \le 0.5 \mid \lambda = 2.5) = 1 - e^{-1.25} = 0.713$$

The value 0.713 was obtained from Table A.9 from the second row by interpolating between the columns headed by 0.2 and 0.3 since λt for this problem is 1.25. Similarly, the probability that the next boat arrives between 2 and 4 hours after the previous boat is

$$P\left(\frac{2}{6} \le t \le \frac{4}{6}\right) = (1 - e^{-2.5 \times 0.67}) - (1 - e^{-2.5 \times 0.33})$$
$$= 0.81 - 0.56$$
$$= 0.25$$

The mean time between arrivals is

$$\mu_t = \frac{1}{2.5} = 0.4$$

which is equal to 2.4 hours (6 × 0.4).

The Poisson distribution is a discrete distribution that computes the probability of x arrivals in a unit time period. In contrast, the exponential is a continuous probability distribution which computes the probability of the time between arrivals. We assume that time is separated into a large number of very short intervals in which at most one arrival can occur. Thus either one or zero arrivals occurs in each interval. The independence assumption implies that the probability of an arrival in one interval does not affect the probability of an arrival in the previous or subsequent intervals. It can be shown using methods beyond this book that the Poisson and exponential distributions are derived from the same basic model and can be derived from each other assuming the same arrival rate, λ. The independent arrivals for the exponential are sometimes called Poisson arrivals.

The number of arrivals per time period should be compared to be sure there are no periods during which the arrival rate is different. The exponential is not appropriate if the rate changes during different times of the day. For example, there might be a rush of people at a bank teller window during the lunch hour in a large office complex, and assumption of a constant arrival rate would be violated. However, it might be possible to model the arrival process at the two time intervals with two different exponential distributions—each with a different arrival rate—provided that the arrivals are independent.

*The probability results are developed using integral calculus:

$$P(t \le t_a) = \int_0^{t_a} \lambda e^{-\lambda t} dt$$

$$= 1 - e^{-\lambda t_a}$$

$$P(t_b \le t \le t_a) = \int_{t_b}^{t_a} \lambda e^{-\lambda t} dt$$

$$= e^{-\lambda t_b} - e^{-\lambda t_a}$$

$$= (1 - e^{-\lambda t_a}) - (1 - e^{-\lambda t_b})$$

Example 6.1   Arrivals at a Car Wash

Bob Jacobson, a successful retailer, has decided to expand his business to include an automatic car wash. He has been negotiating with the manufacturer of an effective, high-quality unit that will do a complete car wash in exactly 6 minutes, including the time to enter and exit. Careful study of the local community indicates that on average 8 cars will seek a car wash each hour during the major usage period from 10 A.M. to 10 P.M. After consulting with him, you agree that the arrivals will be independent, with a stable arrival rate per hour. Bob knows that there is sufficient capacity to meet the average demand because the eight cars per hour would consume only 48 minutes, and thus the car wash would operate only 80% (48/60) of the time. However, he is concerned about the possibility of lines forming and discouraging potential customers from using the car wash. He has asked for your assistance prior to purchasing the equipment. He would like to know the following:

(a) What is the probability that a customer will arrive and need to wait for the previous car to finish its wash cycle?

(b) What is the probability that two cars will arrive within 6 minutes of each other?

(c) What is the probability that a car will arrive between 6 and 12 minutes after the arrival of the previous car?

(d) Bob could also purchase equipment that would complete the car wash in 4 minutes instead of 6 minutes. What benefit could be obtained from this faster equipment, assuming that the mean arrival rate continues to be 8?

Solution   (a) The probability of waiting is the probability that the next car arrives within 6 minutes of the previous car or that the time between arrivals is 6 minutes or less. The exponential distribution has a mean arrival rate $\lambda = 8$ and the time $t_a = 6/60 = 0.1$. Therefore, the probability of having to wait is

$$P(t \leq 0.1 \mid \lambda = 8) = 1 - e^{-0.8}$$
$$= 1 - 0.45$$
$$= 0.55$$

When using Table A.9, the value of $\lambda t = (8)(0.1) = 0.8$ is used to select the probability. In the first row under $\lambda t = 0.8$, the probability is 0.5507, which we round to 0.55. Thus cars can be expected to wait 55% of the time.

(b) The probability of two cars in a row waiting is the product of the probability of one car waiting times the probability of the second car waiting, because the arrivals and the time between arrivals are independent. The probability is 0.30 (0.55×0.55).

(c) The probability that a car arrives between 6 and 12 minutes of the previous car is the area under the probability density function from 0.1 (6/60) to 0.2 (12/60).

$$P(0.1 \leq t \leq 0.2 \mid \lambda = 8) = (1 - e^{-1.6}) - (1 - e^{-0.8})$$
$$= 0.80 - 0.55$$
$$= 0.25$$

(d) The advantage of a faster washing cycle is that the probability of waiting will be reduced. In this case the wash time is reduced from 6 minutes to 4 minutes. Therefore, only cars that arrived within 4 minutes or $(4/60 = 0.067$ hour) of the previous car would have to wait, and this probability is

$$P(t \leq 0.067) = 1 - e^{-8(0.067)}$$
$$= 1 - e^{-0.53}$$
$$= 1 - 0.59$$
$$= 0.41$$

Note that the parameter, $\lambda = 8$, did not change because λ depends on the number of arrivals.

In this case cars would be delayed only 41% of the time. Thus the percent of cars delayed has been reduced from 55% to 41%. The economic value to Bob Jacobson, the owner, of this improvement requires additional judgment. For example, if customers would go to another car wash when Bob's wash was in use, the faster car wash would prevent loss of 14% of his business (55 − 41). This is the maximum loss. With this new information Bob can make a judgment concerning the economic value of a faster car wash.   □

Practice Problem 6.4: Bank Teller Waiting Line

Customers arrive at random intervals at a bank teller window with an average arrival rate of 20 per hour. Determine the probability that:

(a) The next arrival will occur within 3 minutes.
(b) The next arrival will take more than 3 minutes.
(c) The next arrival will take between 2 and 5 minutes.
(d) Two consecutive arrivals will each occur between 2 and 5 minutes.   □

Problem Exercises

6.1   Assume that the time between arrivals at a checkout counter can be modeled by an exponential distribution with a mean arrival rate of 0.6 per minute. Determine the probability:
(a) Of waiting more than 1 minute for the next arrival.
(b) That the next arrival will occur in the next 1.2 minutes.
(c) That the next arrival will occur between 1 and 3 minutes.

6.2   The number of trucks arriving at a warehouse can be modeled by a Poisson distribution with an arrival rate of 6 trucks per hour. Determine the probability:
(a) Of a 15-minute wait between truck arrivals.
(b) That the next truck does not arrive in the next 30 minutes.
(c) That the next truck arrives between 10 and 30 minutes from now.

6.3   The number of service calls in a large apartment can be modeled by a Poisson distribution. Over the past 1000 hours of operating there have been a total of 800 calls. Assume that the same pattern continues. Determine the probability that:
(a) A call will occur within the next hour.
(b) 90 minutes will pass until the next call.
(c) The next call will occur between 30 and 90 minutes of the previous call.

6.4   The time between cars passing on a highway can be modeled by an exponential distribution, with an average rate of 3 cars per minute. Determine the probability that the time between cars is:
(a) At least 30 seconds.
(b) Less than 10 seconds.
(c) Between 20 and 40 seconds.

6.5 NORMAL PROBABILITY DISTRIBUTION

The normal probability distribution (Key Idea 6.7) is the most used continuous random variable probability distribution for economics and business applications. There are many reasons for this.

1. The probability distributions of a wide range of random variables are closely approximated by the normal. For example, the dimensions of parts or the weights of food packages often follow a normal distribution. This leads to quality control applications. Total sales or production often follow a normal distribution, which leads to a large family of applications in marketing and production management. The patterns of stock and bond prices are often modeled using the normal in large computer-based financial trading models. Economic models use the normal distribution for a number of economic measures.
2. Distributions of sample means approach a normal distribution given a large sample size.[2]
3. Computation of probabilities is direct and elegant.
4. The most important reason is that the normal probability distribution has led to good decisions for a number of applications.

Key Idea 6.7: Normal Probability Distribution

The **normal probability distribution** is a model for continuous random variables. It has two parameters, the mean μ and the variance σ^2. Its probability density function is the well-known bell-shaped curve, given by

$$f(x \mid \mu, \sigma^2) = \frac{1}{\sqrt{2\pi}\sigma} e^{-(x-\mu)^2/2\sigma^2}$$

The notation

$$X \sim N(\mu, \sigma^2)$$

is often used to define a normal probability distribution, with actual values for μ and σ^2.

For applied statistical analysis the normal distribution has a number of important characteristics. It is symmetric. Different central tendencies are indicated by differences in μ. In contrast, differences in σ^2 result in density functions of different width.

---

[2] For random variables with a symmetric distribution, a sample size of 25 to 30 is large, whereas for nonsymmetric distributions a sample size of 30 to 50 is large.

By selecting values for μ and σ^2, an analyst can define a large family of normal probability density functions. Figure 6.4 presents six different normal probability density functions with means, μ, equal to 100 and 200 and variances, σ^2, equal to 25, 49, and 100. Differences in the means result in shifts of the entire distribution. In contrast, differences in the variance result in distributions with different widths. Recall from Chapter 2 that as a rough guide, $\mu \pm \sigma$ covers about 68% of the range, while $\mu \pm 2\sigma$ covers about 95% of the range. For all practical purposes almost none of the range is outside $\mu \pm 3\sigma$.

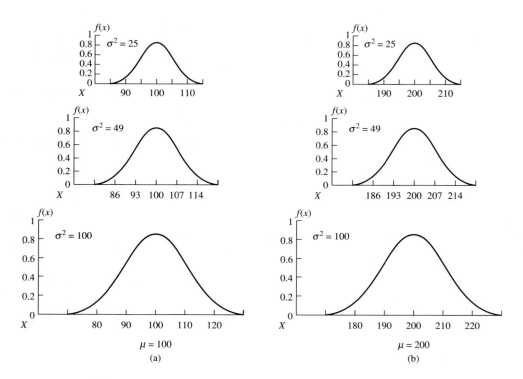

Figure 6.4   Comparison of Normal Probability Density Functions

6.5.1 Computation of Probabilities

The computation of normal distribution probabilities will be developed using an example. Consider a normal probability density function for a random variable X with mean $\mu = 50$ and variance $\sigma^2 = 100$. We want to compute the probability that x is in the interval from 50 to 60. Figure 6.5 is a schematic sketch for this problem. *When determining normal probabilities it is always useful to prepare a sketch, which helps to clearly define the desired probability.* Using the sketch and our understanding of continuous random variables, the desired probability can be computed from

$$P(50 \le X \le 60) = \int_{50}^{60} \frac{1}{\sqrt{2\pi}\,\sigma} e^{-(x-\mu)^2/2\sigma^2} \, dx$$

where $\mu = 50$ and $\sigma^2 = 100$. This is the shaded area under the density function in Figure 6.5.

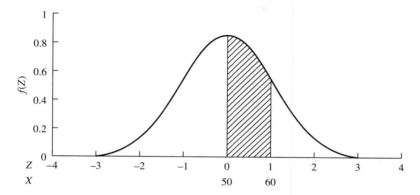

Figure 6.5   Converting X to Z to Compute Normal Probabilities

Unfortunately, the integration required in Key Idea 6.7 is impossible in closed form. Thus the area under the probability density function is determined by using tables for the standard normal distribution (Key Idea 6.8).

Key Idea 6.8: Standard Normal Random Variable

The **standard normal random variable**,

$$Z = \frac{X - \mu}{\sigma}$$

has a normal probability density function with mean 0 and variance 1, where X is any general normal random variable with mean μ and variance σ^2. Z is the distance between the mean μ and X measured in standard deviation units.

This equation can be used to convert any normal random variable to the standard normal random variable. The probabilities for the standard normal are available in Table A.1 and are used to obtain probabilities for the equivalent general normal random variables.

The expected value and variance of Z, the standard normal random variable, are obtained from

$$Z = \frac{X - \mu}{\sigma}$$

$$= \frac{X}{\sigma} - \frac{\mu}{\sigma}$$

Using this form, we find that

$$E[Z] = E\left[\frac{X}{\sigma} - \frac{\mu}{\sigma}\right]$$

$$= \frac{\mu}{\sigma} - \frac{\mu}{\sigma}$$

$$= 0$$

and similarly,

$$\sigma_Z^2 = \text{Var}\left(\frac{X}{\sigma}\right) - \text{Var}\left(\frac{\mu}{\sigma}\right)$$

$$= \frac{\sigma^2}{\sigma^2} - 0$$

$$= 1$$

Now we are ready to determine the probability that the normal random variable X is between 50 and 60 when $\mu = 50$ and $\sigma^2 = 100$. The notation

$$X \sim N(\mu, \sigma^2)$$

is read "the random variable X has a normal probability distribution with mean μ and variance σ^2." For our example problem,

$$X \sim N(50, 100)$$

and for the standard normal random variable

$$Z \sim N(0, 1)$$

Using Key Idea 6.8, convert the X intervals to standard normal or Z intervals.

$$Z_{50} = \frac{X - \mu}{\sigma}$$

$$Z = \frac{50 - 50}{10}$$

$$= 0$$

$$Z_{60} = \frac{60 - 50}{10}$$

$$= 1.0$$

Figure 6.5 shows the conversion from X to Z and indicates the area that represents the desired probability.

Table A.1 presents areas under the standard normal probability density function from the mean, $Z = 0$, up to the indicated value of Z. Each row indicates the value of Z in tenths, and the columns indicate the hundredths position for the value of Z. Thus the first column, headed by 0.00, in the row beginning with $Z = 1.0$ contains the area from $Z = 0.00$ to $Z = 1.00$. As shown, the area is 0.3413. The area from $Z = 0.0$ to $Z = 1.08$ would be found on the same line under the column headed by 0.08. This area, and hence $P(0.00 \leq Z \leq 1.08)$, is 0.3599. Verify that you know how to use the standard normal table by using the table to show that the area from $Z = 0.00$ to $Z = 1.96$ is 0.4750. Also verify that

$$P(0.00 \leq Z \leq \infty) = 0.5000$$

by applying the same reasoning.

The normal distribution is symmetric about the mean, and thus probabilities for negative values of Z are found by using the corresponding positive or absolute values of Z. This idea is shown schematically in Figure 6.6. For example, $P(-1.00 \leq Z \leq 0.00)$ is the area under the standard normal curve from $Z = -1.00$ to $Z = 0.00$, which is exactly equal to the area from $Z = 0.00$ to $Z = 1.00$. As we determined above, the area and the desired probability are 0.3413. Following the same argument, we see that $P(-1.96 \leq Z \leq 0.00)$ is equal to 0.4750; and, of course, $P(-\infty \leq Z \leq 0.00)$ equals 0.5000. Normal probabilities can also be computed in most statistical computer packages.

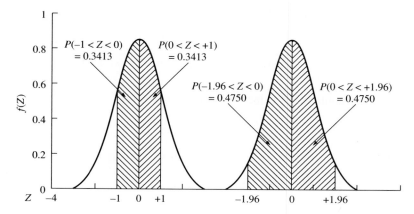

Figure 6.6   Symmetry of $-Z$ and $+Z$ for Standard Normal

Probabilities for ranges of Z that do not begin or end at the mean are computed by subtracting ranges that do. The general equation is

$$P(a \leq Z \leq b) = P(Z \leq b) - P(Z \leq a)$$

Computational examples of this result in various situations are contained in the chapter appendix.

Example 6.2   Light Bulb Maintenance

Charlie Black, the maintenance manager of a large office building, is responsible for 10,000 light bulbs that burn continuously. Each bulb has a mean life of 3000 hours with a standard deviation of 100 hours. The life of the light bulbs in this building is normally distributed. To keep an adequate inventory on hand, he wishes to know how many light bulbs will need replacing before 2850 hours.

Solution   The first step is to determine the probability that a light bulb has a life of less than 2850 hours. This probability is then multiplied by 10,000 to determine the expected number of bulbs that would be burned out. The solution is shown schematically in Figure 6.7.

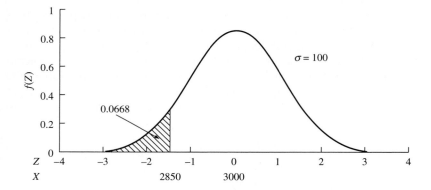

Figure 6.7   Normal Density Function for Example 6.2

Compute the Z value corresponding to 2850:

$$Z = \frac{x - \mu}{\sigma}$$

$$= \frac{2850 - 3000}{100}$$

$$= -1.50$$

The desired probability is

$$
\begin{aligned}
P(X \leq 2850) &= P(Z \leq -1.50) \\
&= P(Z \leq 0.00) - P(-1.50 \leq Z \leq 0.00) \\
&= 0.50 - 0.4332 \\
&= 0.0668
\end{aligned}
$$

Multiplying 0.0668 by 10,000, we find that the expected number of light bulbs that need to be replaced before 2850 hours is 668.   □

Example 6.3   Daily Store Sales

Sally Abercrombie is the manager of a large women's clothing store in Little Apple, Minnesota. To determine ordering patterns and inventory levels, she follows daily sales patterns. From her past experience she knows that daily sales on weekdays are normally distributed with a mean of $10,000 and a variance of 250,000. For the random variable X defined as daily weekday sales,

$$X \sim N(10,000, 250,000)$$

Sally has asked you to prepare a chart that will help her determine if sales on a particular day are very large or very small. She wants the chart to include an interval within which 95% of daily sales X would occur if sales follow their past behavior.

Solution   In this problem we are asked to determine an interval within which the random variable X (daily sales) will occur 95% of the time. In most situations managers or researchers want a symmetric interval such that X is equally likely to be above or below the mean. The symmetric interval for this problem is constructed by assigning a probability of 0.025 to both the upper and the lower tails of the normal probability distribution, as shown in Figure 6.8.

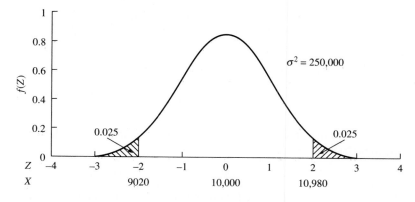

Figure 6.8   Acceptance Interval for Example 6.3

In mathematical form the problem is to find a and b in the equation

$$P(a \le X \le b) = 0.95$$

where

$$\mu - a = b - \mu$$

We will first determine Z_a and Z_b, which are the standardized normal values corresponding to a and b.

$$P(Z_a \leq Z \leq Z_b) = 0.95$$

For the symmetrical acceptance interval

$$P(Z \geq Z_b) = 0.025$$
$$P(Z \leq Z_a) = 0.025$$

Now we need to reverse the process described above for determining the probability when Z is known. The normal distribution, Table A.1, is entered with 0.4750 (0.50–0.025) the desired probability, and Z is the value from the corresponding row and column headings. By this process we find that $Z_b = 1.96$. *Find this result in Table A.1 to be sure that you know how to determine Z_b.* Using symmetry, we see that $Z_a = -1.96$, since the lower tail also has an area of 0.025. Our next step is to determine a and b. From Key Idea 6.8 we know that

$$Z = \frac{X - \mu}{\sigma}$$

Solving this equation for X, we find that

$$X = \mu + Z\sigma$$

For this example problem:

$$b = \mu + Z_b\sigma$$
$$= 10,000 + 1.96 \times 500$$
$$= 10,980$$

and by symmetry,

$$a = \mu + Z_a\sigma$$
$$= 10,000 - 1.96 \times 500$$
$$= 9020$$

By these computations we see that the interval which includes 95% of the X's goes from 9020 to 10,980.

$$P(9020 \leq X \leq 10,980) = 0.95$$

If daily sales began to appear above or below the interval more than about 1 time out of 20, Sally would have evidence that the pattern of sales is increasing or decreasing. This interval is defined as an *acceptance interval* because we accept the conclusion that sales are stable if within this interval. This idea will be developed further in Chapter 9.

Next suppose that Sally wished to have an acceptance interval that had a probability of 0.04 in the lower tail and a probability of 0.01 in the upper tail. This is shown in Figure 6.9. Following the same procedure as that used for the symmetric interval,

$$P(a \leq X \leq b) = 0.95$$

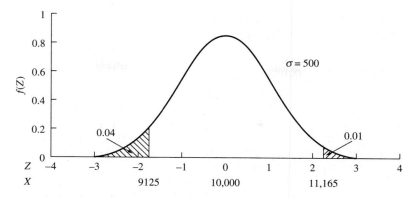

Figure 6.9 Example 6.3 with Nonsymmetric Acceptance Interval

to find a and b we will first determine Z_a and Z_b, which are the standardized normal values corresponding to a and b.

$$P(Z \leq Z_a) = 0.04$$
$$P(Z \geq Z_b) = 0.01$$

From the normal table,

$$Z_a = -1.75$$
$$Z_b = +2.33$$
$$a = \mu + Z_a\sigma$$
$$= 10,000 - 1.75 \times 500$$
$$= 9125$$
$$b = \mu + Z_b\sigma$$
$$= 10,000 + 2.33 \times 500$$
$$= 11,165$$

Thus this interval goes from 9125 to 11,165. The width of the interval is 2040 (11,165 − 9125). In contrast, the width of the symmetric interval was 1960 (10,980 − 9020). Symmetric acceptance intervals will always be narrower than nonsymmetric intervals for a given probability of acceptance. This result can be shown mathematically and you can demonstrate it using examples similar to this problem.

□

Practice Problem 6.5: Casting Weight

National Castings, Inc. produces aluminum wheel castings for a major automobile manufacturer. The weight of the castings has a normal distribution with a mean $\mu = 20$ pounds and a variance $\sigma^2 = 0.04$. Determine the probability that a casting weighs:

(a) More than 20.4 pounds.

(b) Between 19.8 and 20.4 pounds.

(c) Less than 19.95 pounds.   ☐

Problem Exercises

6.5   The daily sales for Foodfast Supermarkets can be modeled using a normal distribution with a mean of $100,000 and a standard deviation of 10,000. Determine the probability that:

(a) Daily sales exceed $115,000.

(b) Sales are less than $80,000.

(c) Sales are between $80,000 and $95,000.

6.6   The miles per gallon for a specific model of semitruck can be modeled by a normal distribution. The mean is 15 and the variance is 2.89. Determine the probability that the miles per gallon are:

(a) Less than 13.

(b) Greater than 17.5.

(c) Between 13.5 and 18.0.

(d) A truck driver claimed that he attained 20.0 miles per gallon with a similar truck. What do you think about that claim?

6.7   The annual cost for snow removal in a large northern city can be modeled by a normal distribution with a mean of $4,000,000 and a variance of 40,000,000,000. The city budget line item for snow removal is set at the mean cost. Determine the probability that the cost is:

(a) Less than $3.5 million.

(b) Between $3,650,000 and $4,250,000.

(c) The city maintains a reserve of $400,000 for emergency expenditures beyond its budget. What is the probability that the city will need to borrow money beyond its reserve for snow removal?

6.8   The product density for cereal, before sugar coating, in the Flowering Sun Cereal Company is 650 grams per liter with a variance of 400. Determine the probability that the density is:

(a) Less than 600.

(b) Greater than 685.

(c) Between 615 and 690.

6.9   The daily closing price of Amalgamated Motors stock can be modeled by a random variable with mean of $81 and a standard deviation of 11. Determine the probability that the price is:

(a) Greater than $100.

(b) Between $48 and $114.

(c) Suppose that one day the closing price was $45. What do you think about the proposed model that we have been using for the stock price?

6.10   Shirley's Variety receives a shipment of wood-cutting saws from its supplier every Monday. Under the present system enough saws are added to the stock to bring the level up to 150 saws. Weekly demand for saws can be modeled by a normal distribution with a mean of 100 and a variance of 900. Determine the probability that:

(a) All 150 saws will be sold by the end of the week.

(b) At least 100 saws are left at the end of the week.

(c) There are 20 or more, and 80 or fewer, saws left at the end of the week.

6.11   Shirley's Variety receives a shipment of wood-cutting saws from its supplier every Monday. Under the present system enough saws are added to the stock to bring the level up to 150 saws. Weekly demand for saws can be modeled by a normal distribution with a mean of 100 and a variance of 900. Customer service level is defined as the percentage of customers whose demand will be met during a particular week. Determine how many saws should be stocked at the beginning of the week so that the customer service level is:

(a) 90%.

(b) 95%.

(c) 100%.

6.12   The end-of-month cash flow for a company can be modeled by the normal distribution with a mean of $10,000 and a standard deviation of $7000. The treasurer is concerned about the possibility of a cash shortage and wishes to develop strategies to manage cash flow.

(a) What is the probability that monthly cash flow becomes negative?

(b) The treasurer wants to establish a reserve fund that can be used in case of negative cash flow. Suppose that she wants to be able to cover all but 1% of the months. How much money should be in the reserve fund?

(c) Determine the upper limit on cash flow that will be exceeded only 5% of the time.

6.13   Monthly sales in Larson's Hardware store are normally distributed with a mean of $8000 and a variance of $4,000,000.

(a) Find a lower boundary such that sales will be lower than this boundary 10% of the time.

(b) Find an upper boundary such that sales will exceed this boundary 8% of the time.

(c) Determine a symmetric interval about the mean that will include 92% of the sales data.

6.6 NORMAL APPROXIMATION FOR BINOMIAL

In this section we show how the normal distribution can be used to approximate the discrete binomial, which is used extensively in business and economics (Key Idea 6.9). This approximation can be used to compute probabilities for larger sample sizes when tables are not readily available. The normal approximation of the binomial also provides a benefit for applied problem solving. Procedures based on the normal distribution which use the mean and variance can also be applied in problems involving binomial and proportion random variables. Thus an analyst can reduce the number of different procedures that she or he needs to know for statistical problem solving in business. Figure 6.10 shows the approximation schematically.

The binomial random variable, X, is the sum of identically distributed Bernoulli random variables, X_i, $i = 1, \ldots, n$.

$$X = X_1 + X_2 + \cdots + X_n$$

Key Idea 6.9: Normal Approximation of Binomial

The binomial probability distribution for the sum X or the proportion $\hat{P}$ can be approximated by a normal with

$$\mu_X = n\pi$$
$$\sigma_X^2 = n\pi(1-\pi)$$

for the sum and

$$\mu_{\hat{P}} = \pi$$
$$\sigma_{\hat{P}}^2 = \frac{\pi(1-\pi)}{n}$$

for the proportion, provided that

$$n\pi(1-\pi) \geq 9$$

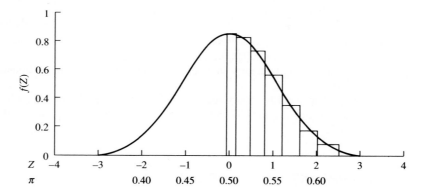

Figure 6.10   Binomial Approximation by the Normal

The normal approximation for X has parameters

$$\mu = n\pi$$
$$\sigma^2 = n\pi(1-\pi)$$

This approximation has been shown to be close enough for most problems when

$$n\pi(1-\pi) \geq 9$$

The proportion random variable, $\hat{P}$, is X divided by n and is thus a mean:

$$\hat{P} = \frac{X_1 + X_2 + \cdots + X_n}{n}$$

The normal approximation for $\hat{P}$ has parameters

$$\mu = \pi$$

$$\sigma^2 = \frac{\pi(1 - \pi)}{n}$$

From the equivalency of the probability distributions for X and $\hat{P}$, we see that the same approximate rule of thumb applies, $n\pi(1 - \pi) \geq 9$.

6.6.1 Continuity Correction

When sample sizes are small, even below those derived by the rule in Key Idea 6.9, the normal approximation can be used if we use the continuity correction factor, which we discuss here. A useful rule of thumb is to use the continuity correction factor when

$$5 \leq n\pi(1 - \pi) < 9$$

Above this interval the correction is not needed, and below the interval the exact binomial values should be used.

There is, of course, some error when we approximate a discrete probability distribution, the binomial, by a continuous probability distribution, the normal. The problem is illustrated in Figure 6.11. The binomial probabilities for each discrete value are represented by the rectangles, while the normal probability density function is a continuous curve. The discrete numbers corresponding to the normal occur at the center of each rectangle. Suppose that we wish to compute the probability $P(X \leq 19)$ at the upper end of an interval. The normal approximation includes only one-half of the rectangle corresponding to 19 and thus understates the binomial probability. Similarly, if we wish to compute $P(X < 19)$, the normal approximation includes one-half of the rectangle corresponding to 19 and thus overstates the binomial probability. To correct for this error we define the normal interval from a point one-half the distance between two integers. Thus for these examples:

Binomial   Normal Approximation

$$P(X \leq 19) \approx P(X \leq 19.5)$$
$$P(X < 19) \approx P(X \leq 18.5)$$

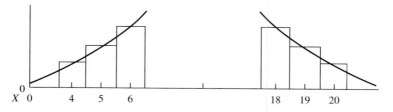

Figure 6.11   Binomial Continuity Correction

When the lower end of the interval is defined, the process is reversed:

$$\text{Binomial} \qquad \text{Normal Approximation}$$
$$P(5 \le X) \approx P(4.5 \le X)$$
$$P(5 < X) \approx P(5.5 \le X)$$

Combining these into intervals we find:

$$\text{Binomial} \qquad\qquad \text{Normal Approximation}$$
$$P(5 \le X \le 19) \approx P(4.5 \le X \le 19.5)$$
$$P(5 < X < 19) \approx P(5.5 \le X \le 18.5)$$

Example 6.4   Sales Contacts

The sales department of a large computer manufacturer is experimenting with the use of telephone contacts with potential customers instead of personal visits. Past data indicate that 30% of personal visits have resulted in a sale. After 3 weeks, telephone calls to 30 potential customers resulted in eight sales. The group of customers contacted by phone had a similar potential for a sale. The manager, Rita Selles, wants to know if the use of phone contacts is decreasing sales.

  Solution   We need to determine if eight sales out of a sample of 30 contacts is reasonable given that sales have a binomial probability distribution with $\pi = 0.30$. As an analyst you would, of course, attempt to determine if the assumptions of independent calls and a similar contact pool have been met. In problems of this type we usually compute the probability of eight or fewer sales given that $n = 30$ and $\pi = 0.30$. That is, we want to know the probability of a result as extreme or more extreme than the one observed. To use the normal approximation, we first check to see if the approximation is suitable by computing $n\pi(1 - \pi) = 30(0.30)(1 - 0.30) = 6.3$. Since this result is greater than 5, the normal approximation can be used. But we should use the continuity correction. The solution is

$$P(X \le 8 \mid n = 30, \pi = 0.30) \approx P(X \le 8.5 \mid \mu = n\pi, \sigma^2 = n\pi(1 - \pi)$$
$$= P(X \le 8.5 \mid \mu = 9, \sigma^2 = 6.3)$$
$$= P\left(Z \le \frac{8.5 - 9}{\sqrt{6.3}}\right)$$
$$= P(Z \le -0.20)$$
$$= 0.5000 - 0.0793$$
$$= 0.4207$$

From this result we see that eight or fewer sales out of 30 calls could be expected 42% of the time. We conclude that the experience does not provide evidence that phone contacts are reducing sales. Of course, the result also does not "prove" that phone contacts have the same sales success. (We will explore the possible conclusions from analyses such as this when we study hypothesis testing in Chapter 11.)

After this analysis, Rita wants to know the number of sales that would have led us to conclude that sales have been reduced. She wants a critical or decision number X_c such that sales at or less than this number would be very unlikely if $\pi = 0.30$. A very unlikely situation can be defined as one that has a small probability: for example, 0.05. We reverse the process of the previous solution:

$$P(X \leq X_c \mid n = 30, \pi = 0.30) = 0.05$$

$$P(X \leq X_c + 0.5 \mid \mu = 9, \sigma^2 = 6.3) = 0.05$$

$$P\left(Z \leq \frac{X_c + 0.5 - 9}{\sqrt{6.3}}\right) = 0.05$$

$$P(Z \leq -1.645) = 0.05$$

and thus

$$\frac{X_c + 0.5 - 9}{\sqrt{6.3}} = -1.645$$

$$X_c = -0.5 + 9 - 1.645\sqrt{6.3}$$

$$= 4.37$$

Statisticians would generally round the answer down to 4. We would report to Rita Selles that if the number of sales had been four or less, she could have concluded that telephone contacts were reducing sales.   ☐

Example 6.5   Economic Development

An economic development project has constructed a well to provide clean water in a remote rural village. Historically, 40% of the children in this village have had a serious stomach disease. Two years after the well began operating, a medical evaluation team discovered that only 8 children out of a sample of 50 had the stomach disease. Do we have evidence that the incidence of stomach disease among children has been reduced?

Solution   We need to determine the probability of 8 or fewer children with disease in the sample of 50, if the probability of any individual child having the disease is 0.40. If that probability is small, we conclude that the incidence of stomach disease has been reduced. If we also know that no other major health improvement programs have occurred in the village, we could state that the new well has improved the health of children. First we check and find that $n\pi(1 - \pi) = 50 \times 0.40 \times 0.60 = 12 > 9$, and thus the normal approximation for the binomial can be used. Computation of the probability is

$$P(X \leq 8 \mid n = 50, \pi = 0.40) \approx P(X \leq 8 \mid \mu = 20, \sigma^2 = 12)$$

$$= P\left(Z \leq \frac{8 - 20}{\sqrt{12}}\right)$$

$$= P(Z \leq -3.46)$$

$$< 0.001$$

The evidence seems very strong that the probability of disease for an individual child is less than 0.40.   □

Example 6.6   Election Forecasting

The success in forecasting elections by television networks is a good example of the success of probability methods in applied problems. Consider how elections can be predicted by using relatively small samples in a simplified example. Daniel Johnson, an election forecaster, has obtained a random sample of 900 voters in which 500 indicate that they will vote for Charlie King. Should Charlie anticipate winning the election?

Solution   In this problem we assume only two candidates, and thus if more than 50% of the population supports Charlie, he will win the election. We will compute the probability that 500 or more voters from a sample of 900 support Charlie under the assumption that exactly 50%, $\pi = 0.50$, of the entire population supports Charlie.

$$P(X \geq 500 \mid n = 900, \pi = 0.50) \approx P(X \geq 500 \mid \mu = 450, \sigma^2 = 225)$$
$$= P\left(Z \geq \frac{500 - 450}{\sqrt{225}}\right)$$
$$= P(Z \geq 3.33)$$
$$= 0.001$$

(Note that we did not use the continuity correction because n is large.) The probability of 500 successes out of 900 trials if $\pi = 0.50$ is very small, and therefore we conclude that π must be greater than 0.50. Hence we predict that Charlie King will win the election.   □

Practice Problem 6.6: Percentage Purchasers

A company knows that its product is purchased by 20% of the people in Dallas, Texas. A random sample of 400 people from Dallas is obtained and the proportion of purchasers, $\hat{P}$, is computed. Determine the probability that $\hat{P}$ is:

(a) Greater than 23%.
(b) Less than 18%.
(c) Between 17% and 24%.   □

Problem Exercises

6.14   The bread produced by Brownstone Bread, Inc. is purchased by 30% of the people in Big Apple, Iowa. Suppose that a random sample of 100 people is selected. Determine the probability that:
(a) More than 37 are purchasers of Brownstone's bread.
(b) Fewer than 25 are purchasers.
(c) From 26 to 35 are purchasers.

6.15   A new computerized claims processing system has been installed by a major health insurance company. Only 20% of the claims require work by a human claims processor when this system is used. On a particular day 500 claims arrived for processing. Determine the probability that:

   (a) More than 120 claims will require processing by a human claims processor.
   (b) Fewer than 75 claims will require human processing.
   (c) Define a symmetric interval for the number of human processed claims such that 95% of those claims will be included in the interval.

6.16   Big Fork Lumber Company buys hardwood logs from neighboring loggers. From past experience they know that 60% of the logs they receive will be No. 1 select and the rest will be No. 2 grade. A shipment of 250 logs has just arrived. Determine the probability that:

   (a) At least 160 logs are No. 1 select grade.
   (b) At least 236 logs are No. 1 select.
   (c) The number of No. 1 select logs is at least 142 but less than 159.

6.17   Suppose that exactly 55% of the voters support an increase in taxes to support local education. A random sample of 300 workers is selected and each person is asked if he or she supports a tax increase. Determine the probability that:

   (a) More than 59% of the sample supports higher taxes.
   (b) 49% or less of the sample supports higher taxes.
   (c) More than 50% of the sample supports higher taxes.

6.18   River Valley Foods believes that their gourmet meat products are preferred by 40% of the families in a large metropolitan area. They have recently obtained a random sample of 350 households and asked them if they prefer River Valley gourmet meat products. Assuming that 40% prefer their product, determine the probability that the sample proportion is:

   (a) Above 0.42.
   (b) Between 0.37 and 0.44.
   (c) Between 0.36 and 0.39.

6.19   Sellitquick, a regional mail-order house, tries to manage its accounts receivable so that a maximum of 20% are older than 30 days. A random sample of 80 accounts receivable are obtained and checked for their age. Assuming that they are meeting their goal, determine the probability that:

   (a) 28% or more are older than 30 days.
   (b) 16% or less are older than 30 days.
   (c) Between 19% and 28% are older than 30 days.

6.7 NORMAL APPROXIMATION FOR POISSON

The Poisson distribution can also be approximated by the normal if the mean λ is greater than 5, but if λ is between 5 and 10, a continuity correction should be used (Key Idea 6.10). Statistical procedures based on the normal distribution provide a rich set of analysis options. If these options can also be applied to problems based on the Poisson distribution, we increase the analysis possibilities. In addition, probabilities can be computed for those problems that have large values of λ. The development of this approximation follows that for the binomial approximation. Here the key differences are developed and an example presented.

Key Idea 6.10: Normal Approximation of Poisson

Given that the number of occurrences X is a Poisson random variable with mean λ, the probability that x is between a and b can be approximated by

$$P(a \leq X \leq b) = P\left(\frac{a - \lambda}{\sqrt{\lambda}} \leq Z \leq \frac{b - \lambda}{\sqrt{\lambda}}\right)$$

with $\mu_x = \lambda$ and $\sigma_x^2 = \lambda$ and $\lambda > 5$.

If λ is between 5 and 10, the continuity correction should be applied and the approximation is

$$P(a \leq X \leq b) = P\left(\frac{a - 0.5 - \lambda}{\sqrt{\lambda}} \leq Z \leq \frac{b + 0.5 - \lambda}{\sqrt{\lambda}}\right)$$

Example 6.7   Quality Improvement

Sheldahl, Inc. is a producer of flexible circuits for the automobile and computer industries made from continuous rolls of copper deposited on a plastic resin film material. In the manufacturing process micrometer-sized bubbles can occur in the thin copper film. Flexible circuit connectors are photoetched on the copper film. That process leaves a set of many small conducting paths for the transfer of electronic signals. If a bubble occurs on one of these paths, the flexible circuit is defective. The number of defective circuits per roll of material depends on the location and frequency of the bubbles. Jean Bronk, manager of quality control, has implemented a number of improvements to reduce the number of bubbles in the copper film. For the past six months the average number of defective circuits per roll was 20. With the new procedures a roll was produced that had only 12 defective circuits. Does this result indicate that an improvement has occurred in the process?

Solution   We want to determine if 12 defective circuits is a typical or unusually low number given a long-term average of 20. Defective circuits result from randomly located bubbles occurring at a critical location in the copper film—a bubble occurs or it does not and the probability of a bubble at any location can be assumed to be the same over the length of the roll. Therefore, it is possible to conclude that the number of defective circuits is a Poisson random variable. By using the normal approximation for the Poisson, we can determine the probability of 12 or fewer defective circuits if the mean is $\lambda = \mu = 20$. If that probability is small, it can be concluded that the process has improved and the average number of defective circuits is lower. For this problem the rate of defective circuits per roll is $\lambda = 20$. The normal approximation thus has $\mu = 20$ and $\sigma^2 = 20$ and the probability is

$$P(X \leq 12 \mid \mu = 20, \sigma = 4.47) = P\left(Z \leq \frac{12 - 20}{4.47}\right)$$

$$= 0.037$$

Since this probability is small, we can tell Jean that there is strong evidence that the number of defects has been reduced by the improvements. □

Problem Exercises

6.20   In Example 6.7, what is the probability that the number of defective circuits is between 22 and 26 if the mean is 20?

6.21   Acme Trucking, Inc. operates a large transfer warehouse in which less-than-truckload shipments are received and combined for shipment to common destinations. Trucks with several partial shipments arrive and are unloaded. The partial shipments are then reloaded on trucks with a common destination. Trucks arrive randomly at a rate of 12 trucks per hour. Determine the probability that:
   (a) More than 16 trucks arrive in a particular hour.
   (b) Between 8 and 15 trucks arrive in a particular hour.

6.22   A large manufacturer of computer memory chips guarantees that shipments of 20,000 chips will have an average of 15 defective chips. A shipment of 20,000 is found to contain 20 defective chips. Can we conclude that this shipment has an average number of defective chips that is greater than the guaranteed mean?

6.8 LINEAR FUNCTIONS OF A RANDOM VARIABLE

Business analysts use mathematical functions to study and solve a wide range of problems. Accountants express total cost and total revenue as functions of the quantity of goods sold. Product managers express the relationship between quantity of goods sold and price as a demand function, which is used to help select the price that will result in the largest revenue and/or profit. In many introductory business textbooks these functions assume that variables such as quantity and price can be determined exactly. However, a more realistic analysis indicates that these variables are random variables.

When a variable such as the number of units produced, X, in a total cost function

$$Y = a + bX$$

is a random variable, the quantity demanded, Y, is also a random variable. (a is the fixed cost and b is the variable cost per unit.)

The objective of this section is to learn how to compute the mean and variance for random variables that are functions of other random variables. Let us begin by considering some examples:

1. A **revenue function** in which the number of units sold, X, is a random variable, the price, b, is a constant, and total revenue, R, is a random variable determined by

$$R = bX$$

2. The **consumption**, C, of a product as a function of income, X:

$$C = a + bX$$

with disposable income represented by the random variable X and consumption represented by the random variable C. The marginal propensity to consume, b, and the intercept, a, are constants.

3. A **production cost function** with the random variable X representing the number of units produced and a random variable T representing the total production cost would be defined by

$$T = a + bX$$

where a is a constant measuring fixed production costs and b is the variable production cost per unit.

In the examples above, the linear combinations of random variables are also random variables. Since a and b are constants, it seems reasonable to conclude that the variation in R, C, or T depends directly on X. In this section we show how the mean and variance of these linear functions can be determined directly from the mean and variance of X using the expected value operator E (Key Idea 6.11).

6.8.1 Making the Algebra Simple

Complicated algebra may be simplified in the expected value E form without having to go through the effort of summing or integration. For example, constants may be moved outside the expectation operator, linear combinations within an operator may be expressed as individual terms, and mathematical operations can be performed within the operator. The rules for the $\sum$ and the $\int$ operators, which were learned in calculus, also apply to the E operator. The following results with a and b as constants can be derived using Key Idea 6.11 and are used frequently in the following sections.

1. Constant times a random variable:

$$E[aX] = aE[X] = a\mu$$

Key Idea 6.11: Expected Values of Functions

The expected value for functions of random variables such as

$$g(X) = a + bX$$

can be computed as

$$E[g(X)] = E[a + bX]$$
$$= \sum g(x_i) \times f(x_i)$$
$$= \sum (a + bx_i) f(x_i) \qquad \text{all } i$$
$$= a \sum f(x_i) + b \sum x_i f(x_i)$$
$$= a + b\mu_x$$

for discrete random variables and*

$$E[g(X)] = E[a + bX]$$
$$= \int g(x) \times f(x)\, dx$$
$$= \int (a + bx) f(x)\, dx$$
$$= a + b\mu_x$$

for continuous random variables.

$f(x)$ is the probability density function for random variable X.

---

2. Expected value of a constant:

$$E[a] = aE[1] = a$$

3. Two linear functions of a random variable:

$$E[aX + bX] = aE[X] + bE[X] = (a + b)E[X] = (a + b)\mu$$

4. Quadratic function of a random variable:

$$E[(a + bX)^2] = E[a^2 + 2abX + b^2X^2]$$
$$= E[a^2] + E[2abX] + E[b^2X^2]$$
$$= a^2 + 2abE[X] + b^2E[X^2]$$
$$= a^2 + 2ab\mu + b^2E[X^2]$$

The examples above apply for both discrete and continuous random variables. The expected value operator is a powerful tool for simplifying the mathematics associated with random variables. It will be helpful to refer to the results above when solving problems.

6.8.2 Mean and Variance of a Function: Expected Value

Revenue function.   The revenue function is a simple linear equation,

$$R = bX$$

where b is a constant and R and X are random variables. The mean, μ, is

$$\begin{aligned}
\mu_R = E[R] &= E[bX] \\
&= bE[X] \\
&= b\mu_X
\end{aligned}$$

Note that the constant b can be moved from within to in front of the E operator.

The variance, σ^2, is

$$\begin{aligned}
\sigma_R^2 = E[(R - \mu_R)^2] \\
= E[(bX - b\mu_X)^2] \\
= E[b^2(X - \mu_X)^2] \\
= b^2 E[(X - \mu_X)^2] \\
= b^2 \sigma_X^2
\end{aligned}$$

Note that the variance of a random variable multiplied by a constant is the variance of the random variable times the constant squared.

The standard deviation is

$$\sigma_R = b\sigma_X$$

The standard deviation of a random variable multiplied by a constant is the standard deviation of the random variable times the constant.

Consumption function.   The consumption function is a linear function with a constant, a, added to the product of a coefficient, b, multiplied times a random variable:

$$C = a + bX$$

The mean, μ, is

$$\begin{aligned}
\mu_C = E[C] &= E[a + bX] \\
&= E[a] + bE[X] \\
&= a + b\mu_X
\end{aligned}$$

Note that the expected value of a constant is a constant.

The variance is

$$\begin{aligned}
\sigma_C^2 &= E[(C - \mu_C)^2] \\
&= E[(a + bX - (a + b\mu_X))^2] \\
&= E[(bX - b\mu_X)^2] \\
&= b^2 E[(X - \mu_X)^2] \\
&= b^2 \sigma_X^2
\end{aligned}$$

Note that adding a constant to a random variable shifts the mean but does not change the variance.

$$\sigma_C = b\sigma_X$$

The results above apply equally to discrete and to continuous random variables since no actual probability distributions were used to develop the results.

Production cost function.   Next consider the production cost function,

$$T = a + bX$$

The mean is

$$\begin{aligned}
\mu_T = E[T] &= E[a + bX] \\
&= a + bE[X] \\
&= a + b\mu_X
\end{aligned}$$

and the variance is

$$\begin{aligned}
\sigma_T^2 &= E[(T - E[T])^2] \\
&= E[(a + bX - (a + b\mu_X))^2] \\
&= b^2 \sigma_X^2
\end{aligned}$$

The results above apply for both discrete and continuous random variables. The expected value operator is a powerful tool for simplifying the mathematics associated with random variables. It will be helpful to refer to these results when solving problems (Key Idea 6.12).

Example 6.8   Production Cost

Arthur Sheldon, the chief accountant for McKenzie Computers Ltd., is developing a budget for the assembly of a new microcomputer. From the company records Arthur knows that the monthly cost consists of a fixed setup cost of $500 plus $200 per hour of operation. From the industrial engineering department Arthur discovers that the assembly of each new microcomputer requires 6 minutes. After some discussion with the marketing department, Arthur receives a report which indicates that monthly demand, X, will have a mean, μ, of 1000 units with a variance,

---

Key Idea 6.12: μ and σ^2 for Linear Functions of Random Variables

Linear functions of random variables are also random variables, which have a mean, μ, and a variance, σ^2. The mean and variance, with a and b as constants, are used frequently in many applications:

1. Constant times a random variable:
$$W = aX$$
$$E[aX] = aE[X] = a\mu_X$$
$$\sigma^2(aX) = a^2\sigma_X^2$$

2. Expected value of a constant:
$$E[a] = aE[1] = a$$
$$\sigma^2(a) = 0$$

3. Constant plus a linear function of a random variable:
$$W = a + bX$$
$$E[a + bX] = a + bE[X] = a + bE[X] = a + b\mu_X$$
$$\sigma^2(a + bX) = b^2\sigma_X^2$$

Note that these means and variances have a similar form to those introduced for linear combinations of sample statistics in Chapter 2. The only difference is that with random variables we use $E[X]$ and σ_X^2 instead of $\bar{X}$ and S_X^2.

σ^2, of 64 units. These values were computed from a probability distribution obtained from a recent market survey. How should he proceed in developing a monthly budget?

Solution With this information Arthur realizes that he has a problem which uses random variables. Monthly cost is a function of the number of units, and the number of units are a function of market demand, X, a random variable. Arthur decides that he will determine the mean and variance of the monthly production cost. The first step is to determine the expected value and variance for the total assembly time. Total assembly time, T, in hours is determined by

$$T = 0.1X$$

The expected value and variance of time, T, are

$$\begin{aligned}
\mu_T = E[T] &= E[0.1X] \\
&= 0.1E[X] \\
&= 0.1 \times 1000 \\
&= 100 \\
\sigma_T^2 = E[(T - \mu_T)^2] \\
&= (0.1)^2 \sigma_X^2 \\
&= 0.01 \times 64 \\
&= 0.64
\end{aligned}$$

The cost of production, C, in dollars is determined by the following linear function of time, T:

$$C = 500 + 200T$$

The expected value and variance of cost, C, are

$$\begin{aligned}
\mu_C = E[C] &= E[500 + 200T] \\
&= 500 + 200\mu_T \\
&= 500 + 200 \times 100 \\
&= 20{,}500 \\
\sigma_C^2 = E[(C - \mu_C)^2] \\
&= E[(500 + 200T - (500 + 200\mu_T))^2] \\
&= (200)^2 \sigma_T^2 \\
&= 40{,}000 \times 0.64 \\
&= 25{,}600 \\
\sigma_C &= 160
\end{aligned}$$

Based on this analysis, Arthur can now express his budget in terms of the mean, $\mu_C = 20{,}500$, and $\sigma_C^2 = 25{,}600$ or $\sigma_C = 160$. This provides more information than merely reporting the budget as a single value and hoping that actual expenditures are close. Later we learn how the mean and variance can be used to determine the probability that the budget will exceed a particular value.

The more mathematically sophisticated readers will have noted that the problem could be simplified by expressing the budget, C, as a function of the number of units, X, demanded by the market.

$$\begin{aligned}
C &= 500 + 200T \\
&= 500 + 200(0.1X) \\
&= 500 + 20X
\end{aligned}$$

The mean and variance of total cost, C, are

$$\mu_C = 500 + 20\mu_X$$
$$= 500 + 20 \times 1000$$
$$= 20,500$$
$$\sigma_C^2 = (20)^2\sigma_X^2$$
$$= 400(64)$$
$$= 25,600 \qquad \square$$

Problem Exercises

6.23   The number of microprocessor chips produced per setup run is a normally distributed random variable, X, with a mean of 2000 and a standard deviation of 200. The fixed setup costs for a run are $5000 and the variable cost per unit is $3.
(a) Write a linear equation for total cost, Y, as a function of the random variable X.
(b) What are the mean and variance of Y?
(c) What is the probability that total cost is greater than $12,000?

6.24   The price for 1 share of Millie Trucks is normally distributed with a mean of $25 and a standard deviation of $2. Suppose that you have 150 shares of this stock. Determine:
(a) The mean and variance of the total value of your stock holding.
(b) The probability that your stock holding has a total value greater than $4000.
(c) The probability that your stocks have a total value less than $3400.

6.25   The monthly budget for a manufacturing plant provides $5000 for spare parts. The cost per day is normally distributed with a mean of $250 and a standard deviation of $25. Determine:
(a) The mean and variance of expenditures for a total of 18 days.
(b) The probability that the monthly budget of $5000 is consumed after 18 days.
(c) The mean and variance of expenditures for a total of 20 days.
(d) The probability that the entire $5000 is not consumed at the end of 20 days.

SUMMARY OF KEY IDEAS

PRACTICE PROBLEM SOLUTIONS

6.1   The first step is to convert the budget numbers into the random variable, which has the range 0 to 5, with each unit interval equal to $10,000. The probability density function is

$$f(x) = 0.4 - 0.08x \qquad 0 \le x \le 5$$

To determine the probability that the project will be completed within a $40,000 budget limit, we need to obtain the area under the probability density function when the random variable, y, is in the range 0 to 4. This can be done by using integral calculus or by using the geometric properties of triangles.

   Geometric solution. Because the total area under the pdf in Figure 6.12 is 1, we can obtain the area from 0 to 4 by subtracting from 1 the area of the small triangle from 4 to 5. The height of this small triangle can be obtained from the pdf:

$$f(4) = 0.4 - 0.08 \times 4 = 0.08$$

and the base is 1. Therefore, the area of the small triangle is 0.04 ($0.5 \times 1.0 \times 0.08$) and the probability that y is less than or equal to 4 is

$$1.0 - 0.04 = 0.96$$

   $\star$ Calculus solution. The solution is obtained by integrating the area under the probability density function from 0 to 4:

$$P(0 \le x \le 4) = \int_0^4 (0.40 - 0.08x)\, dx$$

$$= \left[0.40x - \frac{0.08x^2}{2.0} \right]_0^4$$

$$= \left[0.40 \times 4.0 - \frac{0.08 \times 4^2}{2.0} \right] - 0$$

$$= 1.6 - 0.64$$

$$= 0.96$$

The probability that x is between 2 and 4 can also be solved by both the geometric method and the calculus method as shown in Figure 6.12.

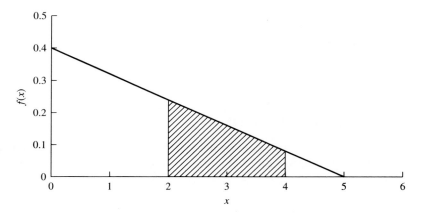

Figure 6.12   Probability Density Function Example for Practice
Problems 6.1, 6.2, 6.3

Geometric method. Subtract the area of the triangle from 4 to 5 from the area of
the triangle from 2 to 5:

area of triangle from 2 to 5 − area of triangle from 4 to 5
$$= [0.5 \times (0.4 - 0.08 \times 2) \times (5 - 2)] - [0.5 \times (0.4 - 0.08 \times 4) \times (5 - 4)]$$
$$= 0.36 - 0.04$$
$$= 0.32$$

* *Calculus method:*

$$P(2 \leq x \leq 4) = \int_2^4 (0.4 - 0.08x)\, dx$$

$$= \left[0.4x - \frac{0.08x^2}{2} \right]_2^4$$

$$= \left[0.4 \times 4 - \frac{0.08 \times 4^2}{2} \right] - \left[0.4 \times 2 - \frac{0.08 \times 2^2}{2} \right]$$

$$= 0.96 - 0.64$$

$$= 0.32$$

*6.2 The expected value for the continuous random variable defined by Figure 6.12 is

$$E(X) = \int_0^5 x f(x)\, dx$$

$$= \int_0^5 x(0.4 - 0.08x)\, dx$$

$$= \int_0^5 (0.4x - 0.08x^2)\, dx$$

$$= \left[\frac{0.4x^2}{2} - \frac{0.08x^3}{3} \right]_0^5$$

$$= \left[\frac{(0.4)(25)}{2} - \frac{(0.08)(125)}{3} \right] - \left[\frac{(0.4)(0)}{2} - \frac{(0.08)(0)}{3} \right]$$

$$= \frac{10}{2} - \frac{10}{3}$$

$$= 1.67$$

6.3 Using the investment example whose probability density function is defined by Figure 6.12:

$$\sigma^2 = E[(X - \mu)^2]$$

$$= \int (x - \mu)^2 f(x)\, dx$$

$$= \int_0^5 (x - 1.67)^2 (0.4 - 0.08x)\, dx$$

The computations can be simplified by first obtaining $E[X^2]$ and then using Key Idea 6.5:

$$E[X^2] = \int x^2 f(x)\, dx$$

$$= \int_0^5 x^2 (0.4 - 0.08x)\, dx$$

$$= \left[\frac{x^3 0.4}{3} - \frac{x^4 0.08}{4} \right]_0^5$$

$$= \left[\frac{5^3 0.4}{3 - \dfrac{5^4 0.08}{4}} \right]$$

$$= 4.167$$

Using this result, the variance is

$$\sigma^2 = E[(X - \mu)^2]$$
$$= E[X^2] - \mu^2$$
$$= 4.167 - 1.67^2$$
$$= 1.389$$

6.4 The time between arrivals at the bank is an exponential distribution with mean $\lambda = 20$ arrivals per hour.

(a) The problem is to find the probability that the time between arrivals is less than or equal to 3 minutes or $3/60 = 0.05$ hour.

$$P(t \le 0.05) = 1 - e^{-\lambda t} = 1 - e^{-(20)(0.05)} = 1 - 0.368 = 0.632$$

(b) The probability that t is greater than 3 minutes is the complement of the probability that t is less than or equal to 3.

$$P(t > 0.05) = 1 - 0.632 = 0.368$$

(c) The probability that the time is between 2 and 5 minutes is equal to the probability that the time is between 0.033 (2/60) hour and 0.0833 (5/60) hour:

$$P(0.033 \le t \le 0.083) = (1 - e^{-(20)(0.083)}) - (1 - e^{-(20)(0.033)})$$
$$= 0.812 - 0.488 = 0.32$$

(d) The probability of two consecutive arrivals between 2 and 5 minutes is the probability of one arrival in the interval squared because arrivals are independent.

$$P(2 \text{ consecutive arrivals between 2 and 5 minutes})$$
$$= (P(0.0333 \le t \le 0.0833))(P(0.0333 \le t \le 0.0833))$$
$$= (0.32)(0.32)$$
$$= 0.1024$$

6.5 The weight of the castings has a normal distribution with mean $\mu = 20$ and variance $\sigma^2 = 0.04$. To compute the required probabilities, we first convert to the standard normal Z and then use Table A.1. A simple sketch of the appropriate normal distribution will assist your solution process.

(a)
$$P(X > 20.4) = P\left(Z > \frac{20.4 - 20.0}{\sqrt{0.04}}\right)$$
$$= P(Z > 2.0)$$
$$= 0.0228$$

(b)
$$P(19.8 < X < 20.4) = P\left(\frac{19.8 - 20.0}{0.2} < Z < \frac{20.4 - 20.0}{0.2}\right)$$
$$= P(-1.0 < Z < 2.0)$$
$$= 0.3413 + 0.4772$$
$$= 0.8185$$

(c)
$$P(X < 19.95) = P\left(Z < \frac{19.95 - 20.0}{0.2}\right)$$
$$= P(Z < -0.25)$$
$$= 0.50 - 0.0987$$
$$= 0.4013$$

6.6 In this problem we approximate the distribution of the sample proportion $\hat{P}$ by the normal distribution with mean $\pi = 0.20$ and standard deviation

$$\sigma = \sqrt{\frac{\pi(1-\pi)}{n}} = \sqrt{\frac{0.2(1-0.2)}{400}} \doteq 0.02$$

Again a sketch of the normal distribution will assist your solution.

(a)
$$P(\hat{P} > 0.23) = P\left(Z > \frac{0.23 - 0.20}{0.02}\right)$$
$$= P(Z > 1.5)$$
$$= 0.50 - 0.4332$$
$$= 0.0668$$

(b)
$$P(\hat{P} < 0.18) = P\left(Z < \frac{0.18 - 0.20}{0.02}\right)$$
$$= P(Z < -1.0)$$
$$= 0.50 - 0.3413$$
$$= 0.1587$$

(c)
$$P(0.17 < \hat{P} < 0.24) = P\left(\frac{0.17 - 0.20}{0.02} < Z < \frac{0.24 - 0.20}{0.02}\right)$$
$$= P(-1.5 < Z < 2.0)$$
$$= 0.4332 + 0.4772$$
$$= 0.9104$$

CHAPTER PROBLEMS

6.1 Rachel Rags, owner of Small Men's Fashions, Inc., has determined that her accounts receivable, in units of $100s, can be modeled as a random variable X, which has the probability density function:

$$f(x) = 0.20 - 0.02x \qquad 0 \le x \le 10$$

(a) Prepare a graphical sketch of the probability density function.
Determine:
(b) $P(X > 5)$.

(c) $P(X \leq 8)$.

(d) $P(2 \leq X \leq 8)$.

(e) $E[X]$ and σ_X^2.

6.2   The probability density function for the number of gallons of gasoline purchased by a customer at Friendly Freddie's Fuel is

$$f(x) = 0.01 \qquad 0 \leq x \leq X_{max}$$

(a) Freddie used a cheap consultant who forgot to tell him the value of X_{max}, and now the consultant has left town with Freddie's check. Please help Freddie by determining X_{max}.

(b) Freddie wants to know the probability that a customer will purchase between 4 and 12 gallons of gasoline.

(c) Compute the probability that a customer purchases more than 5 gallons of gasoline.

* (d) Determine the mean and variance of gasoline purchases.

6.3   Professor Patricia Prob has determined that the probability density function of disposable income is

$$f(x) = 0.2 \qquad 10 \leq X \leq 15$$

The economist Charlie Savetheworld indicates that the savings function is

$$S = -2.0 + 0.2X$$

Determine the mean and variance of savings, S.

6.4   Brown City Auto Repairs, Inc. provides automobile service to persons who drive in without previous appointments. This service results in wide variations in the number of customers who want service at any particular time. They wish to study this problem in greater detail so that they can better plan the number of mechanics that should be scheduled. Based on an analysis of the arrival pattern of customers, you have discovered that the time between customer arrivals can be modeled by the probability density function:

$$f(x) = 2e^{-2x} \qquad 0 \leq x \leq \infty$$

where x is the time in hours between customer arrivals and e is the base for natural logarithms.

(a) Prepare a sketch of the probability density function.

(b) Show that the area under the probability density function is equal to 1. (This requires integral calculus.)

* (c) Develop a mathematical function for $F(x)$. (Requires calculus.)

(d) Compute $P(0 \leq x \leq 2)$.

(e) Compute $P(x \geq 0.4)$.

(f) Compute $P(0.2 \leq x \leq 0.8)$.

(g) A mechanic requires 50 minutes to complete a particular repair. What is the probability that a second customer will have arrived while he is completing the first repair?

6.5   The manager of the Big Hill Sand Company has asked for your help to develop a probability model for the daily demand for sand. He knows that demand varies from 0 to 10 tons, with any value between being equally likely. You decide to model the daily demand for sand as a uniform random variable ranging from 0 to 10.

(a) Write an equation for the probability density function and prepare a graphical sketch.

(b) Compute the mean and variance for this random variable.

(c) What is the probability that demand is between 3 and 8 tons?

(d) The manager schedules enough equipment to deliver 8 tons on a particular day. What is the probability that they will not be able to deliver all of the sand that is ordered?

(e) What is the probability that demand exceeds 4 tons?

6.6 The price, X, for Oven Magic pizza varies from $0 to $2 with a probability density function

$$f(x) = 0.1(x - 2) + 0.6$$

Determine:

(a) The probability that the price is between $0 and $1.

(b) The expected value of X, μ_X.

(c) The variance of X, σ_X^2.

(d) $E[5 + 2X]$.

(e) $\sigma^2(5 + 2X)$.

6.7 Robert Ackley, the director of roads and highways in Copper Harbor, Michigan, has asked for your help in developing plans for snow removal next winter. Daily snowfall in Copper Harbor varies uniformly from 0 to 10 inches and the snowfall is independent from one day to the next. Snowfall patterns are controlled by Lake Superior and the pattern has been observed for many years. Determine the probability that the snowfall:

(a) Ranges from 4 to 8 inches.

(b) Is greater than 8 inches.

(c) Is either less than 2 inches or greater than 8 inches.

6.8 Robert Ackley in Problem 6.7 has asked you to provide summary parameters for the snowfall patterns observed. Daily snowfall varies uniformly from 0 to 10 inches. Determine:

(a) The mean daily snowfall.

(b) The variance of the mean daily snowfall.

(c) The percentage of days that the snowfall is within ±1 standard deviation of the mean.

6.9 Robert Ackley, the director of roads and highways in Copper Harbor, Michigan, has asked for your help in developing plans for snow removal next winter. Daily snowfall in Copper Harbor varies uniformly from 0 to 10 inches and the snowfall is independent from one day to the next. Snowfall patterns are controlled by Lake Superior and the pattern has been observed for many years.

(a) Robert knows that if the snowfall exceeds 7 inches on two consecutive days, it will be necessary to schedule overtime work for the snow removal crews. What is the probability that overtime will need to be scheduled?

(b) Citizens of Copper Harbor are skilled and experienced with driving on snow-covered roads. They have all agreed that if the snowfall is less than 1.6 inches, it is not necessary to plow the roads. What is the probability that the snow-plowing crews can have a free day?

6.10   Consider Problem 6.9 again. The daily cost to plow the roads in Copper Harbor is computed as a fixed cost of $500 and a variable cost of $300 per inch of snowfall. Determine:
(a) The mean and variance of the daily cost of snow removal.
(b) The probability that the daily cost exceeds $2500.

6.11   Kevin Ackley is the maintenance director for a large regional bus company. He has asked for your assistance in studying maintenance costs. Monthly maintenance expenditures vary from 0 to $10,000 with the probability density function

$$f(x) = 0.00020 - 0.00000002x$$

Determine the probability that expenditures:
(a) Exceed $7000.
(b) Exceed $8000 given that expenditures have already exceeded $5000.
(c) Are greater than $2000 and less than $7000.

6.12   Kevin Ackley is the maintenance director for a large regional bus company. He has asked for your assistance in studying maintenance costs. Monthly maintenance expenditures vary from 0 to $10,000 with the probability density function

$$f(x) = 0.00020 - 0.00000002x$$

Determine:
(a) The mean monthly expenditure.
(b) The variance of the monthly expenditure.
(c) The probability that the monthly expenditure is within the interval $\mu \pm 2\sigma$.

6.13   In Problem 6.12, Kevin Ackley has asked for your assistance in analyzing the number of maintenance staff work hours. Your initial analysis indicates that there is a constant assignment of 500 hours and that each additional dollar of maintenance adds 0.05 hour. Determine:
(a) The mean hours of maintenance work.
(b) The variance of the hours of maintenance work.

6.14   A large health insurance company has a staff of customer relations experts who answer telephone calls from customers and provide them with the information requested. The manager of the group has asked you to analyze the pattern of calls and determine if staffing levels are adequate. Calls are independent and the time between calls follows an exponential distribution. During the period from 9:00 A.M. to 12:00 noon an average of 15 calls per hour occur. Determine the probability that the time between calls is:
(a) Less than 3 minutes.
(b) Greater than 10 minutes.
(c) Between 3 and 6 minutes.

6.15   While on a long-distance trip you discover that your car requires an oil change and lubrication. You have arrived in Golden Blade, Nebraska and are going to an important meeting. Suddenly you come upon a new "Quickie Lube" shop, which claims that it will provide rapid oil changes and lubrication. From your past experience you know that these shops complete the task in an average of 10 minutes and that service time is independent. You pull into the shop and discover that they can begin your car immediately. Determine the probability that:

(a) Your car will be finished in less than 8 minutes.

(b) Your car will require more than 12 minutes.

(c) This shop can process eight or more cars in an hour.

6.16 Kevin Lind, the operations manager for a supermarket chain, has asked you to help develop a staffing plan for the customer checkout counters at a new store. Based on the projected sales for the store, he indicates that an average of 3 customers per minute will arrive at the checkout counters and expect to be served rapidly. The arrivals are expected to follow the Poisson model. Determine the probability of:

(a) 10 seconds or less between customer arrivals.

(b) An arrival between 10 and 30 seconds after the previous arrival.

(c) Six or more arrivals in 1 minute.

6.17 Big Ben Thrash, warehouse manager for Floor Mart, a major discount store, has asked for your help in designing and staffing the truck-unloading stations at their stores. Using present procedures it requires 10 minutes to maneuver and prepare a truck for unloading. During this period only one truck can be handled and other trucks arriving during this time will be delayed. Some truckers and store managers have complained about an excessive number of delays. The average number of trucks that arrive each hour is five.

(a) A truck arrives and the crew begins to prepare it for unloading. What is the probability that the next truck will be delayed?

(b) What is the probability that the crew will be idle at least 4 minutes before the next truck arrives?

(c) What is the probability that two trucks in a row will arrive within less than 10 minutes of the previous truck?

(d) What is the probability that 6 or more trucks will arrive in 1 hour?

6.18 For a normally distributed random variable X, with mean $\mu = 400$ and variance $\sigma^2 = 100$, sketch a normal curve that shows schematically the following probabilities and compute the probabilities using appropriate tables.

(a) $P(380 \leq X \leq 390)$.

(b) $P(X \leq 390 \text{ or } X \geq 420)$.

(c) $P(395 \leq X \leq 420)$.

(d) $P(X \geq 430)$.

6.19 The daily sales in a hardware store has a normal distribution with a mean of 2000 and a variance of 40,000. Determine the probability that:

(a) Sales are between 1800 and 2600.

(b) Sales are less than 1500.

(c) Sales are between 2200 and 2500.

(d) Sales are not in the interval between 1800 and 2600.

(e) Five times the sales exceeds 10,600.

6.20 Explain why the normal probability density function is likely to be a good model for total daily sales for a supermarket on Saturdays.

6.21 Given that X is a normally distributed random variable with mean $= 500$ and variance $= 10,000$, compute the following probabilities. Show your procedure with a sketch.

(a) $P(400 < X < 700)$.

(b) $P(X \geq 750)$.

(c) $P(X < 300)$.

(d) $P(300 \leq X < 700)$.

6.22 Betty Thorson is an economist who studies investment expenditures for firms that produce hearing aids for race horses. She reports that annual investment expenditures for these firms have a normal probability distribution with mean of 50,000 and variance of 1,000,000. Determine the probability of expenditures:

(a) In the range 48,500 through 52,000.

(b) Greater than 51,000.

(c) Less than 49,000.

(d) Greater than 48,500 and less than 52,000.

6.23 The breakfast sales for a small restaurant are normally distributed with a mean of 100 and a variance of 400. Determine the probability that a single day's sales are:

(a) Between $70 and $130.

(b) Less than $80.

(c) If you randomly selected 20 days, what is the probability that exactly five days have sales between $100 and $110.50? Assume that daily sales are independent.

6.24 The daily sales in a retail store follow a normal probability distribution with a variance of 100. The mean of the normal distribution is either 110, 120, or 140, with probabilities 0.40, 0.30, and 0.30. For a randomly selected day, what is the probability that sales are greater than or equal to 120?

6.25 Your teacher has indicated that the time in minutes to complete the next hour exam is a random variable X with a mean of 60 and a variance of 25. He also indicates that the probability of correctly answering each of the six questions is 0.60 and that the probabilities of correct solutions to each question are independent. Determine the probability that:

(a) The exam will be completed in less than 55 minutes.

(b) The completion time will be between 55 and 64 minutes.

(c) The completion time will be between 61 and 73 minutes.

(d) Exactly five questions are answered correctly.

(e) Four or more questions are answered correctly.

6.26 Sally Ragseller has discovered that the daily sales at her clothing store are normally distributed with a mean of 5000 and a standard deviation of 500.

(a) Sally likes to celebrate when daily sales are high, but she does not want to celebrate on more than 5% of the days. What is the minimum level of sales that should indicate celebration for Sally?

Determine the probability that daily sales are:

(b) Less than 4000.

(c) Between 3500 and 6000.

(d) Between 3000 and 4500.

6.27 Charlie Cheepsteak raises both brown and black cattle on his ranch in northern South Dakota. Charlie has discovered that the price per pound for brown cattle is a random variable with a mean of 1.00 and a variance of 0.04. He also knows that the price for black cattle is also a random variable with a mean of 1.20 and a variance of 0.16. Assume that the prices are independent. What is the probability that the price of brown cattle is greater than 1.20 and the price of black cattle is less than 0.80?

6.28 The time in hours for 10 people to wash 100 trucks using 20 hoses and 15 sponges is a normal random variable with mean 40 and variance 16. Determine the probability that:

(a) More than 46 hours will be required.

(b) The time is between 42 and 46 hours.

(c) The time required is between 36 and 44 hours.

6.29 The weekly sales for Discount Books, Inc. have a mean of 10,000 and a variance of 1,000,000 based on historical records. You have been asked to develop an analysis of weekly sales for the next year. Your conclusions will be used to help management monitor operations to detect increasing or decreasing sales trends.

(a) What is the probability that weekly sales exceed 11,000?

(b) What is the probability that weekly sales are less than 9000?

(c) What is the probability that sales exceed 13,000 given that we know that they have exceeded 10,000?

(d) Construct a symmetric interval within which 95% of the weekly sales can be expected to occur.

(e) If sales during a particular week drop below 7000, should the management be concerned?

6.30 The daily demand in boxes of cereal for Rust Oats Cereal is distributed normally with mean 5000 and variance 10,000. Determine the probability that:

(a) Sales will exceed 5100.

(b) Sales will be between 4800 and 5300.

(c) Sales will be between 5100 and 5200.

(d) Sales will be between 4800 and 4900.

(e) If the price is $2 per box, what is the probability that total revenue is greater than $10,200?

6.31 Charles Moe, the director of admissions for a business school, has asked for your assistance in analyzing the effects of recent decisions. They have just offered admission to 50 students. From many years of past experience he knows that 80% of students offered admission will decide to enroll. You assume that decisions by students are independent.

(a) What is the probability that more than 45 students will enroll from this group of 50?

(b) What is the probability that fewer than 35 will enroll?

(c) The school has room for only 43 additional students. Should admission be offered to 50 students? Provide a clear rationale for your recommendation, which includes the probability of enrollment.

(d) What is likely to happen if the university offers admission to only 50 students if it has 50 vacancies left for the entering class?

6.32 Suppose that you have 500 independent trials of identically distributed Bernoulli processes each having a probability of success equal to 0.60. Determine the probability that the proportion of successes is:

(a) Greater than or equal to 0.65.

(b) Between 0.55 and 0.60 with the endpoints included.

(c) Greater than or equal to 0.64 or less than or equal to 0.57.

(d) Greater than or equal to 0.65 given that we know that the proportion is greater than or equal to 0.60.

6.33   You have been hired to help design a warehouse loading station for Amalgamated Food
       Distributors, Inc. They have a fleet of 100 delivery trucks that deliver food from your
       warehouse to supermarkets in the region. Each truck requires exactly 1 hour to load.
       The average delivery run requires 5 hours, but they vary uniformly from 1 to 10 hours.
       Therefore, the probability that a randomly selected truck will return to the warehouse in
       any given hour is 0.10. Truck arrivals are also independent. To decide on the number of
       loading stations, they have asked you to determine the following.
       (a) The average number of trucks that will arrive in any hour.
       (b) The probability that more than 15 trucks will arrive in a given hour.
       (c) The probability that fewer than six trucks will arrive in a given hour.
       (d) The probability that at least seven and no more than 14 trucks will arrive in a given
            hour.

6.34   After you completed the analysis for Amalgamated Food Distributors in Problem 6.33,
       you were asked to conduct a similar analysis for Union Food Distributors. Union does
       not have its own trucks; instead, customers contract with private truckers to pick up food
       orders at the warehouse. Union has observed that on average 10 trucks arrive in any
       given hour and that truck arrivals are independent. It also requires 1 hour to load a truck
       at the Union warehouse. Determine:
       (a) The average number of trucks that will arrive in any hour.
       (b) The probability that more than 15 trucks will arrive in a given hour.
       (c) The probability that fewer than six trucks will arrive in a given hour.
       (d) The probability that at least seven and no more than 14 trucks will arrive in a given
            hour.
       (e) Compare the results with those obtained for the Amalgamated warehouse in Prob-
            lem 6.33. What do you conclude concerning the two different probability models
            used for these two problems?

6.35   A recent survey indicates that 20% of the Norwegian population in New York City eat
       bagels regularly.
       (a) In a random sample of 100 New York Norwegians, what is the probability that 20
            eat bagels regularly?
       (b) In the same sample, what is the probability that 37 or fewer eat bagels regularly?

6.36   (Bayes) The Midwest Cereal Company has two factories that prepare their new cereal.
       Factory 1 has produced 6000 cases, in which each cereal box has a mean weight of 20
       ounces with a variance of 4. Factory 2 has produced 4000 cases, with each cereal box
       having a mean weight of 20 ounces and a variance of 16. The weights of cereal boxes
       can be modeled by a normal probability density function.
       (a) Suppose that you receive a randomly selected case of cereal. What is the probability
            that the case came from factory 1?
       (b) You weigh the cereal in the box and discover that the weight is 18 ounces or less.
            Given this new information, what is the probability that the case came from fac-
            tory 1?

6.37   Suppose that 50% of the voters preferred Mr. Lincoln for U.S. President. A random sam-
       ple of 900 voters was obtained and their presidential preference was obtained. Determine
       the probability that:
       (a) More than 55% of the voters in the sample preferred Mr. Lincoln.
       (b) Between 47 and 53% of the sample prefers Mr. Lincoln.

6.38 Harry and Linda Overchest operate a store that sells men's shirts and women's blouses. The number of shirts, X, sold each day follows a binomial probability distribution with $n = 100$ customers and $n = 0.80$. There are 100 women who come to the store each day looking for a blouse. From past experience they know that 60% of the women will purchase a blouse. The contribution to profit is $5 per shirt sold and $10 per blouse sold. The sales of shirts and blouses are independent.

(a) What are the expected value and variance of the profit from selling shirts and blouses each day?

(b) What is the probability that total profit is greater than $1100?

6.39 Total daily sales at Checkers Pizza is normally distributed with a mean of $2000 and a variance of 40,000.

(a) What is the probability that sales are less than $1800?

(b) A new pizza design increases mean sales by $100 per day and also increases the variance from 40,000 to 160,000. What is the probability that sales are less than $1800 per day with the new pizza design?

(c) Is the new pizza design a good idea? Explain why in one or two sentences.

6.40 Eric Ackley, manager of the Harvest Grain Elevator in Thrash, North Dakota, asked for your help in planning the unloading operations during the grain harvest period. The grain elevator has five unloading stations with different grain-handling capacities. Maximum efficiency is achieved if there is a good match between the amount of grain in the truck and the capability of the unloading station. Grain trucks coming from the east have a mean weight of 25 tons with a variance of 16. Their average arrival rate is 10 trucks per hour. Grain trucks coming from the west have a mean weight of 20 tons with a variance of 25. The arrival rate for west trucks is 20 per hour.

(a) A truck arrives. What is the probability that the truck is from the east?

(b) What is the probability that the truck contains more than 28 tons of grain?

(c) The next truck arrives 6 minutes after the previous truck. What is the probability that the truck came from the east? What is the probability that the truck came from the west?

(d) Given the answer to part (c), what is the probability that the truck contains more than 28 tons?

APPENDIX: COMPUTATION OF NORMAL PROBABILITIES

The following examples, which are shown schematically in Figures 6.13 through 6.17, illustrate this application.

1. Both a and b are greater than 0.00 (Figure 6.13).

$$
\begin{aligned}
P(1.00 \leq Z \leq 2.00) &= P(Z \leq 2.00) - P(Z \leq 1.00) \\
&= P(Z \leq 0.00) + P(0.00 \leq Z \leq 2.00) \\
&\quad - (P(Z \leq 0.00) + P(0.00 \leq Z \leq 1.00)) \\
&= P(0.00 \leq Z \leq 2.00) - P(0.00 \leq Z \leq 1.00) \\
&= 0.4772 - 0.3413 \\
&= 0.1359
\end{aligned}
$$

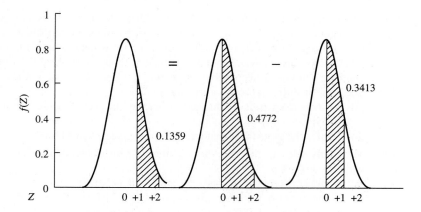

Figure 6.13   Both a and b Are Above 0.00.

2. Both a and b are less than 0.00 (Figure 6.14).

$$
\begin{aligned}
P(-2.00 \leq Z \leq -1.00) &= P(Z \leq -1.00) - P(Z \leq -2.00) \\
&= P(Z \leq 0.00) - P(-1.00 \leq Z \leq 0.00) \\
&\quad - (P(Z \leq 0.00) - P(-2.00 \leq Z \leq 0.00)) \\
&= - P(-1.00 \leq Z \leq 0.00) + P(-2.00 \leq Z \leq 0.00) \\
&= - 0.3413 + 0.4772 \\
&= 0.1359
\end{aligned}
$$

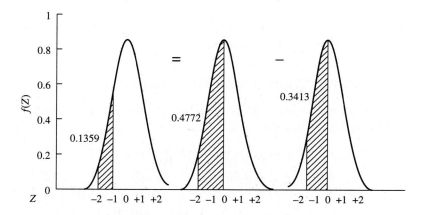

Figure 6.14   Both a and b Are Below 0.00.

3. a is less than 0.00 and b is greater than 0.00 (Figure 6.15).

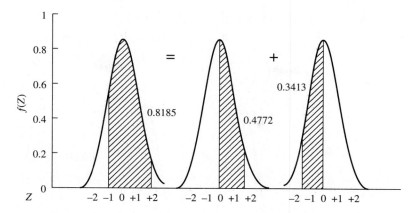

Figure 6.15   Here a Is Less Than 0.00 and b Is Greater Than 0.00.

$$
\begin{aligned}
P(-1.00 \leq Z \leq 2.00) &= P(Z \leq 2.00) - P(Z \leq -1.00) \\
&= P(Z \leq 0.00) + P(0.00 \leq Z \leq 2.00) \\
&\quad - (P(Z \leq 0.00) - P(-1.00 \leq Z \leq 0.00)) \\
&= P(0.00 \leq Z \leq 2.00) + P(-1.00 \leq Z \leq 0.00) \\
&= 0.4772 + 0.3413 \\
&= 0.8185
\end{aligned}
$$

4. a is greater than 0.00 and b is ∞ (Figure 6.16).

$$
\begin{aligned}
P(Z \geq 1.00) &= P(1.00 \leq Z \leq \infty) \\
&= P(Z \geq 0.00) - P(0.00 \leq Z \leq 1.00) \\
&= 0.5000 - 0.3413 \\
&= 0.1587
\end{aligned}
$$

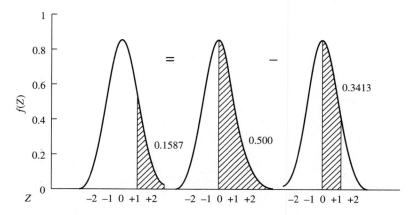

Figure 6.16   Here a Is Greater Than 0.00 and b Is ∞.

5. *a* is $-\infty$ and *b* is less than 0.00 (Figure 6.17).

$$P(Z \leq -1.00) = P(Z \geq 1.00)$$
$$= 0.1587$$

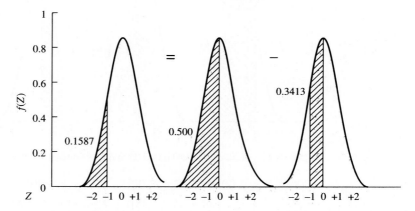

Figure 6.17   Here *a* Is $-\infty$ and *b* Is Less Than 0.00.

7

Two Random Variables

Analysis of the relationship between variables is fundamental to the work of business people and economists.

7.1 COMBINING RANDOM VARIABLES

In this chapter we extend the ideas developed in Chapters 5 and 6 to provide models for a broader set of business and economics problems. Chapter 5 developed discrete random variables and probability distribution functions. In Chapter 6 continuous random variables and probability density functions were developed. Here we study problems that combine two random variables.

Analysis of the relationship between variables is fundamental to the work of business people and economists. A manager proposes an investment and wants to know the profit or sales for various levels of investment. The project could require different levels of investment, depending on the feasible design options and the project scope desired. For each level of investment there are a number of different levels of sales, depending on factors such as market conditions, the strength of the overall economy, and the actions of competitors. The random variable X representing the level of investment and the random variable Y representing the level of sales need to be combined in the probability model.

Wall Street financial traders seek portfolios with the appropriate balance of return (mean) and risk (variance). These portfolios contain, for example, shares of different stocks, and the prices of these stocks are random variables. The total value of these portfolios is determined by combining two or more random variables. In this chapter you will learn how the values of such portfolios are determined.

Total revenue for a business is computed by multiplying the number of units of each of several products by their selling prices. Often, the number of units sold is a random variable. Lessons learned in this chapter can be used to compute total revenue.

Typical more detailed applications include the following:

1. Stock portfolios contain a number of stocks whose individual prices are random variables. A simple stock portfolio can be modeled by assuming only two stocks.

This simple model, in which the price of both stocks are random variables, demonstrates important characteristics that are directly applicable to more complex portfolios. For example, consider a stock portfolio with total value W, which is composed of a units of stock 1, with a price of X, and b units of stock 2, with a price of Y. The total value of the portfolio is

$$W = aX + bY$$

If the stock prices X and Y are random variables, W is also a random variable. We learn how to compute the mean and variance of W and the probability that the portfolio value is above or below specific values. Using these methods, you will learn to compute measures of expected return and risk for the portfolio.

2. Economic planners in developing countries are concerned with both agricultural and industrial development. Total economic development results from a combination of these and other sectors. A simple model could contain a units of agricultural and b units of industry. We define the random variable X as the output of individual agricultural units and the random variable Y as the output of individual industrial units. Total output W would be represented by

$$W = aX + bY$$

The expected value and variance of W can be used to compute the probability that the economy will reach certain target levels.

7.2 JOINT RANDOM VARIABLES AND PROBABILITY DISTRIBUTIONS

Sarah Smith is studying the pattern of sales of bread machines for various age groups. Both the decision to purchase and the age group for a person can be modeled as random variables. To complete her study she needs to develop probability models that combine these random variables. In Chapter 4 the definition of probability based on two different characteristics was developed. This was done using two-way tables. That definition of probability using two-way tables will be combined with random variables and probability distribution functions to create joint probability distribution functions (Key Idea 7.1).

Key Idea 7.1: Joint Probability Distribution Function

A **joint probability distribution** $f(x, y)$ generates the probability for all combinations of two random variables X and Y and is defined mathematically as

$$f(x, y) = P(X = x \cap Y = y)$$

The analysis procedures for joint probability distributions are developed using a series of examples. Careful attention to the details of these examples will help you develop the important analysis tools.

Example 7.1   Market Research

Sarah Smith has participated in a number of focus group discussions about bread machines. Based on those discussions, she believes that age influences the purchase of her company's bread machines.

Solution   To study the market, she initially proposes a model that considers purchase behavior for three age subgroups. The development of her study proceeds as follows. First, she develops the following definitions for the subsets of the random variables:

$X = 1$ refers to persons aged 16–25.
$X = 2$ refers to persons aged 26–45.
$X = 3$ refers to persons aged 46–65.
$Y = 1$ refers to persons who will buy the product.
$Y = 2$ refers to persons who will not buy the product.

Next, she collects a random sample of 10,000 persons aged 16–65 and records their age and purchase intentions. Based on the sample, she computes the joint probability distribution shown in Table 7.1. For Table 7.1 the joint probability distribution, $f(x, y)$, for the combination of $X = 1$ and $Y = 1$ is

$$f(1, 1) = P(X = 1 \cap Y = 1)$$
$$= 0.10$$

and

$$f(2, 2) = 0.25 \qquad \square$$

TABLE 7.1   Joint Distribution of Age Group (X) Versus Purchase Decision (Y)

| | Age, X | | | |
Decision, Y	1 (16–25)	2 (26–45)	3 (46–65)	$h(y)$
1 (buy)	0.10	0.20	0.10	0.40
2 (not buy)	0.25	0.25	0.10	0.60
$g(x)$	0.35	0.45	0.20	1.00

In any analysis of joint random variables the probability distribution of each variable will be required at some point. The distribution of each random variable will be found in the right-hand column for the random variable defined across the rows and in the bottom row for the random variable defined across the columns. Because these are at the margins of the table the term *marginal probability distributions* has developed in practice (Key Idea 7.2).

Key Idea 7.2: Marginal Probability Function

The **marginal probability functions** $g(x)$ and $h(y)$ are the probability functions for each variable by itself and are defined as

$$g(x) = P(X = x)$$
$$= \sum_{y} P(X = x \cap Y = y)$$
$$= \sum_{y} f(x, y)$$
$$h(y) = P(Y = y)$$
$$= \sum_{x} f(x, y)$$

The probabilities for each value of the individual random variables can be obtained easily by adding the appropriate row or column cell probabilities.

For our Example 7.1 using Table 7.1, the marginal for X is

$$g(2) = f(2, 1) + f(2, 2)$$
$$= 0.20 + 0.25$$
$$= 0.45$$

and the marginal for Y is

$$h(2) = f(1, 2) + f(2, 2) + f(3, 2)$$
$$= 0.25 + 0.25 + 0.10$$
$$= 0.60$$

From these results we see that age group 16–25 ($X = 2$) contains 45% of the sample and that 60% are not buyers ($Y = 2$).

7.3 CONDITIONAL PROBABILITY

The relationship between two random variables in a joint probability distribution can be measured in several ways. Here we consider conditional probability (Key Idea 7.3). As discussed in Chapter 4, a conditional probability is the probability of one random variable when the other random variable is restricted to a single value. This conditional probability is computed by dividing the joint probability by the marginal probability of the conditioning variable.

Key Idea 7.3: Conditional Probability

Conditional probability is defined as the probability of a random variable given a value of a second random variable:

$$g(x \mid y) = \frac{P(X = x \cap Y = y)}{P(Y = y)}$$

$$= \frac{f(x, y)}{h(y)}$$

The conditional probability of X given that we know the value of Y is equal to the joint probability of X and Y divided by the marginal probability of the conditioning variable Y:

$$h(y \mid x) = \frac{f(x, y)}{g(x)}$$

Similarly, the conditional probability of Y given that we know X is the joint probability of X and Y divided by the marginal probability of the conditioning variable X.

By examining the conditional probabilities we can learn how probabilities change with different conditioning variable levels. For example, the probability of a sale given a large store may differ from the probability of a sale in a small store.

To compute conditional probabilities, it is necessary to clearly define X and Y variables and the specific values that are to be included in the conditioning definition. The definitions can be understood more clearly by reading the example that follows carefully.

Example 7.2   Probability of Purchase by Age Group

For the marketing example that uses Table 7.1, determine the conditional probabilities of buying for each age subgroup.

Solution   The probability of purchase given age group 16–25 ($X = 1$) is, from the first column,

$$h(1 \mid 1) = P(Y = 1 \mid X = 1)$$
$$= \frac{f(1, 1)}{g(1)}$$
$$= \frac{0.10}{0.35}$$
$$= 0.286$$

and from the second column the probability of purchase for age group 26–45 $(X = 2)$ is

$$h(1 \mid 2) = \frac{0.20}{0.45}$$
$$= 0.444$$

Finally, from the third column the probability of purchase for age group 46–65 $(X = 3)$ is

$$h(1 \mid 3) = \frac{0.10}{0.20}$$
$$= 0.50$$

We can also note that for age group 16–25 $(X = 1)$ the conditional probabilities are

$$h(1 \mid 1) = \frac{f(1, 1)}{g(1)}$$
$$= 0.286$$
$$h(2 \mid 1) = \frac{f(1, 2)}{g(1)}$$
$$= \frac{0.25}{0.35}$$
$$= 0.714$$

Thus

$$h(1 \mid 1) + h(2 \mid 1) = 0.286 + 0.714$$
$$= 1.0$$

Thus we see that in this example the sum of all the conditional probabilities that are conditional on the same variable equals 1.0. □

This result is always true, as shown in the following general computation:

$$\sum_{y_i} h(y_i \mid x) = \sum_{y_i} \frac{f(x, y_i)}{g(x)}$$
$$= \frac{g(x)}{g(x)}$$
$$= 1.0$$

Conditional probabilities can be combined with marginal probabilities to compute joint probabilities (Key Idea 7.4). These algebraic results are important for studying the relationships between variables and lead to other important analysis techniques. In Chapter 4 we used the relationships between conditional and marginal probabilities to develop overinvolvement ratios and Bayes' theorem. Applying this result to Example 7.2, in the first row of Table 7.1 we have

$$h(1) = f(1, 1) + f(2, 1) + f(3, 1)$$
$$= h(1 \mid 1)g(1) + h(1 \mid 2)g(2) + h(1 \mid 3)g(3)$$
$$= 0.286 \times 0.35 + 0.444 \times 0.45 + 0.50 \times 0.20$$
$$= 0.40$$

Key Idea 7.4: Joint and Marginal Probability

From the definition of conditional probability,

$$g(x \mid y) = \frac{f(x, y)}{h(y)}$$

it follows that

$$f(x, y) = g(x \mid y)h(y)$$

The **joint probability** is equal to the product of the conditional probability multiplied by the probability of the conditioning variable. From the definition of **marginal probability**,

$$h(y) = \sum_x f(x, y)$$
$$= \sum_x h(y \mid x)g(x)$$

The probability of any element of Y is the sum of the probabilities of that element of Y occurring with all possible values of X.

7.4 INDEPENDENCE

When the relationships between random variables are examined it is possible that there is no relationship. That is, the probability of one variable does not depend on the values of the other variables. We define this condition as independence, using the specific definition of Key Idea 7.5 as the test for independence.

Key Idea 7.5: Independence

Two random variables are **independent** if the occurrence of one does not affect the probability of the other. Using conditional probability notation, we have

$$h(y \mid x) = h(y)$$
$$g(x \mid y) = g(x)$$

An alternative form is

$$g(x)h(y) = f(x, y)$$

If two random variables are independent, the value of one cannot be influenced by changing the other. For example, if sales and advertising are independent, expenditures on advertising will not increase or decrease sales. In contrast, if they are dependent and the dependency is positive, increases in advertising will increase the probability of higher sales. The alternative form in Key Idea 7.5 can be derived by using the definition of conditional probability:

$$h(y \mid x) = \frac{f(x, y)}{g(x)}$$

and the first definition of independence:

$$h(y) = h(y \mid x)$$
$$= \frac{f(x, y)}{g(x)}$$

By multiplying both sides by $g(x)$, we see that

$$g(x)h(y) = f(x, y)$$

Independence indicates that information about one random variable, X, does not affect the probability of the other random variable, Y. Both definitions in Key Idea 7.5 are used regularly. Independence is a difficult concept, in part because the word has other meanings in other situations. Independence in a probability sense requires that we test using the definitions.

Example 7.3   Revised Market Research

Consider again the marketing problem. Suppose that instead of the probabilities in Table 7.1, the market could be modeled better using the probabilities in Table 7.2. Determine the conditional probability of purchase for each age group.

TABLE 7.2   Revised Joint Distribution of Age Group
(X) Versus Purchase Decision (Y)

| Decision, Y | Age, X | | | $h(y)$ |
	1 (16–25)	2 (26–45)	3 (46–65)	
1 (buy)	0.14	0.18	0.08	0.40
2 (not buy)	0.21	0.27	0.12	0.60
$g(x)$	0.35	0.45	0.20	1.00

Solution   The conditional probabilities of purchase, $Y = 1$, given age group are

$$h(1 \mid 1) = \frac{0.14}{0.35} = 0.40$$

$$h(1 \mid 2) = \frac{0.18}{0.45} = 0.40$$

$$h(1 \mid 3) = \frac{0.08}{0.20} = 0.40$$

All of the conditional probabilities are equal to 0.40, which is the marginal probability that $Y = 1$. Similar calculations show that the probability of $Y = 2$ is equal to 0.60 for each age group. Therefore, X and Y are independent and information about age groups does not change the probability of purchase.   ☐

Practice Problem 7.1

This problem uses the joint probability distribution in Table 7.3. Determine:

(a) $g(3)$.

(b) $h(2)$.

(c) The probability that X is greater than or equal to 3 and Y is greater than or equal to 2.

(d) The conditional probability of $X = 3$ given that $Y = 2$, that is, $g(3 \mid 2)$.

(e) The conditional probability of $Y = 2$ given that $X = 3$, that is, $h(2 \mid 3)$.

(f) Are X and Y independent?   ☐

TABLE 7.3   Joint Distribution for
Practice Problem 7.1

| Y | X | | | $h(y)$ |
	2	3	4	
1	0.05	0.10	0.15	0.30
2	0.10	0.10	0.10	0.30
3	0.15	0.05	0.20	0.40
$g(x)$	0.30	0.25	0.45	1.00

The solutions for all Practice Problems are given at the end of the chapter.

Problem Exercises

7.1   Big Motors, Inc. is developing a marketing plan to better target advertising and sales promotion to subgroups. As part of the market research they have prepared Table 7.4, which indicates the probabilities for subgroups defined by age of car and owner age group. Determine the following probabilities that are defined in terms of $f(x, y)$.

TABLE 7.4   Joint Distribution of Age Group (X)
Versus Age of Car (Y)

		Age Group, X			
Age of Car, Y		1 (16–25)	2 (26–45)	3 (46–65)	$h(y)$
1	≤ 2	0.05	0.17	0.06	0.28
2	2–4	0.15	0.20	0.07	0.42
3	≥ 5	0.10	0.08	0.12	0.30
$g(x)$		0.30	0.45	0.25	1.00

(a) $f(2, 3)$.
(b) $f(1, 2)$.
(c) $f(3, 1)$.
(d) $f(3, 2)$.

7.2   Continue with the Big Motors, Inc. marketing problem and Table 7.4. Use the conditional probability definition from Key Idea 7.3. Compute each of the following and define the probability in words.
(a) $g(2 \mid 3)$.
(b) $h(3 \mid 1)$.
(c) $g(1 \mid 3)$.
(d) $h(2 \mid 3)$.

7.3   Big Motors, Inc. is developing a marketing plan to better target advertising and sales promotion to subgroups. As part of the market research, they have prepared Table 7.4, which indicates the probabilities for subgroups defined by age of car and owner age group.
(a) Are X and Y independent?
(b) What does your answer in part (a) indicate about the success of the proposed segmented marketing strategy?
(c) Which age group would you concentrate on if you were attempting to sell with cars that are over five years old?

7.4 X and Y are jointly distributed random variables with $X = 1, 2, 3$ and $Y = 2, 4$. The following probability values are given:

$$g(x \mid y) = P(X = x \mid Y = y)$$
$$g(1 \mid 2) = 0.30$$
$$g(2 \mid 2) = 0.40$$
$$h(y) = P(Y = y)$$
$$h(2) = 0.40$$
$$f(x, y) = P(X = x \cap Y = y)$$

Compute:
(a) $f(1, 2)$.
(b) $f(2, 2)$.
(c) $f(3, 2)$.

7.5 X and Y are jointly distributed random variables with $X = 1, 2, 3$ and $Y = 2, 4$. The following probability values are given:

$$g(x \mid y) = P(X = x \mid Y = y)$$
$$g(1 \mid 2) = 0.20$$
$$g(2 \mid 2) = 0.40$$
$$h(y) = P(Y = y)$$
$$h(2) = 0.40$$
$$f(x, y) = P(X = x \cap Y = y)$$

Compute:
(a) $h(2 \mid 1)$.
(b) $h(1 \mid 3)$.
(c) Are X and Y independent?

7.6 X and Y are jointly distributed random variables with $X = 1, 2, 3, 4$ and $Y = 1, 2, 4$. The following probability values are given:

$$g(x \mid y) = P(X = x \mid Y = y)$$
$$g(1 \mid 2) = 0.20$$
$$g(2 \mid 2) = 0.40$$
$$g(3 \mid 2) = 0.20$$
$$g(1 \mid 3) = 0.20$$
$$g(2 \mid 3) = 0.40$$
$$g(3 \mid 3) = 0.20$$
$$h(y) = P(Y = y)$$
$$h(2) = 0.40$$
$$h(3) = 0.30$$
$$f(x, y) = P(X = x \cap Y = y)$$

Compute:
(a) $h(2 \mid 1)$.
(b) $h(1 \mid 3)$.
(c) Are X and Y independent?

7.5 COVARIANCE AND CORRELATION

The covariance and the correlation are both measures of the linear relationship between two random variables. They are properties of the joint probability distribution, just as the mean and variance are properties of a single probability distribution. The covariance, which is analgous to the variance, measures total joint variability. In contrast, the correlation is a standardized measure whose values range from -1 to $+1$.

The covariance is developed next. Then we develop the correlation, which is a standardized measure of the relationship between two random variables. In the next section a number of important applications to business and economics problems are presented.

In Chapter 3 the sample covariance and correlation were presented as important descriptive statistics. Covariance and correlation for jointly distributed random variables have similar properties.

Computation of covariance and correlation uses the means and variances of joint random variables X and Y, which can be computed from the marginal distributions $g(x)$ and $h(y)$. The equations are repeated here for convenience:

$$\mu_x = E[X] = \sum_x x g(x)$$

$$\mu_y = E[Y] = \sum_y y h(y)$$

$$\sigma_x^2 = E[(X - \mu_x)^2] = \sum_x (x - \mu_x)^2 g(x)$$

$$= \sum_x x^2 g(x) - \mu_x^2$$

$$\sigma_y^2 = E[(Y - \mu_y)^2] = \sum_y (y - \mu_y)^2 h(y)$$

$$= \sum_y y^2 h(y) - \mu_y^2$$

7.5.1 Covariance

The formula for computing the covariance (Key Idea 7.6) resembles the variance formula since covariance provides a measure of joint variation for the two random variables. The covariance of a random variable with itself would be the variance.

Example 7.4   Covariance Calculation

Compute the covariance for the joint probability distribution of X and Y defined in Table 7.5.

Key Idea 7.6: Covariance

The **covariance**, σ_{xy}, of two jointly distributed random variables is equal to the expected value of the product of the variable deviations from their respective means:

$$\sigma_{xy} = E[(X - \mu_x)(Y - \mu_y)]$$
$$= E[XY] - \mu_x\mu_y$$

This definition applies for both discrete and continuous random variables. For discrete random variables,

$$E[XY] = \sum_x \sum_y xyf(x, y)$$

TABLE 7.5   Joint Distribution of X and Y

Y	X 1	2	$h(y)$
3	0.10	0.40	0.50
4	0.40	0.10	0.50
$g(x)$	0.50	0.50	1.00

Solution   First compute the means μ_x and μ_y:

$$\mu_x = E[X]$$
$$= \sum_x xg(x)$$
$$= 1 \times 0.50 + 2 \times 0.50$$
$$= 1.5$$
$$\mu_y = E[Y]$$
$$= \sum_y yh(y)$$
$$= 3 \times 0.50 + 4 \times 0.50$$
$$= 3.5$$

Then compute

$$E[XY] = \sum_x \sum_y xyf(x, y)$$

$$= (1)(3)(0.10) + (2)(3)(0.40) + (1)(4)(0.40) + (2)(4)(0.10)$$

$$= 5.1$$

The final computation can now be made:

$$\sigma_{xy} = E[XY] - \mu_x\mu_y$$

$$= 5.1 - (1.5)(3.5)$$

$$= -0.15$$

Notice that in contrast to the variance, the sign of the covariance can be either plus or minus. □

Does It Make Sense?

The population covariance provides a measure of both the size and direction of joint variability. In Table 7.5 we see that when $X = 1$, Y is more likely to be 4, and when $X = 2$, Y is more likely to be 3. Thus as X increases, Y decreases. This is an inverse relationship and the covariance is negative. A direct relationship—X and Y increase together—would have a positive covariance. The size of the covariance depends on both the variances of X and Y and the strength of the relationship between them. Thus the size of the covariance does not provide much intuitive information about the relationship between two variables. □

Covariance for independent random variables is defined in Key Idea 7.7. The result can be shown as follows:

$$E[XY] = \sum_x \sum_y xyf(x, y)$$

Key Idea 7.7: Covariance for Independent Random Variables

When the two random variables X and Y are independent, the covariance is zero. However, a covariance of zero does not imply that X and Y are independent.

---

and from Key Idea 7.5,

$$E[XY] = \sum_x \sum_y xyg(x)h(y)$$

$$= \sum_x xg(x) \sum_y yh(y)$$

$$= \mu_X\mu_Y$$

and

$$\sigma_{xy} = E[XY] - \mu_X\mu_Y$$
$$= \mu_X\mu_Y - \mu_X\mu_Y$$
$$= 0$$

7.5.2 Correlation

The correlation is a standardized measure of joint variability (Key Idea 7.8). It can be used directly to indicate the direction and strength of the relationship between two random variables.

Key Idea 7.8: Correlation

The population **correlation** ρ between two random variables is a standardized ($-1.0 \le \rho \le +1.0$) measure of joint variability. The correlation is defined as

$$\rho_{xy} = \frac{\sigma_{xy}}{\sigma_x\sigma_y}$$

   A positive correlation indicates that both random variables increase or decrease together. A negative correlation occurs when the two random variables move in opposite directions. Independent random variables have a correlation of 0. This definition applies for both discrete and continuous random variables.

Because the correlation varies from -1 to $+1$, it can be used to compare the strength of a linear relationship between two random variables. Two random variables with a correlation of either -1.0 or $+1.0$ are highly correlated because knowledge of one provides precise knowledge of the other. Note also that correlation provides information only about linear relationships between random variables. Random variables could have a nonlinear relationship but still have a correlation close to 0.

   In many cases the correlation is given and the covariance is required. The covariance is easily computed using the relationship

$$\sigma_{xy} = \rho_{xy}\sigma_x\sigma_y$$

Study Example 7.5 carefully to be sure that you understand the computation.

Example 7.5   Correlation Computation

Compute the correlation for the joint probability distribution defined by Table 7.5.

   Solution   First compute the variances for X and Y:

$$\sigma_x^2 = E[X^2] - \mu_X^2$$

where

$$E[X^2] = (1)^2 0.50 + (2)^2 0.50$$
$$= 2.50$$

and therefore

$$\sigma_x^2 = 2.50 - (1.5)^2$$
$$= 0.25$$
$$\sigma_x = 0.50$$

Following the same calculations:

$$\sigma_y^2 = 0.25$$
$$\sigma_y = 0.50$$

Using these results and the covariance computed previously, $\text{Cov}(X, Y) = -0.15$, the correlation is

$$\rho_{xy} = \frac{-0.15}{(0.5)(0.5)} = -0.60$$

This negative correlation indicates that the variables have an inverse relationship.   ☐

Does It Make Sense?

The correlation is more useful than the covariance for describing relationships. With a correlation of +1 we know that the two random variables have a positive linear relationship, and therefore a specific value of one variable, X, predicts the other variable, Y, exactly. A correlation of -1 indicates a negative linear relationship between two variables, with one variable, X, predicting the negative of the other variable, Y. A correlation of 0 indicates no linear relationship between the two variables. Intermediate values indicate that variables tend to be related, with stronger relationships occurring as the absolute value of the correlation approaches 1. Correlation is a term that has moved into common use. In most cases correlation is used to indicate that a relationship exists. However, variables that have nonlinear relationships will not have a correlation close to ± 1. This distinction is important to avoid confusion between correlated random variables and those with nonlinear relationships.   ☐

Practice Problem 7.2

This problem uses the joint probability distribution in Table 7.4. Compute:

(a) The covariance for X and Y.
(b) The correlation for X and Y.   ☐

Problem Exercises

7.7   Refer to Table 7.1, which presents the joint probability distribution of age group X and purchase decision Y. Compute:
(a) The covariance for X and Y.

(b) The variance for X and the variance for Y.

(c) The correlation for X and Y.

7.8   Refer to Table 7.2, which presents the joint probability distribution of age group X and purchase decision Y. Compute:

(a) The covariance for X and Y.

(b) The variance for X and the variance for Y.

(c) The correlation for X and Y.

7.9   Refer to Table 7.5, which presents the joint random variables X and Y and their joint probability distribution function. Compute:

(a) The covariance of X and Y.

(b) The variance of X and the variance of Y.

(c) The correlation for X and Y.

7.10 Refer to Table 7.4, which presents the joint probability distribution of age group X and age of car Y. Compute:

(a) The covariance for X and Y.

(b) The variance for X and the variance for Y.

(c) The correlation for X and Y.

7.11 Refer to Table 7.3, which presents the joint random variables X and Y and their joint probability distribution function. Compute:

(a) The covariance of X and Y.

(b) The variance of X and the variance of Y.

(c) The correlation for X and Y.

7.12 The price per peck for Tolefson's apples from Washington is a random variable X with mean $\mu_X = 4$ and variance $\sigma_X^2 = 4$, and the number of pecks sold is a random variable Y with $\mu_Y = 10,000$ and variance $\sigma_Y^2 = 1,000,000$. The correlation between X and Y is $\rho_{xy} = -0.70$. Compute the covariance.

7.13 The price per gallon for gasoline from George's service station is a random variable X with mean $\mu_X = 1.10$ and variance $\sigma_X^2 = 0.01$, and the number of gallons sold is a random variable Y with $\mu_Y = 10,000$ and variance $\sigma_Y^2 = 1,000,000$. The correlation between X and Y is $\rho_{xy} = -0.62$. Compute the covariance.

7.14 The grades in statistics and starting salaries are correlated with a correlation coefficient equal to $\rho = 0.30$. The standard deviation for grades is 20 and the standard deviation for starting salaries is 2500. What is the covariance?

7.6 LINEAR COMBINATIONS OF RANDOM VARIABLES

There are many applications that require linear combinations of random variables, as defined in Key Idea 7.9. Business and economic examples that involve linear combinations of random variables include the following:

1. Stock portfolios in which the price of each stock is a random variable.

2. Total income for a business is the sum of the incomes from different departments, and the income from each department is a random variable.

3. A nation's balance of trade is the difference between exports and imports, and both are random variables.

Key Idea 7.9: Linear Combination of Random Variables

The general **linear combination of random variables** X and Y is

$$W = aX + bY$$

where a and b are constants. W is also a random variable because it is a linear combination of other random variables.

   This definition applies for both discrete and continuous random variables.

Many business calculations involve differences between income and cost and/or sums of incomes or costs. Costs and incomes are usually the product of a quantity of units multiplied by a price or unit cost. Quantities, prices, or costs are often random variables when future operations are analyzed. We do not know the number of units that will be sold or the number produced. Thus the difference between costs and revenues next year is the difference between random variables, and thus a linear combination of random variables. The difference between cost and revenues is very important for business decisions. Knowing how to derive these random variables as linear combinations is therefore important for business decisions. The examples on the following pages will make these general comments specific.

Example 7.6   Stock Portfolio

Charlie Jones has just purchased five shares of stock in Central Foods Ltd. and 10 shares in Northwest Foods, Inc. The prices for these stocks are known to be jointly distributed random variables whose probability distribution is given by Table 7.5, where X is the price for the Central stock and Y is the price for the Northwest stock. Define the value of Charlie's portfolio as a linear function.

   Solution   The total value W of Charlie's portfolio is a linear combination of the random variables X and Y:

$$W = 5X + 10Y \qquad \qquad \square$$

   In the example above, the value of the portfolio, W, is a random variable because it is a function of the stock prices, which are both random variables. The portfolio value is not known. However, the expected value of W indicates the long-run average and the variance of W provides a measure of risk. The larger the variance, the greater the chance of either very high or very low portfolio values.

Does It Make Sense?

The portfolio problem is an important application of statistical theory to a common decision problem. A decision maker can control her level of risk by carefully choosing the stocks in her portfolio. If she chooses stocks whose prices change in opposite directions (i.e., are negatively correlated), the loss in one will be balanced by a gain in the other. The value of her portfolio will tend to be stable and her risk will be minimized. Alternatively, she could choose stocks whose prices move in the same direction (i.e., are positively correlated); then she will experience either gain in both or loss in both. The value of her portfolio will vary; she will either lose big or gain big. Her risk will be maximized. As a third choice she could select stocks whose prices have no relationship. The risk level would then be between that of the two extremes described previously.   □

The linear combination of two random variables has the same properties as those of other random variables. If the resulting random variable has a normal distribution, the probability of various values can be computed by using the standard normal. However, all of these applications require the mean and variance of linear combination variable W.

In the following discussion we use statistical theory to determine the mean and variance for linear combinations of random variables for the situations described. First the equations are derived and then they are applied to the example problem.

7.6.1 Derivation of the Mean and Variance

The results summarized in Key Ideas 7.10 to 7.12 are derived using only expected value notation and thus apply to both discrete and continuous random variables.

Key Idea 7.10: Mean of a Linear Combination of Random Variables

The mean, μ_W, is derived using expected values:

$$\mu_W = E[W] = E[aX + bY]$$
$$= aE[X] + bE[Y]$$
$$= a\mu_x + b\mu_y$$

The expected value or mean is the linear combination of the means of the individual random variables. This definition applies for both discrete and continuous random variables.

The variance of W can be derived as follows:

$$\sigma_W^2 = E[(W - \mu_W)^2]$$
$$= E[(aX + bY - (a\mu_X + b\mu_Y))^2]$$
$$= E[(a(X - \mu_X) + b(Y - \mu_Y))^2]$$
$$= E[a^2(X - \mu_X)^2 + b^2(Y - \mu_Y)^2 + 2ab(X - \mu_X)(Y - \mu_Y)]$$
$$= a^2 E[(X - \mu_X)^2] + b^2 E[(Y - \mu_Y)^2] + 2ab E[(X - \mu_X)(Y - \mu_Y)]$$

Using the variance and covariance terms for X and Y, we see that

$$\sigma_W^2 = a^2\sigma_x^2 + b^2\sigma_y^2 + 2ab\sigma_{xy}$$

This important result will have application to a number of business and economic problems.

Key Idea 7.11: Variance of a Linear Combination of Random Variables

The variance of W is

$$\sigma_W^2 = E[(W - \mu_W)^2]$$
$$= a^2\sigma_x^2 + b^2\sigma_y^2 + 2ab\sigma_{xy}$$

The variance of W is the sum of the variances of the individual random variables multiplied by their constants squared, plus twice the covariance multiplied by both constants. The correlation ρ_{xy} may also be used to compute the variance of W:

$$\sigma_W^2 = a^2\sigma_x^2 + b^2\sigma_y^2 + 2ab\rho_{xy}\sigma_x\sigma_y$$

This definition applies for both discrete and continuous random variables.

Key Idea 7.12: Variance for Independent Random Variables

If the random variables X and Y are independent, the covariance σ_{xy} is zero and the variance of a linear combination of independent random variables is

$$\sigma_W^2 = a^2\sigma_x^2 + b^2\sigma_y^2$$

This definition applies for both discrete and continuous random variables.

Example 7.6 (Continued)

Now we can complete the computation of the mean and variance for Charlie's portfolio:

$$W = 5X + 10Y$$

Solution From Example 7.4 we know that $\mu_x = 1.5$ and $\mu_y = 3.5$ and therefore, using Key Idea 7.10, we find that

$$E[W] = 5\mu_X + 10\mu_Y$$
$$= 5(1.5) + 10(3.5)$$
$$= 42.5$$

The expected or average value of the portfolio is 42.5. Portfolios are compared using their expected value while recognizing that the value at any point in time is a random variable.

In Example 7.5 we found that $\sigma_x^2 = 0.25$, $\sigma_y^2 = 0.25$, and $\rho_{xy} = -0.60$. Thus the variance of W is computed using Key Idea 7.11:

$$\sigma_W^2 = a^2\sigma_x^2 + b^2\sigma_y^2 + 2ab\rho_{xy}\sigma_x\sigma_y$$
$$= 5^2(0.25) + 10^2(0.25) + 2(5)(10)(-0.60)(0.50)(0.50)$$
$$= 6.25 + 25 - 15.0$$
$$= 16.25$$
$$\sigma_W = 4.03$$

In this example the negative correlation reduces the variance below the variance for the sum of two independent random variables. The variance, σ_W^2, of 16.25 or the standard deviation, σ_W, of 4.03 can be used to compare portfolios in terms of risk. Higher variance implies a higher risk—greater chance for high or low portfolio values. □

Does It Make Sense?

The negative correlation and covariance implies that as one stock price goes up, the other tends to go down. In this portfolio, gains of one stock occur with losses of the other, and hence the variance is smaller. This portfolio would be suitable for an investor who wishes to avoid risk because random variations will not result in large losses or large gains. If an investor were a risk seeker, he or she would seek stocks with a positive correlation. From Key Idea 7.11 we see that a positive correlation would result in a higher variance. Thus larger gains and larger losses would be more likely. □

Example 7.7   Joint Competing Products

The president of Midwest Foods, Inc., Betty Judge, is considering the construction of a pork and beef distribution facility in Soy City. Contribution per pound to profit and overhead is known to be $0.40 for pork and $0.50 for beef. Betty has asked you to compute the mean and variance for total contribution.

Solution First define pounds of pork sold as a random variable X and pounds of beef sold as a random variable Y. Total contribution W is equal to

$$W = 0.40X + 0.50Y$$

A study of the beef and pork market was conducted by a consultant Mark Nelson, who prepared the joint probability distribution of pork and beef sales shown in Table 7.6. From the marginal distributions for Table 7.6, compute

$$\mu_x = 0.30(1000) + 0.40(2000) + 0.30(4000)$$
$$= 2300$$
$$E[X^2] = 0.30(1000)^2 + 0.40(2000)^2 + 0.30(4000)^2$$
$$= 6,700,000$$
$$\sigma_x^2 = E[X^2] - \mu_X^2$$
$$= 6,700,000 - (2300)^2$$
$$= 1,410,000$$
$$\sigma_x = 1187$$

TABLE 7.6   Joint Distribution of Pork Sales (X) Versus Beef Sales (Y)

	X			
Y	1000	2000	4000	$h(y)$
2000	0.00	0.05	0.15	0.20
4000	0.05	0.30	0.15	0.50
6000	0.25	0.05	0.00	0.30
$g(x)$	0.30	0.40	0.30	1.00

Following the same form he also computed

$$\mu_y = 4200$$
$$\sigma_y^2 = 1,960,000$$
$$\sigma_y = 1400$$

The covariance for this joint probability distribution can be computed by first computing

$$E[XY] = (1000)(1000)[(1)(2)(0.00) + (1)(4)(0.05) + (1)(6)(0.25)$$
$$+ (2)(2)(0.05) + (2)(4)(0.30) + (2)(6)(0.05)$$
$$+ (4)(2)(0.15) + (4)(4)(0.15) + (4)(6)(0.00)]$$
$$= 8,500,000$$

which is then used to compute

$$\sigma_{xy} = E[XY] - \mu_x\mu_y$$
$$= 8{,}500{,}000 - (2300)(4200)$$
$$= -1{,}160{,}000$$

$$\rho = \frac{\sigma_{xy}}{\sigma_x\sigma_y}$$
$$= \frac{-1{,}160{,}000}{(1187)(1400)}$$
$$= -0.70$$

The mean and variance for total sales are

$$\mu_W = 0.40\mu_X + 0.50\mu_Y$$
$$= 0.40(2300) + 0.50(4200)$$
$$= 3020$$
$$\sigma_W^2 = (0.40)^2\sigma_x^2 + (0.50)^2\sigma_y^2 + 2(0.40)(0.50)\sigma_{xy}$$
$$= (0.40)^2 1{,}410{,}000 + (0.50)^2 1{,}960{,}000 + 2(0.40)(0.50)(-1{,}160{,}000)$$
$$= 251{,}600$$
$$\sigma_W = 501.6 \qquad \qquad \square$$

Does It Make Sense?

In this example the correlation between X and Y was -0.70. The negative covariance and correlation are consistent with the economic conclusion that beef and pork are competing goods. The negative covariance reduces the variance of total contribution compared to a market in which X and Y were independent. To achieve business stability, the company would market competing goods. $\qquad \square$

Example 7.8   Balance of Trade

Joe Gatt, an economist for a small country, was studying the effect of his country's foreign trade policy. In that project he needed to develop a simple model to describe the behavior of the balance of trade, W:

$$W = X - M$$

where X is total exports, M is total imports, and W is balance of trade.

Solution   Joe knew that both X and M were normally distributed random variables and he conducted a study that provided the following results:

$$\mu_M = 200 \qquad \sigma_M^2 = 900$$
$$\mu_X = 200 \qquad \sigma_X^2 = 625$$
$$\rho_{xm} = -0.50$$

From his study of statistics Joe also knew that W was a linear combination of random variables, and thus he derived the mean and variance for the balance of trade W:

$$\mu_W = a\mu_X + b\mu_M$$
$$= (+1) \times 200 + (-1) \times 200$$
$$= 0$$

Thus we know that, on average, imports and exports are equal, indicating balanced trade. Now consider the risk as measured by the variance:

$$\sigma_W^2 = a^2\sigma_X^2 + b^2\sigma_M^2 + 2ab\rho_{xm}\sigma_X\sigma_M$$
$$= (1)^2 \times 625 + (-1)^2 \times 900 + 2(+1)(-1)(-0.50)\sqrt{625}\sqrt{900}$$
$$= 625 + 900 + 1500$$
$$= 3025$$

and finally,

$$\sigma_W = 55 \qquad \square$$

Computation of probabilities. In this example we can compute the probability that the trade balance is within certain ranges. Random variables X and M are normally distributed, and linear combinations of normally distributed random variables are also normally distributed.

Now consider how we compute the probability that the trade balance is less than -50. The result is shown schematically in Figure 7.1 as the lower tail of the normal distribution. To obtain the probability, the standard normal Z statistic is computed:

$$Z = \frac{-50 - 0}{55} = -0.909$$

The probability, obtained by using Table A.1, is 0.182 (0.50 − 0.318). Similarly, the probability that the trade balance is above +75 is

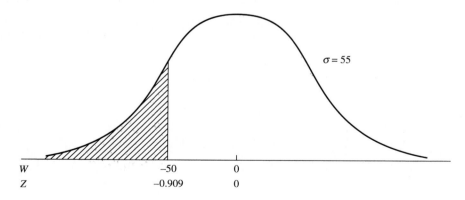

Figure 7.1   Probability of Trade Balance ≤ -50

$$P(W \geq 75 \mid \mu = 0, \sigma = 55) = P\left(Z \geq \frac{75 - 0}{55}\right)$$
$$= P(Z \geq 1.36)$$
$$= 0.087 \qquad \square$$

Does It Make Sense?

Note that in this example a negative correlation increased the variance of the difference between two random variables. In the equation this results from the product of two negatives, $-b$ and $-\rho_{xm}$, which were used to compute the covariance effect. Now consider the actual trade situation. The negative correlation implies that conditions which increase exports tend to decrease imports, and vice versa. This tends to increase the difference between exports and imports (e.g., larger positive trade balance) compared to a situation in which exports and imports were not related. Thus a negative correlation between exports and imports implies that they move in opposite directions, and therefore there will be a higher variance in the balance of trade, W.

A negative correlation could result from changes in the value of a nation's currency unit relative to the rest of the world. Decreased currency value reduces the price of exports, implying that other nations will purchase more and therefore increase exports. However, at the same time the price of imports would increase, which would reduce imports. Thus based on statistical and economic theory, decreases in the value of a nation's currency unit would increase its trade balance—increased exports and decreased imports. Similarly, increased currency value would decrease a nation's trade balance.

In contrast, a positive correlation could result from growth or shrinkage in the world economy, which increased or decreased both exports and imports simultaneously. Thus world economic growth cycles (e.g., patterns of growth followed by decline) would decrease the variance of a nation's trade balance compared to independent import and export changes. $\qquad \square$

Example 7.8 illustrates a very important result for business and economic applications. Many business decision variables result from linear combinations of variables that have a normal distribution. Key Idea 7.13 shows that those decision variables can also benefit from the probability analysis based on the normal distribution.

Example 7.9   Stock Portfolio

Megan Johnson, the account manager for Diversified Investors, is considering a stock portfolio which includes 20 shares of Diversified Machine Tools and 30 shares of Northwest Cereals. The price of Diversified is a normally distributed random variable with a mean $\mu_x = 25$ and a variance $\sigma_x^2 = 81$. The price of Northwest is also a normally distributed random variable with a mean $\mu_y = 40$ and a variance $\sigma_y^2 = 121$. The stock prices have a negative correlation $\rho_{xy} = -0.40$. The value of the portfolio W is

---

Key Idea 7.13: Linear Combinations of Normal Random Variables

The **linear combination of normally distributed random variables** X and Y is defined as

$$W = aX + bY$$

where a and b are constants. The random variable W is also normally distributed with

$$\mu_W = a\mu_X + b\mu_Y$$

and

$$\sigma_W^2 = a^2\sigma_X^2 + b^2\sigma_Y^2 + 2ab\rho_{XY}\sigma_X\sigma_Y$$

or

$$\sigma_W^2 = a^2\sigma_X^2 + b^2\sigma_Y^2$$

if X and Y are independent.

---

a linear combination of two stocks whose market prices are random variables X and Y. The number of shares of each stock are represented by $a = 20$ and $b = 30$. The portfolio value is represented by the linear combination

$$W = aX + bY$$

You have been asked to construct a symmetric interval which includes 95% of the potential portfolio values.

Solution   Since prices, X and Y, are each normally distributed random variables, the total portfolio value W also has a normal distribution. The mean and standard deviation of W are computed using Key Idea 7.13 as follows:

$$\mu_W = a\mu_X + b\mu_Y$$
$$= 20 \times 25 + 30 \times 40$$
$$= 1700$$
$$\sigma_W^2 = a^2\sigma_X^2 + b^2\sigma_Y^2 + 2ab\rho_{XY}\sigma_X\sigma_Y$$
$$= 20^2(81) + 30^2(121) + 2(20)(30)(-0.40)(9)(11)$$
$$= 93,780$$
$$\sigma_W = 306.24$$

The 95% symmetric interval for W, the observed value of the portfolio, can be constructed as follows:

$$P(a \leq W \leq b) = 0.95$$
$$P(W - 1.96\sigma_W \leq W \leq W + 1.96\sigma_W) = 0.95$$
$$P(1700 - 1.96 \times 306.24 \leq W \leq 1700 + 1.96 \times 306.24) = 0.95$$
$$P(1099.77 \leq W \leq 2300.23) = 0.95$$

The probability that value of the portfolio will be in the interval 1100 to 2300 is 0.95. If the prices of the two stocks had a positive correlation ($\rho_{xy} = +0.40$), the standard deviation of W would be $\sigma_W = 434.53$ and the 95% acceptance interval would range from 852 to 2552.

   The latter example with a positive correlation between stock prices would have a larger risk, implying either a chance for a large gain or a large loss.   □

7.6.2 Application to Random Samples

Linear combinations of random variables provide the foundation for developing the properties of sample statistics such as the mean and proportion. We have defined previously a simple random sample as a sample in which each element in the population has an equal probability of being included, and each observation is independent of all others.

   A single observation represents an outcome in the sample space defined by the random sampling plan, and this observation or outcome has a finite probability. Thus each observation in a simple random sample is a random variable.

   Consider the case for a random sample of size 2. Both observations are obtained from the same population, and therefore the probability distribution for both variables is the same. Each observation is a random variable with the same mean and variance. In addition, the covariance and hence the correlation between the two observations is zero because the observations are independent.

   Now we compute the mean and variance for a random sample of size 2. The observations X_i, $i = 1, 2$, are random variables with the same probability distribution, whose mean is μ and whose variance is σ^2. The sample mean for a random sample of size $n = 2$ is

$$\bar{X} = \frac{X_1 + X_2}{2}$$
$$= \frac{X_1}{2} + \frac{X_2}{2}$$

The mean and variance of the sample mean are

$$\mu_{\bar{X}} = E\left[\frac{X_1}{2} + \frac{X_2}{2}\right]$$

$$= \frac{\mu}{2} + \frac{\mu}{2}$$

$$= \mu$$

$$\sigma_{\bar{X}}^2 = \sigma^2\left(\frac{X_1}{2} + \frac{X_2}{2}\right)$$

$$= \sigma^2\left(\frac{X_1}{2}\right) + \sigma^2\left(\frac{X_2}{2}\right)$$

$$= \left(\frac{1}{2}\right)^2 \sigma^2(X_1) + \left(\frac{1}{2}\right)^2 \sigma^2(X_2)$$

$$= \frac{\sigma^2(X_1) + \sigma^2(X_2)}{2^2}$$

$$= \frac{\sigma^2 + \sigma^2}{2^2}$$

$$= \frac{\sigma^2}{2}$$

The covariance terms above are zero because the observations in a random sample are independent random variables. From Key Idea 7.7 we saw that independent random variables have a zero covariance.

This result can be extended directly to random samples of size n as follows:

$$\bar{X} = \frac{\sum_{i=1}^n X_i}{n} = \frac{X_1}{n} + \frac{X_2}{n} + \cdots + \frac{X_n}{n}$$

By following the same steps used for a sample of size $n = 2$, we find that

$$\mu_{\bar{X}} = \mu$$

$$\sigma_{\bar{X}}^2 = n\left(\frac{1}{n}\right)^2 \sigma^2 = \frac{\sigma^2}{n}$$

This discussion provides some important background for the study of sampling distributions in Chapter 9. The expected value of a sample mean is the same as the expected value of the probability distribution from which the observations were obtained. In addition, if the observations are independent, the variance of a sample mean is inversely related to the sample size. Thus with increased sample size the variance of the sample mean becomes smaller, which implies that the sample mean approaches the population mean.

Practice Problem 7.3

The value of a portfolio, W, is a random variable that is a linear combination of random variables, X and Y, with the following relationship:

$$W = 6X + 5Y$$

and the random variables have the following properties:

$$\mu_X = 100 \qquad \sigma_X = 30 \qquad \mu_Y = 200 \qquad \sigma_Y = 40 \qquad \rho_{XY} = -0.40$$

Compute the mean and variance for random variable W.   □

Problem Exercises

7.15   A random variable X has mean $\mu_X = 10$ and variance $\sigma_X^2 = 25$, and a second random variable Y has mean $\mu_Y = 40$ and variance $\sigma_Y^2 = 55$. Determine:
   (a) The mean and variance of the sum of X and Y assuming that they are independent.
   (b) The mean and variance of the sum of X and Y if $\rho_{xy} = 0.5$.

7.16   A random variable X has mean $\mu_X = 10$ and variance $\sigma_X^2 = 25$, and a second random variable Y has mean $\mu_Y = 40$ and variance $\sigma_Y^2 = 55$. There are 5 units of X and 4 units of Y. Determine:
   (a) The mean and variance of the linear combination of 5 units of X and 4 units of Y assuming that they are independent.
   (b) The mean and variance of the linear combination of 5 units of X and 4 units of Y if $\rho_{xy} = 0.5$.

7.17   The mean and variance of the price of GM stock are 15 and 25, while the mean and variance of the price of IBN are 40 and 50. You have a portfolio containing 20 shares of GM and 30 shares of IBN. Assume that the prices are independent. Determine for the portfolio:
   (a) The mean.
   (b) The variance.

7.18   The mean and variance of the price of GM stock are 15 and 25, while the mean and variance of the price of IBN are 40 and 50. You have a portfolio containing 20 shares of GM and 30 shares of IBN. Assume that the prices have a correlation $\rho = -0.50$. Determine:
   (a) The mean of the value of your portfolio.
   (b) The variance of your portfolio value.

7.19   Refer to Problem 7.18 with the portfolio of GM and IBN stock. Now assume that both stock prices are independent.
   (a) Construct a symmetric interval that contains 95% of the stock portfolio values.
   (b) What is the probability that the portfolio value is greater than 1800?
   (c) What is the probability that the portfolio value is less than 1100?

7.20   The mean and variance of the price of GM stock are 15 and 25, while the mean and variance of the price of IBN are 40 and 50. You have a portfolio containing 20 shares of GM and 30 shares of IBN. Assume that the prices are independent and that the prices are normally distributed random variables. Determine:
   (a) The mean of the value of your portfolio.

(b) The variance of your portfolio value.

(c) The probability that the portfolio value is greater than 1800.

(d) The probability that the portfolio value is less than 1100.

7.21   The independent normal random variables X and Y have means and variances equal to $\mu_X = 25$, $\sigma_X^2 = 49$, $\mu_Y = 15$, and $\sigma_Y^2 = 25$. Determine:

(a) The mean of the difference X minus Y.

(b) The variance of the difference.

7.22   The independent normal random variables X and Y have means and variances equal to $\mu_X = 25$, $\sigma_X^2 = 49$, $\mu_Y = 15$, and $\sigma_Y^2 = 25$. Determine the probability that:

(a) The difference X minus Y is less than 0.

(b) The difference is greater than 20.

7.23   Consider the linear combination W of independent normal random variables X and Y:

$$W = 5X + 10Y$$

and X and Y have means and variances $\mu_X = 25$, $\sigma_X^2 = 49$, $\mu_Y = 15$, and $\sigma_Y^2 = 25$. Determine:

(a) The mean of W.

(b) The variance of W.

7.24   Refer to Problem 7.23 and assume that X and Y are independent. Determine the probability that:

(a) W is greater than 400.

(b) W is between 200 and 400.

(c) W is less than 150.

SUMMARY OF KEY IDEAS

PRACTICE PROBLEM SOLUTIONS

7.1

(a)
$$g(3) = \sum_y f(3, y) = 0.10 + 0.10 + 0.05 = 0.25$$

(b)
$$h(2) = \sum_x f(x, 2) = 0.10 + 0.10 + 0.10 = 0.30$$

(c)
$$P(X \geq 3 \cap Y \geq 2) = \sum_{x=3}^{4} \sum_{y=2}^{3} f(x, y)$$
$$= 0.10 + 0.05 + 0.10 + 0.20$$
$$= 0.45$$

(d)
$$g(3 \mid 2) = \frac{f(3, 2)}{h(2)} = \frac{0.10}{0.30} = 0.33$$

(e)
$$h(2 \mid 3) = \frac{f(3, 2)}{g(3)} = \frac{0.10}{0.25} = 0.40$$

(f)
$$f(x, y) \neq g(x)h(y)$$
$$f(2, 1) = 0.05 \neq g(2)h(1) = (0.30)(0.30)$$
$$\longrightarrow X \text{ and } Y \text{ are not independent.}$$

7.2

(a) $\sigma_{XY} = E[XY] - \mu_X \mu_Y$

$$E[XY] = \sum_x \sum_y f(x, y)$$
$$= (1)(2)(0.05) + (1)(3)(0.10) + (1)(4)(0.15)$$
$$+ (2)(2)(0.10) + (2)(3)(0.10) + (2)(4)(0.10)$$
$$+ (3)(2)(0.15) + (3)(3)(0.05) + (3)(4)(0.20)$$
$$= 0.10 + 0.30 + 0.60 + 0.40 + 0.60 + 0.80 + 0.90 + 0.45 + 2.40$$
$$= 6.55$$
$$\mu_X = \sum_y xg(x)$$
$$= (2)(0.30) + (3)(0.25) + (4)(0.45)$$
$$= 0.60 + 0.75 + 1.80$$
$$= 3.15$$

$$\mu_Y = \sum_x yh(y)$$

$$= (1)(0.30) + (2)(0.30) + (3)(0.40)$$

$$= 0.30 + 0.60 + 1.20$$

$$= 2.10$$

$$\sigma_{XY} = 6.55 - (3.15)(2.10)$$

$$= 6.55 - 6.62$$

$$= -0.07$$

(b)

$$\rho_{XY} = \frac{\sigma_{XY}}{\sigma_X \sigma_Y}$$

$$\sigma_X^2 = E[X^2] - \mu_X^2$$

$$E[X^2] = \sum_y x^2 g(x)$$

$$= (4)(0.30) + (9)(0.25) + (16)(0.45)$$

$$= 1.20 + 2.25 + 7.20$$

$$= 10.65$$

$$\sigma_X^2 = 10.65 - (3.15)^2$$

$$= 0.73$$

$$\sigma_X = 0.85$$

$$\sigma_Y^2 = E[Y^2] - \mu_X^2$$

$$E[Y^2] = \sum_x y^2 h(y)$$

$$= (1)(0.30) + (4)(0.30) + (9)(0.40)$$

$$= 0.30 + 1.20 + 3.60$$

$$= 5.10$$

$$\sigma_Y^2 = 5.10 - (2.10)^2$$

$$= 0.69$$

$$\sigma_Y = 0.83$$

$$\rho_{XY} = \frac{-0.07}{(0.85)(0.83)}$$

$$= -0.10$$

7.3   The mean μ for W is

$$\mu_W = 6\mu_X + 5\mu_Y$$

$$= 6(100) + 5(200)$$

$$= 1600$$

The variance σ^2 for W is

$$\sigma_W^2 = (6)^2\sigma_X^2 + (5)^2\sigma_Y^2 + (2)(6)(5)\rho_{XY}\sigma_X\sigma_Y$$
$$= (36)(900) + (25)(1600) + (2)(6)(5)(-0.4)(30)(40)$$
$$= 32{,}400 + 40{,}000 - 28{,}800$$
$$= 43{,}600$$

CHAPTER PROBLEMS

7.1   Given the following:

$$P(X = x) = g(x) \qquad x = 1, 2, 3 \qquad g(1) = 0.30 \qquad g(2) = 0.40$$
$$P(Y = y) = h(y) \qquad y = 1, 2 \qquad h(1) = 0.40$$
$$P(X = x \cap Y = y) = f(x, y) \qquad P(X = x \mid Y = y) = g(x \mid y)$$
$$P(Y = y \mid X = x) = h(y \mid x) \qquad h(1 \mid 1) = h(1 \mid 2) = 0.50$$

Find:
(a) $f(3, 2)$.
(b) $h(2 \mid 3)$.
(c) $g(1 \mid 2)$.
(d) $g(2 \mid 2)$.

7.2   Theresa Hill, president of Natural Foods, wishes to study the purchase patterns of cold and hot breakfast cereals. From her staff she discovers that sales of cold cereals per week are either 2, 4, or 6 units and that sales of hot cereals are either 1, 2, or 3 units per week. She decides to define the sales of cold cereals by the random variable X and sales of hot cereals by the random variable Y. She then asks her staff to determine the joint probabilities $f(x, y)$ for all combinations of cold and hot cereal sales and the marginal probabilities $g(x) = \sum_y f(x, y)$ and $h(y) = \sum_x f(x, y)$ and $g(x \mid y) = P(x \mid y)$ and $h(y \mid x) = P(y \mid x)$. Unfortunately, they only provide her with the following probabilities:

$$f(2, 1) = 0.10 \qquad f(6, 1) = 0.20 \qquad f(2, 2) = 0.20$$
$$f(6, 2) = 0.15 \qquad f(4, 3) = 0.10$$
$$g(2) = 0.30 \qquad h(1) = 0.40 \qquad h(2) = 0.40$$

(a) Construct the joint probability distribution table and compute the missing values.
(b) Compute the conditional probabilities $g(2 \mid 2)$ and $h(3 \mid 4)$.
(c) Compute the means and variances for X and Y.

7.3   Compute the covariance for the joint random variables in Problem 7.2.

7.4   Charlie Johnson, sales manager for Rogers Foods, maintains careful records of weekly sales performance to provide data for studying his sales operation. From these records he has developed the joint probability distribution of number of sales versus number of business lunches for the sales staff. Table 7.7 contains the joint probability distribution of the number of sales (random variable Y) and number of business lunches (random variable X). He has asked you to analyze these data and make recommendations regarding a policy for expense accounts for his sales staff.

TABLE 7.7   Joint Distribution of
Number of Lunches (X) Versus Number
of Units Sold (Y)

Y	1	2	3	$h(y)$
		X		
1	0.10	0.05	0.10	0.25
2	0.20	0.10	0.10	0.40
3	0.15	0.10	0.10	0.35
$g(x)$	0.45	0.25	0.30	1.00

(a) Compute $E[X]$, $E[Y]$, σ_X^2, and σ_Y^2.
(b) Compute the covariance of X and Y, σ_{xy}.
(c) What is the expected value of sales when $X = 1$?
(d) What is the expected value of sales when $X = 3$?
(e) What recommendations would you make to Charlie concerning a policy for sales staff expense accounts?

7.5   Given the random variables X, Y, and Z defined as

$$f(x): \quad f(0) = 0.30, \quad f(1) = 0.40, \quad f(2) = 0.30$$
$$f(y): \quad f(0) = 0.50, \quad f(1) = 0.50$$
$$f(z): \quad f(1) = 0.50, \quad f(2) = 0.50$$

In addition, we note that $\rho(y, z) = 0.00$, $\rho(x, z) = 0.50$, and $\rho(x, y) = 0.50$. Define $W = X + Y - Z$. Determine:
(a) The mean and variance of W.
(b) $E[0.5W]$ and $\sigma^2(0.5W)$.

7.6   The probability distribution function for the joint random variables X and Y is $f(x_i, y_j) = 0.10$ with $y_j = 1, 2, 3, 4, 5$ and $x_i = 1, 2$. Determine:
(a) The covariance of X and Y.
(b) The mean of $X + Y$.
(c) The variance of $X + Y$.

7.7   Agricultural Commodities, Inc. sells soybean flour and grain oil. The probability distribution for soybean flour is

$$f(2) = 0.20 \qquad f(4) = 0.50 \qquad f(6) = 0.30$$

The probability distribution function for grain oil is

$$f(1) = 0.40 \qquad f(2) = 0.60$$

The correlation between sales of the two products is $\rho = 0.50$. Soybean flour sells for $1 per unit and grain oil sells for $2 per unit. Determine:
(a) The mean for total sales revenue.
(b) The variance for total sales revenue.

7.8   Given the random variables

$$X_1: \quad f(1) = 0.40, \quad f(2) = 0.20, \quad f(3) = 0.40$$
$$X_2: \quad g(10) = 0.30, \quad g(0) = 0.40, \quad g(-10) = 0.30$$

The correlation $\rho_{X_1, X_2} = 0.50$. For the function $Y = 5X_1 - 8X_2$, compute the mean and variance for Y.

7.9   Shirley Trump has an investment portfolio consisting of 10 shares of stock in Consolidated Electronics, manufacturer of memory chips, and 20 shares of stock in Northwest Products, manufacturers of 8468 processor chips. She believes that the prices of these shares are random variables with their probability distribution function presented in Table 7.8. You have been asked to provide advice regarding her portfolio. Determine:
(a) The covariance of the prices X and Y.
(b) The expected value and variance of the total portfolio value.

TABLE 7.8   Probability
Distribution of Consolidated
Price (X) Versus Northwest
Price (Y)

		X	
Y	2	4	$h(y)$
5	0.10	0.20	0.30
10	0.20	0.50	0.70
$g(x)$	0.30	0.70	1.00

7.10   Gale McDavis, a former olympic skier, is considering her new career as owner of a ski shop. She has decided that she will either sell cross-country skis and boots or downhill skis and boots. You have been asked to analyze the potential profit and risks for these two options. As a first step, you gather information on the two markets. First you investigate the market for cross-country equipment. You find that daily sales of skis are expected to be either 0 with probability 0.30, 1 with probability 0.40, or 2 with probability 0.30. For boots the daily sales are expected to be either 0 with probability 0.40, 1 with probability 0.30, or 2 with probability 0.30. In addition, the correlation between sales of skis and boots is 0.80. The profit for each pair of skis and for each pair of boots is $10. Next, you investigate the market for downhill equipment. You find that daily sales of skis are expected to be either 0 with probability 0.40, 1 with probability 0.20, or 2 with probability 0.40. For boots the daily sales are expected to be either 0 with probability 0.30, 1 with probability 0.50, or 2 with probability 0.20. In addition, the correlation between sales of skis and boots is 0.50. The profit for each pair of skis and for each pair of boots is $10.
(a) Compute the mean and variance for profit from the sale of cross-country equipment.
(b) Compute the mean and variance for profit from the sale of downhill equipment.

(c) Prepare a recommendation for Gale concerning which business she should undertake. Support your analysis using the results of the previous work on this
problem.

7.11 Peter Chang wishes to open a Chinese pizza restaurant in which the principal items
would be pizza and tea. He hires Sherry Wong to conduct a marketing study to determine the potential demand for tea and pizza. He identifies two locations and develops
the joint probability distribution function for the number of pizzas sold per day (X)
and the number of pitchers of tea sold per day (Y) in each location. The results are
given in Tables 7.9 and 7.10. Each pizza is sold for $4 and each pitcher of tea is sold
for $2.

TABLE 7.9   Joint Distribution
of X and Y for Location A

| | X | | |
Y	10	20	$h(y)$
5	0.20	0.20	0.40
10	0.30	0.30	0.60
$g(x)$	0.50	0.50	1.00

TABLE 7.10   Joint
Distribution of X and Y for
Location B

| | X | | |
Y	10	20	$h(y)$
5	0.10	0.30	0.40
10	0.40	0.20	0.60
$g(x)$	0.50	0.50	1.00

(a) Compute the expected value of total revenue for both locations A and B.
(b) Compute the covariance of X and Y for each location.
(c) Compute the variance of total revenue for each location.
(d) Based on the description of this problem, would you conclude that Peter is a risk
seeker or a risk averter?
(e) Using the answers to parts (a) to (d), which location would you recommend?

7.12 Define X_1, X_2, and X_3 as Bernoulli random variables with $E[X_1] = 0.20$, $E[X_2] =$
0.40, and $E[X_3] = 0.70$ and $\rho(X_1, X_2) = 0.50$, $\rho(X_1, X_3) = 0.00$, and $\rho(X_2, X_3) =$
0.00. Bernoulli random variables have only two values, $X = 0$ and $X = 1$. For example
in this problem, $P(X_1 = 0) = 0.80$ and $P(X_1 = 1) = 0.20$. The variance for a Bernoulli
random variable is equal to $E[X](1 - E[X])$. Thus in this problem, $\sigma^2(X_1) = 0.20 \times$
0.80.

(a) Find the mean and variance of Y, where $Y = X_1 + X_2 + X_3$.

(b) Find the mean and variance of $\bar{Y}$, where

$$\bar{Y} = \frac{X_1 + X_2 + X_3}{3}$$

7.13 Consider the joint probability distribution for X and Y in Table 7.11. Determine:

TABLE 7.11   Probability
Distribution of X Versus Y

		X	
Y	0	1	2
0	0.25	0.00	0.25
1	0.00	0.00	0.00
2	0.25	0.00	.25

(a) $E[X]$ and $E[Y]$.

(b) σ_X^2 and σ_Y^2.

(c) $E[Z]$ and σ_Z^2 where $Z = aX + bY$.

(d) $E[W]$ and $\sigma^2(W)$ where $W = X - Y$.

7.14 Douglas Brown, marketing vice-president for Tada Computers, Inc., is developing alternative marketing plans for the coming sales year. Total sales for computers and disk drives are modeled by the random variables X and Y as shown in the Table 7.12. The correlation between computer and disk drive sales is 0.60. The profit for computers is 10 per unit and for disk drives it is 5 per unit.

TABLE 7.12   Probability
Distributions for Computers
(X) and Disk Drives (Y)

X	$f(x)$	Y	$f(y)$
1	0.30	1	0.30
2	0.40	2	0.40
3	0.30	3	0.30

(a) What are the expected value and variance for total profit from both computers and disk drives?

(b) For the same marketing cost, we can change the sales probabilities for computers to

$$f(x): \quad f(1) = 0.25, \quad f(2) = 0.50, \quad f(3) = 0.25$$

or we can change the sales probabilities for disk drives to

$$g(y): \quad g(1) = 0.20, \quad g(2) = 0.60, \quad g(3) = 0.20$$

Which change would you recommend if the objective is to maximize profit?

7.15 Given the joint probability distribution function in Table 7.13 and the linear function $W = 5X + 2Y$, compute $E[X]$, $E[Y]$, σ_X^2, σ_Y^2, $\sigma_{X,Y}$, $E[W]$, and σ_W^2.

TABLE 7.13   Joint
Probability Distribution
for Problem 7.15

	X	
Y	1	2
0	0.30	0.20
1	0.20	0.30

7.16 George Elgar, president of Natural Foods, is considering the introduction of two new cake mixes. These products appeal to somewhat different market segments, but there is some overlap. Therefore, the marketing consultant believes that sales will be negatively correlated, with $\rho = -0.3$. The expected first-year sales for cake mix 1 has a mean $\mu_1 = 10,000$ and a variance $\sigma_1^2 = 64,000$. For cake mix 2 the mean $\mu_2 = 20,000$ with a standard deviation $\sigma_2 = 300$. Cake mix 1 will contribute \$0.20 to profit and overhead. Cake mix 2 will contribute \$0.30 to profit and overhead. What are the mean and variance for total contribution to profit and overhead from the two cake mixes?

7.17 Red Heart, Inc. produces fast rotary lawn mowers with organically neutral composting systems and hydrodynamic vertical suspension for easier mowing. Monthly sales for these mowers is normally distributed with mean 100 and variance 64. The selling price is \$100 per unit. The number of units produced per month is also normally distributed with mean 100, and variance of 25. Each unit produced has a variable cost of \$80. Sales and units produced have a correlation of 0.50. What are the mean and variance for the contribution margin (total income minus total variable cost) for lawn mowers?

7.18 Shirley Smith, the manager of computer sales for Fox Valley Computers, has asked you to help with the analysis of computer sales activity. Fox Valley sells both a standard desktop microcomputer and a lightweight notebook computer for analysts who travel. Table 7.14 is the probability distribution function for daily computer sales over the past six months. The number of notebook computers is indicated by the random variable X,

TABLE 7.14   Probability
Distributions for Desktop
(Y) and Notebook (X)
Computers

	Y		
X	2	3	4
2	0.30	0.10	0.10
3	0.20	0.10	0.20

and the number of desktop computers is indicated by the random variable Y. Determine the probability of selling:

(a) Exactly 3 desktop computers given that exactly 2 notebook computers have been sold.

(b) Exactly 2 notebook computers given that exactly 3 desktop computers have been sold.

(c) Either 3 desktop computers or 3 notebook computers.

(d) Both 3 desktop computers and 3 notebook computers.

7.19 Shirley Smith, the manager of computer sales for Fox Valley Computers, has asked you to help with the analysis of computer sales activity. Fox Valley sells both a standard desktop microcomputer and a lightweight notebook computer for analysts who travel. Table 7.14 is the probability distribution function for daily computer sales over the past six months. The number of notebook computers is indicated by the random variable X and the number of desktop computers is indicated by the random variable Y. Compute:

(a) The mean and variance for desktop computer sales.

(b) The mean and variance for notebook computer sales.

(c) The covariance and correlation for desktop and notebook computer sales.

7.20 Shirley Smith from Problem 7.19 has asked you to analyze the sales revenue. The selling price for desktop computers is $1200 per unit and the selling price for notebook computers is $1600 per unit. Using these figures, what are the mean and the variance for daily sales revenue?

7.21 Consider again Problem 7.19 involving daily computer sales. Now you are asked to study the contribution to profit and overhead. Contribution is total revenue minus total costs. The fixed daily costs are $1000. Each desktop computer costs $1000 and each notebook computer costs $1400.

(a) Write an equation for contribution in terms of computer sales and reduce it to a compact form.

(b) Compute the mean and variance for the contribution margin.

7.22 Shirley Johnson, the portfolio manager, has asked you to analyze a newly acquired portfolio to determine its mean value and variability. The portfolio consists of 50 shares of Xylophone Music and 40 shares of Yankee Workshop. Analysis of past history indicates that the share price of Xylophone Music has a mean of 25 and a variance of 121. A similar analysis indicated that Yankee has a mean share price of 40 with a variance of 225. Your best evidence indicates that the share prices have a correlation of $+0.5$.

(a) Compute the mean and variance of the portfolio.

(b) Suppose that the correlation between share prices was actually -0.5. Now what are the mean and variance of the portfolio?

7.23 The Acme Manufacturing Company of Lower Fork, North Dakota, produces a variety of high-quality lawn and patio furniture. The vice-president of finance, Aaron Ackley, has asked you to analyze the monthly cash flow, which is defined as total revenue minus total cost. In particular, he wants you to determine the mean and variance of monthly cash flow. The direct costs per unit produced are $15 and the fixed cost per month is $2000. The selling price is $20 per unit. The quantity sold per month is a random variable with mean equal to 500 and variance equal to 2500. The quantity produced is also a random variable with mean 500 but with variance 1600. Production quantity and quantity sold have a correlation of 0.40. What are the mean and variance of monthly cash flow?

7.24   Financial Managers, Inc. buy and sell a large number of stocks routinely for the various accounts that they manage. The portfolio manager Andrea Carlson has asked for your assistance in the analysis of the Johnson Fund. A portion of this portfolio consists of 10 shares of stock A and 8 shares of stock B. The price of A has a mean $\mu = 10$ and a variance $\sigma^2 = 16$, while the price of B has a mean of 12 and a variance of 9. The correlation between prices is $\rho = 0.3$.

(a) What are the mean and variance of the portfolio value?

(b) Andrea has been asked to reduce the variance (risk) of the portfolio. She offers to trade the 10 shares of stock A and receives two offers from which she can select 1: 10 shares of stock 1, with price mean of 10, variance of 25, and a correlation with the price of stock B equal to $\rho = -0.2$, or 10 shares of stock 2 with a mean price of 10, variance of 9, and a correlation with stock B price of $\rho = +0.6$. Which offer should she select?

7.25   Refer to Problem 7.24 with the portfolio manager Andrea Carlson. She has been offered a trade for the 8 shares of stock B. In return, she would receive 10 shares of stock C with a mean price of 9.6 and a variance of 36. What is the required correlation between the price of stock C and the price of stock A so that the variance of the portfolio remains the same?

7.26   Financial Managers, Inc. buy and sell a large number of stocks routinely for the various accounts that they manage. Portfolio manager Sarah Bloom has asked for your assistance in analysis of the Burde Fund. A portion of this portfolio consists of 10 shares of stock A and 8 shares of stock B. The price of A has a mean $\mu = 12$ and a variance $\sigma^2 = 14$, while the price of B has a mean of 10 and a variance of 12. The correlation between prices is $\rho = 0.5$.

(a) What are the mean and variance of the portfolio value?

(b) Sarah has been asked to reduce the variance (risk) of the portfolio. She offers to trade the 10 shares of stock A and receives two offers from which she can select 1: 10 shares of stock 1, with price mean of 12, variance of 25, and a correlation with the price of stock B equal to $\rho = -0.2$, or 10 shares of stock 2 with a mean price of 10, variance of 9, and a correlation with stock B price of $\rho = +0.6$. Which offer should she select?

7.27   Sunshine Cereals, Inc. has asked you to analyze their raisin flakes cereal production facility. This facility adds raisins to each box of flakes to produce the final product. The amount of flakes has a mean of 14 ounces and a variance of 1. The raisins added have a mean of 2 ounces with a variance of 0.09. Compute the mean and variance of package weight if the correlation between the weight of raisins and the weight of cereal is:

(a) +0.4.

(b) −0.4.

7.28   Heidi Johnson, the quality control manager of Consolidated Motors, has asked for your assistance in the analysis of the dimension of an assembly. The dimension is the sum of the dimensions of parts A and B, which are produced on separate machines. The dimension of part A is a random variable with mean 10 and variance 1, and the dimension of part B is also a random variable with mean 12 and variance 0.25. What are the mean and variance of the completed assembly?

7.29 After completing the computations in Problem 7.28, Heidi has asked you to help with a new problem. Analysis of final component assembly has concluded that the variance of the assembly involving parts A and B is too large. As a result, the quality of final automobiles is below industry standards and customer complaints are increasing. Heidi has proposed that parts A and B should be produced on the same machine, which is designed to produce pairs of parts with correlated measurements. What is the required correlation between the dimensions of parts A and B so that the variance of the final dimension is reduced by 40%?

7.30 The general manager of production for Hygrade Cereals, Inc., John Pautzke, has asked for your assistance in analyzing the density of cereals produced in the main factory. The density of cereals must be controlled within a narrow interval. If the density is too low, a 16-ounce package will contain too much volume for easy packing of the standard 20 packages into a shipping container. If the density is too high, the flavor is degraded and packages appear to be only partially filled. Product density is the sum of the density contributed at process A and the density contributed at process B. The density at A has a mean of 10 and a variance of 0.09, while the density at B has a mean of 12 and a variance of 0.16. The densities contributed at the two steps have a correlation of 0.2. What are the mean and variance of the sum of the two densities?

7.31 Given the joint probability distribution for X and Y in Table 7.15, consider the linear model $W = 2X + 3Y$. Determine:
(a) μ_W.
(b) σ_W^2.

TABLE 7.15   Joint Distribution of Number of X and Y

		X		
Y	2	3	4	$h(y)$
1	0.12	0.16	0.12	0.40
2	0.18	0.24	0.18	0.60
$g(x)$	0.30	0.40	0.30	1.00

7.32 The Acme Manufacturing Company of Lower Fork, North Dakota, produces a variety of high-quality lawn and patio furniture. The vice-president of finance, Robert Ackley, has asked you to analyze the monthly cash flow, which is defined as total revenue minus total cost. In particular, he wants you to determine the mean and variance of monthly cash flow. The direct costs per unit produced are $15, and the fixed cost per month is $2000. The selling price is $20 per unit. The quantity sold per month is a random variable with mean equal to 500 and variance equal to 2500. The quantity produced is also a random variable with mean 500 but with variance 1600. Production quantity and quantity sold have a correlation of 0.40. What are the mean and variance of monthly cash flow?

7.33 Chinpan Imports, Inc. receives high-quality pottery bowls from Pacific basin countries. Shipments are delivered by two different companies. Each shipment crate contains four bowls. The number of crates delivered by each shipping company is the same. Company A breaks 40% of the bowls, and company B breaks 20% of the bowls. The probability of breaking any pot is independent. Let the random variable X indicate the shipping company with $X = 1$ being company A and $X = 2$ being company B. Let Y indicate the number of broken bowls. Assume that the number of broken bowls in any crate can be modeled by a binomial probability distribution.
(a) Construct the joint probability distribution of X and Y.
(b) Are X and Y independent?
(c) What are the expected value and variance of the number of broken bowls?

7.34 Given the random variable Z defined as $Z = 5X + 4Y$, where X is a normal random variable $N(50, 100)$ and Y is a normal random variable $N(50, 64)$, and $\rho(X, Y) = 0$. Note that $\sigma^2(Z) = E[(Z - E[Z])^2]$.
(a) Show that $\sigma^2(Z) = E[Z^2] - (E[Z])^2$.
(b) Compute the numerical values for $E[Z]$ and $\sigma^2(Z)$.

7.35 You have a small store that sells beer and soda. The number of beers sold can be modeled using a random variable, X, which has a normal probability distribution with mean 100 and variance 100. The number of sodas sold can be modeled with a normal random variable, Y, with mean 50 and variance 400. The sales of beer and soda are correlated with a correlation coefficient $\rho = -0.50$. The total sales revenue, W, is given by $W = 2X + Y$. Determine:
(a) The mean and variance of W.
(b) The probability that total sales exceeds 290.

7.36 You have just purchased Ralph's Pretty Good Grocery in Lake Wobegon, Minnesota, and are attempting to determine some operating characteristics. You discover that the cost of goods sold for each week can be modeled as a random variable with mean 100 and variance 400. In addition, sales revenue for each week can be modeled as a normal random variable with mean 400 and variance 900. History also reveals that the correlation between cost of goods sold and sales revenue is 0.50. The operating margin is the difference between sales revenue and cost of goods sold. Determine:
(a) The mean and variance for the operating margin.
(b) The probability that the operating margin is less than 260.

7.37 A large personnel recruiting company believes that success in corporate management depends on academic achievement and participation in extracurricular activities. At a prestigious midwestern college, academic achievement X is measured using a normally distributed random variable with mean 10 and variance 4. Extracurricular activities are measured by a normally distributed random variable Y, which has a mean of 5 and a variance of 9. The correlation coefficient for X and Y is 0.50. The success formula used by the recruiting company is $W = 2X + 4Y$. A score of 30 or more indicates future success. What is the probability that a randomly selected student from the college will experience future success?

7.38 Kris Dale, the financial vice-president of a new specialty retailer, wishes to analyze the corporation's sales, which presently originate at two different retail stores. Based on an analysis of past monthly sales, she develops a model for predicting future monthly sales.

In the model, store 1 has mean sales of 10 units with a variance of 16. The price of each unit sold is $10,000. Store 2 has mean sales of 20 with a variance of 25. The price of each unit sold is $8000. She also discovers that the sales in each store can be modeled by the normal probability distribution and the correlation between sales is -0.50. Determine:

(a) The mean and variance of total sales revenue measured in dollars from the two stores.

(b) The probability that total sales exceed $500,000.

(c) The probability that total sales are less than $250,000.

(d) The probability that total sales from store 1 exceed those from store 2 in any month.

7.39 George Fox, president of Hamburger and Pop Restaurants, Inc., is studying the daily cash flow for one of his new restaurants. In this restaurant the price for a pop is $5 per unit and the price for a hamburger is $10 per unit. He has discovered that the daily sales of pop are distributed normally with a mean of 5000 units and a variance of 10,000. In addition, the daily sales of hamburgers are normally distributed with a mean of 500 units and a variance of 900. The sales of pop and hamburgers have a correlation of -0.60. What is the probability that the total sales revenue exceeds $30,600?

7.40 Amalgamated Agricultural Associates buy and sell grain in an attempt to make a profit. They know from past experience that their purchase price of grain per bushel (X) is normally distributed with a mean of $4 and a variance of 1. They also know that their selling price is normally distributed with a mean of $5 and a variance of 4. The correlation between buying and selling price is 0.5. They have a fixed operating cost of $5000 per month which must be covered by the difference between their sales and purchase revenue.

(a) During the next month they will purchase and sell 5000 bushels of grain. What is their probability of breaking even? (For example, sales revenue exceeds purchase revenue by $5000.)

(b) If they sell 6000 bushels, what is their probability of breaking even?

7.41 You are going to have a book sale. For the sale you have 10 mathematics books and 20 economics books. From past experience you know that the probability of selling a single mathematics book is 0.20 and that the sale of mathematics books are independent. The probability of selling a single economics book is 0.40, and the sales of economics books are also independent. Each economics book has a price of $5.00 and each mathematics book has a price of $8.00.

(a) Compute the mean and variance of total sales in dollars.

(b) What assumption is needed to compute the variance of total sales?

7.42 Kevin Thrash, manager of World Portfolios, has asked for your assistance in analyzing a new portfolio of two stocks. The portfolio consists of 10 shares of Amalgamated Distributors, Inc. and 5 shares of Beta Technologies, Inc. The price of Amalgamated is normally distributed with a mean of 30 and a variance of 16. The price of Beta has a mean of 40 and a variance of 64. The correlation between stock prices is $\rho = +0.5$.

(a) Compute the mean and variance of the portfolio value.

(b) What is the probability that the portfolio value is less than 450?

(c) What correlation between the stock prices would be required to reduce the probability that the portfolio value is less than 450 to 0.05?

8

Sampling and Data Collection

The foundation for good statistical analysis is good data.

8.1 EVALUATING DATA COLLECTION

The foundation for good statistical analysis is good data. In Chapters 2 and 3 we learned some important techniques for describing data. In subsequent chapters statistical inference will be used to obtain additional information from data. Large volumes of data are provided by modern computer and electronic communication systems. However, without proper sampling and measurement, sophisticated technology cannot provide useful data.

The objective of this chapter is to present principles and procedures for good data collection. You will learn how to design studies and to recognize good and bad data collection procedures. We begin with some short examples of poor data collection that can provide misleading results, including:

1. A city wishes to redesign its library so that it will serve more people. It places a set of questionnaires in the library and asks people to evaluate the library operation.

This technique provides input only from people who use the library. If the objective is to serve more people, they need responses from people who do not use the library.

2. A convenience store observes that it is losing customers and wants to make modifications to change this trend. It publishes an advertisement in the local newspaper asking people to write letters to them indicating why they have stopped coming to the store or why they have not.

This technique requires considerable effort from people who may not care about the success or failure of the store. Thus the people who respond could not be considered typical.

3. A candidate for student body president is thinking about a campaign that includes seeking lower prices in the college bookstore. But first she decides to take a sample of 100 students and determine if they think this is an important issue. She asks

each of 10 friends who are on her campaign committee to sample 10 of their friends and ask about the bookstore issue.

This technique is not likely to provide a representative sample of the student body, because most of the students will have no chance of being in the sample. It can only tell her what her friends think.

4. Television news specials often invite people to phone positive or negative responses for important national issues such as: Should we bomb some country? Should the government raise taxes? Should Congress pass stronger gun control laws? The responses are collected by a computer and presented regularly during the news program. Responsible news broadcasters caution that this is not a "scientific sample" but imply by their reporting that the phone poll provides important results.

The problem with those polls is that only people with strong interests who can afford the cost of the phone call will reply. These people often have opinions different from those of the overall population. Thus serious nonresponse biases are likely.

Data are the raw materials that are shaped by statistical tools to provide information products (Key Idea 8.1). The information products can be inferior, dangerous, or just plain junk if the input data are of poor quality or if we use the statistical tools incorrectly. We need to know how to select data carefully so that our sophisticated tools do not produce inferior information products.

Key Idea 8.1: Information

Information consists of data that have been processed into a form that is meaningful to the recipient and is of real or perceived value in current or perspective actions or decisions.

8.2 OBTAINING USEFUL DATA

Statistical studies are conducted with a wide range of objectives.

1. A marketing research team wants to describe the family income of the population surrounding a proposed new shopping center.
2. Store location specialists predict future purchases at the shopping center.
3. Quality control departments conduct continuing studies to determine if a process is producing product that meets guaranteed specifications.
4. Industrial engineers conduct experiments to determine if quality or productivity can be improved by new production procedures.

Data for these studies come from either existing databases or from samples collected specifically to support the study. Existing databases include historical data collected for other purposes, such as accounting or production reports. Also included are research databases collected to support the work of a number of researchers. When data are collected for one purpose, they are often not completely suitable for other purposes. Historical data files such as production or accounting reports should be used with caution because they may include imprecise measurements and/or strange biases. Research databases are usually preferable. However, they may not include all of the variables required for a particular study. Properly designed samples are almost always the best source of data because they are designed to meet the needs of the specific study. However, properly designed samples are usually expensive. Thus analysts will often try to find existing data that will come close to meeting the study requirements. However, cheap data may be worth their price! Analysts must carefully consider a number of alternatives and evaluate the trade-off between data collection cost and data quality.

In Chapter 2 we defined a population by referring to outcomes from a system. This concept is important because it places primary data selection emphasis on the study objective or problem. After we have clearly defined the objectives of our study, we need to select an appropriate population (Key Idea 8.2).

Key Idea 8.2: Populations

A **population** is the set that contains all of the outcomes from a system or process that is being studied.

A **target population** is the set of items that are to be included in the study. Study results will apply to this population.

A **sampling frame** is a listing of all items in the target population that will be represented by the study.

Initially, a target population is defined by indicating the characteristics of the population elements and rules for deciding how an item is included in the population. A target population is the best set of items given the study objectives. For example, a market research team wanted to study the customers in the market area for a small midwestern city. The target population was all customers for the retail shopping area. They defined the sampling frame as those families listed in the local telephone directory. People with unlisted phone numbers and people outside the telephone district were excluded. But the sampling frame included most of the customers and was easy to define, and the sample can be easily obtained.

Target populations may be finite or infinite. The items or elements of finite populations could in theory be listed. Examples include all parts received from a supplier or all people living in China. Infinite populations are defined by describing the process that produces the infinite set of observations. An example could be the monthly crime reports for a particular city or state. Reported crimes are a sample from the population of reported and unreported crimes. This population results from a complex social process which includes variations in the occurrence of crime and errors of under- or overreporting. Another example of an infinite population is the dimension of parts produced by a manufacturing process that is assumed to operate forever.

There are a number of reasons, including cost of data collection, why we may not be able to obtain data from the target population. In those cases a closely related sampling frame is chosen (Key Idea 8.2). For example, David Emery wants to know the percentage of city residents who would purchase from a proposed pizza delivery service. The target population is all people in the city. However, the study budget requires him to contact people by phone. The sampling frame would include only those people who have telephones. A sampling frame that included only those people listed in the phone directory would further exclude those people with unlisted phone numbers. Present survey technology allows interviewers to generate phone numbers randomly, and therefore all people with telephones could be in the sampling frame.

There is a possibility for nonresponse bias. If an important part of the market were college students in dormitories and if their rooms did not have a phone, the sampling frame would exclude an important part of the target population. Even if students have telephones in their rooms, they may not be there when called and could be excluded. In either case the results would be biased.

The definition of a sampling frame requires a careful consideration of the study objectives, the target population, and the resources available to conduct the study. Creative people who understand statistical methods and study objectives can define useful sampling frames. Experience is an important asset in this process.

8.3 SAMPLING METHODS

Most statistical procedures assume a random sample (Key Idea 8.6, page 329) from the sampling frame. It is usually not feasible to obtain the entire population because the cost would be greater than the value of the information. In addition, good sampling methods provide amazingly precise results from relatively small samples. Among the most visible examples are samples used to predict voter preference in political elections. Samples of 1000 to 1500 voters accurately estimate the voting behavior of 60 to 80 million voters. We will examine some of the more important sampling procedures to help us identify and design correct sampling applications.

Many people who are not trained in statistical methods believe that it is better to obtain a census of the entire population, and a sample is always a second-best compromise. In many situations the opposite is true (Key Idea 8.3). When samples are used, more effort can be devoted to ensuring that all items selected for the sample are actually included.

Key Idea 8.3: Sample Versus Census

Even when it is possible to obtain a census, better results are usually obtained by devoting resources to more careful measurement of fewer observations. When a census is obtained from a large population, there are usually not enough resources to ensure precise measurement and to avoid biases that occur because every item in the sampling frame cannot be obtained. The task of managing large data collection efforts is very difficult. Major errors can become part of the results. For example, the census of the U.S. population conducted every 10 years suffers from an inability to contact every person.

A classic case of nonresponse bias (Key Idea 8.4) occurred in the 1936 *Literary Digest* poll to predict the outcome of the 1936 presidential election between Franklin D. Roosevelt and Alf Landon. A sampling frame consisting of 10,000,000 persons was constructed using telephone directories and automobile registration lists. Questionnaire ballots were sent to the entire sampling frame, and 2,000,000 were returned. Based on the results, the *Literary Digest* predicted that Landon would win the election.

Key Idea 8.4: Sources of Bias

Missing observations can often produce serious biases, because they are often different from the target population. Human population samples that use volunteers as subjects are suspect. Volunteers have time and interest in the study topic—most people do not—and those that do will often provide different responses.

However, those responding tended to be employed and generally not suffering as much from the Great Depression. Those who were suffering were either not included in the sampling frame or did not respond to the survey. The latter group, which was larger, tended to vote for Roosevelt, who won the election.

In contrast, note that election results are now routinely predicted within a few percentage points, using samples of 1000 to 1500 voters. Neither a large sample nor a population census is the key to correct determination of population characteristics (Key Idea 8.5).

Key Idea 8.5: Advantages of a Sample

A sample usually provides better results than a census, for two reasons: (1) the probability of each sample observation is known and therefore the sample observations can be combined to obtain approximately the same probability distribution as the population; and (2) each sample observation can be carefully selected and measured because the number of sample observations is small compared to the population size. Sampling theory and experience clearly show that it is much better to obtain a small sample of high-quality observations (i.e., carefully selected and precisely measured) than a large number of low-quality observations. Sampling theory will be developed in Chapter 9.

8.3.1 Simple Random Samples

The designation *scientific sample* is used to identify samples that have been selected by using the methods developed from sampling theory. A few of these methods are discussed below, beginning with the method of simple random sampling (Key Idea 8.6).

Key Idea 8.6: Simple Random Sample

A **simple random sample** has the property that every item in the sampling frame has an equal probability of being selected and that each selection is independent.

    R. A. Fisher, a major developer of modern statistical methods, argued that random samples are an "insurance policy" against all of the many ways that observations can be obtained incorrectly.

    A simple random sample does not imply that we can merely select any item for the sample. Instead, we must select items using a process which ensures that all items are equally likely to be selected. The statistical inference procedures developed in the next several chapters implicitly assume a simple random sample. A simple random sample is the ideal or reference point for comparing other sampling methods.

    Various procedures are used to obtain a simple random sample. For example, we could, directly or implicitly, assign a number to each item in the sampling frame.

A list of uniformly distributed random numbers, which can be generated using your computer statistical program, could then be used to select the sample observations. A starting point in the table is selected randomly, and then the next n random numbers identify the items that should be selected as a sample of size n from the sampling frame. The sample chosen in this way has the property that every item in the sampling frame has an equal probability of being selected. This occurs because uniformly distributed random numbers have the same probability for every random number in the distribution.

Considerable effort should be applied to obtain those items selected by the random numbers. Any item not included implies that a possibly different category is omitted, and thus the sample does not represent the target population. Those not obtained are often different, leading to nonresponse bias.

There are other procedures used to obtain a random sample. A random number generator algorithm can be included in a computer program that is used to generate telephone numbers for a simple random sample of households with phones. Balls can be numbered and mixed in a container. A neutral person can then be asked to select the balls that correspond to the items in the random sample.

If a selected item cannot be obtained and measured, a replacement item is selected using another random number. Failure to obtain a randomly selected observation introduces a nonresponse bias. The seriousness of this bias depends on the number of items that cannot be obtained and on the characteristics of those items not obtained. If all the missing items come from the same subset of the population, the bias could be serious. However, if the missing items have a variety of characteristics, analysts typically assume that the missing items are randomly selected. In that case the nonresponse bias is not a serious problem. Experience, good judgment, and peer review can all help to ensure that a sample which has the properties of a random sample is obtained.

8.3.2 Judgment Samples

So-called "judgment samples" (Key Idea 8.7) are popular in areas such as accounting in which studies are designed to search for specific problems.

Key Idea 8.7: Judgment Sample

A **judgment sample** is one in which the items are selected based on some ad hoc rules or personal insights of the people collecting the sample. The objective is to select items that represent the population being studied. Defenders of judgment samples would argue that persons who know the population are able to choose a representative sample better than a random number table.

In a judgment sample, observers might be instructed to obtain items in various categories, or they might simply choose those items that are easy to obtain. Some judgment samples may give useful results. Unfortunately, the statistical and distribution properties of judgment samples are not clear. We simply cannot tell if the sample provides a good representation, and we cannot provide any probability statement concerning the accuracy of the resulting statistics. Thus we would recommend against using judgment samples. If you do use a judgment sample, it is also incorrect to use the many powerful tools of statistical inference that are presented in Chapters 9 to 11.

8.3.3 Stratified Samples

Stratified samples (Key Idea 8.8) are conducted by first separating the population into subsets and then sampling randomly from each subset. As an example, suppose that we wished to determine average family income in a city. A good stratification variable would be neighborhoods and/or value of the housing unit. We expect that the mean income within each strata would be different. In addition, the sample variance for each strata would be computed using the sample mean for that strata and thus would be smaller than the sample variance, which was computed using the overall population mean. The population mean would be computed by combining the strata means.

Key Idea 8.8: Stratified Samples

Stratified samples are obtained by separating the population into basically homogeneous subsets or strata using a stratification variable that is related to the variable being measured. A random sample is obtained from each stratum and the strata sample mean is computed. If the stratification has been successful, the means from each stratum will be different, and the sample variance within each stratum will be smaller than the sample variance for the entire population. The population sample mean is computed as a linear combination of the strata sample means.

A second important benefit of stratified sampling is that additional information about the strata means can be obtained from the sample. In our example, the comparison of mean family income for each of the neighborhood strata would be an important result from a study of city incomes. For these reasons stratified samples are often used if it is possible to identify stratification variables that are related to the variable being measured. In addition, it must be clear how the items within each strata are to be selected from the sampling frame. The specific computational formulas and analysis procedures for stratified samples are similar to those presented under analysis of variance in Chapter 13.

8.3.4 Systematic Samples

A variation of the simple random sample is described in Key Idea 8.9. Although a systematic sample is not a random sample, it can often be analyzed as if it were a random sample if the first observation in the population is selected randomly. The sample is even more like a random sample if the interval between observations is a random variable selected from a uniform probability distribution with mean equal to the previously defined sampling interval.

Key Idea 8.9: Systematic Samples

A **systematic sample** is obtained by selecting every kth item from a population that is placed in sequential order. Examples of populations suitable for systematic sampling include a telephone directory, a computer list of payments received by a large firm, all of the people passing a store during a month, and automobiles passing through a toll booth. The sampling interval k is obtained by dividing the population size by the desired sample size. Systematic sampling provides a convenient procedure for selecting observations for a sample.

Systematic samples provide a good representation of the population if the sampling interval does not correspond with a cyclical variation in the population. For example, if every tenth car passing through a toll booth was a commercial vehicle and the sampling interval was 10, the sample would be biased. A sample designer can usually avoid such cyclical problems by examining the population carefully. In many cases major cyclical variations do not occur and systematic sampling provides very good samples. Sampling simulation studies by many people, including one of the authors, have indicated that systematic samples provide results similar to those obtained from simple random samples.

8.3.5 Multistage Samples

There are many large sampling studies in which it is impractical first to define a sampling frame that includes all the items in the population and then proceed to select a simple random sample. For example, obtaining a simple random sample from a population defined as all U.S. citizens or even all the citizens of most states would be expensive. Visiting each person selected in a simple random sample would require a very large travel budget.

Another alternative would be to select random subsets from the subpopulations selected in the first stage (Key Idea 8.10).

> ## Key Idea 8.10: Multistage Samples
>
> Many large studies involve some type of **multistage sampling.** First, the large population is divided into subpopulations. For example, the United States can be divided into rural counties and into Standard Metropolitan Statistical Areas (SMSAs), which include large cities and their adjacent suburban counties. A multistage sample could include a random selection of a sample of counties and a sample of SMSAs. Usually, the probability of selection would be proportional to the number of people in the county or SMSA. Then a random sample of people would be selected and interviewed from each county and SMSA selected.

For example, census tracts or other subdivisions could be randomly selected from the counties and SMSAs. Then random samples of people would be obtained from each of the randomly selected second-level subdivisions. These sampling procedures are complex and they require sophisticated analysis procedures. However, the probability of selecting an item in the population is known, and therefore the sample characteristics can be used to estimate the population characteristics.

8.4 ENUMERATIVE VERSUS ANALYTIC STUDIES

In Chapter 1 we explained how statistical studies can be classified in two major groupings, enumerative and analytic, each of which has important differences in assumptions and the strength of the resulting conclusions.[1] Here we repeat and extend this idea, because the enumerative and analytic studies each require different study designs and assumptions concerning how the results are interpreted (Key Idea 8.11).

Enumerative studies reach conclusions about a specific population. A target population is identified and the sampling frame is clearly specified. Then a representative sample is taken from the sampling frame. For example, an election sampling poll measures the present attitudes of voters with respect to a candidate. The key point is that the conclusions refer only to the target population.

In contrast, an analytic study measures one population or subset of items and uses those results to infer characteristics of a second population. For example, we might measure the reaction of a population to a proposed new product. Then from that measurement, infer the number of people in a future population who would buy the product. Enumerative studies are the ideal base from which statistical sampling

---

[1] Gerald J. Hahn and William Q. Meeker, "Assumptions for statistical inference," *The American Statistician*, Vol. 47, No. 1, February 1993.

Key Idea 8.11: Enumerative and Analytic Studies

Statistical studies can be classified in two major groupings, enumerative and analytic, each of which has important differences in assumptions and the strength of the resulting conclusions. **Enumerative studies** reach conclusions about a specific set of items. For example, an election poll measures the present attitudes of voters with respect to a specific candidate. In contrast, an **analytic study** measures one group of items and uses those results to infer characteristics of a second group. For example, we might measure the reaction of a population to a proposed new product. Then from that measurement we could infer the number of people in a future population who would buy the product.

strategies and statistical inference are developed. However, analytic studies are more widely used in business and form the basis for many decisions.

Enumerative studies work with a clearly specified population, and this population is the focus of the analysis and conclusions. Election polls measure a group of voters at a specific time. A shipment of frozen meat packages might be studied for fat content or the absence of dangerous bacteria. A boatload of iron ore could be studied to determine the iron content. In all of these studies the analysis and conclusions refer only to those target populations. As a result, statements based on statistical theory can be made concerning the range of measured population characteristics even though the statements use only data from samples, which are subsets of the population. As we will see, conclusions about a population, based on statistical theory applied to small samples, have a high probability of being correct. Of course, we could also measure every item in the population and obtain an exact measure.

Analytic studies begin with a sample or complete measurement of a population. However, the difference is that we want our conclusions to apply to some other related population. Test marketing studies measure the reaction of a target population to a new product. However, the objective is to determine if a desired percentage of a future population will purchase the new product. A production manager conducts experiments to determine conditions in the factory that result in the highest production and lowest number of defective pieces. These experiments provide conclusions concerning the present factory conditions, and then we infer that the same conditions will result in high production and high quality in future factory operations.

Analytic studies do not have the same level of accuracy as enumerative studies. The measurements on the initial group are in a sense just like enumerative studies and have the same accuracy for the group measured. However, analytic studies require assumptions concerning the link between the population actually measured and the population of interest. These linking assumptions require the judgment of someone who understands the underlying behavior of the groups being studied. These linking assumptions add to the uncertainty of the conclusions for an analytic study.

There are many examples in which expert judgment is used in analytic studies. A marketing analyst can make judgments concerning the behavior of certain related groups. In these analytic studies it is important that the subject expert be available to help decide which groups should be measured to obtain the best understanding of the desired group. A production engineer needs to be consulted when designing experiments whose ultimate objective is increased production and quality.

In the links betweeen the measured population and the population of interest, there are likely to be various errors. These errors can be minimized by careful thought by knowledgeable persons. However, the extent of the errors are based on the quality of the inputs and the design of the study. The errors and variations in enumerative studies can be estimated with precision using statistical procedures. However, the errors in analytic studies are a combination of the statistical variation, which will usually be computed, and the variation and judgment from the linking of the measured population and the population of interest. Careful judgment and design can minimize this latter error. However, we must emphasize that the computed statistical variation is the minimum variation or error for analytic studies (Key Idea 8.11).

Does It Make Sense?

The discussion above emphasizes the importance of a close link between a statistical analyst and a person with subject area understanding. This need is fundamentally important for analytic studies. We should add that in business it is the analytic studies that pay the bills. Statistical studies regularly provide major guidance for decisions and lead to cost reductions and increased sales. However, in most cases these studies are analytic studies and thus require major inputs from subject area experts. The ideal statistical study is composed of a team of area experts working with a statistician. All members of the group become familiar with the insights provided by the others. Statisticians learn about the subject area and engineers, market analysts, and accountants learn about statistics. Extending the principle presented in Chapter 1: Statistics is a team participation sport! This theme is emphasized in this book.   ☐

Problem Exercises

8.1   Define and contrast a target population and a sampling frame.

8.2   Define nonresponse bias and explain why it can be a problem in statistical sampling studies.

8.3   Explain why a sample usually provides better measurements of the characteristics of a large population than does a census.

8.4   Explain why present election polls, with samples of size 1000 to 1500, are so accurate in their predictions when one of the first election polls, conducted by the *Literary Digest* in 1936, using 2,000,000 respondents, was such a failure.

8.5   Explain the advantages of a stratified sample over a simple random sample.

8.6   Explain why a statistician might prefer to use a systematic sample instead of a simple random sample. Include an example in your discussion.

8.7   Judgment samples are often used by accounting auditors. Provide an argument in support of their use of judgment samples.

8.8   Why is it more difficult to make statements about the precision of results from analytic studies compared to enumerative studies?

8.9   Define information and contrast it to data.

8.5 TIME-SERIES AND CROSS-SECTION DATA

Most business and economic studies use either time-series or cross-section data. It is important to understand which data type is being used because the assumptions and possibly even the choice of appropriate analysis may differ.

8.5.1 Time-Series Data

Various government agencies and private organizations routinely gather many thousands of data series, which measure economic activity such as personal income, investment, government spending, interest rates, productivity by economic sector, unemployment, and prices. These data are used in many studies. Because the data are collected over time, the variables include the effect of conditions that vary with time (Key Idea 8.12). Aggregate personal income and many other economic measures are generally increasing over time because of population increases and improvements in productivity. Other series, such as grain stocks or sales for a specific industry, may contain cyclical and/or seasonal variations. Cyclical changes are variations that cover a specific number of time periods. A cycle could cover a period from six months to 100 years or more. Seasonal variations follow the seasons of the year. For example, grain stocks are the largest in August after the yearly crop has been harvested.

Time series cannot be treated as a stable population. Observations from later time periods may be larger. Thus, computing the mean personal income for a quarterly time series that covers 20 years may be misleading. A good alternative would be to compute annual means and use them to show the pattern over time. Observations taken at cyclical or seasonal intervals may be biased because all observations are either above or below the central tendency of the series.

8.5.2 Cross-Section Data

A cross-section of a data set (Key Idea 8.13) may be treated as either a population census or as a random sample, depending on the study assumptions and objectives. As an illustration, suppose that a data set consists of the per capita income from each of the 50 states for a given year. It could be argued that these are the entire set of responses and thus the finite population represents all the information that is available. For example, comparing the incomes for subsets of southern and northern states can be done exactly because all the information is available. Alternatively, it might be

Key Idea 8.12: Time-Series Data

Time-series data are gathered at specific time intervals, such as monthly, quarterly, or annually, and thus include changes in variables that occur over time. One model often used to relate observations from a time series is the additive form

$$Y_t = \mu + T + S + C + \epsilon$$

where μ is the base value of the series, T is the trend or effect of time-related variables, S is the effect of seasonal factors, C is the effect of cyclical factors, and ϵ is the effect of random variation.

Analysis of time-series data must consider the components of the foregoing model. Subset means later in the series may be higher or lower, a peak occurs within each cycle, and one season may be higher or lower than the others. Time-series analysis usually begins by preparing time-series graphs.

argued that the observation from each state is a random sample from a population of possible observations for that state. Each observation is the result of various decisions, compromises, and errors that were part of the complex process of collecting the data and computing the per capita income for each state. Each of these influences can be modeled by a random variable, and thus the combination of all influences is also a random variable. Following that model the state data set is a random sample from an infinite population of per capita incomes that could have been reported.

Key Idea 8.13: Cross-Section Data

Cross-section data consist of measurements that occur at the same nominal point in time. For example, data might be collected from a set of factories, states, cities, or countries for the same time period. Therefore, any influences that change over time will have the same effect on all observations. Frequency distributions, means, and other descriptive measures can be used to describe a particular cross-section data set or to compare one data set with another. Most of the samples in statistical analysis are implicitly assumed to come from cross-section data.

Most of the samples in statistical analysis are implicitly assumed to come from cross-section data. A random sample of potential purchasers obtained for a marketing study assumes a population whose characteristics do not vary over time. The same is true for each sample used to measure voter preference. Random samples obtained for quality control testing are assumed to come from a manufacturing process that does not vary over time.

The examples above might also be modeled as time-series data, depending on the characteristics of the situation. The data may be time-series data, and considerable time may be required to obtain the entire sample. The subjects may change their opinions after the sample measurements have been made and additional samples are needed to trace these changes.

The production of an entire batch of parts for a customer order may require several days or weeks. Parts produced later in the production period may be different, and thus data regarding part quality actually constitute a time series.

Samples should be checked for potential time-series effects. This can be done easily by plotting the measurements against the relative time they were selected. Major time-series effects that could affect the analysis will usually be obvious from such a plot. If an important time-series influence is found, it might be necessary to analyze subsets of the sample grouped by time interval. For example, a sample from a 10-week production run might be divided into 10 weekly subsets. Subset sample means could be used to describe the time-series variations in the population. Samples to obtain voter preference are usually taken at frequent intervals during a political campaign to determine if changes have occurred.

8.6 SOURCES OF ERROR

Measurements on observations are subject to errors defined as either bias or random error (Key Idea 8.14). Bias is a fixed component and we seek to eliminate it. Alternatively, we try to minimize and measure random error.

Key Idea 8.14: Random Error and Bias

Sample measurements can include both random error and bias. **Bias** is a fixed deviation that results from either the measurement instrument or the sampling procedure. **Random error** is different for each observation, and random errors can be modeled by a random variable that has a mean of zero and a finite variance. The magnitude of random error is measured by the variance of the sample statistics.

Sampling methods that produce statistics with smaller variance are preferred given the same bias; in Chapter 9 we will see how random error can be reduced by obtaining larger sample sizes.

Bias reduction is an important consideration for sample design and data collection. Bias can be minimized by correct procedures and increased greatly by incorrect procedures.

1. Nonresponse bias occurs when items in the target population, which have different characteristics, are not included in the sample in the same proportion as they are in the target population. This can occur when certain subsets of people, who have been chosen as part of a random sample, refuse to provide information to an interviewer. It can also occur when the sampling process does not select certain items from the population.

2. Measurement bias results from improper procedures or instruments. An incorrectly adjusted scale will bias the weight of every item weighed. The wording of a question in a survey questionnaire could shift the pattern of responses.

Nonresponse bias is a sample design problem. We presented the *Literary Digest* 1936 presidential poll in Section 8.3. This was a clear example of nonresponse bias. The people who were part of the sample were different from the target population of all voters. From examples such as the *Literary Digest* poll, we have learned to worry about nonresponse bias and to develop procedures for its control.

Prior to 1970, young men in the United States were selected for military service by local county "draft boards." Historically, this process was based on the principle that young men had a responsibility to serve their country in the military. At age 18 all young men were required by law to register for possible selection for military service. As a result of a belief that the system was unfair, a new system was developed. Under this system young men were to be randomly selected for service in a national lottery.

The draft lottery used a container of balls numbered to correspond to the days of the year. The draft officials were supposed to choose a random sample of days, using the balls, and draft males whose birthdays occurred on the days chosen. However, the balls were not properly mixed and birthdates late in the year were more likely to be selected. The random sampling rule was violated because of improper procedures. Examples like this force us to think carefully about our procedures for selecting a random sample.

By using a random sample and devoting considerable effort to finding each item selected by the random process, we can minimize nonresponse bias. Carefully following this rule is fundamental to good sampling. R. A. Fisher's call for random samples as an "insurance policy" against sampling bias is still the best advice we can provide. A sample designer must think carefully about potential sample biases. Experience with sample design is very helpful. In addition, it is important to understand how the system, which produces the sample observations, actually behaves.

Example 8.1   Retail Market Surveys

A city planner wanted to determine the residence communities for people who made retail purchases in his city. After some thinking he decided to obtain a random sample of all checks deposited at one of the three local banks on a specific day. Will this sample meet his objective?

Solution   First let us define the objective. He wants to know the residence of people who purchase in the retail area. Clearly, the check will provide the residence address in most cases. However, customers also pay for purchases with cash or with a credit card. We suspect that residence and the size of purchases will differ for the three forms of payment. That suspicion would have to be tested before we could conclude that the sample of purchases by check is an unbiased sample of all purchases. Another potential problem is that the sample would occur for only one day. This is definitely a bias. The day on which people receive their wages and make purchases is different for various subsets of the potential customers. Certain purchases, such as snowblowers, tend to be seasonal. Based on these concerns we would conclude that the original sample could contain a major bias because it excludes a large fraction of the target population. However, we cannot be certain without actually testing the procedure.   □

Analyses similar to Example 8.1 need to be made for every potential sample design. It may be necessary to discuss the sample design with persons who have special knowledge and experience. Here again the importance of a team is emphasized. In addition, small studies could be conducted to answer questions such as those raised above. Statisticians and sample designers tend to be conservative and thus would probably be more likely to reject a proposed sample design.

My experience suggests that politicians, administrators, and planners tend to be more optimistic and thus would be more likely to accept a proposed sample design. For example, I cannot think of any competent statistician who would recommend collecting a sample by asking newspaper readers to complete and mail a questionnaire. But such sample collection occurs regularly.

Measurement bias can be minimized by careful attention to the details of the measuring process. Physical measurements require high-quality instruments that are well maintained. To avoid biased measurements of package weights a quality control department will implement procedures regularly to maintain, test, and adjust their scales. Studies that use people's responses to questionnaires require careful consideration of the question wording and the sequence of the questions. Professionals who prepare questionnaires have extensive training and experience. They spend considerable time testing the questions using subjects with known characteristics. In addition, the persons who administer the questionnaires must be carefully trained. You should be very skeptical of studies that use measuring instruments that are not designed by professionals and/or are not carefully tested.

An extreme example or folk tale is the World War II general's reaction to a report that the weather forecasts had been incorrect for 200 straight days. In response to this information, he said that the weather forecasts should be continued because we need the forecasts for planning our bombing missions!

Problem Exercises

8.10 Define nonresponse bias and explain why its effect is so difficult to detect in an applied study.

8.11 Why is it easier to assume that one is working with cross-section data instead of time-series data?

8.12 Explain the difference between random error and bias.

8.13 Explain why statisticians are so picky about the details of data collection. Why don't they relax a bit and take the data as they come?

8.14 Why should one hire a professional to write questions for a sampling survey instead of merely using one of the good writers in the office?

8.7 DESIGNS FOR STATISTICAL STUDIES

Statistical studies are designed and implemented to provide useful results. It is important that the study objective is clearly defined during the study design phase. In this section we consider study objectives and indicate design procedures that are useful for achieving these objectives. We discuss descriptive studies and comparative studies. The former concentrate on determining the characteristics of a single population. In contrast, comparative studies typically have an evaluation objective and involve comparisons between two or more subpopulations. The discussion here is introductory and limited. Procedures for conducting these studies and analyzing the data are presented in the chapters that follow. Further study of experimental design and sampling methods is advised for persons who are responsible for designing studies.

8.7.1 Descriptive Studies

Descriptive studies are defined in Key Idea 8.15.

Key Idea 8.15: Descriptive Studies

Descriptive studies are used for exploration and definition of a target population. Studies begin with a search for and an analysis of existing descriptive data. For example, U.S. Census data describe many subpopulations. Next, a measurement instrument such as a questionnaire might be applied to a random sample from the population. Multistage or stratified samples could also be used. Describing and understanding the target population is the primary objective.

As an example, a small city wants to know the extent of retail demand or employment that is being met by local resources. Such a study could provide the basis for an economic development plan. The target population consists of the residents within the geographic boundaries of the community economic area. The study would begin with an examination of the most recent census data. Using this background information, a set of questions based on the study objectives could be prepared and tested. A simple random sample of the population is likely to be the best procedure for obtaining the data. However, other designs might prove to be better after careful analysis of the local situation.

A different example could involve a company that wanted to expand its U.S. service business into another large market such as the European Economic Community, Japan, or China. If its present customers are business firms, the study objective would focus on similar firms in the potential new market area. These firms are the population that is to be studied. It may be possible to obtain some background census information from existing economic studies. However, in a developing country such as China, information might be limited and subject to various data collection problems. A simple random sample is not likely to be a feasible strategy because of the large diverse and geographically dispersed population. A multistage sampling design would be preferred. Complex multistage sampling designs are beyond the scope of this book and usually require the assistance of sampling design professionals.

The objective of this example study would be to determine the importance of the company's service for other firms of different size. They want to know the amount of service required and any special characteristics that are different from the service needs of U.S. companies. They also want to predict the probability that they could provide the service better and at a lower cost than the present service provider. Alternatively, they might wish to know if the service is presently being provided and if they could show the companies that this service would improve performance.

There are many other examples.

1. A school district might want to know the percentage of students from single-parent or low-income families in order to determine the kinds of services that should be provided.
2. A developing country wants to know the number of people in a region who are not obtaining sufficient food so that appropriate agriculture programs can be developed.
3. A manufacturing company wants to know the percentage of substandard parts that are produced in its factories or that it receives from suppliers.

All of these examples involve a single population whose characteristics are to be measured from a descriptive study.

Descriptive studies tend to be enumerative in their methodology. A population exists and a description is required. Thus the focus is on a defined population and measurements are obtained by following one of the sampling methods. However, in some cases we seek a description of a future population but are required to measure a present population. In this case it is necessary to use expert knowledge to help make the link between the population measured and the population of interest.

8.7.2 Comparative Studies

In this section we introduce the principles of comparative study design (Key Idea 8.16) and provide some examples of correct and incorrect designs. The most used simple study designs are parallel group designs (Key Idea 8.17) and before-and-after designs (Key Idea 8.18).

Key Idea 8.16: Comparative Studies

Comparative studies are typically used for evaluation or inference. A *treatment group*, which has been exposed to a change, is compared to a *control group*, which has not. The objective is to determine if the change or treatment results in an improvement in performance compared to groups that have not received the treatment. The two groups are selected to be similar except for the change or treatment that is being studied.

Key Idea 8.17: Parallel Group Studies

For a **parallel group** comparison we select two subgroups that have similar patterns of measurements for variables that might affect the performance measure being studied. One of the subgroups, randomly selected, receives the treatment and the other does not.

Key Idea 8.18: Before-and-After Group Studies

The use of a **before-and-after group** is based on the assumption that the best match for any group is the group itself. In this case the performance measure is recorded for a suitable *control period*, the treatment is applied, and the performance measure is recorded after a suitable *treatment period*.

A control group must be used to determine if the change has resulted from the treatment or from natural causes. In most cases a change in measured performance can result from a number of causes. The only way to obtain evidence that the treatment has caused the change is to be sure that all the other potential causes of the change are the same in both the control and treatment subpopulations.

If all the other important variables have been identified and controlled, one can conclude that significant changes in the performance measure between the control and treatment groups are related to the treatment variable. However, if the matching of control and treatment groups has not been done correctly, one cannot be sure that the treatment variable is related to the performance measure.

The before-and-after design has the advantage that all the variables are matched exactly between the control and the treatment time periods. There are two important disadvantages. First, the group must be measured over both a control and a treatment period, and thus the time required for evaluation will usually be longer. In some cases the performance measure can be obtained immediately and then the treatment applied. This would minimize the time problem. However, there is a more serious problem. Many variables and conditions change over time. Thus without careful controls and/or measurements of other potentially important variables, we cannot be sure that the change has resulted from the treatment variable.

Comparison of health care options.   A study was proposed to determine the least-cost method of providing health care to a population. The research team wishes to compare the use of a new health maintenance organization (HMO)—the treatment group—with traditional medical service using a family physician and other specialists selected by the patient—the control group. In both cases a monthly premium is paid by customers. The HMO plan requires that all services be provided through the HMO, which manages the total health care, including the use of specialists and hospitalization. In the traditional group customers choose when to use medical services and pay a fee of $10 for each first visit to a physician. Specialists and hospital treatment are the joint decision of the customer and the physician. In both the control and treatment groups, costs per patient are billed to an insurance company. The research team wishes to know if the HMO treatment results in lower-cost health care.

The naive design would be to compare an HMO group with a traditional medical practice group. Unfortunately, other studies have shown that people who select HMOs are typically younger and healthier. Therefore, a controlled design is required in which comparable customers are assigned to the two groups. Ideally, customers would be assigned to the two groups by a random process. However, that approach raises many ethical and practical concerns. Most customers in our society want to be able to choose their own type of health care. Typically, the only people who could be forced into a random choice would be those who have low incomes and are thus likely to have different health care needs. Another strategy would be to match a subset of people from both groups on a number of health-related variables. The matched subsets from the HMO and traditional groups would then be used as pseudosamples for purposes of comparison. This option also has a number of potential problems. Clearly, the proposed study would require careful design by an experienced professional.

Comparison of training programs.   A researcher wished to determine which of two company training courses results in the highest student scores on a standard test. All of the students were employees, and thus they were required to take a course as part of their employment. The entire pool of students was matched on variables related to learning. Then one from each pair was randomly assigned to either the treatment or to the control group courses. The control group received the traditional training that has been used for the past five years. The treatment group received a new course, which included interactive projects presented on a microcomputer. Students attended the courses, took the test, and the test scores were compared. This design is a good example of a parallel group comparative study.

Comparison of factory production processes.   A factory manager wanted to know if a new machining technique would increase productivity. The present productivity levels were measured for a group of experienced workers using well-maintained machines. Then the new technique was introduced and the productivity levels measured for the same combinations of workers and machines using the new machining technique. The study was carefully monitored to be certain that worker and machine performance were not influenced by other factors during the second time period. For example, workers could have opposed the new method as an abusive technique that increased worker stress. Alternatively, workers might have enjoyed the attention and worked harder. They might also have increased productivity because the new change was proposed by a respected fellow worker.

With proper controls this study is a good example of a before-and-after study. The evaluation could have been conducted using a parallel design. However, the population of workers who are using both the old and the new techniques would be only one-half as large. This would reduce the precision of the comparison.

The problem of selection bias is a major issue for study designers. People in general do not wish to be arbitrarily placed in groups and/or subjected to treatments by an outside authority. Arbitrary assignment is a violation of freedom of choice. At the same time the choices made by people often influence their performance.

During the 1960s, auto insurance companies provided discounts for young persons who had taken a formal driver education course. Some people interpreted the discount as evidence that driver education resulted in safer drivers. However, insurance companies provided the discount because driver education was selected by those people who had a strong desire to be a safer driver. For this reason persons who elected to take driver education had fewer accidents. Many studies of the safety effectiveness of driver education ignored this important bias and thus the results were misleading. Similar biases occur when people refuse to participate in studies, and these nonparticipants are different.

Comparison of medical treatments.   The evaluation of experimental medical treatments is particularly difficult. Good study design indicates that patients should be randomly assigned to either a group that receives the new treatment or to a control group. However, there is usually some evidence to suggest that the proposed treatment is better than doing nothing. Most physicians follow an oath which requires that they provide the best treatment possible for their patients. Thus they would find it unethical to assign patients to a control group. In contrast, assignment of workers to groups in a factory is usually much easier.

A classic comparative study was the 1954 Salk polio vaccine study, which involved over 200,000 children in a control group and over 200,000 in a treatment group. Paralytic polio was a disease that struck children, often leaving them dead or severely paralyzed. Doctor Jonas Salk identified a vaccine that appeared to have a good chance of being successful. However, the only way to be certain was to conduct a massive study in which the treatment group was inoculated with the vaccine while the control group received inoculation with a neutral saline solution (a placebo). Neither the child nor the nurse providing the inoculation knew if the vaccine or a placebo was being administered. The children were later examined by a physician who did not know if the vaccine or the placebo had been given. This double-blind experiment ensured that there would be no biases in the diagnosis of polio. As a result of the experiment, the Salk vaccine was proven to be successful. It was then administered routinely to all children, with the result that this major childhood disease was virtually eliminated.

The problems of conducting such an experiment were large. First, some very critical ethical issues were involved. Some children who received the placebo died when they might have been saved if they had by chance been assigned to receive the Salk vaccine. However, before the experiment, no one could be certain of that result. Children receiving the vaccine might have contracted polio. The experimental controls had to be very good. Each inoculation had a random code number that was referenced to a child. Only after all the diagnoses were completed was all of the information brought together and analyzed. Many thousands of professional hours were needed for administering the vaccine and for diagnosis. Clearly, a great deal of management was required for a project of this magnitude.

Does It Make Sense?

The result of this experiment was conclusive evidence that the Salk vaccine prevented polio. With this strong evidence a national campaign to inoculate every child was implemented. Polio, a major killer, was essentially eliminated in the United States. However, one suspects that a similar national study would be very difficult if not impossible to implement in the social/political culture of the 1990s. Consider the likelihood of a study involving a vaccine for AIDS.   □

8.8 IMPORTANCE OF MODELS

Good statistical work involves new information gathering and problem solving. Therefore, the data used must be collected with reference to the present understanding of the problem. This understanding can be captured with a model that contains the important features of the problem (Key Idea 8.19). A model provides a reference point for the statistical measurements and therefore provides a basis for conclusions from the data analysis. These models reflect the process that generates the data.

Key Idea 8.19: Data Model

The structure of individual observations can be expressed by the following model:

observation   =   information   +   bias   +   random error

The relative size of these components depends on the data generation and the measurement processes. Any observation could have been produced by one of several different processes. If the information content of the observation is high and the bias and random error are small, it will be possible to choose one model from a small set of possible models. However, as the bias and random error increase, the probability of selecting the correct model using only data becomes small.

Managers and economists use supply-and-demand models to study markets and production functions to study industry behavior. Marketing managers use explicit or implicit models to explain the relative contributions of price, advertising, and distribution to product sales. Statistical studies based on these models reinforce and expand the existing body of knowledge concerning an entire economy, a market, or a specific firm.

A balance between theory (represented by models) and empirical observation (represented by statistical studies) is important for advancing scientific knowledge and for making good business decisions. Economic research is often criticized when it uses deductive analysis from theory that has weak empirical support. There are also managers who make all decisions based only on their personal experience and that of a few trusted colleagues. In contrast, some researchers and managers place excessive emphasis on the most recent data. The need for balance is usually understood by researchers and managers. However, implementation of this understanding in a particular situation is often very difficult.

Chapters 10 and 11 will show how estimation and hypothesis testing are used to help separate random error and information. Identification and elimination of bias require careful design of the sampling and data collection procedure.

Consider a quality control problem in a manufacturing firm. A large number of defective parts result from a particular manufacturing process. To reduce the number of defects, it is necessary to know the causes. Alternative models must be considered. Defective parts could be caused by (1) poorly adjusted production machines, (2) lack of worker skill or motivation, (3) poor-quality raw material, (4) bad part design, or (5) improper manufacturing methods.

The quality control department must construct a model of the process which enables them to test for and isolate these causes using other knowledge and/or various intermediate measurements. This model could result in the conclusion that part design or manufacturing method is a critical issue. A team of experienced engineers would then be asked to evaluate and improve the design and manufacturing method. Alternatively, the process analysis might lead to the conclusion that the quality of raw material should be improved. In that case consultation and negotiation with suppliers would be required. We could go on with other examples. The key point is that a model of the process should be used to guide decisions concerning measurement and data collection. Without such guidance the resulting data analysis, using sophisticated statistical procedures, may not be directed toward answering the appropriate questions.

When economists study markets they begin by noting that combinations of quantities and price result from an equilibrium between supply and demand. The particular set of quantity and price points could represent shifts of supply which resulted from new production facilities being added to a market with a stable demand. The increases in supply could force prices down and the quantity demanded up. The points could be plotted and used to estimate a demand function. Similarly, a stable production system could be subjected to shifts in demand functions. In that case the price and quantity points would trace out a supply function. Alternatively, the market could involve shifts in both supply and demand. In that case sophisticated regression analysis procedures involving instrumental variables would be required for the analysis. These are discussed under regression applications in Chapter 16. Models are needed to provide a clear definition of the problem and to indicate the questions that can be answered by data analysis procedures.

A model is prepared from an understanding of the problem and the system that provides the context for the problem. As we indicated in Chapter 1, a population of data is generated by a system-based process or series of processes. To obtain the required understanding for model building, it is necessary to study the system and the process. This will involve discussions with persons in the system and persons who know about the system. It will also require study of books, technical papers, and special reports that relate to the system and the problem being studied. Some simple preliminary descriptive studies might also be part of model building.

In business and economic applications of statistics, which are most often analytic studies, an understanding of the entire background of the discipline is required to develop models for analysis. The same is true for many other statistical applications. Thus analytic statistical studies must operate in close interaction with the background understanding that comes from the discipline being studied. As a result, many statistical studies are conducted by teams that include statisticians and persons with functional knowledge of the problem being studied.

Problem Exercises

8.15 What is the difference between descriptive and comparative studies?

8.16 Describe how a before-and-after study design would be used for evaluating the effect of a worker training program.

8.17 Discuss the potential problems when a parallel study is used to determine the possible improvement from a worker training program.

8.18   Explain how bias can distort the results of a parallel comparative study.

8.19   Why is it likely that a study such as the Salk polio vaccine study, discussed in this section, would be very difficult to conduct in our time?

8.20   Discuss the ethical implications of the 1970 draft lottery. Is it fair to select people randomly for an undesired activity such as the draft? Discuss the behavior of the people who actually conducted the lottery.

8.21   Explain why a random selection of items provides the best opportunity for obtaining a sample that represents a population.

SUMMARY OF KEY IDEAS

CHAPTER PROBLEMS

8.1   George Apelyard, product manager for Fruity Yogurt, Inc., has asked for your help in determining the percentage of the population of a large midwestern state who would purchase their proposed new yogurt. George originally requests that you conduct a census to obtain the percentage. Prepare a concise and rigorous set of reasons why a random sample would be preferable.

8.2   Explain why nonresponse bias is a major problem in surveys of human populations, and indicate how its effect can be minimized.

8.3   You have been asked to obtain a random sample of 100 ears of corn from a 40-acre cornfield, just prior to harvest. These ears will be used to estimate the output from the entire field. Describe how you would select these ears of corn so that they are a random sample of the field.

8.4   Explain how a multistage sampling plan could be developed to obtain a sample of the United States which represents consumer confidence and the probability that consumer spending will increase over the next year.

8.5   Write a two-paragraph discussion of the differences between descriptive and comparative statistical studies.

8.6   You have been asked by Amalgamated Motors to develop a comparative statistical study to determine which of two assembly processes will achieve the highest productivity and the fewest defects.
        (a) Discuss the advantages of a before-and-after study over a parallel study for this application.
        (b) Discuss the advantages of a parallel study over a before-and-after study for this application.

8.7   The 1954 Salk polio vaccine study is a classic example of a successful major comparative study. Suppose that you were asked to design a similar study to determine the effectiveness of a proposed new vaccine for a major modern disease such as AIDS. Discuss the potential problems that might occur in such a study and indicate your response to these criticisms.

8.8   Explain why the selection of a random sample requires a number of strict rules defining how each item is selected and actually measured. Suppose that someone says to you: "Since the sample is a random sample, why can't I just select the items any way that I want?" Include a response to this criticism in your explanation.

8.9   A student once came to my door and indicated that she was conducting a sampling survey and asked if I would participate. I explained that we were eating dinner but invited her to return later and said that I would participate then. The response was: "Oh, never mind. I will get someone else since I just have to obtain a random sample." Explain how the training for this student was fatally flawed.

8.10   What are the advantages of a stratified sample over a simple random sample?

8.11   You have been asked to develop a study to estimate the percentage of students who prefer meat, poultry, or fish for their evening meal in the college food service facility. Identify two variables that could be used to define strata for a stratified sample. Describe how you would obtain a random sample within each stratum.

8.12   You have been asked to advise Barbara Smith, a prominent local corporate manager, about her chances of being elected mayor of a large city if she would choose to run. Your solution is to collect a sample of voters and determine total support from an analysis of the sample.
        (a) Define the target population and a sampling frame.
        (b) Indicate the type of sample that should be used.
        (c) Discuss the measurement errors that could occur in your study.
        (d) List three sources of potential bias that could occur.

8.13   The city manager of a small city wanted to know the amount of support for a proposed new ice rink and swimming pool. There was no budget for collecting a sample of opinions. However, at the local Rotary club the publisher of the newspaper offered to print a short questionnaire and request that responses be mailed to the city manager. Advise the city manager about the value of this offer. Should the offer be accepted?

8.14   The director of public health for a western state wanted to know the extent of cocaine use in her state. Given a limited budget, she decided to contact a sample of persons by phone and inquire about their use of drugs. Phone calls would be made between 9:00 A.M. and 4:00 P.M. by her staff. Comment on the proposed study, indicating sources of potential bias.

8.15   The director of public safety for a large city decided that it was time to crack down on people who drive while drunk. During the past month a young father of three children and a pregnant mother of one child were killed by drunk drivers who drove into the side of their cars at high speed. Police surveillance of driving behavior near bars was increased by 50% and any driver convicted of driving while intoxicated received a mandatory four-month jail sentence. The director proposes to evaluate the program by determining if there has been a decrease in injury-related automobile accidents during the next six months from the past six months. Critically evaluate the strategy for conducting the evaluation and indicate the major problems.

8.16   The manager of a cereal company wishes to determine the moisture content of the finished cereal. Samples are obtained from every 8-hour work shift and the water content is measured. A sample of 500 observations collected over the last six months is available for determining the moisture content of cereal produced during the past six months. Discuss the potential problems with this sample. How should the sample data be analyzed?

8.17   How would you obtain a multistage random sample of students who live in dormitories on a large university?

8.18   A factory foreman is assigned production goals for each 8-hour work shift. If these goals are not met, a note is added to his evaluation file. However, no recognition is provided if the goals are exceeded. The foreman reports the production for each shift on a production report. Every six months the total incoming materials and total parts shipped are determined and used to check the total reported production. An analyst begins to use the daily production report to study daily production patterns. Comment on the method and value of his study.

8.19   Define a target population for a study to determine if new design changes for the Mercedes automobile will increase sales.

8.20   Define the target population for a study to determine if the increased nutrition levels will increase the sales of Gerber's baby foods.

8.21   A major manufacturer of motor oil for automobiles wishes to determine if a new additive will reduce the time required to start an automobile. He decides to conduct a before-and-after study using two consecutive three-month periods. The control period begins on September 1. The study is to be conducted in Minnesota. Evaluate the research design and indicate potential problems.

9

Distribution of Sample Statistics

Some people use data as the drunk uses a lamppost; for support but not for light.

9.1 CONCLUSIONS FROM DATA

Charlie Thurston, president of Allied Parts, has installed a new production process to produce crankshafts for the popular Laser III automobile, produced by National Motors. This new line can produce 30% more crankshafts per hour than the old line can. However, Charlie needs to certify to National Motors that the crankshafts from this new line meet the weight range and structural stability specifications in the contract. The contract specifies that certification will be based on statistical evidence from scientifically selected samples and appropriate statistical measures. How can he establish sampling and analysis procedures to provide this certification? In this chapter and the two that follow we provide the answer to this and many related statistical analysis problems.

Using our background in descriptive statistics and probability, we are ready to analyze sample data with the objective of drawing conclusions and making statements which include the probability that we are correct. These analyses, which are defined as classical inference, combine an understanding of probability with standard statistics, such as the sample mean, proportion, and standard deviation. Classical inference has two major categories: estimation (Chapter 10) and hypothesis testing (Chapter 11). Estimation provides point and interval measures of population characteristics, such as the mean income, proportion that would purchase a product, and mean weight of cereal packages. Hypothesis testing provides a procedure for answering specific questions based on results computed from a data sample. The ability to describe system behavior and make decisions is based on the probability distribution of sample statistics.

The procedures we learn here have wide application to a number of applications in business and economics. Economists and managers use data regularly to gain understanding and recommend decisions. Examples include:

1. Every month the Current Population Survey is used to estimate the percent unemployed in the United States.
2. Production managers want to know if a new production method will increase productivity over results using the present method.
3. Cereal manufacturers need to be certain that boxes are filled to their correct weight.
4. Political pollsters want to know the percentage of voters who support a particular candidate.
5. Turkey producers use the annual per capita consumption of their product to establish total production.

In each of these examples, measurements are made on a sample of items from a larger population. This population is generated by the system being studied. The key question is

How can we obtain the clearest understanding and make the best recommendations based on our sample of data?

9.2 SAMPLING DISTRIBUTIONS

In Chapter 8 we emphasized the importance of proper sampling, with particular emphasis on random samples as the best sampling method. Once we have obtained a sample, we compute statistics such as the mean, standard deviation, or proportion. These statistics can then be used to describe the sample and to infer characteristics of the population.

Statistical inference (Key Idea 9.1) uses the probability distribution of summary sample statistics, such as the mean, the proportion, and the variance, which are defined as sampling distributions (Key Idea 9.2). Using the sampling distribution, we can compute properties of sample statistics, including:

1. The mean of the sampling distribution
2. The variance of the sampling distribution
3. The probability that the sample statistic occurs within a certain interval

These properties provide the basic components for statistical inference.

But first we need to understand clearly the distribution theory for sample statistics. We begin with a very simple sampling example to explain the idea of sampling distributions. Then we consider an example in which the individual sample observations are assumed to be normally distributed. The resulting sample means are also normally distributed. This is followed by a more general development using the central limit theorem. From that development we will see that the sampling distribution of the sample mean has an approximate normal distribution in many economics and business problems.

Key Idea 9.1: Statistical Inference

Statistical inference is a process used to infer properties of a system by using statistics computed from a sample that represents a population of outcomes from the system. Statistical inference includes procedures to obtain specific values for population parameters—estimation—and to answer questions—hypothesis testing.

Key Idea 9.2: Sampling Distribution

A **sampling distribution** is the probability distribution of a sample statistic, such as the mean, for all possible random samples of the same size from a population. Individual sample observations are random variables, and therefore the sample statistic, which is a function of random variables, is also a random variable.

Example 9.1   A Simple Fish Story

Assume that there is a population of five fish that could be caught from a lake. The weights of the fish are exactly 1, 2, 3, 4, and 5 pounds, thus defining the population. A state biologist wants to know the mean weight μ of the fish in the lake, but she does not know the population.

Solution   If she could obtain the entire population, she could compute the population mean as

$$\mu = \sum_{i=1}^{5} \frac{1}{5}x_i = \frac{1 + 2 + 3 + 4 + 5}{5} = 3$$

Given the difficulty of capturing fish, she decides to obtain a random sample from the population and use the sample mean $\overline{X}$ to compute or "estimate" the population mean μ. If a sample of size 1 is obtained, the estimate could be any integer value from 1 to 5. This seems unsatisfactory, and thus a sample of size $n = 2$ is considered. By sampling without replacement we could obtain a total of $C_2^5 = 10$ different samples as shown in Table 9.1. Each sample has an equal chance of being selected, and the sample means range from 1.5 to 4.5 pounds.

In most applied situations we obtain only one sample and use it to make statistical inferences about the entire population. The study of sampling distributions provides a basis for determining the potential variation in statistics such as the sample mean obtained from random samples. Results based on a sample of size 2 have considerable uncertainty. Reported mean weight could vary from 1.5 to 4.5, depending on the particular sample that was selected. Many decision makers would be unhappy with results that deviated so far from the actual population mean, which we know is 3.0.

TABLE 9.1   Possible
Samples of Fish Weights
($n = 2$)

Observations	Sample Mean
1, 2	1.5
1, 3	2.0
1, 4	2.5
1, 5	3.0
2, 3	2.5
2, 4	3.0
2, 5	3.5
3, 4	3.5
3, 5	4.0
4, 5	4.5

We reason that a larger sample size, implying more information, should reduce the uncertainty of using a sample mean to represent a population mean. This conclusion is true as indicated by Table 9.2, which contains the sampling distributions of sample means for samples of size $n = 2$, 3, and 4. Note that when the sample size is $n = 2$, there are three sample means in the 1.5 to 2.5 interval, four in the 2.5 to 3.5 interval, and two in the 3.5 to 4.5 interval—a total of 10 sample means.

TABLE 9.2   Sampling
Distribution of Sample
Means

		n	
Interval	2	3	4
≤ 1.5	1	0	0
≤ 2.5	3	2	1
≤ 3.5	4	6	4
≤ 4.5	2	2	0
	10	10	5

Notice that as the sample size increases, the sample means cluster more closely about the population mean $\mu = 3$. Our friend the biologist could make statements about the population mean with much greater certainty if she used a sample of size $n = 4$ instead of a single observation or a sample of size $n = 2$. The reason for greater accuracy results from the increased sample size.   □

We can make amazingly accurate inferences from samples that are a very small fraction of the population. Consider, for example, that presidential election results are routinely predicted using samples of size $n = 1000$ to 1500. This general conclusion extends directly to more complex sampling situations.

Does It Make Sense?

This simple example shows that random samples yield a wide range of sample means. Most studies use only one sample, and therefore the statistical conclusion or inference will be based on that single result. We have also seen that as sample sizes increase, the sample means tend to cluster more closely about the population mean. Therefore, we can have more confidence in statistical inferences that are based on larger sample sizes. This principle, which was demonstrated in the simple example with a very small population, also applies in larger populations with more complex probability distributions. Many sampling studies have demonstrated the extension to large populations. Thus the sampling distribution result from this simple example applies to the statistical applications in business and economics. Larger samples provide measurable improvements in the quality of the statistical inferences.   □

In the following sections we learn about the relationship between sample size and the distribution of sample means—sampling distributions—for various populations with different probability distribution models. With this understanding we will be able to use sample statistics to make inferences. Knowledge of sampling distributions will open the doors to many applications. In the next section we study an example in which the underlying population distribution is normal.

9.3 SAMPLING DISTRIBUTION: NORMAL POPULATION

Now that we have seen sampling distributions in a simple context, a more realistic example will be examined. A business analyst is interested in studying the annual sales of small clothing stores (e.g., those with less than 7500 square feet of sales space). The population would be defined as the set of U.S. stores that fit the definition. Annual sales are obtained for a random sample of 30 stores. Based on his experience the analyst assumes that annual sales for these small clothing stores have a normal distribution. He will use the mean sales from his random sample of stores for his study. To obtain results he needs to know the distribution of the sample mean (Key Idea 9.3).

Sample statistics are used to answer questions about the population from which the individual observations were obtained. For example:

1. What is the best estimate of the population mean, and how accurate is our estimate?

Key Idea 9.3: Distribution of Sample Mean

The sampling distribution of the sample mean, where the population of observations x_i are normally distributed with mean μ and variance σ^2, is a normal distribution with mean μ and variance σ^2/n. That is, if

$$X \sim N(\mu, \sigma^2)$$

then

$$\overline{X} = \frac{\sum_i^n x_i}{n} \sim N\left(\mu, \frac{\sigma^2}{n}\right)$$

assuming that the population is countably infinite.

2. What is the probability that the sample mean is greater than a particular value?

Answers to these questions are based on the sampling distribution of the sample mean. We begin by examining the sampling process to determine the sampling distribution. Assume that each observation x_i in the population is a normally distributed random variable. A random sample is selected and the responses are summarized by computing the sample mean. The sample mean $\overline{X}$ is a function of random variables and thus is also a random variable. In Figure 9.1 we represent the population of individual store sales by the set on the left. In the right set we show a population of sample means that could be constructed by obtaining all possible random samples of size n. In the previous fish example we saw that each sample is different and will have a different sample mean. The sampling distribution for very large populations are mathematically more complex, but the principle of sampling distributions is the same as that illustrated by the fish example.

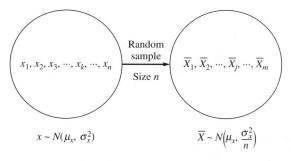

$$x \sim N(\mu_x, \sigma_x^2) \qquad\qquad \overline{X} \sim N\left(\mu_x, \frac{\sigma_x^2}{n}\right)$$

Figure 9.1   Population of x_i and of $\overline{X}_j$

In most applied problems we obtain only one sample and hence make inferences based on a single observation of the sample mean $\bar{X}$. However, in Figure 9.1 we emphasize that a number of different sample means could have resulted from our sampling study. From the distribution of the sample means we can compute the probability that the sample mean will occur in various intervals.

The mean $\bar{X}$ from a random sample is

$$\bar{X} = \frac{1}{n}x_1 + \frac{1}{n}x_2 + \cdots + \frac{1}{n}x_n$$

where the x_i's are individual observations and n is the sample size. From Chapter 7 we know that if the individual observations, x_i's, have a normal distribution, the sample mean, which is a linear combination of normal random variables, will also have a normal distribution.

The expected value or mean of the probability distribution of sample means is

$$\mu_{\bar{X}} = E[\bar{X}]$$

$$= E\left[\frac{1}{n}x_1 + \frac{1}{n}x_2 + \cdots + \frac{1}{n}x_n\right]$$

$$= \mu$$

and the variance is

$$\sigma_{\bar{X}}^2 = \left(\frac{1}{n}\right)^2 \sigma_{x_1}^2 + \left(\frac{1}{n}\right)^2 \sigma_{x_2}^2 + \cdots + \left(\frac{1}{n}\right)^2 \sigma_{x_n}^2$$

$$= \frac{n\sigma^2}{n^2}$$

$$= \frac{\sigma^2}{n}$$

where μ and σ^2 are the mean and variance of the probability distribution of individual store sales x_i; $x_i \sim N(\mu, \sigma^2)$.

If the individual store sales have a normal probability density function, the sample mean also has a normal distribution, with a mean μ and a variance σ^2/n.

9.3.1 Acceptance Intervals

In many statistical applications we would like to compute a range within which a substantial fraction of random sample means will occur given that the population mean is known. For example, quality control acceptance charts are established for almost every production process in modern competitive companies. Acceptance charts are based on a known mean for a properly operating process and established upper and lower bounds for random sample means. Specific procedures for developing these charts are given in Chapter 18. Applications such as these use acceptance intervals (Key Idea 9.4).

> ### Key Idea 9.4: Acceptance Intervals
>
> **Acceptance intervals** are the range within which a sample statistic, such as the mean $\bar{X}$, will occur with a specified probability, assuming a population mean μ and variance σ^2. When the sample mean $\bar{X}$ is in this interval, we accept that the sample came from a population with mean μ and variance σ^2. For a normally distributed random variable, 95% of the sample means would occur in the interval
>
> $$\mu \pm 1.96 \times \frac{\sigma}{\sqrt{n}}$$
>
> This is defined as a *95% acceptance interval*.

Acceptance intervals that have only a lower or an upper limit can also be defined as *one-sided acceptance intervals*. In those cases the probability of being outside the interval is concentrated at one side of the interval. Thus a one-sided 95% upper limit acceptance interval would be

$$\bar{X} \leq \mu + 1.645 \times \frac{\sigma}{\sqrt{n}}$$

where 1.645 is the Z value when the upper tail of the normal distribution is 0.05. Similarly, a one-sided 95% lower limit acceptance interval would be

$$\bar{X} \geq \mu - 1.645 \times \frac{\sigma}{\sqrt{n}}$$

A simple example from our clothing store will be used to clarify this idea. Assume that a population of retail stores had a mean daily sales of $1000 and a variance of 10,000.[1] The probability density function is shown in Figure 9.2. An acceptance interval that contains 95% of the normally distributed observations has been indicated on the graph. An observation that appeared within this interval would be accepted as coming from a population of normal random variables with mean $\mu = 1000$ and variance $\sigma^2 = 10,000$.

The interval is constructed by obtaining the standardized normal Z value for which the probability of being in the tail is 0.025. From Table A.1 we find that $Z_{0.025} = 1.96$. Therefore, the 95% acceptance interval is

$$\mu \pm 1.96 \times \sigma$$
$$1000 \pm 1.96 \times 100$$
$$804 \ \text{to} \ 1196$$

---

[1] If the annual sales have a normal distribution, mean daily sales also have a normal distribution. The mean is merely the total divided by a constant.

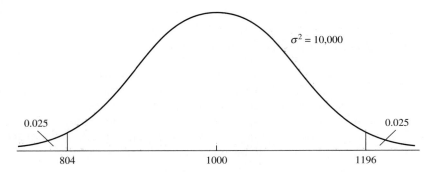

Figure 9.2   Probability Density Function for Store Sales

A single observation within the interval would be in agreement with our accepting the assumption that the population mean is equal to 1000. However, an observation outside the interval would make us question the assumption that the population mean is $\mu = 1000$.

We could also select from the population of stores a random sample of $n = 25$ observations and compute the sample mean. The sample mean will have normal probability density function with mean $\mu = 1000$ and variance $\sigma^2 = 10,000/25$. The probability density function for the sample mean is shown in Figure 9.3 with a 95% acceptance interval. This interval is computed as follows:

$$\mu \pm 1.96 \times \frac{\sigma}{\sqrt{n}}$$

$$1000 \pm 1.96 \times \frac{100}{5}$$

$$960.8 \ \text{to} \ 1039.2$$

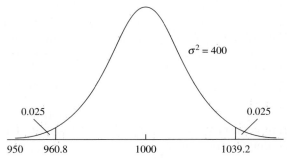

Figure 9.3   Probability Density Function for Mean Store Sales ($n = 25$)

Does It Make Sense?

From the analysis above and comparison of Figures 9.2 and 9.3 we see that the sample mean has a smaller variance and that sample means occur over a smaller interval than that of individual observations. Thus we see that the acceptance intervals become narrower with increased sample size. Acceptance intervals are widely used in quality control work, as we will see in Chapter 18. The customary acceptance interval for quality control is ±3 standard deviations. Those intervals contain over 99.7% of the sample means. A sample mean outside the interval leads to the conclusion that the population mean and/or variance have changed.   □

Example 9.2   Store Sales

Let us consider an application of the results above. Charlie Johnson, a marketing analyst, wishes to determine if the growth of large shopping centers or other factors has reduced the sales for small clothing stores from a previous mean of $1000 per day.

Solution   From an old study he finds that mean daily sales for these stores was 1000 with a variance of 10,000. From the analysis above he knows that if the sales patterns have remained the same, 95% of random sample observations x_i will be in the acceptance interval 804 to 1196. However, if he computes the mean of a random sample ($n = 25$), the probability is 0.95 that the sample mean $\overline{X}$ is in the narrower acceptance interval 960.8 to 1039.2. Charlie obtains a random sample of $n = 25$ daily store sales from the past year and computes the sample mean as 950. Figure 9.3 shows the 95% acceptance interval (960.8 to 1039.2) and the location of the sample mean $\overline{X} = 950$. Since 950 is below the acceptance interval, he cannot accept the assumption that the mean sales for all stores is 1000. He concludes that sales in small clothing stores have been reduced. Charlie could be wrong, but the probability that he is wrong is the probability that $\overline{X}$ is less than or equal to 950, given a population mean $\mu = 1000$, which is less than 0.025. By using the distribution of the sample mean, Charlie has been able to infer that there has been a reduction in the sales for small clothing stores.   □

Practice Problem 9.1: Graduate School Exam

The scores on a graduate school qualifying exam have a mean of 100 and a variance of 225. A random sample of 25 tests are examined and the sample mean test score, $\overline{X}$, is computed. Determine the probability that the sample mean is:

(a) Between 95 and 105.
(b) Less than 94.
(c) Greater than 103.   □

The solutions for all Practice Problems are given at the end of the chapter.

Problem Exercises

9.1   A random sample of size $n = 36$ is obtained from a population having a normal probability distribution with $\mu = 500$ and $\sigma = 20$. The sample mean $\overline{X}$ is computed. Determine:
(a) The 90% acceptance interval for $\overline{X}$.
(b) The probability that $\overline{X}$ is greater than 506.
(c) The probability that $\overline{X}$ is between 498 and 503.

9.2   The price of gasoline is believed to follow a normal distribution with mean $\mu = \$1.10$
        and variance $\sigma^2 = 0.0025$. A random sample is obtained from 16 stations and the sample
        mean price $\bar{X}$ is computed. Determine:
        (a) The 95% acceptance interval for $\bar{X}$.
        (b) The probability that $\bar{X}$ is greater than $1.18.
        (c) The probability that $\bar{X}$ is between $1.02 and $1.13.

9.3   The account receivables for a major parts supplier is believed to follow a normal distri-
        bution with mean $\mu = \$165$ and variance $\sigma^2 = 2500$. A random sample of size $n = 45$
        is obtained by the auditing team to test the receivables.
        (a) If the receivables do follow the distribution, what is the 94% acceptance interval for
            the sample mean?
        (b) What is the upper limit such that only 5% of the sample means exceed this limit?

9.4   The critical dimension of an automobile part has a mean of 2.5 inches and a variance of
        0.0001 and is normally distributed. A random sample of size 5 is taken every 8 hours
        by the quality control inspector and used to determine if the part dimensions are being
        maintained.
        (a) Define an interval such that 95% of the sample means will be included.
        (b) Compute the 3σ interval for the sample mean (i.e., $\mu \pm 3\sigma_{\bar{x}}$). This is a common
            interval used for quality control acceptance charts.
        (c) What is the probability that the sample mean is in this interval if the mean and
            variance remain the same?

9.5   The weights of potato chip packages have a mean of 20 ounces and a variance of 1. The
        weights are normally distributed. A random sample of 28 packages is obtained and the
        sample mean is computed. Determine:
        (a) The lower limit weight such that the probability that the sample mean is less than
            this limit is 0.05.
        (b) The 96% acceptance interval for the sample mean.

9.6   The Speedy Package Delivery (SPD) is a small package delivery firm located in Frank-
        furt, Germany. The weights of the packages delivered are believed to be normally dis-
        tributed with a mean $\mu = 5$ kilograms and a variance of 0.64. A random sample of nine
        packages is obtained. Determine:
        (a) The 98% acceptance interval for the sample mean.
        (b) The probability that the sample mean is less than 4.4 kilograms.
        (c) The probability that the sample mean is greater than 5.3 kilograms.

9.3.2 Finite Population Adjustment

The results developed in this chapter assume random samples from a very large or infinite population. If the population is large, the selection of one observation does not
affect the probability of selecting any other observation. However, there are situations
in which samples are obtained from small populations and selected observations are
not replaced in the population. In these situations the sample may contain 30 or 40%
of the population. Therefore, the probability of selecting later observations will be affected by the selection of previous observations. As a result, the variance and standard

deviation of the sample mean are reduced. The standard deviation reduction is proportional to the finite population correction factor, which is

$$\text{correction factor} = \sqrt{\frac{N-n}{N-1}}$$

where N is the population size and n is the sample size. As a result (Key Idea 9.5) the population standard deviation of the sample mean is

$$\sigma_{\bar{X}} = \sqrt{\frac{N-n}{N-1}}\,\frac{\sigma}{\sqrt{n}}$$

and the sample standard deviation of the sample mean is

$$S_{\bar{X}} = \sqrt{\frac{N-n}{N-1}}\,\frac{S_x}{\sqrt{n}}$$

For example, a sample of size 400 from a population of size 1000 would result in a correction factor of

$$\sqrt{\frac{1000-400}{1000-1}} = 0.775$$

Thus both the population standard deviation and the sample standard deviation would be reduced by about 22% over a sample of 400 obtained from an infinite population. This correction should always be used when sampling from small populations.

Key Idea 9.5: Finite Population Adjustment

If a random sample of size n is obtained from a finite population of size N, the population standard deviation is reduced by the **finite population correction factor** to

$$\sigma_{\bar{X}} = \sqrt{\frac{N-n}{N-1}}\,\frac{\sigma}{\sqrt{n}}$$

and the sample standard deviation of the sample mean is

$$S_{\bar{X}} = \sqrt{\frac{N-n}{N-1}}\,\frac{S_x}{\sqrt{n}}$$

The effect of sample size versus percent of population (Key Idea 9.6) can be seen in the following comparison between the effect of the correction factor and sample size on the standard deviation. Many people who do not have an understanding of statistics assign great importance to the fact that a sample contains 10 or 20% of the population. Using the correction factor, we see that a 10% sample reduces the sample and population standard deviation by 5%, and a 20% sample reduces the standard deviation by 10%. In contrast, the effect of increasing the sample size by a factor of 4 (e.g., from $n = 25$ to $n = 100$) would reduce the standard deviation by $\sqrt{\frac{1}{4}} = \frac{1}{2}$, as seen in the following example:

$$\sigma_{\bar{X}_{25}} = \frac{\sigma}{\sqrt{25}}$$

$$= \frac{\sigma}{5}$$

$$S_{\bar{X}_{25}} = \frac{S_x}{\sqrt{25}}$$

$$= \frac{S_x}{5}$$

$$\sigma_{\bar{X}_{100}} = \frac{\sigma}{\sqrt{100}}$$

$$= \frac{\sigma}{10}$$

$$S_{\bar{X}_{100}} = \frac{S_x}{\sqrt{100}}$$

$$= \frac{S_x}{10}$$

The effect of sample size does not depend on the fraction of the population sampled.

Key Idea 9.6: Sample Size Versus Percent of Population

The standard deviation of a sample mean and hence the acceptance interval is influenced more by the size of the sample than by the percentage of the population contained in the sample. If you want to reduce the variance and the acceptance interval, you should take a larger sample.

9.4 CENTRAL LIMIT THEOREM

The central limit theorem is stated in Key Idea 9.7.

For random variable X with symmetric probability distributions, large n is 25 to 30. For skewed probability distributions, an n from 30 to 50 is usually large enough. In Section 9.5 we show that even the binomial random variable will be approximately normally distributed if the sample size is between 20 and 100.

Key Idea 9.7: Central Limit Theorem

The **central limit theorem** states that the sampling distribution of the sample mean, $\overline{X}$, from a random sample of size n $(x_i, \ i = 1, \ldots, n)$, drawn from a population with mean μ and finite variance σ^2 will approach a normal distribution with mean μ and variance σ^2/n as n becomes large.

These results have been established mathematically and by numerous computer sampling studies. The mathematical proof can be found in any good mathematical statistics textbook. A number of computer-generated random sample simulation studies have also demonstrated this result. In those simulation studies the sample means from many hundreds of random samples, with different sample sizes n, have been used to construct histograms. As the sample size n increases, these histograms—the distribution of sample means—approach a normal distribution.

The central limit theorem provides the rationale for establishing that a number of random variables used in business and economics are normally distributed. For example, daily store sales are the sum of independent purchases by a large number of individual customers. The expenditure by each customer can be modeled as an independent random variable whose probability distribution is unknown. These individual expenditures are not likely to have a normal probability distribution since there are always a few people making very large purchases and the minimum purchase is zero. However, if we add all individual customer expenditures to obtain daily sales, then by the central limit theorem daily sales can be approximated by the normal distribution.

The same argument can be made for a number of aggregate economic variables. Total private investment in a quarter is the sum of independent investments by a large number of businesses. Individual investment expenditures can be modeled as independent random variables that are not likely to have a normal probability distribution. However, aggregate private investment is the sum of random variables and by the central limit theorem is likely to have a normal probability distribution. The same argument can be made for many other economic variables. The examples above show how the central limit theorem can be used to decide a priori if the random variable for a new problem is likely to have a normal probability distribution.

Does It Make Sense?

The central limit theorem is a very useful result for business and economic statistical applications. It provides the basis for using the normal distribution for a wide range of statistical applications. As a result, it is possible to use a few basic analysis procedures and apply them to many seemingly different problems. For most of the business problems, statistical procedures based on the normal will provide a solid and useful analysis. Thus you do not need to understand the entire range of statistical procedures to conduct useful analyses for most of your work. The variety of examples and student problems in future chapters will indicate the range of applications.   □

9.5 DISTRIBUTIONS FOR NONNORMAL POPULATIONS

In many applied economic and business problems the individual random variables do not have a normal distribution. Family incomes and prices of houses usually have a skewed distribution. Contributions to symphony orchestras, churches, colleges, and other charitable organizations are also likely to be skewed. Fortunately, we can use the central limit theorem.

Figure 9.4 presents results from computer simulations that generated empirical distributions of sample means. Several important examples should be noted. When

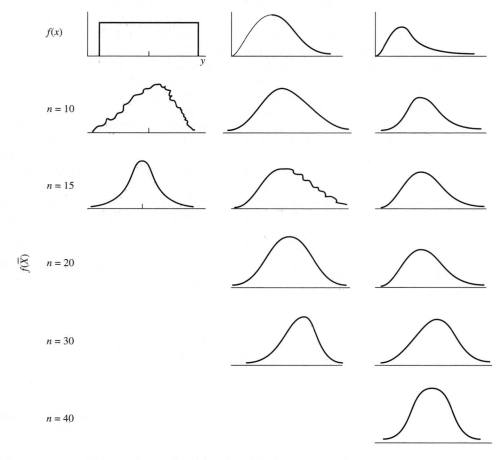

Figure 9.4   Distribution of Sample Means from Various Population
Distributions

the distribution of individual observations is uniform, a sample size of 10 to 15 will be sufficient. For many distributions that are skewed, samples of size 25 to 30 will be sufficient. Even the highly skewed distribution shown on the right will provide normally distributed sample means with a sample of size 30 to 40. Thus we see that the assumption that sample means are normally distributed is robust with respect to the probability distributions that are usually encountered in business and economic applications.

Example 9.3   Per Capita Family Income

Shirley Smith, a market researcher, has been asked to determine if a new slow-food restaurant is likely to be successful in Gourmet City. Based on her economic analysis she concludes that the restaurant would be profitable if the mean per capita family income is greater than $\mu = \$40,000$.

Solution   To determine if per capita family income is greater than $40,000, she decides to obtain a random sample of $n = 50$ families and use the sample mean family income $\overline{X}$ as a decision variable. From other studies she knows that the standard deviation of family incomes is $\sigma = 10,000$. Figure 9.5 shows the probability distribution for the sample mean assuming that the population mean is 40,000. The standard deviation of the distribution of sample means is

$$\sigma_{\overline{X}} = \frac{\sigma}{\sqrt{n}}$$
$$= \frac{10,000}{\sqrt{50}}$$
$$= 1414$$

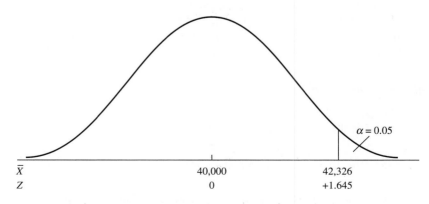

Figure 9.5   Probability Distribution: Sample Mean Income from
Gourmet City

Shirley decides to recommend in favor of the new restaurant only if there is strong evidence that the mean per capita family income is greater than \$40,000. Strong evidence would be a sample mean that is greater than 40,000 and has a small probability ($\alpha \leq 0.05$) of occurring if the population mean is 40,000 or less. For this problem an acceptance level is computed as

$$\mu + Z_\alpha \times \sigma_{\bar{X}} = 40,000 + 1.645 \times 1414 = 42,326$$

where $\alpha = 0.05$. If the sample mean is greater than the acceptance level, we conclude that the population mean is greater than 40,000 because the probability of a sample mean greater than the acceptance level is 0.05 or less if the population mean is 40,000 or less.

In this calculation and in Figure 9.5 we have introduced the symbol α to identify the probability of being outside the acceptance interval. The probability α is usually small and is the probability of error when we conclude that a sample mean did not come from a population with a specified mean when in fact it did.

Thus Shirley will conclude that the restaurant will be successful if the sample mean exceeds 42,326, as shown in Figure 9.5. The probability of a sample mean that is equal to or greater than 42,326 is $\alpha = 0.05$ if the population mean is exactly 40,000. Therefore, $\bar{X} \geq 42,326$ indicates that the population mean is likely to be greater than 40,000. She cannot be certain of her conclusion. But the evidence against a population mean less than or equal to 40,000 is very strong. Thus she decides in favor of a population mean greater than 40,000 if the sample mean, in this problem, exceeds 42,326. Her probability of an incorrect conclusion (i.e., the population mean is 40,000 or less) is less than or equal to $\alpha = 0.05$.   □

Does It Make Sense?

For most applied business problems analysts do not spend much time worrying about the probability distribution of the sample mean. They behave as if the sample mean has a normal distribution. This practice, which is supported by the central limit theorem, makes routine statistical applications easier. In addition, the results have contributed positively to understanding and decision making.   □

Practice Problem 9.2: Package Filling

The packaging machine in a German flour mill is set to fill each package with 250 grams of flour with a variance of 4.

(a) Construct a $\pm 2\sigma$ acceptance interval for the sample mean given a random sample with size of 5.

(b) What proportion of the sample means would occur in the interval from part (a)? What important assumption is needed to answer this question?

(c) Construct a $\pm 3\sigma$ acceptance interval for the sample mean given a sample size of 5.

(d) What proportion of the sample means would occur in the interval from part (c)?

(e) A random sample of size 10 had a mean package weight of 248 grams. What do you conclude about the packaging process?   □

Problem Exercises

9.7   A random sample of 49 house prices is obtained in a small midwestern city. A local real estate broker has claimed that the mean house price is $80,000, with a variance of 100,000,000. If the real estate broker is correct, determine:
(a) The 95% acceptance interval for the sample mean.
(b) The probability that the sample mean is greater than $83,000.
(c) The 90% acceptance interval.

9.8   A random sample of 100 family incomes are obtained in large eastern city and the sample mean income is computed. The mean family income is $25,000 with a standard deviation of $30,000. Determine:
(a) The probability that the sample mean is less than $20,000.
(b) The probability that the sample mean is between $21,000 and $28,000.
(c) The 90% acceptance interval for the sample mean.

9.9   The Speedy Package Delivery (SPD) is a small package delivery firm located in Frankfurt, Germany. The mean time to deliver a package is 90 minutes, with a variance of 900. Individual delivery times are not normally distributed. A random sample of 25 delivery times is obtained and the sample mean is computed.
(a) What is the 95% acceptance interval for the mean delivery time?
(b) What is the probability that the sample mean delivery time is between 80 and 100 minutes?
(c) What assumption was necessary to answer questions (a) and (b)?

9.10   The account receivables for a major parts supplier has a mean $\mu = \$670$ and a variance $\sigma^2 = 2500$. The distribution of individual accounts receivable is skewed to the right. A random sample of size $n = 45$ is obtained by the auditing team to test the receivables.
(a) What is the 94% acceptance interval for the sample mean?
(b) What is the upper limit such that only 5% of the sample means exceed this limit?
(c) What important assumption did you make to answer questions (a) and (b)?

9.11   The distribution of weights of cake mix packages are known to be skewed to the left. The mean package weight is 500 grams with a standard deviation of 5 grams. A random sample of 36 packages was obtained and the sample mean was computed. Determine:
(a) The 98% acceptance interval for the sample mean.
(b) The 90% acceptance interval for the sample mean.
(c) The probability that the sample mean is less than 499 grams.
(d) The probability that the sample mean is over 500 grams.

9.6 BINOMIAL AND PROPORTION RANDOM VARIABLES

The procedure used in Section 9.5 can also be used to obtain the distribution of proportion random variables and the binomial random variable (Key Idea 9.8).

Key Idea 9.8: Binomial Random Variable Distribution

The sampling distribution of the binomial random variable X is developed
by noting that the number of successes with sample size n is merely the
sum of the n independent Bernoulli random variables:

$$X = x_1 + x_2 + \cdots + x_n$$

$$= \sum_{i=1}^{n} x_i$$

The mean for the sampling distribution is

$$\mu = E[Y]$$
$$= n\pi$$

and the variance is

$$\sigma^2 = \sum_{i=1}^{n} \sigma_{x_i}^2$$

$$= \sum_{i=1}^{n} \pi(1 - \pi)$$

$$= n\pi(1 - \pi)$$

In Figure 9.1 we could substitute a Bernoulli (zero or one) random variable for
the original x_i observations and obtain Figure 9.6. The proportion random variable
is computed by using the same equation that was used to compute the sample mean.
The mean and variance of the sample proportion could be derived using the linear
combination of random variables.

Now we consider in detail how to obtain sampling distributions for the binomial
and proportion random variables. From Chapter 5 we know that the binomial random variable is the sum of n independent Bernoulli random variables.[2] Each random

---

[2] Recall from Section 5.5 that the Bernoulli random variable, X, has only two values—0 and 1—with
$P(X = 1) = \pi$ and $P(X = 0) = 1 - \pi$, where π is in the range $0 < \pi < 1$. We showed that the mean $\mu_X = \pi$
and the variance $\sigma_X^2 = \pi(1 - \pi)$.

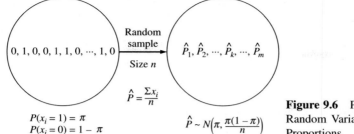

$$P(x_i = 1) = \pi$$
$$P(x_i = 0) = 1 - \pi$$

Figure 9.6   Population of Bernoulli Random Variables and Sample Proportions

sample will contain a different set of Bernoulli random variables and therefore a different number of successes. Thus a sampling distribution of X—binomial successes—would result.

The number of successes X in a random sample of size n from a population modeled by a Bernoulli random variable is merely the sum of the n independent Bernoulli random variables:

$$X = x_1 + x_2 + \cdots + x_n$$

$$= \sum_{i=1}^{n} x_i$$

The mean for the sampling distribution is

$$\mu = E[X]$$

$$= E\left[\sum_{i=1}^{n} x_i\right]$$

$$= E[x_1] + E[x_2] + \cdots + E[x_n]$$

$$= \pi + \pi + \cdots + \pi$$

$$= n\pi$$

For the variance,

$$\sigma^2 = \sigma^2_{x_1} + \sigma^2_{x_2} + \cdots + \sigma^2_{x_n}$$

$$= \sum_{i=1}^{n} \sigma^2_{x_i}$$

$$= \sum_{i=1}^{n} \pi(1 - \pi)$$

$$= n\pi(1 - \pi)$$

A sample proportion could also be computed for each random sample obtained above (Key Idea 9.9). This would provide a sampling distribution of sample proportions as shown in Figure 9.6. The sample proportion is

$$\hat{P} = \frac{\sum_{i=1}^{n} x_i}{n}$$

$$= \frac{x_1}{n} + \frac{x_2}{n} + \cdots + \frac{x_n}{n}$$

Key Idea 9.9: Proportion Random Variable Distribution

The sampling distribution of the proportion random variable is obtained by recognizing that the proportion is the mean for a random sample of n Bernoulli random variables:

$$\hat{P} = \frac{\sum_{i=1}^{n} x_i}{n}$$

$$= \frac{x_1}{n} + \frac{x_2}{n} + \cdots + \frac{x_n}{n}$$

The mean for the sampling distribution is

$$\mu_{\hat{P}} = E\left[\frac{x_1}{n} + \frac{x_2}{n} + \cdots + \frac{x_n}{n}\right]$$

$$= \pi$$

and the variance is

$$\sigma_{\hat{P}}^2 = \frac{\pi(1-\pi)}{n}$$

The mean $\mu_{\hat{P}}$ for the sampling distribution is

$$\mu_{\hat{P}} = E\left[\frac{x_1}{n} + \frac{x_2}{n} + \cdots + \frac{x_n}{n}\right]$$

$$= \frac{1}{n}[E[x_1] + E[x_2] + \cdots + E[x_n]]$$

$$= \frac{1}{n}[\pi + \pi + \cdots + \pi]$$

$$= \pi$$

and the variance, $\sigma_{\hat{P}}^2$, for the sampling distribution is

$$\sigma_{\hat{P}}^2 = \sigma^2 \left(\frac{x_1}{n} + \frac{x_2}{n} + \cdots + \frac{x_n}{n} \right)$$

$$= \frac{\sigma_{x_1}^2}{n^2} + \frac{\sigma_{x_2}^2}{n^2} + \cdots + \frac{\sigma_{x_n}^2}{n^2}$$

$$= \sum_{i=1}^{n} \left(\frac{1}{n} \right)^2 \times \pi(1 - \pi)$$

$$= \frac{\pi(1 - \pi)}{n}$$

By the principle of minimum sample size (Key Idea 9.10), if $\pi = 0.1$, the minimum required sample size is $n > 100$, but if $\pi = 0.5$, the minimum sample size is $n > 36$. At the smaller sample sizes the continuity correction from Section 6.6 is recommended. Based on these results we see that problems involving sample proportions or sums of successes can also be analyzed using the normal assumptions developed in Section 9.2. The only difference is the computation of the means ($\mu_{\hat{P}}$ or μ) and the variances ($\sigma_{\hat{P}}^2$ or σ^2). Thus we are able to solve a set of important problems without having to learn additional probability theory.

Key Idea 9.10: Minimum Sample Size

From Section 6.6 we know that both the sample proportion $\hat{P}$ and the number of successes Y have an approximate normal probability distribution if

$$n\pi(1 - \pi) \geq 9$$

In addition, if

$$5 < n\pi(1 - \pi) < 9$$

we could use the normal approximation if the continuity correction was used.

Example 9.4   New Product Test Market

Sarah Braulick, president of Consumer Products, Inc., is considering the introduction of a new toothpaste. This product has a unique flavor which she hopes will be appealing to teenagers. From the corporate accountants she knows that the new product will be profitable if more than 20% of the people in the market population purchase the product. Should she introduce the new toothpaste?

Solution Sarah obtains a random sample of $n = 1000$ teenagers and finds that 15% of the sample say that they would purchase the toothpaste. The sample proportion $\hat{P}$ is used to make a decision concerning implementation of the new product.

Sarah knows that the sample proportions will differ from the population proportion because of sample variability. To interpret $\hat{P} = 0.15$ she must know its probability distribution model. To construct the probability model she begins with the assumption that $\pi = 0.20$. If her assumption is true, this new product will be profitable.

From her study of the distribution of sample proportions she knows that the decision statistic $\hat{P}$ has a normal distribution with mean and variance

$$\mu_{\hat{P}} = \pi$$
$$= 0.20$$
$$\sigma_{\hat{P}}^2 = \frac{\pi(1 - \pi)}{n}$$
$$= \frac{0.20(1 - 0.20)}{1000}$$
$$= 0.00016$$

and the standard deviation is

$$\sigma_{\hat{P}} = 0.0126$$

The specific mean and variance result from her proposed model, which states that the proportion of buyers is $\pi = 0.20$. She can now compute the probability of obtaining her sample mean $\hat{P} = 0.15$ if the population mean is $\pi = 0.20$. Specifically, she computed a 95% acceptance region, which includes 95% of the sample proportions ($n = 1000$). The normal probability distribution of $\hat{P}$ is shown in Figure 9.7. Using the standardized normal random variable Z and the standard deviation of the sample proportion, we see that if the population proportion $\pi = 0.20$, then 95% of the sample proportions would be in the interval

$$0.20 \pm (1.96) \times (0.0126)$$
$$0.20 \pm 0.0248$$
$$0.175 \text{ to } 0.225$$

Sarah can use this probability distribution and the sample proportion to guide her decision concerning the new product introduction. The interval from 0.175 to 0.225 is a 95% acceptance interval. A sample proportion within this interval would support Sarah's belief that 20% of the people in the market population would purchase her toothpaste. A sample proportion less than 0.175 would be very unusual (probability ≤ 0.025). If such a small sample proportion occurred, Sarah would decide that purchase by 20% of the population was not likely. Thus she would cancel the new product because of potential low sales. However, if the sample proportion were above 0.225, she would decide that it is likely that her initial belief (20% purchase) was conservative. Sales are likely to be higher than anticipated. Thus she would implement the project with enthusiasm.

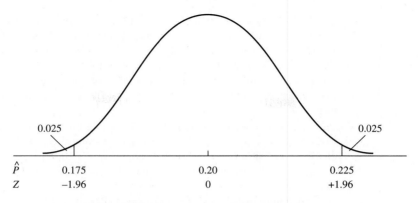

Figure 9.7   Distribution of Sample Proportion

With this analysis procedure she uses the results from her sample, $\hat{P} = 0.15$. Since 0.15 is less than the lower limit, 0.175, the sample does not support her hope that the population proportion of purchasers, π, is equal to 0.20. Thus she decides to cancel the project.   □

Practice Problem 9.3: Proportion Acceptance Interval

Sarah from Example 9.4 asks you to compute a 95% acceptance interval for the proportion from a random sample of size $n = 400$ if the population proportion is $\pi = 0.40$. What is the acceptance interval if $n = 800$?   □

Problem Exercises

9.12   An audit team is checking the age of accounts receivable to a large retailer. The retailer believes that 20% of the receivables are older than 60 days. The team obtains a random sample of 150 receivables and computes the sample proportion of receivables that are older than 60 days. Assuming that the 20% is correct, determine:
(a) The 95% acceptance interval.
(b) The probability that the sample percentage is greater than 25%.
(c) The probability that the sample percentage is less than 14%.

9.13   The marketing manager of Consolidated Products, George Thorson, believes that 30% of the households in Gotham City will react positively to the new taco-flavored turkey burgers that they are planning to introduce. To test this belief, a random sample of $n = 400$ households is obtained and the sample proportion who react positively is computed. Assuming that George is correct, determine:
(a) The 95% acceptance interval for the sample proportion.
(b) The probability that the sample proportion is less than 0.25.
(c) The probability that the sample proportion is greater than 0.33.

9.14   Sally Brown is a candidate for state senator and she believes that she has greater support than her opponent (e.g., at least 50% of the voters support her). However, to test her support she commissions a random sample election poll with $n = 900$ observations. The sample proportion who support her candidacy was computed. Assuming that $\pi = 0.50$, determine:

(a) The 98% acceptance interval for the sample proportion.

(b) The probability that the sample proportion is less than 0.48.

(c) The probability that the percentage of the sample who support her is greater than 56%.

9.15 A local government housing authority has been told by the federal housing authority that 30% of the families in public housing have incomes over \$40,000 per year. They decide to test this by obtaining a random sample of $n = 100$ families and checking their income. The sample proportion with incomes over \$40,000 is computed. Assuming that the federal housing authority is correct, determine:

(a) The probability that the sample percentage is less than 20%.

(b) The probability that the sample percentage is greater than 37%.

(c) The 96% acceptance interval for the sample proportion.

9.16 A company receives a shipment of 100,000 computer storage chips. They believe that 10% are defective. To test this belief, a random sample of 200 chips is obtained and the sample proportion defective is computed. Assuming that there are exactly 10% defective chips, determine:

(a) The 99% confidence interval for the sample proportion.

(b) The probability that the sample proportion is less than 0.06.

(c) The probability that the sample proportion is greater than 0.16.

9.17 A company receives a shipment of 100,000 computer storage chips. They believe that 10% are defective. To test this belief, a random sample of 200 chips is obtained and the number of defectives in the sample is computed. Assuming that there are exactly 10% defective chips, determine:

(a) The 99% confidence interval for the number of defective chips in the sample.

(b) The probability that the number of defective chips is less than 12.

(c) The probability that the number of defective chips in the sample is greater than 32.

9.7 CHI-SQUARE DISTRIBUTION: SAMPLE VARIANCES

In the previous sections of this chapter we have studied the probability distribution of sample means assuming that the population variance σ^2 is known. However, in many applied problems we do not know the population variance. Instead, the sample variance,

$$S_x^2 = \frac{\sum_{i=1}^n (x_i - \bar{X})^2}{n - 1}$$

is computed from the sample (Key Idea 9.11).

Using χ^2 and its probability density function, the probability of obtaining a sample variance S_x^2 or greater given σ^2 and n can be computed. Figure 9.8 shows

---

Key Idea 9.11: Distribution of Sample Variance

The **sample variance** is a random variable that can be modeled using the chi-square (χ^2) probability distribution with $(n-1)$ degrees of freedom. The statistic

$$\chi^2_{(n-1)} = \frac{(n-1)S_x^2}{\sigma^2}$$

has a chi-square probability distribution function with $n-1$ degrees of freedom.

---

the chi-square probability density function for $(n-1) = 24$ degrees of freedom (sample size $n = 25$). Notice that the χ^2 probability density function begins at zero and is skewed to the right. Variances are always positive and thus their ratios are positive.

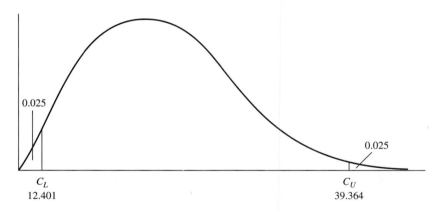

Figure 9.8   Chi-Square Probability Density Function for 24 Degrees of Freedom

There is a chi-square probability distribution for each degree of freedom, $n-1$. Critical values of the chi-square distribution for selected probabilities are presented in Table A.3. Acceptance intervals for each chi-square distribution can be constructed if we know the upper and lower critical values.

Recall that for the standard normal distribution upper and lower critical values could be obtained from a single distribution. For the 95% acceptance intervals used in Figures 9.3 and 9.7, the upper and lower critical values Z were equal to ±1.96. In contrast, upper and lower critical values are different for each chi-square distribution identified by degrees of freedom $n-1$. These critical values have been computed and are contained in the chi-square table, Table A.3. Each row of Table A.3 presents critical chi-square values for a different degree of freedom, $n-1$. For example, with degrees of freedom $n-1=24$, the lower 0.025 critical value is $C_L=12.401$. This value is computed such that 2.5% of the distribution is below 12.401. Similarly, an upper critical value $C_U=39.364$ was computed such that 2.5% of the distribution is above this 39.364. For the chi-square distribution with 24 degrees of freedom the 95% acceptance interval is from 12.401 to 39.364. Intervals with different percentages and different degrees of freedom are shown in the chi-square table. The chi-square value and/or its probability can also be computed in modern computer statistical programs.

Figure 9.9 shows the sampling process schematically. As with the sample mean we obtain a random sample of size n and compute the sample variance S^2. By repeating this process we could construct a probability distribution of sample variances as shown on the right. The sample variances could be multiplied by $n-1$ and divided by the population variance to obtain a χ^2_{n-1} random variable:

$$\chi^2 = \frac{(n-1)S_x^2}{\sigma^2}$$

As a result, we have a sampling distribution for the sample variance S_x^2. The mean and variance of the chi-square distribution are:

$$E[\chi^2] = n-1 \qquad \text{the degrees of freedom}$$
$$\sigma^2(\chi^2) = 2(n-1) \qquad \text{twice the degrees of freedom}$$

As the degrees of freedom increase, the chi-square distribution approaches a symmetric distribution. When the degrees of freedom are greater than about 100, the probability values for the χ^2 can be computed by using a normal approximation with the foregoing mean and variance. Additional theory regarding the development of the chi-square distribution is presented in the chapter appendix.

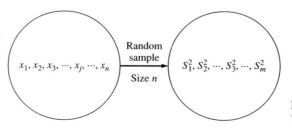

Figure 9.9 Population of Sample Variances

Example 9.5   Cereal Manufacturing

Industrial quality control is concerned with both the variance and the mean of manufacturing processes. In the blending of food products, uniform taste and quality depend on uniform mixtures of ingredients.

The production of flaked breakfast cereals begins with a mixing and cooking process. After cooking the mixture is passed through rollers to produce flakes. The flakes are then baked in an oven while being moved slowly on a conveyor belt. After baking the flakes are packed in boxes for shipment. The recipe for a major brand of flaked breakfast cereal specifies 100 grams of sugar per batch. The quality control department has determined that if the variance of X (grams of sugar added) exceeds 200, the quality of the flakes is reduced. Either the flakes are too brittle, because of too much sugar, and break in the package, or their flavor is not acceptable to customers because of too little sugar.

The quality control department needs an upper acceptance level for monitoring the process. If the sample variance S_x^2 exceeds this level, they would stop the manufacturing process so that the problem can be identified and corrected. Assume that a sample of size $n = 25$ is obtained. How large a sample variance would lead us to question our belief that the population variance is 200 or less? We are willing to accept an error of $\alpha = 0.05$.

Solution   From Table A.3 we find that the upper probability point on the chi-square for $\alpha = 0.05$ is $C_U = 36.42$. Thus we can compute

$$\chi^2 = \frac{(n-1)S_x^2}{\sigma^2}$$

$$36.42 = \frac{24 S_x^2}{200}$$

$$S_x^2 = \frac{36.42}{24} \times 200$$

$$= 303.5$$

$$S_x = 17.42$$

If the sample variance is greater than 303.5, we conclude that the population variance is greater than $\sigma^2 = 200$ and the process should be stopped and corrected. Notice that the upper limit for the variance is about 50% higher than the expected population variance of 200. Sample variances tend to have a wide sampling distribution compared to sample means. In addition, the sample standard deviation has an upper limit of $S_x = 17.42$ compared to the population standard deviation $\sigma = \sqrt{200} = 14.14$.   □

Practice Problem 9.4: Cereal Package Weight

George Melson, the president of Olaf Cereals, Inc., is concerned about the variance of cereal package weights. If the variance is too high, an excessive number of packages will be under the guaranteed weight. This can result in customer complaints and possibly government fines. He knows that the target variance for the weight of cereal packages is 100. He asks you to provide an acceptance interval within which 95% of the sample variances will occur if the sample size is $n = 25$ and the variance is $\sigma^2 = 100$. This acceptance interval will be used by the quality control department to monitor the packaging machines. $\square$

Problem Exercises

9.18   A random sample of size $n = 36$ is obtained from a population having a normal probability distribution with $\mu = 500$ and $\sigma = 20$. The sample variance S^2 is computed. Determine:
(a) The 90% acceptance interval for S^2.
(b) The probability that σ is greater than 25.
(c) The 98% acceptance interval for S^2.

9.19   The price of gasoline is believed to follow a normal distribution with mean $\mu = \$1.10$ and variance $\sigma^2 = 0.0025$. A random sample is obtained from 16 stations and the sample variance S^2 is computed. Determine the following acceptance intervals for S^2.
(a) 95%.
(b) 98%.

9.20   The account receivables for a major parts supplier is believed to follow a normal distribution with mean $\mu = \$165$ and variance $\sigma^2 = 2500$. A random sample of size $n = 51$ is obtained by the auditing team to test the receivables.
(a) If the receivables do follow the distribution, what is the 98% acceptance interval for the sample variance?
(b) What is the upper limit such that only 5% of the sample variances exceed this limit?

9.21   The critical dimension of an automobile part has a mean of 2.5 inches and a variance of 0.0001 and is normally distributed. A random sample of size 5 is taken every 8 hours by the quality control inspector and used to determine if the part dimensions are being maintained.
(a) Define an interval such that 95% of the sample variances will be included.
(b) What is the probability that the sample variance is greater than 0.00015?

9.22   The weights of potato chip packages have a mean of 20 ounces and a variance of 1. The weights are normally distributed. A random sample of 28 packages is obtained and the sample variance is computed. Determine:
(a) The lower limit weight such that the probability that the sample variance is less than this limit is 0.05.
(b) The 96% acceptance interval for the sample variance.

9.8 STUDENT t PROBABILITY DISTRIBUTION

There are many applied problems in which the population standard deviation σ is not known. In these situations we must use the sample standard deviation S_x. When S_x is used we cannot use the normal distribution. Instead we use the Student t probability distribution (Key Idea 9.12), which assumes that we have computed the sample standard deviation instead of the population standard deviation. The Student t distribution is similar to the standard normal. Computation of acceptance intervals follows the same procedure as that used for the normal but with S_x substituted for σ. The sample standard deviation S_x is a random variable, in contrast to the population standard deviation σ, which is a constant. Therefore, acceptance intervals will be wider for a given sample size when the *t* distribution is used instead of the normal.

Key Idea 9.12: Student *t* Statistic

The **Student *t* statistic** is used instead of the normal Z statistic whenever the sample standard deviation S_x is used instead of σ. The *t* statistic is computed using

$$t = \frac{x - \mu}{S_x}$$

or

$$t = \frac{\bar{X} - \mu}{S_x / \sqrt{n}}$$

where x is a normal random variable with mean μ and

$$S_x = \sqrt{\frac{\sum_{i=1}^{n}(x_i - \bar{X})^2}{n - 1}}$$

In contrast, the standard normal random variable Z is computed using

$$Z = \frac{x - \mu}{\sigma}$$

Because the sample mean, from a random sample of normally distributed random variables, is also normally distributed, we can also define the *t* as

$$t = \frac{\bar{X} - \mu}{S_x / \sqrt{n}}$$

or

$$t = \frac{\bar{X} - \mu}{S_{\bar{X}}}$$

Figure 9.10 compares the *t* probability distribution with the normal distribution. The *t* distribution approaches the normal distribution as the sample size increases. Thus there is a separate *t* distribution for each sample size. This result is pictured in Figure 9.11. The parameter for the *t* is the degrees of freedom used to compute the sample variance S_x^2. Table A.2 contains the critical *t* values for selected degrees

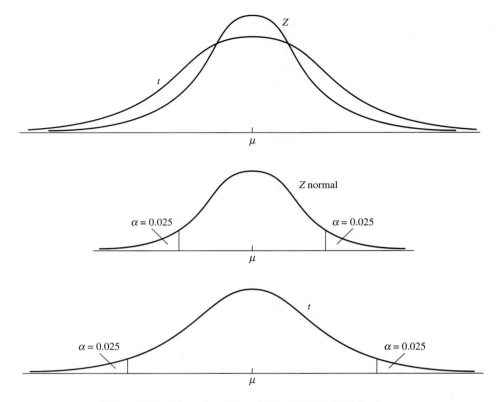

Figure 9.10   Normal and Student t Probability Distributions

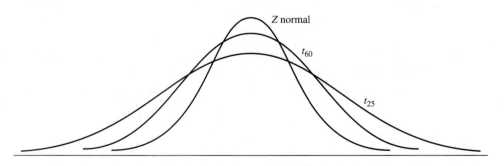

Figure 9.11   Normal and Student t as Degrees of Freedom Increase

of freedom and probabilities in the upper tail. When the degrees of freedom exceed 100, the t and the normal are so close that choosing one or the other will not have a practical effect on the outcome of the statistical analysis. This conclusion is reasonable because as the sample size increases the sample standard variance S_x^2 approaches the population variance σ^2. The chapter appendix presents additional theory related to the Student t.

The Student t distribution was developed by W. S. Gosset, an Irish statistician. Gosset worked for a Dublin brewery that did not allow its employees to publish. Therefore, he wrote under the name "Student," thus the name the *Student t distribution*. We state this bit of history to dispel rumors that the Student t distribution was developed to harass students of statistics.

9.8.1 Student t Tables

Specific values for the Student t distribution are obtained from Table A.2. Each line in this table contains the t statistic for a particular probability α in the upper (or lower) tail of the distribution. These t values can be used in the same way that we used Z values when the standard deviation σ was assumed to be known. For example, if we wanted to compute a 95% acceptance interval using the sample standard deviation S_x computed for a sample of size $n = 26$ (degrees of freedom $n - 1 = 25$), the $t_{0.025}$ value is 2.060. In contrast, if the sample size were $n = 61$, then $t_{0.025} = 2.000$. For cases in which the degrees of freedom do not appear in the table, you may either interpolate between values above and below the desired degrees of freedom or use the conservative strategy of selecting the t value from the table for the degrees of freedom just below that desired. The t value and/or its probability can also be computed in modern statistical computer programs.

Example 9.6   Agricultural Production

Shirley Thorson is the production manager for Johnson Turkey Farms, Inc. Turkey production is a very controlled process for converting grains to meat. She is concerned that the machine that fills the feeding trays for each bird might be underfilling the trays. The desired mean weight for each tray is $\mu = 6.1$ ounces. The machine error could also affect the variance, and thus she cannot assume that the variance can be determined from historical data. How should she proceed to test her concern?

Solution   A random sample of $n = 25$ feeding trays was obtained and each was weighed carefully in the laboratory. The sample mean was $\bar{X} = 5.9$ and the sample variance was $S_x^2 = 0.16$. The distribution of t is shown in Figure 9.12 combined with the minimum acceptance value of the sample mean. If the machine were working properly, the population mean for the sampling distribution would be $\mu = 6.1$. However, if a very small sample mean were obtained, she would doubt that the population mean was 6.1.

Shirley wishes to compute a minimum **acceptance value** such that the probability of a sample mean less than this critical value is $\alpha = 0.05$ if the population mean is $\mu = 6.1$. From the Student t table she finds that the critical value for t with 24 degrees of freedom and $\alpha = 0.05$ is 1.711. Using the definition of t, in Key Idea 9.12 she computed the minimum acceptance value, $\bar{X}_C$, for the sample mean $\bar{X}$.

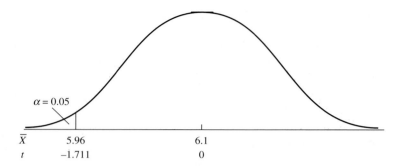

Figure 9.12   Critical Value of Mean Tray Weight Based on Student t
Distribution

The negative value of t is used because the minimum acceptance value is desired.

$$t_{0.05} = \frac{\bar{X}_C - \mu}{S_x / \sqrt{n}}$$

$$\bar{X}_C = \mu - t_{0.05} \frac{S_x}{\sqrt{n}}$$

$$= 6.1 - 1.711 \left(\frac{0.4}{5} \right)$$

$$= 5.96$$

The sample mean, 5.9, is less than $\bar{X}_C = 5.96$. This sample mean would occur less than 5% of the time if the population mean were $\mu = 6.1$. As a result of this evidence, Shirley decides that the feeding machine is likely to be allocating too little feed. The feed level is controlled carefully to produce meat within a cost restriction. Too little feed results in an extended growing cycle, which increases costs. She directs immediately that the machine be repaired. □

9.9 NONNORMAL DISTRIBUTIONS AND THE t DISTRIBUTION

In Section 9.8 we developed the t distribution for problems in which the population variance is not known. The t is derived assuming normally distributed random variables. We have also seen that the central limit theorem provides the result that sample means are approximately normally distributed even if the distribution of individual observations is not normal. Therefore, statistical procedures based on the normal can be applied to sample means from skewed probability distributions such as those for family incomes and housing prices. The development of these results in Section 9.4 assumed that the population variance was known. The central limit theorem allows us to use the sample variance and the t even when the distribution of individual observations is not normal. The sampling distributions of the t were simulated using a computer for two populations with skewed distributions shown in Figures 9.13 and 9.14. Figures 9.15 and 9.16 show the distribution of computed *t* statistics for various random sample sizes obtained from the skewed distributions. Using the computer we obtained 5000 random samples of size *n* from each of the skewed populations. From each of these random samples a *t* statistic was computed using

$$t = \frac{\bar{X} - \mu}{S_x/\sqrt{n}}$$

The distribution of these *t* statistics was then developed. As shown in Figures 9.15 and 9.16, the distribution of these *t* statistics very closely approximates the Student *t* distribution. For this reason we say that the *t* is "robust" with respect to the assumption of a normal probability distribution for the individual observations.

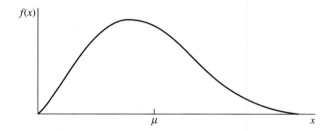

Figure 9.13   Typical Distribution of Family Incomes

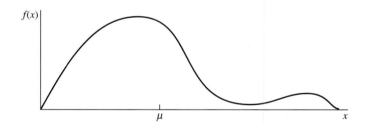

Figure 9.14   Skewed Distribution II

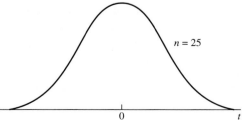

Figure 9.15   Distribution of Sample Student *t*'s; Samples from Figure 9.13

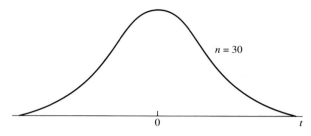

Figure 9.16 Distribution of Sample
Student t's; Samples from Figure 9.14

*9.10 RATIO OF SAMPLE VARIANCES: THE F DISTRIBUTION

Analysts also have an interest in comparing the variances between different populations. An economic policy may change the mean income of a population. However,
at the same time the variance might also change and we need to test for such a
change. Quality control managers seek to control both the mean and the variability of
manufacturing processes. The population of measurements before and after a process
change need to be compared for both stable means and stable variances. Comparison
of different economic systems often considers both the mean level of income and the
variability of income.

The F probability distribution (Key Idea 9.13) is the ratio of two independent
chi-square distributions each of which is divided by its degrees of freedom. When
comparing the variances of two populations, we begin by assuming that the population variances are equal and compute the sample variances S_1^2 and S_2^2 using random
samples from each population:

$$S_1^2 = \frac{\sum_{i=1}^{n}(x_{1i} - \bar{X}_1)^2}{n_1 - 1}$$

$$S_2^2 = \frac{\sum_{i=1}^{n}(x_{2i} - \bar{X}_2)^2}{n_2 - 1}$$

Key Idea 9.13: F Probability Distribution

The ratio of sample variances from normally distributed populations follow an **F distribution** if both population variances are equal, where

$$F = \frac{S_1^2}{S_2^2}$$

with S_1^2 being the larger of the sample variances, so that $F \geq 1$. Using
this result, we can perform analyses that compare the ratio of two sample
variances.

Next we specify the chi-square distributions for each population assuming that the population variances are both equal to σ^2:

$$\chi_1^2 = \frac{(n_1 - 1)S_1^2}{\sigma^2}$$

$$\chi_2^2 = \frac{(n_2 - 1)S_2^2}{\sigma^2}$$

The ratio of two independent chi-square random variables each of which is divided by its degrees of freedom is a random variable that follows an F distribution:

$$
\begin{aligned}
F &= \frac{\chi_{(n_1-1)}^2/(n_1 - 1)}{\chi_{(n_2-1)}^2/(n_2 - 1)} \\
&= \frac{S_1^2/\sigma^2}{S_2^2/\sigma^2} \\
&= \frac{S_1^2}{S_2^2}
\end{aligned}
$$

The analysis is easier if the larger S^2 is in the numerator so that the F ratio exceeds 1. The F probability distribution is shown schematically in Figure 9.17. If the computed value of the F statistic exceeds the acceptance level or critical value, F_c, for a given probability of error α, we would conclude that the assumption that both populations have the same variance is not correct. Table A.4 presents minimum critical values for F with $\alpha = 0.01$ and $\alpha = 0.05$. The acceptance level F_c depends on both the number of degrees in the numerator $(n_1 - 1)$ and the number of degrees of freedom in the denominator $(n_2 - 1)$. Notice how these are specified for the rows and the columns of Table A.4.

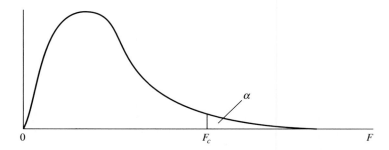

Figure 9.17 F Distribution

For example, with $n_1 - 1 = 40$ degrees of freedom for the numerator and $n_2 - 1 = 25$ degrees of freedom for the denominator, we use the column for 40 degrees of freedom and the row for 25 degrees of freedom, which shows that $F_c = 1.87$ for $\alpha = 0.05$. Similarly, with 39 degrees of freedom for both numerator and denominator, $F_{c,0.05} = 1.69$. The value of F and/or its probability can also be computed in modern statistical computer programs.

Example 9.7 Exports and Imports Analysis

Charlie Baker, an economist, has been studying the patterns of imports and exports for the years 1977 through 1986. He wants to know if the variance of imports is the same as the variance of exports.

Solution From Table 2.2 he finds that the sample variance for imports is 69.4 and the sample variance for exports is 34.2, both with sample sizes of $n = 40$. To provide a comparison, Charlie begins with the assumption that the population of quarterly imports and the population of quarterly exports can be modeled by normal probability distributions with the same variance. Charlie computes the ratio of sample variances:

$$F_{calc} = \frac{S_1^2}{S_2^2}$$
$$= \frac{69.4}{34.2}$$
$$= 2.03$$

From Table A.4 the critical value of the F statistic with 39 degrees of freedom in both the numerator and denominator is 1.69 ($\alpha = 0.05$). Since the calculated $F_{calc} = 2.03$ is greater than the critical value of $F = 1.69$ from Table A.4, Charlie concludes that the population variances for imports and exports are not the same. It appears that the variance of imports is larger for the period 1977–1986. ☐

Problem Exercises

9.23 A population has a mean $\mu = 100$. A random sample of size $n = 25$ is obtained and the sample mean and sample variance equal to 1600 are computed. Determine the following acceptance intervals for the sample mean.
(a) 98%.
(b) 90%.

9.24 The weights of cereal packages from Whole Grain, Inc. are normally distributed with a mean of $\mu = 16$. A random sample of size $n = 36$ packages is obtained and the sample mean and sample variance are computed. The sample variance is 4. Determine:
(a) The 95% acceptance interval for the sample mean.
(b) The probability that the sample mean is less than 15.5.
(c) The probability that the sample mean is greater than 16.7.

9.25 The weights of potato chip packages have a mean of 20 ounces and are normally distributed. A random sample of 28 packages is obtained and the sample mean and sample variance are computed. The sample variance is 4. Determine:
(a) The lower limit weight such that the probability that the sample mean is less than this limit is 0.05.
(b) The 96% acceptance interval for the sample mean.

9.26 The Speedy Package Delivery (SPD) is a small package delivery firm located in Frankfurt, Germany. The weights of the packages delivered are believed to be normally distributed with a mean $\mu = 10$ kilograms. A random sample of nine packages is obtained and the sample mean is computed. The sample variance is 64. Determine:

      (a) The 98% acceptance interval for the sample mean.

      (b) The probability that the sample mean is less than 4.4 kilograms.

      (c) The probability that the sample mean is greater than 16 kilograms.

9.27 Amalgamated manufacturers is considering the purchase of a new machine tool for shaping parts. They are concerned that the variance of the part dimensions is larger for the new machine. A random sample of 36 parts is produced on each machine. The sample of parts produced on the old machine has a variance of 0.0015, and the sample from the new machine has a variance of 0.0025. Based on these sample results, can you conclude that the new machine has a higher variance?

SUMMARY OF KEY IDEAS

PRACTICE PROBLEM SOLUTIONS

9.1 The problem is solved by computing the variance of the sample mean and recognizing that the sample mean has a normal distribution. The standard normal Z values are computed and used to obtain the probability values.

$$\sigma_{\bar{X}}^2 = \frac{225}{25} = 9$$

$$\sigma_{\bar{X}} = \sqrt{9} = 3$$

(a)

$$P(95 \le \bar{X} \le 105) = P\left(\frac{95-100}{3} \le Z \le \frac{105-100}{3}\right)$$

$$= P(-1.67 \le Z \le +1.67)$$

$$= 0.9050$$

(b)
$$P(\bar{X} \leq 94) = P\left(Z \leq \frac{94 - 100}{3}\right)$$
$$= P(Z \leq -2.0)$$
$$= 0.0228$$

(c)
$$P(\bar{X} \geq 103) = P\left(Z \geq \frac{103 - 100}{3}\right)$$
$$= P(Z \geq 1.0)$$
$$= 0.1587$$

9.2 (a) The $\pm 2\sigma$ acceptance interval given a random sample of $n = 5$ and $\sigma^2 = 4$ is computed as follows:

$$\sigma_{\bar{X}} = \frac{2}{\sqrt{5}} = 0.89$$

The interval is

$$250 \pm 2\sigma_{\bar{X}}$$
$$250 \pm 2 \times 0.89$$
$$250 \pm 1.78$$

(b) This interval contains $1 - (2)(0.0228) = 0.9544$ proportion of the data, or 95.44%. We assume a random sample when computing $\sigma_{\bar{X}}$.

(c) The $\pm 3\sigma$ acceptance interval is

$$250 \pm (3)(0.89)$$

or

$$250 \pm 2.67$$

(d) This interval contains $(2)(0.4987) = 0.9974$ proportion, or 99.74%.

(e) In this question we need to determine if the mean package weight equal to 248 is outside the $\pm 3\sigma$ acceptance interval, which is the standard quality control interval. For a sample of size $n = 10$,

$$\sigma_{\bar{X}} = \frac{2}{\sqrt{10}}$$
$$= 0.63$$
$$\pm 3\sigma = \pm 3(0.63)$$
$$\pm 3\sigma = \pm 1.89$$
$$250 \pm 1.89$$
$$248.11 \text{ to } 251.89$$

The sample mean of 248 is outside this interval and we conclude that the process is unlikely to have a mean of $\mu = 250$. The machine should be checked and the problem corrected.

9.3 First we compute the standard deviation of the sample proportion:

$$\sigma_{\hat{P}}^2 = \frac{\pi(1-\pi)}{n}$$

$$= \frac{0.40(1-0.40)}{400}$$

$$= 0.0006$$

$$\sigma_{\hat{P}} = 0.0245$$

The 95% acceptance interval is

$$0.40 - Z_{0.025} \times 0.0245 \text{ to } 0.40 + Z_{0.025} \times 0.0245$$

which is 0.352 to 0.448. If the sample proportion were below 0.352, Sarah would cancel the project, and if it were above 0.448, she would have strong evidence that the population proportion is above 40%. Sample proportions within the acceptance interval would be consistent with a belief that the market population proportion is 0.40 and that she should proceed with the project. If the sample size were 800, the standard deviation would be

$$\sigma_{\bar{X}} = \sqrt{\frac{0.40(1-0.40)}{800}} = 0.0173$$

and the acceptance interval would be between 0.366 and 0.434.

9.4 From Figure 9.8 we know that the lower limit can be computed from

$$C_L = \frac{(n-1)S_x^2}{\sigma^2}$$

$$12.401 = \frac{(25-1)S_x^2}{100}$$

and therefore

$$S_x^2 = 51.67$$

The upper limit can be computed from

$$C_U = \frac{(n-1)S_x^2}{\sigma^2}$$

$$39.364 = \frac{(25-1)S_x^2}{100}$$

and therefore

$$S_x^2 = 164.02$$

Mr. Melson knows that the acceptance interval for the sample variance when $\sigma^2 = 100$ and $n = 25$ is

$$51.67 \leq S_x^2 \leq 164.02$$

The interval for the standard deviation is

$$7.19 \le S_x \le 12.81$$

These intervals can be reduced by using a larger sample size.

CHAPTER PROBLEMS

9.1   In this problem you will conduct a small version of the classic experiments that were
used to establish our present understanding of sampling distributions. The objective is to
help you understand the rich base of research that supports procedures that statisticians
and analysts treat as based on "common sense" or "intuition." We first need a simple
random process whose behavior is easily understood. A six-sided die will serve this
purpose very nicely. You may wish to work on this problem with a friend. Two people
can carry out the work much faster and you will be able to discuss the results.
(a) Roll the die 100 times and prepare a frequency distribution and histogram for the
digit that was on top after each roll. What is the theoretical probability distribution
function for this process? Do the results of your experiment appear to support this
theoretical probability model?
(b) Roll a pair of dice or roll one die twice and note the mean of the two digits that
were on top. Repeat this experiment 100 times and prepare a frequency distribution
and histogram of the means. The means obtained from this experiment are sample
means ($n = 2$) for random samples from a process that has a uniform probability
distribution. Compare the frequency distribution and histogram with those obtained
in part (a). Write a short description of your observations.
(c) Roll five dice or roll one die five times and note the mean of the five digits that appear on top. Repeat this experiment 100 times and prepare a frequency distribution
and histogram of the sample means. Compare the frequency distribution with those
from parts (a) and (b) and write a short description of your observations.
(d) Repeat part (c) by rolling 10 dice or one die 10 times. Compare the frequency
distributions for the random samples of size 1, 2, 5, and 10. Write a short description
of your conclusions.

9.2   In this problem you are asked to describe the likely results of an experiment without
actually carrying out the work. Your answer should be based on your understanding
of probability distributions and sampling distributions. Go to a randomly selected page
of your telephone directory and note the last digit of each telephone number. Prepare
frequency distributions for the means of samples of size 1, 2, 5, 10, and 20 last digits. How would these frequency distributions compare? If you had carried out the experiment, what conclusions concerning the distributions of sample means would you
report?

9.3   A recent national examination was used to select economics and business students for
internships with a major national firm. The test scores were normally distributed with a
mean of 100 and a variance of 225. A random sample of $n = 25$ test scores was obtained
and the mean score computed. Determine the probability that the sample mean is:
(a) Between 95 and 105.
(b) Less than 94.
(c) Greater than 103.

9.4 A complex electronic process generates the following five responses, each with the same probability: $-4, -2, 0, +2, +4$.
(a) Construct the sampling distribution for the sample means given samples of size $n = 2$. Assume sampling without replacement.
(b) Compute the approximate 80% acceptance interval for the distribution of sample means ($n = 2$). Assume sampling without replacement.
(c) Construct the approximate sampling distribution for sample means of size $n = 25$ and compute the approximate 95% acceptance interval. This problem will be much simpler if you recall the central limit theorem.

9.5 The weight of frozen turkeys from the Haugen packing plant is known to have a mean of 20 pounds with a variance of 9.
(a) What is the probability of finding a turkey with weight less than 11 pounds?
(b) A random sample of five turkeys is obtained. What is the probability that the mean weight is between 19 and 21 pounds?
(c) What is the probability that the mean weight from part (b) is greater than 22 pounds?

9.6 The accounts receivable for Midwest Office Supplies, Inc. has a mean of $300 with a variance of 10,000.
(a) A random sample of four accounts is selected. What is the probability that the mean is between $350 and $450?
(b) Another random sample of six accounts had a mean of $250. What is the probability of obtaining a mean of $250 or less?
(c) A random sample of five accounts had a mean of $450. Does this sample seem strange given the population mean and variance?

9.7 Southeast Stampings, Inc. produces refrigerator doors with a width that is normally distributed with $\mu = 28$ inches and $\sigma^2 = 0.04$. Random samples of size $n = 5$ are obtained routinely for quality control monitoring.
(a) Define an interval within which 80% of the sample means should occur.
(b) Define an interval within which 98% of the sample means should occur.
(c) What is the probability that the sample mean is greater than 28.03 inches?

9.8 Charlie Johnson, the economist, wants to study the effect of shopping centers on small hardware stores. From a five-year-old study he finds that mean daily sales for small hardware stores were $2000 with a variance of 40,000. He selects a random sample of 36 small hardware stores and obtains their mean daily sales. The sample mean will be used to determine if there has been a change in the sales level for these stores. All sales are measured in real dollars that have been adjusted for inflation.
(a) Construct a 95% acceptance interval for the sample mean ($n = 36$). Assume no change in sales.
(b) What is the smallest sample mean that would support the belief that small hardware store sales have not been reduced? Use the results from part (a).
(c) Assume that the sample mean is $20 more than the minimum value indicated in part (b). Can you now state that small hardware store sales have not decreased and be quite confident of your conclusion?

9.9 Amalgamated Jelly Beans, Inc. claims that 30% of its jelly beans are black.
(a) A random sample of 100 beans is found to contain 38 black jelly beans. What is the probability of 38 or more black jelly beans in the random sample of 100 given that $P = 0.30$ are black?

(b) Define an interval for the sample proportion of black jelly beans that will include 97% of the samples.

(c) Define an interval that will include 90% of the samples.

9.10 Midwest Office Supplies has an objective of having no more than 10% of its accounts receivable older than 30 days.

(a) A random sample of $n = 121$ accounts receivable contained 16 accounts older than 30 days. What is the probability of this sample result given that their objective is being met?

(b) Define an upper limit proportion, $\hat{P}_c$, such that 99% of the samples would have a sample proportion, $\hat{P}$, less than the upper limit.

(c) Define an upper limit such that 80% of the samples would have a sample proportion, $\hat{P}$, less than the upper limit.

9.11 A recent presidential commission stated that 20% of males had alcoholic tendencies. Dr. Spock has conducted studies in small midwestern cities to determine if they follow the national pattern of male alcoholism.

(a) In city A a random sample of $n = 100$ males found that 14 had alcoholic tendencies. What is the probability of this result given the commission statement?

(b) Define a proportion interval that would include 98% of the sample proportions given $n = 225$ and that the presidential commission is correct.

(c) What is the probability of obtaining a sample proportion between 0.16 and 0.26 using a random sample of size $n = 155$, assuming that the presidential commission is correct?

9.12 A small northern Michigan town has been offered the opportunity to be the location for a nuclear waste disposal facility. The facility would provide 250 jobs with above-average wages. A local group is concerned about the possible environmental effect and has petitioned the county government to have a referendum concerning the necessary zoning approval that would be required for this facility. The company that would build and operate the plant wants to begin preliminary design of the plant. However, it will only do so if there is evidence that at least 50% or more of the citizens will support the plant in the election. The company obtains a random sample of 400 registered voters and asks each if they would support the facility. Using a 95% two-tailed acceptance interval, indicate the minimum sample proportion that would be needed to recommend that the company proceed with its preliminary design. (*Hint:* Construct an acceptance interval and determine the smallest sample proportion greater than 0.50 that would lead you to conclude that more than 50% would support the facility.)

9.13 Larry Smith, the president of Golden Grain Cereals, wishes to study the market for his proposed new cereal Sugar Crunchies. Larry believes that 30% of the people in his city of 1,000,000 would purchase Sugar Crunchies. Based on the assumption that he is correct, answer the following questions:

(a) Define a random variable and a probability model for the response from each person who is asked whether or not he or she would purchase Sugar Crunchies.

(b) Define the exact sampling distribution for the sample mean response given that a random sample of size 10 people are asked if they would purchase Sugar Crunchies and they answer either yes (1) or no (0).

(c) Compute the mean and variance for the sample mean response from part (b).

(d) What is the probability that the sample mean is 0.10 or less?

(e) What is the probability that the sample mean is 0.70 or more?

9.14 After her unsuccessful attempt to market a new toothpaste, Sarah Farrel, president of Magic Tooth, Inc., decides to test market a classical replacement set of teeth for people over age 75. The product would be called Pegatooth. Her accountants tell her that the product must sell to 40% of the target market. She decides to obtain a random sample of 400 persons and ask them if they would purchase Pegatooth. What is the 95% acceptance interval for the sample proportion? Explain how she would use this acceptance interval to make her decision about marketing the new product. If she used a random sample of size 800, what would be the new acceptance interval?

9.15 A noted researcher has obtained what he believes is a random sample of size 2 from a population with a mean $\mu = 100$ and variance $\sigma^2 = 32$.

(a) What is the probability that the sample mean is greater than 105?

(b) You discover that the sample observations have a correlation of $\rho = 0.50$ and thus the sample is not random. Given this new information, what is the probability that the sample mean is greater than 105?

(c) Given these results, present an argument in favor of random samples.

9.16 You have just completed a random sample political poll for your favorite candidate. From the sample of 900 voters a total of 475 indicated that they would vote for your candidate. What can you say about the chances of your candidate winning the election? (She wins if she receives the vote of more than 50% of the voters.)

9.17 It is well known that the population mean family income in Greenbriar City is 50,000. A fellow student claims that he has obtained a random sample of 25 families from Greenbriar City and asks your help in the analysis. You find that the sample mean $\bar{Y} = 25,000$ and the sample standard deviation $S_Y = 10,000$. What do you tell your fellow student about his sample?

9.18 You are interested in determining the mean family income for the residents of Consumption City, a typical midwestern city. The mean family income is a key variable in deciding whether to locate a new shopping center in Consumption City. From a random sample of 100 families, you compute the sample mean $\bar{Y} = 20,000$ and the sample variance $S^2 = 100,000,000$.

(a) What is the approximate probability of obtaining a sample mean of 20,000 or more above the following population means: $\mu = 16,000$, 14,000, 18,000, and 19,000; or 20,000 or less below the following population means: $\mu = 22,000$ and 24,000. [*Hint:* Because the sample size is large ($n = 100$) the normal probability distribution can be used to approximate the t distribution.]

(b) Based on your analysis in part (a), which of the six values of μ would you select as the population mean? Explain your selection.

9.19 A national study has reported that the weekly consumption of fish by college students has a mean of 20 grams per week. You wish to determine if the students on your campus follow the national pattern of fish consumption. A random sample of 25 students is selected and it is found that their total weekly consumption of fish is 250 grams. In addition, the sum of all students' consumption squared is 62,500. Do the students on your campus consume fish according to the national pattern? Clearly define the statistical model and analysis procedures used to answer this question.

9.20 Golden Grain Cereal, Inc. distributes its cereals in 16-ounce plastic bags to minimize packaging costs. The package filling process produces packages whose weight has a normal probability distribution with a standard deviation of 0.3 ounce and a mean of 16.4 ounces. Mean weight is set above the nominal weight to ensure that only a small percentage of the packages weigh less than 16 ounces. Cereal packaging is monitored by obtaining a random sample of 10 packages each day and measuring the exact weight of each package. The sample mean package weights are plotted daily on a chart so that production management can monitor the process and determine if they are deviating from the expected standard.
   (a) What is the probability distribution, including mean and standard deviation, of the sample means?
   (b) Compute a lower acceptance level such that the probability is less than 0.05 that the sample mean is less than this level.
   (c) Compute a 95% acceptance interval for the sample means.

9.21 The Golden Grain Cereal Company (Problem 9.20) also wishes to monitor the variance of package weights by using its random sample of 10 packages. Construct a 95% acceptance interval for the sample variance S^2 computed from the random sample.

9.22 The government has established a complex income maintenance program that is designed to raise annual family incomes to an average level of $15,000. The program planners also believe that the standard deviation of family incomes will be 2000. A random sample of 25 families will be obtained and their annual income will be carefully measured.
   (a) What is the approximate probability distribution of the mean income for the random sample of size 25 given that the program is successful?
   (b) What are the mean and the standard deviation?
   (c) Construct a 95% acceptance interval for the sample mean assuming that the program achieves its objectives.
   (d) Construct a 95% acceptance interval for the sample variance S^2 of the family incomes given that the original assumption about the standard deviation of family incomes is correct.

9.23 Consider again the income maintenance program described in Problem 9.22. At present the mean family income is $10,000, which is below the poverty level.
   (a) Compute an upper acceptance value such that the probability is 0.95 that a sample mean ($n = 25$) is less than this value given the present mean family income of $10,000 with standard deviation of 2000.
   (b) How large a sample mean would be needed to conclude that the program was successful in raising the mean family income above $10,000?
   (c) Construct a 95% acceptance interval for the sample variance.

9.24 The Akimoto Tool Company is considering the purchase of 30 computer-controlled machine tools for use in its production of precision automobile parts. Two models are in final consideration. One is produced by the Kohl Company in West Germany and the other by Smith Tools in the United States. They decide to conduct tests of the two machines to compare the variance of parts produced on the machines. Manufacturers' specifications indicate the same variance for their machining operations. Akimoto obtains a random sample of 25 copies of the same part produced on each of the two machines.

(a) Construct a 90% acceptance interval for the ratio of the sample variances obtained from the two random samples of size $n = 25$.

(b) How would you use this acceptance interval and the results of the two random samples to advise Akimoto Tool with respect to its purchase?

9.25   The Akimoto Tool Company claims that 90% of the parts produced in its factory will meet the rigorous standards imposed by Bayerische Motor Werks. A random sample of 100 parts is obtained and the number of substandard parts is determined.

(a) What is the probability distribution of the number of defective parts?

(b) What is the upper 95% acceptance level for the number of defective parts in the sample?

(c) Assume that only 80% of the parts produced meet the standards. What is the lower 95% acceptance level for the number of defective parts in the sample?

9.26   Write a short discussion that indicates why the Student t distribution should be used to compute acceptance intervals when only the sample variance for a normally distributed random variable is available.

9.27   Write a paragraph that presents the key results from the central limit theorem. Discuss why these results are so important for statistical applications in economics and business.

9.28   The citizens of a small village in southern India have historically been able to consume an average of 2000 calories per day. Government health officials believe that this level is too low for adequate health and human development. As a result, they have established an agricultural assistance plan that will provide the farmers with new seed types, fertilizer, and training for their use. Their goal is to raise the average daily consumption by 100 calories during the first year. After one year a random sample of $n = 25$ citizens is selected and their average daily food consumption is measured. The 25 citizens consumed a total of 53,500 calories per day. A recent major study of food consumption in southern India stated that the population variance in the mean average daily food consumption for a sample of 10 farmers was equal to 1000. (The variance of the sample mean when $n = 10$ is equal to 1000.) Determine the probability of obtaining the food consumption indicated for the people in the sample if:

(a) There had been no change in average daily food consumption in the village population.

(b) Average daily food consumption in the population had increased to 2100 calories per day.

(c) Has the program achieved its one-year goal?

9.29   The mean annual family income in Eagle Gulch has historically been $10,000 with a variance of 1,000,000. A random sample of 16 families was obtained and their average annual family income was $10,400.

(a) What is the probability that these families come from Eagle Gulch? (Assume that the central limit theorem applies for the sample mean.)

(b) A friend has suggested that these people might have come from Green River, where the mean family income is $11,000 with a variance of 1,000,000. What is the probability that they come from Green River?

9.30   Consolidated Parts, Inc. produces pistons for high-performance automobile engines. Piston diameters are known to be normally distributed if the manufacturing process is operating properly. Consolidated guarantees that the diameter of a single piston will have a 95% acceptance interval of 8.0 centimeters plus or minus 0.002 centimeter. The following questions refer to the quality control sampling process for these piston rods:

(a) What are the population standard deviation and variance if the pistons are meeting the specifications?

(b) A random sample of 10 pistons was measured and the average dimension was 8.001 centimeters. Does this result suggest that the manufacturing specification is not being met? [Use the variance from part (a).]

9.31 Consider Problem 9.30 involving Consolidated Parts, Inc.

(a) Construct a 95% acceptance interval for the sample variance obtained from the sample of 10 pistons.

(b) From a second random sample of 25 pistons the sample variance was 0.000002. Does that result cause concern about the variability of the manufacturing process?

9.32 A political candidate obtains a random sample of 900 voters. From this random sample, 47% support her for elected office.

(a) What is the probability that this sample came from a population in which 50% of the total voters support her?

(b) A second random sample was obtained which again showed that 47% of the sample supported her. If the probability of obtaining this sample is 0.04 or less, what was the sample size?

9.33 The admissions department of a prestigious selective liberal arts college has room for 850 students in next year's first-year class. This 850 would provide an ideal balance between dormitory and classroom space and next year's budget requirements. They also know that 60% of those admitted will eventually enroll.

(a) Suppose that 1450 students are admitted. What is the probability that more than 850 will enroll?

(b) What is the probability that 850 or less will enroll?

(c) Repeat parts (a) and (b) assuming first that 1400 are admitted and then that 1500 are admitted.

(d) Which level of admission would you recommend if you are the treasurer?

9.34 A major distributor of mixed nuts is concerned about being cited by a consumer group which claims that companies which distribute mixed nuts are substituting an excessive fraction of low-priced peanuts for cashews, walnuts, and other more expensive nuts. This distributor claims that at least 80% of each 16-ounce package consists of the more expensive nuts. The distributor contacts the consumer group and offers to pay for a random sampling study by an independent and respected quality control consultant. The company agrees to a test in which 25 randomly selected packages will be separated into high-quality nuts and peanuts. The high-quality nuts will be weighed. If the average weight of high-quality nuts is greater than 12.6 ounces, the consumer group will announce that the distributor is selling high-quality mixed nuts that provide good value for the consumer. If the weight is less than or equal to 12.4 ounces, the distributors product will receive negative publicity. Note that 80% of 16 ounces is 12.8 ounces. The distributor knows that the process for placing high-quality nuts in the package has a variance $\sigma^2 = 1$ and it wants the probability of receiving negative publicity to be less than 0.005. The packaging machine can be set for any mean weight μ of high-quality nuts. Determine what weight should be set for the component of the packaging machine:

(a) That adds the high-quality nuts.

(b) If the distributor desires that the probability of favorable publicity is at least 0.95.

9.35   A college offers admission to 500 students and 300 accept. The director of admissions believes that the pattern of acceptances is likely to continue for the rest of the year. Thus she decides to assume that the probability of acceptance by a student offered admission can be computed using the relative frequency argument

$$P = \frac{300}{500} = 0.60$$

(a) If she is correct, what are the sample proportion and variance for the next 100 students offered admission? What critical assumption did you make to answer this question?

(b) Can you conclude that the sample number of students who accept can be approximated by a normal distribution? Present an argument for your conclusion.

(c) Given the results of parts (a) and (b), define an interval that will include 99% of the number who accept given random samples of size $n = 150$.

9.36   The price of XR7 computer chips is known to have a mean $\mu = 5$ with a variance $\sigma^2 = 9$. From past experience it is known that the number of chips ordered by a customer is defined exactly by the demand function $Y = 5000 - 300X$, where Y is the quantity purchased in this order given and X is the price per chip. In this market, prices are set by daily commodity market bidding. Customers understand the distribution of price and adjust their purchases to the foregoing demand model.

(a) What are the mean and variance of the quantity purchased?

(b) What is the probability that a single order will request less than 2000 chips?

(c) A random sample of $n = 10$ orders is obtained. What is the 98% acceptance interval for the sample mean order size?

Problems 9.37 to 9.44 apply methods that are commonly used in quality control applications.

9.37   Consolidated Machining produces gears with a diameter of 10 centimeters and a variance of 0.0001 when the gear cutting machine is working correctly. A random sample of size $n = 5$ is selected.

(a) What interval would include 99% of the sample means given correct operation?

(b) What is the approximate probability that the sample variance is greater than 0.00025?

(c) Define an interval that will include 98% of the sample variance given $n = 5$.

9.38   The variance of a part's dimension in an automobile stamping plant was originally set at 0.0004 inch.

(a) A recent sample of $n = 40$ pieces had a sample standard deviation of $S = 0.025$. Has there been a change from the original machine setting?

(b) Another sample of size $n = 24$ was taken from a parallel process with the same original setting. The sample standard deviation was $S = 0.021$. Does this indicate a change from the original setting?

9.39   The fat content of deluxe hamburger at George's market is advertised as having no more than 25 units of fat. To accomplish this objective the hamburger preparation process has been set at a mean $\mu = 20$ points with a variance $\sigma^2 = 9$. The amount of fat in any single 1-pound package is assumed to be normally distributed with the foregoing mean and variance.

(a) What is the probability that a single package will have a fat content that exceeds the guarantee?

(b) A random sample of 20 packages was selected at a particular store and the sample variance $S^2 = 25.6$. Do they have a problem? If yes, explain what they need to do to correct the problem.

(c) What will happen to the percentage of hamburger packages that exceed the guarantee if the problem in part (b) is not solved? Explain why.

(d) Another random sample taken at a different store had a sample variance $S^2 = 16$. Does this result indicate a problem?

9.40   George's market, from Problem 9.39, decides to set up a quality control sampling procedure to monitor the fat content of their hamburger. The fat content in each 1-pound package is normally distributed with a mean $\mu = 20$ and a variance $\sigma^2 = 9$ when the system is operating properly. They plan to obtain a random sample of $n = 25$ packages every month and measure the fat content of each package.

(a) Compute the upper limit for the sample variance, S^2, such that only 1% of the sample variances will exceed this limit if the process mean and variance are at their original settings.

(b) Compute a similar upper limit such that only 5% of the sample variances will exceed their upper limit.

9.41   Chips Forever, Inc., a regional manufacturer of snack foods, has set the moisture content of its deli chips production line such that the moisture content of each bag of chips is normally distributed with a mean $\mu = 10$ and a variance $\sigma^2 = 4$. These settings are needed to ensure that the weight and the crispness are maintained at satisfactory levels for customers.

(a) What percentage of the bags have a moisture content that exceeds 14?

(b) A random sample of size $n = 14$ bags is obtained and the standard deviation is $S = 2.7$. Is the probability of this sample standard deviation less than 0.05?

(c) A random sample of size $n = 41$ is obtained and the standard deviation is $S = 2.5$. Is the probability of this sample standard deviation less than 0.05?

9.42   Two machines are set to produce parts whose dimension has the same mean and variance. As part of the regular quality control monitoring, a random sample of 25 parts was obtained from each machine and the sample variances were $S_1^2 = 0.16$ and $S_2^2 = 0.20$.

(a) Are these two samples in agreement with the claim that each machine has the same variance?

(b) The sample sizes were each increased to $n = 41$ and the same sample variances were obtained. Are these samples in agreement with the original claim?

(c) Samples were obtained from two other machines with the same mean and variance. The sample sizes were $n_1 = 16$ with a sample variance of $S_1^2 = 0.25$ and $n_2 = 30$ with a sample variance of $S_2^2 = 0.20$. Are these results in agreement with the claim of equal variance?

9.43   The Ace Delivery Service is doing a comparative study of delivery time performance in its two northern districts. Using a sample of size $n_1 = 30$ in district 1, the sample variance $S_1^2 = 9.5$. In district 2 the sample size was $n_2 = 40$ and the sample variance was $S_2^2 = 4.2$.

(a) Are these results likely if the variance in delivery time is supposed to be equal in both districts?

(b) Ten additional random observations were obtained from district 1 and the sample variance for the entire sample of 40 was found to be $S_1^2 = 7.6$. Does this result change your response to part (a)?

9.44 BBW Ltd. produces dark German bread using a variety of recipes originally obtained from Bavaria. The manufacturing process contains a number of interconnected units that mix, knead, and bake the bread. To ensure consistent high quality of their product, they are establishing a quality control system. They have asked for your assistance in designing a quality control acceptance chart for station 4. At station 4 the moisture content of the fixed-size sample should have a mean $\mu = 10$ grams. The variance of moisture content for individual observations is $\sigma^2 = 5$. Each day a random sample of size $n = 5$ will be obtained and the sample mean will be plotted on the acceptance chart. Construct a symmetric acceptance interval using a standard normal Z value equal to ± 3. Use this interval to prepare an acceptance chart with sequential days on the horizontal axis and the sample mean on the vertical axis. Show the interval on the chart.

APPENDIX: THEORY RELATED TO THE STUDENT t

A.1 Distribution Theory for Chi-Square

The chi-square distribution is derived from the standard normal random variable:

$$Z_i = \frac{x_i - \mu}{\sigma}$$

A chi-square with 1 degree of freedom is equal to the square of the standard normal Z:

$$\chi_{(1)}^2 = Z_i^2 = \left(\frac{x_i - \mu}{\sigma}\right)^2$$

If we add n chi-square random variables, each with 1 degree of freedom, we obtain a chi-square with n degrees of freedom:

$$\chi_{(n)}^2 = \sum_{i=1}^{n} Z_i^2 = \sum_{i=1}^{n} \frac{(x_i - \mu)^2}{\sigma^2}$$

Note that the numerator is the sum of squared variability of sample values about the population mean. By a series of algebraic steps we can also show that

$$\chi_{(n-1)}^2 = \sum_{i=1}^{n} \frac{(x_i - \bar{X})^2}{\sigma^2}$$

$$= \frac{(n-1)S_x^2}{\sigma^2}$$

The algebraic steps are

$$\chi_n^2 = \sum_{i=1}^{n} \frac{(x_i - \mu)^2}{\sigma^2}$$

$$= \sum_{i=1}^{n} \frac{(x_i - \bar{X} + \bar{X} - \mu)^2}{\sigma^2}$$

$$= \frac{\sum_{i=1}^{n}(x_i - \bar{X})^2 + \sum_{i=1}^{n}(\bar{X} - \mu)^2}{\sigma^2}$$

$$= \sum_{i=1}^{n} \frac{(x_i - \bar{X})^2}{\sigma^2} + \frac{n(\bar{X} - \mu)^2}{\sigma^2}$$

$$= \sum_{i=1}^{n} \frac{(x_i - \bar{X})^2}{\sigma^2} + \frac{(\bar{X} - \mu)^2}{\sigma^2/n}$$

$$= \chi_{(n-1)}^2 + \chi_{(1)}^2$$

The right-hand term involving $(\bar{X} - \mu)$ is a standard normal squared and hence has 1 degree of freedom. The other right-hand-side term must be a χ^2 with $n - 1$ degrees of freedom, because χ^2 terms are additive. From this analysis we see the link between the standard normal and the chi-square.

A.2 Derivation of the Student t

Gosset sought to develop a probability distribution for normally distributed random variables that did not include the population variance σ^2. As a result, he took the ratio of a standard normal divided by the square root of χ^2, which was divided by its degrees of freedom. In mathematical notation,

$$t = \frac{N(0, 1)}{\sqrt{\chi_{(n-1)}^2/(n - 1)}}$$

$$= \frac{(x - \mu)/\sigma}{\sqrt{S_x^2(n - 1)/\sigma^2(n - 1)}}$$

$$= \frac{x - \mu}{S_x}$$

The resulting t statistic has $n - 1$ degrees of freedom. Notice that the t probability distribution is based on normally distributed random variables. For applications we use the normal Z when the population variance σ^2 is available and the student t when only the sample variance S_x^2 is available. Statistical research using computer-generated random samples has shown that the t can be used to study the distribution of sample means even if the distribution of the individual random variables is not normal.

10

Estimation

*Statistics is a problem-solving discipline that enables us to use data
to understand systems and to answer questions.*

10.1 PARAMETER ESTIMATION

In Chapters 8 and 9 we learned about sampling and probability distributions for sample statistics. Now we are ready to develop procedures for estimating the parameters of probability distributions from sample data. Estimation begins with a random sample and an assumed family of probability distributions. Then the data are used to estimate the value of the probability distribution parameters. The procedures presented in this chapter reduce the probability of misleading conclusions.

George Edwards, production manager of Prairie Flower Cereal, wants to know the mean weight of bags of granola produced in the factory. This population mean can be estimated by using a random sample of packages, each of which is carefully weighed in the quality control laboratory. How should these individual sample results be combined to estimate the population mean weight? How much improvement in the estimate would result from a larger sample size? Are there errors in sampling that could seriously compromise the final estimate? In this chapter we answer questions such as these.

Statistics is a problem-solving discipline that enables us to use data to understand systems and to answer questions. Typical questions include:

1. What percentage of the population would purchase my product?
2. What is the average daily demand for breakfast cereal?
3. What is the per capita income in Egypt?
4. What is the per capita caloric intake for people in China?
5. How many defective computer chips per day would be expected when the production process is in control?

Typically, answers to these questions obtained from a sample of data must apply to an entire population. *Statistical inference*, including estimation and hypothesis testing, is used to help develop correct interpretations from sample data. In this chapter we emphasize estimation, and in Chapter 11, hypothesis testing. Both are developed from the distribution of sample statistics that we studied in Chapter 9, and there is considerable overlap in the applications.

Estimation produces both point estimators and interval estimators. Examples of point estimators include the percentage of people who would purchase a product or the mean family income in Fairmont, Minnesota. Interval estimators assign an interval or range of possible values. For example, the percentage of purchasers could be reported as 20% $\pm$ 5%. Both point estimators and interval estimators are computed using the distribution of sample statistics developed in Chapter 9. We develop this topic beginning with some formal definitions.

10.2 POINT ESTIMATORS

The first objective in a statistical study is to obtain the single number that best represents the population of measurements. Throughout this chapter we use the following notations: θ represents the population parameter that we wish to estimate, and $\hat{\theta}$ is the sample statistic or point estimator of θ. For instance, θ could be the population mean weight of cereal boxes, μ, or the proportion of families that would purchase a particular cereal, π. Thus $\bar{X}$ and $\hat{P}$ are examples of estimators $\hat{\theta}$ of population parameters μ and π. In Chapter 2 these measures were introduced as descriptive statistics. Here we see how these descriptive sample measures can be used as the best estimate of the population mean or proportion.

Using our understanding of probability distributions we develop mathematical equations, called *estimators*, that can be used to compute point *estimates* for parameters (Key Idea 10.1). Given the random sample 5, 6, 7, the point estimate for the population mean is

$$\bar{X} = \frac{5 + 6 + 7}{3} = 6$$

The sample mean and median are examples of estimators for the population mean, μ. The sample mean has a smaller variance than the median for normally distributed random variables. The sample proportion is an estimator for the probability of success in the binomial probability distribution. The most important properties of estimators are presented next.

10.2.1 Properties of Estimators

In this section we define several important properties of good estimators: unbiasedness, efficiency, consistency, and sufficiency. For the business and economic problems emphasized in this book, the most important properties are unbiasedness (Key Idea 10.2) and efficiency (Key Idea 10.3). We include the others for completeness.

No single estimate from a sample will provide the exact value of the parameter. If the expected value of a point estimator, $\hat{\theta}$, is less than the parameter, θ, this indicates that the given point estimator has a high chance of underestimating the population

Key Idea 10.1: Point Estimators

A **point estimator** $\hat{\theta}$ is a function of sample data that provides an estimate of an unknown parameter θ. For example, the sample mean

$$\bar{X} = \frac{\sum_{i=1}^{n} x_i}{n}$$

is a point estimator ($\hat{\theta} = \bar{X}$) of the population mean μ ($\theta = \mu$).

A point estimate is a number that is computed from sample data using the point estimator. Point estimators are random variables because they are functions of sample observations that are random variables.

Key Idea 10.2: Unbiased Estimator

An **unbiased estimator**, $\hat{\theta}$, is an estimator whose expected value or average is the value of the desired parameter. Mathematically, an estimator is unbiased if

$$E[\hat{\theta}] = \theta$$

We use the probability distribution of an estimator to compute its expected value. An estimator is unbiased if the expected value of the estimator is equal to the parameter. Both the sample mean and the sample proportion are unbiased estimators.

Key Idea 10.3: Efficient Estimator

In a set of unbiased estimators the one with the smallest variance is said to be the most **efficient**. The relative efficiency of two estimators is defined as the ratio of the variances of two estimators.

parameter. However, for unbiased estimators, positive and negative deviations tend to cancel over a large number of samples.

Within the set of unbiased estimators we would like to choose the estimator with the smallest variance (Key Idea 10.3). To illustrate the concept, consider a random sample of four observations from a population with mean μ and variance σ^2. Suppose that we consider two estimators of the population mean μ. The first is the sample mean, $\overline{X}$, and the second, X^*, is obtained by multiplying each of the first two observations by 0.10 and each of the last two observations by 0.40. The expected values for the two estimators are

$$\mu_{\overline{X}} = E\left[\frac{x_1}{4} + \frac{x_2}{4} + \frac{x_3}{4} + \frac{x_4}{4}\right]$$

$$= \frac{4 \times \mu}{4}$$

$$= \mu$$

$$\mu_{X^*} = E[0.1x_1 + 0.1x_2 + 0.4x_3 + 0.4x_4]$$

$$= 0.1\mu + 0.1\mu + 0.4\mu + 0.4\mu$$

$$= \mu$$

Thus we see that both $\overline{X}$ and X^* are unbiased. Now consider their variances:

$$\sigma_{\overline{X}}^2 = \frac{\sigma^2}{4}$$

$$= 0.25\sigma^2$$

$$\sigma_{X^*}^2 = 0.1^2\sigma^2 + 0.1^2\sigma^2 + 0.4^2\sigma^2 + 0.4^2\sigma^2$$

$$= (0.01 + 0.01 + 0.16 + 0.16)\sigma^2$$

$$= 0.34\sigma^2$$

Thus we see that the relative efficiency of $\overline{X}$ with respect to X^* is

$$\frac{\sigma_{X^*}^2}{\sigma_{\overline{X}}^2} = \frac{0.34\sigma^2}{0.25\sigma^2} = 1.36$$

We have shown that the sample mean $\overline{X}$ is 36% more efficient than X^*. Estimates obtained by using X^* would require 36% more sample observations to obtain the same variance compared to estimates obtained by using $\overline{X}$. The sample mean uses each observation equally, while the other estimator combines them in a nonuniform way.

Consistency and sufficiency are two additional properties of a good estimator which are more important in higher-level statistics courses and are included here briefly for completeness (Key Ideas 10.4 and 10.5). The difference between an unbiased estimator and a consistent estimator can be seen in the following example. The sample variance,

$$S_x^2 = \frac{\sum_{i=1}^{n}(x_i - \overline{X})^2}{n - 1}$$

Key Idea 10.4: Consistent Estimator

A **consistent estimator** is an estimator that approaches the true value of the parameter as the sample size increases.

Key Idea 10.5: Sufficient Estimator

A **sufficient estimator** is one that uses all the information in a sample.

---

is an unbiased estimator of the population variance σ_y^2. However, the estimator

$$S_*^2 = \frac{\sum_{i=1}^n (x_i - \bar{X})^2}{n}$$

is a biased estimator with the bias equal to

$$\text{bias} = S_x^2 - S_*^2 = \frac{S_x^2}{n}$$

As the sample size n becomes large, the bias approaches zero. Thus S_*^2 is a consistent estimator, whereas S_x^2 is both unbiased and consistent. Note that all unbiased estimators are consistent but not all consistent estimators are unbiased.

In applied statistics the biased estimator that includes division by n instead of by $n - 1$ is often used when the sample size is over 100. In certain advanced econometric work it is not possible to obtain unbiased estimators, but consistent estimators can be obtained and are used.

Consistency is a "large sample" property, in contrast to unbiasedness, which is a "small sample" property. The sample mean and the sample proportion are consistent estimators in addition to being unbiased.

Rigorous mathematical use of the sufficiency property (Key Idea 10.5) is beyond the scope of this book. However, note that the sample median, as an estimator, uses only the rank order of the observations. The sample mean uses both the order and the differences between the observations. Thus the sample mean uses all of the information contained in the sample, whereas the sample median does not. Thus the sample mean is a sufficient estimator but the sample median is not. As we mentioned before, for the business and economic problems emphasized in this book, unbiasedness and efficiency are the most important properties. An unbiased estimator such as the sample mean is preferred because its average based on many samples would approach the population mean. An efficient estimator is preferred because smaller variance implies greater precision.

10.2.2 Mean Square Error

We have emphasized that errors can be either random or fixed for each observation. Random errors are modeled by a probability distribution function and their expected value is zero. Bias is a fixed difference between the expected value of an estimator and the true value of the parameter. For unbiased estimators the magnitude of random error is measured by the variance. The variance for the sample mean and sample proportion decreases with increased sample size. Bias does not always decrease with increased sample size. A broader measure of estimator error, which includes both random error and bias is the mean square error (Key Idea 10.6). Mean square error is included because in practice both random error and bias contribute to a lack of precision in statistical measurements and we need a way to combine both types of error.

Key Idea 10.6: Mean Square Error

The **mean square error** (MSE) is the sum of the variance and the bias squared for an estimator. In mathematical terms,

$$\text{MSE}(\hat{\theta}) = E[(\theta - \hat{\theta})^2]$$
$$= E[(\hat{\theta} - E[\hat{\theta}])^2] + (E[\hat{\theta}] - \theta)^2$$
$$= \sigma_{\hat{\theta}}^2 + (\text{bias})^2$$

A consistent estimator has its mean square error approach zero as the sample size n becomes large.

Example 10.1   Estimating Family Income

Gertrude Jones has been the mayor of a large eastern city for the past 10 years. She is now running for governor. Her campaign emphasizes the high level of family income that resulted from her program to stimulate economic growth in the city. After the program 50% of the families have a mean income of $\mu_1 = \$15,000$ per year while the other 50% have a mean income of $\mu_2 = \$45,000$ per year. The variance of incomes in each group is the same. In her campaign literature Gertrude claims that average family income is $35,150, based on a "scientific sample" of the residents. To obtain the number for her political campaign, Gertrude obtained a random sample of $n = 200$ families, allocated equally to each subpopulation. Unfortunately, only 40% of the people contacted in the low-income group agreed to participate, while 80% of the higher-income group participated. What advice would you give to her opponent, Grace Smith, to help Grace counter the results of Gertrude's income sample survey?

Solution   A reasonable first step would be to determine if Gertrude's income estimate is biased. We suspect that it is because of the unequal response rate for the two subgroups. The city population includes two distinct subpopulations, with mean incomes of $\mu_1 = 15{,}000$ and $\mu_2 = 45{,}000$. The sample means $\bar{X}_1$ and $\bar{X}_2$ from each sector provide unbiased estimates of the sector population means. A random sample allocated equally to each sector would provide an unbiased sample mean $\bar{X}$ as follows:

$$\mu_{\bar{X}} = \frac{100 \times E[\bar{X}_1] + 100 \times E[\bar{X}_2]}{200}$$

$$= 0.50\mu_1 + 0.50\mu_2$$

$$= 0.50(15{,}000) + 0.50(45{,}000)$$

$$= 30{,}000$$

However, the unequal response rates could result in a biased estimator of the mean. We will test for bias by obtaining the expected value of Gertrude's estimate, $\bar{X}_b$, where

$$\bar{X}_b = \frac{40 \times \bar{X}_1 + 80 \times \bar{X}_2}{120}$$

$$E[\bar{X}_b] = \frac{40 \times E[\bar{X}_1] + 80 \times E[\bar{X}_2]}{120}$$

$$= 0.333\mu_1 + 0.667\mu_2$$

$$= 0.333(15{,}000) + 0.667(45{,}000)$$

$$= 35{,}000$$

The nonresponse bias is

$$\text{bias} = E[\bar{X}_b] - \mu_{\bar{X}}$$

$$= 35{,}000 - 30{,}000$$

$$= 5000$$

The biased sample on average overstates the income by 5000. You should advise Grace that Gertrude's income estimates are too high because a greater percentage of high-income people responded to the sampling survey than low-income people. Non-response bias cannot be reduced by taking a larger sample. Thus the biased estimator $\bar{X}_b$ is also not consistent. Grace should conduct her own random sampling study that corrects for the nonresponse bias. For example, the subpopulation sample means could be weighted equally because they each represent 50% of the population.   □

Example 10.2   Estimation of per Capita Agricultural Investment

You have just been appointed director of an economic development project for an economically depressed farming region. An important baseline measurement is the per capita agricultural income in the region to be served by the project. Your predecessor issued contracts to two consulting companies: Eastern Economic Research, Inc. and Burke Associates, Inc. From your previous experience you know that Burke uses poor measurement techniques. Their estimates have a variance that is five times larger than the variance for the estimates provided by Eastern. You receive the reports and find that Eastern estimates the per capita income as $\bar{X}_1 = \$800$ per year, while Burke estimates the per capita income as $\bar{X}_2 = \$1200$ per year. How should you use the estimates to obtain an estimator with the smallest mean square error?

Solution A commonly used approach for obtaining an estimator from two estimates is to compute their simple average. However, this procedure will not provide the most efficient (i.e., minimum variance) estimator when the variance of one estimate is higher than the other. Define the variance for the Eastern estimate as σ^2 and then the variance for the Burke estimate is $5\sigma^2$. The simplistic estimator $\bar{X}$ would be

$$\bar{X} = 0.5\bar{X}_1 + 0.5\bar{X}_2$$

The variance of this estimator is

$$\sigma_{\bar{X}}^2 = (0.5)^2\sigma^2(\bar{X}_1) + (0.5)^2\sigma^2(\bar{X}_2)$$
$$= 0.25\sigma^2 + 0.25 \times 5\sigma^2$$
$$= 1.50\sigma^2$$

if the two estimates are independent.

Notice that a more efficient estimator could be obtained by simply throwing away the Burke estimate. The most efficient estimator can be obtained from the function

$$X^* = a\bar{X}_1 + (1-a)\bar{X}_2$$

by finding the value of a that results in the minimum variance $\sigma_{\bar{X}*}^2$ estimator. Using calculus[1] the value of a can be shown to be $\frac{5}{6}$.[2] The minimum variance estimator is therefore

$$\sigma_{\bar{X}*}^2 = \left(\frac{5}{6}\right)^2\sigma^2 + \left(\frac{1}{6}\right)^2 5\sigma^2$$
$$= \frac{25}{36}\sigma^2 + \frac{5}{36}\sigma^2$$
$$= \frac{5}{6}\sigma^2$$

---

[1] Many of the concepts developed in this and later chapters will include sections that use calculus in the development. These sections are indicated by a star. You can learn the statistical procedures without these sections. However, your understanding will be increased if you can use these calculus-based sections.

[2] The derivation of a is as follows:

$$\sigma_{\bar{X}*}^2 = a^2\sigma^2(\bar{X}_1) + (1-a)^2\sigma^2(\bar{X}_2)$$
$$= a^2\sigma^2 + (1-a)^2 5\sigma^2$$
$$= \sigma^2(5 - 10a + 6a^2)$$
$$\frac{\partial(\sigma^2(X^*))}{\partial a} = \sigma^2(-10 + 12a) = 0$$
$$a = \frac{5}{6}$$

which is an improvement over using the Eastern estimate only. Thus the most efficient point estimate would be

$$X^* = \frac{5}{6}800 + \frac{1}{6}1200$$
$$= 867 \qquad \square$$

Practice Problem 10.1: Estimation of Part Dimension

A manufacturing process produces parts that have a critical dimension of 3.0 inches with a variance $\sigma^2 = 0.001$ when the process is operating properly. For each day's production two inspectors, A and B, each measure two randomly selected observations. The mean of the four observations is used as the estimate of the part dimension for that day.

(a) What is the expected value and the variance of the sample mean?

(b) Suppose that inspector A reads his instrument incorrectly and adds 0.02 inch to each measurement. What are the expected value and variance of the sample mean given this error?

(c) What is the bias for the expected value of the sample mean in part (b)?

(d) What is the mean square error for the expected value of the sample mean in part (b)? $\qquad \square$

The solutions for all Practice Problems are given at the end of the chapter.

Problem Exercises

10.1   A random sample of supermarket retail prices for canned beans provides the following data:

$$0.84 \qquad 0.78 \qquad 0.80 \qquad 0.75 \qquad 0.83$$

(a) Compute an unbiased estimator of the population mean.

(b) If the population variance for individual observations is $\sigma^2 = 10$, what is the variance of your unbiased estimator?

10.2   Return to Problem 10.1 to answer the following questions.

(a) Suppose that the first observation is discarded and the estimator is computed using only the last four observations. What is the efficiency of the estimator?

(b) Is this estimator unbiased?

10.3   A forest community is composed of groundhogs, who make their homes underground, and squirrels, who live in trees. A developer has proposed covering the land with 3 feet of new soil. However, he must submit an environmental impact statement that includes data on the responses of local residents. Thus he distributes a random sample survey instrument. Unfortunately only 50% of the groundhogs respond, while 95% of the squirrels respond. Comment on the expected value, bias, and efficiency of this sample.

10.4   Explain why both variance and bias squared are included in mean square error.

10.5   A random sample of size 4 is obtained from a population with a mean of $\mu = 100$ and a variance of $\sigma^2 = 121$. The population mean has two estimators: $\bar{X}$, which is the mean of all four observations, and X^*, which is computed by multiplying the first observation by one-half, the second by one-fourth, and the third and fourth each by one-eighth.

(a) Are these estimators unbiased?

(b) Does either estimator have a higher efficiency? Compute the efficiency of that estimator relative to the other estimator.

* 10.3 MAXIMUM LIKELIHOOD ESTIMATORS

Now that we have considered properties of estimators, we present one important procedure for obtaining estimators. This optional section is presented for those who seek a more complete understanding of the properties of estimators. The maximum likelihood procedure, developed by R. A. Fisher in the 1920s, is widely used and provides an important intuitive understanding of estimation (Key Idea 10.7). We will show that the sample mean and sample proportion are the desirable maximum likelihood estimators for the population mean and proportion. Thus you will be able to see an important link between sampling distributions and the most used point estimates for business and economics applications.

---

* Key Idea 10.7: Maximum Likelihood Estimators

Maximum likelihood estimators are obtained by finding the parameter value that gives the observed sample the highest probability of occurring.

Maximum likelihood estimators are consistent and approach a normal distribution as the sample size becomes large. They are not always unbiased, but the bias approaches zero as the sample size becomes large.

To understand the procedure, we first develop the idea of a likelihood function and contrast it to a probability distribution function. Before defining the likelihood function we review probability distribution functions.

A probability distribution function computes the probability of obtaining a specific number or range of numbers in a random sample given that we know the parameters of the probability distribution function. For example, assume that a process can be modeled by a binomial probability distribution function with parameter $\pi = 0.40$ and $n = 10$ observations. Suppose that from the 10 observations we have exactly four successes. From the tabulated binomial probabilities in Table A.5, we find that the probability of 4 out of 10 successes when $\pi = 0.40$ is 0.251. Alternatively, if π was assumed to be 0.30, the probability of 4 out of 10 successes would be 0.200. The probability distribution function provides

$$P(\text{data} \mid \text{parameters}) = P(X = 4 \mid \pi, n = 10)$$

For this example the specific function is

$$P(X = 4 \mid \pi = 0.4, n = 10) = C_x^n \pi^x (1 - \pi)^{n-x}$$
$$= C_4^{10} 0.40^4 (1 - 0.40)^{10-4}$$
$$= 0.251$$

Now consider the definition of a likelihood function (see Key Idea 10.8). For example, consider the binomial process, in which we have obtained $X = 4$ successes from a random sample of $n = 10$ trials. The likelihood of $\pi = 0.40$ is equal to the probability of obtaining 4 successes from 10 independent trials, given $\pi = 0.40$, which is 0.251. Similarly, the likelihood of $\pi = 0.30$ is 0.200. We can express the likelihood function L as

$$L(\text{parameter} \mid \text{data}) = L(\pi \mid X = 4, n = 10)$$

For this example the specific function is

$$L(\pi = 0.40 \mid X = 4, n = 10) = C_x^n \pi^x (1 - \pi)^{n-x}$$
$$= C_4^{10} 0.40^4 (1 - 0.40)^{10-4}$$
$$= 0.251$$

---

* Key Idea 10.8: Likelihood Function

A **likelihood function** computes the likelihood or probability of a specific parameter estimate given a sample of known data observations.

One way to implement the maximum likelihood procedure (Key Idea 10.9) is to compute the likelihood function for various values of the parameter and choose the parameter value that results in the largest value for the likelihood function. For the binomial problem with 4 out of 10 successes, the likelihood for selected values of π is

$$L(\pi = 0.10 \mid X = 4, n = 10) = C_4^{10} 0.10^4 0.90^6 = 0.011$$
$$L(\pi = 0.20 \mid X = 4, n = 10) = C_4^{10} 0.20^4 0.80^6 = 0.088$$
$$L(\pi = 0.30 \mid X = 4, n = 10) = C_4^{10} 0.30^4 0.70^6 = 0.200$$
$$L(\pi = 0.40 \mid X = 4, n = 10) = C_4^{10} 0.40^4 0.60^6 = 0.251$$
$$L(\pi = 0.50 \mid X = 4, n = 10) = C_4^{10} 0.50^4 0.50^6 = 0.205$$
$$L(\pi = 0.60 \mid X = 4, n = 10) = C_4^{10} 0.60^4 0.40^6 = 0.111$$

---

* Key Idea 10.9: Maximum Likelihood Procedure

Choose the population parameter to maximize the likelihood function given the sample data.

The probabilities were obtained from the binomial probabilities in Table A.5. By examining these results we see that a value of $\pi = 0.40$ provides the maximum value of the likelihood function. This procedure can be made more precise by graphing the likelihood function for all possible values of π. Figure 10.1 is the likelihood function for the sample with four successes in 10 trials. Examination of the graph shows clearly that $\pi = 0.40$ is the maximum likelihood estimator.

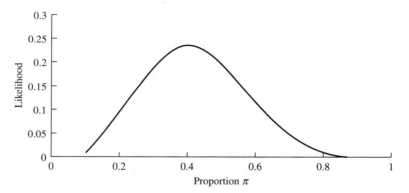

Figure 10.1 Likelihood Function: Binomial with $X = 4$ Successes in $n = 10$ Trials

10.3.1 Maximum Likelihood Estimator for the Binomial Proportion π

The maximum likelihood estimator for π is defined in Key Idea 10.10. Using our results for the distribution of sample statistics, we can show that $\hat{P}_{\mathrm{MLE}}$ is an unbiased estimator.

$$E[\hat{P}_{\mathrm{MLE}}] = \mu_{\hat{P}}$$
$$= \pi$$
$$\sigma^2_{\hat{P}_{\mathrm{MLE}}} = \frac{\pi(1-\pi)}{n}$$

---

*Key Idea 10.10: Maximum Likelihood Estimator: Proportion

The maximum likelihood estimator for the binomial proportion π is equal to the sample proportion:

$$\hat{P}_{\text{MLE}} = \frac{x}{n}$$

where x is the number of successes in a random sample of size n.

---

and that $\hat{P}_{\text{MLE}}$ has a normal distribution given that the sample size meets the assumption $n\pi(1 - \pi) \geq 9$.

Derivation of the MLE for π.   The maximum likelihood estimator for π can also be obtained by using the methods of differential calculus. We want the maximum value for the general likelihood function, which has a form similar to the specific likelihood function in Figure 10.1. The likelihood function for π is

$$L(\pi \mid x, \, n) = C_x^n \pi^x (1 - \pi)^{n-x}$$

To find $\hat{P}_{\text{MLE}}$ we will differentiate the likelihood function L with respect to π and set it equal to zero. Note that we do not have to include the constant C_x^n in this operation because it does not include π.

$$\frac{d(L(\pi \mid x, n))}{d\pi} = x\pi^{x-1}(1 - \pi)^{n-x} + (n - x)(1 - \pi)^{n-x-1}(-1)\pi^x$$

$$= \pi^x (1 - \pi)^{n-x} \left(\frac{x}{\pi} - \frac{n - x}{1 - \pi} \right)$$

$$= 0$$

from which we conclude that

$$0 = \frac{x}{\pi} - \frac{n - x}{1 - \pi}$$

$$x - \pi x = n\pi - \pi x$$

$$x = n\pi$$

$$\hat{P}_{\text{MLE}} = \frac{x}{n}$$

Now we have a general solution for the maximum likelihood estimator for π. In addition, we have an example that shows how the maximum likelihood estimator can be derived for other probability distribution functions.

* 10.3.2 Maximum Likelihood Estimator for the Normal Distribution Mean μ

The maximum likelihood estimator for μ is defined in Key Idea 10.11. The following analysis will also provide another example of the maximum likelihood procedure for obtaining estimators. From Chapter 6 we recall that the normal probability density function for a single observation is

$$f(x \mid \mu, \sigma^2) = \frac{1}{\sqrt{2\pi}\,\sigma} e^{-(x-\mu)^2/2\sigma^2}$$

For a random sample of n observations the joint probability density function is

$$f(x_1, x_2, \ldots, x_n \mid \mu, \sigma^2) = \left(\frac{1}{\sqrt{2\pi}\sigma}\right)^n e^{-\sum_{i=1}^{n}(x_i-\mu)^2/2\sigma^2}$$

The joint probability density function is the product of the density functions for each observation, because the observations are independent random variables. The likelihood function for μ given the random sample and the variance σ^2 is

$$L(\mu \mid x_1, x_2, \ldots, x_n, \sigma^2) = \left(\frac{1}{\sqrt{2\pi}\,\sigma}\right)^n e^{-\sum_{i=1}^{n}(x_i-\mu)^2/2\sigma^2}$$

---

* Key Idea 10.11: Maximum Likelihood Estimator: Normal Mean

The maximum likelihood estimator for the normal distribution mean μ is the sample mean $\bar{X}$:

$$\hat{\mu}_{\mathrm{MLE}} = \frac{\sum_{i=1}^{n} x_i}{n}$$

$$= \bar{X}$$

Note that the likelihood function has the same mathematical form as the joint probability density function (pdf). For the joint pdf the mean μ is known and the pdf indicates the probability of a specific random sample of x_i values. In contrast, the likelihood function has known sample values, because we have the sample, and computes the "likelihood" of a particular value for the parameter μ.

The maximum likelihood estimator $\hat{\mu}_{\mathrm{MLE}}$ is obtained by choosing the value of μ that will maximize the likelihood function. Careful inspection of the function indicates that μ is contained only in the exponent of e and the exponent has a negative sign. Thus maximizing the total likelihood function implies that we minimize the exponent:

$$\frac{\sum_{i=1}^{n}(x_i - \mu)^2}{2\sigma^2}$$

This minimization with respect to μ can be accomplished by minimizing

$$\sum_{i=1}^{n}(x_i - \mu)^2$$

This quantity is minimized if $\bar{X}$ is substituted for μ.

Applying differential calculus we find that

$$\frac{d(\sum_{i=1}^{n}(x_i - \mu)^2)}{d\mu} = \sum_{i=1}^{n} 2(-1)(x_i - \mu)$$

$$= 0$$

from which we obtain

$$\sum_{i=1}^{n} x_i - n\mu = 0$$

$$\hat{\mu}_{\text{MLE}} = \frac{\sum_{i=1}^{n} x_i}{n}$$

$$= \bar{X}$$

The sample mean $\bar{X}$ is the maximum likelihood estimator of the population mean μ for a normally distributed random variable.

The sample mean $\bar{X}$ is an unbiased estimator of μ, the normal distribution mean and thus $\bar{X}$ has a normal distribution with variance

$$\sigma_{\bar{X}}^2 = \frac{\sigma_x^2}{n}$$

10.4 CONFIDENCE INTERVALS

Point estimators provide us with the "best" single number to represent a system or process of interest. However, a more complete understanding of the process that generated the population also requires a measure of variability.

1. The average number of cars produced per day in a factory is an important measure. Wide variations above and below the mean can result in excessive inventory costs or lost sales.

2. A positive average monthly cash balance in a small company indicates solid performance. But if the experience includes several months with negative cash balances, creditors might force bankruptcy.

3. The average daily temperatures in Minneapolis, Minnesota, and Portland, Maine, are very close. However, the summer and winter extremes in Minneapolis result in a very different weather pattern.

Thus we need to have measurements of both central tendency and variability. Numbers contain both information and error. The confidence intervals developed in this section provide a way to include sampling variability, which was developed in Chapter 9, in the estimates provided from analysis of sample data.

The most important measures of variability are the variance and the standard deviation. The standard deviation for normal random variables can be used with the mean to compute the probability that observations will be within designated intervals. We know that probability distributions with higher variances have greater variability. However, even experienced statisticians find it difficult to explain variance to persons without statistical training. In contrast, the mean is easy to explain and to understand. To overcome this communication problem, we use statistical confidence intervals that combine central tendency and variability (Key Idea 10.12). An understanding of confidence intervals can be developed by considering the following example.

Key Idea 10.12: Confidence Intervals

The $1 - \alpha$ **percent confidence interval** is computed as

$$\bar{X} \pm Z_{\alpha/2}\frac{\sigma}{\sqrt{n}}$$

The $1 - \alpha$ percent confidence interval is constructed such that $(1 - \alpha)$ percent of the intervals will include the population mean. Most decision makers behave as if the population mean μ is within the confidence interval. However, they will be wrong α percent of the time.

Example 10.3   Production Rate

We wish to estimate a confidence interval for the mean hourly production rate for a cereal. The variance of the hourly production rate is 100.

Solution   A random sample of 25 hourly production rates is collected. The sample mean was computed to be 90 units per hour. From this information we can construct a 95% confidence interval:

$$90 \pm 3.92$$

The equation for this interval is

$$\bar{X} \pm Z_{0.025}\frac{\sigma}{\sqrt{n}}$$

For this example we find that

$$90 \pm 1.96\frac{\sqrt{100}}{\sqrt{25}}$$

$$90 \pm 3.92$$

The interval is from 86.08 to 93.92 and is interpreted as follows.

Over many attempts, 95% of the confidence intervals constructed using this procedure will contain the population mean μ, given random samples (n = 25) from this population.   □

Each interval constructed from a random sample is centered on the sample mean $\bar{X}$. The sample mean will be different for each sample, and therefore the interval will also be different. Figure 10.2 shows nine different confidence intervals computed using nine different random samples. We see a schematic illustration of the intervals compared with the population mean μ. In most cases the interval includes the mean μ. However, in 5% of cases the complete interval will be either above or below μ. *Note that the mean μ is always the same, even though we do not know its value. It is the intervals that vary.*

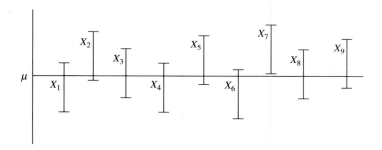

Figure 10.2   Schematic Description of Confidence Intervals

10.4.1 Interpretation

The 95% confidence interval is constructed such that 95% of the intervals will include the true mean. Most decision makers behave as if the population mean μ is within the confidence interval. Note, however, that they will be wrong 5% of the time or once in every 20 times. Arnold Zellner, former president of the American Statistical Association, argues that confidence intervals provide the best interval for μ, given the sample that is the best available information.

Depending on the problem, statisticians compute confidence intervals with different probabilities of error. A 99% confidence interval misses the population mean in only 1% of the cases but is wider than the 95% confidence interval. In contrast, a 90% confidence interval misses the population mean in 10% of cases but is narrower than the 95% confidence interval.

Does It Make Sense?

The confidence interval is useful because it provides both a measure of central tendency and a more intuitive measure of variability. The decision maker can then apply judgment that utilizes both central tendency and variability. We will see how the size of the interval can be changed by either changing the risk (probability of an incorrect interval) or by changing the size of the sample.

Confidence intervals are an important analysis tool. Managers and decision makers generally behave as though the population mean is within the confidence interval. Election polls typically present confidence intervals for the percentage of voters who support a candidate. Campaign managers base their actions on those results. Higher-quality news reports now include confidence intervals. Therefore, analysts who prepare confidence intervals have a responsibility to select and compute the correct interval. □

* 10.4.2 Confidence Interval Derivation

Confidence intervals for a single normally distributed mean are derived, using simple algebra, directly from acceptance intervals, which were defined in Chapter 9. In Figure 10.3 we see that the acceptance interval for a sample mean is defined as

$$P\left(\mu - Z_{\alpha/2}\sigma_{\bar{X}} \leq \bar{X} \leq \mu + Z_{\alpha/2}\sigma_{\bar{X}}\right) = 1 - \alpha$$

The left-hand side of this acceptance interval equation can be transformed to a confidence interval. First, subtract $\bar{X}$ and μ from the left-hand-side terms:

$$P\left(-\bar{X} - Z_{\alpha/2}\sigma_{\bar{X}} \leq -\mu \leq -\bar{X} + Z_{\alpha/2}\sigma_{\bar{X}}\right) = 1 - \alpha$$

Then multiply by -1, which reverses the inequality signs,

$$P\left(\bar{X} + Z_{\alpha/2}\sigma_{\bar{X}} \geq \mu \geq \bar{X} - Z_{\alpha/2}\sigma_{\bar{X}}\right) = 1 - \alpha$$

and then reverse the terms and the inequality signs,

$$P\left(\bar{X} - Z_{\alpha/2}\sigma_{\bar{X}} \leq \mu \leq \bar{X} + Z_{\alpha/2}\sigma_{\bar{X}}\right) = 1 - \alpha$$

The result is the $1 - \alpha$ **percent confidence interval**.

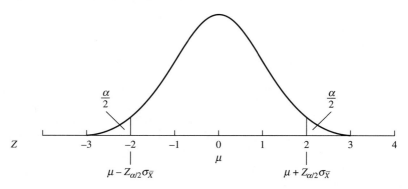

Figure 10.3   Acceptance Interval for Sample Mean

We emphasize that this interval will be different for each sample mean $\bar{X}$. Therefore, a $1 - \alpha$ proportion of the intervals derived using a random sample mean, $\bar{X}$, will include the population mean μ. The population mean μ is always the same, but the

confidence interval is centered on the sample mean, and a different sample mean results from each random sample. Of those sample means, $1 - \alpha$ proportion will be
outside the acceptance interval shown in Figure 10.3. It follows that the $1 - \alpha$ confidence interval constructed using a sample mean outside the acceptance interval will
not include the population mean.

The confidence interval equation is computed using the population standard deviation σ and the sample size n. The standard deviation of the sample mean is the
population standard deviation divided by the square root of the sample size:

$$P \left(\bar{X} - Z_{\alpha/2} \frac{\sigma}{\sqrt{n}} \leq \mu \leq \bar{X} + Z_{\alpha/2} \frac{\sigma}{\sqrt{n}} \right) = 1 - \alpha$$

or

$$\bar{X} \pm Z_{\alpha/2} \frac{\sigma}{\sqrt{n}}$$

This form emphasizes that the confidence interval width varies inversely with the
square root of the sample size. The confidence interval is a measure of an estimate's
precision. Thus larger sample sizes (hence higher sampling cost) lead to narrower
confidence intervals and thus greater precision.

Does It Make Sense?

Confidence intervals are often simplified as

$$\bar{X} \pm 2\sigma_{\bar{X}}$$

This interval is approximately 95% and is easy to compute. Thus the *two-sigma* (2σ)
interval is a good rule for quickly judging the quality of an estimate. This result is the
basis for the empirical rule for symmetric distribution presented in Chapter 2.   □

10.5 SINGLE-SIDED CONFIDENCE INTERVALS

In Section 10.4 we developed symmetric confidence intervals that provide both an upper and a lower limit. But in many situations an analyst wishes to know if a population
mean is greater than a minimum value or less than a maximum value. For example:

1. The product manager will introduce a new product if sales are predicted to
   exceed the minimum break-even quantity.
2. The production manager for a food products company must be certain that the
   average package weight exceeds the guaranteed weight.
3. An agricultural development project has a goal of increasing productivity above
   a minimum level.
4. A quality control manager wants to be certain that the mean number of defective
   parts is below an upper limit.

In the situations above, two-sided confidence intervals are not appropriate. A two-
sided confidence interval assigns probability of error symmetrically to both large and

small extreme values. However, in the examples presented above we are concerned only with values that are either too large or too small but not both. Therefore, the probability of error should be concentrated at either the upper or lower end of the confidence interval. By concentrating the error in one tail, the upper or lower limit is closer to the sample mean. As a result, the confidence interval can be stated with greater precision, for a given probability of error α (Key Idea 10.13).

Key Idea 10.13: Single-Sided Confidence Intervals

Using algebra similar to that used to develop the two-sided confidence interval, we can derive a single-sided confidence interval:

$$P(\mu \leq \bar{X} + Z_\alpha \sigma_{\bar{X}}) = 1 - \alpha$$

or

$$P(\mu \geq \bar{X} - Z_\alpha \sigma_{\bar{X}}) = 1 - \alpha$$

In the abbreviated notation the $1 - \alpha$ percent confidence intervals are

$$\mu \leq \bar{X} + Z_\alpha \sigma_{\bar{X}}$$

$$\mu \geq \bar{X} - Z_\alpha \sigma_{\bar{X}}$$

We say that $1 - \alpha$ percent of these confidence intervals include μ.

The value of Z_α is smaller than $Z_{\alpha/2}$, as can be seen by inspection of Table A.1. Therefore, $Z_\alpha \sigma_{\bar{X}}$ is smaller than $Z_{\alpha/2} \sigma_{\bar{X}}$ and the interval limit is closer to the sample mean.

In the previous cereal manufacturing example, our concern might be the lower limit on productivity. The appropriate confidence interval is

$$\mu \geq 90 - Z_{0.05} \frac{\sigma}{\sqrt{n}}$$

$$\geq 90 - 1.645 \frac{\sqrt{100}}{\sqrt{25}}$$

$$\geq 90 - 3.29$$

$$\geq 86.71$$

The lower limit for this single-sided 95% confidence interval is higher than lower limit for the two-sided confidence interval. This occurs because all of the probability of error, α, is at the lower limit.

Example 10.4   Package Weight Estimation

Freddie Soderlind is president of Aunt Agnes Foods, Inc. He wants to estimate the mean weight of pancake mix boxes packed by the new automatic packer. From the machine specifications and staff experience it is known that the variance between boxes is 0.16. After consultation with Dana Dragseth, the corporate statistician, he decides to ask for a 95% confidence interval based on a random sample of $n = 25$ boxes.

Solution   The random sample mean was $\bar{X} = 16.10$, which can be used to obtain the 95% confidence interval:

$$\bar{X} \pm Z_{\alpha/2} \frac{\sigma}{\sqrt{n}}$$

$$16.10 \pm 1.96 \frac{0.4}{\sqrt{25}}$$

$$16.10 \pm 0.16$$

$$15.94 \leq \mu \leq 16.26$$

Based on these results, Freddie knows that the most likely value for the population mean weight is above 16 ounces. However, there is a possibility that the population mean weight is less than 16 ounces because the interval has a lower limit of 15.94 ounces.

Dana could provide Freddie with an interval of

$$16.10 \pm 0.10$$

whose range did not extend below 16 ounces. However, this interval would have a small Z value and hence a high probability of error. In particular, she would find that

$$0.10 = Z_{\alpha/2} \frac{0.4}{\sqrt{25}}$$

and therefore,

$$Z_{\alpha/2} = 1.25$$

which implies that $\alpha/2 = 0.106$ in the standardized normal distribution (Table A.1). The interval 16.10 ± 0.10 would be a 79% confidence interval. Such intervals would not include the mean population weight, μ, 21% of the time. Most statisticians, including the authors, would advise that confidence intervals with such a large probability of error are misleading and should not be used. Increasing the sample size is a better way to narrow the range of a confidence interval. We know that larger sample sizes provide estimates with greater precision. The confidence interval varies directly with the inverse of the square root of the sample size $1/\sqrt{n}$. If the sample size were increased by a factor of 4, the confidence interval would be reduced by one-half.

$$\pm Z_{\alpha/2} \frac{\sigma}{\sqrt{4n}} = \pm Z_{\alpha/2} \frac{\sigma}{2\sqrt{n}} = \frac{1}{2} \times \pm Z_{\alpha/2} \frac{\sigma}{\sqrt{n}}$$

Thus if Freddie were to obtain a random sample of size $n = 100$, whose sample mean was $\bar{X} = 16.10$, the 95% confidence interval would be

$$\bar{Y} \pm Z_{\alpha/2}\frac{\sigma}{\sqrt{n}}$$

$$16.10 \pm 1.96\frac{0.4}{\sqrt{100}}$$

$$16.10 \pm 0.08$$

$$16.02 \leq \mu \leq 16.18$$

From the larger sample size Freddie can be quite confident that the population mean box weight is above 16 ounces.

If Freddie's primary concern was assurance that the mean package weight was above 16 ounces, he would use a single-sided confidence interval. For a sample size $n = 25$ this interval is

$$\mu \geq \bar{X} - Z_{\alpha}\frac{\sigma}{\sqrt{n}}$$

$$\geq 16.1 - 1.645\frac{0.4}{\sqrt{25}}$$

$$\geq 15.97$$

Because he is only concerned with the lower limit, the single-sided confidence interval has a lower limit of 15.97 instead of the 15.94 computed for the two-sided confidence interval. □

Does It Make Sense?

Confidence intervals can be used to mislead managers. In the example above, the 79% confidence interval had a narrow range, suggesting a small error for the reported statistical result. However, that interval would fail to include the population mean 21% of the time, or 1 in 5 samples. This is not good enough for most statistical work. Many statisticians, including the authors, would consider such a confidence interval as "lying with statistics." As a manager, you need to protect yourself from such lies. Always ask for the error or confidence level when statistical results such as confidence intervals are reported. Good statistical reporting always includes that information. In most situations a 90% confidence interval should be the smallest percentage you should accept—and 95% is preferred. □

Practice Problem 10.2: Sample of Part Dimensions

A process produces parts whose principal dimension—measured in centimeters—has a variance of 0.01. A random sample of size $n = 25$ has a mean of 54 centimeters. Determine:

(a) The 95% confidence interval for the population mean.
(b) The 95% lower confidence limit for the population mean. □

Problem Exercises

10.6   What is the difference between an acceptance interval and a confidence interval?

10.7   A fast-food restaurant, Hamburgers and More, wanted to know the mean weight of cooked burgers. A random sample of 25 hamburgers had a mean of 4.12 ounces. The population variance is 0.25. Determine:
(a) The 95% confidence interval for the population mean weight.
(b) The 98% confidence interval.
(c) The lower limit for a 95% single-sided confidence interval.

10.8   Return to Problem 10.7, dealing with hamburger weights. What sample size would be required to reduce the original confidence intervals by one-half?

10.9   The length of pine boards sold at Sawyer's mill has a variance of 900 inches squared. A random sample of 38 boards had a mean length of 120 inches. Determine:
(a) The 95% confidence interval for the population mean length of boards.
(b) The upper 94% single-sided confidence interval limit.

10.10   The weight of canned tuna in nominal 16-ounce cans has a normal distribution with a variance of 0.75. A random sample of 34 cans are weighed and the sample mean is 16.4 ounces.
(a) What is the 95% confidence interval for the population mean weight?
(b) Can you conclude that the population mean weight is 16 ounces or more using a single-sided 95% confidence interval?

10.11   The weight of canned tuna in nominal 16-ounce cans has a normal distribution with a variance of 0.63. A random sample of 28 cans are weighed and the sample mean is 16.4 ounces.
(a) What is the 95% confidence interval for the population mean weight?
(b) Can you conclude that the population mean weight is 16 ounces or more using a single-sided 95% confidence interval?

10.6 CONFIDENCE INTERVALS FOR PROPORTIONS

Proportions are used widely in economic and business problems. When reporting proportions from a statistical study we should include confidence intervals. In Chapter 9 we presented examples in which analysts are likely to obtain a random sample and compute the sample proportion.

1. Market researchers want to know the proportion of people who would purchase a product.
2. Every political candidate wants to know the proportion of voters who support her or his candidacy.
3. Production managers want to know the percent defective parts in a shipment.
4. Personnel departments want to know the proportion of workers who can perform a complex assembly task.
5. Health insurance companies want to know if the percentage of people filing claims exceeds a control level.

Confidence intervals for proportions can be developed (Key Idea 10.14) if the sample proportion $\hat{P}$ has an approximate normal distribution [e.g., $n\pi(1-\pi) \geq 9$]. We know that the confidence interval has the form

$$P\left(\bar{X} - Z_{\alpha/2}\sigma_{\bar{X}} \leq \mu \leq \bar{X} + Z_{\alpha/2}\sigma_{\bar{X}}\right) = 1 - \alpha$$

In Chapter 9 we showed that the proportion $\hat{P}$ is the sample mean for a sample of $(0, 1)$ or Bernoulli random variables. The standard deviation is[3]

$$\sigma_{\bar{X}} = \sigma_{\hat{P}} = \sqrt{\frac{\hat{P}(1 - \hat{P})}{n}}$$

Key Idea 10.14: Proportion Confidence Intervals

The $1 - \alpha$ percent confidence interval for the proportion is

$$P\left(\hat{P} - Z_{\alpha/2}\sqrt{\frac{\hat{P}(1 - \hat{P})}{n}} \leq \pi \leq \hat{P} + Z_{\alpha/2}\sqrt{\frac{\hat{P}(1 - \hat{P})}{n}}\right) = 1 - \alpha$$

or expressed in the simplified form

$$\hat{P} \pm Z_{\alpha/2}\sqrt{\frac{\hat{P}(1 - \hat{P})}{n}}$$

Does It Make Sense?

A popular application of confidence intervals for proportions is the reporting of candidate support prior to elections. Newscasters often give the point estimate from the election poll (a random sample) and then indicate a "margin of error" as ± 3 or 5%. These intervals are typically 95% confidence intervals.   □

---

[3] Since the population proportion is not known, we typically use the maximum likelihood estimator

$$\hat{P}_{\text{MLE}} = \frac{x}{n}$$

where x is the number of successes, in the computation of the standard deviation.

10.6.1 Single-Sided Confidence Intervals

Single-sided confidence intervals are defined in Key Idea 10.15.

Key Idea 10.15: Single-Sided Proportion Intervals

Single-sided confidence intervals have the form

$$\pi \geq \hat{P} - Z_\alpha \sqrt{\frac{\hat{P}(1 - \hat{P})}{n}}$$

or

$$\pi \leq \hat{P} + Z_\alpha \sqrt{\frac{\hat{P}(1 - \hat{P})}{n}}$$

Example 10.5   Health Care Costs

A large health insurance company is considering a contract bid to provide health insurance for a company with over 100,000 employees. The potential claims cost per employee is related directly to the percent of employees who have the symptoms of a major disease. Before preparing the bid, the senior consultant, Charlotte King, needs to know the percentage who have the symptoms.

Solution   Charlotte decides to obtain a random sample of $n = 400$ employees and have tests conducted to determine the percentage who have the symptoms. In the random sample 30% of the employees test positive. She also computes a 95% confidence interval to provide an indication of the reliability of her estimate. The results are

$$\hat{P} \pm Z_{0.025} \sqrt{\frac{\hat{P}(1 - \hat{P})}{n}}$$

$$0.30 \pm 1.96 \sqrt{\frac{0.30(1 - 0.30)}{400}}$$

$$0.30 \pm 0.045$$

This interval has a probability of 0.95 of including the population proportion. She can expect that the population proportion ranges from 0.255 to 0.345. We could also show that the 99% confidence interval would be

$$0.30 \pm 0.059$$

This interval has a very small probability of missing the population proportion. However, the interval is wider than the 95% interval.

Another approach to this problem could involve determining an upper limit for the occurrence of a disease. The 95% single-sided confidence interval would then be

$$\pi \leq \hat{P} + Z_\alpha \sqrt{\frac{\hat{P}(1 - \hat{P})}{n}}$$

$$\leq 0.30 + 1.645 \sqrt{\frac{0.30(1 - 0.70)}{400}}$$

$$\leq 0.338$$

This upper limit might be more useful for the insurance company because it establishes the maximum potential loss.   □

10.7 CONFIDENCE INTERVALS: σ UNKNOWN

There are many estimation situations in which the population standard deviation is not known.

1. Corporate sales executives employed by retail distributors want to estimate daily sales for their retail stores.
2. Manufacturers estimate the productivity per hour for workers using a particular manufacturing process.
3. A seed producer wishes to estimate the production in bushels per acre for a new variety of corn.

In all of these situations we assume that the statistician is studying a new situation and there is no historical information concerning either the mean or the variance. However, it is reasonable to assume that the variable being measured either has a normal distribution or that the sample mean has a normal distribution. In either case we can use the sample standard deviation and the Student t distribution to develop a confidence interval. The process and theory are similar to previous cases in which the population variance was known (see Key Ideas 10.16 and 10.17).

Development of the confidence interval follows the steps used in Sections 10.4 and 10.5. The confidence interval with σ known is

$$P\left(\bar{X} - Z_{\alpha/2}\sigma_{\bar{X}} \leq \mu \leq \bar{X} + Z_{\alpha/2}\sigma_{\bar{X}}\right) = 1 - \alpha$$

when the population standard deviation is known. From Chapter 9 we know that the Student t and the sample standard deviation S_x are analogous to the standardized normal Z and the population standard deviation σ.

Key Idea 10.16: Confidence Intervals: Variance Unknown

The $1 - \alpha$ percent confidence interval when the population variance is unknown becomes

$$P\left(\bar{X} - t_{\alpha/2}S_{\bar{X}} \leq \mu \leq \bar{X} + t_{\alpha/2}S_{\bar{X}}\right) = 1 - \alpha$$

The t value is based on the degrees of freedom $n - 1$ used to estimate the sample standard deviation S_x. Similar to the other confidence intervals we often express the result as

$$\bar{X} \pm t_{\alpha/2}S_{\bar{X}}$$

This is defined as the $1 - \alpha$ percent confidence interval.

Key Idea 10.17: Single-Sided Confidence Intervals: Variance Unknown

The single-sided confidence interval has either the form

$$\mu \geq \bar{X} - t_{\alpha}S_{\bar{X}}$$

or

$$\mu \leq \bar{X} + t_{\alpha}S_{\bar{X}}$$

In Chapter 9 we learned that the estimated standard deviation of the sample mean is

$$S_{\bar{X}} = \frac{S_x}{\sqrt{n}}$$

where

$$S_x = \sqrt{\frac{\sum_{i=1}^{n}(x_i - \bar{X})^2}{n - 1}}$$

Example 10.6   Food Consumption

Nigel Tada, a development economist, is attempting to determine the daily food consumption for rural village children in western Africa. This work is part of a major agricultural development project. Nigel obtains a random sample of 25 children, and his assistants carefully determine the total calories consumed during a typical day for each child. The sample mean is $\bar{X} = 1950$ and the sum of squared deviations is

$$\sum_{i=1}^{n}(x_i - \bar{X})^2 = 240,000$$

You are asked to advise Dr. Tada concerning appropriate presentation of the results.

Solution   You would first tell Nigel that his maximum likelihood point estimate of the population mean is $\bar{X} = 1950$. However, you also strongly advise him to present an interval estimate so that program developers know the variability of food intake. From the sample data we find that

$$S_x^2 = \frac{\sum_{i=1}^{n}(x_i - \bar{X})^2}{n-1}$$
$$= \frac{240,000}{25-1}$$
$$= 10,000$$
$$S_{\bar{X}} = \frac{S_x}{\sqrt{n}}$$
$$= \sqrt{\frac{10,000}{25}}$$
$$= 20$$

After some discussion you decide to construct a 95% confidence interval. The estimate of S_x^2 has 24 degrees of freedom because the random sample has 25 observations. From Table A.2 we find that for 24 degrees of freedom, $t_{0.025} = 2.06$. Therefore, the 95% confidence interval is

$$\bar{X} \pm t_{\alpha/2}S_{\bar{X}}$$
$$1950 \pm 2.06 \times 20$$
$$1950 \pm 41.2$$

Thus program developers will design their projects based on an average calorie consumption per child between 1909 and 1991. If this interval were too wide, a larger sample size could be used. For example, an additional 75 random observations could be combined with the original 25 to obtain a random sample of 100 observations. If S_x remained at 10,000 and $\bar{X}$ was 1950 for the new, larger sample, the confidence interval would be

$$1950 \pm t_{0.025}\sqrt{\frac{10,000}{100}}$$
$$1950 \pm 1.99 \times 10$$
$$1950 \pm 19.9$$

This narrower interval—1930 to 1970—provides greater precision for the program planners.

Program developers might be more concerned with a lower limit because malnutrition is the critical concern. In that case a single-sided confidence interval would be appropriate. Given a random sample of size $n = 25$, the confidence interval is

$$\mu \geq \bar{X} - t_\alpha S_{\bar{X}}$$
$$\geq 1950 - 1.71 \times 20$$
$$\geq 1915.8$$

compared to the lower limit 1908.2 for the two-sided interval.   □

Does It Make Sense?

From Example 10.6 we see that the 95% confidence interval is approximately

$$\bar{X} \pm 2S_{\bar{X}}$$

This is the same width as the approximate 95% acceptance interval developed in Chapter 9, $\mu \pm 2S_{\bar{X}}$, and the 95% confidence interval when σ is known, $\bar{X} \pm 1.96\sigma_{\bar{X}}$. For many applied statistical studies the interval $\bar{X} \pm 2S_{\bar{X}}$ or $\bar{X} \pm 2\sigma_{\bar{X}}$ is a useful summary.   □

Practice Problem 10.3: Marketing Sampling Study

A marketing study with a random sample of 400 results in 160 subjects reacting positively to the proposed product. Determine:

(a) The 95% confidence interval for the sample proportion.
(b) The 95% lower confidence limit for the population proportion.   □

Problem Exercises

10.12 The marketing research department conducted a random sample test market for a new cheese-flavored snack food. A random sample of $n = 398$ subjects included 143 who said that they would definitely purchase the product. Determine:
   (a) The 96% confidence interval for the population proportion who would purchase.
   (b) The lower limit for the 96% single-tailed confidence interval for the proportion who would purchase.

10.13 A national news program offered people an opportunity to express their reactions to a presidential speech. People could call one number to express positive support and a second number to express opposition. Each call cost the person 50 cents. During the evening, 356,987 calls indicated support and 298,345 indicated opposition. Why is it not possible to develop a 95% confidence interval for the proportion who support the president, by using these data?

10.14 Emily Thorson is a candidate for the U.S. Senate. A recent random sample poll indicated that 475 voters out of 900 supported her candidacy.
   (a) What is the 95% confidence interval for the population proportion who support her candidacy?
   (b) If a single-tailed confidence interval is used, would a 95% confidence interval be entirely above $P = 0.50$?

10.15 Checkitout, Inc., a regional auditing firm, wants to estimate the proportion of accounts receivable that are older than 45 days, as part of its audit of a hospital supply firm. A random sample of 150 receivables included 43 that were older than 45 days.
   (a) What is the 95% confidence interval for the population proportion of receivables that are older than 45 days?
   (b) What is the upper limit for a single-sided 95% confidence interval for the proportion of receivables older than 45 days?
   (c) Write a one- or two-sentence interpretation of your result in part (b) that can be included in the auditing report.

10.16 A random sample of 340 supermarket sales indicated that Cowface yogurt was purchased by 105 of the people. Determine the following confidence intervals for the proportion of the market controlled by Cowface.
   (a) 98%.
   (b) 92%.

10.8 CONFIDENCE INTERVALS: MEAN DIFFERENCES

We have considered estimation of the mean or proportion for a single population. Another important estimation application is the difference between the means or proportions from two different populations. The statistical model for the point and confidence interval estimates of these differences is based on the linear combination of random variables developed in Chapter 7. The basic linear models that we will develop and apply are

$$\Delta \bar{X} = \bar{X}_1 - \bar{X}_2$$
$$\Delta \hat{P} = \hat{P}_1 - \hat{P}_2$$

Differences between sample means are used in a number of comparative studies. Examples include:

1. Production (e.g., units per day) differences between two factories or production units.
2. Differences in student test scores between the first and second examination in a course.
3. Differences in agricultural output between two fields, each treated with a different fertilizer.
4. Differences in length of delivery time for two different small package delivery companies.

The procedure for computing confidence intervals for the difference between population means is similar to that for single means. A key idea is that the difference between sample means is a random variable. This random variable has a standard deviation. Therefore, confidence intervals for differences between means have the same form as confidence intervals for single means. However, the computation of the standard deviation for the difference between sample means is somewhat more complicated. The results described in Key Ideas 10.18 and 10.19 come directly from our understanding of the linear combinations of random variables developed in Chapter 7.

Key Idea 10.18: Confidence Intervals: $\Delta \bar{X} = \bar{X}_1 - \bar{X}_2$

The confidence interval for the difference between population means is

$$P\left(\Delta \bar{X} - Z_{\alpha/2}\sigma_{\Delta \bar{X}} \leq \Delta \mu \leq \Delta \bar{X} + Z_{\alpha/2}\sigma_{\Delta \bar{X}}\right) = 1 - \alpha$$

where

$$\Delta \mu = \mu_1 - \mu_2$$

is the difference between population means μ_1 and μ_2,

$$\Delta \bar{X} = \bar{X}_1 - \bar{X}_2$$

is the difference between sample means $\bar{X}_1$ and $\bar{X}_2$, and

$$\sigma_{\Delta \bar{X}}$$

is the standard deviation of the difference between the sample means.

   If both sample means have normal distributions, their difference also has a normal distribution.

The difference between sample means $\Delta \bar{X}$ is a random variable that is the linear combination of two random variables, $\bar{X}_1$ and $\bar{X}_2$:

$$\Delta \bar{X} = \bar{X}_1 - \bar{X}_2$$

whose expected value is

$$E[\Delta \bar{X}] = E[\bar{X}_1] - E[\bar{X}_2]$$
$$= \mu_1 - \mu_2$$
$$= \Delta \mu$$

Note that the correlation ρ for sample means and for individual observations is the same because the correlation is a standardized measure of relationship that has values between -1.0 and $+1.0$. (See Key Idea 10.19.)

Key Idea 10.19: Variance of $\Delta \bar{X}$

The variance of $\Delta \bar{X}$ results directly from the relationships developed in Chapter 7 for linear combinations of random variables:

$$\sigma^2_{\Delta \bar{X}} = \sigma^2_{\bar{X}_1} + \sigma^2_{\bar{X}_2} - 2\sigma_{\bar{X}_1 \bar{X}_2}$$

where

$$\sigma_{\bar{X}_1 \bar{X}_2} = \rho_{\bar{X}_1 \bar{X}_2} \sigma_{\bar{X}_1} \sigma_{\bar{X}_2}$$
$$= \rho_{X_1 X_2} \sigma_{\bar{X}_1} \sigma_{\bar{X}_2}$$

If the samples are independent, the covariance term $\sigma_{\bar{X}_1 \bar{X}_2}$ is zero, and the variance of the difference between sample means is the sum of the variances of the individual sample means:

$$\sigma^2_{\Delta \bar{X}} = \sigma^2_{\bar{X}_1} + \sigma^2_{\bar{X}_2}$$

The differences between independent sample means can vary from the farthest extremes of the two samples to the nearest extremes. Thus the variance of the difference is the sum of variances from the two samples. When the samples have a positive correlation, the range of differences is reduced because a large or small mean for one sample increases the chances for a large or small mean from the other sample. As the correlation approaches $\rho = +1$, the differences between sample means approach a constant. In the limiting case the variance is $\sigma^2_{\Delta \bar{X}} = 0$ when $\rho = +1$ and $\sigma_1 = \sigma_2$.

Example 10.7 Worker Productivity Differences

A researcher wanted to estimate the difference in worker productivity between a Japanese and a Canadian factory. From each factory a random sample of 25 workers was selected and their productivities in units per hour were recorded. Because samples were obtained from two separate factories, the samples are assumed independent. The mean was computed for each sample. By computing the difference between the two sample means, she obtained a point estimate of the difference between population means. In this way she determined the best single value for the difference in worker productivity. However, our researcher would also like to know the sampling variability for her estimate of the productivity difference. This can be done by using a confidence interval for the difference between population means.

Solution   The two factories are in different countries and have no contact. The workers measured are selected randomly. Therefore, the two samples are independent. We want to estimate the difference between Canadian and Japanese factory workers in a particular industry. Based on other research we can assume that worker productivity has a variance of $\sigma^2 = 100$ for each of the production facilities being studied. From a random sample of 25 Canadian workers, the sample mean was $\overline{X}_c = 240$ units per hour. A random sample of 25 Japanese workers resulted in a sample mean $\overline{X}_j = 232$ units per hour. The point estimate of the difference was

$$\Delta \overline{X} = \overline{X}_c - \overline{X}_j$$
$$= 240 - 232$$
$$= 8.0$$

Independent samples. The confidence interval requires that we first compute the standard deviation of the difference between sample means. We find that

$$\sigma^2_{\Delta \overline{X}} = \sigma^2_{\overline{X}_c} + \sigma^2_{\overline{X}_j}$$
$$= \frac{\sigma^2_c}{n} + \frac{\sigma^2_j}{n}$$
$$= \frac{100}{25} + \frac{100}{25}$$
$$= 8$$
$$\sigma_{\Delta \overline{X}} = 2\sqrt{2}$$
$$= 2.828$$

The 95% confidence interval for the difference in worker productivity is

$$\overline{X}_c - \overline{X}_j \pm Z_{\alpha/2}\sigma_{\Delta \overline{X}}$$
$$8 \pm 1.96 \times 2.828$$
$$8 \pm 5.54$$

The difference in productivity can range between 2.46 and 13.54. This confidence interval does not include zero or negative values. A reasonable interpretation is that mean productivity for Canadian workers is higher. Additional procedures for establishing differences are developed in Chapter 11.

Correlated samples. If the two random samples were correlated with $\rho = 0.60$, the variance of the difference between sample means would be

$$\sigma^2_{\Delta \overline{X}} = \sigma^2_{\overline{X}_c} + \sigma^2_{\overline{X}_j} - 2\rho\sigma_{\overline{X}_c}\sigma_{\overline{X}_j}$$
$$= 8 - 2.0 \times 0.60 \times 2 \times 2$$
$$= 3.20$$
$$\sigma_{\Delta \overline{X}} = 1.79$$

$$\overline{X}_c - \overline{X}_j \pm Z_{\alpha/2}\sigma_{\Delta \overline{X}}$$
$$8 \pm 1.96 \times 1.79$$
$$8 \pm 3.51$$

In this case the difference in productivity is between 4.49 and 11.51. □

The variance of the difference between sample means is reduced if the sample observations are positively correlated. In Example 10.7 the assumption of independent sample observations is the most reasonable. The two factories are in different countries and the raw materials and production tools are different.

Does It Make Sense?

Correlated observations could be obtained if the workers from each country used the same production machines. For example, we could take the random sample of Canadian and Japanese workers to a U.S. factory and randomly assign selected pairs of Canadian and Japanese workers to the same machine. Variability in productivity that resulted from differences between machines would not influence the productivity difference between pairs of workers. The reduced variance in correlated samples results from removing the differences between machines as a component of the total variability. Productivity differences between machines is not removed from the variance if independent samples are used. This idea extends to a number of problems involving paired observations. □

10.8.1 Single-Sided Confidence Intervals

In some cases we are only interested in the possibility that one population mean is larger. In those cases a one-sided confidence interval for the difference in means should be used (Key Idea 10.20). Returning to Example 10.7, we see that the lower confidence interval is

$$\mu_c - \mu_j \geq \Delta \bar{X} - Z_\alpha \sigma_{\Delta \bar{X}}$$
$$\geq 8 - 1.645 \times 1.79$$
$$\geq 2.94$$

In this example we used the standard deviation from the independent samples.

Key Idea 10.20: Single-Sided Confidence Intervals

Single-sided confidence intervals that provide upper or lower limits for the differences between population means, $\Delta \mu = \mu_1 - \mu_2$, can be computed. The form follows from our previous examples:

$$\mu_1 - \mu_2 \geq \Delta \bar{X} - Z_\alpha \sigma_{\Delta \bar{X}}$$
$$\geq \bar{X}_1 - \bar{X}_2 - Z_\alpha \sigma_{\Delta \bar{X}}$$

Example 10.8   Agricultural Productivity

Shirley Brown, an agricultural economist, is attempting to determine the difference in corn productivity between fields that use composted turkey waste versus cow manure. She selects a random sample of $n_1 = 25$ fields and applies cow manure as fertilizer. From past research she knows that the variance in productivity for these fields is $\sigma_1^2 = 400$. Corn is planted and the productivity is $\bar{X}_1 = 100$. A second random sample of $n_2 = 25$ fields is selected, and composted turkey waste is applied as fertilizer. For these fields the variance in productivity is known to be $\sigma_2^2 = 625$. Corn is planted and the productivity is $\bar{X}_2 = 110$. Shirley has asked you to compute a 95% confidence interval for the difference in productivity using the two types of fertilizer.

Solution   The first step is to formulate the difference as a linear combination of the sample means:

$$\Delta \bar{X} = \bar{X}_2 - \bar{X}_1$$
$$= 110 - 100$$
$$= 10$$

Independent samples. We now know the point estimate of the difference and the linear form that will be used to compute the variance. The variance is

$$\sigma_{\Delta\bar{X}}^2 = \frac{\sigma_2^2}{n_2} + \frac{\sigma_1^2}{n_1}$$
$$= \frac{625}{25} + \frac{400}{25}$$
$$= 41$$
$$\sigma_{\Delta\bar{X}} = 6.40$$

She assumed that the samples were independent. The 95% confidence interval is

$$\bar{X}_2 - \bar{X}_1 \pm Z_{\alpha/2}\sigma_{\Delta\bar{X}}$$
$$10 \pm 1.96 \times 6.40$$
$$10 \pm 12.54$$

This confidence interval includes zero, and therefore she could not conclude that the population mean productivities for the two fertilizers were different. The confidence interval for $\Delta\mu = \mu_2 - \mu_1$ extends from -2.54 to $+22.54$. Thus the interval includes both $\mu_2 > \mu_1$ and $\mu_1 > \mu_2$.

Paired samples. Next, she considered the effect of paired samples on the confidence intervals (Key Idea 10.21). Shirley obtained a random sample of 25 fields and divided each into two separate plots. The fertilizers were randomly assigned to each paired plot. In these paired plots the soil and weather conditions were the same. Therefore, the effects of these variables on productivity were the same and productivity differences resulted primarily from the effects of the two fertilizers. The correlation

> ### Key Idea 10.21: Paired Sample Observations
>
> Samples that are positively correlated always have a smaller variance for
> the difference between sample means. Whenever possible, analysts should
> **pair** the sample observations to obtain reduced variances and thus nar-
> rower confidence intervals.

between paired plot productivities was $\rho = +0.50$. The variance of the difference between sample means was

$$\sigma^2_{\Delta \bar{X}} = \frac{\sigma_2^2}{n_2} + \frac{\sigma_1^2}{n_1} - 2\rho \frac{\sigma_2}{\sqrt{n_2}} \frac{\sigma_1}{\sqrt{n_1}}$$

$$= \frac{625}{25} + \frac{400}{25} - 2(0.50)\frac{25}{5}\frac{20}{5}$$

$$= 25 + 16 - 20$$

$$= 21$$

$$\sigma_{\Delta \bar{X}} = 4.58$$

Using this standard deviation of the difference between sample means, the confidence
interval was

$$\bar{X}_2 - \bar{X}_1 \pm Z_{\alpha/2}\sigma_{\Delta \bar{X}}$$

$$10 \pm 1.96 \times 4.58$$

$$10 \pm 8.98$$

This confidence interval did not include zero, and she concluded that composted
turkey dung resulted in higher productivity. ☐

Does It Make Sense?

By using paired observations the variance of the difference between sample means
will be reduced. Paired observations ensure that the effect of differences between individual observations will not contribute to the variance of the difference between populations, $\Delta \bar{X}$. A statistician would design the analysis to include paired observations,
if possible. This example also indicates the importance of consulting an experienced
statistician before beginning to collect data. Smaller variance is often a benefit of careful analysis design. ☐

10.9 CONFIDENCE INTERVALS: σ^2 UNKNOWN

From previous discussion we know that when the population variance σ^2 is unknown,
we must use the sample variance S^2 and the Student t distribution. In this section
we learn how to use those results for computing confidence intervals for differences

between sample means when σ^2 is unknown (Key Idea 10.22). These confidence intervals are based on complex distribution theory, which is influenced by special conditions. Here we develop a standard procedure for these problems. This standard procedure includes various options for computing the standard deviation of the differences between sample means.

Key Idea 10.22: Confidence Intervals: σ^2 Unknown

The basic form of the confidence interval for $\Delta \bar{X} = \bar{X}_1 - \bar{X}_2$ is

$$\Delta \bar{X} \pm t_{\alpha/2} S_{\Delta \bar{x}}$$

The degrees of freedom for the t statistic depend on the procedure used to estimate $S_{\Delta \bar{x}}$.

Selecting the appropriate computational form for $S_{\Delta \bar{x}}$ and the degrees of freedom for the t distribution are complex problems. The chapter appendix indicates the problem for those readers seeking deeper understanding. However, these complexities can be minimized by making certain reasonable assumptions. We first consider the case with two independent samples.

The most common assumption is that the population variances are equal. In most cases where two populations are compared, this assumption is reasonable and valid. Typically, one factor is different between the two populations and this factor might shift the mean while not affecting the variance. For example, we might be interested in the effect of a treatment, such as using a different raw material, on the productivity per worker. The populations compared would be workers in two different factories or the same factory before and after the change. The variance would result from differences in workers and conditions in the work environment that are not influenced by the treatment. Therefore, the variances, σ_1^2 and σ_2^2, can be assumed equal. Similar arguments could be made for other problems that involve the comparison between two populations.

10.9.1 Population Variances Equal and Independent

When the population variances are equal (Key Idea 10.23),

$$\sigma_1^2 = \sigma_2^2 = \sigma^2$$

the two sample variances, S_1^2 and S_2^2, are both estimates of the same population variance. Therefore, we combine the two sample variances to obtain a single pooled estimate S_p^2 for σ^2:

$$S_p^2 = \frac{(n_1 - 1)S_{x_1}^2 + (n_2 - 1)S_{x_2}^2}{(n_1 - 1) + (n_2 - 1)}$$

Key Idea 10.23: Variance for $\Delta \bar{X}$: $\sigma_1^2 = \sigma_2^2$

For independent samples the pooled estimator of population variance,

$$S_p^2 = \frac{(n_1 - 1)S_{x_1}^2 + (n_2 - 1)S_{x_2}^2}{(n_1 - 1) + (n_2 - 1)}$$

is used to replace the individual sample variance estimates when computing the variance of the difference between sample means when we assume that

$$\sigma_1^2 = \sigma_2^2 = \sigma^2$$

With these assumptions the variance of the difference between sample means is

$$S_{\Delta \bar{X}}^2 = \frac{S_p^2}{n_1} + \frac{S_p^2}{n_2}$$

and the degrees of freedom are

$$\text{DOF} = n_1 - 1 + n_2 - 1 = n_1 + n_2 - 2$$

The confidence interval follows the same form presented above:

$$\bar{X}_1 - \bar{X}_2 \pm t_{\alpha/2} S_{\Delta \bar{X}}$$

The pooled sample variance is a weighted average of the individual sample variances, where the weight is the degrees of freedom. Another equivalent form of the pooled variance is

$$S_p^2 = \frac{\sum_{i=1}^{n}(x_{1i} - \bar{X}_1)^2 + \sum_{i=1}^{n}(x_{2i} - \bar{X}_2)^2}{(n_1 - 1) + (n_2 - 1)}$$

The latter form emphasizes that the pooled variance estimator includes the squared variation about each sample mean.

* 10.9.2 Population Variances Not Equal and Independent Samples

The case where the population variances are unequal (Key Idea 10.24) involves some distribution theory problems that are beyond the scope of this book. The form of the problem is shown in the chapter appendix. Important work has been done by various statisticians and we consider how their results can be used. An early paper by Satterthwaite[4] showed that the individual sample variances could be used to compute

---

[4] F. E. Satterthwaite, "On the Behrens–Fisher problem," *Biometrics Bulletin*, Vol. 2, 1946, p. 110.

Key Idea 10.24: Variance for $\Delta \bar{X}$: $\sigma_1^2 \neq \sigma_2^2$

When the population variances for two independent samples, σ_1^2 and σ_2^2, are unknown and not equal,

$$\sigma_1^2 \neq \sigma_2^2$$

a good approximation for the sample variance of the differences is given by

$$S_{\Delta \bar{X}}^2 = \frac{S_{x_1}^2}{n_1} + \frac{S_{x_2}^2}{n_2}$$

The degrees of freedom can be obtained by using the equation

$$DOF = \frac{[(S_1^2/n_1) + (S_2^2/n_2)]^2}{(S_1^2/n_1)^2/(n_1 - 1) + (S_2^2/n_2)^2/(n_2 - 1)}$$

or if the sample size $n_1 = n_2 = n$, this simplifies to

$$DOF = \left(1 + \frac{2}{S_1^2/S_2^2 + S_2^2/S_1^2}\right)(n - 1)$$

$$S_{\Delta \bar{X}}^2 = \frac{S_{x_1}^2}{n_1} + \frac{S_{x_2}^2}{n_2}$$

This $S_{\Delta \bar{X}}^2$ could be used with a t statistic whose degrees of freedom were computed using

$$DOF = \frac{[(S_1^2/n_1) + (S_2^2/n_2)]^2}{(S_1^2/n_1)^2/(n_1 - 1) + (S_2^2/n_2)^2/(n_2 - 1)}$$

The derivation of degrees of freedom is greatly simplified if the sample sizes from the two populations are equal:

$$n_1 = n_2 = n$$

In that case the degrees of freedom reduce to

$$DOF = \left(1 + \frac{2}{S_1^2/S_2^2 + S_2^2/S_1^2}\right)(n - 1)$$

Using this equation we find that the degrees of freedom range from $1.1(n - 1)$ if the variances have a ratio of 20 to 1 ($S_1^2/S_2^2 = 20$) to $2(n - 1)$ if the variances are equal.

If the sample sizes are not equal, DOF can be computed using these more complex equations. Alternatively, the degrees of freedom can be defined conservatively as the smaller of $n_1 - 1$ or $n_2 - 1$. If the smallest sample is above 30 or 40, this approximation will not seriously affect the confidence interval calculation.

Does It Make Sense?

From the discussion above we see the analysis problems that can result when certain assumptions are used. Several important ideas result from this discussion. First, if the variances of two populations being compared are unknown, assuming equal variances makes the analysis easier and better (e.g., more degrees of freedom for error). If that assumption is not possible, one should seek unequal sample sizes from the two populations. It would be ideal if the largest sample variance occurred with the largest sample size. But if the smallest sample resulted in the largest sample variance, $S_{\Delta \bar{X}}$ would be larger than it would be for the other possibilities. Since the population and sample variances are unknown before the data are collected, an experienced analyst would typically select equal sample sizes if possible. $\qquad\square$

Using these options for computing $\sigma_{\Delta \bar{X}}$, it is also possible to construct single-sided confidence intervals. Single-sided confidence intervals have the same form as those presented in Key Idea 10.20, when σ_i^2 is known (Key Idea 10.25).

Key Idea 10.25: Single-Sided Confidence Intervals

Single-sided confidence intervals could also be computed for each of the cases above. The form follows our previous results:

$$\Delta \mu \geq \bar{X}_1 - \bar{X}_2 - t_{\alpha/2} S_{\Delta \bar{X}}$$

10.9.3 Samples Not Independent

We introduced paired observations in Example 10.8. Here we extend the discussion and provide more computational details. In many comparisons between two populations it is possible and desirable to match or pair individual observations before the study begins (Key Idea 10.26). We will see here that this pairing typically reduces $S_{\Delta \bar{X}}^2$ and results in narrower confidence intervals. Examples include:

1. We wish to test the effect of a new lawn fertilizer. A random sample of lawns is selected and each lawn is split into two equal sections. The new fertilizer is applied to one section and the old fertilizer to the other section for each lawn.
2. To test a new drug a random sample of twins would have one receiving the drug and one not receiving the drug.

By using randomly selected pairs—or the same subject before and after—we neutralize the effect of differences beyond the treatment that would increase the vari-

Key Idea 10.26: Paired Differences Between Samples

In cases involving two samples with paired observations the difference between each pair of observations, $\Delta x_i = x_{1i} - x_{2i}$ should be computed. The sample of differences, $\Delta x_i, i = 1, \ldots, n$, is a single random sample with DOF $= n - 1$. Confidence intervals can then be constructed using the procedure for a single sample with sample mean;

$$\Delta \bar{X} = \frac{\sum_{i=1}^{n} \Delta x_i}{n}$$

$$S_{\Delta x_i}^2 = \frac{\sum_{i=1}^{n}(\Delta x_i - \Delta \bar{X})^2}{n - 1}$$

ance. By following the discussion in Example 10.9, you will see the benefits of pairing. By designing the study carefully, the best results—the narrowest confidence interval—can be obtained for a given sample size.

Example 10.9   Paired Samples of Worker Productivity

A small manufacturer of high-quality speakers wanted to evaluate the effect of their new policies on worker productivity. The factory has recently allowed the workers to develop their own work procedures. Table 10.1 contains worker productivity measurements before and after the new policies. Each observation is a worker. The X_1 and X_2

TABLE 10.1   Differences Between Paired Observations

Observation	X_1	X_2	$\Delta X = X_2 - X_1$
1	11	14	3
2	19	21	2
3	22	25	3
4	6	9	3
5	5	8	3
6	16	20	4
7	13	17	4
8	12	10	−2
9	16	18	2
10	23	21	−2
$\bar{X}$	14.3	16.3	2.0
S^2	37.33	33.76	4.89
$S_{\bar{X}}^2$	3.73	3.38	0.489

observations are the productivities for each worker during a randomly selected hour before (X_1) and after (X_2) the new procedures were implemented. You have been asked by the manufacturer to prepare a confidence interval for the before-and-after differences in worker productivity.

Solution   The ΔX column shows the differences in productivity for each worker. The difference between sample means is

$$\Delta \bar{X} = \bar{X}_2 - \bar{X}_1$$
$$= 16.30 - 14.30$$
$$= 2.0$$

The sample variance of the difference between sample means could be computed using

$$S^2_{\Delta \bar{X}} = S^2_{\bar{X}_2} + S^2_{\bar{X}_1} - 2\hat{\rho} S_{\bar{X}_2} S_{\bar{X}_1}$$

The correlation between the two samples is $\hat{\rho} = 0.932$. Using the correlation and the variances from Table 10.1, the variance of the difference between the sample means was

$$S^2(\Delta \bar{X}) = \frac{37.33}{10} + \frac{33.76}{10} - 2(0.932)\sqrt{\frac{33.76}{10}}\sqrt{\frac{37.33}{10}}$$
$$= 3.38 + 3.73 - 2(0.932)\sqrt{3.38}\sqrt{3.73}$$
$$= 0.489$$

This is the same numerical value as the variance computed using the individual observations of Δx_i in the right-hand column of Table 10.1. It is easier to compute the individual paired differences Δx_i and then use those values to compute the variance of the differences. This example reinforces Key Idea 10.21, which we reemphasize here: *If the analysis can be designed to use paired differences instead of two independent random samples, the variance of the difference will be smaller. This will lead to narrower confidence intervals and hence greater precision for the results.*

The confidence interval can then be computed. The degrees of freedom for this example are $n - 1 = 9$ and the Student t for $\alpha = 0.025$ is $t = 2.26$. The 95% confidence interval is

$$\Delta \bar{X} \pm t_{\alpha/2} S_{\Delta \bar{X}}$$
$$2 \pm 2.26\sqrt{0.489}$$
$$2 \pm 1.58$$

This interval does not include zero, and therefore we conclude that worker productivity had increased after the new policies were implemented.

The confidence interval is relatively wide because of the large t statistic, which results from the small sample. However, because it was possible to use paired observations, the variance for the differences is narrower. The resulting confidence interval was narrow enough to allow detection of a change in productivity despite the small sample.   □

Example 10.10   Unequal Law Enforcement

The residents of the small town of Dasdun have complained for many years that they pay higher traffic fines than the residents of Southill when they receive a traffic ticket for speeding. Gertrude Gill agreed to study the problem and indicate if the complaints were reasonable.

Solution   Gertrude obtained a random sample of $n_1 = 25$ residents of Dasdun and a second random sample of $n_2 = 25$ residents of Southill, all of whom had received a speeding ticket. The sample observations could not be paired. For each resident of Dasdun the fine paid, x_{1i}, was obtained. Similarly, the fine paid by each Southill resident, x_{2i}, was also obtained. Sample variances and sample means were computed for both samples. For the Dasdun sample the sample mean was $\bar{X}_1 = 60$ and the sample variance was $S_{x_1}^2 = 144$. The Southill sample mean was $\bar{X}_2 = 50$ and the sample variance was $S_{x_2}^2 = 121$. The population variances were unknown and assumed equal.

Gertrude decided to compute a confidence interval for the difference between the population means for Dasdun and for Southill. The point estimate for the difference was

$$\Delta\bar{X} = \bar{X}_1 - \bar{X}_2$$
$$= 60 - 50$$
$$= 10$$

Because the population variances of traffic fines were the same, the pooled estimator, S_p^2, for the variances was used. The pooled variance estimator is

$$S_p^2 = \frac{(n_1 - 1)S_{x_1}^2 + (n_2 - 1)S_{x_2}^2}{n_1 + n_2 - 2}$$
$$= \frac{(25 - 1)144 + (25 - 1)121}{25 + 25 - 2}$$
$$= 132.5$$

The sample variance of the difference between sample means is then estimated as follows:

$$S_{\Delta\bar{X}}^2 = S_{\bar{X}_2}^2 + S_{\bar{X}_1}^2$$
$$= \frac{S_p^2}{n_1} + \frac{S_p^2}{n_2}$$
$$= \frac{132.5}{25} + \frac{132.5}{25}$$
$$= 10.6$$
$$S_{\Delta\bar{X}} = 3.26$$

The estimated standard deviation $S_{\Delta\bar{X}}$ is the same numerically as the estimate that does not assume equal population variances, as shown below. This result will always occur when the two sample sizes are equal. However, the advantage is that the degrees of freedom are $n_1 + n_2 - 2 = 48$ instead of using the more complicated complex calculation from Key Idea 10.24, as shown below. The 95% confidence interval is

$$\Delta\bar{X} \pm t_{\alpha/2}S_{\Delta\bar{X}}$$
$$60 - 50 \pm 2.01 \times 3.26$$
$$10 \pm 6.55$$

The confidence interval for the difference excluded zero. Therefore, the sample data supported the conclusion that the citizens of Dasdun pay higher traffic fines. $\square$

10.9.4 Variance Computation Without Equal Variances

The sample variance for the difference between sample means if the population variances are not assumed equal is computed as

$$S_{\Delta\bar{X}}^2 = S_{\bar{X}_1}^2 + S_{\bar{X}_2}^2$$
$$= \frac{S_{x_1}^2}{n_1} + \frac{S_{x_2}^2}{n_2}$$
$$= \frac{144}{25} + \frac{121}{25}$$
$$= 10.6$$
$$S_{\Delta\bar{X}} = 3.26$$

The degrees of freedom for this estimate of standard deviation are

$$\text{DOF} = \left(1 + \frac{2}{144/121 + 121/144}\right)(25 - 1)$$
$$= \left(1 + \frac{60}{61}\right)(25 - 1)$$

and is very close to $2n - 2 = 48$. The 95% confidence interval is therefore

$$\Delta\bar{X} \pm t_{\alpha/2}S_{\Delta\bar{X}}$$
$$60 - 50 \pm 2.01 \times 3.26$$
$$10 \pm 6.55$$

Note that both assumptions result in exactly the same variance and confidence interval. This occurred because the sample variances are similar and the sample sizes are equal.

Example 10.11   Analysis of Motor Vehicle Theft

Kevin Hanson, an official for a national police organization, was concerned about motor vehicle theft. Specifically, he wanted to determine if there had been a change in the theft rate (thefts per 100,000 population) between 1982 and 1984. Tony Judge, a statistician, advised him to use a confidence interval for the mean difference between motor vehicle theft rates.

Solution   After some discussion they decided to obtain the motor vehicle theft rates for each state and the District of Columbia for the years 1982 and 1984. These data sets were treated as random samples from two populations of theft rates.[5] The data for this study were obtained from *Statistical Abstracts,*[6] which contains data on a wide variety of topics.

Initially, the two samples were assumed to be independent random samples from populations with equal variances. Tony computed the pooled estimator of variance and the standard deviation for the difference between sample means. Sample means and variances were computed using Minitab applied to the data file. Exhibit 10.1 presents the results from the **Describe** command, which computes sample means and variances. For computer analysis we labeled the 1982 rates as "Ctheft82" and the 1984 rates as "Ctheft84."

EXHIBIT 10.1   Initial Computer Analysis

	N	MEAN	MEDIAN	TRMEAN	STDEV	SEMEAN
Ctheft82	51	351.5	312.0	337.4	194.6	27.2
Ctheft84	51	343.4	296.0	327.4	194.4	27.2

	MIN	MAX	Q1	Q3
Ctheft82	0.0	969.0	191.0	430.0
Ctheft84	109.0	866.0	180.0	427.0

Examination of the initial computer analysis revealed a problem. The minimum theft rate for the 1982 sample was 0.0. We suspected that this result might be an error and proceeded to check the data for each state. The 0.0 rate was reported for the District of Columbia. Tony decided that the reported theft rate was an error and removed it, leaving 50 observations. The revised computer analysis in Exhibit 10.2 provided a better estimator because it excluded an observation that was probably incorrect. Using the Minitab results, the estimate of variance and the confidence interval were computed. The difference between sample means was

$$\Delta \bar{X} = \bar{X}_{82} - \bar{X}_{84}$$
$$= 358.5 - 336.1$$
$$= 22.4$$

---

[5] The reported theft rates result from compilations prepared in different ways by most law enforcement units in a state. It is recognized that these processes contain various reporting errors. In situations like this statisticians often treat the observations as random variables.

[6] *Statistical Abstracts*, U.S. Government Printing Office, Washington, DC, published annually.

EXHIBIT 10.2   Revised Computer Analysis

	N	MEAN	MEDIAN	TRMEAN	STDEV	SEMEAN
Ctheft82	50	358.5	313.5	341.5	189.9	26.9
Ctheft84	50	336.1	294.0	319.1	189.0	26.7

	MIN	MAX	Q1	Q3
Ctheft82	118.0	969.0	215.0	441.5
Ctheft84	109.0	866.0	179.5	424.0

The pooled estimate of the population variance is

$$S_p^2 = \frac{(n_{82}-1)S_{X_{82}}^2 + (n_{84}-1)S_{X_{84}}^2}{n_{82}+n_{84}-2}$$

$$= \frac{(50-1)(189.9)^2 + (50-1)(189.0)^2}{50+50-2}$$

$$= 35{,}891.5$$

The sample variance for the difference between sample means was estimated as

$$S_{\Delta\bar{X}}^2 = S_{\bar{X}_{82}}^2 + S_{\bar{X}_{84}}^2$$

$$= \frac{S_p^2}{n_{82}} + \frac{S_p^2}{n_{84}}$$

$$= \frac{35{,}891.5}{50} + \frac{35{,}891.5}{50}$$

$$= 1435.66$$

$$S_{\Delta\bar{X}} = 37.89$$

The DOF value for the standard deviation was 98 and the confidence interval was

$$\Delta\bar{X} \pm t_{\alpha/2}\sigma_{\Delta\bar{X}}$$

$$\bar{X}_{82} - \bar{X}_{84} \pm t_{\alpha/2}\sigma_{\Delta\bar{X}}$$

$$358.5 - 336.1 \pm 1.98 \times 37.89$$

$$22.4 \pm 75.02$$

This interval included 0 and did not support a difference between the 1982 and 1984 motor vehicle theft rates.

Assume correlated observations. At this point Tony questioned the assumption that the two samples were independent. The 1982 and 1984 sample data came from the same states. This suggested that a paired observation sample would be a better model for computing the variance of the difference. The correlation between the theft rates was computed and the theft rates for 1982 versus those for 1984 were plotted.

Exhibit 10.3 presents the Minitab output for the correlation and graphical plot. These results provide strong evidence that the samples were correlated.

EXHIBIT 10.3   Computer Analysis to Check for Correlated Samples

Correlation of 1982(y-axis) and 1984 (x-axis)theft rates = 0.958

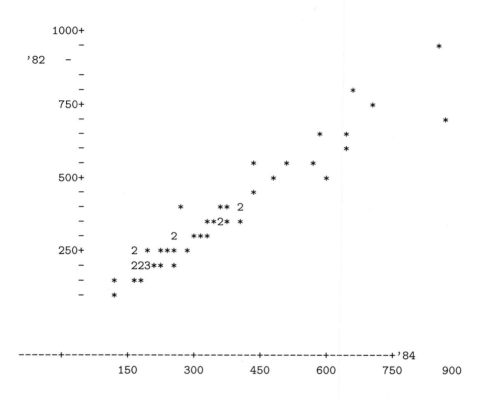

Tony concluded that the analysis procedure should be revised. He computed a new variable, which was the difference between theft rates for each paired observation (e.g., state). Next, the descriptive statistics for the difference variable "Ctheftdf" were computed and presented in Exhibit 10.4. The standard deviation of the mean difference between paired observations was

$$S_{\Delta \bar{x}} = 7.80$$

Note that the standard deviation of the mean is labeled "SEMEAN" in the Minitab output in Exhibit 10.4.

EXHIBIT 10.4   Computer Analysis Assuming Correlated Samples

	N	MEAN	MEDIAN	TRMEAN	STDEV	SEMEAN
Ctheft82	50	358.5	313.5	341.5	189.9	26.9
Ctheft84	50	336.1	294.0	319.1	189.0	26.7
Ctheftdf	50	22.42	20.50	23.77	55.14	7.80

	MIN	MAX	Q1	Q3
Ctheft82	118.0	969.0	215.0	441.5
Ctheft84	109.0	866.0	179.5	424.0
Ctheftdf	-174.00	152.00	0.75	39.00

The 95% confidence interval using paired observations and 49 degrees of freedom was

$$\Delta \bar{X} \pm t_{\alpha/2} S_{\Delta \bar{X}}$$

$$\bar{X}_{82} - \bar{X}_{84} \pm t_{\alpha/2} S_{\Delta \bar{X}}$$

$$358.5 - 336.1 \pm 2.01 \times 7.80$$

$$22.4 \pm 15.68$$

This confidence interval did not include "0" and Tony concluded that motor vehicle theft rates were reduced from 1982 to 1984. We see the importance of using paired correlated samples when they are appropriate.[7]   □

Confidence intervals for differences between sample means follow a pattern. Each confidence interval is based on the method used to compute the variance, $S_{\Delta \bar{X}}^2$, for the difference between sample means. The method selected depends on the assumptions that are appropriate for the comparison. Understanding this pattern will provide you with easy access to an important family of confidence interval estimates.

---

[7] The variance of the difference between the means of correlated samples could also have been computed using the result for correlated random variables:

$$S_{\Delta \bar{X}}^2 = S_{\bar{X}_{82}}^2 + S_{\bar{X}_{84}}^2 - 2\rho_{\bar{X}_{82}\bar{X}_{84}} S_{\bar{X}_{82}} S_{\bar{X}_{84}}$$

$$= \frac{189.9^2}{50} + \frac{189.0^2}{50} - 2(0.958)\left(\frac{189.9}{\sqrt{50}}\right)\left(\frac{189.0}{\sqrt{50}}\right)$$

$$= \frac{36{,}062}{50} + \frac{35{,}721}{50} - \frac{68{,}731}{50}$$

$$= 61.04$$

$$S_{\Delta \bar{X}} = 7.80$$

This calculation is an example showing that paired differences adjust for the covariance effect in the computation of the variance of the difference between dependent sample means.

Does It Make Sense?

Example 10.11 reveals two important results for improving analysis applications involving confidence intervals for the difference between two sample means. First, whenever possible, the analysis should use the differences between paired sample observations. This simplifies the computations and ensures the minimum variance. Second, all data need to be checked carefully to be sure that unusual or incorrect observations are not distorting the results. This checking can be aided by using descriptive statistics, histograms, and scatter plots.   ☐

Practice Problem 10.4: Before-and-After Examination Scores

A random sample of $n = 25$ students is tested before and after studying a unit on competitive markets. Before the study the mean score was 80 with a sample variance of 225. After the study the mean score was 85 and the sample variance 275. Determine the 95% confidence interval if the samples:

(a) Are assumed to be independent.

(b) Have a correlation of 0.50.   ☐

Problem Exercises

10.17 A random sample from two populations provides the following data: $\bar{X}_1 = 150$, $n_1 = 45$, $\bar{X}_2 = 130$, and $n_2 = 34$. In addition, the population variances are known to be $\sigma_1^2 = 900$ and $\sigma_2^2 = 650$. Determine:
(a) The 95% confidence interval for the difference in population means.
(b) The upper limit for the single-tailed 95% confidence interval for the difference between population means.

10.18 Mazdaford, an international automobile manufacturing company, has obtained random samples of 25 production shifts in their U.S. and Australian assembly plants. The number of units produced in 8 hours was obtained for each plant. For the U.S. plant the sample mean was $\bar{X}_1 = 600$ units, and for the Australian plant the sample mean was $\bar{X}_2 = 550$. The variance in units produced is the same for each plant and is equal to 10,000. Determine the following confidence intervals for the difference in productivity between the two plants.
(a) 95%.
(b) 98%.
(c) Based on the analysis above, can you conclude that the population mean productivity is higher?

10.19 Mazdaford, an international automobile manufacturing company, has obtained matched random samples of 25 production shifts in their U.S. and Australian assembly plants. A day and shift were selected randomly and productivity was measured for that day and shift in both plants. The number of units produced in 8 hours was obtained for each plant. Both plants have the same parts suppliers, and therefore the daily productivities in the two plants have a correlation equal to 0.40. For the U.S plant the sample mean was $\bar{X}_1 = 600$ units, and for the Australian plant the sample mean was $\bar{X}_2 = 550$. The variance in units produced is the same for each plant and is equal to 10,000. Determine

the following confidence intervals for the difference in productivity between the two plants.
(a) 95%.
(b) 98%.
(c) Based on the analysis above, can you conclude that the population mean productivity is higher?

10.20 Two random samples from different populations, whose population variances are assumed equal, resulted in the following data: $\bar{X}_1 = 85$, $S_1^2 = 121$, $n_1 = 40$, $\bar{X}_2 = 95$, $S_2^2 = 149$, and $n_2 = 40$. Determine:
(a) The pooled variance estimator.
(b) The 95% confidence interval for the difference between population means.
(c) The upper limit for the single-tailed 95% confidence interval.

10.21 Two random samples from different populations, whose population variances are assumed equal, resulted in the following data: $\bar{X}_1 = 85$, $S_1^2 = 121$, $n_1 = 40$, $\bar{X}_2 = 95$, $S_2^2 = 149$, $n_2 = 40$, and $\hat{\rho}_{x_1,x_2} = 0.42$. Determine:
(a) The pooled variance estimator.
(b) The 95% confidence interval for the difference between population means.
(c) The upper limit for the single-tailed 95% confidence interval.

10.22 Checkitout Auditors, Inc. conducted a random sample of the accounts payable for the east and the west offices of Amalgamated Distributors. From these two independent samples they wanted to determine the difference between the population mean values of the payables. From the east office the sample statistics were $\bar{X} = 240$, $\sigma = 28$, and $n = 28$; from the west office the statistics were $\bar{X} = 290$, $\sigma = 42$, and $n = 28$. The variances of payable values are assumed equal in the two offices. Determine the following confidence intervals for the difference between population means.
(a) 94%.
(b) 98%.

10.10 DIFFERENCE BETWEEN PROPORTIONS

Now that we have developed confidence intervals for differences between sample means it is natural to consider differences between sample proportions. The procedure developed here for differences between proportions has a form similar to that developed for differences between sample means. An important difference is the computation of variance because we are working with differences between proportions.

Estimates of the differences between sample proportions have many applications in business and economics.

1. Market researchers estimate the difference between the percentage of customers who purchase product A versus the percentage who purchase product B.
2. Development economists estimate the change in the proportion of infants who gain weight after a nutrition program is implemented.

3. Politicians and economic policy analysts want to know the change in the unemployment rate from one month to the next.
4. Production managers want to know if the proportion defectives has changed because of manufacturing adjustments.

In the examples above, estimates are computed for both population proportions by using random samples. Two random samples of size n_1 and n_2 are obtained. From each sample the sample proportion $\hat{P}_1$ and $\hat{P}_2$ can be computed. The differences between sample proportions and the variance of the difference are

$$\Delta \hat{P} = \hat{P}_2 - \hat{P}_1$$

$$\sigma_{\Delta \hat{P}}^2 = \sigma_{\hat{P}_1}^2 + \sigma_{\hat{P}_2}^2$$

The variance of $\hat{P}$ requires that we know the population proportion π. However, π is not known in many applied problems. Thus we use $\hat{P}$ as an approximation and compute the estimated variance of $\Delta \hat{P}$ using

$$\hat{\sigma}_{\Delta \hat{P}}^2 = \hat{\sigma}_{\hat{P}_1}^2 + \hat{\sigma}_{\hat{P}_2}^2$$

$$= \frac{\hat{P}_1(1 - \hat{P}_1)}{n_1} + \frac{\hat{P}_2(1 - \hat{P}_2)}{n_2}$$

$$\hat{\sigma}_{\Delta \hat{P}} = \sqrt{\frac{\hat{P}_1(1 - \hat{P}_1)}{n_1} + \frac{\hat{P}_2(1 - \hat{P}_2)}{n_2}}$$

Because $\Delta \hat{P}$ has a normal distribution, the confidence interval follows directly from our previous work:

$$\Delta \hat{P} \pm Z_{\alpha/2} \times \hat{\sigma}_{\Delta \hat{P}}$$

This confidence interval is used for applications similar to those presented above.

Example 10.12   Percent Drinking Drivers

A researcher wanted to know if the percentage of drinking drivers increased during later evening hours. She decided to compare the percentage of drinking drivers from 7:00 to 9:00 P.M. with the percentage from 10:00 to 12:00 P.M.

Solution   This question can be answered with a confidence interval that she proceeded to develop. She obtained a random sample of $n_1 = 250$ drivers from the first time period and a random sample of $n_2 = 200$ drivers from the second. Each driver in both samples was given a breath test and assigned to the category drinking driver or nondrinking driver. From the early period, $\hat{P}_1 = 0.12$ of the drivers were drinking drivers, and from the late period, $\hat{P}_2 = 0.19$ were drinking drivers. The standard deviation for the difference $\Delta \hat{P}$ was

$$\hat{\sigma}^2_{\Delta \hat{P}} = \frac{0.12(1 - 0.12)}{250} + \frac{0.19(1 - 0.19)}{200}$$
$$= 0.0004224 + 0.0007695$$
$$= 0.0011919$$
$$\hat{\sigma}_{\Delta \hat{P}} = 0.0345$$

The 95% confidence interval was

$$\Delta \hat{P} \pm Z_{\alpha/2} \hat{\sigma}_{\Delta \hat{P}}$$
$$0.19 - 0.12 \pm 1.96 \times 0.0345$$
$$0.07 \pm 0.068$$

The interval did not include zero, and she concluded that there was an increase in the percentage of drinking drivers between the early and late periods. $\square$

10.11 SAMPLE SIZE DETERMINATION

In many statistical situations we are asked to determine the appropriate sample size (Key Idea 10.27). Various rules of thumb exist among persons without a clear understanding of statistical concepts. Included in this set of rules is one which says that "10 or 20% of the population should provide a good sample." As we showed in Chapter 9, this rule has two problems: (1) there is no indication that the sample is a random

---

Key Idea 10.27: Sample Size Determination

The choice of sample size depends on the maximum difference that can be tolerated between $\bar{X}$ and μ. Define this maximum difference as

$$\Delta = \bar{X} - \mu$$

Then we compute the sample size n from

$$\Delta = Z_{\alpha/2} \frac{\sigma}{\sqrt{n}}$$

$Z_{\alpha/2}$ depends on the probability of error α selected, and σ is a property of the population from which the random sample will be obtained. The sample size is determined by the maximum difference, Δ:

$$n = Z^2_{\alpha/2} \left(\frac{\sigma}{\Delta} \right)^2$$

sample, and (2) it is sample size and not percentage of the population that determines the precision of the sample result. You now have the necessary statistical background to compute the sample size required for a desired confidence interval width.

Increased sample size yields greater precision for the resulting estimates. Experience provides an intuitive understanding of the benefits from larger samples. The more times we see something occur, the stronger is our belief that it will occur again. This result expressed in statistical terms is the narrower confidence interval from a larger sample size. These narrower intervals strengthen our belief in the point estimate. The width of a confidence interval is inversely related to the square root of the sample size n:

$$\bar{X} \pm Z_{\alpha/2} \frac{\sigma}{\sqrt{n}}$$

Sample size increases as the square of the ratio of the standard deviation σ divided by one-half the confidence interval Δ. Figure 10.4 shows the relationship between sample size and σ/Δ for an approximate 95% confidence interval. This graph could be used as a rough guide for sample size determination. More important, note that sample size increases faster than the ratio of σ/Δ. Using these results, we can determine the appropriate sample size for a given precision measured by Δ. The computed sample size might be larger than the maximum sample possible for the given budget. In that case the maximum difference will be increased to reflect the limited budget for obtaining sample observations.

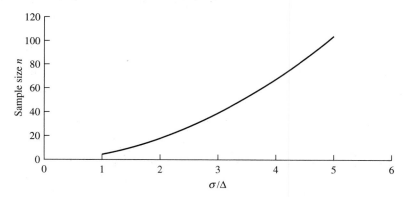

Figure 10.4   Sample Size as a Function of σ/Δ

10.11.1 Sample Size for Proportions

Determining the sample size for proportions (Key Idea 10.28) also uses the concepts developed above. The maximum difference between the sample proportion, $\hat{P}$, and the population proportion, π, is

$$\Delta = \hat{P} - \mu = Z_{\alpha/2} \sqrt{\frac{\pi(1-\pi)}{n}}$$

Key Idea 10.28: Sample Size for Proportions

Defining the maximum difference between μ and $\hat{P}$ as Δ, we obtain

$$\Delta = Z_{\alpha/2}\sqrt{\frac{\pi(1-\pi)}{n}}$$

and the sample size can be computed using

$$n = Z_{\alpha/2}^2 \frac{\pi(1-\pi)}{\Delta^2}$$

Does It Make Sense?

The equation for computing sample size reveals an important relationship between precision and sample size. Consider Δ—which is the maximum difference between μ and $\hat{P}$ and also one-half the confidence interval—as a measure of precision. If you wish to reduce Δ by a factor of $\frac{1}{2}$, the original sample size n_1 and the new sample size n_2 would be

$$n_1 = Z_{\alpha/2}^2 \left(\frac{\sigma}{\Delta}\right)^2$$

$$n_2 = Z_{\alpha/2}^2 \left(\frac{\sigma}{(1/2)\Delta}\right)^2$$

The ratio of the sample sizes is

$$\frac{n_2}{n_1} = \frac{Z_{\alpha/2}^2[\sigma/(1/2)\Delta]^2}{Z_{\alpha/2}^2(\sigma/\Delta)^2}$$

$$= \left(\frac{1}{1/2}\right)^2$$

$$= 4$$

Thus the sample size must be increased fourfold. A similar calculation would show that a reduction of Δ by one-fifth would require a sample size increase by a factor of

$$\frac{1}{(4/5)^2} = \frac{25}{16} = 1.56$$

A major portion of the cost of data collection is related directly to the sample size. Thus an initial computed sample size based on a desired confidence interval may exceed the project budget. In that case managers must either increase the budget or accept a wider confidence interval and hence less precision. Discussions of the trade-off between cost of data and study precision make use of the equations for computing sample size.   □

* 10.11.2 Economic Analysis

The choice of sample size in applied problems involves a trade-off between the benefits of a narrower confidence interval and the cost of larger sample size (Key Idea 10.29). The example presented here shows how this trade-off could be applied. There are other examples, but all require an economic analysis.

Key Idea 10.29: Sample Size: Economic Trade-off

The choice of sample size is an economic trade-off between the cost of more observations and the benefit of better decisions.

1. The cost of obtaining a sample size n can usually be approximated as an increasing linear function of the sample size.
2. Larger sample sizes contribute to better decisions because of improved precision of the sample information. However, the relationship usually contains decreasing returns to scale from increased sample size.

In the preceding two sections we have shown how sample size can be determined given a desired confidence interval of width $2 \times \Delta$. If we were to ask a decision maker for a confidence interval, he or she would like to say: "Give me a confidence interval with width 0." Decision makers know that optimal decisions require perfect knowledge, and perfect knowledge implies a confidence interval of width zero. Unfortunately, such a confidence interval would require a very large sample size (i.e., sample size equals population size) and hence a very large cost. However, there must be a trade-off between the desire for precise, expensive estimates and the desire for low-cost, imprecise estimates.

Data collection usually begins with a fixed cost for study design and management. In addition, there is usually a cost that is related directly to the number of observations. For example, each interview or test has the same marginal cost. Therefore, the marginal cost of larger sample sizes increases linearly with the number of observations.

However, the benefits from narrower confidence intervals are more difficult to determine because the benefits of improved information are difficult to quantify precisely. We consider the economics of sample size in the following example.

Example 10.13   Acme Lumber Company

The Acme Lumber Company is considering the purchase of a large stand of timber to provide inputs for its operations. Before agreeing on a purchase price, Acme can obtain aerial photographs from which the amount of timber can be estimated. Each photograph can be treated as a random observation from which the amount of timber per acre can be computed. Each photograph costs $40 and they can obtain from 1 to 100 observations. The standard deviation of the population of timber computations is 10. Acme has chosen a 95.44% confidence interval, and thus $Z_{\alpha/2} = 2.0$. With a sample of size 1 the confidence interval is ± 20, and with a sample of size 100 the confidence interval is ± 2. Management has asked you to determine the sample size that will minimize the sum of sampling and decision cost.

Solution   After some discussion management concludes that a confidence interval of ± 20 will cost the company $10,000 in added risk and decision effort. We define this cost as decision cost. At the other extreme a confidence interval of ± 2 will have a decision cost of 0 because of the certainty associated with the narrow interval. It is further assumed that decision cost is related directly to the width of the confidence interval. Thus for a confidence interval of ± 11 the cost would be $5000. Figure 10.5 shows the linear relationship between one-half the width of the confidence interval Δ and the decision cost. Figure 10.6 shows the relationship between sample size and decision cost. The decision cost is related directly to Δ. But Δ is related to 1 over the square root of the sample size, $1/\sqrt{n}$. Therefore, decision cost is a function of 1 over the square root of the sample size. Initial increases in sample size result in large decreases in decision cost. The cost of obtaining sample data increases linearly with sample size because each observation has a cost of $10. Figure 10.7 shows the decision cost and sampling cost functions plotted against sample size. We have also shown a total cost function, which is the sum of the decision cost and the sampling cost. The optimal sample size is the value of n that minimizes total cost. For this example the sample size is approximately 25.[8]

The example presents one model for determining the optimal sample size. Other models could be developed. Figure 10.7 provides a schematic representation of the form for the sample size problem.   □

---

[8] The equation for decision cost in this problem can be shown to be

$$\text{decision cost} = \frac{20 - 2\sqrt{n}}{18\sqrt{n}} \times 10{,}000$$

and the sampling cost function is, of course,

$$\text{sampling cost} = 40 \times n$$

The optimal sample size is found where these two functions are equal, as shown in Figure 10.7.

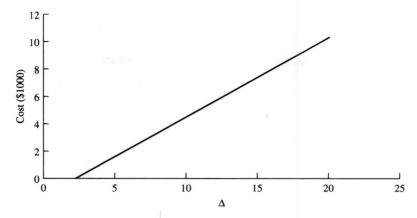

Figure 10.5   Decision Cost as a Function of Δ

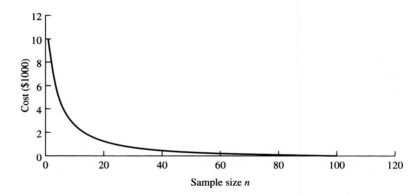

Figure 10.6   Decision Cost as a Function of Sample Size

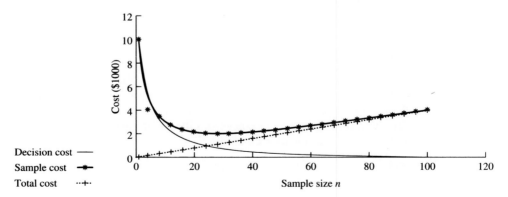

Figure 10.7   Minimum Cost Sample Size

Problem Exercises

10.23 A random sample was obtained from each of two consumer populations, and subjects were asked if they would purchase a new product. From sample 1 a random sample of size $n_1 = 380$ found 160 who would purchase the product. From sample 2 a random sample of size $n_2 = 400$ found 180 who would purchase the product. Determine the following confidence intervals for the difference in proportions.
(a) 95%.
(b) 98%.

10.24 Sarah Box is running for governor and has retained a firm to conduct weekly random sample voter surveys to estimate the proportion of voters who would vote for her. In week 7 of the campaign a random sample of 924 voters resulted in 450 who indicated they would vote for her. In week 8 a random sample of 912 voters contained 490 who would vote for her.
(a) Compute the 95% confidence interval for the difference in the population proportion that would vote for Sarah.
(b) Compute the lower limit of the 95% single-tailed confidence interval for the difference in voter support for Sarah.
(c) Is there any evidence to conclude that the proportion of voters who support Sarah is increasing?

10.25 Joe Morgan, an industrial statistician, has been asked to determine the sample size for a study of manufactured part weights. The variance of the population has a variance of 16. After discussion with the production manager, they decided that the 95% confidence interval for the mean weight should be $\bar{X} \pm 0.8$. Determine the sample size required:
(a) To obtain this confidence interval.
(b) If the production manager wants a confidence interval of $\bar{X} \pm 0.6$.

10.26 The marketing research department of a large consumer goods firm was planning a survey to estimate the proportion of people who would purchase their proposed new product. They would like to have a 95% confidence interval equal to $\hat{P} \pm 0.06$. Use $\pi = 0.50$. Determine the sample size required:
(a) To obtain this confidence interval.
(b) If the desired confidence interval is $\hat{P} \pm 0.08$.

*10.12 CONFIDENCE INTERVALS FOR VARIANCES

The first objective of statistical estimation is usually the mean or proportion and its confidence interval. However, in many cases managers are also interested in the variability of a process. Modern quality assurance requires stable processes with low variance. As a result, sample variances and their confidence intervals are increasingly reported. Important applications include:

1. Quality control systems continually estimate both the central tendency and variation of component dimensions.

2. A small variance of production in units per hour is an important indication of a properly operating manufacturing process.

3. The variance of daily sales in a retail store provides an indication of the ability to maintain a uniform cash flow to cover expenses.

4. The variance of demand is an important parameter used in the design of inventory control systems.

We know that

$$S^2 = \frac{\sum_{i=1}^{n}(x_i - \bar{X})^2}{n - 1}$$

is an unbiased estimator of the population variance σ^2. We will now develop a confidence interval for σ^2 under the assumption that the random variable X has a normal distribution. Confidence intervals for variances are based on the chi-square χ^2 probability density function, developed in Section 9.6. The key result is that

$$\frac{(n - 1)S^2}{\sigma^2} \sim \chi_{n-1}^2$$

The left-hand term involving S^2 has a χ^2 distribution with $(n - 1)$ degrees of freedom. Using this result, we can state the following probability:

$$P\left(\chi_L^2 \leq \frac{(n - 1)S^2}{\sigma^2} \leq \chi_U^2\right) = 1 - \alpha$$

where χ_L^2 and χ_U^2 are the lower and upper $\alpha/2$ probability points as shown in Figure 10.8. From this probability statement we can derive a confidence interval for σ^2 by using a few algebraic steps (Key Idea 10.30).

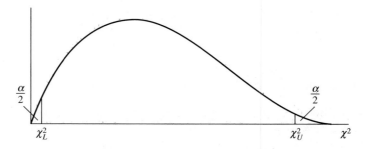

Figure 10.8 Chi-Square Probability Distribution

Example 10.14   Variance of Furnace Temperatures

Robert Saito, manager of Northern Steel, Inc., wants to know the temperature variation in the firm's new electric furnace. He obtains a random sample of 25 temperatures over a one-week period. From this sample he computes the sample variance $S^2 = 100$. He asks you to construct a 95% confidence interval for the population variance temperature.

Key Idea 10.30: Variance Confidence Interval

Confidence intervals for variances are computed using

$$P\left(\frac{(n-1)S^2}{\chi_U^2} \leq \sigma^2 \leq \frac{(n-1)S^2}{\chi_L^2}\right) = 1 - \alpha$$

This interval,

$$\frac{(n-1)S^2}{\chi_U^2} \leq \sigma^2 \leq \frac{(n-1)S^2}{\chi_L^2}$$

includes the population variance with probability $1 - \alpha$. The interval is nonsymmetric.

Solution   You proceed using the distribution of sample variances. From Table A.3 you find that $\chi_L^2 = 12.40$ and that $\chi_U^2 = 39.36$ for $n - 1 = 24$ degrees of freedom and $\alpha = 0.05$. We compute the 95% confidence interval.

$$\frac{(n-1)S^2}{\chi_U^2} \leq \sigma^2 \leq \frac{(n-1)S^2}{\chi_L^2}$$

$$\frac{(25-1)100}{39.36} \leq \sigma^2 \leq \frac{(25-1)100}{12.40}$$

$$60.98 \leq \sigma^2 \leq 193.55$$

You inform Robert that the temperature variance is in the range 61 to 194.   □

* 10.13 CONFIDENCE INTERVAL: RATIO OF VARIANCES

In addition to confidence intervals for single variances, we can obtain confidence intervals for the ratio of variances from two different populations (Key Idea 10.31). Confidence intervals for the ratio of variances are based on the F distribution presented in Section 9.9. From Section 9.9 the F random variable is the ratio of two χ^2 random variables, each of which is divided by its degrees of freedom. The χ^2 random variables for two different populations are

$$\chi_1^2 = \frac{(n_1 - 1)S_1^2}{\sigma_1^2}$$

$$\chi_2^2 = \frac{(n_2 - 1)S_2^2}{\sigma_2^2}$$

Key Idea 10.31: Ratio of Variance Confidence Interval

The confidence interval for the ratio of variances is derived as follows:

$$P\left(F_L \leq \frac{S_1^2/\sigma_1^2}{S_2^2/\sigma_2^2} \leq F_U\right) = 1 - \alpha$$

where F_L and F_U are the lower and upper $\alpha/2$ probability points as shown in Figure 10.9. F_L and F_U assume $n_1 - 1$ degrees of freedom for the numerator and $n_2 - 1$ degrees of freedom for the denominator. A simple transformation leads to the $1 - \alpha$ percent confidence interval:

$$F_L \frac{S_2^2}{S_1^2} \leq \frac{\sigma_2^2}{\sigma_1^2} \leq F_U \frac{S_2^2}{S_1^2}$$

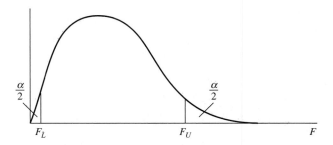

Figure 10.9   *F* Probability Distribution

Then after dividing each χ^2 by its degrees of freedom $(n - 1)$, the F random variable is

$$F = \frac{S_1^2/\sigma_1^2}{S_2^2/\sigma_2^2}$$

Understanding of the confidence intervals described in Key Idea 10.31 will be improved by considering the following example.

Example 10.15   Comparing Temperature Variances

Northern Steel has just opened a second furnace and wants to compare the temperature variances between the old and new furnaces. From Example 10.14 a random sample of size $n_1 = 25$ observations resulted in a sample variance of $S_1^2 = 100$. A second random sample of $n_2 = 31$ temperatures is obtained from the new furnace. The computed variance is $S_2^2 = 75$. After some discussion we agree that a 90% confidence interval for the ratio of the old furnace variance to the new furnace variance, σ_1^2/σ_2^2, will be developed.

Solution   The confidence interval computation follows the foregoing analysis. The upper value of the F distribution F_U is obtained from Table A.4 with $n_1 - 1 = 24$ degrees of freedom for the numerator and $n_2 - 1 = 30$ degrees of freedom for the denominator. The result is

$$F_U = F_{U,(24),(30)} = 1.89$$

For the lower limit we use the reciprocal property of the F distribution to obtain the following identity:

$$F_{L,(n_1-1),(n_2-1)} = \frac{1}{F_{U,(n_2-1),(n_1-1)}}$$

Application to this problem has the result

$$F_{L,(25-1),(31-1)} = \frac{1}{F_{U,(30),(24)}}$$

$$= \frac{1}{1.94}$$

$$= 0.515$$

The 90% confidence interval is

$$F_L \frac{S_1^2}{S_2^2} \le \frac{\sigma_1^2}{\sigma_2^2} \le F_U \frac{S_1^2}{S_2^2}$$

$$0.515 \frac{100}{75} \le \frac{\sigma_1^2}{\sigma_2^2} \le 1.89 \frac{100}{75}$$

$$0.69 \le \frac{\sigma_1^2}{\sigma_2^2} \le 2.52$$

Based on this analysis you report to Mr. Saito that the ratio of variances for furnace 1 temperature to furnace 2 temperature is between 0.69 and 2.52. You also note that if samples of size 61 had been used to estimate each variance, the interval would be

$$F_L \frac{S_1^2}{S_2^2} \le \frac{\sigma_1^2}{\sigma_2^2} \le F_U \frac{S_1^2}{S_2^2}$$

$$0.654 \frac{100}{75} \le \frac{\sigma_1^2}{\sigma_2^2} \le 1.53 \frac{100}{75}$$

$$0.86 \le \frac{\sigma_1^2}{\sigma_2^2} \le 2.03 \qquad \qquad \square$$

Does It Make Sense?

The confidence interval for variances and the ratio of variances is relatively wide compared to confidence intervals for means and proportions. In addition, the confidence interval is not symmetric about the point estimate of the variance or the ratio of variances. These characteristics result from the squared values of random variables compared to the linear values for means and proportions. Typically, there is greater uncertainty about variances compared to means. One or two large sample observations can have a large effect on a sample variance because variances use squared computations. In contrast, the linear deviations of large observations are brought closer to the sample mean by dividing by n. In addition, the confidence intervals for variances are affected more by departures from normality than are confidence intervals for means. Confidence intervals for variances require more judgment when they are used.   □

SUMMARY OF KEY IDEAS

PRACTICE PROBLEM SOLUTIONS

10.1 (a) The expected value of the sample mean for the random sample of size $n = 4$—x_1, x_2, x_3, x_4—is

$$\mu_{\bar{x}} = E\left[\frac{x_1}{4} + \frac{x_2}{4} + \frac{x_3}{4} + \frac{x_4}{4}\right]$$

$$= \frac{3.0}{4} + \frac{3.0}{4} + \frac{3.0}{4} + \frac{3.0}{4}$$

$$= 3.0$$

and the variance of the sample mean is

$$\sigma_{\bar{X}}^2 = \frac{\sigma_{x_1}^2}{16} + \frac{\sigma_{x_2}^2}{16} + \frac{\sigma_{x_1}^2}{16} + \frac{\sigma_{x_2}^2}{16}$$

$$= \frac{4 \times 0.001}{16}$$

$$= \frac{0.001}{4}$$

Note that the sample mean is a minimum variance and unbiased estimator of the population mean.

(b) In this case two of the sample observations have a bias of 0.02 inch, but the fixed shift of the mean does not affect the variance:

$$\mu_{\bar{x}} = E\left[\frac{x_1}{4} + \frac{x_2}{4} + \frac{x_3}{4} + \frac{x_4}{4}\right]$$

$$= \frac{3.02}{4} + \frac{3.02}{4} + \frac{3.0}{4} + \frac{3.0}{4}$$

$$= 3.01$$

and the variance of the sample mean is

$$\sigma_{\bar{X}}^2 = \frac{\sigma_{x_1}^2}{16} + \frac{\sigma_{x_2}^2}{16} + \frac{\sigma_{x_1}^2}{16} + \frac{\sigma_{x_2}^2}{16}$$

$$= \frac{4 \times 0.001}{16}$$

$$= \frac{0.001}{4}$$

(c) The bias in part (b) is the difference between the population mean and the expected value of the sample mean in part (b):

$$\text{bias} = 3.01 - 3.00 = 0.01$$

(d) The mean square error (MSE) is the variance plus the bias squared:

$$\text{MSE} = \frac{0.001}{4} + 0.01^2$$
$$= 0.00025 + 0.001$$
$$= 0.00125$$

Note that the bias portion of the mean square error is not influenced by increased sample size.

10.2 (a) The first task is to compute the standard deviation of the population mean, $\sigma_{\bar{X}}$. A variance of 0.01 implies a standard deviation 0.1 centimeter. Therefore,

$$\sigma_{\bar{X}} = \frac{0.1}{\sqrt{25}} = 0.02$$

The confidence interval is

$$P\left(\bar{X} - Z_{\alpha/2}\sigma_{\bar{X}} \leq \mu \leq \bar{X} + Z_{\alpha/2}\sigma_{\bar{X}}\right) = 1 - \alpha$$
$$P\left(54 - 1.96 \times 0.02 \leq \mu \leq 54 + 1.96 \times 0.02\right) = 0.95$$
$$54 \pm 0.04$$

(b) The lower confidence limit concentrates $\alpha = 0.05$ in one tail and thus uses $Z_\alpha = 1.645$, where $\alpha = 0.05$:

$$\mu \geq \bar{X} - Z_{0.05} \times 0.02$$
$$\geq 54 - 0.0329$$
$$\geq 53.9671$$

10.3 We know that the sample proportion has an approximate normal distribution, and therefore the confidence interval will be developed using the standardized normal Z value from Table A.1. The first tasks are to compute the maximum likelihood estimate of the sample proportion and then to compute the variance of the sample proportion:

$$\hat{P}_{\text{MLE}} = \frac{x}{n} = \frac{160}{400} = 0.40$$

The variance of the sample proportion is computed as

$$\sigma_{\hat{P}} = \sqrt{\frac{\pi(1-\pi)}{n}} = \sqrt{\frac{0.40(1-0.40)}{400}} = 0.024$$

Note that the maximum likelihood estimator for the population proportion, π, was used to compute the variance.

(a) The 95% confidence interval is computed by assigning a probability of 0.025 to each tail of the normal distribution. The Z value from Table A.1 is $Z = 1.96$, and thus the confidence interval is

$$\hat{P} \pm Z_{\alpha/2}\sigma_{\hat{P}}$$
$$0.40 \pm 1.96 \times 0.024$$
$$0.40 \pm 0.048$$

(b) The 95% lower-tail confidence interval concentrates the error in the lower tail, and thus the $Z_{0.05}$ value from Table A.1 is 1.645. The confidence interval is thus

$$\pi \geq \hat{P} - Z_{\alpha}\sigma_{\hat{P}}$$
$$\geq 0.40 - 1.645 \times 0.24$$
$$\geq 0.36$$

10.4 (a) The first step is to compute the difference between the before-and-after test scores:

$$\Delta\bar{X}_1 = \bar{X}_2 - \bar{X}_1$$
$$= 85 - 80$$
$$= 5$$

Next we assume that the population variances are equal because we are using the same students, and we compute

$$S_p^2 = \frac{(n_1 - 1)S_1^2 + (n_2 - 1)S_2^2}{n_1 + n_2 - 2}$$
$$= \frac{(24)(225) + (24)(275)}{24 + 24}$$
$$= 250$$

The standard deviation of the difference if the samples are independent is

$$S_{\Delta\bar{X}}^2 = \frac{250}{25} + \frac{250}{25}$$
$$= 10 + 10$$
$$= 20$$
$$S_{\Delta\bar{X}} = 4.47$$

The confidence interval is

$$5 \pm t_{48,0.025}S_{\Delta\bar{X}}$$
$$5 \pm (2.01)(4.47)$$
$$5 \pm 8.98$$

(b) The standard deviation of the difference between sample means if the sample means have a correlation of 0.5 is

$$S^2_{\Delta \bar{X}} = \frac{225}{25} + \frac{275}{25} - 2(0.5)\sqrt{9}\sqrt{11}$$
$$= 10.05$$
$$S_{\Delta \bar{X}} = 3.17$$

The confidence interval is

$$5 \pm t_{24,0.025}S_{\Delta \bar{X}}$$
$$5 \pm (2.064)(3.17)$$
$$5 \pm 6.54$$

CHAPTER PROBLEMS

10.1 The president of a large research organization has issued a proposed policy memo which states that only unbiased estimators will be presented in its reports. Comment on this policy considering all the properties of estimators discussed in this chapter.

10.2 Explain the difference between an unbiased estimator and a consistent estimator.

10.3 The sample mean is an unbiased estimator of the population mean. However, in some cases other estimators may result in a smaller variance. In those cases an analyst could choose an estimator with the smallest mean square error (MSE) instead of considering only unbiased estimators. Suppose that a population has a probability distribution function as follows:

Y	$f(y)$
0	0.40
1	0.50
5	0.10

In this distribution 90% of the time the random variable will have a value of 0 or 1. However, there will be some extreme outliers with a value of 5. These outliers can have a major effect on the mean from a small sample. To eliminate the effect of outliers, we could use an estimator $\bar{Y}^*$, which is the average of a random sample with the extreme value 5 removed. Compare the estimator $\bar{Y}^*$ with the mean $\bar{Y}$ as the sample size n increases. Use the properties unbiasedness, mean square efficiency, and consistency.

10.4 The famous Dundas probability density function is

$$f(y \mid \theta_1) = \frac{1}{a}K^{(-1/b)(Y-\theta_1)^2}$$

where a, b, and K are constants and θ_1 is a population parameter.
(a) Derive the maximum likelihood estimator for θ_1, a random sample y_i, $i = 1, \ldots, n$. Present the complete analysis that leads to your estimator. Merely presenting the correct answer will not result in full credit.
(b) Use the random sample 5, 6, 4, 7, 8 to compute and estimate for θ_1 using the estimator derived above.

10.5   A random variable X has a probability density function

$$f(x) = K \times 10^{-(x-a)^2}$$

where K and a are unknown parameters.
(a) What is the likelihood function for a assuming that K is known and you have a random sample of n observations for the random variable x?
(b) Derive the maximum likelihood estimator for parameter a.
(c) Given the random sample 100, 110, 120, 115, 125, what is the maximum likelihood estimate for a?

10.6   Derive the maximum likelihood estimators for the mean and variance of a normal distribution given a random sample of size n.

10.7   Based on past research, you know that the time required for a student to finish a statistics exam is defined by an exponential probability distribution whose pdf is $f(t) = \lambda e^{-\lambda t}$.
(a) John George, a randomly selected student, required 25 minutes to complete the exam. Determine the maximum likelihood estimator for λ based on this observation. Derive the estimate for a sample of size 1.
(b) An additional random sample of 10 students was selected, and each of their test completion times were recorded. The additional observations are 20, 21, 24, 35, 50, 65, 80, 10, 29, 35. Derive the maximum likelihood estimator for this random sample and use the data to obtain the maximum likelihood estimate for λ.

10.8   The random variable X is a measure of the "pleasure factor" that occurs when eating Ole rolls. The probability distribution for this continuous random variable is

$$f(x) = K e^{-(2x-3\mu)^2}$$

where K is a constant and μ is the distribution parameter.
(a) Given a sample of n random observations of x, derive the maximum likelihood estimator for the parameter μ.
(b) Given the following observations in the random sample: 5, 7, 4, 8, 3, compute the maximum likelihood estimate using the estimator dervied in part (a).

10.9   The probability that a task will be completed by time t can be modeled using the probability density function $f(t) = \lambda e^{-\lambda t}$ given that the task completion can be modeled by a Poisson process.
(a) Derive the maximum likelihood estimator for the parameter λ given that you have a random sample of size n task completion times.
(b) Given the following randomly selected completion times: 5, 8, 12, 6, 15, 18, compute the point estimate using the estimator derived above.

10.10 The time to repair a car at Acme Auto is modeled by an exponential distribution with parameter λ. If the first car is repaired in 40 minutes, determine the maximum likelihood estimator and the specific estimate for λ. Additional random observations provided the following times to complete repairs on other cars: 50, 30, 20, 45, 60, 75. Derive the maximum likelihood estimator and the estimate for this sample.

10.11 A study of the January weather in Oak Park resulted in a sample mean of 20°F and a sample variance of 79.8. The sample included 25 observations. What is the 95% confidence interval for the mean temperature?

10.12 From a random sample of size $n = 25$, we find that $\sum_{i=1}^{n} y_i = 1000$ and $\sum_{i=1}^{n}(y_i - \bar{Y})^2 = 600$. Given that the y's are normally distributed, compute the maximum likelihood estimate for the population mean μ and a 90% confidence interval for the population mean.

10.13 Speedy Express is a regional delivery service that guarantees delivery within 24 hours or it refunds the cost of delivery. Their delivery process was designed to have a mean $\mu = 19$ and a variance $\sigma^2 = 9$. In the past months the percentage of deliveries eligible for refunds has increased from 5% to 15%. A random sample of $n = 36$ had a mean $\bar{Y} = 19.6$ and a variance $S^2 = 15.6$. Compute the following confidence intervals for the population mean delivery time.
   (a) 95%.
   (b) 98%.
   (c) Based on the results above, would you argue that the mean delivery time has increased?

10.14 The quality control department of a major automobile company was studying the dimensions of parts from a stamping mill.
   (a) A random sample of $n = 36$ pieces had a sample standard deviation of $S = 0.025$. Construct a 95% confidence interval for the population mean.
   (b) A random sample of $n = 21$ pieces from a similar machine has a sample standard deviation of $S = 0.021$. Construct a 95% confidence interval for the population mean from this machine.

10.15 The fat content of deluxe hamburger at George's market is advertised as having no more than 25 units of fat. To assure this guarantee, the hamburger preparation process has been set at a mean of $\mu = 20$ units with variance of $\sigma^2 = 9$. The amount of fat in any single 1-pound package is assumed to be normally distributed with the foregoing mean and variance.
   (a) A random sample of size $n = 30$ is obtained and found to have a mean $\bar{Y} = 21$ and a variance $S^2 = 15$. What is the 95% confidence interval for the population mean based on this sample?
   (b) A second random sample of size $n = 21$ is obtained from a second store and found to have a mean $\bar{Y} = 21.4$ with a variance of $S^2 = 8$. What is the 98% confidence interval for the population mean based on this sample?

10.16 The pollution control manager, Shirley Becker, has issued contracts to four different air quality testing firms to obtain estimates of the pollutant level outside the Mill Creek Foundry. Each testing firm reports the mean pollutant level, $\bar{Y}$, from their random sample and the sample size n. From her secret files Shirley knows the variance, σ^2, of individual observations based on the testing equipment used by each testing firm. The results are:

$$\textit{Firm 1:} \quad \bar{Y}_1 = 50, \quad n_1 = 20, \quad \sigma_1^2 = 200$$
$$\textit{Firm 2:} \quad \bar{Y}_1 = 45, \quad n_1 = 25, \quad \sigma_1^2 = 250$$
$$\textit{Firm 3:} \quad \bar{Y}_1 = 50, \quad n_1 = 20, \quad \sigma_1^2 = 800$$
$$\textit{Firm 4:} \quad \bar{Y}_1 = 45, \quad n_1 = 25, \quad \sigma_1^2 = 1000$$

Shirley asks you to compute a 95% confidence interval for the mean pollutant level. You have been instructed to use the data above to construct the narrowest possible confidence interval. You may use any or all of the results obtained from the four testing firms to accomplish your mission.

10.17 A political candidate obtains a random sample election poll of size $n = 600$. In this random sample, 55% support her candidacy. Using a 95% confidence interval, determine if she has majority support in the population.

10.18 Mike Farrel has asked for your assistance in analyzing a market sampling survey. A random sample of size 400 was obtained. In the sample 200 people responded yes. Each observation is an independent Bernoulli trial with parameter P. What is the 95% confidence interval for P?

10.19 A national nonprofit organization that recruits volunteers to build houses for low-income people has a policy of locating in a community if more than 25% of the residents support their goals and policies.
   (a) A random sample of 400 residents in Pine Creek indicated 40% support. Should they locate in Pine Creek? Explain.
   (b) A random sample of 500 residents in Valley View indicated 32% support. Should they locate in Valley View? Explain.

10.20 John Sellitall, marketing manager of Getitoutfast, a major consumer products firm, wants to know the proportion of the regional population that would purchase his new product. A random sample of size 576 contained 230 who said they would purchase the product.
   (a) What is the MLE estimate of the population proportion who would purchase?
   (b) Compute a 95% one-sided confidence interval for the proportion that indicates a lower limit. Show the derivation starting with a one-tailed acceptance interval. Explain this interval carefully using correct statistical language.
   (c) Explain this interval to the marketing manager, who does not understand statistical methods.

10.21 The food service manager wants to know the mean amount of food waste for the dinner meal. He knows that exactly 10% of the meat served will become waste and exactly 20% of potatoes served will become waste. He also knows that the correlation between meat and potato waste is 0.6. A random sample of 25 dinners is obtained. The mean and variance for the amount of meat and potatoes served are: sample mean for meat is 500 pounds and the sample variance for meat is 2500; sample mean for potatoes is 600 pounds and the sample variance for potatoes is 3600. The population variances are not equal. Determine the 95% confidence interval for the mean amount of waste obtained from meat and potatoes at the dinner meal.

10.22 Governor George Archibald has asked you to compute a 95% confidence interval for the difference between the mean family income in Able City and the mean family income in Baker Town. A random sample of 50 families in Able City resulted in a sample variance of 2500 with a mean of 10,000. A second random sample of 25 families in Baker City resulted in a sample variance of 3600 with a mean of 10,500.

10.23 Marjorie Benson is the production manager for a medium-sized manufacturing firm. She is developing new techniques for increasing productivity in the factory. Under the old method, a random sample of 25 workers had a sample mean productivity of 50 with a sample standard deviation of 25. After the new method was implemented, the same random sample of workers had a mean productivity of 65 with a sample standard deviation of 40. The samples are correlated with $\hat{\rho} = 0.50$. Construct a 95% confidence interval for the change in productivity. What can you tell Marjorie about productivity increase using the new method?

10.24 A major auditing firm has been asked to compare the accounts receivable for the Dallas and Fort Worth stores of a major national retailer. The corporate financial vice-president claims that the mean of the receivables population at both stores is the same. A random sample of size $n = 33$ is obtained from the Dallas store's receivables and found to have a mean of $233 with a sample variance of 500. For the Fort Worth store the mean was $289 with a variance of 650, using a sample of size 33. The population variances can be assumed equal. Construct the following confidence intervals for the difference between the population mean receivables.
 (a) 95%.
 (b) 98%.
 (c) Based on parts (a) and (b), what can you say about the claim by the financial vice-president?

10.25 In the northeast region of a midwestern state the crop production per acre, Y, is a function of the amount of fertilizer per acre, X_1, and the amount of rainfall, X_2, during the growing season. Both X_1 and X_2 can be modeled as normally distributed random variables. The production function is

$$Y = 4X_1 + 5X_2 + W$$

where W is a forecast made by the agricultural extension service each year. W can also be modeled as a normally distributed random variable. The three random variables are assumed to be independent for the farms in this region. A random sample of size 25 farms results in a sample mean $\bar{X}_1 = 20$ and a sample variance $S_{X_1}^2 = 36$. A second random sample of 25 different farms results in a sample mean $\bar{X}_2 = 25$ and a sample variance $S_{X_2}^2 = 64$. The random variable W is obtained from a random sample of experienced farmers, and for this year a random sample of 25 farmers resulted in a sample mean of 140 with a sample variance of 400.
 (a) Based on the information above, obtain the maximum likelihood estimate of the crop production per acre.
 (b) Compute the 95% confidence interval for crop production per year.

10.26 You have been asked to compute a 92% confidence interval for the mean family savings in a developing country. Recall that savings is equal to the difference between disposable income and consumption. Your sampling group has obtained a random sample of size 25 families and found that the sample mean for disposable income was 800. The population variance of disposable income is known to be 10,000. A second random sample of size 75 families was used to obtain data on consumption. The sample mean was 600. It is known that the population variance for consumption is 14,400. Assume that the two samples are independent of each other.
 (a) Construct a 92% confidence interval for mean family savings.
 (b) Assume that each sample had 50 observations instead of different sample sizes. Everything else was the same. Construct the new 92% confidence interval.

10.27 You have been asked to provide an estimate of average family savings in a medium-sized western city. After some initial investigation you discover that individual family disposable income and family consumption can be measured for individual families. However, savings is difficult to obtain. Therefore, you decide to use the economic result that savings, S, is equal to disposable income, Y, minus consumption, C, or $S = Y - C$. You obtain a random sample of households and find that the sum of individual disposable incomes for all 100 households is 2,000,000. The sample standard deviation, $S(Y)$, for individual disposable incomes is 2000. A second random sample 100 households obtains measures of family consumption. The sample mean consumption is 16,000 and the sample standard deviation S is 1500. Past research indicates that the population variances for disposable income and consumption are equal.

   (a) Compute the estimates of mean and variance for disposable income and consumption.

   (b) Derive a 98% confidence interval for savings, S.

10.28 Consider again the problem of obtaining a confidence interval for savings, S. However, now you obtain only one random sample of families and measure both income and consumption for each family. Assume that the sample statistics are exactly the same as those obtained from the two random samples.

   (a) Compute the estimates of mean and variance for disposable income and consumption.

   (b) Derive a 98% confidence interval for savings, S, assuming that Y and C have a correlation of 0.50.

   (c) Carefully explain which sampling strategy, and hence which confidence interval, should be used.

10.29 You are the coach of a famous swimmer. Two coaching strategies are available for your preseason training. Strategy 1 would decrease your swimmer's time for a race, while strategy 2 would reduce the variance of both your swimmer and her opponent. You will choose the strategy that will provide the highest probability of winning.

   The present situation is that the mean time for your swimmer is $\mu_1 = 2.1$ and the mean time for her opponent is $\mu_2 = 2.2$. The population variance of the times for both swimmers is $\sigma^2 = 1$. Coaching strategy 1 will reduce your swimmer's mean time to $\mu_1 = 2.0$. Coaching strategy 2 will reduce the variance of both swimmers to $\sigma^2 = 0.64$. Define the time for your swimmer as the random variable Y_1 and the time for her opponent as Y_2. The difference in scores is $\Delta Y = Y_2 - Y_1$, where the respective population means are μ_2 and μ_1. The random variables Y_2 and Y_1 have a normal distribution and a correlation equal to $\rho = 0.5$. A win occurs when ΔY is greater than 0. Compute the probability of winning before each of the proposed coaching strategies and the new probability of winning after each new coaching strategy is applied by itself. Which new coaching strategy do you recommend?

10.30 Walter Akimoto is the coordinator of government statistics in Japan. He has asked you to compute a 95% confidence interval for the change in unemployment between month 1 and month 2. Unemployment is estimated each month using a random sample of $n = 50,000$ households. Assume that the samples are independent from one month to the next. For month 1 the sample estimated unemployment rate was 9.8%. For month 2 the estimated unemployment rate was 10.2%.

(a) Compute the 95% confidence interval for the change in unemployment.

(b) What can you advise Mr. Akimoto concerning the change in unemployment? Could the change result from statistical variation?

10.31 You are the study director of the president's office of political affairs. Among your responsibilities is the monitoring of public opinion regarding the president's popularity rating. To obtain data for this purpose, a new random sample of 400 households is obtained each week. Each household is contacted by phone and asked if they approve of the president's overall performance. In the first week 300 people respond positively, and in the second week 280 people respond positively.

(a) Construct a 98% confidence interval for the change in the president's support level.

(b) Is there evidence that the president's popularity has decreased from week 1 to week 2?

10.32 Robert Archer, the county administrator, has asked you to estimate the percentage of voters who would support a property tax increase to build a new solid waste processing facility. The county has 30,000 urban voters and 20,000 rural voters. You obtain a random sample of 150 urban voters and 100 rural voters. The percentage positive support for the urban sample of voters is 0.70, and for the rural sample of voters it is 0.25.

(a) Construct a 95% confidence interval for the voter support in the entire county by weighting the rural and urban samples by the percentage of voters in the county.

(b) Construct a 95% confidence interval by using the combined sample of 250 voters from both rural and urban areas.

(c) Repeat part (b) assuming that only two-thirds of the urban voters respond while all the rural voters respond, and thus your confidence interval is based on only 200 voters.

(d) Explain any differences observed between the various confidence intervals. Which procedure provides the best result?

10.33 A random sample poll conducted for a political candidate results in 40% of the sample favoring the candidate, with a margin of error of $\pm 3\%$. (*Note:* Some news reports use the term *margin of error* when reporting confidence intervals.)

(a) Assuming that we have a 95% confidence interval, what is the sample size? (Show your analysis.)

(b) A second random sample poll conducted two weeks later with $n = 900$ observations indicated support from 46% of the sample. Using a 95% confidence interval, determine if there has been a change in the percent of the population who support the candidate.

10.34 You have been asked to obtain a 95% confidence interval for μ such that

$$P(\bar{Y} - 1 \leq \mu \leq \bar{Y} + 1) = 0.95$$

Y and $\bar{Y}$ are normally distributed with $\sigma^2 = 25$. What sample size should be used?

10.35 The Nelson Market Research Company has been asked to design a random sample to estimate the proportion of people who would purchase a new toothpaste. Initial judgment is that between 20 and 40% of the population would purchase the toothpaste. The toothpaste manufacturer wishes to have a confidence interval of $\pm 5\%$ regarding the estimated percentage of purchasers. How large a sample size should be used?

10.36 Howard Rand, the quality control manager of Northeast Parts, Inc., is establishing a quality monitoring procedure for the production of a new part that is being produced for an automobile company. The contract requires that a critical part dimension must have a mean greater than 1.50 inches. The variance of the manufacturing process is known to be $\sigma^2 = 0.0025$. To meet the contract, the production machine is set to produce parts with the mean of the critical dimension set at 1.52 inches. A random sample of parts will be selected and measured each day. If the sample mean dimension is less than 1.50 inches, the entire day's production will be scrapped. How large a sample size should be used so that the probability is less than 0.05 that the production will be scrapped if the population mean is 1.52 inches or more?

10.37 A cereal manufacturing company guarantees that each package has at least 16 ounces of cereal. To provide a margin for error, the mean package weight is set at 16.4 ounces. The variance of package weights is $\sigma^2 = 0.25$. A consumer testing group routinely obtains a random sample of packages and measures the weight using high-precision scales. If the sample mean package weight is less than 16 ounces, a news report is prepared which indicates that the company routinely sells packages that have less than 16 ounces of cereal. What sample size should be used so that the probability is less than 0.01 that the sample mean is less than 16 ounces given that the mean weight of all packages is 16.4 ounces?

10.38 A study of January weather in Oak Park, Illinois, found that daytime high temperatures are approximately normally distributed. A random sample of $n = 20$ January days resulted in a sample variance of 79.8. Construct a 95% confidence interval for the population variance.

10.39 Speedy Express is a regional delivery service that guarantees delivery within 24 hours or it refunds the cost of delivery. Their delivery process was designed to have a mean $\mu = 19$ and a variance $\sigma^2 = 9$. In the past months the percentage of deliveries eligible for refunds has increased from 5% to 15%. A random sample of $n = 36$ had a mean $\bar{Y} = 19.6$ and a variance $S^2 = 15.6$. Compute the following lower confidence limits for the population variance of the delivery time.
(a) 95%.
(b) 97.5%.
(c) Based on the results above, would you argue that the variance of the delivery time has increased?

10.40 The quality control department of a major automobile company was studying the dimensions of parts from a stamping mill.
(a) A random sample of $n = 36$ pieces had a sample standard deviation of $S = 0.025$. Construct a 95% confidence interval for the population variance.
(b) A random sample of $n = 21$ pieces from a similar machine has a sample standard deviation of $S = 0.021$. Construct a 95% confidence interval for the population variance from this machine.
* (c) Construct a 95% confidence interval for the ratio of the population variances.

10.41 The fat content of deluxe hamburger at George's market is advertised as having no more than 25 units of fat. To assure this guarantee, the hamburger preparation process has been set at a mean of $\mu = 20$ units with variance of $\sigma^2 = 9$. The amount of fat in any single 1-pound package is assumed to be normally distributed with the foregoing mean and variance.

(a) A random sample of size $n = 30$ is obtained and found to have a mean $\bar{Y} = 21$ and a variance $S^2 = 15$. What is the 98% confidence limit for the population variance based on this sample?

(b) A second random sample of size $n = 21$ is obtained from a second store and found to have a mean $\bar{Y} = 21.4$ with a variance of $S^2 = 8$. What is the 95% confidence limit for the population variance based on this sample?

*(c) What is the 95% confidence interval for the ratio of the two population variances based on the sample results from parts (a) and (b)?

Problems 10.42 to 10.46 require use of a statistical computer package and computer-accessible data sets. Your instructor will provide specific instructions for accessing the statistical package and data sets on your computer.

10.42 This problem uses the data set "Student" on your computer. Variable names and descriptions are provided in Appendix B at the end of the book. The faculty of an economics department wanted to analyze the academic performance of their graduating majors. As part of the analysis they have asked you to prepare the following 95% confidence intervals.

(a) Student grade-point average and grade-point average in economics courses.

(b) Student grade-point average and economics grade-point average for both men and women. Note that the variable "Gender" is coded "0" for men and "1" for women.

(c) The difference between men's overall GPA and women's overall GPA and the difference between men's economics GPA and women's economics GPA.

(d) The differences between men and women on the individual SAT scores and the total SAT score.

10.43 This problem uses the data set "Crime" on your computer. Variable names and descriptions are provided in Appendix B at the end of the book. George Hoff of the National Association of Police Chiefs has asked you to compare the state-level crime data for the years 1982 and 1984. He is particularly interested in total crime, violent crime (murder, rape, assault, and robbery), and property crime (burglary, larceny, and motor vehicle theft). In particular you have been asked to determine the following 95% confidence intervals.

(a) Total crime, violent crime, and property crime for each of the years 1982 and 1984.

(b) Differences between total crime, violent crime, and property crime (1984 crime rate minus 1982 crime rate).

(c) Prepare a one-paragraph discussion of the changes in crime rate between 1982 and 1984.

10.44 Use the sample of 112 students in the data file "Student" on your computer for the following problem. Variable names and descriptions are provided in Appendix B at the end of the book. Construct a 95% confidence interval for the difference in mean GPA between male and female students assuming a random sample of 112 students. Student gender is labeled "0" for males and "1" for females.

10.45 BBW Ltd. does quality control work on the final loaves of bread produced in its factory. Part of this work includes a comparison with the products of their competitors. The data file named "BBWltd" contains data collected as part of its analysis of the market. The variables in the file are:
   1. "Dbread," which contains a random sample of weights, in grams, of their dark bread collected from supermarket shelves.
   2. "Sbread," which contains a random sample of weights, in grams, of their specialty bread collected from supermarket shelves.
   3. "Csbread," which contains a random sample of weights, in grams, of their competitor's specialty bread collected from supermarket shelves.
   Compute a 95% confidence interval for the difference in population mean weight of BBW's specialty bread and the population mean weight of their competitor's specialty bread.

10.46 Thrash Busters, Inc. manufactures fertilizers and herbicides for the grain farming industry. They have conducted an extensive advertising campaign to gain recognition for their brand A herbicide. Now they want to know if farmers recognize their brand A herbicide more than farmers recognize their competitor's brand B herbicide. In a random sample of 423 farmers, 100 indicated that they recognized brand A. In a separate independent sample of 388 farmers, a total of 98 recognized brand B.
   (a) Construct a 98% confidence interval for the difference in population proportions that recognize brand A compared to brand B.
   (b) After the foregoing interval was computed, additional random sample results came in for each sample. For the first brand A sample, 15 out of 49 recognized brand A. For the second brand B sample, 13 out of 65 recognized brand B. Assume that these data are each a random sample whose observations are independent of the first sample. What is the new 98% confidence interval as a result of these additional data?

APPENDIX: STUDENT t FOR DIFFERENCES BETWEEN POPULATIONS WITH σ^2 UNKNOWN

The Student t statistic is defined as

$$t = \frac{Z}{\sqrt{\chi^2/\nu}}$$

where Z is a standard normal random variable and χ^2 is a chi-square random variable with ν degrees of freedom.

For the difference between two populations we use

$$Z = \frac{(\bar{X}_1 - \bar{X}_2) - (\mu_1 - \mu_2)}{\sqrt{\sigma_1^2/n_1 + \sigma_2^2/n_2}}$$

and

$$\chi^2 = \chi_1^2 + \chi_2^2$$

is the sum of two independent chi-square random variables from the two independent random samples

$$\chi_1^2 = \frac{(n_1 - 1)S_1^2}{\sigma_1^2}$$

$$\chi_2^2 = \frac{(n_2 - 1)S_2^2}{\sigma_2^2}$$

with $n_1 - 1$ and $n_2 - 1$ degrees of freedom, respectively. The degrees of freedom for χ^2 is the sum of the component degrees of freedom, $n_1 - 1$ plus $n_2 - 1$.

Bringing these pieces together, we see that

$$t = \frac{(\bar{X}_1 - \bar{X}_2) - (\mu_1 - \mu_2)/\sqrt{\sigma_1^2/n_1 + \sigma_2^2/n_2}}{\sqrt{[(n_1 - 1)S_1^2/\sigma_1^2 + (n_2 - 1)S_2^2/\sigma_2^2]/(n_1 + n_2 - 2)}}$$

If

$$\sigma_1^2 = \sigma_2^2$$

this reduces to

$$t = \frac{(\bar{X}_1 - \bar{X}_2) - (\mu_1 - \mu_2)}{\sqrt{S_p^2/n_1 + S_p^2/n_2}}$$

If the population variances cannot be assumed equal, the more complex form of the Student t, from Section 10.9.1, must be used with reduced degrees of freedom.

11

Hypothesis Testing

Hypothesis testing is a formal statistical procedure for making decisions in the face of random variability.

11.1 CHOOSING BETWEEN ALTERNATIVES

In this chapter we present hypothesis testing, the other major component of classical statistical inference. In Chapter 10 we presented estimation, which provides procedures to obtain numerical values for parameters such as the population mean and the population proportion. In contrast, we now develop procedures for asking specific questions that can be answered by comparing sample statistics—such as the sample mean or proportion—with critical decision values. The objective is to choose between alternatives, which are stated in terms of parameters such as the mean or the proportion. We will see many similarities to estimation as we develop methods for hypothesis testing. Both depend on the distribution of sample statistics, developed in Chapter 9.

Robert Clinton is the marketing manager for New Design Electronics. He has been informed that his new television model will be successful if 20% of future purchasers buy his model. To determine success, a random sample of future purchasers will be asked if they would purchase his model. What procedure should he use with the sample to determine if the population proportion is greater than 20%? How large a sample size is needed? What decision rule should be used? In this chapter we provide answers to these questions.

Hypothesis testing is a formal statistical procedure for making decisions in the face of random variability. The problem is to choose between two options. For example, the average weight of cereal packages is greater than 16 ounces or it is not. The decision is made by comparing a sample mean with a critical value. If the sample mean exceeds the critical value, we conclude that the average weight of the population of packages is greater than 16 ounces. This decision involves risk because the sample mean has a probability distribution. A formal procedure for handling the risk is developed in this chapter. This procedure will be applied using means or proportions from single populations or differences between two populations.

We begin by developing the formal hypothesis-testing procedure using a sample mean from a single population. Similar procedures are developed for sample proportions. A formal analysis will indicate the probability of error when decisions are made using measurements that contain variability. Finally, the testing procedures are extended to comparisons between two populations.

Hypothesis testing has applications to business and economic problems by providing specific information to guide decision making:

1. *Transportation safety.* Transportation safety planners want to know if highway death rates are decreasing.
2. *Economic development.* Development economists need to know if per capita income is above a subsistence level and if unemployment is below a target maximum.
3. *Sales forecasting.* Product managers need to know if new product sales will exceed the break-even level.
4. *Engineering specifications.* Production managers need to know if product dimensions are at the design specification.
5. *Economic policy.* Economic policymakers need to know if exports and imports are increasing or decreasing.

Hypothesis testing provides a formal objective procedure for analyzing the data to provide answers.

11.2 DECISION MAKING: ELEMENTS AND PROCESS

Decision processes in modern business and government organizations are data dependent. Managers and executives want to know: "What do the data tell us?" Given the importance of data, analysts must use appropriate procedures for carrying out their analyses. It is easy to obtain a variety of conclusions, many of them wrong, using incorrect procedures. Statistical hypothesis testing provides an objective and comprehensive procedure for decision making (Key Idea 11.1).

The basic elements of hypothesis testing are developed here. In the following section, specific forms of the procedure are applied to a variety of problems. As a result, you will know how hypothesis testing can help you answer a number of questions by using data.

A useful analogy for statistical hypothesis testing is a jury trial.

1. In a criminal trial a person is either guilty or innocent of the charge. In civil suits the plaintiff either receives or does not receive a settlement from the defendant.
2. The legal system has an extensive process for accumulating evidence regarding the alternatives. In the legal system highly trained judges and lawyers are required to ensure correct accumulation of evidence in the trial.
3. The decision rule is that a jury of peers will listen to and evaluate the evidence and reach a unanimous decision.

4. Variability is minimized by providing a sufficient body of evidence whose interpretation is established by the adversarial process of a trial. In a criminal trial a person is assumed innocent unless the evidence establishes guilt beyond a reasonable doubt. We are aware that this rule results in a conviction only when the evidence strongly favors a conviction. Thus the probability of convicting an innocent person is small. However, this rule does result in a higher probability that a guilty person will not be convicted. In contrast, civil suits require that a majority of the evidence is in favor of the plaintiff. With this rule, convictions in a criminal trial require stronger evidence than damage awards in a civil trial.

Statistical hypothesis testing has a number of similarities to the trial procedure.

Key Idea 11.1: Hypothesis-Testing Components

Hypothesis testing is a formal decision-making procedure that includes the following components:

1. A carefully defined set of alternatives. The alternatives must be mutually exclusive. Thus when one is true the other is false, and vice versa.

2. A specific measurable and comparable criterion for determining the performance or outcome for each alternative.

3. A decision rule for selecting alternatives based on the performance criterion measurement.

4. A procedure for handling variability in the criterion measurement, including:
  (a) Appropriate statistical models for the criterion.
  (b) A rule for deciding which alternative will be favored by the uncertainty of the measurement process.

11.3 HYPOTHESIS TESTING FOR A SINGLE POPULATION

Hypothesis testing is a procedure for choosing between alternatives using sample data that include random error (Key Idea 11.2). Typically, two options are defined:

H_0: The null hypothesis is the presumed condition that will be accepted unless there is strong evidence against.

H_1: The alternative hypothesis will be accepted with a small probability of error if H_0 is rejected.

Key Idea 11.2: Hypothesis-Testing Procedure

1. We begin by stating a null hypothesis, H_0, which we accept unless contrary evidence is very strong, and an alternative hypothesis, H_1, which we accept when the evidence against H_0 is strong. Single-tailed tests can refer either to the upper or lower tail of the probability distribution.

   The upper tail test has the form

$$H_0: \mu \leq \mu_0$$
$$H_1: \mu > \mu_0$$

   Rejection of H_0 provides strong evidence that the population mean, μ, is greater than μ_0. [Probability of Type I error (accept H_1 when H_0 is true) is less than α.] For the upper-tail test the critical value $\bar{X}_c$ is

$$\bar{X}_c = \mu_0 + Z_\alpha \frac{\sigma}{\sqrt{n}}$$

   The lower-tail test has the form

$$H_0: \mu \geq \mu_0$$
$$H_1: \mu < \mu_0$$

   Rejection of H_0 provides strong evidence that the population mean, μ, is less than μ_0. The lower-tail test has the form

$$\bar{X}_c = \mu_0 - Z_\alpha \frac{\sigma}{\sqrt{n}}$$

   where α is the probability of Type I error.

2. To test the null hypothesis, H_0, we use a test statistic. The probability distribution of the random variable test statistic is defined assuming that the null hypothesis is true.

3. The upper tail alternative hypothesis

$$H_1: \mu > \mu_0$$

   is accepted if

$$\bar{X} > \bar{X}_c$$

   and the lower tail alternative hypothesis

$$H_1: \mu < \mu_0$$

   is accepted if

$$\bar{X} < \bar{X}_c$$

To choose between H_0 and H_1, a random sample is selected and a sample statistic, such as the mean $\bar{X}$ or the proportion $\hat{P}$, is computed. If, for example, the statistic is greater than a critical value, H_1 is selected; if not, H_0 is selected. We want to choose correctly and avoid choosing H_1 when H_0 is true or choosing H_0 when H_1 is true. By adjusting the critical value, either alternative can have a greater probability of being selected.

Classical hypothesis testing seeks a decision that provides strong support for H_1, the alternative hypothesis, if H_1 is selected. Strong support is obtained by using a decision rule that chooses H_1 only if the probability of obtaining the observed sample statistic given H_0 (is correct) is very small. Therefore, if H_1 is chosen, there is strong evidence in its favor. However, H_1 may be correct but not chosen because the decision rule is too severe. Note the analogy to a criminal trial in which conviction occurs only when there is strong evidence to support a guilty verdict. Given that rule, some guilty people avoid conviction—a decision in favor of their guilt—but few innocent people are convicted. Hypothesis testing has the same characteristic.

These ideas will be developed with a simple example. A manufacturer seeks strong evidence that cereal boxes have an average weight greater than 16 ounces.

1. The null hypothesis, H_0, is that the average package weight μ is less than or equal to 16 ounces, while the alternative hypothesis, H_1, is that the mean weight, μ, is greater than 16. The formal statement is

$$H_0: \mu \leq 16.0$$

$$H_1: \mu > 16.0$$

Included in H_0 is a probability distribution for the test statistic, in this case $\bar{X}$. This form is called a *composite hypothesis* because each alternative includes a range of values for μ. As we will see, it is conceptually easier to test hypotheses when H_0 and H_1 are defined as point values. However, composite hypotheses usually provide better decision-making information.

2. The test statistic, $\bar{X}$, is computed from a sample of size $n = 25$, which was randomly selected from a normal population with $\sigma^2 = 0.16$. Therefore, given H_0, the test statistic $\bar{X}$ has a normal distribution with mean

$$\mu = 16.0$$

and variance

$$\sigma_{\bar{X}}^2 = \frac{\sigma^2}{n}$$

$$= \frac{0.16}{25}$$

$$\sigma_{\bar{X}} = 0.08$$

The extreme value of μ from H_0 that is closest to the values of μ for H_1 (e.g., $\mu = 16.0$) is selected as a point value for μ so that a test rule can be developed. The sample mean, $\bar{X}$, will be used to choose between H_0 and H_1. If $\bar{X}$ is significantly larger than 16, we have evidence to reject H_0 and accept H_1.

The hypothesis-testing options can be represented in the matrix shown in Table 11.1. The actual situation is either H_0 or H_1; unfortunately, we do not know which one is true. We choose one of the options using a decision rule. There are four combinations of decision and truth, as shown in Table 11.1. Two of the combinations are correct; accept H_0 when it is true or accept H_1 when it is true. However, if we accept H_1, that is, $\mu > 16.0$, when H_0 ($\mu \leq 16.0$) is true, we have committed a *Type I error*, whose probability is α. If we accept H_0 when H_1 is true, we have committed a *Type II error*, whose probability is β. Statistical hypothesis tests are set up to ensure a small probability of *Type I error*, α. In many situations either $\alpha = 0.01$ or $\alpha = 0.05$ is used.

TABLE 11.1   Types of Hypothesis-Testing Errors

Sample Decision	H_0 Is True	H_1 Is True
Accept H_0	Correct conclusion	Type II error (probability = β)
Accept H_1	Type I error (probability = α)	Correct conclusion

The decision rule is designed so that the alternative assigned to H_0 will have a very small probability of being rejected if it is true. The null hypothesis can be rejected if there is strong evidence to do so. If we reject H_0 and accept H_1, there is a small probability of error, α. However, failing to reject H_0 leads to the conclusion that either H_0 is true or that the decision procedure is not precise enough to accept H_1 in preference to H_0. We prefer to define the null and alternative hypotheses so that our decision—in this example to conclude that cereal packages contain more than 16 ounces—is reached by rejecting H_0. That decision has a known small error.

Failing to reject H_0 is analogous to failing to convict a person in a criminal trial. In that case the person is either innocent or the evidence was not strong enough to overcome the initial presumption of innocence.

3. The decision rule is to reject H_0 when the sample mean $\bar{X}$ is greater than a critical value $\bar{X}_c$. We chose $\mu \leq 16.0$ as the null hypothesis because we want to have a small probability of error if we decide that $\mu > 16.0$ (i.e., the cereal weight is above 16 ounces). The decision rule includes a high probability of committing a Type II error (choose H_0 when H_1 is true) when μ is only slightly larger than 16.0.

A careful examination of the hypothesis test indicates that the critical value $\bar{X}_c$ will be greater than 16.0. The critical value given that we have chosen $\alpha = 0.05$ is

$$\bar{X}_c = \mu_0 + Z_\alpha \sigma_{\bar{X}}$$
$$= 16.0 + 1.645 \times 0.08$$
$$= 16.13$$

as shown in Figure 11.1. We choose a critical value such that the probability of a larger sample mean is α. In this case if the population mean, $\mu = 16.0$, the probability is very small that the sample mean is greater than the critical value, $\bar{X}_c = 16.13$. Therefore, if the sample mean is greater than the critical value, we conclude that μ is not less than or equal to 16.0 and reject H_0. We have strong evidence in favor of H_1—the sample mean is greater than 16.0. The inequality associated with the alternative hypothesis H_1 always points to the critical value. The formal decision rule is

$$\text{choose } H_1 \text{ if } \bar{X} > 16.13,$$

where $\bar{X}$ is the sample mean for the random sample of size $n = 25$.

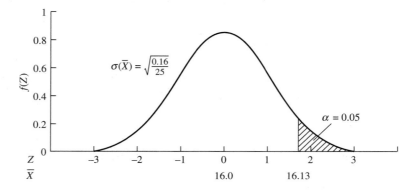

Figure 11.1   Critical Value for Sample Mean: $\mu = 16.0$

Does It Make Sense?

Hypothesis testing uses rules that make it difficult to reject the null hypothesis, H_0, if the null hypothesis is true. The probability of obtaining a sample mean greater or equal to the critical value, $\bar{X}_c = 16.13$, is α if $\mu = 16$. If μ is less than the upper limit of 16, the probability that the sample mean is greater than 16.13 is smaller than α. Discussion of Type II error in the next section will provide additional understanding.   □

The decision rule accepts H_1 incorrectly when $\mu < 16.0$ with a probability less than $\alpha = 0.05$. When μ is less than 16.0, the probability that the sample mean $\bar{X}$ is greater than the critical decision value $\bar{X}_c = 16.13$ is less than 0.05. For example, if $\mu = 15.9$ the probability of Type I error is computed as follows:

$$Z_\alpha = \frac{16.13 - 15.90}{0.08}$$
$$= 2.88$$

and therefore

$$\alpha = 0.002$$

This result is shown in Figure 11.2.

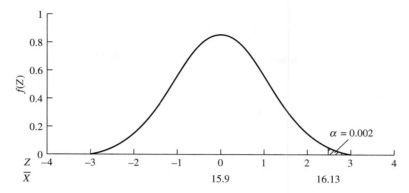

Figure 11.2   Probability of Type I Error When $\mu = 15.9$

In the following example the hypothesis-testing situation will be placed in a more realistic setting and its contribution to an important management problem—product quality—will be demonstrated. In addition, we provide some extensions to broaden our understanding of hypothesis testing.

Example 11.1   Cereal Package Weight

John Pautzke, president of Cereals Unlimited, Inc., wants to be very certain that the mean weight μ of packages satisfies the package label weight of 16 ounces. The packages are filled by a machine that is set to fill each package to a specified weight. However, the machine has random variability measured by σ^2. John would like to have strong evidence that the mean package weight is above 16 ounces. In this problem he must consider two possibilities. The mean package weight, μ, is either less than or equal to 16 ounces, or it is greater than 16 ounces.

   Solution   George Williams, quality control manager, advises him to test these options using the mean for a random sample of packages. George instructs his staff to obtain a random sample of 25 packages of cereal. George chose 25 observations because of his desire to balance increased sampling cost against his desire for a small value of

$$\sigma_{\bar{X}} = \frac{\sigma}{\sqrt{n}}$$

Each package is carefully weighed in the laboratory and the weight is recorded. The sample mean will be used to decide if the population mean weight is above 16 ounces.

   The decision rule developed for statistical hypothesis testing is based on the probability distribution of the test statistic—the sample mean in this example. From previous experience we assume that the sample mean has a normal distribution. The variance for individual package weights is $\sigma^2 = 0.16$. Mr. Pautzke wants to have a decision rule that will protect his company against the possibility of underweight cereal boxes. If packages are underweight, the government could impose a large fine and the unfavorable publicity could lead to lost sales. Thus he will initially assume that the mean package weight μ is less than or equal to 16 ounces unless there is strong evidence to reject that assumption. Thus the null hypothesis, H_0: $\mu \leq 16$, will be rejected if there is strong evidence against it. A large sample mean is strong evidence against H_0. His commonsense judgment indicates that the sample mean must be greater than 16 ounces in order to decide against his initial assumption and to conclude that the mean for all boxes is more than 16 ounces.

The specific decision rule is based on the probability distribution of the sample mean given $\mu \leq 16$. Figure 11.1 indicates that the sample mean will exceed 16.13 with probability $\alpha = 0.05$ given the initial assumption ($\mu = 16$, $\sigma^2 = 0.16$). The critical value $\bar{X}_c$ is computed using our decision objective and the normal probability distribution model:

$$\bar{X}_c = \mu + Z_\alpha \frac{\sigma}{\sqrt{n}}$$

$$= 16 + 1.645 \times \frac{\sqrt{0.16}}{\sqrt{25}}$$

$$= 16.13$$

The standardized normal value, $Z_{0.05} = 1.645$, is obtained from Table A.1 in Appendix A at the end of the book. It is very unlikely that the sample mean will be greater than 16.13 if the population mean μ is less than 16.0.

Based on this analysis, we inform Mr. Pautzke that he should reject his initial assumption—mean package weight less than or equal to 16.0—if the sample mean $\bar{X}$ is greater than 16.13 (Figure 11.1). His operational decision rule is therefore:

If $\bar{X} \leq 16.13$:   The population mean package weight is $\mu \leq 16$ ounces.

If $\bar{X} > 16.13$:   The population mean package weight is $\mu > 16$ ounces.

$P(\bar{X} \leq 16.13 \mid \mu = 16.0) = 0.95$

$P(\bar{X} > 16.13 \mid \mu = 16.0) = 0.05$

This decision rule protects the company against incorrectly deciding that the mean μ is greater than 16.0 when it is not. Such an incorrect decision would result in maintaining the bag-filling process when it should be changed. However, note that the rule could easily lead Mr. Pautzke to conclude that the population mean μ is less than or equal to 16 ounces even if μ is slightly greater than 16. In that case the process would be changed when it should not. For example, in Figure 11.3 with $\mu = 16.1$, we would incorrectly conclude that the population mean is less than or equal to 16 with probability equal to 0.646.

$$P(\bar{X} \leq 16.13 \mid \mu = 16.1) = 0.646$$

$$P(\bar{X} > 16.13 \mid \mu = 16.1) = 0.354$$

Failure to reject H_0 in this case would be a Type II error with probability $\beta = 0.646$. The probability that the sample mean is less than 16.13 is the probability that H_0 is chosen and hence that a Type II error has occurred. Type II errors are explored in greater depth in Section 11.6.   □

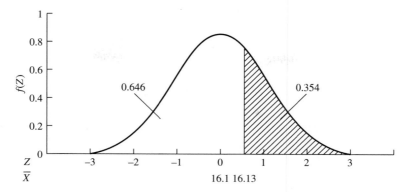

Figure 11.3   Normal Distribution of Sample Mean Weights: $\mu = 16.1$

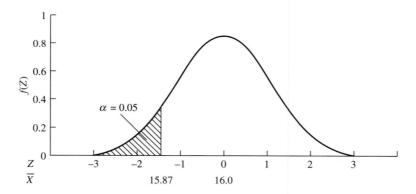

Figure 11.4   Normal Distribution with Alternative Decision Rule: $\mu = 16.0$

Analysis extension: What if?   In contrast to the decision above, suppose that John Pautzke wanted strong evidence that mean package weight was below 16 ounces. In that case he would initially assume that mean package weight was at or above 16 ounces. This assumption would be rejected only if the sample mean were less than $\bar{X}_c = 15.87$, as shown in Figure 11.4. Rejection of the assumption would lead to the conclusion that the mean population weight μ was less than 16 ounces.

This rule would result in missing cases where the mean weight was less than 16 ounces. For example, in Figure 11.5 we see that if the population mean was $\mu = 15.9$, our rule would fail to identify that the mean was under 16 ounces with probability 0.646. Again this would be a Type II error with probability $\beta = 0.646$. From this discussion we see that the decision maker's objective has a great influence on the decision rule and on its performance under various assumptions.

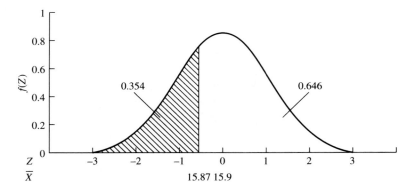

Figure 11.5   Normal Distribution with Alternative Decision Rule: $\mu = 15.9$

11.3.1 Two-Tailed Hypothesis Tests

There are situations defined by a single value for the population mean. In these cases an error can occur if the population mean is either too large or too small. The two-tailed hypothesis test is defined in Key Idea 11.3.

Key Idea 11.3: Two-Tailed Hypothesis Test

The hypothesis test has the form

$$H_0: \ \mu = \mu_0$$
$$H_1: \ \mu \neq \mu_0$$

The upper and lower limits are computed using

$$\bar{X}_c = \mu_0 \pm Z_{\alpha/2} \frac{\sigma}{\sqrt{n}}$$

The decision rule is

$$\text{Reject } H_0 \text{ if } \bar{X} > \mu_0 + Z_{\alpha/2} \frac{\sigma}{\sqrt{n}} \text{ or if } \bar{X} < \mu_0 - Z_{\alpha/2} \frac{\sigma}{\sqrt{n}}.$$

A common application involves quality control charts in manufacturing facilities. Component parts must have a specific dimension or they will not fit. Parts that are too big or too small must be rejected. The quality control example that follows is important because of the large and increasing number of quality control applications in business and industry.

Example 11.2   Quality Control: Part Dimension

A quality control department needs a procedure to determine if the mean dimension of a part has shifted away from the design specification as parts are produced over time. Assume that the design specification requires a mean dimension of $\mu_0 = 2.50$. From past history we know that the variance is $\sigma^2 = 0.00015$. Each week a random sample of 38 parts is obtained and used to determine if the mean dimension of parts is close enough to the design specification. The sample mean is assumed to have a normal distribution.

Solution   The quality control hypothesis test is

$$H_0: \; \mu = 2.500$$
$$H_1: \; \mu \neq 2.500$$

In this test the null hypothesis will be rejected if the sample mean is either too large or too small. Using the population mean and variance, we can compute upper and lower limits ($\bar{X}_{cU}$ and $\bar{X}_{cL}$) for rejecting H_0. The probability of Type I error α is allocated equally to both the upper and lower tails of the normal distribution, as shown in Figure 11.6.

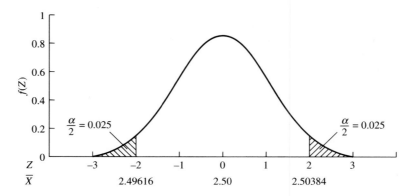

Figure 11.6   Distribution of Sample Mean for Part Dimensions

The upper and lower limits are computed using

$$\bar{X}_c = \mu_0 \pm Z_{\alpha/2} \frac{\sigma}{\sqrt{n}}$$

In this problem we have chosen $\alpha = 0.05$, and thus the error probabilities for each tail are 0.025. From Table A.1 the standardized normal values are $Z = \pm 1.96$.

The upper and lower critical values are therefore

$$\bar{X}_{cU} = 2.500 + 1.96 \times \sqrt{\frac{0.00015}{38}}$$

$$= 2.50387$$

$$\bar{X}_{cL} = 2.500 - 1.96 \times \sqrt{\frac{0.00015}{38}}$$

$$= 2.49613$$

The decision rule is

Reject H_0 if the sample mean is less than 2.49613 or greater than 2.50387.

If we reject H_0, we conclude that the manufacturing process is not producing parts whose mean dimension is 2.500. Using quality control language, we conclude that the process is out of control and thus the manufacturing process should be examined carefully and corrected. The interval

$$\mu_0 \pm Z_{\alpha/2}\frac{\sigma}{\sqrt{n}}$$

is an acceptance interval as developed in Chapter 9. A sample mean within this interval leads us to accept the conclusion that the process is in control and producing acceptable part dimensions. In Chapter 18 we see that acceptance intervals are used as control charts to monitor manufacturing and service projects.   □

11.3.2 p or Probability Values

There is another related statistic, the p or probability value, that can be used to perform the hypothesis test (Key Idea 11.4). Its use is strongly advocated by some statisticians, who argue that its use provides more information from the statistical analysis.

Example 11.3   Cereal Package Weight Revisited

Consider again the cereal package problem with the hypothesis

$$H_0: \mu \le 16.0$$
$$H_1: \mu > 16.0$$

The population variance $\sigma^2 = 0.16$ and the sample size $n = 25$. The decision rule was to reject H_0 if $\bar{X} \ge 16.13$. Suppose that the sample mean, $\bar{X}$, were 16.15. The value of p would then be computed as follows:

$$Z_p = \frac{16.15 - 16.0}{\sqrt{0.16}/\sqrt{25}}$$

$$= 1.875$$
$$p = 0.03$$

Key Idea 11.4: p or Probability Values

The **p value** for a hypothesis test is the probability of observing a sample value as exteme as that observed given that the null hypothesis is true.
  Beginning with a hypothesis test of the form

$$H_0: \mu \le \mu_0$$
$$H_1: \mu > \mu_0$$

If the sample mean is $\bar{X}$, the Z value, Z_p, for the sample result is

$$Z_p = \frac{\bar{X} - \mu_0}{\sigma/\sqrt{n}}$$

Then Z_p is used with the normal table to obtain the probability of the sample mean, $\bar{X}$, given H_0. If p is less than the probability of Type I error α, H_0 is rejected and H_1 is accepted. By comparing p and α it is possible to determine the strength of the rejection of H_0 (e.g., if $\alpha = 0.05$, then $p = 0.009$ is a stronger rejection than $p = 0.04$).

If the sample mean had instead been 16.11, the value of p would be computed as

$$Z_p = \frac{16.11 - 16.0}{\sqrt{0.16}/\sqrt{25}}$$
$$= 1.375$$
$$p = 0.085$$

Similarly, if $\bar{X}$ were 16.24, then $p \approx 0$.   □

Discussion.   Advocates of the p statistic method argue that a smaller value of p implies much stronger evidence in support of H_1. Thus the p of 0.03 is stronger evidence than if $\bar{X}$ had been 16.131 and hence p were just 0.05. And, of course, a value of $p \approx 0.0$ when the sample mean is 16.24 is even stronger evidence. Finally, in the case with $\bar{X} = 16.11$, H_0 could not be rejected with $\alpha = 0.05$, but would be rejected if α had been 0.09. By reporting p it is argued that more information is provided to the client who will use the results of the hypothesis test.

  The counterargument is that the sample mean, $\bar{X}$, is the result of one sample and the next sample will provide a different p value. Thus we recommend that one should either accept or reject the null hypothesis. Trying to infer too much from a single random sample is risky. Random sample means could easily generate p values from 0.04 to 0.10 merely from random variability. To argue that one random sample mean gives stronger results is misleading.

The use of p values for testing hypotheses is just as correct as using the critical value rule. Thus, use the p value for hypothesis testing if you feel that it is appropriate and as long as you understand that the p value will be different for every random sample.

11.4 PRODUCER'S VERSUS PURCHASER'S RISK

Hypothesis testing requires a choice between two alternatives. One is defined as the null hypothesis, H_0, and the other as the alternative hypothesis, H_1. If we reject the null hypothesis, the probability of error is at or less than the specified level α. Thus if we reject H_0, we have strong evidence to support the alternative hypothesis. Unfortunately, the reverse is not true. Failure to reject H_0 does not provide strong support for H_0.

In applied problems there is often confusion about the choice between the null and alternative hypotheses. This confusion regarding the specification of the null and alternative hypotheses results from different perspectives regarding the decision objective. In the jury trial analogy, the prosecution and the defense have different perspectives. They would each like to modify the rules of evidence in their favor. For example, the prosecution would prefer a prior assumption of guilt unless proven innocent. In this section we consider the effect of different perspectives on the hypothesis-testing decision rule. An example of this problem is the decision perspectives of producers versus purchasers as they evaluate the quality of a shipment of goods (Key Idea 11.5).

Example 11.4   Ground Turkey Weight

Consider the problem of correct weights for 16-ounce packages of ground turkey. A large shipment is sent from the producer to the purchaser. A random sample of 25 packages is selected from the shipment and each package is carefully weighed. The mean weight of these packages will be used to decide if the mean weight for all packages is 16 ounces. From previous experience we know that the variance is $\sigma^2 = 0.04$.

Solution   *Producer's rule.* The producer would favor a decision rule such as:

Ship the turkey unless there is strong evidence that the mean weight of the packages is less than 16 ounces.

The resulting hypothesis test is

$$H_0: \mu \geq 16$$
$$H_1: \mu < 16$$

Key Idea 11.5: Producer's Versus Purchaser's Risk

A producer and consumer agree that the population mean for a shipment of goods should be at or above μ_0. The decision to transfer the shipment will be based on the sample mean, $\bar{X}$, from a random sample of items from the shipment.

1. The producer would prefer the rule "ship to the purchaser unless there is strong evidence that the population mean μ is less than μ_0." The hypothesis is

$$H_0: \mu \geq \mu_0$$
$$H_1: \mu < \mu_0$$

   and goods would be shipped if the sample mean

$$\bar{X} > \mu_0 - Z_\alpha \sigma_{\bar{X}}$$

2. The purchaser would prefer the rule "accept the shipment from the producer only if there is strong evidence that the population mean μ is greater than or equal to μ_0." The hypothesis is

$$H_0: \mu \leq \mu_0$$
$$H_1: \mu > \mu_0$$

   and goods would be accepted if the sample mean

$$\bar{X} > \mu_0 + Z_\alpha \sigma_{\bar{X}}$$

The specification of null (H_0) and alternative (H_1) hypotheses implicitly favors the null hypothesis in a decision. In decisions that have inherent difference of view, one side will be favored. Correct decisions will result only if both sides understand the test specification and have informed negotiations.

The critical value in this option would be less than 16 ounces, as shown in Figure 11.7. It is calculated as

$$\bar{X}_c = \mu - Z_\alpha \frac{\sigma}{\sqrt{n}}$$

$$= 16.0 - 1.645 \frac{0.2}{\sqrt{25}}$$

$$= 16.0 - 0.066$$

$$= 15.934$$

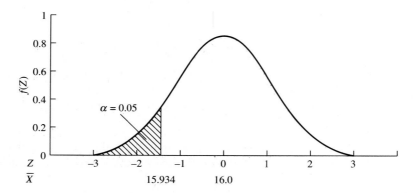

Figure 11.7   Producer's Decision Rule

The decision rule is

Reject H_0 and do not ship if $\bar{X}$ is less than 15.934.

Purchaser's rule. The purchaser would favor a decision rule such as:

Accept the turkey only if there is strong evidence that the mean weight of the packages is greater than 16 ounces.

The resulting hypothesis test is

$$H_0: \mu \leq 16$$
$$H_1: \mu > 16$$

The critical value in this option will be greater than 16 ounces, as shown in Figure 11.8. It is calculated as

$$\bar{X}_c = \mu + Z_\alpha \frac{\sigma}{\sqrt{n}}$$

$$= 16.0 + 1.645 \frac{0.2}{\sqrt{25}}$$

$$= 16.0 + 0.066$$

$$= 16.066$$

The decision rule is

Reject H_0 and accept the shipment if $\bar{X}$ is greater than 16.066.   □

Does It Make Sense?

Careful study of these rules indicates that the producer would ship if the sample mean is greater than 15.934 ounces, but the purchaser would accept the shipment only if the sample mean is greater than 16.066. Both decision rules are based on sound statistical reasoning. Note how the perspective of the decision maker influences the rule. The

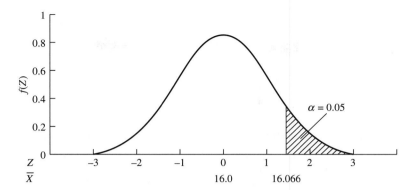

Figure 11.8 Purchaser's Decision Rule

difference between the two decision values is a region of uncertainty. We could reduce uncertainty by increasing the sample size. However, a choice would ultimately have to be made using additional criteria. Negotiation of this difference would be influenced by market power. If the purchaser has more supplier options than the producer has customers, the purchaser could obtain a more favorable decision rule. The reverse would move the decision closer to the producer's favor.

   Managers should understand the options presented above. Too often decision rules are supported because they are "statistically" or "scientifically" valid. Every statistically correct decision rule includes assumptions that precede the development of an objective rule. These assumptions must be made clear to the decision maker and included in the decision process.   □

11.5 HYPOTHESIS TESTS WHEN THE VARIANCE IS UNKNOWN

In many applied problems we do not know the population variance σ^2, and therefore the critical value cannot be computed using the standardized normal distribution. We faced a similar problem in constructing confidence intervals in Chapter 10. Recall that the solution was to compute the sample standard deviation and use the Student t distribution. The same solution applies to hypothesis testing. The basic methodology is the same with substitution of the t distribution for the normal and the use of S_x^2 in place of σ^2 (Key Idea 11.6). Thus we do not need to learn an entirely new approach.

11.5.1 p Values

Hypothesis tests when the variance is unknown can also be performed using p values. The procedure is similar to that used when the variance is known, except that the sample variance, S^2, and the t distribution are substituted for the population variance, σ^2, and the normal distribution:

$$t_p = \frac{\bar{X} - \mu}{S/\sqrt{n}}$$

Key Idea 11.6: Hypothesis Test: Variance Unknown

We begin with a hypothesis test of the form

$$H_0: \mu \geq \mu_0$$
$$H_1: \mu < \mu_0$$

and a test statistic $\overline{X}$. The critical value for the test statistic is

$$\overline{X}_c = \mu_0 - t_\alpha S_{\overline{X}}$$
$$= \mu_0 - t_\alpha \frac{S_x}{\sqrt{n}}$$

where t_α with $n - 1$ degrees of freedom is obtained from Table A.2. The decision rule is:

Reject H_0 and accept H_1 if $\overline{X} < \overline{X}_c$.

When H_0 is rejected, the probability of Type I error is less than α.

The value of t_p is then used with the t table to determine the value of p. The following example demonstrates hypothesis testing when the variance is unknown.

Example 11.5   Income Program

A statistical consultant, George Judge, is responsible for evaluating a complex new training and work program designed to help people escape from the welfare system and become self-sufficient. An important measure of program success is the income level of participants. If the participants earn less total income than they receive from public assistance payments, they will be discouraged away from participating in the new program. In the year before the program was initiated, public assistance payments averaged $10,000 per year to heads of households. The Secretary of Health, Education, and Welfare is inclined to expand the program unless there is strong evidence that earnings under the program are less than welfare payments. The program has now been operating for 18 months. George has been asked to determine if there is strong evidence that annual incomes for heads of households are less than the $10,000 welfare payment.

Solution   Given this objective, George forms the hypothesis

$$H_0: \mu \geq 10,000$$
$$H_1: \mu < 10,000$$

The null hypothesis assumes that mean incomes are at least $10,000 under the new program. If we reject H_0, the probability that H_0 is true will be less than α. This result—rejection of H_0 with small probability of error—provides strong evidence in favor of the remaining alternative:

H_1: Earnings are less than welfare payments.

George decided to set the probability of Type I error α at 0.05. A random sample of $n = 29$ participants was selected. With α equal to 0.05 and the degrees of freedom, $n - 1$, equal to 28, the critical value of $t = 1.701$ is obtained from Table A.2. For each randomly selected participant he examines their income sources and determines their annual incomes. The sample mean is $\bar{X} = 8000$ and the sample variance $S_x^2 = 29{,}000{,}000$. Figure 11.9 shows the t distribution given 28 degrees of freedom. The critical value of the sample mean,

$$\bar{X}_c = \mu - t_{0.05}\sqrt{\frac{S_x^2}{n}}$$

$$= 10{,}000 - 1.701 \times \sqrt{\frac{29{,}000{,}000}{29}}$$

$$= 8299$$

is shown in Figure 11.9. Thus the decision rule is

Reject H_0 if $\bar{X}$ is less than 8299. Rejecting H_0 implies that incomes are less than \$10,000.

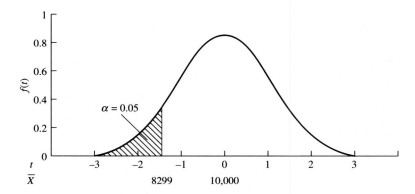

Figure 11.9   Student t Distribution for Example 11.5

Because the sample mean $\bar{X} = 8000$, George concludes that mean incomes have decreased and reports his conclusion to the program secretary. In this example the secretary was committed to the program and would cancel only if there was strong evidence that incomes were reduced from \$10,000. Since the sample mean, 8000, was less than the critical value, there was strong evidence to conclude that incomes were reduced. The program could be rejected with confidence that it was not meeting the objective of increasing incomes.

The p value for the sample mean of 8000 is

$$t_p = \frac{8000 - 10{,}000}{\sqrt{29{,}000{,}000/29}}$$

$$= -2.0$$

$$p \approx 0.03$$

The exact value of p requires some interpolation in the t table. Since 0.03 is less than $\alpha = 0.05$, H_0 is rejected and H_1 is accepted. □

Does It Make Sense?

Example 11.5 follows the form of hypothesis tests based on the normal with σ^2. A probability model is specified for the null hypothesis and used to construct a decision rule. We need to emphasize that the probability of Type I error must be set before the sample data are collected and the sample mean and variance are computed. Of course, the critical value cannot be computed before the sample standard deviation S_x is computed. However, because the t value is determined before obtaining the data, the critical value cannot be changed after the data are examined. Two-tailed t tests can also be constructed that follow the form of two-tailed tests based on the normal, as shown in Section 11.3. □

Example 11.6   Store Sales Analysis

Barbara Anderson has just completed four years of college at a medium-sized liberal arts college, where she majored in economics with a concentration in business. During her college years she was a star swimmer, achieving All-American ranking in her last two years. She has always enjoyed sports and upon graduation was offered an opportunity to operate and eventually purchase a sporting goods store in a small city.

Before deciding to pursue this venture, she wanted to analyze the past operations of the store. Examination of the financial statements indicated that basic operating expenses, including a subsistence salary for the manager, were \$55,000 per year. She consulted an accountant who works with sporting goods stores and he indicated that the cost of goods sold for stores of this type was approximately 65% of total sales. Using these numbers, she concluded that the break-even annual sales for the store had to be \$157,143 [55,000/(1 − 0.65)] (i.e., a gross profit of 35% multiplied by 157,143 would provide operating expenses of \$55,000).

Discussions with the present owners indicated that the store was open six days per week and closed on major holidays. Thus the store would be open 300 days per year (6 days per week times 52 weeks equals 312 less 12 holidays). As a result, she concluded that to cover basic expenses, average daily sales must be $157{,}143/300 = 523.81$, or about $\mu = 525$. Does the past daily sales experience provide strong evidence that the store can at least cover basic expenses?

Solution   Using her knowledge of statistical hypothesis testing, she formulated a hypothesis test to determine if sales were high enough to operate the store successfully. She believes that she can expand sales using her knowledge of business practice and sports. Therefore, she decided that she will operate the store if mean daily sales in the past have covered break-even costs. This led to the hypothesis test

$$H_0: \mu \leq 525$$
$$H_1: \mu > 525$$

She chose a probability of Type I error $\alpha = 0.05$. The population standard deviation was not known and thus she used a t test, with a random sample of size $n = 25$ observations. As a result, the decision rule was

Reject H_0 if the sample mean $\overline{X}$ is greater than

$$525 + t_{0.05,24} \times \frac{S_x}{\sqrt{25}}$$

where S_x is the sample standard deviation.

Using the random sample, Barbara prepared the computer analysis shown in Exhibit 11.1. The standard error of the sample mean $S_{\overline{X}}$ is shown under "SEMEAN." The critical value is

$$\begin{aligned}
\overline{X}_c &= 525 + t_{0.05,24} \times \frac{S_x}{\sqrt{25}} \\
&= 525 + t_{0.05,24} \times S_{\overline{X}} \\
&= 525 + 1.711 \times 115 \\
&= 721.8
\end{aligned}$$

EXHIBIT 11.1   Analysis of Daily Store Sales: Minitab Output

	N	MEAN	MEDIAN	TRMEAN	STDEV	SEMEAN
C26	25	913	801	882	574	115

	MIN	MAX	Q1	Q3
C26	246	2294	403	1335

Midpoint	Count	
200	2	**
400	6	******
600	2	**
800	5	*****
1000	2	**
1200	2	**
1400	1	*
1600	3	***
1800	0	
2000	1	*
2200	1	*

The sample mean was $\bar{\bar{X}} = 913$, which is greater than $\bar{X}_c = 721.8$. She concluded that mean daily store sales were greater than 525, which provided strong evidence that sales were above the break-even level.

In Exhibit 11.1 she also obtained descriptive statistics and a copy of the sample histogram to check for unusual observations. The distribution was somewhat skewed, with a few days having very large sales. Recall from Chapter 2 that skewness is apparent since the mean exceeds the median. The observed patterns were not unusual and did not compromise her conclusion.[1]

Additional analysis. Because we have the actual population for this problem, we can carry out additional analyses to extend our experience with applied hypothesis testing. We illustrate changes in Barbara's results had she chosen a sample of size $n = 50$. However, in practice the sample size is determined first, and one does not change the sample size to obtain the results desired.

First, let us assume that Barbara decided to obtain a random sample of size $n = 50$. This would reduce her probability of Type II error. In addition, the daily store sales were skewed to the right and the mean for a random sample of size $n = 50$ was more likely to be normally distributed. The analysis results are presented in Exhibit 11.2. Using the computer output, the critical value is

$$\bar{X}_c = 525 + t_{0.05,49} \times \frac{S_x}{\sqrt{50}}$$
$$= 525 + t_{0.05,49} \times S_{\bar{Y}}$$
$$= 525 + 1.678 \times 65.4$$
$$= 634.7$$

The sample mean, $\bar{X} = 750$, is above the critical value. She would decide with even greater confidence that mean store sales are above the break-even level. The histogram indicates somewhat greater concentration near the mean compared to the sample of size 25. Skewness is still apparent, but there were no unusual observations that might affect the conclusion.   □

11.6 HYPOTHESIS TESTS USING PROPORTIONS

Hypothesis tests involving proportions are usually conducted by assuming that the sample proportion $\hat{P}$ has a normal distribution [i.e., $n\pi(1 - \pi) \geq 9$]. From previous work we know that the population mean and variance for the proportion is

$$\mu_{\hat{P}} = \pi$$
$$\sigma_{\hat{P}}^2 = \frac{\pi(1 - \pi)}{n}$$

---

[1] For example, if each of the two outliers had been 500 dollars smaller, the sample mean would have been reduced by $(2 \times 500)/25 = 40$. The resulting mean $913 - 40 = 873$ would still have been well above the critical value $\bar{X}_c = 721.8$ and the decision would have remained the same.

EXHIBIT 11.2   Analysis of Daily Store Sales with $n = 50$: Minitab Output

	N	MEAN	MEDIAN	TRMEAN	STDEV	SEMEAN
C31	50	750.0	667.0	698.1	462.8	65.4

	MIN	MAX	Q1	Q3
C31	155.0	2217.0	441.2	880.0

```
Midpoint   Count
     200     6   ******
     400     9   *********
     600    13   *************
     800    10   **********
    1000     4   ****
    1200     2   **
    1400     2   **
    1600     1   *
    1800     1   *
    2000     0
    2200     2   **
```

With the mean and variance of $\hat{P}$ and the assumption that $\hat{P}$ has a normal distribution, hypothesis tests can be specified. These hypothesis tests follow the pattern in Key Idea 11.2. Hypothesis tests involving proportions are developed using Key Idea 11.7 and Example 11.7.

Example 11.7   New Product Market Testing

Nellie Wahl, a market research consultant, has been asked to develop a decision procedure to determine if a new product is likely to be successful. After analyzing the production cost and potential gross profit, she concludes that a profitable introduction would require purchases by 20% of the households, given a retail price of $1.00 per unit. A random sample of $n = 400$ households was selected.

Solution   The decision process uses the hypothesis test

$$H_0: \pi \leq 0.20$$
$$H_1: \pi > 0.20$$

Introduction of the new product would be recommended only if there is strong evidence that more than 20% of the households would purchase. A Type I error in this decision implies introduction of a product that is doomed to failure. The company has many new products scheduled for introduction next year and thus decides to set the probability of Type I error $\alpha = 0.01$.[2] As a result, the standardized normal is

---

[2] With a small probability of Type I error $\alpha = 0.01$ compared to $\alpha = 0.05$, the probability of Type II error will be larger. Thus some potentially successful products will not be introduced. As indicated, the company has many product opportunities and this rule will select only those with the highest potential for success.

Key Idea 11.7: Hypothesis Tests for Proportions

The form of hypothesis tests is similar to those presented previously:

$$H_0: \pi \leq \pi_0$$
$$H_1: \pi > \pi_0$$

Given this form of the hypothesis test, we compute a critical value $\hat{P}_c$ using the normal distribution of the sample statistic $\hat{P}$:

$$\hat{P}_c = \pi_0 + Z_\alpha \sigma_{\hat{P}}$$
$$= \pi_0 + Z_\alpha \sqrt{\frac{\pi_0(1 - \pi_0)}{n}}$$

The variance is computed using π_0, which is the largest value of π in the null hypothesis. The decision rule would be

Reject H_0 if $\hat{P}$ is greater than $\hat{P}_c$.

$Z_{0.01} = 2.33$ from Table A.1. The critical decision proportion $\hat{P}_c$ is located to the right of 0.20, as shown in Figure 11.10. Computation of $\hat{P}_c$ is as follows:

$$\hat{P}_c = \pi_0 + Z_\alpha \sigma_{\hat{P}}$$
$$= 0.20 + 2.33\sqrt{\frac{0.20(1 - 0.20)}{400}}$$
$$= 0.247$$

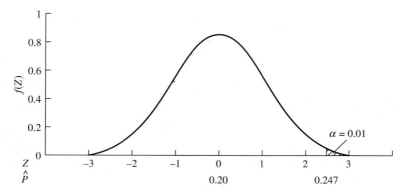

Figure 11.10   Distribution of Sample Proportion for Example 11.7

The decision rule is:

Reject H_0 if the sample proportion $\hat{P}$ is greater than 0.247.

Rejecting H_0 results in the conclusion that the new product will be purchased by more than 20% of the households. ☐

Does It Make Sense?

Hypothesis testing provides a decision rule before data are collected. This decision rule is based on objective statistical criteria as discussed in this chapter. Thus it avoids the temptation to seek data that support one's initial opinion. The choice of α should provide similar risk over many decisions. Thus $\alpha = 0.05$ is a useful rule, with $\alpha = 0.01$ reserved for choices where very strong evidence is desired. At times one may prefer to use $\alpha = 0.07$, 0.02, or 0.005. The important point for a decision maker is that the choice of α be the same for problems with similar risk. We strongly believe that stable rules, based on a solid rationale, will produce better decisions over a long time horizon. ☐

Practice Problem 11.1: Delivery Time

Speedy Bike delivery company guarantees that it will complete its deliveries in the downtown area of Metropolis within 90 minutes after a pickup. A statistical consultant is hired to evaluate their performance. He collects the following data: $n = 36$, $S_x^2 = 109$, and $\bar{X} = 86$ minutes. Can you conclude that there is strong evidence to support the conclusion that mean delivery time is less than 90 minutes?

(a) State the hypothesis.
(b) What are the decision rule and the critical value?
(c) What is your conclusion?

The solutions for all Practice Problems are given at the end of the chapter.

Problem Exercises

11.1   Given the hypothesis test

$$H_0: \mu \leq 100$$
$$H_1: \mu > 100$$

with X distributed normal and a variance of 64, a random sample of size 28 is obtained and the sample mean is used to test the hypothesis. Determine the critical value with:
(a) $\alpha = 0.05$.
(b) $\alpha = 0.02$.

11.2   Given the hypothesis test

$$H_0: \mu = 100$$
$$H_1: \mu \neq 100$$

with X distributed normal and a variance of 64. A random sample of size 28 is obtained and the sample mean is used to test the hypothesis. Determine the critical values with:
(a) $\alpha = 0.05$.
(b) $\alpha = 0.02$.

11.3   Given the hypothesis test

$$H_0: \mu \geq 350$$
$$H_1: \mu < 350$$

with X distributed normal and a variance of 100, a random sample of size 25 is obtained and the sample mean is used to test the hypothesis. Determine the critical value with:
(a) $\alpha = 0.05$.
(b) $\alpha = 0.02$.
(c) What is your conclusion if $\bar{X} = 346$ and the rule from part (a) is used?
(d) What is the p value if $\bar{X} = 346$?

11.4   Given the hypothesis test

$$H_0: \mu = 50$$
$$H_1: \mu \neq 50$$

with X distributed normal and a variance of 75, a random sample of size 34 is obtained and the sample mean is used to test the hypothesis. Determine the critical values with:
(a) $\alpha = 0.08$.
(b) $\alpha = 0.04$.

11.5   Jerusalem Stone, Inc. sells cut stone for yard construction. They claim that the average weight of their stones is less than 40 pounds with a variance of 100. A random sample of 25 stones is used to test their claim.
(a) What is the critical value with $\alpha = 0.05$ that would provide strong evidence to support their claim?
(b) The sample mean weight was 37 pounds. What is your conclusion?
(c) What is the p value for part (b)?

11.6   A consumer products company claims that its packages weigh 400 grams with a variance of 150 and the package weights have a normal distribution. A random sample of size 33 is used to test this claim.
(a) Define the hypothesis test and write a definition of the null and alternative hypotheses.
(b) What is the critical value for the test if $\alpha = 0.05$?
(c) What is the p value if the sample mean is 395?

11.7   Given the hypothesis test

$$H_0: \pi \leq 0.60$$
$$H_1: \pi > 0.60$$

a random sample of size 400 is obtained and the sample proportion is used to test the hypothesis. Determine the critical value with:
(a) $\alpha = 0.05$.
(b) $\alpha = 0.02$.
(c) What is your conclusion if $\hat{P} = 0.67$ and the rule from part (a) is used?
(d) What is the p value if $\hat{P} = 0.65$?

11.8   A political candidate wishes to know if more than 50% of the population supports her candidacy. Using a random sample of 900 voters, she finds that 55% would vote for her.
(a) Write the hypothesis test and indicate the critical value with $\alpha = 0.05$.
(b) What is your conclusion?
(c) What is the p value for this test?

11.9   A market research study is designed to determine if 30% or more of the people in a large southern state would purchase a new brand of frozen spiced chicken. A random sample of 500 persons is obtained. They are given a portion to eat and then asked if they would purchase the product.
(a) Define the hypothesis test and compute the critical value if $\alpha = 0.05$. Assume that they want strong evidence before they would introduce the product.
(b) Compute the critical value if $\alpha = 0.01$.

11.7 DETERMINING THE PROBABILITY OF TYPE II ERROR

In this section we learn how to compute the probability of Type II error when we fail to reject the null hypothesis (Key Idea 11.8). In Section 11.3 we learned how to develop decision rules using hypothesis tests. If we reject this null hypothesis, the probability model indicates that error is less than a predetermined small value α. However, if we fail to reject, we know that either the null hypothesis is true or that our decision process is not sensitive enough to detect that the null hypothesis should be rejected. We defined a Type II error as the probability of failing to reject the null hypothesis when we should.

Type II error indicates how well our hypothesis test discriminates between the alternatives. Consider the jury trial analogy. We want to protect innocent people from conviction, and therefore we assume that a person is innocent until proven guilty. We have confidence that a guilty verdict has a small probability of error given the way that we have dealt with the uncertainty. But suppose that we have a weak prosecuting attorney who prepares poor cases and that most people are judged innocent. We have protected the innocent. However, it is likely that we have a large Type II error that results in no punishment for many guilty people. The criminal justice decision process is not well served by such a result.

Key Idea 11.8: Probability of Type II Error and Power

The formal process for determining the probability of Type II error uses the following definitions:

1. A Type II error is defined as failing to reject H_0, the null hypothesis, when H_0 is false. The **probability of Type II error** is defined as β.
2. The **power** of a hypothesis test is the probability that we will reject H_0 when we should.
3. Combining these definitions leads to the result that

$$\beta + \text{power} = 1.0$$

Type II errors are computed and used to judge the quality of the hypothesis test. We present the method for computing the probability β of a Type II error (Key Idea 11.9) in an extended example.

Example 11.8 Cereal Package Weight: Type II Error

In Section 11.2 we developed a decision rule that enabled John Pautzke to determine if cereal boxes were being filled properly.

$$H_0: \mu \le 16.0$$

$$H_1: \mu > 16.0$$

The null hypothesis mean was $\mu \le 16$ ounces. He used a random sample of $n = 25$ boxes and the variance of box weights was $\sigma^2 = 0.16$. As a result, his decision rule, with $\alpha = 0.05$, was to reject H_0 and conclude that weight was over 16 ounces if the sample mean exceeded $\bar{X}_c = 16.13$. Now we ask: How good is this rule?

Solution   To answer this question, consider some specific alternatives. Suppose that the mean weight of all cereal boxes is actually $\mu = 16.13$ ounces. The correct decision would be to reject H_0 and conclude that the mean weight exceeds 16 ounces. Unfortunately, in a decision situation the mean weight of all boxes is not known. Figure 11.11 shows the normal distribution for the sample mean when $\mu = 16.13$ ounces. When the population mean is 16.13, 50% of the sample means are greater than 16.13. The power of the test when $\mu = 16.13$ is 0.50.

Using the decision rule "reject H_0 if $\bar{X} > 16.13$," H_0 is rejected only 50% of the time. The probability of a correct decision (power) is only 0.50, and hence the probability of a Type II error $\beta = 0.50$. Thus a system that is not filling boxes properly would be identified correctly 50% of the time. A Type II error—deciding that boxes are properly filled when they are not—would occur with a probability $\beta = 0.50$ (1 − power).

In this example the power was 0.50 and $\beta = 1 - \text{power} = 0.50$. The power and β depend on the specific value for the alternative hypothesis H_1, which was $\mu = 16.13$

Key Idea 11.9: Compute Probability of Type II Error

The probability of Type II error for the hypothesis test

$$H_0: \mu \le \mu_0$$
$$H_1: \mu > \mu_0$$

and a proposed mean, μ_*, which is in the H_1 region, can be computed as follows:

1. Compute the Z_β value for the critical value, $\overline{X}_c$, given a mean μ_*, where Z_β is the normal value for the critical decision value, $\overline{X}_c$, given a mean μ_* that is in the H_1 region.

$$Z_\beta = \frac{\overline{X}_c - \mu_*}{\sigma_{\overline{X}}}$$

2. Use the computed Z_β to determine the probability of Type II error β and the power for the specific value of $\mu = \mu_*$ contained in H_1.
3. Sketch a normal curve that shows the probability of Type II error β and the power for the alternative μ_* and the critical value $\overline{X}_c$.
4. Repeat this process for various values of μ_* that are included in the alternative hypothesis H_1.

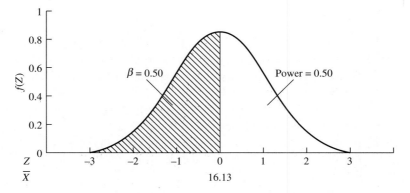

Figure 11.11   Power of Test When $n = 25$, $\alpha = 0.05$, $\mu = 16.13$

in this case. Note that the decision rule is based on $\alpha = 0.05$ and the original null hypothesis.

Now consider the effect of different values of μ on the power of the test. If μ is actually 16.08, as shown in Figure 11.12, a correct decision would reject H_0. The power and probability of Type II error for the test are computed as follows:

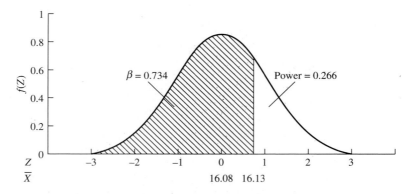

Figure 11.12   Power of Test When $n = 25$, $\alpha = 0.05$, $\mu = 16.08$

1. Compute the Z_β value for 16.13 given a population mean $\mu = 16.08$, where Z_β is the normal value for the critical decision value, $\bar{X}_c$, given a mean μ that is in the H_1 region.

$$Z_\beta = \frac{\bar{X}_c - \mu}{\sigma_{\bar{X}}}$$
$$= \frac{16.13 - 16.08}{\sqrt{0.16/25}}$$
$$= \frac{16.13 - 16.08}{0.08}$$
$$= 0.625$$

2. Use the computed Z_β to determine the probability of Type II error β and the power for the specific value of $\mu = 16.08$ contained in H_1. From the standard normal Table A.1, we find that the probability of $\bar{X}$ less than 16.13 is $\beta = 0.734$, and thus the power is 0.266.
3. Construct Figure 11.12, which shows the probability of Type II error β and the power for the alternative $\mu = 16.08$.
4. Repeat this process for various values of μ that are included in the alternative hypothesis H_1. For example, if $\mu = 16.23$, then

$$Z_\beta = \frac{16.13 - 16.23}{0.08}$$
$$= -1.25$$

From Table A.1 and Figure 11.13 we find that $\beta = 0.106$, and the power equals 0.894.   □

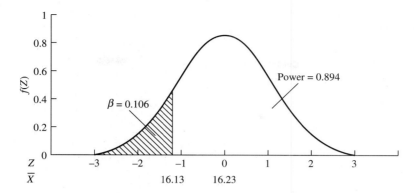

Figure 11.13   Power of Test When $n = 25$, $\alpha = 0.05$, $\mu = 16.23$

11.7.1 Power Curve

We have now seen how to compute the probability of Type II error and the power of a statistical hypothesis test. These results depend on the value μ contained in the alternative hypothesis. But we do not know the value of μ. Given this problem, analysts typically compute Type II error for several different values of the unknown parameter. This process is known as *sensitivity analysis*, sometimes called *what-if analysis* in business applications. For hypothesis testing we perform this analysis using the power curve (Key Idea 11.10).

Key Idea 11.10: Power Curve

The **power curve** presents the relationship between the power of a test and values of μ_* that are contained in the alternative hypothesis, H_1. It is used to evaluate the hypothesis test for ranges of the unknown parameter μ_*.

Figure 11.14 presents the power curve for our example problem. We see that the power increases and the probability of Type II error decreases as the actual value of the population mean μ increases. This result is intuitively reasonable because higher average package weights increase the likelihood of our concluding that the mean is greater than 16 ounces. The power curve provides a rationale for that conclusion and indicates specific probability results.

By examining the power curve, an analyst can make judgments concerning the quality of the hypothesis test for decision making. For example, suppose that the mean package weights were only slightly above 16 ounces (e.g., 16.05 or 16.10). Then the hypothesis test result has a small probability of being correct because the probability

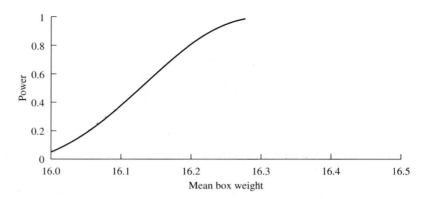

Figure 11.14   Power Curve with $\alpha = 0.05$, $n = 25$, for Cereal Packaging
Hypothesis Test

of concluding that mean package weights exceed 16 ounces is less than 0.50. If correct decisions concerning weights, 16.05 or 16.10, are important, we need to redesign the test. We could increase the probability of Type I error α or we could increase the sample size. The first alternative exchanges one type of error for another, while the second lowers the probability of both errors. However, increasing sample size also increases the cost of analysis.

If we change the probability of Type II error from $\alpha = 0.05$ to $\alpha = 0.10$, the critical value is changed to

$$\bar{X}_c = \mu_0 + Z_{0.10}\sigma_{\bar{X}}$$
$$= 16.00 + 1.28 \times 0.08$$
$$= 16.10$$

In this case the decision rule is "reject H_0 if $\bar{X}$ is greater than 16.10 and conclude that the mean package weights exceed 16 ounces."

Figure 11.15 presents the power curve for the hypothesis test with $\alpha = 0.10$. The power curve has shifted to the left and thus, for example, when $\mu = 16.13$, β decreases from 0.50 to 0.354 as the power increases from 0.50 to 0.656. Also, when $\mu = 16.23$ the power increases from 0.894 to 0.948, reducing β from 0.106 to 0.052. These reductions in Type II error come at the expense of an increase in Type I error α.

Reducing Type II error reduces the chance of deciding incorrectly that mean weight is less than 16 ounces when it is not. In addition, by increasing α to 0.10, we increased the probability of failing to identify correctly that the mean is under 16 ounces.[3]

---

[3] In this example, selecting H_0 implies that the company will increase the mean weight of all packages. This option may be more costly than risking a Type I error.

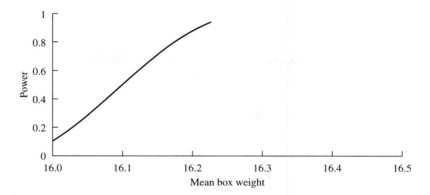

Figure 11.15   Power Curve with $\alpha = 0.10$, $n = 25$, for Cereal Packaging
Hypothesis Test

Computer computation of power curves.   Exhibit 11.3 indicates how the computations for power curves can be made using a statistical package such as Minitab. Similar calculations could be made using a spreadsheet. The process is as follows:

1. Define the critical value $\bar{X}_c$ as a constant, K1, and the standard deviation, $\sigma_{\bar{X}}$, as a constant, K2.

        Let K1=16.13
        Let K2=0.08

2. Enter the desired values of the mean, μ^*, that are included in the alternative hypothesis H_1, into column 1.

        Set C1
        16.05 16.10 16.15 . . .

3. Compute the Z values for each μ^* in H_1.

        Let c2=(k1 - c1)/k2

4. Compute the probability of Type II error β and store in c3.

        CDF c2 c3

5. Compute the power for each mean, μ^*, and store in column 4.

        Let c4 = 1 - c3

6. Plot the power in column 4 versus the means in column 1.

        Plot C4 C1

EXHIBIT 11.3   Computation of Power Curve Using Minitab

```
MTB > Let K1=16.13  # Critical Value
MTB > Let K2=0.08   # Standard deviation of sample mean
MTB > Set C1     # Enter values of mean in H1
DATA> 16.05 16.10 16.15 16.20 16.25 16.30 16.35 16.40
DATA> end
MTB > name c1 'mu_beta'
MTB > Let c2=(k1-c1)/k2  # Compute Z values for means in H1
MTB > name c2 'Z_beta'
MTB > CDF c2 c3        # Compute cumulative distribution  Beta
MTB > name c3 'beta'
MTB > let c4=1-c3      # Compute the Power
MTB > name c4 'Power'
MTB > plot c4 c1       # Plot the Power Curve
```

```
             -                                                     *       *
             -                                         *       *
      0.90+
             -
Power    -                                    *
             -
             -
      0.60+                        *
             -
             -
             -              *
      0.30+
             -
             -     *
             -
             -
          +---------+---------+---------+---------+---------+---mu_beta
        16.030     16.100    16.170    16.240    16.310   16.380
```

```
MTB > print c1-c4
 ROW  mu_beta     Z_beta       beta        Power
   1    16.05    1.00000   0.841344    0.158656
   2    16.10    0.37498   0.646164    0.353836
   3    16.15   -0.25001   0.401292    0.598708
   4    16.20   -0.87502   0.190781    0.809219
   5    16.25   -1.50001   0.066806    0.933194
   6    16.30   -2.12500   0.016793    0.983207
   7    16.35   -2.75002   0.002980    0.997020
   8    16.40   -3.37501   0.000369    0.999631
```

Does It Make Sense?

A decision maker is always more confident of a decision if the null hypothesis is rejected because the probability of making a Type I error is set small. If the null hypothesis is accepted, then either H_0 is true or there is a Type II error.

Because of the large probability of Type II errors, precautions must be taken. In Example 11.7 the decision required that the sample mean exceed 16.13, in order to conclude that the population mean was greater than 16. From Figure 11.13 and the related calculation it is necessary to set the population mean—the machine setting—at 16.23 so that 89.4% of the time the sample mean exceeds 16.13. This additional 0.23 ounce of cereal is a safety factor, which adds to the cost of cereal production. The size of the safety factor increases as the probability of Type II error is reduced. Note that the safety factor could be reduced if the packaging machine had a smaller standard deviation. □

11.7.2 Type II Error for Proportions

Computations for Type II error and the power curve for proportions are similar to those that we have presented for other random variables. The major difference is that the variance for a sample proportion $\sigma_{\hat{P}}^2$ is a function of the population mean π. This effect is small, but it must be recognized in the calculations. We will present the method using the market research problem from Section 11.7.

Example 11.9   New Product Market Testing Revisited

Our objective is to determine if more than 20% of the population would purchase a new product. The hypothesis test is

$$H_0: \pi \leq 0.20$$

$$H_1: \pi > 0.20$$

The hypothesis is tested by using the sample proportion $\hat{P}$ from a random sample of size $n = 400$. The probability of Type I error is $\alpha = 0.01$. The resulting decision rule is "reject H_0 if the sample proportion $\hat{P}$ is greater than $\hat{P}_c = 0.247$."

Solution   To determine the power and the probability of Type II error, we first compute Z_β for values of π contained in the alternative hypothesis H_1. The computation is made using

$$Z_\beta = \frac{\hat{P}_c - \pi}{\sigma_{\hat{P}}}$$

$$= \frac{\hat{P}_c - \pi}{\sqrt{\pi(1-\pi)/n}}$$

If we assume that $\pi = 0.26$, the result is

$$Z_\beta = \frac{0.247 - 0.26}{\sqrt{0.26(1 - 0.26)/400}}$$

$$= -0.59$$

From Table A.1 we find that the power of the test for $\pi = 0.26$ is 0.722 and the probability of Type II error $\beta = 0.278$. Figure 11.16 shows the power and β when $\pi = 0.26$.

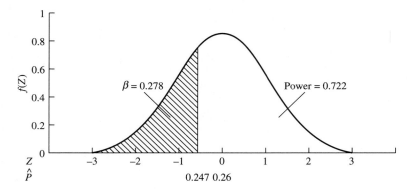

Figure 11.16   Power of Test for Proportions $\pi_0 = 0.20$, $\pi = 0.26$, $n = 400$, and $\alpha = 0.01$

Similar computations can be made for other values of π contained in the alternative hypothesis, H_1. For example, when $\pi = 0.22$, we find that

$$Z_\beta = \frac{0.247 - 0.22}{\sqrt{0.22(1 - 0.22)/400}}$$

$$= 1.29$$

From Table A.1 the power of the test for $\pi = 0.22$ is 0.098 and the probability of Type II error $\beta = 0.902$.

When $\pi = 0.30$ the results are

$$Z_\beta = \frac{0.247 - 0.30}{\sqrt{0.30(1 - 0.30)/400}}$$

$$= -2.30$$

From Table A.1 the power of the test for $\pi = 0.30$ is 0.989 and the probability of Type II error $\beta = 0.011$. These results are summarized in the power curve presented in Figure 11.17.   □

11.7.3 Power Curve: Increased Sample Size

The effect on the power curve of a larger α value was examined earlier. A larger α shifted the power curve, resulting in higher power and smaller β. However, this was done at the cost of a larger probability of Type I error α. Here it will be shown that larger sample sizes make the power curve steeper and thus reduce β without changing α; in addition, the critical value is closer to the hypothesized mean (Key Idea 11.11).

For example, consider the cereal packaging hypothesis test with a sample size of $n = 100$. The critical decision value for $\alpha = 0.05$, $\bar{X}_c$, is computed as

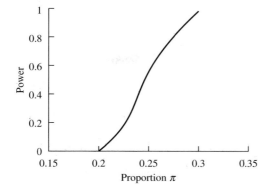

Figure 11.17   Power Curve for Proportion Hypothesis Test When $\pi_0 = 0.20$, $n = 400$, and $\alpha = 0.01$

Key Idea 11.11: Power Curve and Larger Samples

Increased sample size will decrease the probability of Type II error β and increase the power for a given Type I error α. This occurs because larger sample size decreases the variance of the sample mean. The difference, $Z_\alpha \sigma_{\bar{X}}$, between the hypothesized mean, μ_0, and the critical value will be smaller. The decision has greater precision but at an increased cost for more observations.

$$\bar{X}_c = 16.0 + 1.645\sqrt{\frac{0.16}{100}}$$

$$= 16.07$$

With $n = 100$ we decide that the mean weight of packages is greater than or equal to 16 ounces if $\bar{X}$ is greater than 16.07. Figure 11.18 indicates the probability of Type II error and the power of the test when $\mu = 16.08$. Computation of the power began with the calculation of

$$Z_\beta = \frac{\bar{X}_c - \mu}{\sigma_{\bar{X}}}$$

$$= \frac{16.07 - 16.08}{0.04}$$

$$= -0.25$$

Using Table A.1, the probability of Type II error $\beta = 0.401$ and thus the power is 0.599. This contrasts with $\beta = 0.734$ and a power of 0.266 when the sample size is $n = 25$ and $\alpha = 0.05$.

Continuing with calculations for $n = 100$ and various values of μ for the alternative hypothesis, we develop the power curve shown in Figure 11.19. Note that the

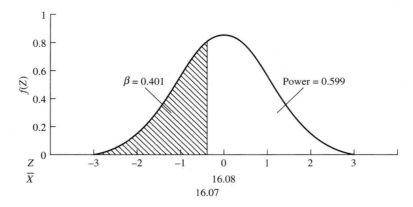

Figure 11.18   Power of Test When $n = 100$, $\alpha = 0.05$, and $\mu = 16.08$

power curve is much steeper and thus the hypothesis test is better able to discriminate between the alternative values of μ.

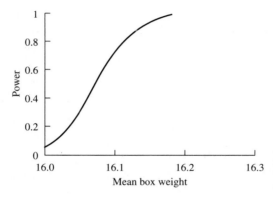

Figure 11.19   Power Curve for Cereal Packaging Hypothesis Test When $n = 100$ and $\alpha = 0.05$

Does It Make Sense?

The power and the probability of Type II error indicate the capability of a test to choose between alternatives. In addition, the benefits of increased sample size and/or smaller variance are related directly to the power. $\square$

Example 11.10   Analysis of Store Sales: Five Samples

Barbara Anderson (Example 11.6) was attempting to determine if mean daily sales were high enough to cover the operating expenses of a store whose management and possible purchase she was considering. As part of the analysis we also obtained four additional random samples of size $n = 25$ from the population of daily store sales. Descriptive statistics for these samples are shown in Exhibit 11.4 together with the results for the random sample labeled "sample 1," which was used previously in this example. If we compute the critical value for each sample, we will find that the null

EXHIBIT 11.4   Additional Samples of Daily Sales: Minitab Output

	N	MEAN	MEDIAN	TRMEAN	STDEV	SEMEAN
Sample 1	25	913	801	882	574	115
Sample 2	25	737.0	577.0	711.2	478.8	95.8
Sample 3	25	698	546	631	645	129
Sample 4	25	625.0	577.0	606.9	402.0	80.4
Sample 5	25	775.1	697.0	769.6	413.6	82.7

	MIN	MAX	Q1	Q3
Sample 1	246	2294	403	1335
Sample 2	117.0	1950.0	386.0	1154.5
Sample 3	117	2817	307	797
Sample 4	17.0	1648.0	263.5	849.5
Sample 5	78.0	1599.0	378.5	1102.0

hypothesis was rejected for all samples except the one labeled "sample 4." In that case the critical value would be

$$\bar{X}_c = + t_{0.05,24} \times \frac{S_x}{\sqrt{25}}$$

$$= 525 + 1.711 \times \frac{402}{\sqrt{25}}$$

$$= 662.6$$

The sample mean was $\bar{X} = 625$, which is less than the critical value. If Barbara had obtained the "c29" random sample as the only sample, she would have accepted the null hypothesis and concluded that mean store sales were less than or equal to 525. Because we have the entire population, we know that the population mean is $\mu = 742.7$ and $\sigma^2 = 537.1$. Therefore, the decision not to reject would be a Type II error.

Figure 11.20 shows the power and the probability of Type II error β when $\mu = 742.7$. The computation of Type II error begins with

$$Z_\beta = \frac{\bar{X}_c - \mu}{\sigma/\sqrt{n}}$$

$$= \frac{662.6 - 742.7}{537.1/\sqrt{25}}$$

$$= -0.746$$

From the standard normal distribution probabilities in Table A.1 we find that the power is 0.772 and that $\beta = 0.228$. Recall that we obtained five random samples of size $n = 25$ and that using one of the five resulted in a Type II error.

Given the probability of Type II error ($\beta = 0.228$) for the actual population mean ($\mu = 742.7$), we see that failing to reject H_0—a Type II error—would be expected in one case out of five (i.e., 20%). Thus the empirical results from the five random

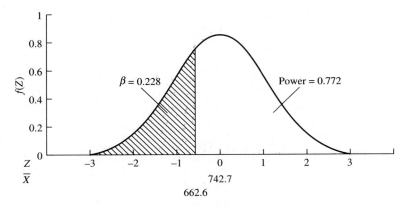

Figure 11.20   Power of Test for Store Sales When $n = 25$, $\alpha = 0.05$, and
$\mu = 742.7$

samples are very close to the results based on statistical theory. If 100 or 1000 random
samples had been used, the results would have been even closer.   □

Does It Make Sense?

In applied problems we do not know the population mean and therefore must make
our decisions based on the sample. This example demonstrates that we can reach
incorrect conclusions using our hypothesis testing procedure with random samples.
Mature decision makers understand that some decisions will be in error regardless of
the procedure used.   □

* 11.8 ECONOMIC ANALYSIS OF ERRORS

The choice between Type I and Type II errors is difficult because a clear understanding
of the balancing of these errors is often not available. In some situations we can
provide a basis for the choice by attempting to determine the cost of each type of error
for important values of μ. Define the cost of a Type I error as C_α and the cost of a
Type II error as $C_\beta(\mu)$ for various values of μ. These costs can be combined into a
total cost function of the form

$$\text{TC}(\mu) = \alpha C_\alpha + \beta C_\beta(\mu)$$

where $\text{TC}(\mu)$ is the expected total cost as a function of μ.

This equation can be computed for various values of α and the associated β over
the range of μ. By examining the computed values, more information to guide the
choice of α can be obtained.

This analysis could be expanded to include the effect of sample size. Increased sample size reduces both Type I and Type II error, but it also increases the cost of obtaining data. The new equation, which includes the cost of sample data $C(n)$, is

$$TC(\mu) = \alpha C_\alpha + \beta C_\beta(\mu) + C(n)$$

The values of $TC(\mu)$ could be computed for different values of α and n and the minimum cost combination could be used for the hypothesis test.

You can use this equation to select the best test design. Realistic application would require an algorithm that could be written in the language of a statistical package such as Minitab or in a spreadsheet such as Lotus.

Practice Problem 11.2

In Practice Problem 11.1, Speedy Bike's delivery service was evaluated. From the data collected, $n = 36$, $S_x^2 = 109$, and $\bar{X} = 86$, we found that there was strong evidence that the mean delivery time was less than 90 minutes. The critical value for the hypothesis test was $\bar{X}_c = 87.14$ and $S_{\bar{X}} = 1.74$. Now you are asked to determine the sensitivity of the hypothesis-testing process. What is the probability of Type II error if the population mean is actually:

(a) $\mu_* = 87.14$.
(b) $\mu_* = 89$.
(c) $\mu_* = 84$.   □

Problem Exercises

11.10 Given the hypothesis test

$$H_0: \mu \leq 100$$
$$H_1: \mu > 100$$

with X distributed normal and a variance of 64, a random sample of size 28 is obtained and the sample mean is used to test the hypothesis.
(a) What is the critical value with $\alpha = 0.05$?
(b) What is the probability of Type II error given $\mu = 105$?

11.11 Given the hypothesis test

$$H_0: \mu = 100$$
$$H_1: \mu \neq 100$$

with X distributed normal and a variance of 64, a random sample of size 28 is obtained and the sample mean is used to test the hypothesis.
(a) What are the critical values with $\alpha = 0.05$?
(b) What is β if $\mu = 105$?

11.12 Given the hypothesis test

$$H_0: \mu \geq 350$$
$$H_1: \mu < 350$$

with X distributed normal and a variance of 100, a random sample of size 25 is obtained and the sample mean is used to test the hypothesis.
(a) What is the critical value with $\alpha = 0.05$?
(b) What is the probability of Type II error if $\mu = 347$?

11.13 Given the hypothesis test

$$H_0: \ \mu = 50$$
$$H_1: \ \mu \neq 50$$

with X distributed normal and a variance of 75, a random sample of size 34 is obtained and the sample mean is used to test the hypothesis.
(a) What are the critical values with $\alpha = 0.10$?
(b) What is probability of Type II error if $\mu = 54$?

11.14 Jerusalem Stone, Inc. sells cut stone for yard construction. They claim that the average weight of their stones is less than 40 pounds with a variance of 100. A random sample of 25 stones is used to test their claim.
(a) What is the critical value with $\alpha = 0.05$ that would provide strong evidence to support their claim?
(b) What is the probability of Type II error if $\mu = 38$?

11.15 A consumer products company claims that its packages weigh 400 grams with a variance of 150 and the package weights have a normal distribution. A random sample of size 33 is used to test the claim that package weights are at least 400 grams.
(a) What is the critical value for the test if $\alpha = 0.05$?
(b) What is the probability of Type II error if $\mu = 403$?

11.16 Given the hypothesis test

$$H_0: \ \pi \leq 0.60$$
$$H_1: \ \pi > 0.60$$

a random sample of size 400 is obtained and the sample mean is used to test the hypothesis.
(a) What is the critical value with $\alpha = 0.05$?
(b) What is the probability of Type II error if $\pi = 0.66$?

11.17 A political candidate wishes to know if more than 50% of the population supports her candidacy. Using a random sample of 900 voters, she finds that 55% would vote for her.
(a) Write the hypothesis test and indicate the critical value with $\alpha = 0.05$.
(b) What is your conclusion?
(c) What is the probability of Type II error for the rule in part (a) and $\pi = 0.52$?

11.18 A market research study is designed to determine if 30% or more of the people in a large southern state would purchase a new brand of frozen spiced chicken. A random sample of 500 persons is obtained. They are given a portion to eat and then asked if they would purchase the product.
(a) Define the hypothesis test and compute the critical value if $\alpha = 0.05$. Assume that they want strong evidence before they would introduce the product.
(b) Compute the critical value if $\alpha = 0.01$.
(c) What is the probability of Type II error if $\pi = 0.34$ and $\alpha = 0.01$?

11.9 HYPOTHESIS TESTS FOR COMPARING TWO POPULATIONS

11.9.1 Two-Population Tests: σ^2 Known

There are a number of hypothesis-testing situations in which we do not know the exact value of a population mean. Instead, the problem involves the comparison of two population means using a random sample from each (Key Idea 11.12). Among the numerous examples are the following:

1. Management wants to compare worker productivity levels for two different groups. The goal is to identify the group with the highest productivity, in contrast to determining if productivity exceeds a specific level.

Key Idea 11.12: Hypothesis Tests for Two Populations

The hypothesis tests for problems involving two populations have the form

$$H_0: \mu_1 \leq \mu_2$$
$$H_1: \mu_1 > \mu_2$$

where μ_1 and μ_2 are the population means. Lower-tail and two-tailed hypothesis tests can be specified as simple modifications of this form. This form cannot be utilized because a known value of the mean is not available. However, a simple transformation converts the hypothesis to the form

$$H_0: \mu_1 - \mu_2 \leq 0$$
$$H_1: \mu_1 - \mu_2 > 0$$

or

$$H_0: \Delta\mu \leq 0$$
$$H_1: \Delta\mu > 0$$

where

$$\Delta\mu = \mu_1 - \mu_2$$

The test statistic for this hypothesis test will be

$$\Delta\bar{X} = \bar{X}_1 - \bar{X}_2$$

If the two sample means are normally distributed, $\Delta\bar{X}$ will also be normally distributed because linear combinations of normal random variables have a normal distribution. The critical decision value is

$$\Delta\bar{X}_c = 0 + Z_\alpha \sigma_{\Delta\bar{X}}$$

---

2. Economists are assigned to compare per capita incomes between geographic regions. The comparison would be made using random samples of income from each region.

3. Government evaluators seek to determine if crime rates have fallen after a major crime prevention program has been operating for a year. They would compare population means from two different time periods.

4. Marketing managers want to determine which geographic region has the highest proportion of persons who would purchase a new product. This result would be used to determine the appropriate region for introducing the product.

The major difference between two-population hypothesis tests and one-population hypothesis tests is the computation of the variance of the test statistic. Figure 11.21 shows the normal distribution for the two-population hypothesis test. Key Idea 11.13 shows that the critical value for the hypothesis test is directly related to the standard deviation of the difference between the sample means, $\sigma_{\Delta\bar{X}}$.

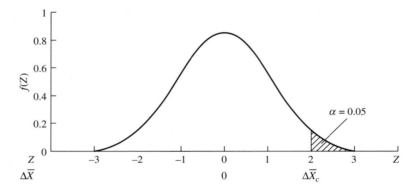

Figure 11.21   Critical Value for Differences Between Sample Means

In Section 10.8 we learned how to compute the variance and standard deviation for the difference between sample means, to develop confidence intervals. Hypothesis tests for differences between population means use these same variances and standard deviations for differences between sample means—$\sigma^2_{\Delta\bar{X}}$ and $\sigma_{\Delta\bar{X}}$.

Example 11.11   Agricultural Experiment

Let us consider again the example in Section 10.8 in which Shirley Brown, an agricultural economist, was comparing cow manure and turkey dung as fertilizers. Both fertilizers were applied to a sample of randomly selected cornfields and the productivity was measured. In the original problem she computed a 95% confidence interval for the difference between mean productivity using the two fertilizers.

Historically, farmers had used cow manure on their cornfields. However, recently a major turkey farm offered to sell composted turkey dung at a favorable price. The farm association decided that they would use this new fertilizer only if there was

---

Key Idea 11.13: Variance for Difference Between Sample Means

In Section 10.8 we showed that the variance of $\Delta \bar{X}$ is computed by using

$$\sigma^2_{\Delta \bar{X}} = \sigma^2_{\bar{X}_1} + \sigma^2_{\bar{X}_2} - 2\sigma_{\bar{X}_1 \bar{X}_2}$$

where

$$\sigma_{\bar{X}_1 \bar{X}_2} = \rho_{\bar{X}_1 \bar{X}_2} \sigma_{\bar{X}_1} \sigma_{\bar{X}_2}$$
$$= \rho_{Y_1, Y_2} \sigma_{\bar{X}_1} \sigma_{\bar{X}_2}$$

This equation assumes that the samples used to compute $\bar{X}_1$ and $\bar{X}_2$ are correlated with a correlation coefficient ρ_{X_1, X_2}. If the samples are independent, the variance is

$$\sigma^2_{\Delta \bar{X}} = \sigma^2_{\bar{X}_1} + \sigma^2_{\bar{X}_2}$$

because the correlation between samples is equal to zero.

---

strong evidence that productivity increased over the productivity that occurred with cow manure. Therefore, the hypothesis test was specified as

$$H_0: \mu_2 - \mu_1 \leq 0$$
$$H_1: \mu_2 - \mu_1 > 0$$

where μ_1 is the productivity using cow manure and μ_2 is the productivity using turkey dung. H_1 indicates that turkey dung results in higher productivity. The farmers will not change their fertilizer unless there is strong evidence for increased productivity.

   Solution   Using this design Shirley implemented an experiment to test the hypothesis. Cow manure was applied to one set of $n_1 = 25$ randomly selected fields. The sample mean productivity was $\bar{X}_1 = 100$. From past experience, the variance in productivity for these fields was assummed to be $\sigma^2_1 = 400$. Turkey dung was applied to a second random sample of $n_2 = 25$ fields and the sample mean productivity was $\bar{X}_2 = 110$. Based on published research reports, the variance for these fields was assumed to be $\sigma^2_2 = 625$. The two sets of random samples were independent. To compute the critical value, she first computed the mean and variance of the test statistic $\Delta \bar{X}$, where

$$\Delta \bar{X} = \bar{X}_2 - \bar{X}_1$$
$$= 110 - 100$$
$$= 10$$

The variance was

$$\sigma^2_{\Delta\bar{X}} = \frac{\sigma^2_2}{n_2} + \frac{\sigma^2_1}{n_1}$$

$$= \frac{625}{25} + \frac{400}{25}$$

$$= 41$$

$$\sigma_{\Delta\bar{X}} = 6.40$$

The critical value $\Delta\bar{X}_c$ can be computed as shown in Figure 11.22.

$$\Delta\bar{X}_c = 0 + Z_\alpha \times \sigma_{\Delta\bar{X}}$$

$$= 0 + 1.645 \times 6.40$$

$$= 10.53$$

where

$$\Delta\bar{X} = \bar{X}_2 - \bar{X}_1$$

The decision rule was

Reject H_0, and decide in favor of increased productivity, if $\Delta\bar{X} = \bar{X}_2 - \bar{X}_1$ is greater than 10.53.

The observed value of the difference $\Delta\bar{X}$ is 10.00, and therefore the null hypothesis could not be rejected. The test did not provide strong evidence in favor of turkey dung fertilizer.

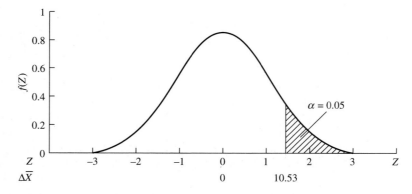

Figure 11.22   Critical Value: Difference Between Productivity for Two
Fertilizers

Correlated samples. In Section 10.8, Shirley also considered the effect of the assumption that the samples were correlated. Correlated samples would result from splitting each field and applying cow manure to one portion and turkey dung to the other. Under this experimental design using a correlation of $\rho = 0.50$, the same population variances, and the same sample sizes, the standard deviation for the difference was

$$\sigma^2_{\Delta \bar{X}} = \frac{\sigma^2_2}{n_2} + \frac{\sigma^2_1}{n_1} - 2\hat{\rho}_{12} \frac{\sigma_2}{\sqrt{n_2}} \frac{\sigma_1}{\sqrt{n_1}}$$

$$= \frac{625}{25} + \frac{400}{25} - 2.0(0.50)\left(\frac{25}{5}\right)\left(\frac{20}{5}\right)$$

$$= 21$$

$$\sigma_{\Delta \bar{X}} = 4.58$$

With this assumption the critical value for $\Delta \bar{X} = \bar{X}_2 - \bar{X}_1$ was

$$\Delta \bar{X}_c = 0 + 1.645 \times 4.58$$

$$= 7.53$$

With correlated samples,

$$\Delta \bar{X} = \bar{X}_2 - \bar{X}_1 = 10$$

is greater than $\Delta \bar{X}_c = 7.53$. We would reject the null hypothesis and conclude that turkey dung provided greater productivity.   ☐

Does It Make Sense?

Whenever possible, researchers and statisticians should try to use matched or correlated samples to obtain smaller variances for the differences. We say that the test using matched samples has more power because of its smaller variance. Recall that power curves indicate smaller Type II error when larger samples are used to obtain a smaller variance. Smaller variances obtained from correlated samples have the same effect on the power curve.   ☐

11.9.2 Two-Population Tests: σ^2 Unknown

By this point in our study of statistics we know that when the population variance is unknown, it will be estimated from the sample data and the Student t statistic will be used instead of the standardized normal Z. This same approach applies for two population tests. In Section 10.9 confidence intervals for differences between the means of two populations were developed using variance estimators based on various assumptions. Those results will be presented here and you are encouraged to review Section 10.9 to strengthen your understanding of the derivations and assumptions.

Independent samples.   In most situations involving the comparison of two populations, we assume that the population variances are equal: $\sigma^2_1 = \sigma^2_2 = \sigma^2$ (see Key Idea 11.14).

Key Idea 11.14: Two-Population Test: σ^2 Unknown but Equal

The critical value for the hypothesis

$$H_0: \mu_2 - \mu_1 \leq 0$$
$$H_1: \mu_2 - \mu_1 > 0$$

would be

$$\Delta \bar{X}_c = 0 + t_\alpha S_{\Delta \bar{X}}$$

where the degrees of freedom for t are $n_1 + n_2 - 2$.
    The variance for the difference between sample means is

$$S^2_{\Delta \bar{X}} = \frac{S^2_p}{n_1} + \frac{S^2_p}{n_2}$$

where the pooled estimator S^2_p for the population variance is

$$S^2_p = \frac{(n_1 - 1)S^2_1 + (n_2 - 1)S^2_2}{(n_1 - 1) + (n_2 - 1)}$$

Population variances not equal: $\sigma^2_1 \neq \sigma^2_2$.   If it is not possible to assume equal population variances, then we compute

$$S^2_{\Delta \bar{X}} = \frac{S^2_1}{n_1} + \frac{S^2_2}{n_2}$$

and the degrees of freedom are computed using

$$\text{DOF} = \left(1 + \frac{2}{S^2_1/S^2_2 + S^2_2/S^2_1}\right)(n - 1)$$

if the sample sizes are equal, $n_1 = n_2 = n$, or

$$\text{DOF} = \frac{[(S^2_1/n_1) + (S^2_2/n_2)]^2}{(S^2_1/n_1)^2/(n_1 - 1) + (S^2_2/n_2)^2/(n_2 - 1)}$$

if the sample sizes are not equal. These alternatives are discussed in detail in Section 10.9. As we indicated in that discussion, there are often strong arguments for assuming that the two populations being compared have equal variances. Thus the latter option should be used only when the assumption of equal variance is clearly incorrect.

Correlated samples.   The sample variance of the difference between sample means is reduced (see Key Idea 11.15) just as it was earlier where variances are known. The resulting $S_{\Delta \bar{X}}$ is used to compute critical values.

Key Idea 11.15: $S^2_{\Delta \bar{X}}$ for Correlated Samples: σ^2 Unknown

If the samples are correlated, the variance for the difference would be computed using

$$S^2_{\Delta \bar{X}} = S^2_{\bar{X}_1} + S^2_{\bar{X}_2} - 2\hat{\rho}_{12} S_{\bar{X}_1} S_{\bar{X}_2}$$

$$= \frac{S^2_1}{n_1} + \frac{S^2_2}{n_2} - 2\hat{\rho}_{12} \frac{S_1}{\sqrt{n_1}} \frac{S_2}{\sqrt{n_2}}$$

where $\hat{\rho}_{12}$ is the sample correlation between the two samples.

Does It Make Sense?

As we saw in Section 10.9, we can compute the variance by using the differences between paired observations from two different samples. This is the easiest way to compute the variance for the difference between sample means. In addition, the co-variance effect is removed without a separate calculation. Whenever possible, you should try to design comparisons between populations, to obtain paired observations. For more details, review Example 10.9.   □

11.9.3 Two-Population Tests: Proportions

A new product manager is attempting to choose between two geographic regions for the introduction of a new product. Both regions have the same population and per capita income. Therefore, the region with maximum potential sales is the one with the highest proportion of people who would purchase the product. The region with the highest proportion of potential purchasers can be identified by the hypothesis test

$$H_0: \pi_1 - \pi_2 = 0$$
$$H_1: \pi_1 - \pi_2 \neq 0$$

where π_1 and π_2 are the proportions of potential purchasers in each geographic region. The null hypothesis assumes that both regions have the same proportion of purchasers. We have formulated this problem as a two-tailed hypothesis test because we have no prior information that leads us to prefer either region. If we reject H_0, we will also conclude that either region 1 or region 2 has the larger proportion. The upper and lower critical values are shown in Figure 11.23. A random sample of n observations will be obtained from each region (see Key Idea 11.16).

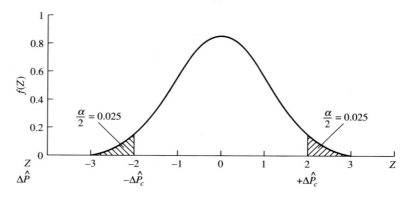

Figure 11.23   Two-Tailed Hypothesis Test for Difference Between Proportions

The two random sample surveys each contained 400 observations, and the sample proportions were $\hat{P}_1 = 0.40$ and $\hat{P}_2 = 0.50$. Using the relationships above, we find that the test statistic is

$$\Delta\hat{P} = \hat{P}_1 - \hat{P}_2$$
$$= 0.40 - 0.50$$
$$= -0.10$$

The average of the sample proportions is

$$\bar{P} = \frac{400(0.40) + 400(0.50)}{400 + 400}$$
$$= 0.45$$

The variance for the difference in proportions is

$$\sigma^2(\Delta\hat{P}) = \frac{\bar{P}(1-\bar{P})}{n_1} + \frac{\bar{P}(1-\bar{P})}{n_2}$$
$$= \frac{0.45(1-0.45)}{400} + \frac{0.45(1-0.45)}{400}$$
$$= 0.0012374$$
$$\sigma_{\Delta\hat{P}} = 0.035$$

The critical values are therefore

$$\Delta\hat{P}_c = \pm Z_{\alpha/2}\sigma_{\Delta\hat{P}}$$
$$= \pm 1.96 \times 0.035$$
$$= \pm 0.069$$

Key Idea 11.16: Two-Population Tests for Proportions

$$H_0: \pi_1 - \pi_2 = 0$$
$$H_1: \pi_1 - \pi_2 \neq 0$$

or

$$H_0: \Delta\pi = 0$$
$$H_1: \Delta\pi \neq 0$$

The sample proportions from each population are $\hat{P}_1$ and $\hat{P}_2$. The test statistic is the difference between sample proportions,

$$\Delta\hat{P} = \hat{P}_1 - \hat{P}_2$$

The variance for $\Delta\hat{P}$ is the variance of the linear combination of the two proportions computed from independent samples,

$$\sigma^2_{\Delta\hat{P}} = \sigma^2_{\hat{P}_1} + \sigma^2_{\hat{P}_2}$$

Under the null hypothesis, π_1 and π_2 are equal and a best estimate would be the weighted average of the two sample proportions:

$$\bar{P} = \frac{n_1\hat{P}_1 + n_2\hat{P}_2}{n_1 + n_2}$$

The variance of $\Delta\hat{P}$ is therefore

$$\sigma^2_{\Delta\hat{P}} = \frac{\bar{P}(1 - \bar{P})}{n_1} + \frac{\bar{P}(1 - \bar{P})}{n_2}$$

$$\Delta\hat{P}_c = \pm Z_{\alpha/2}\sigma_{\Delta\hat{P}}$$

Decision Rule

If $\Delta\hat{P} = \hat{P}_1 - \hat{P}_2$ is greater than $\Delta\hat{P}_c$, reject H_0 and conclude that a difference exists.

The decision rule is

Reject H_0 if $\Delta\hat{P}$ is less than -0.069 or greater than $+0.069$; choose region 1 if $\Delta\hat{P}$ is greater than $+0.069$ and choose region 2 if $\Delta\hat{P}$ is less than -0.069.

From the sample data we found that the difference $\Delta\hat{P}$ was -0.10 and therefore we chose region 2.

Single-tailed hypothesis tests can also be specified using the standard forms that we have presented. We emphasize that the differences between the various hypothesis tests occur mainly in the variance computation. The variance computation is based on the linear combination of random variables. Detailed development of variance estimators was presented in Chapter 10.

Example 11.12   Retail Sales Differences

After Barbara Anderson decided to begin operating the sporting goods store, she needed to establish work schedules. She decided to spend five days per week in the store. However, she was uncertain about which day to be away. After some consideration of business operations and personal needs she concluded that either Saturday or Monday would be appropriate. Discussion with the previous store operators and other small-business people led her to conclude that she should be in the store on Saturday unless Monday sales were significantly higher. This led to a hypothesis test of the form

$$H_0: \mu_S - \mu_M \geq 0$$
$$H_1: \mu_S - \mu_M < 0$$

where μ_S is the mean sales for Saturdays and μ_M is the mean sales for Mondays.

Solution   Using a probability of Type I error $\alpha = 0.05$, her decision rule would be to reject H_0 if $\Delta \bar{X}$ is less than $\Delta \bar{X}_c$, where

$$\Delta \bar{X} = \bar{X}_S - \bar{X}_M$$
$$\Delta \bar{X}_C = -t_{0.05} S_{\Delta \bar{X}}$$

To test the hypothesis, she obtained random samples of daily sales from both Monday and Saturday operations. The results of the analysis are shown in Exhibit 11.5.

Based on her understanding of the store operation, she assumed that the population variances for Monday and Saturday were the same and used the pooled estimator S_p^2 to compute the sample variances.

$$S_p^2 = \frac{(25-1)S_S^2 + (25-1)S_M^2}{(25-1) + (25-1)}$$
$$= \frac{(25-1)(469.8)^2 + (25-1)(633)^2}{25 + 25 - 2}$$
$$= 310,700$$

The degrees of freedom are 48 ($48 = 25 + 25 - 2$). The standard deviation of the differences between sample means $S_{\Delta \bar{X}}$ were calculated as

$$S_{\Delta \bar{X}} = \sqrt{\frac{S_p^2}{n_1} + \frac{S_p^2}{n_1}}$$
$$= \sqrt{\frac{310,700}{25} + \frac{310,700}{25}}$$
$$= 157.7$$

EXHIBIT 11.5   Analysis of Monday and Saturday Daily Sales

	N	MEAN	MEDIAN	TRMEAN	STDEV	SEMEAN
Monsamp	25	1078	786	1042	633	127
Satsamp	25	908.2	791.0	878.5	469.8	94.0

	MIN	MAX	Q1	Q3
Monsamp	272	2710	628	1555
Satsamp	312.0	2187.0	556.5	1271.0

Histogram of Monsamp   N = 25

```
Midpoint   Count
     200       2  **
     400       1  *
     600       6  ******
     800       5  *****
    1000       1  *
    1200       1  *
    1400       2  **
    1600       2  **
    1800       2  **
    2000       2  **
    2200       0
    2400       0
    2600       0
    2800       1  *
```

Histogram of Satsamp   N = 25

```
Midpoint   Count
     400       4  ****
     600       8  ********
     800       4  ****
    1000       1  *
    1200       2  **
    1400       3  ***
    1600       2  **
    1800       0
    2000       0
    2200       1  *
```

The critical value is

$$\Delta \bar{X}_C = -t_{0.05,48} S_{\Delta \bar{x}}$$
$$= -1.68 \times 157.7$$
$$= -264.9$$

The difference between sample means is

$$\Delta \bar{X} = \bar{X}_S - \bar{X}_M$$
$$= 908.2 - 1078$$
$$= -169.2$$

Since the difference between sample means (-169.2) is not less than the critical difference (-264.9), we cannot conclude that Monday sales are significantly higher. Therefore, Barbara will follow her initial intuition and be away from the store on Mondays.

Examination of other descriptive statistics shows that while the mean for Monday is larger, the medians are almost equal. Thus the Monday distribution is more highly skewed. Monday sales also have a higher variance, indicating that more extreme sales occur on Mondays.   □

Example 11.13   Differences Between Paired Observations

George Smith has been hired to determine if total crime rates have declined between 1982 and 1984. There has been a major reduction in the number of persons in the high-crime ages (i.e., 16 to 25). National policy planners want to know if this demographic change is associated with a change in the total crime rate.

Solution   George decides to use the state crime rates for 1982 and 1984 to answer the question. Because of many reporting sources and their associated errors, which can be assumed to be random, statisticians often use samples of states and cities as random samples. Historically, crime rates have been increasing, and therefore George specifies in his null hypothesis that 1982 crime rates are lower than 1984 rates.

$$H_0: \mu_{82} - \mu_{84} \leq 0$$
$$H_1: \mu_{82} - \mu_{84} > 0$$

The decision rule is to reject H_0 if the difference in crime rates,

$$\Delta \bar{X} = \bar{X}_{82} - \bar{X}_{84}$$

is greater than

$$\Delta \bar{X}_c = t_\alpha S_{\Delta \bar{x}} = t_\alpha S_{\bar{X}_{82} \bar{X}_{84}}$$

To perform the analysis, George prepared the computer output in Exhibits 11.6 and 11.7, which contain the descriptive statistics for the 1982 and 1984 crime rates for the sample of 50 states and the District of Columbia. The 1982 crime rates are contained in the variable named "Totcri82" and the 1984 crime rates are contained in the variable named "Totcri84."

EXHIBIT 11.6   Analysis of 1982 and 1984 Total Crime Rates: Minitab Output

	N	MEAN	MEDIAN	TRMEAN	STDEV	SEMEAN
totcri82	51	5253	5215	5203	1501	210
totcri84	51	4680	4588	4643	1331	186
Totcrdif	51	573.0	568.0	554.0	363.4	50.9

	MIN	MAX	Q1	Q3
totcri82	2511	10600	4256	6302
totcri84	2336	8799	3784	5577
Totcrdif	-320.0	1801.0	333.0	724.0

Histogram of totcri82   N = 51

Midpoint	Count	
3000	4	****
4000	14	**************
5000	14	**************
6000	9	*********
7000	8	********
8000	1	*
9000	0	
10000	0	
11000	1	*

Histogram of totcri84   N = 51
1 Obs. below the first class

Midpoint	Count	
3000	8	********
4000	16	****************
5000	13	*************
6000	9	*********
7000	3	***
8000	0	
9000	1	*

An inexperienced statistician might assume that the 1982 and 1984 samples are independent and compute $S_{\Delta\bar{x}}$ similar to the method used in Example 11.12. If that had been done, the result would have been

$$S_{\Delta\bar{x}} = \sqrt{\frac{(1501)^2}{51} + \frac{(1331)^2}{51}}$$
$$= 280.9$$

EXHIBIT 11.7   Analysis of 1982 and 1984 Crime Rates (*continued*)

```
Histogram of Totcrdif    N = 51

Midpoint    Count
   -400        1    *
   -200        0
      0        3    ***
    200        6    ******
    400       10    *********
    600       17    *****************
    800        8    ********
   1000        1    *
   1200        2    **
   1400        2    **
   1600        0
   1800        1    *
```

Plot of '82 and '84 crime rates:

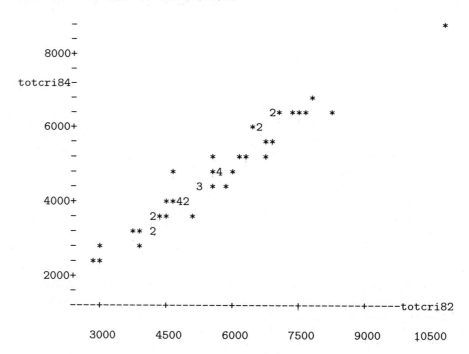

```
Correlation of totcri82 and totcri84 = 0.974
```

However, based on our study of paired samples and variances in Section 10.9, we know that the state samples from 1982 and 1984 should be treated as paired observations. The differences between the individual state crime rates were computed using Minitab and stored in the variable named "Totcrdif," where

$$\text{Totcrdif} = \Delta x_i = x_{82,i} - x_{84,i}$$

The standard error of the differences between means is therefore

$$S_{\Delta \bar{x}} = 50.9$$

from Exhibit 11.6. Using this result, the critical value is computed as

$$\begin{aligned}
\Delta \bar{X}_c &= t_{0.05,50} S_{\Delta \bar{x}} \\
&= 1.68 \times 50.9 \\
&= 85.5
\end{aligned}$$

Exhibit 11.6 also shows that the mean difference between 1982 and 1984 crime rates is

$$\begin{aligned}
\Delta \bar{X} &= \bar{X}_{82} - \bar{X}_{84} \\
&= 5253 - 4680 \\
&= 573
\end{aligned}$$

Therefore, George rejects the null hypothesis and concludes that total crime rates actually were reduced from 1982 to 1984. The histograms in Exhibit 11.6 show similar patterns of crime rates for the individual years, with the distributions being somewhat skewed toward higher rates. The histogram for the differences in Exhibit 11.7 is somewhat more symmetric. Finally, the plot of 1982 versus 1984 total crime rates indicates a strong linear relationship with a computed correlation of 0.974. This large correlation explains the large difference between the standard deviation for the difference between independent sample means (280.9) and the standard deviation for correlated or matched samples (50.9).   □

Does It Make Sense?

Whenever two populations are being compared, the analyst should design the analysis to use paired observations. This will result in more powerful hypothesis tests. Hypothesis tests based on differences between paired observations reduce the variance of the difference between subgroup means. This increases the power of the test. The variance reduction occurs because the variability between individual observations within each subgroup is removed.   □

Practice Problem 11.3: Comparing Auto Repair Procedures

A national chain of auto service centers wanted to know if the procedures used for brake repair in its Moorhead, Minnesota, center resulted in less time than brake repairs in its Boston, Massachusetts, center. Because the Boston center was near corporate headquarters, the operations vice-president, George Lodge, believed that the times were shorter at the Boston center. However, he would switch to the Moorhead procedures if there was strong evidence of shorter times in the Moorhead center. A comparative study was conducted with 25 randomly selected brake repair jobs measured in each center. In the Moorhead center the sample variance $S_2^2 = 250$ and the mean time $\bar{X}_2 = 110$ minutes. In the Boston center $S_1^2 = 200$ and the mean time $\bar{X}_1 = 120$ minutes. Assume that the population variances are equal. Can you conclude that there is strong evidence that the Moorhead center procedure requires less time?

(a) State the hypothesis test.

(b) Compute the critical value and state your conclusion.

Problem Exercises

11.19 Test the hypothesis

$$H_0: \mu_1 \le \mu_2$$
$$H_1: \mu_1 > \mu_2$$

given the following data from two random samples: $\sigma_1^2 = 120$, $\sigma_2^2 = 76$, $n_1 = n_2 = 25$, $\bar{X}_1 = 110$, and $\bar{X}_2 = 103$. Use $\alpha = 0.05$.

11.20 Test the hypothesis

$$H_0: \mu_1 \le \mu_2$$
$$H_1: \mu_1 > \mu_2$$

given the following data from two random samples: $\sigma_1^2 = 240$, $\sigma_2^2 = 176$, $n_1 = n_2 = 25$, $\bar{X}_1 = 110$, $\bar{X}_2 = 100$, and $\rho_{1,2} = 0.6$. Use $\alpha = 0.05$.

11.21 The Acme production company wishes to know if the mean strength of pieces from a proposed new stamping press exceeds that of the old press. Their old press has a variance of 121, and the new press has a variance of 86. They have arranged to run a random sample of 25 parts on the new press and another random sample of 25 parts on their old press.

(a) Write the hypothesis test.

(b) Compute the variance for the difference in strength between pieces run on the two machines.

(c) Compute the critical value and state the decision rule given $\alpha = 0.05$.

11.22 Test the hypothesis

$$H_0: \pi_1 \le \pi_2$$
$$H_1: \pi_1 > \pi_2$$

given $\alpha = 0.05$, $n_1 = n_2 = 400$, $\hat{P}_1 = 0.44$, and $\hat{P}_2 = 0.38$.

11.23 A market research firm has been hired to test the sales effectiveness of a new design feature on a snowblower. A random sample of 400 people indicated that 25% would

purchase the old snowblower. A second random sample of 450 people indicated that 30% would purchase the new snowblower.
(a) State the hypothesis test.
(b) Compute the variance of the difference between the proportions and the critical value for the hypothesis test.
(c) Do they have strong evidence to conclude that a larger percentage would purchase the new snowblower?

11.24 Given the hypothesis

$$H_0: \mu_1 \leq \mu_2$$
$$H_1: \mu_1 > \mu_2$$

and the following data from two random samples: $S_1^2 = 129$, $S_2^2 = 98$, $n_1 = n_2 = 25$, $\overline{X}_1 = 110$, and $\overline{X}_2 = 103$, and using $\alpha = 0.05$, compute:
(a) The pooled variance estimator.
(b) The critical value and state the decision rule.
(c) What is your conclusion?

11.25 Given the hypothesis

$$H_0: \mu_1 \leq \mu_2$$
$$H_1: \mu_1 > \mu_2$$

and the following data from two random samples: $S_1^2 = 240$, $S_2^2 = 176$, $n_1 = n_2 = 25$, $\overline{X}_1 = 110$, $\overline{X}_2 = 100$, and $\hat{\rho}_{1,2} = 0.6$, and using $\alpha = 0.05$, compute:
(a) The pooled variance estimator.
(b) The critical value and state the decision rule.
(c) What is your conclusion?

11.26 Given the hypothesis

$$H_0: \mu_1 \geq \mu_2$$
$$H_1: \mu_1 < \mu_2$$

and the following data from two random samples: $S_1^2 = 229$, $S_2^2 = 198$, $n_1 = 35$, $n_2 = 25$, $\overline{X}_1 = 110$, and $\overline{X}_2 = 121$, and using $\alpha = 0.05$, compute:
(a) The pooled variance estimator.
(b) The critical value and state the decision rule.
(c) What is your conclusion?

11.10 CONTROLLING TYPE I AND TYPE II ERROR

Hypothesis tests have been developed that are based on a selected probability of Type I error. These tests use a critical value to choose between H_0 and H_1. Unfortunately, this procedure often results in large probabilities of Type II error if H_0 is not rejected. Here a test is presented that controls Type I and Type II error simultaneously (Key Idea 11.17). However, this test requires that we specify an interval between H_0 and H_1 within which no conclusion can be reached.

Key Idea 11.17: Controlling Type I and Type II Error

Hypothesis tests that control Type I and Type II error simultaneously can be specified. The specification has the form

$$H_0\colon \mu \leq \mu_0$$
$$H_1\colon \mu \geq \mu_1$$

The distance between μ_0 and μ_1 is the distance to the critical value for rejecting $H_0\colon \mu \leq \mu_0$ plus the distance to the critical value for rejecting $H_1\colon \mu \geq \mu_1$ as defined by the following relationship:

$$\mu_1 - \mu_0 = Z_\alpha \frac{\sigma}{\sqrt{n}} + Z_\beta \frac{\sigma}{\sqrt{n}}$$

$$\Delta\mu = \frac{\sigma}{\sqrt{n}}(Z_\alpha + Z_\beta)$$

This expression can be solved for the sample size that will balance the desired error probabilities with the standard deviation and the difference between the population means.

$$n = \left(\frac{\sigma}{\Delta\mu}\right)^2 (Z_\alpha + Z_\beta)^2$$

The difference between the population means is defined as the minimum critical difference.

The alternative hypothesis-testing procedure presented in this section computes the sample size required to choose between two population means while controlling both Type I and Type II error. Discussion begins with a review of classical hypothesis tests, which use a composite single-tailed test. Those tests separate the range for the population mean into two subranges using a hypothesis of the form

$$H_0\colon \mu \geq \mu_0$$
$$H_1\colon \mu < \mu_0$$

The test is performed by choosing a probability of Type I error, α, and computing a critical value. If the test statistic is less than the critical value, H_0 is rejected and H_1 is accepted and we conclude that μ is less than μ_0.

This test has a fundamental weakness. If the value of μ is slightly less than that of μ_0, the test is most likely to choose H_0 incorrectly. We saw this when computing the probability of Type II error in Section 11.7. The hypothesis test is not useful when μ is slightly less than μ_0.

Now consider a test that has three regions instead of two. One region is defined by H_0 and a second by H_1, just like the classical test. Now add a third region in the center which will be ignored by the hypothesis test. The hypothesis is now stated as

$$H_0: \mu \geq \mu_0$$
$$H_1: \mu \leq \mu_1$$

The difference between μ_0 and μ_1 is the new region, which is ignored by the test. Previously, we showed that the test is not likely to be correct in this ignored region. Thus, in reality, little has been lost by this modification. However, this hypothesis form does force the test designer to think more realistically about H_0 and H_1, as will be shown in the examples that follow.

This new formulation provides a modification of the classical test. Type I error is still the probability of rejecting H_0 incorrectly and is specified before data are collected. But now Type II error can be viewed as the probability of rejecting H_1 incorrectly and is also specified before data are collected. With these two parameters, α and β, specified, the sample size and the critical value can be computed. This formulation is developed next using a set of examples.

Example 11.14   Production Facility Closing

Consider a typical hypothesis-testing example. A microcomputer manufacturer is attempting to determine if a particular production facility should remain open. The alternative is to have the units produced in a Latin American country using lower-cost workers. The accounting and industrial engineering departments have determined that if mean productivity is less than 1000 units per 8-hour shift, the plant should be closed and production moved. Alternatively, if productivity is at or above 1100 units per shift, this plant is the lowest-cost producer and should remain open. We also know from past experience that the standard deviation of productivity is $\sigma = 200$.

Solution   The hypothesis test can be specified as

$$H_0: \mu \leq 1000$$
$$H_1: \mu \geq 1100$$

The test is shown schematically in Figure 11.24. In contrast to previous procedures, the extreme of each hypothesis implies a different population. The problem is to choose which one of two populations is the source of the sample data. The populations associated with H_0 have their means at or less than 1000, while the populations associated with H_1 have their means at or above 1100. Any populations whose means are between 1000 and 1100 cannot be selected by this hypothesis test and is ignored.

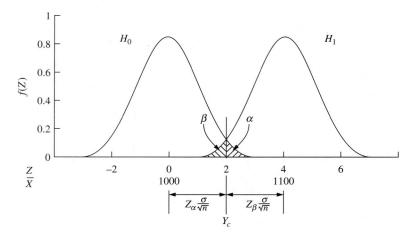

Figure 11.24   Hypothesis Test Controlling Type I and Type II Error

The assignment of the null H_0 and alternative H_1 hypotheses is arbitrary since both Type I and Type II error are specified. In this formulation Type I error α is the probability that the mean is 1000 or less and we decide that it is 1100 or more. Type II error β is the probability that the mean is 1100 or more and we decide that it is 1000 or less.

From Figure 11.24 we can state the following relationship:

$$\mu_1 - \mu_0 = Z_\alpha \frac{\sigma}{\sqrt{n}} + Z_\beta \frac{\sigma}{\sqrt{n}}$$

$$\Delta\mu = \frac{\sigma}{\sqrt{n}}(Z_\alpha + Z_\beta)$$

where $\mu_1 = 1100$ and $\mu_0 = 1000$. This expression can be solved for the sample size that will balance the desired error probabilities with the standard deviation and the difference between the population means. The difference between the population means is defined as the minimum critical difference since it indicates the minimum difference between population means that can be detected by the hypothesis test. The required sample size is

$$\sqrt{n} = \frac{\sigma}{\Delta\mu}(Z_\alpha + Z_\beta)$$

$$n = \left(\frac{\sigma}{\Delta\mu}\right)^2 (Z_\alpha + Z_\beta)^2$$

By examining this equation, we see how the various parameters affect the determination of sample size. The ratio of the standard deviation σ divided by the minimum critical difference $\Delta\mu$ is an important parameter. The standard deviation is a measure of the inherent variability of the process being studied. Minimum critical difference, $\Delta\mu$, is the detectable difference set by the decision maker. However, there is a cost in terms of sample size. Note that the sample size increases as the square of $\sigma/\Delta\mu$. Thus, attempts to detect small differences have a large cost in terms of increased sample size. In addition, decreasing either α or β increases Z_α or Z_β and thus increases the sample size. For a given sum of $\alpha + \beta$, a minimum sample size results when α and β are equal.

Figure 11.25 presents the relationship between sample size and β given that $\alpha = 0.05$. The same relationship would occur between sample size and α given that $\beta = 0.05$. Note how the sample size increases rapidly as we decrease β.

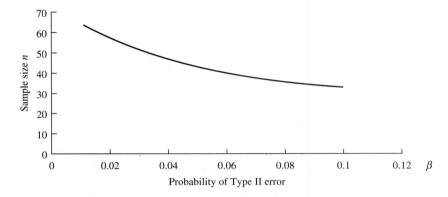

Figure 11.25   Sample Size Versus β for $\alpha = 0.05$ and $\sigma/\Delta = 2.0$

The critical decision value $\overline{X}_c$ can be computed using the sample size derived. From Figure 11.24 and our previous work we see that the critical decision value is

$$\overline{X}_c = 1000 + Z_\alpha \frac{\sigma}{\sqrt{n}}$$

or

$$\overline{X}_c = 1100 - Z_\beta \frac{\sigma}{\sqrt{n}}$$

Using these equations, we can show that if α and β are equal, the critical decision value will be exactly halfway between $\mu_0 = 1000$ and $\mu_1 = 1100$.

With this background let us return to the original example. The standard deviation was $\sigma = 200$ and the minimum critical difference was $\Delta\mu = 100$. In addition, we will set $\alpha = \beta = 0.05$. Therefore, the sample size is equal to

$$n = \left(\frac{\sigma}{\Delta\mu}\right)^2 (Z_\alpha + Z_\beta)^2$$

$$= \left(\frac{200}{100}\right)^2 (1.645 + 1.645)^2$$

$$= 43.30$$

Since n must be an integer, we usually round the sample size to the next highest integer, and therefore $n = 44$. The critical value is

$$\bar{X}_c = \mu_0 + Z_\alpha \frac{\sigma}{\sqrt{n}}$$

$$= 1000 + 1.645 \frac{200}{\sqrt{44}}$$

$$= 1049.6$$

The critical value, $\bar{X}_c = 1049.6$, is slightly less than the middle point 1150 because the sample size was rounded to the next-highest integer. Note also that

$$\bar{X}_c = \mu_1 - Z_\beta \frac{\sigma}{\sqrt{n}}$$

$$= 1100 - 1.645 \frac{200}{\sqrt{44}}$$

$$= 1050.4$$

In cases such as this we would use 1050 as the critical value. The decision rule is

If $\bar{X}$ is less than or equal to 1050, accept H_0 ($\mu \leq 1000$), and if $\bar{X}$ is greater than 1050, accept H_1 ($\mu \geq 1100$). $\qquad\square$

Does It Make Sense?

This rule provides a decision that controls both Type I and Type II error at desired levels. However, the disadvantage is that the test does not apply if the population mean is between μ_0 and μ_1.

In most cases we do not know if the population mean is between these limits. Thus we must depend on other information that will allow us to eliminate these options. In the example problem the accounting analysis was not precise enough to indicate appropriate action if the mean productivity was between 1000 and 1100. Thus options in this interval could not be used and were eliminated from the hypothesis test. The size of the difference between μ_1 and μ_2 can also be reduced. However, recall that reduced intervals increase the sample size and thus the cost of gathering information. $\qquad\square$

11.10.1 Tests Using Proportions

Hypothesis tests for proportions can also be designed to control Type I and Type II error. The format is similar to the one presented above except for the variance computation. An example will be used to develop the procedure.

Example 11.15   Product Test Marketing

Susan Emery is the market manager for a new cake mix. She has analyzed the costs and potential profit for her new product. Combining this information with the population of the market area, she concludes that the product will be profitable if more than 25% of the households will purchase it regularly. However, if less than 20% will purchase it regularly, the product will be a failure.

Solution   The hypothesis test is

$$H_0: \pi \le 0.20$$
$$H_1: \pi \ge 0.25$$

The test is described by Figure 11.26. The sample size is determined as follows:

$$\pi_2 - \pi_1 = Z_\alpha \sqrt{\frac{\pi_1(1 - \pi_1)}{n}} + Z_\beta \sqrt{\frac{\pi_2(1 - \pi_2)}{n}}$$

$$\Delta\pi = \frac{1}{\sqrt{n}}\left[Z_\alpha\sqrt{\pi_1(1 - \pi_1)} + Z_\beta\sqrt{\pi_2(1 - \pi_2)} \right]$$

$$n = \left(\frac{1}{\Delta\pi}\right)^2 \left[Z_\alpha\sqrt{\pi_1(1 - \pi_1)} + Z_\beta\sqrt{\pi_2(1 - \pi_2)} \right]^2$$

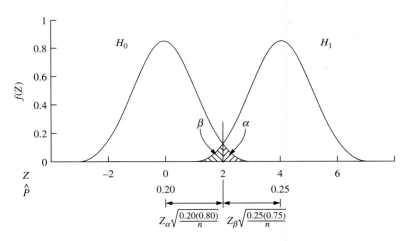

Figure 11.26   Proportion Hypothesis Test Controlling Both Type I and
Type II Error

For the cake mix example we choose $\alpha = 0.02$ because we want to have a small probability of a product failure. In addition, we choose $\beta = 0.10$ because we have many new product choices and are not concerned about losing a potentially successful project. The sample size is

$$n = \left(\frac{1}{0.05}\right)^2 \left[2.05\sqrt{0.20(1 - 0.20)} + 1.28\sqrt{0.25(1 - 0.25)} \right]^2$$
$$= 755.56$$

Following our convention of rounding up to the next integer, we will use a sample size of 756. The critical decision point π_c is

$$\pi_c = 0.20 + Z_\alpha \sqrt{\frac{0.20(1 - 0.20)}{756}}$$
$$= 0.20 + 2.05 \times 0.0145$$
$$= 0.230$$

A random sample of $n = 756$ households will be contacted and asked if they would purchase the new cake mix. If more than 23% indicate purchase, the new cake mix will be introduced. If less than 23% indicate purchase, the project will be abandoned. ◻

Problem Exercises

11.27 Determine the sample size and critical value to test the following hypothesis:

$$H_0: \mu \geq 120$$
$$H_1: \mu \leq 100$$

$$\sigma^2 = 900 \text{ and } \alpha = \beta = 0.05.$$

11.28 Determine the sample size and critical value to test the following hypothesis:

$$H_0: \mu \leq 250$$
$$H_1: \mu \geq 260$$

$$\sigma^2 = 900, \alpha = 0.06, \text{ and } \beta = 0.04.$$

11.29 Determine the sample size and critical value to test the following hypothesis:

$$H_0: \pi \geq 0.60$$
$$H_1: \pi \leq 0.50$$

$$\alpha = \beta = 0.05.$$

11.30 Determine the sample size and critical value to test the following hypothesis:

$$H_0: \pi \leq 0.20$$
$$H_1: \pi \geq 0.32$$

$$\alpha = 0.06 \text{ and } \beta = 0.04.$$

11.31 Mark Thorson, product manager for Consolidated Cereals, Inc., must decide on the introduction of a new sugar-coated cereal product. Company policy is to introduce new products if more than 30% of the test market indicates that they will purchase the product, and not to introduce if 20% or less indicate that they will purchase. He has asked you to design a random sampling study to select between the two ranges of market acceptance. The probability of failing to introduce a product when they should is 0.04, and the probability of introducing a product when they should not is 0.06. Compute:
   (a) The sample size required.
   (b) The critical value.
   (c) State the decision rule.

SUMMARY OF KEY IDEAS

See also Charts 11.1 to 11.4 (pages 548 to 551).

PRACTICE PROBLEM SOLUTIONS

11.1 (a) The null hypothesis should state that the mean delivery time is greater than 90 minutes and thus they are not meeting their guarantee on average. Rejecting the null hypothesis will provide strong evidence that the mean delivery time is less than 90. However, it does not lead to the conclusion that every delivery is less than 90 minutes.

$$H_0: \mu \geq 90$$
$$H_1: \mu < 90$$

(b) The decision rule is:

Reject H_0 if $\bar{X} < \bar{X}_c$.

With the critical value

$$\bar{X}_c = 90 - Z_{0.05} \times S_{\bar{X}}$$
$$= 90 - 1.645 \times \frac{\sqrt{109}}{\sqrt{36}}$$
$$= 87.14$$

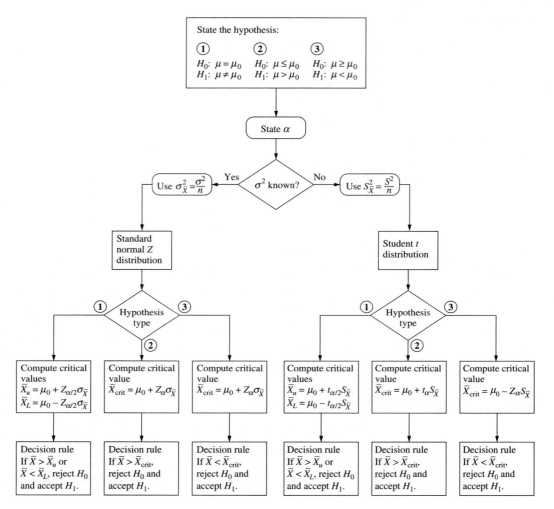

Chart 11.1   One Population $\bar{X}$

    (c) The sample mean $\bar{X} = 86$ is less than the critical value $\bar{X}_c = 87.14$, and therefore H_0 is rejected and we conclude that the mean delivery time is less than 90 minutes.

11.2   (a) Type II error occurs when the sample mean is greater than the critical value $\bar{X}_c = 87.14$ even though the population mean μ_* is in the subset defined by H_1. With $\mu_* = 87.14$ the probability that

$$\bar{X} > \bar{X}_c = 87.14$$

is $\beta = 0.50$.

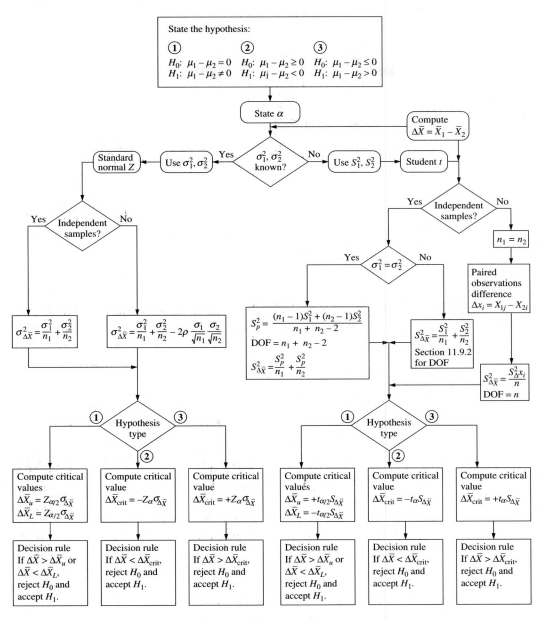

Chart 11.2   Two Populations $\Delta \bar{X} = \bar{X}_1 - \bar{X}_2$

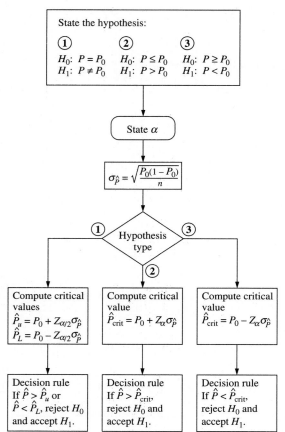

Chart 11.3   One Population $\hat{P}$

(b) In this case $\bar{X}_c = 87.14$ but $\mu_* = 89$. The Z_β value for determining β is computed as

$$Z_\beta = \frac{\bar{X}_c - \mu_*}{S_{\bar{X}}}$$

$$= \frac{87.14 - 89}{1.74}$$

$$= -1.07$$

and therefore

$$\beta = 0.8577$$

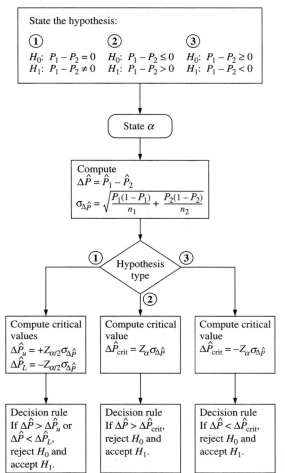

State the hypothesis:

① ② ③

H_0: $P_1 - P_2 = 0$ H_0: $P_1 - P_2 \leq 0$ H_0: $P_1 - P_2 \geq 0$
H_1: $P_1 - P_2 \neq 0$ H_1: $P_1 - P_2 > 0$ H_1: $P_1 - P_2 < 0$

State α

Compute
$\Delta \hat{P} = \hat{P}_1 - \hat{P}_2$

$$\sigma_{\Delta \hat{P}} = \sqrt{\frac{P_1(1-P_1)}{n_1} + \frac{P_2(1-P_2)}{n_2}}$$

Hypothesis type ① ② ③

Compute critical values
$\Delta \hat{P}_u = +Z_{\alpha/2}\sigma_{\Delta \hat{P}}$
$\Delta \hat{P}_L = -Z_{\alpha/2}\sigma_{\Delta \hat{P}}$

Compute critical value
$\Delta \hat{P}_{crit} = Z_{\alpha}\sigma_{\Delta \hat{P}}$

Compute critical value
$\Delta \hat{P}_{crit} = -Z_{\alpha}\sigma_{\Delta \hat{P}}$

Decision rule
If $\Delta \hat{P} > \Delta \hat{P}_u$ or $\Delta \hat{P} < \Delta \hat{P}_L$, reject H_0 and accept H_1.

Decision rule
If $\Delta \hat{P} > \Delta \hat{P}_{crit}$, reject H_0 and accept H_1.

Decision rule
If $\Delta \hat{P} < \Delta \hat{P}_{crit}$, reject H_0 and accept H_1.

Chart 11.4 Two Populations
$\Delta \hat{P} = \hat{P}_1 - \hat{P}_2$

(c) In this case $\bar{X}_c = 87.14$ but $\mu_* = 84$. The Z_β value for determining β is computed as

$$Z_\beta = \frac{\bar{X}_c - \mu_*}{S_{\bar{X}}}$$

$$= \frac{87.14 - 84}{1.74}$$

$$= +1.80$$

and therefore

$$\beta = 0.0359$$

11.3   (a) The problem states that a change will occur only if there is strong evidence that the mean time required is less in Moorhead. Thus the null hypothesis should assume that mean Boston repair time is less than or equal to the mean Moorhead time:

$$H_0: \mu_2 - \mu_1 \geq 0$$
$$H_1: \mu_2 - \mu_1 < 0$$

The critical value will have a negative sign.

(b) Because the population variances are assumed equal, we first compute the pooled variance estimator, S_p^2, using the equation

$$S_p^2 = \frac{(n_1 - 1)S_1^2 + (n_2 - 1)S_2^2}{n_1 + n_2 - 2}$$
$$= \frac{(25 - 1)200 + (25 - 1)250}{25 + 25 - 2}$$
$$= 225$$

This estimate of S_p^2 has 48 degrees of freedom. Using this result, compute the estimated variance for the difference between sample means:

$$S_{\Delta \bar{X}}^2 = \frac{S_p^2}{n_1} + \frac{S_p^2}{n_2}$$
$$= \frac{225}{25} + \frac{225}{25}$$
$$= 18$$

and therefore

$$S_{\Delta \bar{X}} = 4.243$$

The critical value is therefore

$$\Delta \bar{X}_c = -t_{48,0.05} S_{\Delta \bar{X}}$$
$$= (-1.671)(4.243)$$
$$= -7.09$$

The difference between sample means is

$$\bar{X}_2 - \bar{X}_1 = 110 - 120 = -10$$

Therefore, since $\Delta \bar{X} = \bar{X}_2 - \bar{X}_1 = -10$ is less than the critical value, $\Delta \bar{X}_2 = -7.09$, we conclude that there is strong evidence to support the conclusion that the procedure used for brake repair in Moorhead requires less time than the procedure used in Boston.

CHAPTER PROBLEMS

11.1 Design a hypothesis test to determine if the mean of a normally distributed random variable is greater than 100. The variance is $\sigma^2 = 100$.
   (a) Using a random sample of size 50, state the hypothesis and the decision rule.
   (b) How would you handle this problem if you could not assume that the random variable has a normal distribution?

11.2 You are in charge of location analysis for an expanding chain of ethnic restaurants. Market studies indicate that these restaurants have great appeal in midwestern cities with a population above 15,000 and a mean family income at or above $50,000. The variance of family incomes is 100,000,000. You typically obtain a random sample of 25 families and determine the sample mean income. This sample mean will be used to decide if the income level is satisfied.
   (a) Develop a hypothesis test such that the probability of recommending a community when you should not is 0.05 or less. State the decision rule.
   (b) Repeat part (a) using a sample size of $n = 100$. Why might you use this test instead of the one developed in part (a)?

11.3 The Sunshine Juice Company sells juice in 32-ounce bottles. They wish to establish a quality control procedure to monitor their bottle-filling operation to ensure that the bottles contain at least 32 ounces with a probability of error of 0.05 or less. The bottle-filling machine has a variance of 1. Their quality control policy states that monitoring procedures will use random samples of size $n = 25$. The contents of each bottle is measured precisely and the sample mean is computed.
   (a) State the hypothesis test that should be used and indicate the critical value for the test.
   (b) If the sample mean on a particular day is 32.35 ounces, what action do you recommend?

11.4 Frank Fillemup is distribution manager for a flour manufacturer. He is concerned that the 30-ounce package is not being completely filled. From past experience he knows that the variance for individual package weight is $\sigma^2 = 0.16$. A random sample of size $n = 25$ packages is obtained and carefully weighed. If he concludes that packages are being filled properly, he wishes the probability of error to be $\alpha = 0.05$ or less.
   (a) State an appropriate hypothesis test and provide an interpretation.
   (b) Compute the critical value and state the decision rule.

11.5 You are the chief statistician for the Manitou Headlight Works. Present production is 400 lights per shift, with a variance of 1600. A new process to increase productivity is being tested. The production manager indicates that the new process may be tested during 16 randomly selected 8-hour production shifts over the next month.
   (a) Develop a decision procedure that will indicate if the new production process actually increases productivity.
   (b) Discuss the comparison between a decision rule based on $\alpha = 0.05$ versus a rule based on $\alpha = 0.10$ for this problem. Assume that the new production process has a very small additional cost.

11.6 A cereal manufacturing company guarantees that each package has at least 16 ounces of cereal. A consumer testing group routinely conducts unannounced random inspections of 25 packages and checks their weight. If the sample mean does not exceed 16 ounces, the testing group reports that the entire lot is under the guaranteed weight. The variance of package weights is $\sigma^2 = 0.25$. The company wishes to ensure that the probability of packages being reported as under weight is less than 0.05.
(a) What mean weight should be set for the packaging machine?
(b) State the hypothesis test and the decision rule that should be used by the testing group.

11.7 An active competitive market exists for Dundas Donoughts, which are produced by spinster Norwegian farmers using grain that is stone ground by a secret process somewhere in the ancient city of Dundas. Dundas Donoughts are advertised to have an average weight of 4 pounds each with a standard deviation of 0.16. A sales contract is being negotiated between you, a local retailer with a reputation for high-quality products, and Dundas Donoughts, Inc. The guarantee of average weight is an important issue in the negotiations. The contract states that a random sample of 25 will be obtained from each shipment. The sample mean will be used to decide if the shipment meets the contracted mean weight. The probability of Type I error will be 0.05.
(a) Determine the decision rule that will be used by Dundas Donoughts to ensure compliance with the contract.
(b) Determine the decision rule that you the retailer will use to ensure compliance with the contract.
(c) If the rules are different, explain why this difference exists despite the high-priced lawyers who were used to write the contract.

11.8 You are trying to determine if the mean weight of a large shipment of hogs is greater than 100 pounds or less than 60 pounds. The standard deviation of the weighing process is 100. However, it is possible to reduce the standard deviation by purchasing various levels of repair for the scale. The standard deviation can be reduced by one for each dollar spent up to 80 dollars. Thus an expenditure of $80 would reduce the standard deviation from 100 to 20. Each sample observation costs $2. You wish to choose between the two weights with a probability of error of 0.05 for missing either alternative.
(a) Design a hypothesis-testing procedure and indicate the decision rule.
(b) Determine the amount of money that should be spent to improve the scale and the sample size so that the test is conducted at minimum cost. (*Hint:* Compute total costs for scale expenditures at selected points, such as $0, $20, $40, $60, and $80. Then choose narrower intervals until you obtain the lowest-cost combination.)

11.9 Frank's Deli sells a premium hamburger that it guarantees will contain less than 25 units of fat in each 1-pound package. The hamburger grinding process has been set so that the distribution of fat in each pound has a mean $\mu = 20$ and a variance $\sigma^2 = 9$.
(a) What proportion of the 1-pound packages will exceed the guarantee?
(b) A sample of size $n = 16$ is obtained and the sample mean was 18. Do you have strong evidence that the process has changed?
(c) A second sample of size $n = 25$ was obtained and the sample mean was 21. Has a change occurred? Use a two-tailed test.

(d) What is the probability of Type II error in part (c) if the mean actually increased to $\mu_* = 20.5$?

11.10 The measurements for a new plastic part are produced on a process whose mean $\mu = 10$ and variance $\sigma^2 = 25$. The process is monitored by selecting a random sample of size 5 each day, and the sample mean is computed. Set up a two-tailed hypothesis test with $\alpha = 0.01$.

(a) State the upper and lower critical values for the sample mean.

(b) What are the upper and lower critical values for the sample mean if the probability of Type I error is changed to 0.05?

11.11 The long-run historical mean production of beans using conventional seeds is 100 bushels per acre. A new seed is used in 25 randomly selected 1-acre fields, and the total production is 2700 bushels for the 25 fields. In addition, the sum of the square of each field's production, $\sum Y_i^2$, is 301,200. Based on these data, do we have strong evidence that the new seed increases production above the historical mean?

11.12 The Proctor Soap Company has sold its product to 20% of the households for a number of years. They have recently conducted an extensive advertising campaign to increase the percentage of households who purchase their product. After the campaign was completed, a random sample of $n = 400$ households was asked if they have purchased Proctor soap. This proportion of positive responses will be used to decide if the advertising campaign increased sales.

(a) State the null and alternative hypotheses in terms of π, the proportion of households who purchase the product.

(b) After some thought it is decided that the advertising campaign will be considered successful if at least 92 of the 400 households interviewed have responded positively. Determine the probability of Type I error, α.

(c) What is the actual percentage of households who purchase Proctor soap after the advertising campaign if the probability of Type II error is 0.10 and the decision rule from part (b) is used?

11.13 George Mellard is a candidate for a major elective office in a two-candidate election. As his political consultant, you obtain a random sample of 400 voters on the night before the election. In the sample 224 indicate that they will vote for George. What advice should you provide to George regarding his chances of election? Your past practice in this election is to provide hypothesis test results that have a probability of Type I error equal to 0.05.

11.14 George Mel, a statistician, was interested in determining the likelihood that he could be elected mayor of South Hill. George obtained a random sample of size n from the population of voters in South Hill. The sample proportion was equal to 0.54 when voters were asked if they would vote for George for mayor.

(a) Given a probability of type I error, $\alpha = 0.05$, what is the minimum sample size that would enable George to feel confident of winning the election? (He will win if more than 50% of the voters support him.)

(b) Suppose that 56% of all voters in the population would vote for George. What is the probability of Type II error in the decision situation above if a critical value of 0.54 and a sample size as determined above are used?

11.15 You are in charge of market research for a large consumer foods company. A new breakfast food has been developed for the college market. It can be eaten from the box while running to or sitting in an early morning class. Production and marketing cost analyses developed by the accounting department indicate that the product will be profitable if at least 25% of the college students in a five-state region would purchase the product at least once per week. In a recent random sample survey you found that 98 college students out of a random sample of 342 said they would purchase your new product at least once a week.

(a) Design a hypothesis test to determine if the new product should be introduced. Present a rationale for the selection of the probability of Type I error, α.

(b) Using the test and the sampling results, make a recommendation about adoption of the product.

11.16 Frank Lewis, the marketing manager, has asked you to conduct a random sampling survey to determine if a new product will be successful if it is introduced. You compute the fixed and variable production and marketing costs. After some discussion a decision is made that the wholesale price must be $0.50 and the fixed costs must be recovered in two years. As a result, you determine that 50% of the families in the market area must be willing to purchase the product at least once over the next two years. Your budget allows you to obtain a random sample of 144 families who will be asked if they would purchase the product at least once. You will compute the proportion, $\hat{P}$, of the sample who respond positively to the new product. Develop a hypothesis-testing procedure. State the hypothesis, the probability model, the test statistic, the critical value, and the decision rule. Use a probability of Type I error equal to 0.05.

11.17 Return to Problem 11.16, in which Frank Lewis has asked for a sampling study for a new product. Compute values for the power of the test for various proportions above 0.50. Draw the power curve. Briefly explain the power curve to Frank Lewis, who does not understand Type II error.

11.18 You are a political analyst who designs sampling studies to determine voter preference for candidates. A candidate has asked you to determine if she is preferred to more than 50% of the voters. She wants you to obtain a random sample of size n and use the following decision rules:

1. If the sample proportion is above 0.51, decide that she has the support of more than 50% of the voters.

2. If the sample proportion is below 0.49, decide that she has the support of less than 50% of the voters.

3. If the sample proportion is between 0.49 and 0.51, decide that she has exactly 50% of the voters.

(a) State the hypothesis test and indicate the sample size if $\alpha = 0.05$.

(b) Compute the power of the test if the actual proportion of support is 0.55 and if it is 0.46.

11.19 Ruth Smith, the new plant manager, has implemented new manufacturing procedures that she hopes will increase mean productivity per 8-hour shift above the present 100 units. She asks you to evaluate the new procedures. A random sample of 25 shifts is obtained. The total production on these shifts was 2600 units. The sample variance of production is $S^2 = 100$.

(a) Using a probability of Type I error equal to 0.05, design a hypothesis test that will provide strong evidence in favor of an increase if it has occurred. Show the probability model and the decision rule.

(b) Determine the probability of Type II error if the actual mean production level has increased to 105 units per shift.

11.20 The marketing research department has asked you to evaluate the effect on customer taste of adding wheat germ to their yogurt. In a random sample of 200 people, 80 state that they like the flavor of the present yogurt. In a second random sample of size 200 people, 110 state that they like the flavor of the new yogurt, which contains wheat germ.

(a) Can the company conclude that there is a statistically significant increase in consumer acceptance for the new yogurt compared to the old yogurt? Use a probability of Type I error equal to 0.05.

(b) Prepare the power curve for the test.

(c) Now assume that a random sample of $n = 400$ were used for each test group and the same proportion of positive responses were obtained (i.e., 160 out of 400 and 220 out of 400). Prepare the power curve for this second test design.

(d) Assume that the actual population increase in the proportion of customers who like the new product is 0.10. If this increase is not detected, the company will lose $100,000 in gross profit (selling price minus variable cost). How much additional money could the company afford to spend to increase both sample sizes from 200 people to 400 people?

11.21 A new computer program for processing health care claims is supposed to process 70% of the claims without human intervention if the input data are prepared properly. Develop a hypothesis test that would detect an increase in the number of unprocessed claims with a probability of Type I error equal to 0.01 and a random sample of size 100 claims.

(a) What is the upper critical value?

(b) Given the decision rule from part (a), what is the probability of Type II error if the number of processed claims actually drops to 67%?

(c) What is the upper critical value if $\alpha = 0.05$?

(d) Given the decision rule from part (c), what is the power of the test if the number of processed claims actually drops to 67%?

(e) What is β in part (d)?

11.22 A manufacturer of coated insulated glass deposits an ionized metal coating one-half the thickness of a smoke particle on window glass. This coating reduces the heat transfer for insulated glass. If the coating is too thin, insulating capability is lost, and if it is too thick, the glass is cloudy and customers complain. The thickness is measured by the light-transmission capabilities of the glass. The process is set so that the mean $\mu = 50$ units of light transmission and the variance $\sigma^2 = 16$. If these standards are met, the product is ideal for the market. Each day a random sample of 10 pieces of coated glass is selected and the light transmission is measured precisely. The manufacturing vice-president, Kevin Ackley, has asked you to develop quality control procedures for their process.

(a) On the seventh day the sample mean was $\bar{Y} = 53$. Using a two-tailed hypothesis test with probability of error equal to 0.05, determine if the production process has a problem on the seventh day.

(b) Compute the critical upper and lower values for the light transmission given a probability of error equal to 0.01. State the hypothesis test clearly.

(c) Using the critical values from part (b), compute the probability of Type II error if the mean has actually shifted to $\mu_* = 48$.

11.23 You have been asked to determine if a new manufacturing process produces stronger parts than the present process. Define the present process as process 1 and the new process as process 2. Random samples of parts from each process were obtained and the strength was measured. The following statistics were obtained from the two random samples:

$$\bar{Y}_1 = 100 \qquad S_1^2 = 10 \qquad n_1 = 11$$
$$\bar{Y}_2 = 105 \qquad S_2^2 = 20 \qquad n_2 = 16$$

Assume that strength is normally distributed and that the variance of strengths for the two processes are equal. Using $\alpha = 0.05$, can you conclude that process 2 produces stronger parts?

11.24 Educational psychologists are interested in identifying characteristics that affect academic performance in college. In a recent study the objective was to determine the effect of automobile ownership on academic performance. Two random samples of size 100 were obtained from a population of student car owners and from a population of students who do not own cars. The sample mean grade-point average for the non-car owners was 2.70 and the sample variance was 0.36. For the car owner sample the mean was 2.54 with a sample variance of 0.40. Do these data provide evidence that car owners have lower grade-point averages? Indicate the hypothesis test, decision rule, and your conclusion. Use $\alpha = 0.05$.

11.25 You are responsible for recommending one of two production management strategies for a large manufacturing firm. The choice is between strategy A, which is preferred by the president of the labor union and several of the top executives of the firm, and strategy B, which has been recommended because of its success in another firm.

(a) Develop a hypothesis-testing strategy that includes the pre-judgments concerning strategies A and B and a probability of Type I error equal to 0.05. You will take a random sample of 25 observations using each strategy and measure the production in units per hour. The experiments will be run in separate factories whose productivities are independent of each other. The sample observations are random variables from a population that can be modeled as a normal probability distribution. The probability distributions for strategies A and B have the same variance.

(b) The sample statistics from the experiments were

$$\bar{Y}_A = 100 \qquad S_{Y_A}^2 = 250 \qquad n_A = 25$$
$$\bar{Y}_B = 110 \qquad S_{Y_B}^2 = 200 \qquad n_A = 25$$

Using these sample results and your hypothesis test, develop a recommendation.

11.26 Roger Sweetfield is conducting a series of agricultural experiments designed to increase the production of sugar beets measured in bushels per hour. He plans to compare the output of n randomly selected fields that are planted with standard beet seeds and n randomly selected fields that are planted with the new improved variety of seeds. It is well known that the variance of individual field production is 2500 for both the present and the new seed variety. He wishes to conclude that a statistically significant (with probability of Type I error equal to 0.04) increase has occurred if the difference between the standard and improved seed sample means is 4. Determine the sample size n for each type of seed given that:

(a) The fields are selected randomly.

(b) The field samples are correlated with the correlation equal to $+0.5$.

11.27 A developing country is implementing a number of innovations to increase the efficiency of food production. You have been asked to determine if the productivity of food under a new trickle irrigation system is as high as the productivity under the old spray irrigation system. The new system uses less water because of lower evaporation losses. However, it will be implemented only if food production per acre is at least as great or greater than under the old system. In your experimental design you have a random sample of 25 fields that are split into a plot for trickle irrigation and a second for spray irrigation. The production between fields is correlated, with the sample correlation being equal to $\rho = 0.40$. In the fields using spray irrigation, the sample mean production is 100 and the sample variance, S^2, is 1600. However, in the fields with trickle irrigation the sample mean production is 115 with a sample variance of $S^2 = 900$. The population variances cannot be assumed to be equal. Should the new trickle irrigation system be implemented? Present evidence based on a hypothesis test.

11.28 A health insurance company is trying to determine if it should raise the monthly premium charged for its standard individual insurance package. The decision will be based on the average size of the increase in claims paid to individual policyholders from 1989 (year 1) to 1990 (year 2). A random sample of n policyholders will be selected and their total claims will be obtained for years 1 and 2. The difference between the sample means for year 2 and those for year 1 will be used as a test statistic. The known population variance for each year is 10,000, and the samples have a correlation of 0.50. If the mean difference between the population means for years 2 and 1 is greater than 50, a premium increase will be implemented. If the mean difference between the population means is zero or negative, a premium increase will not be made. Any changes in population mean between 0 and 50 will be ignored.

(a) What sample size should be used for the sample that will be measured in both 1989 and 1990? The probability of missing an increase of 50 should be 0.06, and the probability of missing no change should be 0.04. Remember that you are choosing between two population differences.

(b) What is the critical value for selecting between the two alternatives?

11.29 Consolidated Auto Parts, Inc. has a contract to supply bumper assemblies to a major automobile manufacturer. The assemblies consist of a 90-pound part and a 180-pound part. The contract guarantees that the total weight of the assembly will not exceed 270 pounds. If there is strong evidence that the assemblies exceed this limit (e.g., $\alpha = 0.05$), the entire shipment will be rejected. Random samples of $n = 25$ are obtained for each part. The random sample for the first part had a mean of $\bar{Y}_1 = 100$, and for the second part the sample mean was $\bar{Y}_2 = 200$. The variance for individual pieces of each component part is known to be $\sigma^2 = 2500$. Because of the manufacturing process and the way samples were selected, there is a correlation, $\rho = 0.50$, between the samples of component part weights.

(a) Assuming that the sample means are normally distributed, what is the probability that the population mean of the assembly exceeds the contract guarantee?

(b) Given the result from part (a), should Consolidated worry about the shipment?

11.30 You are the consulting statistician for a Department of Labor contract to investigate the benefits of a complex training, counseling, and referral program. One of the program's objectives is to increase the income of the principal wage earner in low-income families who are not eligible for supplemental benefits. A pilot program, which applies the new complex training program, has been run for the past year on a test group of 60 families, and a second program using conventional services was run for a group of 50 families with similar economic, social, and cultural backgrounds. For the pilot program group the mean weekly income was 300 with a sample variance of 8100. For the second group the mean income was 250 and the sample variance was 10,000. Based on this information, can you conclude that there is strong evidence to support the conclusion that the new program is significantly better than the conventional program?

11.31 You are the product manager for brand 4 in a large food company. The company president has complained that a competing brand, called brand 2, has higher average sales. The data services group has stored the latest product sales and price data in a file named "Storet," which is contained on your data disk or local computer system and described in the appendix.

(a) Based on a statistical hypothesis test, does the president have strong evidence to support his complaint? Show all statistical work and reasoning.

(b) After analyzing the data you note that a large outlier of value 971 is contained in the sample for brand 2. Repeat part (a) with this extreme observation removed. What do you now conclude about the president's complaint?

11.32 The product manager, Kevin Ackley, for a major consumer product line has just completed a major advertising campaign and wishes to know if there is strong evidence to conclude that the campaign was successful. Before the campaign began a random sample of 500 households resulted in 100 respondents who were regular users of the consumer product line. After the advertising campaign a random sample of 1300 households resulted in 325 respondents who were regular users of the consumer product line.

(a) Using these data, can you conclude that the proportion of regular users has increased?

(b) Given the same number of total observations for both samples ($500 + 1300 = 1800$)—essentially the same total cost—could this study have been designed to provide a test with higher power (i.e., a smaller Type II error for various values in the alternative hypothesis)?

11.33 A proposed new procedure for knee reconstruction is being evaluated at a major research hospital. The new procedure would reduce costs by 40%, but there is concern that the recovery time will be longer. A comparative study was undertaken with 40 randomly selected patients treated with the old procedure and 25 randomly selected patients treated with the new procedure. For the new procedure the mean recovery time for the 25 patients was 35 days, with a sample variance equal to 36. In contrast, the mean recovery time for the 40 patients who received the old procedure was 34.2 days with a sample variance of 49.

(a) The new procedure will be adopted because of its lower cost unless there is strong evidence that the recovery time has increased significantly. Prepare a hypothesis test that indicates clearly your recommendation concerning adoption of the proposed new medical procedure. Show all steps and follow appropriate statistical testing methods.

(b) Suppose that the new procedure actually increased recovery time by an average of two days for all patients. Compute the probability of Type II error using your hypothesis test and an actual increase of two days. (*Note:* Use the normal distribution to approximate the Student t.)

11.34 You are conducting a market research study to determine the location for a new shopping mall. The choice has been narrowed to cities A and B. Both cities have approximately the same population and the same total disposable income. There is some preference for city A because it is closer to the other malls owned by your company. You decide that you will choose city A unless the proportion of people in city B who want the mall exceed the proportion who want the mall in city A by 5% or more. You will conduct a random sample of size n in each city to estimate the proportion who want the mall. Determine the sample size n for the random sample in each city and the critical value of the proportion that you will use to choose between a difference of zero and a difference of 5%. Assume that around 50% of people in each city want the mall for purposes of estimating the variance. You want the probability of choosing B when A should be chosen to be 0.06 or less. In addition, you want the probability of choosing A when B is correct to be 0.04 or less.

11.35 You are a political analyst who has been asked to determine voter preference for a particular candidate. The candidate wishes to know if more than 51% or less than 49% would vote for her. She wishes the probability of missing either alternative to be 0.06 or less. Indicate the sample size and the decision rule for this study.

11.36 You are in charge of research for the president's budget committee. The president has decided that he will go ahead with his economic program if a "substantial" proportion of the people are in agreement with his economic program. He will not go ahead if only a "small" number are in favor. After considerable discussion he agrees that a "substantial" proportion is 30% or more and a "small" proportion is 26% or less. You are assigned to design a random sampling study to determine the level of public support for the proposed program.

(a) State a formal hypothesis test for the study.

(b) Compute the sample size assuming that both Type I and Type II error are equal to 0.05.

(c) State the decision rule that will be used with the sample results to prepare a recommendation for the president.

11.37 You have been assigned the task of evaluating a new advertising campaign for a new frozen vegetable product. Your study will use a random sample of size n from each of two populations of households. Each household has a cable TV connection, and thus separate ads can be transmitted to each household. The n households in sample A will receive the new ads, and the n households in sample B will receive the old ads. The new ads will be considered successful if the average household consumption of the product is at least six boxes higher over the next six months in families that have seen the new ads. Households have agreed to keep accurate records of their purchases for this and many other products. If the consumption difference is zero or decreases, ads will be considered unsuccessful.

(a) Design a hypothesis-testing procedure that can be used to make a decision concerning the new ads. Indicate the assumptions, the model, and the specific hypothesis.

(b) Show how you would determine the sample size n for each group of households and how you would obtain a decision rule.

(c) From past experience you know that the variance of individual household consumption is $\sigma^2 = 250$. In addition, the probability of deciding that an increase has occurred when it has not will be 0.10 or less. The probability of deciding that an increase has not occurred when it has will be 0.05 or less.

11.38 The marketing research director of a large cereal company wants to know if the company should introduce its new cereal. From past experience the company has decided that cereals that appeal to at least 25% of the people will be very profitable and cereals that appeal to 20% or less of the people will lose money. The company wants you to design a study such that the probability of missing a profitable cereal is 0.05 or less and the probability of introducing an unprofitable cereal is 0.10 or less. Design the study indicating the sample size and the decision rule that satisfies the objectives.

11.39 A large market research company is designing a study to determine if customer support for a new breakfast cereal is increasing. The cereal contains both oatmeal and reconstituted protein. Increased customer interest is anticipated because of recent health articles in national magazines. Determine the sample size for each of the following set of assumptions.

(a) In the past, 20% of the population liked the cereal. What sample size is required to conclude that a significant increase has occurred if the sample proportion is 0.25 or greater? Use a probability of Type I error equal to 0.05.

(b) The researchers want to know if the percent who like the cereal has increased by 5%. They will take a random sample of size n before a new advertising campaign and a second random sample of size n after the new advertising campaign has been conducted. Use a probability of Type I error and the probability of Type II error both equal to 0.05. What is the sample size n for both the before and after samples? Use $P = 0.20$ to compute the variance before the advertising campaign.

11.40 The manufacturers of Sleepy Eye reconstituted wheat germ have created a new version of their product by adding Harcourt's *brotchen mit kase* as a vitamin and flavor enhancer. They hope that this will increase sales to persons with northern European ancestry. The present product is consumed by 25% of the population. They hope that the new version will increase the consumption percentage by 5%. A random sample will be obtained and each person will be asked if they would purchase the new product. How large a sample should be taken to determine if the percent purchasers have remained at 25% or if the percentage has increased to 30%? The probability of incorrectly concluding that there has been an increase from 25% when an increase has not occurred is to be 0.06. The probability of missing an increase is to be 0.03. What are the decision rule and the critical value?

11.41 A new drug is being tested against the standard drug. If the new drug results in an increase of at least 5% in the percentage of people cured, the new drug will be adopted (e.g., an increase from 20% cured for the old drug to 25% cured for the new drug would lead to the conclusion that the new drug is better). You have been asked by the marketing director, Eric Lind, to design an experiment to determine if either a 5% or greater increase in the percent cured or a 0% or less increase has occurred. Note that 0% or less implies that the old drug has a higher cure rate. The probability of incorrectly rejecting the old drug should be 0.02, while the probability of failing to detect an improvement for the new drug, if it occurred, should be 0.05. To compute the variance, assume that the average percent cured for drugs of this type is about 20%. You will obtain a random sample of size n subjects who will be treated using the new drug and a second random sample of the same size n of subjects who will be treated with the old drug. You are to compute the sample size n and the minimum critical difference that will be used in a decision rule to decide if an improvement has occurred. State the decision rule. [*Hint:* The variance for the difference between sample proportions can be approximated using

$$\sigma_{\Delta \hat{P}} = \sqrt{\frac{(0.20)(0.80)}{n} + \frac{(0.20)(0.80)}{n}}.]$$

11.42 The city of Dirtyneck, New Jersey, has implemented a massive plan to reduce air pollution. The plan includes severe restrictions on industry and on wood-burning fireplaces in homes. In addition, the number of parking lots in the center of the city has been reduced by 50% and the parking fee raised to $10 per hour. A high-volume bus system has been developed to bring people from various residential and commercial neighborhoods and from parking lots on the exterior of the city. They have asked you to evaluate the effect of this program on reducing air pollution. A set of 25 randomly located monitoring stations were installed before the plan was implemented to obtain baseline measurements of pollution levels. The measurements obtained before the plan was implemented indicated a mean level of 1000 parts per million with a sample variance of 10,000. Two years after the plan was implemented, measurements were again obtained at the 25 monitoring stations. This time the sample mean was 957 parts per million with a sample variance of 12,100. The samples have a correlation of 0.50. Can you conclude that the plan to reduce pollution level has been successful? Assume stable population variances between the two periods studied. Develop a hypothesis test that will provide strong evidence of a reduction in pollution levels if reduction has actually occurred. Indicate clearly each of your steps and write a one- or two-sentence conclusion based on your analysis.

11.43 You have been asked to design a study that will choose between two worker training programs. A random sample of n workers will be assigned to training program A and a second random sample of n workers will be assigned to training program B. The number of workers assigned to each program will be the same. Daily productivity of these workers will be measured on a randomly selected day at least two weeks after they have completed their training. If program B has a population mean productivity that is at least 4 units per day higher than program A, program B will be selected. Alternatively, if program A has a population mean productivity that is at least 4 units per day higher than program B, program A will be selected. The variance in productivity for each program is

$\sigma^2 = 100$. Select the sample size and decision rule such that the probability of missing B as the best program is 0.04 and the probability of missing A as the best program is 0.05. Show all of your work and clearly indicate how the analysis should be conducted.

11.44 Ackley Associates has offered to sell you a portfolio for $540. This portfolio contains 10 shares of Amalgamated Butter, Inc. (stock 1) and 5 shares of Blowing Inthewind, Inc. (stock 2). You decide that you will accept their offer if there is strong evidence that the value of the portfolio is greater than $540. In this case strong evidence implies a probability of Type I error, α, less than or equal to 0.05. To help in your decision, you have obtained a random sample of each stock price for the same randomly selected weeks. From these two samples the following statistics were computed.

$$Stock\ 1: \quad \bar{Y}_1 = 50, \quad S_1^2 = 121, \quad n_1 = 25$$
$$Stock\ 2: \quad \bar{Y}_2 = 20, \quad S_2^2 = 144, \quad n_2 = 25$$

and the sample correlation between the prices was

$$r_{Y_1 Y_2} = +0.47$$

Given the data and conditions above, should you accept the offer? Present a complete analysis and explain your conclusion.

11.45 BBW Ltd. does quality control work on the final loaves of bread produced. The data file named "BBWltd," which is stored on the data disk, contains data collected as part of its analysis of the market. The variables in the file are:
1. "Dbread," which contains a random sample of weights, in grams, of their dark bread collected from supermarket shelves.
2. "Sbread," which contains a random sample of weights, in grams, of their specialty bread collected from supermarket shelves.
3. "Csbread," which contains a random sample of weights, in grams, of their competitor's specialty bread collected from supermarket shelves.

The file can be accessed by using the Minitab retrieve command. The company guarantees that its dark bread will have a weight of 100 grams or more. Based on the sample, do they have strong evidence, $\alpha = 0.05$, that the guarantee is being met? Provide an appropriate hypothesis test result as evidence.

11.46 Integrated Hardwoods purchases logs from Cutemall Associates, loggers of high-quality timber. The contract states that at least 70% of the logs will be No. 1 grade, with the remainder being No. 2 grade. You have been asked to design an acceptance sampling strategy for Integrated Hardwoods. From each large shipment floated to the mill, a random sample of $n = 100$ logs is obtained.
   (a) Compute the critical value and state a decision rule that Integrated Hardwoods would develop and apply (assume that they control the contract) to decide if the shipment should be accepted at full price.
   (b) What is the probability that the shipment will be accepted if the population proportion of No. 1 grade logs is $P = 0.75$? $P = 0.77$? $P = 0.80$? $P = 0.83$?
   (c) What would you tell Cutemall Associates about the rule and how they should behave to meet it?

11.47 Magic Circuits, Inc. manufactures a microprocessor that is used in computer-controlled gas furnaces for homes. It is anticipated that new energy efficiency laws will require computer-controlled furnaces in new homes within two years. Thus Magic Circuit wishes to expand its production to meet the anticipated increase in demand. They will either expand their present production facilities or build an entirely new factory in another state, depending on the quality level of their present production facilities. A national standards board has developed an extensive and complex testing procedure for these microprocessors. This procedure will be required by all furnace manufacturers who are the customers for the Magic Circuit microprocessor. The test provides a numerical score from 0 to 100. A score of 85 or better indicates that the unit will provide good service and is the acceptance level that furnace manufacturers will use. The variance of this test procedure is $\sigma^2 = 10$. The company decides to expand its present factory if the mean quality score on its microprocessor units is greater than or equal to 88. Alternatively, they will build a new factory if the mean quality is less than or equal to 86. They have also decided that the probability of failing to choose the higher level if it is correct should be 0.04 or less, while the probability of failing to select the lower level, if it is correct, and building a new factory should be 0.07. Develop a sampling and analysis plan that can be used to determine which quality level exists for the present factory. Indicate the number of randomly selected microprocessors that will need to be tested and the decision rule that will be used to choose between the two subsets, by using the sample mean.

is the same for the five production facilities located in different regions of the country. (contingency table)

None of these problems can be analyzed using statistical procedures based on means and variances. They do not involve continuous normally distributed random variables. Instead, they contain nominal or ordinal variables and there are no assumptions concerning their probability distributions. Therefore, a different set of statistical procedures is required.

In goodness-of-fit problems the objective is to determine if a specific probability distribution is an appropriate model for the problem. Subgroups are defined that cover all possible values for the random variable. The probability model is used to compute the expected number of sample observations in each subgroup. The number of observations expected are compared with the number of observations for each subgroup. If the frequencies are close, we accept the hypothesis that the sample fits the probability distribution.

Contingency table analysis is used to determine if there is a relationship between two nominal or ordinal variables. In Chapter 14 regression and correlation analysis are used to identify relationships between continuous variables. Contingency table tests have the same objective for qualitative variables. The analysis begins with a two-way table defined by using all possible combinations of the discrete intervals for the two variables. The null hypothesis is that the two variables are independent. Using that hypothesis, the probability for each of the cells in the two-way table is computed. The cell probabilities are then used to compute the expected number of observations in each cell given the null hypothesis. The observed number of observations from the sample are then compared with the expected number and a chi-square test statistic is computed. This statistic is used to test the null hypothesis that the two variables are independent.

12.2 GOODNESS-OF-FIT TESTS

Goodness-of-fit tests (Key Idea 12.2) are used to determine if a sample of data could have come from a population that has a given probability distribution. For example, a Poisson distribution describes the occurrence of defective units. The number of units purchased by consumer groups could follow a binomial distribution if purchases are independent and identically distributed. If brands are equally preferred, the number of randomly selected individuals selecting each brand follows a uniform distribution. The applications of goodness-of-fit tests is developed in the following extended examples.

Example 12.1   Taste Preference Test

Christine Whitney is a product manager for Eastern Cola, which produces a generic brand of cola soft drink. She wants to know if people can tell the difference between colas.

Solution   To answer the question, she decided to conduct a taste test in which the three major brands of cola, *A*, *B*, and *C*, were compared with another generic

Key Idea 12.2: Goodness-of-Fit Test

The following steps are used to test the hypothesis that a random sample, $x_i, i = 1, \ldots, n$, comes from a population with a probability distribution $f(x)$:

H_0: The probability distribution is $f(x)$.

H_1: The probability distribution is not $f(x)$.

1. Divide the range of the random variable, x, into m subgroups—usually, five to 10—defined conveniently by the probability distribution.

2. Count the number of sample observations, f_{oj}, in each subgroup j; $f_{oj}, j = 1, \ldots, m$. Compute the expected number, f_{ej}, of sample observations in each subgroup:

$$f_{ej} = P_{ej} \times n$$

where P_{ej} is the probability for subgroup j and n is the total number of observations. (*Note:* $f_{ej} \geq 5$ for all j.)

3. Compute the chi-square statistic:

$$\chi^2 = \sum_{j=1}^{m} \frac{(f_{oj} - f_{ej})^2}{f_{ej}}$$

$$\text{DOF} = m - p - 1$$

where p is the number of probability distribution parameters estimated from the sample data.

4. If the χ^2 value computed is greater than the critical value from Table A.3, reject H_0 and conclude that the data do not support the specified probability distribution, $f(x)$.

5. Failure to reject provides support for the specified probability distribution. However, we emphasize that accepting H_0 could include a large Type II error, β. This error can be reduced by choosing a larger Type I error (i.e., $\alpha = 0.10$), but the computation of β is very difficult.

brand, D, and the cola from her company, E. A random sample of 1000 persons was asked to taste each of the five brands and indicate which brand they preferred. Subjects washed their mouth with distilled water between each taste. In addition, the brands were presented in random order to avoid any bias associated with the order in which a brand was tasted. The frequency with which each brand A through E was preferred is as follows:

$$190 \ (A) \qquad 230 \ (B) \qquad 191 \ (C) \qquad 161 \ (D) \qquad 228 \ (E)$$

Inspection of the frequencies observed for each brand indicates differences in brand preference. However, these differences could result from random variation and not from an actual difference in preference. Therefore, a formal hypothesis-testing procedure should be used.

For this problem the null hypothesis is that all brands of cola are preferred equally. If this hypothesis is rejected, there is evidence to conclude that people can tell the difference between colas and that some brands are preferred to others. The null hypothesis of equal preferences implies a uniform probability distribution with $P = 0.20$ for each brand.

The question of equal brand preference can be answered by comparing the observed and expected number of subjects who preferred each brand. The null and alternative hypotheses are:

H_0: All brands are equally preferred.

$$P_1 = P_2 = \cdots = P_5 = 0.20$$

H_1: All brands are not equally preferred.

The null hypothesis is tested by using the χ^2 test statistic, which is equal to

$$\chi^2 = \sum_j^m \frac{(f_{0j} - f_{ej})^2}{f_{ej}}$$

where f_{oj} is the observed frequency in subgroup j, f_{ej} is the expected frequency in subgroup j, and m is the number of subgroups.

The χ^2 test statistic has an approximate chi-square distribution if the null hypothesis is true. This approximation is compromised if there are several cells with small expected frequencies. A small expected subgroup frequency will result in a large contribution to the χ^2 value calculated. The rule of thumb generally used is that expected frequencies should be 5 or greater. This rule can be relaxed a little if there are 15 or 20 subgroups. In that case, one or possibly two subgroups could have expected frequencies less than 5.

The degrees of freedom are computed by subtracting the number of restrictions on the data from the number of subgroups m into which the observations can be assigned. For this example there are five possible subgroups and the number of observations is restricted to exactly 1000. Therefore, the degrees of freedom are

$$\text{DOF} = m - 1 = 5 - 1 = 4$$

If the χ^2 computed exceeds the critical value for the chi-square probability distribution, the null hypothesis is rejected.

Rejection of the null hypothesis implies that certain brands are preferred to others. The expected frequency for each cell is $f_{ej} = 200$, because the probability for each cell given H_0 is $P_j = 0.20$ and $f_{ej} = 0.20 \times 1000 = 200$. The value of χ^2 is computed as follows:

$$\chi^2 = \sum_j^m \frac{(f_{oj} - f_{ej})^2}{f_{ej}}$$

$$= \frac{(190 - 200)^2}{200} + \frac{(230 - 200)^2}{200} + \frac{(191 - 200)^2}{200}$$

$$+ \frac{(161 - 200)^2}{200} + \frac{(228 - 200)^2}{200}$$

$$= 0.50 + 4.50 + 0.405 + 7.605 + 3.92$$

$$= 16.93$$

The critical value for the chi-square distribution with 4 degrees of freedom and a probability of error $\alpha = 0.01$ is 13.277, as shown in Table A.3. Because the computed value, 16.93, is larger, the null hypothesis is rejected and it is concluded that some brands are preferred by more people. Inspection of the data indicates that in the sample, brand B (230) and brand E (228) are preferred by more, and brand D (161) is preferred by fewer, than would be expected if all brands were equally preferred in the population.

The calculations for the chi-square goodness-of-fit test are summarized in Table 12.1. The fifth column contains the ratio of the frequency observed divided by the frequency expected if the null hypothesis is true. This ratio provides an indication of the relative size of observed and expected frequencies. Note the large preference for brands B and E and the small preference for brand D. In addition, the contribution of each subgroup to the overall χ^2 statistic is shown.

TABLE 12.1   Chi-Square Computations for Cola Taste Test

Cola Brand	f_o	f_e	$\dfrac{(f_o - f_e)^2}{f_e}$	$\dfrac{f_o}{f_e}$
A	190	200	0.500	0.950
B	230	200	4.500	1.150
C	191	200	0.405	0.955
D	161	200	7.605	0.805
E	228	200	3.920	1.140
	1000	1000	16.930	

Based on this analysis, Christine knows that cola brands are not viewed the same by consumers. In addition, she noted that brand E, her brand, was preferred by approximately the same percentage as was one of the nationally advertised brands. □

Example 12.2   Normal Distribution of Daily Rice Sales

A store in a medium-sized Chinese city sells rice by the kilogram. The store owner believes that daily sales of rice are normally distributed with a mean $\mu = 50$ kilograms and a variance $\sigma^2 = 100$. She has asked you to determine if her assumption is correct.

Solution   A random sample of 100 daily sales in kilograms per day is available for testing the normal distribution hypothesis.

The null and alternative hypotheses for this problem are

H_0: Daily rice sales have a normal distribution: $\mu = 50$, $\sigma^2 = 100$.

H_1: Daily rice sales do not have a normal probability distribution.

This is a goodness-of-fit problem for a continuous probability distribution. The chi-square test requires discrete subgroups. Therefore, the normal is used to define subgroup boundaries. Subgroup boundaries were established by first obtaining the standardized normal Z's that define the boundaries. When defining boundaries it is usually best to obtain subgroups with approximately the same probability that an observation will be included. For this problem, 10 subgroups, each with an equal probability of 0.10, were chosen for the goodness-of-fit test. This will ensure that the subgroup expected values are all greater than 5 since 100 observations are assigned to the 10 subgroups.

From the standard normal distribution the Z values for the 0.10 subgroups are shown in Table 12.2. The lower interval boundary $Z = -1.28$ is the value such that 10% of the population would be below -1.28. Similarly, the next boundary, $Z = -0.84$, has 20% of the population below it. In the second column the intervals are

TABLE 12.2 χ^2 Computations for Normal Goodness of Fit

Z Interval	Kilogram Interval	f_o	f_e	$\dfrac{(f_o - f_e)^2}{f_e}$
≤ -1.280	≤ 37.20	8	10	0.40
$-1.280 \leq -0.840$	$37.20 \leq 41.60$	14	10	1.60
$-0.840 \leq -0.525$	$41.60 \leq 44.75$	7	10	0.90
$-0.525 \leq -0.255$	$44.75 \leq 47.45$	15	10	2.50
$-0.255 \leq 0.000$	$47.45 \leq 50.00$	9	10	0.10
$0.000 \leq +0.255$	$50.00 \leq 52.55$	8	10	0.40
$0.255 \leq +0.525$	$52.55 \leq 55.25$	7	10	0.90
$0.525 \leq +0.840$	$55.25 \leq 58.40$	11	10	0.10
$0.840 \leq +1.280$	$58.40 \leq 62.80$	12	10	0.40
> 1.280	> 62.80	9	10	0.10
		100	100	
χ^2				7.40

converted to a normal distribution with mean $\mu = 50$ and variance $\sigma^2 = 100$. The resulting boundaries are computed using

$$X = \mu + Z \times \sigma$$
$$= 50 + Z \times 10$$

As a result the lowest boundary is

$$50 + (-1.28) \times 10 = 37.2$$

The remaining subgroup intervals are shown in Table 12.2. The expected frequencies in each cell are all equal to 10 because the normal probability is 0.10 and there are $n = 100$ observations. The observed frequencies and the contributions to χ^2 are shown in the remaining columns.

The degrees of freedom required to compute the critical value of χ^2 are computed using

$$\text{DOF} = m - 1 - p$$

where m is the number of subgroups or rows in the table and p is the number of parameters estimated from the sample. For this problem, 1 degree of freedom is lost because we have a specified sample size and therefore only $m - 1$ of the subgroups can be determined independently.

In some problems we may estimate from the data one or more parameters, such as the mean and/or the variance for the normal distribution. These parameters are used to compute the cell probabilities and expected frequencies. If that is done, the degrees of freedom are reduced further by the number of parameters estimated from the data.

Using the results from Table 12.2, the hypothesis test can be completed. The computed value of $\chi^2 = 7.40$. The degrees of freedom are equal to 9, since the parameters μ and σ^2 were given. From the tabulated chi-square critical values in Table A.3, we find that the critical value for $\alpha = 0.05$ and 1 degree of freedom is $\chi^2 = 16.919$. The critical value for $\alpha = 0.10$ is 14.68. Therefore, we cannot reject the null hypothesis, even with $\alpha = 0.10$. At this point many analysts would conclude that the distribution is normal. However, recall from the discussions of hypothesis testing in Chapter 11 that "failure to reject" does not imply strong evidence in favor of the null hypothesis. It is extremely difficult to define a method for computing the probability of Type II error for the chi-square test, and thus it is usually not done. We are still left with the possibility that other probability models could have generated the sample data for this example. As a result of the hypothesis test, we know that the data could have come from a normal distribution. This provides greater support for the normal than a rejection of the null hypothesis. Thus without any further information, we would continue to assume that the data were generated by a normal probability model.   □

Does It Make Sense?

In these examples we have seen how the chi-square test can be used to determine if a sample of data could have been obtained from a specified probability distribution function. The hypothesis-testing procedure follows the approach presented in Chapter 11:

1. The hypothesis that includes a probability model for the data is specified.
2. The data are collected and a test statistic is computed.
3. If the test statistic exceeds a critical value, the null hypothesis is rejected.   □

Problem Exercises

12.1   Could the following frequency data for four groups have come from a uniform distribution? Group A, 39 units; group B, 45 units; group C, 35 units; group D, 32 units.

12.2   Could the following frequency data for four groups have come from a binomial distribution with $\pi = 0.5$ and $n = 3$? Group A (0 successes), 40 units; group B (1 success), 140 units; group C (2 successes), 125 units; group D (3 successes), 36 units.

12.3   A cheese store has four cheese types available. Each customer can either purchase or not purchase 1 unit of each cheese type. The number of units of all cheese types purchased by a customer is believed to follow a binomial distribution with $\pi = 0.4$. The purchases for 100 randomly selected customers were examined and the frequencies for each number of units purchased were 0, 5; 1, 30; 2, 40; 3, 20; and 4, 5. Do the data support the assumption of a binomial distribution? Note that when expected frequencies are less than 5, subgroups should be combined.

12.4   The number of defective disk drives in each shipment of 1000 microcomputers is believed to follow a Poisson distribution with a mean of one defect per shipment. For a random sample of 200 shipments of 1000 computers each, the frequency of defective disk drives was 0, 100; 1, 50; 2, 40; 3, 7; and ≥ 4, 3. Do the data support the assumption of a Poisson with:
   (a) $\lambda = 1.0$?
   (b) $\lambda = 0.6$?

12.5   The market for bread machines has historically been dominated by three brands with the following market shares: brand A, 40%; brand B, 30%; brand C, 20%; all others, 10%. The product manager for brand C wants to determine if a major design change is likely to result in increased market share. A random sample of bread machine users is asked to compare brands A, B, the new brand C, and all other brands and indicate a preference. The frequencies of preference were as follows: brand A, 60; brand B, 55; new brand C, 70; all others, 15. Is the new design likely to change the market share significantly for brand C?

12.3 CONTINGENCY TABLES: INDEPENDENCE

The second important application of the chi-square test is to determine if two nominal or ordinal variables are independent. Many problems involving these data occur in political science, sociology, psychology, marketing, and other studies of human populations. Business applications occur frequently in marketing and human resources. When the data are continuous, we use correlation and regression analysis to study relationships between variables. With nominal or ordinal data, the concept of a relationship between variables is not as clearly defined. Therefore, the linear models used with continuous variables are not appropriate for categorical variables.

In this section we see how the χ^2 statistic is used to test for the independence of two variables in a contingency table (Key Idea 12.3). The chi-square test is not always the best procedure, but it is the most widely used.

The procedure begins by placing the frequency data for all combinations of the two variables in two-way tables called *contingency tables*. Both variables define each observation in terms of a category or level. One variable has c categories, which define the columns of the table, and the second has r categories, which define the rows of the table. The table is called an $r \times c$ *contingency table*. The number of cells in the table into which an observation could be classified is equal to the number of columns c multiplied by the number of rows r.

The hypotheses are

H_0: The two variables are independent.

H_1: The two variables are not independent.

In Chapter 4 we learned that if two variables are independent, the probability for a particular cell, defined by unique levels for each of the two variables, is equal to the product of the marginal probabilities for the two variables. This result can be used to determine the probability and the expected value for each table cell when the null hypothesis is true. The row marginal probabilities are computed by dividing the number of observations in each row category by the total number of observations. Similarly, the column marginal probabilities are computed by dividing the number of observations in each column category by the total number of observations. The product of the marginal probabilities is multiplied by the total number of observations to obtain the expected frequency for each cell.

A simple example will be used to show the method.

Example 12.3   Graduate School Choice

The economics department of a private liberal arts college wanted to understand the graduate school choices of its alumni.

Solution   Survey information was obtained from a random sample of alumni. Table 12.3 compares the graduate school field before and after 1970. The graduate school subgroups were masters of business administration (MBA) and economics, law, and other (E & L). In addition to the frequencies, Table 12.3 includes the marginal probabilities for the rows and columns. The row marginal probability for the MBA subgroup is

$$P_1 = \frac{37}{85} = 0.435$$

Key Idea 12.3: Contingency Table Tests for Independence

The hypothesis that two qualitative variables are independent can be tested using two-way contingency tables and the chi-square distribution.

1. Given two variables defined by discrete values, $X_j, j = 1, \ldots, c$ subgroups and $Y_i, i = 1, \ldots, r$ subgroups. The hypothesis test is:

   H_0: The two variables X and Y are independent.

   H_1: The two variables are not independent.

2. Obtain a random sample of n observations identified by X_j and Y_i. Arrange the data in a two-way table for all combinations of X_j, $j = 1, \ldots, c$ and $Y_i, i = 1, \ldots, r$. The table contains c columns and r rows, for a total of $r \times c$ distinct cells. The frequency observed for each cell is f_{oij}. Compute the probabilities for each column, $P_j, j = 1, \ldots, c$ and each row, $P_i, i = 1, \ldots r$:

$$P_j = \frac{\sum_{i=1}^{r} f_{oij}}{n} \qquad j = 1, \ldots, c$$

$$P_i = \frac{\sum_{j=1}^{c} f_{oij}}{n} \qquad i = 1, \ldots, r$$

$$\sum_{j=1}^{c} P_j = \sum_{i=1}^{r} P_i = 1$$

3. If X and Y are independent, the cell probabilities P_{ij} are the product of the column and row marginal probabilities,

$$P_{ij} = P_i \times P_j$$

   and therefore the expected cell probabilities f_{eij} are

$$f_{eij} = P_{ij} \times n$$

   f_{eij} should be greater than 5 for each cell.

4. Compute the chi-square statistic,

$$\chi^2 = \sum_{i=1}^{r} \sum_{j=1}^{c} \frac{(f_{oij} - f_{eij})^2}{f_{eij}}$$

$$\text{DOF} = (c - 1) \times (r - 1)$$

If the computed χ^2 is greater than the critical χ^2 from the chi-square table, reject H_0 and accept H_1; X and Y are not independent.

TABLE 12.3   Alumni Survey: Observed Frequencies

Graduate Field	Before 1971	After 1970	Total	Marginal Probability
MBA	13	24	37	0.435
E & L	36	12	48	0.565
	49	36	85	
Marginal probability	0.576	0.424		1.00

and for the E & L category it is

$$P_2 = \frac{48}{85} = 0.565$$

Similarly, the before 1971 column marginal probability is 0.576 (49/85), and the 1971 and after marginal probability is 0.424 (36/85).

Beginning with the null hypothesis—the rows and columns are independent—the row and column marginal probabilities are used to compute the expected probabilities in each table cell. This computation is shown in Table 12.4. For example, assuming independence, the probability for the upper left table cell (MBA and before 1971) is equal to the row marginal probability 0.435 (MBA) multiplied by the column probability marginal probability 0.576 (before 1971), which is equal to 0.251 (0.435 × 0.576). The remaining cell probabilities are computed in a similar manner.

TABLE 12.4   Alumni Survey: Cell Probabilities

Graduate Field	Before 1971	After 1970	Marginal Probability
MBA	(0.435)(0.576) = 0.251	(0.435)(0.424) = 0.184	0.435
E & L	(0.565)(0.576) = 0.325	(0.565)(0.424) = 0.240	0.565
Marginal probability	0.576	0.424	1.00

The expected cell probabilities are used to compute cell expected values under the assumption of independent rows and column variables. These computations are shown in Table 12.5. For example, the value expected in the upper left table cell is equal to the cell probability (0.251) multiplied by the total number of observations in

TABLE 12.5   Alumni Survey: Expected Values

Graduate Field	Before 1971	After 1970	Total	Marginal Probability
MBA	(0.251)(85) = 21.3	(0.184)(85) = 15.7	37	0.435
E & L	(0.325)(85) = 27.7	(0.240)(85) = 20.3	48	0.565
	49	36	85	
Marginal probability	0.576	0.424		1.00

the table (85), which equals 21.3. The remaining cell expected values are shown in Table 12.5.

The observed and expected cell frequencies are used to compute the χ^2 test statistic as follows:

$$\chi^2 = \sum_i^c \sum_j^r \frac{(f_o - f_e)^2}{f_e}$$

$$= \frac{(13 - 21.3)^2}{21.3} + \frac{(24 - 15.7)^2}{15.7} + \frac{(36 - 27.7)^2}{27.7} + \frac{(12 - 20.3)^2}{20.3}$$

$$= 3.25 + 4.43 + 2.51 + 3.41$$

$$= 13.60$$

The degrees of freedom for a contingency table is equal to the number of rows minus 1 multiplied by the number of columns minus 1:

$$DOF = (r - 1)(c - 1)$$

The total number of observations is fixed, and therefore only $(r - 1)$ rows and $(c - 1)$ columns could be set independently. The product of the number of rows that can be set independently times the number of columns that can be set independently indicates the number of cells that can be set independently, which is equal to the degrees of freedom. For this example the degrees of freedom are

$$DOF = (r - 1)(c - 1) = (2 - 1)(2 - 1) = 1$$

The critical value of the χ^2 with 1 degree of freedom and $\alpha = 0.01$ is, from Table A.3, equal to 6.63. Since the χ^2 value computed is 13.60, the null hypothesis that the rows and columns are independent is rejected. There is strong evidence of different patterns of graduate school attendance before and after 1970. By comparing the observed and expected cell frequencies, we see that MBA programs became more popular after 1970, and law and economics graduate study became less popular.

Additional descriptive information is provided by the ratios of the observed to expected frequencies for each cell. Table 12.6 shows the ratios for the example problem. Comparison of these ratios indicates which combinations deviate high and which deviate low from the assumption that the row and column variables are independent. The combination of ratios provides an indication of relationship between the variables.

TABLE 12.6   Alumni Survey: Ratio of Observed to Expected Frequencies

Graduate Field	Before 1971	After 1970	Total
MBA	$\frac{13}{21.3} = 0.61$	$\frac{24}{15.7} = 1.53$	37
E & L	$\frac{36}{27.7} = 1.30$	$\frac{12}{20.3} = 0.59$	48
Total	49	36	85

In Table 12.6 the ratios over 1 indicate that economics and law were more popular before 1970, and MBAs were more popular after 1970.   □

Example 12.4   Grades and Driving Violations

Sociologists have a continuing interest in the relationship between different kinds of deviant behavior. In the example presented here, the research team was interested in the relationship between traffic violations and the deviation of college grades from grades predicted using standard test scores.[1] They wanted to know if students who were underperforming in school had more traffic violations than did students who were overperforming in school.

Solution   A large sample of college students was obtained. For each student the number of driving convictions and his or her academic performance were measured. The academic performance variable was an ordinal variable defined as

1. Student grade-point average (GPA) was substantially below the predicted grade-point average.
2. Student GPA was slightly below the predicted GPA.
3. Student GPA was the same as the predicted GPA.
4. Student GPA was slightly above the predicted GPA.
5. Student GPA was substantially above the predicted GPA.

The number of traffic convictions varied from 0 to 4 or more for each student. The subgroup levels are

1. Zero traffic convictions (C1)
2. One traffic conviction (C2)
3. Two traffic convictions (C3)
4. Three traffic convictions (C4)
5. Four or more traffic convictions (C5)

The data for this study are shown in Table 12.7. The five columns indicate the number of driving convictions. The five rows represent the five levels of the academic performance variable. The null hypothesis is

H_0: Convictions and academic performance are independent.

In contrast, the alternative hypothesis is

H_1: Convictions and academic performance are not independent.

If the null hypothesis is rejected, there is evidence that college students who are underperforming in school also have more driving violations.

---

[1] W. L. Carlson and D. Klein, "Familial versus institutional socialization of the young traffic offender," *Journal of Safety Research*, March 1970, Vol. 2, No. 1.

TABLE 12.7   Academic Performance and Driving Convictions

	Convictions					
Grade Deviation	0	1	2	3	4+	Total
1	85	38	21	6	8	158
2	673	371	163	84	59	1350
3	1406	673	247	112	91	2529
4	711	225	68	30	16	1050
5	174	57	13	6	3	253
	3049	1364	512	238	177	5340

The chi-square computations were made using Minitab and the results are pre-sented in Exhibit 12.1. The rows, corresponding to grade deviation, are identified as 1 through 5. Columns, which indicate the number of convictions, are labeled C1 through C5. Each cell contains the values observed and expected. The χ^2 computation is shown at the bottom of the table. The degrees of freedom are equal to 16 $[(5-1)(5-1)]$. From Table A.3 the critical value of χ^2 for 16 degrees of freedom and $\alpha = 0.01$ is 32.00. The computed value of 116.80 (from Exhibit 12.1) exceeds the critical value, and therefore the null hypothesis is rejected. Academic performance and driving convictions are not independent. Comparison of the observed and expected frequencies indicates that the college students who were performing below their academic potential also had more driving convictions. In contrast, students who were performing above their academic potential tended to have fewer driving convictions. Based on these results, the researchers concluded that there was a relationship between these two types of deviant behavior.   □

Does It Make Sense?

In some applications each of the variables have many levels (≥ 6). As a result, the contingency table has a large number of cells. In those cases some cells may have expected values of less than 5. Because this would bias the χ^2 value computed, the chi-square test would not be appropriate. However, it may be possible to combine levels for one or both of the row and column variables. The decision to combine levels can only be made by a person who understands the variables and the objective of the statistical analysis. However, combining levels may provide the opportunity to answer at least some of the questions that are being addressed by the statistical study.   □

Practice Problem 12.1: Automobile Choice Patterns

Motors magazine conducted a random sample survey of automobile preference among men and women in a large southern city. Of the 24 men in the survey, 14 preferred Honda, 7 Nissan, and 3 Saturn. For the 24 women, 5 preferred Honda, 7 Nissan, and 12 Saturn. Is there evidence that men and women have different car preference patterns?   □

The solution is given at the end of the chapter.

EXHIBIT 12.1   Chi-Square Analysis: Academic Performance Versus Convictions

```
MTB > Read C1-C5
DATA> 85 38 21 6 8
DATA> 673 371 163 84 59
DATA> 1406 673 247 112 91
DATA> 711 225 68 30 16
DATA> 174 57 13 6 3
DATA> END
MTB > chisquare analysis on data in c1-c5
```

Expected counts are printed below observed counts

	C1	C2	C3	C4	C5	Total
1	85	38	21	6	8	158
	90.2	40.4	15.1	7.0	5.2	
2	673	371	163	84	59	1350
	770.8	344.8	129.4	60.2	44.7	
3	1406	673	247	112	91	2529
	1444.0	646.0	242.5	112.7	83.8	
4	711	225	68	30	16	1050
	599.5	268.2	100.7	46.8	34.8	
5	174	57	13	6	3	253
	144.5	64.6	24.3	11.3	8.4	
Total	3049	1364	512	238	177	5340

```
ChiSq =   0.30 +   0.14 +   2.26 +   0.15 +    1.46 +
         12.41 +   1.99 +   8.70 +   9.44 +    4.54 +
          1.00 +   1.13 +   0.08 +   0.00 +    0.61 +
         20.73 +   6.96 +  10.60 +   6.03 +   10.16 +
          6.04 +   0.90 +   5.22 +   2.47 +    3.46 = 116.80
df = 16
```

Problem Exercises

12.6   A manufacturer of yogurt has three factories located across the United States. There are three major causes of defects in yogurt, which we will identify as A, B, and C. During a recent week the reported occurrences of product defects in the three factories were as follows:

Factory 1: A, 15; B, 25; C, 23
Factory 2: A, 10; B, 12; C, 21
Factory 3: A, 32; B, 28; C, 44

Based on these frequencies, can we conclude that the defect patterns in the different factories are the same? Use $\alpha = 0.05$.

12.7   The human resources department is attempting to determine if the performance of its employees is influenced by their undergraduate major. The majors considered are business, economics, mathematics, and all others. Personnel ratings are grouped as excellent, strong, and average. The classifications based on employees with two to four years of experience as follows:

Business major: excellent, 21;   strong, 18;   average, 10
Economics major: excellent, 19;   strong, 15;   average, 5
Mathematics major: excellent, 10;   strong, 5;   average, 5
Other major: excellent, 5;   strong, 15;   average, 13

Do these data indicate that there is a difference in ratings based on undergraduate major? Use $\alpha = 0.01$.

12.8   A random sample of people from three different job classifications labeled A, B, and C were asked to indicate their preferences for three brands of camping lanterns: Big Star, Lone Star, and Bright Star. The preferences were as follows:

Group A: Big Star, 54;   Lone Star, 67;   Bright Star, 39
Group B: Big Star, 23;   Lone Star, 13;   Bright Star, 44
Group C: Big Star, 69;   Lone Star, 53;   Bright Star, 59

Do these data indicate that there is a difference in ratings for the three different groups? Use $\alpha = 0.05$.

12.9   George Peterson, vice-president of marketing for Chicken George, Inc., a poultry processor, is attempting to determine if there are regional differences in the purchases of its three major products: whole chickens, chicken breasts, and thighs and legs. For their study the country is divided into three segments: east, middle, and west. The frequencies of sales units by market segment were as follows:

East: whole, 45;   breasts, 76;   thighs and legs, 60
Middle: whole, 80;   breasts, 34;   thighs and legs, 50
West: whole, 32;   breasts, 98;   thighs and legs, 75

Do these data indicate regional differences in the demand for chicken products? Use $\alpha = 0.01$.

12.4 TEST USING PROPORTIONS

When 2×2 contingency tables are used in a statistical study, there is a good alternative to the chi-square test for independence. We can use the two sample tests for equality of proportions presented in Chapter 11. In the graduate school example, the two populations could be defined as alumni who graduate in 1970 or before and alumni who graduated after 1970. Then the proportions for the two populations can be defined as

π_1:   the proportion of early graduates with MBA degrees

π_2:   the proportion of recent graduates with MBA degrees

Using this definition, the test for independence could be based on the following hypotheses:

$$H_0: \pi_1 = \pi_2$$
$$H_1: \pi_1 \neq \pi_2$$

The test statistic would be

$$\Delta \hat{P} = \hat{P}_1 - \hat{P}_2$$

and $\Delta \hat{P}$ would have an approximate normal distribution with variance

$$\sigma^2_{\Delta \hat{P}} = \sigma^2_{\hat{P}_1} + \sigma^2_{\hat{P}_2}$$

For the example problem, the sample proportions are

$$\hat{P}_1 = \frac{13}{49} = 0.265$$

$$\hat{P}_2 = \frac{24}{36} = 0.667$$

$$\Delta \hat{P} = 0.265 - 0.667 = -0.402$$

The variance for the test statistic is estimated using

$$\sigma^2_{\Delta \hat{P}} = \frac{0.435(1 - 0.435)}{49} + \frac{0.435(1 - 0.435)}{36}$$
$$= 0.0050158 + 0.006827$$
$$= 0.0118428$$

Note that under the null hypothesis, the two samples and therefore $\hat{P}_1$ and $\hat{P}_2$ are assumed to be independent. Therefore, the variance is estimated using the row marginal probabilities. The standard deviation is estimated as

$$\sigma_{\Delta \hat{P}} = 0.1088$$

The Z statistic is equal to

$$Z = \frac{\hat{P}_1 - \hat{P}_2}{\sigma_{\Delta \hat{P}}}$$
$$= \frac{0.265 - 0.667}{0.1088}$$
$$= 3.69$$

Comparing this value of $Z = 3.69$ with the critical value of 2.33 when $\alpha = 0.01$, we would reject the assumption of independence.

Using the difference between proportions provides exactly the same probability of rejecting the hypothesis that the row and column variables are independent as that of the chi-square test for 2×2 contingency tables. However, the test using proportions and the normal distribution has greater power, and it is possible to compute the probability of Type II error. Therefore, we would prefer to use the test involving the comparison of proportions.

Does It Make Sense?

There are a number of business studies that use qualitative variables. Marketing studies are often directed toward identifying market segments that have a favorable response toward a particular brand of a product type. These segments are often identified by qualitative demographic variables such as age group, job classification, ethnic group, education level, and residential area (zip code). Geographic regions are also used. Many direct-mail retailers maintain large customer databases that contain classification variables such as these. These databases are used to direct specific product brands and/or marketing strategies to narrow market segments.

The analysis of these qualitative data to identify the segments makes use of nonparametric statistical procedures. The study of nonparametric procedures requires another statistics course. However, a large fraction of problems that use qualitative variables can be analyzed using the contingency table procedures presented in this chapter. Thus in this chapter we have presented a very useful tool without requiring a high price in terms of learning time.   □

Problem Exercises

12.10 A recent study of promotion patterns in a large manufacturing company indicated that 67 men out of 120 were promoted and 100 women out of 310 were promoted. The men and women were equally qualified for promotion.

(a) Use a chi-square contingency table test to determine if there are differences in promotion patterns based on gender. What is the probability of this pattern being observed if the promotion patterns are the same?

(b) Compare the proportion of men and women promoted using a hypothesis test that compares the proportion. What is the probability of the results observed if there is no discrimination?

(c) If you were a member of the group of women, would you challenge the company's promotion policies?

12.11 Amalgamated manufacturing has concluded that for factory A there were 45 out of 148 units that required postmanufacturing adjustments. For factory B, 84 out of 400 units required postmanufacturing adjustments. Is there a difference in the quality performance of the two factories? Use $\alpha = 0.05$.

SUMMARY OF KEY IDEAS

PRACTICE PROBLEM SOLUTION

12.1 The first step is to arrange the data as shown in Table 12.8. The hypotheses to be tested are

H_0: Gender and automobile preference are independent.

H_1: Gender and automobile preference are not dependent.

TABLE 12.8   Automobile Preference: Observed Frequencies

| Gender | Automobile | | | Total | Marginal Probability |
	Honda	Nissan	Saturn		
Men	14	7	3	24	0.50
Women	5	7	12	24	0.50
	19	14	15	48	
Marginal probability	0.396	0.292	0.312		1.00

The row and column frequencies are computed and used to compute the cell probabilities under H_0 in Table 12.9. Finally, in Table 12.10 we have the expected cell frequencies, which are the product of the expected cell probabilities times the total number of observations, $n = 48$. Table 12.8 contains the observed cell frequencies, f_{oij}, and Table 12.10 contains the expected cell frequencies, f_{eij}, given H_0. The chi-square computation is

$$\chi^2 = \sum_{i=1}^{r} \sum_{j=1}^{c} \frac{(f_{oij} - f_{eij})^2}{f_{eij}}$$

$$= \frac{(14 - 9.5)^2}{9.5} + \frac{(7 - 7)^2}{7} + \frac{(3 - 7.5)^2}{7.5} + \frac{(5 - 9.5)^2}{9.5} + \frac{(7 - 7)^2}{7} + \frac{(12 - 7.5)^2}{7.5}$$

$$= 2.13 + 0 + 2.7 + 2.13 + 0 + 2.7$$

$$= 9.66$$

TABLE 12.9   Automobile Preference: Expected Probabilities

| Gender | Automobile | | | Marginal Probability |
	Honda	Nissan	Saturn	
Men	(0.50)(0.396) = 0.198	(0.50)(0.292) = 0.146	(0.50)(0.312) = 0.156	0.50
Women	(0.50)(0.396) = 0.198	(0.50)(0.292) = 0.146	(0.50)(0.312) = 0.156	0.50
Marginal probability	0.396	0.292	0.312	1.00

TABLE 12.10   Automobile Preference: Expected Frequencies

Gender	Automobile			Total	Marginal Probability
	Honda	Nissan	Saturn		
Men	9.5	7	7.5	24	0.50
Women	9.5	7	7.5	24	0.50
	19	14	15	48	
Marginal probability	0.396	0.292	0.312		1.00

With two rows and three columns there are two degrees of freedom. The critical value of χ^2 with $\alpha = 0.01$ is 9.21. Thus the null hypothesis is rejected and we conclude that car preferences are different for men and women. Casual inspection of the tables would indicate that women tend to prefer the Saturn and men the Honda. These results do not necessarily agree with national surveys.

CHAPTER PROBLEMS

12.1   A liberal arts college was interested in determining if there were different graduate school patterns for students with undergraduate majors in history and economics. They surveyed a random sample of recent graduates and found that a large number obtained graduate degrees in business, law, and theology. The frequency of persons in the various combinations are shown in Table 12.11. Based on these results, is there evidence that undergraduate economics and history majors pursue different graduate school programs? Present a hypothesis test and base your answer on a probability of Type I error $\alpha = 0.01$.

TABLE 12.11   Frequencies for Graduate Study

Undergraduate	Graduate		
	Business	Law	Theology
Economics	30	20	10
History	6	34	20

12.2   Suppose that you have collected the data in Table 12.12 from a market survey. Perform a chi-square test to determine if there is a different probability of purchase among men and women. Include in your answer the expected cell values under the null hypothesis. Perform the test using sample proportions from two samples. Show that both tests have the same power. That is, they have the same probability of rejecting the null hypothesis. (Yes, you do need to determine the correct null hypothesis for both methods!)

TABLE 12.12   Market Survey
Data

	Men	Women
Purchase	150	150
Nonpurchase	50	250

12.3   Sally Smith is a long-time political campaign manager from Chicago. In the primary election there are four candidates. She wishes to determine if voter preference is different over the four major districts. A random sample survey results in the candidate preference frequencies by district shown in Table 12.13. Perform an appropriate statistical test to determine if candidate preference is related to the district.

TABLE 12.13   Candidates for Primary Election

District	Candidate A	B	C	D	Total
1	52	34	80	34	200
2	33	15	78	24	150
3	66	54	141	39	300
	151	103	299	97	650

12.4   The economic development agency in a small African country has received a grant from the World Bank to train farmers in the use of natural fertilizers to increase production. The training program uses one instructor to work with groups of three farmers working on their own fields. Designers of the program indicate that 50% of the farmers trained will increase production within two years. They further claim that production increases are independent of a farmer's background. If that is true, the number of successful farmers from each group trained should follow a binomial probability distribution. For 50 subgroups, each with 3 farmers, the following numbers were successful in each group:

1, 2, 2, 1, 1, 2, 0, 1, 2, 3, 0, 3, 2, 1, 1, 2, 1, 2, 1, 2
3, 2, 1, 2, 1, 0, 1, 2, 2, 1, 0, 1, 2, 2, 1, 1, 2, 2, 1, 2
0, 1, 2, 2, 1, 0, 1, 2, 1, 2

Perform a hypothesis test to determine if the assumption of a binomial probability distribution is supported by the data.

12.5   The director of admissions for a prestigious college uses a complex judgmental analysis to predict median grades of graduates. The analysis uses the information contained in the original student application. The combinations of predicted and actual grades is given in Table 12.14. Perform a hypothesis test to determine if the judgmental analysis is successful in predicting a student's academic performance in the college.

TABLE 12.14   Predicted and
Observed Median Grades

Grade Predicted	Grade Observed		
	A	B	C
A	10	7	8
B	10	20	5
C	5	10	20

12.6   The market research department of a large consumer goods company was conducting an extensive study of coupon redemption behavior. They were interested in identifying a number of variables potentially related to the percentage of coupons that would be redeemed. As part of that study, they compared the coupon redemption patterns on weekdays versus weekends. Observation of 30 randomly selected weekend shoppers indicated that 5 out of the 30 redeemed coupons and the remainder did not. In addition, 70 randomly selected weekday shoppers were observed, 40 of whom redeemed coupons. Based on these results, can you conclude that weekend and weekday shoppers have different coupon redemption patterns? State the hypothesis test, perform the necessary computations, and indicate your conclusion. Which groups are more likely to redeem coupons?

12.7   A manufacturer of household appliances wanted to determine if there was a relationship between family size and the size of washing machine purchased. They were preparing guidelines for sales personnel and wanted to know if the sales staff should make specific recommendations to customers. A random sample of 300 families was asked about family size and size of washing machine. For the 40 families with one or two people, 25 had an 8-pound washer, 10 had a 10-pound washer, and five had a 12-pound washer. The 140 families with three or four people included 37 with the 8-pound, 62 with the 10-pound, and 41 with the 12-pound. For the remaining 120 families with five or more people, eight had an 8-pound, 53 had a 10-pound, and 59 had a 12-pound. Based on these results, what can be concluded about family size and size of washer? Construct a two-way table, state the hypothesis, compute the statistics, and state your conclusion.

12.8   Susan Chison, a Norwegian economist, is conducting research to determine if Danes, Germans, and British prefer their own beer to that of their neighbors. The null hypothesis is that they have no preference for any of the three beers. A random sample of 100 people are selected from each of the three countries and are asked to rank each of the three beers by taste. The beer is served in unmarked glasses in random order to each person. After each taste their mouth is washed with distilled water. Of the 100 Danes, 40 prefer Danish beer, 35 German, and 25 British beer. Of the 100 Germans, 30 prefer Danish beer, 40 German beer, and 30 British beer. Of the 100 British, 30 prefer Danish beer, 32 German beer, and 38 prefer British beer. Perform a statistical hypothesis test to answer the research question. Use the appropriate procedure in your statistical computer system to compute the appropriate statistics for your hypothesis test.

12.9   You are attempting to determine if there is a relationship between the rating scores assigned by the Master Raters and the consumption expenditure category for a family. The Master Raters inspect the garbage cans and recycling bins for households and rate them in categories *A*, *B*, and *C*. Following this a detailed survey of household expenditures is conducted, and from this survey households are classified in either a low-, average-, or high-expenditure category. You are to determine if there is a relationship between the Master Raters garbage scale and the household expenditure category. Data in Table 12.15 were collected for a random sample of households. The number of households in each category is defined by the rating and the household consumption expenditure category. Perform an appropriate statistical hypothesis test and indicate the conclusions from your analysis. Carefully explain what you have done and indicate clearly the conclusion regarding the value of the garbage rating as a way to obtain an indication of expenditure category.

TABLE 12.15   Households by Rating and Expenditure

Rating	Expenditure Category	Number of Households
A	Low	50
B	Low	10
C	Low	20
A	Average	20
B	Average	50
C	Average	10
A	High	10
B	High	10
C	High	60

12.10 Allied Distributors has added 220 new sales personnel to its staff of 300. All of the new people have been with the company between one and two years. The sales department has asked you to compare the selling performance of the new and old sales staff to determine if the new people are performing at the same level as the old people. Of the 220 new sales staff, 150 had high sales, 60 average sales, and 10 low sales. In contrast, of the 300 old sales staff, 100 had high sales, 80 had average sales, and 120 had low sales.
   (a) Can you conclude that the sales performance is the same for the old and new sales staff?
   (b) Prepare a short statement to answer the question concerning the capability of the new staff to keep up with the old sales staff.

12.11 Return to Problem 12.10 concerning the sales performance of Allied Distributors' old and new sales staff. To analyze the question of sales performance further, the data were divided between the eastern and western territories. For the eastern territory 150 new staff and 80 old staff had high sales, 50 new staff and 20 old staff had average sales, and none of the old or new staff had low sales. But for the western territory 0 of the new staff and 20 of the old staff had high sales, while 10 of the new staff and 60 of the old staff had average sales, and 10 new sales staff had low sales and 120 old sales staff had low sales.

(a) Perform additional analyses, using these data, to compare the sales performance of old and new sales staff for each region. Have you discovered anything new as the result of this analysis?

(b) Explain clearly, based on your entire analysis, the reason for the apparent difference in results between the analysis of the combined sales force and the analysis divided by sales territories.

12.12 The frequency distribution and histogram in Exhibit 12.2 were prepared using Minitab. The 12 intervals have uniform width and correspond to Z intervals of width 0.50 beginning with $Z = -3.0$ and extending to $Z = 3.0$. The expected probabilities in each cell can be determined from a standard normal distribution. The sample contains 200 random observations. Perform a goodness-of-fit test to determine if the data could have come from a population with a normal distribution.

EXHIBIT 12.2   Empirical Frequency Distribution for Problem 12.12

```
The Center of the lower interval is;
K8         2.39867
The Mean of the population is;
K1         3.92000
The Center of the upper interval is;
K9         5.44133
The Population standard deviation of the mean is;
K4         0.468103


Histogram of mean    N = 200
1 Obs. above the last class

Midpoint    Count
   2.633        0
   2.867        6    ******
   3.101       11    **********
   3.335       26    ************************
   3.569       32    ******************************
   3.803       39    ***************************************
   4.037       22    *********************
   4.271       24    ***********************
   4.505       22    *********************
   4.739       13    *************
   4.973        1    *
   5.207        3    ***
```

12.13 Suppose that you perform a goodness-of-fit test and find that you cannot reject the hypothesis that the data were obtained from a normally distributed population. Do you have strong evidence that the data were obtained from a normally distributed population? Explain your answer.

12.14 Kirby Puckett had a 300 batting average (30% of the time, he hit safely). Over a 100-game period he was at bat exactly four times in each game. Examining the statistics we find that he had 0 hits in 30 games, 1 hit in 34 games, 2 hits in 25 games, 3 hits in eight games, and 4 hits in 3 games. Do the data support the conclusion that Mr. Puckett's hits per game follow a binomial distribution?

12.15 The gear cutting department in a large manufacturing firm produces high-quality gears. The number produced per hour by a single machinist is either 1, 2, or 3, as shown in Table 12.16. Company management is interested in determining the effect of worker experience on the number of units produced per hour. Worker experience is classified in three subgroups: less than 1 year, 2 to 5 years, and more than 5 years. Use the data in Table 12.16 to determine if experience and the number of parts produced per hour are independent.

TABLE 12.16   Worker Experience Versus Gear Production

| Experience | X | | | Total |
	1	2	3	
≤ 1	10	30	10	50
2–5	10	20	20	50
≥ 5	10	10	30	50
	30	60	60	150

12.16 Amalgamated Cereals, Inc. has asked for your assistance in their study of consumer response to their ready-to-eat cereals. As part of that study you are to determine if there are different cereal consumption patterns related to income level. Based on sampling survey data you prepare Table 12.17, which shows the frequency of consumption of the three ready-to-eat cereals by income level. Perform a hypothesis test to determine if there is any relationship between cereal type and income group.

TABLE 12.17   Cereal Demand by Income Group

| Income Group | Cereal | | | Total |
	O's	Flakes	Puffed	
Low	10	19	21	50
Medium	10	20	20	50
High	10	21	19	50
	30	60	60	150

12.17 Agnes Larson has been working on a plan for new store locations as part of her regional expansion. In one city proposed for expansion there are three possible locations: north, east, or west. From past experience she knows that the three major profit centers in her stores are tools, lumber, and paint. In selecting a location, the demand patterns in the different parts of the city were important. She commissioned a sampling study of the city, which resulted in Table 12.18, a two-way table for the variables "residential location" versus "product purchased." This table was prepared by the market research department using data obtained from the random sample of households in the three major residential areas of the city. Each residential area had a separate phone number prefix, and the last four digits were chosen using a computer random number generator. Is there a difference in the demand patterns for the three major items among the different areas of the city?

TABLE 12.18   Two-Way Table of Household Demand for Products by Residential Area

Area	Product				Total
	Tools	Lumber	Paint	None	
East	100	50	50	50	250
North	50	95	45	60	250
West	65	70	75	40	250
	215	215	170	150	750

12.18 In a study of alcohol and driving the research staff prepared Table 12.19, which shows the relationship between blood alcohol concentration and the location of first drinking episode for night drivers who had been drinking. The data for this table were obtained from a random sample of drivers in Washtenaw County, Michigan, collected during the hours 7 P.M. to 3 A.M. The columns indicate the blood alcohol concentration (BAC) of the driver, obtained from a breath test. Common interpretations of these concentrations are: $\leq 0.02\%$, essentially no blood alcohol and no driving impairment; 0.03 to 0.04%, social drinking with no impairment for most drivers; 0.05 to 0.09%, almost all drivers will have noticeable impairment and could be convicted by a court; $\geq 0.10\%$, all drivers are seriously impaired and represent a threat to other vehicles and pedestrians. The rows indicate the source of the most recent drinking episode.
(a) Is there a difference in the blood alcohol levels based on the different drinking locations?
(b) Which location produces the largest percentage of high blood alcohol levels?

TABLE 12.19   Two-Way Table of Driver BAC by Location of First Drinking Episode

Location	Driver BAC (%)				Total
	≤ 0.02	0.03–0.04	0.05–0.09	≥ 0.10	
Bar	22	25	17	14	78
Own home	45	16	11	10	82
Another home	42	10	6	0	58
	120	54	43	25	242

12.19 Apple Packers Ltd. conducts regular sampling inspections of apples shipped to the pack-ing plant from its various orchard suppliers. The contract with Molson Orchards states that shipments will not contain more than 30% grade 2 apples. Over the past two weeks 100 samples of size $n = 6$ were obtained from shipments received from Molson Or-chards. In these 100 samples they found that 4 contained 0 grade 2 apples, 18 contained 1, 31 contained 2, 28 contained 3, 14 contained 4, 4 contained 5, and 1 contained 6 grade 2 apples.

(a) Based on these sample data can you conclude that the contract requirement for grade 2 apples has been met?

(b) One of the warehouse managers suggested that the shipments actually contained 40% grade 2 apples. Does the sample evidence support that suggestion?

12.20 Fitzger's Breweries wanted to determine how its new light beer compared to other light beers in a blind sample taste test. They decided to compare their brand with the follow-ing other brands: (1) Rainer Light, (2) Maccabee Light, and (3) Stella Light. The study used 300 randomly selected taste testers. Each subject was asked to taste four different unlabeled beers and indicate which they preferred. The number of subjects who pre-ferred each beer was: Fitzger's Light, 105; Rainer Light, 60; Maccabee Light, 65; Stella Light, 70.

(a) Based on the data from this study, can you conclude that all four beers are preferred equally?

(b) Which beer appears to have the highest percentage of support based on these data?

12.21 The automobile assembly division of Mazdaford Motors constantly monitors the quality of its body-painting operations. Jennifer Smith, the quality control manager for the paint division, has prepared Table 12.20. This table compares the frequency of three major paint defects: burrs, paint chips, and bubbles over the division's three painting operations. These studies are conducted regularly to identify problems that should be singled out for special action by the quality control staff. Are the defect patterns uniform over the three paint operations?

TABLE 12.20 Paint Defects by Painting Line

Line	Defect			Total
	Burrs	Paint Chips	Bubbles	
1	5	10	8	23
2	11	8	6	25
3	12	6	7	25
	28	24	21	73

12.22 The Speedi-Flex delivery service is conducting a study of its delivery operations. As part of this study they collected data on package type by originating source for one day's operation for one district office in the southeast. These data are shown in Table 12.21. The major originating sources were identified as (1) small cities (towns), (2) central business districts (CBDs), (3) light manufacturing districts (factory), or (4) suburban residential communities (suburbs). The items handled are classified by size and rate with

TABLE 12.21   Package Size by Originating Source

Package Source	Package Size (lb)			Total
	≤ 3	4–10	11–75	
Towns	40	40	20	100
CBDs	119	63	18	200
Factory	18	71	111	200
Suburbs	69	64	17	150
	246	238	166	650

three major categories. Overnight envelopes must weigh less than 3 pounds and have a fixed charged of $12 anywhere in the United States. Small packages weigh less than 10 pounds and have dimension restrictions. Large packages can weigh up to 75 pounds and have the lowest rate per pound and the longest delivery time.

(a) Are there any differences in the patterns of packages originated at the various locations?

(b) Which two combinations have the largest percentage deviation from a uniform pattern?

13

Analysis of Variance

We want to determine if subgroups have different means for a dependent variable.

13.1 ANALYSIS OVER SEVERAL POPULATIONS

In this chapter we introduce statistical analysis of variance procedures. In Chapter 11, hypothesis tests for comparing two populations were developed. But there are problems in which several populations are compared. Analysis of variance methods are used to compare these populations. There are many examples, including:

1. A manufacturer wants to know if the productivity per hour is different for the five production machines located in her factory.
2. The director of an agricultural development project wants to know which of four different fertilizers provides the highest productivity of raggi grain measured in bushels per acre.
3. The marketing manager wants to know if any of the five different advertising strategies results in a higher level of sales.
4. A police department wants to know if crime rates are significantly different among various neighborhoods.
5. A plant manager wants to know if the number of defective pieces per shift is different between production units, between raw material suppliers, or between combinations of production units and suppliers.

In each of these problems there is a discrete variable or factor that separates a population into a set of subpopulations or subgroups. We want to determine if the subgroups have different means for a dependent variable. In Chapter 11 we presented a method to determine if two-subgroup means were different. Analysis of variance provides the same results when more than two subgroups are compared.

Analysis of variance procedures were originally developed to support agricultural experiments in the early part of the twentieth century. Agricultural experiments require an entire growing season and utilize considerable input resources to prepare fields, apply different treatments, harvest crops, and measure the results. Typically, the objective was to compare seeds, fertilizers, irrigation levels, tillage methods, and other factors to determine which levels and combinations of factor levels resulted in the highest crop productivity. These experiments were also affected by factors such as soil condition and weather, which could not be controlled by the researchers.

Given the problem, statisticians such as R. A. Fisher and many others developed experimental design procedures. These procedures provided a way to handle the many factors that could affect the outcome. In addition, they provided a way to obtain a number of results simultaneously from a single set of experimental observations. These efforts had considerable impact on the early development of applied statistical methods. In the United States, many of the early statistical research and education programs grew at universities such as Iowa State, Michigan State, Wisconsin, and North Carolina State, which emphasized agricultural research programs.

Experimental design using analysis of variance has spread to a number of applied fields. Psychologists discovered that their experiments had many of the same problems as those faced by agricultural researchers. Thus they have adopted and extended experimental design and analysis of variance methods to their discipline. Another area of major application has been industrial experiments to increase productivity and improve product quality.

Experimental design and statistical methods were very important in the rapid growth of Japanese industry after World War II. The work of W. Edwards Deming and his associates in Japan is legendary. Industrial experiments have experienced considerable recent growth in the United States because of the interest in increased productivity and higher quality. Other areas of business also use experimental design and analysis of experiments.

Economists have not tended to be users of these procedures because of their emphasis on continuous variable models. Their work in econometrics has tended to use regression analysis and various nonlinear estimation procedures. However, the work in applied areas such as economic development has made considerable use of experimental design and analysis of variance procedures. Evaluation of development and environmental projects often involves comparisons of different programs with the present or base condition. For example, program administrators want to know which procedures provide the highest income or the cleanest water.

The techniques of regression analysis and analysis of variance have a number of applications in common. Regression develops continuous linear relationships between independent variables and dependent variables. In contrast, analysis of variance works with discrete subgroups. Applied problems do not always separate nicely into discrete or continuous problems. Continuous variables can be separated into subgroups by specifying discrete ranges, such as age groups 16–20, 21–25, and so on. In contrast, discrete independent variables, with many levels, are sometimes approximated by continuous variables. For example, automobile weight is often used as a continuous variable for predicting fuel consumption or accident injury severity. However, vehicle weight also identifies a discrete model and style. Analysis of variance uses simpler computational procedures and thus was the technique of choice before computers were readily available. Now computers are almost always used for analysis of variance computations.

As we will see in Chapters 15 and 16, the development of dummy variable regression has meant that all analysis of variance computations can also be performed using regression analysis. In addition, problems involving both discrete and continuous independent variables can easily be analyzed using multiple regression models.

We present the basic ideas of experimental design and analysis of variance in this chapter. In addition to providing problem solutions, analysis of variance provides background for the study of regression analysis.

13.2 ONE-WAY ANALYSIS OF VARIANCE

In this section multilevel comparisons between subgroups defined by one factor are presented. The problem is to determine if discrete subgroups are different with respect to a dependent or criterion variable. Applications include:

1. Do certain fertilizers result in higher production of corn?
2. Do some neighborhoods in a city have families with higher incomes?
3. Which of the production facilities has the highest productivity?
4. Can we expect greater sales gains from some advertising techniques?
5. Data collected from stratified samples, discussed in Section 8.3, are analyzed using the procedures of one-way analysis of variance.

Example 13.1   Production Levels by Machine

Shirley Anderson, the production manager, wishes to determine if any of the three machines in her factory have higher production levels when they are producing A struts for a new domestic automobile. Production is measured by the number of pieces produced per hour.

Solution   To develop the formal analysis we identify each of the three machines as $j = 1$, $j = 2$, and $j = 3$. For each machine a sample of $i = 1, \ldots, n$ observations is obtained. Each observation of production i for machine j is designated Y_{ij}. For example,

$$Machine\ j = 1: \quad Y_{11} = 1, \quad Y_{21} = 2$$
$$Machine\ j = 2: \quad Y_{12} = 4, \quad Y_{22} = 5$$
$$Machine\ j = 3: \quad Y_{13} = 8, \quad Y_{23} = 10$$

Sample means for each machine could be computed and used to compare the machines. After developing some analysis methodology, we will return to complete this example.   □

13.2.1 Data Model and Hypothesis Test

A formal data model can be used to provide a description of the analysis of variance problem (see Key Idea 13.1). If there are only $r = 2$ subgroups, the two-population hypothesis test presented in Chapter 11 is the preferred test.

Key Idea 13.1: One-Way Analysis-of-Variance Model

Within each of the $j = 1, \ldots, r$ subgroups, n_j observations are obtained for the dependent variable Y_{ij} ($i = 1, \ldots, n_j$). The data model for one-way analysis of variance is

$$Y_{ij} = \mu + \theta_j + \epsilon_{ij}$$

where μ is the population mean for all observations, θ_j is the difference between the mean for subgroup j and μ, and ϵ_{ij} is the random error for observation i within subgroup j. ϵ_{ij} has a mean of 0 and a constant variance σ^2 for all subgroups. If there are no differences between the subgroups, the θ_j is zero for all of the $j = 1, \ldots, r$ subgroups.

Using this model, it is possible to conclude that the means for one or more subgroups are different by rejecting the null hypothesis,

$$H_0: \theta_1 = \theta_2 = \cdots = \theta_r = 0$$

and accepting the alternative hypothesis,

$$H_1: \text{At least two } \theta_j\text{'s are not equal.}$$

The hypothesis for differences between subgroups is tested by comparing the variability between subgroup sample means with the variability within the subgroups. This idea for the hypothesis test is shown schematically in Figure 13.1. In both the left and right columns the distributions of observations from subgroups (a), (b), and (c) are compared. The differences between the subgroup means are exactly the same. The subgroup distributions on the left have a large variance within their subgroup and the distributions have considerable overlap. By contrast, the subgroup distributions on the right have a small variance within their subgroup and do not tend to overlap. Using the analysis of variance hypothesis test, the subgroups on the right would lead us to reject the null hypothesis and conclude that the subgroup means are not equal. This occurs because the variability between subgroup means is large compared to the variability within subgroups. However, the same test applied to the subgroups on the left would not result in rejecting H_0. The variability within the subgroups is too large compared to the variability between the subgroup means.

13.2.2 Partitioning the Variance

Now that we have seen the basic idea, we will return to the example problem. Shirley Anderson, production supervisor, wants to know if the three machines under her supervision have different mean productivity measured in units per hour. From the production reports she randomly selects two different production hours for each machine

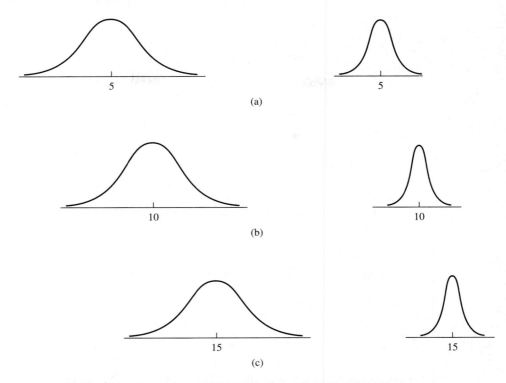

Figure 13.1   Comparison of High-Variance and Low-Variance Subgroups

and records the number of units produced. Table 13.1 presents the observations combined with the subgroup sample mean production for each machine.

TABLE 13.1   Observed Production for
Machines

Machine, j	Observation, i		Subgroup Mean
	1	2	
1	1	2	1.5
2	4	5	4.5
3	8	10	9.0

Inspection of the numbers observed suggests that the productivity levels for the three machines are different. This difference can be seen easily by examining Figure 13.2. The variability of observations within the subgroups for each machine is small compared to the variability between the subgroup means. In Key Idea 13.2 we have the analysis of variance algorithm that will provide a formal hypothesis test (Key Idea 13.3).

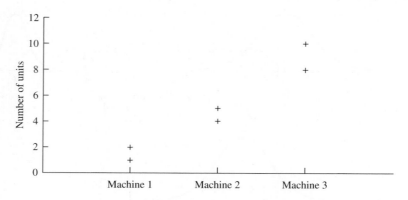

Figure 13.2 Observed Production for Each Machine

Key Idea 13.2: Analysis of Variance Computational Algorithm

The one-way analysis of variance model is

$$Y_{ij} = \mu + \theta_j + \epsilon_{ij}$$

where $j = 1, \ldots, r$ subgroups, and $i = 1, \ldots, n_j$ observations in subgroup j. The total variability, defined as *total sum of squares* (TSS), can be partitioned into variability within subgroups, defined as *error sum of squares* (ESS), and the variability between subgroups, defined as *between-group sum of squares* (BSS). The components of variance are

$$\text{TSS} = \sum_{j=1}^{r} \sum_{i=1}^{n_j} (Y_{ij} - \bar{Y})^2$$

$$\text{BSS} = \sum_{j=1}^{r} n_j (\bar{Y}_j - \bar{Y})^2$$

$$\text{ESS} = \sum_{j=1}^{r} \sum_{i=1}^{n_j} (Y_{ij} - \bar{Y}_j)^2$$

$$\text{TSS} = \text{BSS} + \text{ESS}$$

$\bar{Y}$ is the overall mean for all observations and $\bar{Y}_j$ is the mean for observations in subgroup j. These results are developed in the appendix to this chapter.

Key Idea 13.3: Analysis-of-Variance Hypothesis Test

The hypothesis that all subgroup means are equal:

$$H_0: \theta_1 = \theta_2 = \cdots = \theta_j$$

is tested against the hypothesis that at least one of the subgroup means is different:

$$H_1: \theta_k \neq \theta_l \quad \text{at least one pair} \quad k, l$$

The hypothesis test uses the calculated F statistic

$$F = \frac{\text{MSB}}{\text{MSE}}$$

with MSB and MSE computed from the sums of squares,

$$\text{MSB} = \frac{\text{BSS}}{r - 1}$$

$$\text{MSE} = \frac{\text{ESS}}{n - r}$$

If the null hypothesis is true, both MSE and MSB are estimates of the variance σ^2. From our previous work with the F distribution in Section 9.10, we know that the ratio of two estimates of variance has an F distribution.

This calculated F has $r - 1$ degrees of freedom for the numerator and $n - r$ degrees of freedom for the denominator. If the F calculated is greater than the critical value of F for a chosen α with $r - 1$ over $n - r$ degrees of freedom, then H_0 is rejected and we conclude that at least one of the subgroup means is different.

ESS and BSS are measures of total variability that can be converted to mean square error terms with division by their respective degrees of freedom. The degrees of freedom for BSS is the number of subgroups r minus 1, because the overall mean $\bar{Y}$ is used. The degrees of freedom for ESS is the total observations, n, minus the number of subgroups r.

The overall grand mean is

$$\bar{Y} = \frac{\sum_{j=1}^{r} \sum_{i=1}^{n_j} Y_{ij}}{n}$$

where

$$n = \sum_{j=1}^{r} n_j$$

is the total number of observations for all subgroups.

The subgroup means are

$$\bar{Y}_j = \frac{\sum_{i=1}^{n_j} Y_{ij}}{n_j}$$

Computations for Example 13.1. In the example problem, there are $r = 3$ machines with $n_j = 2$ observations for each machine. The overall mean is

$$
\begin{aligned}
\bar{Y} &= \frac{\sum_{j=1}^{3} \sum_{i=1}^{2} Y_{ij}}{3 \times 2} \\
&= \frac{1 + 2 + 4 + 5 + 8 + 10}{6} \\
&= 5
\end{aligned}
$$

The total sum of squares TSS is

$$
\begin{aligned}
\text{TSS} &= \sum_{j=1}^{3} \sum_{i=1}^{2} (Y_{ij} - \bar{Y})^2 \\
&= (1 - 5)^2 + (2 - 5)^2 + \cdots + (10 - 5)^2 \\
&= (-4)^2 + (-3)^2 + (-1)^2 + 0^2 + 3^2 + 5^2 \\
&= 60.0
\end{aligned}
$$

The between-group sum of squares BSS is

$$
\begin{aligned}
\text{BSS} &= \sum_{j=1}^{3} \sum_{i=1}^{2} (\bar{Y}_j - \bar{Y})^2 \\
&= \sum_{j=1}^{3} [2(1.5 - 5)^2 + 2(4.5 - 5)^2 + 2(9 - 5)^2] \\
&= 2(12.25 + 0.25 + 16) \\
&= 57.0
\end{aligned}
$$

The within-group sum of squares ESS is

$$\text{ESS} = \sum_{j=1}^{3} \sum_{i=1}^{2} (Y_{ij} - \bar{Y}_j)^2$$

$$= (1 - 1.5)^2 + (2 - 1.5)^2 + (4 - 4.5)^2 + (5 - 4.5)^2$$
$$+ (8 - 9.0)^2 + (10 - 9.0)^2$$
$$= (-0.5)^2 + 0.5^2 + (-0.5)^2 + 0.5^2 + (-1.0)^2 + 1.0^2$$
$$= 3.0$$

Note that the basic identity,

$$\text{TSS} = \text{BSS} + \text{ESS}$$
$$60.0 = 57.0 + 3.0$$

is satisfied in this problem.

The next step is to compute the mean square error terms and the F statistic for the hypothesis test.

$$\text{MSB} = \frac{\text{BSS}}{r - 1}$$
$$= \frac{57.0}{3 - 1}$$
$$= 28.5$$
$$\text{MSE} = \frac{\text{ESS}}{n - r}$$
$$= \frac{3.0}{6 - 3}$$
$$= 1.0$$

The computed F statistic for this problem is

$$F = \frac{\text{MSB}}{\text{MSE}}$$
$$= \frac{28.5}{1.0}$$
$$= 28.5$$

From Table A.4 the critical value of F with 2 degrees of freedom for the numerator and 3 degrees of freedom for the denominator and $\alpha = 0.05$ is

$$F_{2,3,\alpha=0.05} = 9.55$$

Since the computed value of F exceeds the critical value ($F = 9.55$), the null hypothesis

$$H_0: \theta_1 = \theta_2 = \theta_3 = 0$$

is rejected and we conclude that the machines have different productivity levels.

The analysis of variance calculations are usually summarized in an *ANOVA* table, as shown in Table 13.2. In most applications the above calculations will be made by a computer, as in Example 13.2. However, the above computations indicate how the ANOVA table is computed. For the machine productivity problem the ANOVA table is shown in Table 13.3.

TABLE 13.2   ANOVA Table Description

Source	Sum of Squares	DOF	Mean Square	F
Between groups	BSS	$r - 1$	MSB	$\dfrac{\text{MSB}}{\text{MSE}}$
Within groups	ESS	$n - r$	MSE	
Total	TSS	$n - 1$		

TABLE 13.3   ANOVA Table for Machine Productivity

Source	Sum of Squares	DOF	Mean Square	F
Between groups	57.0	2	28.5	28.5
Within groups	3.0	3	1.0	
Total	60.0	5		

Example 13.2   Analysis of Store Sales

In Chapter 11 we presented the problem of Barbara Anderson, who was analyzing the sales data for a sporting goods store that she had recently acquired. In this example Barbara wants to determine if sales are significantly different over the six days that the store is normally open. Thus she decides to perform an analysis of variance in which the days Monday through Saturday identify the subgroups and the dependent variable is daily sales.

Solution   Exhibit 13.1 presents the Minitab output for the analysis of variance. The null hypothesis is that all six days (1 = Monday, 6 = Saturday) have the same sales. In contrast to the previous example, there are a total of 468 observations spread approximately equally over the six days. All of the computations could have been made using the basic equations presented above. However, hand calculation would be very time consuming, and thus we used the Minitab computer output. The analysis of

EXHIBIT 13.1   Analysis of Variance for Daily Store Sales

```
MTB > oneway ANOVA on 'sales' groups in 'dayweek'

ANALYSIS OF VARIANCE ON sales
SOURCE       DF         SS         MS         F
dayweek       5   21331880    4266376     17.38
ERROR       462  113395240     245444
TOTAL       467  134727120
                                   INDIVIDUAL 95 PCT CI'S FOR MEAN
                                   BASED ON POOLED STDEV
  LEVEL        N      MEAN     STDEV
--+---------+---------+---------+----
    1        78     1168.2     661.3                        (----*---)
    2        78      576.6     408.2    (---*---)
    3        79      605.8     603.2    (---*----)
    4        76      588.4     332.6    (----*---)
    5        79      652.9     380.5      (---*---)
    6        78      863.0     495.6         (----*---)

--+---------+---------+---------+----
POOLED STDEV =     495.4          500       750      1000      1250
```

variance table has the same format as that presented in Table 13.2. The row labeled "dayweek" contains the between-group analysis (BSS) and the row labeled "ERROR" contains the within-group analysis (ESS). The six subgroups (days) result in 5 degrees of freedom for the between-group sum of squares. Note that

$$TSS = BSS + ESS$$
$$134{,}727{,}120 = 21{,}331{,}880 + 113{,}395{,}240$$

The degrees of freedom for the within-group sum of squares is equal to the total number of 478 observations minus the number of subgroups. Using the ratio of mean squares, the F value, from Exhibit 13.1, is 17.38. From Table A.4 the critical value of F for $\alpha = 0.01$, 5 degrees of freedom for the numerator, and 462 degrees of freedom for the denominator is $F_{\alpha=0.01,5,462} = 3.02$. Since $F = 17.38$ is greater than $F_{crit} = 3.02$, the null hypothesis—equal daily sales—is rejected.

The computer ouput also presents a graphical display of the subgroup means. A simple 95% confidence interval is computed and plotted for each mean to provide a rough basis for comparison. Examination of the graph and the subgroup means indicates that Monday sales are substantially larger than those for any other day, with Saturday sales being somewhat different from those for the other four weekdays.   □

13.3 MULTIPLE COMPARISONS

Using the analysis of variance procedure, we conclude that the subgroups identified by factor levels are either equal or not equal. In Example 13.2 we concluded that store sales were not equal for the six days of the week. After establishing that the subgroup means are not equal, it is natural to ask which subgroup means are significantly larger than others. If there were only two subgroups, the hypothesis tests for differences between population means developed in Chapter 11 would be used. However, that test cannot be used for multiple comparisons between pairs when there are more than two subgroups. The hypothesis test for differences between population means assumes that only two means are being compared. However, if r subgroups are being compared, the number of possible comparisons are equal to the number of combinations of r items taken 2 at a time. In Chapter 4 we found that

$$C_2^r = \frac{r!}{(r-2)!\,2!}$$

Thus when there are $r = 6$ subgroups, we have $(6 \times 5)/2 = 15$ different comparisons. With one comparison the probability of error is set at α and the minimum significant difference (MSD) between a pair of subgroups each with the same number of observations, n, and a common sample estimate of variance, S_p, is computed using

$$\text{MSD} = t_{\alpha/2} S_p \sqrt{\frac{2}{n}}$$

However, with more than one simultaneous comparison, the probability of error becomes larger than α.[1] The problem of multiple comparisons has been studied by a number of statisticians. We present Tukey's multiple comparison test for equal-sized groups because it solves the problem and is easy to use.

John Tukey proposed a method that is similar to the comparison between two subgroups but provides a larger MSD to control for the many possible comparisons (Key Idea 13.4). This method uses a factor q that depends on the number of groups being compared and the number of degrees of freedom used to estimate the common error standard deviation, S_p.

Example 13.3   Analysis of Store Sales Revisited

In Example 13.2 we found that the average sales per day were different over the six days Monday through Friday. Now we would like to know which days are actually different from the others.

---

[1] If the comparisons were independent, the probability of error would be approximately

$$1 - (1 - \alpha)^k$$

where k is the number of multiple comparisons.

Key Idea 13.4: Multiple Comparisons

The minimum significant difference between multiple means is computed using

$$\Delta = q \frac{S_p}{\sqrt{n}}$$

where n is the number of observations in each subgroup. The factor q is given in Table A.12 for $\alpha = 0.01$ and $\alpha = 0.05$. The rows in Table A.12 are the degrees of freedom for S_p and the columns are the number of treatments. The difference Δ can be used to compare any pair of means. The null hypothesis is that the subgroup means are equal. If the specific difference observed is greater than Δ, we conclude that the subgroup means are different. The probability that this decision would be incorrect is less than α.

Solution   Our first step is to compute the minimum difference, Δ. From Exhibit 13.1 we see that the standard deviation is $S_p = 495.4$ with 462 degrees of freedom. From Table A.12 for $\alpha = 0.05$, degrees of freedom > 120 (Table A.12 rows) and six treatment means (Table A.12 columns), the factor is $q = 4.03$. Therefore, the minimum difference is

$$\Delta = q \frac{S_p}{\sqrt{n}}$$
$$= 4.03 \frac{495.4}{\sqrt{78}}$$
$$= 226.05$$

Using this critical value of $\Delta = 226.05$, we find that statistically significant differences between factor levels can be identified. First note that Monday mean sales exceed sales on all other days. To see this, subtract $\Delta = 226.05$ from the Monday sales of $\bar{Y} = 1168.2$. The result is 942.15 $(1168.2 - 226.05)$, which exceeds the mean daily sales for all other days. Note also that the mean daily sales for day 6, $\bar{Y}_6 = 863.0$, exceeds the sales for days 2, 3, and 4. Subtract $863.0 - 226.05 = 636.95$ and note that 636.95 exceeds $\bar{Y}_2 = 576.6$, $\bar{Y}_3 = 605.8$, and $\bar{Y}_4 = 588.4$. As this example shows, the minimum significant difference Δ provides a way to determine which subgroups are different, after the hypothesis test indicates that a least one is different.   □

Does It Make Sense?

The analysis of variance procedure provides a hypothesis test to determine if any of the subgroup means are different. This is an important result and is obtained by comparing the explained variability (between groups) and the error variability (within groups). Multiple comparison procedures, such as those presented here, indicate which of the subgroup means are significantly different in a statistical sense. Identifying the subgroups that are different is an important result in applied statistics. These differences between subgroups are identified because the differences between subgroup means exceed the minimum critical difference, Δ. ☐

Practice Problem 13.1

The sports medicine department at a major medical center was interested in comparing procedures for treatment of a particular type of knee injury. They wanted to know if any of the three common procedures has a significantly reduced time for total recovery. The treatment procedures evaluated were:

1. Surgery
2. Injections and heat
3. Physical therapy

Injured athletes were randomly assigned to one of the three procedures to minimize the effect of injury severity differences. The recovery times in days for each of the treatments are

1. 24,   26,   28
2. 24,   22,   23
3. 15,   17,   19

Can you conclude that there are differences in recovery time among the three procedures? ☐

The solution is given at the end of the chapter.

Problem Exercises

13.1   The number of units produced on three randomly selected days for each of four different machines are
       Machine 1:   58,   62,   66
       Machine 2:   72,   68,   76
       Machine 3:   48,   52,   56
       Machine 4:   54,   56,   58
       Are the production levels on the four machines different?

13.2   Numbercheckers, Inc., a regional accounting team, wishes to compare the levels of accounts receivables for three different retail stores. Random samples were obtained from each of the three stores and the receivable values were

> *Store 1:*   145,   126,   118
> *Store 2:*   110,   120,   128
> *Store 3:*   135,   128,   150

Do the three stores have differences in the mean receivables?

13.3   Numbercheckers, Inc. has also compared the age in days of accounts receivables for three different retail stores. Random samples were obtained from each of the three stores and the receivable ages were

> *Store 1:*   10,   8,   12,   9
> *Store 2:*   16,   17,   19,   15
> *Store 3:*   26,   28,   24,   27

Do the three stores have differences in the age of their receivables?

13.4   Return to Problem 13.3, in which Numbercheckers, Inc. is analyzing the age of receivables. Which stores have mean age of receivables significantly different from the other stores?

13.5   Deep Zero, Inc. has developed a new snow ski design that it intends to bring to market. First, they tested it with three different age groups of skiers. As part of the survey they asked randomly selected individuals in each age group the price that they would be willing to pay for this new ski. The results were

> *Age group 16–25:*   300,   320,   330
> *Age group 26–45:*   200,   230,   250
> *Age group 46–60:*   250,   260,   270

Do the three age groups have different responses in terms of a market price for this new ski?

13.6   Return to Problem 13.5, in which Deep Zero, Inc. is studying the possible price level for its new ski.

(a) Which, if any, of the age groups have a different perception of a fair market price?

(b) How could the results of this problem help Deep Zero market its new ski?

13.4 TWO-WAY ANALYSIS OF VARIANCE

In the previous sections we have shown how analysis of variance can be used to determine if there are differences between subgroups defined by a single factor. There are a number of problems in which more than one factor is important. In this section we present analysis of variance when two factors are used. Two-way analysis of variance partitions variability into portions due to each of the factors and a portion that is unexplained and thus assigned to random error. The computational equations are more complex than those seen previously.

There are many important applications of two-way analysis of variance.

1. Agricultural experiments are conducted to compare the effect of different fertilizers or different herbicides on crop productivity while including factors such as soil type, which also influence productivity. Typically, agricultural experiments will use several fields, each defined as a *block*. Each block has approximately uniform soil conditions. However, the soil conditions are different between the various blocks. The blocks are separated into individual plots and the different fertilizer treatments are

applied to each plot. The process is repeated on the other blocks so that the fertiliz-ers are compared directly under a variety of soil conditions. As a result of the original agricultural experiments, the term *blocking variable* has become common usage in the literature of statistical experimental design, which now extends far beyond agricultural applications. A blocking variable is used to help reduce the unexplained or error vari-ance by assigning this variance to a factor. With a smaller error variance, experimental comparisons can be made with greater precision.

2. Industrial experiments also have need for more than one factor to identify subgroups. Experiments that compare the effect of different machines on productivity or number of defective units must control for differences between workers. Processes that are less dependent on workers may be influenced by the source of raw materials, the time of day, or the ambient temperature. Any of these variables might be used as a blocking variable in experiments attempting to compare different machines or different production methods. Alternatively, experimenters may be interested in the effects of these other variables on productivity when they are used with different machines. The designation of a variable as a blocking variable does not influence the required computations or the amount of information that can be obtained concerning the variable.

3. Market researchers design experiments to look at the combined effect of price level and advertising copy design on product sales. Some marketing experiments are more difficult to control because they must use human subjects. Thus in some cases, population subgroups, identified by age, sex, race, education, neighborhood, or in-come, are used as blocking variables in a marketing study. The experimenters might also want to know how different subgroups are influenced by marketing approaches. In those cases blocking variables become one of the independent variables in the analysis.

4. The evaluation of economic development projects can utilize experimental design and two-way analysis of variance. Programs designed to help people increase their income involve different job training strategies and different programs to create more jobs. The job training options can be treated as one factor and the different job creation programs as a second. Each observation in the experiment could be a city neighborhood or census tract that has a specific combination of a job training option and a job creation program.

13.4.1 Two-Factor Model and Analysis

The two-factor model is described in Key Idea 13.5. An important new term in this model is *interaction effect*, which results from the unique combination of two-factor levels, which is different from the simple additive effect of the two factors by them-selves. Interaction is common to many processes.

1. In agriculture the combination of fertilizer and water has a much greater effect than the sum of effects for the two factors taken individually.

Key Idea 13.5: Two-Factor Model

Two-factor analysis of variance uses a data model similar to the one-factor model in Key Idea 13.1. The two-factor model is

$$Y_{ijk} = \mu + \alpha_j + \beta_k + \gamma_{jk} + \epsilon_{ijk}$$

where μ is the overall base mean, α_j the shift from μ that results from level j for the α factor, β_k the shift from μ that results from level k for the β factor, γ_{kj} the shift from $\mu + \alpha_j + \beta_k$ that results from the interaction between levels j and k for the two factors, and ϵ_{ijk} the random error term for observations i, j, k.

An important assumption for hypothesis testing is that

$$\sigma^2(\epsilon_{ijk}) = \sigma^2$$

indicating that the error variance is uniform over all the combinations of the two factors. In the model there are $j = 1, \ldots, r$ levels for α, $k = 1, \ldots, p$ for β, $i = 1, \ldots, m$ observations for each combination of the two-factor levels and n $(r \times p \times m)$ total observations in the entire analysis.

The total variability can be partitioned into its major components:

$$\text{TSS} = \text{ASS} \quad + \quad \text{BSS} \quad + \quad \text{ISS} \quad + \quad \text{ESS}$$

where TSS is the total sum of squares, ASS is the sum of squares for the α factor, BSS is the sum of squares for the β factor, ISS is the sum of squares for interaction, and ESS is the sum of squares for error.

2. Worker productivity is often much higher with the combination of good wages and supportive management, compared to the sum of effects from these two factors treated separately.

3. Management literature uses the term *synergism* to define those unique combinations of factors whose interaction results in successful organizations.

The two-factor hypothesis test is described in Key Idea 13.6. The computational details for these equations are shown in the chapter appendix.

13.4.2 Factor-Level Effects

The two-way analysis of variance can be understood intuitively by examining Figures 13.3 and 13.4. In Figure 13.3 the three levels of factor A have different means, and each of those means have approximately the same distance between levels 1 and

Key Idea 13.6: Two-Factor Hypothesis Test

Hypothesis testing for two-factor analysis of variance follows a similar form except that there are several different hypotheses. The effect of the first factor is tested using the null hypothesis

$$H_0: \alpha_1 = \alpha_2 = \cdots = \alpha_r = 0$$

The effect of the second factor is tested by

$$H_0: \beta_1 = \beta_2 = \cdots = \beta_p = 0$$

The test for interaction effect follows the same form with more terms:

$$H_0: \gamma_{1,1} = \gamma_{1,2} = \cdots = \gamma_{j,k} = \cdots = \gamma_{r,p} = 0$$

Hypothesis testing is performed by computing the ratios of mean squares for the main effects (α_j or β_k) and the interactions γ_{jk} divided by the mean square for error.

$$MSA = \frac{ASS}{r-1}$$

$$MSB = \frac{BSS}{p-1}$$

$$MSI = \frac{ISS}{(r-1)(p-1)}$$

$$MSE = \frac{ESS}{n-rp}$$

The first factor is tested with

$$F_a = \frac{MSA}{MSE}$$

with $(r-1)$ over $(n-rp)$ degrees of freedom; the second factor is tested with

$$F_b = \frac{MSB}{MSE}$$

with $(p-1)$ over $(n-rp)$ degrees of freedom; and the interaction effect is tested with

$$F_i = \frac{MSI}{MSE}$$

with $(r-1)(p-1)$ over $(n-rp)$ degrees of freedom.

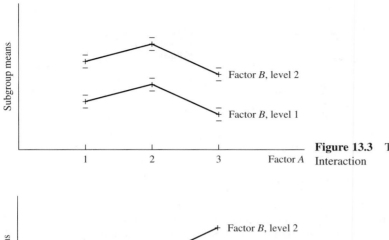

Figure 13.3   Two-Factor Effects: No Interaction

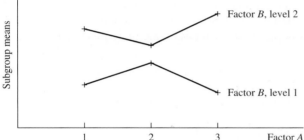

Figure 13.4   Two-Factor Effects with Interaction

2 for factor B. This figure is an idealized example of a two-way analysis of variance with both factors significant and a nonsignificant interaction term.

Figure 13.4 presents different results for a two-way analysis of variance. There are significant differences overall between the three levels of factor A and between the two levels of factor B. However, the differences do not follow the balanced pattern shown in Figure 13.3. Differences between the factor B levels are small when factor A is at level 2 and large when factor A is at level 3. This is an example of an interaction effect. Note that the combined effects of different factor-level combinations in Figure 13.4 are different from the simple factor-level effects shown in Figure 13.3.

The two-way analysis of variance computations are summarized in the ANOVA table, whose format is shown in Table 13.4. The form for the two-way ANOVA table is similar to that for the one-way ANOVA table. The difference is the increased number of variance components. The variance associated with each factor separately and with their interaction is a separate portion of the unexplained variability. The degrees of freedom for the main effects are equal to the number of levels minus 1. The degrees of freedom for the interaction is the product of the main-effects degrees of freedom. The degrees of freedom for the within-group or error sum of squares is computed as the difference between the degrees of freedom for TSS minus the degrees of freedom for the various explained components.

TABLE 13.4   Two-Way ANOVA Table Description

Source	Sum of Squares	DOF	Mean Square	F
Factor A	ASS	$r - 1$	MSA	$\dfrac{\text{MSA}}{\text{MSE}}$
Factor B	BSS	$p - 1$	MSB	$\dfrac{\text{MSB}}{\text{MSE}}$
Interaction	ISS	$(r - 1)(p - 1)$	MSI	$\dfrac{\text{MSI}}{\text{MSE}}$
Within groups	ESS	$n - rp$	MSE	
Total	TSS	$n - 1$		

Example 13.4   Machine Productivity

Lori Becker is the production manager for a company that produces integrated circuit boards for commercial aircraft. The company has three different machines, which have a number of automated operations controlled by a highly skilled worker. She wants to know if there are differences in productivity between the three machines.

Solution   From her experience she knows that worker skill makes a major contribution to productivity. Therefore, she conducts an experiment in which each worker is assigned to each machine for two different 8-hour shifts in random sequence. The resulting productivity in units per hour is shown in Table 13.5.

TABLE 13.5   Results from Machine Productivity Experiment

Machine	Worker 1	2	3	Row Mean
1	4	9	15	
	6	11	17	10.33
2	7	13	16	
	6	15	18	12.50
3	4	12	18	
	6	13	20	12.17
Column mean	5.50	12.17	17.33	
Overall mean				11.67

From Table 13.5 we see that there are differences in productivity between the three machines. However, even more apparent are the large productivity differences between the three workers. Therefore, it seems apparent that "worker" should be a blocking variable that is used to reduce the unexplained variability. The analysis of variance output for this problem, prepared using Minitab, is shown in Exhibit 13.2. The F statistics for the main effects and interactions are as follows.

EXHIBIT 13.2   ANOVA for Machine Productivity Experiment

```
MTB > twoway data in c3 subscripts c1, c2

ANALYSIS OF VARIANCE  output

SOURCE          DF          SS          MS
machine          2       16.33        8.17
worker           2      422.33      211.17
INTERACTION      4       12.33        3.08
ERROR            9       15.00        1.67
TOTAL           17      466.00
```

For the machine:

$$F = \frac{\text{MSA}}{\text{MSE}}$$
$$= \frac{8.17}{1.67}$$
$$= 4.89$$

For the worker:

$$F = \frac{\text{MSB}}{\text{MSE}}$$
$$= \frac{211.17}{1.67}$$
$$= 126.4$$

For the interaction:

$$F = \frac{\text{MSI}}{\text{MSE}}$$
$$= \frac{3.08}{1.67}$$
$$= 1.84$$

These computed values of F are compared with the critical values of F from Table A.4 for different error levels α and the appropriate degrees of freedom for numerator and denominator. The critical value of $F_{\alpha=0.05,2/9} = 4.26$, and therefore the machine productivities, are significantly different at the $\alpha = 0.05$ error level. The critical value of $F_{\alpha=0.01,2/9} = 8.02$, and therefore the operator effect, is significant at the $\alpha = 0.01$

error level. The critical value of $F_{\alpha=0.05,4/9} = 3.63$ and therefore the interaction is not significant at the $\alpha = 0.05$ level.[2]

In this example we see the importance of including the worker variable as a blocking variable. Without the blocking variable the error mean square would have been much larger, and we would not have been able to conclude that the machines have different productivity levels. In Exhibit 13.3 the analysis of variance using only one factor is presented. The differences between workers contribute to the error term, and the mean square for error is 30 instead of the mean square error of 1.67 that occurred when workers were included in the two-factor analysis of variance, presented in Exhibit 13.2.   □

EXHIBIT 13.3   One-Way ANOVA for Machine Productivity

```
MTB > oneway data in c3 levels in c1

ANALYSIS OF VARIANCE ON output
SOURCE       DF        SS          MS          F
machine       2       16.3         8.2        0.27
ERROR        15      449.7        30.0
TOTAL        17      466.0
                                    INDIVIDUAL 95 PCT CI'S FOR MEAN
                                    BASED ON POOLED STDEV
LEVEL    N      MEAN      STDEV
-----+---------+---------+---------+-----------+---------+--------+-----
1        6     10.333     5.046    (------------*------------)
2        6     12.500     4.930          (-------------*-----------)

3        6     12.167     6.338          (-------------*-----------)

-----+---------+---------+---------+-POOLED----+---------+--------+-----
STDEV =     5.475                      7.0        10.5      14.0     17.5
```

The examples that we have presented up to this point have had the same number of observations for each factor level and for cells defined by combinations of factor levels. In many situations, especially with larger problems, such balance is not possible. The basic analysis strategy is the same if the cell sizes are not equal. However, the computational equations become more complex, even though they follow the same reasoning used to develop the equations for balanced problems. These computational complexities are handled in all good statistical computer programs.

---

[2] Some statisticians would recommend including interaction effects that are not statistically significant with the error mean square. If that recommendation were followed in this problem, the interaction sum of squares would be combined with the error sum of squares. As a result, the mean square for error would be increased along with the degrees of freedom for error. These changes would not have changed the conclusions regarding the effect of machine or worker on productivity.

Problem Exercises

13.7   The weight of raw peanuts in a nominal 100-pound bag is believed to depend on the supplier and on the length of time since delivery. To test this, randomly selected bags from different suppliers and length of time since delivery were weighed. The time since delivery was grouped into group I, less than 45 days, and group II, more than 45 days. The results were

   Supplier 1:   I, 101.1, 100.5;   II, 99.4, 99.8
   Supplier 2:   I, 101.9, 102.1;   II, 100.6, 100.9
   Supplier 3:   I, 98.6, 99.0;   II, 98.1, 98.3

   (a) Is there evidence to support the claim that weight differences exist between suppliers and/or between length of time since delivery?
   (b) Is there an interaction effect?

13.8   Numbercheckers, Inc., a regional accounting team, wishes to compare the levels of accounts receivables grouped by hardware and clothing sales for three different retail stores. Random samples were obtained from each of the three stores and the receivable values were

   Store 1, clothing: 145,   126,   118
   Store 1, hardware: 198,   204,   192
   Store 2, clothing: 110,   120,   128
   Store 2, hardware: 172,   176,   180
   Store 3, clothing: 135,   128,   150
   Store 3, hardware: 156,   159,   163

   (a) Do the three stores have differences in the mean receivables?
   (b) Are there differences in mean receivables between clothing and hardware sales?
   (c) Are there interactions between stores and type of merchandise?

13.9   Numbercheckers, Inc. has also compared the age in days of accounts receivables grouped by clothing and hardware sales for three different retail stores. Random samples were obtained from each of the three stores and the receivable ages were

   Store 1, clothing: 10,   8,   12,   9
   Store 1, hardware: 11,   9,   8,   13
   Store 2, clothing: 16,   17,   19,   15
   Store 2, hardware: 14,   18,   16,   20
   Store 3, clothing: 26,   28,   24,   27
   Store 3, hardware: 24,   26,   22,   20

   (a) Do the three stores have differences in the age of their receivables?
   (b) Are there differences in the age of receivables by product group?
   (c) Are there interaction effects?

13.10 Deep Zero, Inc. has developed a new snow ski design that it intends to bring to market. They have tested it for men and women in three different age groups of skiers. As part of the survey, they asked randomly selected individuals in each age group the price that they would be willing to pay for this new ski. The results were

   Age group 16–25, men: 300,   320,   330
   Age group 16–25, women: 280,   270,   275
   Age group 26–45, men: 200,   230,   250

Age group 26–45, women: 180,   185,   190
Age group 46–60, men: 250,   260,   270
Age group 46–60, women: 190,   200,   180

(a) Do the three age groups have different responses in terms of a market price for this new ski?
(b) Do men and women differ in their responses?
(c) Are there interaction terms?

13.5 EXPERIMENTAL DESIGN

There are many analysis of variance applications in which two factors are not sufficient. In addition, a number of complex experimental design models have been developed for a wide variety of applications. To obtain a good understanding of analysis of variance, one must take several courses.

If you have need for analysis of variance models with more than two factors, I suggest that you prepare the analysis using dummy variable multiple regression. This approach is presented in Chapter 16. Any analysis of variance problem can be modeled using dummy variables. At this level of your statistical development it is better to use a few tools effectively instead of trying to have a minimal knowledge of the entire range of possible analysis techniques.

SUMMARY OF KEY IDEAS

PRACTICE PROBLEM SOLUTION

13.1   First, we compute the subgroup means and the overall grand mean:

$$\bar{Y}_1 = \frac{24 + 26 + 28}{3} = 26$$

$$\bar{Y}_2 = \frac{22 + 23 + 24}{3} = 23$$

$$\bar{Y}_3 = \frac{15 + 17 + 19}{3} = 17$$

$$\bar{Y} = \frac{26 + 23 + 17}{3} = 22$$

Next, the between-group sum of squares is computed:

$$\text{BSS} = \sum_{j=1}^{3} \sum_{i=1}^{3} 3(\bar{Y}_j - \bar{Y})^2$$

$$= 3[(26 - 22)^2 + (23 - 22)^2 + (17 - 22)^2]$$

$$= 3(16 + 1 + 25)$$

$$= 42$$

$$\text{DOF} = 3 - 1 = 2$$

and then the within-group error sum of squares:

$$\text{ESS} = \sum_{j=1}^{3} \sum_{i=1}^{3} (Y_{ij} - \bar{Y}_j)^2$$

$$= (24 - 26)^2 + (26 - 26)^2 + (28 - 26)^2 + (22 - 23)^2 + (23 - 23)^2$$

$$+ (24 - 23)^2 + (15 - 17)^2 + (17 - 17)^2 + (19 - 17)^2$$

$$= 18$$

$$\text{DOF} = 9 - 3 = 6$$

The mean square errors are

$$\text{MSB} = \frac{42}{2}$$

$$= 21$$

$$\text{MSE} = \frac{18}{6}$$

$$= 3$$

and the calculated F statistic is

$$F_{2,6} = \frac{\text{MSB}}{\text{MSE}}$$

$$= \frac{21}{3}$$

$$= 7$$

The critical value of F from Table A.4 is $F_{0.05,2,6} = 5.14$, and therefore we reject H_0 and conclude that there is a difference in recovery time for the procedures.

CHAPTER PROBLEMS

13.1   A manufacturer receives shipments of component parts for its lawnmower assembly from four different suppliers. Experienced internal inspectors rate the quality of parts using a complex evaluation procedure. The results of their ratings, on a scale from 1 to 20, are

Supplier 1:   18,   17,   16

Supplier 2:   19,   18,   18
Supplier 3:   14,   15,   16
Supplier 4:   18,   19,   20

(a) Compute the variance partitioning and prepare an analysis of variance table.

(b) Is there a difference between suppliers?

13.2 A large regional restaurant chain wanted to know if the family income levels of employees were different in three restaurants in different parts of a large urban area. Three employees were randomly selected in each of the three restaurants and asked a series of questions about family income. The resulting family income sample results are

Restaurant 1:   30,000,   40,000,   36,000
Restaurant 2:   50,000,   48,000,   51,000
Restaurant 3:   42,000,   44,000,   46,000

(a) Compute the variance partitioning and prepare an analysis of variance table.

(b) Is there a difference between employee incomes in the three restaurants?

13.3 A high-circulation personal computer magazine was preparing a story that compared major suppliers of microcomputer repair service. Four microcomputers with similar defects were taken randomly to facilities of each of the three major repair vendors in a region over a one-month period. Independent repair specialists agreed that the costs for the repairs should have been approximately equal. The resulting repair bills in dollars were as follows:

Repair service 1:   38,   50,   40,   46
Repair service 2:   70,   80,   60,   50
Repair service 3:   48,   44,   54,   56

(a) Prepare the analysis of variance table.

(b) Are the service costs the same?

(c) Are any of the three suppliers significantly more expensive?

13.4 A large graduate school of business was studying the performance of students from various undergraduate colleges. In one comparison of four selective liberal arts schools, the final MBA grade-point averages were compared. A random sample of three graduates of each of the four liberal arts colleges were chosen and their final MBA grade-point averages were

College 1:   3.80,   3.81,   3.76
College 2:   3.70,   3.60,   3.50
College 3:   3.50,   3.40,   3.60
College 4:   3.74,   3.40,   3.30

(a) Prepare the analysis of variance table.

(b) Are the students from the different colleges the same with respect to MBA grade-point averages?

(c) Do the students from any of the individual colleges have a significantly higher grade-point average?

13.5 An economic development program in East Africa wanted to determine the relative wood consumption of different cooking devices. With population increases, people are stripping trees from much of the terrain. Thus reforestation efforts must also include efforts to reduce wood consumption. The three stove options considered in this experiment are (1) open fire, (2) traditional mud brick stove, and (3) low-technology metal stove produced in the local economy. Twelve families were selected to participate in the experiment and they were randomly assigned to one of the three stove options. Wood consumption was measured in pounds per week, with the results being:

Open fire: 26, 28, 32, 30
Brick stove: 20, 22, 24, 20
Metal stove: 14, 16, 18, 16

(a) Prepare the analysis of variance table.
(b) Are there differences in the wood consumption among the three cooking devices?
(c) Is there a significant difference between the brick and metal stove?

13.6 An economist is studying post–World War II investment. She decides to compare investment rates for the following 10-year periods: 41–50; 51–60; 61–70; 71–80; 81–90; 91– . Note that you will not have a complete 10 years of data for the first and last intervals. Use the data in the file "Macrel95," which is available on your data disk. Use the routines in your computer statistical package to code the six time intervals as 1, 2, 3, 4, 5, and 6. Also use your statistical package to compute the investment rate—investment divided by GNP.

(a) Use your statistical package to prepare the one-way analysis of variance of investment rate over the year groups.
(b) Was there a difference in investment rate over the six 10-year intervals?

13.7 After completing the previous analysis of investment rate by 10-year periods, the economist wondered if there were differences between Republican and Democratic administrations. Use the data file "Macrel95" and prepare a discrete variable to identify each of the four-year presidential intervals beginning with 1945–48, 1949–52, through 1993– . This may require some additional research on U.S. elections.

(a) Use your computer package to prepare the analysis of variance.
(b) Is there an investment rate difference between presidential administrations?

13.8 After completing the investment rate study in Problem 13.7 the economist was asked to examine government expenditure rates over the same variables. Use your computer statistical package and the data file "Macrel95" to compute government spending rate—government spending divided by gross national product. Compute codes for the four-year presidential intervals as described in earlier problems.

(a) Use your computer package to prepare the analysis of variance.
(b) Is the government spending rate influenced by the presidential administrations?

13.9 An economic development study in South Asia is seeking to identify the best combinations for growing ragii, a local grain. They are interested in comparing three fertilizer strategies: no fertilizer, cow dung, and chemical fertilizer. In addition, the fertilizers were compared with and without irrigation. Table 13.6 contains the production in bushels per acre with two observations per combination.

(a) Compute the two-way analysis of variance.
(b) Are there differences in bushels per acre for the three types of fertilizer?
(c) Does irrigation result in a difference in output?
(d) Is there an interaction between fertilizer and irrigation?

TABLE 13.6   Production of Ragii per Acre

Fertilizer	No Irrigation	Irrigation
No fertilizer	50	58
	60	62
Cow dung	90	110
	100	120
Chemical	70	90
	80	100

13.10 The human resources department of an electronics manufacturing firm is working to improve its training program for production employees. They have developed a plan to compare three training options:
1. The traditional training program used for many years.
2. A computer-assisted interactive training program marketed by a vendor.
3. A vendor-marketed program that uses videotapes and a series of case projects.

They are also interested in knowing if it is better to conduct the training in three concentrated days away from the firm or in six half-day sessions, one per week, conducted on site. They measured the weekly output one month after the completion of training. Table 13.7 contains the data from four observations of each combination. Enter the data into a statistical computer program and compute the analysis of variance.
(a) Is there any difference in worker production for the three training options?
(b) Is it better to conduct concentrated training off site or spread over six weeks on site?

TABLE 13.7   Production for Workers with Training Options

Training Program	Off Site		On Site	
Traditional	10	11	12	8
	9	12	13	14
Computer-assisted	14	16	16	17
	17	19	19	20
Videotape	15	14	17	21
	16	18	15	18

13.11 A Minnesota policy planning agency is seeking to identify variables that influence the tax rate (tax per unit of property value) in small cities in Minnesota. You have been asked to determine the influence of city size and value of housing. City development theory argues that larger cities will have a wider range of problems and generally higher wages for employees. Both of these effects would lead to higher tax rates. Market value of housing could be related in two ways. First, higher average housing values imply a larger total assessed property value, and therefore the same amount of total tax revenue can be obtained with a lower tax rate. An alternative model argues that higher property value is associated with higher income and a demand for more and higher-quality municipal services, which require higher taxes. The data for this study are in a file called "Citydat" which is on your data disk, and the variables are described in the data dictionary. The subsetting variables "Pop73" and "Hseval" are divided into four levels at their quartile points. The intervals for Pop73 are $X_1 \leq 7573$, $7573 < X_2 \leq 9972$, $9972 < X_3 \leq 14,218$, $14,218 < X_4$. The intervals for Hseval, in thousands, are $Z_1 \leq 17.665$; $17.665 < Z_2 \leq 20.301$, $20.301 < Z_3 \leq 24.046$, and $24.046 < Z_4$. Group the observations into four subgroups for each of the variables Pop73 and Hseval using your statistical program system on the computer. Prepare the analysis of variance table for each of the two variables using one-way analysis of variance and answer the following questions:

(a) Does population influence tax rate?

(b) Does the market value of housing influence tax rate?

13.12 The policy planning agency in Problem 13.11 was also interested in the influence of population and housing value on per capita local government expenditures. Repeat the analysis design from Problem 13.11 using "Totexp," total government expenditures, divided by "Pop73," 1973 population, instead of tax rate. "Totexp" is also found in the data file "Citydat" which is on your data disk. You will need to use your statistics package to compute the expenditure rate, by dividing "Totexp" by "Pop73." Then use your statistics package to compute the analysis of variance for each of the classification variables, population and housing value. Then answer the following questions:

(a) Does population influence per capita local government expenditures?

(b) Does average house value influence per capita local government expenditures?

13.13 A Minnesota policy planning agency is seeking to identify variables that influence the tax rate (tax per unit of property value) in small cities in Minnesota. You have been asked to determine the influence of commercial and industrial property on tax rate. City development theory argues that commercial and industrial enterprises increase the amount of assessed property value and hence the base for taxation. However, commercial and industrial activities also increase the demand for city services. They can generate increased traffic volume, which increases the demand for law enforcement and road services. In addition, depending on the business, there might be special needs for the employees, including low-cost housing and social services. These effects could lead to higher tax rates. For this study you will use the percent commercial property and the percent industrial property to measure the relative intensity of commercial and industrial development in the city. The data for this study are in a file called "Citydat" which is on your data disk, and the variables are described in the data dictionary. The subsetting variables "Comper," percent commercial property, and "Indper," percent industrial property, are divided into four levels at their quartile points. The intervals for Comper, expressed in proportions, are $X_1 \leq 0.11388$, $0.11388 < X_2 \leq 0.15930$, $0.15930 < X_3 \leq 0.20826$, and $0.20826 < X_4$. The intervals for Indper, in proportions, are $Z_1 \leq 0.02656$; $0.02656 < Z_2 \leq 0.04657$, $0.04657 < Z_3 \leq 0.09623$, and $0.09623 < Z_4$. Group the observations into four subgroups for each of the variables "Comper" and "Indper," using your statistical program system on the computer. Prepare the analysis of variance table for each of the two variables and answer the following questions:

(a) Does the amount of commercial property influence tax rate?

(b) Does the amount of industrial property influence tax rate?

13.14 The policy planning agency in Problem 13.13 was also interested in the influence of commercial and industrial property on per capita local government expenditures. Repeat the analysis design from Problem 13.13 using "Totexp," total government expenditures, divided by "Pop73," 1973 population, instead of tax rate. "Totexp" is also found in the data file "Citydat" which is on your data disk. You will need to use your statistics package to compute the expenditure rate, by dividing "Totexp" by "Pop73." Then use your statistics package to compute the analysis of variance for each of the classification variables, percent commercial and percent industrial property.

(a) Does the amount of commercial property influence per capita local government expenditures?

(b) Does the amount of industrial property influence per capita local government expenditures?

13.15 The international trade section of the U.S. Department of Commerce is interested in studying the import and export patterns since World War II. They decide that appropriate measures for this study are (1) imports divided by gross domestic product, both in 1987 dollars, and (2) exports divided by gross domestic product, both in 1987 dollars. These data are contained in the data file "Macrel95," which is stored on the data disk and described in Appendix B at the end of the book. You are asked to subset the data into four time periods and test for differences using analysis of variance. The time periods are 1951–1960, 1961–1970, 1971–1980, and 1981–1990. Use your local statistical computer package to assign these selected years to their appropriate subgroup.

(a) Is there a significant difference in imports and exports as a percentage of GDP over the four time periods?

(b) Identify any subgroups that are significantly different from others using a statistical hypothesis test.

13.16 The agricultural research agency in a midwest farming state is conducting a major study of farming methods that are less capital and energy intensive than are conventional procedures. As part of that study, you are asked to determine if there are significant differences in grain production per acre using different tillage procedures. Specifically, you are asked to compare conventional full tillage, modified tillage, and minimal surface tillage. Use the data in Table 13.8 to conduct your analysis.

TABLE 13.8   Grain Production per Acre by Tillage Method

Tillage Method	Trial			
	1	2	3	4
Full	110	105	90	85
Modified	98	96	86	92
Minimal	99	108	88	94

(a) Is there a significant difference in productivity per acre among the three tilling procedures?

(b) Identify any tillage methods that are significantly different from the others.

13.17 After completing the analysis in Problem 13.16, you discover that trials 1 and 2 also used composted turkey dung fertilizer, while trials 3 and 4 used conventional chemical fertilizers. Repeat the analysis above using this new information. Indicate and explain any differences in your conclusions.

13.18 Pelland Windows produces energy-efficient windows in three separate factories in the northern midwest. The production levels, plant size, and workforce characteristics have been essentially the same over the past 10 years. Arthur Olson, production vice-president, wants to reduce the number of defects in the window assembly operations in the three factories. He has asked you to conduct an experiment to determine if defects could be reduced by modifying the work procedures. You decide to compare three different procedures: (1) conventional supervisor/worker procedure, (2) quality circles, and (3) group-led worker teams. The three procedures were randomly assigned to the three factories for a two-month period. Table 13.9 contains the average number of defective windows per 8-hour shift for each month over two shifts. Trials 1 and 2 are from months 1 and 2 for the night shift, while trials 3 and 4 are from months 1 and 2 for the day shift.

(a) Are there significant differences in the number of defective windows among the three workforce procedures?

(b) Identify any procedures that have significantly different levels of defects.

TABLE 13.9   Number of Defective Windows by Work Procedure

		Trial		
Workforce Procedure	1	2	3	4
Supervisor/worker	25	30	28	32
Quality circles	22	24	26	23
Worker teams	16	15	18	22

13.19 After completing the analysis in Problem 13.18, you discover that the general foremen of the night shifts offered their workers a bottle of wine each if their number of defects was below that of the day shift. Repeat the analysis in Problem 13.18 using this new information.

13.20 The Whole Grain, Inc. cereal company is seeking to reduce the number of underweight cereal packages produced in its factory. You have been asked to conduct experiments to determine the method that will have the greatest effect on reducing underweight packages. The factory has three identical production lines and you randomly assign one of the following three procedures to each line:

1. Monitor and control product density at four key processing locations on the line.
2. Adjust mean package weight on the filling machines upward by 2%.
3. Overhaul packaging machine to reduce variance. To estimate underweight packages, you obtain random samples of size 100 packages from the three production lines at four different times. The times are randomly selected and the plant operators are not

notified in advance when the samples are obtained. The percentage of underweight packages are recorded based on careful weighing of the packages. The proportion underweight statistic can be treated as a random variable and used in the standard analysis of variance procedure. Table 13.10 contains the data from the samples.

(a) Are there significant differences in the percentage of defective packages among the three procedures?
(b) Identify any procedure that is significantly different from the others.

TABLE 13.10   Percent Underweight Packages by Procedure

| | | Trial | | |
Procedure	1	2	3	4
Control density	18	16	14	15
Increase mean	22	21	17	19
Overhaul machine	14	16	13	12

13.21 After you have finished the analysis in Problem 13.20, the plant manager informs you that new cereal drying units were installed on all three lines after the trial 2 data were obtained. Thus the data from trials 1 and 2 used the old drying units, while trials 3 and 4 used the new units. Repeat the analysis as follows:

(a) Are there significant differences in the percentage of defective packages among the three procedures?
(b) Identify any procedure that is significantly different from the others.
(c) Do the new dryers have any effect on underweight packages? How does the effect of the new dryers compare with the effect of the three experimental modifications?

13.22 Central Industries produces circuit boards for a major manufacturer of small process control computers. Central is facing severe price competition from Asian manufacturers. The quality of the Central boards is generally better than that of the competitors, but the price issue must be faced by increasing the number of units produced per hour. The present manufacturing process uses machines by three manufacturers: Benz Ltd., Mashida, and Smith Brothers. You are asked to determine if one of the three machines yields significantly higher productivity. You collect production data for three randomly selected hours on each of the three machines. These are labeled trials 1, 2, and 3 in Table 13.11.

(a) Are there significant differences in productivity for the three machines?

TABLE 13.11   Production (Units per Hour)

| | | Trial | |
Machine Producer	1	2	3
Benz Ltd.	19	18	17
Mashida	16	18	19
Smith Brothers	22	23	24

(b) Is it possible to identify clearly that one machine is significantly better than the other two by using a statistical test?

13.23 Return to Problem 13.22 involving Central Industries. After you complete the analysis above, the company installs a computer-controlled parts transfer system to replace its conventional system, which used a forklift and containers. You are asked to repeat the experiment by collecting production data from the three machines and combining them with the data from the previous analysis. Thus you are to test the effects of both machine type and the material-handling system. The data collected using the new material-handling system is shown as trials 4, 5, and 6 in Table 13.12.

(a) Are there significant differences in productivity among the three machines?

(b) Is it possible to identify clearly that one machine is significantly better than the other two by using a statistical test?

(c) Does the new material-handling system increase productivity?

(d) Is there a significant interaction between machine type and the material-handling system?

(e) Based on the analysis in this problem, which machine would you recommend?

TABLE 13.12 Production (Units per Hour)

Machine Producer	Trial		
	4	5	6
Benz Ltd.	22	18	20
Mashida	22	18	19
Smith Brothers	25	26	27

APPENDIX: ANALYSIS-OF-VARIANCE COMPUTATIONS

A.1 Partition Variance Components

The partitioning of variance is determined as follows:

$$\text{TSS} = \sum_{j=1}^{r} \sum_{i=1}^{n_j} (Y_{ij} - \bar{Y})^2$$

$$= \sum_{j=1}^{r} \sum_{i=1}^{n_j} (Y_{ij} - \bar{Y}_j + \bar{Y}_j - \bar{Y})^2$$

$$= \sum_{j=1}^{r} \sum_{i=1}^{n_j} [(Y_{ij} - \bar{Y}_j)^2 + 2(Y_{ij} - \bar{Y}_j)(\bar{Y}_j - \bar{Y}) + (\bar{Y}_j - \bar{Y})^2]$$

$$= \sum_{j=1}^{r} \sum_{i=1}^{n_j} (Y_{ij} - \bar{Y}_j)^2 + \sum_{j=1}^{r} (\bar{Y}_j - \bar{Y}) \sum_{i=1}^{n_j} (Y_{ij} - \bar{Y}_j) + \sum_{j=1}^{r} n_j (\bar{Y}_j - \bar{Y})^2$$

$$= \text{ESS} + 0 + \text{BSS}$$

A.2 Computational Equations for Two-Way Analysis of Variance

The equations presented here show the form for deriving the various sum of square terms. Because of their complexity, most of the computations will be performed on a computer. The computational equations include the following subgroup means:

$$\bar{Y} = \frac{\sum_{j=1}^{r} \sum_{k=1}^{p} \sum_{i=1}^{m} Y_{jki}}{n}$$

$$\bar{Y}_j = \frac{\sum_{k=1}^{p} \sum_{i=1}^{m} Y_{jki}}{p \times m}$$

$$\bar{Y}k = \frac{\sum_{j=1}^{r} \sum_{i=1}^{m} Y_{jki}}{r \times m}$$

$$\bar{Y}_{jk} = \frac{\sum_{i=1}^{m} Y_{jki}}{m}$$

The components of variance are computed using the following equations:

$$\text{TSS} = \sum_{j=1}^{r} \sum_{k=1}^{p} \sum_{i=1}^{m} (Y_{jki} - \bar{Y})^2$$

$$\text{ASS} = pm \sum_{j=1}^{r} (\bar{Y}_j - \bar{Y})^2$$

$$\text{BSS} = rm \sum_{k=1}^{p} (\bar{Y}_k - \bar{Y})^2$$

$$\text{ISS} = m \sum_{j=1}^{r} \sum_{k=1}^{p} [(\bar{Y}_{jk} - \bar{Y}) - (\bar{Y}_j - \bar{Y}) - (\bar{Y}_k - \bar{Y})]^2$$

$$= m \sum_{j=1}^{r} \sum_{k=1}^{p} [\bar{Y}_{jk} - \bar{Y}_j - \bar{Y}_k + \bar{Y}]^2$$

$$\text{ESS} = \sum_{j=1}^{r} \sum_{k=1}^{p} \sum_{i=1}^{m} (Y_{jki} - \bar{Y}_{jk})^2$$

14

Simple Least-Squares Regression

The power of regression modeling tools provides the motivation to learn more.

14.1 USES OF LINEAR REGRESSION

In this chapter we present simple regression, followed in Chapter 15 by multiple regression. The development in Chapter 3 of regression as a description of the relationship between two variables is extended to develop regression as a statistical inference tool.

John Holden, president of Holden Farms, is responsible for purchasing mixed feed for his turkey producing operation. In the past he has picked a quantity and then added a safety factor to be sure that they would not run out of feed. As a result, there is typically an excess supply, and a portion of the feed routinely spoils and must be destroyed. John would like a better procedure for determining the amount of feed to be ordered. For the past two years he has collected weekly data on the quantity of feed consumed and the number of live turkeys under production. In this chapter we learn how to help John prepare a better model to predict the amount of feed to be ordered.

Linear relationships are used extensively in business and economics. In business, linear relationships are used routinely to estimate output as a function of inputs (Key Idea 14.1). Product sales as a function of price or disposable income for various regions are important for planning production and distribution schedules. Government policymakers want to know the relationship between marginal tax rates and savings or investment.

For example, the production manager wants to know the predicted sales given that the price is set. In contrast, the vice-president of finance wants to know the change in sales that would result from a $1 increase or decrease in price per unit. The former result would be used to schedule the required production and distribution facilities. In contrast, the marginal rate of change could be used to determine the effect of price changes on total revenue. In Chapter 3 we introduced correlation and regression

---

Key Idea 14.1: Linear Regression Outcomes

Linear regression provides two important results:

1. Predicted values for the dependent or endogenous variable as a function of independent or exogenous variables.
2. Marginal change of the dependent variable that results from a one-unit change of the independent or exogenous variable.

---

analysis and developed a simple demand function (plywood sales versus price) and then used a computer to develop the relationship between quantity sold and price for a food product. That example used data from a supermarket over a one-year period. In this chapter we extend the descriptive model and develop procedures for statistical inference. The presentation will build on the ideas in Chapter 3, which you may wish to review.

Linear models of the form

$$Y = \beta_0 + \beta_1 X_1$$

can be very useful for representing many processes. For example, if X_1 is the number of workers in a factory and Y is the total output, the model could be used to determine the number of units of output that would be produced given different numbers of workers. The coefficient β_1 is the change in Y given a 1-unit change in X. In this example β_1 is the marginal productivity of labor and β_0 is a constant that adjusts the equation to the observed values of Y. To use the model we must know the values of β_0 and β_1, which are estimated using regression analysis (Key Idea 14.2).

Key Idea 14.2: Least-Squares Regression

Least-squares regression is a procedure for estimating the coefficients β_0 and β_1 from a set of X_1, Y points that have been measured at various levels of system operation.

Development of a linear model requires both data and a theory to support the model. For example, it is possible to discover that the number of sidewalk cracks in urban blocks predicts the death rate. Further investigation does not support the theory that old people trip and hit their heads. Instead, both measures are related to the age of the neighborhood. The relationship between sidewalk cracks and death rate is called a *spurious correlation*.

For a number of years auto insurance companies gave discounts if young drivers had taken a course in driver education. Evidence from reduced claims supported this position. What they did not realize is that when driver education was voluntary it attracted young people whose parents insisted that they drive safely. Thus, when driver education became mandatory, the selection effect was removed and reduced claims ceased. The initial spurious relationship was actually used as evidence to support a business policy. Regression analysis will always give the best fit to a given set of data. However, unless the data represent an underlying system that is related to your problem, the resulting regression equation will not help your analysis.

Our development of regression begins with a previous example. From Chapter 3 we recall that Agnes Larson and her friend Sally Goldberg developed a demand function to estimate the quantity of plywood sold as a function of price. The data for this problem are shown in Table 14.1 and a graphical plot is presented in Figure 14.1.

TABLE 14.1   Plywood Sales Versus Price

Observation, i	Price per Piece, X_1	Number of Pieces, Y
1	6	80
2	7	60
3	8	70
4	9	40
5	10	0

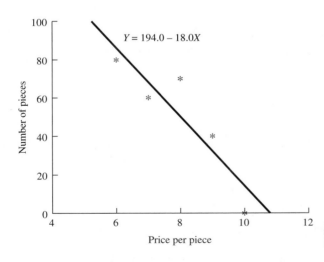

$Y = 194.0 - 18.0X$

Figure 14.1   Plywood Demand Function: Quantity Versus Price

From that analysis we found that the linear regression model was

$$\hat{Y} = 194.0 - 18.0X_1$$

where $\hat{Y}$ is the number of sheets of plywood sold and X_1 is the price per sheet in dollars.

Now we begin a formal study of regression analysis. As you learn to use regression you will begin to identify many applications from other courses and from your experience. The power of regression modeling tools provides motivation to learn more and to try different options in business and economic problems.

As you study the material there are several things to keep in mind. First, the applications use sampling distributions, estimation, and hypothesis testing—that is, statistical inference. You will need to use concepts developed in previous chapters. Second, the study of relationships between variables is greatly assisted by preparing simple graphical sketches and computer-generated plots. These pictures assist learning and provide important insights into actual problems.

In applying regression analysis (Key Idea 14.3), we first determine if there is a relationship between the variables. A small factory owner might believe that there is a relationship between ambient temperature in the factory and the number of units produced. However, effort devoted to developing a temperature-based production model would be wasted if temperature and production are not related. Finding that a relationship exists is often the most important study result. Graphs such as Figure 14.1 and the correlation coefficient can be used to identify linear relationships, as we learned in Chapter 3. We also develop several hypothesis-testing procedures.

Key Idea 14.3: Results from Regression Analysis

The process of regression analysis provides answers to three important questions:

1. Is there a relationship between the variables being considered?
2. What is the relationship?
3. What is the associated variability?

Next, the coefficients β_0 and β_1, which define the relationship, are estimated using the least-squares algorithm. Finally, variance estimators such as $S_{\hat{\beta}_1}^2$ are developed to provide measures of variability. These will be used to prepare confidence intervals and to test various regression model hypotheses.

14.2 LEAST-SQUARES COEFFICIENT ESTIMATORS

Our goal is to determine, using a set of (x_i, y_i) observations, the "best" equation for the linear relationship between X and Y. As shown in the example in Figure 14.1, the points do not lie exactly on a straight line. Thus we need to find the line that best fits the data observed (Key Idea 14.4). The least-squares method chooses this line to

---

Key Idea 14.4: Linear Population Equation Model

The linear model, including a measure of unexplained variability ϵ, is

$$y_i = \beta_0 + \beta_1 x_{1i} + \epsilon_i$$

where the pairs of observations x_{1i}, y_i are designated by an index $i = 1, \ldots, n$. β_1 is the change in Y for each unit change in X_1, and β_0 is a constant that adjusts the linear equation to the data. The new term, ϵ_i, is the measure of random and unexplained variability, which is assumed to have a mean of zero and a variance of σ^2. Initially, we assume that ϵ has a normal distribution, so that we can perform statistical inference procedures. Later that assumption will be dropped and replaced by the central limit theorem.

---

minimize the sum of the squared deviation of points from the line. By squaring the deviation of each point from the line, we avoid adding positive and negative deviations. Since deviations from the line are squared, the method is influenced more by points that are a longer distance from the equation line. Least squares provides coefficient estimators with excellent statistical properties. In addition, these estimators make sense intuitively. The combination of inherent simplicity and useful results explains the continued popularity of least squares for deriving linear equations for business and economic applications.

14.2.1 Regression Procedure

The structure of the model and its error distribution are shown in Figure 14.2. Each value of X_1 (where $X_1 = 1, 2, 3, 4, 5$) is assumed to have an associated random variable Y. The mean for this random variable is given by the equation

$$E[Y \mid X] = \mu_Y = \beta_0 + \beta_1 X_1$$

In addition, Y contains an error component ϵ which is assumed initially to have a normal distribution. The resulting value of y_i, for every x_{1i}, is given by the equation

$$y_i = \beta_0 + \beta_1 x_{1i} + \epsilon_i$$

Thus y_i contains two parts:

1. The "information" supplied by the linear component, $\beta_0 + \beta_1 X_1$.
2. The error ϵ_i, which is a single observation from a population of normally distributed values of ϵ.

The least-squares assumptions are summarized in Key Idea 14.5.

Since the value of $\beta_0 + \beta_1 X_1$ is fixed but unknown, we can say that Y given X_1 has the same variance, σ^2, as ϵ_i. Recall from Chapter 6 that adding a constant to a

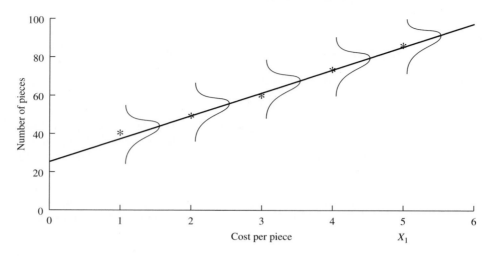

Figure 14.2   Linear Model with Error Distribution

Key Idea 14.5: Least-Squares Assumptions

The least-squares estimation and inference procedure uses the following assumptions:

1. The X_1's are known exactly without random error.
2. The variance σ^2 is constant over the range of the independent variable X_1. This is defined as *homoscedasticity*.
3. $\epsilon_i \sim N(0, \sigma^2)$.
4. ϵ_i and x_{1i} are independent.
5. The ϵ_i's from each observation are independent.

---

random variable results in a new random variable with a different mean but the same variance. Thus the data model assumes a set of X_1's, each of which has a normally distributed dependent variable Y. The mean for this Y depends on the value of X_1. If the Y's did not contain a random error term, all the X_1, Y points would lie on a straight line. But they do contain an error term, and therefore we typically have a plot of the data point that looks like Figure 14.3. This example shows the quantity of plywood that would be supplied given various market prices. For the plywood supply example the data points have the following x_{1i}, y_i coordinates:

$$(1, 10) \qquad (2, 40) \qquad (3, 80) \qquad (4, 60) \qquad (5, 90)$$

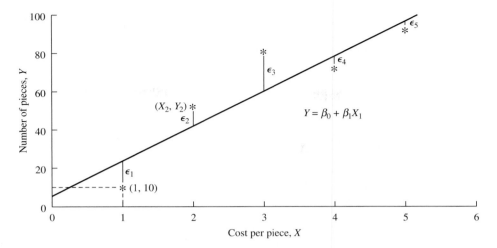

Figure 14.3   Population Supply Model with Data

In Figure 14.3 the population equation

$$Y = \beta_0 + \beta_1 X_1$$

is shown together with the observed data points. Here the equation with its coefficients β_0 and β_1 are defined as being known exactly. Note that the ϵ_i is the difference between the observed value and the linear population equation. There is a different value of ϵ_i for each data point. The entire set of ϵ_i's are random variables from a population with mean 0 and variance σ^2.

To have a useful model, we need to compute estimates for β_0 and β_1. These estimates will be computed from the data using estimators, which compute $\hat{\beta}_0$ and $\hat{\beta}_1$ as functions of x_i, y_i data. The resulting estimates have error and therefore we never obtain the exact equation:

$$y_i = \beta_0 + \beta_1 x_{1i} + \epsilon_i$$

However, using the estimates $\hat{\beta}_0$ and $\hat{\beta}_1$ we can obtain an approximation (Key Idea 14.6):

$$\hat{Y}_i = \hat{\beta}_0 + \hat{\beta}_1 x_{1i}$$

The observed values of y_i are then equal to

$$y_i = \hat{\beta}_0 + \hat{\beta}_1 x_{1i} + \hat{e}_i$$

where the residual, $\hat{e}_i$, is the observed difference between y_i and the esimated value, $\hat{Y}_i$. (Note that $\epsilon_i \neq \hat{e}_i$.) The supply model derived using least squares in shown in Figure 14.4 with the data points and their residuals.

To obtain the estimates, we first define

$$\hat{e}_i = y_i - \hat{Y}_i$$

Key Idea 14.6: Least-Squares Procedure

The least-squares line is obtained by estimating the coefficients of the function

$$\hat{Y}_i = \hat{\beta}_0 + \hat{\beta}_1 x_{1i}$$

so that the resulting equation is a best linear approximation of the relationship between Y and X_1 using the least-squares principle.

Select the coefficient estimators $\hat{\beta}_0$ and $\hat{\beta}_1$ to minimize the sum of squared deviations of the observed values of the dependent variable y_i from the predicted values $\hat{Y}_i$.

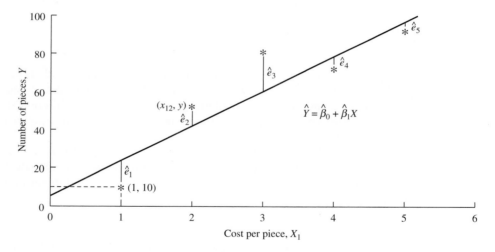

Figure 14.4   Least-Squares Supply Model with Data

the observed deviation or *residual* of the observed value y_i from the predicted equation value $\hat{Y}_i$, as shown in Figure 14.4. Then using simple algebra we develop the exact definition of the function to be minimized. The least-squares algorithm is stated in Key Idea 14.7.

The derivation of the coefficient estimators $\hat{\beta}_0$ and $\hat{\beta}_1$ is shown in the chapter appendix. Students that understand differential calculus are encouraged to study that development. It provides important additional understanding of the least-squares procedure. However, the remainder of this chapter can be understood without a complete understanding of the derivation in the appendix.

Key Idea 14.7: Least-Squares Algorithm

Minimize

$$\text{ESS} = \sum_{i=1}^{n} \hat{e}_i^2$$

$$= \sum_{i=1}^{n} (y_i - \hat{Y}_i)^2$$

$$= \sum_{i=1}^{n} [y_i - (\hat{\beta}_0 + \hat{\beta}_1 x_{1i})]^2$$

where ESS is the error sum of squares, or the sum of the squared Y deviations from the estimated least-squares equation, and

$$\hat{e}_i = y_i - \hat{Y}_i$$

The least-squares estimators $\hat{\beta}_0$ and $\hat{\beta}_1$ are derived by applying differential calculus (see the chapter appendix) to the ESS equation. The partial derivatives with respect to the unknown coefficients $\hat{\beta}_0$ and $\hat{\beta}_1$ provide two "normal equations" that can be solved for the coefficients as functions of the observed data.

$$\hat{\beta}_1 = \frac{\sum_{i=1}^{n}(x_{1i} - \bar{X}_1)(y_i - \bar{Y})}{\sum_{i=1}^{n}(x_{1i} - \bar{X}_1)^2}$$

$$= \frac{\sum_{i=1}^{n}(x_{1i} - \bar{X}_1)y_i}{\sum_{i=1}^{n}(x_{1i} - \bar{X}_1)^2}$$

which can also be expressed as

$$\hat{\beta}_1 = r_{xy}\frac{S_Y}{S_{X_1}}$$

and then we can show that

$$\hat{\beta}_0 = \bar{Y} - \hat{\beta}_1 \bar{X}_1$$

The coefficient estimators, $\hat{\beta}_0$ and $\hat{\beta}_1$, and the resulting linear equations are valid only over the range of the X_1 observations used for the estimates. Attempts to extrapolate beyond the data are based entirely on the additional knowledge of the analyst.

The results of the derivation in the appendix are the coefficient estimators

$$\hat{\beta}_1 = \frac{\sum_{i=1}^{n}(x_{1i} - \bar{X}_1)(y_i - \bar{Y})}{\sum_{i=1}^{n}(x_{1i} - \bar{X}_1)^2}$$

$$= \frac{\sum_{i=1}^{n}(x_{1i} - \bar{X}_1)y_i}{\sum_{i=1}^{n}(x_{1i} - \bar{X}_1)^2}$$

$$\hat{\beta}_0 = \bar{Y} - \hat{\beta}_1\bar{X}_1$$

$\hat{\beta}_1$ measures the change in Y as X_1 changes by 1 unit. This rate of change is an important parameter for many business and economic problems.

Additional understanding of the regression coefficient can be obtained by algebraically transforming the estimator for $\hat{\beta}$ to[1]

$$\hat{\beta}_1 = r_{xy}\frac{S_Y}{S_{X_1}}$$

where r_{xy} is the simple correlation coefficient between X and Y, S_Y is the standard deviation of Y:

$$S_Y = \sqrt{\frac{\sum_{i=1}^{n}(y_i - \bar{Y})^2}{n-1}}$$

and S_{X_1} is the standard deviation of X_1:

$$S_{X_1} = \sqrt{\frac{\sum_{i=1}^{n}(x_{1i} - \bar{X})^2}{n-1}}$$

Does It Make Sense?

The estimator

$$\hat{\beta}_1 = r_{xy}\frac{S_Y}{S_{X_1}}$$

---

[1] The transformation is as follows:

$$\sum_{i=1}^{n}(x_{1i} - \bar{X}_1)(y_i - \bar{Y}) = (n-1)\text{cov}(X_1, Y)$$

$$= (n-1)r_{xy}S_{X_1}S_Y$$

$$\sum_{i=1}^{n}(x_{1i} - \bar{X}_1)^2 = (n-1)S_{X_1}^2$$

$$\hat{\beta}_1 = \frac{r_{xy}(n-1)S_{X_1}S_Y}{(n-1)S_{X_1}^2}$$

$$= r_{xy}\frac{S_Y}{S_{X_1}}$$

is shown to be directly related to the correlation coefficient multiplied by the ratio of the standard deviations in Y and X. From Chapters 3 and 7 we recall that the correlation coefficient, r_{xy}, is a standardized measure of the strength of relationship between two variables. The correlation ranges from -1, which indicates a perfect inverse relationship, to $+1$, which indicates a perfect direct relationship, with 0 indicating no relationship. This link between the correlation coefficient, r_{xy}, and the slope coefficient, $\hat{\beta}_1$, is an important connection.

The properties of the coefficient estimator indicate its strength and value. The chapter appendix shows that the coefficient estimator, $\hat{\beta}_1$, is unbiased. It can also be shown that the least-squares estimators have the smallest variance of any estimator that is a linear function of the y_i's. Thus statisticians say that the least-squares estimators are the best linear unbiased estimators (BLUE). □

In Chapter 3 the coefficient estimates were computed from the data as

$$\hat{\beta}_1 = r_{xy} \frac{S_Y}{S_{X_1}}$$

$$= (-0.90) \times \frac{31.61}{1.58}$$

$$= -18.0$$

$$\hat{\beta}_0 = \bar{Y} - \hat{\beta}_1 \bar{X}_1$$

$$= 50.0 - (-18.0) \times 8.0$$

$$= 194.0$$

and therefore the equation is

$$\hat{Y} = 194.0 - 18.0 X_1$$

where $\hat{Y}$ is the quantity of plywood in number of sheets and X_1 is the price per sheet in dollars.

In some cases people interpret the standard form constant, $\hat{\beta}_0$, as the mean value or intercept when X_1 is zero. Although this is true mathematically, caution should be used before attempting to infer behavior of real systems based on extrapolating X_1 back to zero (Key Idea 14.8). Unless the system has been measured at $X_1 = 0$, one can only infer this behavior based on knowledge beyond the data.

Practice Problem 14.1: Cereal Demand Function

John Smith, director of sales for Rolled Oats Cereal, has asked you to develop a demand function for weekly cereal sales. You obtain a sample of the past 40 weeks for use in your analysis. After data entry the computer staff prepares the following summary statistics:

$$r_{xy} = -0.70 \qquad \bar{Y} = 1000 \qquad \bar{X} = 120 \qquad S_y = 100 \qquad S_x = 50$$

Key Idea 14.8: Alternative Linear Regression Equation Form

The regression equation is sometimes presented in the form

$$\hat{Y} = \bar{Y} + \hat{\beta}_1(X_1 - \bar{X})$$

to emphasize that the regression equation goes through the sample means of Y and X_1. This form shows that the estimated equation is "centered" on the sample means and applies only over the range of the X_1's and Y's used to estimate the coefficients.

---

where Y is the total sales in 100-pound cartons and X is the price in dollars. Using these data, prepare responses to the following questions.

(a) Compute the constant and slope coefficient and write the least-squares estimate for the linear demand function.

(b) If the carton price were increased from \$90 to \$120, what would be the change in total demand?

***(c)** What price would provide the maximum total revenue from cereal sales?[2]

☐

The solutions for all Practice Problems are given at the end of the chapter.

Problem Exercises

14.1   Why should an analyst be concerned about an observation that has a large residual from a linear regression model?

14.2   Describe and compare the information provided by a correlation coefficient and a least-squares regression slope coefficient.

14.3   Using the least-squares estimator in Key Idea 14.7, explain why the variance of $\hat{\beta}_1$ is a linear function of the model error, ϵ.

14.4   Why do business and economic analysts often express the regression model in terms of the sample means instead of using the intercept $\hat{\beta}_0$?

14.5   Explain why all of the regression output can be computed if we know the sample size, the two-variable sample means and sample variances, and the sample correlation coefficient.

14.6   Given the regression equation

$$Y = 10 + 5X$$

---

[2] Many of the concepts developed in this and later chapters will include sections that use calculus in the development. These sections are indicated by a star. You can learn the statistical procedures without these sections. However, your understanding will be increased if you can use these calculus-based sections.

(a) How much does Y increase when X increases by 3?

(b) What is the predicted value of Y when $x = 20$?

(c) Suppose that one of the observed data points is $(x = 10, y = 65)$. What is the residual for that observation?

14.7   The Brown Manufacturing Company is analyzing its processes to identify strategies for reducing the number of defects produced per hour. As part of its analysis the following regression model was prepared: $Y = 150 - 7X$, where Y is the number of defects produced per hour and X is the number of hours spent setting up and adjusting the manufacturing process $(10 \leq X \leq 20)$. This regression model is used to improve their manufacturing process.

(a) How much reduction in defects results when X increases by 3?

(b) What is the predicted number of defects when $x = 18$?

(c) Suppose that one of the observed data points is $(x = 10, y = 70)$. What is the residual for that observation?

14.8   Acme Cabinet Works has studied the relationship between price per base cabinet and the number of units sold per week during the past year. The summary statistics for the $n = 52$ observations are $r_{xy} = -0.70$, $\bar{Y} = 400$, $\bar{X} = 100$, $S_y = 80$, and $S_x = 40$, where Y is the total number of base cabinets sold in a week and X is the price in dollars for that week.

(a) What are the constant and slope coefficient for the regression model? Write the equation.

(b) Write the equation in the alternative form using the sample means instead of the intercept.

(c) What is the increase in sales for each $1 decrease in price?

14.9   The cost of new houses in a small college town is believed to be related to the number of square feet of floor space. A sample of 30 new houses provided the following summary statistics: $r_{xy} = 0.80$, $\bar{Y} = 60,000$, $\bar{X} = 1200$, $S_y = 8000$, and $S_x = 80$, where X is the total square feet of floor space and Y is the price in dollars.

(a) What are the constant and slope coefficient for the regression model? Write the equation.

(b) Write the equation in the alternative form using the sample means instead of the intercept.

(c) What is the increase in price for each additional square foot?

(d) A 1300-square-foot house has a price of $80,000. What is the residual price for that house?

14.10 The construction cost for turkey growing sheds, complete with automated feeding equipment, is believed to be linearly related to the number of turkeys grown in the shed. A study of 40 recently constructed sheds in Minnesota and South Dakota provided the following results: $r_{xy} = 0.60$, $\bar{Y} = 160,000$, $\bar{X} = 1200$, $S_y = 8000$, and $S_x = 80$, where X is the number of turkeys that can be grown in the shed and Y is the price in dollars.

(a) What are the constant and slope coefficient for the regression model? Write the equation.

(b) Write the equation in the alternative form using the sample means instead of the intercept.

(c) What is the increase in price for each additional turkey?

(d) A 1500-turkey shed has a price of $240,000. What is the residual price for that shed?

14.3 PARTITIONING VARIABILITY

In Section 14.2 we showed how to estimate the coefficients of the regression line. In this section we study the variability of the dependent variable Y and indicate how it can be partitioned into "information" and "error." In the regression model only Y is assumed to have variability and the X_1's are fixed. If we did not know about the X_1's, we might use the mean, $\bar{Y}$, to represent the sample of observed y_i's. Then the deviations of points from the mean would be used to estimate the sample variance, S_Y^2, or the total variability about the mean, $\sum_{i=1}^{n}(y_i - \bar{Y})^2$. If there is a relationship between Y and X_1, such as seen in Figure 14.4, the deviations from the regression line will be smaller than the deviations about the sample mean. Thus the regression line provides "information" that reduces "error."

In the regression model the dependent variable Y contains both an information component, $\beta_0 + \beta_1 X_1$, which is a function of X_1, and a random error component, ϵ. Using the method of analysis of variance, we separate the total variability of Y into a component related to the variability of the regression line, $\hat{Y}$, about the mean, $\bar{Y}$, and a component related to the variability about the regression line, $\hat{Y}$. The latter component is an estimate for the variance, σ^2, in the least-squares model. This variance is used to develop confidence intervals and hypothesis tests.

Assume for a moment that we only had a sample of the y_i's instead of the (x_{1i}, y_i) pairs. In that case the sample mean, $\bar{Y}$, would be a measure of the information content in the Y's. In Figure 14.5 we see that there are large deviations from the line $Y = \bar{Y} = 60$.

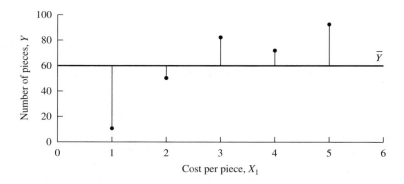

Figure 14.5 Components of Total Sum of Squares

The sample variance would be

$$S_Y^2 = \frac{\sum_{i=1}^{n}(y_i - \bar{Y})^2}{n - 1}$$

The numerator of the sample variance is defined as the total sum of squares (TSS), where

$$\text{TSS} = \sum_{i=1}^{n}(y_i - \bar{Y})^2$$

The variation of the Y's about the mean line in Figure 14.5 is equal to TSS. The least-squares estimates of the coefficients were obtained by minimizing the error sum of squares,

$$\text{ESS} = \sum_{i=1}^{n}(y_i - \hat{Y}_i)^2$$

In Figure 14.6, ESS is the total variation of the points about the least-squares regression line. The difference between TSS and ESS is the reduction in variability from using the regression line instead of using the sample mean $\bar{Y}$. We say that the regression line has "explained" some of the variability and increased our understanding.

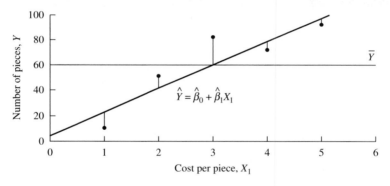

Figure 14.6   Variation of y_i's from $\hat{Y}$

Each x_{1i} has three measures of Y: the observed value y_i, the predicted value $\hat{Y}_i$ (on the regression line), and the sample mean $\bar{Y}$. These three measures are used to develop the analysis of variance or partitioning of variability.

$$\begin{aligned}
\text{TSS} &= \sum_{i=1}^{n}(y_i - \bar{Y})^2 \\
&= \sum_{i=1}^{n}(y_i - \hat{Y}_i + \hat{Y}_i - \bar{Y})^2 \\
&= \sum_{i=1}^{n}(y_i - \hat{Y}_i)^2 + \sum_{i=1}^{n}(\hat{Y}_i - \bar{Y})^2 + 2\sum_{i=1}^{n}(y_i - \hat{Y}_i)(\hat{Y}_i - \bar{Y}) \\
&= \text{ESS} + \text{RSS}
\end{aligned}$$

The new term RSS is defined as the regression sum of squares[3] and indicates the amount of variability that is "explained" by the regression (Key Idea 14.9).

Key Idea 14.9: Partitioning of Variability

The summary identity is

$$TSS = RSS + ESS$$

total variability of y_i about $\bar{Y}$ = variability of $\hat{Y}_i$ about $\bar{Y}$

$$+ \text{ variability of } y_i \text{ about } \hat{Y}_i$$

where[4]

$$TSS = \text{total sum of squares}$$

$$= \sum_{i=1}^{n}(y_i - \bar{Y})^2$$

$$RSS = \text{regression sum of squares}$$

$$= \sum_{i=1}^{n}(\hat{Y}_i - \bar{Y})^2$$

$$ESS = \text{error sum of squares}$$

$$= \sum_{i=1}^{n}(y_i - \hat{Y}_i)^2$$

---

[3] $\displaystyle\sum_{i=1}^{n}(y_i - \hat{Y})(\hat{Y}_i - \bar{Y}) = \sum_{i=1}^{n}(y_i - \hat{Y}_i)(\bar{Y} + \hat{\beta}_1(x_{1i} - \bar{X}_1) - \bar{Y})$

$$= \hat{\beta}_1 \sum_{i=1}^{n}((x_{1i} - \bar{X}_1)y_i - (x_{1i} - \bar{X}_1)(\hat{Y}_i))$$

$$= \hat{\beta}_1 \sum_{i=1}^{n}((x_{1i} - \bar{X}_1)y_i - (x_{1i} - \bar{X}_1)(\hat{\beta}_0 + \hat{\beta}_1(x_{1i} - \bar{X}_1)))$$

$$= \hat{\beta}_1 \sum_{i=1}^{n}((x_{1i} - \bar{X}_1)y_i - \hat{\beta}_0(x_{1i} - \bar{X}_1) - \hat{\beta}_1(x_{1i} - \bar{X}_1)^2$$

$$= 0$$

[4] The last result comes from the least-squares derivation in the chapter appendix.

14.3.1 Coefficient of Determination

The coefficient of determination is defined in Key Idea 14.10. Some writers assign great importance to the result that a regression model explains 50% or 90% of the total variability. However, R^2 depends not only on the explained variability RSS but also on the initial total variability TSS. Thus a high R^2 indicates either that the regression equation is close to all the points or that the Y variables have a wide range. Using R^2 to compare several different regression models that all have the same set of Y observations, and thus the same TSS, is particularly useful because high R^2 implies small ESS.

Key Idea 14.10: Coefficient of Determination, R^2

A measure of regression effectiveness is the **coefficient of determination** or R^2, which is equal to

$$R^2 = \frac{\text{RSS}}{\text{TSS}}$$

$$= \frac{\text{TSS} - \text{ESS}}{\text{TSS}}$$

$$= 1 - \frac{\text{ESS}}{\text{TSS}}$$

Careful analysis shows that R^2 can have values from 0 to 1. Values close to 1 imply a smaller ESS and thus an equation that is close to the data points. R^2 is often interpreted as the *percent explained variability*. R^2 can be used to compare regression equations for goodness of fit to the data if the same y_i observations are used for each equation.

Hazards of R^2.   The problem with using R^2 as an absolute measure of the quality of a regression equation can be seen in the following simple example. The regression equation in Figure 14.7 has TSS equal to 4000 and ESS equal to 760. Therefore,

$$R^2 = 1 - \frac{\text{ESS}}{\text{TSS}}$$

$$= 1 - \frac{760}{4000}$$

$$= 0.81$$

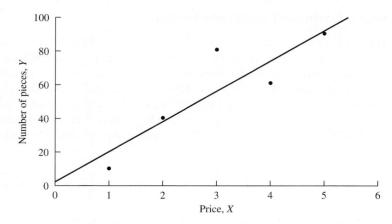

Figure 14.7   Regression with Larger TSS

Now consider the regression line in Figure 14.8. Each point is the same distance from the regression line, and thus ESS is equal to 760, which is the same as the former regression. However, TSS is only 1400. The smaller TSS results from a narrower range in the original Y's and a smaller slope for the regression line. Therefore,

$$R^2 = 1 - \frac{\text{ESS}}{\text{TSS}}$$

$$= 1 - \frac{760}{1400}$$

$$= 0.46$$

which is smaller than the R^2 from the former equation. If we had compared only the R^2 for the two equations, we would have concluded that the equation in Figure 14.7

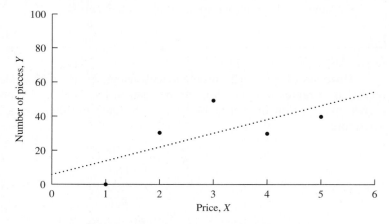

Figure 14.8   Regression with Smaller TSS

had a much better fit. However, each equation has the same distance from the data points. Thus the equations have the same fit.

Does It Make Sense?

Based on the analysis above, we should be careful about assigning too much importance to the absolute value of R^2 (Key Idea 14.11). Statements such as "The regression model explained only 40% of the variability" can be misleading. After all, the real concern should be with the differences between the regression line and the individual points as measured by ESS. As a general observation, regression equations for economic time-series data generally have R^2 above 0.80, while cross-section data will have R^2 around 0.40 to 0.60, and data on individual human behavior will be between 0.10 and 0.20.   □

Key Idea 14.11: Correlation and R^2

The multiple coefficient of determination, R^2, for simple regression is equal to the simple correlation squared:

$$R^2 = r_{xy}^2$$

as shown in the chapter appendix. Thus the simple correlation coefficient r_{xy}, which measures the strength of the relationship between variables, is equal to the square root of the percent explained variability for the regression equation. This provides an important link between correlation and the concept of partitioning variability into explained and unexplained portions.

14.3.2 Variance Estimator: $\hat{\sigma}^2$

The partitioning of variability also provides an estimator for model variance. Recall that in the linear model

$$y_i = \beta_0 + \beta_1 x_{1i} + \epsilon_i$$

we assumed that ϵ_i had a uniform variance σ^2. This variance provides the basis for all confidence intervals and hypothesis tests associated with the estimated regression model.

Since σ^2 is in general unknown, an estimator is needed. See Key Idea 14.12. Note that the divisor is $n - 2$ because two parameters, $\hat{\beta}_0$ and $\hat{\beta}_1$, are estimated in the regression process, in contrast to only one parameter, $\bar{Y}$, used to compute S_Y^2. If there were only two observations, the regression line would go through both of them and variance could not be estimated. In contrast, two points would provide data for estimating the variance about the mean, $\bar{Y}$.

Key Idea 14.12: $S^2_{Y|X_1}$: Estimator for σ^2

The estimator for σ^2 is

$$S^2_{Y|X} = \frac{\text{ESS}}{n-2}$$

$$= \frac{\sum_{i=1}^{n}(y_i - \hat{Y}_i)^2}{n-2}$$

defined as the **variance of the estimate** and $S_{Y|X}$ as the **standard error of the estimate**. This notation emphasizes the standard error of Y given that the effect of X_1 has been removed. Degrees of freedom $= n - 2$.

There are many different variances associated with Y in regression analysis, and special notation will help to keep them separate. Recall that at this point we also have S_Y, which is the sample standard deviation about the sample mean.

14.3.3 *F* Test

Now that we know about partitioning explained variability and error variance, we can develop hypothesis tests for the linear relationship between Y and X_1 (Key Idea 14.13). The slope coefficient, β_1, defines the linear relationship. If β_1 is equal to zero, changes in X_1 cannot affect Y.

The mean square for regression (MSR) is defined as RSS divided by the 1 degree of freedom used for the slope estimate $\hat{\beta}_1$, and thus in simple regression,

$$\text{MSR} = \frac{\text{RSS}}{1} = \text{RSS}$$

In addition, we also define the mean square for error (MSE) as

$$\text{MSE} = \frac{\text{ESS}}{n-2} = S^2_{Y|X}$$

If the null hypothesis is true, both MSR and MSE are estimates of the variance of the regression model error.

In Chapter 9 we showed that the F distribution is the ratio of independent estimates of variance. For simple regression the null hypothesis that there is no relationship between X_1 and Y implies that both MSR and MSE are estimates of variance and thus

$$F = \frac{\text{MSR}}{\text{MSE}}$$

has an F distribution with 1 degree of freedom for the numerator and $n - 2$ degrees of freedom for the denominator. If the calculated value of F exceeds the critical value of

---

Key Idea 14.13: Overall F Hypothesis Test

The hypothesis test

$$H_0: \beta_1 = 0$$
$$H_1: \beta_1 \neq 0$$

uses

$$F = \frac{\text{RSS}/1}{\text{ESS}/n - 2} = \frac{\text{RSS}}{S_{Y|X}^2}$$

If $F > F_{\text{crit}}$, we reject H_0 and accept H_1. F_{crit} is obtained from Table A.4 with 1 degree of freedom for the numerator and $n - 2$ degrees of freedom for the denominator. The null hypothesis H_0 implies that there is no relationship between Y and X_1. Rejection of H_0 leads us to conclude that there is a relationship.

F from Table A.4, for a given α we reject the null hypothesis and conclude that there is a relationship between X_1 and Y. Another interpretation is that a large value of the calculated F implies that a significant amount of variability RSS has been explained by the regression model.

These results can be applied to Agnes Larson's demand function. Table 14.2 shows the original data and the computation of the components of variance. We note that the basic identity

$$\text{TSS} = \text{RSS} + \text{ESS}$$
$$4000 = 3240 + 760$$

applies to this problem. We also see that the coefficient of determination is

$$R^2 = \frac{\text{RSS}}{\text{TSS}} = \frac{3240}{4000} = 0.81$$

TABLE 14.2   Analysis of Variance for Demand Function

Observation	X_1	Y	$\hat{Y}$	$(y_i - \hat{Y}_i)^2$	$(\hat{Y}_i - \bar{Y})^2$	$(y_i - \bar{Y}_i)^2$
1	6	80	86	36	1296	900
2	7	60	68	64	324	100
3	8	70	50	400	0	400
4	9	40	32	64	324	100
5	10	0	14	196	1296	2500
				760	3240	4000

Therefore, this regression explains 81% of the variability of sales about the mean. Finally, she decides to compute the standard error of the estimate $S_{Y|X}$ using the data from Table 14.2.

$$S^2_{Y|X} = \frac{\sum_{i=1}^{n}(y_i - \hat{Y}_i)^2}{n-2}$$

$$= \frac{760}{5-2}$$

$$= 253.3$$

$$S_{Y|X} = \sqrt{\frac{\sum_{i=1}^{n}(y_i - \hat{Y}_i)^2}{n-2}}$$

$$= \sqrt{253.3}$$

$$= 15.92$$

which is the standard deviation of Y given that the effect of X_1 has been removed. The degrees of freedom for the variance estimate are equal to $n - 2 = 3$. In simple regression two parameters, $\hat{\beta}_0$ and $\hat{\beta}_1$, are used to compute ESS and hence $S_{Y|X}$. Each parameter uses 1 degree of freedom, which leaves $n - 2$ degrees of freedom for error. In later sections we will learn that all the estimated variance terms have $n - 2$ degrees of freedom because they are derived from $S^2_{Y|X}$.

There is a simpler way to compute the variance components if the correlation between the two variables r_{xy} has been computed (see Key Idea 14.14).

Key Idea 14.14: Simplified Partitioning of Variability

As shown in Key Idea 14.11, the multiple correlation coefficient R^2 is equal to the simple correlation squared. Thus we have the identity

$$R^2 = r^2_{xy} = \frac{\text{RSS}}{\text{TSS}}$$

The total sum of squares TSS is easier to compute than either of the partitioned components. Using the results above, we find that

$$\text{RSS} = r^2_{xy} \times \text{TSS}$$

$$\text{ESS} = \text{TSS} - \text{RSS} = (1 - r^2_{xy})\text{TSS}$$

In the demand function example, TSS was 4000, and from Chapter 3 the simple correlation was $r_{xy} = -0.90$. Using these results, we can compute the partitioned variability explained by the regression line,

$$\text{RSS} = (-0.90)^2 \times 4000 = 3240$$

and the unexplained variability,

$$\text{ESS} = \text{TSS} - \text{RSS} = 4000 - 3240 = 760$$

Finally, the standard error of the estimate can be calculated using ESS.

To test for a significant relationship between price X_1 and quantity sold Y, use the hypothesis

$$H_0: \beta_1 = 0$$
$$H_1: \beta_1 \neq 0$$

and the F test. The calculated F statistic is

$$F = \frac{\text{MSR}}{\text{MSE}} = \frac{3240}{760/3} = 12.79$$

The critical value of F for $\alpha = 0.05$, 1 degree of freedom for the numerator, and 3 degrees of freedom for the denominator is, from Table A.4, equal to 10.13. Therefore, we reject the null hypothesis and conclude that there is a relationship between price and quantity sold.

14.3.4 Analysis of Computer Output

Exhibit 14.1 is a copy of the regression analysis computer output prepared using Minitab. You are encouraged to prepare a similar regression analysis using the data from Table 14.1 and the statistical package that is being used for your course. Regression applications are always done using a computer. Thus it is important that you understand clearly how to find each of the statistics on the computer output.

The computer output indicates the coefficients $\hat{\beta}_0 = 194$ and $\hat{\beta}_1 = -18.0$, first in equation form and then under the column headed "Coef." We note that the standard error of the estimate $S_{Y|X} = 15.92$ is labeled "s" on the computer output. Similarly, $R^2 = 0.81$ is labeled "R-sq" and expressed as a percentage. The analysis of variance table presents RSS, ESS, and TSS under the column labeled "SS." The "MS" column presents the sums of squares divided by the degrees of freedom ("DOF"). These results are commonly called "mean squares," and in particular the mean square for error, MSE, is $S_{Y|X}^2 = 253.3$. The lower portion of the output is a simple plot showing observed values of Y designated by A's and the predicted values of Y designated by B's. This plot provides an immediate intuitive description of the relationship between price and quantity of plywood. We will refer to this output in the next section as we develop inference procedures.

Does It Make Sense?

The computation of regression statistics is almost always done with a computer, using either a statistical package, such as Minitab, or a spreadsheet, such Lotus, Quatro, or Excel. In previous sections considerable effort has been spent on the algebraic and computational details. This was done so that you will understand how regression results are computed. With that knowledge you can explain the results and you will be able to identify reasons why actual results do not always agree with anticipated

EXHIBIT 14.1   Demand Function Regression: Minitab Output

```
The regression equation is
Y = 194 - 18.0 X1
```

Predictor	Coef	Stdev	t-ratio
Constant	$194.00(\hat{\beta}_0)$	$40.89(S_{\hat{\beta}_0})$	4.74
X1	$-18.000(\hat{\beta}_1)$	$5.033(S_{\hat{\beta}_1})$	$-3.58(t)$

$s = 15.92(S_{Y|X})$ R-sq = $81.0(R^2)$ R-sq(adj) $=74.7$

Analysis of Variance

SOURCE	DF	SS	MS
Regression	1	3240.0(RSS)	3240.0(MSR)
Error	3	760.0(ESS)	253.3(MSE)
Total	4	4000.0(TSS)	

```
MTB > mplot c2 on c1, and c3 on c1


        -
        -    B
        -    A
     75+
        -              B              A
        -
        -              A
        -
     50+                              B
        -
        -                                      A
        -
        -                                      B
     25+
        -
        -                                              B
        -

        -
        -
      0+                                                      A
        --------+---------+---------+---------+---------+--------
             6.40      7.20      8.00      8.80      9.60


        A = Y vs. X1                   B = Yhat vs. X1
```

results. Professionals know how to use sophisticated tools and they know how they work.   □

Practice Problem 14.2

Using the data from Practice Problem 14.1 ($r_{xy} = -0.70$, $\bar{Y} = 1000$, $\bar{X} = 120$, $S_y = 100$, $S_x = 50$, $n = 40$), compute the following regression statistics.

(a) The multiple coefficient of determination, R^2.

(b) The variance components; TSS, RSS, and ESS.

(c) The estimate of the model standard deviation, σ^2.   □

Problem Exercises

14.11 Explain why the error sum of squares will always be less than or equal to the total sum of squares in regression.

14.12 Explain how the coefficient of determination, R^2, should be used to analyze a regression model and show how it can be misinterpreted.

14.13 Explain the reasoning used for the F test and indicate what the test tells you the analyst.

14.14 Acme Cabinet Works has studied the relationship between price per base cabinet and the number of units sold per week during the past year. The summary statistics for the $n = 52$ observations are $r_{xy} = -0.70$, $\bar{Y} = 400$, $\bar{X} = 100$, $S_y = 80$, and $S_x = 40$, where Y is the total number of base cabinets sold in a week and X is the price in dollars for that week.

(a) What are the constant and slope coefficient for the regression model? Write the equation.

(b) Compute the multiple coefficient of determination, R^2.

(c) Compute the variance components: TSS, RSS, and ESS.

(d) Compute the sample standard deviation, $S_{Y|X}^2$.

14.15 The cost of new houses in a small college town is believed to be related to the number of square feet of floor space. A sample of 30 new houses provided the following summary statistics: $r_{xy} = 0.80$, $\bar{Y} = 60{,}000$, $\bar{X} = 1200$, $S_y = 8000$, and $S_x = 80$, where X is the total square foot of floor space and Y is the price in dollars. Determine:

(a) The constant and slope coefficient for the regression model. Write the equation.

(b) The multiple coefficient of determination, R^2.

(c) The variance components: TSS, RSS, and ESS.

(d) The sample standard deviation, $S_{Y|X}^2$.

14.16 The construction cost for turkey growing sheds, complete with automated feeding equipment, is believed to be linearly related to the number of turkeys grown in the shed. A study of 40 recently constructed sheds in Minnesota and South Dakota provided the following results: $r_{xy} = 0.60$, $\bar{Y} = 160{,}000$, $\bar{X} = 1200$, $S_y = 8000$, and $S_x = 80$, where X is the number of turkeys that can be grown in the shed and Y is the price in dollars. Determine:

(a) The constant and slope coefficient for the regression model. Write the equation.

(b) The multiple coefficient of determination, R^2.

(c) The variance components: TSS, RSS, and ESS.

(d) The sample standard deviation, $S_{Y|X}^2$.

14.17 The Brown Manufacturing Company is analyzing its processes to identify strategies for reducing the number of defects produced per hour. As part of its analysis the following regression model was prepared: $Y = 150 - 7X$, where Y is the number of defects produced per hour and X is the number of hours spent setting up and adjusting the manufacturing process ($10 \leq X \leq 20$). The regression model was prepared using $n = 40$ observations. The means and variances were $\bar{X} = 15$, $S_Y = 140$, and $S_X = 10$. This regression model is used to improve their manufacturing process. Determine:

(a) The constant and slope coefficient for the regression model.

(b) The multiple coefficient of determination, R^2.

(c) The variance components: TSS, RSS, and ESS.

(d) The sample standard deviation, $S_{Y|X}^2$.

(e) Do we have evidence that the slope coefficient is not equal to zero?

14.18 The human resources department of a large corporation is trying to determine if the women employees' wages are comparable to those of male employees. As part of their analysis they want to develop a regression model to predict wages as a function of years of experience. The following summary statistics have been prepared for a sample of 32 women employees: $r_{xy} = 0.70$, $\bar{Y} = 30,000$, $\bar{X} = 10$, $S_y = 3000$, and $S_x = 4$, where X is the number of years of experience and Y is the wage in dollars. Determine:

(a) The constant and slope coefficient for the regression model. Write the equation.

(b) The multiple coefficient of determination, R^2.

(c) The variance components: TSS, RSS, and ESS.

(d) The sample standard deviation, $S_{Y|X}^2$.

(e) Do we have evidence that the slope coefficient is not equal to zero?

14.19 The human resources department of a large corporation is trying to determine if the women employees' wages are comparable to those of male employees. As part of their analysis they want to develop a regression model to predict wages as a function of years of experience. The following summary statistics have been prepared for a sample of 32 male employees: $r_{xy} = 0.68$, $\bar{Y} = 39,000$, $\bar{X} = 14$, $S_y = 3600$, and $S_x = 4$, where X is the number of years of experience and Y is the wage in dollars. Determine:

(a) The constant and slope coefficient for the regression model. Write the equation.

(b) The multiple coefficient of determination, R^2.

(c) The variance components: TSS, RSS, and ESS.

(d) The sample standard deviation, $S_{Y|X}^2$.

(e) Do we have evidence that the slope coefficient is not equal to zero?

14.20 Briefly indicate why the regression sum of squares (RSS) cannot exceed the total sum of squares (TSS).

14.4 STATISTICAL INFERENCE

In previous sections we have developed the estimators for the model coefficients and predictions. Our next task is to learn how to compute confidence intervals and perform hypothesis tests. We begin by developing variance estimators.

14.4.1 Variance of $\hat{\beta}_1$

The slope coefficient $\hat{\beta}_1$ is a very important analysis and decision variable. When a manager predicts quantity sold as a function of price, she knows that the slope indicates the rate of change in quantity as a function of price, or the change in the number sold for every \$1 decrease in price. The slope of a consumption function indicates the increase in consumption for each unit increase in disposable income. Production function slopes indicate the marginal increase in output for each 1-unit increase in an input variable X_1. Given the importance of the slope coefficient, it follows that confidence intervals and hypotheses tests related to $\hat{\beta}_1$ are also important.

The variance of $\hat{\beta}_1$ (Key Idea 14.15) is computed by using the result that $\hat{\beta}_1$ is a linear combination of the y_i random variables. First consider the linear estimator,

$$\hat{\beta}_1 = \sum_{i=1}^{n} \frac{(x_{1i} - \bar{X}_1)}{\sum_{i=1}^{n}(x_{1i} - \bar{X}_1)^2} y_i$$

where

$$y_i = \beta_0 + \beta_1 x_{1i} + \epsilon_i$$

The random variable, ϵ_i, has a variance equal to σ^2. Since the β's and X's are fixed, the random variable y_i also has variance equal to σ^2. All of the x_{1i} terms are fixed (not random variables) and thus we could state the function as

$$\hat{\beta}_1 = \sum_{i=1}^{n} a_i y_i$$

Key Idea 14.15: Variance of $\hat{\beta}_1$

Statistical inference procedures for $\hat{\beta}_1$ require an estimate of the slope coefficient standard deviation $\sigma_{\hat{\beta}_1}$, which is

$$\sigma_{\hat{\beta}_1}^2 = \frac{\sigma^2}{\sum_{i=1}^{n}(x_{1i} - \bar{X}_1)^2}$$

and the sample variance estimator is

$$S_{\hat{\beta}_1}^2 = \frac{S_{Y|X}^2}{\sum_{i=1}^{n}(x_{1i} - \bar{X}_1)^2}$$

If the x_{1i} values are concentrated near the mean of X_1, the slope estimate will have a larger variance. Thus we should always try to maximize $\sum_{i=1}^{n}(x_{1i} - \bar{X})^2$ by selecting points whose X_1 values are spread over the entire model application range.

where

$$a_i = \frac{x_{1i} - \bar{X}_1}{\sum_{i=1}^{n}(x_{1i} - \bar{X}_1)^2}$$

is also a constant. We see that $\hat{\beta}_1$ is a linear combination of independent random variables y_i, because the ϵ_i's and thus the y_i's are assumed independent. Using the variance for linear combinations of independent random variables from Chapter 7, we see that

$$\sigma_{\hat{\beta}_1}^2 = \sum_{i=1}^{n} a_i^2 \sigma^2$$

which after some algebra is[5]

$$\sigma_{\hat{\beta}_1}^2 = \frac{\sigma^2}{\sum_{i=1}^{n}(x_{1i} - \bar{X}_1)^2}$$

Using the same approach, the sample variance estimator is

$$S_{\hat{\beta}_1}^2 = \frac{S_{Y|X}^2}{\sum_{i=1}^{n}(x_{1i} - \bar{X}_1)^2}$$

Examination of these equations shows that the variance of $\hat{\beta}_1$, the slope coefficient, is directly related to σ^2 and inversely related to the dispersion of the independent variable.

Does It Make Sense?

A decision maker who is using the slope will have greater confidence in her analysis if the sample points are close to the line. However, note that she should also be concerned about the location of the X_1 values. If the x_{1i} values are concentrated near the mean of X_1, the slope estimate will have a larger variance. Thus she should try to obtain points whose X_1 values are spread over the entire model application range.

Comparison of Figure 14.9a and b provides an intuitive understanding of the effect of the dispersion of X_1 on the variance of the slope. In Figure 14.9a the X_1 values are spread uniformly over the range and all contribute to determining the slope. In Figure 14.9b most of the data are narrowly concentrated and the single extreme point determines the slope coefficient $\hat{\beta}_1$. In the second example the slope coefficient estimate would be unstable because of sampling variations for the single extreme point. The variance of the slope $\sigma_{\hat{\beta}_1}^2$ would be substantially larger in the Figure 14.9b example. This example emphasizes the importance of a wide range for the independent variables.

---

[5] The derivation is as follows:

$$\sigma_{\hat{\beta}_1}^2 = \sum_{i=1}^{n} \left[\frac{x_{1i} - \bar{X}_1}{\sum_{i=1}^{n}(x_{1i} - \bar{X}_1)^2} \right]^2 \sigma^2 = \frac{\sum_{i=1}^{n}(x_{1i} - \bar{X}_1)^2 \sigma^2}{\left[\sum_{i=1}^{n}(x_{1i} - \bar{X}_1)^2\right]^2} = \frac{\sigma^2}{\sum_{i=1}^{n}(x_{1i} - \bar{X}_1)^2}$$

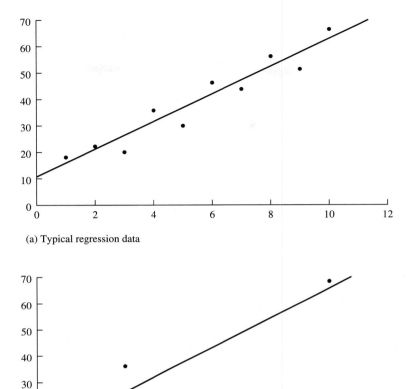

(a) Typical regression data

(b) Data with outlier

Figure 14.9   Effect of X_1 Values on the Slope

If we assume that the deviations ϵ about the regression line have a normal distribution, $\hat{\beta}_1$ will have a normal distribution because $\hat{\beta}_1$ is a linear function of normally distributed random variables. Even when the errors are not normal, the central limit theorem leads to the conclusion that $\hat{\beta}_1$ has an approximate normal distribution.   □

14.4.2 Confidence Intervals for $\hat{\beta}_1$

The slope coefficient, $\hat{\beta}_1$, is an important decision variable for many business and economics problems. For that reason decision makers must know the precision of the estimated $\hat{\beta}_1$ (Key Idea 14.16).

Key Idea 14.16: Confidence Intervals for $\hat{\beta}_1$

Confidence intervals follow the form presented in Chapter 10. Thus the two-sided $1 - \alpha$ percent confidence interval is

$$\hat{\beta}_1 \pm t_{(n-2,\alpha/2)} S_{\hat{\beta}_1}$$

The degrees of freedom for t are determined by the degrees of freedom for the standard error of the estimate $S_{Y|X}$.

Single-sided $(1 - \alpha)$ confidence intervals are defined following the form presented in Chapter 10:

$$\beta_1 \geq \hat{\beta}_1 - t_{(n-2,\alpha)} S_{\hat{\beta}_1}$$

Returning to the demand function example, Agnes wanted a 95% confidence interval for the slope coefficient. The estimated coefficient $\hat{\beta}_1 = -18.0$ indicated that each \$1 decrease in price would increase daily sales by 18 sheets. But what is a reasonable interval for the estimate of the slope coefficient? From Exhibit 14.1 we see that the standard deviation of the slope coefficient is $S_{\hat{\beta}_1} = 5.033$. The number is located in the column headed "Stdev" and the row indicated by "X1," next to the slope coefficient estimate. With only 3 degrees of freedom the t value is 3.182. Therefore, the 95% confidence interval is

$$\hat{\beta}_1 \pm t_{(n-2),\alpha/2} S_{\hat{\beta}_1}$$
$$-18.0 \pm 3.182 \times 5.033$$
$$-18.0 \pm 16.0$$

This confidence interval is quite wide, because we have only five data points and three degrees of freedom.

Computation of $S_{\hat{\beta}_1}$ is simplified by using the identity

$$\sum_{i=1}^{n}(x_{1i} - \bar{X}_1)^2 = (n - 1)S_{X_1}^2$$

From the calculations in Chapter 3, $S_{X_1}^2 = 2.5$ and therefore

$$\sum_{i=1}^{n}(x_{1i} - \bar{X}_1)^2 = 4 \times 2.5 = 10$$

Then, using $S^2_{Y|X_1} = 253.3$, we compute

$$S_{\hat{\beta}_1} = \sqrt{\frac{S^2_{Y|X}}{\sum_{i=1}^{n}(x_{1i} - \bar{X}_1)^2}}$$

$$= \sqrt{\frac{253.3}{10}}$$

$$= 5.033$$

14.4.3 Hypothesis Tests for $\hat{\beta}_1$

Hypothesis testing for the slope coefficient is also an important decision-making tool (see Key Idea 14.17). Most modern regression computer programs compute the t statistic automatically. The t statistic is usually located on the same line as the estimated coefficient $\hat{\beta}_1$ and the estimated coefficient standard deviation $S_{\hat{\beta}_1}$ (see Exhibit 14.1). Most analysts look at the computed t statistic in their computer output to determine if a relationship exists. The F test for this hypothesis, presented in Section 14.3.3, provides the same conclusion because $F = t^2$, as shown in the chapter appendix.

Returning again to the plywood demand function, Agnes Larson wishes to determine if plywood prices affect the number of pieces sold. After consultation with her friend Sally Goldberg, she states her question in the form of the standard hypothesis test:

$$H_0: \beta_1 = 0$$
$$H_1: \beta_1 \neq 0$$

To test the hypothesis, most statisticians compute a t statistic for their particular sample:

$$t = \frac{\hat{\beta}_1 - 0}{S_{\hat{\beta}_1}}$$

$$= \frac{-18.0 - 0}{5.033}$$

$$= -3.58$$

The value of $t = -3.58$ computed is less than the critical value $t_c = -3.182$, which was obtained from Table A.2. Therefore, Agnes rejects the null hypothesis and concludes that a relationship exists between price and quantity sold.

Agnes could also have asked if there was a negative slope for the regression equation (e.g., does the quantity sold increase as the price is lowered?). Then the hypothesis test would be

$$H_0: \beta_1 \geq 0$$
$$H_1: \beta_1 < 0$$

Key Idea 14.17: Hypothesis Test for $\hat{\beta}_1$

The hypothesis test

$$H_0: \beta_1 = 0$$
$$H_1: \beta_1 \neq 0$$

is used to determine if there is a significant relationship between the variables. The null hypothesis proposes a slope of zero, implying that Y does not change with changes in X_1. If H_0 is rejected, there is evidence that a relationship exists.

This hypothesis is usually tested by computing a sample Student t statistic using

$$t = \frac{\hat{\beta}_1 - 0}{S_{\hat{\beta}_1}}$$

When the degrees of freedom are above 40, the critical value of t is approximately 2.0 (i.e., two-sided test with $\alpha = 0.05$). This leads to the common rule of thumb:

If the coefficient t has an **absolute value** greater than 2, the coefficient is significant in a statistical sense.

It is also possible to test the hypothesis that β_1 is equal to or less than a specific value (equal to or greater than).

$$H_0: \beta_1 \leq \beta_*$$
$$H_1: \beta_1 > \beta_*$$

We use the standard rule "reject H_0 and accept H_1 if $t > t_{\alpha,n-2}$," where $t_{\alpha,n-2}$ is obtained from Table A.2 for this single-tailed test.

This is a single-tailed test with the lower critical value being $t_c = -2.353$. The computed value $t = -3.58$ is much less than the critical value and we reject H_0 and conclude that quantity sold does increase with decreasing prices. As we saw in Chapter 11, single-tailed hypothesis tests do have higher power.

14.4.4 Variance of $\hat{\beta}_0$

The constant β_0 merely shifts the regression line up or down and is usually less important than the slope β_1. The variance is computed by first noting that

$$\hat{\beta}_0 = \bar{Y} - \hat{\beta}_1 \bar{X}_1$$

Thus $\hat{\beta}_0$ is a linear combination of $\hat{\beta}_1$ and $\bar{Y}$ that are independent random variables and functions of ϵ, the model error. $\hat{\beta}_1$, $\bar{Y}$, and therefore $\hat{\beta}_0$ all have normal distributions either because ϵ is normal or because of the central limit theorem. Therefore, we can develop confidence intervals and perform hypothesis tests similar to those presented for $\hat{\beta}_1$, provided that we have an estimator for the standard deviation $S_{\hat{\beta}_0}$ (Key Idea 14.18).

Key Idea 14.18: Variance for Constant $\hat{\beta}_0$

The population and sample variances of $\hat{\beta}_0$ can be derived using the linear combination of random variables. The results are

$$\sigma_{\hat{\beta}_0}^2 = \left[\frac{1}{n} + \frac{\bar{X}^2}{\sum_{i=1}^{n}(x_{1i} - \bar{X}_1)^2} \right] \sigma^2$$

$$\sigma_{\hat{\beta}_0} = \sqrt{\sigma_{\hat{\beta}_0}^2}$$

$$S_{\hat{\beta}_0}^2 = \left[\frac{1}{n} + \frac{\bar{X}^2}{\sum_{i=1}^{n}(x_{1i} - \bar{X}_1)^2} \right] S_{Y|X}^2$$

$$S_{\hat{\beta}_0} = \sqrt{S_{\hat{\beta}_0}^2}$$

Confidence intervals and hypothesis tests follow the form presented for the slope using these variances and standard deviations.

14.4.5 Predicted Value of Y

The third and very important regression estimator is the predicted or mean value $\hat{Y}$ for a given X_1 (Key Idea 14.19). The prediction of Y at a given X_1^* using the regression equation is

$$\hat{Y}^* = \hat{\beta}_0 + \hat{\beta}_1 X_1^*$$

or

$$\hat{Y}^* = \bar{Y} + \hat{\beta}_1(X_1^* - \bar{X}_1)$$

The second form is used to obtain the variance estimator because $\bar{Y}$ and $\hat{\beta}_1$ are independent, while $\hat{\beta}_0$ is not independent of $\hat{\beta}_1$.

From Key Idea 14.19 we see that the variance of the predicted value is smallest at the mean $\bar{X}_1$. It increases quadratically as the prediction moves in either a positive

Key Idea 14.19: Variance for Predicted Value, $\hat{Y}^*$

The variance for the predicted value of Y, $\hat{Y}^*$, for a specific value of X_1, X_1^*, is

$$\sigma_{\hat{Y}^*}^2 = \sigma_{\bar{Y}}^2 + (X_1^* - \bar{X}_1)^2 \sigma_{\hat{\beta}_1}^2$$

$$= \left[\frac{1}{n} + \frac{(X_1^* - \bar{X}_1)^2}{\sum_{i=1}^{n}(x_{1i} - \bar{X}_1)^2} \right] \sigma^2$$

The sample estimator, which is used in most applied work, is

$$S_{\hat{Y}^*}^2 = S_{\bar{Y}}^2 + (X_1^* - \bar{X}_1)^2 S_{\hat{\beta}_1}^2$$

$$= \left[\frac{1}{n} + \frac{(X_1^* - \bar{X}_1)^2}{\sum_{i=1}^{n}(x_{1i} - \bar{X}_1)^2} \right] S_{Y|X}^2$$

This is the variance for the expected or predicted value of Y for a given value of X_1^*. The variance for a single-point observation would also have to include variability about $\hat{Y}$. Therefore, the sample variance for a point observation Y^* would be

$$S_{Y^*}^2 = \left[1 + \frac{1}{n} + \frac{(X_1^* - \bar{X}_1)^2}{\sum_{i=1}^{n}(x_{1i} - \bar{X}_1)^2} \right] S_{Y|X}^2$$

The variances for either the expected value or point observation of Y can be used for both hypothesis testing and confidence intervals.

or negative direction from the mean, $\bar{X}_1$. This result is intuitively reasonable when we analyze the problem. The regression equation goes through the mean point $(\bar{X}_1, \bar{Y})$, and the regression line "rotates" about the mean point. Therefore, at the mean, $\bar{X}_1$, variations in the slope do not affect the predicted value. However, as we move away from the mean, variation in the slope coefficient affects the prediction. The effect of the variation is the product of the slope multiplied by the distance from the mean.

In the plywood demand problem, suppose that Agnes Larson wanted to know if the expected sales of plywood exceeded 50 sheets when the price was $X_1 = \$6.50$. The formal hypothesis test would be

$$H_0: Y^* \leq 50$$

$$H_1: Y^* > 50$$

If H_0 is rejected, we conclude that expected sales are greater than 50 when the price, X_1, is $\$6.50$. The hypothesis can be tested by either computing the sample Student t or by computing a critical value for $X_1 = 6.5$. First we compute the variance using Key Idea 14.19:

$$S_{Y*}^2 = \left[\frac{1}{n} + \frac{(X_1^* - \bar{X}_1)^2}{\sum_{i=1}^{n}(x_{1i} - \bar{X}_1)^2} \right] S_{Y|X_1}^2$$

$$= \left[\frac{1}{5} + \frac{(6.5 - 8.0)^2}{4 \times 2.5} \right] 253.3$$

$$= 107.65$$

$$S_{\hat{Y}*} = 10.38$$

The critical value of t for a one-tailed test with $\alpha = 0.05$ and 3 degrees of freedom[6] is 2.353. Therefore, the critical value for the hypothesis test is

$$Y_c = 50 + t_{0.05} \times S(\hat{Y}^*)$$

$$= 50 + 2.353 \times 10.38$$

$$= 74.42$$

Thus the decision rule is:

Reject H_0 if $\hat{Y}_{x_1=6.5}$ is greater than 74.42.

The predicted value of Y is

$$\hat{Y}_{x_1=6.5} = 194 - 18 \times 6.5$$

$$= 77.0$$

Since the predicted value exceeds the critical value, we conclude that the expected number of sales does exceed 50. Note that in this example problem the degrees of freedom are only 3, and therefore the value of t is large compared to more typical analyses with at least 25 degrees of freedom. Thus the critical value is much larger than the hypothesized value of 50, compared to an analysis with $n > 25$.

Hypothesis test for a single observation.   Agnes might also be interested in determining if a single observation of quantity sold is below the lower acceptance interval of an assumed sales level of $Y = 80$ when the price is $X_1 = \$6.50$. In that case the hypothesized value is $\$80$. The hypothesis test would be

$$H_0: Y^* \geq 80$$

$$H_1: Y^* < 80$$

If H_0 is rejected, we conclude that the single observed sales level is less than would be expected when the price, X_1, is $\$6.50$ and the mean demand is 80. The hypothesis can

---

[6] The degrees of freedom for t tests in regression is always associated with $S_{Y|X}^2$, which is $n - 2$ for simple regression.

be tested by either computing the sample Student t or by computing a lower critical value for $X_1 = 6.5$. First we compute the variance using Key Idea 14.19:

$$S_{Y*}^2 = \left[1 + \frac{1}{n} + \frac{(X_1^* - \bar{X}_1)^2}{\sum_{i=1}^{n}(x_{1i} - \bar{X}_1)^2} \right] S_{Y|X_1}^2$$

$$= \left[1 + \frac{1}{5} + \frac{(6.5 - 8.0)^2}{4 \times 2.5} \right] 253.3$$

$$= 360.95$$

$$S_{Y*} = 19$$

The critical value of t for a one-tailed test with $\alpha = 0.05$ and 3 degrees of freedom is 2.353. Therefore, the critical value for the hypothesis test is

$$Y_c = 80 - t_{0.05} \times S(Y^*)$$

$$= 80 - 2.353 \times 19$$

$$= 35.29$$

Thus the decision rule is

Reject H_0 if $Y_{x_1=6.5}$ is less than 35.29.

Note that for a single observation the lower critical acceptance level is substantially below the predicted mean level of sales. Thus, attempting to accept or reject a regression model based on a single point would have large Type II error.

Confidence intervals.　Confidence intervals can also be computed for the predicted and point values of Y. The form for a $1 - \alpha$ symmetric confidence interval is

$$\hat{Y}^* \pm t_\alpha \times S_{\hat{Y}*}$$

This confidence interval is smallest at the mean, $\bar{X}_1$, $\bar{Y}$, and expands as X_1 moves away from the mean.

Figure 14.10 presents a schematic representation of the $1 - \alpha$ percent confidence interval for $\hat{Y}$. Observe how the confidence interval increases as we move away from the mean $\bar{X}_1$. Predictions of Y at the extreme points of the X_1 range have high variance. This variance can be decreased by having a large sample size and a wide spread of the data. We want the quantity $\sum_{i=1}^{n}(x_{1i} - \bar{X}_1)^2$ to be large, because this reduces the variance of $S_{\hat{\beta}_1}^2$ and therefore also the variance of the predicted value $S_{\hat{Y}*}^2$.

Does It Make Sense?

It is very risky to use regression equations for predictions outside the range of the data used to fit the equation. The confidence intervals increase rapidly as we move away from the mean. In addition, predictions outside the X_1 range do not have support

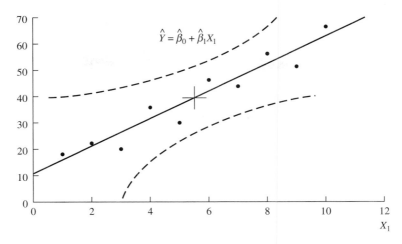

Figure 14.10   Confidence Interval for Regression Prediction

from the data. When a linear function is estimated we assume a linear relationship between the independent and dependent variables. This assumption can be tested by using plots of observed and predicted values. However, outside the X_1 range we have no information about the function, and predictions of Y must assume that the analyst has special knowledge that supports the assumption of a linear function.   □

Practice Problem 14.3

Use the data and results from Practice Problems 14.1 and 14.2 ($r_{xy} = -0.70$, $\bar{Y} = 1000$, $\bar{X} = 120$, $S_y = 100$, $S_x = 50$, $n = 40$) to answer the following questions.

(a) Compute the sample estimate of the slope coefficient standard deviation, $S_{\hat{\beta}_1}$

(b) Is there evidence to support a statistically significant relationship between X and Y?

(c) What is the 95% confidence interval for sales, Y, when price, X, is set at $100? □

Problem Exercises

14.21 Explain why the variance of the slope coefficient estimator is linearly related to the model variance.

14.22 Explain why better estimates of the slope coefficient are obtained when the independent variables are spread uniformly over a wider range.

14.23 Why can the Student t distribution, which assumes a normal distribution of random variables, be used to compute confidence intervals and hypothesis test critical values for the slope coefficient, $\hat{\beta}_1$?

14.24 Why does the variance of the predicted value, $\hat{Y}$, have its smallest variance at the mean of the independent variable, $\bar{X}$?

14.25 Acme Cabinet Works has studied the relationship between price per base cabinet and the number of units sold per week during the past year. The summary statistics for the $n = 52$ observations are $r_{xy} = -0.70$, $\bar{Y} = 400$, $\bar{X} = 100$, $S_y = 80$, and $S_x = 40$, where Y is the total number of base cabinets sold in a week and X is the price in dollars for that week. Determine:
(a) The constant and slope coefficient for the regression model. Write the equation.
(b) The standard deviation of $\hat{\beta}_1$.
(c) The 95% confidence interval for the slope coefficient $\hat{\beta}_1$.
(d) The 95% confidence interval for the number of cabinets sold, Y, when $X = 110$.

14.26 The cost of new houses in a small college town is believed to be related to the number of square feet of floor space. A sample of 30 new houses provided the following summary statistics: $r_{xy} = 0.80$, $\bar{Y} = 60,000$, $\bar{X} = 1200$, $S_y = 8000$, and $S_x = 80$, where X is the total square feet of floor space and Y is the price in dollars. Determine:
(a) The constant and slope coefficient for the regression model. Write the equation.
(b) The standard deviation of $\hat{\beta}_1$.
(c) The 95% confidence interval for the slope coefficient $\hat{\beta}_1$.
(d) The 95% confidence interval for the price of houses, Y, when $X = 1100$.

14.27 The construction cost for turkey growing sheds, complete with automated feeding equipment, is believed to be linearly related to the number of turkeys grown in the shed. A study of 40 recently constructed sheds in Minnesota and South Dakota provided the following results: $r_{xy} = 0.60$, $\bar{Y} = 160,000$, $\bar{X} = 1200$, $S_y = 8000$, and $S_x = 80$, where X is the number of turkeys that can be grown in the shed and Y is the price in dollars. Determine:
(a) The constant and slope coefficient for the regression model. Write the equation.
(b) The standard deviation of $\hat{\beta}_1$.
(c) The 95% confidence interval for the slope coefficient $\hat{\beta}_1$.
(d) The 95% confidence interval for the construction cost for turkey growing sheds, Y, when $X = 1300$.

14.28 The Brown Manufacturing Company is analyzing its processes to identify strategies for reducing the number of defects produced per hour. As part of its analysis the following regression model was prepared:

$$Y = 150 - 7X,$$

where Y is the number of defects produced per hour and X is the number of hours spent setting up and adjusting the manufacturing process ($10 \leq X \leq 20$). The regression model was prepared using $n = 40$ observations. The means and variances were $\bar{X} = 15$, $S_Y = 140$, and $S_X = 10$. This regression model is used to improve their manufacturing process. Determine:
(a) The constant and slope coefficient for the regression model.
(b) The standard deviation of $\hat{\beta}_1$.
(c) The 95% confidence interval for the slope coefficient $\hat{\beta}_1$.

    (d) The 95% confidence interval for the number of defects produced per hour, Y, when $x = 14$.

    (e) Do we have evidence that the slope coefficient is not equal to zero?

14.29 The human resources department of a large corporation is trying to determine if the women employees' wages are comparable to those of male employees. As part of their analysis they want to develop a regression model to predict wages as a function of years of experience. The following summary statistics have been prepared for a sample of 32 women employees: $r_{xy} = 0.70$, $\bar{Y} = 30{,}000$, $\bar{X} = 10$, $S_y = 3000$, and $S_x = 4$, where X is the number of years of experience and Y is the wage in dollars. Determine:

    (a) The constant and slope coefficient for the regression model. Write the equation.

    (b) The standard deviation of $\hat{\beta}_1$.

    (c) The 95% confidence interval for the slope coefficient $\hat{\beta}_1$.

    (d) The 95% confidence interval for the wages, Y, when $x = 13$.

    (e) Do we have evidence that the slope coefficient is not equal to zero?

14.30 The human resources department of a large corporation is trying to determine if the women employees' wages are comparable to those of male employees. As part of their analysis they want to develop a regression model to predict wages as a function of years of experience. The following summary statistics have been prepared for a sample of 32 male employees: $r_{xy} = 0.68$, $\bar{Y} = 39{,}000$, $\bar{X} = 14$, $S_y = 3600$, and $S_x = 4$, where X is the number of years of experience and Y is the wage in dollars. Determine:

    (a) The constant and slope coefficient for the regression model. Write the equation.

    (b) The standard deviation of $\hat{\beta}_1$.

    (c) The 95% confidence interval for the slope coefficient $\hat{\beta}_1$.

    (d) The 95% confidence interval for the wages, Y, when $x = 13$.

    (e) Do we have evidence that the slope coefficient is not equal to zero?

14.5 CORRELATION ANALYSIS

In Chapter 3 the correlation coefficient was used to indicate linear relationships between variables. When using the correlation it is not necessary to assume that X is the independent variable and Y is the dependent variable. However, to develop a hypothesis test for a linear relationship, the procedures from regression analysis will be used (Key Idea 14.20).

    Correlations have wide applications in business and economics. Do sales increase when prices are reduced? Do stock prices increase when major banks announce lower prime interest rates? Do the number of defective parts increase with the number of consecutive hours that the machine has been running? In some applied economic problems it is difficult to argue that there is an independent variable X whose values are "fixed" by activities outside the economic system being modeled. When driving a car we can set the accelerator at different positions and the speed will respond directly. However, "driving" an economic system is a more complex task. In many cases

Key Idea 14.20: Hypothesis Tests Using the Sample Correlation

The correlation hypothesis test

$$H_0: \rho_{xy} = 0$$
$$H_1: \rho_{xy} \neq 0$$

can be performed using a Student t statistic calculated as

$$t = \frac{r_{xy}\sqrt{n-2}}{\sqrt{1-r_{xy}^2}}$$

where r_{xy}^2 is the sample correlation. This result is developed in the chapter appendix. If t is greater than the critical value of t, t_c (from Table A.2), we reject H_0 and accept H_1. Accepting the null hypothesis leads to the conclusion that there is not a relationship between X and Y. Rejecting H_0 would lead to the conclusion that there is a relationship. These conclusions are the same if both X and Y are random variables or if the X's are not random variables.

The minimum absolute critical value of the sample correlation, r_c, can also be used to test the hypothesis. It can be calculated using

$$r_c = \sqrt{\frac{t_c^2}{t_c^2 + n - 2}}$$

where t_c is the critical value of t for a specific α and degrees of freedom. The minimum absolute critical value is approximately

$$r_c \simeq \frac{2}{\sqrt{n}}$$

when $t_c = 2.0$. If the observed correlation is greater than r_c, H_0 is rejected and we conclude that a linear relationship exists.

both X and Y may be determined simultaneously by factors that are outside the economic system being modeled. Therefore, a model in which both X and Y are random variables is often more realistic.

In those cases the correlation coefficient, ρ_{xy}, is used to indicate a linear relationship without implying that one variable is independent and the other is dependent. One of the important results is that the least-squares estimators for β_0 and β_1 apply even when both X and Y are random variables. Therefore, least-squares regression can be used to test for linear relationships between two jointly distributed random variables. In Chapter 7 the correlation coefficient ρ_{xy} was developed as a measure of the relationship between two random variables X and Y. If both X and Y are jointly distributed random variables with correlation ρ_{xy}, the coefficient estimators for the linear model,

$$Y = \beta_0 + \beta_1 X_1$$

are the same as the least-squares regression estimators.[7]

We can develop a rough rule of thumb for screening correlations to see if a relationship exists. Begin with the equation to compute t from Key Idea 14.20:

$$t_c = \frac{r_c \sqrt{n-2}}{\sqrt{1-r_c^2}}$$

and the absolute critical value of r_c is

$$r_c = \sqrt{\frac{t_c^2}{t_c^2 + n - 2}}$$

where t_c is the critical value for a two-tailed test with a given probability of error, α, and n is the sample size. If the sample size is above $n = 40$ the critical value of t for $\alpha = 0.05$ is approximately 2. If we substitute $t_c = 2$, we find that

$$r_c = \sqrt{\frac{4}{4 + n - 2}}$$

$$= \frac{2}{\sqrt{2 + n}}$$

Further simplification can be obtained because the denominator is dominated by n and thus

$$r_c \simeq \frac{2}{\sqrt{n}}$$

Thus if n is 64, the critical value of the correlation r_{xy} is approximately 0.25, and if n is 49, the critical value of the correlation is approximately 0.28.

---

[7] It can be shown that the coefficients for the linear model when X and Y are joint random variables are

$$\beta_1 = \rho_{xy} \frac{\sigma_Y}{\sigma_X}$$

$$\beta_0 = \mu_y - \beta_1 \mu_x$$

The estimators are

$$\hat{\beta}_1 = r_{xy} \frac{S_Y}{S_X}$$

$$\hat{\beta}_0 = \bar{Y} - \hat{\beta}_1 \bar{X}$$

Does It Make Sense?

If the absolute value of the correlation between two quantitative variables is greater than $2/\sqrt{n}$ the population correlation is not zero and there is a linear relationship between the variables. This rule of thumb is useful when screening a correlation matrix to identify linear relationships between variables.   □

14.6 GRAPHICAL ANALYSIS

We have developed the basic tools for obtaining simple regression estimates and for determining their statistical significance. These tools are based on the least-squares assumptions. The results are generally robust with respect to the assumptions. Therefore, we have a powerful tool for analyzing a number of applied problems. However, there are situations in which the available data do not meet the assumptions, and errors can occur. Fortunately, many of these situations can be identified by simple scatter plots (Key Idea 14.21).

Key Idea 14.21: Two-Variable Scatter Plots

Least-squares regression provides the best linear equation estimates given the assumptions. However, it is also important to examine relationships between Y and X using scatter plots. These plots can reveal violations of the assumptions and/or unusual data patterns that may compromise the analysis.

Figure 14.11 presents the ideal case that is implicitly assumed when performing regression analysis. The points are spread over the range of the independent variable and have a linear pattern with uniform variation.

Figure 14.12 provides typical examples of nonlinear relationships. In Figure 14.12a least squares would result in a statistically significant linear approximation. However, the plot suggests a quadratic function that would be missed by simple regression. In Figure 14.12b least squares would indicate no relationship when there is an important quadratic relationship with an intermediate minimum. The relationship between production cost per unit and size of plant often follows such a relationship. The economically efficient plant size would be missed if a simple linear model were used. In Chapter 15 we learn how to estimate quadratic functions. Figure 14.12c indicates a cyclical model with a definite increasing trend. In some situations a linear

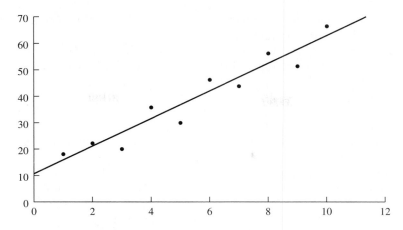

Figure 14.11   Ideal Data Pattern for Regression Analysis

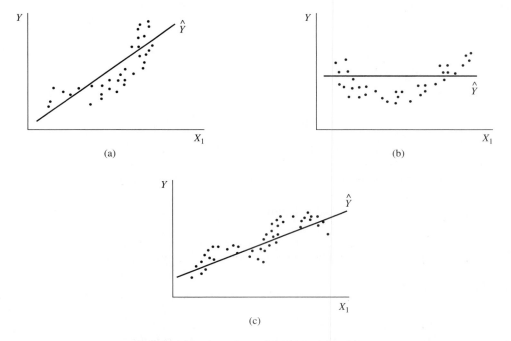

Figure 14.12   Examples of Nonlinearity in Data

approximation of this process might be satisfactory. However, a more complex model would be more accurate.[8]

Figure 14.13 demonstrates a common problem when using historical data from systems with stable operations. For example, these data could come from a factory where Y is the daily production and X_1 is the number of workers. The coefficient β_1 is the change in Y given a 1-unit change in X_1. In this example β_1 is the marginal productivity of labor and β_0 is a constant. The factory normally operates with a very narrow range of workers and subsequent output. However, there are some unusual situations that result in a much larger or smaller workforce. The reported output on these unusual days has a major influence on the regression slope. It does not seem reasonable that a production model for a stable factory operation should be based primarily on the few days that have unusual operating conditions.

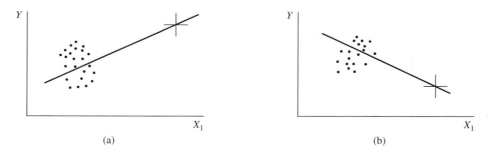

(a)   (b)

Figure 14.13   Outliers from a Nonvarying System

Figure 14.14 indicates a generally linear pattern of data with a few outliers. These few outliers will tend to "pull" the slope of the least-squares regression line either up or down. The analyst must decide whether these points represent real situations that occur as part of the system being studied or if they result from reporting error or other unusual situations. In the former case the points should be included in the regression and allowed to have their influence. After all, they do represent reality. However, in the latter case they should be removed. We emphasize that unusual observations should be removed from a data set only when there is a good reason.

Does It Make Sense?

Scatter plots are an important step in regression analysis. Examination of the plots can indicate unusual patterns in the data. Scatter plots indicate points that deviate greatly from a linear pattern and thus can suggest the possibility of nonlinear relationships.

---

[8] We should note that there is a potential danger in using complex models because they can be influenced by random errors or biases in the data. The separation of error from real effects is difficult in applied problems. Experience with data analysis is extremely beneficial. Experienced analysts generally advocate the use of the simplest model that will meet the needs of the problem.

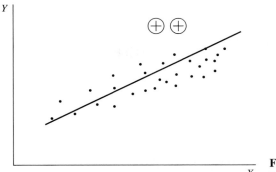

Figure 14.14 Typical Regression Data with Outliers

Extreme points indicate either measurement error or an unusual situation that should be investigated further. Such investigations will often identify unusual problems or influences.   □

Problem Exercises

14.31 Explain why we can conclude that a linear relationship exists between two variables if the absolute value of the sample correlation exceeds $2/\sqrt{n}$.

14.32 Explain why scatter plots should be used as part of regression analysis.

14.33 Olson Manufacturing wishes to study the relationship between the number of workers, X, and the number of chairs, Y, produced in its Fergus Falls plant. They have obtained a random sample of 10 days of production. The following (x, y) combination of points were obtained:

(12, 200)	(32, 620)	(15, 270)	(24, 500)	(14, 210)
(18, 300)	(26, 590)	(26, 540)	(19, 320)	(27, 570)

Enter the data into a statistical computer program and use the computer to do the following:

(a) Prepare a scatter plot of the points.
(b) Compute the regression constant, $\hat{\beta}_0$, and slope coefficient, $\hat{\beta}_1$.
(c) Find the predicted number of tables when there are 20 workers.
(d) Calculate the 95% confidence interval for the slope coefficient.
(e) Determine the standard error of the estimate.

14.34 Northfield Hospital is interested in determining the effectiveness of a new drug for reducing the time required for complete recovery from knee surgery. Complete recovery is measured by a series of strength tests that compare the treated knee with the untreated knee. The drug was given in varying amounts to 15 patients over a six-month period.

674

Simple Least-Squares Regression   Ch. 14

For each patient the number of drug units, X, and the days for complete recovery, Y, are given in the following (x, y) data:

(6, 53)	(21, 66)	(12, 44)	(11, 66)	(9, 46)	(4, 56)
(7, 53)	(21, 57)	(17, 49)	(14, 66)	(9, 54)	(7, 56)
(9, 53)	(21, 52)	(13, 49)	(14, 56)	(9, 59)	(4, 56)

Enter the data into your statistical computer package and do the following:
(a) Prepare a scatter plot of the points.
(b) Compute the regression constant, $\hat{\beta}_0$, and slope coefficient, $\hat{\beta}_1$.
(c) Compute the 95% confidence interval for the slope coefficient.
(d) Determine the percent explained variability and the correlation coefficient.
(e) Decide whether or not you recommend larger doses of the drug for a patient seeking rapid recovery.

14.35 Consolidated Delivery offers three different shipping rates for packages under 5 pounds delivered from Maine to the west coast: regular, $3; fast, $5; and lightning, $10. To test the quality of these services a major mail-order retailer shipped 15 packages at randomly selected times from Maine to Tacoma, Washington. The packages were shipped in groups of three by the three services at the same time to reduce variation resulting from the shipping day. The following data show the shipping cost, x, and the number of days, y, in (x, y) pairs.

| (3, 7) | (5, 6) | (10, 3) | (3, 9) | (5, 6) | (10, 5) | (3, 6) | (5, 6) |
| (10, 1) | (3, 11) | (5, 7) | (10, 4) | (3, 5) | (5, 6) | (10, 4) |

Use your local statistical computer package to do the following:
(a) Prepare a scatter plot of the points.
(b) Compute the regression constant, $\hat{\beta}_0$, and slope coefficient, $\hat{\beta}_1$.
(c) Compute the predicted delivery time for each of the three delivery categories.
(d) Compute the 95% confidence interval for the predicted delivery times in part (c).
(e) Discuss the value of the higher-priced services in terms of quicker delivery.

14.36 The human resources department of a large firm conducted a study of its salary structure. As part of this study the years of experience and monthly wages were collected for a sample of 12 employees. These employees were in various administrative and management positions. The first number in the following pairs is the years of experience.

| (6, 2600) | (8, 6200) | (14, 8000) | (12, 6400) | (2, 2200) | (6, 4000) |
| (6, 4500) | (10, 6600) | (15, 10,000) | (11, 6900) | (1, 2000) | (8, 4800) |

Use your statistical computer program to do the following:
(a) Prepare a scatter plot of the points.
(b) Compute the regression constant, $\hat{\beta}_0$, and slope coefficient, $\hat{\beta}_1$.
(c) Find the expected increase in monthly salary for each year of experience and the 95% confidence interval for that increase.
(d) Determine the percent explained variability.
(e) Calculate the predicted monthly salary for someone with 10 years of experience.
(f) State whether or not it is correct for the company to conclude that wages tend to increase directly with years of experience.

14.37 Johnson Foods, Inc. wishes to evaluate the effectiveness of its advertising expenditures. Advertising effectiveness is measured by the percentage of randomly selected households that have seen the advertisement and purchased the product. Expenditures are measured by the cost per 10,000 viewers in a region. The following data were collected in 10 major urban markets, with the first number being the expenditures and the second being the effectiveness.

| (50, 10.4) | (40, 7.9) | (68, 11.4) | (74, 14.7) | (66, 13.8) |
| (36, 6.1) | (55, 15.0) | (62, 12.1) | (48, 10.8) | (59, 14.8) |

Use your statistical computer program to do the following:
(a) Prepare a scatter plot of the points.
(b) Compute the regression constant, $\hat{\beta}_0$, and slope coefficient, $\hat{\beta}_1$.
(c) Find the predicted effectiveness when the expenditure is 50 and find the 95% confidence interval.
(d) Calculate the increase in advertising effectiveness for each unit of expenditure and the 95% confidence interval.
(e) Discuss the relationship between advertising cost and effectiveness for Consumer Foods, Inc.

14.7 REGRESSION EXAMPLE: FACULTY SALARIES

The faculty association coordinating committee representing select midwestern private liberal arts colleges was interested in developing a fair and equitable faculty salary structure. As a first step they commissioned a noted labor economist, Gary Frank, to study the present salaries using a random sample of salaries from the combined colleges.[9]

After some discussion the committee asked Dr. Frank to answer the following questions:

1. What, if any, is the relationship between salary and years of teaching experience?

2. What, if any, is the relationship between salary and age?

3. Is there a difference in salary for male and female faculty members after adjusting for experience?

4. Is there a difference in salary between senior faculty (full and associate professors) and junior faculty (instructors and assistant professors)?

Dr. Frank discussed the project with the committee to become familiar with their concerns and to develop a complete understanding of the questions. He then obtained

---

[9] The motivation and data for this example were provided by Frank Gery of the St. Olaf College Economics Department. The data have been modified by adding a constant to the salaries to protect confidentiality. Reference: Frank Gery, "A faculty salary model," *Papers and Proceedings of the 1987 National Meeting of the Association of Human Resources Management and Organizational Behavior*, Philadelphia, November 1987.

data for a random sample of 150 faculty from the various colleges. For each faculty member he obtained salary, age, experience, faculty rank, and gender.

Salary versus years of experience.   The first step was to study the relationship between salary and years of experience. Exhibit 14.2 presents a plot of salary versus years of experience ("Yrsexper") and a copy of the regression analysis computer output. From the plot we see a strong linear relationship, with a good spread of points over the range from 0 to 40 years. This suggests that regression analysis will provide a good estimate of the relationship between experience and salary. Using the computer output in Exhibit 14.2, we see that the estimated regression equation is

$$\hat{Y} = \hat{\beta}_0 + \hat{\beta}_1 X_1$$
$$= 20{,}545 + 616 X_1$$
$$\quad (41.9) \quad \quad (22.9)$$
$$S_{Y|X} = 3118 \quad \quad R^2 = 0.78 \quad \quad n = 150$$

where $\hat{Y}$ is the faculty salary and X_1 is years of teaching experience. (The numbers under the constant and the slope coefficient are the calculated t statistics.)

The regression model is presented in a standard form that communicates directly the estimated relationship and its measures of error. This format should be used whenever regression results are presented. The t statistic for the slope coefficient (22.93) indicates a significant linear relationship. The slope coefficient $\hat{\beta}_1 = 616$ indicates that on average, each year of experience increases salary by \$616. Dr. Frank also computed a 95% confidence interval for $\hat{\beta}_1$ using the coefficient standard deviation $S_{\hat{\beta}_1} = 26.87$.

$$\hat{\beta}_1 \pm 1.96 S_{\hat{\beta}_1}$$
$$616 \pm 1.96 \times 26.87$$
$$616 \pm 52.67$$

Thus the interval 563 to 669 includes the slope with probability 0.95. The $R^2 = 0.78$ indicates that 78% of the variability in salaries is explained by years of experience.

The regression output in Exhibit 14.2 also presents a list of "unusual observations" that have a large residual or deviation from the predicted value. We have previously defined the residual as

$$\hat{e}_i = y_i - \hat{Y}_i$$

Examination of observations with either large positive or negative residuals can provide important additional information about the regression model and about the particular set of observations that are being studied. The faculty members represented by observations 2, 122, 131, and 147 have salaries that are substantially below the amount predicted by their years of experience. Similarly, observations 48, 58, and 130 are much higher than predicted. A dean or department chair should examine these cases individually and decide, using other information, if these people should be that far from the predicted salary. Unusual circumstances could explain their deviation, or

EXHIBIT 14.2   Salary Versus Experience

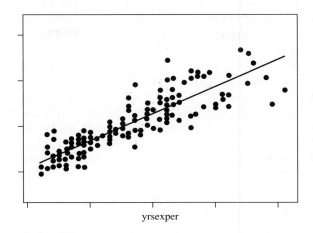

yrsexper

```
The regression equation is
salary = 20545 + 616 yrsexper
Predictor        Coef          Stdev      t-ratio
Constant       20544.5         490.2        41.91
yrsexper        616.11         26.87        22.93
s = 3118        R-sq = 78.0%      R-sq(adj) = 77.9%
Analysis of Variance
SOURCE         DF           SS              MS
Regression      1     5109486592      5109486592
Error         148     1438740224         9721218
Total         149     6548227072
Unusual Observations
Obs.yrsexper      salary      Fit Stdev.Fit   Residual    St.Resid
  2      26.0       30150     36563      378      -6413      -2.07R
 48      22.0       45000     34099      307      10901       3.51R
 58      22.0       40400     34099      307       6301       2.03R
122      41.0       38500     45805      729      -7305      -2.41RX
130      17.0       39500     31018      257       8482       2.73R
131      39.0       35300     44573      679      -9273      -3.05RX
147      38.0       41200     43957      654      -2757      -0.90X
```
R denotes an obs. with a large st. resid.
X denotes an obs. whose X value gives it large influence.

salary adjustments might be needed. Alternatively, there could be some other factor associated with these people that should be included in the analysis. This possibility will be considered in Chapters 15 and 16 as we study multiple regression.

Salary versus age. Examination of the computer output in Exhibit 14.3 indicates clearly that salary is a function of age. However, age is not as good a predictor as years of experience. This is seen in the wider spread of points in the plot and $R^2 = 0.56$ compared to $R^2 = 0.78$ for the experience model. In addition, the standard error of the estimate $S_{Y|X} = 4411$, compared to 3118 when years of experience is used. Note also that the t statistic is highly significant, but the Student t is much smaller than that observed in the regression that uses experience.

Based on this analysis and his experience as a labor economist, Dr. Frank recommends that age not be used as a predictor in the salary model. The observed rela-

EXHIBIT 14.3   Salary Versus Age

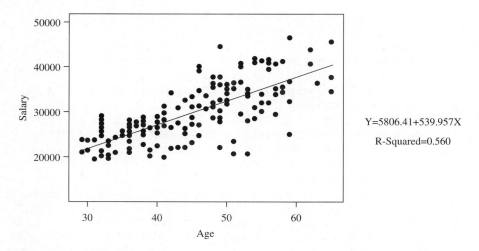

$Y=5806.41+539.957X$

R-Squared=0.560

```
The regression equation is
salary = 5806 + 540 age
Predictor        Coef         Stdev       t-ratio
Constant         5806         1809          3.21
age             539.96        39.32         13.73
s = 4411          R-sq = 56.0%      R-sq(adj) = 55.7%

Analysis of Variance
SOURCE         DF          SS              MS
Regression      1      3669210624      3669210624
Error         148      2879016192        19452812
Total         149      6548227072
```

tionship between salary and age results from the correlation between age and years of experience.

Experience versus salary for men and women.   The sample was divided into two subsets—male faculty and female faculty—and separate regression models were fitted to each subset. The regression output is shown in Exhibits 14.4 and 14.5. By comparing these two regression models, Dr. Frank was able to identify differences between the salary structure for male and female faculty. Comparison of the plots indicates that men are more likely to be at the higher experience and salary levels. In addition, we see a few women with limited experience whose salaries are substantially above the central tendency for their age group.

The male and female regression analyses provide an opportunity to test for differences in the salary structure. In the regression models the constant $\hat{\beta}_0$ can be interpreted as a base salary for persons with no experience, and the slope $\hat{\beta}_1$ can be interpreted as the incremental increase for each additional year of experience. To determine if women have a lower starting salary, we can test the hypothesis

$$H_0: \beta_{0w} - \beta_{0m} \geq 0$$
$$H_1: \beta_{0w} - \beta_{0m} < 0$$

where β_{0w} is the constant in the women's salary regression and β_{0m} is the constant in the men's salary regression. The null hypothesis H_0 is that women's base salaries are equal to or greater than those for men. Rejection of H_0 leads to the conclusion that women have significantly lower starting salaries.

The test statistic for this hypothesis test is

$$\Delta\hat{\beta}_0 = \hat{\beta}_{0w} - \hat{\beta}_{0m}$$
$$-461 = 20{,}695 - 21{,}156$$

If we assume that the constants have a normal distribution, as we typically do, $\Delta\hat{\beta}_0$ also has a normal distribution and the hypothesis can be tested using the Student t test. The sample standard error for the difference between the two regression constants, assuming independent regressions, is

$$S_{\Delta\hat{\beta}_0} = \sqrt{S_{\hat{\beta}_{0w}}^2 + S_{\hat{\beta}_{0m}}^2}$$
$$= \sqrt{(605.7)^2 + (669.4)^2}$$
$$= 902.8$$

The t statistic for the hypothesis test is thus

$$t = \frac{\Delta\hat{\beta}_0 - 0}{S_{\Delta\hat{\beta}_0}}$$
$$= -0.51$$

Clearly, we cannot reject the hypothesis and thus we cannot conclude that women faculty have lower base salaries.

EXHIBIT 14.4   Salary Versus Experience for Women

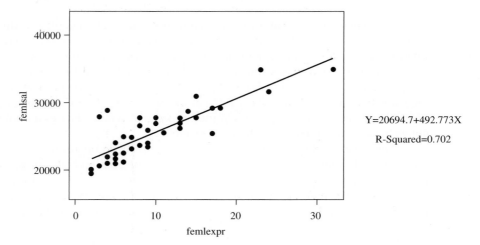

$$Y = 20694.7 + 492.773X$$

$$R\text{-Squared} = 0.702$$

```
The regression equation is
femlsal = 20695 + 493 femlexpr
Predictor        Coef        Stdev        t-ratio
Constant      20694.7        605.7          34.17
femlexpr       492.77        52.10           9.46
s = 2136       R-sq = 70.2%     R-sq(adj) = 69.4%
```

Another important hypothesis test would compare the slopes or rates of increase for each additional year of experience. To determine if women receive smaller increases for each year of experience, we use

$$H_0: \beta_{1w} - \beta_{1m} \geq 0$$
$$H_1: \beta_{1w} - \beta_{1m} < 0$$

where β_{1w} is the slope coefficient in the women's salary regression and β_{1m} is the slope coefficient in the men's salary regression. The null hypothesis H_0 states that the salary increment per year for women's teaching experience is equal to or greater than the increment per year for men. Rejection of H_0 leads to the conclusion that women receive smaller increases for each year of experience. The test statistic for this hypothesis test is

$$\Delta\hat{\beta}_1 = \hat{\beta}_{1w} - \hat{\beta}_{1m}$$
$$-110 = 493 - 603$$

If we assume that the slopes have a normal distribution, as we typically do, $\Delta\hat{\beta}_1$ also has a normal distribution and the hypothesis can be tested using the Student t test. The sample standard error for the difference between the two regression slopes, assuming independent regressions, is

EXHIBIT 14.5   Salary Versus Experience for Men

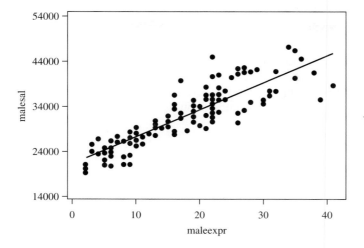

$Y=21155.7+602.982X$

R-Squared=0.752

```
The regression equation is
malesal = 21156 + 603 maleexpr
Predictor        Coef         Stdev        t-ratio
Constant       21155.7        669.4          31.61
maleexpr        602.98        33.28          18.12
s = 3304        R-sq = 75.2%      R-sq(adj) = 75.0%
```

$$S_{\Delta\hat{\beta}_1} = \sqrt{S^2_{\hat{\beta}_{1w}} + S^2_{\hat{\beta}_{1m}}}$$
$$= \sqrt{(52.10)^2 + (33.28)^2}$$
$$= 61.82$$

The t statistic for the hypothesis test is thus

$$t = \frac{\Delta\hat{\beta}_1 - 0}{S_{\Delta\hat{\beta}_1}}$$
$$= \frac{-110}{61.82}$$
$$= -1.78$$

From Table A.2 the critical value of t for 38 degrees of freedom and $\alpha = 0.05$ is 1.685.[10] Therefore, he rejected the null hypothesis. As a result, Dr. Frank reported that

---

[10] To determine degrees of freedom for the t statistic, we used the conservative rule of choosing the smallest degrees of freedom from the two standard deviations that were combined. Recall the discussion in Chapter 10.

there was evidence to conclude that the amount of increase for each year of experience for women faculty was less than that for men. At this point we do not know if the differences in salary increase reflect differences in education, academic rank, or other relevant variables, or if they resulted from sex discrimination. Careful examination of Exhibit 14.4 shows that women faculty members with high levels of experience appear to have lower salaries than would be expected from a linear projection of salaries for women with less experience. These points located toward the right side of the graph could be responsible for the lower slope coefficient for women faculty. Further analysis will occur after we have studied multiple regression.

Practice Problem 14.4: Interpreting Computer Output

Use the computer outputs in Exhibits 14.6 and 14.7 to compare the salary structures for junior and senior faculty. Include the following specific comparisons.

(a) Ranges of experience and salary.

EXHIBIT 14.6   Salary Versus Experience for Junior Faculty

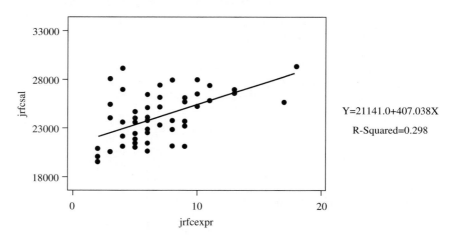

Y=21141.0+407.038X

R-Squared=0.298

```
The regression equation is
Jrfcsal = 21141 + 407 Jrfcexp
Predictor        Coef            Stdev       t-ratio
Constant        21141.0          625.1        33.82
Jrfcexp          407.04          83.46         4.88
s = 2162         R-sq = 29.8%      R-sq(adj) = 28.6%

Analysis of Variance
SOURCE          DF              SS              MS
Regression       1          111133912       111133912
Error           56          261668336         4672649
Total           57          372802240
```

EXHIBIT 14.7   Salary Versus Experience for Senior Faculty

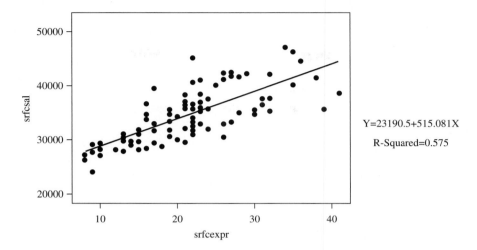

$$Y = 23190.5 + 515.081X$$

$$R\text{-Squared} = 0.575$$

```
The regression equation is
Srfcsal = 23191 + 515 Srfcexp
Predictor        Coef         Stdev       t-ratio
Constant         23191         1051         22.07
Srfcexp         515.08        46.66         11.04
s = 3389        R-sq = 57.5%     R-sq(adj) = 57.0%


Analysis of Variance
SOURCE          DF            SS              MS
Regression       1       1399522560      1399522560
Error           90       1033597952        11484422
Total           91       2433120512
```

(b) Regression constants or "base" salaries.

(c) Regression slopes or "experience" increments.

SUMMARY OF KEY IDEAS

PRACTICE PROBLEM SOLUTIONS

14.1   (a) Compute the slope coefficient, $\hat{\beta}_1$ and the equation constant, $\hat{\beta}_0$.

$$\hat{\beta}_1 = r_{xy} \frac{S_Y}{S_X}$$
$$= -0.70 \frac{100}{50}$$
$$= -1.40$$
$$\hat{\beta}_0 = \bar{Y} - \hat{\beta}_1 \bar{X}$$
$$= 1000 - (-1.40)120$$
$$= 1168$$

and the resulting equation is

$$Y = \hat{\beta}_0 + \hat{\beta}_1 X$$
$$= 1168 - 1.40X$$

(b) The increase in price from \$90 to \$120 would change sales by

$$(120 - 90) \times \hat{\beta}_1 = 30(-1.40) = -42 \qquad \text{100-pound boxes}$$

This reduction would be from

$$\bar{Y}_{90} = 1168 - 1.40(90) = 1042$$

to

$$\bar{Y}_{120} = 1168 - 1.40(120) = 1000$$

(c) This problem represents an important application of demand functions in microeconomics. The first step is to express the total revenue—price times quantity— in terms of price alone. This can be done by multiplying price X times the quantity Y,

$$\begin{aligned} \text{TR} &= XY \\ &= X(\hat{\beta}_0 + \hat{\beta}_1 X) \\ &= \hat{\beta}_0 + \hat{\beta}_1 X^2 \end{aligned}$$

The price that maximizes TR is found using calculus:

$$\frac{d(\text{TR})}{dX} = \hat{\beta}_0 + 2\hat{\beta}_1 X = 0$$

$$\begin{aligned} X &= \frac{\hat{\beta}_0}{2(-\hat{\beta}_1)} \\ &= \frac{1168}{2 \times -(-1.40)} \\ &= \$417 \end{aligned}$$

This price is clearly beyond the range of the data and thus this result is suspicious. The rational analyst would select the highest price within the range of the data as a more reasonable and practical answer. Note that this problem could also have been solved by using the computer to compute and plot total revenue predicted by the model versus price.

14.2 (a) We know that the multiple coefficient of determination, R^2, is for simple regression equal to the correlation squared and thus

$$R^2 = r_{xy}^2 = (-0.70)^2 = 0.49$$

This regression explains 49% of the variability.

(b) Note that

$$\text{TSS} = \sum_{i=1}^{n}(y_i - \bar{Y})^2 = (n-1)S_Y^2$$

from the definition of sample variance and

$$\begin{aligned} \text{TSS} &= (40-1)(100)^2 \\ &= 390{,}000 \end{aligned}$$

Then using the definition of R^2,

$$\begin{aligned} \text{RSS} &= R^2 \times \text{TSS} \\ &= 0.49(390{,}000) \\ &= 191{,}100 \end{aligned}$$

and ESS is found as the difference,

$$\begin{aligned} \text{ESS} &= \text{TSS} - \text{RSS} \\ &= 390{,}000 - 191{,}100 \\ &= 198{,}900 \end{aligned}$$

(c) The estimator for σ^2 is the variance of the estimate, $S_{Y|X}^2$.

$$S_{Y|X}^2 = \frac{\text{ESS}}{n-2} = \frac{198{,}900}{40-2} = 5234$$

14.3   (a) The estimated standard deviation of the slope coefficient is computed as

$$\begin{aligned} S_{\hat{\beta}_1}^2 &= \frac{S_{Y|X}^2}{\sum_{i=1}^{n}(x_i - \bar{X})^2} \\ &= \frac{S_{Y|X}^2}{(n-1)S_X^2} \\ &= \frac{5234}{(39)2500} \\ &= 0.0537 \end{aligned}$$

(b) Testing for a statistically significant relationship can be accomplished by following the procedure in Key Idea 14.17. The hypothesis test

$$\begin{aligned} H_0 &: \beta_1 = 0 \\ H_1 &: \beta_1 \neq 0 \end{aligned}$$

We compute the Student t,

$$t = \frac{\hat{\beta}_1 - 0}{S_{\hat{\beta}_1}}$$

$$= \frac{-1.40}{0.0537}$$

$$= -26.07$$

Since the absolute value of t is above the critical value, $t_{0.025,38} = 2.021$, which is found in Table A.2, we reject H_0 and conclude that a statistically significant relationship exists.

(c) To compute the confidence interval we first need to obtain the predicted value of Y and its standard error, $S_{\hat{Y}}$, when the price is $100 per 100-pound box. The predicted value

$$\hat{Y}_{100} = 1168 + (-1.40)100 = 1028$$

The estimated variance for $\hat{Y}$ is given by

$$S_{\hat{Y}^*}^2 = S_{\bar{Y}}^2 + (X_1^* - \bar{X}_1)^2 S_{\hat{\beta}_1}^2$$

$$= \left[\frac{1}{n} + \frac{(X_1^* - \bar{X}_1)^2}{\sum_{i=1}^{n}(x_{1i} - \bar{X}_1)^2} \right] S_{Y|X}^2$$

$$S_{\hat{Y}=100}^2 = \left[\frac{1}{40} + \frac{(100 - 120)^2}{97,500} \right] 5234$$

$$= 151.79$$

$$S_{Y=100} = 12.32$$

The 95% confidence interval is

$$\hat{Y}_{X=100} \pm t_{\alpha/2,\text{DOF}} S_{\hat{Y}_{100}}$$

$$1028 \pm 2.02(12.32)$$

$$1011.6 \pm 24.89$$

14.4 (a) From the graphs we see that the experience of junior faculty ranges from 0 to 18 years, while their salaries range from about $12,000 to $30,000. In contrast, the senior faculty experience goes from 8 to 40 years and their salaries from $24,000 to $50,000.

(b) The constant, β_0, for junior faculty was 21,141 and for senior faculty it was 23,191. By using the sample variance for the junior faculty, $S_{\hat{\beta}_0} = 625.1$, and for senior faculty, $S_{\beta_0} = 1051$, we can compute the standard deviation of the difference between these constants as

$$S^2_{\Delta \hat{\beta}_0} = S^2_{\hat{\beta}_{0jf}} + S^2_{\hat{\beta}_{0sf}}$$

$$= (625.1)^2 + (1051)^2$$

$$= 1,495,351$$

$$S_{\Delta \hat{\beta}_0} = 1222.8$$

Thus the difference between equation constants $23,191 - 21,141 = 2050$ is less than twice the standard deviation of the difference, $S_{\Delta \hat{\beta}_0} = 1222.8$. Thus the hypothesis of equal constants could not be rejected.

(c) The slope coefficient, β_1, for junior faculty was 407.04, and for senior faculty it was 515.08. By using the sample variance for the junior faculty, $S_{\hat{\beta}_1} = 83.46$, and for senior faculty, $S_{\beta_1} = 46.66$, we can compute the standard deviation of the difference between these constants as

$$S^2_{\Delta \hat{\beta}_1} = S^2_{\hat{\beta}_{1jf}} + S^2_{\hat{\beta}_{1sf}}$$

$$= (83.46)^2 + (46.66)^2$$

$$= 9142.73$$

$$S_{\Delta \hat{\beta}_0} = 95.61$$

Thus the difference between equation constants $515.08 - 407.04 = 108.04$ is less than twice the standard deviation of the difference, $S_{\Delta \hat{\beta}_1} = 95.61$. Thus the hypothesis of equal constants could not be rejected.

CHAPTER PROBLEMS

14.1 A small manufacturer of lawn furniture conducted experiments in two stores, located in different cities, to determine the relationship between weekly sales and price per unit. The experiments were conducted over the same time period to avoid any differences due to seasonal effects. The data collected from store A were:

Price: 11,   14,   13,   16,   19,   20,   24

Sales: 27,   32,   39,   38,   44,   52,   55

The data collected from store B were:

Price: 14,   15,   18,   16,   17,   15,   16

Sales: 36,   37,   42,   40,   42,   40,   38

(a) Plot the data from stores A and B on separate graphs. Visually sketch a best-fit line for each graph. Compare the graphs and indicate which would be more useful.

(b) Compute the correlation coefficients for both the store A and store B data sets. Use your calculator or type the data into your computer statistical package. Compare the correlations and indicate which data set provides the best linear model.

(c) Compute the regression coefficients for the linear model for both stores. Compute the standard error of the estimate, $S_{Y|X}$, and the standard error of the slope coefficient, $S_{\hat{\beta}_1}$. Which linear model provides the smallest estimate of model variance σ^2? Which linear model provides the smallest standard error of the slope coefficient $S_{\hat{\beta}_1}$? Compare the graphical plots with the regression statistics and state why the plots support your choice of a best prediction model.

14.2   This problem is based on an article by Frank Anscombe, who wanted to emphasize the importance of examining data using graphical plots.[11] Use your local computer package to estimate the regression models using the data in Table 14.3. The following four regression models should be estimated:

$$\hat{Y}_1 = \hat{\beta}_0 + \hat{\beta}_1 X_1$$

$$\hat{Y}_2 = \hat{\beta}_0 + \hat{\beta}_1 X_1$$

$$\hat{Y}_3 = \hat{\beta}_0 + \hat{\beta}_1 X_1$$

$$\hat{Y}_4 = \hat{\beta}_0 + \hat{\beta}_1 X_2$$

In addition, plot the points using the computer package. Compare the regression estimates and other statistics with the graphical plots. Note and discuss any unusual observations.

TABLE 14.3   Data for Problem 14.2

X_1	X_2	Y_1	Y_2	Y_3	Y_4
10.0	8.0	8.04	9.14	6.77	6.58
8.0	8.0	6.95	8.14	6.77	5.76
13.0	8.0	7.58	8.74	12.74	7.71
9.0	8.0	8.81	8.77	7.11	8.84
11.0	8.0	8.33	9.26	7.81	8.47
14.0	8.0	9.96	8.10	8.84	7.04
6.0	8.0	7.24	6.13	6.08	5.25
4.0	19.0	4.26	3.10	5.39	12.50
12.0	8.0	10.84	9.13	8.15	5.56
7.0	8.0	4.82	7.26	6.42	7.91
5.0	8.0	5.68	4.74	5.73	6.89

14.3   Show that

$$\sum_{i=1}^{n} (x_i - \bar{X})(y_i - \bar{Y}) = \sum_{i=1}^{n} (x_i - \bar{X})y_i$$

[*Hint:* What is the value of $\sum_{i=1}^{n} (x_i - \bar{X})\bar{Y}$?]

14.4   Frank George, the production manager of a powerboat manufacturer, seeks to develop a model to predict monthly output as a function of the number of workers scheduled. The boats are custom built to customer specifications, and therefore there is considerable

---

[11] F. Anscombe, "Graphs in statistical analysis," *The American Statistician*, Vol. 27, pp. 17–21, 1973.

variation in the work required for each boat. Because of this variation he has found it very difficult to predict the number of boats that a given size of work crew will produce. This has caused problems in failing to meet customer order deadlines and in having a shortage of work. Frank has collected the data in Table 14.4 from the past 12 months of operation. Your assignment is to prepare a regression model and help him to interpret the results. You may enter the data into a computer program or use graph paper and a calculator.

(a) Plot the data and indicate if there is a linear relationship.
(b) Prepare a simple regression analysis including the model coefficients, the standard error of the estimate, and R^2.
(c) How many units can he expect to produce during a typical month with 12 workers? With 16 workers?
(d) Compute a 95% confidence interval for the predictions in part (c).
(e) Explain the benefits and cautions for using this regression model to predict output.

TABLE 14.4   Powerboat Production Data

Month	Number of Workers, X	Number of Boats, Y
January	10	50
February	12	70
March	14	80
April	15	90
May	12	62
June	13	68
July	14	92
August	16	106
September	14	65
October	15	76
November	17	85
December	19	110

14.5 Given the following descriptive statistics:

$$S_Y = 66.51 \qquad S_X = 285.3 \qquad n = 51$$
$$\bar{Y} = 178.78 \qquad \bar{X} = 1178.0 \qquad \hat{\rho}_{X,Y} = 0.86$$

(a) Compute the various Minitab output statistics for the simple regression

$$Y = \beta_0 + \beta_1 X$$

and display the statistics in the Minitab output format. It is not necessary to prepare residuals analysis.
(b) Compute the 95% confidence interval for the predicted value of $\hat{Y}$ when $X = 2178.0$.

14.6 Given the simple regression equation

$$Y = 10 + 8X,$$

Student t for the slope coefficient of 4, sample size of 32, and standard deviation of Y of 10, determine:

(a) $S_{Y|X}$.

(b) The simple correlation between X and Y.

(c) The multiple coefficient of determination R^2.

14.7 Use the computer outputs in Exhibits 14.6 and 14.7 to compare the salary structures for junior and senior faculty. Include the following specific requirements:

(a) Compare the ranges of experience and salary.

(b) Compare the regression constants or base salaries. Do we have strong evidence that base salaries are different?

(c) Compare the regression slopes or experience increments. Do we have strong evidence that the experience increments are different?

(d) Write a short comparison of junior and senior faculty salary structures based on your analysis.

14.8 Derive the variances and 95% confidence interval for the estimated coefficient, $\hat{\beta}_1$, and the predicted value, $\hat{Y}^0$, at a given value of x, defined as x^0 for the regression equation

$$Y = \beta_0 + \beta_1 X_1 + \epsilon$$

$$\epsilon \sim N(0, \sigma^2)$$

(a) Define the estimator $\hat{\beta}_1$.

(b) Derive $\sigma^2_{\hat{\beta}_1}$ using the linear relationship between $\hat{\beta}_1$ and ϵ.

(c) Derive $\sigma^2_{\hat{Y}^0}$ using the linear relationship between $\hat{Y}^0$ and $\bar{X}_1$ and $\hat{\beta}_1$.

(d) Present the arguments for not using $\hat{Y}$ beyond the range of the given x's.

(e) Present a set of assumptions and problem conditions that would allow you to extrapolate $\hat{Y}$ beyond the range of the x's.

14.9 The manager of a mail-order clothing store is attempting to determine the best variable for predicting total sales per order. One analyst argues that a linear equation using age is the best predictor. A second analyst claims that the average family income for people in the buyer's census tract is the best predictor. Both statistics can be easily obtained for each customer. Two regression models were obtained:

$$Y = 100 + 10X_1$$

$$(4)$$

$$Y = 50 + 0.5X_2$$

$$(0.1)$$

where X_1 is the customer's age and X_2 is the average family income. The numbers below the coefficients are the coefficient standard errors, $S(\hat{\beta})$.

(a) Compare the two models and indicate which would provide better predictions.

(b) Compute R^2 for each model if the sample size for each was 100.

14.10 Derive the following identities.

(a) $t = \dfrac{\hat{\rho}(X, Y)\sqrt{n - 2}}{\sqrt{1 - \hat{\rho}^2(X, Y)}}$.

(b) $t^2 = F$.

(c) $R^2 = \hat{\rho}^2(X, Y)$.

(d) $R^2 = \dfrac{F}{F + n - 2}$.

14.11 Using a random sample of 51 observations, we have obtained the following regression results. The estimated equation is

$$Y = 10 + 5X$$

$$S^2(X) = 100$$

$$S^2(Y) = 3000$$

(a) Compute the values for R^2, $S^2(Y \mid X)$, and the simple correlation between X and Y.

(b) Compute the overall F statistic and the Student t for the regression slope coefficient.

(c) Present the analysis of variance table with all entries.

14.12 For the simple linear regression model

$$Y = \hat{\beta}_0 + \hat{\beta}_1 X_1$$

(a) Show that the simple correlation between X and Y is equal to the square root of the ratio of RSS divided by TSS.

(b) Show that the ratio of the estimated $\hat{\beta}_1$ divided by its standard error is equal to the square root of the overall F for the model.

$\star$ (c) Derive the estimator for the variance of the predicted value of Y at $X_1 = X_1^*$.

14.13 A college economics department is attempting to determine if verbal or mathematical proficiency is more important for predicting academic success in the study of economics. They have decided to use the grade-point average in economics courses for graduates as a measure of success. Measurement of verbal proficiency is available in the SAT verbal and the ACT English entrance examination test scores. Mathematical proficiency is measured by the SAT mathematics and the ACT mathematics entrance examination scores. The data for 112 students are available in a data file named "Student," which is available on your data disk. The designation of the variable columns is presented at the beginning of the data file. You should use your local statistical computer program to perform the analysis for this problem.

(a) Prepare a graphical plot of economics GPA versus each of the two verbal proficiency scores and each of the two mathematical proficiency scores. Which variable is a better predictor? Note any unusual patterns in the data.

(b) Compute the linear model coefficients and the regression analysis statistics for the models that predict economics GPA as a function of each verbal and each mathematical score. Using both the SAT mathematics and verbal measures and the ACT measures, determine whether mathematical or verbal proficiency is the best predictor of economics GPA.

(c) Compare the descriptive statistics—mean, standard deviation, upper and lower quartiles, range—for the predictor variables. Note the differences and indicate how these differences affect the capability of the linear model to predict.

14.14 The administrator of the National Highway Traffic Safety Administration (NHTSA) wants to know if the different types of vehicles in a state have a relationship to the highway death rate in the state. She has asked you to perform several regression analyses to determine if average vehicle weight, percentage imported cars, percentage light trucks, or average car age are related to "crash deaths in automobiles and pickups." The data for the analysis are located in the data file named "Crash," which is located on your data disk. The variable descriptions and locations are contained in the data file dictionary in Appendix B at the end of the book.

(a) Prepare graphical plots of crash deaths versus each of the potential predictor variables. Note the relationship and any unusual patterns in the data points.

(b) Prepare a simple regression analysis of crash deaths on the potential predictor variables. Determine which, if any, of the regressions indicate a significant relationship.

(c) State the results of your analysis and rank the predictor variables in terms of their relationship to crash deaths.

14.15 The department of transportation wishes to know if states with a larger percentage of urban population have higher automobile and pickup crash death rates. In addition, they want to know if the average speed on rural roads or the percentage of rural roads that are surfaced are related to crash death rates. Data for this study are included in the file "Crash" stored on your data disk and described in the data file dictionary in Appendix B at the end of the book.

(a) Prepare graphical plots of crash deaths versus each of the potential predictor variables. Note the relationship and any unusual patterns in the data points.

(b) Prepare a simple regression analysis of crash deaths on the potential predictor variables. Determine which, if any, of the regressions indicate a significant relationship.

(c) State the results of your analysis and rank the predictor variables in terms of their relationship to crash deaths.

14.16 An economist wishes to predict the market value of owner-occupied homes in small midwestern cities. He has collected a set of data from 45 small cities for a two-year period and wants you to use this as the data source for the analysis. The data are in the file "Citydat," which is stored on your data disk and described in the data file dictionary in Appendix B at the end of the book. He wants you to develop two prediction equations: one that uses the size of the house as a predictor and a second that uses tax rate as a predictor.

(a) Plot the market value of houses versus size of house and tax rate. Note any unusual patterns in the data.

(b) Prepare regression analyses for the two predictor variables. Which variable is the stronger predictor of the value of houses?

(c) A business developer in a midwestern state has stated that local property tax rates in small towns need to be lowered because if they are not, no one will purchase a house in these towns. Based on your analysis in this problem, evaluate the business developer's claim.

14.17 George Holt, the vice-president of purchasing for a large national retailer, has asked you to prepare an analysis of retail sales by state. He wants to know if either the percent unemployment or the per capita personal income are related to per capita retail sales. Data for this study are in the data file named "Retail," which is stored on your data disk and described in the data file dictionary in Appendix B at the end of the book.

(a) Prepare graphical plots and regression analyses to determine the relationships between per capita retail sales and unemployment and personal income. Compute 95% confidence intervals for the slope coefficients in each regression equation.

(b) What is the effect of a $1000 decrease in per capita income on per capita sales?

(c) For the per capita income regression equation, what is the 95% confidence interval for retail sales at the mean per capita income and at $1000 above the mean per capita income?

14.18 A major national supplier of building materials for residential construction is concerned about total sales for next year. It is well known that the company's sales are directly related to the total national residential investment. Several New York bankers are predicting that interest rates will rise about 2 percentage points next year. You have been asked to develop a regression analysis that can be used to predict the effect of interest-rate changes on residential investment. The time-series data for this study are contained in the data file named "Macro95," which is stored on your data disk and described in the data file dictionary in Appendix B at the end of the book.

(a) Develop two regression models to predict residential investment using prime interest rate for one and federal funds interest rate for the other. Analyze the regression statistics and indicate which equation provides the best predictions.

(b) Determine the 95% confidence interval for the slope coefficient in both regression equations.

(c) Based on each model, predict the effect of a 2-percentage-point increase in interest rates on residential investment.

(d) Using both models, compute 95% confidence intervals for the change in residential investment that results from a 2-percentage-point increase in interest rates.

* 14.19 For the simple regression model

$$Y = \beta_0 + \beta_1 X_1$$

derive the normal equations using the least-squares principle. The following summary statistics have been collected:

$$\bar{Y} = 5536 \qquad \bar{X}_1 = 12{,}227 \qquad S_y = 812 \qquad S_{x_1} = 1851 \qquad n = 51$$

$$\hat{\rho}(X_1, Y) = 0.633$$

Compute:

(a) Estimates for $\hat{\beta}_0$ and $\hat{\beta}_1$.

(b) The coefficient of determination, R^2.

(c) The standard error of the estimate, $S_{Y|X_1}$.

(d) The standard error for the coefficient estimate, $S_{\hat{\beta}_1}$.

(e) The Student t for the coefficient estimate.

14.20 Shirley Matson, production manager of Amalgamated Electronics, wants to develop a linear equation to predict the number of control boards assembled as a function of the number of hours worked. She has obtained a random sample of 41 production shifts and recorded the number of hours worked and the number of units produced on each shift. From these data the following summary statistics have been computed:

$$S_{x_1} = 10 \qquad S_y = 30 \qquad \hat{\rho}(X_1, Y) = 0.80 \qquad \bar{X}_1 = 100 \qquad \bar{Y} = 300$$

(a) She has asked you to compute the regression coefficients, the Student t for the slope coefficient, the standard error of the estimate, and the percent explained variability, R^2, for the regression model.

(b) What is the predicted production and its 95% confidence interval when the number of hours worked is 110?

14.21 Prove the following identities.

(a) Conditional Student t squared for the coefficient β_1 is equal to conditional F in the simple regression

$$Y = \beta_0 + \beta_1 X_1$$

(b) In the same simple regression, show that the percent explained variability is equal to the correlation between Y and X_1 squared.

(c) Beginning with

$$t = \frac{\hat{\beta}_1}{S(\hat{\beta}_1)}$$

show that

$$t = \frac{\hat{\rho}(X_1, y)\sqrt{n-2}}{\sqrt{1 - \hat{\rho}^2(X_1, y)}}$$

14.22 Given the estimated regression model

$$Y = 10 + 6.25 X_1$$

$$(3.0)\ (9.33)$$

$$S_{Y|X_1} = 10.0 \qquad R^2 = 0.64 \qquad n = 51$$

The Student t statistic for the coefficient of X_1 is 9.33. Compute the remaining statistics and prepare the Minitab computer output, using the ANOVA table.

14.23 Carefully explain how R^2 can provide misleading results if you are trying to select a regression model with the smallest $S^2_{Y|X}$.

14.24 Derive the approximate screening test

$$r_{xy} > \frac{2}{\sqrt{n}}$$

for identifying variables that have statistically significant linear relationships, where r_{xy} is the simple correlation between X and Y.

APPENDIX: COEFFICIENT ESTIMATORS

A.1 Derivation of Coefficient Estimators $\hat{\beta}_0$ and $\hat{\beta}_1$

Partial derivatives of the error sum of squares function are performed:

$$\sum_{i=1}^{n} \left[y_i - (\hat{\beta}_0 + \hat{\beta}_1 x_{1i}) \right]^2$$

The normal equations and resulting least-squares estimators are as follows:

$$\frac{\partial \text{ESS}}{\partial \hat{\beta}_0} = 0$$

$$2 \sum_{i=1}^{n} \left[y_i - (\hat{\beta}_0 + \hat{\beta}_1 x_{1i}) \right] (-1) = 0$$

$$\sum_{i=1}^{n} y_i - n\hat{\beta}_0 - \hat{\beta}_1 \sum_{i=1}^{n} x_{1i} = 0$$

$$n\hat{\beta}_0 + \hat{\beta}_1 \sum_{i=1}^{n} x_{1i} = \sum_{i=1}^{n} y_i$$

$$\frac{\partial \text{ESS}}{\partial \hat{\beta}_1} = 0$$

$$2 \sum_{i=1}^{n} \left[y_i - (\hat{\beta}_0 + \hat{\beta}_1 x_{1i}) \right] (-x_{1i}) = 0$$

$$\sum_{i=1}^{n} x_{1i} y_i - \hat{\beta}_0 \sum_{i=1}^{n} x_{1i} - \hat{\beta}_1 \sum_{i=1}^{n} x_{1i}^2 = 0$$

$$\hat{\beta}_0 \sum_{i=1}^{n} x_{1i} + \hat{\beta}_1 \sum_{i=1}^{n} x_{1i}^2 = \sum_{i=1}^{n} x_{1i} y_i$$

The normal equations

$$n\hat{\beta}_0 + \hat{\beta}_1 \sum_{i=1}^{n} x_{1i} = \sum_{i=1}^{n} y_i$$

$$\hat{\beta}_0 \sum_{i=1}^{n} x_{1i} + \hat{\beta}_1 \sum_{i=1}^{n} x_{1i}^2 = \sum_{i=1}^{n} x_{1i} y_i$$

can be solved simultaneously to obtain the coefficient estimator, $\hat{\beta}_1$, and the equation constant, $\hat{\beta}_0$. First consider $\hat{\beta}_1$:[12]

---

[12] The following transformation leads directly to the second form:

$$\sum_{i=1}^{n} (x_{1i} - \bar{X}_1)(y_i - \bar{Y}) = \sum_{i=1}^{n} (x_{1i} - \bar{X}_1) y_i - \bar{Y} \sum_{i=1}^{n} (x_{1i} - \bar{X}_1)$$

$$= \sum_{i=1}^{n} (x_{1i} - \bar{X}_1) y_i - 0$$

$$\hat{\beta}_1 = \frac{\sum_{i=1}^{n}(x_{1i} - \bar{X}_1)(y_i - \bar{Y})}{\sum_{i=1}^{n}(x_{1i} - \bar{X}_1)^2}$$

$$= \frac{\sum_{i=1}^{n}(x_{1i} - \bar{X}_1)y_i}{\sum_{i=1}^{n}(x_{1i} - \bar{X}_1)^2}$$

This is the typical standard form of the regression slope coefficient found in most books. The deviations in X and Y are multiplied and summed and in turn divided by the sum of square deviations in X.

The constant $\hat{\beta}_0$ is also obtained from the normal equations:

$$\hat{\beta}_0 = \bar{Y} - \hat{\beta}_1 \bar{X}_1$$

A.2 Coefficient Estimators Are Unbiased

In Chapter 10 we developed the properties of estimators and indicated how the best estimators could be selected using these properties. We showed in particular why the sample mean $\bar{Y}$ is the best estimate for the population mean μ. Using these properties we can also show that the least-squares coefficients are the best linear unbiased estimators (BLUE) for the population coefficients.

Given the model

$$y_i = \beta_0 + \beta_1 x_{1i} + \epsilon_i$$

the expected value of the slope coefficient is

$$E[\hat{\beta}_1] = E\left[\frac{\sum_{i=1}^{n}(x_{1i} - \bar{X}_1)y_i}{\sum_{i=1}^{n}(x_{1i} - \bar{X}_1)^2}\right]$$

$$= E\left[\frac{\sum_{i=1}^{n}(x_{1i} - \bar{X}_1)(\beta_0 + \beta_1 x_{1i} + \epsilon_i)}{\sum_{i=1}^{n}(x_{1i} - \bar{X}_1)^2}\right]$$

$$= E\left[\frac{\sum_{i=1}^{n}(x_{1i} - \bar{X}_1)(\beta_0)}{\sum_{i=1}^{n}(x_{1i} - \bar{X}_1)^2}\right] + E\left[\frac{\sum_{i=1}^{n}(x_{1i} - \bar{X}_1)(x_{1i})\beta_1}{\sum_{i=1}^{n}(x_{1i} - \bar{X}_1)^2}\right]$$

$$+ E\left[\frac{\sum_{i=1}^{n}(x_{1i} - \bar{X}_1)(\epsilon_i)}{\sum_{i=1}^{n}(x_{1i} - \bar{X}_1)^2}\right]$$

$$= 0 + \beta_1 + 0$$

$$= \beta_1$$

Therefore, the least-squares estimators are unbiased.

The first term on the right-hand side is zero because we are summing the deviations of X_1 from the mean, and this sum is always zero. In the second term the summations involving X_1 in the numerator and denominator are equal, and thus their ratio is 1. The third term goes to zero because we have assumed that the independent variable X_1 and the error ϵ are independent. In addition to being unbiased, the least-squares estimator $\hat{\beta}_1$ is equal to the maximum likelihood estimator when the error is normally distributed. Using methods beyond the level of this book, we can also show that the coefficient estimators have the minimum variance compared to all possible estimators. Thus they are efficient or "best."

A.3 Correlation and R^2

The relationship between the coefficient of determination and the simple correlation coefficient provides an important link between regression analysis and correlation analysis. The result is

$$R^2 = r_{xy}^2$$

To demonstrate this result we will first develop some important identities for RSS and TSS.

$$\text{RSS} = \sum_{i=1}^{n}(\hat{Y}_i - \bar{Y})^2$$

$$= \sum_{i=1}^{n}\left[\hat{\beta}_0 + \hat{\beta}_1 X_i - (\hat{\beta}_0 + \hat{\beta}_1 \bar{X})\right]^2$$

$$= \hat{\beta}_1^2 \sum_{i=1}^{n}(X_i - \bar{X})^2$$

$$= \hat{\beta}_1^2(n-1)S_X^2$$

$$\text{TSS} = \sum_{i=1}^{n}(y_i - \bar{Y})^2$$

$$= (n-1)S_Y^2$$

We should also recall that

$$\hat{\beta}_1 = r_{xy}\frac{S_Y}{S_X}$$

Using these results, we can show that

$$R^2 = \frac{\text{RSS}}{\text{TSS}}$$

$$= \frac{\hat{\beta}_1^2 (n-1) S_X^2}{(n-1) S_Y^2}$$

$$= \hat{\beta}_1^2 \frac{S_X^2}{S_Y^2}$$

$$= \left(r_{xy} \frac{S_Y}{S_X} \right)^2 \frac{S_X^2}{S_Y^2}$$

$$= r_{xy}^2$$

A.4 Student t and F Statistics

The t test for the slope coefficient and the F test for explained variability are both used to test for a relationship between the dependent variable Y and the independent variable X. The equivalency of these tests is demonstrated by showing that

$$t^2 = F$$

From the definitions in the chapter,

$$t = \frac{\hat{\beta}_1}{S_{\hat{\beta}_1}}$$

$$F = \frac{\text{RSS}}{S_{Y|X}^2}$$

Using these results we show that

$$t^2 = \frac{\hat{\beta}_1^2}{S_{\hat{\beta}_1}^2}$$

$$= \frac{\hat{\beta}_1^2}{S^2(Y \mid X_1) / \sum_{i=1}^{n} (x_{1i} - \bar{X}_1)^2}$$

$$= \frac{\hat{\beta}_1^2 \sum_{i=1}^{n} (x_{1i} - \bar{X}_1)^2}{S_{Y|X}^2}$$

$$= \frac{\text{RSS}}{S_{Y|X}^2}$$

$$= F$$

A.5 Student t Test for Correlation

The correlation coefficient can be tested to determine if it is significantly different from "0," indicating no relationship, using the relationship

$$t = \frac{r_{x_1y}\sqrt{n-2}}{\sqrt{1-r_{x_1y}^2}}$$

This relationship is demonstrated by first showing that

$$S_{Y|X}^2 = \frac{\text{ESS}}{n-2}$$

$$= \frac{\text{TSS}(1-r_{x_1y}^2)}{n-2}$$

$$= \frac{(n-1)S_Y^2(1-r_{x_1y}^2)}{n-2}$$

This result is then substituted into the t ratio for testing the slope coefficient:

$$t = \frac{\hat{\beta}_1}{S_{\hat{\beta}_1}}$$

$$= \frac{r_{x_1y}(S_Y/S_{X_1})}{S_{Y|X}/\sqrt{(n-1)S_{X_1}^2}}$$

$$= \frac{r_{x_1y}(S_Y/S_{X_1})}{\sqrt{(n-1)S_Y^2(1-r_{x_1y}^2)/(n-1)S_{X_1}^2(n-2)}}$$

$$= \frac{r_{x_1y}\sqrt{n-2}}{\sqrt{1-r_{x_1y}^2}}$$

15

Multiple Regression

Our objective is to learn how to use multiple regression for creating and analyzing models.

15.1 SIMULTANEOUS EFFECTS OF SEVERAL VARIABLES

Stephanie Smith is the production manager for Flexible Circuits, Inc. Flexible circuits are produced from a continuous roll of flexible resin with a thin film of copper conducting material bonded to its surface. Copper is bonded by passing the resin through a copper-based solution. The thickness of the copper is critical for high-quality circuits. Copper thickness depends in part on the temperature of the copper solution, speed of the production line, density of the solution, and thickness of the flexible resin. To control the thickness, Stephanie needs to know the precise effect of each of these variables. Multiple regression will provide estimates of the effect of each variable.

In Chapter 14 we learned how to use least-squares regression to estimate and analyze relationships between two variables: for example, total sales as a function of price. However, in many situations several independent variables jointly influence a dependent variable. Multiple regression enables us to determine the simultaneous effect of several independent variables on a dependent variable using the least-squares principle. Many of the concepts studied in Chapter 14 are extended in this chapter.

Our objective is to learn how to use multiple regression to create and analyze models. We will learn how multiple regression works and some rules for interpretation. A good understanding provides the flexibility for solving a wide range of applied problems. Our study begins with some important mathematical and graphical relationships. Then we study examples, using computer output, to learn how multiple regression is applied.

There are many examples of multiple regression applications:

1. The quantity of goods sold is a function of price, income, advertising, price of substitute goods, and other variables.

2. Capital investment occurs when a businessperson believes that a profit can be made. Thus capital investment is a function of variables related to the potential

independent variables change simultaneously, it is difficult to determine the effect of each independent variable on the dependent variable.

15.2 ESTIMATION OF COEFFICIENTS

Multiple regression coefficients are computed using estimators obtained by the least-squares procedure. This procedure is similar to that presented in Chapter 14 for simple regression. The estimators are complicated by the relationships between the independent X variables which occur simultaneously with the relationships between the independent and dependent variables. The estimates of coefficients and their variances are always obtained using a computer. However, we spend considerable effort studying the algebra and computational forms in least-squares regression. This study provides you with the background to understand the procedure and to determine how different data patterns influence the results. We begin with a definition of the model and the assumptions used for estimating coefficients (Key Idea 15.2).

Key Idea 15.2: Multiple Regression Model

Multiple regression is a procedure for determining the simultaneous linear effect of several independent variables on a dependent variable. This is done by estimating the coefficients of the linear equation

$$Y = \beta_0 + \beta_1 X_1 + \beta_2 X_2 + \cdots + \beta_k X_k + \epsilon$$

using the principle of least squares. The assumptions are similar to those presented in Chapter 14 for simple regression:

1. The X's are known exactly without error.
2. $\epsilon \sim N(0, \sigma^2)$.
3. The variance σ^2 is constant over the range of all the independent variables.
4. ϵ and X_j, $j = 1, \ldots, k$, are independent.
5. The ϵ's from each observation are independent.
6. An exact relationship does not exist between the independent variables.

Using these assumptions, we develop estimators, $\hat{\beta}_j$'s, of the coefficients in the linear model

$$\hat{Y}_i = \beta_0 + \hat{\beta}_1 x_{1i} + \hat{\beta}_2 x_{2i} + \cdots + \hat{\beta}_k x_{ki}$$

so that the resulting equation is a best approximation of the relationship. In multiple regression the coefficient estimators are selected using the *least-squares principle:* Select the coefficient estimators to minimize the sum of squared deviations of the observed values of the dependent variable y_i from the predicted values $\hat{Y}_i$ (Key Idea 15.3).

Key Idea 15.3: Basic Least-Squares Algorithm

The formal development begins by defining the residual

$$\hat{e}_i = y_i - \hat{Y}_i$$

as the deviation between the predicted value $\hat{Y}_i$ and the observed value y_i of the dependent variable. Then the coefficient estimators $\hat{\beta}_j$'s are chosen to minimize ESS, the error sum of squares:

$$\text{ESS} = \sum_{i=1}^{n} \hat{e}_i^2$$

$$= \sum_{i=1}^{n} (y_i - \hat{Y}_i)^2$$

$$= \sum_{i=1}^{n} \left[y_i - (\hat{\beta}_0 + \hat{\beta}_1 x_{1i} + \cdots + \hat{\beta}_k x_{ki}) \right]^2$$

The coefficient estimators are obtained by applying differential calculus to this function for each coefficient in the linear equation. (See the chapter appendix.)

15.2.1 Three-Dimensional Graphing

Your understanding of the multiple regression procedure might be helped by considering a simplified graphical image. Look at the corner of the room. The lines formed by two walls and the floor represent the axis for two independent variables, X_1 and X_2. The corner between these two walls is the dependent variable, Y, axis. To estimate a regression line we collect sets of points (x_{1i}, x_{2i}, and y_i). Now picture these points plotted in your room using the two walls and floor corners as the three axes. With these points hanging in your room, we find a plane in space that comes close to all of them. This plane is the geometric form of the least-squares equation.

Geometric interpretations of multiple regression become increasingly complex as the number of independent variables increases. However, the analogy to simple regression is extremely useful. We are minimizing the sum of squared deviations in the

Y dimension about a linear function of the independent variables. In simple regression the function is a straight line on a two-dimensional graph. With two independent variables the function is a plane in three-dimensional space. Beyond two independent variables we have various complex hyperplanes.

To learn more about the multiple regression procedure, we examine the coefficient estimators for the linear equation

$$\hat{Y}_i = \hat{\beta}_0 + \hat{\beta}_1 X_{1i} + \hat{\beta}_2 X_{2i}$$

The application of partial differential calculus results in three equations that can be solved to obtain the coefficient estimators.

This derivation is presented in the chapter appendix. Students who understand differential calculus are encouraged to study the derivation. The coefficients that result from the least-squares analysis are presented in Key Idea 15.4.

Key Idea 15.4: Least-Squares Coefficient Estimators

For the linear model, $\hat{Y}_i = \hat{\beta}_0 + \hat{\beta}_1 X_{1i} + \hat{\beta}_2 X_{2i}$, the normal equations can be solved to obtain the following estimators:

$$\hat{\beta}_1 = \frac{S_Y(r_{x_1y} - r_{x_1x_2}r_{x_2y})}{S_{X_1}(1 - r_{x_1x_2}^2)}$$

$$\hat{\beta}_2 = \frac{S_Y(r_{x_2y} - r_{x_1x_2}r_{x_1y})}{S_{X_2}(1 - r_{x_1x_2}^2)}$$

$$\hat{\beta}_0 = \bar{Y} - \hat{\beta}_1 \bar{X}_1 - \hat{\beta}_2 \bar{X}_2$$

where r_{x_1y} is the sample correlation between x_1 and y, r_{x_2y} is the sample correlation between x_2 and y, $r_{x_1x_2}$ is the sample correlation between x_1 and x_2, S_Y is the sample standard deviation of Y, and S_{X_j} is the sample standard deviation of X_j. It can be shown that the regression equation passes through the means of all variables: $\bar{Y}, \bar{X}_j, j = 1, \ldots, k$.

$$r_{x_1y} = \frac{S_{x_1,y}}{S_{X_1}S_Y}$$

$$S_{x_1,y} = \frac{\sum_{i=1}^{n}(x_{1i} - \bar{X}_1)(y_i - \bar{Y})}{n-1}$$

$$r_{x_1x_2} = \frac{S_{x_1,x_2}}{S_{X_1}S_{X_2}}$$

$$S_{x_1, x_2} = \frac{\sum_{i=1}^{n}(x_{1i} - \bar{X}_1)(x_{2i} - \bar{X}_2)}{n - 1}$$

$$S_Y = \sqrt{\frac{\sum_{i=1}^{n}(y_i - \bar{Y})^2}{n - 1}}$$

$$S_{X_1} = \sqrt{\frac{\sum_{i=1}^{n}(x_{1i} - \bar{X}_1)^2}{n - 1}}$$

The estimator for $\hat{\beta}_1$ in Key Idea 15.4 provides some important insights concerning multiple regression coefficients. $\hat{\beta}_1$ has a complex relationship with all of the variables in the model

$$Y = \beta_0 + \beta_1 X_1 + \beta_2 X_2$$

The slope coefficient estimator, $\hat{\beta}_1$, depends not only on the correlation between X_1 and Y, $r_{x_1 y}$, but also on the correlations between the other variables, $r_{x_1 x_2}$ and $r_{x_2 y}$. Consider first the special case where the correlation $r_{x_1 x_2}$ equals zero. Then $\hat{\beta}_1$ is exactly the same as the simple regression coefficient in

$$Y = \beta_0 + \beta_1 X_1$$

which is

$$\hat{\beta}_1 = r_{x_1 y} \frac{S_Y}{S_{X_1}}$$

However, if $r_{x_1 x_2}$ is not equal to zero—the typical case for business and economics data—$\hat{\beta}_1$ will be influenced by the linear relationships between X_1 and X_2, $r_{x_1 x_2}$ and between X_2 and Y, $r_{x_2 y}$. If the correlation between X_1 and X_2, $r_{x_1 x_2}$, equals 1, it is not possible to compute $\hat{\beta}_1$ or $\hat{\beta}_2$. We say that the coefficients are conditional on all variables in the analysis, as discussed in Key Idea 15.5.

Key Idea 15.5: Conditional Coefficient Estimators

$\hat{\beta}_1$ is an estimator of the linear relationship between X_1 and Y conditional on the effect of other independent variables, X_j.

As a result, we usually find that the simple regression coefficient—for x_1 and Y—will not be the same as the multiple regression coefficient. In some cases the signs will even be reversed. Such a result is not surprising because the simple relationship between Y and X_1 is different from the conditional relationship between Y and X_1 given X_j, $j = 1, \ldots, k$.

The regression constant, $\hat{\beta}_0$, is a function of the slope coefficients and the variable means. A simple manipulation of this equation will also show that the estimated regression line goes through the mean of all the variables.

Does It Make Sense?

Economic demand functions provide a good example of the conditional effect. Usually, we expect that the simple regression coefficient between quantity demanded and price will be negative. However, the effect of income can change the relationship. Income changes shift the demand function. Therefore, if we only examined the relationship between quantity and price, we might find no relationship. A logical explanation is that price changes along the demand function occur simultaneously with shifts in the demand function—caused by income. In that case only the multiple regression of quantity, Y, on both price, X_1, and income, X_2, will provide the correct slope—the conditional relationship between quantity and price.

Another good example is the use of linear equations to predict employee wages. In almost all cases the years of experience is one of the important predictors. However, this linear relationship can be shifted by education, job classification, demand and supply for job skills, geographic area, and possibly gender and race.[1] The latter factors have the effect of shifting the wage versus experience model and possibly changing its slope. Simple regression does not include the effect of income, and thus the slope coefficient, $\hat{\beta}_1$, would be distorted. Thus in some cases a simple linear regression of wage on experience may not indicate a significant relationship. However, by adding the other variables in a multiple regression analysis, the wage versus experience relationship may become significant.   □

The effect of the independent variable correlations on the slope coefficients is an important result (Key Idea 15.6) as indicated by the following simplified cases for the model

$$Y = \beta_0 + \beta_1 X_1 + \beta_2 X_2 + \epsilon$$

1. Assume that between observations, X_1 changes by 1 unit ($\Delta X_1 = 1$), X_2 does not change ($\Delta X_2 = 0$), and Y changes by 2 units ($\Delta Y = 2$). We would conclude that the slope coefficient was equal to

$$\hat{\beta}_1 = \frac{\Delta Y}{\Delta X_1} = 2$$

2. Assume that X_2 changes by 2 units ($\Delta X_2 = 2$), X_1 does not change ($\Delta X_1 = 0$), and Y changes by 8 units ($\Delta Y = 8$). We would conclude that the slope coefficient was equal to

---

[1] Identification of significant gender and/or race variables have provided the basis for winning a number of important wage discrimination lawsuits. As a result, sensitive and wise employers test for race and gender effects in their wage prediction models.

Key Idea 15.6: Effect of Correlated Independent Variables

If the absolute value of the correlation between X_1 and X_2 is equal to 1, the slope coefficients $\hat{\beta}_1$ and $\hat{\beta}_2$ are undefined. When the independent variables are highly correlated, we cannot determine which of the independent variable changes are related to the change in the dependent variable.

$$\hat{\beta}_2 = \frac{\Delta Y}{\Delta X_2} = 4$$

3. In a third case, assume that both X_1 and X_2 change while Y also changes; $\Delta X_1 = 1$, $\Delta X_2 = 2$, and $\Delta Y = 5$. In this case we cannot determine which of the variables X_1 or X_2 affected the change in Y, because they changed simultaneously.

Case 3 contains a high correlation between X_1 and X_2. A high correlation between two variables implies that they move together in a predictable pattern. When two independent variables move together, we cannot determine whether one or the other or both influenced the change in the dependent variable.

Example 15.2   Multiple Regression Computation: Demand for Plywood

When we last visited Agnes Larson she had developed a simple regression model to predict sales as a function of price. Of course, the model did not predict sales exactly, but it was a useful tool. Recently, she noticed that when her competitor had a high price for plywood, her sales were greater than predicted. But when her competitor had a low price, her sales were lower. Therefore, she wondered if the competitor's price would improve her sales prediction.

   Solution   Agnes asked her friend Sally Goldberg for help. Sally suggested that she apply multiple regression to the data in Table 15.1, which contained the previous

TABLE 15.1   Data for the Plywood Demand Example

Price, X_1	Competitor's Price, X_2	Quantity, Y	Residual, $\hat{e}_i$
6	5	80	−6
7	6	60	−8
8	10	70	+20
9	10	40	+8
10	8	0	−14

data relating quantity and price and, in addition, the competitor's price, X_2, for the same day. Sally told Agnes to use the multiple regression model

$$y_i = \beta_0 + \beta_1 x_{1i} + \beta_2 x_{2i} + \epsilon_i$$

where y_i is the number of plywood sheets sold, x_{1i} is the price per sheet charged, and x_{2i} is the competitor's price per sheet.

Sally first used the simple regression equation from Chapter 14 and computed the residual $\hat{e}_i$:

$$\hat{Y}_i = 194.0 - 18.0 x_1 i$$

$$\hat{e}_i = y_i - \hat{Y}_i$$

Residuals were computed and added to Table 15.1. In addition, Sally prepared Figure 15.1, which shows the relationship between competitor's price, X_2, and the residual, $\hat{e}_i$. The residual is the quantity demanded, Y, with the linear effect of price X_1 removed. Thus the relationship between X_2 and the residual is the same as the relationship between Y and X_2 conditional on X_1. In a multiple regression model the coefficient of X_2 would be positive because there is a direct relationship between the residual and X_2.

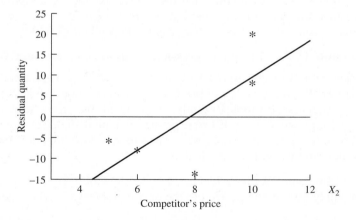

Figure 15.1   Simple Regression Residual Versus Competitor's Price

Ms. Larson then proceeded to compute the various correlations, sample means, and sample standard deviations. The results are

$$\bar{Y} = 50 \qquad \bar{X}_1 = 8 \qquad \bar{X}_2 = 7.8$$

$$S_Y = 31.62 \qquad S_{X_1} = 1.58 \qquad S_{X_2} = 2.28$$

$$r_{x_1 y} = -0.90 \qquad r_{x_2 y} = -0.312 \qquad r_{x_1 x_2} = 0.693$$

Using these descriptive statistics, she computed the regression coefficients:

$$\hat{\beta}_1 = \frac{S_Y(r_{x_1y} - r_{x_1x_2}r_{x_2y})}{S_{X_1}(1 - r_{x_1x_2}^2)}$$

$$= \frac{31.62[-0.90 - (0.693)(-0.312)]}{1.58[1 - (0.693)^2]}$$

$$= -26.33$$

$$\hat{\beta}_2 = \frac{S_Y(r_{x_2y} - r_{x_1x_2}r_{x_1y})}{S_{X_2}(1 - r_{x_1x_2}^2)}$$

$$= \frac{31.62[-0.312 - (0.693)(-0.90)]}{2.28[1 - (0.693)^2]}$$

$$= 8.33$$

$$\hat{\beta}_0 = \bar{Y} - \hat{\beta}_1\bar{X}_1 - \hat{\beta}_2\bar{X}_2$$

$$= 50 - (-26.33)(8) - (8.33)(7.8)$$

$$= 195.67$$

The new equation for predicting plywood sales is

$$\hat{Y} = 195.67 - 26.33X_1 + 8.33X_2$$

Comparing this equation with the simple regression equation

$$\hat{Y} = 194 - 18.0X_1$$

we see that conditional on the competitor's prices, the effect of price changes is even greater. Note also that the simple correlation between Y and X_2 is negative and very small, $r_{x_2y} = -0.312$. However, conditional on the X_1 price, the coefficient $\hat{\beta}_2$ has a positive sign. As we discussed above, conditional regression coefficients are usually different from simple coefficients. □

Practice Problem 15.1

Explain why the multiple regression coefficients for the independent variables are usually not the same as the simple regression coefficients. □

The solutions for all Practice Problems are given at the end of the chapter.

Practice Problem 15.2

Using your understanding of the least-squares algorithm, explain why a point far away from the other points will have a greater effect on the slope coefficients than a point nearer all the others.

(a) Consider first a point with a large deviation in the Y direction.
(b) Consider second a point with a large deviation in the X direction. □

Problem Exercises

15.1   What is the correlation between the independent variables, X_j's, and the model error, ϵ_j? Explain the reasoning behind your answer.

15.2   Explain why correlations between independent variables have an influence on the slope coefficients that indicate the relationship between the dependent and independent variables.

15.3   Express the linear regression model

$$Y = \hat{\beta}_0 + \hat{\beta}_1 X_1 + \hat{\beta}_2 X_2$$

as a function that includes the sample means instead of the constant, $\hat{\beta}_0$. What is the advantage of this form of the model?

15.4   George Treloar has been conducting a series of studies of the effect of grain moisture level on the productivity of a flour production process. In his study he discovered that the line speed also changed over the various experiments. In some cases the line speed was highly correlated with moisture level and in others it was not. The following variables were used:

   Y: productivity in units per hour
   X_1: moisture level as a percentage
   X_2: line speed in feet per minute

The data collected from three experiments are approximately as follows: $S_y = 100$, $S_{x_1} = 50$, $S_{x_2} = 40$, $r_{x_1 y} = 0.70$, and $r_{x_2 y} = -0.60$. The correlation $r_{x_1 x_2}$ varied over three experiments. Determine the slope coefficient for moisture for experiment 1 when:

   (a) $r_{x_1 x_2} = 0.2$.
   (b) $r_{x_1 x_2} = 0.6$.
   (c) $r_{x_1 x_2} = 0.9$.

15.5   George Treloar conducted a second series of studies of the effect of grain moisture level on the productivity of a flour production process. In this study he discovered that the line speed also changed over the various experiments. In some cases the line speed was highly correlated with moisture level and in others it was not. The following variables were used:

   Y: productivity in units per hour
   X_1: moisture level as a percentage
   X_2: line speed in feet per minute

The data collected from three experiments are approximately as follows: $S_Y = 100$, $S_{X_1} = 50$, $S_{X_2} = 40$, $r_{x_1 y} = 0.50$, and $r_{x_2 y} = 0.60$. The correlation $r_{x_1 x_2}$ varied over three experiments. Determine the slope coefficient for moisture for experiment 1 when:

   (a) $r_{x_1 x_2} = 0.2$.
   (b) $r_{x_1 x_2} = 0.6$.
   (c) $r_{x_1 x_2} = 0.9$.

15.6   Refer to Problem 15.5. Use your statistical package or an electronic spreadsheet to compute the estimated slope coefficients $\hat{\beta}_1$ and $\hat{\beta}_2$ as a function of the correlation between independent variables, $r_{x_1 x_2}$. Compute the coefficients for $r_{x_1 x_2}$ at 0.05 increments over the range 0.05 to 0.95. Then prepare a graphical plot of the relationship between $r_{x_1x_2}$ and each of the slope coefficients. Explain and interpret the results.

15.7   Describe a process from your experience that would be suitable for multiple regression analysis. Define the variables and interpret the slope coefficients. Indicate important questions that might be answered by using the regression analysis model.

15.8   Explain in your own words how the multiple regression normal equations are obtained, and how they are used to obtain the coefficient estimators.

15.3 PARTITIONING OF VARIABILITY

Chapter 14 showed how the total variability in the dependent variable Y could be partitioned into a component that was "explained" by the regression model and a component that was unexplained or error. The resulting identity,

$$\text{TSS} = \text{RSS} + \text{ESS}$$

also holds for multiple regression (Key Idea 15.7).

Key Idea 15.7: Analysis of Variance

Analysis of variance,

$$\text{TSS} = \text{RSS} + \text{ESS}$$

is used in multiple regression to determine:

1. The amount of explained variability, RSS, and the amount of unexplained variability, ESS
2. An estimate of the error variance
3. The components of variability explained by each of the independent variables given the variability explained by the other variables

---

In the multiple regression model,

$$y_i = \beta_0 + \beta_1 x_{1i} + \beta_2 x_{2i} + \cdots + \beta_k x_{ki} + \epsilon_i$$

the error term ϵ_i is assumed to have a uniform variance σ^2. The estimate of σ^2 can be computed from the error sum of squares (Key Idea 15.8),

$$\text{ESS} = \sum_{i=1}^{n} (y_i - \hat{Y}_i)^2$$

Key Idea 15.8: Standard Error of the Estimate

The estimator for the linear model variance, σ^2, is

$$S_{Y|X}^2 = \frac{\text{ESS}}{n - k - 1}$$

which is defined as the **variance of the estimate**. ESS divided by the degrees of freedom, $n - k - 1$, with $k > 1$ independent variables,

$$S_{Y|X} = \sqrt{\frac{\text{ESS}}{n - k - 1}}$$

is the **standard error of the estimate**. The X represents all the independent variables. This is the variance in Y after the effect of all the independent variables has been removed.

which is minimized in multiple regression. The computation is similar to the one used in simple regression and uses the equation

$$\hat{\sigma}^2 = \frac{\text{ESS}}{n - k - 1}$$

where k is the number of independent variables in the regression.

In multiple regression R^2 is also interpreted as the percent explained variability, just as it was in simple regression (Key Idea 15.9). One must be careful to avoid assigning global significance to R^2 because a large value can result from either a small ESS or a large TSS. The simple regression example in Chapter 14 that showed the dangers of using R^2 globally also applies to multiple regression. Using R^2 to compare models with the same set of observed Y's is always useful because a higher R^2 implies a smaller ESS.

Key Idea 15.9: Multiple Coefficient of Determination, R^2

For multiple regression equations we can also compute the **multiple coefficient of determination**, or R^2, as the ratio of total explained variability divided by total variability:

$$R^2 = \frac{\text{RSS}}{\text{TSS}} = 1 - \frac{\text{ESS}}{\text{TSS}}$$

Different data sources generally lead to regression models having R^2 in certain ranges. Multiple regression models using time-series data tend to have R^2 between 0.70 and 0.99, while cross-section models tend to have R^2 in the range 0.50 to 0.70. Models fitted to individual human behavior will tend to have a large error and hence R^2 in the range 0.10 to 0.20.

A number of analysts prefer to use R_a^2 adjusted for degrees of freedom to compare equations with different independent variables. R_a^2 is defined as

$$R_a^2 = 1 - \frac{S_{Y|X}^2}{S_Y^2}$$

$$= 1 - \frac{\text{ESS}/(n-k-1)}{\text{TSS}/n-1}$$

$$= 1 - \frac{\text{ESS}(n-1)}{\text{TSS}(n-k-1)}$$

$$= 1 - (1 - R^2)\frac{n-1}{n-k-1}$$

The adjusted R_a^2 is computed using 1 minus the ratio of the variance estimates $S_{Y|X}^2$ and S_Y^2 instead of using ESS and TSS. R_a^2 is thus adjusted for degrees of freedom and will be slightly smaller than R^2. An important advantage is that R_a^2 will increase only if $S_{Y|X}^2$ decreases. In contrast, R^2 increases whenever ESS decreases and ESS decreases even when nonsignificant variables are added. For that reason R_a^2 is a more useful statistic for comparing regression models. The difference between R^2 and R_a^2 is small and they approach each other as the sample size increases. Thus the general discussion of R^2 applies also to R_a^2.

15.4 CONDITIONAL EXPLAINED VARIABILITY

The first question we ask about a multiple regression model is: Does the model explain a significant amount of variability? If it does not, we conclude that none of the independent variables are individually or in combination important predictors of the dependent variable. This implies that the model specification needs to be redefined (see Key Idea 15.10).

15.4.1 Statistical Significance of Individual X's

Determining the contribution of each variable in a multiple regression model is complicated because the effect of an independent variable is conditional on the other variables in the model. We begin our discussion with the simple case in which there is no correlation between independent variables and then proceed to the more typical case where the independent variables are correlated.

Key Idea 15.10: Overall F Test

The test for the significance of the entire regression can be performed using an F test similar to the one used in simple regression. The null hypothesis,

$$H_0: \beta_1 = \beta_2 = \cdots = \beta_k = 0$$

states that all the coefficients are simultaneously equal to zero. The alternative hypothesis,

$$H_1: \beta_j \neq 0 \quad \text{at least one } j$$

states that at least one of the coefficients is not equal to zero. The calculated F ratio is

$$F = \frac{\text{RSS}/k}{\text{ESS}/(n-k-1)}$$

$$= \frac{\text{MSR}}{S_{Y|X}^2}$$

The explained sum of squares RSS is divided by the number of predictor variables, and the error sum of squares is divided by the degrees of freedom for error. The numerator RSS/k is defined as the **mean square of the regression** (MSR). The calculated F ratio has k degrees of freedom for the numerator and $n-k-1$ degrees of freedom for the denominator. To test the hypothesis we compare the calculated F with the critical F_c obtained from Table A.4. The critical F_c selected will have k degrees of freedom for the numerator and $n-k-1$ degrees of freedom for the denominator.

Rule: Reject H_0 if F calculated is greater than F_c.

15.4.2 Significance When X's Are Not Correlated

When the independent variables are not correlated the estimated coefficients are equivalent to those that would be obtained by running a set of simple regressions for each independent variable. Examination of the coefficient estimators in Key Idea 15.4 shows this result. The variability explained by each independent variable X_j could be obtained by multiplying the total sum of squares TSS by the percent explained variability, for X_j, $R_{x_j}^2 = r_{x_j y}^2$. We could then partition the explained variability RSS into a component explained by each variable as follows:

$$RSS = RSS_{X_1} + RSS_{X_2} + \cdots + RSS_{X_k}$$
$$= r_{x_1y}^2 TSS + r_{x_2y}^2 TSS + \cdots + r_{x_ky}^2 TSS$$
$$= (r_{x_1y}^2 + r_{x_2y}^2 + \cdots + r_{x_ky}^2)TSS$$

Thus, in this case, the total explained variability RSS is partitioned into components that are uniquely related to each of the independent variables. This unique partitioning is shown schematically in Figure 15.2. Each partition, RSS_{X_j}, depends only on the relationship between X_j and Y. The overall percent explained variability R^2 for the multiple regression model would be equal to the sum of the simple correlations squared, as shown in Figure 15.2.

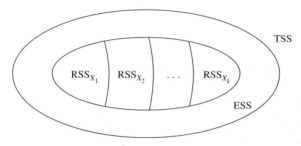

Figure 15.2 Partitioning of Variance When Independent Variables Have Zero Correlation

A conditional F test (Key Idea 15.11) could be performed to determine if an independent variable contributed significantly to explained variability, given the variability explained by the other independent variables. If the conditional regression coefficient is not zero, the variable contributes significantly to explained variability. The hypothesis test would be

$$H_0: \beta_j = 0 \mid \beta_l \neq 0, j \neq l$$
$$H_1: \beta_j \neq 0 \mid \beta_l \neq 0, j \neq l$$

This complex notation emphasizes that the significance of a particular independent variable in multiple regression depends on the other variables in the model. The conditional F statistic for this hypothesis test is (no correlation between X_j's)

$$F_{x_j} = \frac{RSS_{X_j}}{S_{Y|X}^2} = \frac{r_{x_jy}^2 TSS}{S_{Y|X}^2}$$

This computed value is compared with the critical F from Table A.4 with 1 degree of freedom for the numerator and $n - k - 1$ degrees of freedom for the denominator. Note that as the number of significant independent variables increases and hence $S_{Y|X}^2$ decreases, the computed conditional F_{x_j} will increase. Thus a variable is more likely to be significant.

Example 15.3   Variance Partitioning for the Plywood Problem

Agnes Larson developed a regression equation to predict the demand for plywood, Y, as a function of her price, X_1, and her competitor's price, X_2:

$$\hat{Y} = 195.67 - 26.33X_1 + 8.33X_2$$

This equation was used to compute the explained variability RSS and the unexplained variability ESS in Table 15.2.

TABLE 15.2   Partitioning of Variability for Plywood Demand Model

X_1	X_2	Y	$\hat{Y}$	$(y_i - \hat{Y}_i)^2$	$(\hat{Y}_i - \bar{Y})^2$	$(y_i - \bar{Y})^2$
6	5	80	79.33	0.44	860.45	900
7	6	60	61.33	1.78	128.44	100
8	10	70	68.33	2.78	336.11	400
9	10	40	42.00	4.00	64.00	100
10	8	0	−1.00	1.00	2601	2500
				10.0	3990.0	4000
				ESS	RSS	TSS

The partitioning of variability identity is satisfied with

$$TSS = RSS + ESS$$

$$\sum_{i=1}^{n}(y_i - \bar{Y})^2 = \sum_{i=1}^{n}(\hat{Y}_i - \bar{Y})^2 + \sum_{i=1}^{n}(y_i - \hat{Y}_i)^2$$

$$4000 = 3990 + 10$$

The variance of the estimate can be computed using ESS and the degrees of freedom $5 - 2 - 1 = 2$.

$$S_{Y|X}^2 = \frac{ESS}{n - k - 1}$$

$$= \frac{10}{2}$$

$$= 5$$

$$S_{Y|X} = 2.236$$

The multiple coefficient of determination R^2 is

$$R^2 = \frac{RSS}{TSS} = \frac{3990}{4000} = 0.997$$

The final task is to determine if both variables are important in the multiple regression model. This will be done by determining their contributions to explained variability. The contribution of price X_1 by itself to explained variability can be computed using

$$RSS_{X_1} = R_{x_1}^2\,TSS = r_{x_1 y}^2\,TSS = (-0.90)^2 \times 4000 = 3240$$

where $r_{xy} = -0.90$ is the simple correlation between X_1 and Y. This result was also computed in Table 14.2. The conditional contribution of competitor's price X_2 given X_1 can be computed by subtracting the variability explained by price X_1 from the variability explained by both X_1 and X_2:

$$\text{RSS}(X_2 \mid X_1) = \text{RSS}(X_1, X_2) - \text{RSS}_{X_1}$$

$$= 3990 - 3240$$

$$= 750$$

We can then compute the conditional F to test the hypothesis

$$H_0: \beta_2 = 0 \mid \beta_1 \neq 0$$

$$H_1: \beta_2 \neq 0 \mid \beta_1 \neq 0$$

The conditional F is

$$F_{x_2} = \frac{\text{RSS}(X_1, X_2) - \text{RSS}_{X_1}}{S_{Y \mid X}^2}$$

$$= \frac{3990 - 3240}{5}$$

$$= 150$$

The critical value of F for $\alpha = 0.05$, with 1 degree of freedom for the numerator and 2 degrees of freedom for the denominator, is, from Table A.4, $F_{0.05, 1, 2} = 18.51$. Since 150 is greater than 18.51, we conclude that competitor's price X_2 is a significant variable given the effect of X_1.

A simple regression with X_2 could be used to compute the conditional explained variability and F test for X_1 given X_2. In all cases the conditional significance of a variable depends on the other variables in the model.

The computer outputs for simple and multiple regression in Exhibit 15.1 could have been used to obtain $\text{RSS}(X_1, X_2)$ and RSS_{X_1}. In the multiple regression output conditional explained variability for competitor's price has been computed. Examine the output from your computer to understand clearly where the various statistics used in the analysis are presented. $\square$

15.5 STATISTICAL INFERENCE

A great deal of emphasis is placed on the slope coefficients, $\hat{\beta}_j$'s, in multiple regression. They are the conditional marginal effect of a particular variable given a model containing several other independent variables. Conditional slope coefficients, $\hat{\beta}_j$, estimate how much a dependent variable—sales, production, total income—changes for each 1-unit change of an independent policy or decision variable—price, labor units, or tax rate. Thus they provide important information for economic decision making.

Because coefficient estimates are so important, we need to estimate the coefficient variances, $\sigma_{\hat{\beta}_j}^2$, and the standard deviations, $\sigma_{\hat{\beta}_j}$. The standard deviation of the slope coefficient $S_{\hat{\beta}_j}$ is used for confidence intervals and hypothesis tests (Key Idea 15.12). Decision makers need to know the precision of important decision variables, and therefore we analyze the basic standard deviation estimator.

EXHIBIT 15.1   Simple and Multiple Regression: Plywood Demand

```
MTB > regress c3 on 1 independent variable c1

The regression equation is
quantity = 194 - 18.0 price


Predictor         Coef           Stdev        t-ratio
Constant        194.00           40.89           4.74
price           -18.000           5.033         -3.58


s = 15.92        R-sq = 81.0%     R-sq(adj) = 74.7%

Analysis of Variance
SOURCE          DF            SS              MS
Regression       1          3240.0          3240.0
Error            3           760.0           253.3
Total            4          4000.0


MTB > corr c1-c3


         price comprice
comprice  0.693
quantity -0.900    -0.312


MTB > regress c3 on 2 independent variables c1,c2

The regression equation is
quantity = 196 - 26.3 price + 8.33 comprice


Predictor         Coef           Stdev        t-ratio
Constant        195.667          5.746          34.05
price           -26.3333         0.9813        -26.83
comprice          8.3333         0.6804         12.25


s = 2.236        R-sq = 99.7%     R-sq(adj) = 99.5%

Analysis of Variance
SOURCE          DF            SS              MS
Regression       2          3990.0          1995.0
Error            2            10.0             5.0
Total            4          4000.0


SOURCE          DF         SEQ SS
price            1          3240.0
comprice         1           750.0
```

Key Idea 15.12: Coefficient Variances

The estimator of the coefficient standard deviation is a complex linear function of the standard error of the estimate. We develop some insights by considering a multiple regression with two independent variables:

$$\hat{Y} = \beta_0 + \hat{\beta}_1 X_1 + \hat{\beta}_2 X_2$$

For this model the population variance and standard deviation for the slope coefficient are

$$\sigma_{\hat{\beta}_1}^2 = \frac{\sigma^2}{\left[\sum_{i=1}^{n}(x_{1i} - \bar{X}_1)^2 \right](1 - r_{x_1 x_2}^2)}$$

$$\sigma_{\hat{\beta}_1} = \sqrt{\frac{\sigma^2}{\left[\sum_{i=1}^{n}(x_{1i} - \bar{X}_1)^2 \right](1 - r_{x_1 x_2}^2)}}$$

The sample variance and standard deviation are

$$S_{\hat{\beta}_1}^2 = \frac{S_{Y|X}^2}{\left[\sum_{i=1}^{n}(x_{1i} - \bar{X}_1)^2 \right](1 - r_{x_1 x_2}^2)}$$

$$S_{\hat{\beta}_1} = \sqrt{\frac{S_{Y|X}^2}{\left[\sum_{i=1}^{n}(x_{1i} - \bar{X}_1)^2 \right](1 - r_{x_1 x_2}^2)}}$$

The coefficient variance is directly related to the variance σ^2 of the model error ϵ. If the observations are closer to the regression model, we have lower variance estimates of the slope coefficients. A wider spread of the independent variables, X_j, provides smaller coefficient variances. If two independent variables have a strong linear relationship $|r_{x_j x_l}| \rightarrow 1$, their coefficient estimates have a larger variance and are subject to large errors. Experienced analysts examine the correlations between all independent variables and know that high correlations between independent variables will result in unstable coefficient estimates.

15.5.1 Confidence Intervals for $\hat{\beta}_j$

Results of multiple regression analysis are typically presented by providing both point and interval estimates for the coefficients. These provide the decision maker with an understanding of how much certainty she can have in using the $\hat{\beta}_j$ coefficients.

The conditional confidence interval for β_j (Key Idea 15.13) is conditional on the other independent variables. The standard deviation and hence the confidence interval increases as the correlation between the independent variables increases.

Key Idea 15.13: Conditional Confidence Interval for $\hat{\beta}_j$

Confidence intervals for the slope coefficient follow the standard form:

$$\hat{\beta}_j \pm t_{(n-k-1),\alpha/2} S_{\hat{\beta}_j}$$

15.5.2 Hypothesis Tests for $\hat{\beta}_j$

Managers use statistical results in a wide variety of decision situations. In many cases decisions deal with rates of change. Hypothesis tests on rates of change provide important inputs to these decisions (Key Idea 15.14).

Key Idea 15.14: Conditional Hypothesis Test for $\hat{\beta}_j$

The conditional hypothesis test

$$H_0: \beta_j = 0 \mid \beta_l \neq 0 \quad j \neq l$$
$$H_1: \beta_j \neq 0 \mid \beta_l \neq 0 \quad j \neq l$$

is used to determine if a specific independent variable is related to the dependent variable given the effects of the other independent variables. If we accept H_0, we conclude that the independent variable X_j contributes nothing to the multiple regression model conditional on the other variables. This hypothesis can be tested using the conditional F test. Another test uses the conditional t statistic:

$$t = \frac{\hat{\beta}_j}{S_{\hat{\beta}_j}}$$

which is routinely computed by most computer programs. The calculated value of t is compared with the critical value in Table A.2 for $n - k - 1$ degrees of freedom.

If the absolute value of the calculated t is greater than the critical value, the null hypothesis is rejected and we conclude that the variable X_j has a significant effect and should be included in the multiple regression model.

The conditional hypothesis test is more complex because the test for a given independent variable is influenced by the set of independent variables in the multiple regression model. Each time an independent variable is added or subtracted, the conditional t statistic changes because both the coefficient estimator $\hat{\beta}_j$ and the coefficient standard error estimator $S_{\hat{\beta}_j}$ are different. A nonsignificant variable can result because it either has no relationship to the dependent variable or because it is highly correlated with another strongly significant independent variable.

Useful Guideline

Many analysts use the following rule when initially screening hypothesis tests. If the absolute value of the student t is greater than 2, the slope coefficient, β_j, is not equal to zero and the variable X_j is a conditional predictor of Y.

15.5.3 Comparison of t and F Tests

There are two common tests for significant slope coefficients, the conditional F test and the conditional t test (Key Idea 15.15). The algebraic demonstration is beyond the scope of this book. However, we can demonstrate the result numerically by comparing regressions that include and exclude the independent variable being considered. In the plywood example in the preceding section, we showed that the conditional F for variable X_2 was $F_{x_2} = 150$. From the computer output in Exhibit 15.1, the conditional t for variable X_2 is 12.25. Therefore, we see that

$$F_{x_2} = t_{x_2}^2$$
$$150 = (12.25)^2$$

You should repeat this demonstration in one of the regression models that are part of your project work for this course. Most analysts use the Student t to determine if a variable is significant and hence should be included in the multiple regression model.

Key Idea 15.15: Conditional F and t Tests

It can be shown that the conditional F test is exactly the same as the conditional t test given the same α and degrees of freedom. The identity

$$F_{x_j} = t_{x_j}^2$$

holds in all multiple regressions.

   The understanding of regression is substantially increased by an understanding of conditional explained variability and the F test. Conditional explained variability depends on both the relationship between the independent and dependent variables and the correlation between independent variables.

15.5.4 Multicollinearity

The interpretation of multiple regression coefficients is complicated by the multicollinearity, which is the correlations between independent variables (Key Idea 15.16). Recall the estimators for the coefficient and its variance when there are two independent variables:

$$\hat{\beta}_1 = \frac{S_Y(r_{x_1y} - r_{x_1x_2}r_{x_2y})}{S_{X_1}(1 - r_{x_1x_2}^2)}$$

$$S_{\hat{\beta}_1}^2 = \frac{S_{Y|X}^2}{\sum_{i=1}^{n}(x_{1i} - \bar{X}_1)^2(1 - r_{x_1x_2}^2)}$$

Key Idea 15.16: Multicollinearity

The general results from the two-independent-variable case continues to hold with k independent variables:

1. Correlations between independent variables change the estimated slope coefficients $\hat{\beta}_j$ compared to simple regression coefficients.
2. Correlations between independent variables increase the estimated standard deviation of the slope coefficients $S_{\hat{\beta}_j}$.

   When the two independent variables have a correlation of zero, simple regression and multiple regression coefficient estimators are exactly the same. The coefficient variance estimators, $S_{\hat{\beta}_1}^2$ for simple and multiple regression coefficient variances are equal when there is zero correlation between independent variables. At the other extreme, a correlation of 1 between independent variables results in undefined coefficient estimators and coefficient variances. With $r_{x_1x_2}^2 = 1$, both denominators are zero and division by zero is not defined.

   For intermediate correlations the effect can be determined from the estimators above. For example, the coefficient variance increases with increased correlation between independent variables. With more than two independent variables, the effect of correlations between independent variables becomes more complex.

Does It Make Sense?

The two conclusions of Key Idea 15.16 imply that the estimated coefficients, $\hat{\beta}_j$'s, their estimated standard deviations, $S_{\hat{\beta}_j}$, and the associated Student t_j's all depend on the set of independent variables included in a particular equation.

The analyst is faced with an important problem when creating multiple regression models for applied studies. Retaining two highly correlated independent variables in a model increases the variance of the slope coefficients, which results in less reliable coefficients. However, arbitrarily eliminating an independent variable when it is conditionally significant causes a biased coefficient estimate.

Statisticians devote considerable effort to the multicollinearity problem. However, many statistical solutions based on specialized assumptions and conditions have limited value in applied problems. If two or more independent variables are highly correlated, we simply cannot determine the unique effects of the correlated independent variables on Y. Solutions for multicollinearity usually involve changes in the equation specification—that is, including different variables and/or different mathematical forms.

Given the complications above, careful model specification is very important. The purpose of each variable in the model needs to be defined carefully. If one of two highly correlated independent variables can be eliminated without seriously affecting the study objectives, this should be done. If two independent variables are likely to be correlated in future applications, the conditional coefficient estimated using the correlated variables provides the most useful estimate. However, note in the example which follows that high variance estimators can lead to unreliable conclusions. All of these problems are more serious when coefficient interpretation is our principal concern. When the model objective is predicting the dependent variable, $\hat{Y}$, multicollinearity is not a serious problem as long as the correlations between independent variables continue to apply in future data.

Figure 15.5 presents an example of multicollinearity to help you understand the concept. There are three subsets of data, each of which has a single value for the variable X_2 (e.g., $X_2 = 1$, $X_2 = 2$, and $X_2 = 3$). The $+$ in each data set indicates the mean for Y and X_1 for that subset. Note that X_1 and X_2 increase together and thus have a positive correlation. Within each of the subsets, with a common value for X_2, there is a negative conditional correlation between Y and X_1. However, a simple regression between Y and X_1 would result in a positive correlation. By fitting a multiple regression of Y on both X_1 and X_2, a negative slope coefficient would result for X_1. The sign for the estimated coefficient $\hat{\beta}_1$ would be positive for simple regression and negative for multiple regression. As indicated by Figure 15.5, the negative sign for the conditional coefficient is the correct sign. If the correlation between X_1 and X_2 had been close to 1, the multiple regression would not have provided a useful model. This would have occurred because the slope coefficient variances, $S_{\hat{\beta}_1}^2$ and $S_{\hat{\beta}_2}^2$, would have been very large. Note the effect of the $1 - r_{x_1 x_2}^2$ term in the denominator of the coefficient variance estimator. $\square$

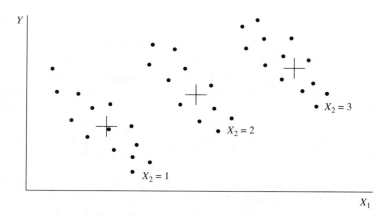

Figure 15.5   Example Showing Multicollinearity

Example 15.4   Electrical Generation

Arnie Rogers wanted to study the operations of an electrical generating plant using input and output data. The plant used bulk crude oil and natural gas as fuels at various times in its operation. Arnie developed a regression model using energy output as the dependent variable and the fuels as two of the input variables.

Solution   Unfortunately, after developing his model specification he was informed that during normal plant operations either crude oil or natural gas were used, depending on price and availability. Thus his weekly fuel consumption figures contained high negative correlations between the quantities of the two fuels. He ran the regression on one set of data and found that natural gas was a more important variable and its coefficient was statistically significant, whereas the coefficient for crude oil was not. When he added observations the analysis indicated that bulk fuel oil was significant, whereas natural gas was not. He was understandably frustrated and disappointed by these results. However, given the data generation process, the results are not surprising. There was no way that good estimates of the coefficients could be obtained. His only solution would be a series of experiments in which one of the fuels was held constant while the second varied. This would be followed by experiments in which the second fuel was held constant while the first was varied. Such experiments often interfere with plant operations and thus are difficult, if not impossible, to schedule.   □

Whenever two independent variables change simultaneously we cannot determine which variable causes the change in the dependent variable. Competent analysts check their data for multicollinearity. Severe multicollinearity, $r_{x_1 x_2} = 1$, makes it impossible to compute coefficient estimates. Strong multicollinearity can result in high variance and hence misleading coefficient estimates. Thus it is important to examine all of the correlations between independent variables as part of a multiple regression analysis. When we examine the coefficient estimators we will see that simple correlations around 0.60 or larger seriously affect the coefficient estimates and their variances.

In models with five or six independent variables it is possible to have a strong relationship between the combination of three or four independent variables, even though none of the individual variables are strongly correlated with each other. For example, a regression of the form

$$X_1 = \alpha_0 + \alpha_1 X_2 + \alpha_2 X_3 + \alpha_3 X_4$$

could have an $R^2 = 0.90$, which indicates a severe multicollinearity problem in the regression model

$$Y = \beta_0 + \beta_1 X_1 + \beta_2 X_2 + \beta_3 X_3 + \beta_4 X_4$$

The latter problem can only be detected by running multiple regressions between several independent variables. A good understanding of the problem can suggest appropriate intermediate regressions as candidates for investigation. In the example above, perhaps only X_1 needs to be included in the linear equation, thus simplifying the analysis and model interpretation.

Does It Make Sense?

When multicollinearity is discovered, modifications need to be made. One solution is to eliminate one or more highly correlated variables from the model. However, eliminating an important predictor variable results in biased estimates for the coefficients of the remaining variables. This problem is discussed in Section 16.8. We are faced with the classic statistical problem of balancing estimator bias and higher estimator variance.

Another solution is to create a new variable that is a function of several independent variables, which requires a careful study of the problem. For example, when determining the conditional relationship between quantity demanded and price, we would not omit price or combine it with other variables.   □

15.5.5 Prediction of $\hat{Y}$

Multiple regression models are often used to predict the dependent or endogenous variable as a function of the independent or exogenous variables. Predictions are made using the estimated equation

$$\hat{Y}_i = \hat{\beta}_0 + \hat{\beta}_1 x_{1i} + \hat{\beta}_2 x_{2i} + \cdots + \hat{\beta}_k x_{ki}$$

Previously, we stressed that it is risky to use points outside the original data range because we do not have any information about the relationship between the independent and dependent variables. However, in some cases forecasters must obtain forecasts beyond the range of the data-independent variable. The basis for these estimates is a belief that the model relationships continue to hold outside the original range of the X's.

The variance of model predictions is a function of the error variance σ^2. However, the relationship is complex because $\hat{Y}$ is a function of the estimated slope coefficients $\hat{\beta}_j$'s, which are all correlated. We present the form of the prediction variance estimator in the chapter appendix. The variance of $\hat{Y}$ increases with the variances of the slope coefficients, with the distance of the prediction from the sample means, and with increased correlations between independent variables. Most modern statistical programs have procedures to compute the prediction variance estimator. If such a feature is not available, a statistician can generally write a short procedure using the capabilities of your statistical system.

Practice Problem 15.3

Explain how you would like to collect data on the X_j's and Y to obtain narrow slope coefficient confidence intervals.   ☐

Practice Problem 15.4

Compare the conditional t and conditional F tests for independent variable coefficients.

(a) Explain intuitively the criteria used by each test to determine significance.
(b) Explain why it is not surprising that both tests are equivalent.   ☐

Problem Exercises

15.9 Explain the overall F statistic in multiple regression and indicate how it should be used.

15.10 Explain the difference between the overall F test and the conditional F test for $\hat{\beta}_j$ in multiple regression.

15.11 How does the correlation between independent variables affect the conditional explained variability associated with a single independent variable?

15.12 George Treloar has been conducting a series of studies of the effect of grain moisture level on the productivity of a flour production process. In his study he discovered that the line speed also changed over the various experiments. In some cases the line speed was highly correlated with moisture level, and in others it was not. The following variables were used:

   Y: productivity in units per hour
   X_1: moisture level as a percentage
   X_2: line speed in feet per minute

The data collected from three experiments are approximately as follows: $S_{Y|X} = 10$, $S_{X_1} = 50$, $S_{X_2} = 40$, $r_{x_1y} = 0.70$, $r_{x_2y} = -0.60$, and $n = 50$. The correlation $r_{x_1x_2}$ varied over three experiments.

(a) For experiment 1, $r_{x_1x_2} = 0.2$. What is the estimated variance of the estimated slope coefficient for moisture?

(b) For experiment 1, $r_{x_1x_2} = 0.6$. What is the estimated variance of the estimated slope coefficient for moisture?

(c) For experiment 1, $r_{x_1 x_2} = 0.9$. What is the estimated variance of the estimated slope coefficient for moisture?

15.13 George Treloar conducted a second series of studies of the effect of grain moisture level on the productivity of a flour production process. In this study he discovered that the line speed also changed over the various experiments. In some cases the line speed was highly correlated with moisture level, and in others it was not. The following variables were used:

Y: productivity in units per hour
X_1: moisture level as a percentage
X_2: line speed in feet per minute

The data collected from three experiments are approximately as follows: $S_{Y|X} = 10$, $S_{X_1} = 50$, $S_{X_2} = 40$, $r_{x_1 y} = 0.50$, $r_{x_2 y} = 0.60$, and $n = 50$. The correlation $r_{x_1 x_2}$ varied over three experiments. Determine the estimated variance of the estimated slope coefficient for line speed for experiment 1 when $r_{x_1 x_2}$ is:

(a) 0.2.
(b) 0.6.
(c) 0.9.

15.14 Refer to Problem 15.13. Use your statistical package or an electronic spreadsheet to compute the estimated variance of the estimated slope coefficients $\hat{\beta}_1$ and $\hat{\beta}_2$ as a function of the correlation between independent variables, $r_{x_1 x_2}$. Compute the coefficients for $r_{x_1 x_2}$ at 0.05 increments over the range from 0.05 to 0.95. Then prepare a graphical plot of the relationship between $r_{x_1 x_2}$ and each of the estimated slope coefficient variances. Explain and interpret the results.

15.15 Explain why the computed Student t statistics for each independent variable in multiple regression are different when the number of independent variables increases or decreases.

15.16 Explain why a Student t equal to 2 is often used to identify important independent variables in multiple regression analysis.

15.17 Describe an example from your experience in which multicollinearity would have an influence on the estimated regression slope coefficients and on their estimated variances.

15.18 Given a typical business or economics application of multiple regression, explain why the total explained variability, RSS, in multiple regression is not equal to the sum of the explained variability from simple regressions between Y and each of the independent variables.

15.6 TRANSFORMATION OF NONLINEAR MODELS

Up to this point we have considered only linear relationships between a dependent variable, Y, and a set of independent variables, X_j's. Now we will show how multiple regression can be used for a broader set of nonlinear applications. We will consider quadratic functions, exponential functions, and categorical or dummy variable functions. Then in Chapter 16, these will be extended to more complex examples.

Examination of the least-squares algorithm indicates that by careful manipulation of nonlinear models it is possible to use least squares for a broader set of applied problems. The assumptions concerning independent variables in multiple regression are not very restrictive. Independent variables define points at which we measure a random variable Y. We assume that there is a linear relationship between the levels of the independent variables X_j, $j = 1, \ldots, k$, and the dependent variable Y. We can take advantage of this freedom to expand the set of models that can be estimated. Thus we can move beyond linear models in our multiple regression applications.

15.6.1 Quadratic Transformations

A number of business and economic relationships can be modeled as a quadratic function (Key Idea 15.17):

$$Y = \beta_0 + \beta_1 X_1 + \beta_2 X_1^2 + \epsilon$$

Three examples are shown in Figure 15.6:

(a) Supply functions may be nonlinear.
(b) The relationship between total output and number of workers may become flatter at higher levels of production.

Key Idea 15.17: Quadratic Model Transformations

The quadratic function

$$Y = \beta_0 + \beta_1 X_1 + \beta_2 X_1^2 + \epsilon$$

can be transformed into a linear multiple regression model by defining new variables,

$$z_1 = x_1$$
$$z_2 = x_1^2$$

and then specifying the model

$$Y_i = \beta_0 + \beta_1 z_{1i} + \beta_{2i} z_{2i} + \epsilon$$

which is linear in the transformed variables. Transformed quadratic variables can be combined with other variables in a multiple regression model. Thus we could even fit a multiple quadratic regression using transformed variables.

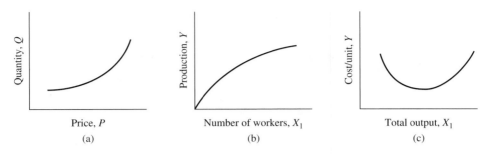

Figure 15.6   Examples of Quadratic Functions

(c) Costs per unit produced are often minimized at an intermediate level of production.

By transforming the variables we can estimate a linear multiple regression model and use the results as a nonlinear model. Inference procedures on transformed quadratic models are those used for linear models. In this way we avoid confusion between separate statistical procedures for linear versus quadratic models. We can also perform a simple hypothesis test to determine if a quadratic model is an improvement over a linear model. The Z_2 or X_1^2 variable is merely an additional variable whose coefficient can be tested using the conditional t or F statistic. If a quadratic model fits the data better than a linear model, the coefficient of the quadratic variable—$Z_2 = X_1^2$— will be conditionally significant.

Example 15.5   Production Costs

George Lapik, production manager of Consolidated Manufacturing, Inc., was interested in estimating the mathematical relationship between the number of electronic assemblies produced during an 8-hour shift and the average cost per assembly. This function would then be used to estimate cost for various production order bids and to determine the production level that would minimize average cost.

Solution   George collected data from nine shifts, during which the number of assemblies ranged from 100 to 900. In addition, he obtained the average cost per unit for those days from the accounting department. From his study of economics and his experience, George suspected that the function might be quadratic with an intermediate minimum average cost. He designed his analysis to consider both a linear and a quadratic average production cost function.

Exhibit 15.2 presents a summary of the computer analysis to obtain the average production cost function. First, the variable values are listed; "avecost" is the average cost per unit produced on that shift, "numassem" is the number of units assembled on that shift, and "numsqrd" is the number of units squared. George entered the average cost and number assembled data and used the computer transformation routine to compute the squared value.

should be used for further analysis. Using this model and calculus, George found that the minimum cost occurred when 510 units were produced during a shift. This result and the average production cost function were included in the procedures manual for bidding on new jobs. □

15.6.2 Exponential Models

Several important economic relationships are modeled by an exponential function (Key Idea 15.18):

$$Y = \beta_0 X_1^{\beta_1} X_2^{\beta_2} \epsilon_i$$

These relationships include constant elasticity of substitution (CES) production functions and demand functions.

Key Idea 15.18: Exponential Model Transformations

Regression estimation of the coefficients of an exponential model,

$$Y = \beta_0 X_1^{\beta_1} X_2^{\beta_2} \epsilon_i$$

requires the use of logarithmic transformations applied to both sides of the equation. The results are

$$\log(y_i) = \log(\beta_0 x_{1i}^{\beta_1} x_{2i}^{\beta_2} \epsilon_i)$$
$$\log(y_i) = \log(\beta_0) + \beta_1 \log(x_{1i}) + \beta_2 \log(x_{2i}) + \log(\epsilon_i)$$

The exponential function is linear in the logarithms of the dependent and independent variables. The coefficients β_1 and β_2 are estimated directly in the transformed regression. However, the transformed model constant, β_0, is the logarithm of the original equation constant. Thus the antilogarithm must be computed. In the transformed model, the error is the logarithm of the original error ϵ_i. For obtaining confidence intervals and performing hypothesis tests we assume that $\log(\epsilon_i)$ has a normal distribution or that ϵ_i has a **log normal distribution**.

A special case of CES production functions has the form

$$Q = \beta_0 L^{\beta_1} K^{\beta_2}$$

where Q is the quantity produced, L is the amount of labor used, and K is the amount of capital used. β_1 and β_2 are the relative contributions of changes in labor and capital to changes in the quantity produced. In one special case, the Cobb–Douglas production function, the sum of coefficients β_1 and β_2 is equal to 1.0. Therefore, β_1 and β_2 are the percent contributions of labor and capital to productivity increase.

Exponential demand functions have the form

$$Q = \beta_0 P^{\beta_1}$$

where Q is the quantity demanded and P is the price. Exponential demand functions have constant elasticity and thus a 1% change in price results in the same percent change in quantity demanded for all price levels. This is not true for linear demand functions. Therefore, in many cases exponential demand functions provide a more realistic model of actual demand.

Exponential functions have broad application in applied economics and business. They are good models for a number of real processes and can easily be manipulated mathematically. One feature of exponential functions is that the coefficients β_j are the elasticities e of Y with respect to X_j,

$$e_{X_j} = \frac{\partial Y / Y}{\partial X_j / X_j} = \beta_j$$

This result is developed in most microeconomics books and in the chapter appendix.

This transformation assumes that the random error term multiplies the true value of Y to obtain the observed value. Thus in the exponential model the error is a percentage of the true value. This implies that the width of the error distribution increases with increases in Y. If this result is not true, the log transformation is not correct. In that case a much more complex nonlinear estimation technique must be used. Those models and the analysis of their statistical properties are considerably beyond the scope of this book.

Cobb–Douglas production function.   Estimation of the Cobb–Douglas function provides a good example of the procedure for estimating restricted functions. The equation in Key Idea 15.18 is modified by the restriction

$$\beta_1 + \beta_2 = 1$$

and therefore a substitution of the form

$$\beta_2 = 1 - \beta_1$$

is made and the new equation is

$$\log(y_i) = \log(\beta_0) + \beta_1 \log(x_{1i}) + (1 - \beta_1)\log(x_{2i}) + \log(\epsilon_i)$$

$$\log(y_i) - \log(x_{2i}) = \log(\beta_0) + \beta_1 \left[\log(x_{1i}) - \log(x_{2i})\right] + \log(\epsilon_i)$$

which reduces to

$$\log\left(\frac{y_i}{x_{2i}}\right) = \log(\beta_0) + \beta_1 \log\left(\frac{x_{1i}}{x_{2i}}\right) + \log(\epsilon_i)$$

The β_2 coefficient is then computed by subtracting β_1 from 1.0. Therefore, estimation of the Cobb–Douglas function coefficients can be accomplished by regressing $\log(Y/X_2)$ on $\log(X_1/X_2)$. A parallel development indicates that we could also regress

$\log(Y/X_1)$ on $\log(X_2/X_1)$ and obtain first an estimate of β_2, followed by subtracting β_2 from 1 to obtain β_1.

Example 15.6   Exponential Production Function

The Dollar Bay Boat Works began producing small fishing boats in the middle 1970s for northern Wisconsin fishermen. George and Susan Peterson, the owners, developed a low-cost production method for producing high-quality boats. As a result, they have experienced increased demand over the years. The production method uses a workstation with a set of jigs and power tools that can be operated by a varying number of workers. Over the years the number of workstations (units of capital) have grown from 1 to 15 to meet the demand for boats. At the same time the workforce has grown from 2 person-years (George and Susan) to 20.9 person-years. They are considering expanding their sales to potential markets in Michigan and Minnesota. Therefore, they need to decide how much to increase the number of workstations and number of workers to achieve various levels of increased production.

Their daughter Heidi, a senior economics major, suggested that they should estimate a Cobb–Douglas production function using data from previous years of operation. She explains that this production function would enable them to predict the number of boats produced for different levels of workstations and workers. George and Susan agree that such an analysis would be a good idea and ask Heidi to prepare the analysis.

Solution   Heidi begins the analysis by collecting production data, shown in Table 15.3, from old company records. To obtain the coefficient estimates, she must first transform the original model specification to a form that can be estimated by least-squares regression. The Cobb–Douglas production function model is

$$Y = \beta_0 X_1^{\beta_1} X_2^{\beta_2} \epsilon$$

with the restriction

$$\beta_2 = 1 - \beta_1$$

where Y is the number of boats produced each year, X_1 is the number of production stations (units of capital) used each year, and X_2 is the number of workers used each year.

Using the series of algebraic steps shown above, the model of the production function was converted to

$$\log\left(\frac{Y}{X_1}\right) = \log(\beta_0) + \beta_2\log\left(\frac{X_2}{X_1}\right)$$

The data in Table 15.3 were transformed to obtain $\log(Y/X_1)$ and $\log(X_2/X_1)$, which were then used in a linear regression to obtain the estimated regression model:

$$\log\left(\frac{Y}{X_1}\right) = 3.0 \qquad + 0.870\log\left(\frac{X_2}{X_1}\right)$$

$$(58.1) \qquad (8.66)$$

$$S_{Y|X} = 0.119 \qquad R^2 = 0.807 \qquad n = 20$$

TABLE 15.3   Production Data for Dollar Bay Boat Works

Year	Production Units	Number of Workers	Number of Boats	Predicted Boats
1976	1.0	2.0	40	36.7
1977	1.2	2.1	45	39.2
1978	1.2	2.7	52	48.8
1979	1.1	3.0	57	52.9
1980	2.0	3.1	65	58.9
1981	3.0	3.6	75	70.7
1982	4.0	4.0	86	80.4
1983	4.5	6.0	95	116.2
1984	4.5	7.1	100	134.5
1985	4.5	8.5	130	157.3
1986	4.1	8.9	161	161.7
1987	6.0	10.0	215	188.1
1988	8.1	13.9	260	260.4
1989	7.9	16.1	265	295.0
1990	11.0	14.0	275	272.7
1991	12.0	14.0	282	275.8
1992	13.2	15.6	300	306.8
1993	14.0	17.0	340	333.2
1994	14.8	18.0	370	352.7
1995	15.0	20.9	405	387.2

After applying the algebraic transformations, the final form of the estimated production function is

$$Y = 20.1 X_1^{0.13} X_2^{0.87}$$

The last column of Table 15.3 contains the predicted number of boats computed from the Cobb–Douglas production function. Exhibit 15.3 compares the actual and predicted production over time. In addition, by regressing the observed number of boats on the predicted number of boats it is possible to compute $S_{Y|X}$ and R^2 in terms of the original data. The resulting model has an equivalent R^2 of 0.983, which indicates a good fit. As shown by the statistical results from the regression analysis and the comparison of observed and predicted production, the Cobb–Douglas production function is a good model for the boat production.

The resulting Cobb–Douglas production function can now be used as a tool for studying the boat production operation. The effect of changes in production that result from changes in capital and labor can be predicted. The estimated model coefficients $\beta_2 = 0.87$ and $\beta_1 = 0.13$ indicates that 87% of the value of the production comes from labor and 13% from capital. In addition, the combinations of labor and capital that provide the most efficient production can be estimated. This analysis provides an important tool for studying the proposed expansion.   □

EXHIBIT 15.3   Observed Versus Predicted Number of Boats per Year

```
MTB > mplot c4 vs c1 c17 vs c1
```

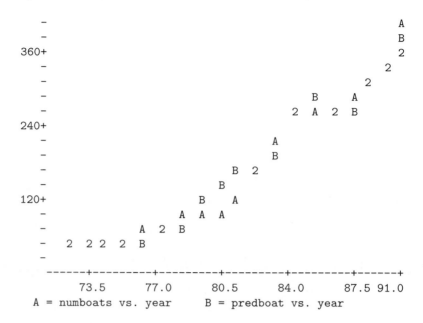

```
          A = numboats vs. year      B = predboat vs. year


MTB > regress c4 on 1 c17

The regression equation is
numboats = - 3.27 + 1.01 predboat

Predictor       Coef        Stdev      t-ratio          p
Constant       -3.266       6.835       -0.48        0.639
predboat       1.01485      0.03177     31.94        0.000

s = 16.42       R-sq = 98.3%      R-sq(adj) = 98.2%
```

15.6.3 Dummy Variables

Linear functions can shift between two different conditions as shown in Figure 15.7.
One condition generates the upper set of points, while the second condition generates
the lower set of points (Key Idea 15.19). There are many examples of models with
shifting functions, including:

1. The relationship between salary and experience may be different for men and
   women because of a historical pattern of discrimination.
2. The relationship between quantity produced and the variable cost per unit will
   shift if a second factory is added to the production facility.

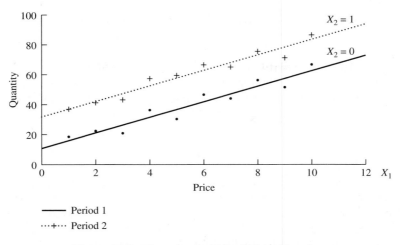

Figure 15.7   Example of a Shifted Linear Function

Key Idea 15.19: Dummy Variable Model

The relationship between Y and X_1,

$$\hat{Y} = \hat{\alpha}_0 + \hat{\alpha}_1 X_1$$

can shift in response to a changed condition. The shift effect can be estimated by using a **dummy variable** which has values of 0 (condition not present) and 1 (condition present). As shown in Figure 15.7, all of the observations from one set of data have the dummy variable $X_2 = 1$, and the observations from the other set of data have $X_2 = 0$. In these cases the relationship between Y and X_1 is specified by the multiple regression model

$$\hat{Y}_i = \hat{\beta}_0 + \hat{\beta}_2 X_2 + \hat{\beta}_1 X_1$$

The coefficient $\hat{\beta}_2$ represents the shift of the function between the upper set of points and the lower set in Figure 15.7. The functions for each set of points are

$$\hat{Y} = \hat{\beta}_0 + \hat{\beta}_1 X_1 \qquad \text{when } X_2 = 0$$

and

$$\hat{Y} = (\beta_0 + \hat{\beta}_2) + \hat{\beta}_1 X_1 \qquad \text{when } X_2 = 1$$

In the first function the constant is $\hat{\beta}_0$, while in the second the constant is $\hat{\beta}_0 + \hat{\beta}_2$. Dummy variables are also called indicator variables.

3. A consumption function may shift because of a war or other political change.

4. The demand function for a product will shift if the marketing area is doubled.

This simple specification of the regression model is a very powerful tool for problems that involve a shift of the linear function by identifiable factors. We can perform a hypothesis test to determine if there is a statistically significant difference between the two subsets of data. The hypothesis test is

$$H_0: \beta_2 = 0 \mid \beta_1 \neq 0$$
$$H_1: \beta_2 \neq 0 \mid \beta_1 \neq 0$$

Rejection of the null hypothesis H_0 leads to the conclusion that the constant is different between the two subsets of data. In the faculty salary example (Section 15.8), you will see how the test has been used to study wage discrimination. Similar procedures have also been used to compare housing prices in different neighborhoods and to determine if an advertising campaign shifted the demand function.

15.6.4 Differences in Slope

Dummy variables can also be used to model and test for differences in the slope coefficient. Figure 15.8 is a typical example. Both the constant and the slope are different in the two subsets of data. The regression model is more complex:

$$\hat{Y} = \hat{\beta}_0 + \hat{\beta}_2 X_2 + (\hat{\beta}_1 + \hat{\beta}_3 X_2) X_1$$

The slope coefficient for X_1 contains two components, $\hat{\beta}_1$ and $\hat{\beta}_3 X_2$. When X_2 equals zero, the slope is the usual $\hat{\beta}_1$. However, when X_2 equals 1, the slope is equal to the

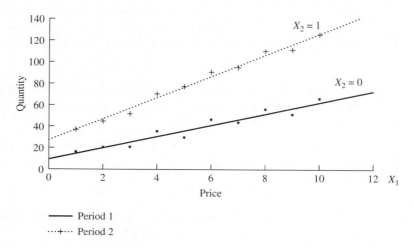

Figure 15.8 Examples of Subsets with Different Slopes

algebraic sum $\hat{\beta}_1 + \hat{\beta}_3$. The model is actually estimated by changing the equation to the form

$$\hat{Y} = \hat{\beta}_0 + \hat{\beta}_2 X_2 + \hat{\beta}_1 X_1 + \hat{\beta}_3 X_2 X_1$$

The *interaction variable*, $X_1 X_2$, is equal to 0 when $X_2 = 0$ and to X_1 when $X_2 = 1$. Therefore, its coefficient, $\hat{\beta}_3$, is the difference in the coefficient of X_1 when $X_2 = 1$ compared to $X_2 = 0$. The t statistic for $\hat{\beta}_3$ can be used to test for differences in slope. The t statistic for $\hat{\beta}_2$ can be used to test for differences in the constant.

Dummy variables provide a powerful tool for studying an expanded set of applied analysis problems. In Chapter 16 we expand the dummy variable applications.

Example 15.7   Machine Production

George Moline, production manager for Allied Machinery, has asked for your assistance in estimating the effect of computer control technology on the output from its new corn cutting machine. This machine cuts the corn from cobs in preparation for canning or frozen-food packing. The traditional machine without computer control has a fixed setting for each corn ear and slices the corn uniformly from the ear. In contrast, the computer-controlled machine has a sensor that measures the size of each ear and adjusts the cutting heads so that each ear is cut at exactly the appropriate level. The rationale for this design is that the adjustments should result in higher corn yield from each ear and lead to increased total output of corn for the same period. Allied Machinery custom manufactures corn cutters of different size. Generally, the output is linearly related to the capital cost for each machine. George wishes to know if the computer-controlled machines have a uniformly higher production for an 8-hour shift. Production data have been collected for 30 machines in various factories; 15 of these machines have computer control and 15 do not.

Solution   This is a problem that can be handled with dummy variables. The data are organized into the following variables:

X_1 ("Capinvst"): capital cost of the machine in thousands of dollars
X_2 ("Comcontr"): dummy variable with values of 0 for conventional machines and 1 for computer-controlled machines
Y ("Productn"): total corn production for an 8-hour shift in kilograms

After discussion with the corporate engineers and with various production managers, the following model was proposed:

$$Y = \beta_0 + \beta_1 X_2 + (\beta_2 + \beta_3 X_2) X_1$$

In this model the coefficient β_1 is an estimate of the overall change in output given computer-controlled machines. Similarly, β_2 is the rate of change in production for each dollar increase in capital cost, and β_3 is the difference in the slope for computer-controlled machines compared to conventional machines. Thus for conventional machines the slope coefficient is β_2, and for computer-controlled machines the slope coefficient is $\beta_2 + \beta_3$. If the rate of output increase per dollar of capital cost is greater for computer-controlled machines, β_3 will be greater than zero.

Exhibit 15.4 presents the output from the regression analysis using the 30 observations. As indicated, the capital investment variable ("Capinvst") has a coefficient (β_2) of 36.547 and a t ratio greater than 2 and thus is a significant variable. This slope coefficient for capital investment is shifted by +37.327, as indicated by the coefficient (β_3) of ("Capxcom"), which is the interaction term (X_2 by X_1). In addition, the regression equation constant is lower by 221.2, as indicated by the coefficient (β_1) of the dummy variable "Comcontr" (X_2).

EXHIBIT 15.4   Regression of Production on Capital and Computer

```
MTB > regress c3 on 3 c2 c1 c4

The regression equation is
Productn = 323 - 221 Comcontr + 36.5 Capinvst + 37.3 Capxcom
    Y                        X_2                X_1              X_2 by X_1
Predictor        Coef        Stdev      t-ratio        p
Constant        323.2        396.6         0.81     0.423
Comcontr       -221.2        496.1        -0.45     0.659
Capinvst       36.547        6.052         6.04     0.000
Capxcom        37.327        7.773         4.80     0.000

s = 284.9        R-sq = 95.6%       R-sq(adj) = 95.1%

Analysis of Variance

SOURCE          DF           SS            MS           F           p
Regression       3      45832416      15277472      188.25     0.000
Error           26       2110045         81156
Total           29      47942460

SOURCE          DF       SEQ SS
Comcontr         1      24260838
Capinvst         1      19700230
Capxcom          1       1871348

Unusual Observations
Obs.Comcontr  Productn        Fit Stdev.Fit   Residual    St.Resid
  1     1.00     4044.5     3426.4     101.0      618.1       2.32R
 27     0.00     1594.4     1638.9     187.0      -44.5      -0.21 X

R denotes an obs. with a large st. resid.
X denotes an obs. whose X value gives it large influence.
```

EXHIBIT 15.4   Regression of Production on Capital and Computer (*Continued*)

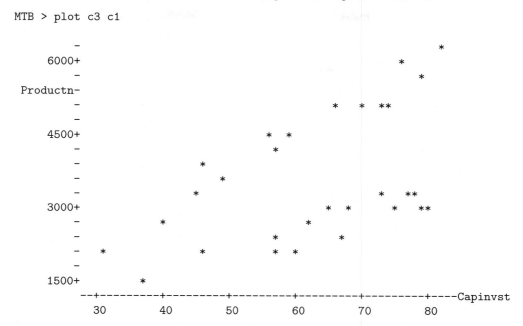

```
MTB > plot c3 c1

          -                                                              *
     6000+                                                         *
          -                                                            *
 Productn-
          -                                                *    *   **
     4500+                                     *    *
          -                                       *
          -                          *
          -                             *
          -                       *                            *     **
     3000+                                          *    *         *    **
          -               *                          *
          -                                    *            *
          -         *                  *          *    *
          -
     1500+             *
        --+---------+---------+---------+---------+---------+----Capinvst
          30        40        50        60        70        80
```

The major difference between the computer-controlled machines and conventional machines is in the coefficient for capital investment. Thus production as a function of capital investment, which represents machine size, increases faster for computer-controlled machines. As a result, larger machines obtain comparatively greater production increases than do small machines. The graphical plot provides a further indication of the pattern of the relationship between production and capital cost for the machines.   □

15.7 RESIDUALS ANALYSIS

Regression analysis provides the best coefficient estimates for the specified model and available data. However, there is no guarantee that the specification is correct or that the data represent the system of interest. Therefore, analysts try to examine the data and the estimators in various ways to test the model specification and assumptions about the data. Residuals analysis is a very important tool for this examination (Key Idea 15.20).

Scatter plots of residuals versus the independent variables and the predicted value of Y should be prepared routinely and examined after a regression model has been estimated. The independent variable plots are used to test the stability of the model fit over the ranges of the independent variables. All residuals should be within

Key Idea 15.20: Residuals Analysis

The **residual** is the difference between the observed value of the dependent variable and the value predicted by the regression equation:

$$\hat{e}_i = y_i - \hat{Y}_i$$

The residual indicates how far each point is from the estimated regression equation. By examining the residuals using scatter plots, we can check the agreement between the model and the actual data.

the range $\pm 3 S_{Y|X}$. Outliers beyond this range should be investigated. Residuals plots that indicate a functional pattern can result from an incorrectly specified model. Residuals plotted against the predicted value are used to test for overall model stability.

If the model has a good fit to the data and the assumptions are reasonable, we expect a plot like Exhibit 15.5. The residuals are spread uniformly over the range

EXHIBIT 15.5   Residuals When Assumptions Are Correct

```
MTB > plot c2 on c1
```

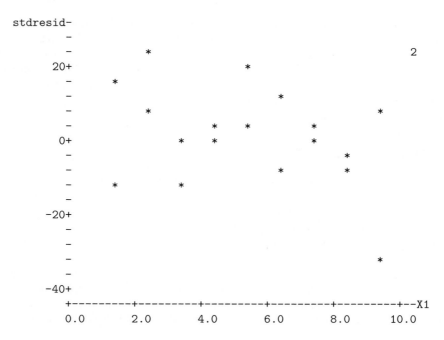

of an independent variable, and there are no unusual patterns. The choice of residual plots depends on the situation and the skill and experience of the analyst in searching for unusual deviations from the assummed model. The characteristics of a Sherlock Holmes are useful for residuals analysis.

There are many examples of graphs that indicate violations of assumptions or unusual relationships in the data. Exhibit 15.6 indicates a quadratic effect for variable X_j. The linear model predicts too low at lower and higher values of X_j and too high at the intermediate values. Thus the model should be modified to include a quadratic effect for X_j. Exhibit 15.7 indicates either a quadratic or possibly an exponential relationship. The latter could be modeled with a transformation of the form

$$Z = e^{X_j}$$

and the model would be

$$\hat{Y} = \hat{\beta}_0 + \hat{\beta}_1 Z$$

where e is the base for natural logarithms.

EXHIBIT 15.6   Residuals Given a Quadratic Relationship

```
MTB > plot c4 on c1
```

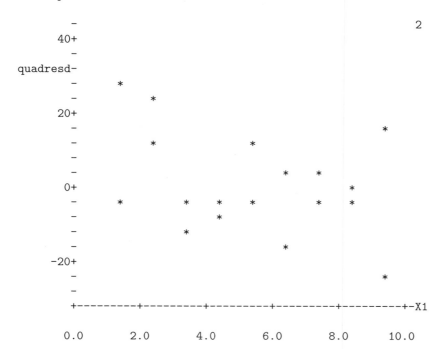

EXHIBIT 15.7   Residuals Given a Quadratic or an Exponential Relationship

MTB > plot c6 on c1

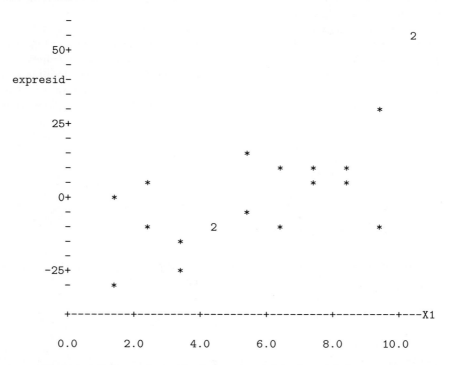

Some analysts study residuals by computing the statistics,

$$\Delta X_{ji} = \hat{\beta}_j X_{ji} + \hat{e}_i$$

Plotting ΔX_j versus X_j provides a picture of the conditional relationship between X_j and Y after the effects of other variables have been removed. Such a picture can provide additional guidance for selecting an appropriate transformation for X_j.

   Exhibit 15.8 shows a plot of residuals versus time. Whenever we fit models using time-series data, a check should be made to determine if there are unusual patterns over time. In this example, with the dependent variable being consumption or investment, the normal business cycle effects are generating residuals that follow a cyclical pattern.[2]

---

[2] In this case we might wish to include a transformation such as

$$Z = A \sin \omega t$$

where A is the amplitude and ω is the frequency of the cycle using the variable t to represent time. This transformation is presented in Chapter 17.

EXHIBIT 15.8   Residuals with Cyclical Time-Series Pattern

```
MTB > plot c12 on c1
```

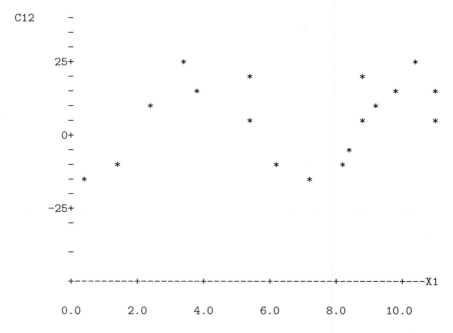

Exhibit 15.9 shows a pattern that indicates residuals spread uniformly over the range of X_j. However, there are two residuals that deviate from the pattern (outside the $\pm 3 S_{Y|X}$ interval). These points, called *outliers*, should be investigated individually by going back to the original data. Outliers may be the result of errors in measuring or recording data. However, they may also indicate an important characteristic of the system being modeled. In the latter case, important management insights can be gained by careful investigation of these unusual situations.

Problem Exercises

15.19 Describe an example from your experience in which a quadratic model would be better than a linear model.

15.20 You are asked to estimate the coefficients of the model

$$Y = \beta_0 + \beta_1 X_1 + \beta_2 X_1^2 + \beta_3 X_2$$

given that the coefficients are restricted such that

$$\beta_1 + \beta_2 = 2$$

Describe how you would estimate the model coefficients using least squares.

EXHIBIT 15.9   Residuals with Two Outliers

MTB > plot c8 on c1

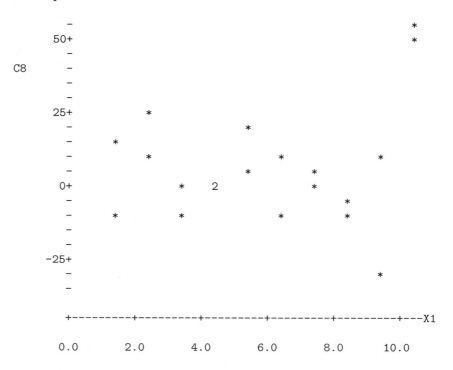

15.21 Least-squares regression results in the best linear unbiased estimators (BLUE). Then why do we examine various plots of residuals when working on applied business and economics problems?

15.22 Why do economists often use exponential functions of the form

$$Y = \beta_0 X_1^{\beta_1} \epsilon$$

to estimate demand curves? (*Note:* Y is the quantity demanded and X_1 is the price.)

15.23 Is it possible to use a dummy variable in a model that includes a quadratic term? Provide an example and interpret the results.

15.24 You have been asked to develop a regression model that predicts the number of strike-outs in a game by a major league starting pitcher as a function of the number of innings pitched in the game. Why might you consider using a combination of linear and quadratic terms for innings pitched in the model?

15.8 REGRESSION EXAMPLE: FACULTY SALARY (PART II)

In Chapter 14 the work of Dr. Gary Frank was introduced. His study considered variables that have an effect on faculty salaries. Based on the simple regression analysis,
he concluded that there was a strong relationship between salary and years of teaching
experience. He also discovered that the annual increase for women was less than the
increase for men. The previous work used only simple regression, but now multiple
regression can be used to increase our understanding of the variables that affect salary.

As he began his study, Dr. Frank prepared a list of all variables that he considered important in the study.

1. Y ("salary"): annual salary in U.S. dollars received by the faculty member
2. X_1 ("yrsexper"): number of years teaching full time at the college
3. X_2 ("female"): dummy variable that has a 1 for female faculty and a 0 for male
   faculty
4. X_3 ("yrsasoc"): number of years as an associate professor
5. X_4 ("yresfull"): number of years as a full professor
6. X_5 ("market"): dummy variable that has a 1 for faculty in a field that includes
   a market premium, because of high demand and limited supply, and a zero
   otherwise

These variables were collected because Dr. Frank believed that they were important factors in determining the salary level. The names in parentheses are the iden-
tifiers assigned in the Minitab program. They are used to identify the variables in
the computer outputs. The first step was to compute descriptive statistics and prepare
histograms using his computer package. These outputs were examined carefully to determine the spread of the data and to check for unusual observations. These descriptive
statistics will also be important as he prepares the final report.

In Exhibit 15.10 the correlation matrix is presented for all of the variables in the
study. This matrix contains one additional variable, "femxexpr," which is the product
of X_2 ("female") times X_1 ("yrsexper"), and is used to test the relationship between
experience and salary for males and for females. We note a large correlation of $r_{x_1 y} =$
0.88 between salary and experience. Thus a regression model that contains only X_1 as

EXHIBIT 15.10   Correlation Matrix for Salary Study

```
MTB > corr c6 c2 c5 c25 c3 c4 c9


          salary yrsexper    female femxexpr  yrsasoc yresfull
yrsexper   0.883
female    -0.429   -0.378
femxexpr  -0.183   -0.079     0.787
yrsasoc    0.698    0.803    -0.367   -0.113
yresfull   0.777    0.674    -0.292   -0.214    0.312
market    -0.007   -0.195    -0.038   -0.099   -0.134   -0.047
```

a predictor would explain $R^2 = (0.88)^2 = 0.78$ or 78% of the variability, as we saw in the Chapter 14 example. Thus any multiple regression model will have an R^2 value greater than 0.78 if the additional variables are important. We also note that X_3 and X_4, experience as an associate and a full professor, are strongly correlated with salary. This result is obvious given the strong relationship between salary and experience.

In addition, the correlation matrix can be used to check for the presence of multicollinearity. We note that X_3 ("yrsasoc") and X_4 ("yresfull") are strongly correlated with experience, which could cause some multicollinearity problems. However, these correlations are typical characteristics of a faculty salary structure, because promotions depend on experience to develop teaching skills and publications. Therefore, the conditional coefficients are appropriate. There is also a high correlation between X_2 ("female"), the dummy variable for gender, and the product of "female" times the experience variable X_1. This occurs because both the variable "female" and the variable "femxexpr" have a value of zero for all male faculty members in the sample. The other independent variables have small correlations and thus will not cause multicollinearity problems. The correlations noted are typical for a faculty salary system. Thus those variables should be included.

15.8.1 Effect of Experience and Gender

In the simple regression example Dr. Frank concluded that the annual increase in salary for each year of experience was significantly lower for female compared to male faculty members. Using dummy variables, a multiple regression model was specified to test this conclusion:

$$Y = \beta_0 + \beta_2 X_2 + (\beta_1 + \beta_3 X_2)X_1$$

The application of multiple regression requires that the variables be transformed to individual linear terms as follows:

$$Y = \beta_0 + \beta_2 X_2 + \beta_1 X_1 + \beta_3 X_2 X_1$$

The final term, $X_2 X_1$, is the variable "femxexpr," which was included in the Exhibit 15.10 correlation matrix.

The regression analysis for this model is presented in the Exhibit 15.11 computer output. The estimated regression model is

$$\hat{Y} = \hat{\beta}_0 + \hat{\beta}_2 X_2 + \hat{\beta}_1 X_1 + \hat{\beta}_3 X_2 X_1$$
$$= 21{,}156 - 461 X_2 + 603 X_1 - 110 X_2 X_1$$
$$(34.3) \quad (-0.43) \quad (19.7) \quad (-1.37)$$
$$S_{Y|X} = 3044 \qquad R^2 = 0.793 \qquad n = 150$$

(Conditional Student t statistics are presented below the coefficients.) In the model, Y is the annual salary in U.S. dollars received by the faculty member, X_1 is the number of years teaching full time at the college, and X_2 is a dummy variable that has a 1 for female faculty and a 0 for male faculty.

EXHIBIT 15.11   Regression Analysis: Salary Versus Experience and Gender

```
MTB > regress c6 on 3 independent variables c2 c5 c25

The regression equation is
salary = 21156 + 603 yrsexper - 461 female - 110 femxexpr

Predictor        Coef          Stdev      t-ratio
Constant       21155.7         616.6        34.31
yrsexper        602.98         30.66        19.67
female            -461          1061        -0.43
femxexpr       -110.21         80.31        -1.37

s = 3044        R-sq = 79.3%     R-sq(adj) = 78.9%

Analysis of Variance
SOURCE          DF          SS              MS
Regression       3     5195758080      1731919360
Error          146     1352468864         9263485
Total          149     6548227072

SOURCE          DF        SEQ SS
yrsexper         1     5109486592
female           1       68827592
femxexpr         1       17443734


MTB > regress c6 on 2 independent variables c2 c25

The regression equation is
salary = 21000 + 610 yrsexper - 139 femxexpr

Predictor        Coef          Stdev      t-ratio
Constant       20999.9         500.3        41.98
yrsexper        609.82         26.24        23.24
femxexpr       -138.83         45.84        -3.03

s = 3035        R-sq = 79.3%     R-sq(adj) = 79.0%

Analysis of Variance
SOURCE          DF          SS              MS
Regression       2     5194008064      2597004032
Error          147     1354218752         9212372
Total          149     6548227072

SOURCE          DF        SEQ SS
yrsexper         1     5109486592
femxexpr         1       84521376
```

We see that both of the variables involving male versus female, X_2 and X_2X_1, have small t statistics indicating that neither of these coefficients are significantly different from zero. However, we recall that these variables were highly correlated, and thus the lack of significance for either variable may result from multicollinearity—the high correlation between independent variables. Therefore, we decide to drop the X_2 dummy variable and fit another multiple regression model using only the remaining variables.

The lower part of Exhibit 15.11 shows this second regression as

$$\hat{Y} = 21{,}000 + 610X_1 - 139X_2X_1$$

$$(42.0) \qquad (23.2) \qquad (-3.0)$$

$$S_{Y|X} = 3035 \qquad R^2 = 0.793 \qquad n = 150$$

In this revised regression model all of the coefficients are significantly different from zero. As a result of the analysis, we conclude that there is no difference in the constant or starting salary between male and female faculty. But there is a significant difference in the salary increase per year of experience for male and female faculty. The amount of increase per year for male faculty is $610. However, the increase for women faculty is $139 less per year of experience, or $610 - 139 = 471$. In contrast, the analysis in Chapter 14, which used two separate regression models, showed that the salary increase per year of experience for female faculty was $110 less. The multiple regression analysis has more degrees of freedom for error, and therefore most analysts would prefer the multiple regression estimate over the estimate that used two simple regression models.

Conclusion 1.   At this point we conclude that female faculty have the same starting salary, but their increase per year of experience is significantly less than for male faculty.

15.8.2 Faculty Rank and Market Variables

The next step in the analysis was to determine if the smaller increase in faculty salaries for women could be "explained" by faculty rank and/or market conditions. This was done by adding variables X_3, years as an associate professor, X_4, years as a full professor, and X_5, a dummy variable equal to 1 if there was a shortage of faculty in this discipline and 0 if there was not. The resulting model is specified as

$$Y = \beta_0 + (\beta_1 + \beta_2 X_2)X_1 + \beta_3 X_3 + \beta_4 X_4 + \beta_5 X_5$$

The results of the first regression are shown in Exhibit 15.12. We see that the t statistic for the experience times gender ("femxexpr") variable is $t = -0.80$. Therefore, Dr. Frank concluded that this variable was not significant after we adjusted for the effect of faculty rank and disciplines with higher salaries because of market demand. The regression model was run again and the results are shown in Exhibit 15.13. Here we see that all of the coefficients are significant.

EXHIBIT 15.12   Multiple Regression: Faculty Rank and Market Variables

```
MTB > regress c6 on 5 independent variables c2 c25 c3 c4 c9
```

```
The regression equation is
salary = 22073 + 329 yrsexper - 30.4 femxexpr + 274 yrsasoc
         + 501 yresfull + 2129 market
```

Predictor	Coef	Stdev	t-ratio
Constant	22072.8	524.7	42.07
yrsexper	328.52	54.75	6.00
femxexpr	-30.43	38.22	-0.80
yrsasoc	274.33	77.99	3.52
yresfull	501.02	63.02	7.95
market	2128.6	506.4	4.20

```
s = 2395        R-sq = 87.4%     R-sq(adj) = 86.9%
```

Analysis of Variance

SOURCE	DF	SS	MS
Regression	5	5721981952	1144396416
Error	144	826244800	5737811
Total	149	6548226560	

SOURCE	DF	SEQ SS
yrsexper	1	5109486592
femxexpr	1	84521376
yrsasoc	1	5278668
yresfull	1	421320928
market	1	101374416

The resulting model was

$$\hat{Y} = \hat{\beta}_0 + \hat{\beta}_1 X_1 + \hat{\beta}_3 X_3 + \hat{\beta}_4 X_4 + \hat{\beta}_5 X_5$$
$$= 22{,}038 + 319 X_1 + 288 X_3 + 516 X_4 + 2157 X_5$$
$$\quad\quad (42.2) \quad (6.0) \quad\quad (3.8) \quad\quad (8.6) \quad\quad (4.3)$$
$$S_{Y|X} = 2392 \quad\quad R^2 = 0.873 \quad\quad n = 150$$

(Student t statistics are shown below each coefficient.) In the model, Y is the annual salary in U.S. dollars received by the faculty member, X_1 is the number of years teaching full time at the college, X_3 is the number of years as an associate professor, X_4 is the number of years as a full professor, and X_5 is a dummy variable that has a 1 for faculty in a field that includes a market premium, because of high demand and limited supply, and a zero otherwise.

EXHIBIT 15.13   Multiple Regression Model: Experience, Rank, and Market Variables

```
MTB > regress c6 on 4 independent variables c2 c3 c4 c9;
 SUBC> residuals in c31.
```

The regression equation is
 salary = 22038 + 319 yrsexper + 288 yrsasoc + 516 yresfull +
2157 market

Predictor	Coef	Stdev	t-ratio
Constant	22037.9	522.2	42.20
yrsexper	318.62	53.25	5.98
yrsasoc	288.40	75.87	3.80
yresfull	515.75	60.17	8.57
market	2156.9	504.5	4.28

s = 2392   R-sq = 87.3%   R-sq(adj) = 87.0%

Analysis of Variance

SOURCE	DF	SS	MS
Regression	4	5718344704	1429586176
Error	145	829881728	5723323
Total	149	6548226560	

SOURCE	DF	SEQ SS
yrsexper	1	5109486592
yrsasoc	1	2333422
yresfull	1	501920800
market	1	104604224

Unusual Observations

Obs.	yrsexper	salary	Fit	Stdev.Fit	Residual	St.Resid
13	35.0	40000	45069	616	-5069	-2.19R
16	24.0	37150	31127	582	6023	2.60R
17	27.0	33000	36985	859	-3985	-1.78 X
22	34.0	47200	48227	805	-1027	-0.46 X
48	22.0	45000	36451	410	8549	3.63R
122	41.0	38500	42339	838	-3839	-1.71 X
123	32.0	37300	41989	536	-4689	-2.01R
130	17.0	39500	31536	278	7964	3.35R
131	39.0	35300	42006	645	-6706	-2.91R
147	38.0	41200	46768	713	-5568	-2.44R

R denotes an obs. with a large st. resid.
X denotes an obs. whose X value gives it large influence.

This model has all coefficients significant. The slope coefficient for experience $\hat{\beta}_1 = 319$ is substantially smaller than the simple regression slope coefficient. Years spent at the senior faculty ranks are significant contributors to larger annual salary increases, and there is a significant market effect on salary $\hat{\beta}_5 = 2157$ dollars.

Conclusion 2.   The lower rate of increase for women's salaries is removed when the effect of faculty rank and market are included. Thus the lower rate of increase appears to be associated with fewer promotions for women and/or fewer women in high-demand disciplines.

The performance of this extended regression model was analyzed using residuals analysis. Dr. Frank computed the residuals for all observations and stored them as a separate variable. This is generally done in most regression studies. Exhibit 15.14 includes a list of observations that have large residuals $\hat{e}_i = y_i - \hat{Y}_i$. This list indicates faculty whose salaries are substantially below or above the expected salary as predicted by the regression model. A dean or department chair should consider each case individually and judge if such a large deviation is appropriate given the faculty member's capability and contributions. It is not unusual to have a set of persons with large deviations from the standard in any salary system. Such deviations would indicate that star performers are being rewarded and weak performers are not.

EXHIBIT 15.14   Residuals Versus Years of Experience

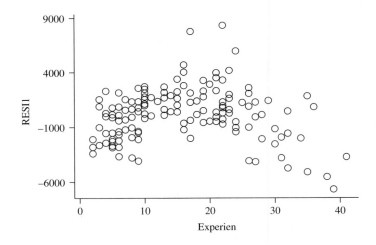

Dr. Frank prepared a number of residual plots and other analyses to determine if the model represents the data adequately. Included in the set of plots prepared by Dr. Frank is Exhibit 15.14, which shows the residuals versus years of experience.

Careful examination of this plot suggests a quadratic relationship between experience and salary. At the higher levels of experience most of the residuals are negative. At intermediate levels of years of experience the residuals tend to be positive. These are clear indications of a quadratic relationship. As a result, Dr. Frank created a new variable that was a quadratic transformation of the years of experience variable. This variable, named "expsqrd," was added to the list of independent variables used in the final regression included in Exhibit 15.15. We see that both the linear and quadratic terms are significant. We also note that the linear coefficient is much larger than the previous regression model without the quadratic term.

EXHIBIT 15.15   Multiple Regression: Quadratic Experience Variable

```
MTB > let c26=c2*c2
MTB > name c26 'expsqrd'
MTB > regress c6 on 5 independent variables c2 c26 c3 c4 c9
```

The regression equation is
salary = 18828 + 848 yrsexper - 15.4 expsqrd + 246 yrsasoc
              + 630 yresfull + 2155 market

Predictor	Coef	Stdev	t-ratio
Constant	18828.2	565.9	33.27
yrsexper	847.55	75.22	11.27
expsqrd	-15.413	1.790	-8.61
yrsasoc	245.61	62.05	3.96
yresfull	630.50	50.83	12.40
market	2154.6	411.3	5.24

s = 1950   R-sq = 91.6%   R-sq(adj) = 91.3%

Analysis of Variance

SOURCE	DF	SS	MS
Regression	5	6000434688	1200086912
Error	144	547791808	3804110
Total	149	6548226560	

SOURCE	DF	SEQ SS
yrsexper	1	5109486592
expsqrd	1	91663416
yrsasoc	1	15948822
yresfull	1	678958848
market	1	104377272

EXHIBIT 15.15   Multiple Regression: Quadratic Experience Variable (*Continued*)

Unusual Observations

Obs.	yrsexper	salary	Fit	Stdev.Fit	Residual	St.Resid
16	24.0	37150	31519	77	5631	2.98R
17	27.0	33000	35879	712	-2879	-1.59 X
30	3.0	27950	23387	446	4563	2.40R
32	4.0	29000	24126	414	4874	2.56R
48	22.0	45000	38423	405	6577	3.45R
99	9.0	21000	25208	249	-4208	-2.18R
122	41.0	38500	35553	1043	2947	1.79 X
123	32.0	37300	41343	443	-4043	-2.13R
130	17.0	39500	33023	285	6477	3.36R
131	39.0	35300	35627	908	-327	-0.19 X
147	38.0	41200	43353	704	-2153	-1.18 X

R denotes an obs. with a large st. resid.
X denotes an obs. whose X value gives it large influence.

The final regression model is

$$\hat{Y} = 18{,}828 + 848X_1 - 15.4X_1^2 + 246X_3 + 630X_4 + 2155X_5$$
$$(33.3) \quad (11.3) \quad (-8.6) \quad (4.0) \quad (12.4) \quad (5.2)$$
$$S_{Y|X} = 1950 \qquad R^2 = 0.916 \qquad n = 150$$

where X_1 is the years of experience teaching, X_3 is the number of years as an associate professor, X_4 is the number of years as a full professor, and X_5 is a dummy variable; 1 the discipline has a high demand. The numbers under the coefficients are the coefficient Student t statistics. From the correlation matrix in Exhibit 15.10, we noted the high correlations between independent variables X_1, X_3, and X_4. Thus there is the potential for multicollinearity problems, in particular higher variances for the slope coefficient estimates. However, all of the coefficients are conditionally significant. These correlations are an anticipated characteristic of the data. Faculty with experience as associate and full professors generally have more years of total experience than faculty at lower ranks. Typically, faculty have at least six years of experience before promotion to associate professor and a similar interval before promotion to full professor. Therefore, in this example the coefficients for experience at higher ranks are always conditional on considerable total experience.

From labor market theory, Dr. Frank notes that salaries typically increase with experience, due to the effect of accumulated human capital. However, there is eventually a leveling off as worker skills become obsolete and productivity increases do not continue. Thus Dr. Frank has developed a multiple regression model that is consistent with the economic theories of the labor market. The final model has an $R^2 = 0.916$

value, which is a substantial improvement over the initial model. Also, the standard error of the estimate has been reduced from $S_{Y|X} = 3035$ to $S_{Y|X} = 1950$. Note that the observations with large residuals are approximately the same observations as those resulting from the previous regression model. Thus it appears that the salaries for these faculty truly deviate from a standard model and they must be treated as special cases.

Conclusion 3.   The rate of increase in faculty salaries with experience begins to decline at higher levels of experience. This result is supported by other studies. A few people have salaries that deviate greatly from the overall pattern.

Final comments.   The final model does not include the previous conclusion that the annual salary increases for women faculty are lower than those for men. Multiple regression shows that when we include experience at higher faculty ranks, the difference between male and female faculty does not appear.

Does It Make Sense?

Given the early conclusion of gender differences and their removal by including faculty rank, we now need to focus on the issue of promotion. Why are women at lower ranks? Has there been discrimination in terms of promotion? Do women faculty have less education, or are they less productive in terms of teaching and professional activity? We have discovered that the differences are not merely the result of less experience as faculty. The relationships between ability, discrimination, and promotion are difficult issues that cannot be answered completely using regression analysis and the data available for Dr. Frank's study. However, the regression analysis has brought us considerable understanding and has focused on additional questions. As a result we see that examination of individual faculty career patterns would be needed to answer the gender discrimination question.   □

SUMMARY OF KEY IDEAS

PRACTICE PROBLEM SOLUTIONS

15.1 Simple regression coefficients indicate the relationship between a single independent variable and the dependent variable. Thus it corresponds to a two-variable graphical plot. In contrast, multiple regression computes conditional coefficients, which correspond to shifts of simple relationships as a result of the influence of other variables. Conditional coefficients indicate the unique effect of a variable given that other variables are having simultaneous effects.

15.2 (a) Large Y deviation. The least-squares algorithm minimizes squared deviations in the Y direction. The algorithm would attempt to reduce the distance to the deviant point because large deviations squared contribute much more to the sum of squares than do several small deviation points (e.g., consider $2^2 = 4$ with $5^2 = 25$; six deviations of size 2 squared equal one deviation of size 5 squared).

(b) A point with a large X deviation would "attract" the least-squares line because shifts in slope would require small deviations from the central group of points and avoid a large Y deviation from the point with the large X deviation.

15.3 Narrower confidence intervals result primarily from smaller variance of the slope coefficient estimate, $S_{\hat{\beta}_j}$. This variance is reduced if we have large samples, wide dispersion of X_j, small correlations between the X variables, and points close to the linear regression equation.

(a) Observations of each X_j variable would be selected with as wide a range as possible. The objective would be to obtain a maximum value for $S_{X_j}^2$.

(b) Observations would be selected to minimize the correlations between the independent variables.

(c) It is difficult to select the data a priori so that the points will be close to the regression equation. However, careful problem analysis and review of existing knowledge will increase the chances that all of the significant predictor variables are included. Correct model specification will ensure that the points are as close to the regression equation as possible.

15.4 (a) The t test uses the ratio of the estimated coefficient, $\hat{\beta}_j$, divided by the standard error of the coefficient, $S_{\hat{\beta}_j}$. Thus a variable is significant if its effect measured by the coefficient is significantly greater than its error. The F test uses the contribution to explained variability that results from adding the variable X_j to the set of variables in the regression model. If the contribution is significantly greater than the estimated variance of the regression model, $S^2_{Y|X}$, the F test concludes that the variable is significant.

(b) If a variable has a significant coefficient as measured by the t test, that variable will move the equation closer to the observed data points. This occurs because the coefficient effect is significantly larger than the random error. The result of moving the equation closer to the data will be a large explained variability and hence a significant F test.

CHAPTER PROBLEMS

15.1   Derive the normal equations for the model

$$Y = \beta_0 + \beta_1 X_1 + \beta_2 X_2 + \beta_3 X_3$$

Assume that you have n observations defined as:

$$y_i^*, \quad x_{1i}^*, \quad x_{2i}^*, \quad x_{3i}^*, \qquad i = 1, \ldots, n$$

(*Hint:* Use transformations of the form

$$x_{ji} = x_{ji}^* - \bar{X}_j^* \qquad y_i = y_i^* - \bar{Y}^*$$

given that

$$\sum_{i=1}^{n} x_{1i} x_{3i} = 0 \quad \text{and} \quad \sum_{i=1}^{n} x_{2i} x_{3i} = 0 \qquad \sum_{i=1}^{n} x_{1i} x_{2i} = 0$$

Discuss how you would derive the coefficient estimators.)

15.2   You have been assigned the task of analyzing the data in Table 15.4, which were collected from an industrial experiment. The experiment was designed to determine the effect of the following variables on the number of units, Y, produced per shift:

X_2: new lighting ($X_2 = +1$) versus old lighting ($X_2 = -1$)
X_3: worker training ($X_3 = +1$) versus no training ($X_3 = -1$)
X_4: day shift ($X_4 = +1$) versus night shift ($X_4 = -1$)

(a) Derive the least-squares normal equations.

TABLE 15.4   Data for Problem 15.2

X_1	X_2	X_3	X_4	Y
1	-1	-1	-1	1
1	$+1$	-1	0	10
1	-1	0	$+1$	17
1	$+1$	0	-1	7
1	-1	$+1$	0	14
1	$+1$	$+1$	$+1$	22

(b) Using the normal equations and the data, compute the regression coefficients.

(c) Compute ESS, RSS, and TSS and the R^2.

(d) Enter the data into your computer program and prepare a regression analysis standard output.

(e) Which of the independent variables have a significant effect on productivity?

15.3   You have obtained the regression output for the linear model

$$Y = \beta_0 + \beta_1 X_1 + \beta_2 X_2$$

Among the regression statistics you discover that TSS $= 100{,}000$, $R^2 = 0.80$, and $S^2(Y \mid X_1, X_2) = 1000$. You decide to add an additional variable X_3 to the model and obtain a second regression analysis. From this analysis, which includes X_3, you discover that $R^2 = 0.805$, and $S^2(Y \mid X_1, X_2, X_3) = 1026.3$. Is this result strange? Yes, it is! Explain how the percent explained variability could go up when the estimated variance has also increased.

15.4   Based on some careful market analysis, you have hypothesized that the demand for breakfast cereal can be modeled as

$$Y = \beta_0 X_1^{\beta_1} X_2^{\beta_2} X_3^{\beta_3}$$

where Y is the monthly consumption of cereal for a family of four, X_1 is the price of cereal per pound, X_2 is the family income, and X_3 is the price of eggs per dozen. You have a random sample of 200 families which contains measurements of the variables for each family. Explain how you would determine the effect of the price of eggs on the sale of breakfast cereal given the effects of family income and the price of breakfast cereal.

15.5   The economics department wishes to develop a multiple regression model to predict student GPA for economics courses. They have collected data for 112 graduates, which include the variables economics GPA, SAT verbal, SAT mathematics, ACT English, ACT social science, and high school percentile rank. The data are stored in a file named "Student" on your data disk. Appendix B contains a description of the variables.

(a) Use the SAT variables and class rank to determine the best prediction model. Remove any independent variables that are not significant. What are the coefficients, their Student t statistics, and the model R^2?

(b) Use the ACT variables and class rank to determine the best prediction model. Remove any independent variables that are not significant. What are the coefficients, their Student t statistics, and the model R^2?

(c) Which model predicts economics GPA better? Present the evidence to support your conclusion.

15.6   The data file "Salmod," which is stored on your data disk and described in Appendix B, contains a dependent variable and seven independent variables. You are to obtain the best regression model that predicts Y as a function of the seven independent variables.

The dependent variable is named "Y" in the file, and the independent variables are also appropriately labeled. Use regression analysis to determine which variables should be in the final model and to estimate the coefficients. Show the conditional F test and the conditional t test for any variables removed. Analyze the model residuals using plots. Show your results and discuss your conclusions. Transform variables if the residuals indicate a nonlinear relationship. Present your final model clearly, showing the coefficients and the coefficient Student t statistics.

15.7 You have been asked to estimate the coefficients for the linear model

$$Y = \hat{\beta}_1 X_1 + \hat{\beta}_2 X_2 + \hat{\beta}_3 X_3 + \hat{e}$$

using a sample of n_i observations. In the sample data the variable means

$$\bar{Y} = \bar{X}_1 = \bar{X}_2 = \bar{X}_3 = 0$$

and therefore the constant parameter is zero.
(a) Derive the normal equations.
(b) You have been given the sample standard deviations $S(X_j)$ for all the X_j and Y variables, the simple correlations $\hat{\rho}(X_j, Y)$ and $\hat{\rho}(X_j, X_k)$ for all combinations of the X's and Y, and the sample size n. Show how you would use this information to derive the coefficient estimators, $\hat{\beta}_j$'s.
(c) Indicate how you would test the null hypothesis that $\hat{\beta}_3$ is equal to zero versus the hypothesis that it is not equal to zero. Use the conditional F test. Draw a sketch to indicate how this test works.

15.8 Use the data in the file "Citydat," which is stored on your data disk and described in Appendix B, to estimate a regression equation that can be used to determine the marginal effect of the percent commercial property on the market value per owner-occupied residence. Include in your multiple regression equation percent owner-occupied residences, percent industrial property, the median rooms per residence, and per capita income as additional predictor variables. Indicate which of the variables are conditionally significant. Your final equation should include only significant variables. Discuss and interpret your final regression model, including an indication of how you would select a community for your house.

15.9 The Minitab output in Exhibit 15.16 presents the multiple regression analysis for Y as a function of X_1, X_2, and X_3. The developer has decided that she really wants the regression analysis for Y as a function of X_1 and X_3. Unfortunately, the computer crashed just as the regression results were to appear. Therefore, you must compute the regression results for Y as a function of X_1 and X_3 using the available computer output. Find the coefficient estimates for β_0, β_1, and β_2. Find the standard errors for $\hat{\beta}_1$ and $\hat{\beta}_2$. Compute $S(Y \mid X_1, X_3)$. Prepare the analysis of variance table. Compute the adjusted R^2 for the new regression. (*Note:* β_2 is the coefficient of X_{30})

15.10 Define and describe conditional explained variability using words, equations, and/or sketches. Indicate how you would determine the conditional explained variability and conditional F for X_1 and for X_2 in the equation

$$Y = \beta_0 + \beta_1 X_1 + \beta_2 X_2 + \beta_3 X_3 + \beta_4 X_4 + \epsilon$$

15.11 Given the correlation matrix in Table 15.5, discuss the possible statistical significance for the coefficients in the following equations. Your comments should reflect the

EXHIBIT 15.16

```
MTB > corr 'Y' 'X1' 'X2' 'X3'

              Y         X1        X2
     X1     0.633
     X2     0.475     0.743
     X3     0.544     0.524     0.765


MTB > describe  'Y' 'X1' 'X2' 'X3'

       N      MEAN    MEDIAN    TRMEAN     STDEV    SEMEAN
  Y   51      5536      5336      5483       812       114
  X1  51     12277     12314     12166      1851       259
  X2  51     22751     22064     22486      3899       546
  X3  51      2301      2008      2042      1486       208
MTB > regress 'Y'   on 3 variables 'X1' 'X2' 'X3'


The regression equation is
  Y = 3232 + 0.297 X1 - 0.0871 X2 + 0.279 X3


Predictor         Coef          Stdev       t-ratio
Constant        3231.6          667.3          4.84
    X1         0.29683        0.06752          4.40
    X2        -0.08706        0.04240         -2.05
    X3         0.27859        0.08740          3.19


s = 587.9        R-sq = 50.7%      R-sq(adj) = 47.6%

Analysis of Variance

SOURCE         DF           SS            MS
Regression      3     16716562       5572188
Error          47     16244709        345632
Total          50     32961272


SOURCE         DF       SEQ SS
   X1           1     13203228
   X2           1         1465
   X3           1      3511869
```

TABLE 15.5   Correlation
Matrix for Problem 15.11

	Y	X_1	X_2
X_1	0.68		
X_2	0.20	0.20	
X_3	0.80	0.79	0.10

relationships between variables as presented in the correlation matrix. Assume that the sample size is $n = 51$.

(a) $Y = \beta_0 + \beta_1 X_1$.
(b) $Y = \beta_0 + \beta_2 X_2$.
(c) $Y = \beta_0 + \beta_3 X_3$.
(d) $Y = \beta_0 + \beta_1 X_1 + \beta_3 X_3$.
(e) $Y = \beta_0 + \beta_1 X_1 + \beta_2 X_2 + \beta_3 X_3$.

15.12 Given the multiple regression equation

$$Y = \beta_0 + \beta_1 X_1 + \beta_2 X_2 + \epsilon$$

and the following statistics:

$$\bar{Y} = 0 \qquad \bar{X}_1 = 0 \qquad \bar{X}_2 = 0,$$

$$S_Y^2 = 400 \qquad S_{X_1}^2 = 20 \qquad S_{X_2}^2 = 40$$

$$S_{X_1, Y} = 50 \qquad S_{X_2, Y} = 80 \qquad S_{X_1, X_2} = 10$$

$$n = 51$$

(a) Derive the normal equations to estimate the coefficients. Express the normal equations in terms of variances and covariances. Use the normal equations to compute the coefficient estimates.

(b) Derive an equation for regression sum of squares (RSS) as a function of the variances, covariances, and sample size.

(c) Use the RSS to compute the standard error of the estimate, $S(Y \mid X_1, X_2)$, and then compute the Student t's for the coefficient estimates.

(d) Determine the conditional F for X_2 given X_1.

15.13 Estimate the regression coefficients, their Student t's, and the analysis of variance table for the regression model

$$Y = \hat{\beta}_0 + \hat{\beta}_1 X_1 + \hat{\beta}_2 X_2$$

Unfortunately, you do not have the original data and a computer. However, you do have the descriptive statistics in Tables 15.6 and 15.7.

15.14 The "true model" for a particular system is

$$Y = \beta_0 + \beta_1 X_1 + \beta_2 X_2 + \epsilon$$

but an analyst incorrectly estimated the simple regression of Y on X_1.

TABLE 15.6 Sample Means
and Standard Deviations
(Problem 15.13)

Variable	Mean	Standard Deviation
Y	1779.75	290.453
X_1	106.814	6.11378
X_2	7.525	7.32776

TABLE 15.7 Correlation
Matrix (Problem 15.13)

	Y	X_1
X_1	−0.94986	
X_2	0.29111	−0.43927
	$n = 28$	

(a) Show that the coefficient of X_1 is biased.

(b) How is the bias changed if the correlation between X_1 and X_2 is equal to zero?

(c) What is the effect of this specification error on the variance of the coefficient estimator for X_1? (Indicate if the variance is larger, smaller, unchanged, or you cannot tell. Explain your answer carefully.)

15.15 The following regression model predicts the depth of snow, Y, as a function of the distance to be traveled, X_1, and the intensity of the desire to complete the trip, X_2. The estimated model is

$$Y = 5.0X_1 + 10.0X_2$$
$$(2.5) \qquad (2.0)$$

The numbers beneath the coefficient estimates are the coefficient Student t statistics. In addition, the correlation between $\hat{\beta}_1$ and $\hat{\beta}_2$ is 0.5. Find the 95% confidence interval for the predicted value of Y when $X_1 = 4$ and $X_2 = 5$. Use the standard normal Z.

15.16 Write a two-page guide for developing a linear equation using multiple regression. Include a discussion of model formulation, variable selection and model specification, analysis assumptions, procedures for analysis, statistical hypothesis tests, and hints for examining the data and checking model validity.

15.17 The administrator of the National Highway Traffic Safety Administration (NHTSA) wants to know if the different types of vehicles in a state have a relationship to the highway death rate in the state. She has asked you to develop multiple regression analyses to determine if average vehicle weight, percentage imported cars, percentage light trucks, and average car age are related to "crash deaths in automobiles and pickups." The data for the analysis are located in the data file named "Crash," which is located on your data disk. The variable descriptions and locations are contained in the data file dictionary in Appendix B.

(a) Prepare a correlation matrix for crash deaths and the predictor variables. Note the simple relationships between crash deaths and the predictor variables. In addition, indicate any potential multicollinearity problems between the predictor variables.

(b) Prepare a multiple regression analysis of crash deaths on the potential predictor variables. Remove any nonsignificant predictor variables, one at a time, from the regression model. Indicate your best final model.

(c) State the conclusions from your analysis and discuss the conditional importance of the variables in terms of their relationship to crash deaths.

15.18 The department of transportation wishes to know if the variable "states with a larger percentage of urban population" is related to "higher automobile and pickup crash death rates." In addition, they want to know if the average speed on rural roads or the percentage of rural roads that are surfaced are conditionaly related to crash death rates given the percentage of urban population. Data for this study are included in the file "Crash" stored on your data disk and described in the data file dictionary in Appendix B.

(a) Prepare a correlation matrix and descriptive statistics for crash deaths and the potential predictor variables. Note the relationships and any potential problems of multicollinearity.

(b) Prepare a multiple regression analysis of crash deaths on the potential predictor variables. Determine which of the variables should be retained in the regression model because they have a conditionally significant relationship.

(c) State the results of your analysis in terms of your final regression model. Indicate which variables are conditionally significant.

15.19 An economist wishes to predict the market value of owner-occupied homes in small midwestern cities. He has collected a set of data from 45 small cities for a two-year period and wants you to use this as the data source for the analysis. The data are stored in the file "Citydat," which is stored on your data disk and described in the data file dictionary in Appendix B. He wants you to develop a multiple regression prediction equation. The potential predictor variables include the size of the house, tax rate, percent commercial property, per capita income, and total city government expenditures.

(a) Compute the correlation matrix and descriptive statistics for the market value of residences and the potential predictor variables. Note any potential problems of multicollinearity. Define the approximate range for your regression model by the variable means ±2 standard deviations.

(b) Prepare multiple regression analyses using the predictor variables. Remove any variables that are not conditionally significant. Which variable, size of house or tax rate, has the stronger conditional relationship to the value of houses?

(c) A business developer in a midwestern state has stated that local property tax rates in small towns need to be lowered because if they are not, no one will purchase a house in these towns. Based on your analysis in this problem, evaluate the business developer's claim.

15.20 George Holt, the vice-president of purchasing for a large national retailer, has asked you to prepare an analysis of retail sales by state. He wants to know if the percent unemployment and the per capita personal income are jointly related to per capita retail sales. Data for this study are stored in the data file named "Retail," which is stored on your data disk and described in the data file dictionary in Appendix B.

(a) Prepare a correlation matrix, compute descriptive statistics, and obtain a regression analysis of per capita retail sales on unemployment and personal income. Compute 95% confidence intervals for the slope coefficients in each regression equation.

(b) What is the conditional effect of a $1000 decrease in per capita income on per capita sales?

(c) Would the prediction equation be improved by adding the state population as an additional predictor variable?

15.21 A major national supplier of building materials for residential construction is concerned about total sales for next year. It is well known that the company's sales are related directly to the total national residential investment. Several New York bankers are predicting that interest rates will rise about 2 percentage points next year. You have been asked to develop a regression analysis that can be used to predict the effect of interest rate changes on residential investment. In addition to interest rate, you also believe that GNP, money supply, government spending, and the price index for finished goods might also be predictors of residential investment. Therefore, you decide that two multiple regression models will be needed. One will include prime interest rate and important additional variables. The second will include federal funds interest rate and important additional variables. The time-series data for this study are contained in the data file named "Macro95," which is stored on your data disk and described in the data file dictionary in Appendix B.

(a) Develop two multiple regression models to predict residential investment using prime interest rate for one and federal funds interest rate for the other. The final regression models should include only predictor variables that have a significant conditional effect. Analyze the regression statistics and indicate which equation provides the best predictions.

(b) Determine the 95% confidence interval for the interest rate conditional slope coefficient in both regression equations.

15.22 The Congressional Budget Office (CBO) was interested in determining if state-level infant death rates are related to the level of medical resources available in the state. Data for the study are contained in the data file named "State87," which is stored on your data disk and described in the data file dictionary in Appendix B. The measure of infant deaths is infant deaths under 1 year per 100 live births. The set of possible predictor variables includes physicians per 100,000 population, per capita personal income, and total expenditures for hospitals (this variable should be expressed on a per capita base by dividing by the state population).

(a) Prepare the multiple regression analysis and determine which of the predictor variables should be included in the multiple regression model. Interpret your final regression model, including a discussion of the coefficients, their Student t's, the standard error of the estimate, and R^2.

(b) Identify two additional variables that might be additional predictors if added to the multiple regression model. Test their effect in a multiple regression analysis and indicate if your initial suspicions were correct.

15.23 Given a sample of n observations $(y_i, X_{1i}, X_{2i}, i = 1, \ldots, n)$, two regression models are estimated:

$$\text{I: } Y = \beta_0 + \beta_1 X_1$$
$$\text{II: } Y = \alpha_0 + \alpha_1 X_1 + \alpha_2 X_2$$

(a) Would you expect the coefficient estimate of X_1 in equation I (i.e., β_1) to be equal to the coefficient of X_1 in equation II (i.e., α_1)? Explain your answer carefully and completely using words and appropriate mathematics.

(b) Explain the concept of conditional explained variability using Venn diagrams. Compare an example with a large correlation between X_1 and X_2 and a case with a small correlation between X_1 and X_2.

15.24 Given the correlation matrix

$$
\begin{array}{c}
\\
X_1 \\
X_2 \\
X_3 \\
X_4
\end{array}
\begin{array}{cccc}
Y & X_1 & X_2 & X_3 \\
\left(\begin{array}{cccc}
0.60 & & & \\
0.65 & 0.95 & & \\
0.50 & 0.60 & 0.10 & \\
0.50 & 0.40 & 0.20 & 0.0
\end{array} \right)
\end{array}
$$

and

$$S_{X_1} = S_{X_2} = S_{X_3} = S_{X_4}$$

two regression models are proposed:

$$\text{I: } Y = \beta_0 + \beta_1 X_1 + \beta_2 X_2$$
$$\text{II: } Y = \beta_0 + \beta_3 X_3 + \beta_4 X_4$$

(a) Which model will have the smallest variances for the slope coefficients? Explain using appropriate variance estimators (equations) and the correlation matrix above.

(b) Which model will have the largest R^2? Explain using the correlation matrix above.

(c) Which three independent variables will result in a model with an even larger R^2 than either model I or II? Explain using the correlation matrix and your understanding of conditional explained variability.

The following two problems are extensions of Problem 14.20.

15.25 Shirley Matson, production manager of Acme Electronics, wants to develop a linear equation to predict the number of control boards assembled as a function of the number of hours worked. She has obtained a random sample of 41 production shifts and recorded the number of hours worked and the number of units produced on each shift. From these data the following summary statistics have been computed:

$$S_{x_1} = 10 \qquad S_y = 30 \qquad \hat{\rho}(X_1, Y) = 0.80$$
$$\bar{X}_1 = 100, \qquad \bar{Y} = 300$$

(a) She has asked you to compute the regression coefficients, the Student t for the slope coefficient, the standard error of the estimate, and the percent explained variability, R^2, for the regression model.

(b) What is the predicted production and its 95% confidence interval when the number of hours worked is 110?

The production operation is also supported by a set of material-handling robots that help position parts for the workers. Because the robotic system is new, the production crew is experimenting with various strategies for using the system. The contribution of the robotic material-handling system is measured in the number of unit hours for all the robots assigned to the production operation. By defining the number of hours contributed by the robots as X_2, Shirley modeled a new production equation as

$$Y = \hat{\beta}_0 + \hat{\beta}_1 X_1 + \hat{\beta}_2 X_2$$

where Y is the number of units produced and X_1 the number of hours worked as collected above. She also obtained the number of hours for the robots for each of the 41 shifts and estimated a regression equation. For this new multiple regression equation, the following additional statistics were obtained:

$$R^2 = 0.81 \qquad S^2_{x_2} = 40 \qquad \hat{\rho}(X_1, X_2) = 0.0 \qquad \bar{X}_2 = 30$$

In addition, the correlation, $\hat{\rho}_{X_2,Y}$, is positive.

(c) Compute the conditional sum of squares and conditional t for the effect of robots, X_2, on the number of units produced.
(d) Compute the coefficients $\hat{\beta}_0$, $\hat{\beta}_1$, and $\hat{\beta}_2$ for the regression equation.
(e) Compute the Student t statistics for coefficients $\hat{\beta}_1$ and $\hat{\beta}_2$.
(f) Write the final equation for the regression of total output on labor hours and robot hours, in standard form.

15.26 Repeat Problem 15.25 with the following changes:

$$R^2 \neq 0.81 \qquad \hat{\rho}(X_2, Y) = 0.76 \qquad \hat{\rho}(X_1, X_2) = 0.50$$

[Note: The solutions for parts (a) and (b) are exactly the same, part (c) can be omitted, and therefore only parts (d) through (f) require additional work. After completing parts (d) through (f), answer part (g) below.]

(g) Compare the final equations for Problems 15.25 and 15.26. What is the effect of the nonzero correlation between the two independent variables?

15.27 The following summary statistics were computed as part of a routine analysis of a data set:

$$S_{x1} = 8 \qquad S_{x2} = 5 \qquad S_y = 10 \qquad n = 52$$
$$\bar{X}_1 = 5 \qquad \bar{X}_2 = 6 \qquad \bar{Y} = 10$$
$$\hat{\beta}_1 = 1 \qquad \hat{\rho}(X_2, Y) = 0.40 \qquad \hat{\rho}(X_1, X_2) = 0.0$$

For the regression of Y on X_1 and X_2, compute:
(a) The regression coefficients.
(b) The ANOVA table and R^2 for the regression.
(c) The coefficient standard errors and the Student t statistics for the coefficients.
(d) Write the regression equation in standard form.

15.28 You have been asked to prepare an exponential production function for the Dollar Bay Boat Works. Your model is to predict the number of boats produced per year as a function of the number of production units and the number of workers. The Dollar Bay Boat Works has collected the production data in Table 15.8.

(a) Specify the production function model for this problem.
(b) Estimate the coefficients β_1 and β_2 in the exponential model.
(c) Compute the predicted values using your production function.

TABLE 15.8   Production Data for Dollar Bay Boat Works

Year	Production Units	Number of Workers	Number of Boats
1976	1.0	2.0	40
1977	1.2	2.1	45
1978	1.2	2.7	52
1979	1.1	3.0	57
1980	2.0	3.1	65
1981	3.0	3.6	75
1982	4.0	4.0	86
1983	4.5	6.0	95
1984	4.5	7.1	100
1985	4.5	8.5	130
1986	4.1	8.9	161
1987	6.0	10.0	215
1988	8.1	13.9	260
1989	7.9	16.1	265
1990	11.0	14.0	275
1991	12.0	14.0	282
1992	13.2	15.6	300
1993	14.0	17.0	340
1994	14.8	18.0	370
1995	15.0	20.9	405

15.29 Given the model

$$Y = \beta_0 + \beta_1 X_1 + \beta_2 X_2 + \beta_3 X_3 + \beta_4 X_4 + \epsilon$$

and the correlation matrix shown in Table 15.9, answer the following questions.

(a) Are there any potential problems of major influences of multicollinearity on the coefficient estimates? Explain your answer carefully and concisely.
(b) If X_2 were regressed on X_3, what would be the percent explained variability?
(c) If X_2 were regressed on X_4, what would be the percent explained variability?
(d) If X_4 were regressed on X_1, X_2, and X_3, what would be the percent explained variability (R^2)?

TABLE 15.9 Correlation Matrix for Problem 15.29

	X_1	X_2	X_3	X_4
X_2	0.0	1.0	0.0	0.5
X_3	0.0	0.0	1.0	-0.5
X_4	-0.6	0.5	-0.5	1.0

15.30 Given the correlation matrix shown in Table 15.10, answer the following questions.
   (a) Which two of the three independent, X, variables will result in a model with the highest R^2 and the smallest standard error of the estimate when Y is regressed on these two independent variables?
   (b) Given the statistics

$$n = 101 \qquad S_{X_1} = 20 \qquad S_{X_2} = 100 \qquad S_{X_3} = 40 \qquad S_Y = 100$$

$$\bar{Y} = 10 \qquad \bar{X}_1 = 20 \qquad \bar{X}_2 = 30 \qquad \bar{X}_3 = 30$$

compute the coefficient estimators and their standard errors for the regression equation selected in part (a). Omit the standard error for the constant β_0 in the regression equation.

TABLE 15.10 Correlation Matrix for Problem 15.30

	Y	X_1	X_2
X_1	0.60		
X_2	0.70	0.95	
X_3	0.50	0.0	0.90

15.31 Develop a multiple regression model to predict salary as a function of other independent variables, using the data in the file "Salmod," which is stored on your data disk and described in Appendix B. For this problem, do not use years of experience; instead, use age as a surrogate for experience.
   (a) Describe the steps used to obtain the final regression model.
   (b) Test the hypothesis that the rate of change in female salaries as a function of age are less than the rate of change for male salaries as a function of age. Your hypothesis test should be set up to provide strong evidence of discrimination against females if it exists. [*Note:* Females are indicated by a "1" for the variable "sex" in column 5. The test should be made conditional on the other significant predictor variables from part (a).]

15.32 Given the regression equation

$$Y = \beta_1 X_1 + \beta_2 X_2 + \epsilon$$

   (a) Derive the least-squares normal equations for estimating the coefficients β_1 and β_2, assuming a sample of n observations containing Y, X_1, and X_2.

(b) Given the following statistics from an analysis of the sample data:

$$n = 101 \qquad \bar{X}_1 = \bar{X}_2 = \bar{Y} = 0$$
$$S_Y = 10 \qquad S_{X_1} = 10 \qquad S_{X_2} = 8$$
$$\rho(X_1, Y) = 0.8 \qquad \rho(X_2, Y) = 0.7 \qquad \rho(X_1, X_2) = 0.5$$

compute the coefficient estimators using the normal equations developed in part (a). (*Hint:* Carefully review the definition of covariance and variance given the specific data for this problem and your normal equations.)

(c) Compute the statistics in the analysis of variance table, the percent explained variability, and the standard error of the estimate, $S(Y \mid X)$.

15.33 Given the Minitab computer output in Exhibit 15.17 for the regression model

$$Y = \beta_0 + \beta_1 X_1 + \beta_2 X_2$$

compute the following regression output statistics.

(a) The two coefficient estimators, $\hat{\beta}_1$ and $\hat{\beta}_2$.

(b) The regression sum of squares for the combined effect of both independent variables.

(c) The conditional regression sum of squares for the second variable, X_2, given the effect of X_1.

(d) The conditional F for X_2 and for X_1. (*Note:* Derive these conditional F statistics by first computing the conditional regression sum of squares and then the conditional F.)

(e) The Student t statistics based on the null hypothesis that these coefficients are equal to zero.

EXHIBIT 15.17   Computer Output for Problem 15.33

	N	MEAN	MEDIAN	TRMEAN	STDEV	SEMEAN
X(1)	51	12277	12314	12166	1851	259
Y	51	5536	5336	5483	812	114
X(2)	51	7.335	7.000	7.196	2.216	0.310

	MIN	MAX	Q1	Q3
X(1)	8857	17148	10689	13218
Y	4250	8348	5059	6037
X(2)	4.300	15.000	5.600	9.100

MTB > corr c2,c3,c5

	X(1)	Y
Y	0.633	
X(2)	-0.232	-0.370

15.34 For the regression model $Y = 12 + \hat{\beta}_1 X_1$ and the following statistics: $S_y = 10$, $S_{x_1} = 5$, $\rho(x_1, y) = 0.60$, $n = 100$, and mean of $X_1 = 10$:

(a) Compute the 98% two-sided confidence interval for β_1.

(b) Compute the 95% two-sided confidence interval for the predicted value of Y when $X_1 = 5$ and when $X_1 = 15$.

(c) What is the elasticity of Y with respect to X_1?

(d) Based on the following correlation matrix in Exhibit 15.18, which variable, X_2 or X_3, will make the largest contribution to RSS when combined in a regression model with X_1? Explain your rationale.

EXHIBIT 15.18   Correlation Matrix for Problem 15.34

	Y	X(1)	X(2)
X(1)	0.70		
X(2)	0.40	0.20	
X(3)	0.70	0.95	0.35

15.35 This problem will use the data file "Citydat," which is stored on your data disk and whose variables are defined in Appendix B. A group of activists in Camelot, Minnesota, are seeking increased development for this pristine enclave, which has received some national recognition on the television program, "Four Dirty Old Men." They claim that increased commercial and industrial development will bring new prosperity and lower taxes to Camelot. Specifically, they claim that an increased percentage of commercial and industrial development will decrease the property tax rate and increase the market value for owner-occupied residences.

You have been hired to analyze their claims. For this purpose you have obtained the data file "Citydat," which is stored on your data disk and described in Appendix B at the end of the book. It contains data from 45 small Minnesota cities. From these data you will first develop regression models that predict average value of owner-occupied housing and the property tax rate. Then you will determine if and how the addition of percent commercial property and then percent industrial property affects the variability explained in these regression models. The basic model for predicting market value of houses (C10) includes size of house (C4), tax rate (C7), per capita income (C9), and percent owner-occupied residence (C12) as independent variables. The basic model for predicting tax rate (C7) includes the tax assesment base (C6), current city expenditures per capita (C5/C8), and percent owner-occupied residence (C12) as independent variables.

Determine if the percent commercial (C14) and the percent industrial (C15) variables improve the explained variability in each of the two models. Perform conditional F tests for each of these additional variables. First estimate the conditional effect of percent commercial property by itself and then the conditional effect of percent industrial property by itself. Carefully explain the results of your analysis. Include in your report an explanation of why it was important to include all of the other variables in the regression model instead of just examining the effect of the direct and simple relationship between percent commercial property and percent industrial property on the tax rate and market value of housing.

15.36 Consider the following two regression models:

Model I: $Y_i = \beta_0 + \beta_1 X_{1i} + \beta_2 X_{2i} + \epsilon_{1i}$

Model II: $Y_i = \alpha_0 + \alpha_1 X_{1i} + \alpha_2 X_{2i} + \alpha_3 X_{3i} + \epsilon_{2i}$

The following regression statistics were computed using Minitab:

$$S_Y^2 = 1000 \qquad n = 51 \qquad R_I^2 = 0.60$$

$$R_{II}^2 = 0.80 \qquad r_{X_3 Y} = 0.75$$

(a) What are the conditional F and conditional t for the coefficient of X_3, $\hat{\alpha}_3$?

(b) Is there a correlation between X_3 and X_1 and/or X_2? Sketch an approximate Venn diagram. Explain the reasoning for your conclusion.

(c) Compare regression model I with the simple regression model

$$Y_i = \gamma_0 + \gamma_1 X_{3i} + \epsilon_{3i}$$

in terms of how well each model "fits" the data (e.g., consider the standard error of the estimate).

15.37 Given the correlation matrix in Table 15.11 and

$$S_Y = 100 \qquad S_{X_1} = 50 \qquad S_{X_2} = 80 \qquad S_{X_3} = 70 \qquad n = 51$$

$$\bar{Y} = 100 \qquad \bar{X}_1 = 10 \qquad \bar{X}_2 = 20 \qquad \bar{X}_3 = 30$$

compute the coefficient estimates, their standard error estimates, the standard error of the estimate, and R^2 for the regression model

$$Y = \beta_0 + \beta_1 X_1 + \beta_2 X_2 + \beta_3 X_3$$

TABLE 15.11
Correlation Matrix for
Problem 15.37

	Y	X_2	X_3
X_1	0.30	0	0
X_2	0.50	1.0	0
X_3	0.60	0	1.0

15.38 Use the data in the data file named "Student," which is stored on your data disk and described in Appendix B, to develop a model to predict a student's grade-point average in economics. Begin with the variables ACT scores, gender, and HSpct.

(a) Use appropriate statistical procedures to choose a subset of statistically significant predictor variables. Describe your strategy and define your final model carefully.

(b) Discuss how this model might be used as part of the college's decision process to select students for admission.

15.39 Explain the conditional F test for an independent variable in a multiple regression model. Be careful and complete. Provide an example using data from Minitab outputs and include the computer output with your answer.

15.40 Given the correlation matrix and descriptive statistics in Exhibit 15.19:
  (a) Write the Minitab output through the analysis of variance table.
  (b) Compute the conditional F for X_1 given X_2.

EXHIBIT 15.19   Minitab Output for Problem 15.40

MTB > describe c1 c2 c3

	N	MEAN	MEDIAN	TRMEAN	STDEV	SEMEAN
Y	27	2340	1602	2110	2252	433
X1	27	401.3	259.9	366.6	333.9	64.3
X2	27	2725	1697	2372	3072	591

	MIN	MAX	Q1	Q3
Y	593	9849	1004	3175
X1	105.8	1564.8	211.4	521.7
X2	280	13990	812	3289

MTB > corr c1-c3

	Y	X1
X1	0.900	
X2	0.400	0.500

15.41 Explain why high correlation between two independent variables results in a high variance for the slope coefficient. Present your explanation both mathematically and in words.

15.42 Explain how the addition of another independent variable to a multiple regression model could result in an increase in the standard error of the estimate, $S_{Y|X}$, even though R^2 increased.

15.43 Consider the multiple regression model

$$Y = 100 - 10X_1 + 9X_2$$

where Y is the quantity of an item that is sold, X_1 the price per unit for the item, and X_2 the price per unit for a competing item. The Student t statistics for the coefficients of X_1 and X_2 are -5.0 and $+4.8$. The simple correlations between Y and X_1 and between Y and X_2 are both less than 0.20 ($n = 50$), while the correlation between X_1 and X_2 is 0.87. Explain why the simple correlations between Y and the X's are not significant but the conditional coefficients in the multiple regression model are statistically significant.

APPENDIX: DERIVATION OF REGRESSION RELATIONSHIPS

A.1 Least-Squares Derivation of Estimators

The derivation of coefficient estimators for a model with two predictor variables is as follows:

$$\hat{Y}_i = \hat{\beta}_0 + \hat{\beta}_1 x_{1i} + \hat{\beta}_2 x_{2i}$$

Minimize

$$\text{ESS} = \sum_{i=1}^{n} \left[y_i - (\hat{\beta}_0 + \hat{\beta}_1 x_{1i} + \hat{\beta}_2 x_{2i}) \right]^2$$

Applying differential calculus, we obtain a set of three normal equations that can be solved for the coefficient estimators.

$$\frac{\partial \text{ESS}}{\partial \hat{\beta}_0} = 0$$

$$2 \sum_{i=1}^{n} \left[y_i - (\hat{\beta}_0 + \hat{\beta}_1 x_{1i} + \hat{\beta}_2 x_{2i}) \right] (-1) = 0$$

$$\sum_{i=1}^{n} y_i - n\hat{\beta}_0 - \hat{\beta}_1 \sum_{i=1}^{n} x_{1i} - \hat{\beta}_2 \sum_{i=1}^{n} x_{2i} = 0$$

$$n\hat{\beta}_0 + \hat{\beta}_1 \sum_{i=1}^{n} x_{1i} + \hat{\beta}_2 \sum_{i=1}^{n} x_{2i} = \sum_{i=1}^{n} y_i$$

$$\frac{\partial \text{ESS}}{\partial \hat{\beta}_1} = 0$$

$$2 \sum_{i=1}^{n} \left[y_i - (\hat{\beta}_0 + \hat{\beta}_1 x_{1i} + \hat{\beta}_2 x_{2i}) \right] (-x_{1i}) = 0$$

$$\sum_{i=1}^{n} x_{1i} y_i - \hat{\beta}_0 \sum_{i=1}^{n} x_{1i} - \hat{\beta}_1 \sum_{i=1}^{n} x_{1i}^2 - \hat{\beta}_2 \sum_{i=1}^{n} x_{1i} x_{2i} = 0$$

$$\hat{\beta}_0 \sum_{i=1}^{n} x_{1i} + \hat{\beta}_1 \sum_{i=1}^{n} x_{1i}^2 + \hat{\beta}_2 \sum_{i=1}^{n} x_{1i} x_{2i} = \sum_{i=1}^{n} x_{1i} y_i$$

$$\frac{\partial \text{ESS}}{\partial \hat{\beta}_2} = 0$$

$$2 \sum_{i=1}^{n} \left[y_i - (\hat{\beta}_0 + \hat{\beta}_1 x_{1i} + \hat{\beta}_2 x_{2i}) \right] (-x_{2i}) = 0$$

$$\sum_{i=1}^{n} x_{2i} y_i - \hat{\beta}_0 \sum_{i=1}^{n} x_{2i} - \hat{\beta}_1 \sum_{i=1}^{n} x_{1i} x_{2i} - \hat{\beta}_2 \sum_{i=1}^{n} x_{2i}^2 = 0$$

$$\hat{\beta}_0 \sum_{i=1}^{n} x_{2i} + \hat{\beta}_1 \sum_{i=1}^{n} x_{1i} x_{2i} + \hat{\beta}_2 \sum_{i=1}^{n} x_{2i}^2 = \sum_{i=1}^{n} x_{2i} y_i$$

As a result of applying the least-squares algorithm, we have a system of three linear equations in three unknowns: $\hat{\beta}_0$, $\hat{\beta}_1$, and $\hat{\beta}_2$.

$$n\hat{\beta}_0 + \hat{\beta}_1 \sum_{i=1}^{n} x_{1i} + \hat{\beta}_2 \sum_{i=1}^{n} x_{2i} = \sum_{i=1}^{n} y_i$$

$$\hat{\beta}_0 \sum_{i=1}^{n} x_{1i} + \hat{\beta}_1 \sum_{i=1}^{n} x_{1i}^2 + \hat{\beta}_2 \sum_{i=1}^{n} x_{1i} x_{2i} = \sum_{i=1}^{n} x_{1i} y_i$$

$$\hat{\beta}_0 \sum_{i=1}^{n} x_{2i} + \hat{\beta}_1 \sum_{i=1}^{n} x_{1i} x_{2i} + \hat{\beta}_2 \sum_{i=1}^{n} x_{2i}^2 = \sum_{i=1}^{n} x_{2i} y_i$$

The normal equations are solved for the desired coefficients by first computing the various X and Y squared and cross-product terms.

A.2 Total Explained Variability

The explained variability RSS term in multiple regression is more complex than the term in simple regression. For the two-independent-variable regression model

$$Y = \beta_0 + \beta_1 X_1 + \beta_2 X_2$$

we find that

$$
\begin{aligned}
\text{RSS} &= \sum_{i=1}^{n} (\hat{Y}_i - \bar{Y})^2 \\
&= \sum_{i=1}^{n} \left[\hat{\beta}_0 + \hat{\beta}_1 x_{1i} + \hat{\beta}_2 x_{2i} - (\hat{\beta}_0 + \hat{\beta}_1 \bar{X}_1 + \hat{\beta}_2 \bar{X}_2) \right]^2 \\
&= \sum_{i=1}^{n} \left[\hat{\beta}_1^2 (x_{1i} - \bar{X}_1)^2 + \hat{\beta}_2^2 (x_{2i} - \bar{X}_1)^2 + 2\hat{\beta}_1 \hat{\beta}_2 (x_{1i} - \bar{X}_1)(x_{2i} - \bar{X}_2) \right] \\
&= (n-1) \left(\hat{\beta}_1^2 S_{X_1}^2 + \hat{\beta}_2^2 S_{X_2}^2 + 2 r_{x_1 x_2} \hat{\beta}_1 \hat{\beta}_2 S_{X_1} S_{X_2} \right)
\end{aligned}
$$

We see that the explained variability has a portion directly associated with each of the independent variables and a portion associated with the correlation between the two variables. Compare this result with Figure 15.3 and note that both the graphical and algebraic forms show variability explained by the variables individually and by the combination of the variables.

A.3 Variance of Prediction

In multiple regression applications we often want to construct confidence intervals or test hypotheses using the predicted value $\hat{Y}_*$. Assume that Y_* is estimated using independent variables $X_1 = X_{1*}$ and $X_2 = X_{2*}$. The estimated variance of the value predicted is computed in a number of the better statistical packages. We present the results for the two-variable multiple regression model

$$Y_* = \hat{\beta}_0 + \hat{\beta}_1 X_{1*} + \hat{\beta}_2 X_{2*}$$

which is used to estimate Y_* given X_{1*} and X_{2*}. The predicted value is a linear combination of the coefficient estimators, which are random variables, and the values of the independent variables. Therefore, using the results from Chapter 7, we find that

$$S_{Y_*}^2 = S_{\hat{\beta}_0}^2 + X_{1*}^2 S_{\hat{\beta}_1}^2 + X_{2*}^2 S_{\hat{\beta}_2}^2$$
$$+ 2X_{1*}\text{cov}(\hat{\beta}_0, \hat{\beta}_1) + 2X_{2*}\text{cov}(\hat{\beta}_0, \hat{\beta}_2) + 2X_{1*}X_{2*}\text{cov}(\hat{\beta}_1, \hat{\beta}_2)$$

The variance and covariance terms involving the estimated coefficients can be obtained from the *variance–covariance matrix of coefficients*, which can be computed as an option in many computer packages.

16

Multiple Regression Extensions

Know thy data and thy problem specification.

16.1 AN EXTENDED VIEW OF REGRESSION ANALYSIS

In this chapter we present a number of topics that are normally covered in econometrics or other statistical modeling courses. These topics are selected and presented here to provide increased understanding of regression analysis and its applications. In contrast to other chapters, we have developed each topic as a separate unit. Thus topics can be pursued selectively in courses or for independent study. Section 16.2 provides a background for model development, and we encourage its reading in addition to other selected sections.

The topics included in this chapter are:

1. Polynomial transformations
2. Dummy variables and experimental design
3. Heteroscedasticity
4. Serial correlation
5. Bias from specification error
6. Random independent variables

The topics in this chapter can be grouped into three major categories. In Section 16.2 we present a general discussion of the process of model development. This is followed by transformations and dummy variables that enable us to apply regression models in situations where a linear model is not appropriate. In Chapter 15 we introduced the topic with a presentation of dummy variable adjustments, quadratic models, and exponential models. The third category of topics deals with procedures for handling situations in which the basic assumptions are violated. The most important of these relate to assumptions regarding the distribution of the error term. When the assumption of uniform and independent error is violated, estimates of variance terms are no longer correct and coefficient estimates are not efficient. We show how to

781

detect and adjust for nonuniform error—heteroscedasticity—and for correlations between the error terms—serial correlation. In another section we indicate the problems that occur when the independent variables are random variables. The biases that result from incorrect model specification and from correlations between the independent variables and the error are also analyzed.

16.2 ART AND PRACTICE OF MODEL DEVELOPMENT

Regression models are developed in business and economic applications to increase understanding and guide decisions and/or to predict an outcome or dependent variable as a function of input or independent variables[1] (Key Idea 16.1). The pursuit of this objective must be based on an understanding of the system in which the problem occurs. Statistical theory applied to the data provides the link between the theory and understanding of the system and the observed behavior as defined by the data. Both an understanding of the problem context and the methods of statistics are necessary for developing the best model. This often implies that interdisciplinary teams are organized to study the problem. An experienced production manager and an analyst familiar with regression analysis might work together on model development. Their likelihood of success is greatly increased if all members of the team learn from each other about the system operation and about appropriate statistical methods.

From a statistical perspective regression model objectives can be divided into either prediction of the dependent variable or estimation of one or more slope coefficients—the relationship between dependent and independent variables. Real problem objectives are usually not so clear, but these alternatives identify important options.

If the objective is prediction, we want a model that has a small standard error of the estimate $S_{Y|X}$. We are not as concerned about correlated independent variables because we know that a number of different combinations of correlated variables will result in the same prediction precision. We do need to know that the correlations between independent variables continue to hold in future applications. A wide spread for the independent variables is needed to ensure small prediction variance over the desired range of model application.

Alternatively, estimation of slope coefficients leads us to consider a wider range of issues. Slope coefficient variance is influenced by the standard error of the estimate $S_{Y|X}$. A wide spread of the independent variable is also important. Multicollinearity is of greater concern because high correlations between independent variables increase the coefficient variance $\sigma_{\hat{\beta}_j}^2$. We will also see in Section 16.7 that incorrect

---

[1] Economists use the term *endogenous variables* to identify variables that are determined by the system, and *exogenous variables* to identify variables that are determined outside the system and affect the endogenous variables. As such, endogenous variables correspond to dependent variables and exogenous variables correspond to independent variables.

Key Idea 16.1: Regression Model Development

Model development is a complex process requiring a broad range of inputs. The process generally includes the following components:

1. Interdisciplinary teams that combine substantial knowledge of the process with an understanding of analysis tools such as multiple regression that are needed for model development.
2. Ideal data for regression models have independent variables with a wide range and small correlations between independent variables. Correct model specification based on process knowledge is important and should proceed data collection.
3. Theory, experience, and historical knowledge are the foundation for analysis and problem solving. Rigorous statistical analysis of available and collected data using the procedures learned in this book complete the problem-solving process.
4. An understanding based on experience that data contain both information and error. Analysis and modeling seek to enhance information and minimize error.

specification—failure to include important independent variables—leads to biased coefficient estimates. We may be faced with a dilemma. Do we include correlated independent variables in the model and thus increase the coefficient variance $\sigma^2_{\hat{\beta}_j}$, or do we exclude significant independent variables, with the result that the remaining coefficient estimates are biased?

Statistical measures do not provide the complete answer to the model specification question. Mean square error—variance plus biased squared—should be minimized. In applied problems we do not always have a good measure of bias. Most statisticians would select the model with the smallest coefficient standard error, $S_{\hat{\beta}_j}$. However, that strategy could ignore important relationships between variables in the problem model, which could help resolve specification problems. For example, omitting the price variable when the dependent variable is quantity demanded would raise serious questions by most economists.

Does It Make Sense?

Model development can be enhanced by the use of evidence from both theory and data. For this discussion, *theory* will refer to the accumulated knowledge concerning a particular process or problem. An important knowledge source for the solution of applied business problems is the accumulated experience of managers and other senior persons. *Data*, for this discussion, are sets of measured variables that are suitable for analysis by statistical procedures. Ideally, the data comprise a random sample. However, we often have data sets—not necessarily random samples—that are believed to represent the system being studied. Some economists and business analysts tend to favor either theory or data as the final authority. Theoreticians develop arguments based on past research. Some managers make all of their decisions using analyses based on their accumulated knowledge and experience. Other, more empirical managers base their conclusions on the analysis of numbers. In a sense they view results based on the analysis of data as factual and objective, while other results are subjective.

Economic and business theory represents the accumulated knowledge from many thinkers who have observed society through history. This knowledge has resulted from many "experiments" and debates that have been observed and analyzed by great thinkers, such as Smith, Marx, and Keynes. More recently, results have come from rigorous econometric work and the use of high-level mathematics. The political debates and the comparisons of policies used by successful and unsuccessful firms also contribute to the knowledge base. Applied studies of production, marketing, and organizational behavior benefit from the insights of experienced practitioners. Certainly, we cannot ignore this accumulated knowledge. However, today's problems are in many senses unique and require factual understanding of the situation. The common wisdom may be wrong. The interpretation of theory in the context of the current problem may be incorrect. Society moves ahead as the result of new insights and new discoveries based on the analysis of new evidence. However, its foundation is a large body of accumulated knowledge. But well-built problem solutions also require careful and rigorous data analysis.

Sample data provide objective observations of present and historical system behavior. These observations define points that represent specific occurrences. These points can be linked together using techniques such as multiple regression analysis. The result is a model of the system expressed in mathematical form. This form can then be used with a number of optimization and decision-making techniques to increase understanding and to make better decisions. Data collection techniques and statistical data models that are based on probability theory provide reliable data. On this foundation we apply well-developed statistical inference techniques such as estimation and hypothesis testing. We cannot ignore the factual results that come from data through the use of statistical methods. However, some data are collected with no thought given to appropriate sample and/or measurement techniques. Conclusions based on such data should be viewed with great suspicion.

Experienced analysts approach data with an understanding of the potential problems. All sample data contain information and error. In some cases the error is so large that information is hidden or seriously obscured. Data sets contain variables that are linked together by various complex correlation structures. These structures can lead to high variance for estimators, which in turn can obscure important results. Data collection and estimation techniques can produce biased results if not performed carefully using the best judgment about the error and correlation structure in the system that produces the data.

The contrast between procedures that emphasize theory versus those that emphasize data is a fundamental issue in scientific research. In business and policy activities there is a parallel contrast between experience and the observation of new phenomena. In business and economic study these issues lead to more difficult problems than is usually the case in the natural sciences. Human behavior is complex, and individual behavior has considerable variability about group norms. This can lead to large error terms and complex correlations. Thus it may be difficult to make inferences from the data. For the same reasons, theory may not be as well defined as we would like. The contribution of particular historical results and/or experience to the problem solutions is sometimes unclear.

Resolution of these problems separate professional from amateur analysts. A good understanding of the system is the beginning. We must also understand the statistical methods that apply to the problem being studied. Peer review and discussion of analysis techniques and conclusions with other competent professionals is important. Ultimately, analysts combine the statistical analysis and the theory to reach a conclusion. For applied work this conclusion is often a recommendation that must be communicated in both oral and written forms. Finally, the recommendation must be defended. This process is complex and not precisely defined. It contains many checks and balances. Given the foregoing difficulties, professional analysis must be performed within a highly interactive process. However, persons with good statistical understanding and the ability to communicate their results will perform well.   □

Problem Exercises

16.1   Refer to the salary prediction model in Chapter 15. A senior college administrator once said that the salary prediction model would be improved if the R^2 were closer to 1.0. Assume that the proposed model improvement does not imply adding many additional predictor variables. Comment on the administrator's statement.

16.2   A business analyst was examining a data set that contained data from large cities, with each observation representing a four-square-block area. In those data he noted that the frequency of cracks in the sidewalk was a statistically significant predictor of death rate and of per capita health care costs in the neighborhood. He then proposed a major sidewalk repair program, arguing that the cost of the sidewalks could be paid for with reduced health care expenditures. Comment on this conclusion from his regression analysis work. Would you support his argument?

16.3 TRANSFORMATIONS: POLYNOMIAL MODELS

Linear models do not provide an adequate approximation of the relationship in many situations. Total sales do not always increase linearly as prices are reduced. Total production does not increase continually at the same rate when workers are added to a production process. Instead, there are frequently examples of increasing or decreasing returns at different staffing levels. Economic theory argues that productivity for a given plant increases with increased size until the optimal size is passed and decreasing returns to scale occur.

For multiple regression analysis a number of nonlinear models such as the quadratic function can be represented as linear models through appropriate transformations of the variables. Using multiple regression with transformations for modeling nonlinear relationships has several important advantages. First, multiple regression is widely used and understood. This provides a common lanquage for problem analysis. In addition, computer software for regression analysis is readily available. Thus it is not necessary to find and learn a new algorithm for estimating many nonlinear models. Finally, the multiple regression approach, which minimizes error variability, provides an easy method for comparing a variety of linear and nonlinear models. We have seen how models with increasing numbers of independent variables can be compared using conditional explained sum of squares. The same analysis can be applied to compare linear and polynomial nonlinear models (Key Idea 16.2).

Key Idea 16.2: Polynomial Models

Polynomial models have always had great appeal for applied work because they can be used to approximate a wide range of functions. In Chapter 15 we saw that a quadratic model is linear in the squared term X_1^2. Using the same reasoning, we can take a general polynomial,

$$Y = \beta_0 + \beta_1 X_1 + \beta_2 X_1^2 + \beta_3 X_1^3 + \cdots + \beta_k X_1^k$$

and represent it as a linear function,

$$Y = \beta_0 + \beta_1 Z_1 + \beta_2 Z_2 + \beta_3 Z_3 + \cdots + \beta_k Z_k$$

where

$$Z_j = X_1^j$$

Any good statistical computer program will have the capability to make these computations or transformations.

The coefficients estimated using the transformed regression model are the coefficient estimates for the polynomial model. An important advantage is that we can use conditional t or F tests to determine the degree k of the polynomial. If the term X_1^k is conditionally significant given the variability explained by the lower-degree terms, we conclude that the polynomial is of at least degree k. Higher-degree terms can be added and tested until they no longer contribute significantly to explained variability. In this example, if X_1^{k+1} is not conditionally significant and X_1^k is, the polynomial is of degree k.

This same logic can be used for polynomials in several variables, such as

$$Y = \beta_0 + \beta_1 X_1 + \beta_2 X_1^2 + \cdots + \beta_k X_1^k + \alpha_1 X_2 + \alpha_2 X_2^2 + \cdots + \alpha_k X_2^k + \gamma_1 X_1 X_2$$
$$+ \gamma_2 X_1 X_2^2 + \gamma_3 X_1^2 X_2 + \cdots$$

The various terms in this equation can be represented by transformed Z_j variables. Conditional t or F tests can be used to determine the number of polynomial and cross-product terms that should be in the model.

It appears that we have an approach that is ideally suited for multiple regression analysis. Any equation can be approximated by a polynomial of high-enough degree. It seems that the model development opportunities are too good to be true. As you have learned by this time, when something is too good to be true, it is either not true or it is not as good as it appears. Such is the case with polynomial regression. First, each additional coefficient requires a degree of freedom, and an excessive number of parameters can result in high variance estimates. Higher-order polynomial models can also follow random movements in the dependent variable, resulting in models that fit the sample data but are not suitable for estimating new situations. In the past there was considerable interest in polynomial models for time-series forecasting. A polynomial using time as the independent variable would be proposed and fitted to the historical time series as shown in Figure 16.1. However, forecasts can be quite unreliable because polynomial models "explode"—increase or decrease rapidly—outside the range of the data observed. In Figure 16.1, the best fit uses a fifth-degree polynomial in time t, which has the form

$$\hat{Y}_t = \hat{\beta}_0 + \hat{\beta}_1 t + \hat{\beta}_2 t^2 + \cdots + \hat{\beta}_5 t^5$$

Note the problem that would occur if a forecast were made by extrapolation of the polynomial function in Figure 16.1 using higher values of t.

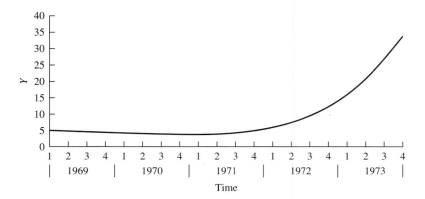

Figure 16.1   Polynomial Models for Time-Series Forecasting

Does It Make Sense?

Experience suggests that second- or third-degree polynomials provide useful models for some complex systems. In a few situations a fourth-degree model provides additional understanding. However, you should be very suspicious of claims that a fourth-degree or higher polynomial added important insights beyond those obtained using lower-degree models. Analysts must understand the problem before attempting to fit various complex regression models. *Know thy data and thy problem specification.*   □

Problem Exercise

16.3   Explain why a tenth-degree polynomial model estimated by using multiple regression applied to transformed variables would not be very useful if only 11 to 15 data points were available for the regression analysis.

16.4 DUMMY VARIABLES: EXTENDED APPLICATIONS

Dummy variables were introduced in Chapter 15 in applications involving regression models applied to two different subsets of data. We saw how they could be used to test for sex discrimination in the faculty salary example.

In this section we expand the potential applications of dummy variables (Key Idea 16.3). First, we present an application in which a regression model is applied to more than two subsets of data. Next, we show how dummy variables can be used to estimate the seasonal effects on a regression model applied to time-series data. Finally, we show how dummy variables can be used to analyze data from experimental situations that are defined by multiple-level categorical variables.

Example 16.1   Cross-Section Analysis

Wendy Thorson is a senior marketing analyst for the American Wool Producers Association. She is interested in estimating the demand for wool products in various cities as a function of total disposable income in the city. Data were gathered from 150 Standard Metropolitan Statistical Areas (SMSAs). As a first step, Wendy estimates a regression model for the relationship between sales and disposable income:

$$\hat{Y} = \hat{\beta}_0 + \hat{\beta}_1 X_1$$

where X_1 is the per capita annual disposable income for a city and Y is the per capita sales of wool products in the city. After some additional discussions she wonders if the regression model might have different coefficients in different geographic regions: north, central, and south.

Solution   The analysis begins by placing each of the cities in one of the three regions. Figure 16.2 indicates the situation schematically if the sales level is different

Key Idea 16.3: Dummy Variable Model

The relationship between Y and X_1,

$$\hat{Y} = \hat{\alpha}_0 + \hat{\alpha}_1 X_1$$

can shift in response to a changed condition. The shift effect can be estimated by using a **dummy variable**, X_2, which has values of 0 (condition not present) and 1 (condition present). In these cases the relationship between Y and X_1 is specified by the multiple regression model

$$\hat{Y}_i = \hat{\beta}_0 + \hat{\beta}_2 X_2 + \hat{\beta}_1 X_1$$

The coefficient $\hat{\beta}_2$ represents the shift of the function between the two sets of data points. The functions for each set of points are

$$\hat{Y} = \hat{\beta}_0 + \hat{\beta}_1 X_1 \qquad \text{when } X_2 = 0$$

and

$$\hat{Y} = (\hat{\beta}_0 + \hat{\beta}_2) + \hat{\beta}_1 X_1 \qquad \text{when } X_2 = 1$$

In the first function the constant is just $\hat{\beta}_0$, while in the second the constant is $\hat{\beta}_0 + \hat{\beta}_2$.

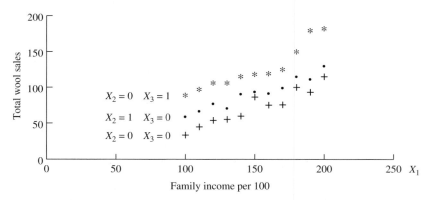

• Central
+ South
* North

Figure 16.2   Sales Versus Income by Geographic Region

between the geographic regions. Note that combinations of two dummy variables have been used to identify each of the three regions. The identifications are

$$\text{North:} \quad X_2 = 0, \quad X_3 = 1$$
$$\text{Central:} \quad X_2 = 1, \quad X_3 = 0$$
$$\text{South:} \quad X_2 = 0, \quad X_3 = 0$$

In general, k distinct regions or subsets could be identified uniquely with $k - 1$ dummy variables.

Shifts in the model constant could be estimated using the model

$$Y = \beta_0 + \beta_2 X_2 + \beta_3 X_3 + \beta_1 X_1$$

Applying this model to the north, it becomes

$$Y = \beta_0 + \beta_2(0) + \beta_3(1) + \beta_1 X_1$$
$$= (\beta_0 + \beta_3) + \beta_1 X_1$$

In the central states we find

$$Y = \beta_0 + \beta_2(1) + \beta_3(0) + \beta_1 X_1$$
$$= (\beta_0 + \beta_2) + \beta_1 X_1$$

Finally, for the southern states the model is

$$Y = \beta_0 + \beta_2(0) + \beta_3(0) + \beta_1 X_1$$
$$= \beta_0 + \beta_1 X_1$$

Summarizing these results, we find that the constants for the various regions are

$$\text{North:} \quad \beta_0 + \beta_3$$
$$\text{Central:} \quad \beta_0 + \beta_2$$
$$\text{South:} \quad \beta_0$$

This formulation defines the south as the base constant, with β_3 and β_2 defining the shift of the function for northern and central cities, respectively. Hypothesis tests using the coefficient Student t statistic could be used to determine if there are significant differences between the constants that represent the regions. For additional regions, constants could be modeled by using dummy variables that continued the pattern shown above.

The model with differences in slope coefficients and constants is

$$Y = \beta_0 + \beta_2 X_2 + \beta_3 X_3 + (\beta_1 + \beta_4 X_2 + \beta_5 X_3) X_1$$
$$= \beta_0 + \beta_2 X_2 + \beta_3 X_3 + \beta_1 X_1 + \beta_4 X_2 X_1 + \beta_5 X_3 X_1$$

Applying this model to the northern states, we see that

$$Y = \beta_0 + \beta_2(0) + \beta_3(1) + (\beta_1 + \beta_4(0) + \beta_5(1))X_1$$
$$= (\beta_0 + \beta_3) + (\beta_1 + \beta_5)X_1$$

For the central states the model is

$$Y = \beta_0 + \beta_2(1) + \beta_3(0) + (\beta_1 + \beta_4(1) + \beta_5(0))X_1$$
$$= (\beta_0 + \beta_2) + (\beta_1 + \beta_4)X_1$$

Finally, for the southern states,

$$Y = \beta_0 + \beta_2(0) + \beta_3(0) + (\beta_1 + \beta_4(0) + \beta_5(0))X_1$$
$$= \beta_0 + (\beta_1)X_1$$

The X_1 slope coefficient for cities in different regions are

$$\textit{North:} \quad \beta_1 + \beta_5$$
$$\textit{Central:} \quad \beta_1 + \beta_4$$
$$\textit{South:} \quad \beta_1$$

Again the south is the base condition, with slope β_1. Hypothesis tests can be used to determine the statistical significance of slope coefficient differences. Using this dummy variable regression model, Ms. Thorson can estimate the relationship between sales and disposable income by region of the country. $\qquad\qquad\qquad\square$

Example 16.2   Seasonal Time Series

After finishing the regional analysis, Wendy Thorson decides to study the relationship between sales and disposable income using time-series data. After some discussion she realized that sales are different for each quarter of the year. For example, during the fourth quarter sales were high in anticipation of holiday season gifts and colder weather.

Solution   She decided to define a set of three dummy variables to estimate shifts in sales among the various quarters. Notice that this problem has a similar formulation to the regional subset problem discussed above. Ms. Thorson decided to define the quarterly dummy variables as follows:

$$\textit{First quarter:} \quad X_2 = 0, \quad X_3 = 0, \quad X_4 = 0$$
$$\textit{Second quarter:} \quad X_2 = 1, \quad X_3 = 0, \quad X_4 = 0$$
$$\textit{Third quarter:} \quad X_2 = 0, \quad X_3 = 1, \quad X_4 = 0$$
$$\textit{Fourth quarter:} \quad X_2 = 0, \quad X_3 = 0, \quad X_4 = 1$$

The dummy variable coefficients are estimates of shifts in wool consumption function between quarters in the model

$$Y = \beta_0 + \beta_2 X_2 + \beta_3 X_3 + \beta_4 X_4 + \beta_1 X_1$$

where Y is the total sales of wool products and X_1 is disposable income. The constants for the various quarters are as follows:

First quarter: β_0

Second quarter: $\beta_0 + \beta_2$

Third quarter: $\beta_0 + \beta_3$

Fourth quarter: $\beta_0 + \beta_4$

Hypothesis tests using the Student t statistic can be made to determine if there are significant differences in sales, conditional on disposable income, among quarters.

$\square$

16.5 EXPERIMENTAL DESIGN MODELS

Experimental design procedures have been a major area of statistical research and practice for a number of years. Early work dealt with agricultural research. The efforts of statisticians such as R. A. Fisher and O. L. Davies in England during the 1920s provided the foundation for experimental design methodology and for statistical practice in general (Key Idea 16.4). Agricultural experiments require an entire growing

Key Idea 16.4: Experimental Design

Dummy variable regression can be used as a tool in **experimental design** work. The experiments have a single outcome variable, which contains all the random error. Each experimental outcome or response is measured at discrete combinations of experimental (independent) variables, X_j.

There is an important difference in philosophy for experimental designs in comparison to most of the problems we have considered. Experimental design attempts to identify causes for the changes in the dependent variable. This is done by prespecifying combinations of discrete independent variables at which the dependent variable will be measured. An important objective is to choose experimental points defined by independent variables that provide minimum variance estimators. The order in which the experiments are performed is chosen randomly to avoid biases from variables not included in the experiment.

season to obtain data. Thus it was important to develop procedures that could answer a number of questions and ensure great precision. In addition, most of the experiments defined activity using variables with discrete as opposed to continuous levels. Experimental design methods have also been used extensively in the study of human behavior and in various industrial experiments. The recent emphasis on improving quality and productivity has spawned increased activity in this area of statistics, with important contributions from groups such as the Center for Quality and Productivity led by George Box at the University of Wisconsin.

16.5.1 Experimental Design and Dummy Variables

Experimental outcomes, Y, are measured under specific conditions defined by combinations of levels for the treatment and blocking variables, $Z_l, l = 1, \ldots, m$. Determining the effect of treatment variable levels on the outcome is the primary objective. Blocking variables are included to reduce variance. Each treatment and blocking variable, Z_l, with K_l discrete levels is represented by $(K_l - 1), 0, 1$ dummy variables, $X_{lj}, j = 2, \ldots, K_l$. All of these variables are included in a multiple regression model whose coefficients are estimates of the effect of that variable level on the outcome, Y.

$$Y = \beta_0 + \sum_{l=1}^{m} (\beta_{l2}X_{l2} + \beta_{l3}X_{l3} + \cdots + \beta_{lk_l}X_{lk_l}) + \epsilon$$

Level 1 for each categorical variable, Z_l, is represented by 0 values for the dummy variables representing Z_l. Level 2 is represented by $X_{l2} = 1$ and the other $X_{lj} = 0$. Level 3 is represented by $X_{l3} = 1$ and the other $X_{lj} = 0$. This pattern continues for all levels of the categorical variable Z_l. Continuous treatment variables, Z_q, defined as covariates, are represented by a single continuous variable X_q which is added to the model. In many cases several replications of the basic design are conducted to provide sufficient degrees of freedom for error. This process is demonstrated in the example that follows.

Example 16.3   Experimental Design for Worker Training Program

Mary Manyunit is the production manager for a large auto parts factory. She is interested in determining the effect of a new training program on worker productivity. Considerable research supports the conclusion that productivity is also influenced by the machine type and by the amount of education a worker has received.

Solution   Mary defines the following variables for the experiment:

Y: Number of units produced per 8-hour shift

Z_1: Type of training
  1. Traditional classroom lecture and film presentation
  2. Interactive computer-assisted instruction

Z_2: Machine type
  1. Machine type 1

   2. Machine type 2
   3. Machine type 3
Z_3: Worker's educational level
   1. High school education
   2. At least one year of post–high school education

The variable Z_1 is called a *treatment variable* because the major study objective is an evaluation of the training program. The variables Z_2 and Z_3 are called *blocking variables* because they are included to help reduce or block out some of the unexplained variability. In this way the variance is reduced and the test for the main treatment effects has greater power. The term *blocking variable* is a carryover from the agricultural experiments, where fields were separated into small blocks each of which had different soil conditions. We will see that it is also possible to estimate the effect of the blocking variables. Thus one does not lose information by calling certain variables blocking variables instead of treatment variables.

Experimental design observations are predefined using the independent variables. Table 16.1 presents a list of the observations, with each observation designated using levels of the Z variables. In this design, which is called a *full factorial design,* there are 12 observations, one for each combination of the treatment and blocking variables. The y_i's represent the measured responses at each of the experimental conditions. In the data model y_i contains the effect of the treatment and blocking variables plus random error. In many experimental designs this pattern of 12 observations would be replicated (repeated) to provide more degrees of freedom for error and lower variance estimates of the effects of the design variables. This design could be analyzed using analysis of variance. However, we show how the analysis can be performed using dummy variable regression.

TABLE 16.1   Experimental Design for Productivity Study

Observation	Product, Y	Training, Z_1	Machine, Z_2	Education, Z_3
1	y_1	1	1	1
2	y_2	1	1	2
3	y_3	1	2	1
4	y_4	1	2	2
5	y_5	1	3	1
6	y_6	1	3	2
7	y_7	2	1	1
8	y_8	2	1	2
9	y_9	2	2	1
10	y_{10}	2	2	2
11	y_{11}	2	3	1
12	y_{12}	2	3	2

The levels for each of the three design variables, Z_1, Z_2, and Z_3, can be expressed as a set of dummy variables. Define the following dummy variables:

$$Z_1 = 1 \rightarrow X_1 = 0$$
$$Z_1 = 2 \rightarrow X_1 = 1$$
$$Z_2 = 1 \rightarrow X_2 = 0 \ \& \ X_3 = 0$$
$$Z_2 = 2 \rightarrow X_2 = 1 \ \& \ X_3 = 0$$
$$Z_2 = 3 \rightarrow X_2 = 0 \ \& \ X_3 = 1$$
$$Z_3 = 1 \rightarrow X_4 = 0$$
$$Z_3 = 2 \rightarrow X_4 = 1$$

Using these relationships, the experimental design model in Table 16.1, which uses the Z variables, can be represented by dummy variables as shown in Table 16.2. Using these dummy variables we can define a multiple regression model:

$$Y_i = \beta_0 + \beta_1 X_{1i} + \beta_2 X_{2i} + \beta_3 X_{3i} + \beta_4 X_{4i} + \epsilon_i$$

The regression coefficients would be estimated using the variables as specified above. The 12 experiments or observations shown in Tables 16.1 and 16.2 are defined as one replication of the experimental design. A replication contains all of the individual experiments that are included in the experimental design. Often, several replications of the design would be made to provide greater accuracy for the coefficient estimates and to provide sufficient degrees of freedom for estimating the variance. In the dummy variable model we estimate four coefficients and a constant, leaving $n - 4 - 1$ degrees of freedom for estimating the variance. With one replication, $n = 12$ and we have 7 degrees of freedom for estimating the variance. With two replications of the design,

TABLE 16.2   Experimental Design Model Using Dummy Variables

Observation	Product, Y	X_1	X_2	X_3	X_4
1	y_1	0	0	0	0
2	y_2	0	0	0	1
3	y_3	0	1	0	0
4	y_4	0	1	0	1
5	y_5	0	0	1	0
6	y_6	0	0	1	1
7	y_7	1	0	0	0
8	y_8	1	0	0	1
9	y_9	!	1	0	0
10	y_{10}	1	1	0	1
11	y_{11}	1	0	1	0
12	y_{12}	1	0	1	1

$n = 24$, leaving 19 degrees of freedom for estimating the variance, and with three replications we have 31 degrees of freedom. Usually, at least 15 or 20 degrees of freedom are required to obtain stable estimates of variance. Using the definitions of the dummy variables, we find that the regression coefficients would be interpreted as follows:

1. $\hat{\beta}_1$ is the productivity increase for the new CAI training compared to the standard classroom training.
2. $\hat{\beta}_2$ is the productivity increase for machine type 2 compared to machine type 1.
3. $\hat{\beta}_3$ is the productivity increase for machine type 3 compared to machine type 1.
4. $\hat{\beta}_4$ is the productivity increase for the post–high school education compared to high school alone.

Any of these "increases" could be negative, implying a decrease.

The significance of each of these effects can be tested using our standard hypothesis-testing procedures. Note that if an experimental observation were lost or failed, the same regression model could still be used to estimate the coefficients. However, we would have a larger variance and hence the hypothesis tests would have lower power.

It is also possible to add continuous variables or covariates to the model. Suppose that Mary suspects that the number of years of worker experience and the ambient temperature also influence productivity. These two variables could be measured for each experiment and added to the dummy variable regression model. The regression model would then become

$$Y_i = \beta_0 + \beta_1 X_{1i} + \beta_2 X_{2i} + \beta_3 X_{3i} + \beta_4 X_{4i} + \beta_5 X_{5i} + \beta_6 X_{6i} + \epsilon_i$$

where X_5 is the years of experience and X_6 is the ambient temperature. If the latter variables have a linear effect, they will reduce the variance and increase the power of the hypothesis tests for the effects of other variables.

Another possible extension is the inclusion of interaction effects. Suppose that Mary suspects that the CAI training would provide greater benefits for workers working with machine type 3. To test for this effect she could include an interaction variable, $X_7 = X_1 X_3$. The values for X_7 would be merely the product of the X_1 and the X_3 variables. Thus, in Table 16.2, we would have a column for X_7 that had 1's for observations 11 and 12 and 0's for the remaining observations. If she also suspected that the CAI training would benefit workers with more education, she could define another interaction variable, $X_8 = X_1 X_4$. This variable would add another column to Table 16.2, with 1's for observations 8, 10, and 12 and 0's for the remaining observations. It is possible to add other variables and interaction terms. Thus the number of options with these experimental designs is very large.

With all of these additions, the regression model would be

$$Y_i = \beta_0 + \beta_1 X_{1i} + \beta_2 X_{2i} + \beta_3 X_{3i} + \beta_4 X_{4i} + \beta_5 X_{5i} + \beta_6 X_{6i} + \beta_7 X_{7i} + \beta_8 X_{8i} + \epsilon_i$$

In this equation there are eight coefficients and a constant to estimate, leaving only 3 degrees of freedom for estimating the variance if only one replication of the design was performed. In situations where measurements can be made accurately and the various effects are large, this design with even one replication could provide useful information about the factors that influence productivity. In most cases more than one replication would be desirable. More observations provide better coefficient estimates and a smaller coefficient variance. However, in an industrial situation experiments may involve the entire factory and thus can be very expensive. Analysts try to maximize the understanding gained from each set of experiments.   □

Does It Make Sense?

In this section we have introduced experimental designs and their analysis using dummy variables. Experimental design is a major area for applied statistics that can be studied in many other courses and books. However, even with the introduction presented here, you have a powerful tool for handling some important productivity problems.

Applications of experimental design have become increasingly important in manufacturing and other business operations. Experiments to identify variables related to increased production and decreased number of defects are important in efforts to improve production operations. The use of dummy variables and multiple regression for experimental design analysis extends the problem types that you can handle without learning additional analysis techniques. This is an important additional advantage for dummy variable procedures.   □

Problem Exercises

16.4   Write the model specification and define the variables for a multiple regression model to predict college GPA as a function of entering SAT scores and the year in college: first year, sophomore, junior, and senior.

16.5   Write the model specification and define the variables for a multiple regression model to predict wages in U.S. dollars as a function of years of experience and country of employment, indicated as Germany, Great Britain, Japan, United States, and Turkey.

16.6   Write the model specification and define the variables for a multiple regression model to predict the cost per unit produced as a function of factory type, indicated as classic technology, computer-controlled machines, computer-controlled machines and computer-controlled material handling, and a function of country, indicated as Colombia, South Africa, and Japan.

16.6 HETEROSCEDASTICITY TRANSFORMATIONS

This section and those that follow indicate the problems (and their solutions) that result when the regression model assumptions are not satisfied. In this section we consider the effect of nonuniform error over the range of the model. A definition of heteroscedasticity is given in Key Idea 16.5.

Key Idea 16.5: Heteroscedasticity

The linear model for regression analysis,

$$Y_i = \beta_0 + \beta_1 X_{1i} + \cdots + \beta_k X_{ki} + \epsilon_i$$

assumes the error term has a constant variance over the range of the independent variables. This is the property of **homoscedasticity**:

$$\sigma^2_{\epsilon_i} = \sigma^2 \qquad \text{for all } i$$

$$\epsilon_i \sim N(0, \sigma^2)$$

However, there are a number of situations in business and economics where the data do not meet the assumption of homoscedasticity, and error has the property of **heteroscedasticity**. For example, suppose that the error term is

$$\epsilon_i = Z_i u_i$$

where

$$u_i \sim N(0, \sigma^2)$$

In this expression Z_i represents any variable that is related to the error. The variance of ϵ_i is $Z_i^2 \sigma^2$, and thus ϵ_i does not have a constant variance.

Examples of heteroscedasticity include:

1. Aggregate consumption is often modeled as a linear function of aggregate disposable income. However, when this model is applied to family data, we find that families with higher incomes have more flexibility in choosing between consumption and saving. Thus we expect higher variances at higher levels of family disposable income.

2. Sales in retail stores are often a linear function of the total square feet of sales area. However, larger stores are likely to have greater sales losses during weeks when sales conditions are bad and greater gains during weeks with special promotions. Thus we expect that weekly sales in larger stores will have a greater variance.

When model errors show heteroscedasticity—nonuniform variance—the estimated regression variances will be biased. However, *the coefficient estimates are still unbiased.* Recall that the estimated variance for σ^2, $S^2_{Y|X}$, was computed by dividing the error sum of squares (ESS) by the degrees of freedom. This calculation assumed that the true variance σ^2 was uniform over the range of the model. With a biased estimate of the variance, the estimated coefficients are not efficient estimates. In addition, we do not know which variance to use for confidence intervals and hypothesis tests. Thus our *statistical inference procedures are suspect.* Given these problems, we would like to be able to detect and correct for heteroscedasticity.

Heteroscedasticity can be identified in several ways. First we may be able to infer from other knowledge that the data produced by a system do not have constant variance. We presented two examples using consumption and retail sales. There are others. Residuals analysis can also be used to detect heteroscedasticity. Figure 16.3 presents a residual plot with the errors showing a heteroscedastic pattern. We see that the spread of the residuals appears to increase with larger values of the independent variable X_1. This is the most typical example of heteroscedasticity. However, residuals whose range decreases or whose range is larger for intermediate values of X_1 are also possible and lead to the same problems. A third way to detect heteroscedasticity is to use a hypothesis-testing procedure. We will present the Goldfield–Quandt test, which is easy to use and interpret.

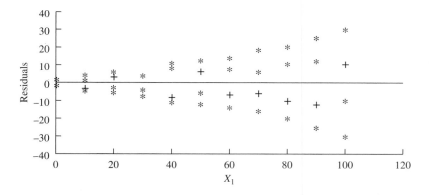

Figure 16.3   Residual Plot When Errors Are Nonuniform

16.6.1 Goldfield–Quandt Test for Heteroscedasticity

The Goldfield–Quandt test is described in Key Idea 16.6. The specific steps in applying the Goldfield–Quandt test, given a sample of n observations, are as follows:

1. Rank order the n observations on the Z variable that is suspected of being related to the nonuniform error. Remove c—approximately 10 to 20%—of the observations from the center of the ordered observations.
2. Define the subsample with the largest sample variance, $S^2_{Y|X}$, as sample 1. Define the subsample with the smallest sample variance, $S^2_{Y|X}$, as sample 2.

Key Idea 16.6: Goldfield–Quandt Test for Heteroscedasticity

The **Goldfield–Quandt** (GQ) **test** can detect situations in which the residuals increase or decrease with respect to an ordering variable such as the Z in Key Idea 16.5. The sample is separated into two subsets that we suspect have different error variances. The regression model is fitted using each subset, and the resulting error sums of squares are used to estimate the variance for each sample. If there is heteroscedasticity, the variance estimates for each subset will be significantly different. An F test is used to test for differences between the variance estimates and hence for the presence of heteroscedasticity.

---

3. Define the hypothesis test as

$$H_0: \sigma_1^2 = \sigma_2^2$$
$$H_1: \sigma_1^2 \neq \sigma_2^2$$

If H_0 is rejected, we conclude that there is heteroscedasticity.

4. The hypothesis is tested by fitting a separate regression model to each subset using the same k independent variables. The variances of the estimate, $S_{1Y|X}^2$ and $S_{2Y|X}^2$, are computed for each regression. If the null hypothesis H_0 is true, both $S_{1Y|X}^2$ and $S_{2Y|X}^2$ are estimates of the model variance σ^2. In that case,

$$F = \frac{S_{1Y|X}^2}{S_{2Y|X}^2}$$

has an F distribution with $((n-c)/2) - k - 1$ degrees of freedom for both the numerator and the denominator. Note that $S_{1Y|X}^2$ is the largest error variance, so that $F \geq 1$. If the value of F computed exceeds the critical value of F from Table A.4, we reject H_0 and conclude that there is heteroscedasticity.

16.6.2 Correcting for Heteroscedasticity

The usual way to correct for heteroscedasticity is to transform the model variables to a form that has uniform variance. Suppose that the regression model with heteroscedasticity has the form

$$Y_i = \beta_0 + \beta_1 X_{1i} + \cdots + \beta_k X_{ki} + Z_i u_i$$

where u_i has a uniform variance

$$u_i \sim N(0, \sigma^2)$$

To remove the nonuniform error, we divide both sides of the model equation by Z_i. The resulting model is

$$\frac{Y_i}{Z_i} = \frac{1}{Z_i}\beta_0 + \beta_1\frac{X_{1i}}{Z_i} + \cdots + \beta_k\frac{X_{ki}}{Z_i} + u_i$$

Note that the error term is u_i, which has a uniform variance. The regression model is estimated using a standard multiple regression computer program with the following transformed variables:

$$Y_i^* = \frac{Y_i}{Z_i}$$

$$X_{0i}^* = \frac{1}{Z_i}$$

$$X_{1i}^* = \frac{X_{1i}}{Z_i}$$

$$X_{ki}^* = \frac{X_{ki}}{Z_i}$$

The regression model that is estimated is therefore

$$Y_i^* = \beta_0 X_{0i}^* + \beta_1 X_{1i}^* + \cdots + \beta_k X_{ki}^* + u_i$$

The estimated coefficients of the original model are obtained directly from the transformed model regression. The statistics computed from the error estimate, including R^2, t, and the various variance estimates, cannot be compared with similar statistics obtained from the untransformed model. We no longer have the same set of dependent variable observations in the transformed regression model.

In many applications the Z variable is actually one of the independent variables in the regression. This leads to results such as the following for a simple regression model:

$$Y_i = \beta_0 + \beta_1 X_{1i} + X_{1i} + u_i$$

which when transformed becomes

$$Y_i^* = \beta_0 \frac{1}{X_{1i}} + \beta_1 + u_i$$

When a regression analysis is computed, the coefficient of X_1 in the original model is the constant in the transformed equation, while the constant in the original equation is the coefficient of $1/X_1$ in the transformed equation.

Does It Make Sense?

This technique is often called *weighted least squares* because each variable observation is "weighted" or multiplied by $1/Z_i$. Those observations with a large Z_i receive the smallest weight and thus have less influence on the regression estimates. Observations with a large Z_i have the largest error variance. Thus weighted least squares gives more importance to observations with smaller variances.   □

Problem Exercises

16.7   Define an example where a regression model application is likely to include heteroscedasticity.

16.8   Provide an intuitive rationale for the weighted least-squares estimation strategy that gives greater influence to those observations that have a smaller variance.

16.7 SERIAL CORRELATION TRANSFORMATIONS

Whenever time-series data are used for regression models, there is a possibility of serial correlation, which is the correlation between random errors ϵ_t's from adjacent time periods (Key Idea 16.7). Serial correlation indicates that the assumption of independent errors is violated. The effect is that standard regression analysis produces biased estimates of the variances, which in turn implies that hypothesis test conclusions and confidence intervals are incorrect. However, *the coefficient estimates are unbiased.* One important problem involves the t test to determine if slope coefficients

---

Key Idea 16.7: Serial Correlation

Serial correlation may occur when time-series data are used in regression analysis. Serial correlation for simple regression is defined by

$$Y_t = \beta_0 + \beta_1 X_{1t} + \epsilon_t$$
$$\epsilon_t = \rho \epsilon_{t-1} + u_t$$
$$u_t \sim N(0, \sigma^2)$$

where ρ is defined as the serial correlation coefficient. The t subscripts refer to the location of an observation in time. The subscript $t-1$ refers to an observation that occurs just before observation t. The errors are correlated with the error for the previous observation in time.

   With positive serial correlation we could conclude that a relationship is significant when it is not. Exactly the opposite effect occurs when we have negative serial correlation.

are significant. When positive serial correlation occurs, the t statistics computed using regression are biased high. Thus we might conclude that variables are significant when in fact they are not. Given these potential problems, we need to detect and correct for serial correlation.

An understanding of serial correlation can be developed by thinking about the processes that generate economic and business data over time.

1. Aggregate consumption is a function of disposable income and a number of variables related to overall societal behavior, such as anticipated inflation, change of political attitudes, or fear of world unrest. These later variables are difficult to measure and include in the model and thus their effect becomes part of the model error. However, it is likely that the effects of these excluded variables will hold for several time periods and result in positively correlated errors.

2. Many economic measures are generated using information reported by private groups to government agencies. Activity near the end of one time period may not be reported until the beginning of the next period. Thus the first period has a negative error and the second a positive error, resulting in negatively correlated errors.

3. More generally, various societal phenomena change over time and it is not possible to capture all of these changes in a model. The composite of these changes results in errors that are serially correlated.

Serial correlation can be recognized in residual plots as shown in Figure 16.4, which shows typical positive serial correlation, and Figure 16.5, which shows typical negative serial correlation.

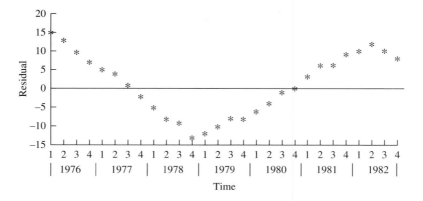

Figure 16.4   Residual Plot for Positive Serial Correlation

Positive serial correlation is indicated by residuals that tend to be close to each other as a result of the positive correlations between adjacent residuals. Negative serial correlation is indicated by residuals that jump back and forth from positive

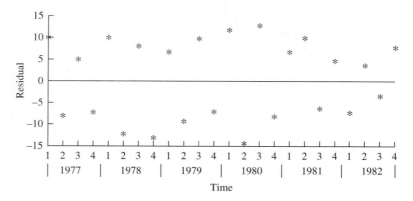

Figure 16.5   Residual Plot for Negative Serial Correlation

to negative. These results can be seen by examining the defining equation for serial correlation,

$$\epsilon_t = \rho\epsilon_{t-1} + u_t$$

A positive serial correlation ρ will result in errors that are close to each other. In contrast, a negative serial correlation will have errors that alternate in sign.

Serial correlation leads to a bias in the estimate of slope coefficient variances. From Chapter 14 we recall that the slope coefficient estimator is a linear combination of the dependent variable observations, Y_i,

$$\hat{\beta}_1 = \sum_{i=1}^{n} a_i Y_i$$

where

$$a_i = \frac{X_{1i} - \bar{X}_1}{\sum_{i=1}^{n}(X_{1i} - \bar{X}_1)}$$

The variance estimator $\sigma_{\hat{\beta}_1}^2$ assumes that the errors ϵ_i's and therefore the Y_i's are independent. The resulting variance is

$$\sigma_{\hat{\beta}_1}^2 = \sum_{t=1}^{T} a_t^2 \sigma_{Y|X_1}^2 = \frac{\sigma_{Y|X_1}^2}{\sum_{t=1}^{T}(X_{1t} - \bar{X}_1)^2}$$

where σ^2 is the variance of ϵ_t. The variance estimator is

$$S_{\hat{\beta}_1}^2 = \sum_{t=1}^{T} a_t^2 S_{Y|X_1}^2 = \frac{S_{Y|X_1}^2}{\sum_{t=1}^{T}(X_{1t} - \bar{X}_1)^2}$$

This is the estimator that is used to compute $S_{\hat{\beta}_1}^2$ in the standard computer packages. When the errors are correlated, the covariance effects must be added to obtain the correct variance estimator:

$$\sigma_{\hat{\beta}_1}^2 = \sum_{t=1}^{T} a_i^2 \sigma_{Y|X_1}^2 + 2 \sum_{t=1}^{T} \sum_{l=t+1}^{T-1} a_t a_l \rho \sigma_{Y|X_1} \sigma_{Y|X_1}$$

From this equation we see that positive serial correlation ρ implies that $\sigma_{\hat{\beta}_1}^2$ and its estimator $S_{\hat{\beta}_1}^2$ are actually larger than the value computed in standard regression programs. Thus the computed value, $S_{\hat{\beta}_1}^2$, presented in the regression output has a negative bias when serial correlation is positive. Decisions regarding the significance of a relationship between Y and X_1 are made using the Student t statistic,

$$t = \frac{\hat{\beta}_1}{S_{\hat{\beta}_1}}$$

When $S_{\hat{\beta}_1}^2$ has a negative bias, the Student t has a positive bias. For example, assume a problem in which $\hat{\beta}_1 = 10$ and the "correct" estimate of $S_{\hat{\beta}_1}$—including the covariance term—is 8. However, failure to include the positive covariance of 4 results in a biased estimate, $S_{\hat{\beta}_1}^* = 4$. The correct t would be $1.25(10/8)$, but instead, the biased t^* is $2.5 \, (10/4)$.

Does It Make Sense?

Positive serial correlation could lead us to conclude that a relationship is significant when it is not. Exactly the opposite effect occurs when we have negative serial correlation. If positive serial correlation exists, a covariance term should be added to the estimated coefficient variance, $S_{\hat{\beta}_j}^2$. However, the least-squares algorithm assumes independence and does not include the covariance term. Thus if there is positive serial correlation, the covariance is not included and the computed coefficient variance is biased low and the coefficient Student t is biased high. Negative serial correlation yields the opposite effect.   □

16.7.1 Durbin–Watson Test for Serial Correlation

The Durbin–Watson test is described in Key Idea 16.8. Critical values of the d statistic are presented in Table A.10 for various sample sizes n and number of predictor variables k. Notice that two critical values are given for each hypothesis test: d_L or d lower, and d_U or d upper. The interpretation of the hypothesis test using these critical values can be assisted by examining Figure 16.6. If the d computed is less than d_L, we conclude that there is positive serial correlation. If d is between d_L and d_U, we cannot tell if there is positive serial correlation or no serial correlation. Between d_U and $4 - d_U$, we have no serial correlation. Between $4 - d_U$ and $4 - d_L$, we cannot tell if there is negative serial correlation or no serial correlation. Finally, a value of d above $4 - d_L$ indicates negative serial correlation.

Key Idea 16.8: Durbin–Watson Test for Serial Correlation

Serial correlation can be detected by testing the hypothesis:

$$H_0: \rho = 0$$
$$H_1: \rho \neq 0$$

If we reject H_0, we conclude that serial correlation is present.

The hypothesis is most often tested using the **Durbin–Watson** (DW) **test**. This test uses the d statistic, which is computed as a function of the standard regression residuals $\hat{e}_t$'s:

$$d = \frac{\sum_{t=2}^{T}(\hat{e}_t - \hat{e}_{t-1})^2}{\sum_{t=1}^{T} \hat{e}_t^2}$$

$$= \frac{\sum_{t=2}^{T}(\hat{e}_t^2 - 2\hat{e}_t\hat{e}_{t-1} + \hat{e}_{t-1}^2)}{\sum_{t=1}^{T} \hat{e}_t^2}$$

$$\approx 1 - 2\hat{\rho} + 1$$

$$= 2 - 2\hat{\rho}$$

When the estimated serial correlation $\hat{\rho}$ is zero, the d statistic is 2. With strong positive serial correlation, d approaches zero, and with strong negative correlation, d approaches 4. Durbin and Watson individually studied the probability distribution of the d statistic and computed critical values for rejecting the null hypothesis $H_0: \rho = 0$. Critical values for d are in Table A.10.

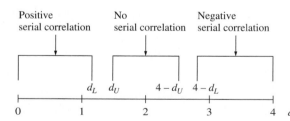

Figure 16.6   The Durbin–Watson d Statistic

16.7.2 Correcting for Serial Correlation

The adjustment for serial correlation can be made by transforming the original variables into forms that have the serial correlation effect removed. The transformation is developed by multiplying the equation for observation $t - 1$ by ρ and subtracting from the equation for observation t as follows:

$$t: \quad Y_t = \beta_0 + \beta_1 X_{1t} + \rho \epsilon_{t-1} + u_t$$
$$t - 1: \quad Y_{t-1} = \beta_0 + \beta_1 X_{1t-1} + \epsilon_{t-1}$$
$$Y_t - \rho Y_{t-1} = (1 - \rho)\beta_0 + \beta_1(X_{1t} - \rho X_{1t-1}) + u_t$$

The regression analysis is performed by first obtaining the transformed dependent and independent variables:

$$Y_t^* = Y_t - \rho Y_{t-1}$$
$$X_{1t}^* = X_{1t} - \rho X_{1,t-1}$$

Additional independent variables would be transformed in the same way. Using the transformed variables, the regression

$$\hat{Y}_t^* = \hat{\beta}_0 + \hat{\beta}_1 X_{1t}^*$$

is estimated using multiple regression. The slope coefficient is the slope coefficient for the original untransformed model. However, the constant β_0 in the transformed model is the original model constant multiplied by $1 - \rho$.

The value of ρ can be estimated from the Durbin–Watson d statistic.[2]

$$d = 2 - 2\hat{\rho}$$
$$\hat{\rho} = 1 - \frac{d}{2}$$

A procedure developed by Cochrane and Orcutt recommends that the transformations above be applied repeatedly until the computed serial correlation coefficient is stabilized. The transformed variables Y^* and X_1^* are used to compute new coefficient estimates. These coefficient estimates are then used to compute a new set of predicted values $\hat{Y}_t$, and in turn a second set of residuals are computed. These residuals are used to compute a new estimated serial correlation coefficient,

$$\rho_2 = \frac{\sum_{t=2}^{T} \hat{e}_t \hat{e}_{t-1}}{\sum_{t=2}^{T} \hat{e}_{t-1}^2}$$

This process is repeated until the serial correlation coefficient has only a very small change from one iteration to the next.[3]

Does It Make Sense?

The discussion above of the adjustment for serial correlation is presented so that you will understand the basic adjustment process. A number of regression packages have procedures that automatically make the transformations and apply appropriate adjustments to compute multiple regression coefficients with the effect of serial correlation

---

[2] Justification for this estimate is provided later in the text in Key Idea 16.10.

[3] D. Cochrane and G. H. Orcutt, "Application of least squares regressions to relationships containing auto correlated error terms," *Journal of the American Statistical Association*, Vol. 44, pp. 32–61, 1949.

removed. These computer routines use a number of special techniques whose details are beyond the scope of this book. However, the discussion above illustrates the fundamental process. We strongly recommend using the procedure in the statistical computer program to adjust for serial correlation.   □

Problem Exercises

16.9 Provide an example from your own experience in which a least squares regression analysis is likely to exhibit positive serial correlation.

16.10 Consider a least-squares regression in which the observations are in order from smallest to largest values of the independent or predictor variable X_1. Suppose that the relationship between Y and X_1 is quadratic and you fit a linear model. What value would you expect for the Durbin–Watson d statistic? (*Hint:* A two-way scatter plot might prove helpful.)

16.8 SPECIFICATION BIAS: EXCLUDED VARIABLES

In applied regression analysis we cannot always be certain that we have identified all of the significant variables. The initial model specification, including the designation of independent variables, is based on prior knowledge that is not perfect. In addition, it is likely that there are significant variables that should be in the original specification but cannot or have not been measured in the available data set (Key Idea 16.9). If we begin with variables that are not significant, they will generally be eliminated by conditional hypothesis tests that use the t or F statistics. However, the effect of omitting significant variables is a bias in the estimate for the other coefficients. The bias can be seen by analyzing the result of using one predictor variable when there are two significant predictor variables.

Key Idea 16.9: Bias from Excluding Significant Variables

If significant exogenous variables are excluded from a regression model, the coefficients of the other variables will be biased and the effect of that variable will be added to the error variance.

This biased coefficient estimator has important implications for regression analysis. In applied work there are likely to be significant variables that are not included in the model. In those cases the coefficients for the remaining variables will be biased. This bias will be reduced if the excluded variables are not strongly correlated with the variables in the model.

Example 16.4   Specification Bias

Melvin Smith, manager of Electronic Sound, Inc., wants to develop a regression model to predict sales of high-quality speakers. Sales records indicate the number of units sold per week and the prices charged during that week for the past 18 months. The market for speakers is very competitive and prices have varied considerably. In a meeting with Sally Rice, the assistant manager, she points out that different levels of advertising have been used. She argues that advertising is also a significant variable and should be included in the regression. Unfortunately, Melvin is lazy and does not understand multiple regression. He decides to predict sales using only price. What is the effect on the slope coefficient for price if Sally is correct?

Solution   The model proposed by Sally is

$$Y_t = \beta_0 + \beta_1 X_{1t} + \beta_2 X_{2t} + \epsilon_t$$

where Y is the total number of speakers sold during the week, X_1 is the price charged per speaker, and X_2 is the week's advertising expenditures. Instead Melvin uses the model

$$Y_t = \alpha_0 + \alpha_1 X_{1t} + \delta_t$$

The slope coefficient estimator for Melvin's model is

$$\hat{\alpha}_1 = \frac{\sum_{t=1}^{T}(X_{1t} - \bar{X}_1)Y_t}{\sum_{t=1}^{T}(X_{1t} - \bar{X}_1)^2}$$

By substituting the two-variable model for Y, we can determine the expected value of the slope coefficient for price $\hat{\alpha}_1$ in Melvin's model:

$$E[\hat{\alpha}_1] = E\left[\frac{\sum_{i=1}^{n}(X_{1t} - \bar{X}_1)Y_t}{\sum_{i=1}^{n}(X_{1t} - \bar{X}_1)^2}\right]$$

$$= E\left[\frac{\sum_{i=1}^{n}(X_{1t} - \bar{X}_1)(\beta_0 + \beta_1 X_{1t} + \beta_2 X_{2t} + \epsilon_t)}{\sum_{i=1}^{n}(X_{1t} - \bar{X}_1)^2}\right]$$

$$= E\left[\frac{\sum_{i=1}^{n}(X_{1t} - \bar{X}_1)\beta_1 X_{1t}}{\sum_{i=1}^{n}(X_{1t} - \bar{X}_1)^2}\right] + E\left[\frac{\sum_{i=1}^{n}(X_{1t} - \bar{X}_1)\beta_2 X_{2t}}{\sum_{i=1}^{n}(X_{1t} - \bar{X}_1)^2}\right]$$

$$+ E\left[\frac{\sum_{i=1}^{n}(X_{1t} - \bar{X}_1)\epsilon_t}{\sum_{i=1}^{n}(X_{1t} - \bar{X}_1)^2}\right]$$

$$= \beta_1 + \beta_2 E\left[\frac{\sum_{i=1}^{n}(X_{1t} - \bar{X}_1)X_{2t}}{\sum_{i=1}^{n}(X_{1t} - \bar{X}_1)^2}\right] + 0$$

Thus we see that if β_2 is not equal to zero or if the correlation between X_1 and X_2 is not equal to zero, the coefficient estimator for price $\hat{\alpha}_1$ is biased.   □

Does It Make Sense?

Applied analysts are often faced with difficult choices between the increased variance for $\hat{\beta}_j$ that results from correlated independent variables and the bias effect on $\hat{\beta}_j$ that results from excluded variables. Without knowing the exact model, the choice above is typically guided by experience and intuition. Often, the choice leads to uncertainty about the model. The analyst needs to be aware of this potential problem. The problem can be reduced if we have a good understanding of the system that generated the data and the analysis objectives. In this way the most significant variables can be included and we can avoid severe biases: *Know thy data and thy problem specification!* Despite the potential problems of high variance and bias, analysts have produced many very useful models. It is important that these problems are recognized and understood. Then one must go on and find the best solution given these problems.   □

Problem Exercises

16.11 Explain why regression model coefficients will be biased if an important independent predictor variable is left out of the set of independent predictor variables used in the analysis.

16.12 Suppose you are estimating a regression model that predicts computer processing time, Y, for a statistical analysis as a function of the number of observations, X_1. A variety of data sets with different numbers of observations are used. Unfortunately, the person who collected the data failed to note the type of computer used. The variety of computers included Macintosh, 286-based PC, 386-based PC, 486-based PC, Cray supercomputer, and a large minicomputer. Explain why the coefficient for X_1 is likely to be biased.

16.9 RANDOM INDEPENDENT VARIABLES

Regression analysis assumes that the independent X variables do not contain a random component. However, in applied business and economics this assumption is not very realistic. In many cases a variable may be modeled as a random dependent variable in one example and an independent variable in another example. We often use price as an independent variable to predict quantity demanded. However, there are also situations in which price is predicted as a dependent variable and assumed to contain a random component. Given this potential problem, we would like to know if our estimates are seriously biased if the independent variables contain random error.

    We can determine the potential bias by deriving the expected value of the coefficient estimator when the independent variable X contains a random component. The situation in mathematical language is

$$Y_i = \beta_0 + \beta_1 X_{1i} + \epsilon_i$$
$$\epsilon_i \sim N(0, \sigma_y^2)$$

where

$$X_{1i} = \mu_i + \delta_i$$
$$\delta_i \sim N(0, \sigma_x^2)$$
$$\rho(\epsilon_i, \delta_i) = 0$$

Using these assumptions, we derive and examine the expected value for $\hat{\beta}_1$.

$$E[\hat{\beta}_1] = E\left[\frac{\sum_{i=1}^n (X_{1i} - \bar{X}_1)Y_i}{\sum_{i=1}^n (X_{1i} - \bar{X}_1)^2}\right]$$

$$= E\left[\frac{\sum_{i=1}^n (X_{1i} - \bar{X}_1)(\beta_0 + \beta_1 X_{1i} + \epsilon_i)}{\sum_{i=1}^n (X_{1i} - \bar{X}_1)^2}\right]$$

$$= 0 + \beta_1 E\left[\frac{\sum_{i=1}^n (X_{1i} - \bar{X}_1)X_{1i}}{\sum_{i=1}^n (X_{1i} - \bar{X}_1)^2}\right] + E\left[\frac{\sum_{i=1}^n (X_{1i} - \bar{X}_1)\epsilon_i}{\sum_{i=1}^n (X_{1i} - \bar{X}_1)^2}\right]$$

$$= \beta_1 + E\left[\frac{\sum_{i=1}^n (X_{1i} - \bar{X}_1)\epsilon_i}{\sum_{i=1}^n (X_{1i} - \bar{X}_1)^2}\right]$$

If X_1 is not correlated with the model error ϵ_i, the last term is zero and $\hat{\beta}_1$ is unbiased. If there is zero correlation between the model error ϵ_i and the random error δ_i in X_1, $\hat{\beta}_1$ will be unbiased. We can also show that the variance estimates are unbiased and that the coefficient estimators are efficient (Key Idea 16.10).

Key Idea 16.10: Exogenous Variables with Random Error

The assumption of no random error for the independent variables is not a major concern. An exogenous variable, X_j, with a random error term will still produce unbiased least-squares coefficients unless there are correlations between the model error ϵ_i and the independent X_j variables.

SUMMARY OF KEY IDEAS

CHAPTER PROBLEMS

16.1 Explain the problem of serial correlation. Include the following considerations.
  (a) Indicate why the least-squares coefficient estimators are unbiased while the least-squares coefficient variance estimators are biased.
  (b) Given the Durbin–Watson statistic, derive an estimator for the serial correlation.
  (c) Present an intuitive explanation that indicates why the R^2 from the regression analysis for the data transformed to remove serial correlation is smaller than the R^2 from the regression using the original data. (*Hint:* What happens to TSS?)

16.2 The U.S. Department of Commerce has asked you to develop a regression model to predict quarterly investment in production and durable equipment. The suggested predictor variables include GNP, prime interest rate, price index for industrial commodities, and government spending. The data for your analysis are provided in the data file "Macro95," which is stored on your data disk and described in the data dictionary in Appendix B.
  (a) Estimate a regression model using only interest rate to predict the investment. Use the Durbin–Watson statistic to test for serial correlation.
  (b) Find the best multiple regression equation to predict investment using the predictor variables indicated above. Use the Durbin–Watson statistic to test for serial correlation.
  (c) What are the differences between the regression models in parts (a) and (b) in terms of goodness of fit, prediction capability, serial correlation, and contributions to understanding the investment problem?

16.3 An economist has asked you to develop a regression model to predict consumption of service goods as a function of GNP and other important variables. The data for your analysis are given in the data file "Macro95," which is stored on your data disk and described in Appendix B.
  (a) Estimate a regression model using only GNP to predict consumption of service goods. Test for serial correlation using the Durbin–Watson test.
  (b) Estimate a multiple regression model using GNP, total consumption lagged 1 period, and prime interest rate as additional predictors. Test for serial correlation. Does this multiple regression model reduce the problem of serial correlation?

16.4 George Wong, a Hong Kong investor, is considering plans to develop a primary steel plant in China. After reviewing the initial design proposal he is concerned about the proposed mix of capital and labor. He has asked you to prepare several production functions using some historical data from the United States. The data file "Metals" contains 27 observations of value-added output, labor input, and the gross value of plant and equipment per factory. The file description is contained in the data dictionary in Appendix B.

(a) Use multiple regression to estimate a linear production function with value added regressed on labor and capital. Plot the residuals versus labor and equipment. Note any unusual patterns.

(b) Use multiple regression with transformed variables to estimate a second production function of the form

$$Y = \beta_0 L^{\beta_1} K^{\beta_2}$$

where Y is the value added, L is the labor input, and K is the capital input.

(c) Use multiple regression transformed variables to estimate a Cobb–Douglas production function. Note that a Cobb–Douglas production function has the same form as the function estimated in part (b), but it has the additional restriction that $\beta_1 + \beta_2 = 1$. To develop the transformed regression model, substitute β_2 as a function of β_1 and convert to a regression format.

(d) Compare the three production functions using residual plots and a standard error of the estimate that is expressed in the same scale. You will need to convert the predicted values from parts (b) and (c) (which are in logarithms) back to the original units. Then you can subtract the predicted values from the original values of Y to obtain the residuals. Use the residuals to compute comparable standard errors of the estimate.

16.5 You have been asked to develop a regression model to predict factory output for the Truth Manufacturing Company, which produces portable two-way radios. Initial research leads you to the hypothesis that factory output is a function of day of week (Monday–Friday), number of workers, product grade (A, B, or C), season (winter, spring, summer, or fall), and the number of machines operating.

(a) Develop a regression model, including complete variable specification, which can be used to predict factory output.

(b) Define each of the variables and indicate how you will collect the data.

(c) Indicate how you will analyze the data and how you will decide which variables should be included in your model.

(d) Suggest additional variables that might be included in your model.

16.6 You are interested in estimating a linear model to predict family expenditures as a function of family income. You have obtained a random sample of 100 families and measured the following variables for each:

Y: monthly expenditure for the family
X_1: monthly family income
X_2: dummy variable indicating that the family has both parents
X_3: dummy variable indicating that at least one parent has a college degree
X_4: dummy variable indicating that the family has at least one dependent child

You estimate two regression models:

Model I: $Y = \beta_1 X_1 + \beta_2 X_2 + \beta_3 X_3 + \beta_4 X_4$
Model II: $Y = \alpha_0 + \alpha_1 X_1 + \alpha_2 X_2 + \alpha_3 X_3$

Interpret the regression coefficients in the two different models. (Clearly define the contribution of each coefficient to monthly expenditure.)

16.7   Explain how serially correlated errors of the form $\epsilon_t = \rho\epsilon_{t-1} + u$ can be detected using a hypothesis test.

(a) Explain in detail how the test statistic is computed and interpreted.

(b) Explain in detail how regression coefficients should be estimated given serial correlation.

16.8   Charlie Knowitall, a small-town brain surgeon, has been estimating some regression functions using time-series data. He noted that the regression output includes a Durbin–Watson statistic equal to 1.0. As a small-town brain surgeon who works part time as a grave digger, he has learned to appreciate the beauty of 1.0. He often sits on his back porch and contemplates 1.0 as he watches the sun set over the new Wal-Mart store. However, being a practical man, he seeks your advice on the meaning of this Durbin–Watson equal to 1.0. His regression model has 57 observations and three predictor variables. Explain carefully the meaning of the Durbin–Watson statistic, how it is derived, and the importance of serial correlation. Also show how you would estimate the coefficient of serial correlation and then do it, given the Durbin–Watson equal to 1.0.

16.9   The administrator of a small city has asked you to identify variables that influence the market value of houses in small midwestern cities. You have obtained data from a number of small cities which are stored in the data file "Citydat.mtw" and described in the data file dictionary in Appendix B. The candidate predictor variables are median size of house, property tax rate (tax levy divided by total assessment), total expenditures for city services, and the percent commercial property.

(a) Estimate the multiple regression model using all of the predictor variables indicated. Select only statistically significant variables for your final equation.

(b) An economist stated that since the data came from cities of different population, your model is likely to contain heteroscedasticity. He argued that data from larger cities would have a smaller variance. Sort the data on population and perform the Goldfield–Quandt test for heteroscedasticity.

(c) Estimate the multiple regression equation using weighted least squares with population as the weighting variable. Compare the coefficients for the weighted and the unweighted multiple regression model.

16.10 Explain how you would use a multiple regression model to test the effectiveness of a new computerized quality control system on reducing the number of defective parts produced in a factory per 8-hour shift, defined as Y. The number of defective parts is also a function of:

X_1: number of parts produced on the shift

X_2: temperature of the processing furnace [the number of defective parts is a quadratic (second-degree polynomial) function of temperature]

X_3: number of tons of input material

X_4: number of labor hours used per shift

Discuss how you would collect the data, define and explain your regression model specification, and indicate how you would perform a hypothesis test to determine the effectiveness of the new quality control system.

16.11 Don Baker, manager of store development for a convenience store corporation, wishes to have a model to help predict annual sales for potential convenience food store (CFS) locations. You have been hired to collect and analyze data from the existing stores and to prepare a prediction model. Initial discussions with company staff indicates that the following variables are likely to be important as predictors:

1. Number of people living within $\frac{1}{4}$ mile of the store.
2. Number of people living within 1 mile of the store.
3. Per capita income of people living within 1 mile of the store.
4. Existence of a competing store within 100 yards.

(a) Indicate at least two additional independent variables that are possible predictors of store sales.
(b) Prepare a model specification using the original variables plus your additional variables. Define each variable carefully.
(c) Indicate how you would obtain your final model.
(d) How would you test your final model?

16.12 You have been asked to develop a multiple regression equation that will predict total retail expenditures, Y, for individual families. A random sample of families will be obtained and asked to provide responses to a survey. You are to indicate variables that you will need for your model. Based on a literature review you have identified the following candidate variables:

1. Disposable family income
2. Occupation in the following subgroups: (a) laborer, (b) skilled worker, (c) nurse, (d) company president, and (e) college professor.
3. Number of hours watching television. (*Note:* The literature suggests that with some television watching, purchases increase. However, persons who watch a great deal of television actually have lower purchases.)
4. Neighborhood in the city: (a) east, (b) west, (c) south.

Indicate clearly how you would specify the model including these variables. Discuss how you would carry out the analysis.

16.13 You have been assigned the task of evaluating the effect of a project sponsored by the German government to improve agriculture in Tanzania. Specifically, you are to determine if a new irrigation project has increased grain productivity, measured in bushels per acre. Your task is to design an experiment that will determine if the irrigation project has increased productivity where it has been implemented compared to areas where it has not been implemented. The analysis is complicated because farmers in both areas use one of five fertilizer options: 1, no fertilizer; 2, chemical fertilizer; 3, cow dung; 4, human waste; and 5, old government reports. There are also different levels of rainfall on the individual farms, and the soil conditions are defined by one of three different types. You are to select farm fields in both irrigated and nonirrigated areas. The fields should be selected equally from the three soil condition categories. You will be able to assign the fertilizer type that will be used on each field. The experimental design should use a dummy variable regression model to carry out the analysis. In the model the variable X_1 should have a value of 1 when irrigation is in place and 0 when it is not. Present the experimental design model using dummy variables where appropriate. Carefully indicate how you will assign fertilizers to fields and what you will measure for each field selected for your experiment. Indicate how you will test the effectiveness of the irrigation project.

16.14 You have been hired as an educational consultant to develop a regression model that can be used to predict grade-point averages at graduation for students at a prestigious midwestern liberal arts college. From your vast experience you believe that SAT math scores, SAT verbal scores, and high school percentile rank will be good linear predictor variables. A student's major department is also believed to have an equal effect on all students in the department. Students in your sample come from the following major departments: economics, chemistry, mathematics, classics, and education. Other research indicates that a student's gender also influences the grade-point average. Finally, you hypothesize that the geographic region from which the student entered college also influences the college grade-point average because of different secondary quality. You choose to use three regions: east, midwest, and west. Other research indicates that the slope coefficients for SAT math and SAT verbal will be different for males and females. Finally, a faculty member wants you to determine if chemistry majors from the midwest have a higher grade-point average than would be predicted by the direct additive effects of chemistry major and midwest origin alone. He suspects that midwestern secondary education prepares students better for the study of science. Formulate a regression model that would allow you to estimate all of the foregoing effects. Define each variable used and indicate how you would test for the significance of the various variables conditional on the other variables in the model.

16.15 Shirley Smith, the vice-president of manufacturing, has asked you to conduct a set of experiments that will determine the effect of operating conditions on that number of units produced per 8-hour shift in the factory. The production process begins with an operation to machine castings and is followed by an assembly operation. The time required for assembly is believed to be a factor of both the supplier of the castings and the machining process. You are to prepare an experimental design that will simultaneously estimate the effect of the following factors on the number of units produced per 8-hour shift:
1. Casting suppliers: A, B, and C
2. Machine units: the Smith–Wright unit and the Sperry–Olson unit
3. Assembly teams: Ashman, Lillemoe, and Zimmerman
4. The total number of hours worked by all workers on the 8-hour shift

(a) Prepare an analysis design that would enable you to estimate the effect of each condition relative to a base condition in each category. Describe how you would perform a statistical hypothesis test to determine if the effect relative to a base condition is significantly different from zero.

(b) Show how you would include a test for the interaction between supplier C and the Sperry–Olson machine unit. Also show how you would include a test for the interaction of supplier B and the Zimmerman assembly team. The effect of both of these interactions on the production in units per hour are to be estimated.

16.16 Your consulting company has been asked to develop a regression equation to predict the sale of wine as a function of a set of variables that are believed to be important. The data for this model will be collected from weekly sales at wine stores that are located in different areas of the country. Data collection will take place over the next year. Weekly sales for red and white wine will be collected each week at each store you select. In addition, you may ask that data for additional variables be collected from the selected stores.

You begin your research design by talking to Pepo, the Heidelberg wine consultant. He indicates that in his research he has found that the following variables influence wine sales: price, red versus white wine, season (winter, spring, summer, fall), outdoor temperature (quadratic function), income of customers, percentage of female customers coming into the store, and geographic region of the country.

Prepare a research plan which indicates specific data that are to be collected at each store. Show the form of your regression model and provide a clear definition of each variable in the equation. Indicate how you would select the best set of variables for your final model.

After your data have been collected and the final regression model developed, you are asked to determine if an 8-week media campaign during the year of data collection had an effect on wine sales. Discuss how you would use your model to answer that question. Assume that you know the exact 8 weeks of the media campaign. Your conclusion should be conditional on the effects of variables identified in your original model.

16.17 The wages of factory workers in the textile industry in a developing country are supposed to be determined as a function of years of experience and number of hours of education. All workers receive a starting wage that is composed of a fixed base adjusted for experience and education. In addition, the supervisor may award an additional cumulative increase each year based on his judgment concerning work performance. The labor force can be identified by three distinct ethnic groups: G(1), G(2), and G(3), and by gender. The three ethnic groups each represent approximately one-third of the workforce, and each group is one-half female.

Recently, there have been claims of wage discrimination by one of the ethnic groups. You have been hired as a consultant to determine if there is wage discrimination against any of the three groups or against women. You are supplied with a random sample of data from individual workers. The data for each worker include present wages, years of experience, number of hours of education, ethnic group, and gender.

Prepare an analysis design that will allow you to test for wage discrimination of any kind against any of the three ethnic groups and against women. Clearly specify your model and identify all variables. Indicate how you will carry out your analysis to test rigorously for wage discrimination. Define the statistics and the specific statistical tests that you will use. Discuss how your analysis will meet the objectives of your consulting contract.

16.18 Explain the difference between serial correlation and heteroscedasticity.

16.19 Explain how you would test for serial correlation and why serial correlation is a problem.

16.20 Suppose that the Durbin–Watson statistic equals 3. What is the serial correlation?

16.21 Derive the expected value for the slope coefficient, B_1, in a simple regression when the model errors for the observations are serially correlated.

16.22 Assume that the college food service adopted a demand-based food service plan. Under this plan students would purchase and pay only for meals they consumed. The food service management has asked you to develop and estimate multiple regression models that can be used to predict demand, set prices, and choose menus. Food service management would like to maintain a high level of demand to achieve economies of scale and to continue employing its entire workforce.

(a) Specify the predictor variables for a model to predict the total number of dinner meals sold each day. Indicate the type of variable form (i.e., linear, nonlinear, dummy variables) and describe the exact form.

(b) Discuss how you would collect data and conduct experiments to obtain low variance estimates of coefficients.

(c) Discuss the strengths and weaknesses of your model. Indicate how it would be used by the food service management.

16.23 You are to develop the specifications for a multiple regression model and indicate how you would obtain data and carry out the analysis. The objective is to develop a model to predict the number of pounds of dry ready-to-eat cereal sold each week by Malt O Meal, Inc., a small cereal manufacturer that produces a full line of generic dry cereals and its own full-line brand. The company has been very successful with continual annual increases in sales. These items are sold in durable plastic bags that are lower in cost than standard cereal boxes. Their cereals are typically priced lower than comparable major cereal brands. The corporate philosophy is to sell high-quality product at a low price, with minimum major advertising expenditures.

Indicate the variables that you would include in your model as predictor variables. Define the functional form for the variables and provide a short discussion of how each variable contributes to the model. Indicate experiments that you would recommend to obtain low variance estimators of the coefficients. Discuss how your model could be used to help increase sales in supermarkets.

16.24 You have been asked to serve as a consultant and expert witness for a wage discrimination lawsuit. A group of Latino and black women have filed the suit against their company, Amalgamated Distributors, Inc. The women, who have between 5 and 25 years of service with the company, allege that their average annual rate of wage increase has been significantly less than that of a group of white males and a second group of white females. The jobs for all three groups contain a variety of administrative, analytical, and managerial components. All of the employees began with a bachelor's degree, and years of experience is an important factor for predicting job performance and worker productivity. You have been provided with the present monthly wage and the number of years of experience for all workers in the three groups. In addition, the data indicate those in all three groups who have obtained an MBA degree. You do not perform any data analysis for this problem.

(a) Develop a statistical model and analysis that can be used to analyze the data. Indicate hypothesis tests that can be used to provide strong evidence of wage discrimination, if it exists. The company has also hired a statistician as a consultant and expert witness. Describe your analysis completely and clearly.

(b) Assume that your hypothesis test results in strong evidence that supports your client's claim. Summarize briefly the key points that you will make in your expert witness testimony to the court. The company's lawyer can be expected to cross examine you with the help of their statistician, who teaches statistics at a prestigious liberal arts college.

16.25 Explain how positive serial correlation results in Student t statistics that are biased high.

16.26 Suppose that Y is a random variable that is a linear function of X_1 and X_2. You have estimated the coefficient of X_1 by regressing Y on only X_1. Show that the resulting coefficient of X_1 is biased.

17

Time Series and Forecasting

The study of history helps us to avoid repeating mistakes.

17.1 HOW TO ANTICIPATE THE FUTURE

Forecasting is an important activity for business and government. Modern businesses invest in production facilities and various managerial procedures based on the assumption of future profits. Small and large retail stores are built and operated assuming that future sales will be sufficient to cover expenses and yield a profit. Airlines commit to contracts exceeding half a billion dollars for new airplanes to be delivered three to five years in the future. Energy companies spend money for 5 to 10 years to develop future energy sources. Large retailers establish inventory levels based on anticipated sales levels. All of these activities require forecasts of economic conditions and social environments that have never been experienced. Judgments and decisions must be made based on an anticipated future. Forecasts based on time-series (Key Idea 17.1) models are one important tool for helping to anticipate the future and make better decisions. Examples of time series include:

1. Monthly interest rates
2. Quarterly investment in plant and equipment
3. Monthly sales for a good
4. Quarterly stock market indices
5. Daily air quality measurements

Analysts study the properties of time series with the objective of developing forecasting models. There are many methods used to obtain forecasts. For example, a set of experts can be asked to provide a forecast based on their best judgment of all available information. Other forecasters will examine the leading economic indicator time series, which are prepared by the U.S. Department of Commerce, and relate these series to their forecasting problems. Other analysts use econometric models, such as those developed in Chapters 15 and 16, to develop forecasts based on exogenous or independent variables.

Key Idea 17.1: Time Series

A **time series** is a set of time-ordered measurements of a continuous process obtained at discrete time intervals.

The forecasts developed in this chapter use only the series itself to forecast the future. Historical patterns are assumed to repeat in the future, but often, these patterns are very complex. Thus the analyst must use a variety of tools to identify the historical patterns and then use the patterns to obtain a forecast. *The study of history helps us to avoid repeating mistakes.*

In this chapter we develop basic approaches to time-series analysis and forecasting. In Section 17.2 we present index numbers, which are used to isolate the effect on a time series of underlying influences such as inflation. In Section 17.3 we show how to identify model components, and in Section 17.4 we present statistical measures for comparing time series. Several extended application examples are presented in Section 17.5. We can only begin to explore time-series forecasting in this book. If you wish to increase your understanding and develop strong forecasting skills, consider courses and books that emphasize time-series analysis.

17.2 INDEX NUMBERS

Time-series measurements in dollars contain both changes over time and the effect of inflation. For most analyses we would like to remove the effect of inflation and concentrate on changes in quantity. Inflation effects are removed by using price indices that measure the inflation level relative to a base year. The two most used indices are the *consumer price index* (CPI) and the *GDP implicit price deflator*. Indices convert economic series to *real dollars* referenced to a base year. For example, many of the national income measures are adjusted using the implicit price deflator with 1987 as the base year. Adjusted series would be identified as being measured in *1987 dollars* or "1987$."

The *consumer price index*, prepared by the U.S. Bureau of Labor Statistics, is widely used for a number of public policy applications in addition to adjusting consumption measures to real dollars. Government payments for Social Security and many labor contracts include a cost-of-living adjustment. The logic of these adjustments is that people should receive regular payments with the same purchasing power. The CPI is constructed by using a *market basket* of 300 carefully selected consumption items. The price changes in each of these items is measured monthly, by surveying a large number of retail establishments. These prices are then used to compute the total cost of the 300 consumption items for that month. The total cost of the basket of items for the present month is divided by the total cost of the same basket of items in the base year. The result of this division is the CPI for that month.

The *implicit price deflator* represents prices for all items in the economy instead of just consumption items. Prices for all economic goods are used to develop a total cost for the base year and the present year. The index or deflator for the present year is thus the ratio of the total present year cost divided by the total base year cost. This deflator is widely used to provide the same adjustment for a broad set of economic measures that are used together in an economic study.

17.2.1 Computation of Indices

Simple price index.   The *simple aggregate price index* is computed as the ratio of the sum of prices in year k divided by the sum of prices in the base year:

$$I_k = \frac{\sum_{i=1}^{n} P_{ki}}{\sum_{i=1}^{n} P_{0i}} \times 100$$

where P_{ki} is the price for good i in year k, P_{0i} is the price for good i in year 0, and n is the number of items used to develop the index. The ratio is multiplied by 100 to express the index as a percentage of the base year. This simple index assumes that each item contributes equally to the change in economic value between the base year and year k.

Weighted price index.   To reflect the change in total purchasing power or economic value, it is necessary to consider the relative quantities of the various goods used to construct the index. Therefore, most price indices are weighted aggregate or Laspeyres indices. The *Laspeyres price index* is computed as

$$I_k = \frac{\sum_{i=1}^{n} q_{0i} P_{ki}}{\sum_{i=1}^{n} q_{0i} P_{0i}} \times 100$$

where P_{ki} is the price for good i in year k, P_{0i} is the price for good i in year 0, q_{0i} is the quantity of good i used in base year 0, and n is the number of items used to develop the index. The ratio is also multiplied by 100 to express the result in percentage terms. This index assumes that there will be a constant quantity of each good between the base year and year k. This assumption of a constant quantity of each good raises important questions, which we discuss below. However, determining the quantities is often a very large and expensive task. Thus changes in quantities are usually not made at frequent intervals. But the relative quantities in the basket of goods used for the CPI are changed periodically.

Example 17.1   Index Computation

A state agency in a rapidly developing country has asked you to compute a consumer price index to be used for adjusting government employee wages. You begin by conducting an extensive survey of consumer purchasing patterns and prices for the base year 0. In a related study the prices for these items was also obtained for year 2. The results of both of these studies are presented in Table 17.1. Using these data, compute a simple price index for year 2 and a weighted price index for year 2. After computing the price indices, you are also asked to adjust total consumption expenditures of $12.5 billion for year 2 to "real" units relative to the base year 0.

TABLE 17.1   Simple Basket of Goods

Item	Number of Units	Price Year 0	Price Year 2
Food	8	1.00	1.10
Clothing	2	2.00	2.30
Housing	10	2.00	2.10
Transportation	4	1.00	1.20
Travel	1	2.00	2.40
Entertainment	1	2.00	2.20

Solution   1. *Simple price index.* First we use the data above to compute a simple unweighted price index. This computation is

$$I_2 = \frac{1.10 + 2.30 + 2.10 + 1.20 + 2.40 + 2.20}{1.00 + 2.00 + 2.00 + 1.00 + 2.00 + 2.00} \times 100$$

$$= 113.0$$

Using this index, one would conclude that prices have risen by 13% from the base year to year 2.

2. *Weighted price index.* These data can also be used to compute the weighted or Laspeyres price index as follows:

$$I_2 = \frac{(8)1.10 + (2)2.30 + (10)2.10 + (4)1.20 + (1)2.40 + (1)2.20}{(8)1.00 + (2)2.00 + (10)2.00 + (4)1.00 + (1)2.00 + (1)2.00} \times 100$$

$$= 109.5$$

The weighted price index indicates that prices have risen by 9.5% from the base year to year 2. Careful examination of Table 17.1 indicates why these indices are different. Note that the items whose prices increased the most, such as clothing and travel, are a small part of the total quantity of goods consumed. Weighted price indices are dominated by price changes for goods that are consumed in the largest quantities.

The total consumption of $12.5 billion in year 2 terms can be adjusted for inflation by converting to real dollars in year 0 units. This is done by dividing consumption expenditures by the price index and multiplying by 100. Therefore, using the weighted price index, year 2 consumption in real dollars is

$$C_R = \frac{12.5}{109.5} \times 100$$

$$= 11.42 \qquad \qquad \square$$

The objective in constructing indices such as the CPI is to measure changes in the overall cost of consumption goods. To achieve this objective those who prepare indices define a constant basket of goods. This basket is assumed to represent the average consumption pattern and to remain stable over the time period of the index.

Does It Make Sense?

Indices are sometimes criticized because they may not represent basic changes in consumption patterns that occur over time. It should be noted that the relative quantities of the goods used to construct the CPI are changed periodically, but possibly not often enough to satisfy critics. This is another case of the trade-off between cost and quality of data.

Another criticism, based on economic theory, is that goods whose prices increase relative to others are purchased in lesser quantities. For example, the rapid increases in the price of gasoline in the 1970s resulted in the purchase of many more-fuel-efficient automobiles. In contrast, the lack of gasoline price increases in the late 1980s and early 1990s resulted in more larger and less-fuel-efficient automobiles. Certainly, many of these criticisms are valid. However, indices such as the CPI are widely accepted as a useful standard. As such, they are a major improvement over the option of not adjusting for price changes. Their use is clearly an important part of a high-quality economic analysis.   □

Production indices.   In addition to the price indices discussed above, quantity indices are used to provide a measure of relative change. The index is computed by dividing the quantity in year k by the quantity in the base year:

$$I_k = \frac{Q_k}{Q_0} \times 100$$

where Q_0 is the quantity in the base year 0 and Q_k is the quantity in the year k. This index is also presented in percentage terms relative to the base year. For example, if a country produced 50 million tons of steel in the base year and 60 million tons in year k, the steel production index for year k would be

$$I_k = \frac{60}{50} \times 100 = 120.0$$

Production indices are widely used in many sectors of the economy to indicate relative growth. These indices indicate change, not the basic level of a sector. They are quite useful for comparing changes in various sectors, such as education and agricultural output.

Index numbers are summarized in Key Idea 17.2.

Practice Problem 17.1

The agency in the country in Example 17.1 and Table 17.1 has asked you to compute the weighted price index for year 5. You conduct a survey of prices in year 5 and find the following results: food, 1.40; clothing, 2.80; housing, 2.40; transportation, 1.50; travel, 3.00; and entertainment, 3.00. Compute the weighted price index for year 5.

The solution is given at the end of the chapter.

Key Idea 17.2: Index Numbers

1. *Price indices.* The simple unweighted price index relative to base year 0 is defined as

$$I_k = \frac{\sum_{i=1}^{n} P_{ki}}{\sum_{i=1}^{n} P_{0i}} \times 100$$

where P_{ki} is the price for good i in year k, P_{0i} is the price for good i in base year 0, and n is the number of items used to develop the index. The weighted or Laspeyres price index is defined as

$$I_k = \frac{\sum_{i=1}^{n} q_{0i} P_{ki}}{\sum_{i=1}^{n} q_{0i} P_{0i}} \times 100$$

where P_{ki} is the price for good i in year k, P_{0i} is the price for good i in base year 0, q_{0i} is the quantity of good i used in base year 0, and n is the number of items used to develop the index.

2. *Production indices.* Quantity indices are used to express relative change in quantity with respect to base year 0:

$$I_k = \frac{Q_k}{Q_0} \times 100$$

where Q_0 is the quantity in the base year 0 and Q_k is the quantity in the year k.

Problem Exercises

17.1 Consider the simple economy of Sunnyisle, which produces 500 units of consumption goods, 300 units of investment goods, and 200 units of government goods. In 1990, consumption goods had a price of $350, investment goods had a price of $600, and government goods had a price of $500. In 1994, consumption goods had a price of $400, investment goods a price of $700, and government goods a price of $550. Compute the price index for 1994 in 1990 dollars.

17.2 Consider the simple economy of Frigidisle, which produces 800 units of consumption goods, 400 units of investment goods, and 250 units of government goods. In 1990 consumption goods had a price of $300, investment goods had a price of $500, and government goods a price of $450. In 1994 consumption goods had a price of $450, investment goods a price of $650, and government goods a price of $550. Compute the price index for 1994 in 1990 dollars.

17.3 In 1980 the price of suspenders was $11 and the price of high-heeled shoes was $60. By 1992 the price of suspenders was $15 and the price of shoes was $75. The price index in 1980 was $120 and in 1992 it was $165.

(a) Compute the 1992 prices of suspenders and high-heeled shoes in 1980 dollars.

(b) Which item has experienced the largest price increase?

17.4   In 1978 the price of paperback books was $11 and the price of hardcover books was $30. By 1993 the price of paperback books was $16 and the price of hardcover books was $70. The price index in 1978 was $110 and in 1993 it was $170.

(a) Compute the 1993 prices of paperback books and hardcover books in 1978 dollars.

(b) Which item has experienced the largest price increase?

17.3 ANALYSIS OF TIME SERIES

Time-series analysis uses only the information in the time series. In contrast, regression or econometric models predict a dependent variable, which can be a time-series variable, as a function of other independent variables. When regression models are used for forecasting, values of the independent variables must be available for each future period being forecast. In addition, there are methodological problems when regression models are used to predict—or forecast—beyond the range of the original data. The latter two problems provide considerable motivation for developing forecasting procedures that use only the past history of the time series. Time-series forecasting assumes that a time series has an identifiable structure and that knowledge of that structure can be used to obtain forecasts.

The study of a time series begins with an examination of graphical plots. Figures 17.1 and 17.2 present time-series plots of quarterly data prepared using Minitab. Figure 17.1 shows the time series for aggregate consumption, and Figure 17.2 presents the plant and equipment investment time series. The data in these examples, which are in billions of 1987 dollars, begin with the first quarter of 1981 and end with the second quarter of 1993. Notice that the consumption series in Figure 17.1 tends to move upward with a few "flat" intervals. In contrast, the investment series in Figure 17.2 also moves upward, but in addition it has a cyclical variation about the upward trend.

In addition to examining time-series plots, a good forecaster also considers other available information about the series. For example, from economic theory we know that consumption is equal to total income less withdrawals for savings and taxes. Thus increased income will increase consumption. Reductions in savings rates such as occurred during the 1980s will also increase consumption. Tax increases—a government policy decision—would reduce consumption. In Figure 17.1 we see that consumption was flat during 1981 and the first half of 1982. An upward trend began in 1982 and continued through 1990. This trend resulted in part from the federal tax decrease and expanded money supply. Consumption flattened until late 1992 and then began to rise again. Because the trend is steadily increasing for most of the time period, a model that assumed a linear increase of consumption versus time should provide a good fit to the series. Examination of consumption over longer time periods indicates a similar pattern. Generally, consumption increases with increased population and an expanding economy. Therefore, a forecast that used a linear regression model would be a good first approximation. More careful analysis would look at the periods of stagnant

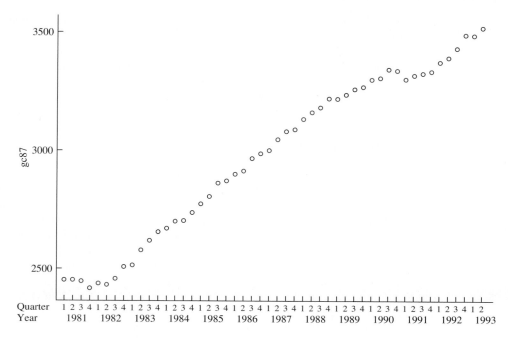

Figure 17.1   Time-Series Plot: Consumption 1981–1993 (1987$)

growth and attempt to forecast those periods also. In addition, other information about economic activity and policy could be used to refine the forecast further.

Figure 17.2 shows private domestic investment in plant and equipment measured in 1987 dollars. The cyclical pattern here contrasts dramatically with the previous example. Investment usually follows cycles in response to overall economic activity. Factories reach their capacity and are expanded in anticipation of increasing demand. Eventually, excess capacity is generated and investment levels are reduced. This cyclical pattern of investment can be included in forecasting models by using a number of different techniques. There is also a trend that would be included in a forecasting model. The graphical plot provides a picture of the time-series pattern.

Time-series plots provide valuable information and should always be used as part of any time-series analysis and model development. A "picture" of the time-series pattern provides intuitive insights that are important for model development. In many applied forecasts time-series plots are an important part of the analysis.

17.3.1 Forecasting Problem

Before beginning a formal analysis of time series and the development of models, let us consider the general issues associated with forecasting (Key Idea 17.3). Suppose that you were interested in forecasting the difficulty of the final examination in this course. (We leave you to judge the importance of this question!) An initial consideration of this problem might generate some data about the teacher, including characteris-

Figure 17.2   Time-Series Plot of Plant and Equipment Investment 1981–1993
(1987$)

tics such as white hair, beard, beautiful face, youthful appearance, or ownership of an old Plymouth station wagon. Based on your experience, most of you would conclude that this information will not provide much help for the forecasting problem. However, you might ask other students or alumni who have taken this course for their judgment about the difficulty of past examinations in this course. Copies of previous examinations could also be obtained and their difficulty determined. Patterns of increasing or decreasing difficulty over the years could be recorded. You should also be aware of recent college policies to lower or raise grades, or statements by the department chair that final examinations have been too easy in the past. All of these sources of relevant information could be used to obtain a forecast.

A forecaster would classify all available information according to its useful-ness for forecasting. Information about a teacher's appearance is independent of the question and is thus not useful for forecasting. The information about policy changes should be considered. However, its effect would be to modify past patterns and would not be the only information. You would like to have as much information as possi-ble about the difficulty of past examinations. A time-series graph could be constructed if data were available from all of the past final examinations prepared by the teacher for this course. From that time series you might feel comfortable in forecasting the difficulty of the examination. This could be done by extending the graph into the fu-ture. After examining the time-series graph the forecast might be modified by using

---

Key Idea 17.3: Forecasting Concepts

Time-series forecasting uses the past pattern of the series to predict future values. Forecasting begins with a time-series graphical plot, followed by the application of specific analysis tools. Forecasting is more of an art than are other statistical procedures.

Forecasters use experience and understanding of the process that generates the series to help in the analysis. Judgment, intuition, and common sense are also important tools. Good forecasters are guided by the principle that the ultimate evaluation criterion is the accuracy of the forecast, not the elegance of the analysis or the model.

---

information about policy changes or information logically related to the next point in the time series, the difficulty of the next examination.

Now let us consider some alternatives that could occur in your forecast. The historical time series might indicate that examinations are always difficult or always easy. In that case you would feel confident that your forecast should be the same as the past stable pattern. But you might observe patterns of increasing and decreasing difficulty over a number of years—a cyclical pattern. In that case you might attempt to determine if recent examinations are on an increasing or decreasing part of the pattern. Another possibility is that fall-semester examinations are always difficult and spring-semester examinations easy—a seasonal pattern. A seasonal adjustment would be made in response to this observation. You might also find that exams have become increasingly difficult—a trend pattern. In contrast, a series that had widely fluctuating levels of difficulty, with no apparent pattern, would lead to considerable uncertainty about the forecast. In the scenario above, forecasts were based on the assumption that past patterns will continue in the future. However, there is no guarantee that history will repeat itself. The teacher could have a sudden sickness or a personal problem. Another teacher might prepare the examination. The teacher might have changed her mind about the benefit of difficult or easy examinations.

Does It Make Sense?

Major changes in the environment of the forecast can greatly change the series being forecast. In 1989 the Berlin Wall came down. As you might suspect, forecasts of European economic variables were adjusted rapidly. Some critics of forecasting argue that economic forecasting is similar to driving a car by constantly looking at the road behind while trying to keep the car on the road. Clearly, any additional information about the future is useful for either providing confidence in the time-series forecast or for modifying the forecast.   □

17.4 TIME-SERIES COMPONENTS

Time-series forecasting models are based on the assumption that the past history of a time series provides valuable information about future values of the time series. This assumption implies that there is a time-related structure in the series. If the structure is identified, a time-series model would be specified and its parameters estimated. The resulting time-series model is used to forecast future values of the series. In this section we identify structural components of a time series. In the next section we show how the parameters of the components can be estimated and a model constructed.

A time series can be separated into structural components and irregular components (Key Idea 17.4). One approach for developing forecasting models is first, to identify and estimate structural components. Next, the residual variation from the structural components, defined as the irregular component, is computed. Separate forecasting models are developed for the irregular components. Next, structural and irregular component forecasts are combined to obtain an overall forecast. The resulting forecast is then tested. Regression analysis can be used as one of the tools for estimating structural component parameters. Regression is often used as a descriptive estimation technique because regression assumptions are often not met by time-series data.

Key Idea 17.4: Time-Series Components

Time-series components can be classified as structural and irregular. The structural components are analogous to the information part of numbers, and the irregular components are analogous to the error. Three structural components are

1. Trend components
2. Cyclical components
3. Seasonal components

17.4.1 Structural Components

An important part of model development is the specification of the component forms. This is usually done by a combination of process analysis and time-series graphs.

Trend components.   Trends (Key Idea 17.5) are typically modeled as *linear*, which assumes a constant rate of increase or decrease over time, or *quadratic*, which assumes a rate of increase that is either increasing or decreasing. The plot in Figure 17.1 shows that the aggregate consumption trend increases approximately linearly over time.

Key Idea 17.5: Trend Component

The **trend component** is an effect that is either increasing or decreasing over time. Thus one structural component of the consumption series would be a linear trend, which could be modeled by

$$E[Y_t] = \beta_0 + \beta_1 \times t$$

where Y_t is the consumption for time period t and β_0 and β_1 are the model parameters, which are estimated by using the historical data.

Does It Make Sense?

Better forecasting models are obtained if we have an understanding of the process that generates the time series. For example, economic theory indicates that aggregate consumption will grow as a result of population growth and per capita growth in gross national product. In developed economies such as the United States, growth will be approximately linear over long periods of time. Similar arguments could be made for sales by a company that is maintaining a constant share of a growing product market.

Figure 17.3 presents a schematic representation of three trend options. A firm that is obtaining an increasing share of a growing market would have its sales modeled by an increasing quadratic function. A firm with decreasing market share in a decreasing market would have its sales modeled by a decreasing quadratic function. □

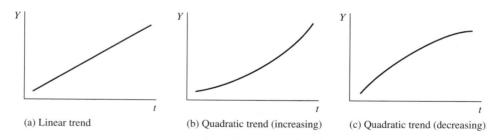

(a) Linear trend   (b) Quadratic trend (increasing)   (c) Quadratic trend (decreasing)

Figure 17.3   Schematic Forms of Trend Component

* **Cyclical component.**   The cyclical component (Key Idea 17.6) represents an effect that moves repeatedly from high to low levels over the time interval. Figure 17.4 is a good example of a cyclical time-series component. As shown in Figure 17.4, p is the time period over which the cycle repeats. In many applied problems the amplitude and the period may not be the same over the entire series. Therefore, the forecaster must apply good judgment to select a model that provides the best compromise.

Key Idea 17.6: Cyclical Component

Cyclical components are typically modeled by a combination of sine and cosine functions. There are two important characteristics of cyclical components: the amplitude or range from high to low values and the period or time required to move from high to low and return. One form of a cyclical component would be

$$E[Y_t] = \beta_0 + \beta_1 \sin\frac{2\pi t}{p} + \beta_2 \cos\frac{2\pi t}{p}$$

where $E[Y_t]$ is the forecast at time t, β_0 is the series mean, β_1 and β_2 are the coefficients of the sine and cosine components, and p is period of the cycle. The coefficients $\hat{\beta}_0$, $\hat{\beta}_1$, and $\hat{\beta}_2$ can be estimated using regression, but p must be specified by the analyst.

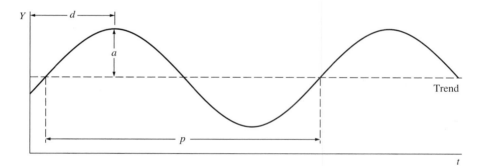

Figure 17.4   Schematic Time-Series Model: Cyclical Components

The parameters β_1 and β_2 provide estimates for the amplitude, a, and displacement, d, of the maximum point from the origin, as shown in Figure 17.4. The amplitude of the cycle is equal to

$$a = \sqrt{\beta_1^2 + \beta_2^2},$$

while the maximum point of the curve is displaced by a distance equal to

$$d = \arctan\frac{\beta_1}{\beta_2}$$

from the origin $t = 0$.

Cyclical variations over time occur in a number of economic processes. The example in Figure 17.2 is typical for aggregate investment. Investment will increase when businesses anticipate increased demand as a result of economic growth and factories that are nearing capacity. After a period of increasing investment, excess production capacity will occur and businesses will reduce their investment. Alternatively, reduced economic growth will cause businesses to reduce their investment levels. The combined effect of these factors results in *business cycles*, which are common in developed economies. Sales of consumer products, especially durable goods, often follow a cyclical pattern because of replacement schedules.

A number of other series, such as interest rates, a firm's inventory levels, and the expenditures for equipment replacement, may also follow cyclical patterns. Thus cyclical models have applications to many business forecasting problems.

It is difficult to predict the period of future cycles accurately from historical data. Thus applied forecasters have tended to use other techniques. Cyclical models such as those presented here are useful for developing models of historical series. However, their use for forecasting the future requires understandings considerably beyond the ideas presented here. Having said all that, you should note the example in the chapter appendix, which indicates a very good forecast for a cyclical time series.

Seasonal components.   The third major structural component of time-series models is the seasonal component (Key Idea 17.7). Seasonal components are quarterly or monthly variations whose pattern is repeated each year (Figure 17.5). Grain prices tend to be lowest during the harvest season when supplies are the largest. Retail sales for many stores are highest during the Christmas season. Retail prices for cars are highest just after new models are introduced. The number of housing units sold and their prices are usually higher during the spring and early summer when demand is high. Unemployment numbers are higher in June and July as high school and college graduates enter the job market for the first time.

The seasonal component is similar to a cyclical component whose period is one year. However, its origins are related to factors that vary with annual calendars instead of some longer-term condition such as a business cycle. In addition, seasonal patterns may have only one or two higher or lower periods each year instead of the uniform variation modeled by a sine or cosine function.

Note that dummy variables are used for only three of the four quarters or 11 of the 12 months, to avoid the dummy variable trap (Chapter 15). The time interval not included can be chosen arbitrarily, and the coefficient β_0 provides the measure for the excluded interval. Then all other coefficients are estimates of the differences relative to the interval not included. Figure 17.5 presents a schematic form of a seasonal model assuming quarterly data. A monthly model would differ because of more intervals within each year.

Estimates of the seasonal adjustments, $\hat{\beta}_j$'s, can be obtained using regression analysis. A matrix of dummy variables would be specified for either four quarters or 12 months. The coefficients for the regression model

$$\hat{Y}_t = \hat{\beta}_0 + \hat{\beta}_2 X_{2t} + \hat{\beta}_3 X_{3t} + \hat{\beta}_4 X_{4t}$$

would be estimated using quarterly data. The variable X_2 would be 1 for the second quarter and 0 otherwise, X_3 would be 1 for the third quarter and 0 otherwise, and X_4 would be 1 for the fourth quarter and 0 otherwise. Trend components should be

Key Idea 17.7: Seasonal Component

Seasonal components are estimated using a dummy variable regression model which has 0 or 1 values for each of the time periods during the year. A quarterly model has the form

$$\hat{Y}_{tF} = \hat{\beta}_0 + \sum_{j=2}^{4} \hat{\beta}_j X_{jt}$$

where $\hat{Y}_{tF}$ is the time-series value for period t, $\hat{\beta}_0$ is the series mean, the β_j's are the estimated seasonal adjustments, and the X_{jt}'s are 1 for quarter j and 0 for other quarters. The model for monthly data has the form

$$\hat{Y}_{tF} = \hat{\beta}_0 + \sum_{j=2}^{12} \hat{\beta}_j X_{jt}$$

The only difference is that the $\hat{\beta}_j$'s and X_{jt}'s represent 12 months instead of four quarters.

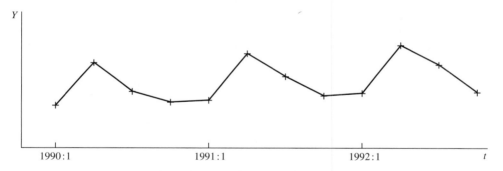

Figure 17.5   Schematic Time-Series Model: Seasonal Components

removed before obtaining the seasonal estimates. However, one should not attempt to combine seasonal and cyclical component estimates in the same model because the results would be confusing.

    Combined components.   Many time-series models will contain more than one of the structural components. Therefore, the analysis of components is often a several-step process. The analysis begins with a graphical plot. Discussions with persons who understand the process being modeled are of great value. For example, if we wish to forecast the sale of airline tickets, it would be useful to interview some travel agents. Many processes contain a trend, and therefore fitting a linear or quadratic regression model would be a good first step. The residuals, or differences between observed and trend predictions, would be plotted as a second time series. This time series might indicate a cyclical or seasonal structure. If that occurs, the regression model would be expanded to include this additional component. The new residuals would be plotted as a time series to determine if additional structural components should be included. Figure 17.6 indicates a model with both linear trend and cyclical components.

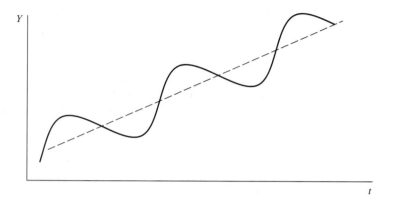

Figure 17.6   Schematic Time-Series Model: Linear Trend and Seasonal
Components

17.4.2 Irregular Components

After the structural components have been identified and estimated, differences between observed and predicted values of the time series will usually remain. These differences are defined as *irregular components*. Irregular components are similar to the residuals discussed in regression analysis. For purposes of forecasting we would like to know if the irregular components contain any patterns that can be used to improve the forecast. For example, serial correlation between residuals, as presented in Chapter 16, provides a useful model for forecasting future residuals from previous observed residuals.

We consider several models used to analyze irregular components. If regression analysis has been used to obtain models for the structural components, the mean of the irregular components will be zero. This results from the fact that regression analysis will always provide the minimum variance fit for any set of data. The analysis objective is to determine if it is possible to identify a pattern in the observed time-series plot of the irregular components. Three formal estimation procedures for forecasting irregular components will be considered. They are (1) random walk, (2) autoregressive process, and (3) exponential smoothing.

Random walk.   Figure 17.7 is a time-series graph that has a random walk pattern (Key Idea 17.8). This pattern resembles regression residual plots for models with the correct mathematical form.

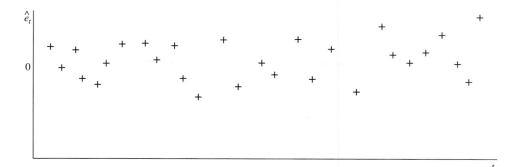

Figure 17.7   Schematic Time-Series Model: Random Walk Irregular
Component

Key Idea 17.8: Random Walk

The terms $\hat{e}_t$ in a random walk are independent, and previous observations do not provide information about subsequent observations. If the irregular component follows a random walk model, it is not possible to improve the forecast by considering the irregular component. The forecast of this component would be zero, its mean. In algebraic model form we have

$$E[\hat{e}_t] = 0$$

The random walk model implies that there is no relationship between observations in a time series. The irregular components, $\hat{e}_t$'s, are assumed to be independent random variables. The model is that of a drunken man who is attempting to walk from the street to his door. Each step can go either right or left, with no relationship to the previous step. He does eventually arrive at the door, but it is not possible to predict his path.

Some analysts argue that daily stock market prices are a random walk. This derives from the hypothesis that buyers and sellers have perfect information and thus all sales decisions are independent. The random walk model assumes that the selling price is not influenced by previous selling prices.

Autoregressive process.   Figure 17.8 presents an example of the data pattern for an autoregressive (AR) model. The model presented in Key Idea 17.9 is an AR(1) model. This model uses only the most recent observation to produce a prediction for the next observation. It is also possible to have an AR(2) model that has the form

$$\hat{e}_{tF} = \beta_0 + \beta_1 \hat{e}_{t-1} + \beta_2 \hat{e}_{t-2}$$

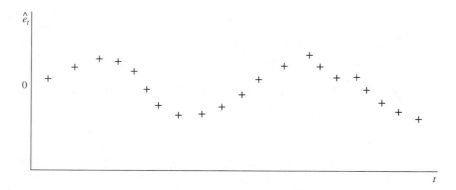

Figure 17.8   Schematic Time-Series Model: Autoregressive Irregular
Component

Key Idea 17.9: Autoregressive Process

An **autoregressive** (AR) **process** contains correlations between observations that are separated by a given time interval. For example, knowledge of the component at time $t - 1$ could provide information to forecast the component at time t. The simplest form of the autoregressive model is

$$\hat{e}_{tF} = \beta_0 + \beta_1 \hat{e}_{t-1}$$

where $\hat{e}_{tF}$ is the forecast for period t; β_1 is the linear coefficient, which is related to the observed correlation between irregular components; and β_0 is the constant. In this model the irregular component $\hat{e}_t$ is a linear function of the previous observation in the time series. The component $\hat{e}_{t-1}$ is said to be lagged one period. Serial correlation of errors in the regression model from Chapter 16 is another example of an autoregressive process.

In this model the forecast is a linear function of the two most recent lagged observations. Following this pattern, we can also develop AR(3), AR(4), ..., AR(k) autoregressive models. In most cases one, two, or three lagged periods will be sufficient. Additional lagged periods usually only add to model complexity without important improvements in the forecast.

Seasonal autoregressive models, SAR(1), SAR(2), ..., SAR(k), can also be developed. The SAR(2) seasonal model has the form

$$\hat{e}_{tF} = \beta_0 + \beta_1 \hat{e}_{t-4} + \beta_2 \hat{e}_{t-8}$$

for quarterly data. If monthly data were used, $\hat{e}_{t-12}$ and $\hat{e}_{t-24}$ would be substituted as the predictor variables on the right-hand side of this equation. In seasonal models we assume that irregular components from the same season have an observed correlation. Examination of the time-series plot and/or knowledge of the process can provide motivation for trying to use a seasonal autoregressive model.

The autoregressive model is part of a sophisticated time-series modeling and forecasting technique developed by George Box and Gwendylin Jenkins.[1] This approach, often called the *Box–Jenkins method*, is presented in most books on time-series analysis.

Stationary series.   Stationarity is an important concept from Box and Jenkins that is useful for our present level of analysis. A stationary time series consists of T random variables at discrete time intervals that have a constant expected value and variance for each observation. In addition, the correlation between two observations separated by k periods, $k = 1, \ldots, T$, depends only on k, the number of periods, not on the location of the observations in the time series. For example, the irregular components of a time series could be treated as a stationary series.

Autoregressive models assume that correlations between observations are stationary. Using the stationarity property, the correlations between observations separated by k periods can be used to forecast future observations of the time series.

In the approach presented here, using the irregular components from regression analysis, the regression residuals have a mean of zero and are assumed to have a constant variance. However, if the irregular components are not a stationary series, use of the autoregressive model can lead to incorrect forecast models. In particular, the assumption that the correlations between components separated by one or two observations is critical for good forecasts of the irregular component.

In a number of cases, stationarity can be established by using the first differences between observations,

$$\Delta \bar{Y} = y_t - y_{t-1}$$

as the series to be forecast. Most statistical packages provide an option for obtaining first differences—and even second and third differences.

Examination of the time-series plot can provide some guidance. The forecaster must ask if adjacent observations appear to follow a repeating pattern. If they do not, the autoregressive model will not provide good forecasts. In that case a procedure such as exponential smoothing, which is discussed next, should be used. A forecaster who is uncertain about stationarity—and we often are in applied forecasting situations—should try both the autoregressive method and exponential smoothing on the available data and determine which provides the best forecasts. With modern computer packages little effort is required to try a variety of models to determine the model that best fits the data. Methods for testing forecasts are presented below.

---

[1] G. E. P. Box and G. M. Jenkins, *Time Series Analysis, Forecasting and Control*, 2nd ed., Holden-Day, San Francisco, 1976.

The autoregressive model is one technique used in the Box–Jenkins method to forecast irregular components from a stationary series. Various techniques are used to test for stationarity and to adjust nonstationary time series to stationary time se-ries. These methods involve a combination of sophisticated statistical procedures and considerable experience. Thus they are not presented here.

Exponential smoothing.   Exponential smoothing (Key Idea 17.10) is a heuristic forecasting procedure for time series that do not contain a trend, which has been used extensively in applied forecasting. It has proven to be very useful in a number of situations, including the forecasting of irregular components. Exponential smoothing is easy to understand and to apply. In addition, the specific forecasting model can easily be modified in response to changes in the characteristics of the process that generates the time series.

Key Idea 17.10: Exponential Smoothing

The **exponential smoothing forecasting model** is

$$\hat{e}_{tF} = \alpha\hat{e}_{t-1} + (1 - \alpha)\hat{e}_{t-1,F}$$

$$0 < \alpha < 1.0$$

where $\hat{e}_{tF}$ is the forecast value for time period t, $\hat{e}_{t-1}$ is the observed value for time period $t - 1$, $\hat{e}_{t-1,F}$ is the forecast value for time period $t - 1$, and α is a smoothing constant. The forecast is a linear combination of the forecast and the value observed for the previous time period. The smooth-ing constant indicates the weight that is given to each item of information. Higher values of α assign more weight to $\hat{e}_{t-1}$, the most recent observation. The coefficient α is determined by examining the historical time series and testing several different values to obtain a value that provides the "best" forecast, based on the measures of forecast accuracy.

Key Idea 17.10 shows that the most recent observation of the series is multiplied by α and the most recent forecast is multiplied by $1 - \alpha$. This most recent forecast is given by

$$\hat{e}_{t-1,F} = \alpha\hat{e}_{t-2} + (1 - \alpha)\hat{e}_{t-2,F}$$

Repeated applications of this equation would indicate that the previous forecast is ob-tained from the entire past history of the time series. Thus the forecast is a combination of the most recent observation and the entire past history. If the time series has erratic variations, we would choose a small value of α that provides a forecast that is strongly influenced by the entire past history. However, if the time series has smooth variations over time, we would choose a larger value of α so that the most recent observation receives more weight.

Another form for exponential smoothing is

$$\hat{e}_{tF} = \hat{e}_{t-1,F} + \alpha(\hat{e}_{t-1} - \hat{e}_{t-1,F})$$

The forecast for time period t is composed of the forecast for period $t - 1$ adjusted by a fraction, α, of the difference between the observed and forecast values for period $t - 1$. Exponential smoothing is viewed as containing a historical component, $\hat{e}_{t-1,F}$, which is adjusted using the deviation between observed and forecast values from the most recent time period. The amount of adjustment is determined by the deviation and the smoothing constant, α. The forecaster controls the process by her choice of the smoothing constant. Exponential smoothing provides considerable opportunity for using the forecaster's experience and special insights in combination with the observed patterns of historical time series. In Section 17.5 we present some procedures for determining the quality of the forecast. These can be used to help guide the choice of an appropriate smoothing constant.

Model comparisons.   The three models presented for analyzing the irregular component provide considerable flexibility for combining the forecaster's experience with the data available in the historical time series. The random walk model assumes that the historical series contains no information that can be used for forecasting. Thus the forecast is the mean, which is zero for the irregular component. In contrast, the autoregressive model provides a forecast that is a linear function of the most recent values observed in the time series. The coefficients are determined using regression analysis. Forecaster judgment is limited to choosing the number of lagged values included in the autoregressive model. Exponential smoothing forecasts are based on a combination of recent and historical information. Forecasts are dependent on the choice of the smoothing constant α. The forecaster has considerable control over the forecasting model.

We need to emphasize again that the forecasting methods presented in this chapter do not include the assumptions of random variables required for statistical inference. Therefore, our analysis has not included discussion of hypothesis testing and confidence intervals. In more advanced work with time-series models, such as the methods developed by Box and Jenkins, the properties of random variables are included and more sophisticated models are developed.

Problem Exercises

17.5   Define the three structural components of a time series and provide an example of each.

17.6   Explain why time-series forecasting models are different from multiple regression models used to forecast.

17.7   Discuss the differences between seasonal and cyclical effects in a time-series model.

17.8   Compare and contrast irregular components in a time-series model and residuals in a multiple regression model.

17.9   Explain how exponential smoothing combines recent time-series information and the past history of the time series.

17.10   Compare and contrast the methodology of exponential smoothing and autoregressive procedures for developing time-series forecasting models.

17.5 SMOOTHING FORECASTS

Another approach to forecasting is to develop a forecasting model directly from the original series. The resulting forecast model would combine the structural and the irregular components directly. That approach, which has been used successfully in a number of applications, is developed here. Here the application of three techniques—exponential smoothing, autoregression, and moving averages—is developed.

17.5.1 Exponential Smoothing

Exponential smoothing is a very flexible procedure that combines recent and historical information. In addition, it is simple to understand and apply. The model is

$$Y_{tF} = \alpha y_{t-1} + (1 - \alpha)Y_{t-1,F} \qquad 0 < \alpha < 1.0$$

where Y_{tF} is the forecast value for time period t, y_{t-1} is the observed value for time period $t - 1$, $Y_{t-1,F}$ is the forecast value for time period $t - 1$, and α is a smoothing constant. The forecast is a linear combination of the forecast and observed values for the previous time period. The smoothing constant indicates the weight that is given to each item of information. Higher values of α assign more weight to $\hat{e}_{t-1}$, the most recent observation. The coefficient α is determined by examining the historical time series and testing several different values to obtain a value that provides the best forecast, based on the measures of forecast accuracy.

Exponential smoothing combines the most recent value of the series and the most recent forecast. The most recent forecast contains components from the entire past history of the series. Careful selection of the smoothing constant, α, provides the opportunity to choose the best combination of recent information and the stability of the past history of the series. A dynamic series with substantial real changes occurring regularly would be forecast best by using a high value of α. In contrast, a series with many random fluctuations, which do not follow a pattern, would require a small value of α. Small values of α lead to stable forecasts because those forecasts depend much more on the past history of the series.

17.5.2 Autoregressive Forecast

The autoregressive forecast uses regression analysis to estimate coefficients that relate one or more recent observations to the next period's forecast. For example, a forecast, Y_{tF}, using three past observations could be made using the model

$$Y_{tF} = \beta_0 + \beta_1 y_{t-1} + \beta_2 y_{t-2} + \beta_3 y_{t-3}$$

where the y_t's are observed values of the series at time period t. The β_j's would be estimated using multiple regression analysis. This forecast procedure assumes that there is a stable relationship between observations that are separated by the same interval in a time series. In most cases first differences would be used. They can be obtained by using an option in most statistical packages. If there is not a stable relationship, the estimated β_j coefficients will have a large variance and the forecast model will not be useful. The entire past history is used to estimate the coefficients;

however, without a stable relationship between observations the forecast will have a large error.

17.5.3 Moving Average

The moving average forecast is an old technique that uses the most recent observations for computing the forecast. A forecast is made by obtaining the average of the most recent observations. The number of observations typically vary from $m = 3$ to $m = 12$, depending on the amount of random instability in the series. In mathematical terms the forecast, Y_{tF}, is

$$Y_{tF} = \frac{y_{t-1} + y_{t-2} + \cdots + y_{t-m}}{m}$$

If the series is dynamic and contains a minimum of random instability, values near $m = 3$ would provide the best forecast.

However, if there is considerable instability, the period of the moving average should be extended to remove the positive and negative fluctuations. Clearly, there is considerable experience and intuition required to obtain useful moving average forecasts.

17.5.4 Comparison of Forecasting Procedures

The three forecasting procedures discussed above require considerable experience and art. Forecasters typically try different variations of each method and then test how well the procedure follows the past history of the series. In the next section techniques for measuring and evaluating a forecast are presented. Those techniques are used to compare different forecast procedures to determine which approach provides the best forecast. The selection criterion is to choose the procedure that provides the best forecast.

17.6 EVALUATING TIME-SERIES FORECASTS

The ultimate benefit of the forecasting procedures presented above is a good forecast. In this section we present criteria for judging the quality of the forecast. In the next section we present some applications of the time-series models and show how these criteria can be used to compare the forecasting models. Three basic criteria will be used in this book: (1) root mean square error, (2) mean deviation, and (3) time-series plots. In the presentation that follows, the observed values of the series will be defined as Y_t and the predicted or forecast values as $\hat{Y}_t$ for every period t. This is the same notation as that used for dependent variables in regression models.

17.6.1 Root Mean Square Error

If regression is used to obtain the forecasting model, RMSE is minimized for the model form used. RMSE provides a useful measure of the variation of observations about the forecast value (Key Idea 17.11). We would like to have a forecast with the smallest possible RMSE. Note that points which are distant from the forecast have a great deal of influence on RMSE because the deviations are squared.

Key Idea 17.11: Root Mean Square Error

Root mean square error (RMSE) is the square root of the sum of the squared deviations between observed, Y_t, and predicted, $\hat{Y}_t$, values divided by the number of observations, T, in the series.

$$\text{RMSE} = \sqrt{\frac{\sum_{t=1}^{T}(Y_t - \hat{Y}_t)^2}{T}}$$

RMSE is a measure that resembles the population standard deviation. Thus a few extreme values in the time series could make RMSE quite large.

17.6.2 Mean Deviation

The mean deviation is described in Key Idea 17.12. The bias is the average deviation between the observed and forecast series. In some cases forecasters will add or subtract a constant equal to the bias from every forecast point to obtain a new forecast with zero bias. This approach is reasonable if there has been a shift in the process that generates the time series.

Key Idea 17.12: Mean Deviation

The **mean deviation** (MD) is the average of the algebraic sum of deviations between the observed and forecast values.

$$\text{MD} = \frac{\sum_{t=1}^{T}(Y_t - \hat{Y}_t)}{T}$$

The MD will be zero if the observed values are equally spaced above and below the forecast. A positive value of MD indicates that the forecasts tend to be too low. Conversely a negative value of MD indicates that the forecasts tend to be too high. We attempt to obtain an MD that is close to zero by using various model adjustments. The mean deviation (MD) multiplied by (-1) is defined as the forecast bias.

17.6.3 Graphical Plots

The use of graphical plots (Key Idea 17.13) requires the use of more judgment and experience than are needed in using the statistical measures RMSE and MD. Both the observed and predicted values are plotted over time, as shown in Figure 17.9. This plot shows a time series that combines trend and cyclical components. The forecast has a good fit to the time series and there are no large deviations. The RMSE would be small and the MD very close to zero. Also note that the forecast "anticipates" upward or downward shifts in the actual time series. These changes from upward or downward movement are defined as *turning points*.

Key Idea 17.13: Time-Series Plots: Observed and Predicted

Time-series plots of observed and predicted values are an important tool for evaluating forecasts. An important question when examining graphical plots is the prediction of turning points. Forecasts that can accurately predict turning points are of great importance. A firm can make timely decisions to avoid shortages or excess inventories by predicting upward and downward movements in sales. Government policymakers can implement timely policies to ensure a continuation of stable economic growth and avoid severe unemployment or rapid inflation. Most forecasters would sacrifice RMSE and MD measurements if the forecasting model consistently predicts turning points.

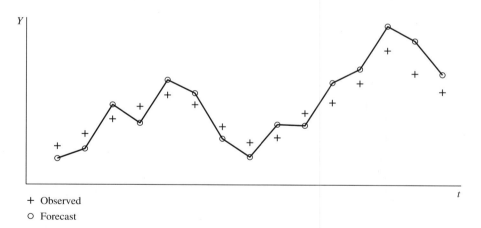

+ Observed
o Forecast

Figure 17.9   Observed and Forecast Time Series: Good Forecast Model

Knowing when a change is about to occur can provide very important guidance for an organization. Thus a forecast that identifies turning points may be more useful than a forecast with a smaller RMSE. Organizations that make timely changes are those that are most successful. History contains numerous examples of business failures and declining nations that resulted from a failure to adapt to change. In most of those examples leaders did not anticipate the change and thus failed to react.

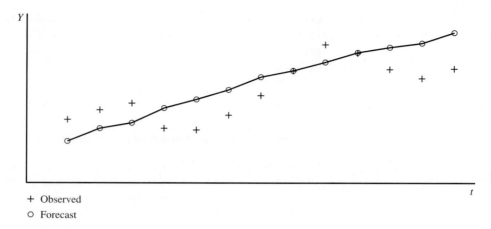

Figure 17.10   Observed and Forecast Time Series: Turning Points Missed

There are many other characteristics of a forecast that can be seen by examining a graphical plot. Figure 17.10 indicates a forecast that would have a small RMSE and an MD close to zero. However, note that the forecast shows an increasing trend and does not identify important turning points. In contrast, the forecast in Figure 17.11 would have poor values for RMSE and MD. However, it does reflect the turning points in the actual series. A fixed positive adjustment would provide an excellent forecasting model.

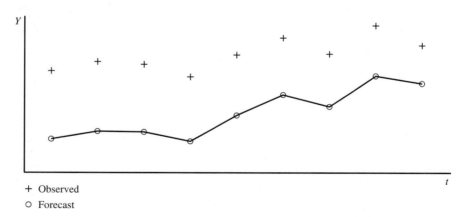

Figure 17.11   Observed and Forecast Time Series: Forecast Bias

Does It Make Sense?

Points that have a large deviation from the forecast should be examined carefully. These points could have resulted from a reporting error. They might also provide an indication of an important factor that occurs infrequently. Knowledge of this factor could be used to improve the forecast. Graphical plots should be examined carefully to discover potential improvements to your forecast model.   ☐

Problem Exercises

17.11 Explain the difference between the information provided by the root mean square error and the mean deviation statistics for evaluating time-series forecasting models.

17.12 Explain why you should examine the turning points when evaluating a time-series forecasting model.

17.13 Time-series models are often tested by applying them to "fresh data" that were not used in developing the model. How does this test compare to applying the model to the data used to fit the model?

17.14 In evaluating a time-series forecasting model, what are the most important criteria that should be examined?

17.7 APPLICATION OF FORECASTING METHODS

We are now ready to apply the methods that have been developed in previous sections. Examples showing the development of time-series models (Key Idea 17.14) will be presented using Minitab computer outputs.

Example 17.2   Aggregate Consumption (1981–1993)

In this example a time-series model for aggregate consumption, measured in real 1987 dollars, is developed.

Solution   Examination of a graphical plot is usually the first step in developing a time-series forecasting model. Figure 17.1 presents the graphical plot, which indicates a strong increasing trend with some flat periods, as discussed in Section 17.3. Based on that analysis, the first step was to obtain an estimate of the linear trend using regression analysis. The linear trend model and its graph are shown in Figure 17.12.

Key Idea 17.14: Forecast Model Development

The development of time-series forecasts consists of three steps:

1. Model development and estimation
2. Model testing
3. Application to obtain forecasts

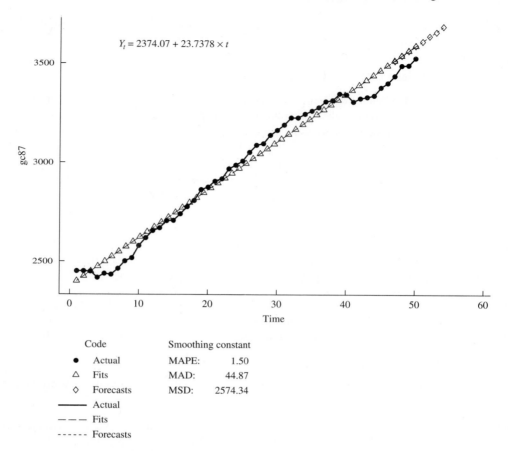

$$Y_t = 2374.07 + 23.7378 \times t$$

Code		Smoothing constant	
●	Actual	MAPE:	1.50
△	Fits	MAD:	44.87
◇	Forecasts	MSD:	2574.34
——	Actual		
– – –	Fits		
- - - - - -	Forecasts		

Figure 17.12   Linear Trend Forecast of Consumption 1981–1993

The regression analysis indicates a linear trend that can be estimated using the equation[2]

$$\hat{Y}_t = 2364.43 + 24.3238 \times t$$

This result can be used to obtain the linear trend forecast for period 47 (1992:3) as follows:

$$\hat{Y}_{47} = 2364.43 + 24.3238 \times 47 = 3507.65$$

---

[2] Note that this equation is slightly different than the equation in Figure 17.12. This results from the way Minitab has chosen to display its output. The equation in Figure 17.12 is based on the entire available series of 50 observations. However, in this example the forecasts are based on only the first 46 observations in the time series. Thus the actual trend equation is not shown. To obtain the trend equation used here it was necessary to delete observations 47 through 50 from the series and then run the trend analysis using only the actual 46 observations used to develop the forecasts.

The root mean square error (RMSE) for this time-series model was obtained by computing the square root of the mean square deviation (MSD):

$$\text{RMSE} = \sqrt{\text{MSD}} = \sqrt{2574.34} = 50.74$$

The next step in the forecasting process is to determine if an improved forecast can be obtained by forecasting the irregular components. If the irregular components follow a pattern, information about a previous component can be used to obtain an improved forecast. Figure 17.13 shows the residuals or irregular components from the linear trend forecast.

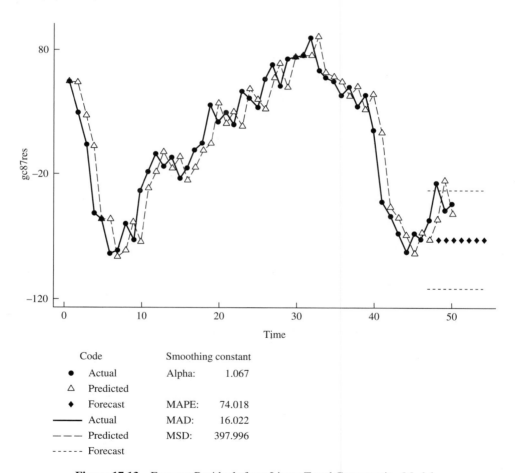

Code		Smoothing constant	
●	Actual	Alpha:	1.067
△	Predicted		
◆	Forecast	MAPE:	74.018
——	Actual	MAD:	16.022
— — —	Predicted	MSD:	397.996
- - - - -	Forecast		

Figure 17.13   Forecast Residuals from Linear Trend Consumption Model

After removing the linear trend, we next examined the residual time series that remained after the trend effect was removed. Both exponential smoothing and autoregressive models, AR(1), were used to forecast the residuals in order to obtain an improved forecast of aggregate consumption. Figure 17.13 shows the residuals, the fitted model, and the forecast using exponential smoothing. The forecast was developed using an optimal α computed by the Minitab exponential smoothing routine. This resulted in a value of $\alpha = 1.067$.[3] The root mean square error (RMSE) for the combined trend/exponential smoothing time-series model was obtained by computing the square root of the mean square deviation (MSD),

$$\text{RMSE} = \sqrt{\text{MSD}} = \sqrt{397.996} = 19.9$$

The final model used a value of $\alpha = 1.067$ and computed the forecast of the irregular component using

$$E[\hat{e}_t] = 1.067 \times \hat{e}_{t-1} + (1 - 1.067) \times E[\hat{e}_{t-1}]$$

For example, to forecast the residual for period 47 (1992:3), we would use the observed residual for period 46 (1992:2), which was $\hat{e}_{46} = -74.86$, and the forecast for period 46, which was $E[\hat{e}_{46}] = -69.17$. The forecast value for the residual is thus

$$\begin{aligned} E[\hat{e}_{47}] &= 1.067 \times \hat{e}_{46} + (1 - 1.067) \times E[\hat{e}_{46}] \\ &= 1.067 \times (-74.85) + (1 - 1.067) \times (-69.17) \\ &= -75.24 \end{aligned}$$

This forecast was then combined with the previous forecast, $\hat{Y}_{tr,t}$, to obtain the final forecast, $\hat{Y}_{f,t}$:

$$\hat{Y}_{f,t} = \hat{Y}_{tr,t} + E[\hat{e}_t]$$

Using the results generated above for observation 47, the result is

$$\begin{aligned} \hat{Y}_{f,47} &= \hat{Y}_{tr,47} + E[\hat{e}_{47}] \\ &= 3507.65 + (-75.24) \\ &= 3432.41 \end{aligned}$$

This combined forecast for the third quarter of 1992 (1992:3) is shown in the fourth column of Table 17.2. The results for all eight time periods forecast are presented in Table 17.2.

The AR(1) model was also applied to the residuals. The forecast model was prepared by regressing the residuals on their lagged values. The regression output is shown in Exhibit 17.1. Figure 17.14 presents a plot of the residuals and their lags with the fitted model. For this regression the RMSE was

$$\text{RMSE} = \sqrt{\text{MSD}} = \sqrt{404} = 20.10$$

---

[3] If the time series has an increasing trend, it is possible that a value of α slightly greater than 1.0 will provide the forecast with the smallest mean square deviation. Minitab has an optimization feature which selects the value of α that provides the smallest mean square deviation. In this example the optimal α is greater than 1.0.

TABLE 17.2   Comparison of Consumption Forecasts

Time Period	Observed	Trend	Trend/Exponential Smoothing	Trend/Autoregression
1992:3	3429.95	3507.65	3432.41	3437.35
1992:4	3482.98	3531.98	3456.74	3465.96
1993:1	3484.35	3556.30	3481.06	3494.31
1993:2	3513.79	3580.63	3505.39	3522.43
1993:3		3604.95	3529.71	3541.52
1993:4		3629.27	3554.03	3565.84
1994:1		3653.60	3578.36	3590.16
1994:2		3677.92	3602.68	3614.48

EXHIBIT 17.1   Autoregressive Forecast of Consumption Model Residuals

Regression Analysis

The regression equation is
gc87res = - 2.00 + 0.919 gc87resl

49 cases used 1 cases contain missing values

```
Predictor        Coef        Stdev     t-ratio         p
Constant       -1.996        2.871       -0.70     0.490
gc87resl      0.91864      0.05651       16.26     0.000

s = 20.10      R-sq = 84.9%     R-sq(adj) = 84.6%
```

Analysis of Variance

```
SOURCE         DF           SS          MS          F          p
Regression      1       106707      106707     264.23     0.000
Error          47        18981         404
Total          48       125688
```

The regression equation to forecast residuals was

$$\hat{e}_t = -2.00 + 0.919\hat{e}_{t-1}$$

Residuals were forecast for each observation in the series and then added to the trend analysis following the same procedure as that described above for the trend and exponential smoothing forecast. The autoregressive forecast provided essentially the same results as the exponential smoothing forecast. Therefore, the final forecast was prepared using a combination of a linear trend and exponential smoothing. The results of the combined forecast are presented in Table 17.2.   □

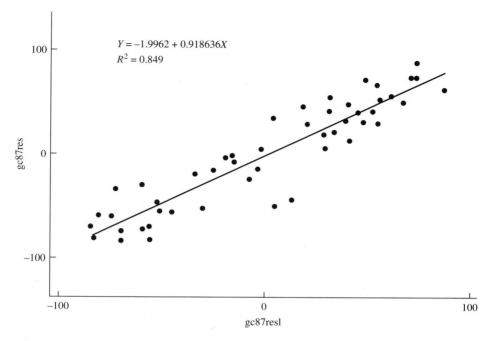

Figure 17.14   AR(1) Forecast of Consumption Trend Residuals

17.7.1 Forecast Model Testing

In the discussion above we developed a time-series model for consumption using data from the first quarter of 1981 through the second quarter of 1992. This model was shown to provide a very close fit to the historical data used for its development (1981:1–1992:2). However, a forecast model must be able to predict or forecast for time periods that are beyond the historical data used to develop the model (Key Idea 17.15).

Table 17.2 presents the forecasts using the trend, the trend plus exponential smoothing, and the trend plus autoregressive model forecasts for the time period 1992:3–1994:2. In addition, the series observed for the first four periods is presented to provide a comparison between the observed and forecast series.

Table 17.3, which contains the deviations (observed minus forecast) between the observed and forecast series, is presented to compare and evaluate the three forecasts. The mean deviation (MD) for each series was computed using

$$\text{MD} = \frac{\sum_{i=1}^{4} \hat{e}_t}{4}$$

and the root mean square error (RMSE) was computed using

$$\text{RMSE} = \frac{\sum_{i=1}^{4} \hat{e}_t^2}{4}$$

Key Idea 17.15: Forecast Model Testing

When a model is developed, the most recent data are left out of the model development and estimation phase. The forecasting model is applied to this fresh data to determine how well the model fits beyond the range of the data used to develop the model. A model can almost always be developed that will fit the historical data quite closely. However, as we have indicated previously, the ultimate test of a time-series forecasting model is: How close is the forecast to the actual data?

TABLE 17.3   Deviations (Observed − Forecast) from Consumption Forecasts

Time Period	Trend	Trend/Experimental Smoothing	Trend/Autoregression
1992:3	−77.70	−2.46	−7.40
1992:4	−49.00	26.24	17.02
1993:1	−71.95	3.29	−9.96
1993:2	−66.84	8.40	−8.64
MD	−66.37	8.87	−2.25
RMSE	67.23	13.93	11.38

These measures are shown for each of the three forecasts. The trend model has the worst performance based on the mean deviation and the root mean square error. The combined trend/autoregressive (AR) model has the smallest mean deviation because, in part, its deviations are both positive and negative. The AR model also has the smallest root mean square error. Thus, based on these two measures, the AR model appears to provide the best forecast of these periods. However, examination of the individual deviations indicates that the trend/exponential smoothing model has the smallest deviations in three of four quarters. Thus the smaller measures for the AR model result from a much better forecast for the 1992:4 period.

For this example the models that combine the forecast of both a structural and an irregular component provide the best forecasts. However, it is difficult to choose between the models based on their test forecast of four time periods. The selection is complicated further because the trend/exponential smoothing model had a slightly smaller RMSE over the model development period.

Does It Make Sense?

Based on the comparisons of the two structural and irregular component forecasting models, we find that both models provided a good forecast. I would choose the exponential smoothing model over the trend/autoregressive model because three out of four of its test forecasts were closer. This example has shown the procedures used to develop and test time-series forecasting models. Note in particular that a number of different model forms were attempted and tested for goodness of fit during the model development phase. Residuals analysis and graphical analysis were very important.   □

Example 17.3   Forecast Federal Funds Interest Rate

Arnold Smith, president of Amalgamated Banks, is interested in forecasting the federal funds interest rate. In particular, he has asked Susan Edwards to develop a model that can provide regular forecasts that would be used for planning loan and savings instruments for the bank.

Solution   After some discussion they decide that a forecast of quarterly interest rates would be appropriate. Initial model development will use data from the time period 1981:1–1993:2.

Figure 17.15 presents a plot of quarterly interest rates from 1981:1 to 1993:2. This plot indicates a sharp drop in the early 1980s followed by another drop in the early 1990s. The first step was to fit a quadratic trend model to the series as shown in Figure 17.16. The trend model is

$$Y_t = 14.88 - 0.373t + 0.00355t^2$$

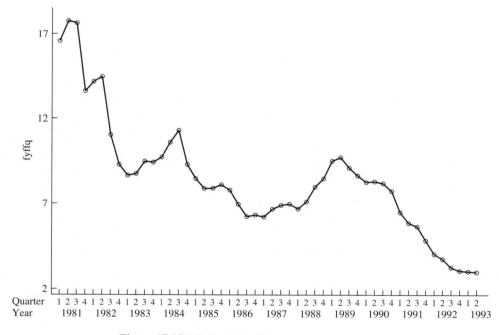

Figure 17.15   Federal Funds Rates: 1981:1–1993:2

This model follows the pattern of the series as shown in the graph. In addition, the trend would begin to increase at a future point. This structural trend model

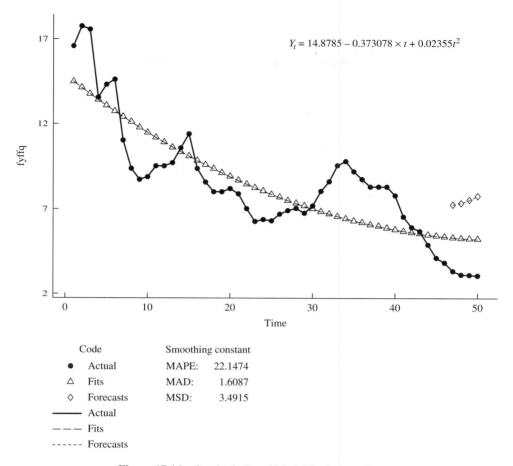

Figure 17.16   Quadratic Trend Model for Interest Rates

provides a good fit for the time period used. However, there is no guarantee that the structural trend will continue for a long period into the future. Thus at some point it might become necessary to use a different structural model. Some early time-series forecasts attempted to use structural trend models to forecast far—10 to 15 periods—into the future. In some cases these forecasts resulted in major errors because the series did not maintain its historic trend. Structural models can be very useful in forecasting. However, caution and experience are needed to ensure that the model is not used to replace reality. Time-series forecasting involves extrapolation of model predictions beyond the range of the data used for their development. Extrapolation of models is risky business and should only be undertaken by experienced analysts who use a variety of different information sources.

The residuals from the quadratic trend model were used to develop an exponential smoothing residuals forecasting model. This model uses an optimal value of

α, which is equal to 1.462. The plot of residuals and the model forecasts are shown in Figure 17.17. The combined trend and exponential smoothing model reduced the MSD from 3.4915 (trend model) to 0.860 (combined model). Note also how closely this combined model follows the actual series. Turning points in the actual and forecast series are very close to each other. This combined quadratic trend and exponential smoothing model provides a close fit to the existing series and appears to be a useful forecasting model.   □

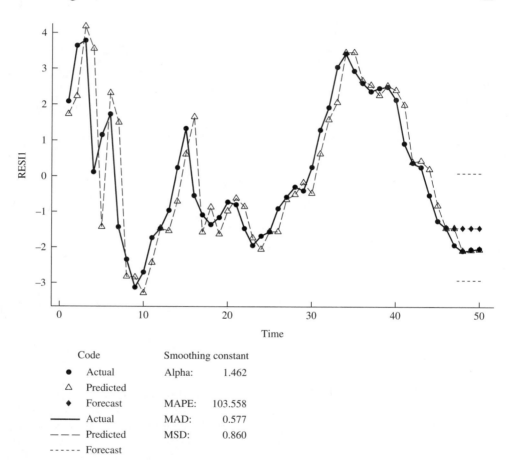

Code		Smoothing constant	
●	Actual	Alpha:	1.462
△	Predicted		
◆	Forecast	MAPE:	103.558
——	Actual	MAD:	0.577
– – –	Predicted	MSD:	0.860
- - - -	Forecast		

Figure 17.17   Residuals from Quadratic Trend Model

17.7.2 Exponential Smoothing Forecast

The forecasting model could also be developed by applying exponential smoothing to the original series. Figure 17.18 presents the observed and predicted values using an optimal exponential smoothing forecast with $\alpha = 1.514$. The MSD for this model

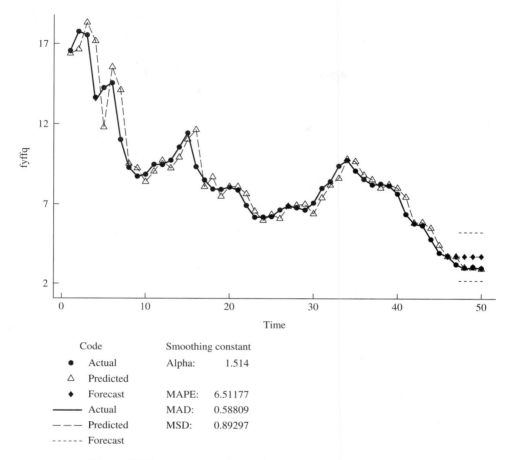

Figure 17.18   Exponential Smoothing Forecast: Federal Funds Rate

is 0.893, which compares favorably to the MSD of 0.860 for the combined structural trend and exponential smoothing model. In addition, examination of the plot of observed and predicted values indicates a good fit that follows the turning points of the original series. In this case the structure of the series is not considered and the forecast is developed by finding a parameter, α, that results in a good forecast. Thus efforts are focused on using the historical pattern to forecast future values in the series.

17.7.3 Summary

The choice of a forecasting method should be based on an understanding of the underlying system that generates the data, combined with an understanding of forecasting procedures. If the series contains a structural component, such as a trend or seasonal effect, that effect should be removed by an appropriate model. After that has occurred the deviations from the structure can be fitted using a procedure such as exponential smoothing or autoregression. Another popular approach for removing structural components is to obtain differences between observations in the series. A forecasting model for the differences is developed and the resulting forecast differences are used to construct the final forecast. In other cases, forecasts are obtained by direct application of a forecasting model.

There is an extensive set of rigorous literature that presents considerable theory and numerous application procedures. However, applied forecasting involves considerable art and experience. Certainly one should try several different models and determine which provides the best forecast. The choice of the best model should be based on the time-series model statistics, such as the mean square deviation (MSD) and the mean deviation (MD), which result from the model fitted to the historical series. In addition, comparison of graphs of observed and fitted points for the historical period is also useful. The final step is to forecast values for points not included in the development of the model. These points are then compared with actual observed points to determine how well the model forecasts new data points in the series.

In this chapter we presented an introduction to time series. With this background you can prepare some basic forecasting models using the wide range of available statistical software. In addition, you can discuss forecasting strategies with more experienced forecasters. However, there is much more to learn, and persons interested in time-series forecasting should pursue additional courses to provide a broader perspective and to develop a larger set of tools.

SUMMARY OF KEY IDEAS

PRACTICE PROBLEM SOLUTION

17.1   The price index for year 5 is

$$I_2 = \frac{(8)1.40 + (2)2.80 + (10)2.40 + (4)1.50 + (1)3.00 + (1)3.00}{(8)1.00 + (2)2.00 + (10)2.00 + (4)1.00 + (1)2.00 + (1)2.00} \times 100$$
$$= 132.0$$

CHAPTER PROBLEMS

17.1   The new director of economic planning in a small developing country, Abdal Fahri, has asked for your assistance in establishing a database for economic analysis. Your first assignment is to develop a consumer price index to be used for adjusting data for analysis and for guiding economic assistance programs. You discover that in 1985, consumers purchased 10 million tons of food, 5 million tons of clothing, 50,000 new houses, and 500,000 bus tickets. From 1985 to 1990, prices for food increased from 110 to 260 per ton, clothing from 250 to 340 per ton, houses from 10,000 to 14,500 per house, and bus tickets from 0.12 to 0.13 per ticket.
(a) Compute a simple price index.
(b) Develop a Lespeyres price index.
(c) Per capita income increased by 25% in nominal currency units between 1985 and 1990. Is the economic situation improving for the average citizen?

17.2   During 1990 a typical student at a major university made the following nonacademic purchases: 26 pizzas, 250 drinks, 14 CDs, one pair of shoes, one pair of pants, 10 shirts, and four pairs of earrings. The prices in 1990 were pizzas $5.00, drinks $0.50, CDs $7.00, shoes $45, pants $22, shirts $15, and earrings $4.50. In 1993 the prices were pizzas $5.60, drinks $0.55, CDs $6.00, shoes $47, pants $22, shirts $16, and earrings $4.20. Student wages were increased from $4.75 per hour in 1990 to $5.25 in 1993.
(a) Compute the weighted student consumer price index for 1993 using 1990 as the base year.
(b) Were students better off in terms of purchasing power in 1993 or in 1990?

17.3   An analysis of major national income accounts for a small country indicated that from 1990 to 1993, consumer prices increased by 13%, housing prices increased by 10%, plant and equipment prices increased by 8%, inventory prices increased by 12%, and government spending per unit of output increased by 7%. In 1990 consumption was 50% of economic activity, housing was 8%, inventory was 6%, plant and equipment was 16%, and government spending was 20%. Nominal GDP increased by 15% from 1990 to 1993.
(a) Compute a Lespeyres GDP implicit price deflator.
(b) Is the country better off in 1993 than it was in 1990?

17.4   A medium-sized Asian country found that from 1988 to 1992 the consumer price index increased by 15%, the investment index increased by 17%, and its government spending index increased by 9%. In 1988 consumption was 50% of GDP, government spending was 20% of GDP, and investment was 30% of GDP. During the same period nominal GDP increased by 25%.

(a) Compute the weighted GDP implicit price deflator.

(b) Compute the percent economic growth in real terms from 1988 to 1992.

17.5   Annual steel production in millions of tons for a 10-year period was

| 98 | 97 | 101 | 99 | 104 | 106 | 107 | 109 | 110 | 114 |

Construct a steel production index.

17.6   Microcomputer production in thousands of units was

| 0.2 | 0.8 | 2 | 6 | 15 | 20 | 23 | 24 | 27 | 31 |

Construct a microcomputer production index.

17.7   Table 17.1 contains the consumer price index and nominal consumption for a 10-year period.

(a) Convert nominal consumption to real consumption in 1981 units.

(b) Develop a new consumer price index with 1986 as the base year.

(c) Convert nominal consumption to real consumption using the 1986 base consumer price index.

17.8   Write a one-paragraph discussion about the philosophy of forecasting, including basic assumptions, choice of data, and evaluation of the forecast model.

17.9   Write a one-paragraph discussion concerning the role of history in developing time-series forecasting models.

17.10 Show that an exponential smoothing forecast,

$$\hat{Y}_t = \alpha Y_{t-1} + (1 - \alpha)\hat{Y}_{t-1}$$

is a weighted average of the observed value of the last period and a function of the entire past history of the series.

17.11 Discuss the difference in forecasting assumptions between an autoregressive model and an econometric multiple regression model such as that developed using the procedures in Chapters 15 and 16.

17.12 Apply an autoregressive model to develop the next observation in the series

| 10 | 12 | 15 | 13 | 12 | 14 | 15 | 16 |

first using $\alpha = 0.3$ and then using $\alpha = 0.8$.

In several of the following exercises you will use the data file named "Macrel95," which is on your data disk. The variables are described and named in Appendix B at the end of the book. The quarterly data cover the period from 1946 through the second quarter of 1995. You will need to select certain periods using your statistical computer system.

17.13 Smith Brothers Builders constructs residential housing in the southeast region of the United States. They have asked you to prepare a forecast of the demand for housing and mortgage interest rates in their business region for 1977. As part of previous work, you have developed a multiple regression model for forecasting housing starts in the southeastern United States. This model uses a forecast for national residential investment. Because Smith Brothers is a large company, they obtain mortgage financing nationally. From previous work you know that the interest rates that they will pay will be based on the prime interest rate. As you begin your work you will prepare time-series plots for U.S. residential investment ("GIR87") and for the prime interest rate ("Fyprq") for the period 1960–1976.

(a) Examine the plots and describe in words the pattern observed for each series.

(b) Can you identify any structural components? What are they?

(c) Based on your observations of the series, what would be your 1977 forecast?

17.14 Smith Brothers Builders constructs residential housing in the southeast region of the United States. They have asked you to prepare a forecast of the demand for housing and mortgage interest rates in their business region for 1993. As part of previous work, you have developed a multiple regression model for forecasting housing starts in the southeastern United States. This model uses a forecast for national residential investment. Because Smith Brothers is a large company, they obtain mortgage financing nationally. From previous work you know that the interest rates that they will pay will be based on the prime interest rate. As you begin your work you will prepare a time-series plot for U.S. residential investment ("GIR87") and for the prime interest rate ("Fyprq") for the period 1977–1992.

(a) Examine the plot and describe in words the pattern observed for each series.

(b) Can you identify any structural components? What are they?

(c) Based on your observations of the series, what would be your 1993 forecast?

17.15 The International Trade Division of the U.S. Department of Commerce has been asked to study U.S. trade patterns and determine if new treaties and/or policies are needed to ensure balanced trade. As part of this large study you have been asked to forecast imports and exports for 1977. To begin your forecast you will prepare a time-series plot for U.S. exports ("Gex87") and for U.S. imports ("Gim87") for the period 1960–1976.

(a) Examine the plot and describe in words the pattern observed for each series.

(b) Can you identify any structural components? What are they?

(c) Based on your observations of the series, what would be your 1977 forecast?

17.16 The International Trade Division of the U.S. Department of Commerce has been asked to study U.S. trade patterns and determine if new treaties and/or policies are needed to ensure balanced trade. As part of this large study you have been asked to forecast imports and exports for 1993. To begin your forecast you will prepare a time-series plot for U.S. exports ("Gex87") and for U.S. imports ("Gim87") for the period 1977–1992.

(a) Examine the plot and describe in words the pattern observed for each series.

(b) Can you identify any structural components? What are they?

(c) Based on your observations of the series, what would be your 1993 forecast?

17.17 A national retail chain is seeking to determine the size of its store expansion budget for the next three years. The company's budget is a function of the expected future growth of retail spending for their product groups. A complex model has been developed to predict retail spending. This model is a function of total national disposable personal income and the money supply, M1. You have been asked to prepare a forecast model for these two series. As a first step you will prepare a time-series plot for the money supply, M1 ("Fm1q87"), and disposable personal income ("Gyd87") for the period 1960–1976.

(a) Examine the plot and describe in words the pattern observed for each series.

(b) Can you identify any structural components? What are they?

(c) Based on your observations of the series, what would be your 1977 forecast?

17.18 A national retail chain is seeking to determine the size of its store expansion budget for the next three years. The company's budget is a function of the expected future growth of retail spending for their product groups. A complex model has been developed to predict retail spending. This model is a function of total national disposable personal income and the money supply, M1. You have been asked to prepare a forecast model for these two series. As a first step you will prepare a time-series plot for the money supply, M1 ("Fm1q87"), and disposable personal income ("Gyd87") for the period 1977–1992.

(a) Examine the plot and describe in words the pattern observed for each series.

(b) Can you identify any structural components? What are they?

(c) Based on your observations of the series, what would be your 1993 forecast?

17.19 Consolidated Office Furniture was evaluating the option to build two new factories to produce modular office components. These components were used in many new office buildings, and thus they believe that the construction of new office buildings is an important predictor of future sales. They have asked you to prepare a time-series model for forecasting office construction. The data file "Mondat2" contains a monthly series for office building construction put in place in millions of dollars ("Conno"). These data cover the years 1987–1993. The data file is on your data disk and is described in Appendix B at the end of the book.

(a) Plot the series and discuss the pattern. Does the series appear to have a trend, cyclical, or quadratic pattern?

(b) Fit a combined trend, cyclical, or quadratic model and compute the root mean square error (RMSE).

(c) Plot the residuals and develop an exponential smoothing model to predict the residuals.

(d) Combine the two models and compute the RMSE for the overall model.

17.20 Refer to Problem 17.19, in which a components forecasting model was prepared. In this problem you will use the same data and prepare an exponential smoothing model and an autoregressive model directly with the original data. The data file is "Mondat2" and the series to be forecast is "Conno." The data file is on your data disk and is described in Appendix B at the end of the book.

(a) Develop an exponential smoothing model and compute its RMSE.

(b) Develop an autoregressive model and compute its RMSE.

(c) Compare these two models using the RMSE and plots of the observed and predicted values. Recommend one of the two models and indicate the reasons for your recommendation.

17.21 Consolidated Building Materials, Inc. is a national supplier of building materials used primarily in industrial and commercial construction. They have asked you to develop a time-series forecasting model for industrial building construction. For this task you will use the quarterly data contained in the data file "Constr," which is on your data disk and described in Appendix B at the end of the book. This data covers the period from 1972 through the second quarter of 1993.

(a) Plot the data and discuss the pattern of the series.

(b) Fit a trend and cyclical components model to the data using the 20 years of data from 1972 through 1991. Compute the RMSE and prepare a plot of observed and predicted values.

(c) Use the model to prepare a forecast for 1992 and the first two quarters of 1993. Compute the RMSE for the forecast period.

(d) Compare the RMSE for the period used to estimate the model with the RMSE for the forecast period. Discuss your reasons for any differences.

17.22 Consolidated Office Furniture has asked you to prepare another forecast model for office construction using quarterly data. The data are contained in the data file "Constr," which is on your data disk and described in Appendix B at the end of the book. The data cover the period from 1972 through the second quarter of 1993. The variable "Connoq" contains the amount of office buildings put in place in millions of dollars.

(a) Plot the data and discuss the pattern of the series.

(b) Fit a trend, cyclical, and exponential smoothing model to the data using the 20 years of data from 1972 through 1991. Compute the RMSE and prepare a plot of observed and predicted values.

17.23 Acme Motor, a large national manufacturer of automobiles, has asked you to prepare a forecasting model for domestic cars, using quarterly data. For this model you will use the data file "Auto," which is contained on your data disk and described in Appendix B at the end of the book. The variable "Rcardq" is the millions of cars sold in the quarter, expressed in annual figures.

(a) Plot the data and discuss the pattern of the series.

(b) Fit an exponential smoothing model to the data using the 20 years of data from 1972 through 1991. Compute the RMSE and prepare a plot of observed and predicted values.

17.24 Acme Motors from Problem 17.23 now asks you to prepare a forecasting model for foreign cars, using quarterly data. These data are contained in the file "Auto," which is on your data disk and described in Appendix B at the end of the book. Imported car sales are in the variable "Rcarfq." The data are measured in millions of units sold expressed in annual terms.

(a) Plot the data and discuss the pattern of the series.

(b) Fit an autoregressive model to the data using the 20 years of data from 1972 through 1991. Compute the RMSE and prepare a plot of observed and predicted values.

APPENDIX: FORECAST EUROPEAN DEPOSIT INTEREST RATES

In this appendix, an example forecast that uses a cyclical structure estimate is presented. The variable to be forecast is "European Deposit Interest Rates in London." The original series contained monthly data that we converted to quarterly data by obtaining the average for each quarter. Interest rates are more difficult to forecast than consumption. Observed interest rates result from a complex combination of economic, market, and policy variables, and therefore the time-series patterns tend to lack stability.

Model development followed the procedure used above. A subset of the time-series data set was used for model development, with the remainder used for model testing. The available data cover the period from the first quarter of 1973 through the second quarter of 1988. The model was developed using data from the first quarter of 1973 through the second quarter of 1986. Model testing used data from the third quarter of 1986 through the second quarter of 1988. Exhibit 17.2 presents a plot of the entire time series. From the plot we see that there is no apparent trend but there is a cyclical pattern. The cycle period appears to be variable. After examining the data we decided to use a period of 28 quarters, or seven years. One might argue that there could be an "economic cycle" that had an influence on European interest rates.

EXHIBIT 17.2   Time Series: European Interest Rate

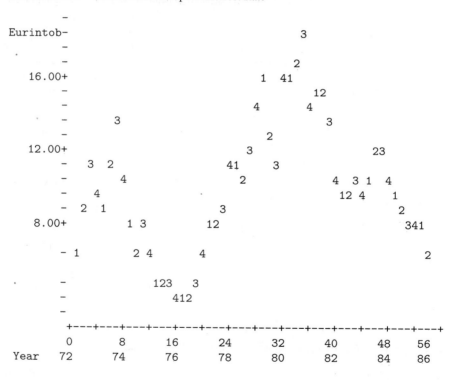

The forecasting model for the cyclical component was estimated using least squares with the following result:

$$\hat{Y}_t = 10.3 + 2.18 \sin\frac{2\pi t}{28} + 1.28 \cos\frac{2\pi t}{28}$$

The amplitude of the cyclical model was

$$a = \sqrt{\beta_1^2 + \beta_2^2}$$
$$= \sqrt{(2.18)^2 + (1.28)^2}$$
$$= 2.53$$

and the displacement was

$$d = \arctan \frac{\beta_1}{\beta_2}$$
$$= \arctan \frac{2.18}{1.28}$$
$$= \arctan 1.704$$
$$= 1.04$$

The RMSE was equal to 2.64. Exhibit 17.3 compares the observed and predicted values using the cyclical forecasting model. The forecast follows a smooth cyclical

EXHIBIT 17.3   Interest Rate Observed and Predicted: Cyclical Model

```
          -
Eurinto2-                                           3
          -
          -                                       2
  16.00+                                     1    41
          -                                              12
          -                                4         4
          -         3                                        3
          -   ZZZZZZ                              +ZZZZZ
  12.00+ Z          ZZ                       3 Z      ZZ           23
          -   3   2    Z                   41 ZZ   3       Z
          -        4   ZZ                       +        Z+  3 1   4      Z
          -    4          Z                  ZZ              +2 4    1   ZZ
          -  2   1          ZZ      Z+                        ZZ         +Z
   8.00+           1 3       ZZZZZ+2                          ZZZZZZ 341
          - 1            2 4        4                                    2
          -            123    3
          -            412
          -
          +---+---+---+---+---+---+---+---+---+---+---+---+---+---+
          0       8      16      24      32      40      48      56
  Year   72      74      76      78      80      82      84      86
          Z = cycpred   (Predicted Value)
```

function, but the observed values have some large deviations, especially in the later periods. This pattern suggests that a forecasting model for the irregular components could improve the forecast considerably.

The irregular component model used exponential smoothing. A number of different values for α were tried. Comparing the options, we chose a value of $\alpha = 0.6$ for the final model. By combining the cyclical and exponential smoothing forecasts, we obtained a final model with RMSE equal to 1.60, which is a considerable improvement over the 2.64 obtained for the cyclical model alone. Exhibit 17.4 compares observed and predicted values over the entire period through the second quarter of 1988. As seen, the final model provides a close approximation to the data observed. The forecasts for the test period appear to predict the observed values quite well.

EXHIBIT 17.4   Interest Rate Observed and Predicted: Cyclical and Exponential Smoothing Model

```
         -
Eurintob                                      3       Model        |
Test
         -                                            Development |
Period
         -                                   2 Z      Period       |
  16.00+                                 1Z 41 Z                    |
         -                                   Z   +2                 |
         -                               4Z Z Z   4 ZZ              |
         -          3                             3                 |
         -                                 2 Z       Z             |
  12.00+          Z                    Z+Z                  23Z     |
         -      3  2                  4+     3              Z Z     |
         -      Z  Z4Z                  2             4Z 3 1  4 Z   |
         -       4ZZ                    Z            1+ +ZZ  1 ZZ |
         -     2Z 1      Z               +              Z     2 ZZ
   8.00+  Z        1 3             1+                       341 Z   4Z
         - +          2Z+Z        4Z                        2ZZ++Z1+
         -             123    3Z                                3 1
         -            ZZ+++Z                                     4
         -
         -
         +---+---+---+---+---+---+---+---+---+---+---+---+---+---+---+---+
         0       8      16      24      32      40      48      56     64
        72      74      76      78      80      82      84      86     88
        Z = C12     (Predicted Value)
```

The final analysis deals with the values forecast and observed during the test period. Exhibit 17.5 presents a graphical plot for the comparison. Note that the vertical scale shows a finer precision, and thus we are magnifying the test period to emphasize

EXHIBIT 17.5   Interest Rate Observed and Predicted Test Period

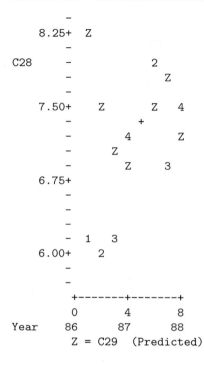

```
           –
   8.25+   Z
           –
C28        –                    2
           –                      Z
           –
   7.50+   Z          Z    4
           –             +
           –         4        Z
           –       Z
           –       Z     3
   6.75+
           –
           –
           –
           –   1   3
   6.00+       2
           –
           –
           +-------+-------+
           0       4       8
Year      86      87      88
          Z = C29   (Predicted)
```

the pattern of differences. As can be seen, the forecasts are close to the observed values and tend to pick up the turning points. The RMSE is 1.02, which is actually smaller than the 1.60 observed during the model development period. As a result of this analysis, we have gained some confidence in the capability of our model to provide good forecasts.

18

Quality

It is not necessary to do any of these things . . . survival is not compulsory.

W. Edwards Deming

18.1 PERSPECTIVES ON QUALITY

Since the early to mid-1980s, quality control has become an extremely important function for all business managers. More recently, quality has become a major concern of such organizations as educational institutions, health care facilities, government agencies, the legal environment, the entertainment industry, and service-oriented industries, such as hotel management and transportation. The application of quality control methods requires a clear understanding of statistical concepts and procedures. For example, in our visits to many factories, managers have told us that they wish that they knew and understood statistics better, as they are the ones who teach statistical techniques to the workers. In fact, a vigorous education of all employees in basic statistical quality control techniques is common in many organizations striving to compete in the global economy.

In this chapter we develop the basic principles of quality assurance and study the related statistical techniques. First we discuss methods used to analyze processes and bring them into control. These efforts are devoted to reducing variability by eliminating the effects of controllable factors. As a result, the process variation is minimal and cannot be reduced by additional cost-effective actions. Next, the use of control charts to monitor processes is discussed. Control charts are designed to detect the occurrence of controllable factors that increase product variability and result in defective products. These factors need to be eliminated as soon as detected.

Many definitions have been given for the term *quality*. The customer's perceptions are expressed in the following definition by Gitlow:[1] "Quality is a judgment by

---

[1] Howard Gitlow et al., *Tools and Methods for the Improvement of Quality*, Boston, Irwin, 1989.

customers or users of a product or service; it is the extent to which the customers or users believe the product or service surpasses their needs and expectations." For example, a person who purchases a new computer has certain expectations; a tourist arrives at a major attraction (say DisneyWorld) and has certain expectations; a student has certain expectations in his or her statistics class. Each will somehow measure the "quality" of the computer, the vacation, or the classroom by some set of standards and determine whether or not it is considered to be a quality product or service.

Quality is also seen by the manufacturer or service provider in terms of a continuous effort at improvement. Suppliers of raw goods must also be considered in the chain for never-ending improvement. Together, suppliers, designers, manufacturers, and customers all contribute to the concept of a quality product or service.

The United States was a world industrial leader following World War II through the 1960s, but a lack of commitment to quality issues during this period was a key factor contributing to the decline of the United States in global markets in the 1970s. Quality control became a central component of the subsequent economic rebound in the late 1980s and into the 1990s.

Quality control was at the heart of Japan's rise to world economic leadership. During the 1950s and 1960s customers would choose American products over Japanese products because Japanese products were of much lower quality and everyone knew it. However, in the 1970s and early 1980s Americans purchased Japanese cars and other products because their quality was much better than those produced in the United States. Many blamed the American worker and claimed that they were lazy or lacked pride in their work. More careful analysis has shown that the problem resulted mainly from a failure of management to apply modern quality and production improvement methods.

Beginning in the mid-1980s a major change occurred in U.S. business. Management emphasis on quality and the expansion of business courses dealing with quality is clear evidence of the change. Success of Ford Motor Company's Taurus, General Motor's Saturn, and Chrysler's Minivan are clear evidence of the effect of these management changes.

These are only a few examples that demonstrate how quality control has fundamentally affected modern business. Many of the quality control procedures, especially control charts and process analysis, developed for manufacturing have application in the service sector of the economy. In all cases these businesses have customers and these customers demand high-quality goods and services. Quality control is also rapidly spreading to government and nonprofit agencies that are sensitive to customer desires. The reduction of errors in documents such as customer invoices can decrease losses from charges that are too low and from excessive processing time. Insurance companies are improving the accuracy of claims and customer billing. Delivery companies and airlines monitor on-time arrival of packages and planes. Fast-food restaurants monitor the quality and preparation times for their various meal products.

18.2 QUALITY ASSURANCE PHILOSOPHY

The work of a statistician, W. Edwards Deming, immediately after World War II was important for Japan's quality program and later for the renewed emphasis on quality in the United States[2] (Key Idea 18.1).

Key Idea 18.1: Quality Control Concepts

Two of Deming's important concepts are:

1. Quality results from a careful study of the entire production process and direct action by management to correct all of the small problems that contribute to defects.
2. Data need to be collected regularly and analyzed by appropriate statistical procedures to ensure that the process has a stable operation with minimum variance. Whenever deviations from standard are identified, they need to be corrected immediately.

The work of W. Edwards Deming and many others has led to an important change in the philosophy of quality control. Traditional quality control practice emphasized inspection of final product units—either all units or a random sample. By this inspection defective units would be identified, removed, and either repaired or scrapped.

Some organizations used acceptance sampling to either accept or reject a shipment of output units based on a random sample from the shipment. For example, a batch would be accepted if it had less than 10% defective units. This traditional practice was very expensive and led to poor-quality products in the marketplace. Acceptance sampling requires a choice between producer's versus purchaser's risk (see Section 11.8) and has large Type II errors. Thus a company would either scrap and/or repair a large percentage of batches that met the standard or would ship a large number of batches that did not meet the standard. This occurred even though proper sampling and statistical procedures were used to accept or reject a batch.

Deming was critical of this approach, as he indicated in an interview with Mary Walton.[3] Deming said: "Inspection with the aim of finding the bad ones and throwing them out is too late, ineffective, and costly. In the first place, you can't find the bad ones, not all of them. Second it costs too much. Quality comes not from inspection but

---

[2] W. E. Deming, *Out of Crisis*, MIT Press, Cambridge, MA, 1986.

[3] Mary Walton, *The Deming Management Method*, The Putnam Publishing Group, New York, 1986.

from improvement of the process." Other problems occur when attempts are made to ensure quality by final-stage inspection.

1. The repair or destruction of a finished part implies that the labor and other resources used to produce the unit are partially or totally lost. This resulted in a very large hidden expense.

2. Another more subtle problem occurred in large production processes. Quality was the responsibility of the inspectors at the end, and thus no one worried about sloppy work or defects built in at various stages of the process. Quality was not the responsibility of everyone.

The modern philosophy "preached" by Deming and others argued that quality was the responsibility of everyone in the organization and that management had to organize the process to ensure uniform high quality. Deming suggested that the traditional method that emphasized the *detection* of errors should be replaced by the new philosophy of *prevention* of errors. This led to Deming's famous 14 points for quality organizations.[4]

18.2.1 Deming's 14 Points

1. Constancy of purpose.   Create constancy of purpose for continual improvement of products and service, allocating resources to provide for long-range needs rather than only short-term profitability, with a plan to become competitive, to stay in business, and to provide jobs.

2. The new philosophy.   Adopt the new philosophy. We are in a new economic age, created in Japan. We can no longer live with commonly accepted levels of delays, mistakes, defective materials, and defective workmanship. Transformation of Western management style is necessary to halt the continued decline of industry.

3. Cease dependence on mass inspection.   Eliminate the need for mass inspection as a way to achieve quality by building quality into the product in the first place. Require statistical evidence of built-in quality in both manufacturing and purchasing functions. Again quoting from Deming: "Even inspection at various stages of production rather than at the very end is not the answer. No one likes to do rework. All too often, the pile of defects grows until, in desperation, the parts are used as is."

4. End lowest-tender contracts.   End the practice of awarding business solely on the basis of price tag. Instead, require meaningful measures of quality along with price. Reduce the number of suppliers for the same item by eliminating those that do not qualify with statistical evidence of quality. Move toward a single supplier for any one item, on a long-term relationship of loyalty and trust. The aim is to minimize total costs, not merely initial cost. Purchasing managers have a new job, and must learn it. Again from Deming: "Purchasing should be a team effort, and one of the most

---

[4] Ibid.

important people on the team should be the chosen supplier—if you have a choice—picked on the basis of his record of improvement and of his efforts to learn and to follow the Fourteen Points."

5. Improve every process.   Improve constantly and forever every process for planning, production, and service. Search continually for problems in order to improve every activity in the company, to improve quality and productivity, and thus to decrease costs constantly. It is management's job to work on the system continually (design, incoming materials, maintenance, improvement of machines, supervision, training, retraining).

6. Institute training on the job.   Institute modern methods of training on the job for all, including management, to make better use of every employee. New skills are required to keep up with changes in materials, methods, product design, machinery, techniques, and service.

7. Institute leadership.   Adopt and institute leadership aimed at helping people to do a better job. The responsibility of managers and supervisors must be changed from sheer numbers to quality. Improvement of quality will improve productivity automatically. Management must ensure that immediate action is taken on reports of inherited defects, maintenance requirements, poor tools, fuzzy operational definitions, and other conditions detrimental to quality.

8. Drive out fear.   Encourage effective two-way communication and other means to drive out fear throughout the organization so that everybody may work effectively and more productively for the company.

9. Break down barriers.   Break down barriers between departments and staff areas. People in different areas, such as research, design, sales, administration, and production, must work in teams to tackle problems that may be encountered with products or service.

10. Eliminate exhortations.   Eliminate the use of slogans, posters, and exhortations for the workforce, demanding zero defects and new levels of productivity, without providing methods. Such exhortations only create adversarial relationships; the bulk of the causes of low quality and low productivity belong to the system and thus lie beyond the power of the workforce.

11. Eliminate arbitrary numerical targets.   Eliminate work standards that prescribe quotas for the workforce and numerical goals for people in management. Substitute aid and helpful leadership to achieve continual improvement of quality and productivity.

12. Permit pride of workmanship.   Remove the barriers that rob hourly workers, and people in management, of their right of pride of workmanship. This implies, *inter alia*, abolition of the annual merit rating (appraisal of performance) and of management by objective. Again, the responsibility of managers, supervisors, and foremen must be changed from sheer numbers to quality. Again from Deming: " . . . communication. I said, Tell me about it. His machine had gone out of order and would make only defective items. He had reported it, but the maintenance men could not come for a long time. Meanwhile, he was trying to repair it himself. The foreman came along and said to run it. In other words he told me to make defective items. 'Where is my pride of workmanship?' he asked me. 'If the foreman would give me as much respect as he does the machine I'd be better off.' He didn't want to get paid for making defective items. . . . "

13. Encourage education.   Institute a vigorous program of education, and encourage self-improvement for everyone. What an organization needs is not just good people; it needs people who are improving with education. Advances in competitive position will have their roots in knowledge. From Deming: "How do you help people to improve? What do you mean by improve? If you ask me, I would say that I find a general fear of education. People are afraid to take a course. It might not be the right one. My advice is take it. Find the right one later. And how do you know it is the wrong one? Study, learn, improve. . . . Who knows what is practical?"

14. Define top management commitment and action.   Clearly define top management's permanent commitment to ever-improving quality and productivity and their obligation to implement all of these principles. Create a structure in top management that will push every day on the preceding 13 points, and take action to accomplish the transformation. Support is not enough; action is required.

Implementation of this modern philosophy requires exhaustive and detailed work at every step of the production process. In this chapter we present some tools for studying processes and identifying potential sources of problems. Processes are monitored at intermediate points to identify problems when they occur and not after considerable work has gone into a unit and many defective units have been produced. We will see how control charts, which are used extensively, are prepared and used.

Management combines with workers to minimize process variability by removing sources of variability that can be identified and controlled. Finally, there is a continuing effort to reduce the number of defects and improve process quality. Customers are asked their impressions of product quality. Managers talk routinely to customers and workers and examine finished products for even minor defects. The result has been substantial quality improvements for companies practicing these modern procedures. For the others we again quote Deming: "Survival is not mandatory."

18.3 PROCESS ANALYSIS

In the early chapters of this book we laid the foundation on which to build quality concepts. For example, in Chapter 1 we defined both a process and a system (Key Idea 1.4), and repeat them here for review and emphasis (see Key Idea 18.2).

Key Idea 18.2: System and Process

A **system** is a number of components that are logically and sometimes physically linked together for some purpose.

A **process** is a set of activities operating on a system that transforms inputs to outputs.

In Chapter 1 we presented examples of systems. For instance, your computer is a system consisting of a chip that performs simple tasks, other chips that store information, a keyboard, a screen, a disk storage drive, possibly a printer, and/or connections to the world. Another example was an automobile assembly line with machine and human components linked together.

Examples of processes included entering numbers and/or instructions into your statistical computer program. A number of steps transform data from a raw list into output such as a graph or regression analysis. Similarly, steel, plastic, paint, energy, and human efforts are part of the inputs to an automobile assembly line; automobiles are the outputs.

Quality begins with a complete analysis of the system and process used to produce the good or service. The objective is to identify all of the factors that contribute to the production of the final product and hence contribute to product quality. Problems that result in product defects must be identified and corrected. In this phase, management must set high standards and encourage everyone to work toward a stable process with minimum defects. The result is a system and process that is in control.

It is important to understand that variation that exists in all processes is the result of either common causes or assignable causes (Key Idea 18.3).

Key Idea 18.3: Causes of Process Variation

Common causes (also called *random* or *uncontrollable causes*) of variation are those causes that are random in occurrence and are inherent in all processes. Management, not the workers, are responsible for these causes.

Assignable causes (also called *special causes*) of variation are the result of external sources outside the system. These causes can and must be detected, and corrective action must be taken to remove them from the process. Failing to do so will increase variation and lower quality.

Examples of common causes include minor variations in raw materials, random human error, or unpleasant working conditions (too hot or too cold). Examples of assignable causes are operator errors or machine setting errors. A process is said to be stable, or in control, if all assignable causes have been detected and removed from the process, so that only common causes remain.

The quality of the product produced in a factory is improved by detailed lines analysis and small corrections of the system and process contained in the factory. Improved customer service by a package delivery company such as Federal Express requires detailed analysis of every unit that handles each package in the delivery process. Most improvements result from many small changes and not some major problem correction. If there were only a few major problems, they would have been solved long ago. Instead, the tools presented in this chapter will be used extensively to help improve specific subprocesses and thus improve the entire process.

A number of techniques have been developed for organizing and assisting this initial analysis. Among the most popular are process flow diagrams, Pareto charts, and cause-and-effect diagrams. These will be introduced in the following sections. There are other techniques which may be equally useful.

18.3.1 Process Flow Diagrams

The process flow diagram is described in Key Idea 18.4. Process analysis is used to help understand the process, eliminate potential problems, and identify locations to monitor the process.

Key Idea 18.4: Process Flow Diagrams

Process analysis is often greatly assisted by using **process flow diagrams** (see Figure 18.1). This diagram indicates the system components and the flow of product units through various activities that transform inputs to final products. Analysis of process flow helps the analyst prepare a comprehensive list of important factors. These graphs also indicate listening places in the process where intermediate measurements can be made to determine if the process is operating properly.

The analysis begins by preparing a set of sequential activities or operations that are required to prepare a good or service. For example, the production of a ready-to-eat flake breakfast cereal requires the following activities:

1. Mix the required ingredients, such as flour, sugar, water, vitamin supplements, and so on.
2. Cook the mixture.

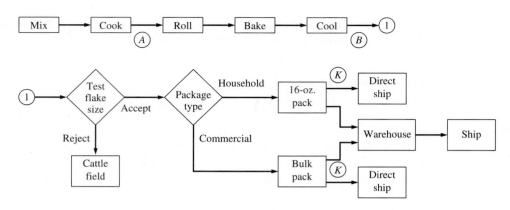

Figure 18.1   Process Flow for Cereal Production

3. Roll the mixture into uniform flakes.

4. Bake the flakes until crisp and resistant to breakage.

5. Cool the flakes.

6. Place the flakes in packages and cartons for shipment.

7. Deliver packages to distributors and/or retail outlets.

The objective is to place a high-quality product in the retail outlets. To achieve this objective, each step of the process must have a stable operation that produces output which meets specification standards with minimum variance.

Process analysis to obtain a diagram like Figure 18.1 should be conducted by an interdisciplinary team with each member familiar with the operation of the production process.[5] This team will include the production line manager, a production engineer, a quality control representative, a product design specialist, and possibly representatives from marketing and finance. In this analysis the process is separated into logical modules or stages.

Regular measurements after each stage provide immediate identification and correction of problems at that stage. In that way defects are eliminated before additional labor and materials are added. Measurements of product quality might be performed at points A and B prior to the measurement of the final product at point K. The analysts define the range of measurements at points A and B that will be consistent with a high-quality final product at point K. This approach provides the opportunity to identify and correct problems before they result in a defective final product. This approach is defined as the *prevention approach*. In contrast, older quality control procedures measured only the final product and either accepted or rejected the final product. That approach, called the *detection approach*, can provide feedback to improve the process at various intermediate stages. However, the correction occurs only

---

[5] The diagram for an actual cereal process would be more detailed and extensive. By using more detail it would be possible to identify additional places for potential process improvement.

after a number of defective parts have been produced. Thus modern managers prefer to use the prevention approach, but there are situations where intermediate measures are not possible or are very expensive.

18.3.2 Pareto Charts

In Chapter 2 we introduced another quality technique known as the Pareto chart (Figure 18.2), a graph used to describe qualitative data. We summarize the Pareto concepts in Key Idea 18.5.

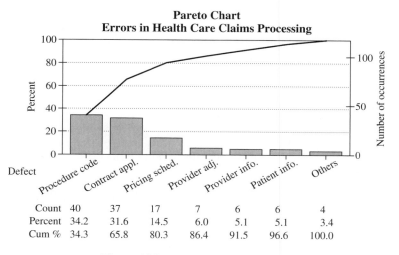

	Procedure code	Contract appl.	Pricing sched.	Provider adj.	Provider info.	Patient info.	Others
Count	40	37	17	7	6	6	4
Percent	34.2	31.6	14.5	6.0	5.1	5.1	3.4
Cum %	34.3	65.8	80.3	86.4	91.5	96.6	100.0

Figure 18.2   Example Pareto Chart

Key Idea 18.5: Pareto Chart

The **Pareto chart** is a bar chart that displays the frequency of defect causes. The bar at the left indicates the most frequent cause and bars to its right indicate causes in decreasing frequency. Using Pareto charts, the analyst can quickly identify the factors that are most often involved in process failure.

We saw that Pareto analysis, named for an Italian economist, Vilfredo Pareto (1848–1923), is used to search for significant causes of problems, separating the vital few from the trivial many. Pareto recognized that in most cases a small number of factors are responsible for most problems. Pareto's result applies to a wide variety of behavior over many systems; it is sometimes referred to as the 80–20 rule—80%

of the problems result from 20% of the causes. Quality control managers seek first to identify the major causes of problems and attempt to correct them quickly at minimum cost. The use of a Pareto chart can also improve communication with employees, management, and within production teams.

A cumulative frequency line graph is often sketched above the various bars in the Pareto chart. The increase in this cumulative frequency line clearly indicates the relative improvement that would result from correcting each of the most frequent problems. In most cases the vertical axis on the Pareto chart indicates the frequency or percentage of problems that resulted from this cause. However, the vertical axis could also be scaled in terms of total costs incurred because of problems associated with each factor. By examining the Pareto chart, the analyst can quickly determine which causes should receive most of the problem correction effort.

In Chapter 2 we used a Pareto chart to study the errors in health care claims processing. Figure 18.2 is the Pareto chart that we found to assist the insurance company to quickly determine which factors should receive most of the attention in problem correction. You are encouraged to review this application in Example 2.2.

18.3.3 Cause-and-Effect Diagrams

One of the easiest but most effective quality tools is the cause-and-effect, or Fishbone, diagram (Key Idea 18.6). The first step in the development of a quality assurance process is the removal of all problems (assignable causes) that can result in a process that is out of control. The cause-and-effect diagrams are a useful tool to identify problems.

Key Idea 18.6: Cause-and-Effect Diagram or Fishbone Diagram

Cause-and-effect diagrams are used to help identify factors that could cause quality control problems and to organize the identification and correction of problems.

The central spine of the diagram is directed toward the problem being analyzed. Major possible causes are shown on arrows directed to the main spine. Quality control teams often brainstorm a problem and then categorize the major possible causes into one of several areas such as personnel, method, materials, machines, measurements, and environment.

Next, subcauses related to each of the major problems are attached to the major cause arrows. The appearance of the final diagram provides the basis for the popular term "Fishbone" diagram.

A cause-and-effect diagram is often referred to as an Ishikawa diagram in honor of its developer, Kaoru Ishikawa, the driving force behind Japan's QC circle movement. Ishikawa authored several books and was involved in efforts to promote quality in Japan. In 1994 the American Society for Quality Control (ASQC) established an Ishikawa Medal, an annual award to be given to a "nominee or team of nominees who has demonstrated the most outstanding leadership in improving the human aspects of quality."[6]

A typical cause-and-effect diagram is shown in Figure 18.3 and in Figure 18.4 there is a cause-and-effect diagram for the health care claims processing example from Chapter 2. The Fishbone diagram, prepared by the people who know and understand the process, was used to help identify the factors that might be a cause of error.

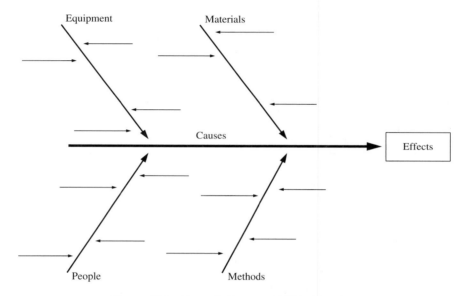

Figure 18.3   Example Cause and Effect Diagram

Does It Make Sense?

Process flow diagrams, Pareto charts, and cause-and-effect diagrams are useful tools for helping to identify all factors that could affect quality. Most improvements in quality result from many small corrections. Thus careful study with attention to detail is critical. These efforts need to be organized and comprehensive. The graphical tools used by people who understand the process provide a way of organizing the quality control effort and ensuring that it is comprehensive. Management must include everyone, especially production workers, and ensure that their efforts are used efficiently and contribute to the goal of quality improvement.   □

---

[6] "Medal to honor leadership in 'soft' quality," *On Q*, Vol. VIII, October, 1993, p. 1.

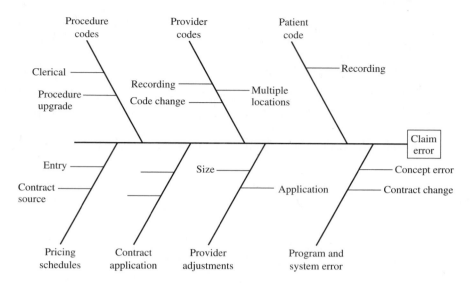

Figure 18.4   Cause and Effect Diagram for Insurance Claims

18.4 CONTROL CHARTS

The theory and application of control charts were developed by Walter A. Shewart in the 1920s and 1930s.[7] Shewart's classic work emphasized two kinds of mistakes:

1. One could treat a complaint, defect, or accident as if it came from an assignable or controllable cause when in fact it was part of the common or uncontrollable variation in the system operating under control.

2. One could treat a complaint or accident as if it resulted from a common or uncontrollable process variation when it actually was due to an assignable or controllable cause.

He argued correctly that it is very important to differentiate between these possibilities. If the process is constantly changed in response to uncontrollable variation, the process variance will increase, resulting in greater instability and more process defects. In contrast, failure to detect and correct a controllable cause will lead to a steady production of defective products. This is the classic problem in hypothesis testing of controlling both Type I and Type II errors. Using the hypothesis-testing procedure, we assume that the process is in control unless there is strong evidence to reject that assumption. Thus identifying a controllable cause when in fact the defect resulted from uncontrollable process variation would be a Type I error. Similarly, failure to detect a controllable cause when it occurred would be a Type II error.

---

[7] Walter A. Shewart, *Economic Quality of Manufactured Product*, reproduced ed., American Society for Quality Control, Milwaukee, WI, 1980

Quality control procedures typically seek a small probability of Type I error—that is, identifying a controllable cause for a defect when the defect resulted from uncontrollable system variation. The standard device used is a control chart, as shown in Figure 18.5. This control chart is an acceptance interval, as discussed in Chapter 10. However, in this case the acceptance or control interval is used in graphical form over a time scale (Key Idea 18.7).

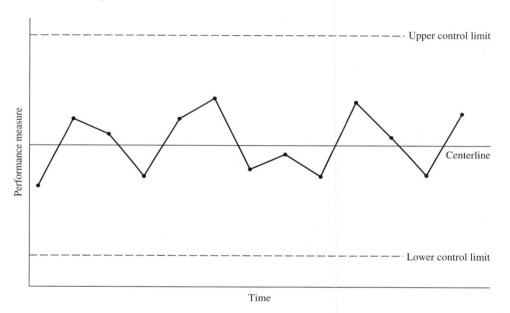

Figure 18.5   Statistical Control Chart

Key Idea 18.7: Stable, or In-Control Process

A process is stable or in control if all assignable causes are removed; thus the variation results only from common causes.

After a process is in control, control charts can be developed and installed. The mean, variance, and standard deviation of the process are established from historical data and other available information, such as manufacturer's specifications for the machines used in the process. Using the mean, μ, and standard deviation, σ, an acceptance or control limit of ± 3 standard deviations is established:

$$\mu \pm 3\sigma$$

From the normal probability distribution we know that the probability of a number outside this interval when the mean is μ is less than 0.01. The *lower control limit* is the mean μ minus 3 standard deviations, while the *upper control limit* is the mean μ plus 3 standard deviations.

A quality control analyst wishes to have both the mean and the variation of a process under control. From each sample both the sample mean $\bar{X}$ and sample range R are computed. Control charts are prepared for both the mean—$\bar{X}$ chart—and the range—R chart. Both charts are examined together routinely to determine if the process is in control (Key Idea 18.8).

Key Idea 18.8: Control Charts

Control charts are graphs that indicate the upper and lower control limits for random samples of process measures over time. The limits are typically computed using the standard $\mu \pm 3\sigma$ interval. Thus they indicate the interval of variation for a process whose variation is due only to uncontrollable factors. The following control charts are used most frequently:

1. The $\bar{X}$ **chart** is a plot of random sample means used to monitor the process central tendency.
2. The R or **range chart** is a plot of the sample ranges for the random samples taken at regular intervals used to monitor process variability.
3. The p and np **charts** are used to plot the fraction and number of items with a particular defect.

After a process has been brought into control with all controllable sources of error removed, control charts can be prepared. The process mean and variance are computed from controlled process operation and used to establish the control limits. Samples are obtained regularly and used to monitor the process for any assignable or controllable factors that might be contributing to error.

One indication that a process is *out of control* (an assignable cause is present) is a sample measure outside the control limits. When a sample measure is outside the control limits, the process needs to be examined to identify and to remove the assignable cause of variation. There are several other indications or rules to determine the stability of a process. The analysis of these control chart patterns is beyond the scope of this book.

Control charts are used to monitor processes to determine if the process is in control or is experiencing a problem. Charts are prepared by selecting samples at frequent intervals. A quality performance characteristic (e.g., size, length of service time, number of defects) is measured for each unit observed. For each sample, statistics such as the mean, range, proportion defective, or number of defects are plotted on a control chart such as Figure 18.5. Quality product requires that each of the process steps are operating in control. If the process is operating in control, sample measurements such as means and ranges will occur between the boundaries of the control range, which are included on each chart. If sample means are outside the boundaries, there is strong evidence that a controllable factor is causing the increased number of errors or defects. In that case the process should be examined and the problem corrected. Using the language of hypothesis testing, a control chart is a continuous acceptance interval based on the probability distribution of the sample mean or the sample range.

Quality control analysts have usually favored small sample sizes ($n = 3$ to 5) taken at shorter intervals instead of larger samples obtained at longer intervals. This strategy makes it possible quickly to detect instability resulting from assignable causes. The wide control intervals minimize the likelihood of detecting a problem when it does not exist. However, when conditions change and a problem results, rapid detection and correction is very important so that the number of defective units is minimized. Samples should also be taken from subgroups that are logically different, to maximize the chances of detecting changes or differences that could result in problems. For example, samples from different shifts, different production lines, or from production runs that use materials from different suppliers should be obtained whenever possible. There is always a need to allocate the resources available for sampling to minimize product defects. These strategies are a good starting point. Careful analysis of the local situation must be used to obtain the best results.

Now you might ask the obvious question. Why choose such a wide control interval when we are trying to identify and correct defects in the process? The answer is based on the modern quality control practice discussed above. A process is first brought into control by removing all controllable factors that contribute to defects. However, if a controllable cause of defects is introduced, the number of defects would increase and the process would be out of control. Implicit in the $\mu \pm 3\sigma$ control limits is the strong assumption that the process continues to be in control. Thus a point outside the control limits provides very strong evidence that a controllable cause of defects has been introduced. Deming and others would also argue that standard operating conditions are established by management and are the responsibility of management. Included in regular operation might be poorly trained workers, poor-quality raw materials, or poorly maintained equipment. Deming emphasized that these negative process characteristics result from management failure. Establishing a process in control requires procedures for training workers, obtaining high-quality raw materials, and preventive maintenance.

Failure to correct such problems is a management failure which results in a process that is not in control. If a process is not in control, control charts will not properly detect controllable causes because they will be confused with process instability.

Management failure contributes to a high variance and hence wide control intervals. If the control intervals are too wide, management must modify the process by improving management leadership and/or investing in new equipment or training. In this way a new and improved state of process control is established. Control charts to identify controllable causes that need correction should be established only after all cost-effective management improvements have been made.

18.4.1 Process Capability

The ultimate objective of any manufacturing or service process is to produce products that exceed customer expectations. Product design engineers define product specifications or tolerances which ensure that the performance is obtained. These specifications include an interval within which important dimensions must occur. Upper and lower specification limits define the interval for all units in order to meet customer expectations. *Specification limits* are established outside the process, in contrast to *control limits*, which are based on the uncontrollable variation in the process. The pistons in modern high-performance engines must have diameters within a very small range if the engine is to operate properly. A particular piston might have specification limits of 8 centimeters $\pm$ 2 millimeters. A delivery service guarantees delivery within 24 hours. In this case the specification focuses on the upper limit.

Specification limits and control limits are combined to determine process capability (Key Idea 18.9). A process is *capable* if its control limits for a single unit, $\mu \pm 3\sigma$, are included within the specification or tolerance limits. Figure 18.6 is a control chart for a process that is capable of producing high-quality parts. The interval for a single unit, $\mu \pm 3\sigma$, is included within the specification limits. Less than 1% of the units produced would be outside this limit. Since the specification limits are even wider, the process is capable of producing high-quality parts. In contrast, Figure 18.7 is a control chart for a process that is not capable because the $\mu \pm 3\sigma$ interval includes the upper and lower specification limits.

Key Idea 18.9: Process Capability Index

A **process capability index** (PCI) is computed for many processes:

$$PCI = \frac{USL - LSL}{6\sigma}$$

where USL is the upper specification limit, LSL is the lower specification limit, and σ is the process standard deviation from uncontrollable factors.

If PCI > 1, the process is capable of producing the product with the required precision, but if PCI < 1, the process is not capable. If the process is not capable, it must be rebuilt or the specification limits widened. It would be expensive and foolish to continue operations.

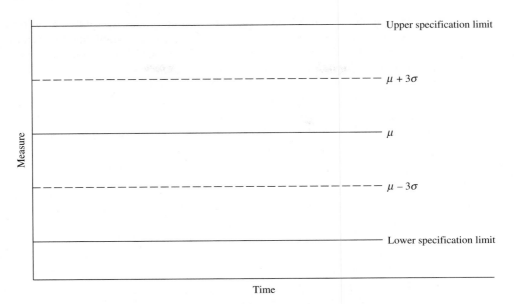

Figure 18.6   Control Chart for a Capable Process

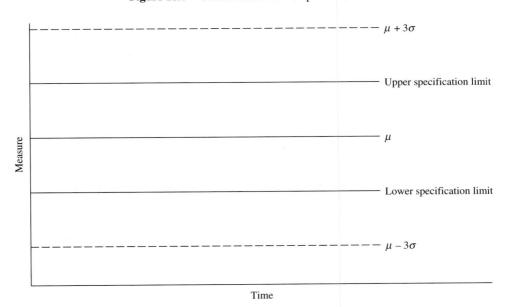

Figure 18.7   Control Chart for a Noncapable Process

One of the benefits of specification limits is that they prevent the product and/or process engineers from sticking workers with a job that they cannot consistently do well. If the process is not deemed capable, the engineers have three options: (1) loosen the specification, (2) redesign the process, or (3) redesign the product.

Quality control procedures must produce products that satisfy customer needs. For example, suppose that a component machine part must have dimension of 2.5 inches $\pm$ 0.00001 inch or the machine will not operate properly. Thus the specification limits are

$$2.5 \pm 0.00001$$

In this case the lower specification limit is $2.5 - 0.00001$ and the upper specification limit is $2.5 + 0.00001$. Previously, we discussed control limits, $\mu \pm 3\sigma$, which could be computed for a process in control. There is no guarantee that the control limits will be contained within the required specification limits. If the control limits, which are based on the manufacturing process capability, are wider than the specification limits, which are based on the requirements of the product user, the manufacturing process will be prone to produce defective parts.

This problem can only be solved by management efforts to improve the manufacturing process, thus reducing the process variance and establishing narrower control limits. Failure to solve this problem is clearly a management failure, included in Deming's 85% of defects that are the responsibility of management.

Problem Exercises

18.1 Explain the difference between assignable and common causes of defects.

18.2 What is implied when a manager says that a process is in control?

18.3 The diameter of a front axle shaft has a mean of 10 centimeters and a variance of 0.01. What are the control limits for the sample mean when the sample size is $n = 4$?

18.4 Speedy Package Delivery, Inc. has found that the mean time to deliver a package in the city is 6 hours with a variance of 0.25. To monitor the quality of its service, a random sample of size $n = 5$ deliveries is obtained each day and the mean delivery time is computed. Compute the control limits and sketch the control chart.

18.5 Explain the difference between specification limits and control limits.

18.6 The engineering designer has indicated that the diameter of the front axle shaft must be in the interval 10 centimeters $\pm$ 0.2 centimeter. Based on an initial pilot test run, the axle shafts produced have a mean of 10 centimers and a variance of 0.01. Is this manufacturing process capable?

18.7 Speedy Package Delivery, Inc. promises to deliver every package in the city within 7 hours. Analysis of their delivery times indicates a mean delivery time of 6 hours with a variance of 0.25. Is the delivery process capable of meeting the promise?

18.5 CONTROL CHARTS FOR MEAN AND RANGE

The mean ($\bar{X}$) and range (R) control charts are described in Key Idea 18.10.

Key Idea 18.10: $\bar{X}$ and R Control Charts

The most used control charts are the $\bar{X}$ and R charts. The $\bar{X}$ chart shows the plot of sample means and is used to determine if the central tendency is being influenced by assignable or controllable causes. Similarly, the R or range chart is used to determine if the process variability is being influenced by assignable or controllable causes. A process is in control if both its mean and its variability are stable or in control.

Example 18.1   Quality Pistons for Allied Motors

The engine components department of Allied Motors, Inc. wants to maintain high-quality engines, thus requiring that the pistons produced have closely monitored dimensions. The specification limits require that the piston diameter be in the range 3.5 inches $\pm$ 0.035 inch.

Solution   The process for manufacturing the pistons was analyzed carefully and brought into control with a mean of 3.5 inches and a standard deviation of 0.01 inch. The process capability index is

$$\text{PCI} = \frac{\text{USL} - \text{LSL}}{6\sigma}$$
$$= \frac{3.535 - 2.465}{6 \times 0.01}$$
$$= 1.2$$

The PCI is greater than 1, and therefore the process is capable of producing pistons that meet the required specification limits.

To monitor the process a random sample of five pistons is obtained each day, and the mean and range are plotted as shown in Figure 18.8. Routine examination of these $\bar{X}$ and R charts will provide a signal if the process is out of control.

After each sample is obtained, the sample mean ($\bar{X}$) and range (R) are computed using the standard equations

$$\bar{X} = \frac{\sum_{i=1}^{n} x_i}{n}$$
$$R = x_{\max} - x_{\min}$$

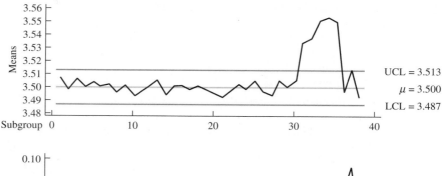

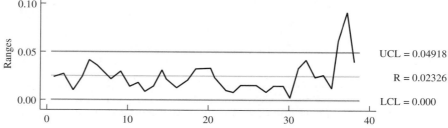

Figure 18.8 $\bar{X}$ and R Charts for Allied Engine Pistons

The resulting $\bar{X}$ and R for each day are plotted in Figure 18.8. For the $\bar{X}$ chart, the mean μ equal to 3.5 is shown as a horizontal line across the graphs. In addition, horizontal lines are drawn at ± 3 standard deviations: (3.0SL = 3.513) and (-3.0SL = 3.487). Computation of these limits uses the standard deviation of the sample mean with $n = 5$ and $\sigma = 0.01$:

$$\sigma_{\bar{X}} = \frac{\sigma_X}{\sqrt{n}} = \frac{0.01}{\sqrt{5}} = 0.0045$$

Using this standard deviation, the upper control limit (UCL) is computed as

$$UCL = \mu + 3.0 \times \sigma_{\bar{X}}$$
$$= 3.5 + 3.0 \times 0.0045$$
$$= 3.513$$

Similarly, the lower control limit (LCL) is computed as

$$LCL = \mu - 3.0 \times \sigma_{\bar{X}}$$
$$= 3.5 - 3.0 \times 0.0045$$
$$= 3.487$$

The upper and lower statistical control limits define an acceptance interval that covers 3σ above and below the mean μ. Figure 18.8 also includes the R chart for the piston manufacturing process. The range from each sample is plotted as shown. In addition, horizontal lines are drawn for the mean range and the upper and lower control limits. Computation of the mean and standard deviation of the range requires statistical theory beyond the scope of this book. Therefore, quality control analysts typically make use of the factors $d_2(n)$ and $d_3(n)$, which are given in Table A.11 for various sample sizes. These factors are defined as:

1. $d_2(n)$: expected value or mean of the range for n normally distributed random sample observations with the standard deviation equal to 1. The expected value of the range $\bar{R}$ when the population standard deviation is σ is $\bar{R} = d_2(n) \times \sigma$.

2. $d_3(n)$: standard deviation of the range for n normally distributed random sample observations with standard deviation equal to 1. The standard deviation of the range σ_R when the population standard deviation is σ is $\sigma_R = d_3(n) \times \sigma$.

For our example the mean range is

$$\bar{R} = d_2(n) \times \sigma$$
$$= 2.326 \times 0.01$$
$$= 0.02326$$

where the value of $d_2(n)$ for $n = 5$ was obtained from Table A.11. A horizontal line was drawn for this mean in Figure 18.8.

The standard deviation of the range is

$$\sigma_R = d_3(n) \times \sigma$$
$$= 0.864 \times 0.01$$
$$= 0.00864$$

where the value of $d_3(n)$ for $n = 5$ was obtained from Table A.11. Using the standard deviation of the range σ_R, the upper and lower control limits for the range were computed:

$$\text{UCL} = \bar{R} + 3.0 \times \sigma_R$$
$$= 0.02326 + 3.0 \times 0.00864$$
$$= 0.04918$$
$$\text{LCL} = \bar{R} - 3.0 \times \sigma_R$$
$$= 0.02326 - 3.0 \times 0.00864$$
$$= 0.00000$$

(Note that the lower control limit for the range cannot logically be less than 0.000.)

Control limits can also be computed using the population range and appropriate tabulated factors, which are based on statistical theory. A description of that procedure can be found in quality control manuals and production management books.[8]

By examining the $\bar{X}$ control chart and the R control chart in Figure 18.8, the analyst can determine if the process is in control—that is, the observed variation results from common uncontrollable causes that are expected when the process is operating under control. The production operation appears to be operating properly for days 1 through 30. Both the sample mean and sample range are within the control limits.

---

[8] N. Gaither, *Production and Operations Management*, 5th ed., Dryden Press, Fort Worth, TX, 1992.

However, beginning with day 31 the sample mean begins to increase dramatically and jumps above the upper control limit. These high values continue for several more days. Since the probability of being outside the control limits is less than 0.01, there is clear evidence that the manufacturing process is no longer in control. Extreme deviations are probably the result of an assignable cause.

An out-of-control process can also be identified by various patterns of sample means near the upper or lower limits. The use of pattern analysis is a more sophisticated and complex procedure for identifying an out-of-control process and is not described in this book. However, the rule presented here is very useful.

Examining the R control chart in Figure 18.8, the analyst can see that the range is in control until day 35. On day 36 a range outside the control limit occurred, followed by a large value on day 37 and another range outside the control limits on day 38. From the $\bar{X}$ chart the sample means appear to have greater variability beginning with day 36, which is also an indication that the variability is out of control. A sample range outside the control limits shows that the process is operating erratically and producing pieces that are both too large and too small.

Given these problem signals, the production operation should be stopped and the assignable and controllable causes identified and corrected. The large sample mean beginning on day 31 indicates that the process is producing too many parts whose diameters are larger than required. Then beginning on day 36, the range is out of control because of increased variability in the process. The large variability is identified by both sample ranges beyond the control limits in the R chart (Figure 18.8) and sample means with greater variability in the $\bar{X}$ chart. A large variability also causes the sample mean to be unstable. This is, of course, what we would expect from our knowledge of random variables. We emphasize that process monitoring requires simultaneous examination of the $\bar{X}$ and R charts.   □

Problem Exercises

18.8   What is the difference between an $\bar{X}$ chart and an R chart?

18.9   Explain why one should stop a process and attempt to identify and correct the problem whenever a sample mean or range is outside the control limits.

18.10   The diameter of a front axle shaft has a mean of 10 centimeters and a variance of 0.015. What are the $\bar{X}$ and the R control limits for the sample mean when the sample size is $n = 5$? Sketch the control charts.

18.11   Speedy Package Delivery, Inc. has found that the mean time to deliver a package in the city is 6.5 hours with a variance of 0.35. To monitor the quality of its service, a random sample of size $n = 4$ deliveries is obtained each day and the mean delivery time is computed. Compute the $\bar{X}$ and R control limits and sketch the control charts.

18.12   Oat Cereals, Inc. has asked you to prepare $\bar{X}$ and R charts for its new cereal packing process. The mean weight of packages is to be 15 ounces with a variance of 0.09. Marketing has indicated that all packages packed should weigh between 14 and 16 ounces.
(a) Is the process capable?
(b) Compute the control limits, $n = 5$, and sketch the control charts.

18.6 CONTROL CHARTS FOR PROPORTIONS

Another measure of performance for a process is the proportion of output that does not satisfy a standard. In this case a random sample of n products is obtained and tested to determine if they meet the standard. The proportion that do not are plotted on a p control chart and compared against control limits established for the process after it is in control (Key Idea 18.11).

Key Idea 18.11: Proportion p Control Charts

The control limits for p charts are usually established by assuming that the proportions have a distribution that is approximately normal when the process is in control. Thus the mean for the normal distribution is the population proportion p when the process is in control. The standard deviation for the sample proportion using a random sample of size n is

$$\sigma_{\hat{p}} = \sqrt{\frac{p(1-p)}{n}}$$

The control limits are usually set at $\pm 3\sigma_{\hat{p}}$ to ensure that the process is interrupted only when there is strong evidence that the process is not in control.

In some cases it is not convenient or possible to obtain the same sample size each day. With computer-generated control charts different control intervals can be computed for each different sample size. Alternatively, some analysts prefer to compute an average or typical sample size, which is then used to compute a uniform control interval.

Example 18.2   Health Care Claims Processing

A large health insurance company has recently installed a new, sophisticated claims processing system. The payment of health insurance claims is complex because of the many procedure and diagnosis codes and policy limitations, which are defined in terms of authorized procedures and health care providers. The previous computer processing system could process 40% of the claims successfully without special analysis by an experienced claims processor. The new system was designed to process 80% of the claims without human intervention. Thus it is expected that 20% of the claims will require some human intervention if the process is in control. If there are an excessive number of claims for human processing, claims processing costs will increase and payments will be delayed. The process is to be studied and the claims processing system modified.

Solution   Each day a random sample of 200 claims is selected and their disposition checked. The sample proportion of the claims assigned for human processing is plotted daily as shown in Figure 18.9. For this sample the standard deviation of the sample proportion is

$$\sigma_{\hat{p}} = \sqrt{\frac{p(1-p)}{n}}$$

$$= \sqrt{\frac{0.20(1-0.20)}{200}}$$

$$= 0.028$$

The control limits are thus equal to

$$P \pm 3.0 \times \sigma_{\hat{p}}$$

$$0.20 \pm 3.0 \times 0.0283$$

$$0.20 \pm 0.0849$$

$$\text{LCL} = 0.1151$$

$$\text{UCL} = 0.2849$$

From Figure 18.9 the process appears to be in control through day 30. However, following day 30 the proportion of human processing claims appears to be increasing. Upon investigating, the process analysts discovered that on day 31 new medical procedure and diagnosis codes were introduced that were not coded into the claims processing system. Thus any claim with the new codes was automatically sent for human processing. Note that in this example the sample proportion did not exceed the control limits until day 33. The $\pm 3\sigma$ control limits do have a greater chance of not detecting a change compared to a procedure that used narrower limits.   □

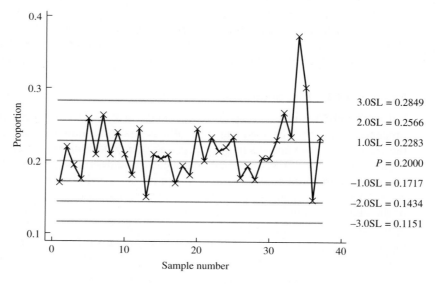

Figure 18.9   Proportion of Claims with Special Conditions

Problem Exercises

18.13 The U.S. Department of Transportation has ruled that states must control speed on expressways so that the overall proportion of cars exceeding the speed limit does not exceed 15%. To monitor this ruling, a random sample of 250 cars is checked to determine if they are exceeding the speed limit. Prepare a control chart for these samples and indicate the upper control limit.

18.14 The Pluto Motor Company monitors the quality of customer service by randomly calling 300 service customers each week and asking them to rate the service. Their target goal is to obtain at least 60% who rate the service excellent (e.g., the customer would be willing to tell their friends that the service is great). Prepare a control chart to monitor these weekly data.

18.7 *C* CHARTS

In some quality problems the analyst is concerned with the total number of defects in a unit of production. Examples include the number of surface blemishes in a roll of steel, the number of packages delivered late each day from a specific office of a national delivery service, the number of customer complaints at a large department store each day, the number of warranty complaints filed for each car sold at a particular dealership, and the number of errors in customer invoices. *C* charts are developed for this type of analysis (Key Idea 18.12).

The first step in constructing a *C* chart is to choose the inspection unit for each sample. For example, the total number of late deliveries might be recorded each day. In this case the sampling unit is the entire daily activity for the particular office. In another case the sampling unit could be a random sample of 10 customer invoices obtained each day and for which the number of errors are identified and counted. The sampling unit could also be a large roll of cloth or a computer network. These error counts would be plotted daily on a control chart and examined to ensure that the number of errors indicated a process that was in control.

Example 18.3   Microprocessor Chips for Dishwashers

Consolidated Electronics produces microprocessor chips for a major manufacturer of dishwashers. These chips control the washing cycles. An added feature is that the microprocessors also use information collected from sensors to make real-time adjustments of the washing cycle that improve the appearance of the dishes. The state of control of the process is to be determined.

Solution   Each chip produced passes through an electronic test to check its performance reliability. This test ensures that only error-free chips are shipped and provides a check on the process. If an excessive number of defective chips are produced, the process is stopped, analyzed, and the problem corrected. The number of defective chips is counted each day and plotted on the control chart (Figure 18.10). After the process was established and adjusted to remove sources of defects, quality control analysts found that a mean of five defective chips per day would be produced.

Key Idea 18.12: C Control Charts

Control charts for C, the number of defects, are developed using the Poisson probability distribution presented in Chapter 7. The number of errors for the sampling unit follows a Poisson distribution if there are a large number of independent events that could lead to an error and the probability of an error is stable and small for each event. The Poisson distribution has a single parameter μ for the sampling unit, which is both the mean and variance of the distribution. This parameter can be estimated using data collected from stable in-control operation of the process:

$$\hat{\mu} = \bar{C} = \frac{\sum_{i=1}^{n} c_i}{n}$$

where c_i is the number of defects for observation i, where $i = 1, \ldots, n$. Then the variance can be estimated using

$$\hat{\sigma}_C^2 = \bar{C}$$

Using these results, upper and lower control limits are computed using a normal approximation for the Poisson distribution:

$$\text{UCL} = \bar{C} + 3 \times \sqrt{\bar{C}}$$
$$\text{LCL} = \bar{C} - 3 \times \sqrt{\bar{C}}$$

After additional work it was concluded that this mean could not be reduced further without substantially increasing production costs. Thus a mean of five defects per day represented the process in control.

Figure 18.10 is a C control chart for microprocessor production. The process is assumed to be operating under control, with the mean number of defective chips per day being 5. The upper control limit is

$$\text{UCL} = 5 + 3\sqrt{5} = 11.71$$

and the lower control limit,

$$\text{LCL} = 5 - 3\sqrt{5} = -1.71 = 0$$

The lower limit of the chart cannot be less than zero, and thus the control interval above the mean is wider.

By examining the control chart we see that during the first 30 days the process appears to be operating properly with the number of defects within the control region. However, beginning with day 31 the number of defects increased greatly. There was strong evidence that the process was no longer in control.

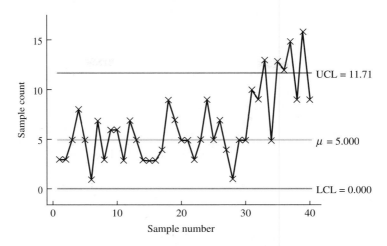

Figure 18.10   Frequency of Microprocessor Failures

As a result of the signal that the process was out of control, an investigation was conducted to identify the cause. After carefully inspecting every step in the process, they found the problem. Three filters located behind an etching machine were found to be damaged. These damaged filters allowed small dust particles to enter the room, and they occasionally attached to a chip, creating a defect. The filters were replaced. In addition, the preventive maintenance procedures were modified to include more frequent inspection of all filters. After removing the special cause, the process returned to its previous state of control.   □

Problem Exercises

18.15 Marvelous Computers, Inc. sells 10,000 microcomputers each month through its national dealer network. Their design goal is that an average of no more than eight computers will have a major defect in the first 30 days of operation. Defective computers are reported directly by customers using a free national hot-line number. Prepare a control chart to monitor the number of defects reported each month.

18.16 The Minnesota Twins baseball team has established a standard of less than one fielding error per game: more specifically, no more than four errors in every five games. The total number of errors for each set of five games is plotted on a control chart. Compute the upper control limit and sketch the control chart.

18.8 PRODUCT RELIABILITY

In this final section product quality will be analyzed from a system perspective. You will see how simple probability concepts provide important guidance for improving product quality. Product reliability analysis provides guidance for product design and for higher-quality manufacturing and service systems (Key Idea 18.13).

Key Idea 18.13: Product Reliability

Product reliability is the probability that a product will operate according to specification during a given period of time. The reliability for a system containing m components is

$$SR = CR_1 \times CR_2 \times \cdots \times CR_m$$

where SR is the system reliability and CR_j is the reliability for component j.

System reliability may be increased by increasing individual component reliability and/or by decreasing the number of components. The reliability of a single component can be increased substantially by installing a copy of the component that takes over in case the original component fails. Component reliability with redundancy CR_r is

$$CR_r = CR + CR \times (1 - CR)$$

Product reliability is the probability that a product will operate according to specification during a given period. Thus if 99 out of 100 lightbulbs of a particular type are operating at the end of 1000 hours of use, lightbulbs of that type have a reliability of 0.99. If 100 power antennas fail in the first three years out of 100,000 automobiles, the power antenna has a reliability of 0.999. The following definitions are useful in developing product reliability concepts:

1. *Failure rate (FR)*:

$$FR = \frac{\text{number of failures}}{\text{number in operation}}$$

2. *Component reliability (CR)*:

$$CR = 1 - FR$$

3. *System reliability (SR)*: System reliability is the probability that a system composed of m parts will operate according to specification during a given period. This implies that each of the individual parts operates correctly.

$$SR = CR_1 \times CR_2 \times \cdots \times CR_m$$

The probability of every part operating correctly is the product of each part's reliability, given that failures are independent.

Most consumer products—cars, computers, CD players—contain many components linked together as a system. High component reliability is the goal for every component. However, achieving that goal may still not ensure customer satisfaction, as can be seen from a few simple computations.

1. A product contains 5 components, each of which has a component reliability of $CR = 0.99$. The system reliability is

$$SR = CR_1 \times CR_2 \times \cdots \times CR_5$$
$$= CR^5$$
$$= 0.99^5$$
$$= 0.951$$

2. Now suppose that a similar product contained 20 components with $CR = 0.99$ for each component. The reliability is

$$SR = 0.99^{20} = 0.818$$

This level of reliability would be unacceptable for almost any product.

Many companies have examined results such as these and concluded that they must either simplify their products by reducing the number of components or by increasing the reliability of each component. The design of the popular Taurus model by Ford Motor Co. included a reduction in the number of components. The benefits of this simplification are clear. Reducing from 20 to 10 components with a reliability of 0.99 raises the system reliability from 0.818 to 0.904. Further reduction to 5 components would raise it to 0.951.

Companies also have worked hard to increase the reliability of individual components. If the component reliability were increased to 0.999, the 20-component system would have a system reliability $SR = 0.98$ (0.999^{20}), while the 10-component system would have a reliability of $SR = 0.99$, and the 5-component system would be $SR = 0.995$. Thus we see clearly the benefits of very high levels of reliability for individual components given that most consumer products are complex systems.

Another strategy used to improve system reliability is component redundancy. A second duplicate component is installed and the system is designed to switch automatically to the second component if the first one fails. The improvement in reliability is computed as follows:

$$CR_r = CR + CR \times (1 - CR)$$

where CR_r is the component reliability given redundancy and CR is the single-component reliability.

The reliability is equal to the single-unit reliability plus the single-unit reliability multipled times the failure rate, $1 - CR$. For example, suppose that we had a low-cost part with a reliability of 0.95, but the cost per unit of increasing reliability to 0.99 was three times higher. If, instead, we doubled the cost by including a redundant part, the reliability would be

$$CR_r = 0.95 + 0.95(1 - 0.95) = 0.998$$

Thus we see that redundancy would provide higher reliability at a lower cost for this example. Redundancy is not always the lowest-cost solution. The point of this example is that the cost versus reliability increase for both options should be obtained and the option that provides the required reliability for minimum cost should be selected.

SUMMARY OF KEY IDEAS

CHAPTER PROBLEMS

18.1   Consolidated Pistons has a contract which specifies that each piston delivered will have a mean of 2.5 inches $\pm$ 0.03 inch. The process is known to have a variance $\sigma^2 = 0.0001$.
   (a) Prepare $\bar{X}$ and R charts for the process assuming a random sample of size $n = 5$.
   (b) Does the process have the capability to meet the contract?
   (c) The following sample means and ranges were obtained on 10 consecutive days:

2.51, 0.025	2.504, 0.021	2.492, 0.020	2.484, 0.026
2.511, 0.023	2.509, 0.018	2.498, 0.024	2.497, 0.022
2.523, 0.021	2.525, 0.022		

   Plot these on the control chart and identify any problems.

18.2   A manufacturer of precision bolts is required to produce bolts for a luxury automobile that have a mean strength of 60,000 psi with a standard deviation of 300.
   (a) Prepare $\bar{X}$ and R charts for the process assuming random samples of size $n = 4$ and that the process is capable.
   (b) Table 18.1 contains the random sample observations for 12 consecutive random samples. Plot the sample results on the control charts and comment on any unusual patterns.

TABLE 18.1   Random Samples of Bolt Dimensions

Sample	Observation 1	2	3	4
1	60,500	60,600	60,100	60,700
2	60,200	60,300	60,500	60,400
3	59,750	59,900	60,050	60,200
4	59,500	59,400	59,800	59,900
5	60,100	59,900	59,600	60,400
6	59,550	60,500	60,100	60,050
7	59,700	60,600	60,200	59,900
8	60,300	60,400	60,500	60,100
9	59,900	60,200	60,300	60,100
10	59,500	59,600	59,900	59,600
11	59,900	59,400	59,500	59,300
12	59,800	59,400	59,600	59,200

18.3 Amalgamated Plastics has a contract to produce lenses for a trailer light. The contract specifies that the lense diameter must be 10 inches $\pm$ 0.2 inch. Their manufacturing process has a standard deviation of 0.06 inch. Their standard practice is to obtain random samples of size $n = 5$ to monitor the controls on their operation.
   (a) Compute the control limits for this process.
   (b) Compute the process capability index and indicate if this process is capable of meeting the contract specifications.
   (c) The purchaser of the lenses has developed a problem with the light assembly that uses the lens. They have asked that the specification limits be reduced to ± 0.15 inch. Compute the new process capability index. What action do you recommend to the management of Amalgamated Plastics?

18.4 Speedy Bike Delivery, Inc. delivers small packages in a major metropolitan area. It guarantees that all packages will be delivered within 2.5 hours or the delivery charge will be refunded. A careful study of their operation indicates that delivery times have a mean of 90 minutes with a variance of 400. They monitor their operation using a random sample of size $n = 6$ every week to be certain that their standards are being maintained.
   (a) Compute the control limits and the process capability index. Is the process capable of meeting their guarantee?
   (b) During the past several weeks the percentage of late delivery refund claims has risen to 5% from almost no claims. Do they have a problem? Explain your answer.
   (c) A new competitor that guarantees delivery within 2.2 hours or a refund of charges. Is Speedy Bike Delivery capable of meeting that guarantee with their present process? If not, what should they do?

18.5 Best Place Electronics offers a special price to clean and adjust VCRs. As a result, they have considerable business. To continue this offer and make a profit, the service time must have a mean of 45 minutes with a standard deviation of 6 minutes. They monitor the repair process using a daily random samples of 5 VCRs.

(a) Compute the $\bar{X}$ and R control limits for the sample mean.

(b) Suppose that on three consecutive days the sample means are 52 minutes, 53 minutes, and 54 minutes. Do they have a problem? Explain your answer.

(c) During a different period the sample means were 52, 40, and 51. Do they have a problem? Explain your answer.

18.6 The Green Valley Dental Clinic is facing competition from a number of branch clinics that are opening in shopping centers. Most of the clients are covered by insurance and price competition is not possible. Thus Green Valley is seeking to provide a higher level of service. The clinic administrator has proposed that clients coming for routine teeth cleaning and examination will spend no more than one hour—waiting time plus service time—in the clinic. They have asked you to study the clinic's operations and recommend strategies for meeting this guarantee. Your study indicates that the mean waiting time is 15 minutes with a standard deviation of 4 minutes, and the service time is 30 minutes with a standard deviation of 2 minutes.

(a) Is the process capable of meeting the guarantee? Answer the question first by assuming that waiting time and service time are independent. Then answer by assuming that they have a correlation of 0.40.

(b) A random sample of five waiting times and five service times is taken every week to monitor the process. Compute the control limits for the $\bar{X}$ and R charts for both the waiting and service processes.

(c) You have been asked to recommend strategies for reducing the number of times that the guarantee is not met, assuming that waiting and service times have a correlation of 0.40. Indicate where you would focus your search for improvements and suggest possible improvements.

18.7 Karin's Supermarkets, Inc. has opened a new high-volume store. To encourage customers, they promise that customers will not spend more than 15 minutes waiting in line and checking out their order. If more than 15 minutes is required, the customer is given a free item from a selected list. Examination of the process indicates that the mean is 8 minutes and the variance is 9. A random sample of size $n = 4$ is obtained daily to monitor the checkout process.

(a) Is the process capable of meeting the guarantee?

(b) Compute the control limits for $\bar{X}$ and R charts.

(c) Prepare a cause-and-effect diagram for the checkout process and recommend possible improvements that will increase the chances of meeting the guarantee.

18.8 Direct Marketing, Inc. contacts households by phone and offers to sell magazines at a special price. Callers are trained to follow a script that has proven successful. The persons called are screened from large mailing lists using a variety of selection rules that are correlated with a positive sales response. Based on their past experience and industry performance, Direct Marketing, Inc. expects to sell to 30% of the people contacted. A random sample of 100 calls are monitored each week and the sample proportion of sales is plotted on a p control chart.

(a) Compute the control limits for the p control chart.

(b) Compute the p chart limits if the sample size is reduced to 60.

18.9   The director of admissions at Sweet Water College is concerned about the number of accepted students who actually attend. Historically, 60% of the students accepted actually attend. However, competition for students is increasing. The director would like to know if any changes have occurred in the percentage attending. The college has a rolling admissions policy that admits qualified students shortly after their application is complete. Each 100 students admitted are treated as a random sample, and the percent who accept admission after one month and after three months is recorded.
   (a) Historical data show that 40% accept in the first month when they eventually reach 60% acceptance. Construct the p chart limits for the first-month acceptances.
   (b) Three-month acceptances are 60% if the acceptance ratio is being maintained. Construct the p chart limits for the three-month acceptances.
   (c) Prepare a cause-and-effect diagram and use it to make recommendations for increasing the acceptance proportion.

18.10 A large manufacturer of computer chips expects that 90% of the chips will pass the performance test if the process is operating properly. Random samples of 150 are tested each day. Compute the p chart limits if the process is operating under control.

18.11 A mail-order distribution house has designed a computer processing and inventory control system that will process 70% of the orders on the same day they are received. However, customer order patterns can change and inventory levels may need adjustment. Therefore, the company monitors its operation by checking 100 randomly selected orders each day to determine if the 70% level is being maintained.
   (a) Compute the p chart limits for this process.
   (b) What would you conclude if the sample percent of orders processed in one day for a 10-day period had the following pattern?

   71   73   69   68   71   67   72   61   58   55

18.12 Data First, Inc., a manufacturer of microcomputers, does a function test of all computers before shipment. If their process is in control, they expect to find an average of 5 defective floppy disk drives each day.
   (a) Compute the control limits and prepare a C chart.
   (b) The following number of defective disk drives per day were observed over a three-week period:

3	4	6	7	5
7	4	3	6	5
4	6	8	11	10

   Plot these data and discuss any need for intervention in the process.

18.13 The Minnesota Twins commit an average of 0.8 fielding error per game. The master fielding coach, Jake "Hands" Tolefson, claims that any time a team commits four errors in a game they will lose.
   (a) Compute the upper and lower control limits for the Twins' fielding performance.
   (b) Given the rule of Jake, are the Twins capable of winning games based on their fielding?

18.14 The Gravel Gulch Rattlers have a mean of 1.4 fielding errors per game.
   (a) Given the "rule of Jake" from Problem 18.13, are the Rattlers capable of winning?

(b) During a recent 60-game stretch the Rattlers had an average of 2 errors per game. You attend a game and they commit 0 errors. Should you cheer wildly to recognize the team for its vastly improved performance? Explain your answer.

18.15 The Federal Emergency Management Agency (FEMA) employs analysts to prepare damage claims for flood relief payments. The claim process is complex and over the years the mean number of errors per completed claim has been 0.40.
(a) Prepare a C control chart for the number of errors per claim.
(b) Suppose that a new employee prepares a claim that has two errors. Should you be highly concerned about this employee and recommend that she immediately attend a two-week course on preparing these claims?
(c) Suppose that the next day she submits a claim that contains zero errors. Do you commend her for her significant improvement and buy her a rose?

18.16 Cardinal Glass, Inc. deposits a thin metallic film on window glass to improve the insulating characteristics of the glass. Defects in the glass supplied to their coating line produce a defect in the final product and the glass must be scrapped. On average, five pieces of glass will be scrapped during each 8-hour shift.
(a) Prepare a C control chart for the number of pieces of defective glass.
(b) Suppose that on a certain 8-hour shift 10 pieces of glass had to be scrapped because of defects in the glass supplied. Should you call the supplier, complain with vigor, and threaten to cancel future orders?
(c) You discover that there have been 10 or 11 pieces of glass scrapped for defects on each of the five previous 8-hour shifts. Should you have a discussion with the supplier?

18.17 Circuits Unlimited produces specialized microprocessor controls for specialized manufacturing applications. Their basic system contains four electronic components, which have a reliability of 0.99 each, and a microprocessor with a reliability of 0.95.
(a) What is the system reliability?
(b) A potential purchaser has indicated great interest but desires a higher reliability. How would you increase the reliability? Show the computations that indicate the increased reliability from your revised system design.

18.18 The assembly process for a new medical appliance has five critical steps that must be completed correctly or the equipment will not work. The probability of step 1 being done correctly is 0.98, for step 2 the probability is 0.99, for step 3, 0.94, for step 4, 0.97, and for step 5 the probability is 0.95.
(a) What is the overall probability of the complete appliance being assembled correctly?
(b) Suppose that you could replicate two of the steps and that if either replication was successful, the entire appliance would function correctly. Which two steps would you replicate? Compute the resulting probability of successful assembly as a result of your modification of the procedure.

18.19 The Acme Distribution Company has recently installed a new computerized order processing system that is supposed to process 80% of the electronically submitted orders without intervention by an order processor. The system was developed by analyzing the pattern of existing orders and developing standard response procedures. Each incoming order is analyzed by the computer system and processed if its information is complete and if it meets the standard conditions for an order. If information is not complete and/or the order is nonstandard, it will be diverted to an order processing analyst. The company has asked you to design a quality control acceptance interval procedure that will indicate if there is a deviation above or below the target of 80% automatic processing. A random sample of 150 orders will be examined each week and classified as either processed automatically or diverted to an order processing analyst. Develop an acceptance interval such that the probability of falsely rejecting the hypothesis of 80% automatic processing is less than 0.005. Sketch an acceptance chart that shows the interval over time and that could be used to plot the weekly percentage of automatically processed orders.

18.20 Burde's Supermarkets offer high-quality hamburger with a low fat content. They advertise that their hamburger has only 3.2 ounces of fat per pound compared to the 4.8 ounces per pound in regular hamburger. Joseph Burde, manager of meats, knows that the variance of fat content is 0.50. To ensure that quality is maintained, a random sample of 5 pounds of hamburger is obtained each day and the fat content is measured.
(a) Compute the acceptance limits for a standard quality control.
(b) Explain the use of these limits to Joseph.

18.21 Mazdaford Motors has developed quality control charts for the size dimensions of automobile parts. One of the key dimensions on the fender stampings has a mean of $\mu = 6.2$ inches and a variance of $\sigma^2 = 0.0025$. The quality control monitoring procedures state that random samples of size $n = 5$ will be obtained and the sample mean will be plotted on a control chart. During a recent week the following sample means were observed:

6.19	6.22	6.21	6.25	6.64	6.70	6.71	6.69

(a) Prepare a control chart and plot the sample means.
(b) Based on the analysis in part (a), what recommendations would you make?

18.22 American Manufacturing, Inc. has recently installed a complex local area computer network (LAN). From the experience on similar networks, Jane Erickson, manager of network systems, has planned for an average of two system breakdowns per week. During the first 10 weeks of operation, the number of breakdowns per week were

3	1	4	2	5	4	6	7	6	8

You have been asked to design a control chart system to monitor system breakdowns.
(a) Prepare a control chart and plot the breakdowns observed over the 10-week period.
(b) Examine the plot and make a recommendation to Jan concerning the breakdowns.

18.23 Applesweet Orchards has a contract for sale of its apples to United Fruit Growers. Included in the contract is a provision that at least 60% of the apples delivered will be grade A. United checks each shipment by obtaining a random sample of 200 apples and determining the sample percentage of grade A apples. Over a period of 10 days the sample percentage of grade A apples are as follows:

58	61	57	52	56	65	51	59	50	64

(a) Prepare a control chart and plot the observed breakdowns over the 10-day period.
(b) Examine the plot and make a recommendation to United Fruit Growers regarding the capability of Applesweet to meet the contract.

18.24 Millcreek Grains is a regional manufacturer of natural granola. They have just begun to establish quality control procedures and have asked for your assistance. Their package filling machine is set at a mean of 16 ounces. After careful adjustment they have set the variance of the package filling machine at 0.01. Random samples of size $n = 5$ were obtained for a 10-day period and they have asked for your assistance in analyzing the data. The means for the 10 samples were

| 15.94 | 15.89 | 16.09 | 15.88 | 16.02 | 16.12 | 16.11 | 15.87 |
| 16.06 | 16.10 | | | | | | |

The ranges for the 10 samples were

| 0.200 | 0.228 | 0.451 | 0.401 | 0.398 | 0.345 | 0.475 | 0.482 |
| 0.491 | 0.498 | | | | | | |

(a) Prepare $\bar{X}$ and R charts and plot the data.

(b) Based on the charts above, what recommendations would you make to the management of Millcreek Grains?

18.25 Northern Steel has a rolling mill that prepares sheet steel for the automobile industry. The automobile manufacturers use the sheet steel in stamping mills to prepare body parts. If a surface defect occurs in the sheet, a defective stamping will be produced. Thus it is important to minimize the number of defects. Northern has a reputation for producing quality steel with only 2 defects per 1000-foot roll. The number of defects in 10 randomly selected rolls are as follows:

| 3 | 1 | 2 | 4 | 5 | 7 | 9 | 6 | 8 | 7 |

(a) Prepare a control chart for the number of defects and plot the data.

(b) What are your conclusions based on an analysis of the chart above?

Appendix A

Probability Tables

903

TABLE A.1   Standard Normal Distribution

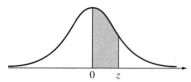

z	0.00	0.01	0.02	0.03	0.04	0.05	0.06	0.07	0.08	0.09
0.0	0.0000	0.0040	0.0080	0.0120	0.0160	0.0199	0.0239	0.0279	0.0319	0.0359
0.1	0.0398	0.0438	0.0478	0.0517	0.0557	0.0596	0.0636	0.0675	0.0714	0.0753
0.2	0.0793	0.0832	0.0871	0.0910	0.0948	0.0987	0.1026	0.1064	0.1103	0.1141
0.3	0.1179	0.1217	0.1255	0.1293	0.1331	0.1368	0.1406	0.1443	0.1480	0.1517
0.4	0.1554	0.1591	0.1628	0.1664	0.1700	0.1736	0.1772	0.1808	0.1844	0.1879
0.5	0.1915	0.1950	0.1985	0.2019	0.2054	0.2088	0.2123	0.2157	0.2190	0.2224
0.6	0.2257	0.2291	0.2324	0.2357	0.2389	0.2422	0.2454	0.2486	0.2517	0.2549
0.7	0.2580	0.2611	0.2642	0.2673	0.2704	0.2734	0.2764	0.2794	0.2823	0.2852
0.8	0.2881	0.2910	0.2939	0.2967	0.2995	0.3023	0.3051	0.3078	0.3106	0.3133
0.9	0.3159	0.3186	0.3212	0.3238	0.3264	0.3289	0.3315	0.3340	0.3365	0.3389
1.0	0.3413	0.3438	0.3461	0.3485	0.3508	0.3531	0.3554	0.3577	0.3599	0.3621
1.1	0.3643	0.3665	0.3686	0.3708	0.3729	0.3749	0.3770	0.3790	0.3810	0.3830
1.2	0.3849	0.3869	0.3888	0.3907	0.3925	0.3944	0.3962	0.3980	0.3997	0.4015
1.3	0.4032	0.4049	0.4066	0.4082	0.4099	0.4115	0.4131	0.4147	0.4162	0.4177
1.4	0.4192	0.4207	0.4222	0.4236	0.4251	0.4265	0.4279	0.4292	0.4306	0.4319
1.5	0.4332	0.4345	0.4357	0.4370	0.4382	0.4394	0.4406	0.4418	0.4429	0.4441
1.6	0.4452	0.4463	0.4474	0.4484	0.4495	0.4505	0.4515	0.4525	0.4535	0.4545
1.7	0.4554	0.4564	0.4573	0.4582	0.4591	0.4599	0.4608	0.4616	0.4625	0.4633
1.8	0.4641	0.4649	0.4656	0.4664	0.4671	0.4678	0.4686	0.4693	0.4699	0.4706
1.9	0.4713	0.4719	0.4726	0.4732	0.4738	0.4744	0.4750	0.4756	0.4761	0.4767
2.0	0.4772	0.4778	0.4783	0.4788	0.4793	0.4798	0.4803	0.4808	0.4812	0.4817
2.1	0.4821	0.4826	0.4830	0.4834	0.4838	0.4842	0.4846	0.4850	0.4854	0.4857
2.2	0.4861	0.4864	0.4868	0.4871	0.4875	0.4878	0.4881	0.4884	0.4887	0.4890
2.3	0.4893	0.4896	0.4898	0.4901	0.4904	0.4906	0.4909	0.4911	0.4913	0.4916
2.4	0.4918	0.4920	0.4922	0.4925	0.4927	0.4929	0.4931	0.4932	0.4934	0.4936
2.5	0.4938	0.4940	0.4941	0.4943	0.4945	0.4946	0.4948	0.4949	0.4951	0.4952
2.6	0.4953	0.4955	0.4956	0.4957	0.4959	0.4960	0.4961	0.4962	0.4963	0.4964
2.7	0.4965	0.4966	0.4967	0.4968	0.4969	0.4970	0.4971	0.4972	0.4973	0.4974
2.8	0.4974	0.4975	0.4976	0.4977	0.4977	0.4978	0.4979	0.4979	0.4980	0.4981
2.9	0.4981	0.4982	0.4982	0.4983	0.4984	0.4984	0.4985	0.4985	0.4986	0.4986
3.0	0.4987	0.4987	0.4987	0.4988	0.4988	0.4989	0.4989	0.4989	0.4990	0.4990

Source: Abridged from Table I of A. Hald, *Statistical Tables and Formulas* (New York: Wiley), 1952. Reproduced by permission of A. Hald and the publisher, John Wiley & Sons, Inc.

TABLE A.2 Student t for Selected Upper-Tail Probabilities

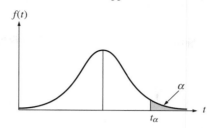

DOF	α					
	0.25	0.10	0.05	0.025	0.01	0.005
1	1.000	3.078	6.314	12.706	31.821	63.657
2	0.816	1.886	2.920	4.303	6.965	9.925
3	0.765	1.638	2.353	3.182	4.541	5.841
4	0.741	1.533	2.132	2.776	3.747	4.604
5	0.727	1.476	2.015	2.571	3.365	4.032
6	0.718	1.440	1.943	2.447	3.143	3.707
7	0.711	1.415	1.895	2.365	2.998	3.499
8	0.706	1.397	1.860	2.306	2.896	3.355
9	0.703	1.383	1.833	2.262	2.821	3.250
10	0.700	1.372	1.812	2.228	2.764	3.169
11	0.697	1.363	1.796	2.201	2.718	3.106
12	0.695	1.356	1.782	2.179	2.681	3.055
13	0.694	1.350	1.771	2.160	2.650	3.012
14	0.692	1.345	1.761	2.145	2.624	2.977
15	0.691	1.341	1.753	2.131	2.602	2.947
16	0.690	1.337	1.746	2.120	2.583	2.921
17	0.689	1.333	1.740	2.110	2.567	2.898
18	0.688	1.330	1.734	2.101	2.552	2.878
19	0.688	1.328	1.729	2.093	2.539	2.861
20	0.687	1.325	1.725	2.086	2.528	2.845
21	0.686	1.323	1.721	2.080	2.518	2.831
22	0.686	1.321	1.717	2.074	2.508	2.819
23	0.685	1.319	1.714	2.069	2.500	2.807
24	0.685	1.318	1.711	2.064	2.492	2.797
25	0.684	1.316	1.708	2.060	2.485	2.787
26	0.684	1.315	1.706	2.056	2.479	2.779
27	0.684	1.314	1.703	2.052	2.473	2.771
28	0.683	1.313	1.701	2.048	2.467	2.763
29	0.683	1.311	1.699	2.045	2.462	2.756
30	0.683	1.310	1.697	2.042	2.457	2.750

TABLE A.2   Student t for Selected Upper-Tail
Probabilities (*continued*)

DOF	α					
	0.25	0.10	0.05	0.025	0.01	0.005
31	0.682	1.309	1.696	2.040	2.453	2.744
32	0.682	1.309	1.694	2.037	2.449	2.738
33	0.682	1.308	1.692	2.035	2.445	2.733
34	0.682	1.307	1.691	2.032	2.441	2.728
35	0.682	1.306	1.690	2.030	2.438	2.724
36	0.681	1.306	1.688	2.028	2.434	2.719
37	0.681	1.305	1.687	2.026	2.431	2.715
38	0.681	1.304	1.686	2.024	2.429	2.712
39	0.681	1.304	1.685	2.023	2.426	2.708
40	0.681	1.303	1.684	2.021	2.423	2.704
41	0.681	1.303	1.683	2.020	2.421	2.701
42	0.680	1.302	1.682	2.018	2.418	2.698
43	0.680	1.302	1.681	2.017	2.416	2.695
44	0.680	1.301	1.680	2.015	2.414	2.692
45	0.680	1.301	1.679	2.014	2.412	2.690
46	0.680	1.300	1.679	2.013	2.410	2.687
47	0.680	1.300	1.678	2.012	2.408	2.685
48	0.680	1.299	1.677	2.011	2.407	2.682
49	0.680	1.299	1.677	2.010	2.405	2.680
50	0.679	1.299	1.676	2.009	2.403	2.678
51	0.679	1.298	1.675	2.008	2.402	2.676
52	0.679	1.298	1.675	2.007	2.400	2.674
53	0.679	1.298	1.674	2.006	2.399	2.672
54	0.679	1.297	1.674	2.005	2.397	2.670
55	0.679	1.297	1.673	2.004	2.396	2.668
56	0.679	1.297	1.673	2.003	2.395	2.667
57	0.679	1.297	1.672	2.002	2.394	2.665
58	0.679	1.296	1.672	2.002	2.392	2.663
59	0.679	1.296	1.671	2.001	2.391	2.662
60	0.679	1.296	1.671	2.000	2.390	2.660
61	0.679	1.296	1.670	2.000	2.389	2.659
62	0.678	1.295	1.670	1.999	2.388	2.658
63	0.678	1.295	1.669	1.998	2.387	2.656
64	0.678	1.295	1.669	1.998	2.386	2.655
65	0.678	1.295	1.669	1.997	2.385	2.654
66	0.678	1.295	1.668	1.997	2.384	2.652

TABLE A.2   Student t for Selected Upper-Tail
Probabilities (*continued*)

DOF	α					
	0.25	0.10	0.05	0.025	0.01	0.005
67	0.678	1.294	1.668	1.996	2.383	2.651
68	0.678	1.294	1.668	1.995	2.382	2.650
69	0.678	1.294	1.667	1.995	2.382	2.649
70	0.678	1.294	1.667	1.994	2.381	2.648
71	0.678	1.294	1.667	1.994	2.380	2.647
72	0.678	1.293	1.666	1.993	2.379	2.646
73	0.678	1.293	1.666	1.993	2.379	2.645
74	0.678	1.293	1.666	1.993	2.378	2.644
75	0.678	1.293	1.665	1.992	2.377	2.643
76	0.678	1.293	1.665	1.992	2.376	2.642
77	0.678	1.293	1.665	1.991	2.376	2.641
78	0.678	1.292	1.665	1.991	2.375	2.640
79	0.678	1.292	1.664	1.990	2.375	2.640
80	0.678	1.292	1.664	1.990	2.374	2.639
81	0.678	1.292	1.664	1.990	2.373	2.638
82	0.677	1.292	1.664	1.989	2.373	2.637
83	0.677	1.292	1.663	1.989	2.372	2.636
84	0.677	1.292	1.663	1.989	2.372	2.636
85	0.677	1.292	1.663	1.988	2.371	2.635
86	0.677	1.291	1.663	1.988	2.371	2.634
87	0.677	1.291	1.663	1.988	2.370	2.634
88	0.677	1.291	1.662	1.987	2.369	2.633
89	0.677	1.291	1.662	1.987	2.369	2.632
90	0.677	1.291	1.662	1.987	2.369	2.632
91	0.677	1.291	1.662	1.986	2.368	2.631
92	0.677	1.291	1.662	1.986	2.368	2.630
93	0.677	1.291	1.661	1.986	2.367	2.630
94	0.677	1.291	1.661	1.986	2.367	2.629
95	0.677	1.291	1.661	1.985	2.366	2.629
96	0.677	1.290	1.661	1.985	2.366	2.628
97	0.677	1.290	1.661	1.985	2.365	2.627
98	0.677	1.290	1.661	1.984	2.365	2.627
99	0.677	1.290	1.660	1.984	2.365	2.626
100	0.677	1.290	1.660	1.984	2.364	2.626
101	0.677	1.290	1.660	1.984	2.364	2.625
102	0.677	1.290	1.660	1.984	2.363	2.625

TABLE A.2   Student t for Selected Upper-Tail
Probabilities (*continued*)

DOF	α					
	0.25	0.10	0.05	0.025	0.01	0.005
103	0.677	1.290	1.660	1.983	2.363	2.624
104	0.677	1.290	1.660	1.983	2.363	2.624
105	0.677	1.290	1.659	1.983	2.362	2.623
106	0.677	1.290	1.659	1.983	2.362	2.623
107	0.677	1.290	1.659	1.982	2.362	2.623
108	0.677	1.289	1.659	1.982	2.361	2.622
109	0.677	1.289	1.659	1.982	2.361	2.622
110	0.677	1.289	1.659	1.982	2.361	2.621
111	0.677	1.289	1.659	1.982	2.360	2.621
112	0.677	1.289	1.659	1.981	2.360	2.620
113	0.677	1.289	1.658	1.981	2.360	2.620
114	0.677	1.289	1.658	1.981	2.360	2.620
115	0.677	1.289	1.658	1.981	2.359	2.619
116	0.677	1.289	1.658	1.981	2.359	2.619
117	0.677	1.289	1.658	1.980	2.359	2.619
118	0.677	1.289	1.658	1.980	2.358	2.618
119	0.677	1.289	1.658	1.980	2.358	2.618
120	0.677	1.289	1.658	1.980	2.358	2.617

TABLE A.3 Chi Square Values for Selected Upper-Tail Probabilities

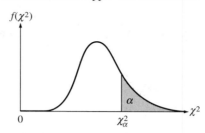

DOF	0.99	0.975	0.95	0.90	0.10	0.05	0.025	0.01
1	0.000	0.001	0.004	0.016	2.706	3.841	5.024	6.635
2	0.020	0.051	0.103	0.211	4.605	5.991	7.378	9.210
3	0.115	0.216	0.352	0.584	6.251	7.815	9.348	11.345
4	0.297	0.484	0.711	1.064	7.779	9.488	11.143	13.277
5	0.554	0.831	1.145	1.610	9.236	11.070	12.833	15.086
6	0.872	1.237	1.635	2.204	10.645	12.592	14.449	16.812
7	1.239	1.690	2.167	2.833	12.017	14.067	16.013	18.475
8	1.646	2.180	2.733	3.490	13.362	15.507	17.535	20.090
9	2.088	2.700	3.325	4.168	14.684	16.919	19.023	21.666
10	2.558	3.247	3.940	4.865	15.987	18.307	20.483	23.209
11	3.053	3.816	4.575	5.578	17.275	19.675	21.920	24.725
12	3.571	4.404	5.226	6.304	18.549	21.026	23.337	26.217
13	4.107	5.009	5.892	7.042	19.812	22.362	24.736	27.688
14	4.660	5.629	6.571	7.790	21.064	23.685	26.119	29.141
15	5.229	6.262	7.261	8.547	22.307	24.996	27.488	30.578
16	5.812	6.908	7.962	9.312	23.542	26.296	28.845	32.000
17	6.408	7.564	8.672	10.085	24.769	27.587	30.191	33.409
18	7.015	8.231	9.390	10.865	25.989	28.869	31.526	34.805
19	7.633	8.907	10.117	11.651	27.204	30.143	32.852	36.191
20	8.260	9.591	10.851	12.443	28.412	31.410	34.170	37.566
21	8.897	10.283	11.591	13.240	29.615	32.671	35.479	38.932
22	9.542	10.982	12.338	14.041	30.813	33.924	36.781	40.290
23	10.196	11.689	13.091	14.848	32.007	35.172	38.076	41.638
24	10.856	12.401	13.848	15.659	33.196	36.415	39.364	42.980
25	11.524	13.120	14.611	16.473	34.382	37.653	40.647	44.314
26	12.198	13.844	15.379	17.292	35.563	38.885	41.923	45.642
27	12.879	14.573	16.151	18.114	36.741	40.113	43.195	46.963
28	13.565	15.308	16.928	18.939	37.916	41.337	44.461	48.278
29	14.256	16.047	17.708	19.768	39.087	42.557	45.722	49.588
30	14.953	16.791	18.493	20.599	40.256	43.773	46.979	50.892

TABLE A.3   Chi Square Values for Selected Upper-Tail Probabilities (*continued*)

DOF	0.99	0.975	0.95	0.90	0.10	0.05	0.025	0.01
40	22. 64	24.433	26.509	29.051	51.805	55.759	59.342	63.691
50	29 707	32.357	34.764	37.689	63.167	67.505	71.420	76.154
60	37 485	40.482	43.188	46.459	74.397	79.082	83.298	88.381
70	45.442	48.758	51.739	55.329	85.527	90.531	95.023	100.424
80	53.540	57.153	60.391	64.278	96.578	101.879	106.628	112.328
90	61.754	65.647	69.126	73.291	107.565	113.145	118.135	124.115
100	70.065	74.222	77.930	82.358	118.499	124.343	129.563	135.811

TABLE A.4   *F* for Selected Upper-Tail Probabilities, $\alpha = 0.10$

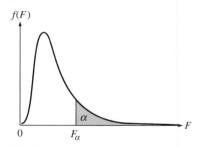

Denominator DOF	Numerator Degrees of Freedom								
	1	2	3	4	5	6	7	8	9
1	39.86	49.50	53.59	55.83	57.24	58.20	58.91	59.44	59.86
2	8.53	9.00	9.16	9.24	9.29	9.33	9.35	9.37	9.38
3	5.54	5.46	5.39	5.34	5.31	5.28	5.27	5.25	5.24
4	4.54	4.32	4.19	4.11	4.05	4.01	3.98	3.95	3.94
5	4.06	3.78	3.62	3.52	3.45	3.40	3.37	3.34	3.32
6	3.78	3.46	3.29	3.18	3.11	3.05	3.01	2.98	2.96
7	3.59	3.26	3.07	2.96	2.88	2.83	2.78	2.75	2.72
8	3.46	3.11	2.92	2.81	2.73	2.67	2.62	2.59	2.56
9	3.36	3.01	2.81	2.69	2.61	2.55	2.51	2.47	2.44
10	3.29	2.92	2.73	2.61	2.52	2.46	2.41	2.38	2.35
11	3.23	2.86	2.66	2.54	2.45	2.39	2.34	2.30	2.27
12	3.18	2.81	2.61	2.48	2.39	2.33	2.28	2.24	2.21
13	3.14	2.76	2.56	2.43	2.35	2.28	2.23	2.20	2.16
14	3.10	2.73	2.52	2.39	2.31	2.24	2.19	2.15	2.12
15	3.07	2.70	2.49	2.36	2.27	2.21	2.16	2.12	2.09
16	3.05	2.67	2.46	2.33	2.24	2.18	2.13	2.09	2.06
17	3.03	2.64	2.44	2.31	2.22	2.15	2.10	2.06	2.03
18	3.01	2.62	2.42	2.29	2.20	2.13	2.08	2.04	2.00
19	2.99	2.61	2.40	2.27	2.18	2.11	2.06	2.02	1.98
20	2.97	2.59	2.38	2.25	2.16	2.09	2.04	2.00	1.96
21	2.96	2.57	2.36	2.23	2.14	2.08	2.02	1.98	1.95
22	2.95	2.56	2.35	2.22	2.13	2.06	2.01	1.97	1.93
23	2.94	2.55	2.34	2.21	2.11	2.05	1.99	1.95	1.92
24	2.93	2.54	2.33	2.19	2.10	2.04	1.98	1.94	1.91
25	2.92	2.53	2.32	2.18	2.09	2.02	1.97	1.93	1.89
26	2.91	2.52	2.31	2.17	2.08	2.01	1.96	1.92	1.88
27	2.90	2.51	2.30	2.17	2.07	2.00	1.95	1.91	1.87
28	2.89	2.50	2.29	2.16	2.06	2.00	1.94	1.90	1.87
29	2.89	2.50	2.28	2.15	2.06	1.99	1.93	1.89	1.86

TABLE A.4   *F* for Selected Upper-Tail Probabilities, $\alpha = 0.10$ (*continued*)

Denominator DOF	Numerator Degrees of Freedom								
	1	2	3	4	5	6	7	8	9
30	2.88	2.49	2.28	2.14	2.05	1.98	1.93	1.88	1.85
40	2.84	2.44	2.23	2.09	2.00	1.93	1.87	1.83	1.79
60	2.79	2.39	2.18	2.04	1.95	1.87	1.82	1.77	1.74
120	2.75	2.35	2.13	1.99	1.90	1.82	1.77	1.72	1.68
∞	2.71	2.30	2.08	1.94	1.85	1.77	1.72	1.67	1.63

Source: From M. Merrington and C. M. Thompson, "Tables of Percentage Points of the Inverted Beta *F*-Distribution," *Biometrika,* 1943, 33, 73–88. Reproduced by permission of the *Biometrika* Trustees.

TABLE A.4   *F* for Selected Upper-Tail Probabilities, $\alpha = 0.10$ (*continued*)

Denominator DOF	Numerator Degrees of Freedom									
	10	12	15	20	24	30	40	60	120	∞
1	60.19	60.71	61.22	61.74	62.00	62.26	62.53	62.79	62.06	63.33
2	9.39	9.41	9.42	9.44	9.45	9.46	9.47	9.47	9.48	9.49
3	5.23	5.22	5.20	5.18	5.18	5.17	5.16	5.15	5.14	5.13
4	3.92	3.90	3.87	3.84	3.83	3.82	3.80	3.79	3.78	3.76
5	3.30	3.27	3.24	3.21	3.19	3.17	3.16	3.14	3.12	3.10
6	2.94	2.90	2.87	2.84	2.82	2.80	2.78	2.76	2.74	2.72
7	2.70	2.67	2.63	2.59	2.58	2.56	2.54	2.51	2.49	2.47
8	2.54	2.50	2.46	2.42	2.40	2.38	2.36	2.34	2.32	2.29
9	2.42	2.38	2.34	2.30	2.28	2.25	2.23	2.21	2.18	2.16
10	2.32	2.28	2.24	2.20	2.18	2.16	2.13	2.11	2.08	2.06
11	2.25	2.21	2.17	2.12	2.10	2.08	2.05	2.03	2.00	1.97
12	2.19	2.15	2.10	2.06	2.04	2.01	1.99	1.96	1.93	1.90
13	2.14	2.10	2.05	2.01	1.98	1.96	1.93	1.90	1.88	1.85
14	2.10	2.05	2.01	1.96	1.94	1.91	1.89	1.86	1.83	1.80
15	2.06	2.02	1.97	1.92	1.90	1.87	1.85	1.82	1.79	1.76
16	2.03	1.99	1.94	1.89	1.87	1.84	1.81	1.78	1.75	1.72
17	2.00	1.96	1.91	1.86	1.84	1.81	1.78	1.75	1.72	1.69
18	1.98	1.93	1.89	1.84	1.81	1.78	1.75	1.72	1.69	1.66
19	1.96	1.91	1.86	1.81	1.79	1.76	1.73	1.70	1.67	1.63
20	1.94	1.89	1.84	1.79	1.77	1.74	1.71	1.68	1.64	1.61
21	1.92	1.87	1.83	1.78	1.75	1.72	1.69	1.66	1.62	1.59
22	1.90	1.86	1.81	1.76	1.73	1.70	1.67	1.64	1.60	1.57
23	1.89	1.84	1.80	1.74	1.72	1.69	1.66	1.62	1.59	1.55
24	1.88	1.83	1.78	1.73	1.70	1.67	1.64	1.61	1.57	1.53
25	1.87	1.82	1.77	1.72	1.69	1.66	1.63	1.59	1.56	1.52
26	1.86	1.81	1.76	1.71	1.68	1.65	1.61	1.58	1.54	1.50
27	1.85	1.80	1.75	1.70	1.67	1.64	1.60	1.57	1.53	1.49
28	1.84	1.79	1.74	1.69	1.66	1.63	1.59	1.56	1.52	1.48
29	1.83	1.78	1.73	1.68	1.65	1.62	1.58	1.55	1.51	1.47
30	1.82	1.77	1.72	1.67	1.64	1.61	1.57	1.54	1.50	1.46
40	1.76	1.71	1.66	1.61	1.57	1.54	1.51	1.47	1.42	1.38
60	1.71	1.66	1.60	1.54	1.51	1.48	1.44	1.40	1.35	1.29
120	1.65	1.60	1.55	1.48	1.45	1.41	1.37	1.32	1.26	1.19
∞	1.60	1.55	1.49	1.42	1.38	1.34	1.30	1.24	1.17	1.00

TABLE A.4   *F* for Selected Upper-Tail Probabilities, $\alpha = 0.05$ (*continued*)

Denominator DOF	Numerator Degrees of Freedom								
	1	2	3	4	5	6	7	8	9
1	161.4	199.5	215.7	224.6	230.2	234.0	236.8	238.9	240.5
2	18.51	19.00	19.16	19.25	19.30	19.33	19.35	19.37	19.38
3	10.13	9.55	9.28	9.12	9.01	8.94	8.89	8.85	8.81
4	7.71	6.94	6.59	6.39	6.26	6.16	6.09	6.04	6.00
5	6.61	5.70	5.41	5.19	5.05	4.95	4.88	4.82	4.77
6	5.99	5.14	4.76	4.53	4.39	4.28	4.21	4.15	4.10
7	5.59	4.74	4.35	4.12	3.97	3.87	3.79	3.73	3.68
8	5.32	4.46	4.07	3.84	3.69	3.58	3.50	3.44	3.39
9	5.12	4.26	3.86	3.63	3.48	3.37	3.29	3.23	3.18
10	4.96	4.10	3.71	3.48	3.33	3.22	3.14	3.07	3.02
11	4.84	3.98	3.59	3.36	3.20	3.09	3.01	2.95	2.90
12	4.75	3.89	3.49	3.26	3.11	3.00	2.91	2.85	2.80
13	4.67	3.81	3.41	3.18	3.03	2.92	2.83	2.77	2.71
14	4.60	3.74	3.34	3.11	2.96	2.85	2.76	2.70	2.65
15	4.54	3.68	3.29	3.06	2.90	2.79	2.71	2.64	2.59
16	4.49	3.63	3.24	3.01	2.85	2.74	2.66	2.59	2.54
17	4.45	3.59	3.20	2.96	2.81	2.70	2.61	2.55	2.49
18	4.41	3.55	3.16	2.93	2.77	2.66	2.58	2.51	2.46
19	4.38	3.52	3.13	2.90	2.74	2.63	2.54	2.48	2.42
20	4.35	3.49	3.10	2.87	2.71	2.60	2.51	2.45	2.39
21	4.32	3.47	3.07	2.84	2.68	2.57	2.49	2.42	2.37
22	4.30	3.44	3.05	2.82	2.66	2.55	2.46	2.40	2.34
23	4.28	3.42	3.03	2.80	2.64	2.53	2.44	2.37	2.32
24	4.26	3.40	3.01	2.78	2.62	2.51	2.42	2.36	2.30
25	4.24	3.39	2.99	2.76	2.60	2.49	2.40	2.34	2.28
26	4.23	3.37	2.98	2.74	2.59	2.47	2.39	2.32	2.27
27	4.21	3.35	2.96	2.73	2.57	2.46	2.37	2.31	2.25
28	4.20	3.34	2.95	2.71	2.56	2.45	2.36	2.29	2.24
29	4.18	3.33	2.93	2.70	2.55	2.43	2.35	2.28	2.22
30	4.17	3.32	2.92	2.69	2.53	2.42	2.33	2.27	2.21
40	4.08	3.23	2.84	2.61	2.45	2.34	2.25	2.18	2.12
60	4.00	3.15	2.76	2.53	2.37	2.25	2.17	2.10	2.04
120	3.92	3.07	2.68	2.45	2.29	2.17	2.09	2.02	1.96
∞	3.84	3.00	2.60	2.37	2.21	2.10	2.01	1.94	1.88

TABLE A.4   *F* for Selected Upper-Tail Probabilities, $\alpha = 0.05$ (*continued*)

Denominator DOF	Numerator Degrees of Freedom									
	10	12	15	20	24	30	40	60	120	∞
1	241.9	243.9	245.9	248.0	249.1	250.1	251.1	252.2	253.3	254.3
2	19.40	19.41	19.43	19.45	19.45	19.46	19.47	19.48	19.49	19.50
3	8.79	8.74	8.70	8.66	8.64	8.62	8.59	8.57	8.55	8.53
4	5.96	5.91	5.86	5.80	5.77	5.75	5.72	5.69	5.66	5.63
5	4.74	4.68	4.62	4.56	4.53	4.50	4.46	4.43	4.40	4.36
6	4.06	4.00	3.94	3.87	3.84	3.81	3.77	3.74	3.70	3.67
7	3.64	3.57	3.51	3.44	3.41	3.38	3.34	3.30	3.27	3.23
8	3.35	3.28	3.22	3.15	3.12	3.08	3.04	3.01	2.97	2.93
9	3.14	3.07	3.01	2.94	2.90	2.86	2.83	2.79	2.75	2.71
10	2.98	2.91	2.85	2.77	2.74	2.70	2.66	2.62	2.58	2.54
11	2.85	2.79	2.72	2.65	2.61	2.57	2.53	2.49	2.45	2.40
12	2.75	2.69	2.62	2.54	2.51	2.47	2.43	2.38	2.34	2.30
13	2.67	2.60	2.53	2.46	2.42	2.38	2.34	2.30	2.25	2.21
14	2.60	2.53	2.46	2.39	2.35	2.31	2.27	2.22	2.18	2.13
15	2.54	2.48	2.40	2.33	2.29	2.25	2.20	2.16	2.11	2.07
16	2.49	2.42	2.35	2.28	2.24	2.19	2.15	2.11	2.06	2.01
17	2.45	2.38	2.31	2.23	2.19	2.15	2.10	2.06	2.01	1.96
18	2.41	2.34	2.27	2.19	2.15	2.11	2.06	2.02	1.97	1.92
19	2.38	2.31	2.23	2.16	2.11	2.07	2.03	1.98	1.93	1.88
20	2.35	2.28	2.20	2.12	2.08	2.04	1.99	1.95	1.90	1.84
21	2.32	2.25	2.18	2.10	2.05	2.01	1.96	1.92	1.87	1.81
22	2.30	2.23	2.15	2.07	2.03	1.98	1.94	1.89	1.84	1.78
23	2.27	2.20	2.13	2.05	2.01	1.96	1.91	1.86	1.81	1.76
24	2.25	2.18	2.11	2.03	1.98	1.94	1.89	1.84	1.79	1.73
25	2.24	2.16	2.09	2.01	1.96	1.92	1.87	1.82	1.77	1.71
26	2.22	2.15	2.07	1.99	1.95	1.90	1.85	1.80	1.75	1.69
27	2.20	2.13	2.06	1.97	1.93	1.88	1.84	1.79	1.73	1.67
28	2.19	2.12	2.04	1.96	1.91	1.87	1.82	1.77	1.71	1.65
29	2.18	2.10	2.03	1.94	1.90	1.85	1.81	1.75	1.70	1.64
30	2.16	2.09	2.01	1.93	1.89	1.84	1.79	1.74	1.68	1.62
40	2.08	2.00	1.92	1.84	1.79	1.74	1.69	1.64	1.58	1.51
60	1.99	1.92	1.84	1.75	1.70	1.65	1.59	1.53	1.47	1.39
120	1.91	1.83	1.75	1.66	1.61	1.55	1.50	1.43	1.35	1.25
∞	1.83	1.75	1.67	1.57	1.52	1.46	1.39	1.32	1.22	1.00

TABLE A.4   *F* for Selected Upper-Tail Probabilities, $\alpha = 0.025$ (*continued*)

Denominator DOF	Numerator Degrees of Freedom								
	1	2	3	4	5	6	7	8	9
1	647.8	799.5	864.2	899.6	921.8	937.1	948.2	956.7	963.3
2	38.51	39.00	39.17	39.25	39.30	39.33	39.36	39.37	39.39
3	17.44	16.04	15.44	15.10	14.88	14.73	14.62	14.54	14.47
4	12.22	10.65	9.98	9.60	9.36	9.20	9.07	8.98	8.90
5	10.01	8.43	7.76	7.39	7.15	6.98	6.85	6.76	6.68
6	8.81	7.26	6.60	6.23	5.99	5.82	5.70	5.60	5.52
7	8.07	6.54	5.89	5.52	5.29	5.12	4.99	4.90	4.82
8	7.57	6.06	5.42	5.05	4.82	4.65	4.53	4.43	4.36
9	7.21	5.71	5.08	4.72	4.48	4.32	4.20	4.10	4.03
10	6.94	5.46	4.83	4.47	4.24	4.07	3.95	3.85	3.78
11	6.72	5.26	4.63	4.28	4.04	3.88	3.76	3.66	3.59
12	6.55	5.10	4.47	4.12	3.89	3.73	3.61	3.51	3.44
13	6.41	4.97	4.35	4.00	3.77	3.60	3.48	3.39	3.31
14	6.30	4.86	4.24	3.89	3.66	3.50	3.38	3.29	3.21
15	6.20	4.77	4.15	3.80	3.58	3.41	3.29	3.20	3.12
16	6.12	4.69	4.08	3.73	3.50	3.34	3.22	3.12	3.05
17	6.04	4.62	4.01	3.66	3.44	3.28	3.16	3.06	2.98
18	5.98	4.56	3.95	3.61	3.38	3.22	3.10	3.01	2.93
19	5.92	4.51	3.90	3.56	3.33	3.17	3.05	2.96	2.88
20	5.87	4.46	3.86	3.51	3.29	3.13	3.01	2.91	2.84
21	5.83	4.42	3.82	3.48	3.25	3.09	2.97	2.87	2.80
22	5.79	4.38	3.78	3.44	3.22	3.05	2.93	2.84	2.76
23	5.75	4.35	3.75	3.41	3.18	3.02	2.90	2.81	2.73
24	5.72	4.32	3.72	3.38	3.15	2.99	2.87	2.78	2.70
25	5.69	4.29	3.69	3.35	3.13	2.97	2.85	2.75	2.68
26	5.66	4.27	3.67	3.33	3.10	2.94	2.82	2.73	2.65
27	5.63	4.24	3.65	3.31	3.08	2.92	2.80	2.71	2.63
28	5.61	4.22	3.63	3.29	3.06	2.90	2.78	2.69	2.61
29	5.59	4.20	3.61	3.27	3.04	2.88	2.76	2.67	2.59
30	5.57	4.18	3.59	3.25	3.03	2.87	2.75	2.65	2.57
40	5.42	4.05	3.46	3.13	2.90	2.74	2.62	2.53	2.45
60	5.29	3.93	3.34	3.01	2.79	2.63	2.51	2.41	2.33
120	5.15	3.80	3.23	2.89	2.67	2.52	2.39	2.30	2.22
∞	5.02	3.69	3.12	2.79	2.57	2.41	2.29	2.19	2.11

TABLE A.4   *F* for Selected Upper-Tail Probabilities, $\alpha = 0.025$ (*continued*)

Denominator DOF	Numerator Degrees of Freedom									
	10	12	15	20	24	30	40	60	120	∞
1	968.6	976.7	984.9	993.1	997.2	1001	1006	1010	1014	1018
2	39.40	39.41	39.43	39.45	39.46	39.46	39.47	39.48	39.49	39.50
3	14.42	14.34	14.25	14.17	14.12	14.08	14.04	13.99	13.95	13.90
4	8.84	8.75	8.66	8.56	8.51	8.46	8.41	8.36	8.31	8.26
5	6.62	6.52	6.43	6.33	6.28	6.23	6.18	6.12	6.07	6.02
6	5.46	5.37	5.27	5.17	5.12	5.07	5.01	4.96	4.90	4.85
7	4.76	4.67	4.57	4.47	4.42	4.36	4.31	4.25	4.20	4.14
8	4.30	4.20	4.10	4.00	3.95	3.89	3.84	3.78	3.73	3.67
9	3.96	3.87	3.77	3.67	3.61	3.56	3.51	3.45	3.39	3.33
10	3.72	3.62	3.52	3.42	3.37	3.31	3.26	3.20	3.14	3.08
11	3.53	3.43	3.33	3.23	3.17	3.12	3.06	3.00	2.94	2.88
12	3.37	3.28	3.18	3.07	3.02	2.96	2.91	2.85	2.79	2.72
13	3.25	3.15	3.05	2.95	2.89	2.84	2.78	2.72	2.66	2.60
14	3.15	3.05	2.95	2.84	2.79	2.73	2.67	2.61	2.55	2.49
15	3.06	2.96	2.86	2.76	2.70	2.64	2.59	2.52	2.46	2.40
16	2.99	2.89	2.79	2.68	2.63	2.57	2.51	2.45	2.38	2.32
17	2.92	2.82	2.72	2.62	2.56	2.50	2.44	2.38	2.32	2.25
18	2.87	2.77	2.67	2.56	2.50	2.44	2.38	2.32	2.26	2.19
19	2.82	2.72	2.62	2.51	2.45	2.39	2.33	2.27	2.20	2.13
20	2.77	2.68	2.57	2.46	2.41	2.35	2.29	2.22	2.16	2.09
21	2.73	2.64	2.53	2.42	2.37	2.31	2.25	2.18	2.11	2.04
22	2.70	2.60	2.50	2.39	2.33	2.27	2.21	2.14	2.08	2.00
23	2.67	2.57	2.47	2.36	2.30	2.24	2.18	2.11	2.04	1.97
24	2.64	2.54	2.44	2.33	2.27	2.21	2.15	2.08	2.01	1.94
25	2.61	2.51	2.41	2.30	2.24	2.18	2.12	2.05	1.98	1.91
26	2.59	2.49	2.39	2.28	2.22	2.16	2.09	2.03	1.95	1.88
27	2.57	2.47	2.36	2.25	2.19	2.13	2.07	2.00	1.93	1.85
28	2.55	2.45	2.34	2.23	2.17	2.11	2.05	1.98	1.91	1.83
29	2.53	2.43	2.32	2.21	2.15	2.09	2.03	1.96	1.89	1.81
30	2.51	2.41	2.31	2.20	2.14	2.07	2.01	1.94	1.87	1.79
40	2.39	2.29	2.18	2.07	2.01	1.94	1.88	1.80	1.72	1.64
60	2.27	2.17	2.06	1.94	1.88	1.82	1.74	1.67	1.58	1.48
120	2.16	2.05	1.94	1.82	1.76	1.69	1.61	1.53	1.43	1.31
∞	2.05	1.94	1.83	1.71	1.64	1.57	1.48	1.39	1.27	1.00

TABLE A.4   *F* for Selected Upper-Tail Probabilities, $\alpha = 0.01$ (*continued*)

Denominator DOF	Numerator Degrees of Freedom								
	1	2	3	4	5	6	7	8	9
1	4052	4999.5	5403	5625	5764	5859	5928	5982	6022
2	98.50	99.00	99.17	99.25	99.30	99.33	99.36	99.37	99.39
3	34.12	30.82	29.46	28.71	28.24	27.91	27.67	27.49	27.35
4	21.20	18.00	16.69	15.98	15.52	15.21	14.98	14.80	14.66
5	16.26	13.27	12.06	11.39	10.97	10.67	10.46	10.29	10.16
6	13.75	10.92	9.78	9.15	8.75	8.47	8.26	8.10	7.98
7	12.25	9.55	8.45	7.85	7.46	7.19	6.99	6.84	6.72
8	11.26	8.65	7.59	7.01	6.63	6.37	6.18	6.03	5.91
9	10.56	8.02	6.99	6.42	6.06	5.80	5.61	5.47	5.35
10	10.04	7.56	6.55	5.99	5.64	5.39	5.20	5.06	4.94
11	9.65	7.21	6.22	5.67	5.32	5.07	4.89	4.74	4.63
12	9.33	6.93	5.95	5.41	5.06	4.82	4.64	4.50	4.39
13	9.07	6.70	5.74	5.21	4.86	4.62	4.44	4.30	4.19
14	8.86	6.51	5.56	5.04	4.69	4.46	4.28	4.14	4.03
15	8.68	6.36	5.42	4.89	4.56	4.32	4.14	4.00	3.89
16	8.53	6.23	5.29	4.77	4.44	4.20	4.03	3.89	3.78
17	8.40	6.11	5.18	4.67	4.34	4.10	3.93	3.79	3.68
18	8.29	6.01	5.09	4.58	4.25	4.01	3.84	3.71	3.60
19	8.18	5.93	5.01	4.50	4.17	3.94	3.77	3.63	3.52
20	8.10	5.85	4.94	4.43	4.10	3.87	3.70	3.56	3.46
21	8.02	5.78	4.87	4.37	4.04	3.81	3.64	3.51	3.40
22	7.95	5.72	4.82	4.31	3.99	3.76	3.59	3.45	3.35
23	7.88	5.66	4.76	4.26	3.94	3.71	3.54	3.41	3.30
24	7.82	5.61	4.72	4.22	3.90	3.67	3.50	3.36	3.26
25	7.77	5.57	4.68	4.18	3.85	3.63	3.46	3.32	3.22
26	7.72	5.53	4.64	4.14	3.82	3.59	3.42	3.29	3.18
27	7.68	5.49	4.60	4.11	3.78	3.56	3.39	3.26	3.15
28	7.64	5.45	4.57	4.07	3.75	3.53	3.36	3.23	3.12
29	7.60	5.42	4.54	4.04	3.73	3.50	3.33	3.20	3.09
30	7.56	5.39	4.51	4.02	3.70	3.47	3.30	3.17	3.07
40	7.31	5.18	4.31	3.83	3.51	3.29	3.12	2.99	2.89
60	7.08	4.98	4.13	3.65	3.34	3.12	2.95	2.82	2.72
120	6.85	4.79	3.95	3.48	3.17	2.96	2.79	2.66	2.56
∞	6.63	4.61	3.78	3.32	3.02	2.80	2.64	2.51	2.41

TABLE A.4   *F* for Selected Upper-Tail Probabilities, $\alpha = 0.01$ (*continued*)

Denominator DOF	Numerator Degrees of Freedom									
	10	12	15	20	24	30	40	60	120	∞
1	6056	6106	6157	6209	6235	6261	6287	6313	6339	6366
2	99.40	99.42	99.43	99.45	99.46	99.47	99.47	99.48	99.49	99.50
3	27.23	27.05	26.87	26.69	26.60	26.50	26.41	26.32	26.22	26.13
4	14.55	14.37	14.20	14.02	13.93	13.84	13.75	13.65	13.56	13.46
5	10.05	9.89	9.72	9.55	9.47	9.38	9.29	9.20	9.11	9.02
6	7.87	7.72	7.56	7.40	7.31	7.23	7.14	7.06	6.97	6.88
7	6.62	6.47	6.31	6.16	6.07	5.99	5.91	5.82	5.74	5.65
8	5.81	5.67	5.52	5.36	5.28	5.20	5.12	5.03	4.95	4.86
9	5.26	5.11	4.96	4.81	4.73	4.65	4.57	4.48	4.40	4.31
10	4.85	4.71	4.56	4.41	4.33	4.25	4.17	4.08	4.00	3.91
11	4.54	4.40	4.25	4.10	4.02	3.94	3.86	3.78	3.69	3.60
12	4.30	4.16	4.01	3.86	3.78	3.70	3.62	3.54	3.45	3.36
13	4.10	3.96	3.82	3.66	3.59	3.51	3.43	3.34	3.25	3.17
14	3.94	3.80	3.66	3.51	3.43	3.35	3.27	3.18	3.09	3.00
15	3.80	3.67	3.52	3.37	3.29	3.21	3.13	3.05	2.96	2.87
16	3.69	3.55	3.41	3.26	3.18	3.10	3.02	2.93	2.84	2.75
17	3.59	3.46	3.31	3.16	3.08	3.00	2.92	2.83	2.75	2.65
18	3.51	3.37	3.23	3.08	3.00	2.92	2.84	2.75	2.66	2.57
19	3.43	3.30	3.15	3.00	2.92	2.84	2.76	2.67	2.58	2.49
20	3.37	3.23	3.09	2.94	2.86	2.78	2.69	2.61	2.52	2.42
21	3.31	3.17	3.03	2.88	2.80	2.72	2.64	2.55	2.46	2.36
22	3.26	3.12	2.98	2.83	2.75	2.67	2.58	2.50	2.40	2.31
23	3.21	3.07	2.93	2.78	2.70	2.62	2.54	2.45	2.35	2.26
24	3.17	3.03	2.89	2.74	2.66	2.58	2.49	2.40	2.31	2.21
25	3.13	2.99	2.85	2.70	2.62	2.54	2.45	2.36	2.27	2.17
26	3.09	2.96	2.81	2.66	2.58	2.50	2.42	2.33	2.23	2.13
27	3.06	2.93	2.78	2.63	2.55	2.47	2.38	2.29	2.20	2.10
28	3.03	2.90	2.75	2.60	2.52	2.44	2.35	2.26	2.17	2.06
29	3.00	2.87	2.73	2.57	2.49	2.41	2.33	2.23	2.14	2.03
30	2.98	2.84	2.70	2.55	2.47	2.39	2.30	2.21	2.11	2.01
40	2.80	2.66	2.52	2.37	2.29	2.20	2.11	2.02	1.92	1.80
60	2.63	2.50	2.35	2.20	2.12	2.03	1.94	1.84	1.73	1.60
120	2.47	2.34	2.19	2.03	1.95	1.86	1.76	1.66	1.53	1.38
∞	2.32	2.18	2.04	1.88	1.79	1.70	1.59	1.47	1.32	1.00

Source: From M. Merrington and C. M. Thompson, "Tables of Percentage Points of the Inverted Beta (*F*)-Distribution," *Biometrika,* 1943, 33, 73–88. Reproduced by permission of the *Biometrika* Trustees.

TABLE A.5   Individual Binomial Probabilities

						π					
x	0.05	0.10	0.15	0.20	0.25	0.30	0.35	0.40	0.45	0.50	
					a. $n = 2$						
0	0.9025	0.81	0.7225	0.64	0.5625	0.49	0.4225	0.36	0.3025	0.25	2
1	0.0950	0.18	0.2550	0.32	0.3750	0.42	0.4550	0.48	0.4950	0.50	1
2	0.0025	0.01	0.0225	0.04	0.0625	0.09	0.1225	0.16	0.2025	0.25	0
	0.95	0.90	0.85	0.80	0.75	0.70	0.65	0.60	0.55	0.50	
					b. $n = 3$						
0	0.8574	0.7290	0.6141	0.5120	0.4219	0.3430	0.2746	0.2160	0.1664	0.1250	3
1	0.1354	0.2430	0.3251	0.3840	0.4219	0.4410	0.4436	0.4320	0.4084	0.3750	2
2	0.0071	0.0270	0.0574	0.0960	0.1406	0.1890	0.2389	0.2880	0.3341	0.3750	1
3	0.0001	0.0010	0.0034	0.0080	0.0156	0.0270	0.0429	0.0640	0.0911	0.1250	0
	0.95	0.90	0.85	0.80	0.75	0.70	0.65	0.60	0.55	0.50	
					c. $n = 4$						
0	0.8145	0.6561	0.5220	0.4096	0.3164	0.2401	0.1785	0.1296	0.0915	0.0625	4
1	0.1715	0.2916	0.3685	0.4096	0.4219	0.4116	0.3845	0.3456	0.2995	0.25	3
2	0.0135	0.0486	0.0975	0.1536	0.2109	0.2646	0.3105	0.3456	0.3675	0.3750	2
3	0.0005	0.0036	0.0115	0.0256	0.0469	0.0756	0.1115	0.1536	0.2005	0.25	1
4	0.00	0.0001	0.0005	0.0016	0.0039	0.0081	0.0150	0.0256	0.0410	0.0625	0
	0.95	0.90	0.85	0.80	0.75	0.70	0.65	0.60	0.55	0.50	
					d. $n = 5$						
0	0.7738	0.5905	0.4437	0.3277	0.2373	0.1681	0.1160	0.0778	0.0503	0.0312	5
1	0.2036	0.3281	0.3915	0.4096	0.3955	0.3601	0.3124	0.2592	0.2059	0.1562	4
2	0.0214	0.0729	0.1382	0.2048	0.2637	0.3087	0.3364	0.3456	0.3369	0.3125	3
3	0.0011	0.0081	0.0244	0.0512	0.0879	0.1323	0.1811	0.2304	0.2757	0.3125	2
4	0.00	0.0005	0.0022	0.0064	0.0146	0.0284	0.0488	0.0768	0.1128	0.1563	1
5	0.00	0.00	0.0001	0.0003	0.0010	0.0024	0.0053	0.0102	0.0185	0.0313	0
	0.95	0.90	0.85	0.80	0.75	0.70	0.65	0.60	0.55	0.50	

TABLE A.5   Individual Binomial Probabilities (*continued*)

						π					
x	0.05	0.10	0.15	0.20	0.25	0.30	0.35	0.40	0.45	0.50	
						e. $n = 6$					
0	0.7351	0.5314	0.3771	0.2621	0.1780	0.1176	0.0754	0.0467	0.0277	0.0156	6
1	0.2321	0.3543	0.3993	0.3932	0.3560	0.3025	0.2437	0.1866	0.1359	0.0937	5
2	0.0305	0.0984	0.1762	0.2458	0.2966	0.3241	0.3280	0.3110	0.2780	0.2344	4
3	0.0021	0.0146	0.0415	0.0819	0.1318	0.1852	0.2355	0.2765	0.3032	0.3125	3
4	0.0001	0.0012	0.0055	0.0154	0.0330	0.0595	0.0951	0.1382	0.1861	0.2344	2
5	0.00	0.0001	0.0004	0.0015	0.0044	0.0102	0.0205	0.0369	0.0609	0.0938	1
6	0.00	0.00	0.00	0.0001	0.0002	0.0007	0.0018	0.0041	0.0083	0.0156	0
	0.95	0.90	0.85	0.80	0.75	0.70	0.65	0.60	0.55	0.50	
						f. $n = 7$					
0	0.6983	0.4783	0.3206	0.2907	0.1335	0.0824	0.0490	0.0280	0.0152	0.0078	7
1	0.2573	0.3720	0.3960	0.3670	0.3115	0.2471	0.1848	0.1306	0.0872	0.0547	6
2	0.0406	0.1240	0.2097	0.2753	0.3115	0.3177	0.2985	0.2613	0.2140	0.1641	5
3	0.0036	0.0230	0.0617	0.1147	0.1730	0.2269	0.2679	0.2903	0.2918	0.2734	4
4	0.0002	0.0026	0.0109	0.0287	0.0577	0.0972	0.1442	0.1935	0.2388	0.2734	3
5	0.00	0.0002	0.0012	0.0043	0.0115	0.0250	0.0466	0.0774	0.1172	0.1641	2
6	0.00	0.00	0.0001	0.0004	0.0013	0.0036	0.0084	0.0172	0.0320	0.0547	1
7	0.00	0.00	0.00	0.00	0.0001	0.0002	0.0006	0.0016	0.0037	0.0078	0
	0.95	0.90	0.85	0.80	0.75	0.70	0.65	0.60	0.55	0.50	

TABLE A.5   Individual Binomial Probabilities (*continued*)

x	0.05	0.10	0.15	0.20	0.25	π 0.30	0.35	0.40	0.45	0.50	
						g. $n = 8$					
0	0.6634	0.4305	0.2725	0.1678	0.1001	0.0576	0.0319	0.0168	0.0084	0.0039	8
1	0.2793	0.3826	0.3847	0.3355	0.2670	0.1977	0.1373	0.0896	0.0548	0.0312	7
2	0.0515	0.1488	0.2376	0.2936	0.3115	0.2965	0.2587	0.2090	0.1569	0.1094	6
3	0.0054	0.0331	0.0839	0.1468	0.2076	0.2541	0.2786	0.2787	0.2568	0.2187	5
4	0.0004	0.0046	0.0185	0.0459	0.0865	0.1361	0.1875	0.2322	0.2627	0.2734	4
5	0.00	0.0004	0.0026	0.0092	0.0231	0.0467	0.0808	0.1239	0.1719	0.2188	3
6	0.00	0.00	0.0002	0.0011	0.0038	0.01	0.0217	0.0413	0.0703	0.1094	2
7	0.00	0.00	0.00	0.0001	0.0004	0.0012	0.0033	0.0079	0.0164	0.0313	1
8	0.00	0.00	0.00	0.00	0.00	0.0001	0.0002	0.0007	0.0017	0.0039	0
	0.95	0.90	0.85	0.80	0.75	0.70	0.65	0.60	0.55	0.50	
						h. $n = 9$					
0	0.6302	0.3874	0.2316	0.1342	0.0751	0.0404	0.0207	0.0101	0.0046	0.0020	9
1	0.2985	0.3874	0.3679	0.3020	0.2253	0.1556	0.1004	0.0605	0.0339	0.0176	8
2	0.0629	0.1722	0.2597	0.3020	0.3003	0.2668	0.2162	0.1612	0.1110	0.0703	7
3	0.0077	0.0446	0.1069	0.1762	0.2336	0.2668	0.2716	0.2508	0.2119	0.1641	6
4	0.0006	0.0074	0.0283	0.0661	0.1168	0.1715	0.2194	0.2508	0.26	0.2461	5
5	0.00	0.0008	0.0050	0.0165	0.0389	0.0735	0.1181	0.1672	0.2128	0.2461	4
6	0.00	0.0001	0.0006	0.0028	0.0087	0.0210	0.0424	0.0743	0.1160	0.1641	3
7	0.00	0.00	0.00	0.0003	0.0012	0.0039	0.0098	0.0212	0.0407	0.0703	2
8	0.00	0.00	0.00	0.00	0.0001	0.0004	0.0013	0.0035	0.0083	0.0176	1
9	0.00	0.00	0.00	0.00	0.00	0.00	0.0001	0.0003	0.0008	0.0020	0
	0.95	0.90	0.85	0.80	0.75	0.70	0.65	0.60	0.55	0.50	

TABLE A.5   Individual Binomial Probabilities (*continued*)

						π					
x	0.05	0.10	0.15	0.20	0.25	0.30	0.35	0.40	0.45	0.50	
						i. $n = 10$					
0	0.5987	0.3487	0.1969	0.1074	0.0563	0.0282	0.0135	0.0060	0.0025	0.0010	10
1	0.3151	0.3874	0.3474	0.2684	0.1877	0.1211	0.0725	0.0403	0.0207	0.0098	9
2	0.0746	0.1937	0.2759	0.3020	0.2816	0.2335	0.1757	0.1209	0.0763	0.0439	8
3	0.0105	0.0574	0.1298	0.2013	0.2503	0.2668	0.2522	0.2150	0.1665	0.1172	7
4	0.0010	0.0112	0.0401	0.0881	0.1460	0.2001	0.2377	0.2508	0.2384	0.2051	6
5	0.0001	0.0015	0.0085	0.0264	0.0584	0.1029	0.1536	0.2007	0.2340	0.2461	5
6	0.00	0.0001	0.0012	0.0055	0.0162	0.0368	0.0689	0.1115	0.1596	0.2051	4
7	0.00	0.00	0.0001	0.0008	0.0031	0.0090	0.0212	0.0425	0.0746	0.1172	3
8	0.00	0.00	0.00	0.0001	0.0004	0.0014	0.0043	0.0106	0.0229	0.0439	2
9	0.00	0.00	0.00	0.00	0.00	0.0001	0.0005	0.0016	0.0042	0.0098	1
10	0.00	0.00	0.00	0.00	0.00	0.00	0.00	0.0001	0.0003	0.0010	0
	0.95	0.90	0.85	0.80	0.75	0.70	0.65	0.60	0.55	0.50	
						j. $n = 11$					
0	0.5688	0.3138	0.1673	0.0859	0.0422	0.0198	0.0088	0.0036	0.0014	0.0005	11
1	0.3293	0.3835	0.3248	0.2362	0.1549	0.0932	0.0518	0.0266	0.0125	0.0054	10
2	0.0867	0.2131	0.2866	0.2953	0.2581	0.1998	0.1395	0.0887	0.0513	0.0269	9
3	0.0137	0.0710	0.1517	0.2215	0.2581	0.2568	0.2254	0.1774	0.1259	0.0806	8
4	0.0014	0.0158	0.0536	0.1107	0.1721	0.2201	0.2428	0.2365	0.2060	0.1611	7
5	0.0001	0.0025	0.0132	0.0388	0.0803	0.1321	0.1830	0.2207	0.2360	0.2256	6
6	0.00	0.0003	0.0023	0.0097	0.0268	0.0566	0.0985	0.1471	0.1931	0.2256	5
7	0.00	0.00	0.0003	0.0017	0.0064	0.0173	0.0379	0.0701	0.1128	0.1611	4
8	0.00	0.00	0.00	0.0002	0.0011	0.0037	0.0102	0.0234	0.0462	0.0806	3
9	0.00	0.00	0.00	0.00	0.0001	0.0005	0.0018	0.0052	0.0126	0.0269	2
10	0.00	0.00	0.00	0.00	0.00	0.00	0.0002	0.0007	0.0021	0.0054	1
11	0.00	0.00	0.00	0.00	0.00	0.00	0.00	0.00	0.0002	0.0005	0
	0.95	0.90	0.85	0.80	0.75	0.70	0.65	0.60	0.55	0.50	

TABLE A.5   Individual Binomial Probabilities (*continued*)

x	0.05	0.10	0.15	0.20	0.25	0.30	0.35	0.40	0.45	0.50	
						π					

k. $n = 12$

x	0.05	0.10	0.15	0.20	0.25	0.30	0.35	0.40	0.45	0.50	
0	0.5404	0.2824	0.1422	0.0687	0.0317	0.0138	0.0057	0.0022	0.0008	0.0002	12
1	0.3413	0.3766	0.3012	0.2062	0.1267	0.0712	0.0368	0.0174	0.0075	0.0029	11
2	0.0988	0.2301	0.2924	0.2835	0.2323	0.1678	0.1088	0.0639	0.0339	0.0161	10
3	0.0173	0.0852	0.1720	0.2362	0.2581	0.2397	0.1954	0.1419	0.0923	0.0537	9
4	0.0021	0.0213	0.0683	0.1329	0.1936	0.2311	0.2367	0.2128	0.17	0.1208	8
5	0.0002	0.0038	0.0193	0.0532	0.1032	0.1585	0.2039	0.2270	0.2225	0.1934	7
6	0.00	0.0005	0.0040	0.0155	0.0401	0.0792	0.1281	0.1766	0.2124	0.2256	6
7	0.00	0.00	0.0006	0.0033	0.0115	0.0291	0.0591	0.1009	0.1489	0.1934	5
8	0.00	0.00	0.0001	0.0005	0.0024	0.0078	0.0199	0.0420	0.0762	0.1208	4
9	0.00	0.00	0.00	0.0001	0.0004	0.0015	0.0048	0.0125	0.0277	0.0537	3
10	0.00	0.00	0.00	0.00	0.00	0.0002	0.0008	0.0025	0.0068	0.0161	2
11	0.00	0.00	0.00	0.00	0.00	0.00	0.0001	0.0003	0.0010	0.0029	1
12	0.00	0.00	0.00	0.00	0.00	0.00	0.00	0.00	0.0001	0.0002	0
	0.95	0.90	0.85	0.80	0.75	0.70	0.65	0.60	0.55	0.50	

l. $n = 13$

x	0.05	0.10	0.15	0.20	0.25	0.30	0.35	0.40	0.45	0.50	
0	0.5133	0.2542	0.1209	0.0550	0.0238	0.0097	0.0037	0.0013	0.0004	0.0001	13
1	0.3512	0.3672	0.2774	0.1787	0.1029	0.0540	0.0259	0.0113	0.0045	0.0016	12
2	0.1109	0.2448	0.2937	0.2680	0.2059	0.1388	0.0836	0.0453	0.0220	0.0095	11
3	0.0214	0.0997	0.19	0.2457	0.2517	0.2181	0.1651	0.1107	0.0660	0.0349	10
4	0.0028	0.0277	0.0838	0.1535	0.2097	0.2337	0.2222	0.1845	0.1350	0.0873	9
5	0.0003	0.0055	0.0266	0.0691	0.1258	0.1803	0.2154	0.2214	0.1989	0.1571	8
6	0.00	0.0008	0.0063	0.0230	0.0559	0.1030	0.1546	0.1968	0.2169	0.2095	7
7	0.00	0.0001	0.0011	0.0058	0.0186	0.0442	0.0833	0.1312	0.1775	0.2095	6
8	0.00	0.00	0.0001	0.0011	0.0047	0.0142	0.0336	0.0656	0.1089	0.1571	5
9	0.00	0.00	0.00	0.0001	0.0009	0.0034	0.0101	0.0243	0.0495	0.0873	4
10	0.00	0.00	0.00	0.00	0.0001	0.0006	0.0022	0.0065	0.0162	0.0349	3
11	0.00	0.00	0.00	0.00	0.00	0.0001	0.0003	0.0012	0.0036	0.0095	2
12	0.00	0.00	0.00	0.00	0.00	0.00	0.00	0.0001	0.0005	0.0016	1
13	0.00	0.00	0.00	0.00	0.00	0.00	0.00	0.00	0.00	0.0001	0
	0.95	0.90	0.85	0.80	0.75	0.70	0.65	0.60	0.55	0.50	

TABLE A.5   Individual Binomial Probabilities (*continued*)

						π					
x	0.05	0.10	0.15	0.20	0.25	0.30	0.35	0.40	0.45	0.50	

m. $n = 14$

0	0.4877	0.2288	0.1028	0.0440	0.0178	0.0068	0.0024	0.0008	0.0002	0.0001	14
1	0.3593	0.3559	0.2539	0.1539	0.0832	0.0407	0.0181	0.0073	0.0027	0.0009	13
2	0.1229	0.2570	0.2912	0.2501	0.1802	0.1134	0.0634	0.0317	0.0141	0.0056	12
3	0.0259	0.1142	0.2056	0.2501	0.2402	0.1943	0.1366	0.0845	0.0462	0.0222	11
4	0.0037	0.0349	0.0998	0.1720	0.2202	0.2290	0.2022	0.1549	0.1040	0.0611	10
5	0.0004	0.0078	0.0352	0.0860	0.1468	0.1963	0.2178	0.2066	0.1701	0.1222	9
6	0.00	0.0013	0.0093	0.0322	0.0734	0.1262	0.1759	0.2066	0.2088	0.1833	8
7	0.00	0.0002	0.0019	0.0092	0.0280	0.0618	0.1082	0.1574	0.1952	0.2095	7
8	0.00	0.00	0.0003	0.0020	0.0082	0.0232	0.0510	0.0918	0.1398	0.1833	6
9	0.00	0.00	0.00	0.0003	0.0018	0.0066	0.0183	0.0408	0.0762	0.1222	5
10	0.00	0.00	0.00	0.00	0.0003	0.0014	0.0049	0.0136	0.0312	0.0611	4
11	0.00	0.00	0.00	0.00	0.00	0.0002	0.0010	0.0033	0.0093	0.0222	3
12	0.00	0.00	0.00	0.00	0.00	0.00	0.0001	0.0005	0.0019	0.0056	2
13	0.00	0.00	0.00	0.00	0.00	0.00	0.00	0.0001	0.0002	0.0009	1
14	0.00	0.00	0.00	0.00	0.00	0.00	0.00	0.00	0.00	0.0001	0
	0.95	0.90	0.85	0.80	0.75	0.70	0.65	0.60	0.55	0.50	

n. $n = 15$

0	0.4633	0.2059	0.0874	0.0352	0.0134	0.0047	0.0016	0.0005	0.0001	0.00	15
1	0.3658	0.3432	0.2312	0.1319	0.0668	0.0305	0.0126	0.0047	0.0016	0.0005	14
2	0.1348	0.2669	0.2856	0.2309	0.1559	0.0916	0.0476	0.0219	0.0090	0.0032	13
3	0.0307	0.1285	0.2184	0.2501	0.2252	0.17	0.1110	0.0634	0.0318	0.0139	12
4	0.0049	0.0428	0.1156	0.1876	0.2252	0.2186	0.1792	0.1268	0.0780	0.0417	11
5	0.0006	0.0105	0.0449	0.1032	0.1651	0.2061	0.2123	0.1859	0.1404	0.0916	10
6	0.00	0.0019	0.0132	0.0430	0.0917	0.1472	0.1906	0.2066	0.1914	0.1527	9
7	0.00	0.0003	0.0030	0.0138	0.0393	0.0811	0.1319	0.1771	0.2013	0.1964	8
8	0.00	0.00	0.0005	0.0035	0.0131	0.0348	0.0710	0.1181	0.1647	0.1964	7
9	0.00	0.00	0.0001	0.0007	0.0034	0.0116	0.0298	0.0612	0.1048	0.1527	6
10	0.00	0.00	0.00	0.0001	0.0007	0.0030	0.0096	0.0245	0.0515	0.0916	5
11	0.00	0.00	0.00	0.00	0.0001	0.0006	0.0024	0.0074	0.0191	0.0417	4
12	0.00	0.00	0.00	0.00	0.00	0.0001	0.0004	0.0016	0.0052	0.0139	3
13	0.00	0.00	0.00	0.00	0.00	0.00	0.0001	0.0003	0.0010	0.0032	2
14	0.00	0.00	0.00	0.00	0.00	0.00	0.00	0.00	0.0001	0.0005	1
15	0.00	0.00	0.00	0.00	0.00	0.00	0.00	0.00	0.00	0.00	0
	0.95	0.90	0.85	0.80	0.75	0.70	0.65	0.60	0.55	0.50	

TABLE A.5   Individual Binomial Probabilities (*continued*)

x	0.05	0.10	0.15	0.20	0.25	π 0.30	0.35	0.40	0.45	0.50	
						o. *n* = 16					
0	0.4401	0.1853	0.0743	0.0281	0.01	0.0033	0.0010	0.0003	0.0001	0.00	16
1	0.3706	0.3294	0.2097	0.1126	0.0535	0.0228	0.0087	0.0030	0.0009	0.0002	15
2	0.1463	0.2745	0.2775	0.2111	0.1336	0.0732	0.0353	0.0150	0.0056	0.0018	14
3	0.0359	0.1423	0.2285	0.2463	0.2079	0.1465	0.0888	0.0468	0.0215	0.0085	13
4	0.0061	0.0514	0.1311	0.2001	0.2252	0.2040	0.1553	0.1014	0.0572	0.0278	12
5	0.0008	0.0137	0.0555	0.1201	0.1802	0.2099	0.2008	0.1623	0.1123	0.0667	11
6	0.0001	0.0028	0.0180	0.0550	0.1101	0.1649	0.1982	0.1983	0.1684	0.1222	10
7	0.00	0.0004	0.0045	0.0197	0.0524	0.1010	0.1524	0.1889	0.1969	0.1746	9
8	0.00	0.0001	0.0009	0.0055	0.0197	0.0487	0.0923	0.1417	0.1812	0.1964	8
9	0.00	0.00	0.0001	0.0012	0.0058	0.0185	0.0442	0.0840	0.1318	0.1746	7
10	0.00	0.00	0.00	0.0002	0.0014	0.0056	0.0167	0.0392	0.0755	0.1222	6
11	0.00	0.00	0.00	0.00	0.0002	0.0013	0.0049	0.0142	0.0337	0.0667	5
12	0.00	0.00	0.00	0.00	0.00	0.0002	0.0011	0.0040	0.0115	0.0278	4
13	0.00	0.00	0.00	0.00	0.00	0.00	0.0002	0.0008	0.0029	0.0085	3
14	0.00	0.00	0.00	0.00	0.00	0.00	0.00	0.0001	0.0005	0.0018	2
15	0.00	0.00	0.00	0.00	0.00	0.00	0.00	0.00	0.0001	0.0002	1
16	0.00	0.00	0.00	0.00	0.00	0.00	0.00	0.00	0.00	0.00	0
	0.95	0.90	0.85	0.80	0.75	0.70	0.65	0.60	0.55	0.50	
						p. *n* = 17					
0	0.4181	0.1668	0.0631	0.0225	0.0075	0.0623	0.0007	0.0002	0.00	0.00	17
1	0.3741	0.3150	0.1893	0.0957	0.0426	0.0169	0.0060	0.0019	0.0005	0.0001	16
2	0.1575	0.28	0.2673	0.1914	0.1136	0.0581	0.0260	0.0102	0.0035	0.0010	15
3	0.0415	0.1556	0.2359	0.2393	0.1893	0.1245	0.0701	0.0341	0.0144	0.0052	14
4	0.0076	0.0605	0.1457	0.2093	0.2209	0.1868	0.1320	0.0796	0.0411	0.0182	13
5	0.0010	0.0175	0.0668	0.1361	0.1914	0.2081	0.1849	0.1379	0.0875	0.0472	12
6	0.0001	0.0039	0.0236	0.0680	0.1276	0.1784	0.1991	0.1839	0.1432	0.0944	11
7	0.00	0.0007	0.0065	0.0267	0.0668	0.1201	0.1685	0.1927	0.1841	0.1484	10
8	0.00	0.0001	0.0014	0.0084	0.0279	0.0644	0.1134	0.1606	0.1883	0.1855	9
9	0.00	0.00	0.0003	0.0021	0.0093	0.0276	0.0611	0.1070	0.1540	0.1855	8
10	0.00	0.00	0.00	0.0004	0.0025	0.0095	0.0263	0.0571	0.1008	0.1484	7
11	0.00	0.00	0.00	0.0001	0.0005	0.0026	0.0090	0.0242	0.0525	0.0944	6
12	0.00	0.00	0.00	0.00	0.0001	0.0006	0.0024	0.0081	0.0215	0.0472	5
13	0.00	0.00	0.00	0.00	0.00	0.0001	0.0005	0.0021	0.0068	0.0182	4
14	0.00	0.00	0.00	0.00	0.00	0.00	0.0001	0.0004	0.0016	0.0052	3
15	0.00	0.00	0.00	0.00	0.00	0.00	0.00	0.0001	0.0003	0.0010	2
16	0.00	0.00	0.00	0.00	0.00	0.00	0.00	0.00	0.00	0.0001	1
17	0.00	0.00	0.00	0.00	0.00	0.00	0.00	0.00	0.00	0.00	0
	0.95	0.90	0.85	0.80	0.75	0.70	0.65	0.60	0.55	0.50	

TABLE A.5 Individual Binomial Probabilities (*continued*)

x	0.05	0.10	0.15	0.20	0.25	0.30	0.35	0.40	0.45	0.50	
						π					
					q. $n = 18$						
0	0.3972	0.1501	0.0536	0.0180	0.0056	0.0016	0.0004	0.0001	0.00	0.00	18
1	0.3763	0.3002	0.1704	0.0811	0.0338	0.0126	0.0042	0.0012	0.0003	0.0001	17
2	0.1683	0.2835	0.2556	0.1723	0.0958	0.0458	0.0190	0.0069	0.0022	0.0006	16
3	0.0473	0.1680	0.2406	0.2297	0.1704	0.1046	0.0547	0.0246	0.0095	0.0031	15
4	0.0093	0.07	0.1592	0.2153	0.2130	0.1681	0.1104	0.0614	0.0291	0.0117	14
5	0.0014	0.0218	0.0787	0.1507	0.1988	0.2017	0.1664	0.1146	0.0666	0.0327	13
6	0.0002	0.0052	0.0301	0.0816	0.1436	0.1873	0.1941	0.1655	0.1181	0.0708	12
7	0.00	0.0010	0.0091	0.0350	0.0820	0.1376	0.1792	0.1892	0.1657	0.1214	11
8	0.00	0.0002	0.0022	0.0120	0.0376	0.0811	0.1327	0.1734	0.1864	0.1669	10
9	0.00	0.00	0.0004	0.0033	0.0139	0.0386	0.0794	0.1284	0.1694	0.1855	9
10	0.00	0.00	0.0001	0.0008	0.0042	0.0149	0.0385	0.0771	0.1248	0.1669	8
11	0.00	0.00	0.00	0.0001	0.0010	0.0046	0.0151	0.0374	0.0742	0.1214	7
12	0.00	0.00	0.00	0.00	0.0002	0.0012	0.0047	0.0145	0.0354	0.0708	6
13	0.00	0.00	0.00	0.00	0.00	0.0002	0.0012	0.0045	0.0134	0.0327	5
14	0.00	0.00	0.00	0.00	0.00	0.00	0.0002	0.0011	0.0039	0.0117	4
15	0.00	0.00	0.00	0.00	0.00	0.00	0.00	0.0002	0.0009	0.0031	3
16	0.00	0.00	0.00	0.00	0.00	0.00	0.00	0.00	0.0001	0.0006	2
17	0.00	0.00	0.00	0.00	0.00	0.00	0.00	0.00	0.00	0.0001	1
18	0.00	0.00	0.00	0.00	0.00	0.00	0.00	0.00	0.00	0.00	0
	0.95	0.90	0.85	0.80	0.75	0.70	0.65	0.60	0.55	0.50	
					r. $n = 19$						
0	0.3774	0.1351	0.0456	0.0144	0.0042	0.0011	0.0003	0.0001	0.00	0.00	19
1	0.3774	0.2852	0.1529	0.0685	0.0268	0.0093	0.0029	0.0008	0.0002	0.00	18
2	0.1787	0.2852	0.2428	0.1540	0.0803	0.0358	0.0138	0.0046	0.0013	0.0003	17
3	0.0533	0.1796	0.2428	0.2182	0.1517	0.0869	0.0422	0.0175	0.0062	0.0018	16
4	0.0112	0.0798	0.1714	0.2182	0.2023	0.1491	0.0909	0.0467	0.0203	0.0074	15
5	0.0018	0.0266	0.0907	0.1636	0.2023	0.1916	0.1468	0.0933	0.0497	0.0222	14
6	0.0002	0.0069	0.0374	0.0955	0.1574	0.1916	0.1844	0.1451	0.0949	0.0518	13
7	0.00	0.0014	0.0122	0.0443	0.0974	0.1525	0.1844	0.1797	0.1443	0.0961	12
8	0.00	0.0002	0.0032	0.0166	0.0487	0.0981	0.1489	0.1797	0.1771	0.1442	11
9	0.00	0.00	0.0007	0.0051	0.0198	0.0514	0.0980	0.1464	0.1771	0.1762	10
10	0.00	0.00	0.0001	0.0013	0.0066	0.0220	0.0528	0.0976	0.1449	0.1762	9
11	0.00	0.00	0.00	0.0003	0.0018	0.0077	0.0233	0.0532	0.0970	0.1442	8
12	0.00	0.00	0.00	0.00	0.0004	0.0022	0.0083	0.0237	0.0529	0.0961	7
13	0.00	0.00	0.00	0.00	0.0001	0.0005	0.0024	0.0085	0.0233	0.0518	6
14	0.00	0.00	0.00	0.00	0.00	0.0001	0.0006	0.0024	0.0082	0.0222	5
15	0.00	0.00	0.00	0.00	0.00	0.00	0.0001	0.0005	0.0022	0.0074	4
16	0.00	0.00	0.00	0.00	0.00	0.00	0.00	0.0001	0.0005	0.0018	3
17	0.00	0.00	0.00	0.00	0.00	0.00	0.00	0.00	0.0001	0.0003	2
18	0.00	0.00	0.00	0.00	0.00	0.00	0.00	0.00	0.00	0.00	1
19	0.00	0.00	0.00	0.00	0.00	0.00	0.00	0.00	0.00	0.00	0
	0.95	0.90	0.85	0.80	0.75	0.70	0.65	0.60	0.55	0.50	

TABLE A.5   Individual Binomial Probabilities (*continued*)

x	0.05	0.10	0.15	0.20	0.25	0.30	0.35	0.40	0.45	0.50	
					s. $n = 20$						
0	0.3585	0.1216	0.0388	0.0115	0.0032	0.0008	0.0002	0.00	0.00	0.00	20
1	0.3774	0.2702	0.1368	0.0576	0.0211	0.0068	0.0020	0.0005	0.0001	0.00	19
2	0.1887	0.2852	0.2293	0.1369	0.0669	0.0278	0.01	0.0031	0.0008	0.0002	18
3	0.0596	0.1901	0.2428	0.2054	0.1339	0.0716	0.0323	0.0123	0.0040	0.0011	17
4	0.0133	0.0898	0.1821	0.2182	0.1897	0.1304	0.0738	0.0350	0.0139	0.0046	16
5	0.0022	0.0319	0.1028	0.1746	0.2023	0.1789	0.1272	0.0746	0.0365	0.0148	15
6	0.0003	0.0089	0.0454	0.1091	0.1686	0.1916	0.1712	0.1244	0.0746	0.0370	14
7	0.00	0.0020	0.0160	0.0545	0.1124	0.1643	0.1844	0.1659	0.1221	0.0739	13
8	0.00	0.0004	0.0046	0.0222	0.0609	0.1144	0.1614	0.1797	0.1623	0.1201	12
9	0.00	0.0001	0.0011	0.0074	0.0271	0.0654	0.1158	0.1597	0.1771	0.1602	11
10	0.00	0.00	0.0002	0.0020	0.0099	0.0308	0.0686	0.1171	0.1593	0.1762	10
11	0.00	0.00	0.00	0.0005	0.0030	0.0120	0.0336	0.0710	0.1185	0.1602	9
12	0.00	0.00	0.00	0.0001	0.0008	0.0039	0.0136	0.0355	0.0727	0.1201	8
13	0.00	0.00	0.00	0.00	0.0002	0.0010	0.0045	0.0146	0.0366	0.0739	7
14	0.00	0.00	0.00	0.00	0.00	0.0002	0.0012	0.0049	0.0150	0.0370	6
15	0.00	0.00	0.00	0.00	0.00	0.00	0.0003	0.0013	0.0049	0.0148	5
16	0.00	0.00	0.00	0.00	0.00	0.00	0.00	0.0003	0.0013	0.0046	4
17	0.00	0.00	0.00	0.00	0.00	0.00	0.00	0.00	0.0002	0.0011	3
18	0.00	0.00	0.00	0.00	0.00	0.00	0.00	0.00	0.00	0.0002	2
	0.95	0.90	0.85	0.80	0.75	0.70	0.65	0.60	0.55	0.50	

TABLE A.5   Individual Binomial Probabilities (*continued*)

x	0.05	0.10	0.15	0.20	0.25	0.30	0.35	0.40	0.45	0.50	
					π						
					t. $n = 21$						
0	0.3406	0.1094	0.0329	0.0092	0.0024	0.0006	0.0001	0.00	0.00	0.00	21
1	0.3764	0.2553	0.1221	0.0484	0.0166	0.0050	0.0013	0.0003	0.0001	0.00	20
2	0.1981	0.2837	0.2155	0.1211	0.0555	0.0215	0.0072	0.0020	0.0005	0.0001	19
3	0.0660	0.1996	0.2408	0.1917	0.1172	0.0585	0.0245	0.0086	0.0026	0.0006	18
4	0.0156	0.0998	0.1912	0.2156	0.1757	0.1128	0.0593	0.0259	0.0095	0.0029	17
5	0.0028	0.0377	0.1147	0.1833	0.1992	0.1643	0.1085	0.0588	0.0263	0.0097	16
6	0.0004	0.0112	0.0540	0.1222	0.1770	0.1878	0.1558	0.1045	0.0574	0.0259	15
7	0.00	0.0027	0.0204	0.0655	0.1265	0.1725	0.1798	0.1493	0.1007	0.0554	14
8	0.00	0.0005	0.0063	0.0286	0.0738	0.1294	0.1694	0.1742	0.1442	0.0970	13
9	0.00	0.0001	0.0016	0.0103	0.0355	0.0801	0.1318	0.1677	0.1704	0.1402	12
10	0.00	0.00	0.0003	0.0031	0.0142	0.0412	0.0851	0.1342	0.1673	0.1682	11
11	0.00	0.00	0.0001	0.0008	0.0047	0.0176	0.0458	0.0895	0.1369	0.1682	10
12	0.00	0.00	0.00	0.0002	0.0013	0.0063	0.0206	0.0497	0.0933	0.1402	9
13	0.00	0.00	0.00	0.00	0.0003	0.0019	0.0077	0.0229	0.0529	0.0970	8
14	0.00	0.00	0.00	0.00	0.0001	0.0005	0.0024	0.0087	0.0247	0.0554	7
15	0.00	0.00	0.00	0.00	0.00	0.0001	0.0006	0.0027	0.0094	0.0259	6
16	0.00	0.00	0.00	0.00	0.00	0.00	0.0001	0.0007	0.0029	0.0097	5
17	0.00	0.00	0.00	0.00	0.00	0.00	0.00	0.0001	0.0007	0.0029	4
18	0.00	0.00	0.00	0.00	0.00	0.00	0.00	0.00	0.0001	0.0006	3
	0.95	0.90	0.85	0.80	0.75	0.70	0.65	0.60	0.55	0.50	

TABLE A.6   Cumulative Binomial Probabilities

					π					
x	0.05	0.10	0.15	0.20	0.25	0.30	0.35	0.40	0.45	0.500
					a. $n=2$					
0	0.902	0.81	0.722	0.64	0.562	0.49	0.422	0.36	0.302	0.25
1	0.998	0.99	0.978	0.96	0.937	0.91	0.877	0.84	0.797	0.75
2	1.00	1.00	1.00	1.00	1.00	1.00	1.00	1.00	1.00	1.00
					b. $n=3$					
0	0.857	0.729	0.614	0.512	0.422	0.343	0.275	0.216	0.166	0.125
1	0.993	0.972	0.939	0.896	0.844	0.784	0.718	0.648	0.575	0.500
2	1.00	0.999	0.997	0.992	0.984	0.973	0.957	0.936	0.909	0.875
3	1.00	1.00	1.00	1.00	1.00	1.00	1.00	1.00	1.00	1.000
					c. $n=4$					
0	0.815	0.656	0.522	0.41	0.316	0.24	0.179	0.13	0.092	0.062
1	0.986	0.948	0.89	0.819	0.738	0.652	0.563	0.475	0.391	0.312
2	1.00	0.996	0.988	0.973	0.949	0.916	0.874	0.821	0.759	0.687
3	1.00	1.00	0.999	0.998	0.996	0.992	0.985	0.974	0.959	0.937
4	1.00	1.00	1.00	1.00	1.00	1.00	1.00	1.00	1.00	1.000
					d. $n=5$					
0	0.774	0.59	0.444	0.328	0.237	0.168	0.116	0.078	0.05	0.031
1	0.977	0.919	0.835	0.737	0.633	0.528	0.428	0.337	0.256	0.187
2	0.999	0.991	0.973	0.942	0.896	0.837	0.765	0.683	0.593	0.500
3	1.00	1.00	0.998	0.993	0.984	0.969	0.946	0.913	0.869	0.812
4	1.00	1.00	1.00	1.00	0.999	0.998	0.995	0.99	0.982	0.969
5	1.00	1.00	1.00	1.00	1.00	1.00	1.00	1.00	1.00	1.000
					e. $n=6$					
0	0.735	0.531	0.377	0.262	0.178	0.118	0.075	0.047	0.028	0.016
1	0.967	0.886	0.776	0.655	0.534	0.42	0.319	0.233	0.164	0.109
2	0.998	0.984	0.953	0.901	0.831	0.744	0.647	0.544	0.442	0.344
3	1.00	0.999	0.994	0.983	0.962	0.93	0.883	0.821	0.745	0.656
4	1.00	1.00	1.00	0.998	0.995	0.989	0.978	0.959	0.931	0.891
5	1.00	1.00	1.00	1.00	1.00	0.999	0.998	0.996	0.992	0.984
6	1.00	1.00	1.00	1.00	1.00	1.00	1.00	1.00	1.00	1.000

TABLE A.6 Cumulative Binomial Probabilities (*continued*)

x	0.05	0.10	0.15	0.20	0.25	0.30	0.35	0.40	0.45	0.500
					f. $n=7$					
0	0.698	0.478	0.321	0.21	0.133	0.082	0.049	0.028	0.015	0.008
1	0.956	0.85	0.717	0.577	0.445	0.329	0.234	0.159	0.102	0.062
2	0.996	0.974	0.926	0.852	0.756	0.647	0.532	0.42	0.316	0.227
3	1.00	0.997	0.988	0.967	0.929	0.874	0.80	0.71	0.608	0.500
4	1.00	1.00	0.999	0.995	0.987	0.971	0.944	0.904	0.847	0.773
5	1.00	1.00	1.00	1.00	0.999	0.996	0.991	0.981	0.964	0.937
6	1.00	1.00	1.00	1.00	1.00	1.00	0.999	0.998	0.996	0.992
7	1.00	1.00	1.00	1.00	1.00	1.00	1.00	1.00	1.00	1.000
					g. $n=8$					
0	0.663	0.43	0.272	0.168	0.10	0.058	0.032	0.017	0.008	1.004
1	0.943	0.813	0.657	0.503	0.367	0.255	0.169	0.106	0.063	0.035
2	0.994	0.962	0.895	0.797	0.679	0.552	0.428	0.315	0.22	0.145
3	1.00	0.995	0.979	0.944	0.886	0.806	0.706	0.594	0.477	0.363
4	1.00	1.00	0.997	0.99	0.973	0.942	0.894	0.826	0.74	0.637
5	1.00	1.00	1.00	0.999	0.996	0.989	0.975	0.95	0.912	0.855
6	1.00	1.00	1.00	1.00	1.00	0.999	0.996	0.991	0.982	0.965
7	1.00	1.00	1.00	1.00	1.00	1.00	1.00	0.999	0.988	0.996
8	1.00	1.00	1.00	1.00	1.00	1.00	1.00	1.00	1.00	1.000
					h. $n=9$					
0	0.63	0.387	0.232	0.134	0.075	0.04	0.021	0.01	0.005	0.002
1	0.929	0.775	0.599	0.436	0.30	0.196	0.121	0.071	0.039	0.020
2	0.992	0.947	0.859	0.738	0.601	0.463	0.337	0.232	0.15	0.090
3	0.999	0.992	0.966	0.914	0.834	0.73	0.609	0.483	0.361	0.254
4	1.00	0.999	0.994	0.98	0.951	0.901	0.828	0.733	0.621	0.500
5	1.00	1.00	0.999	0.997	0.99	0.975	0.946	0.901	0.834	0.746
6	1.00	1.00	1.00	1.00	0.999	0.996	0.989	0.975	0.95	0.910
7	1.00	1.00	1.00	1.00	1.00	1.00	0.999	0.996	0.991	0.980
8	1.00	1.00	1.00	1.00	1.00	1.00	1.00	1.00	0.999	0.998
9	1.00	1.00	1.00	1.00	1.00	1.00	1.00	1.00	1.00	1.000

TABLE A.6   Cumulative Binomial Probabilities (*continued*)

					π					
x	0.05	0.10	0.15	0.20	0.25	0.30	0.35	0.40	0.45	0.500
					i. $n = 10$					
0	0.599	0.349	0.197	0.107	0.056	0.028	0.013	0.006	0.003	0.001
1	0.914	0.736	0.544	0.376	0.244	0.149	0.086	0.046	0.023	0.011
2	0.988	0.93	0.82	0.678	0.526	0.383	0.262	0.167	0.10	0.055
3	0.999	0.967	0.95	0.879	0.776	0.65	0.514	0.382	0.266	0.172
4	1.00	0.998	0.99	0.967	0.922	0.85	0.751	0.633	0.504	0.377
5	1.00	1.00	0.999	0.994	0.98	0.953	0.905	0.834	0.738	0.623
6	1.00	1.00	1.00	0.999	0.996	0.989	0.974	0.945	0.898	0.828
7	1.00	1.00	1.00	1.00	1.00	0.998	0.995	0.988	0.973	0.945
8	1.00	1.00	1.00	1.00	1.00	1.00	0.999	0.998	0.995	0.989
9	1.00	1.00	1.00	1.00	1.00	1.00	1.00	1.00	1.00	0.999
10	1.00	1.00	1.00	1.00	1.00	1.00	1.00	1.00	1.00	1.000
					j. $n = 11$					
0	0.569	0.314	0.167	0.086	0.042	0.02	0.009	0.004	0.001	0.000
1	0.898	0.697	0.492	0.322	0.197	0.113	0.061	0.03	0.014	0.006
2	0.985	0.91	0.779	0.617	0.455	0.313	0.20	0.119	0.065	0.033
3	0.998	0.981	0.931	0.839	0.713	0.57	0.426	0.296	0.191	0.113
4	1.00	0.997	0.984	0.95	0.885	0.79	0.668	0.533	0.397	0.274
5	1.00	1.00	0.997	0.988	0.966	0.922	0.851	0.753	0.633	0.500
6	1.00	1.00	1.00	0.998	0.992	0.978	0.95	0.901	0.826	0.726
7	1.00	1.00	1.00	1.00	0.999	0.996	0.988	0.971	0.939	0.887
8	1.00	1.00	1.00	1.00	1.00	0.999	0.998	0.994	0.985	0.967
9	1.00	1.00	1.00	1.00	1.00	1.00	1.00	0.999	0.998	0.994
10	1.00	1.00	1.00	1.00	1.00	1.00	1.00	1.00	1.00	1.000
11	1.00	1.00	1.00	1.00	1.00	1.00	1.00	1.00	1.00	1.000

TABLE A.6   Cumulative Binomial Probabilities (*continued*)

x	0.05	0.10	0.15	0.20	0.25	0.30	0.35	0.40	0.45	0.500
					k. $n = 12$					
0	0.54	0.282	0.142	0.069	0.032	0.014	0.006	0.002	0.001	0.000
1	0.882	0.659	0.443	0.275	0.158	0.085	0.042	0.02	0.008	1.003
2	0.98	0.889	0.736	0.558	0.391	0.253	0.151	0.083	0.042	0.019
3	0.998	0.974	0.908	0.795	0.649	0.493	0.347	0.225	0.134	0.073
4	1.00	0.996	0.976	0.927	0.842	0.724	0.583	0.438	0.304	0.194
5	1.00	0.999	0.995	0.981	0.946	0.882	0.787	0.665	0.527	0.387
6	1.00	1.00	0.999	0.996	0.986	0.961	0.915	0.842	0.739	0.613
7	1.00	1.00	1.00	0.999	0.997	0.991	0.974	0.943	0.888	0.806
8	1.00	1.00	1.00	1.00	1.00	0.998	0.994	0.985	0.964	0.927
9	1.00	1.00	1.00	1.00	1.00	1.00	0.999	0.997	0.992	0.981
10	1.00	1.00	1.00	1.00	1.00	1.00	1.00	1.00	0.999	0.997
11	1.00	1.00	1.00	1.00	1.00	1.00	1.00	1.00	1.00	1.000
12	1.00	1.00	1.00	1.00	1.00	1.00	1.00	1.00	1.00	1.000
					l. $n = 13$					
0	0.513	0.254	0.121	0.055	0.024	0.01	0.004	0.001	0.00	0.000
1	0.865	0.621	0.398	0.234	0.127	0.064	0.03	0.013	0.005	0.002
2	0.975	0.866	0.692	0.502	0.333	0.202	0.113	0.058	0.027	0.011
3	0.997	0.966	0.882	0.747	0.584	0.421	0.278	0.169	0.093	0.046
4	1.00	0.994	0.966	0.901	0.794	0.654	0.501	0.353	0.228	0.133
5	1.00	0.999	0.992	0.97	0.92	0.835	0.716	0.574	0.427	0.291
6	1.00	1.00	0.999	0.993	0.976	0.938	0.871	0.771	0.644	0.50
7	1.00	1.00	1.00	0.999	0.994	0.982	0.954	0.902	0.821	0.709
8	1.00	1.00	1.00	1.00	0.999	0.996	0.987	0.968	0.93	0.867
9	1.00	1.00	1.00	1.00	1.00	0.999	0.997	0.992	0.98	0.954
10	1.00	1.00	1.00	1.00	1.00	1.00	1.00	0.999	0.996	0.989
11	1.00	1.00	1.00	1.00	1.00	1.00	1.00	1.00	0.999	0.998
12	1.00	1.00	1.00	1.00	1.00	1.00	1.00	1.00	1.00	1.000

TABLE A.6   Cumulative Binomial Probabilities (*continued*)

x	0.05	0.10	0.15	0.20	0.25	0.30	0.35	0.40	0.45	0.500
					m. $n = 14$					
0	0.488	0.229	0.103	0.044	0.018	0.007	0.002	0.001	0.00	0.000
1	0.847	0.585	0.357	0.198	0.101	0.047	0.012	0.008	0.003	0.001
2	0.97	0.842	0.648	0.448	0.281	0.161	0.084	0.04	0.17	0.006
3	0.996	0.956	0.853	0.698	0.521	0.355	0.22	0.124	0.063	0.029
4	1.00	0.991	0.953	0.87	0.742	0.584	0.423	0.279	0.167	0.090
5	1.00	0.999	0.988	0.956	0.888	0.781	0.641	0.486	0.337	0.212
6	1.00	1.00	0.998	0.988	0.962	0.907	0.816	0.692	0.546	0.395
7	1.00	1.00	1.00	0.998	0.99	0.969	0.925	0.85	0.741	0.605
8	1.00	1.00	1.00	1.00	0.998	0.992	0.976	0.942	0.881	0.788
9	1.00	1.00	1.00	1.00	1.00	0.998	0.994	0.982	0.957	0.910
10	1.00	1.00	1.00	1.00	1.00	1.00	0.999	0.996	0.989	0.971
11	1.00	1.00	1.00	1.00	1.00	1.00	1.00	0.999	0.998	0.994
12	1.00	1.00	1.00	1.00	1.00	1.00	1.00	1.00	1.00	0.999
13	1.00	1.00	1.00	1.00	1.00	1.00	1.00	1.00	1.00	1.000
					n. $n = 15$					
0	0.463	0.206	0.087	0.035	0.013	0.005	0.002	0.00	0.000	0.000
1	0.829	0.549	0.319	0.167	0.08	0.035	0.014	0.005	0.002	0.000
2	0.964	0.816	0.604	0.398	0.236	0.127	0.062	0.027	0.011	0.004
3	0.995	0.944	0.823	0.648	0.461	0.297	0.173	0.091	0.042	0.018
4	0.999	0.987	0.938	0.836	0.686	0.515	0.352	0.217	0.12	0.059
5	1.00	0.998	0.983	0.939	0.852	0.722	0.564	0.403	0.261	0.151
6	1.00	1.00	0.996	0.982	0.943	0.869	0.755	0.61	0.452	0.304
7	1.00	1.00	0.999	0.996	0.983	0.95	0.887	0.787	0.654	0.500
8	1.00	1.00	1.00	0.999	0.996	0.985	0.958	0.905	0.818	0.696
9	1.00	1.00	1.00	1.00	0.999	0.996	0.988	0.966	0.923	0.849
10	1.00	1.00	1.00	1.00	1.00	0.999	0.997	0.991	0.975	0.941
11	1.00	1.00	1.00	1.00	1.00	1.00	1.00	0.998	0.994	0.982
12	1.00	1.00	1.00	1.00	1.00	1.00	1.00	1.00	0.999	0.996
13	1.00	1.00	1.00	1.00	1.00	1.00	1.00	1.00	1.00	1.000

TABLE A.6   Cumulative Binomial Probabilities (*continued*)

					π					
x	0.05	0.10	0.15	0.20	0.25	0.30	0.35	0.40	0.45	0.500
					o. $n = 16$					
0	0.44	0.185	0.074	0.028	0.01	0.003	0.001	0.00	0.00	0.000
1	0.811	0.515	0.284	0.141	0.063	0.026	0.01	0.003	0.001	0.000
2	0.957	0.789	0.561	0.352	0.197	0.099	0.045	0.018	0.007	0.002
3	0.993	0.932	0.79	0.598	0.405	0.246	0.134	0.065	0.028	0.011
4	0.999	0.983	0.921	0.798	0.63	0.45	0.289	0.167	0.085	0.038
5	1.00	0.997	0.976	0.918	0.81	0.66	0.49	0.329	0.198	0.105
6	1.00	0.999	0.994	0.973	0.92	0.825	0.688	0.527	0.366	0.227
7	1.00	1.00	0.999	0.993	0.973	0.926	0.841	0.716	0.563	0.402
8	1.00	1.00	1.00	0.999	0.993	0.974	0.933	0.858	0.744	0.598
9	1.00	1.00	1.00	1.00	0.998	0.993	0.977	0.942	0.876	0.773
10	1.00	1.00	1.00	1.00	1.00	0.998	0.994	0.981	0.951	0.895
11	1.00	1.00	1.00	1.00	1.00	1.00	0.999	0.995	0.985	0.962
12	1.00	1.00	1.00	1.00	1.00	1.00	1.00	0.999	0.997	0.989
13	1.00	1.00	1.00	1.00	1.00	1.00	1.00	1.00	0.999	0.998
14	1.00	1.00	1.00	1.00	1.00	1.00	1.00	1.00	1.00	1.000
					p. $n = 17$					
0	0.418	0.167	0.063	0.023	0.008	0.002	0.001	0.00	0.00	0.000
1	0.792	0.482	0.252	0.118	0.05	0.019	0.007	0.002	0.001	0.000
2	0.95	0.762	0.52	0.31	0.164	0.077	0.033	0.012	0.004	0.001
3	0.991	0.917	0.756	0.549	0.353	0.202	0.103	0.046	0.018	0.006
4	0.999	0.978	0.901	0.758	0.574	0.389	0.235	0.126	0.06	0.025
5	1.00	0.995	0.968	0.894	0.765	0.597	0.42	0.264	0.147	0.072
6	1.00	0.999	0.992	0.962	0.893	0.775	0.619	0.448	0.29	0.166
7	1.00	1.00	0.998	0.989	0.96	0.895	0.787	0.641	0.474	0.315
8	1.00	1.00	1.00	0.997	0.988	0.96	0.901	0.801	0.663	0.500
9	1.00	1.00	1.00	1.00	0.997	0.987	0.962	0.908	0.817	0.685
10	1.00	1.00	1.00	1.00	0.999	0.997	0.988	0.965	0.917	0.834
11	1.00	1.00	1.00	1.00	1.00	0.999	0.997	0.989	0.97	0.928
12	1.00	1.00	1.00	1.00	1.00	1.00	0.999	0.997	0.991	0.975
13	1.00	1.00	1.00	1.00	1.00	1.00	1.00	1.00	0.998	0.994
14	1.00	1.00	1.00	1.00	1.00	1.00	1.00	1.00	1.00	0.999
15	1.00	1.00	1.00	1.00	1.00	1.00	1.00	1.00	1.00	1.00

TABLE A.6 Cumulative Binomial Probabilities (*continued*)

x	π 0.05	0.10	0.15	0.20	0.25	0.30	0.35	0.40	0.45	0.500
					q. $n = 18$					
0	0.397	0.015	0.054	0.018	0.006	0.002	0.00	0.00	0.00	0.000
1	0.774	0.45	0.224	0.099	0.039	0.014	0.005	0.001	0.00	0.000
2	0.942	0.734	0.48	0.271	0.135	0.06	0.024	0.008	0.003	0.001
3	0.989	0.902	0.72	0.501	0.306	0.165	0.078	0.033	0.012	0.004
4	0.998	0.972	0.879	0.716	0.519	0.333	0.189	0.094	0.041	0.015
5	1.00	0.994	0.958	0.867	0.717	0.534	0.355	0.209	0.108	0.048
6	1.00	0.999	0.988	0.949	0.861	0.722	0.549	0.374	0.226	0.119
7	1.00	1.00	0.997	0.984	0.943	0.859	0.728	0.563	0.391	0.240
8	1.00	1.00	0.999	0.996	0.981	0.94	0.861	0.737	0.578	0.407
9	1.00	1.00	1.00	0.999	0.995	0.979	0.94	0.865	0.747	0.593
10	1.00	1.00	1.00	1.00	0.999	0.994	0.979	0.942	0.872	0.760
11	1.00	1.00	1.00	1.00	1.00	0.999	0.994	0.98	0.946	0.881
12	1.00	1.00	1.00	1.00	1.00	1.00	0.999	0.994	0.982	0.952
13	1.00	1.00	1.00	1.00	1.00	1.00	1.00	0.999	0.995	0.985
14	1.00	1.00	1.00	1.00	1.00	1.00	1.00	1.00	0.999	0.996
15	1.00	1.00	1.00	1.00	1.00	1.00	1.00	1.00	1.00	0.999
16	1.00	1.00	1.00	1.00	1.00	1.00	1.00	1.00	1.00	1.000
					r. $n = 19$					
0	0.377	0.135	0.046	0.014	0.004	0.001	0.00	0.00	0.00	0.000
1	0.755	0.42	0.198	0.083	0.031	0.01	0.003	0.001	0.00	0.000
2	0.933	0.705	0.441	0.237	0.111	0.046	0.017	0.005	0.002	0.000
3	0.987	0.885	0.684	0.455	0.263	0.133	0.059	0.023	0.008	0.002
4	0.998	0.965	0.856	0.673	0.465	0.282	0.15	0.07	0.028	0.010
5	1.00	0.991	0.946	0.837	0.668	0.474	0.297	0.163	0.078	0.032
6	1.00	0.998	0.984	0.932	0.825	0.666	0.481	0.308	0.173	0.084
7	1.00	1.00	0.996	0.977	0.923	0.818	0.666	0.488	0.317	0.180
8	1.00	1.00	0.999	0.993	0.971	0.916	0.815	0.667	0.494	0.324
9	1.00	1.00	1.00	0.998	0.991	0.967	0.913	0.814	0.671	0.500
10	1.00	1.00	1.00	1.00	0.998	0.989	0.965	0.912	0.816	0.676
11	1.00	1.00	1.00	1.00	1.00	0.997	0.989	0.965	0.913	0.820
12	1.00	1.00	1.00	1.00	1.00	0.999	0.997	0.988	0.966	0.916
13	1.00	1.00	1.00	1.00	1.00	1.00	0.999	0.997	0.989	0.968
14	1.00	1.00	1.00	1.00	1.00	1.00	1.00	0.999	0.997	0.990
15	1.00	1.00	1.00	1.00	1.00	1.00	1.00	1.00	0.999	0.998
16	1.00	1.00	1.00	1.00	1.00	1.00	1.00	1.00	1.00	1.000

TABLE A.6   Cumulative Binomial Probabilities (*continued*)

x	0.05	0.10	0.15	0.20	0.25	0.30	0.35	0.40	0.45	0.500
						π				
					s. $n = 20$					
0	0.358	0.122	0.039	0.012	0.003	0.001	0.00	0.00	0.00	0.000
1	0.736	0.392	0.176	0.069	0.024	0.008	1.002	0.001	0.00	0.000
2	0.925	0.677	0.405	0.206	0.091	0.035	0.012	0.004	0.001	0.000
3	0.984	0.867	0.648	0.411	0.225	0.107	0.044	0.016	0.005	0.001
4	0.997	0.957	0.83	0.63	0.415	0.238	0.118	0.051	0.019	0.006
5	1.00	0.989	0.933	0.804	0.617	0.416	0.245	0.126	0.055	0.021
6	1.00	0.998	0.978	0.913	0.786	0.608	0.417	0.25	0.13	0.058
7	1.00	1.00	0.994	0.968	0.898	0.772	0.601	0.416	0.252	0.132
8	1.00	1.00	0.999	0.99	0.959	0.887	0.762	0.596	0.414	0.252
9	1.00	1.00	1.00	0.997	0.986	0.952	0.878	0.755	0.591	0.412
10	1.00	1.00	1.00	0.999	0.996	0.983	0.947	0.872	0.751	0.588
11	1.00	1.00	1.00	1.00	0.999	0.995	0.98	0.943	0.869	0.748
12	1.00	1.00	1.00	1.00	1.00	0.999	0.994	0.979	0.942	0.868
13	1.00	1.00	1.00	1.00	1.00	1.00	0.998	0.994	0.979	0.942
14	1.00	1.00	1.00	1.00	1.00	1.00	1.00	0.998	0.994	0.979
15	1.00	1.00	1.00	1.00	1.00	1.00	1.00	1.00	0.998	0.994
16	1.00	1.00	1.00	1.00	1.00	1.00	1.00	1.00	1.00	0.999
17	1.00	1.00	1.00	1.00	1.00	1.00	1.00	1.00	1.00	1.000

TABLE A.7   Individual Poisson Probabilities

	Mean Arrival Rate λ									
x	0.1	0.2	0.3	0.4	0.5	0.6	0.7	0.8	0.9	1.0
0	0.9048	0.8187	0.7408	0.6703	0.6065	0.5488	0.4966	0.4493	0.4066	0.3679
1	0.0905	0.1637	0.2222	0.2681	0.3033	0.3293	0.3476	0.3595	0.3659	0.3679
2	0.0045	0.0164	0.0333	0.0536	0.0758	0.0988	0.1217	0.1438	0.1647	0.1839
3	0.0002	0.0011	0.0033	0.0072	0.0126	0.0198	0.0284	0.0383	0.0494	0.0613
4	0.0	0.0001	0.0003	0.0007	0.0016	0.0030	0.0050	0.0077	0.0111	0.0153
5	0.0	0.0	0.0	0.0001	0.0002	0.0004	0.0007	0.0012	0.0020	0.0031
6	0.0	0.0	0.0	0.0	0.0	0.0	0.0001	0.0002	0.0003	0.0005
7	0.0	0.0	0.0	0.0	0.0	0.0	0.0	0.0	0.0	0.0001

	Mean Arrival Rate λ									
x	1.1	1.2	1.3	1.4	1.5	1.6	1.7	1.8	1.9	2.0
0	0.3329	0.3012	0.2725	0.2466	0.2231	0.2019	0.1827	0.1653	0.1496	0.1353
1	0.3662	0.3614	0.3543	0.3452	0.3347	0.3230	0.3106	0.2975	0.2842	0.2707
2	0.2014	0.2169	0.2303	0.2417	0.2510	0.2584	0.2640	0.2678	0.2700	0.2707
3	0.0738	0.0867	0.0998	0.1128	0.1255	0.1378	0.1496	0.1607	0.1710	0.1804
4	0.0203	0.0260	0.0324	0.0395	0.0471	0.0551	0.0636	0.0723	0.0812	0.0902
5	0.0045	0.0062	0.0084	0.0111	0.0141	0.0176	0.0216	0.0260	0.0309	0.0361
6	0.0008	0.0012	0.0018	0.0026	0.0035	0.0047	0.0061	0.0078	0.0098	0.0120
7	0.0001	0.0002	0.0003	0.0005	0.0008	0.0011	0.0015	0.0020	0.0027	0.0034
8	0.0	0.0	0.0001	0.0001	0.0001	0.0002	0.0003	0.0005	0.0006	0.0009
9	0.0	0.0	0.0	0.0	0.0	0.0	0.0001	0.0001	0.0001	0.0002

	Mean Arrival Rate λ									
x	2.1	2.2	2.3	2.4	2.5	2.6	2.7	2.8	2.9	3.0
0	0.1225	0.1108	0.1003	0.0907	0.0821	0.0743	0.0672	0.0608	0.0550	0.0498
1	0.2572	0.2438	0.2306	0.2177	0.2052	0.1931	0.1815	0.1703	0.1596	0.1494
2	0.2700	0.2681	0.2652	0.2613	0.2565	0.2510	0.2450	0.2384	0.2314	0.2240
3	0.1890	0.1966	0.2033	0.2090	0.2138	0.2176	0.2205	0.2225	0.2237	0.2240
4	0.0992	0.1082	0.1169	0.1254	0.1336	0.1414	0.1488	0.1557	0.1622	0.1680
5	0.0417	0.0476	0.0538	0.0602	0.0668	0.0735	0.0804	0.0872	0.0940	0.1008
6	0.0146	0.0174	0.0206	0.0241	0.0278	0.0319	0.0362	0.0407	0.0455	0.0504
7	0.0044	0.0055	0.0068	0.0083	0.0099	0.0118	0.0139	0.0163	0.0188	0.0216
8	0.0011	0.0015	0.0019	0.0025	0.0031	0.0038	0.0047	0.0057	0.0068	0.0081
9	0.0003	0.0004	0.0005	0.0007	0.0009	0.0011	0.0014	0.0018	0.0022	0.0027
10	0.0001	0.0001	0.0001	0.0002	0.0002	0.0003	0.0004	0.0005	0.0006	0.0008
11	0.0	0.0	0.0	0.0	0.0	0.0001	0.0001	0.0001	0.0002	0.0002
12	0.0	0.0	0.0	0.0	0.0	0.0	0.0	0.0	0.0	0.0001

TABLE A.7   Individual Poisson Probabilities (*continued*)

	Mean Arrival Rate λ									
x	3.1	3.2	3.3	3.4	3.5	3.6	3.7	3.8	3.9	4.0
0	0.0450	0.0408	0.0369	0.0334	0.0302	0.0273	0.0247	0.0224	0.0202	0.0183
1	0.1397	0.1304	0.1217	0.1135	0.1057	0.0984	0.0915	0.0850	0.0789	0.0733
2	0.2165	0.2087	0.2008	0.1929	0.1850	0.1771	0.1692	0.1615	0.1539	0.1465
3	0.2237	0.2226	0.2209	0.2186	0.2158	0.2125	0.2087	0.2046	0.2001	0.1954
4	0.1733	0.1781	0.1823	0.1858	0.1888	0.1912	0.1931	0.1944	0.1951	0.1954
5	0.1075	0.1140	0.1203	0.1264	0.1322	0.1377	0.1429	0.1477	0.1522	0.1563
6	0.0555	0.0608	0.0662	0.0716	0.0771	0.0826	0.0881	0.0936	0.0989	0.1042
7	0.0246	0.0278	0.0312	0.0348	0.0385	0.0425	0.0466	0.0508	0.0551	0.0595
8	0.0095	0.0111	0.0129	0.0148	0.0169	0.0191	0.0215	0.0241	0.0269	0.0298
9	0.0033	0.0040	0.0047	0.0056	0.0066	0.0076	0.0089	0.0102	0.0116	0.0132
10	0.0010	0.0013	0.0016	0.0019	0.0023	0.0028	0.0033	0.0039	0.0045	0.0053
11	0.0003	0.0004	0.0005	0.0006	0.0007	0.0009	0.0011	0.0013	0.0016	0.0019
12	0.0001	0.0001	0.0001	0.0002	0.0002	0.0003	0.0003	0.0004	0.0005	0.0006
13	0.0	0.0	0.0	0.0	0.0001	0.0001	0.0001	0.0001	0.0002	0.0002
14	0.0	0.0	0.0	0.0	0.0	0.0	0.0	0.0	0.0	0.0001

	Mean Arrival Rate λ									
x	4.1	4.2	4.3	4.4	4.5	4.6	4.7	4.8	4.9	5.0
0	0.0166	0.0150	0.0136	0.0123	0.0111	0.0101	0.0091	0.0082	0.0074	0.0067
1	0.0679	0.0630	0.0583	0.0540	0.0500	0.0462	0.0427	0.0395	0.0365	0.0337
2	0.1393	0.1323	0.1254	0.1188	0.1125	0.1063	0.1005	0.0948	0.0894	0.0842
3	0.1904	0.1852	0.1798	0.1743	0.1687	0.1631	0.1574	0.1517	0.1460	0.1404
4	0.1951	0.1944	0.1933	0.1917	0.1898	0.1875	0.1849	0.1820	0.1789	0.1755
5	0.1600	0.1633	0.1662	0.1687	0.1708	0.1725	0.1738	0.1747	0.1753	0.1755
6	0.1093	0.1143	0.1191	0.1237	0.1281	0.1323	0.1362	0.1398	0.1432	0.1462
7	0.0640	0.0686	0.0732	0.0778	0.0824	0.0869	0.0914	0.0959	0.1002	0.1044
8	0.0328	0.0360	0.0393	0.0428	0.0463	0.0500	0.0537	0.0575	0.0614	0.0653
9	0.0150	0.0168	0.0188	0.0209	0.0232	0.0255	0.0281	0.0307	0.0334	0.0363
10	0.0061	0.0071	0.0081	0.0092	0.0104	0.0118	0.0132	0.0147	0.0164	0.0181
11	0.0023	0.0027	0.0032	0.0037	0.0043	0.0049	0.0056	0.0064	0.0073	0.0082
12	0.0008	0.0009	0.0011	0.0013	0.0016	0.0019	0.0022	0.0026	0.0030	0.0034
13	0.0002	0.0003	0.0004	0.0005	0.0006	0.0007	0.0008	0.0009	0.0011	0.0013
14	0.0001	0.0001	0.0001	0.0001	0.0002	0.0002	0.0003	0.0003	0.0004	0.0005

TABLE A.7   Individual Poisson Probabilities (*continued*)

					Mean Arrival Rate λ					
x	5.1	5.2	5.3	5.4	5.5	5.6	5.7	5.8	5.9	6.0
0	0.0061	0.0055	0.0050	0.0045	0.0041	0.0037	0.0033	0.0030	0.0027	0.0025
1	0.0311	0.0287	0.0265	0.0244	0.0225	0.0207	0.0191	0.0176	0.0162	0.0149
2	0.0793	0.0746	0.0701	0.0659	0.0618	0.0580	0.0544	0.0509	0.0477	0.0446
3	0.1348	0.1293	0.1239	0.1185	0.1133	0.1082	0.1033	0.0985	0.0938	0.0892
4	0.1719	0.1681	0.1641	0.1600	0.1558	0.1515	0.1472	0.1428	0.1383	0.1339
5	0.1753	0.1748	0.1740	0.1728	0.1714	0.1697	0.1678	0.1656	0.1632	0.1606
6	0.1490	0.1515	0.1537	0.1555	0.1571	0.1584	0.1594	0.1601	0.1605	0.1606
7	0.1086	0.1125	0.1163	0.1200	0.1234	0.1267	0.1298	0.1326	0.1353	0.1377
8	0.0692	0.0731	0.0771	0.0810	0.0849	0.0887	0.0925	0.0962	0.0998	0.1033
9	0.0392	0.0423	0.0454	0.0486	0.0519	0.0552	0.0586	0.0620	0.0654	0.0688
10	0.0200	0.0220	0.0241	0.0262	0.0285	0.0309	0.0334	0.0359	0.0386	0.0413
11	0.0093	0.0104	0.0116	0.0129	0.0143	0.0157	0.0173	0.0190	0.0207	0.0225
12	0.0039	0.0045	0.0051	0.0058	0.0065	0.0073	0.0082	0.0092	0.0102	0.0113
13	0.0015	0.0018	0.0021	0.0024	0.0028	0.0032	0.0036	0.0041	0.0046	0.0052
14	0.0006	0.0007	0.0008	0.0009	0.0011	0.0013	0.0015	0.0017	0.0019	0.0022

					Mean Arrival Rate λ					
x	6.1	6.2	6.3	6.4	6.5	6.6	6.7	6.8	6.9	7.0
0	0.0022	0.0020	0.0018	0.0017	0.0015	0.0014	0.0012	0.0011	0.0010	0.0009
1	0.0137	0.0126	0.0116	0.0106	0.0098	0.0090	0.0082	0.0076	0.0070	0.0064
2	0.0417	0.0390	0.0364	0.0340	0.0318	0.0296	0.0276	0.0258	0.0240	0.0223
3	0.0848	0.0806	0.0765	0.0726	0.0688	0.0652	0.0617	0.0584	0.0552	0.0521
4	0.1294	0.1249	0.1205	0.1162	0.1118	0.1076	0.1034	0.0992	0.0952	0.0912
5	0.1579	0.1549	0.1519	0.1487	0.1454	0.1420	0.1385	0.1349	0.1314	0.1277
6	0.1605	0.1601	0.1595	0.1586	0.1575	0.1562	0.1546	0.1529	0.1511	0.1490
7	0.1399	0.1418	0.1435	0.1450	0.1462	0.1472	0.1480	0.1486	0.1489	0.1490
8	0.1066	0.1099	0.1130	0.1160	0.1188	0.1215	0.1240	0.1263	0.1284	0.1304
9	0.0723	0.0757	0.0791	0.0825	0.0858	0.0891	0.0923	0.0954	0.0985	0.1014
10	0.0441	0.0469	0.0498	0.0528	0.0558	0.0588	0.0618	0.0649	0.0679	0.0710
11	0.0244	0.0265	0.0285	0.0307	0.0330	0.0353	0.0377	0.0401	0.0426	0.0452
12	0.0124	0.0137	0.0150	0.0164	0.0179	0.0194	0.0210	0.0227	0.0245	0.0263
13	0.0058	0.0065	0.0073	0.0081	0.0089	0.0099	0.0108	0.0119	0.0130	0.0142
14	0.0025	0.0029	0.0033	0.0037	0.0041	0.0046	0.0052	0.0058	0.0064	0.0071

TABLE A.7   Individual Poisson Probabilities (*continued*)

| | Mean Arrival Rate λ | | | | | | | | | |
x	7.1	7.2	7.3	7.4	7.5	7.6	7.7	7.8	7.9	8.0
0	0.0008	0.0007	0.0007	0.0006	0.0006	0.0005	0.0005	0.0004	0.0004	0.0003
1	0.0059	0.0054	0.0049	0.0045	0.0041	0.0038	0.0035	0.0032	0.0029	0.0027
2	0.0208	0.0194	0.0180	0.0167	0.0156	0.0145	0.0134	0.0125	0.0116	0.0107
3	0.0492	0.0464	0.0438	0.0413	0.0389	0.0366	0.0345	0.0324	0.0305	0.0286
4	0.0874	0.0836	0.0799	0.0764	0.0729	0.0696	0.0663	0.0632	0.0602	0.0573
5	0.1241	0.1204	0.1167	0.1130	0.1094	0.1057	0.1021	0.0986	0.0951	0.0916
6	0.1468	0.1445	0.1420	0.1394	0.1367	0.1339	0.1311	0.1282	0.1252	0.1221
7	0.1489	0.1486	0.1481	0.1474	0.1465	0.1454	0.1442	0.1428	0.1413	0.1396
8	0.1321	0.1337	0.1351	0.1363	0.1373	0.1381	0.1388	0.1392	0.1395	0.1396
9	0.1042	0.1070	0.1096	0.1121	0.1144	0.1167	0.1187	0.1207	0.1224	0.1241
10	0.0740	0.0770	0.08	0.0829	0.0858	0.0887	0.0914	0.0941	0.0967	0.0993
11	0.0478	0.0504	0.0531	0.0558	0.0585	0.0613	0.0640	0.0667	0.0695	0.0722
12	0.0283	0.0303	0.0323	0.0344	0.0366	0.0388	0.0411	0.0434	0.0457	0.0481
13	0.0154	0.0168	0.0181	0.0196	0.0211	0.0227	0.0243	0.0260	0.0278	0.0296
14	0.0078	0.0086	0.0095	0.0104	0.0113	0.0123	0.0134	0.0145	0.0157	0.0169
15	0.0037	0.0041	0.0046	0.0051	0.0057	0.0062	0.0069	0.0075	0.0083	0.0090
16	0.0016	0.0019	0.0021	0.0024	0.0026	0.0030	0.0033	0.0037	0.0041	0.0045
17	0.0007	0.0008	0.0009	0.0010	0.0012	0.0013	0.0015	0.0017	0.0019	0.0021
18	0.0003	0.0003	0.0004	0.0004	0.0005	0.0006	0.0006	0.0007	0.0008	0.0009
19	0.0001	0.0001	0.0001	0.0002	0.0002	0.0002	0.0003	0.0003	0.0003	0.0004

| | Mean Arrival Rate λ | | | | | | | | | |
x	8.1	8.2	8.3	8.4	8.5	8.6	8.7	8.8	8.9	9.0
0	0.0003	0.0003	0.0002	0.0002	0.0002	0.0002	0.0002	0.0002	0.0001	0.0001
1	0.0025	0.0023	0.0021	0.0019	0.0017	0.0016	0.0014	0.0013	0.0012	0.0011
2	0.01	0.0092	0.0086	0.0079	0.0074	0.0068	0.0063	0.0058	0.0054	0.0050
3	0.0269	0.0252	0.0237	0.0222	0.0208	0.0195	0.0183	0.0171	0.0160	0.0150
4	0.0544	0.0517	0.0491	0.0466	0.0443	0.0420	0.0398	0.0377	0.0357	0.0337
5	0.0882	0.0849	0.0816	0.0784	0.0752	0.0722	0.0692	0.0663	0.0635	0.0607
6	0.1191	0.1160	0.1128	0.1097	0.1066	0.1034	0.1003	0.0972	0.0941	0.0911
7	0.1378	0.1358	0.1338	0.1317	0.1294	0.1271	0.1247	0.1222	0.1197	0.1171
8	0.1395	0.1392	0.1388	0.1382	0.1375	0.1366	0.1356	0.1344	0.1332	0.1318
9	0.1256	0.1269	0.1280	0.1290	0.1299	0.1306	0.1311	0.1315	0.1317	0.1318
10	0.1017	0.1040	0.1063	0.1084	0.1104	0.1123	0.1140	0.1157	0.1172	0.1186
11	0.0749	0.0776	0.0802	0.0828	0.0853	0.0878	0.0902	0.0925	0.0948	0.0970
12	0.0505	0.0530	0.0555	0.0579	0.0604	0.0629	0.0654	0.0679	0.0703	0.0728
13	0.0315	0.0334	0.0354	0.0374	0.0395	0.0416	0.0438	0.0459	0.0481	0.0504

TABLE A.7   Individual Poisson Probabilities (*continued*)

| | | | | | Mean Arrival Rate λ | | | | | |
x	8.1	8.2	8.3	8.4	8.5	8.6	8.7	8.8	8.9	9.0
14	0.0182	0.0196	0.0210	0.0225	0.0240	0.0256	0.0272	0.0289	0.0306	0.0324
15	0.0098	0.0107	0.0116	0.0126	0.0136	0.0147	0.0158	0.0169	0.0182	0.0194
16	0.0050	0.0055	0.0060	0.0066	0.0072	0.0079	0.0086	0.0093	0.0101	0.0109
17	0.0024	0.0026	0.0029	0.0033	0.0036	0.0040	0.0044	0.0048	0.0053	0.0058
18	0.0011	0.0012	0.0014	0.0015	0.0017	0.0019	0.0021	0.0024	0.0026	0.0029
19	0.0005	0.0005	0.0006	0.0007	0.0008	0.0009	0.0010	0.0011	0.0012	0.0014

| | | | | | Mean Arrival Rate λ | | | | | |
x	9.1	9.2	9.3	9.4	9.5	9.6	9.7	9.8	9.9	10.0
0	0.0001	0.0001	0.0001	0.0001	0.0001	0.0001	0.0001	0.0001	0.0001	0.0000
1	0.0010	0.0009	0.0009	0.0008	0.0007	0.0007	0.0006	0.0005	0.0005	0.0005
2	0.0046	0.0043	0.0040	0.0037	0.0034	0.0031	0.0029	0.0027	0.0025	0.0023
3	0.0140	0.0131	0.0123	0.0115	0.0107	0.01	0.0093	0.0087	0.0081	0.0076
4	0.0319	0.0302	0.0285	0.0269	0.0254	0.0240	0.0226	0.0213	0.0201	0.0189
5	0.0581	0.0555	0.0530	0.0506	0.0483	0.0460	0.0439	0.0418	0.0398	0.0378
6	0.0881	0.0851	0.0822	0.0793	0.0764	0.0736	0.0709	0.0682	0.0656	0.0631
7	0.1145	0.1118	0.1091	0.1064	0.1037	0.1010	0.0982	0.0955	0.0928	0.0901
8	0.1302	0.1286	0.1269	0.1251	0.1232	0.1212	0.1191	0.1170	0.1148	0.1126
9	0.1317	0.1315	0.1311	0.1306	0.13	0.1293	0.1284	0.1274	0.1263	0.1251
10	0.1198	0.1210	0.1219	0.1228	0.1235	0.1241	0.1245	0.1249	0.1250	0.1251
11	0.0991	0.1012	0.1031	0.1049	0.1067	0.1083	0.1098	0.1112	0.1125	0.1137
12	0.0752	0.0776	0.0799	0.0822	0.0844	0.0866	0.0888	0.0908	0.0928	0.0948
13	0.0526	0.0549	0.0572	0.0594	0.0617	0.0640	0.0662	0.0685	0.0707	0.0729
14	0.0342	0.0361	0.0380	0.0399	0.0419	0.0439	0.0459	0.0479	0.05	0.0521
15	0.0208	0.0221	0.0235	0.0250	0.0265	0.0281	0.0297	0.0313	0.0330	0.0347
16	0.0118	0.0127	0.0137	0.0147	0.0157	0.0168	0.0180	0.0192	0.0204	0.0217
17	0.0063	0.0069	0.0075	0.0081	0.0088	0.0095	0.0103	0.0111	0.0119	0.0128
18	0.0032	0.0035	0.0039	0.0042	0.0046	0.0051	0.0055	0.0060	0.0065	0.0071
19	0.0015	0.0017	0.0019	0.0021	0.0023	0.0026	0.0028	0.0031	0.0034	0.0037

| | | | | | Mean Arrival Rate λ | | | | | |
x	10.1	10.2	10.3	10.4	10.5	10.6	10.7	10.8	10.9	11.0
0	0.00	0.00	0.00	0.00	0.00	0.00	0.00	0.00	0.00	0.0000
1	0.0004	0.0004	0.0003	0.0003	0.0003	0.0003	0.0002	0.0002	0.0002	0.0002
2	0.0021	0.0019	0.0018	0.0016	0.0015	0.0014	0.0013	0.0012	0.0011	0.0010
3	0.0071	0.0066	0.0061	0.0057	0.0053	0.0049	0.0046	0.0043	0.0040	0.0037

Probability Tables   943

TABLE A.7   Individual Poisson Probabilities (*continued*)

	Mean Arrival Rate λ									
x	10.1	10.2	10.3	10.4	10.5	10.6	10.7	10.8	10.9	11.0
4	0.0178	0.0168	0.0158	0.0148	0.0139	0.0131	0.0123	0.0116	0.0109	0.0102
5	0.0360	0.0342	0.0325	0.0309	0.0293	0.0278	0.0264	0.0250	0.0237	0.0224
6	0.0606	0.0581	0.0558	0.0535	0.0513	0.0491	0.0470	0.0450	0.0430	0.0411
7	0.0874	0.0847	0.0821	0.0795	0.0769	0.0743	0.0718	0.0694	0.0669	0.0646
8	0.1103	0.1080	0.1057	0.1033	0.1009	0.0985	0.0961	0.0936	0.0912	0.0888
9	0.1238	0.1224	0.1209	0.1194	0.1177	0.1160	0.1142	0.1124	0.1105	0.1085
10	0.1250	0.1249	0.1246	0.1241	0.1236	0.1230	0.1222	0.1214	0.1204	0.1194
11	0.1148	0.1158	0.1166	0.1174	0.1180	0.1185	0.1189	0.1192	0.1193	0.1194
12	0.0966	0.0984	0.1001	0.1017	0.1032	0.1047	0.1060	0.1072	0.1084	0.1094
13	0.0751	0.0772	0.0793	0.0814	0.0834	0.0853	0.0872	0.0891	0.0909	0.0926
14	0.0542	0.0563	0.0584	0.0604	0.0625	0.0646	0.0667	0.0687	0.0708	0.0728
15	0.0365	0.0383	0.0401	0.0419	0.0438	0.0457	0.0476	0.0495	0.0514	0.0534
16	0.0230	0.0244	0.0258	0.0272	0.0287	0.0303	0.0318	0.0334	0.0350	0.0367
17	0.0137	0.0146	0.0156	0.0167	0.0177	0.0189	0.0200	0.0212	0.0225	0.0237
18	0.0077	0.0083	0.0089	0.0096	0.0104	0.0111	0.0119	0.0127	0.0136	0.0145
19	0.0041	0.0045	0.0048	0.0053	0.0057	0.0062	0.0067	0.0072	0.0078	0.0084
20	0.0021	0.0023	0.0025	0.0027	0.0030	0.0033	0.0036	0.0039	0.043	0.0046

	Mean Arrival Rate λ									
x	11.1	11.2	11.3	11.4	11.5	11.6	11.7	11.8	11.9	12.0
0	0.0000	0.0000	0.0000	0.0000	0.0000	0.0000	0.0000	0.0000	0.0000	0.0000
1	0.0002	0.0002	0.0001	0.0001	0.0001	0.0001	0.0001	0.0001	0.0001	0.0001
2	0.0009	0.0009	0.0008	0.0007	0.0007	0.0006	0.0006	0.0005	0.0005	0.0004
3	0.0034	0.0032	0.0030	0.0028	0.0026	0.0024	0.0022	0.0021	0.0019	0.0018
4	0.0096	0.0090	0.0084	0.0079	0.0074	0.0069	0.0065	0.0061	0.0057	0.0053
5	0.0212	0.0201	0.0190	0.0180	0.0170	0.0160	0.0152	0.0143	0.0135	0.0127
6	0.0393	0.0375	0.0358	0.0341	0.0325	0.0310	0.0295	0.0281	0.0268	0.0255
7	0.0623	0.0600	0.0578	0.0556	0.0535	0.0514	0.0494	0.0474	0.0455	0.0437
8	0.0864	0.0840	0.0816	0.0792	0.0769	0.0745	0.0722	0.0700	0.0677	0.0655
9	0.1065	0.1045	0.1024	0.1003	0.0982	0.0961	0.0939	0.0917	0.0895	0.0874
10	0.1182	0.1170	0.1157	0.1144	0.1129	0.1114	0.1099	0.1082	0.1066	0.1048
11	0.1193	0.1192	0.1189	0.1185	0.1181	0.1175	0.1169	0.1161	0.1153	0.1144
12	0.1104	0.1112	0.1120	0.1126	0.1131	0.1136	0.1139	0.1142	0.1143	0.1144
13	0.0942	0.0958	0.0973	0.0987	0.1001	0.1014	0.1025	0.1036	0.1046	0.1056
14	0.0747	0.0767	0.0786	0.0804	0.0822	0.0840	0.0857	0.0874	0.0889	0.0905
15	0.0553	0.0572	0.0592	0.0611	0.0630	0.0649	0.0668	0.0687	0.0706	0.0724
16	0.0384	0.0401	0.0418	0.0435	0.0453	0.0471	0.0489	0.0507	0.0525	0.0543

TABLE A.7   Individual Poisson Probabilities (*continued*)

| | | | | | Mean Arrival Rate λ | | | | | |
x	11.1	11.2	11.3	11.4	11.5	11.6	11.7	11.8	11.9	12.0
17	0.0250	0.0264	0.0278	0.0292	0.0306	0.0321	0.0336	0.0352	0.0367	0.0383
18	0.0154	0.0164	0.0174	0.0185	0.0196	0.0207	0.0219	0.0231	0.0243	0.0255
19	0.0090	0.0097	0.0104	0.0111	0.0119	0.0126	0.0135	0.0143	0.0152	0.0161
20	0.0050	0.0054	0.0059	0.0063	0.0068	0.0073	0.0079	0.0084	0.0091	0.0097

| | | | | | Mean Arrival Rate λ | | | | | |
x	12.1	12.2	12.3	12.4	12.5	12.6	12.7	12.8	12.9	13.0
4	0.0050	0.0046	0.0043	0.0041	0.0038	0.0035	0.0033	0.0031	0.0029	0.0027
5	0.0120	0.0113	0.0107	0.0101	0.0095	0.0089	0.0084	0.0079	0.0074	0.0070
6	0.0242	0.0230	0.0219	0.0208	0.0197	0.0187	0.0178	0.0169	0.0160	0.0152
7	0.0419	0.0402	0.0385	0.0368	0.0353	0.0337	0.0323	0.0308	0.0295	0.0281
8	0.0634	0.0612	0.0591	0.0571	0.0551	0.0531	0.0512	0.0493	0.0475	0.0457
9	0.0852	0.0830	0.0808	0.0787	0.0765	0.0744	0.0723	0.0702	0.0681	0.0661
10	0.1031	0.1013	0.0994	0.0975	0.0956	0.0937	0.0918	0.0898	0.0878	0.0859
11	0.1134	0.1123	0.1112	0.1100	0.1087	0.1074	0.1060	0.1045	0.1030	0.1015
12	0.1143	0.1142	0.1139	0.1136	0.1132	0.1127	0.1121	0.1115	0.1107	0.1099
13	0.1064	0.1072	0.1078	0.1084	0.1089	0.1093	0.1096	0.1098	0.1099	0.1099
14	0.0920	0.0934	0.0947	0.0960	0.0972	0.0983	0.0994	0.1004	0.1013	0.1021
15	0.0742	0.0759	0.0777	0.0794	0.0810	0.0826	0.0841	0.0856	0.0871	0.0885
16	0.0561	0.0579	0.0597	0.0615	0.0633	0.0650	0.0668	0.0685	0.0702	0.0719
17	0.0399	0.0416	0.0432	0.0449	0.0465	0.0482	0.0499	0.0516	0.0533	0.0550
18	0.0268	0.0282	0.0295	0.0309	0.0323	0.0337	0.0352	0.0367	0.0382	0.0397
19	0.0171	0.0181	0.0191	0.0202	0.0213	0.0224	0.0235	0.0247	0.0259	0.0272
20	0.0103	0.0110	0.0118	0.0125	0.0133	0.0141	0.0149	0.0158	0.0167	0.0177

| | | | | | Mean Arrival Rate λ | | | | | |
x	13.1	13.2	13.3	13.4	13.5	13.6	13.7	13.8	13.9	14.0
5	0.0066	0.0062	0.0058	0.0055	0.0051	0.0048	0.0045	0.0042	0.0040	0.0037
6	0.0144	0.0136	0.0129	0.0122	0.0115	0.0109	0.0103	0.0097	0.0092	0.0087
7	0.0269	0.0256	0.0245	0.0233	0.0222	0.0212	0.0202	0.0192	0.0183	0.0174
8	0.0440	0.0423	0.0407	0.0391	0.0375	0.0360	0.0345	0.0331	0.0318	0.0304
9	0.0640	0.0620	0.0601	0.0582	0.0563	0.0544	0.0526	0.0508	0.0491	0.0473
10	0.0839	0.0819	0.0799	0.0779	0.0760	0.0740	0.0720	0.0701	0.0682	0.0663
11	0.0999	0.0983	0.0966	0.0949	0.0932	0.0915	0.0897	0.0880	0.0862	0.0844
12	0.1091	0.1081	0.1071	0.1060	0.1049	0.1037	0.1024	0.1011	0.0998	0.0984
13	0.1099	0.1098	0.1096	0.1093	0.1089	0.1085	0.1080	0.1074	0.1067	0.1060

TABLE A.7 Individual Poisson Probabilities (*continued*)

				Mean Arrival Rate λ						
x	13.1	13.2	13.3	13.4	13.5	13.6	13.7	13.8	13.9	14.0
14	0.1028	0.1035	0.1041	0.1046	0.1050	0.1054	0.1056	0.1058	0.1060	0.1060
15	0.0898	0.0911	0.0923	0.0934	0.0945	0.0955	0.0965	0.0974	0.0982	0.0989
16	0.0735	0.0751	0.0767	0.0783	0.0798	0.0812	0.0826	0.0840	0.0853	0.0866
17	0.0567	0.0583	0.0600	0.0617	0.0633	0.0650	0.0666	0.0682	0.0697	0.0713
18	0.0412	0.0428	0.0443	0.0459	0.0475	0.0491	0.0507	0.0523	0.0539	0.0554
19	0.0284	0.0297	0.0310	0.0324	0.0337	0.0351	0.0365	0.0380	0.0394	0.0409
20	0.0186	0.0196	0.0206	0.0217	0.0228	0.0239	0.0250	0.0262	0.0274	0.0286

				Mean Arrival Rate λ						
x	14.1	14.2	14.3	14.4	14.5	14.6	14.7	14.8	14.9	15.0
6	0.0082	0.0078	0.0073	0.0069	0.0065	0.0061	0.0058	0.0055	0.0051	0.0048
7	0.0165	0.0157	0.0149	0.0142	0.0135	0.0128	0.0122	0.0115	0.0109	0.0104
8	0.0292	0.0279	0.0267	0.0256	0.0244	0.0234	0.0223	0.0213	0.0204	0.0194
9	0.0457	0.0440	0.0424	0.0409	0.0394	0.0379	0.0365	0.0351	0.0337	0.0324
10	0.0644	0.0625	0.0607	0.0589	0.0571	0.0553	0.0536	0.0519	0.0502	0.0486
11	0.0825	0.0807	0.0789	0.0771	0.0753	0.0735	0.0716	0.0698	0.0681	0.0663
12	0.0970	0.0955	0.0940	0.0925	0.0910	0.0894	0.0878	0.0861	0.0845	0.0829
13	0.1052	0.1043	0.1034	0.1025	0.1014	0.1004	0.0992	0.0981	0.0969	0.0956
14	0.1060	0.1058	0.1057	0.1054	0.1051	0.1047	0.1042	0.1037	0.1031	0.1024
15	0.0996	0.1002	0.1007	0.1012	0.1016	0.1019	0.1021	0.1023	0.1024	0.1024
16	0.0878	0.0889	0.0900	0.0911	0.0920	0.0930	0.0938	0.0946	0.0954	0.0960
17	0.0728	0.0743	0.0757	0.0771	0.0785	0.0798	0.0811	0.0824	0.0836	0.0847
18	0.0570	0.0586	0.0602	0.0617	0.0632	0.0648	0.0663	0.0677	0.0692	0.0706
19	0.0423	0.0438	0.0453	0.0468	0.0483	0.0498	0.0513	0.0528	0.0543	0.0557
20	0.0298	0.0311	0.0324	0.0337	0.0350	0.0363	0.0377	0.0390	0.0404	0.0418
21	0.0200	0.0210	0.0220	0.0231	0.0242	0.0253	0.0264	0.0275	0.0287	0.0299
22	0.0128	0.0136	0.0143	0.0151	0.0159	0.0168	0.0176	0.0185	0.0194	0.0204
23	0.0079	0.0084	0.0089	0.0095	0.0100	0.0106	0.0113	0.0119	0.0126	0.0133
24	0.0046	0.0050	0.0053	0.0057	0.0061	0.0065	0.0069	0.0073	0.0078	0.0083

				Mean Arrival Rate λ						
x	15.1	15.2	15.3	15.4	15.5	15.6	15.7	15.8	15.9	16.0
7	0.0098	0.0093	0.0088	0.0084	0.0079	0.0075	0.0071	0.0067	0.0063	0.0060
8	0.0186	0.0177	0.0169	0.0161	0.0153	0.0146	0.0139	0.0132	0.0126	0.0120
9	0.0311	0.0299	0.0287	0.0275	0.0264	0.0253	0.0243	0.0232	0.0223	0.0213
10	0.0470	0.0454	0.0439	0.0424	0.0409	0.0395	0.0381	0.0367	0.0354	0.0341

TABLE A.7   Individual Poisson Probabilities (*continued*)

					Mean Arrival Rate λ					
x	15.1	15.2	15.3	15.4	15.5	15.6	15.7	15.8	15.9	16.0
11	0.0645	0.0628	0.0611	0.0594	0.0577	0.0560	0.0544	0.0527	0.0512	0.0496
12	0.0812	0.0795	0.0778	0.0762	0.0745	0.0728	0.0711	0.0695	0.0678	0.0661
13	0.0943	0.0930	0.0916	0.0902	0.0888	0.0874	0.0859	0.0844	0.0829	0.0814
14	0.1017	0.1010	0.1001	0.0993	0.0983	0.0974	0.0963	0.0953	0.0942	0.0930
15	0.1024	0.1023	0.1021	0.1019	0.1016	0.1012	0.1008	0.1003	0.0998	0.0992
16	0.0966	0.0972	0.0977	0.0981	0.0984	0.0987	0.0989	0.0991	0.0992	0.0992
17	0.0858	0.0869	0.0879	0.0888	0.0897	0.0906	0.0914	0.0921	0.0928	0.0934
18	0.0720	0.0734	0.0747	0.0760	0.0773	0.0785	0.0797	0.0808	0.0819	0.0830
19	0.0572	0.0587	0.0602	0.0616	0.0630	0.0645	0.0659	0.0672	0.0686	0.0699
20	0.0432	0.0446	0.0460	0.0474	0.0489	0.0503	0.0517	0.0531	0.0545	0.0559
21	0.0311	0.0323	0.0335	0.0348	0.0361	0.0373	0.0386	0.0400	0.0413	0.0426
22	0.0213	0.0223	0.0233	0.0244	0.0254	0.0265	0.0276	0.0287	0.0298	0.0310
23	0.0140	0.0147	0.0155	0.0163	0.0171	0.0180	0.0188	0.0197	0.0206	0.0216
24	0.0088	0.0093	0.0099	0.0105	0.0111	0.0117	0.0123	0.0130	0.0137	0.0144
25	0.0053	0.0057	0.0061	0.0064	0.0069	0.0073	0.0077	0.0082	0.0087	0.0092

					Mean Arrival Rate λ					
x	16.1	16.2	16.3	16.4	16.5	16.6	16.7	16.8	16.9	17.0
7	0.0057	0.0054	0.0051	0.0048	0.0045	0.0043	0.0040	0.0038	0.0036	0.0034
8	0.0114	0.0108	0.0103	0.0098	0.0093	0.0088	0.0084	0.0080	0.0076	0.0072
9	0.0204	0.0195	0.0187	0.0178	0.0171	0.0163	0.0156	0.0149	0.0142	0.0135
10	0.0328	0.0316	0.0304	0.0293	0.0281	0.0270	0.0260	0.0250	0.0240	0.0230
11	0.0481	0.0466	0.0451	0.0436	0.0422	0.0408	0.0394	0.0381	0.0368	0.0355
12	0.0645	0.0628	0.0612	0.0596	0.0580	0.0565	0.0549	0.0534	0.0518	0.0504
13	0.0799	0.0783	0.0768	0.0752	0.0736	0.0721	0.0705	0.0690	0.0674	0.0658
14	0.0918	0.0906	0.0894	0.0881	0.0868	0.0855	0.0841	0.0828	0.0814	0.0800
15	0.0986	0.0979	0.0971	0.0963	0.0955	0.0946	0.0937	0.0927	0.0917	0.0906
16	0.0992	0.0991	0.0989	0.0987	0.0985	0.0981	0.0978	0.0973	0.0968	0.0963
17	0.0939	0.0944	0.0949	0.0952	0.0956	0.0958	0.0960	0.0962	0.0963	0.0963
18	0.0840	0.0850	0.0859	0.0868	0.0876	0.0884	0.0891	0.0898	0.0904	0.0909
19	0.0712	0.0725	0.0737	0.0749	0.0761	0.0772	0.0783	0.0794	0.0804	0.0814
20	0.0573	0.0587	0.0601	0.0614	0.0628	0.0641	0.0654	0.0667	0.0679	0.0692
21	0.0439	0.0453	0.0466	0.0480	0.0493	0.0507	0.0520	0.0533	0.0547	0.0560
22	0.0322	0.0333	0.0345	0.0358	0.0370	0.0382	0.0395	0.0407	0.0420	0.0433
23	0.0225	0.0235	0.0245	0.0255	0.0265	0.0276	0.0287	0.0297	0.0309	0.0320
24	0.0151	0.0159	0.0166	0.0174	0.0182	0.0191	0.0199	0.0208	0.0217	0.0226
25	0.0097	0.0103	0.0108	0.0114	0.0120	0.0127	0.0133	0.0140	0.0147	0.0154

TABLE A.7   Individual Poisson Probabilities (*continued*)

					Mean Arrival Rate λ					
x	17.1	17.2	17.3	17.4	17.5	17.6	17.7	17.8	17.9	18.0
8	0.0068	0.0064	0.0061	0.0058	0.0055	0.0052	0.0049	0.0046	0.0044	0.0042
9	0.0129	0.0123	0.0117	0.0112	0.0107	0.0101	0.0097	0.0092	0.0088	0.0083
10	0.0221	0.0212	0.0203	0.0195	0.0186	0.0179	0.0171	0.0164	0.0157	0.0150
11	0.0343	0.0331	0.0319	0.0308	0.0297	0.0286	0.0275	0.0265	0.0255	0.0245
12	0.0489	0.0474	0.0460	0.0446	0.0432	0.0419	0.0406	0.0393	0.0380	0.0368
13	0.0643	0.0628	0.0612	0.0597	0.0582	0.0567	0.0553	0.0538	0.0524	0.0509
14	0.0785	0.0771	0.0757	0.0742	0.0728	0.0713	0.0699	0.0684	0.0669	0.0655
15	0.0895	0.0884	0.0873	0.0861	0.0849	0.0837	0.0824	0.0812	0.0799	0.0786
16	0.0957	0.0951	0.0944	0.0936	0.0929	0.0920	0.0912	0.0903	0.0894	0.0884
17	0.0963	0.0962	0.0960	0.0958	0.0956	0.0953	0.0949	0.0945	0.0941	0.0936
18	0.0914	0.0919	0.0923	0.0926	0.0929	0.0932	0.0934	0.0935	0.0936	0.0936
19	0.0823	0.0832	0.0840	0.0848	0.0856	0.0863	0.0870	0.0876	0.0882	0.0887
20	0.0704	0.0715	0.0727	0.0738	0.0749	0.0760	0.0770	0.0780	0.0789	0.0798
21	0.0573	0.0586	0.0599	0.0612	0.0624	0.0637	0.0649	0.0661	0.0673	0.0684
22	0.0445	0.0458	0.0471	0.0484	0.0496	0.0509	0.0522	0.0535	0.0547	0.0560
23	0.0331	0.0343	0.0354	0.0366	0.0378	0.0390	0.0402	0.0414	0.0426	0.0438
24	0.0236	0.0246	0.0255	0.0265	0.0275	0.0286	0.0296	0.0307	0.0318	0.0328
25	0.0161	0.0169	0.0177	0.0185	0.0193	0.0201	0.0210	0.0218	0.0227	0.0237

					Mean Arrival Rate λ					
x	18.1	18.2	18.3	18.4	18.5	18.6	18.7	18.8	18.9	19.0
9	0.0079	0.0075	0.0072	0.0068	0.0065	0.0061	0.0058	0.0055	0.0053	0.0050
10	0.0143	0.0137	0.0131	0.0125	0.0120	0.0114	0.0109	0.0104	0.0099	0.0095
11	0.0236	0.0227	0.0218	0.0209	0.0201	0.0193	0.0185	0.0178	0.0171	0.0164
12	0.0356	0.0344	0.0332	0.0321	0.0310	0.0299	0.0289	0.0278	0.0269	0.0259
13	0.0495	0.0481	0.0468	0.0454	0.0441	0.0428	0.0415	0.0403	0.0390	0.0378
14	0.0640	0.0626	0.0611	0.0597	0.0583	0.0569	0.0555	0.0541	0.0527	0.0514
15	0.0773	0.0759	0.0746	0.0732	0.0719	0.0705	0.0692	0.0678	0.0664	0.0650
16	0.0874	0.0864	0.0853	0.0842	0.0831	0.0820	0.0808	0.0796	0.0785	0.0772
17	0.0931	0.0925	0.0918	0.0912	0.0904	0.0897	0.0889	0.0881	0.0872	0.0863
18	0.0936	0.0935	0.0934	0.0932	0.0930	0.0927	0.0924	0.0920	0.0916	0.0911
19	0.0891	0.0896	0.0899	0.0902	0.0905	0.0907	0.0909	0.0910	0.0911	0.0911
20	0.0807	0.0815	0.0823	0.0830	0.0837	0.0844	0.0850	0.0856	0.0861	0.0866
21	0.0695	0.0706	0.0717	0.0727	0.0738	0.0747	0.0757	0.0766	0.0775	0.0783
22	0.0572	0.0584	0.0596	0.0608	0.0620	0.0632	0.0643	0.0655	0.0666	0.0676
23	0.0450	0.0462	0.0475	0.0487	0.0499	0.0511	0.0523	0.0535	0.0547	0.0559
24	0.0340	0.0351	0.0362	0.0373	0.0385	0.0396	0.0408	0.0419	0.0431	0.0442
25	0.0246	0.0255	0.0265	0.0275	0.0285	0.0295	0.0305	0.0315	0.0326	0.0336

TABLE A.7   Individual Poisson Probabilities (*continued*)

					Mean Arrival Rate λ					
x	19.1	19.2	19.3	19.4	19.5	19.6	19.7	19.8	19.9	20.0
10	0.0090	0.0086	0.0082	0.0078	0.0074	0.0071	0.0067	0.0064	0.0061	0.0058
11	0.0157	0.0150	0.0144	0.0138	0.0132	0.0126	0.0121	0.0116	0.0111	0.0106
12	0.0249	0.0240	0.0231	0.0223	0.0214	0.0206	0.0198	0.0191	0.0183	0.0176
13	0.0367	0.0355	0.0344	0.0333	0.0322	0.0311	0.0301	0.0291	0.0281	0.0271
14	0.0500	0.0487	0.0474	0.0461	0.0448	0.0436	0.0423	0.0411	0.0399	0.0387
15	0.0637	0.0623	0.0610	0.0596	0.0582	0.0569	0.0556	0.0543	0.0529	0.0516
16	0.0760	0.0748	0.0735	0.0723	0.0710	0.0697	0.0684	0.0671	0.0659	0.0646
17	0.0854	0.0844	0.0835	0.0825	0.0814	0.0804	0.0793	0.0782	0.0771	0.0760
18	0.0906	0.0901	0.0895	0.0889	0.0882	0.0875	0.0868	0.0860	0.0852	0.0844
19	0.0911	0.0910	0.0909	0.0907	0.0905	0.0903	0.0900	0.0896	0.0893	0.0888
20	0.0870	0.0874	0.0877	0.0880	0.0883	0.0885	0.0886	0.0887	0.0888	0.0888
21	0.0791	0.0799	0.0806	0.0813	0.0820	0.0826	0.0831	0.0837	0.0842	0.0846
22	0.0687	0.0697	0.0707	0.0717	0.0727	0.0736	0.0745	0.0753	0.0761	0.0769
23	0.0570	0.0582	0.0594	0.0605	0.0616	0.0627	0.0638	0.0648	0.0659	0.0669
24	0.0454	0.0466	0.0477	0.0489	0.0500	0.0512	0.0523	0.0535	0.0546	0.0557
25	0.0347	0.0358	0.0368	0.0379	0.0390	0.0401	0.0412	0.0424	0.0435	0.0446

					Mean Arrival Rate λ					
x	20.1	20.2	20.3	20.4	20.5	20.6	20.7	20.8	20.9	21.0
10	0.0055	0.0053	0.0050	0.0048	0.0045	0.0043	0.0041	0.0039	0.0037	0.0035
11	0.0101	0.0097	0.0092	0.0088	0.0084	0.0080	0.0077	0.0073	0.0070	0.0067
12	0.0169	0.0163	0.0156	0.0150	0.0144	0.0138	0.0132	0.0127	0.0122	0.0116
13	0.0262	0.0253	0.0244	0.0235	0.0227	0.0219	0.0211	0.0203	0.0195	0.0188
14	0.0376	0.0365	0.0353	0.0343	0.0332	0.0322	0.0311	0.0301	0.0292	0.0282
15	0.0504	0.0491	0.0478	0.0466	0.0454	0.0442	0.0430	0.0418	0.0406	0.0395
16	0.0633	0.0620	0.0607	0.0594	0.0581	0.0569	0.0556	0.0543	0.0531	0.0518
17	0.0748	0.0736	0.0725	0.0713	0.0701	0.0689	0.0677	0.0665	0.0653	0.0640
18	0.0835	0.0826	0.0817	0.0808	0.0798	0.0789	0.0778	0.0768	0.0758	0.0747
19	0.0884	0.0879	0.0873	0.0868	0.0861	0.0855	0.0848	0.0841	0.0834	0.0826
20	0.0888	0.0887	0.0886	0.0885	0.0883	0.0881	0.0878	0.0875	0.0871	0.0867
21	0.0850	0.0854	0.0857	0.0860	0.0862	0.0864	0.0865	0.0866	0.0867	0.0867
22	0.0777	0.0784	0.0791	0.0797	0.0803	0.0809	0.0814	0.0819	0.0824	0.0828
23	0.0679	0.0688	0.0698	0.0707	0.0716	0.0724	0.0733	0.0741	0.0748	0.0756
24	0.0568	0.0579	0.0590	0.0601	0.0611	0.0622	0.0632	0.0642	0.0652	0.0661
25	0.0457	0.0468	0.0479	0.0490	0.0501	0.0612	0.0523	0.0534	0.0545	0.0555

TABLE A.8   Cumulative Poisson Probabilities

	Mean Arrival Rate λ									
x	0.1	0.2	0.3	0.4	0.5	0.6	0.7	0.8	0.9	1.0
0	0.9048	0.8187	0.7408	0.6703	0.6065	0.5488	0.4966	0.4493	0.4066	0.3679
1	0.9953	0.9825	0.9631	0.9384	0.9098	0.8781	0.8442	0.8088	0.7725	0.7358
2	0.9998	0.9989	0.9964	0.9921	0.9856	0.9769	0.9659	0.9526	0.9371	0.9197
3	1.0000	0.9999	0.9997	0.9992	0.9982	0.9966	0.9942	0.9909	0.9865	0.9810
4	1.0000	1.0000	1.0000	0.9999	0.9998	0.9996	0.9992	0.9986	0.9977	0.9963
5	1.0000	1.0000	1.0000	1.0000	1.0000	1.0000	0.9999	0.9998	0.9997	0.9994
6	1.0000	1.0000	1.0000	1.0000	1.0000	1.0000	1.0000	1.0000	1.0000	0.9999
7	1.0000	1.0000	1.0000	1.0000	1.0000	1.0000	1.0000	1.0000	1.0000	1.0000

	Mean Arrival Rate λ									
x	1.1	1.2	1.3	1.4	1.5	1.6	1.7	1.8	1.9	2.0
0	0.3329	0.3012	0.2725	0.2466	0.2231	0.2019	0.1827	0.1653	0.1496	0.1353
1	0.6990	0.6626	0.6268	0.5918	0.5578	0.5249	0.4932	0.4628	0.4337	0.4060
2	0.9004	0.8795	0.8571	0.8335	0.8088	0.7834	0.7572	0.7306	0.7037	0.6767
3	0.9743	0.9662	0.9569	0.9463	0.9344	0.9212	0.9068	0.8913	0.8747	0.8571
4	0.9946	0.9923	0.9893	0.9857	0.9814	0.9763	0.9704	0.9636	0.9559	0.9473
5	0.9990	0.9985	0.9978	0.9968	0.9955	0.9940	0.9920	0.9896	0.9868	0.9834
6	0.9999	0.9997	0.9996	0.9994	0.9991	0.9987	0.9981	0.9974	0.9966	0.9955
7	1.0000	1.0000	0.9999	0.9999	0.9998	0.9997	0.9996	0.9994	0.9992	0.9989
8	1.0000	1.0000	1.0000	1.0000	1.0000	1.0000	0.9999	0.9999	0.9998	0.9998
9	1.0000	1.0000	1.0000	1.0000	1.0000	1.0000	1.0000	1.0000	1.0000	1.0000

	Mean Arrival Rate λ									
x	2.1	2.2	2.3	2.4	2.5	2.6	2.7	2.8	2.9	3.0
0	0.1225	0.1108	0.1003	0.0907	0.0821	0.0743	0.0672	0.0608	0.0550	0.0498
1	0.3796	0.3546	0.3309	0.3084	0.2873	0.2674	0.2487	0.2311	0.2146	0.1991
2	0.6496	0.6227	0.5960	0.5697	0.5438	0.5184	0.4936	0.4695	0.4460	0.4232
3	0.8386	0.8194	0.7993	0.7787	0.7576	0.7360	0.7141	0.6919	0.6696	0.6472
4	0.9379	0.9275	0.9162	0.9041	0.8912	0.8774	0.8629	0.8477	0.8318	0.8153
5	0.9796	0.9751	0.9700	0.9643	0.9580	0.9510	0.9433	0.9349	0.9258	0.9161
6	0.9941	0.9925	0.9906	0.9884	0.9858	0.9828	0.9794	0.9756	0.9713	0.9665
7	0.9985	0.9980	0.9974	0.9967	0.9958	0.9947	0.9934	0.9919	0.9901	0.9881
8	0.9997	0.9995	0.9994	0.9991	0.9989	0.9985	0.9981	0.9976	0.9969	0.9962
9	0.9999	0.9999	0.9999	0.9998	0.9997	0.9996	0.9995	0.9993	0.9991	0.9989
10	1.0000	1.0000	1.0000	1.0000	0.9999	0.9999	0.9999	0.9998	0.9998	0.9997
11	1.0000	1.0000	1.0000	1.0000	1.0000	1.0000	1.0000	1.0000	0.9999	0.9999
12	1.0000	1.0000	1.0000	1.0000	1.0000	1.0000	1.0000	1.0000	1.0000	1.0000

TABLE A.8   Cumulative Poisson Probabilities (*continued*)

| | | | | | Mean Arrival Rate λ | | | | | |
x	3.1	3.2	3.3	3.4	3.5	3.6	3.7	3.8	3.9	4.0
0	0.0450	0.0408	0.0369	0.0334	0.0302	0.0273	0.0247	0.0224	0.0202	0.0183
1	0.1847	0.1712	0.1586	0.1468	0.1359	0.1257	0.1162	0.1074	0.0992	0.0916
2	0.4012	0.3799	0.3594	0.3397	0.3208	0.3027	0.2854	0.2689	0.2531	0.2381
3	0.6248	0.6025	0.5803	0.5584	0.5366	0.5152	0.4942	0.4735	0.4532	0.4335
4	0.7982	0.7806	0.7626	0.7442	0.7254	0.7064	0.6872	0.6678	0.6484	0.6288
5	0.9057	0.8946	0.8829	0.8705	0.8576	0.8441	0.8301	0.8156	0.8006	0.7851
6	0.9612	0.9554	0.9490	0.9421	0.9347	0.9267	0.9182	0.9091	0.8995	0.8893
7	0.9858	0.9832	0.9802	0.9769	0.9733	0.9692	0.9648	0.9599	0.9546	0.9489
8	0.9953	0.9943	0.9931	0.9917	0.9901	0.9883	0.9863	0.9840	0.9815	0.9786
9	0.9986	0.9982	0.9978	0.9973	0.9967	0.9960	0.9952	0.9942	0.9931	0.9919
10	0.9996	0.9995	0.9994	0.9992	0.9990	0.9987	0.9984	0.9981	0.9977	0.9972
11	0.9999	0.9999	0.9998	0.9998	0.9997	0.9996	0.9995	0.9994	0.9993	0.9991
12	1.0000	1.0000	1.0000	0.9999	0.9999	0.9999	0.9999	0.9998	0.9998	0.9997
13	1.0000	1.0000	1.0000	1.0000	1.0000	1.0000	1.0000	1.0000	0.9999	0.9999
14	1.0000	1.0000	1.0000	1.0000	1.0000	1.0000	1.0000	1.0000	1.0000	1.0000

| | | | | | Mean Arrival Rate λ | | | | | |
x	4.1	4.2	4.3	4.4	4.5	4.6	4.7	4.8	4.9	5.0
0	0.0166	0.0150	0.0136	0.0123	0.0111	0.0101	0.0091	0.0082	0.0074	0.0067
1	0.0845	0.0780	0.0719	0.0663	0.0611	0.0563	0.0518	0.0477	0.0439	0.0404
2	0.2238	0.2102	0.1974	0.1851	0.1736	0.1626	0.1523	0.1425	0.1333	0.1247
3	0.4142	0.3954	0.3772	0.3594	0.3423	0.3257	0.3097	0.2942	0.2793	0.2650
4	0.6093	0.5898	0.5704	0.5512	0.5321	0.5132	0.4946	0.4763	0.4582	0.4405
5	0.7693	0.7531	0.7367	0.7199	0.7029	0.6858	0.6684	0.6510	0.6335	0.6160
6	0.8786	0.8675	0.8558	0.8436	0.8311	0.8180	0.8046	0.7908	0.7767	0.7622
7	0.9427	0.9361	0.9290	0.9214	0.9134	0.9049	0.8960	0.8867	0.8769	0.8666
8	0.9755	0.9721	0.9683	0.9642	0.9597	0.9549	0.9497	0.9442	0.9382	0.9319
9	0.9905	0.9889	0.9871	0.9851	0.9829	0.9805	0.9778	0.9749	0.9717	0.9682
10	0.9966	0.9959	0.9952	0.9943	0.9933	0.9922	0.9910	0.9896	0.9880	0.9863
11	0.9989	0.9986	0.9983	0.9980	0.9976	0.9971	0.9966	0.9960	0.9953	0.9945
12	0.9997	0.9996	0.9995	0.9993	0.9992	0.9990	0.9988	0.9986	0.9983	0.9980
13	0.9999	0.9999	0.9998	0.9998	0.9997	0.9997	0.9996	0.9995	0.9994	0.9993
14	1.0000	1.0000	1.0000	0.9999	0.9999	0.9999	0.9999	0.9999	0.9998	0.9998

TABLE A.8   Cumulative Poisson Probabilities (*continued*)

					Mean Arrival Rate λ					
x	5.1	5.2	5.3	5.4	5.5	5.6	5.7	5.8	5.9	6.0
0	0.0061	0.0055	0.0050	0.0045	0.0041	0.0037	0.0033	0.0030	0.0027	0.0025
1	0.0372	0.0342	0.0314	0.0289	0.0266	0.0244	0.0224	0.0206	0.0189	0.0174
2	0.1165	0.1088	0.1016	0.0948	0.0884	0.0824	0.0768	0.0715	0.0666	0.0620
3	0.2513	0.2381	0.2254	0.2133	0.2017	0.1906	0.1800	0.1700	0.1604	0.1512
4	0.4231	0.4061	0.3895	0.3733	0.3575	0.3422	0.3272	0.3127	0.2987	0.2851
5	0.5984	0.5809	0.5635	0.5461	0.5289	0.5119	0.4950	0.4783	0.4619	0.4457
6	0.7474	0.7324	0.7171	0.7017	0.6860	0.6703	0.6544	0.6384	0.6224	0.6063
7	0.8560	0.8449	0.8335	0.8217	0.8095	0.7970	0.7841	0.7710	0.7576	0.7440
8	0.9252	0.9181	0.9106	0.9027	0.8944	0.8857	0.8766	0.8672	0.8574	0.8472
9	0.9644	0.9603	0.9559	0.9512	0.9462	0.9409	0.9352	0.9292	0.9228	0.9161
10	0.9844	0.9823	0.9800	0.9775	0.9747	0.9718	0.9686	0.9651	0.9614	0.9574
11	0.9937	0.9927	0.9916	0.9904	0.9890	0.9875	0.9859	0.9841	0.9821	0.9799
12	0.9976	0.9972	0.9967	0.9962	0.9955	0.9949	0.9941	0.9932	0.9922	0.9912
13	0.9992	0.9990	0.9988	0.9986	0.9983	0.9980	0.9977	0.9973	0.9969	0.9964
14	0.9997	0.9997	0.9996	0.9995	0.9994	0.9993	0.9991	0.9990	0.9988	0.9986

					Mean Arrival Rate λ					
x	6.1	6.2	6.3	6.4	6.5	6.6	6.7	6.8	6.9	7.0
0	0.0022	0.0020	0.0018	0.0017	0.0015	0.0014	0.0012	0.0011	0.0010	0.0009
1	0.0159	0.0146	0.0134	0.0123	0.0113	0.0103	0.0095	0.0087	0.0080	0.0073
2	0.0577	0.0536	0.0498	0.0463	0.0430	0.0400	0.0371	0.0344	0.0320	0.0296
3	0.1425	0.1342	0.1264	0.1189	0.1118	0.1052	0.0988	0.0928	0.0871	0.0818
4	0.2719	0.2592	0.2469	0.2351	0.2237	0.2127	0.2022	0.1920	0.1823	0.1730
5	0.4298	0.4141	0.3988	0.3837	0.3690	0.3547	0.3406	0.3270	0.3137	0.3007
6	0.5902	0.5742	0.5582	0.5423	0.5265	0.5108	0.4953	0.4799	0.4647	0.4497
7	0.7301	0.7160	0.7017	0.6873	0.6728	0.6581	0.6433	0.6285	0.6136	0.5987
8	0.8367	0.8259	0.8148	0.8033	0.7916	0.7796	0.7673	0.7548	0.7420	0.7291
9	0.9090	0.9016	0.8939	0.8858	0.8774	0.8686	0.8596	0.8502	0.8405	0.8305
10	0.9531	0.9486	0.9437	0.9386	0.9332	0.9274	0.9214	0.9151	0.9084	0.9015
11	0.9776	0.9750	0.9723	0.9693	0.9661	0.9627	0.9591	0.9552	0.9510	0.9467
12	0.9900	0.9887	0.9873	0.9857	0.9840	0.9821	0.9801	0.9779	0.9755	0.9730
13	0.9958	0.9952	0.9945	0.9937	0.9929	0.9920	0.9909	0.9898	0.9885	0.9872
14	0.9984	0.9981	0.9978	0.9974	0.9970	0.9966	0.9961	0.9956	0.9950	0.9943

TABLE A.8   Cumulative Poisson Probabilities (*continued*)

| | | | | | Mean Arrival Rate λ | | | | | |
x	7.1	7.2	7.3	7.4	7.5	7.6	7.7	7.8	7.9	8.0
0	0.0008	0.0007	0.0007	0.0006	0.0006	0.0005	0.0005	0.0004	0.0004	0.0003
1	0.0067	0.0061	0.0056	0.0051	0.0047	0.0043	0.0039	0.0036	0.0033	0.0030
2	0.0275	0.0255	0.0236	0.0219	0.0203	0.0188	0.0174	0.0161	0.0149	0.0138
3	0.0767	0.0719	0.0674	0.0632	0.0591	0.0554	0.0518	0.0485	0.0453	0.0424
4	0.1641	0.1555	0.1473	0.1395	0.1321	0.1249	0.1181	0.1117	0.1055	0.0996
5	0.2881	0.2759	0.2640	0.2526	0.2414	0.2307	0.2203	0.2103	0.2006	0.1912
6	0.4349	0.4204	0.4060	0.3920	0.3782	0.3646	0.3514	0.3384	0.3257	0.3134
7	0.5838	0.5689	0.5541	0.5393	0.5246	0.5100	0.4956	0.4812	0.4670	0.4530
8	0.7160	0.7027	0.6892	0.6757	0.6620	0.6482	0.6343	0.6204	0.6065	0.5925
9	0.8202	0.8096	0.7988	0.7877	0.7764	0.7649	0.7531	0.7411	0.7290	0.7166
10	0.8942	0.8867	0.8788	0.8707	0.8622	0.8535	0.8445	0.8352	0.8257	0.8159
11	0.9420	0.9371	0.9319	0.9265	0.9208	0.9148	0.9085	0.9020	0.8952	0.8881
12	0.9703	0.9673	0.9642	0.9609	0.9573	0.9536	0.9496	0.9454	0.9409	0.9362
13	0.9857	0.9841	0.9824	0.9805	0.9784	0.9762	0.9739	0.9714	0.9687	0.9658
14	0.9935	0.9927	0.9918	0.9908	0.9897	0.9886	0.9873	0.9859	0.9844	0.9827
15	0.9972	0.9969	0.9964	0.9959	0.9954	0.9948	0.9941	0.9934	0.9926	0.9918
16	0.9989	0.9997	0.9985	0.9983	0.9980	0.9978	0.9974	0.9971	0.9967	0.9963
17	0.9996	0.9995	0.9994	0.9993	0.9992	0.9991	0.9989	0.9988	0.9986	0.9984
18	0.9998	0.9998	0.9998	0.9997	0.9997	0.9996	0.9996	0.9995	0.9994	0.9993
19	0.9999	0.9999	0.9999	0.9999	0.9999	0.9999	0.9998	0.9998	0.9998	0.9997
20	1.0000	1.0000	1.0000	1.0000	1.0000	1.0000	0.9999	0.9999	0.9999	0.9999

| | | | | | Mean Arrival Rate λ | | | | | |
x	8.1	8.2	8.3	8.4	8.5	8.6	8.7	8.8	8.9	9.0
0	0.0003	0.0003	0.0002	0.0002	0.0002	0.0002	0.0002	0.0002	0.0001	0.0001
1	0.0028	0.0025	0.0023	0.0021	0.0019	0.0018	0.0016	0.0015	0.0014	0.0012
2	0.0127	0.0118	0.0109	0.0100	0.0093	0.0086	0.0079	0.0073	0.0068	0.0062
3	0.0396	0.0370	0.0346	0.0323	0.0301	0.0281	0.0262	0.0244	0.0228	0.0212
4	0.0940	0.0887	0.0837	0.0789	0.0744	0.0701	0.0660	0.0621	0.0584	0.0550
5	0.1822	0.1736	0.1653	0.1573	0.1496	0.1422	0.1352	0.1284	0.1219	0.1157
6	0.3013	0.2896	0.2781	0.2670	0.2562	0.2457	0.2355	0.2256	0.2160	0.2068
7	0.4391	0.4254	0.4119	0.3987	0.3856	0.3728	0.3602	0.3478	0.3357	0.3239
8	0.5786	0.5647	0.5507	0.5369	0.5231	0.5094	0.4958	0.4823	0.4689	0.4557
9	0.7041	0.6915	0.6788	0.6659	0.6530	0.6400	0.6269	0.6137	0.6006	0.5874
10	0.8058	0.7955	0.7850	0.7743	0.7634	0.7522	0.7409	0.7294	0.7178	0.7060
11	0.8807	0.8731	0.8652	0.8571	0.8487	0.8400	0.8311	0.8220	0.8126	0.8030

TABLE A.8   Cumulative Poisson Probabilities (*continued*)

	\multicolumn{10}{c}{Mean Arrival Rate λ}
x	8.1	8.2	8.3	8.4	8.5	8.6	8.7	8.8	8.9	9.0
12	0.9313	0.9261	0.9207	0.9150	0.9091	0.9029	0.8965	0.8898	0.8829	0.8758
13	0.9628	0.9595	0.9561	0.9524	0.9486	0.9445	0.9403	0.9358	0.9311	0.9261
14	0.9810	0.9791	0.9771	0.9749	0.9726	0.9701	0.9675	0.9647	0.9617	0.9585
15	0.9908	0.9898	0.9887	0.9875	0.9862	0.9848	0.9832	0.9816	0.9798	0.9780
16	0.9958	0.9953	0.9947	0.9941	0.9934	0.9926	0.9918	0.9909	0.9899	0.9889
17	0.9982	0.9979	0.9977	0.9973	0.9970	0.9966	0.9962	0.9957	0.9952	0.9947
18	0.9992	0.9991	0.9990	0.9989	0.9987	0.9985	0.9983	0.9981	0.9978	0.9976
19	0.9997	0.9997	0.9996	0.9995	0.9995	0.9994	0.9993	0.9992	0.9991	0.9989
20	0.9999	0.9999	0.9998	0.9998	0.9998	0.9998	0.9997	0.9997	0.9996	0.9996

	\multicolumn{10}{c}{Mean Arrival Rate λ}
x	9.1	9.2	9.3	9.4	9.5	9.6	9.7	9.8	9.9	10.0
0	0.0001	0.0001	0.0001	0.0001	0.0001	0.0001	0.0001	0.0001	0.0001	0.0000
1	0.0011	0.0010	0.0009	0.0009	0.0008	0.0007	0.0007	0.0006	0.0005	0.0005
2	0.0058	0.0053	0.0049	0.0045	0.0042	0.0038	0.0035	0.0033	0.0030	0.0028
3	0.0198	0.0184	0.0172	0.0160	0.0149	0.0138	0.0129	0.0120	0.0111	0.0103
4	0.0517	0.0486	0.0456	0.0429	0.0403	0.0378	0.0355	0.0333	0.0312	0.0293
5	0.1098	0.1041	0.0986	0.0935	0.0885	0.0838	0.0793	0.0750	0.0710	0.0671
6	0.1978	0.1892	0.1808	0.1727	0.1649	0.1574	0.1502	0.1433	0.1366	0.1301
7	0.3123	0.3010	0.2900	0.2792	0.2687	0.2584	0.2485	0.2388	0.2294	0.2202
8	0.4426	0.4296	0.4168	0.4042	0.3918	0.3796	0.3676	0.3558	0.3442	0.3328
9	0.5742	0.5611	0.5479	0.5349	0.5218	0.5089	0.4960	0.4832	0.4705	0.4579
10	0.6941	0.6820	0.6699	0.6576	0.6453	0.6329	0.6205	0.6080	0.5955	0.5830
11	0.7932	0.7832	0.7730	0.7626	0.7520	0.7412	0.7303	0.7193	0.7081	0.6968
12	0.8684	0.8607	0.8529	0.8448	0.8364	0.8279	0.8191	0.8101	0.8009	0.7916
13	0.9210	0.9156	0.9100	0.9042	0.8981	0.8919	0.8853	0.8786	0.8716	0.8645
14	0.9552	0.9517	0.9480	0.9441	0.9400	0.9357	0.9312	0.9265	0.9216	0.9165
15	0.9760	0.9738	0.9715	0.9691	0.9665	0.9638	0.9609	0.9579	0.9546	0.9513
16	0.9878	0.9865	0.9852	0.9838	0.9823	0.9806	0.9789	0.9770	0.9751	0.9730
17	0.9941	0.9934	0.9927	0.9919	0.9911	0.9902	0.9892	0.9881	0.9870	0.9857
18	0.9973	0.9969	0.9966	0.9962	0.9957	0.9952	0.9947	0.9941	0.9935	0.9928
19	0.9988	0.9986	0.9985	0.9983	0.9980	0.9978	0.9975	0.9972	0.9969	0.9965
20	0.9995	0.9994	0.9993	0.9992	0.9991	0.9990	0.9989	0.9987	0.9986	0.9984

TABLE A.8   Cumulative Poisson Probabilities (*continued*)

x	\multicolumn{10}{c}{Mean Arrival Rate λ}
	10.1	10.2	10.3	10.4	10.5	10.6	10.7	10.8	10.9	11.0
0	0.0000	0.0000	0.0000	0.0000	0.0000	0.0000	0.0000	0.0000	0.0000	0.0000
1	0.0005	0.0004	0.0004	0.0003	0.0003	0.0003	0.0003	0.0002	0.0002	0.0002
2	0.0026	0.0023	0.0022	0.0020	0.0018	0.0017	0.0016	0.0014	0.0013	0.0012
3	0.0096	0.0089	0.0083	0.0077	0.0071	0.0066	0.0062	0.0057	0.0053	0.0049
4	0.0274	0.0257	0.0241	0.0225	0.0211	0.0197	0.0185	0.0173	0.0162	0.0151
5	0.0634	0.0599	0.0566	0.0534	0.0504	0.0475	0.0448	0.0423	0.0398	0.0375
6	0.1240	0.1180	0.1123	0.1069	0.1016	0.0966	0.0918	0.0872	0.0828	0.0786
7	0.2113	0.2027	0.1944	0.1863	0.1785	0.1710	0.1636	0.1566	0.1498	0.1432
8	0.3217	0.3108	0.3001	0.2896	0.2794	0.2694	0.2597	0.2502	0.2410	0.2320
9	0.4455	0.4332	0.4210	0.4090	0.3971	0.3854	0.3739	0.3626	0.3515	0.3405
10	0.5705	0.5580	0.5456	0.5331	0.5207	0.5084	0.4961	0.4840	0.4719	0.4599
11	0.6853	0.6738	0.6622	0.6505	0.6387	0.6269	0.6150	0.6031	0.5912	0.5793
12	0.7820	0.7722	0.7623	0.7522	0.7420	0.7316	0.7210	0.7104	0.6996	0.6887
13	0.8571	0.8494	0.8416	0.8336	0.8253	0.8169	0.8083	0.7995	0.7905	0.7813
14	0.9112	0.9057	0.9	0.8940	0.8879	0.8815	0.8750	0.8682	0.8612	0.8540
15	0.9477	0.9440	0.9400	0.9359	0.9317	0.9272	0.9225	0.9177	0.9126	0.9074
16	0.9707	0.9684	0.9658	0.9632	0.9604	0.9574	0.9543	0.9511	0.9477	0.9441
17	0.9844	0.9830	0.9815	0.9799	0.9781	0.9763	0.9744	0.9723	0.9701	0.9678
18	0.9921	0.9913	0.9904	0.9895	0.9885	0.9874	0.9863	0.9850	0.9837	0.9823
19	0.9962	0.9957	0.9953	0.9948	0.9942	0.9936	0.9930	0.9923	0.9915	0.9907
20	0.9982	0.9980	0.9978	0.9975	0.9972	0.9969	0.9966	0.9962	0.9958	0.9953

x	\multicolumn{10}{c}{Mean Arrival Rate λ}
	11.1	11.2	11.3	11.4	11.5	11.6	11.7	11.8	11.9	12.0
0	0.0000	0.0000	0.0000	0.0000	0.0000	0.0000	0.0000	0.0000	0.0000	0.0000
1	0.0002	0.0002	0.0002	0.0001	0.0001	0.0001	0.0001	0.0001	0.0001	0.0001
2	0.0011	0.0010	0.0009	0.0009	0.0008	0.0007	0.0007	0.0006	0.0006	0.0005
3	0.0046	0.0042	0.0039	0.0036	0.0034	0.0031	0.0029	0.0027	0.0025	0.0023
4	0.0141	0.0132	0.0123	0.0115	0.0107	0.0100	0.0094	0.0087	0.0081	0.0076
5	0.0353	0.0333	0.0313	0.0295	0.0277	0.0261	0.0245	0.0230	0.0217	0.0203
6	0.0746	0.0708	0.0671	0.0636	0.0603	0.0571	0.0541	0.0512	0.0484	0.0458
7	0.1369	0.1307	0.1249	0.1192	0.1137	0.1085	0.1035	0.0986	0.0940	0.0895
8	0.2232	0.2147	0.2064	0.1984	0.1906	0.1830	0.1757	0.1686	0.1617	0.1550
9	0.3298	0.3192	0.3089	0.2987	0.2888	0.2791	0.2696	0.2603	0.2512	0.2424
10	0.4480	0.4362	0.4246	0.4131	0.4017	0.3905	0.3794	0.3685	0.3578	0.3472
11	0.5673	0.5554	0.5435	0.5316	0.5198	0.5080	0.4963	0.4847	0.4731	0.4616
12	0.6777	0.6666	0.6555	0.6442	0.6329	0.6216	0.6102	0.5988	0.5874	0.5760

TABLE A.8   Cumulative Poisson Probabilities (*continued*)

					Mean Arrival Rate λ					
x	11.1	11.2	11.3	11.4	11.5	11.6	11.7	11.8	11.9	12.0
13	0.7719	0.7624	0.7528	0.7430	0.7330	0.7230	0.7128	0.7025	0.6920	0.6815
14	0.8467	0.8391	0.8313	0.8234	0.8153	0.8069	0.7985	0.7898	0.7810	0.7720
15	0.9020	0.8963	0.8905	0.8845	0.8783	0.8719	0.8653	0.8585	0.8516	0.8444
16	0.9403	0.9364	0.9323	0.9280	0.9236	0.9190	0.9142	0.9092	0.9040	0.8987
17	0.9654	0.9628	0.9601	0.9572	0.9542	0.9511	0.9478	0.9444	0.9408	0.9370
18	0.9808	0.9792	0.9775	0.9757	0.9738	0.9718	0.9697	0.9674	0.9651	0.9626
19	0.9898	0.9889	0.9879	0.9868	0.9857	0.9845	0.9832	0.9818	0.9803	0.9787
20	0.9948	0.9943	0.9938	0.9932	0.9925	0.9918	0.9910	0.9902	0.9893	0.9884

					Mean Arrival Rate λ					
x	12.1	12.2	12.3	12.4	12.5	12.6	12.7	12.8	12.9	13.0
5	0.0191	0.0179	0.0168	0.0158	0.0148	0.0139	0.0130	0.0122	0.0115	0.0107
6	0.0433	0.0410	0.0387	0.0366	0.0346	0.0326	0.0308	0.0291	0.0274	0.0259
7	0.0852	0.0811	0.0772	0.0734	0.0698	0.0664	0.0631	0.0599	0.0569	0.0540
8	0.1486	0.1424	0.1363	0.1305	0.1249	0.1195	0.1143	0.1093	0.1044	0.0998
9	0.2338	0.2254	0.2172	0.2092	0.2014	0.1939	0.1866	0.1794	0.1725	0.1658
10	0.3368	0.3266	0.3166	0.3067	0.2971	0.2876	0.2783	0.2693	0.2604	0.2517
11	0.4502	0.4389	0.4278	0.4167	0.4058	0.3950	0.3843	0.3738	0.3634	0.3532
12	0.5645	0.5531	0.5417	0.5303	0.5190	0.5077	0.4964	0.4853	0.4741	0.4631
13	0.6709	0.6603	0.6495	0.6387	0.6278	0.6169	0.6060	0.5950	0.5840	0.5730
14	0.7629	0.7536	0.7442	0.7347	0.7250	0.7153	0.7054	0.6954	0.6853	0.6751
15	0.8371	0.8296	0.8219	0.8140	0.8060	0.7978	0.7895	0.7810	0.7724	0.7636
16	0.8932	0.8875	0.8816	0.8755	0.8693	0.8629	0.8563	0.8495	0.8426	0.8355
17	0.9331	0.9290	0.9248	0.9204	0.9158	0.9111	0.9062	0.9011	0.8959	0.8905
18	0.9600	0.9572	0.9543	0.9513	0.9481	0.9448	0.9414	0.9378	0.9341	0.9302
19	0.9771	0.9753	0.9734	0.9715	0.9694	0.9672	0.9649	0.9625	0.9600	0.9573
20	0.9874	0.9863	0.9852	0.9840	0.9827	0.9813	0.9799	0.9783	0.9767	0.9750
21	0.9934	0.9927	0.9921	0.9914	0.9906	0.9898	0.9889	0.9880	0.9870	0.9859
22	0.9966	0.9963	0.9959	0.9955	0.9951	0.9946	0.9941	0.9936	0.9930	0.9924
23	0.9984	0.9982	0.9980	0.9978	0.9975	0.9973	0.9970	0.9967	0.9964	0.9960

					Mean Arrival Rate λ					
x	13.1	13.2	13.3	13.4	13.5	13.6	13.7	13.8	13.9	14.0
5	0.0101	0.0094	0.0088	0.0083	0.0077	0.0072	0.0068	0.0063	0.0059	0.0055
6	0.0244	0.0230	0.0217	0.0204	0.0193	0.0181	0.0171	0.0161	0.0151	0.0142
7	0.0513	0.0487	0.0461	0.0438	0.0415	0.0393	0.0372	0.0353	0.0334	0.0316
8	0.0953	0.0910	0.0868	0.0828	0.0790	0.0753	0.0718	0.0684	0.0652	0.0621

TABLE A.8   Cumulative Poisson Probabilities (*continued*)

	Mean Arrival Rate λ									
x	13.1	13.2	13.3	13.4	13.5	13.6	13.7	13.8	13.9	14.0
9	0.1593	0.1530	0.1469	0.1410	0.1353	0.1297	0.1244	0.1192	0.1142	0.1094
10	0.2432	0.2349	0.2268	0.2189	0.2112	0.2037	0.1964	0.1893	0.1824	0.1757
11	0.3431	0.3332	0.3234	0.3139	0.3045	0.2952	0.2862	0.2773	0.2686	0.2600
12	0.4522	0.4413	0.4305	0.4199	0.4093	0.3989	0.3886	0.3784	0.3684	0.3585
13	0.5621	0.5511	0.5401	0.5292	0.5182	0.5074	0.4966	0.4858	0.4751	0.4644
14	0.6649	0.6546	0.6442	0.6338	0.6233	0.6128	0.6022	0.5916	0.5810	0.5704
15	0.7547	0.7456	0.7365	0.7272	0.7178	0.7083	0.6987	0.6890	0.6792	0.6694
16	0.8282	0.8208	0.8132	0.8054	0.7975	0.7895	0.7813	0.7730	0.7645	0.7559
17	0.8849	0.8791	0.8732	0.8671	0.8609	0.8545	0.8479	0.8411	0.8343	0.8272
18	0.9261	0.9219	0.9176	0.9130	0.9084	0.9035	0.8986	0.8934	0.8881	0.8826
19	0.9546	0.9516	0.9486	0.9454	0.9421	0.9387	0.9351	0.9314	0.9275	0.9235
20	0.9732	0.9713	0.9692	0.9671	0.9649	0.9626	0.9601	0.9576	0.9549	0.9521
21	0.9848	0.9836	0.9823	0.9810	0.9796	0.9780	0.9765	0.9748	0.9730	0.9712
22	0.9917	0.9910	0.9902	0.9894	0.9885	0.9876	0.9866	0.9856	0.9845	0.9833
23	0.9956	0.9952	0.9948	0.9943	0.9938	0.9933	0.9927	0.9921	0.9914	0.9907

	Mean Arrival Rate λ									
x	14.1	14.2	14.3	14.4	14.5	14.6	14.7	14.8	14.9	15.0
6	0.0134	0.0126	0.0118	0.0111	0.0105	0.0098	0.0092	0.0087	0.0081	0.0076
7	0.0299	0.0283	0.0268	0.0253	0.0239	0.0226	0.0214	0.0202	0.0191	0.0180
8	0.0591	0.0562	0.0535	0.0509	0.0484	0.0460	0.0437	0.0415	0.0394	0.0374
9	0.1047	0.1003	0.0959	0.0918	0.0878	0.0839	0.0802	0.0766	0.0732	0.0699
10	0.1691	0.1628	0.1566	0.1507	0.1449	0.1392	0.1338	0.1285	0.1234	0.1185
11	0.2517	0.2435	0.2355	0.2277	0.2201	0.2127	0.2054	0.1984	0.1915	0.1848
12	0.3487	0.3391	0.3296	0.3203	0.3111	0.3021	0.2932	0.2845	0.2760	0.2676
13	0.4539	0.4434	0.4330	0.4227	0.4125	0.4024	0.3925	0.3826	0.3728	0.3632
14	0.5598	0.5492	0.5387	0.5281	0.5176	0.5071	0.4967	0.4863	0.4759	0.4657
15	0.6594	0.6494	0.6394	0.6293	0.6192	0.6090	0.5988	0.5886	0.5783	0.5681
16	0.7472	0.7384	0.7294	0.7204	0.7112	0.7020	0.6926	0.6832	0.6737	0.6641
17	0.8200	0.8126	0.8051	0.7975	0.7897	0.7818	0.7737	0.7656	0.7573	0.7489
18	0.8770	0.8712	0.8653	0.8592	0.8530	0.8466	0.8400	0.8333	0.8265	0.8195
19	0.9193	0.9150	0.9106	0.9060	0.9012	0.8963	0.8913	0.8861	0.8807	0.8752
20	0.9492	0.9461	0.9430	0.9396	0.9362	0.9326	0.9289	0.9251	0.9211	0.9170
21	0.9692	0.9671	0.9650	0.9627	0.9604	0.9579	0.9553	0.9526	0.9498	0.9469
22	0.9820	0.9807	0.9793	0.9779	0.9763	0.9747	0.9729	0.9711	0.9692	0.9673
23	0.9899	0.9891	0.9882	0.9873	0.9863	0.9853	0.9842	0.9831	0.9818	0.9805
24	0.9945	0.9941	0.9935	0.9930	0.9924	0.9918	0.9911	0.9904	0.9896	0.9888
25	0.9971	0.9969	0.9966	0.9963	0.9959	0.9956	0.9952	0.9947	0.9943	0.9938

TABLE A.8   Cumulative Poisson Probabilities (*continued*)

	Mean Arrival Rate λ									
x	15.1	15.2	15.3	15.4	15.5	15.6	15.7	15.8	15.9	16.0
7	0.0170	0.0160	0.0151	0.0143	0.0135	0.0127	0.0120	0.0113	0.0106	0.0100
8	0.0355	0.0337	0.0320	0.0304	0.0288	0.0273	0.0259	0.0245	0.0232	0.0220
9	0.0667	0.0636	0.0607	0.0579	0.0552	0.0526	0.0501	0.0478	0.0455	0.0433
10	0.1137	0.1091	0.1046	0.1003	0.0961	0.0921	0.0882	0.0845	0.0809	0.0774
11	0.1782	0.1718	0.1657	0.1596	0.1538	0.1481	0.1426	0.1372	0.1320	0.1270
12	0.2594	0.2514	0.2435	0.2358	0.2283	0.2209	0.2137	0.2067	0.1998	0.1931
13	0.3537	0.3444	0.3351	0.3260	0.3171	0.3083	0.2996	0.2911	0.2827	0.2745
14	0.4554	0.4453	0.4353	0.4253	0.4154	0.4056	0.3959	0.3864	0.3769	0.3675
15	0.5578	0.5476	0.5374	0.5272	0.5170	0.5069	0.4968	0.4867	0.4767	0.4667
16	0.6545	0.6448	0.6351	0.6253	0.6154	0.6056	0.5957	0.5858	0.5759	0.5660
17	0.7403	0.7317	0.7230	0.7141	0.7052	0.6962	0.6871	0.6779	0.6687	0.6593
18	0.8123	0.8051	0.7977	0.7901	0.7825	0.7747	0.7668	0.7587	0.7506	0.7423
19	0.8696	0.8638	0.8578	0.8517	0.8455	0.8391	0.8326	0.8260	0.8192	0.8122
20	0.9128	0.9084	0.9039	0.8992	0.8944	0.8894	0.8843	0.8791	0.8737	0.8682
21	0.9438	0.9407	0.9374	0.9340	0.9304	0.9268	0.9230	0.9190	0.9150	0.9108
22	0.9652	0.9630	0.9607	0.9583	0.9558	0.9532	0.9505	0.9477	0.9448	0.9418
23	0.9792	0.9777	0.9762	0.9746	0.9730	0.9712	0.9694	0.9674	0.9654	0.9633
24	0.9880	0.9871	0.9861	0.9851	0.9840	0.9829	0.9817	0.9804	0.9791	0.9777
25	0.9933	0.9928	0.9922	0.9915	0.9909	0.9902	0.9894	0.9886	0.9878	0.9869

	Mean Arrival Rate λ									
x	16.1	16.2	16.3	16.4	16.5	16.6	16.7	16.8	16.9	17.0
8	0.0208	0.0197	0.0186	0.0176	0.0167	0.0158	0.0149	0.0141	0.0133	0.0126
9	0.0412	0.0392	0.0373	0.0355	0.0337	0.0321	0.0305	0.0290	0.0275	0.0261
10	0.0740	0.0708	0.0677	0.0647	0.0619	0.0591	0.0565	0.0539	0.0515	0.0491
11	0.1221	0.1174	0.1128	0.1084	0.1041	0.0999	0.0959	0.0920	0.0883	0.0847
12	0.1866	0.1802	0.1740	0.1680	0.1621	0.1564	0.1508	0.1454	0.1401	0.1350
13	0.2664	0.2585	0.2508	0.2432	0.2357	0.2285	0.2213	0.2144	0.2075	0.2009
14	0.3583	0.3492	0.3402	0.3313	0.3225	0.3139	0.3054	0.2971	0.2889	0.2808
15	0.4569	0.4470	0.4373	0.4276	0.4180	0.4085	0.3991	0.3898	0.3806	0.3715
16	0.5560	0.5461	0.5362	0.5263	0.5165	0.5067	0.4969	0.4871	0.4774	0.4677
17	0.6500	0.6406	0.6311	0.6216	0.6120	0.6025	0.5929	0.5833	0.5737	0.5640
18	0.7340	0.7255	0.7170	0.7084	0.6996	0.6909	0.6820	0.6730	0.6640	0.6550
19	0.8052	0.7980	0.7907	0.7833	0.7757	0.7681	0.7603	0.7524	0.7444	0.7363
20	0.8625	0.8567	0.8508	0.8447	0.8385	0.8321	0.8257	0.8191	0.8123	0.8055
21	0.9064	0.9020	0.8974	0.8927	0.8878	0.8828	0.8777	0.8724	0.8670	0.8615
22	0.9386	0.9353	0.9319	0.9284	0.9248	0.9210	0.9171	0.9131	0.9090	0.9047

TABLE A.8　Cumulative Poisson Probabilities (*continued*)

	Mean Arrival Rate λ									
x	16.1	16.2	16.3	16.4	16.5	16.6	16.7	16.8	16.9	17.0
23	0.9611	0.9588	0.9564	0.9539	0.9513	0.9486	0.9458	0.9429	0.9398	0.9367
24	0.9762	0.9747	0.9730	0.9713	0.9696	0.9677	0.9657	0.9637	0.9616	0.9594
25	0.9859	0.9849	0.9839	0.9828	0.9816	0.9804	0.9791	0.9777	0.9763	0.9748
26	0.9920	0.9913	0.9907	0.9900	0.9892	0.9884	0.9876	0.9867	0.9858	0.9848

	Mean Arrival Rate λ									
x	17.1	17.2	17.3	17.4	17.5	17.6	17.7	17.8	17.9	18.0
8	0.0119	0.0112	0.0106	0.0100	0.0095	0.0089	0.0084	0.0079	0.0075	0.0071
9	0.0248	0.0235	0.0223	0.0212	0.0201	0.0191	0.0181	0.0171	0.0162	0.0154
10	0.0469	0.0447	0.0426	0.0406	0.0387	0.0369	0.0352	0.0335	0.0319	0.0304
11	0.0812	0.0778	0.0746	0.0714	0.0684	0.0655	0.0627	0.0600	0.0574	0.0549
12	0.1301	0.1252	0.1206	0.1160	0.1116	0.1074	0.1033	0.0993	0.0954	0.0917
13	0.1944	0.1880	0.1818	0.1758	0.1699	0.1641	0.1585	0.1531	0.1478	0.1426
14	0.2729	0.2651	0.2575	0.2500	0.2426	0.2354	0.2284	0.2215	0.2147	0.2081
15	0.3624	0.3535	0.3448	0.3361	0.3275	0.3191	0.3108	0.3026	0.2946	0.2867
16	0.4581	0.4486	0.4391	0.4297	0.4204	0.4112	0.4020	0.3929	0.3839	0.3751
17	0.5544	0.5448	0.5352	0.5256	0.5160	0.5065	0.4969	0.4875	0.4780	0.4686
18	0.6458	0.6367	0.6275	0.6182	0.6089	0.5996	0.5903	0.5810	0.5716	0.5622
19	0.7281	0.7199	0.7115	0.7031	0.6945	0.6859	0.6773	0.6685	0.6598	0.6509
20	0.7985	0.7914	0.7842	0.7769	0.7694	0.7619	0.7542	0.7465	0.7387	0.7307
21	0.8558	0.8500	0.8441	0.8380	0.8319	0.8255	0.8191	0.8126	0.8059	0.7991
22	0.9003	0.8958	0.8912	0.8864	0.8815	0.8765	0.8713	0.8660	0.8606	0.8551
23	0.9334	0.9301	0.9266	0.9230	0.9193	0.9154	0.9115	0.9074	0.9032	0.8989
24	0.9570	0.9546	0.9521	0.9495	0.9468	0.9440	0.9411	0.9381	0.9350	0.9317
25	0.9732	0.9715	0.9698	0.9680	0.9661	0.9641	0.9621	0.9599	0.9577	0.9554
26	0.9838	0.9827	0.9816	0.9804	0.9791	0.9778	0.9764	0.9749	0.9734	0.9718
27	0.9905	0.9898	0.9891	0.9883	0.9875	0.9866	0.9857	0.9848	0.9837	0.9827

	Mean Arrival Rate λ									
x	18.1	18.2	18.3	18.4	18.5	18.6	18.7	18.8	18.9	19.0
9	0.0146	0.0138	0.0131	0.0124	0.0117	0.0111	0.0105	0.0099	0.0094	0.0089
10	0.0289	0.0275	0.0262	0.0249	0.0237	0.0225	0.0214	0.0203	0.0193	0.0183
11	0.0525	0.0502	0.0479	0.0458	0.0438	0.0418	0.0399	0.0381	0.0363	0.0347
12	0.0881	0.0846	0.0812	0.0779	0.0748	0.0717	0.0688	0.0659	0.0632	0.0606
13	0.1376	0.1327	0.1279	0.1233	0.1189	0.1145	0.1103	0.1062	0.1022	0.0984
14	0.2016	0.1953	0.1891	0.1830	0.1771	0.1714	0.1658	0.1603	0.1550	0.1497

TABLE A.8   Cumulative Poisson Probabilities (*continued*)

	Mean Arrival Rate λ									
x	18.1	18.2	18.3	18.4	18.5	18.6	18.7	18.8	18.9	19.0
15	0.2789	0.2712	0.2637	0.2563	0.2490	0.2419	0.2349	0.2281	0.2214	0.2148
16	0.3663	0.3576	0.3490	0.3405	0.3321	0.3239	0.3157	0.3077	0.2998	0.2920
17	0.4593	0.4500	0.4408	0.4317	0.4226	0.4136	0.4047	0.3958	0.3870	0.3784
18	0.5529	0.5435	0.5342	0.5249	0.5156	0.5063	0.4970	0.4878	0.4786	0.4695
19	0.6420	0.6331	0.6241	0.6151	0.6061	0.5970	0.5879	0.5788	0.5697	0.5606
20	0.7227	0.7146	0.7064	0.6981	0.6898	0.6814	0.6729	0.6644	0.6558	0.6472
21	0.7922	0.7852	0.7781	0.7709	0.7636	0.7561	0.7486	0.7410	0.7333	0.7255
22	0.8494	0.8436	0.8377	0.8317	0.8256	0.8193	0.8129	0.8065	0.7998	0.7931
23	0.8944	0.8899	0.8852	0.8804	0.8755	0.8704	0.8652	0.8600	0.8545	0.8490
24	0.9284	0.9249	0.9214	0.9177	0.9139	0.9100	0.9060	0.9019	0.8976	0.8933
25	0.9530	0.9505	0.9479	0.9452	0.9424	0.9395	0.9365	0.9334	0.9302	0.9269
26	0.9701	0.9683	0.9665	0.9646	0.9626	0.9606	0.9584	0.9562	0.9539	0.9514
27	0.9816	0.9804	0.9792	0.9779	0.9765	0.9751	0.9736	0.9720	0.9704	0.9687

	Mean Arrival Rate λ									
x	19.1	19.2	19.3	19.4	19.5	19.6	19.7	19.8	19.9	20.0
10	0.0174	0.0165	0.0157	0.0149	0.0141	0.0134	0.0127	0.0120	0.0114	0.0108
11	0.0331	0.0315	0.0301	0.0287	0.0273	0.0260	0.0248	0.0236	0.0225	0.0214
12	0.0580	0.0556	0.0532	0.0509	0.0488	0.0467	0.0446	0.0427	0.0408	0.0390
13	0.0947	0.0911	0.0876	0.0842	0.0809	0.0778	0.0747	0.0717	0.0689	0.0661
14	0.1447	0.1397	0.1349	0.1303	0.1257	0.1213	0.1170	0.1128	0.1088	0.1049
15	0.2084	0.2021	0.1959	0.1899	0.1840	0.1782	0.1726	0.1671	0.1617	0.1565
16	0.2844	0.2768	0.2694	0.2621	0.2550	0.2479	0.2410	0.2342	0.2276	0.2211
17	0.3698	0.3613	0.3529	0.3446	0.3364	0.3283	0.3203	0.3124	0.3047	0.2970
18	0.4604	0.4514	0.4424	0.4335	0.4246	0.4158	0.4071	0.3985	0.3899	0.3814
19	0.5515	0.5424	0.5333	0.5242	0.5151	0.5061	0.4971	0.4881	0.4792	0.4703
20	0.6385	0.6298	0.6210	0.6122	0.6034	0.5946	0.5857	0.5769	0.5680	0.5591
21	0.7176	0.7097	0.7016	0.6935	0.6854	0.6772	0.6689	0.6605	0.6521	0.6437
22	0.7863	0.7794	0.7724	0.7653	0.7580	0.7507	0.7433	0.7358	0.7283	0.7206
23	0.8434	0.8376	0.8317	0.8257	0.8196	0.8134	0.8071	0.8007	0.7941	0.7875
24	0.8888	0.8842	0.8795	0.8746	0.8697	0.8646	0.8594	0.8541	0.8487	0.8432
25	0.9235	0.9199	0.9163	0.9126	0.9087	0.9048	0.9007	0.8965	0.8922	0.8878
26	0.9489	0.9463	0.9437	0.9409	0.9380	0.9350	0.9319	0.9288	0.9255	0.9221
27	0.9670	0.9651	0.9632	0.9612	0.9591	0.9570	0.9547	0.9524	0.9500	0.9475

TABLE A.8   Cumulative Poisson Probabilities (*continued*)

x	\multicolumn{10}{c}{Mean Arrival Rate λ}
	20.1	20.2	20.3	20.4	20.5	20.6	20.7	20.8	20.9	21.0
10	0.0102	0.0097	0.0092	0.0087	0.0082	0.0078	0.0074	0.0070	0.0066	0.0063
11	0.0204	0.0194	0.0184	0.0175	0.0167	0.0158	0.0150	0.0143	0.0136	0.0129
12	0.0373	0.0356	0.0340	0.0325	0.0310	0.0296	0.0283	0.0270	0.0257	0.0245
13	0.0635	0.0609	0.0584	0.0560	0.0537	0.0515	0.0493	0.0473	0.0453	0.0434
14	0.1010	0.0973	0.0938	0.0903	0.0869	0.0836	0.0805	0.0774	0.0744	0.0716
15	0.1514	0.1464	0.1416	0.1369	0.1323	0.1278	0.1234	0.1192	0.1151	0.1111
16	0.2147	0.2084	0.2023	0.1963	0.1904	0.1847	0.1790	0.1735	0.1682	0.1629
17	0.2895	0.2821	0.2748	0.2676	0.2605	0.2536	0.2467	0.2400	0.2334	0.2270
18	0.3730	0.3647	0.3565	0.3484	0.3403	0.3324	0.3246	0.3168	0.3092	0.3017
19	0.4614	0.4526	0.4438	0.4351	0.4265	0.4179	0.4094	0.4009	0.3926	0.3843
20	0.5502	0.5413	0.5325	0.5236	0.5148	0.5059	0.4972	0.4884	0.4797	0.4710
21	0.6352	0.6267	0.6181	0.6096	0.6010	0.5923	0.5837	0.5750	0.5664	0.5577
22	0.7129	0.7051	0.6972	0.6893	0.6813	0.6732	0.6651	0.6569	0.6487	0.6405
23	0.7808	0.7739	0.7670	0.7600	0.7528	0.7456	0.7384	0.7310	0.7235	0.7160
24	0.8376	0.8319	0.8260	0.8201	0.8140	0.8078	0.8016	0.7952	0.7887	0.7822
25	0.8833	0.8787	0.8739	0.8691	0.8641	0.8591	0.8539	0.8486	0.8432	0.8377
26	0.9186	0.9150	0.9114	0.9076	0.9037	0.8997	0.8955	0.8913	0.8870	0.8826
27	0.9449	0.9423	0.9395	0.9366	0.9337	0.9306	0.9275	0.9242	0.9209	0.9175

x	\multicolumn{10}{c}{Mean Arrival Rate λ}
	21.1	21.2	21.3	21.4	21.5	21.6	21.7	21.8	21.9	22.0
11	0.0123	0.0116	0.0110	0.0105	0.0099	0.0094	0.0090	0.0085	0.0080	0.0076
12	0.0234	0.0223	0.0213	0.0203	0.0193	0.0184	0.0175	0.0167	0.0159	0.0151
13	0.0415	0.0397	0.0380	0.0364	0.0348	0.0333	0.0318	0.0304	0.0291	0.0278
14	0.0688	0.0661	0.0635	0.0610	0.0586	0.0563	0.0540	0.0518	0.0497	0.0477
15	0.1072	0.1034	0.0997	0.0962	0.0927	0.0893	0.0861	0.0829	0.0799	0.0769
16	0.1578	0.1528	0.1479	0.1432	0.1385	0.1340	0.1296	0.1253	0.1211	0.1170
17	0.2206	0.2144	0.2083	0.2023	0.1965	0.1907	0.1851	0.1796	0.1743	0.1690
18	0.2943	0.2870	0.2798	0.2727	0.2657	0.2588	0.2521	0.2454	0.2389	0.2325
19	0.3760	0.3679	0.3599	0.3519	0.3440	0.3362	0.3285	0.3209	0.3134	0.3060
20	0.4623	0.4537	0.4452	0.4367	0.4282	0.4198	0.4115	0.4032	0.3950	0.3869
21	0.5490	0.5403	0.5317	0.5230	0.5144	0.5058	0.4972	0.4887	0.4801	0.4716
22	0.6322	0.6238	0.6155	0.6071	0.5987	0.5902	0.5818	0.5733	0.5648	0.5564
23	0.7084	0.7008	0.6930	0.6853	0.6774	0.6695	0.6616	0.6536	0.6455	0.6374
24	0.7755	0.7687	0.7619	0.7550	0.7480	0.7409	0.7337	0.7264	0.7191	0.7117
25	0.8321	0.8264	0.8206	0.8146	0.8086	0.8025	0.7963	0.7900	0.7836	0.7771
26	0.8780	0.8734	0.8686	0.8638	0.8588	0.8537	0.8486	0.8433	0.8379	0.8324
27	0.9139	0.9103	0.9065	0.9027	0.8988	0.8947	0.8906	0.8863	0.8820	0.8775

TABLE A.9   Cumulative Exponential Distribution for λT[a]

	λ									
T	0.0	0.1	0.2	0.3	0.4	0.5	0.6	0.7	0.8	0.9
0	0.0000	0.0952	0.1813	0.2592	0.3297	0.3935	0.4512	0.5034	0.5507	0.5934
1	0.6321	0.6671	0.6988	0.7275	0.7534	0.7769	0.7981	0.9173	0.8347	0.8504
2	0.8647	0.8775	0.8892	0.8997	0.9093	0.9179	0.9257	0.9328	0.9392	0.9450
3	0.9502	0.9550	0.9592	0.9631	0.9666	0.9698	0.9727	0.9753	0.9776	0.9798
4	0.9817	0.9834	0.9850	0.9864	0.9877	0.9889	0.9899	0.9909	0.9918	0.9926
5	0.9933	0.9939	0.9945	0.9950	0.9955	0.9959	0.9963	0.9967	0.9970	0.9973
6	0.9975	0.9978	0.9980	0.9982	0.9983	0.9985	0.9986	0.9988	0.9989	0.9990
7	0.9991	0.9992	0.9993	0.9993	0.9994	0.9994	0.9995	0.9995	0.9996	0.9996

[a]The rows are the units for T and the columns indicate intervals of 0.2. Table entries are the value for $1 - e^{-\lambda T}$. The cumulative probability computations were made using Minitab.

TABLE A.10   Durbin–Watson Test Bounds ($\alpha = 0.05$)

| | \multicolumn{10}{c}{Number of Independent Variables ($p - 1$)} | | | | | | | | |
| | 1 | | 2 | | 3 | | 4 | | 5 | |
n	d_L	d_U	d_L	d_U	d_L	d_U	d_L	d_U	d_L	d_U
15	1.08	1.36	0.95	1.54	0.82	1.75	0.69	1.97	0.56	2.21
16	1.10	1.37	0.98	1.54	0.86	1.73	0.74	1.93	0.62	2.15
17	1.13	1.38	1.02	1.54	0.90	1.71	0.78	1.90	0.67	2.10
18	1.16	1.39	1.05	1.53	0.93	1.69	0.82	1.87	0.71	2.06
19	1.18	1.40	1.08	1.53	0.97	1.68	0.86	1.85	0.75	2.02
20	1.20	1.41	1.10	1.54	1.00	1.68	0.90	1.83	0.79	1.99
21	1.22	1.42	1.13	1.54	1.03	1.67	0.93	1.81	0.83	1.96
22	1.24	1.43	1.15	1.54	1.05	1.66	0.96	1.80	0.86	1.94
23	1.26	1.44	1.17	1.54	1.08	1.66	0.99	1.79	0.90	1.92
24	1.27	1.45	1.19	1.55	1.10	1.66	1.01	1.78	0.93	1.90
25	1.29	1.45	1.21	1.55	1.12	1.66	1.04	1.77	0.95	1.89
26	1.30	1.46	1.22	1.55	1.14	1.65	1.06	1.76	0.98	1.88
27	1.32	1.47	1.24	1.56	1.16	1.65	1.08	1.76	1.01	1.86
28	1.33	1.48	1.26	1.56	1.18	1.65	1.10	1.75	1.03	1.85
29	1.34	1.48	1.27	1.56	1.20	1.65	1.12	1.74	1.05	1.84
30	1.35	1.49	1.28	1.57	1.21	1.65	1.14	1.74	1.07	1.83
31	1.36	1.50	1.30	1.57	1.23	1.65	1.16	1.74	1.09	1.83
32	1.37	1.50	1.31	1.57	1.24	1.65	1.18	1.73	1.11	1.82
33	1.38	1.51	1.32	1.58	1.26	1.65	1.19	1.73	1.13	1.81
34	1.39	1.51	1.33	1.58	1.27	1.65	1.21	1.73	1.15	1.81
35	1.40	1.52	1.34	1.58	1.28	1.65	1.22	1.73	1.16	1.80
36	1.41	1.52	1.35	1.59	1.29	1.65	1.24	1.73	1.18	1.80
37	1.42	1.53	1.36	1.59	1.31	1.66	1.25	1.72	1.19	1.80
38	1.43	1.54	1.37	1.59	1.32	1.66	1.26	1.72	1.21	1.79
39	1.43	1.54	1.38	1.60	1.33	1.66	1.27	1.72	1.22	1.79
40	1.44	1.54	1.39	1.60	1.34	1.66	1.29	1.72	1.23	1.79
45	1.48	1.57	1.43	1.62	1.38	1.67	1.34	1.72	1.29	1.78
50	1.50	1.59	1.46	1.63	1.42	1.67	1.38	1.72	1.34	1.77
55	1.53	1.60	1.49	1.64	1.45	1.68	1.41	1.72	1.38	1.77
60	1.55	1.62	1.51	1.65	1.48	1.69	1.44	1.73	1.41	1.77
65	1.57	1.63	1.54	1.66	1.50	1.70	1.47	1.73	1.44	1.77
70	1.58	1.64	1.55	1.67	1.52	1.70	1.49	1.74	1.46	1.77
75	1.60	1.65	1.57	1.68	1.54	1.71	1.51	1.74	1.49	1.77
80	1.61	1.66	1.59	1.69	1.56	1.72	1.53	1.74	1.51	1.77
85	1.62	1.67	1.60	1.70	1.57	1.72	1.55	1.75	1.52	1.77
90	1.63	1.68	1.61	1.70	1.59	1.73	1.57	1.75	1.54	1.78
95	1.64	1.69	1.62	1.71	1.60	1.73	1.58	1.75	1.56	1.78
100	1.65	1.69	1.63	1.72	1.61	1.74	1.59	1.76	1.57	1.78

TABLE A.11   Quality Control Values

Number of Observations in Sample	d_2	d_3
2	1.128	0.853
3	1.693	0.888
4	2.059	0.880
5	2.326	0.864
6	2.534	0.848
7	2.704	0.833
8	2.847	0.820
9	2.970	0.808
10	3.078	0.797
11	3.137	0.787
12	3.258	0.778
13	3.336	0.770
14	3.407	0.762
15	3.472	0.755
16	3.532	0.749
17	3.588	0.743
18	3.640	0.738
19	3.689	0.733
20	3.735	0.729
21	3.778	0.724
22	3.819	0.720
23	3.858	0.716
24	3.895	0.712
25	3.931	0.709

Source: Reprinted from ASTM-STP 15D by permission of the American Society for Testing and Materials.

TABLE A.12 Critical Values[a] of the Studentized Range Q

Upper 5% points ($\alpha = .05$)

η

ν	2	3	4	5	6	7	8	9	10	11	12	13	14	15	16	17	18	19	20
1	18.0	27.0	32.8	37.1	40.4	43.1	45.4	47.4	49.1	50.6	52.0	53.2	54.3	55.4	56.3	57.2	58.0	58.8	59.6
2	6.09	8.3	9.8	10.9	11.7	12.4	13.0	13.5	14.0	14.4	14.7	15.1	15.4	15.7	15.9	16.1	16.4	16.6	16.8
3	4.50	5.91	6.82	7.50	8.04	8.48	8.85	9.18	9.46	9.72	9.95	10.15	10.35	10.52	10.69	10.84	10.98	11.11	11.24
4	3.93	5.04	5.76	6.29	6.71	7.05	7.35	7.60	7.83	8.03	8.21	8.37	8.52	8.66	8.79	8.91	9.03	9.13	9.23
5	3.64	4.60	5.22	5.67	6.03	6.33	6.58	6.80	6.99	7.17	7.32	7.47	7.60	7.72	7.83	7.93	8.03	8.12	8.21
6	3.46	4.34	4.90	5.31	5.63	5.89	6.12	6.32	6.49	6.65	6.79	6.92	7.03	7.14	7.24	7.34	7.43	7.51	7.59
7	3.34	4.16	4.68	5.06	5.36	5.61	5.82	6.00	6.16	6.30	6.43	6.55	6.66	6.76	6.85	6.94	7.02	7.09	7.17
8	3.26	4.04	4.53	4.89	5.17	5.40	5.60	5.77	5.92	6.05	6.18	6.29	6.39	6.48	6.57	6.65	6.73	6.80	6.87
9	3.20	3.95	4.42	4.76	5.02	5.24	5.43	5.60	5.74	5.87	5.98	6.09	6.19	6.28	6.36	6.44	6.51	6.58	6.64
10	3.15	3.88	4.33	4.65	4.91	5.12	5.30	5.46	5.60	5.72	5.83	5.93	6.03	6.11	6.20	6.27	6.34	6.40	6.47
11	3.11	3.82	4.26	4.57	4.82	5.03	5.20	5.35	5.49	5.61	5.71	5.81	5.90	5.99	6.06	6.14	6.20	6.26	6.33
12	3.08	3.77	4.20	4.51	4.75	4.95	5.12	5.27	5.40	5.51	5.62	5.71	5.80	5.88	5.95	6.03	6.09	6.15	6.21
13	3.06	3.73	4.15	4.45	4.69	4.88	5.05	5.19	5.32	5.43	5.53	5.63	5.71	5.79	5.86	5.93	6.00	6.05	6.11
14	3.03	3.70	4.11	4.41	4.64	4.83	4.99	5.13	5.25	5.36	5.46	5.55	5.64	5.72	5.79	5.85	5.92	5.97	6.03
15	3.01	3.67	4.08	4.37	4.60	4.78	4.94	5.08	5.20	5.31	5.40	5.49	5.58	5.65	5.72	5.79	5.85	5.90	5.96
16	3.00	3.65	4.05	4.33	4.56	4.74	4.90	5.03	5.15	5.26	5.35	5.44	5.52	5.59	5.66	5.72	5.79	5.84	5.90
17	2.98	3.63	4.02	4.30	4.52	4.71	4.86	4.99	5.11	5.21	5.31	5.39	5.47	5.55	5.61	5.68	5.74	5.79	5.84
18	2.97	3.61	4.00	4.28	4.49	4.67	4.82	4.96	5.07	5.17	5.27	5.35	5.43	5.50	5.57	5.63	5.69	5.74	5.79
19	2.96	3.59	3.98	4.25	4.47	4.65	4.79	4.92	5.04	5.14	5.23	5.32	5.39	5.46	5.53	5.59	5.65	5.70	5.75
20	2.95	3.58	3.96	4.23	4.45	4.62	4.77	4.90	5.01	5.11	5.20	5.28	5.36	5.43	5.49	5.55	5.61	5.66	5.71
24	2.92	3.53	3.90	4.17	4.37	4.54	4.68	4.81	4.92	5.01	5.10	5.18	5.25	5.32	5.38	5.44	5.50	5.54	5.59
30	2.89	3.49	3.84	4.10	4.30	4.46	4.60	4.72	4.83	4.92	5.00	5.08	5.15	5.21	5.27	5.33	5.38	5.43	5.48
40	2.86	3.44	3.79	4.04	4.23	4.39	4.52	4.63	4.74	4.82	4.91	4.98	5.05	5.11	5.16	5.22	5.27	5.31	5.36
60	2.83	3.40	3.74	3.98	4.16	4.31	4.44	4.55	4.65	4.73	4.81	4.88	4.94	5.00	5.06	5.11	5.16	5.20	5.24
120	2.80	3.36	3.69	3.92	4.10	4.24	4.36	4.48	4.56	4.64	4.72	4.78	4.84	4.90	4.95	5.00	5.05	5.09	5.13
∞	2.77	3.31	3.63	3.86	4.03	4.17	4.29	4.39	4.47	4.55	4.62	4.68	4.74	4.80	4.85	4.89	4.93	4.97	5.01

TABLE A.12   Critical Values[a] of the Studentized Range Q (continued)

Upper 1% points ($\alpha = .01$)

η

v''	2	3	4	5	6	7	8	9	10	11	12	13	14	15	16	17	18	19	20
1	90.0	135	164	186	202	216	227	237	246	253	260	266	272	277	282	286	290	294	298
2	14.0	19.0	22.3	24.7	26.6	28.2	29.5	30.7	31.7	32.6	33.4	34.1	34.8	35.4	36.0	36.5	37.0	37.5	37.9
3	8.26	10.6	12.2	13.3	14.2	15.0	15.6	16.2	16.7	17.1	17.5	17.9	18.2	18.5	18.8	19.1	19.3	19.5	19.8
4	6.51	8.12	9.17	9.96	10.6	11.1	11.5	11.9	12.3	12.6	12.8	13.1	13.3	13.5	13.7	13.9	14.1	14.2	14.4
5	5.70	6.97	7.80	8.42	8.91	9.32	9.67	9.97	10.24	10.48	10.70	10.89	11.08	11.24	11.40	11.55	11.68	11.81	11.93
6	5.24	6.33	7.03	7.56	7.97	8.32	8.61	8.87	9.10	9.30	9.49	9.65	9.81	9.95	10.08	10.21	10.32	10.43	10.54
7	4.95	5.92	6.54	7.01	7.37	7.68	7.94	8.17	8.37	8.55	8.71	8.86	9.00	9.12	9.24	9.35	9.46	9.55	9.65
8	4.74	5.63	6.20	6.63	6.96	7.24	7.47	7.68	7.87	8.03	8.18	8.31	8.44	8.55	8.66	8.76	8.85	8.94	9.03
9	4.60	5.43	5.96	6.35	6.66	6.91	7.13	7.32	7.49	7.65	7.78	7.91	8.03	8.13	8.23	8.32	8.41	8.49	8.57
10	4.48	5.27	5.77	6.14	6.43	6.67	6.87	7.05	7.21	7.36	7.48	7.60	7.71	7.81	7.91	7.99	8.07	8.15	8.22
11	4.39	5.14	5.62	5.97	6.25	6.48	6.67	6.84	6.99	7.13	7.25	7.36	7.46	7.56	7.65	7.73	7.81	7.88	7.95
12	4.32	5.04	5.50	5.84	6.10	6.32	6.51	6.67	6.81	6.94	7.06	7.17	7.26	7.36	7.44	7.52	7.59	7.66	7.73
13	4.26	4.96	5.40	5.73	5.98	6.19	6.37	6.53	6.67	6.79	6.90	7.01	7.10	7.19	7.27	7.34	7.42	7.48	7.55
14	4.21	4.89	5.32	5.63	5.88	6.08	6.26	6.41	6.54	6.66	6.77	6.87	6.96	7.05	7.12	7.20	7.27	7.33	7.39
15	4.17	4.83	5.25	5.56	5.80	5.99	6.16	6.31	6.44	6.55	6.66	6.76	6.84	6.93	7.00	7.07	7.14	7.20	7.26
16	4.13	4.78	5.19	5.49	5.72	5.92	6.08	6.22	6.35	6.46	6.56	6.66	6.74	6.82	6.90	6.97	7.03	7.09	7.15
17	4.10	4.74	5.14	5.43	5.66	5.85	6.01	6.15	6.27	6.38	6.48	6.57	6.66	6.73	6.80	6.87	6.94	7.00	7.05
18	4.07	4.70	5.09	5.38	5.60	5.79	5.94	6.08	6.20	6.31	6.41	6.50	6.58	6.65	6.72	6.79	6.85	6.91	6.96
19	4.05	4.67	5.05	5.33	5.55	5.73	5.89	6.02	6.14	6.25	6.34	6.43	6.51	6.58	6.65	6.72	6.78	6.84	6.89
20	4.02	4.64	5.02	5.29	5.51	5.69	5.84	5.97	6.09	6.19	6.29	6.37	6.45	6.52	6.59	6.65	6.71	6.76	6.82
24	3.96	4.54	4.91	5.17	5.37	5.54	5.69	5.81	5.92	6.02	6.11	6.19	6.26	6.33	6.39	6.45	6.51	6.56	6.61
30	3.89	4.45	4.80	5.05	5.24	5.40	5.54	5.65	5.76	5.85	5.93	6.01	6.08	6.14	6.20	6.26	6.31	6.36	6.41
40	3.82	4.37	4.70	4.93	5.11	5.27	5.39	5.50	5.60	5.69	5.77	5.84	5.90	5.96	6.02	6.07	6.12	6.17	6.21
60	3.76	4.28	4.60	4.82	4.99	5.13	5.25	5.36	5.45	5.53	5.60	5.67	5.73	5.79	5.84	5.89	5.93	5.98	6.02
120	3.70	4.20	4.50	4.71	4.87	5.01	5.12	5.21	5.30	5.38	5.44	5.51	5.56	5.61	5.66	5.71	5.75	5.79	5.83
∞	3.64	4.12	4.40	4.60	4.76	4.88	4.99	5.08	5.16	5.23	5.29	5.35	5.40	5.45	5.49	5.54	5.57	5.61	5.65

[a] Range/$S_Y \sim Q_{1-\alpha;\eta,\nu}$. η is the size of the sample from which the range is obtained, and ν is the number of degrees of freedom of S_Y.
Source: Reprinted from E. S. Pearson and H. O. Hartley, eds., Table 29 of *Biometrika Tables for Statisticians*, Vol. 1, 3rd ed., 1966, by permission of the *Biometrika* Trustees, London.

Appendix B

Data Files for Problems and Examples

This appendix contains descriptions of the data files that are used in the textbook examples and problem assignments. Each data file is in three forms on the data disk: ASCII, Minitab, and EXCEL. One or more of these formats can be read into any statistical data package. Descriptions of the variables are also contained at the beginning of each data file.

Anscombe

This data file contains independent and dependent variables prepared by the late Frank Anscombe, a highly competent teacher of statistics and regression. The four regression lines Y1, Y2, and Y3 regressed on X1 and Y4 regressed on X2 provide some interesting and important insights into regression analysis, especially when they are plotted (Table B.1).

TABLE B.1 Data
File Anscombe

Column	Variable Name
C1	X1
C2	X2
C3	Y1
C4	Y2
C5	Y3
C6	Y4

Auto

This data file contains quarterly time-series data for domestic and foreign auto sales in the United States (Table B.2).

TABLE B.2   Data File Auto

Column	Variable Name	Description
C1	Year	Year for each observation
C2	Rcardq	Number of domestic cars (millions) sold during the quarter expressed in annual terms
C3	Rcarfq	Number of foreign manufactured cars (millions) sold during the quarter expressed in annual terms

BBWltd

This data file contains weights of bread, in grams, selected from various supermarkets for quality control assessment (Table B.3).

TABLE B.3   Data File BBWltd

Column	Variable Name	Description
C1	Dbread	Weight in grams of dark bread sampled from supermarkets
C2	Sbread	Weight in grams of specialty bread sampled from supermarkets
C3	Csbread	Weight in grams of competitors' specialty bread sampled from supermarkets

Cereal

This file contains production data from a cereal factory (Table B.4). Each of the 22 observations represents a production run. Each production run lasts from one to two weeks, depending on the demand for this particular cereal. The data were collected for flake cereal production. These data were generously supplied by Malt O Meal, Inc. of Northfield, Minnesota.

TABLE B.4   Data File Cereal

Column	Variable Name	Description
C1	Yieldp	Percent yield of finished product (lb dry cereal/lb wet ingredients)
C2	Pergrit	Percentage of grits and broken cereal diverted from line
C3	Lbsgrit	Total pounds of grits or broken cereal
C4	Totprob	Total pounds cereal produced in production run

Chain

This file contains weekly retail sales data for five competing brands of a food product sold in supermarkets (Table B.5). The data were generously supplied by A. C. Nielsen Inc. They were used in a number of cases that study the effects of price and promotion variables on quantity demanded.

TABLE B.5   Data File Chain

Column	Variable Name	Description
C1	Storenum	Code number for supermarket or chain
C2	Weeknum	Consecutive week number
C3	Saleb1	Total unit sales for brand 1
C4	Apriceb1	Actual retail price for brand 1
C5	Rpriceb1	Regular or recommended price brand 1
C6	Promotb1	Promotion code for brand 1
	0	No promotion
	1	Newspaper advertising only
	2	In-store display only
	3	Newspaper ad and in-store display
C7	Saleb2	Total unit sales for brand 2
C8	Apriceb2	Actual retail price for brand 2
C9	Rpriceb2	Regular or recommended price for brand 2
C10	Promotb2	Promotion code for brand 2
C11	Saleb3	Total unit sales for brand 3
C12	Apriceb3	Actual retail price for brand 3
C13	Rpriceb3	Regular or recommended price for brand 3
C14	Promotb3	Promotion code for brand 3
C15	Saleb4	Total unit sales for brand 4
C16	Apriceb4	Actual retail price for brand 4
C17	Rpriceb4	Regular or recommended price for brand 4
C18	Promotb4	Promotion code for brand 4
C19	Saleb5	Total unit sales for brand 5
C20	Apriceb5	Actual retail price for brand 5
C21	Rpriceb5	Regular or recommended price for brand 5
C22	Promotb5	Promotion code for brand 5

Citydat

This data file contains a cross-section database for project analysis (Table B.6). The file contains data from 45 nonmetropolitan Minnesota cities for the years 1973 and 1974. The data were collected in 1976 as part of a research project to determine the

TABLE B.6   Data File Citydat

Column	Variable Name	Description
C1	Obsnum	Observation sequential number
C2	County	County code
C3	City	MCD code
C4	Sizehse	Median rooms per owner-occupied house
C5	Totexp	Total current city government expenditures
C6	Taxbase	Assessment base in millions of 1972 dollars
C7	Taxrate	Tax levy divided by total assessment
C8	Pop73	1973 population estimate
C9	Incom72	1972 per capita income
C10	Hseval	Market value per owner-occupied residence
C11	Taxhse	Average tax per owner-occupied residence
C12	Homper	Percent of property value: owner-occupied residence
C13	Rentper	Percent of property value: rental residence
C14	Comper	Percent of property value: commercial
C15	Indper	Percent of property value: industrial property
C16	Utilper	Percent of property value: public utility
C17	Year	Year represented by data

effect of economic growth on local city expenditures, tax rates, and housing values. The file contains a total of 90 observations.

Consb

This data file was obtained from a large survey of households conducted by the Survey Research Center at the University of Michigan in 1967 (Table B.7). Because of its size it can be treated as a population from which computer-generated random samples are

TABLE B.7   Data File Consb

Column	Variable Name	Description
C1	Sizpla01	Size of place (1960 census)
C2	Eduhea05	Education of head of family
C3	Income19	Total family income

obtained for analysis. Thus it is useful for applied projects involving data analysis and sampling distributions.

Constr

This file contains quarterly time-series data on office and industrial construction (Table B.8). The series are measured in millions of real dollars of construction for the quarter indicated.

TABLE B.8   Data File Constr

Column	Variable Name	Description
C1	Year	Year of the observation
C2	Quarter	Quarter of the observation
C3	Time	Sequential time variable beginning with 1
C4	Conniq	Total construction expenditures on industrial buildings
C5	Connoq	Total construction expenditures on office buildings

Cotton

This file contains quarterly data that deal with cotton production for the years 1966–1972 (Table B.9).

TABLE B.9   Data File Cotton

Column	Variable Name	Description
C1	Quarter	Quarter of year
C2	Year	Year of observation
C3	Cotprod	Cotton production
C4	Whopri	Wholesale price
C5	Impfab	Imported fabric
C6	Expfab	Exported fabric

Crash

This data file contains observations by state, with one state missing (Tables B.10 and B.11). The data were used to develop regression models to predict motor vehicle death rate per state as a function of the characteristics of the state population, road system, and motor vehicle mix. A variety of interesting models can be developed using these data. All of the data were collected for the year 1976.

TABLE B.10   Data File Crash

Column	Variable Name	Description
C1	State	State code
C2	Carage	Average age of automobiles
C3	Vehwt	Average weight of automobiles (lb)
C4	F1	Computed variable that represents the relative size of cars; larger value implies greater difference in vehicle size
C5	Wtstd	Standard deviation of automobile weight
C6	PrurPop	Proportion rural population
C7	Deaths	Crash deaths in automobiles and pickups divided by population
C8	Lghttrks	Percent light trucks
C9	Impcars	Percent imported automobiles
C10	Popdens	Population per square mile
C11	DRm76Mi	Deaths per mile driven in 1976
C12	Hschool	Percent high school graduates
C13	Doctors	Physicians per 100,000 population
C14	Ruspeed	Average measured speed on rural two-lane roads
C15	Prsurf	Proportion of rural roads surfaced
C16	Tpopdeth	Total motor vehicle deaths divided by population (equal to C7 times 100)

Crime

This data file contains 1982 and 1984 crime rate data for individual states and the District of Columbia (Tables B.12 and B.13). The data were obtained from the 1986 edition of *Statistical Abstract of the United States*. The crime rates are expressed in reported crimes per 100,000 population as collected by the Federal Bureau of Investigation. The data use the same state codes and the same observation sequence as the State87 data file.

Labor2

This data file contains variables collected from the 1980 census for 150 Standard Metropolitan Statistical Areas (Table B.14). The data describe women's labor force participation as a function of age and family status.

TABLE B.11   State Codes for Data File Crash

Code	State	Code	State	Code	State
1	Alabama	18	Kentucky	35	North Dakota
2	Alaska	19	Louisiana	36	Ohio
3	Arizona	20	Maine	37	Oklahoma
4	Arkansas	21	Maryland	38	Oregon
5	California	22	Massachusetts	39	Pennsylvania
6	Colorado	23	Michigan	40	Rhode Island
7	Connecticut	24	Minnesota	41	South Carolina
8	Delaware	25	Mississippi	42	South Dakota
9	Dist of Colum	26	Missouri	43	Tennessee
10	Florida	27	Montana	44	Texas
11	Georgia	28	Nebraska	45	Utah
12	Hawaii	29	Nevada	46	Vermont
13	Idaho	30	New Hampshire	47	Virginia
14	Illinois	31	New Jersey	48	Washington
15	Indiana	32	New Mexico	49	West Virginia
16	Iowa	33	New York	50	Wisconsin
17	Kansas	34	North Carolina	51	Wyoming

Macrel95

This quarterly data file contains the same variables as "Macro95." However, "Macrel95" contains data beginning with the first quarter of 1946.

Macro95

This data file contains a number of popular quarterly economic data series that are routinely collected by the U.S. Department of Commerce (Table B.15). The data series all begin in the first quarter of 1959.

Metals

This data file was prepared by G. Hilderbrand and T. Liu, *Manufacturing Production Functions in the United States* (Ithaca, NY, Cornell University Press, 1957). The data are statewide observations on SIC 33 Primary Metals Industry (Table B.16). The data are useful for estimating production functions.

TABLE B.12 Data File Crime

Column	Variable Name	Description
C1	Code	State code
C2	Totcri82	Total crime rate 1982
C3	Totcri84	Total crime rate 1984
C4	Murd82	Murder rate 1982
C5	Murd84	Murder rate 1984
C6	Rape82	Rape rate 1982
C7	Rape84	Rape rate 1984
C8	Asslt82	Assault rate 1982
C9	Asslt84	Assault rate 1984
C10	Rober82	Robbery rate 1982
C11	Rober84	Robbery rate 1984
C12	Burgl82	Burglary rate 1982
C13	Burgl84	Burglary rate 1984
C14	Larcny82	Larceny rate 1982
C15	Larcny84	Larceny rate 1984
C16	Mrtveh82	Motor vehicle theft rate 1982
C17	Mrtveh84	Motor vehicle theft rate 1984

Mondat2

This file stores monthly time-series data from 1987 through 1993 that is used for a number of forecasting problems (Table B.17).

Retail

This small data file is a subset of the State87 data file. It contains observations for 50 states and the District of Columbia (Table B.18). The data, for the year 1984, were obtained from the 1986 *Statistical Abstract*.

Salmod

This data file contains salary data for college faculty, adjusted to protect confidentiality. See Table B.19.

TABLE B.13   State Codes for Data File Crime and for State87

Code	State	Code	State	Code	State
1	Maine	18	North Dakota	35	Arkansas
2	New Hampshire	19	South Dakota	36	Louisiana
3	Vermont	20	Nebraska	37	Oklahoma
4	Massachusetts	21	Kansas	38	Texas
5	Rhode Island	22	Delaware	39	Montana
6	Connecticut	23	Maryland	40	Idaho
7	New York	24	Dist of Colum	41	Wyoming
8	New Jersey	25	Virginia	42	Colorado
9	Pennsylvania	26	West Virginia	43	New Mexico
10	Ohio	27	North Carolina	44	Arizona
11	Indiana	28	South Carolina	45	Utah
12	Illinois	29	Georgia	46	Nevada
13	Michigan	30	Florida	47	Washington
14	Wisconsin	31	Kentucky	48	Oregon
15	Minnesota	32	Tennessee	49	California
16	Iowa	33	Alabama	50	Alaska
17	Missouri	34	Mississippi	51	Hawaii

TABLE B.14   Data File Labor2

Column	Variable Name	Description
C1	Smsa	Code identifying the SMSA
C2	East	1 = eastern states, 0 = else
C3	Norcent	1 = north central states, 0 = else
C4	Soucent	1 = south central states, 0 = else
C5	West	1 = Pacific and mountain states, 0 = else
C6	Par15t24	Labor participation, wife's age 15–24
C7	Par25t34	Labor participation, wife's age 25–34
C8	Par35t44	Labor participation, wife's age 35–44
C9	Par45t54	Labor participation, wife's age 45–54
C10	Par55t64	Labor participation, wife's age 55–64
C11	Parnoch	Labor participation, wife, no child
C12	Prclt6	Labor participation, wife, child > 6
C13	Prc6to17	Labor participation, wife, child 6–17

TABLE B.15   Data File Macro95

Column	Variable Name	Description
C1	Year.qtr	Year for data fraction is quarter
C2	Fm1qq	Money supply M2, 1987$
C3	Fyffq	Federal funds interest rate
C4	Fyprq	Prime interest rate, short-term loans
C5	Gcdq	Consumption of durables, 1987$
C6	Gcompq	National income; compensation of employees, 1987$
C7	Gcq	Total consumption, 1987$
C8	Gcsq	Consumption of service, 1987$
C9	Gdpq	Gross domestic product, 1987$
C10	Gdpd	GDP deflator, 1987 base
C11	Gexq	Exports of goods and services, 1987$
C12	Ggeq	Total government spending: federal, state, local
C13	Gimq	Imports goods and services, 1987$
C14	Gipd	Investment products and durable equipment, 1987$
C15	Girq	Residential investment, 1987$
C16	Gnpq	Gross national product, 1987$
C17	Gpiq	Total investment, 1987$
C18	Gydq	Disposable personal income, 1987$
C19	Gyq	National income total, 1987$
C20	Pwfq	Product price index finished goods, 1987 base
C21	Pwicq	Price index industrial commodities, 1987 base
C22	Totalq	Gc87 + gpi87 + gge87 + gex87 − gim87

TABLE B.16   Data File Metals

Column	Variable Name	Description
C1	Value added	Total value added (Index)
C2	Labor	Labor usage (Index)
C3	Capital	Capital usage (Index)

State87

This cross-section data file for statistics projects was obtained from the 1986 *Statistical Abstract* (Table B.20). The table number from the *Statistical Abstract* for each variable is noted in this table. The file was developed for use by students and faculty

Data Files for Problems and Examples

TABLE B.17   Data File Mondat2

Column	Variable Name	Description
C1	Year	Year for each observation
C2	Month	Month for each observation
C3	Time	Sequential time variable beginning with 1
C4	Conni	Expenditures on industrial construction in millions of real dollars, annual rate
C5	Conno	Expenditures on office construction in millions of real dollars, annual rate
C6	Exrger	German exchange rate in deutschemark, per U.S. dollar
C7	Exrjan	Japanese exchange rate in yen per U.S. dollar
C8	Rcard	Number of domestic cars (millions) sold during the month expressed in annual terms
C9	Rcarf	Number of foreign manufactured cars (millions) sold during the quarter expressed in annual terms

TABLE B.18   Data File Retail

Column	Variable Name	Description
C1	Perinc84	Per capita personal income for 1984
C2	Retsal84	Per capita retail sales for 1984
C3	Totpop84	Total population for 1984
C4	Unemp84	Percent unemployment for 1984

TABLE B.19   Data File Salmod

Column	Variable Name	Description
C1	Age	Age of person
C2	Experien	Years experience
C3	Yrs_Assoc	Years associate professor
C4	Yrs_Full	Years full professor
C5	Gender_F1	Gender 1 = female
C6	Salary	Annual salary
C7	Market	Special market

TABLE B.20   Data File State87

Name	Table	Description
State		Name of state
Code		Code number assigned to state
Totpop84	12	Total state population 1984
Birth83	85	Registered births/1000 population by place of residence, excludes births to non-U.S. residents, 1983
Infmrt82	113	Infant deaths under 1 year per 100 live births, excludes fetal deaths, 1982
Helexp82	152	Personal health care expenditures per capita, 1982
Phys82	164	Physicians per 100,000 population, 1982, American Medical Association
Tecsal85	227	Average teacher salaries, public elementary and secondary schools, 1985, National Education Association
Pupexp85	233	Current expenditures per pupil in attendance, 1985, National Education Association
Welper84	645	Public aid recipients as percent of population, 1984, ADC + FSSI payments
Emper84	662	Civilian employment as percent of civilian noninstitutional population, 1984, BLS
Unemp84	662	Unemployment percentage of civilian labor force, 1984, BLS
Perinc84	735	Per capita personal income, 1984
Peren84	959	Per capita energy consumption, 1983, U.S. Energy Information Administration
Vehdet82	1047	Motor vehicle death rate per 100,000 population, 1982, U.S. Center for Health Statistics
Retsal84	1397	Retail sales per capita, 1984
Totcri82	281	Total reported crime per 100,000 population, 1982
Totcri84	281	Total reported crime per 100,000 population, 1984
Heart82	116	Deaths per 100,000 population, heart disease, 1982
Acid82	116	Deaths per 100,000 population, accidents, 1982
Pulmon82	116	Deaths per 100,000 population, chronic obstructive pulmonary diseases and allied conditions, 1982
Suicid82	116	Deaths per 100,000 population, suicide, 1982
Cirrh82	116	Deaths per 100,000 population, chronic liver disease, cirrhosis, 1982

TABLE B.20   Data File State87 (*Continued*)

Name	Table	Description
Homici82	116	Deaths per 100,000 population, homicide and legal intervention, 1982
Police83	303	Police per 100,000 population, 1983; state and local government revenues and expenditures, 1983
Enfexp83	303	Police and prison expenditures per capita, 1983
Reven83	455	Total revenue per capita, 1983
Educ83	455	Total expenditures for education, million $
Hiway83	455	Total expenditures for highways, million $
Pubwel83	455	Total expenditures for public welfare, million $
Hosp83	455	Total expenditures for hospitals, million $

in the Department of Economics at St. Olaf College. The state codes are defined in Table B.13 and are the same as those in the crime data file.

Stordata

The file stores retail sales data during the years 1986 and 1987 for a small sporting goods store located in a midwestern city (Table B.21). The data were collected by William L. Carlson, Department of Economics, St. Olaf College (1988), as part of a special study.

TABLE B.21   Data File Stordata

Column	Variable Name	Description
C1	Month	Month numerical order with January = 1
C2	Dayweek	Day of week with Monday = 1 through Saturday = 6
C3	Salesrev	Total daily sales revenue, dollars

Stortet

The variable list for this file is the same as the list for "Chain." However, this file has only 52 observations from a single store.

Student

This data file contains academic information for 112 students who were economics majors at a high-quality midwestern liberal arts college (Table B.22). The data can be used in a variety of projects that analyze or predict student performance. It should be noted that all students did not take both entrance tests.

TABLE B.22　Data File Student

Column	Variable Name	Description
C1	Gender	1 if female, 0 else
C2	GPA	Overall grade-point average in all courses
C3	SATverb	SAT entrance score on verbal section
C4	SATmath	SAT entrance score on mathematics section
C5	ACTeng	ACT entrance score on English section
C6	ACTmath	ACT entrance score on mathematics section
C7	ACTss	ACT entrance score on social studies section
C8	ACTcomp	ACT entrance score comprehensive
C9	HSPct	High school percentile rank
C10	EconGPA	Grade-point average in economics courses

Selected Answers to Problem Exercises

Chapter 1

1.1 Essentially, the term *information age* refers to the ever-increasing focus on and use of processed data. Furthermore, fewer people are needed, in this day and age, to undertake physical labor: more people are needed to analyze data and make "knowledgeable" decisions as to, say, the production methods of goods, and so forth. Statistically speaking, this present age will truly test the power and capability of current applied statistical practice and reasoning.

1.2 The role of statistical analysis within the framework of information is to evaluate accumulated data, which in turn provide hopefully relevant information. Ultimately, this information is used to gain heightened knowledge or insight into a particular issue or area of research. If the statistical procedures or inferences are carried out poorly, it follows that the information and hence the knowledge gained will also be doomed to be inadequate. The process of data collection is also extremely important; statistical analyses are only as effective as the data. Errors in data processing and/or collection will also skew results of information or knowledge.

1.3 Analytic study

1.4 Enumerative study

1.5 Answers will vary.

Chapter 2

2.10 (a) 5.79%
     (b) 12.95 years

2.11 (a) 2.5%
     (b) Yes, AID should attempt to increase annual food production: if the mean population growth rate continues at 2.5% (and the expected food growth rate is just 2%), there will be ever-increasing malnourishment over time if food production is not increased.

2.12 (a) 10.18%
     (b) 7.37 years

2.13 (a) 4.40%
     (b) 3.73%
     (c) Yes, Ms. Treloar does, in fact, have a predicament: she will continue to lose money since her mean employee wage increases are greater than her mean price

increases. Based on this information alone, and supposing that this trend continues, Ms. Treloar might eventually bankrupt her accounts.

2.14 (a) $\bar{X} = 449.9$
      (b) $S_X^2 = 31.49$; $S_X = 5.61$
      (c) $X_m = 450$
      (d) $CV = 0.0125$
      (e) Range $= 17$

2.15 (a) $\bar{X} = 2075$
      (b) $S_X = 349.35$
      (c) $CV = 0.168$
      (d) $X_m = 2100$ [i.e., $(2200 + 2000)/2$]
      (e) Percentile $= 42$nd

2.16 (a) $\bar{X} = 11$; $X_m = 10.5$
      (b) $S_X^2 = 15.68$; $S_X = 3.96$

2.17 (a) $X_m = 14$;   interquartile range $= 6$
      (b) 16 days
      (c) 10%
      (d) 40%

2.18 (a) 50th percentile $= 115$; $X_m = 117$
      (b) 20th percentile $= 95$
      (c) 80th percentile $= 13$
      (d) ca. 56th percentile

2.21 (a) $\bar{X} = 117.9$; $X_m = 117$
      (b) $S_X = 21.76$;   range $= 75$
      (c) 100%

2.22 (a) $\bar{X} = 12.75$; $X_m = 14$;   trimodal:14, 15, 16
      (b) $S_X^2 = 12.83$; $S_X = 3.58$
      (c) 100%
      (d) 12.75 ± 7.16
      (e) 12.75 ± 9.24

2.23 (a) $\bar{X} = 2.91$; $X_m = 2.4$
      (b) $S_X^2 = 2.77$; $S_X = 1.66$
      (c) $CV = 0.573$
      (d) 2.91 ± 3.32
      (e) 2.91 ± 5.25
      (f) The first interval is narrower because the curve is postulated to be symmetric—the data are balanced about the mean. A skewed distribution of observations, as postulated by Chebyshev, demands a larger "acceptance" interval since more observations are farther away from the mean than if the curve were symmetric.

2.24 (a) $\bar{X} = 113$
      (b) $S_X^2 = 698.63$; $S_X = 26.43$
      (c) 113 ± 52.86

2.25 (a) $\bar{X} = 1660$

(b) $S_X = 279.48$
(c) $CV = 0.1684$

2.26   (a) $\bar{X} = 1745$
     (b) $S_X = 209.4$
     (c) $CV = 0.12$

2.27 $\bar{X} = 2500$; $S_X = 850$

2.28 $\bar{X} = 2200$ (i.e., $1000 + 1200$); $S_X^2 = 15{,}625$

2.29 $\bar{X} = 937$; $S_X = 100.5$

2.30   (a) $\bar{X} = 113$
     (b) $S_X^2 = 698.63$; $S_X = 26.43$
     (c) $\bar{X} = 11{,}170$
     (d) $S_X = 2378.85$

2.31   (a) $\bar{X} = 117.9$; $X_m = 117$
     (b) $S_X = 21.76$;   range $= 66$
     (c) $\bar{X} = 276.85$; $S_X = 32.64$
     (d) 276.85 ± 65.28

2.32   (a) $\bar{X} = 12.75$
     (b) $S_X = 3.58$
     (c) $\bar{X} = 1275$; $S_X = 358.18$
     (d) $\bar{X} = 305$; $S_X = 71.64$

Chapter 3

3.1   (b) Covariance $= 1069.33$
    (c) Correlation $= 0.989$
    (d) The number of workers and number of tables produced have a nearly perfect positive linear relationship: as more workers are employed, the greater the number of tables produced.

3.2   (b) Covariance $= 4.27$
    (c) Correlation $= 0.128$
    (d) The relationship between number of drug units and recovery time is quite minute. In effect, the correlation tends to suggest almost no relationship whatsoever; however, mind you, the relationship is positive. Generally speaking, a dosage of 9 drug units would be recommended. A case could, of course, be argued for other varying numbers of units prescribed.

3.3   (b) Covariance $= -5.5$
    (c) Correlation $= -0.776$
    (d) There exists an adequately strong negative linear relationship between service price and delivery time to warrant paying more for "speedier" delivery.

3.4   (b) Covariance $= 10{,}299.2$
    (c) Correlation $= 0.956$
    (d) Yes, the company would be correct in concluding that monthly wages tend to increase directly with years of experience.

3.5   (b) Covariance $= 30.31$
        (c) Correlation $= 0.818$
        (d) The advertising costs incurred by Consumer Foods, Inc. have a quite strong positive linear relationship with effectiveness. With a correlation of 0.818, effectiveness and advertising costs can typically be shown to increase with one another.

3.6   (a) Δsales $= 6$ for a 1-cent reduction in price
        (b) 204 units
        (c) Predicted total revenue $= \$162.32$
        (d) Predicted total revenue $= \$194.16$
        (e) A price of 57 cents will result in the maximum predicted total revenue.

3.7   (a) Predicted quantity sold $= 86$
        (b) Predicted quantity sold $= 23$
        (c) Predicted total revenue $= \$442.5$
        (d) Predicted total revenue $= \$218.5$

3.8   (b) $\hat{\beta}_0 = -130.16; \quad \hat{\beta}_1 = 25.45$
        (c) 379 tables
        (d) As the number of workers increases, so does the number of tables produced.

3.9   (b) $\hat{\beta}_0 = 53.67; \quad \hat{\beta}_1 = 0.134$
        (c) When the drug dosage is 6 units, the predicted recovery time is 54 days. A dosage of 15 units gives a predicted recovery time of 56 days.
        (d) Given the regression information, one can deduce that a much larger dose tends not to speed up the recovery time by any worthwhile measure. Also, from this initial analysis, a dosage of 9 drug units seems to provide the greatest effect for the least amount of medicine.

3.10 (b) $\hat{\beta}_0 = 9.09; \quad \hat{\beta}_1 = -0.59$
        (c) Regular delivery $= 7$ days; fast delivery $= 6$ days; lightning delivery $= 3$ days
        (d) Regular and fast delivery rates tend not to be distinguishable from one another (7 vs. 6 days), whereas if one were able to afford the $10 lightning rate, the delivery rate would be much more expedient.

3.11 (b) $\hat{\beta}_0 = 820.7; \quad \hat{\beta}_1 = 537.14$
        (c) Predicted monthly wage increase for each successive year of experience $= \$537$
        (d) Predicted annual wage increase for each year of experience $= \$6444$
        (e) Given 10 years of experience, the predicted monthly wage $= \$6191$.
        (f) Yes, the company would be correct in concluding that monthly wages tend to increase directly with years of experience.

3.12 (b) $\hat{\beta}_0 = 0.58; \quad \hat{\beta}_1 = 0.2$
        (c) Predicted effectiveness $= 10.6$
        (d) For each unit of expenditure, the increased effectiveness $= 0.2$.
        (e) The greater the advertising expenditure, the greater the effectiveness

Chapter 4

4.1   (a) $P = 0.15$
        (b) $P = 0.35$
        (c) $P = 0.40$

4.2   (a) $P = 0.346$
      (b) $P = 0.208$
      (c) $P = 0.979$

4.3   (a) $P = 0.073$
      (b) $P = 0.1077$
      (c) $P = 0.1077$
      (d) $P = 0.0046$

4.4   (a) $P = 0.03$
      (b) $P = 0.052$
      (c) $P = 0.015$

4.5   (a) $P = 0.52$
      (b) $P = 0.504$

4.6   (a) $P = 0.04$
      (b) $P = 0.218$
      (c) $P = 0.204$

4.7 $P = 0.07$

4.8   (a) $P(A_1 \cap B_1) = 0.20$
      (b) $P(A_1) = 0.60$
      (c) $P(A_2 \cap B_3) = 0.15$
      (d) $P(B_2) = 0.35$
      (e) $P(A_2 \cap B_1) = 0.10$

4.9   (a) $P(A_1 \cap B_2) = 0.20$
      (b) $P(A_1) = 0.60$
      (c) $P(A_2 \cap B_3) = 0.05$
      (d) $P(B_2) = 0.45$
      (e) $P(A_2 \cap B_1) = 0.10$

4.10 (a) $P(A_2 \cap B_2) = 0.10$
      (b) $P(A_1) = 0.60$
      (c) $P(A_2 \cap B_2) = 0.10$
      (d) $P(B_3) = 0.35$

4.11 $P(A_1 \cup B_1) = 0.60$

4.12 (a) $P = 0.30$
      (b) $P = 0.10$
      (c) $P = 0.35$

4.13 $P = 0.35$

4.14 $P = 0.15$

4.15 (a) $P(A_1 \mid B_1) = 0.44$
      (b) $P(A_2 \mid B_1) = 0.56$
      (c) $P(B_2 \mid A_2) = 0.55$
      (d) No, they are not independent.

4.16 (a) $P(A_1 \mid B_1) = 0.44$
      (b) $P(A_2 \mid B_3) = 0.57$

(c) $P(B_3 \mid A_2) = 0.36$

(d) No, they are not independent.

4.17   (a) $P(A_2 \mid B_2) = 0.50$

      (b) $P(B_2 \mid A_1) = 0.38$

      (c) $P(B_2 \mid A_2) = 0.71$

      (d) No, they are not independent.

4.18   (a) $P(A_1 \mid B_1) = 0.33$

      (b) $P(A_2 \mid B_3) = 0.20$

      (c) $P(B_3 \mid A_2) = 0.14$

      (d) No, they are not independent.

4.19 $P = 0.78$

4.20   (b) $P = 0.78$

      (c) The odds are 3.55 to 1.

4.21   (a) $P(A_1 \mid T_1) = 0.64$

      (b) $P(A_2 \mid T_2) = 0.45$

4.22   (a) $P(A_2 \mid T_2) = 0.68$

      (b) $P(A_1 \mid T_1) = 0.28$

4.23 $P = 0.40$

4.24   Yes, the advertising is effective because the overinvolvement ratio is greater than 1.0 (i.e., $0.50/0.30 = 1.67$).

4.25   (a) $P = 0.57$

      (b) $P = 0.94$

Chapter 5

5.1   (c) $P = 0.64$

5.2   (a) $\mu = 1.9$

     (b) $\sigma^2 = 1.45$, $\sigma = 1.20$

5.3   (c) $P = 0.40$

5.4   (a) $\mu = 2.31$

     (b) $\sigma^2 = 1.914$, $\sigma = 1.383$

5.5   (a) The probability distribution function is as follows: for either 0 or 3 heads, $f(y) = 0.125$; for either 1 or 2 heads, $f(y) = 0.375$.

     (b) Answers will vary.

     (c) Actual results from your various trials will differ from the expected, "probable" results in the short run. One should recognize the fact that as the sample size approaches ∞, the actual results will approach the probability distribution, as stated in part (a).

5.6   (a) $\mu = 1.5$

     (b) $\sigma^2 = 0.75$

5.7   (a) The probability distribution function is as follows: for either 0 or 3 classical CDs, $f(y) = 0.125$; for either 1 or 2 classical CDs, $f(y) = 0.375$.

     (c) $P = 0.50$

5.8   (a) The mean μ or expected value $E[Y] = 1.5$.
       (b) $\sigma^2 = 0.75$

5.9   (a) $P = 0.21$
       (b) $P = 0.21$
       (c) $P = 0.38$
       (d) $P = 0.17$

5.10   (a) $P = 0.13$
       (b) $P = 0.53$

5.11   (a) $P = 0.16$
       (b) $P = 0.12$
       (c) $P = 0.49$

5.12 $P = 0.25$

5.13   (a) $P = 0.11$
       (b) $P = 0.85$
       (c) $P = 0.01$
       (d) From his experience with Great Planes Air, Mr. George Brown should most defi-
           nitely find the claim of 80% on-time flights to be ludicrous.

5.14   (a) $P = 0.23$
       (b) $P = 0.61$
       (c) $P = 0.18$

5.15 $P = 0.68$

5.16   (a) $\mu = 6$
       (b) $\sigma^2 = 4.2$

5.17   (a) $\mu = 12.5$
       (b) $\sigma^2 = 9.38$

5.18   (a) $P = 0.867$
       (b) $P = 0.411$
       (c) $P = 0.107$

5.19   (a) $P = 0.19$
       (b) $P = 0.18$
       (c) $P = 0.29$
       (d) $P = 0.52$

5.20   (a) $P = 0.18$
       (b) $P = 0.38$
       (c) $P = 0.13$

5.21   (a) $P = 0.11$
       (b) The fact that 12 computers experienced software problems on a certain day, of
           course, seems quite unusual.
       (c) Assuming a binomial probability distribution: $\mu = 4$; $\sigma^2 = 3.84$.
       (d) Assuming a Poisson probability distribution: $\mu = 4$; $\sigma^2 = 4$. The mean and vari-
           ance are approximately the same using either the binomial or the Poisson approxi-
           mation.

5.22   (a) $P = 0.10$

(b) $P = 0.05$
(c) $P = 0.45$

5.23 (a) $\mu = 6$
(b) $\sigma^2 = 6$
(c) $P = 0.9574 - 0.0174 = 0.94$
(d) $P = 0.9964$

5.24 (a) $P = 0.30$
(b) $P = 0.03$
(c) $P = 0.12$

5.25 (a) $\mu = 1$
(b) $\sigma^2 = 1$
(c) $P = 0.981$
(d) $P = 0.996$

5.26 (a) $P = 0.04$
(b) $P = 0.17$
(c) $P = 0.35$

5.27 (a) $\mu = 3.2$
(b) $\sigma^2 = 3.2$
(c) $P = 0.955$
(d) $P = 0.994$

Chapter 6

6.1 (a) $P = 0.55$
(b) $P = 0.51$
(c) $P = 0.38$

6.2 (a) $P = 0.22$
(b) $P = 0.05$
(c) $P = 0.32$

6.3 (a) $P = 0.55$
(b) $P = 0.30$
(c) $P = 0.37$

6.4 (a) $P = 0.22$
(b) $P = 0.39$
(c) $P = 0.23$

6.5 (a) $P = 0.067$
(b) $P = 0.023$
(c) $P = 0.286$

6.6 (a) $P = 0.119$
(b) $P = 0.071$
(c) $P = 0.771$
(d) The truck driver's claim of 20.0 miles per gallon seems, according to the normal probability distribution, quite improbable (i.e., $P = 0.0016$).

6.7   (a) $P = 0.006$
      (b) $P = 0.854$
      (c) $P = 0.023$

6.8   (a) $P = 0.006$
      (b) $P = 0.04$
      (c) $P = 0.937$

6.9   (a) $P = 0.042$
      (b) $P = 0.997$
      (c) Since the probability of the stock price being $45 is less than 0.001 (given the current model), one could justifiably discredit the model as inadequate.

6.10 (a) $P = 0.0475$
      (b) $P = 0.0475$
      (c) $P = 0.6826$

6.11 (a) 139 saws
      (b) 150 saws
      (c) 220 saws (using 4.0 as the Z value)

6.12 (a) $P = 0.0764$
      (b) The following amount should be left in the reserve fund: $6310.
      (c) The upper limit, which would be exceeded only 5% of the time, is $21,515.

6.13 (a) This lower boundary equals $5440 (i.e., $Z \approx 1.28$).
      (b) This upper boundary equals $10,810 (i.e., $Z \approx 1.405$).
      (c) The following is the 92% symmetric acceptance interval for the Y's: $P(4500 \leq Y \leq 11,500) = 0.92$.

6.14 The continuity correction is used in this problem.
      (a) $P = 0.0401$
      (b) $P = 0.0951$
      (c) $P = 0.6699$

6.15 (a) $P = 0.0094$
      (b) $P = 0.0018$
      (c) $P(82 \leq X \leq 118) = 0.95$

6.16 (a) $P = 0.0985$
      (b) Approximately 0.00
      (c) $P = 0.6970$

6.17 (a) $P = 0.0655$
      (b) $P = 0.0183$
      (c) $P = 0.9474$

6.18 (a) $P = 0.1922$
      (b) $P = 0.8119$
      (c) $P = 0.289$

6.19 (a) $P = 0.0367$
      (b) $P = 0.1867$
      (c) $P = 0.5504$

6.20 $P = 0.2363$

6.21   (a) $P = 0.0735$
       (b) $P = 0.6848$

6.22 $P = 0.0985$. Since the probability of such a number of defects occurring is fairly minute with respect to the expected (mean) number, one can then conclude that this particular shipment has a larger average number of defective chips than the "guaranteed mean."

6.23   (a) $Y = 5000 + 3X$
       (b) $\mu = \$11{,}000;$ $\sigma^2 = 360{,}000$
       (c) $P = 0.0475$

6.24   (a) $\mu = \$3750;$ $\sigma^2 = 90{,}000$
       (b) $P = 0.2033$
       (c) $P = 0.121$

6.25   (a) $\mu = \$4500;$ $\sigma^2 = 202{,}500$
       (b) $P = 0.1335$
       (c) $\mu = \$5000;$ $\sigma^2 = 250{,}000$
       (d) $P = 0.50$

Chapter 7

7.1   (a) $f(2, 3) = 0.08$
     (b) $f(1, 2) = 0.15$
     (c) $f(3, 1) = 0.06$
     (d) $f(3, 2) = 0.07$

7.2   (a) $g(2 \mid 3) = 0.2667$
     (b) $h(3 \mid 1) = 0.3333$
     (c) $g(1 \mid 3) = 0.3333$
     (d) $h(2 \mid 3) = 0.28$

7.3   (a) No, X and Y are not independent.
     (b) The proposed marketing strategy most likely will succeed since the variables are dependent on one another. In short, sales can be increased through various marketing venues since the subgroups are better able to be identified.
     (c) For cars over five years old, one would concentrate on those in the subgroup ranging from 46 to 65 years of age.

7.4   (a) $f(1, 2) = 0.12$
     (b) $f(2, 2) = 0.16$
     (c) $f(3, 2) = 0.12$

7.5   (a) $h(2 \mid 1) = 0.40$
     (b) $h(2 \mid 3) = 0.40$
     (c) Yes, X and Y are independent.

7.6   (a) $h(2 \mid 1) = 0.40$
     (b) $h(1 \mid 3) = 0.30$
     (c) Yes, X and Y are independent.

7.7   (a) $\sigma_{XY} = -0.06$
     (b) $\sigma_X^2 = 0.5275;$ $\sigma_Y^2 = 0.24$
     (c) $\rho_{XY} = -0.1686$

7.8   (a) $\sigma_{XY} = 0$
       (b) $\sigma_X^2 = 0.5275;$ $\sigma_Y^2 = 0.24$
       (c) $\rho_{XY} = 0$

7.9   (a) $\sigma_{XY} = -0.15$
       (b) $\sigma_X^2 = 0.25;$ $\sigma_Y^2 = 0.25$
       (c) $\rho_{XY} = -0.6$

7.10   (a) $\sigma_{XY} = 0.011$
       (b) $\sigma_X^2 = 0.5475;$ $\sigma_Y^2 = 0.5796$
       (c) $\rho_{XY} = 0.0195$

7.11   (a) $\sigma_{XY} = -0.065$
       (b) $\sigma_X^2 = 0.7275;$ $\sigma_Y^2 = 0.69$
       (c) $\rho_{XY} = -0.0917$

7.12 $\sigma_{XY} = -1400$

7.13 $\sigma_{XY} = -62$

7.14 $\sigma_{XY} = 15,000$

7.15   (a) $\mu_W = 50;$ $\sigma_W^2 = 80$
       (b) $\mu_W = 50;$ $\sigma_W^2 = 117.1$

7.16   (a) $\mu_W = 210;$ $\sigma_W^2 = 1505$
       (b) $\mu_W = 210;$ $\sigma_W^2 = 2246.62$

7.17   (a) $\mu_W = \$1500$
       (b) $\sigma_W^2 = 55,000$

7.18   (a) $\mu_W = \$1500$
       (b) $\sigma_W^2 = 33,786.8$

7.19   (a) $\$1139.73 \le Y \le \$1860.27$
       (b) $P = 0.0516$
       (c) $P = 0.0146$

7.20   (a) $\mu_W = \$1500$
       (b) $\sigma_W^2 = 55,000$
       (c) $P = 0.1003$
       (d) $P = 0.0436$

7.21   (a) $\mu_W = 10$
       (b) $\sigma_W^2 = 24$

7.22   (a) $P = 0.0207$
       (b) $P = 0.0207$

7.23   (a) $\mu_W = 275$
       (b) $\sigma_W^2 = 3725$

7.24   (a) $P = 0.0202$
       (b) $P = 0.8705$
       (c) $P = 0.0202$

Chapter 8

8.1   A target population is a set of items (e.g., people) that are to be included in a certain study. A sampling frame, on the other hand, is a listing of the items within the target population (e.g., a telephone directory).

8.2   Nonresponse bias is the occurrence whereby certain items are excluded in a target population because the methodology of the sampling frame was not successful in obtaining responses from each item in the said population. The obvious dilemma surrounding nonresponse bias is that the results of the study will be different than the "beliefs" of the population.

8.3   A sample tends to provide more accurate measurements of large population characteristics than does a census for the following reasons: each sample observation can be meticulously analyzed and "measured," whereas in a census the quality of measurement methodology is in question. In addition, the probability of each sample distribution is known, thereby enabling one to configure the population probability distribution with relative precision.

8.4   Election polls with sample sizes of just 1000 to 1500 are considerably more accurate than the infamous *Literary Digest* poll of 1936, for the following reasons: small-sample election polls are readily able to identify and delineate each sample observation and then make assumptions about the entire population; also, small-sample polls do not suffer from the gross effects of nonresponse bias as did the 1936 *Digest* poll.

8.5   The advantages of stratified samples as opposed to simple random samples are as follows: first, the results from stratified samples will (hopefully) provide a statistician with various strata, each possessing different sample means and variances. This being the case, each stratum (having been delineated from the others) can be better "dealt with," for example, by marketing schemes or any other basis for such a study. It is also important to note that each stratum's mean and variance can be manipulated mathematically to arrive at the approximate population mean.

8.6   A statistician might opt for systematic sampling since obtaining sample observations is quite easy. An example would include the sampling of every fifth person to enter a grocery store. However, the caveat of using systematic sampling techniques is that one must be aware of possible systematic tendencies within the population: that is, if every fifth person entering the store were from the same wealthy district (stratum) within the target population. Also, one should watch for sample observation overlap such that the same person happened to regularly be the fifth person to enter the store—the probability of this being the case, however, is quite minute and therefore can typically be discounted.

8.7   In the case of accounting auditors, judgment samples might, in fact, be more accurate than a simple random sample: expert experience can often account for variations and tendencies in a certain study that are otherwise overlooked by pure statistical analysis.

8.8   The precision of analytic studies cannot as readily be "analyzed" as the precision of enumerative studies in that analytic studies are based on inference. An analytic study, in essence, takes a certain enumerative study, and from there attempts to make judgments about a population other than that being studied initially.

8.9   Information is simply the organization and processing of data into a form that provides us with a (hopefully) valuable and accurate microcosm of a certain target population.

8.10   Nonresponse bias is the deviation from projecting the true population characteristics because of the exclusion (due to refusal to respond or lack of communication) of certain sample observations within the target population. It follows that if the observations were included in the study, the descriptive statistics of the population would be better approximated.

8.11   One is able to assume the use of cross-section data because most studies use random samples (of a certain target population) whose characteristics do not change over the course of time.

8.12   Random error differs from bias in that it is not a fixed deviation stemming from the "measuring" or sampling procedure; for each sample observation the random error is different. One should also note that the random error is measured by the variance of the sample statistics.

8.13   All in all, statisticians must be picky when it comes to the process of data collection because, very simply, data and the resulting information are the lifeblood of any effective study. No matter how genius-like the statistical and mathematical manipulation of the data might be, the quality of the data remains the most key component to either the success or failure of a certain study.

8.14   A professional questionnaire writer is, of course, experienced in focusing on the objective of a certain study. This expertise, if you will, reduces the amount of measurement error and hence maximizes the analytic potential of the study. The probability of nonresponse bias is also minimized since an experienced writer realizes what type of questionnaires are most likely to be answered adequately and ultimately returned.

8.15   Descriptive studies describe target population. Comparative studies involve the comparison of two different populations: one such population can be termed the "treatment group" and the other the "control group."

8.16   In analyzing a worker training program under a before-and-after format, it is necessary that the same test group, in fact, be used "before and after." Naturally, analysis of the test group takes place before the institution of the training program and the results are compared to those compiled after the program has been completed.

8.17   A possible dilemma stemming from the use of parallel studies when analyzing the effectiveness of a worker training program is as follows: since there exist two different test groups, the differences between groups could result from differences between the groups and not the training program. The results of the training program could be misleading since one group might improve at a rate greater than that of the other.

8.18   Measurement bias could ultimately play a very influential role during the course of a parallel comparative study. If the measurement bias is different for each test group, the overall results from the study are biased.

8.19   A study such as the one surrounding the Salk polio vaccine would be very unlikely today for various reasons: first, our society lacks the patience to "sit idly by" for many months awaiting the study results. Also, the use of a placebo injection would be labeled as insufficient—if a possible cure for the AIDS virus were to be proclaimed, it seems all but certain that most victims of the virus would demand immediate injections. Many other ethical and practical reasons exist, however.

8.20   In the case of a draft lottery, the most ethical method in choosing people is, in fact, through the use of random selection. This holds true only if the process of selection is carried out properly. In the case of the 1970 draft, the behavior of those conducting the selection process was terribly incoherent, due to the fact that the process ultimately was not by any means random.

8.21   A random sample is selected such that each item has the same probability of being selected and the selection of each item is independent. Thus the sample distribution will approximate the population distribution.

Chapter 9

9.1   (a) $494.5 \leq \bar{X} \leq 505.5$
        (b) $P = 0.0359$
        (c) $P = 0.5416$

9.2   (a) $1.08 \leq \bar{X} \leq 1.12$
        (b) $P = 0.0$
        (c) $P = 0.9918$

9.3   (a) $151 \leq \bar{X} \leq 179$ (i.e., $Z \approx 1.88$)
        (b) The upper limit is 177.3.

9.4   (a) $2.491 \leq \bar{X} \leq 2.509$
        (b) $2.487 \leq \bar{X} \leq 2.513$
        (c) $P = 0.9974$

9.5   (a) The lower limit is 19.689.
        (b) $19.362 \leq \bar{X} \leq 20.638$ (i.e., $Z \approx 2.055$)

9.6   (a) $4.379 \leq \bar{X} \leq 5.621$ (i.e., $Z \approx 2.33$)
        (b) $P = 0.0122$
        (c) $P = 0.1292$

9.7   (a) $\$77{,}200 \leq \bar{X} \leq \$82{,}800$
        (b) $P = 0.0179$
        (c) $\$77{,}650 \leq \bar{X} \leq \$82{,}350$

9.8   (a) $P = 0.0475$
        (b) $P = 0.7495$
        (c) $\$20{,}065 \leq \bar{X} \leq \$29{,}935$

9.9   (a) $78 \leq \bar{X} \leq 102$
        (b) $P = 0.905$
        (c) The necessary assumption is that the distribution of the sample mean is approximately normal, based on the central limit theorem.

9.10   (a) $\$656 \leq \bar{X} \leq \$684$
        (b) The upper limit is $682.
        (c) We assume that the sample mean has a normal distribution.

9.11   (a) $498.06 \leq \bar{X} \leq 501.94$

      (b) $498.63 \leq \bar{X} \leq 501.37$
      (c) $P = 0.1151$
      (d) $P = 0.50$

9.12   (a) $0.14 \leq \hat{P} \leq 0.26$
      (b) $P = 0.0630$
      (c) $P = 0.0329$

9.13   (a) $0.255 \leq \hat{P} \leq 0.345$
      (b) $P = 0.0146$
      (c) $P = 0.0951$

9.14   (a) $0.46 \leq \hat{P} \leq 0.54$
      (b) $P = 0.1151$
      (c) $P = 0.0011$

9.15   (a) $P = 0.0146$
      (b) $P = 0.0630$
      (c) $0.21 \leq \hat{P} \leq 0.39$

9.16   (a) $0.05 \leq \hat{P} \leq 0.15$
      (b) $P = 0.0294$
      (c) $P = 0.0023$

9.17   (a) $9 \leq \bar{X} \leq 31$
      (b) $P = 0.0294$
      (c) $P = 0.0023$

9.18   (a) For $\mu = 16{,}000$, $z = +0.40$ and $p \simeq 0.34, 0.27, 0.42, 0.46, 0.42, 0.34$.
      (b) 19,000 has the highest probability.

9.19   (a) $0.0010 \leq S^2 \leq 0.0046$
      (b) $0.00087 \leq S^2 \leq 0.0051$

9.20   (a) 1485, 3807
      (b) 3375

9.21   (a) $0.000012 \leq S^2 \leq 0.00028$
      (b) $P \approx 0.05$

9.22   (a) Lower limit weight is 19.227.
      (b) $0.513 \leq S^2 \leq 1.6$

9.23   (a) $80.06 \leq \bar{X} \leq 119.94$
      (b) $86.34 \leq \bar{X} \leq 113.66$

9.24   (a) $15.32 \leq \bar{X} \leq 16.68$
      (b) $P \approx 0.075$
      (c) $P \approx 0.025$

9.25   (a) The lower limit weight is 19.36 ounces.
      (b) $19.22 \leq \bar{X} \leq 20.78$

9.26   (a) $2.28 \leq \bar{X} \leq 17.72$
      (b) ~ 0.035
      (c) $\simeq 0.025$

9.27   No. $F_{0.05} \sim 1.76$.

Chapter 10

10.1 (a) $\mu_{\bar{X}} = 0.8$
      (b) $\sigma_{\bar{X}}^2 = 2.0$

10.2 (b) No, it would then be biased.

10.5 (a) Yes, both are unbiased.
      (b) The estimator, $\bar{X}$, has a higher efficiency (i.e., $\bar{X}$ is 37.5% more efficient).

10.7 (a) $3.91 \leq \mu \leq 4.33$
      (b) $3.887 \leq \mu \leq 4.353$
      (c) The lower limit is 3.95.

10.8 A sample size of 100 would be needed.

10.9 (a) $110.46 \leq \mu \leq 129.54$
      (b) The upper limit is 127.57.

10.10 (a) $16.11 \leq \mu \leq 16.69$
      (b) Yes, we conclude that the population mean weight is greater than 16 ounces.

10.11 (a) $16.11 \leq \mu \leq 16.69$
      (b) Yes, since 16.4 is greater than 16.24.

10.12 (a) Note that a 96% cofidence interval has a $Z \approx 2.055$. Thus the interval is as follows:
          $0.31 \leq \hat{P} \leq 0.41$
      (b) The lower limit is 0.32.

10.13 It is not possible to develop a 95% confidence interval because the sample is not random and thus the assumptions are not satisfied.

10.14 (a) $0.50 \leq \hat{P} \leq 0.56$
      (b) Yes, the entire interval would be above 0.50 given the use of a 95% confidence interval.

10.15 (a) $0.21 \leq \hat{P} \leq 0.36$
      (b) The upper limit is 0.35.

10.16 (a) $0.25 \leq \hat{P} \leq 0.37$
      (b) $0.26 \leq \hat{P} \leq 0.35$

10.17 (a) 7.74 to 32.26
      (b) The upper limit is 30.29.

10.18 (a) 0 to 105.44
      (b) 0 to 115.9
      (c) Given the preceding information, one cannot conclude that the population mean productivity is higher since the intervals above include 0.

10.19 (a) 7.06 to 92.94
      (b) -1.05 to 101.05
      (c) No, because the interval in part (b) includes 0.

10.20 (a) $S_P^2 = 135$
      (b) 4.83 to 15.17
      (c) The upper limit is 14.33.

10.21 (a) The pooled variance estimator is the same as in Problem 10.20 (i.e., 135). However, given the correlation, the sample variance for the difference in sample means will be smaller.
  (b) 6.06 to 13.94
  (c) The upper limit is 13.29.

10.22 (a) 32.07 to 67.93
  (b) 27.77 to 72.73

10.23 (a) -0.041 to 0.099
  (b) 0.0 to 0.112

10.24 (a) 0.0033 to 0.0947
  (b) The lower limit is 0.0117.
  (c) Yes, there is strong evidence that her voter support is increasing since the interval above does not include 0.

10.25 (a) $n = 97$
  (b) $n = 171$

10.26 (a) 267
  (b) 151

Chapter 11

11.1 (a) $\bar{X}_c = 102.487$
  (b) $\bar{X}_c = 103.107$

11.2 This problem uses $\alpha/2$.
  (a) $\bar{X}_c = 102.963$ and 97.037
  (b) $\bar{X}_c = 103.523$ and 96.477

11.3 (a) $\bar{X}_c = 346.71$
  (b) $\bar{X}_c = 345.89$
  (c) Our conclusion is that the population mean is less than or equal to 350 (i.e., the probability of $\mu \le 350$ is less than α).
  (d) $P = 0.0228$

11.4 (a) $\bar{X}_c = 52.6$ and 47.4
  (b) $\bar{X}_c = 53.05$ and 46.95

11.5 (a) $\bar{X}_c = 36.71$
  (b) With $\alpha = 0.05$, one cannot reasonably state that the population mean is less than 40 pounds.
  (c) $P = 0.0668$

11.6 (a) H_0: $\mu = 400$, H_1: $\mu \neq 400$. If $\bar{X}$ is greater than the upper limit or less than the lower limit, H_0 can be rejected and H_1 is to be accepted.
  (b) $\bar{X}_c = 404.18$ and 395.82
  (c) $P = 0.0188$

11.7 (a) $\hat{P}_c = 0.64$
  (b) $\hat{P}_c = 0.65$
  (c) If $\hat{P} = 0.67$, we would conclude that the population proportion is greater than 0.60.
  (d) $P = 0.0207$

11.8 (a) H_0: $P < 0.50$, H_1: $P \geq 0.50$. The critical value is 0.5274.
      (b) The conclusion is that she will win the election.
      (c) $P = 0.0013$

11.9 (a) H_0: $P < 0.30$, H_1: $P \geq 0.30$. The critical value is 0.32.
      (b) $\hat{P}_c = 0.348$

11.10 (a) $\bar{X}_c = 102.49$
      (b) $\beta = 0.0485$

11.11 (a) $\bar{X}_c = 102.963$ and 97.037
      (b) $\beta = 0.0885$

11.12 (a) $\bar{X}_c = 346.71$
      (b) Since $Z_\beta = -0.145$, $\beta \approx 0.5577$.

Concerning Problems 11.12 and 11.14, the region of β probability lies to the right of the power. In effect, the decision rule is testing whether a particular value is less than the expected value as opposed to greater than the expected value. Thus the probability of incorrectly accepting the null hypothesis is the region to the right of the power.

11.13 (a) $\bar{X}_c = 52.44$ and 47.56
      (b) $\beta = 0.1469$

11.14 (a) $\bar{X}_c = 36.71$
      (b) Since $Z_\beta = -0.645$, $\beta = 0.7405$.

11.15 (a) $\bar{X}_c = 403.51$
      (b) $\beta = 0.5948$

11.16 (a) $\hat{P}_c = 0.64$
      (b) $\beta = 0.2061$

11.17 (a) H_0: $P < 0.50$, H_1: $P \geq 0.50$. The critical value is 0.5274.
      (b) The conclusion is that she will win the election.
      (c) Since $Z_\beta = 0.4444$, it follows that $\beta = 0.6718$.

11.18 (a) $\hat{P}_c = 0.334$
      (b) $\hat{P}_c = 0.348$
      (c) With $\alpha = 0.01$, since $Z_\beta \approx 0.38$, it follows that $\beta = 0.6480$.

11.19 Conclusion: reject H_0, accept H_1.

11.20 Conclusion: reject H_0, accept H_1.

11.21 (a) H_0: $\mu_2 < \mu_1$, H_1: $\mu_2 \geq \mu_1$
      (b) $\sigma^2_{\Delta\bar{x}} = 8.28$
      (c) $\bar{X}_c = 5.64$; therefore, reject H_0, accept H_1.

11.22 Conclusion: reject H_0, accept H_1.

11.23 (a) H_0: $\mu_1 < \mu_2$, H_1: $\mu_1 \geq \mu_2$
      (b) $\sigma^2_{\Delta\hat{P}} = 0.0009446$; $\hat{P}_c = 0.051$
      (c) No, they do not have strong evidence that a larger percentage of the population would buy the new snowblower.

11.24 (a) $S^2_P = 113.5$

(b) $\bar{X}_c = 5.05$; if $\Delta\bar{X} \geq \bar{X}_c$, then reject H_0 and accept H_1.
(c) Conclusion: reject H_0, accept H_1.

11.25 (a) $S_p^2 = 208$
(b) $\bar{X}_c = 11.16$; if $\Delta\bar{X} \geq \bar{X}_c$, then reject H_0 and accept H_1.
(c) Conclusion: accept H_0.

11.26 (a) $S_p^2 = 216.17$
(b) $\bar{X}_c = 6.46$; if $\Delta\bar{X} \leq \bar{X}_c$, then reject H_0 and accept H_1.
(c) Conclusion: reject H_0, accept H_1.

In Problems 11.27 to 11.30, approximate values of $\bar{X}_c$ are given for the reason given just before Key Idea 11.17. Critical values were found for both populations and then simply averaged. Furthermore, values for n are also simply rounded up.

11.27 $n = 25$, $\bar{X}_c \approx 110$
11.28 $n = 99$, $\bar{X}_c \approx 254.8$
11.29 $n = 265$, $\bar{X}_c \approx 0.55$
11.30 $n = 144$, $\bar{X}_c \approx 0.252$
11.31 (a) $n = 203$
(b) $\bar{X}_c = 0.2437$. Therefore, Mr. Thorson should decide to introduce the new cereal product if more than 24.37% of the sample population responded favorably. The opposite decision would be ruled, of course, if less than 24.37% were to respond favorably.

Chapter 12

12.1 The following is the hypothesis test: H_0: The frequency data follow a uniform distribution; H_1: The frequency data do not follow a uniform distribution. With $\alpha = 0.05$, $\chi^2_{calc} = 2.51$ and $\chi^2_{crit} = 7.82$—we thus accept the null hypothesis, H_0, since $\chi^2 < \chi^2_{crit}$. Therefore, the frequency data do follow a uniform distribution.

12.2 H_0: The frequency data are from a binomial distribution; H_1: The frequency data are not from a binomial distribution. With a probability of error, α, of 0.05, $\chi^2 = 2.41$ and $\chi^2_{crit} = 5.99$. Because of the χ^2_{crit} value, the null hypothesis is accepted.

12.3 The hypothesis test is as follows: H_0: The data support the assumption of a binomial distribution; H_1: The data do not support the assumption of a binomial distribution. Given: $\alpha = 0.05$. Ultimately, the null hypothesis, H_0, is accepted and H_1 rejected because χ^2 of 9.15 is less than χ^2_{crit} of 9.49. The data do support the assumption of a binomial distribution.

12.4 (a) The following is the hypothesis test for both parts (a) and (b): H_0: The data support the assumption of a Poisson distribution; H_1: The data do not support the assumption of Poisson distribution. Given $\alpha = 0.05$ and $\mu = 1.0$, the null hypothesis, H_0, is rejected and H_1 accepted. $\chi^2 = 19.02$ and is greater than the χ^2_{crit} value of 7.815.
(b) Given $\alpha = 0.05$, $\mu = 0.6$. H_1 is accepted since $\chi^2 = 31.61$ and is greater than the χ^2_{crit} of 7.815.

12.5 H_0: The implementation of the new design change will follow the given market share distribution; H_1: The implementation of the new design change will not follow the given market share distribution. Given the random sample after the implementation of the new machine, $\chi^2 = 29.17$—thus greater than the χ^2_{crit} value of 7.815, with $\alpha = 0.05$ and DOF $= 3$. Hence the null hypothesis, H_0, can be rejected and H_1 accepted. This result leads us to believe that the new market share is "significantly" different than the previous distribution.

12.6 H_0: Factories and defect patterns are independent; H_1: Factories and defect patterns are dependent. Given: $\alpha = 0.05$, DOF $= 4$. Since $\chi^2 = 4.16$ and is less than the χ^2_{crit} value of 9.49, the null hypothesis is rejected and H_1 accepted. We can conclude that the defect patterns in the different factories are, in fact, the same.

12.7 H_0: Personnel rating and undergraduate major are independent; H_1: Personnel rating and undergraduate major are dependent. Given: $\alpha = 0.01$, DOF $= 6$. Since $\chi^2 = 13.648$ and is less than the χ^2_{crit} value of 16.812, we must then accept the null hypothesis, H_0. Therefore, we cannot deduce that ratings are different according to undergraduate major.

12.8 H_0: The ratings among the three groups are the same; H_1: The ratings among the three groups are different. $\chi^2 = 28.04$ and $\chi^2_{crit} = 9.49$. Given: $\alpha = 0.05$, DOF $= 4$. From these results, we can most certainly deduce that there exist differences between the three groups and their corresponding ratings—H_0 is rejected and H_1 accepted.

12.9 H_0: Region and demand for chicken products are independent; H_1: Region and demand for chicken products are dependent. Given: $\alpha = 0.01$, DOF $= 4$. Since $\chi^2 = 56.33$ and is greater than the χ^2_{crit} value of 13.28, we can reject H_0 and accept H_1. Thus the data indicate regional differences in demand for chicken products.

12.10 (a) By using a chi-square contingency table, we find χ^2 to be 20.242. This computed value is considerably larger than the χ^2_{crit} value of 3.841 with $\alpha = 0.05$ and DOF $= 1$. Therefore, we can reject the null hypothesis, H_0: gender and promotion possibility are independent, and accept H_1: gender and promotion are dependent. The probability of the observed data occurring, given that discrimination does not apply, is less than 0.01.

(b) The computed Z value, using a hypothesis test that compares the proportions, is equal to 4.5—considerably greater than the Z_{crit} value of 1.96. Thus we can deduce that the two variables are not independent of one another (i.e., accept H_1). The probability of the results observed is less than 0.001. The probability of H_0 being true is the same for both the X_2 and the Z tests.

12.11 The computed Z value is equal to 2.30—this value exceeds the critical value of 1.96. Hence we can rule out independence and accept H_1: factory and performance are dependent on one another (with $\alpha = 0.05$). If $\alpha = 0.01$ ($Z_{crit} = 2.33$), the null hypothesis, H_0, would be accepted.

Chapter 13

13.1 Since the computed F value of 17.46 is greater than the critical value of 4.07 (for 3 DOF in the numerator and 8 DOF in the denominator), the production levels are thus different on the four machines.

13.2   In this case, however, the critical F value of 5.14 is greater than the computed value of
       1.9—hence the three stores have no "differences" in the mean receivables.

13.3   The computed F value of 94.06 is considerably larger than the critical value of 4.26.
       Therefore, the age of the receivables is, in fact, different.

13.4   Essentially, each subgroup has a noticeably different mean age of receivables.

13.5   The computed F value of 19.28 is larger than the critical value of 5.14—thus the three
       groups do, in fact, have different responses according to the pricing of new skis.

13.6   (a) The youngest age group, 16–25, has a different perception of a fair market price than
           do the two other subgroups.
       (b) The results of the survey allow Deep Zero, Inc. to better focus their various market-
           ing schemes as to the age of the skier: perhaps cheaper models of the same ski are
           necessary for the age group 26–45 (they are more price conscious and, dare we say,
           stingy). Ultimately, potential profits from this new ski can be suggested to be the
           greatest for the 16–25 age group—this assumes, nonetheless, that these people have
           equal purchasing power relative to the two older-aged subgroups.

13.7   (a) Yes, there is evidence to suggest that weight differences exist between both suppliers
           and the length of delivery time. In effect, the computed F statistics for suppliers and
           delivery time are 107.15 and 43.80, respectively (2 DOF in numerator for suppliers
           and 1 DOF for delivery time; 6 DOF in the denominator for both). Their related
           critical values are 5.14 and 5.99. Thus the null hypothesis can be rejected, and the
           hypothesis of different weights can be accepted because the computed F statistics
           are greater than the corresponding critical values.
       (b) No, there is not an interaction effect—the critical F value of 5.14 is greater than the
           computed value of 1.85—accept the null hypothesis.

13.8   (a) Yes, the three stores have differences in mean receivables—the computed F statistic
           of 6.42 is greater than the critical value of 3.89 (12 DOF in the denominator, 2 DOF
           in the numerator).
       (b) Yes, there exist differences between mean receivables and clothing and hardware
           sales. F computed $= 138.96$ (1 DOF in numerator); F critical $= 4.75$.
       (c) There is an interaction effect since the computed F value of 11.43 is greater than the
           critical value of 3.89 (2 DOF in numerator).

13.9   (a) Yes, the three stores do have differences in the age of their receivables. This can be
           shown since the F computed value of 95.18 is greater than the F critical value of
           3.55 (2 DOF in numerator, 18 DOF in denominator).
       (b) No, there are not any differences in the age of receivables as they relate to product
           group—the computed F statistic of 0.93 is less than the critical value of 4.41 (1 DOF
           in numerator). Thus the null hypothesis is accepted.
       (c) No, there are not any interaction effects. The computed F value of 1.95 is less than
           the critical value of 3.55 (2 DOF in numerator), and thus the null hypothesis cannot
           be rejected.

13.10 (a) Yes, the three age groups do indeed have different perceptions of a fair market price.
           The computed F value of 72.5 is greater than the critical value of 3.89 (2 DOF in
           numerator, 12 DOF in denominator)—thus, reject the null hypothesis.

(b) Yes, it has been shown that men and women do differ in terms of their responses since the F computed value of 63.20 is greater than the critical value of 4.75 (1 DOF in numerator).

(c) No, there are not any interaction terms because the F computed value of 2.16 is less than the critical value of 3.89 (2 DOF in numerator).

Chapter 14

14.1   An observation with a large residual can distort a linear regression model immensely (i.e., a terribly large residual will alter the slope of the regression line, thereby distorting the overall picture and "worth" of the linear model). Often, measurement error, sampling error, or other unexplained error account for observations with such striking residuals— as a statistician or analyst, one must utilize professional judgment in either including or excluding the observations in question.

14.2   A correlation coefficient provides one with a sense of how strong a relationship is between two variables. This measuring tool is standardized (i.e., a perfectly direct relationship is given by $+1$, whereas a perfectly inverse relationship is given by -1). Conversely, a value of 0 indicates that no relationship whatsoever exists between the two variables. The least-squares regression slope coefficient, in a way, expands on the premise of the correlation coefficient—one can find the change in the endogenous variable, Y, with the addition or subtraction of 1 unit of an exogenous variable, X_i. Therefore, the least-squares coefficient provides one with a sense of relational strength, but also a method of strength valuation. Note that $\hat{\beta}_1 = r_{xy}(S_Y/S_{X_1})$.

14.3   The variance of $\hat{\beta}_1$ is a linear function of the model error ϵ because the dependent variable Y is a linear function of ϵ and $\hat{\beta} - 1$ is a linear function of Y.

14.4   The use of sample means within the regression equation, rather than the intercept, $\hat{\beta}_0$, provides an easier mental visualization of the linear model at hand. In applied problems the model is centered at the mean of X and Y and covers the range of the data. Extrapolating beyond the range of the data, especially trying to interpret β_0 as the intercept when $X = 0$ can often be misleading.

14.5   Once having obtained the sample size, means, variances, and the correlation coefficient, one is readily able to construct the linear regression equation by means of simple algebraic transformations in obtaining the slope coefficients.

14.6   (a) Y increases by 15 when X increases by 3.
       (b) The predicted value of Y equals 110 when X is 20.
       (c) The residual value equals the observed value minus the expected value (i.e., $65 - 60 = 5$).

14.7   (a) The reduction in defects equals 21 when X increases by 3.
       (b) The predicted number of defects equals 24 when X is 18.
       (c) The residual is computed as follows: $80 - 70 = 10$.

14.8   (a) The constant of the regression model, $\hat{\beta}_0$, equals 540. The slope coefficient, $\hat{\beta}_1$, is -1.4. The equation, then, is as follows: $\hat{Y} = 540 - 1.4X_1$.
       (b) $\hat{Y} = 400 - 1.4(X_1 - 100)$
       (c) The increase in sales is 1.4 units for each \$1 decrease in price.

14.9   (a) The constant, $\hat{\beta}_0$, equals $-36,000$. The slope coefficient, $\hat{\beta}_1$, equals 80. Thus the equation looks as follows: $\hat{Y} = -36,000 + 80X_1$.

     (b) $\hat{Y} = 60,000 + 80(X_1 - 1200)$

     (c) The increase in price equals \$80 for each additional square foot.

     (d) The residual is computed in the following manner: first, the predicted price is computed as \$68,000 [i.e., $-36,000 + 80(1300)$]. The difference, then, between the observed and predicted price is equal to \$12,000—namely, the residual.

14.10 (a) The constant, $\hat{\beta}_0$, is equal to 88,000. The slope coefficient, $\hat{\beta}_1$, is equal to 60. The regression equation looks thus: $\hat{Y} = 88,000 + 60X_1$.

     (b) $\hat{Y} = 160,000 + 60(X_1 - 1200)$

     (c) The increase in price for each additional turkey is \$60.

     (d) The residual price of the shed equals $240,000 - 178,000$: \$62,000.

14.11 In least-squares regression, variability is partitioned into explained and unexplained components. The total sum of squares is partitioned into regression sum of squares, RSS (explained error), and error sum of squares, ESS (unexplained error). By using the regression line in place of the mean, $\bar{Y}$, the regression line comes closer to the data points and ESS is minimized and unexplained error will always be less than or equal to the TSS.

14.12 Generally, R^2 indicates the percent explained variability. This would dictate that the higher the R^2 value, the better the model. However, one must be cautioned as to the misleading potential lying within the R^2 philosophy: a high R^2 suggests either points lying close to the regression line or Y's over a large range. This suggests that a model might have the same ESS as another despite having a higher or lower R^2 value. Refer to pp. 19–21 for further explanation.

14.13 The purpose of the F test is to test for a relationship between Y and X_1. If there is no relationship, RSS and ESS both measure unexplained error. However, if the mean square regression (RSS/1) is significantly greater than the mean square error $[(\text{ESS}/(n-2)]$, it is concluded that RSS does not measure unexplained error and a relationship exists between Y and X_1.

14.14 (a) $\hat{\beta}_1 = -1.4$ and $\hat{\beta}_0 = 540$. The equation, then, is as follows: $\hat{Y} = 540 - 1.4X_1$.

     (b) $R^2 = 0.49$

     (c) TSS $= 326,400$;   RSS $= 159,936$;   ESS $= 166,464$

     (d) $S^2_{Y|X} = 3329.28$

14.15 (a) The constant, $\hat{\beta}_0$, equals $-36,000$. The slope coefficient, $\hat{\beta}_1$, equals 80. Thus the equation looks as follows: $\hat{Y} = -36,000 + 80X_1$.

     (b) $R^2 = 0.64$

     (c) TSS $= 1.856 \times 10^9$;   RSS $= 1.188 \times 10^9$;   ESS $= 6.682 \times 10^9$

     (d) $S^2_{Y|X} = 2.386 \times 10^7$

14.16 (a) The constant, $\hat{\beta}_0$, is equal to 88,000. The slope coefficient, $\hat{\beta}_1$, is equal to 60. The regression equation looks thus: $\hat{Y} = 88,000 + 60X_1$.

     (b) $R^2 = 0.36$

     (c) TSS $= 2.496 \times 10^9$;   RSS $= 8.986 \times 10^8$;   ESS $= 1.597 \times 10^9$

     (d) $S^2_{Y|X} = 4.204 \times 10^7$

14.17 (a) The constant for the regression model, $\hat{\beta}_0$, is 150, and the slope coefficient, $\hat{\beta}_1$, is -7.

(b) $R^2 = 0.25$

(c) TSS $= 764,400$; RSS $= 191,100$; ESS $= 573,300$

(d) $S_{Y|X}^2 = 15,086.84$

(e) Yes, we do have evidence that the slope coefficient is not equal to zero. Since the computed F value of 12.67 is greater than the critical value, which is approximately equal to 4.10, we can reject the null hypothesis, H_0: $\hat{\beta}_1 = 0$, and accept H_1: $\hat{\beta}_1 \neq 0$.

14.18 (a) The constant for the regression model, $\hat{\beta}_0$, is 24,750, and the slope coefficient, $\hat{\beta}_1$, is 525.

(b) $R^2 = 0.49$

(c) TSS $= 2.79 \times 10^8$; RSS $= 1.367 \times 10^8$; ESS $= 1.423 \times 10^8$

(d) $S_{Y|X}^2 = 4.743 \times 10^6$

(e) Yes, we do have evidence that the slope coefficient is not equal to zero. Since the computed F value of 28.82 is greater than the critical value, which is 4.17, we can reject the null hypothesis, H_0: $\hat{\beta}_1 = 0$, and accept H_1: $\hat{\beta}_1 \neq 0$.

14.19 (a) The constant for the regression model, $\hat{\beta}_0$, is 30,432, and the slope coefficient, $\hat{\beta}_1$, is 612.

(b) $R^2 = 0.4624$

(c) TSS $= 4.018 \times 10^8$; RSS $= 1.858 \times 10^8$; ESS $= 2.1603 \times 10^8$

(d) $S_{Y|X}^2 = 7.2 \times 10^6$

(e) Yes, we do have evidence that the slope coefficient is not equal to zero. Since the computed F value of 25.8 is greater than the critical value, which is 4.17, we can reject the null hypothesis, H_0: $\hat{\beta}_1 = 0$, and accept H_1: $\hat{\beta}_1 \neq 0$.

14.20 Since there is a given, finite amount of variability, TSS, the value of RSS (explained variability) simply could never exceed that of TSS.

14.21 The variance of the slope coefficient estimator, $\hat{\beta}_1$, is linearly related to the model variance because (1) $\hat{\beta}_1$ is a linear combination of the independent random variables (Y's) since the ϵ's and Y's are postulated to be independent from one another; (2) using linear combinations of random variables (Chapter 6), it can be seen that σ^2 is directly related (linearly, of course) to the variance of $\hat{\beta}_1$.

14.22 When the independent variables, X's, are spread out over the entire range of the data, the variance of the slope coefficient is minimized. The reasoning behind this is that the regression line is simply fitting the data to the utmost level. In other words, if the X's were concentrated around the mean, $\overline{X}$, and the observations farther away from the mean were not taken into consideration, the variance of $\hat{\beta}_1$ is likely to be much larger.

14.23 Mathematically speaking, $\hat{\beta}_1$ and other regression estimators are related to the estimators in Chapter 10—thus it follows that the t-statistic can also be used.

14.24 Since the variance of the predicted value, $\hat{Y}$, increases quadratically as the X's move away from the mean, $\overline{X}_1$, it follows that at the mean, $\overline{X}$, the variance of the predicted value would be the least. Furthermore, at $\overline{X}_1$ deviations in the slope of the regression line do not alter the predicted value.

14.25 (a) The constant of the regression model, $\hat{\beta}_0$, equals 540. The slope coefficient, $\hat{\beta}_1$, is -1.4. The equation, then, is as follows: $\hat{Y} = 540 - 1.4X_1$.

(b) $S_{\hat{\beta}_1} = 0.202$

(c) Given $\alpha/2 = 0.025$, DOF $= n - 2 = 50$. Therefore, the 95% confidence interval, $\hat{\beta}_1 \pm (t_{(n-2,\alpha/2)})(S_{\hat{\beta}_1})$, is as follows: $-1.4 \pm (2.009)(0.202) = -1.4 \pm 0.041$.

(d) Given $\alpha/2 = 0.025$, DOF $= n - 2 = 50$. Therefore, the 95% confidence interval, $\hat{Y}_{X=110} \pm t_{(n-2,\alpha/2)} S_{\hat{Y}_{110}}$, is as follows: $694 \pm (2.009)(9.41) = 694 \pm 18.91$.

14.26 (a) The constant, $\hat{\beta}_0$, equals $-36,000$. The slope coefficient, $\hat{\beta}_1$, equals 80. Thus the equation looks as follows: $\hat{Y} = -36,000 + 80X_1$.

(b) $S_{\hat{\beta}_1} = 11.34$

(c) Given $\alpha/2 = 0.025$, DOF $= n - 2 = 28$. Therefore, the 95% confidence interval, $\hat{\beta}_1 \pm t_{(n-2,\alpha/2)} S_{\hat{\beta}_1}$, is as follows: $80 \pm (2.048)(11.34) = 80 \pm 23.22$.

(d) Given $\alpha/2 = 0.025$, DOF $= n - 2 = 28$. Therefore, the 95% confidence interval, $\hat{Y}_{X=1,100} \pm t_{(n-2,\alpha/2)} S_{\hat{Y}_{1,100}}$, is as follows: $52,000 \pm (2.048)(1442.5) = 52,000 \pm 2954.3$.

14.27 (a) The constant, $\hat{\beta}_0$, is equal to 88,000. The slope coefficient, $\hat{\beta}_1$, is equal to 60. The regression equation looks thus: $\hat{Y} = 88,000 + 60X_1$.

(b) $S_{\hat{\beta}_1} = 12.98$

(c) Given $\alpha/2 = 0.025$, DOF $= n - 2 = 38$. Therefore, the 95% confidence interval, $\hat{\beta}_1 \pm t_{(n-2,\alpha/2)} S_{\hat{\beta}_1}$, is as follows: $60 \pm (2.024)(12.98) = 60 \pm 26.27$.

(d) Given $\alpha/2 = 0.025$, DOF $= n - 2 = 38$. Therefore, the 95% confidence interval, $\hat{Y}_{X=1,300} \pm t_{(n-2,\alpha/2)} S_{\hat{Y}_{1,300}}$, is as follows: $166,000 \pm (2.024)(1653.9) = 166,000 \pm 3347.4$.

14.28 (a) The constant for the regression model, $\hat{\beta}_0$, is 150, and the slope coefficient, $\hat{\beta}_1$, is -7.

(b) $S_{\hat{\beta}_1} = 1.967$

(c) Given $\alpha/2 = 0.025$, DOF $= n - 2 = 38$. Therefore, the 95% confidence interval, $\hat{\beta}_1 \pm t_{(n-2,\alpha/2)} S_{\hat{\beta}_1}$, is as follows: $-7 \pm (2.024)(1.967) = -7 \pm 3.98$.

(d) Given $\alpha/2 = 0.025$, DOF $= n - 2 = 38$. Therefore, the 95% confidence interval, $\hat{Y}_{X=14} \pm t_{(n-2,\alpha/2)} S_{\hat{Y}_{14}}$, is as follows: $52 \pm (2.024)(19.52) = 52 \pm 39.51$.

(e) Yes, the confidence interval for the slope does not include 0.

14.29 (a) The constant for the regression model, $\hat{\beta}_0$, is 24,750, and the slope coefficient, $\hat{\beta}_1$, is 525.

(b) $S_{\hat{\beta}_1} = 97.79$

(c) Given $\alpha/2 = 0.025$, DOF $= n - 2 = 30$. Therefore, the 95% confidence interval, $\hat{\beta}_1 \pm t_{(n-2,\alpha/2)} S_{\hat{\beta}_1}$, is as follows: $525 \pm (2.042)(97.79) = 525 \pm 199.68$.

(d) Given $\alpha/2 = 0.025$, DOF $= n - 2 = 30$. Therefore, the 95% confidence interval, $\hat{Y}_{X=13} \pm t_{(n-2,\alpha/2)} S_{\hat{Y}_{13}}$, is as follows: $31,575 \pm (2.042)(484.03) = 31,575 \pm 988.38$.

(e) Yes, the confidence interval does not include 0.

14.30 (a) The constant for the regression model, $\hat{\beta}_0$, is 30,432, and the slope coefficient, $\hat{\beta}_1$, is 612.

(b) $S_{\hat{\beta}_1} = 120.48$

(c) Given $\alpha/2 = 0.025$, DOF $= n - 2 = 30$. Therefore, the 95% confidence interval, $\hat{\beta}_1 \pm t_{(n-2,\alpha/2)} S_{\hat{\beta}_1}$, is as follows: $612 \pm (2.042)(120.48) = 612 \pm 246.03$.

(d) Given $\alpha/2 = 0.025$, DOF $= n - 2 = 30$. Therefore, the 95% confidence interval, $\hat{Y}_{X=13} \pm t_{(n-2,\alpha/2)} S_{\hat{Y}_{13}}$, is as follows: $38,388 \pm (2.042)(489.4) = 38,388 \pm 999.36$.

(e) Yes, the confidence interval does not include 0.

14.31 (a) This rule of thumb stems from the initial hypothesis test, involving the t statistic, which tests that the correlation between two variables is not equal to zero. By manipulating the equation in Key Idea 14.20, one can ultimately arrive at the simple expression of 2 divided by the square root of n. The value "2" is essentially the critical t statistic of the initial equation.

14.32 Scatter plots are very useful in regression analysis. First, one can analyze the residuals of the model and, if necessary, transform the function accordingly (scatter plots are very readily able to indicate the "presence" of, say, heteroscedasticity). Second, one might simply wish to analyze the simple relationship between two variables—perhaps both exogenous, or one exogenous variable and the endogenous variable. (Other more involved reasons do, of course, stand behind the value of scatter plots.)

14.33 (b) The regression constant, $\hat{\beta}_0$, is -113.55. The slope coefficient, $\hat{\beta}_1$, is 24.674.
(c) When there are 20 workers, the predicted number of tables produced is 380.
(d) The t statistic, given that DOF $= 8$ $(n-2)$ and $\alpha/2 = 0.025$, is 2.306. Therefore, the 95% confidence interval is as follows: $20.36 \le \hat{\beta}_1 \le 28.99$.
(e) The standard error of the estimate, $S_{Y|X}$, is 37.13.

14.34 (b) The regression constant, $\hat{\beta}_0$, is 53. The slope coefficient, $\hat{\beta}_1$, is 0.176.
(c) The t statistic, given that DOF $= 18$ $(n-2)$ and $\alpha/2 = 0.025$, is 2.101. Therefore, the 95% confidence interval is as follows: $20.36 \le \hat{\beta}_1 \le 28.99$.
(d) The percent explained variability, R^2, is 2.4%. The correlation coefficient is 0.154.
(e) No, the regression output suggests little value in taking larger increments of medication.

14.35 (b) The regression constant, $\hat{\beta}_0$, is 9.29. The slope coefficient, $\hat{\beta}_1$, is -0.592.
(c) For the $3 shipping rate, the predicted delivery time is 7 to 8 days (i.e., 7.51). For the $5 rate, the predicted time until delivery is approximately 6 days (i.e., 6.33). For the $10 rate, the predicted delivery time is 3 to 4 days (i.e., 3.37).
(d) The t statistic, given that DOF $= 13$ $(n-2)$ and $\alpha/2 = 0.025$, is 2.160. Therefore, the 95% confidence intervals for the three delivery costs are as follows: (a) 1.80 to 4.20; (b) 4.37 to 5.63; (c) 8.25 to 11.75.
(e) There seems, in fact, to be evidence pointing toward adequately quicker times of delivery given the increase in price.

14.36 (b) The regression constant, $\hat{\beta}_0$, is 953.3. The slope coefficient, $\hat{\beta}_1$, is 532.94.
(c) The expected increase in monthly salary per year of experience is $533. The t statistic, given that DOF $= 10$ $(n-2)$ and $\alpha/2 = 0.025$, is 2.228. Therefore, the 95% confidence interval is as follows: $\$411.28 \le \hat{\beta}_1 \le \$654.72$.
(d) The percent explained variability, R^2, is 90.5%.
(e) The expected monthly salary for a person in the company with 10 years of experience is $6282.4.
(f) Yes, the company would be correct in stating that experience very much influences monthly salary.

14.37 (b) The regression constant, $\hat{\beta}_0$, is 0.80. The slope coefficient, $\hat{\beta}_1$, is 0.195.
(c) When expenditures $= 50$, the expected effectiveness is 10.55. The t statistic, given that DOF $= 8$ $(n-2)$ and $\alpha/2 = 0.025$, is 2.306. Therefore, the 95% confidence interval is as follows: 9.62 to 11.47.

(d) The increase in advertising effectiveness is 0.195 for each additional unit of expenditure. The t statistic, given that DOF $= 8$ $(n - 2)$ and $\alpha/2 = 0.025$, is 2.306. Therefore, the 95% confidence interval is as follows: $0.074 \leq \hat{\beta}_1 \leq 0.316$.

(e) In all, the relationship between advertising cost and effectiveness is significant. Each additional unit spent per 10,000 viewers will increase the effectiveness by 0.195 (MLE).

Chapter 15

15.1 The multiple regression models assume no correlation between the X_j's and ϵ_j.

15.2 Correlation (especially a high correlation) influences the slope coefficients in such a way that one cannot determine precisely whether one or both of the independent variables caused the change in the dependent variable, Y. Correlation between independent variables increases the variance of the estimated coefficient, $\hat{\beta}_j$.

15.3 A two-variable regression model, expressed in terms of sample means, looks as follows: $\hat{Y} = \bar{Y} + B_1(X_1 - \bar{X}_1) + B_2(X_2 - \bar{X}_2)$. This notation emphasizes that the model is centered on the means of the X and Y variables.

15.4 (a) $\hat{\beta}_1 = 1.708$
      (b) $\hat{\beta}_1 = 3.313$
      (c) $\hat{\beta}_1 = 13.053$

15.5 (a) $\hat{\beta}_1 = 0.792$
      (b) $\hat{\beta}_1 = 0.438$
      (c) $\hat{\beta}_1 = -0.421$

15.6 Plot the estimator functions in Key Idea 15.4 versus $r_{X_1 X_2}$.

15.7 Answers will vary.

15.8 The normal equations are obtained by minimizing the sum of squared residuals with respect to each of the β_j coefficients in the multiple linear model. This is accomplished using calculus, as shown in the chapter appendix. Normal equations include both the observed data from the sample and the unknown coefficient estimates. The system of normal equations—one for each coefficient—are then solved simultaneously to obtain the coefficient estimates.

15.9 In multiple regression, the overall F test determines whether a certain model (with any number of predictor variables) is statistically significant based on the amount of variability it is able to explain. If the F computed value is greater than that of the F critical value, we are led to believe that at least one of the slope coefficients (β's) is not equal to zero.

15.10 The overall F test determines whether or not a multiple regression model, as a whole, is significant. On the other hand, the conditional F test tests the significance (essentially, the contribution that the variable makes within the model to the total explained variability) of a certain independent variable, X_j, given the effect of the other independent predictor variables.

15.11 When independent predictor variables are correlated, they share a certain amount of explained variability—the higher the correlation, the higher the amount of explained variability shared. Therefore, the conditional explained variability of a certain variable,

X_j, is the total explained variability of the model minus the total explained variability of the model excluding that particular variable (i.e., $\text{RSS}_j - \text{RSS}_{j-1}$).

15.12 (a) 0.00085
(b) 0.00128
(c) 0.00429

15.13 (a) 0.00133
(b) 0.00199
(c) 0.00671

15.14 Plot the estimator functions for the coefficient variance $S^2_{\beta_j}$ shown in Key Idea 15.12 versus the correlation $r_{X_1 X_2}$.

15.15 The t statistic for each independent variable differs with the addition or subtraction of other independent variables for the following reason: the significance of each variable (i.e., the t value) is conditional on the effect of the other variables within the model (also bringing into account the degrees of freedom of the equation). If different variables are used, the t statistic will change accordingly.

15.16 To identify an independent variable as being significant, the slope coefficient must not be zero. Within the necessary hypothesis testing, $H_0: \beta_j = 0$ must be rejected, and $H_1: \beta_j \neq 0$ accepted. With $\alpha = 0.05$, the critical t value is approximately 2, when there are 60 degrees of freedom.

15.17 Answers will vary.

15.18 In most business and economic applications of multiple regression models, the independent predictor variables involved are correlated, to some degree, with one another. This causes the conditional explained variability of each variable to be smaller than the amount of explained variability for each independent variable in simple regression. Therefore, the sum of explained variability for the independent variables and Y in simple regressions would be less than the total explained variability provided by the multiple regression model.

15.19 Answers will vary.

15.20 Note that the restriction implies that $\beta_1 = 2 - \beta_2$ and substitute this result for β_1 in the equation. Reduce the model algebraically to

$$Y - 2X_1 = \beta_0 + \beta_2(X_1^2 - X_1) + \beta_3 X_2$$

Compute the transformed value for the X_1 variable and apply least squares.

15.21 Least-squares estimation methodology does, indeed, provide one with a best linear unbiased estimator. Residual plots help us identify cases in which the model assumptions are not satisfied. For example, if the process being analyzed or estimated is not linear, it is necessary to transform the regression equation mathematically to best fit the data points.

15.22 Exponential functions provide constant elasticities equal to the estimated coefficient β_j, and also indicate nonlinear demand functions. Economists like these properties.

15.23 Yes, the inclusion of a dummy variable is feasible within a function having a quadratic term. Answers will vary.

15.24 The consideration of a quadratic function in predicting the number of strikeouts revolves around the notion that starting pitchers might strike out more batters during certain stretches of the game. For example, either batters or pitchers might suffer from fatigue. Since a pitcher probably does not strike out a constant number of batters over the course of the game, one should consider a quadratic transformation equation since, for example, more batters might be struck out during the fourth, fifth, and sixth innings. Of course, other variables might be considered and/or used within the model, and it is very plausible to transform other such variables quadratically.

Chapter 16

16.1   This statement would raise some serious concerns. If the R^2 were close to 1.0, it would imply that all salaries were exactly on the regression line. However, the predictor variables are not sufficient to identify individual differences above and below the regression line. Thus such a salary structure would fail to recognize individual differences.

16.2   The proposition of a major sidewalk repair program, as it relates to the death rate and per capita health care costs, epitomizes the meaning of a spurious relationship. Such a conclusion is flawed in a myriad of ways, the first being: sidewalk cracks relate directly to the overall age of a community, which is in turn correlated with the death rate and health care programming. Ultimately, the suggestion that sidewalk repairs be deemed absolutely necessary is simply a gross error in judgment.

16.3   In the case of using a tenth-degree polynomial in order to estimate just 11 to 15 data points, the following problems arise: (1) By incorporating so many parameters (and "unnecessary" DOFs), the variance of the estimates are most likely to be extremely high; (2) the polynomial would fit the data set quite well. However, future or additional studies (of the same system), with a different data set, probably will not produce the same estimated model.

16.4   The regression model would look thus: $Y_i = \beta_0 + \beta_1 X_{1i} + \beta_2 X_{2i} + \beta_3 X_{3i} + \beta_4 X_{4i} + \epsilon_i$. The exogenous variables are designated as follows: Y = college GPA; X_1 = SAT score; $X_2 = 1$ if the student is a sophomore; $X_3 = 1$ if the student is a junior; and $X_4 = 1$ if the student is a senior. Otherwise X_2, X_3, and $X_4 = 0$. Note that just three dummy variables are used—the status of being a first-year student is the base condition, and is thus excluded in the regression model.

16.5   The regression model would look thus: $Y_i = \beta_0 + \beta_1 X_{1i} + \beta_2 X_{2i} + \beta_3 X_{3i} + \beta_4 X_{4i} + \beta_5 X_{5i} + \epsilon_i$. The exogenous variables are designated as follows: Y = wage; X_1 = years of experience; $X_2 = 1$ if the country is Great Britain; $X_3 = 1$ if the country is Japan; $X_4 = 1$ if the country is the United States; $X_5 = 1$ if the country is Turkey; else these latter variables equal 0. Note that just four dummy variables are used—the status of being employed in Germany is the base condition and is thus excluded in the regression model.

16.6   The regression model would look thus: $Y_i = \beta_0 + \beta_1 X_{1i} + \beta_2 X_{2i} + \beta_3 X_{3i} + \beta_4 X_{4i} + \epsilon_i$. The exogenous variables are designated as follows: Y = cost per unit; $X_1 = 1$ if computer-controlled machines; $X_2 = 1$ if computer-controlled material handling; $X_3 = 1$ if South Africa; $X_4 = 1$ if Japan. Note that there are two different sets of dummy variables, each with two variables within the regression model—the status of using classic technology and being based in Colombia are the two separate base conditions and are thus excluded in the regression model.

16.7   Answers will vary.

16.8   Weighted least squares is used to adjust for heteroscedasticity or nonuniform error over the range of the data. Heteroscedasticity results in coefficient estimates that are not efficient. Weighted least squares results in greater weight for observations with a smaller error variance in the dependent variable. As a result the coefficient estimates are efficient.

16.9   Answers will vary.

16.10 The question suggests positive serial correlation, because the residuals would begin positive (or negative) then become negative (or positive) for some observations and then revert to the initial sign. This pattern would be the same as that generated by a time-series model with serial correlation. Therefore, the d statistic must be less than d_L in order to signify such positive correlation.

16.11 If a significant exogenous variable is omitted from a regression model, then the other coefficients will need to be adjusted to account for the effect of the excluded variable when the sum of squares of deviation of the regression plane from the data points is minimized. These adjustments will result in biased coefficient estimates.

16.12 The coefficient for X_1 is likely to be biased since the specification of computer make and model will directly affect the computer processing time (i.e., the endogenous variable, Y). Given the exclusion of the make and model variable, the other coefficients will need to adjust for the missing effect of computer model. Thus the slope coefficient estimator for X_1 will have a different value and ultimately be biased.

Chapter 17

17.1   1.14

17.2   1.37

17.3   (a) Suspenders $10.91, shoes $54.55
       (b) Suspenders had the largest increase.

17.4   (a) Paperback $10.35, hardcover $45.29
       (b) Hardcover books had the largest increase.

17.5   Trend national consumption, cyclical national investment, and monthly retail toy sales

17.6   Time-series models use only the information in the series to predict the future, in contrast to multiple regression models, which use additional exogenous variables.

17.7   Cyclical effects follow a pattern over an unspecified time period. Seasonal effects occur in the same pattern over a year.

17.8   Residuals are assumed to be independent in the standard regression assumptions. Generally, irregular components in a time-series model are related. Time-series forecasting models attempt to take advantage of the relationship between the irregular components.

17.9   Exponential smoothing is essentially a linear combination of the observed and forecast values for the preceding period. The forecast for the previous period includes information from the past history of the series.

17.10 Autoregressive models use information from recent observations in the series to generate the forecast. In contrast, exponential smoothing essentially uses the entire history of the time series.

17.11 The root mean square error provides a measure of variability between the forecast and observed values of the time series. The mean deviation indicates a positive or negative bias in the forecast (e.g., does the model forecast error equal in both the positive and negative directions?).

17.12 Turning points indicate a change in direction—up or down—of a series, which in turn suggests that the management tactics should change in response (e.g., do not increase production if sales have turned downward).

17.13 A forecast model will always work best on the data used for its development. Thus structural biases might be missed. Application to fresh data will test both model structure and goodness of fit.

17.14 Does the model forecast satisfactorily? The elegance of the estimation procedure or the model form are less important for any applied work in management.

Chapter 18

18.1 The difference between assignable and common causes of defects is very simply that assignable defects can be pinpointed, identified, and controlled, whereas common defects are those which are uncontrollable within the system.

18.2 When a process is labeled as being in control, the implication is that as many steps as possible have been taken in analyzing and improving the overall system, including not only machinery but also employee productivity, efficiency, welfare, and others.

18.3 The control limits are as follows: LCL = 9.85; UCL = 10.15.

18.4 The control limits are as follows: LCL = 5.33 hours; UCL = 6.67 hours.

18.5 Control limits provide an interval for data that indicate whether or not a system is in control (refer to answer 18.2). Specification limits are based on customer expectations or prescribed mandates for the system. For a system to be labeled as "capable," the control limits must be contained within the specification limits—in other words, the process capability index (PCI) must exceed 1 for a system to be termed capable.

18.6 No, the manufacturing process is not capable. First, we calculate the control limits and find that the interval is 10 centimeters $\pm$ 0.3 centimeter. This interval is outside the given specification limits of 10 ± 0.2 and thus the system is found to be incapable. Also, the PCI could be calculated as such: (PCI $=$ USL $-$ LSL)$/6\sigma$; the result is 0.67. For a capable system, the PCI must be greater than 1.

18.7 No, Speedy Package Delivery, Inc. cannot meet its promise of delivering a package within 7 hours. Calculation of the control limits yields an interval of 6 ± 3 hours. These limits, however, are contained within the specification limits 6 ± 1 hour, and thus the system is incapable. Also, the PCI $=$ 0.67.

18.8 An $\bar{X}$ chart provides an analyst with a plot of sample means, whereas an R chart provides one with a plot of the data range. Note that both charts attempt to identify variability caused by assignable causes.

18.9 Whenever a sample mean or range exceeds its control bounds, the process should be halted so that either assignable or uncontrollable causes can be corrected before the entire system begins to go haywire—over time, the defects will most likely increase exponentially, and thus is the reasoning behind stopping the system as quickly as possible in order to bring it back into control.

18.10 The limits for the front axle shaft are as follows: $\bar{X}$ chart: LCL = 9.836, UCL = 10.164. R chart: LCL = 0.0, UCL = 0.602.

18.11 The limits for the delivery time are as follows: $\bar{X}$ chart: LCL = 5.6 hours, UCL = 7.4 hours. R chart: LCL = 0.0, UCL = 2.78.

18.12 (a) Yes, overall the process is capable because the control limits of 15 ± 0.9 are within the required specification limits of 15 ± 1—in addition, the PCI = 1.1.
(b) With $n = 5$, the control limits for the $\bar{X}$ chart are: UCL = 16.21, LCL = 13.79. For the R chart: UCL = 0.6598, LCL = 0.0.

18.13 The upper control limit is 0.218.

18.16 The upper control limit is 10 errors for every five games.

Index

Student *t* for Selected Upper-Tail Probabilities *(continued)*

DOF	α					
	0.25	0.10	0.05	0.025	0.01	0.005
31	0.682	1.309	1.696	2.040	2.453	2.744
32	0.682	1.309	1.694	2.037	2.449	2.738
33	0.682	1.308	1.692	2.035	2.445	2.733
34	0.682	1.307	1.691	2.032	2.441	2.728
35	0.682	1.306	1.690	2.030	2.438	2.724
36	0.681	1.306	1.688	2.028	2.434	2.719
37	0.681	1.305	1.687	2.026	2.431	2.715
38	0.681	1.304	1.686	2.024	2.429	2.712
39	0.681	1.304	1.685	2.023	2.426	2.708
40	0.681	1.303	1.684	2.021	2.423	2.704
41	0.681	1.303	1.683	2.020	2.421	2.701
42	0.680	1.302	1.682	2.018	2.418	2.698
43	0.680	1.302	1.681	2.017	2.416	2.695
44	0.680	1.301	1.680	2.015	2.414	2.692
45	0.680	1.301	1.679	2.014	2.412	2.690
46	0.680	1.300	1.679	2.013	2.410	2.687
47	0.680	1.300	1.678	2.012	2.408	2.685
48	0.680	1.299	1.677	2.011	2.407	2.682
49	0.680	1.299	1.677	2.010	2.405	2.680
50	0.679	1.299	1.676	2.009	2.403	2.678
51	0.679	1.298	1.675	2.008	2.402	2.676
52	0.679	1.298	1.675	2.007	2.400	2.674
53	0.679	1.298	1.674	2.006	2.399	2.672
54	0.679	1.297	1.674	2.005	2.397	2.670
55	0.679	1.297	1.673	2.004	2.396	2.668
56	0.679	1.297	1.673	2.003	2.395	2.667
57	0.679	1.297	1.672	2.002	2.394	2.665
58	0.679	1.296	1.672	2.002	2.392	2.663
59	0.679	1.296	1.671	2.001	2.391	2.662
60	0.679	1.296	1.671	2.000	2.390	2.660
61	0.679	1.296	1.670	2.000	2.389	2.659
62	0.678	1.295	1.670	1.999	2.388	2.658
63	0.678	1.295	1.669	1.998	2.387	2.656
64	0.678	1.295	1.669	1.998	2.386	2.655
65	0.678	1.295	1.669	1.997	2.385	2.654
66	0.678	1.295	1.668	1.997	2.384	2.652

Student *t* for Selected Upper-Tail Probabilities *(continued)*

DOF	0.25	0.10	0.05	0.025	0.01	0.005
67	0.678	1.294	1.668	1.996	2.383	2.651
68	0.678	1.294	1.668	1.995	2.382	2.650
69	0.678	1.294	1.667	1.995	2.382	2.649
70	0.678	1.294	1.667	1.994	2.381	2.648
71	0.678	1.294	1.667	1.994	2.380	2.647
72	0.678	1.293	1.666	1.993	2.379	2.646
73	0.678	1.293	1.666	1.993	2.379	2.645
74	0.678	1.293	1.666	1.993	2.378	2.644
75	0.678	1.293	1.665	1.992	2.377	2.643
76	0.678	1.293	1.665	1.992	2.376	2.642
77	0.678	1.293	1.665	1.991	2.376	2.641
78	0.678	1.292	1.665	1.991	2.375	2.640
79	0.678	1.292	1.664	1.990	2.375	2.640
80	0.678	1.292	1.664	1.990	2.374	2.639
81	0.678	1.292	1.664	1.990	2.373	2.638
82	0.677	1.292	1.664	1.989	2.373	2.637
83	0.677	1.292	1.663	1.989	2.372	2.636
84	0.677	1.292	1.663	1.989	2.372	2.636
85	0.677	1.292	1.663	1.988	2.371	2.635
86	0.677	1.291	1.663	1.988	2.371	2.634
87	0.677	1.291	1.663	1.988	2.370	2.634
88	0.677	1.291	1.662	1.987	2.369	2.633
89	0.677	1.291	1.662	1.987	2.369	2.632
90	0.677	1.291	1.662	1.987	2.369	2.632
91	0.677	1.291	1.662	1.986	2.368	2.631
92	0.677	1.291	1.662	1.986	2.368	2.630
93	0.677	1.291	1.661	1.986	2.367	2.630
94	0.677	1.291	1.661	1.986	2.367	2.629
95	0.677	1.291	1.661	1.985	2.366	2.629
96	0.677	1.290	1.661	1.985	2.366	2.628
97	0.677	1.290	1.661	1.985	2.365	2.627
98	0.677	1.290	1.661	1.984	2.365	2.627
99	0.677	1.290	1.660	1.984	2.365	2.626
100	0.677	1.290	1.660	1.984	2.364	2.626
101	0.677	1.290	1.660	1.984	2.364	2.625
102	0.677	1.290	1.660	1.984	2.363	2.625